GW00602787

SIPRI Yearbook 2006
Armaments, Disarmament and International Security

sipri
Stockholm International Peace Research Institute

SIPRI is an independent international institute for research into problems of peace and conflict, especially those of arms control and disarmament. It was established in 1966 to commemorate Sweden's 150 years of unbroken peace.

The Institute is financed mainly by a grant proposed by the Swedish Government and subsequently approved by the Swedish Parliament. The staff and the Governing Board are international. The Institute also has an Advisory Committee as an international consultative body.

The Governing Board is not responsible for the views expressed in the publications of the Institute.

Governing Board

Ambassador Rolf Ekéus, Chairman (Sweden)
Sir Marrack Goulding, Vice-Chairman (United Kingdom)
Dr Alexei G. Arbatov (Russia)
Jayantha Dhanapala (Sri Lanka)
Dr Willem F. van Eekelen (Netherlands)
Dr Nabil Elaraby (Egypt)
Rose E. Gottemoeller (United States)
Professor Helga Haftendorn (Germany)
Professor Ronald G. Sutherland (Canada)
The Director

Director

Alyson J. K. Bailes (United Kingdom)

Alyson J. K. Bailes, Director, *Yearbook Editor and Publisher*
Ian Anthony, *Executive Editor*
Connie Wall and D. A. Cruickshank, *Managing Editors*
Coordinators
Ian Anthony, Alyson J. K. Bailes, Björn Hagelin
Editors
D. A. Cruickshank, Tom Gill, Jetta Gilligan Borg, Connie Wall

sipri
Stockholm International Peace Research Institute
Signalistgatan 9, SE-169 70 Solna, Sweden
Cable: SIPRI
Telephone: 46 8/655 97 00
Telefax: 46 8/655 97 33
Email: sipri@sipri.org
Internet URL: http://www.sipri.org

SIPRI Yearbook 2006

Armaments, Disarmament and International Security

Stockholm International Peace Research Institute

OXFORD UNIVERSITY PRESS
2006

OXFORD

UNIVERSITY PRESS

Great Clarendon Street, Oxford OX2 6DP

Oxford University Press is a department of the University of Oxford.
It furthers the University's objective of excellence in research, scholarship,
and education by publishing worldwide in

Oxford New York

Auckland Cape Town Dar es Salaam Hong Kong Karachi
Kuala Lumpur Madrid Melbourne Mexico City Nairobi
New Delhi Shanghai Taipei Toronto

With offices in

Argentina Austria Brazil Chile Czech Republic France Greece
Guatemala Hungary Italy Japan Poland Portugal Singapore
South Korea Switzerland Thailand Turkey Ukraine Vietnam

Oxford is a registered trade mark of Oxford University Press
in the UK and in certain other countries

Published in the United States
by Oxford University Press Inc., New York

© SIPRI 2006

*Yearbooks before 1987 were published under the title
'World Armaments and Disarmament:
SIPRI Yearbook [year of publication]'*

All rights reserved. No part of this publication may be reproduced,
stored in a retrieval system, or transmitted, in any form or by any means,
without the prior permission in writing of SIPRI,
or as expressly permitted by law, or under terms agreed with the appropriate
reprographics rights organizations. Enquiries concerning reproduction
outside the scope of the above should be sent to
SIPRI, Signalistgatan 9, SE-169 70 Solna, Sweden

You must not circulate this book in any other binding or cover
and you must impose the same condition on any acquirer

British Library Cataloguing in Publication Data
Data available

Library of Congress Cataloging in Publication Data
Data available

Typeset and originated by Stockholm International Peace Research Institute
Printed and bound in Great Britain
on acid-free paper by
Biddles Ltd, King's Lynn, Norfolk

ISSN 0953–0282
ISBN 0–19–929873–4 978–0–19–929873–0

Contents

Part II. Military spending and armaments, 2005

Part III. Non-proliferation, arms control and disarmament, 2005

Annexes

Preface

The Stockholm International Peace Research Institute initiated its work 40 years ago, in July 1966. Three years later the first edition of the SIPRI Yearbook was published.

Compared to the challenges to peace and security in 1966, the contemporary political environment is radically different. Even since the end of the cold war, in 1989, the geopolitical and geo-strategic realities—especially as regards Europe, transatlantic relations and the Middle East—have shifted from manifest optimism, witnessed in the 1990 Charter of Paris for a New Europe and the Barcelona Process for peace in the Middle East, to a situation of troubled concern.

The process of globalization, although difficult to define in precise terms, implies that powers of economic and political significance have moved from the authority of states to international institutions, economic conglomerates and other non-state actors, including terrorist networks. The IT revolution and the opportunities presented by the Internet have profoundly influenced communications, opinion building and, dramatically, the speed of news distribution. This has had an impact on intercultural and inter-religious relations and made the 'clash of civilizations' less of a geopolitical notion and more of a phenomenon of internal and societal significance.

In her Introduction to this edition of the Yearbook, SIPRI's Director, Alyson J. K. Bailes, describes the main trends following the end of the East–West confrontation and reflects on the responses to the challenges by the main international actors, especially the United States. She also addresses the shift of emphasis since 1990 from arms control to security building in international affairs, including the changing role of NATO and the expansion of the European Union's security agenda.

This edition of the Yearbook illustrates the change from strict peacekeeping operations under UN mandate to the variety of types of peace mission executed by an increasingly wide array of international organizations and demonstrates the necessity of adjusting the means of peace-building to new realities.

The magnitude and impact of ongoing armed conflicts are described and analysed from different perspectives. As regards arms control and the proliferation of weapons of mass destruction (WMD), especially nuclear weapons, the passivity and lack of attention in Europe and elsewhere since 1990 has, in recent years, turned into a matter of major international concern. The chapters on these issues should be of special interest to politicians and decisions makers. The potential for terrorist acts involving WMD should put arms control and non-proliferation on the top of the international agenda. The appendix devoted to the complex questions of Islam, conflict and terrorism is more topical than ever.

The chapters on the SIPRI speciality of military spending and armaments are unique and indispensable expressions of SIPRI's traditional and leading role in these contexts.

This edition of the Yearbook, marking the 40th anniversary of SIPRI, constitutes a significant contribution by the research staff under the leadership of the Director to the search for responses to new and complex challenges to international peace and security. As always with the SIPRI Yearbook, the careful reader will enjoy the quality and professionalism of the contributions, since the outset a characteristic of SIPRI publications.

Rolf Ekéus
Chairman, SIPRI Governing Board
May 2006

Acknowledgements

SIPRI continues to seek ways to make best use of this Yearbook and its contents as a tool of transparency. We are seeking means to continue the translation of the entire text into Arabic, Chinese, Russian and Ukrainian, and (with the help of various partners) we shall continue to produce translations of a pocket-sized summary version in Dutch, French, German, Russian, Spanish and Swedish. (The latter short texts are available on the SIPRI website at http://www.sipri.org/contents/publications/pocket/pocket_yb.html.) All proposals for further translations and ways of reaching a wider audience with this publication will be welcome.

As always, production of this Yearbook has been a truly collective endeavour. While warmly thanking all SIPRI colleagues and outside contributors, I would like to make special mention of the invaluable work of the team of editors—Connie Wall, David Cruickshank, Jetta Gilligan Borg and Tom Gill; Nenne Bodell and the SIPRI Library staff, who take the lead in producing much of the volume's reference material; Gerd Hagmeyer-Gaverus and the IT Department; Peter Rea, the indexer; and my Assistant, Cynthia Loo.

Alyson J. K. Bailes
Director, SIPRI
May 2006

Glossary

NENNE BODELL and CONNIE WALL

Abbreviations

ABM	Anti-ballistic missile	CFSP	Common Foreign and Security Policy
ACV	Armoured combat vehicle		
AG	Australia Group	CICA	Conference on Interaction and Confidence-building Measures in Asia
ALCM	Air-launched cruise missile		
APEC	Asia–Pacific Economic Forum	CIS	Commonwealth of Independent States
APM	Anti-personnel mine	CNCI	Civil Nuclear Cooperation Initiative
APT	ASEAN Plus Three	CSBM	Confidence- and security-building measure
ARF	ASEAN Regional Forum		
ASEAN	Association of South East Asian Nations	CSCAP	Council for Security Cooperation in the Asia Pacific
ATTU	Atlantic-to-the Urals (zone)		
AU	African Union	CSTO	Collective Security Treaty Organization
BMD	Ballistic missile defence	CTBT	Comprehensive Nuclear-Test-Ban Treaty
BSEC	Organization of Black Sea Economic Cooperation		
BTWC	Biological and Toxin Weapons Convention	CTBTO	Comprehensive Nuclear-Test-Ban Treaty Organization
BW	Biological weapon/warfare	CTR	Co-operative Threat Reduction
CADSP	Common African Defence and Security Policy	CW	Chemical weapon/warfare
CAR	Central African Republic	CWC	Chemical Weapons Convention
CBM	Confidence-building measure	DDR	Disarmament, demobilization, and reintegration
CBW	Chemical and biological weapon/warfare		
CD	Conference on Disarmament	DPKO	Department of Peacekeeping Operations
CEI	Central European Initiative	DRC	Democratic Republic of the Congo
CEMAC	Communauté Economique et Monétaire d'Afrique Centrale (Economic Community of Central African States)	EAEC	European Atomic Energy Community (*also* Euratom)
		EAPC	Euro-Atlantic Partnership Council
CFE	Conventional Armed Forces in Europe (Treaty)	ECOMOG	ECOWAS Monitoring Group

ECOWAS	Economic Community of West African States	INF	Intermediate-range Nuclear Forces (Treaty)
EMU	European Monetary Union	INFCE	International Nuclear Fuel Cycle Evaluation
ESA	European Space Agency		
ESDP	European Security and Defence Policy	INPRO	International Project on Innovative Nuclear Reactors and Fuel Cycles
EU	European Union		
FP	Framework Programme	IRBM	Intermediate-range ballistic missile
FSC	Forum for Security Co-operation	JCG	Joint Consultative Group
FY	Financial year	JHA	Justice and Home Affairs
FYROM	Former Yugoslav Republic of Macedonia	LEU	Low-enriched uranium
		MANPADS	Man-portable air defence system
G8	Group of Eight	MDGs	Millennium Development Goals
GAERC	General Affairs and External Relations Council		
GCC	Gulf Cooperation Council	MER	Market exchange rate
GDP	Gross domestic product	MERCOSUR	Mercado Común del Sur (Southern Common Market)
GLCM	Ground-launched cruise missile		
GNEP	Global Nuclear Energy Partnership	MIRV	Multiple, independently targetable re-entry vehicle
GNI	Gross national income	MTCR	Missile Technology Control Regime
GNP	Gross national product	NAC	New Agenda Coalition
GTRI	Global Threat Reduction Initiative	NAM	Non-Aligned Movement
HCOC	Hague Code of Conduct	NATO	North Atlantic Treaty Organization
HCNM	High Commissioner on National Minorities	NBC	Nuclear, biological and chemical (weapons)
HEU	Highly enriched uranium	NGO	Non-governmental organization
IAEA	International Atomic Energy Agency	NNWS	Non-nuclear weapon state
ICBM	Intercontinental ballistic missile	NPT	Non-Proliferation Treaty
		NRF	NATO Response Force
ICC	International Criminal Court	NSG	Nuclear Suppliers Group
		NWS	Nuclear weapon state
IGAD	Intergovernmental Authority on Development	OAS	Organization of American States
IGC	Intergovernmental Conference	OCCAR	Organisme Conjoint de Coopération en Matière d'Armement
IMF	International Monetary Fund		
INDA	International non-proliferation and disarmament assistance	ODA	Official development assistance

OECD	Organisation for Economic Co-operation and Development	UAV	Unmanned air vehicle
		UCAV	Unmanned combat air vehicle
OIC	Organization of the Islamic Conference	USAID	US Agency for International Development
OPCW	Organisation for the Prohibition of Chemical Weapons	UN	United Nations
		UNDP	UN Development Programme
OPEC	Organization of the Petroleum Exporting Countries	UNHCR	UN High Commissioner for Refugees
OSCC	Open Skies Consultative Commission	UNMOVIC	UN Monitoring, Verification and Inspection Commission
OSCE	Organization for Security and Co-operation in Europe	UNROCA	UN Register of Conventional Arms
PFP	Partnership for Peace	UNSCOM	UN Special Commission on Iraq
PPP	Purchasing power parity	WA	Wassenaar Arrangement
PSI	Proliferation Security Initiative	WEAO	Western European Armaments Organisation
R&D	Research and development	WEU	Western European Union
SAARC	South Asian Association for Regional Co-operation	WMD	Weapon(s) of mass destruction
SADC	Southern African Development Community		
SALW	Small arms and light weapons		
SAM	Surface-to-air missile		
SCO	Shanghai Cooperation Organization		
SECI	Southeast European Cooperative Initiative		
SLBM	Submarine-launched ballistic missile		
SLCM	Sea-launched cruise missile		
SORT	Strategic Offensive Reductions Treaty		
SRBM	Short-range ballistic missile		
SSM	Surface-to-surface missile		
SSR	Security sector reform		
START	Strategic Arms Reduction Treaty		
TLE	Treaty-limited equipment		
UAE	United Arab Emirates		

Intergovernmental bodies and international organizations

The main organizations and export control regimes discussed in this Yearbook are described in the glossary. Members or participants are listed on pages xxviii–xxxv. On the arms control and disarmament agreements mentioned in the glossary, see annex A in this volume.

African Union (AU)	The Constitutive Act of the African Union entered into force in 2001, formally establishing the AU. Its headquarters are in Addis Ababa, Ethiopia, and it is open for membership of all African states. In 2002 it replaced the Organization for African Unity. The AU promotes unity, security and conflict resolution, democracy, human rights, and political, social and economic integration in Africa. *See* the list of members.
Agency for the Prohibition of Nuclear Weapons in Latin America and the Caribbean (OPANAL)	Established by the 1967 Treaty of Tlatelolco to resolve, together with the IAEA, questions of compliance with the treaty. Its seat is in Mexico D.F., Mexico.
Andean Community of Nations	Established in 1969 (as the Andean Pact), the Andean Community promotes the economic and social development and integration of its member states. Its seat is in Lima, Peru. *See* the list of members.
Arab League	The League of Arab States, established in 1945, with Permanent Headquarters in Cairo, Egypt. Its principal objective is to form closer union among Arab states and foster political and economic cooperation. An agreement for collective defence and economic cooperation among the members was signed in 1950. *See* the list of members.
Association of South East Asian Nations (ASEAN)	Established in 1967 to promote economic, social and cultural development as well as regional peace and security in South-East Asia. The seat of the Secretariat is in Jakarta, Indonesia. The ASEAN Regional Forum (ARF) was established in 1994 to address security issues. Cooperation on political and security issues in the ASEAN Plus Three (APT) forum started in 1997 and was institutionalized in 1999. *See* the lists of the members of ASEAN, ARF and ASEAN Plus Three.
Australia Group (AG)	Group of states, formed in 1985, which meets informally each year to monitor the proliferation of chemical and biological products and to discuss chemical and biological weapon-related items which should be subject to national regulatory measures. *See* the list of participants.
Black Sea Economic Cooperation (BSEC)	*See* Organization of the Black Sea Economic Cooperation.
Central European Initiative (CEI)	Established in 1989 to promote cooperation among members in the political and economic spheres. It provides support to its non-EU members in their process of accession to the EU. The seat of the Executive Secretariat is in Trieste, Italy. *See* the list of members.

Collective Security Treaty Organization (CSTO)

Formally established in 2003, the CSTO emanates from the 1992 Collective Security Treaty for the promotion of cooperation among the parties, mainly states in Central Asia. An objective is to provide a more efficient response to strategic problems such as terrorism and narcotics trafficking in the region. Its seat is in Moscow, Russia. *See* the list of members.

Commonwealth of Independent States (CIS)

Established in 1991 as a framework for multilateral cooperation among former Soviet republics, with headquarters in Minsk, Belarus. *See* the list of members.

Commonwealth of Nations

An organization, established in 1949, of developed and developing countries whose aim is to advance democracy, human rights, and sustainable economic and social development within its member states and beyond. Its Secretariat is in London, UK. *See* the list of members.

Comprehensive Nuclear-Test-Ban Treaty Organization (CTBTO)

Established by the 1996 CTBT to resolve questions of compliance with the treaty and as a forum for consultation and cooperation among the states parties. Its seat is in Vienna, Austria.

Conference on Disarmament (CD)

A multilateral arms control negotiating body, set up in 1961 as the Eighteen-Nation Committee on Disarmament; it has been enlarged and renamed several times and has been called the Conference on Disarmament since 1984. It reports to the UN General Assembly and is based in Geneva, Switzerland. *See* the list of members under United Nations.

Conference on Interaction and Confidence-building Measures in Asia (CICA)

Initiated in 1992, and established by the 1999 Declaration on the Principles Guiding Relations among the CICA Member States, as a forum to enhance security cooperation and confidence-building measures among the member states. It also promotes economic, social and cultural cooperation. *See* the list of members.

Council for Security Cooperation in the Asia Pacific (CSCAP)

Established in 1993 as an informal, non-governmental process for regional confidence building and security cooperation through dialogue and consultation in Asia–Pacific security matters. *See* the list of member committees.

Council of Europe

Established in 1949, with its seat in Strasbourg, France, the Council is open to membership of all the European states that accept the principle of the rule of law and guarantee their citizens' human rights and fundamental freedoms. Among its organs are the European Court of Human Rights and the Council of Europe Development Bank. *See* the list of members.

Council of the Baltic Sea States (CBSS)

Established in 1992 as a regional intergovernmental organization for cooperation among the states of the Baltic Sea region. Its secretariat is located in Stockholm, Sweden. *See* the list of members.

Economic Community of West African States (ECOWAS)	A regional organization established in 1975, with its Executive Secretariat in Lagos, Nigeria, to promote trade and cooperation and contribute to development in West Africa. In 1981 it adopted the Protocol on Mutual Assistance in Defence Matters. The ECOWAS Monitoring Group (ECOMOG) was established in 1990 as a multinational peacekeeping/peace-enforcement force. *See* the list of members.
European Atomic Energy Community (Euratom, or EAEC)	Created by the 1957 Treaty Establishing the European Atomic Energy Community (Euratom Treaty) to promote the development of nuclear energy for peaceful purposes and to administer the multinational regional safeguards system covering the EU member states. Euratom is located in Brussels, Belgium. The members of Euratom are the EU member states.
European Union (EU)	Organization of European states, with its headquarters in Brussels, Belgium. The 2000 Treaty of Nice entered into force on 1 February 2003. The three EU 'pillars' are: the Community dimension, including the Single European Market, the Economic and Monetary Union (EMU) and the Euratom Treaty; the Common Foreign and Security Policy (CFSP); and cooperation in Justice and Home Affairs (JHA). The Treaty establishing a Constitution for Europe was signed by the EU heads of state or government in October 2004, but it will not enter into force until all the EU governments have ratified it, by a parliamentary vote or a referendum. *See* the list of members and *see also* European Atomic Energy Community.
Group of Eight (G8)	Group of eight (originally seven) leading industrialized nations which have met informally, at the level of heads of state or government, since the 1970s. *See* the list of members.
Gulf Cooperation Council (GCC)	The Cooperation Council for the Arab States of the Gulf, known as the GCC and with its headquarters in Riyadh, Saudi Arabia, was created in 1981 to promote regional integration in such areas as economy, finance, trade, administration and legislation and to foster scientific and technical progress. The members also cooperate in areas of foreign policy and military and security matters. The Supreme Council is the highest GCC authority. *See* the list of members.
Hague Code of Conduct Against Ballistic Missile Proliferation (HCOC)	The 2002 HCOC is subscribed to by a group of states which recognize its principles, primarily the need to prevent and curb the proliferation of ballistic missile systems capable of delivering weapons of mass destruction and the importance of strengthening multilateral disarmament and non-proliferation mechanisms. The Austrian Ministry of Foreign Affairs, Vienna, Austria, acts as the HCOC Secretariat. *See* the list of subscribing states.
Intergovernmental Authority on Development (IGAD)	Established in 1996 to promote peace and stability in the Horn of Africa and to create mechanisms for conflict prevention, management and resolution. Its Secretariat is in Djibouti, Djibouti. *See* the list of members.

International Atomic Energy Agency (IAEA)	An intergovernmental organization within the UN system, with headquarters in Vienna, Austria. The IAEA is endowed by its Statute, which entered into force in 1957, to promote the peaceful uses of atomic energy and ensure that nuclear activities are not used to further any military purpose. Under the NPT and the nuclear weapon-free zone treaties, non-nuclear weapon states must accept IAEA nuclear safeguards to demonstrate the fulfilment of their obligation not to manufacture nuclear weapons. *See* the list of IAEA members under United Nations.
Joint Compliance and Inspection Commission (JCIC)	The forum established by the 1991 START I Treaty in which the two parties (Russia and the United States) exchange data, resolve questions of compliance, clarify ambiguities and discuss ways to improve implementation of the START treaties. It convenes at the request of at least one of the parties.
Joint Consultative Group (JCG)	Established by the 1990 CFE Treaty to promote the objectives and implementation of the treaty by reconciling ambiguities of interpretation and implementation.
Mercado Común del Sur (MERCOSUR)	*See* Southern Common Market.
Missile Technology Control Regime (MTCR)	An informal military-related export control regime which in 1987 produced the Guidelines for Sensitive Missile-Relevant Transfers (subsequently revised). Its goal is to limit the spread of weapons of mass destruction by controlling ballistic missile delivery systems. *See* the list of participants.
NATO–Russia Council	Established in 2002 as a mechanism for consultation, consensus building, cooperation, and joint decisions and action on security issues, focusing on areas of mutual interest identified in the 1997 NATO–Russia Founding Act on Mutual Relations, Cooperation and Security and new areas, such as terrorism, crisis management and non-proliferation.
NATO–Ukraine Commission	Established in 1997 for consultations on political and security issues, conflict prevention and resolution, non-proliferation, arms exports and technology transfers, and other subjects of common concern.
Non-Aligned Movement (NAM)	Established in 1961 as a forum for consultations and coordination of positions in the United Nations on political, economic and arms control issues among non-aligned states. *See* the list of members.
North Atlantic Treaty Organization (NATO)	Established in 1949 by the North Atlantic Treaty (Washington Treaty) as a Western defence alliance. Article 5 of the treaty defines the members' commitment to respond to an armed attack against any party to the treaty. Its institutional headquarters are in Brussels, Belgium. The NATO Euro-Atlantic Partnership Council (EAPC), established in 1997, is the forum for bilateral cooperation between NATO and its Partnership for Peace partners. *See* the list of NATO and EAPC members.

Nuclear Suppliers Group (NSG)	Established in 1975 and also known as the London Club, the NSG coordinates national export controls on nuclear materials according to its Guidelines for Nuclear Transfers (London Guidelines), which contain a 'trigger list' of materials that should trigger IAEA safeguards when they are to be exported for peaceful purposes to any non-nuclear weapon state, and the Guidelines for Transfers of Nuclear-Related Dual-Use Equipment, Materials, Software and Related Technology (Warsaw Guidelines). *See* the list of participants.
Open Skies Consultative Commission (OSCC)	Established by the 1992 Open Skies Treaty to resolve questions of compliance with the treaty.
Organisation for Economic Co-operation and Development (OECD)	Established in 1961, its objectives are to promote economic and social welfare by coordinating policies among the member states. Its headquarters are in Paris, France. *See* the list of members.
Organisation for the Prohibition of Chemical Weapons (OPCW)	Established by the 1993 Chemical Weapons Convention as a body for the parties to oversee implementation of the convention and resolve questions of compliance. Its seat is in The Hague, the Netherlands.
Organisme Conjoint de Coopération en Matière d'Armement (OCCAR)	Established in 1996, with headquarters in Bonn, Germany, as a management structure for international cooperative armaments programmes between France, Germany, Italy and the UK. It is also known as the Joint Armaments Cooperation Organization (JACO).
Organization for Security and Co-operation in Europe (OSCE)	Initiated in 1973 as the Conference on Security and Co-operation in Europe (CSCE), in 1995 it was renamed the OSCE and transformed into an organization, with headquarters in Vienna, Austria, as a primary instrument for early warning, conflict prevention and crisis management. Its Forum for Security Co-operation (FSC), located in Vienna, Austria, deals with arms control and CSBMs. The OSCE comprises several institutions, all located in Europe. *See* the list of members, and *see also* Stability Pace for South Eastern Europe.
Organization of American States (OAS)	Group of states in the Americas which adopted its charter in 1948, with the objective of strengthening peace and security in the western hemisphere. The General Secretariat is in Washington, DC, USA. *See* the list of members.
Organization of the Black Sea Economic Cooperation (BSEC)	Established in 1992, with its Permanent Secretariat in Istanbul, Turkey. Its aims are to ensure peace, stability and prosperity in the Black Sea region and to promote and develop economic cooperation and progress. *See* the list of members.
Organization of the Islamic Conference (OIC)	Established in 1971 by Islamic states to promote cooperation among the members and to support peace, security and the struggle of the people of Palestine and all Muslim people. Its Secretariat is in Jeddah, Saudi Arabia. *See* the list of members.

Pacific Islands Forum	Founded in 1971, a group of South Pacific states that proposed the South Pacific Nuclear Free Zone, embodied in the 1985 Treaty of Rarotonga, and contribute to monitoring implementation of the treaty. The Secretariat is in Suva, Fiji. *See* the list of members.
Proliferation Security Initiative (PSI)	Based on a US initiative announced in 2003, the PSI is a multilateral activity focusing on law enforcement cooperation for the interdiction and seizure of illegal weapons of mass destruction, missile technologies and related materials when in transit on land, in the air or at sea. The PSI has a 'core group' of 11 participants plus at least 60 supporting states. The PSI Statement of Interdiction Principles was issued in 2003.
Shanghai Cooperation Organization (SCO)	The predecessor group the Shanghai Five was founded in 1996; it was renamed the SCO in 2001 and opened for membership of all states that support its aims. The member states cooperate on confidence-building measures and regional security and in the economic sphere. The SCO Secretariat is in Beijing, China. *See* the list of members.
South Asian Association for Regional Co-operation (SAARC)	Created in 1985 as an association of states to promote political and economic regional cooperation, with its secretariat in Kathmandu, Nepal. *See* the list of members.
Southeast European Cooperative Initiative (SECI)	An initiative launched by the USA in 1996 to promote cooperation and stability among the countries of southern Europe and facilitate their accession to the European Union. The SECI Secretariat is located in the OSCE offices in Vienna. *See* the list of members.
Southern African Development Community (SADC)	Established in 1992 to promote regional economic development and fundamental principles of sovereignty, peace and security, human rights and democracy. The Secretariat is in Gaborone, Botswana. *See* the list of members.
Southern Common Market (MERCOSUR)	Established in 1991 to achieve economic integration between the member states. In 1996 it adopted a decision that only countries with democratic, accountable institutions in place would be allowed to participate. The Common Market Council is the highest decision-making body, and the Common Market Group is the permanent executive body. The Secretariat is in Montevideo, Uruguay. *See* the list of members.
Stability Pact for South Eastern Europe	Initiated by the EU at the 1999 Conference on South Eastern Europe and subsequently placed under OSCE auspices, the Pact is intended to provide the sub-region with a comprehensive, long-term conflict prevention strategy by promoting political and economic reforms, development and enhanced security, and integration of South-East European countries into the Euro-Atlantic structures. Its activities are coordinated by the South Eastern Europe Regional Table and chaired by the Special Co-ordinator of the Stability Pact. The seat of the Special Co-ordinator is in Brussels, Belgium. *See* the list of partners.

Sub-Regional Consultative Commission (SRCC)	Established by the 1996 Agreement on Sub-Regional Arms Control concerning Yugoslavia (Florence Agreement) as the forum in which the parties resolve questions of compliance with the agreement.
United Nations (UN)	The world intergovernmental organization with headquarters in New York, USA. It was founded in 1945 through the adoption of its Charter. The six principal UN organs are the General Assembly, the Security Council, the Economic and Social Council (ECOSOC), the Trusteeship Council, the International Court of Justice (ICJ) and the Secretariat. The UN also has a large number of specialized agencies and other autonomous bodies. *See* the list of members.
Visegrad Group (V4)	A group four Central European states formed in 1991 as a forum for cooperation in the process of European integration. *See* the list of members.
Wassenaar Arrangement (WA)	The Wassenaar Arrangement on Export Controls for Conventional Arms and Dual-Use Goods and Technologies was formally established in 1996. It aims to prevent the acquisition of armaments and sensitive dual-use goods and technologies for military uses by states whose behaviour is cause for concern to the member states. *See* the list of participants.
Western European Union (WEU)	Established by the 1954 Modified Brussels Treaty. The seat of the WEU is in Brussels, Belgium. WEU operational activities (the 'Petersberg Tasks') were transferred to the EU in 2000. The Interparliamentary European Security and Defence Assembly, seated in Paris, France, scrutinizes intergovernmental cooperation in the Western European Armaments Organisation (WEAO). *See* the list of members.
Zangger Committee	Established in 1971, the Nuclear Exporters Committee, called the Zangger Committee, is a group of nuclear supplier countries that meets informally twice a year to coordinate export controls on nuclear materials according to its regularly updated trigger list of items which, when exported, must be subject to IAEA safeguards. It complements the work of the NSG (*see* Nuclear Suppliers Group). *See* the list of participants.

Membership of intergovernmental bodies and international organizations as of 1 January 2006

The UN member states and organizations within the UN system are listed first, followed by all other organizations in alphabetical order. Note that not all members or participants of the organizations are UN member states. Membership is as of 1 January 2006. The address of an Internet site with information about each organization is provided where available.

United Nations members (191) and year of membership
<http://www.un.org>

Afghanistan, 1946
Albania, 1955
Algeria, 1962
Andorra, 1993
Angola, 1976
Antigua and Barbuda, 1981
Argentina, 1945
Armenia, 1992
Australia, 1945
Austria, 1955
Azerbaijan, 1992
Bahamas, 1973
Bahrain, 1971
Bangladesh, 1974
Barbados, 1966
Belarus, 1945
Belgium, 1945
Belize, 1981
Benin, 1960
Bhutan, 1971
Bolivia, 1945
Bosnia and Herzegovina, 1992
Botswana, 1966
Brazil, 1945
Brunei Darussalam, 1984
Bulgaria, 1955
Burkina Faso, 1960
Burundi, 1962
Cambodia, 1955
Cameroon, 1960
Canada, 1945
Cape Verde, 1975
Central African Republic, 1960
Chad, 1960
Chile, 1945
China, 1945
Colombia, 1945
Comoros, 1975
Congo, Democratic Republic of the, 1960
Congo, Republic of the, 1960
Costa Rica, 1945
Côte d'Ivoire, 1960
Croatia, 1992
Cuba, 1945
Cyprus, 1960

Czech Republic, 1993
Denmark, 1945
Djibouti, 1977
Dominica, 1978
Dominican Republic, 1945
Ecuador, 1945
Egypt, 1945
El Salvador, 1945
Equatorial Guinea, 1968
Eritrea, 1993
Estonia, 1991
Ethiopia, 1945
Fiji, 1970
Finland, 1955
France, 1945
Gabon, 1960
Gambia, 1965
Georgia, 1992
Germany, 1973
Ghana, 1957
Greece, 1945
Grenada, 1974
Guatemala, 1945
Guinea, 1958
Guinea-Bissau, 1974
Guyana, 1966
Haiti, 1945
Honduras, 1945
Hungary, 1955
Iceland, 1946
India, 1945
Indonesia, 1950
Iran, 1945
Iraq, 1945
Ireland, 1955
Israel, 1949
Italy, 1955
Jamaica, 1962
Japan, 1956
Jordan, 1955
Kazakhstan, 1992
Kenya, 1963
Kiribati, 1999
Korea, Democratic People's Republic of (North Korea), 1991

Korea, Republic of (South Korea), 1991
Kuwait, 1963
Kyrgyzstan, 1992
Laos, 1955
Latvia, 1991
Lebanon, 1945
Lesotho, 1966
Liberia, 1945
Libya, 1955
Liechtenstein, 1990
Lithuania, 1991
Luxembourg, 1945
Macedonia, Former Yugoslav Republic of, 1993
Madagascar, 1960
Malawi, 1964
Malaysia, 1957
Maldives, 1965
Mali, 1960
Malta, 1964
Marshall Islands, 1991
Mauritania, 1961
Mauritius, 1968
Mexico, 1945
Micronesia, 1991
Moldova, 1992
Monaco, 1993
Mongolia, 1961
Morocco, 1956
Mozambique, 1975
Myanmar (Burma), 1948
Namibia, 1990
Nauru, 1999
Nepal, 1955
Netherlands, 1945
New Zealand, 1945
Nicaragua, 1945
Niger, 1960
Nigeria, 1960
Norway, 1945
Oman, 1971
Pakistan, 1947
Palau, 1994
Panama, 1945
Papua New Guinea, 1975

Paraguay, 1945
Peru, 1945
Philippines, 1945
Poland, 1945
Portugal, 1955
Qatar, 1971
Romania, 1955
Russia, 1945
Rwanda, 1962
Saint Kitts and Nevis, 1983
Saint Lucia, 1979
Saint Vincent and the
  Grenadines, 1980
Samoa, 1976
San Marino, 1992
Sao Tome and Principe, 1975
Saudi Arabia, 1945
Senegal, 1960
Serbia and Montenegro, 2000
Seychelles, 1976

Sierra Leone, 1961
Singapore, 1965
Slovakia, 1993
Slovenia, 1992
Solomon Islands, 1978
Somalia, 1960
South Africa, 1945
Spain, 1955
Sri Lanka, 1955
Sudan, 1956
Suriname, 1975
Swaziland, 1968
Sweden, 1946
Switzerland, 2002
Syria, 1945
Tajikistan, 1992
Tanzania, 1961
Thailand, 1946
Timor-Leste, 2002
Togo, 1960

Tonga, 1999
Trinidad and Tobago, 1962
Tunisia, 1956
Turkey, 1945
Turkmenistan, 1992
Tuvalu, 2000
Uganda, 1962
UK, 1945
Ukraine, 1945
United Arab Emirates, 1971
Uruguay, 1945
USA, 1945
Uzbekistan, 1992
Vanuatu, 1981
Venezuela, 1945
Viet Nam, 1977
Yemen, 1947
Zambia, 1964
Zimbabwe, 1980

UN Security Council
<http://www.un.org/Docs/sc/>

Permanent members (the P5): China, France, Russia, UK, USA

Non-permanent members in 2006 (elected by the UN General Assembly for two-year terms; the year in brackets is the year at the end of which the term expires): Argentina (2006), Congo, Republic of the (2007), Denmark (2006), Ghana (2007), Greece (2006), Japan (2006), Peru (2007), Qatar (2007), Slovakia (2007), Tanzania (2006)

Conference on Disarmament (CD)
<http://disarmament2.un.org/cd>

Algeria, Argentina, Australia, Austria, Bangladesh, Belarus, Belgium, Brazil, Bulgaria, Cameroon, Canada, Chile, China, Colombia, Congo (Democratic Republic of the), Cuba, Ecuador, Egypt, Ethiopia, Finland, France, Germany, Hungary, India, Indonesia, Iran, Iraq, Ireland, Israel, Italy, Japan, Kazakhstan, Kenya, Korea (North), Korea (South), Malaysia, Mexico, Mongolia, Morocco, Myanmar (Burma), Netherlands, New Zealand, Nigeria, Norway, Pakistan, Peru, Poland, Romania, Russia, Senegal, Slovakia, South Africa, Spain, Sri Lanka, Sweden, Switzerland, Syria, Tunisia, Turkey, UK, Ukraine, USA, Venezuela, Viet Nam, Zimbabwe

International Atomic Energy Agency (IAEA)
<http://www.iaea.org>

Afghanistan, Albania, Algeria, Angola, Argentina, Armenia, Australia, Austria, Azerbaijan, Bangladesh, Belarus, Belgium, Benin, Bolivia, Bosnia and Herzegovina, Botswana, Brazil, Bulgaria, Burkina Faso, Cameroon, Canada, Central African Republic, Chad, Chile, China, Colombia, Congo (Democratic Republic of the), Costa Rica, Côte d'Ivoire, Croatia, Cuba, Cyprus, Czech Republic, Denmark, Dominican Republic, Ecuador, Egypt, El Salvador, Eritrea, Estonia, Ethiopia, Finland, France, Gabon, Georgia, Germany, Ghana, Greece, Guatemala, Haiti, Holy See, Honduras, Hungary, Iceland, India, Indonesia, Iran, Iraq, Ireland, Israel, Italy, Jamaica, Japan, Jordan, Kazakhstan, Kenya, Korea (South), Kuwait, Kyrgyzstan, Latvia, Lebanon, Liberia, Libya, Liechtenstein, Lithuania, Luxembourg, Macedonia (Former Yugoslav Republic of), Madagascar, Malaysia, Mali, Malta, Marshall Islands, Mauritania, Mauritius, Mexico, Moldova, Monaco, Mongolia, Morocco, Myanmar (Burma), Namibia, Netherlands, New Zealand, Nicaragua, Niger, Nigeria, Norway, Pakistan, Panama, Paraguay, Peru, Philippines, Poland, Portugal, Qatar, Romania, Russia, Saudi Arabia, Senegal, Serbia and Montenegro, Seychelles, Sierra Leone, Singapore, Slovakia, Slovenia, South Africa, Spain, Sri Lanka, Sudan, Sweden, Switzerland, Syria, Tajikistan, Tanzania, Thailand, Togo, Tunisia,

Turkey, Uganda, UK, Ukraine, United Arab Emirates, Uruguay, USA, Uzbekistan, Venezuela, Viet Nam, Yemen, Zambia, Zimbabwe

Note: North Korea was a member of the IAEA until June 1994. Cambodia withdrew its membership as of March 2003.

African Union (AU)
<http://www.africa-union.org>

Algeria, Angola, Benin, Botswana, Burkina Faso, Burundi, Cameroon, Cape Verde, Central African Republic, Chad, Comoros, Congo (Democratic Republic of the), Congo (Republic of the), Côte d'Ivoire, Djibouti, Egypt, Equatorial Guinea, Eritrea, Ethiopia, Gabon, Gambia, Ghana, Guinea, Guinea-Bissau, Kenya, Lesotho, Liberia, Libya, Madagascar, Malawi, Mali, Mauritania, Mauritius, Mozambique, Namibia, Niger, Nigeria, Rwanda, Western Sahara (Sahrawi Arab Democratic Republic, SADR), Sao Tome and Principe, Senegal, Seychelles, Sierra Leone, Somalia, South Africa, Sudan, Swaziland, Tanzania, Togo, Tunisia, Uganda, Zambia, Zimbabwe

Andean Community of Nations
<http://www.comunidadandina.org>

Bolivia, Colombia, Ecuador, Peru, Venezuela

Arab League
<http://www.arableagueonline.org/>

Algeria, Bahrain, Comoros, Djibouti, Egypt, Iraq, Jordan, Kuwait, Lebanon, Libya, Mauritania, Morocco, Oman, Palestine, Qatar, Saudi Arabia, Somalia, Sudan, Syria, Tunisia, United Arab Emirates, Yemen

Association of South East Asian Nations (ASEAN)
<http://www.aseansec.org>

Brunei Darussalam, Cambodia, Indonesia, Laos, Malaysia, Myanmar (Burma), Philippines, Singapore, Thailand, Viet Nam

ASEAN Regional Forum (ARF)
<http://www.aseanregionalforum.org>

The ASEAN member states plus Australia, Canada, China, European Union, India, Japan, Korea (North), Korea (South), Mongolia, New Zealand, Pakistan, Papua New Guinea, Russia, Timor-Leste, USA

ASEAN Plus Three
<http://www.aseansec.org/16580.htm>

The ASEAN member states plus China, Japan and Korea (South)

Australia Group (AG)
<http://www.australiagroup.net>

Argentina, Australia, Austria, Belgium, Bulgaria, Canada, Cyprus, Czech Republic, Denmark, Estonia, European Commission, Finland, France, Germany, Greece, Hungary, Iceland, Ireland, Italy, Japan, Korea (South), Latvia, Lithuania, Luxembourg, Malta, Netherlands, New Zealand, Norway, Poland, Portugal, Romania, Slovakia, Slovenia, Spain, Sweden, Switzerland, Turkey, UK, Ukraine, USA

Central European Initiative (CEI)
<http://www.ceinet.org>

Albania, Austria, Belarus, Bosnia and Herzegovina, Bulgaria, Croatia, Czech Republic, Hungary, Italy, Macedonia (Former Yugoslav Republic of), Moldova, Poland, Romania, Serbia and Montenegro, Slovakia, Slovenia, Ukraine

Collective Security Treaty Organization (CSTO)

Armenia, Belarus, Kazakhstan, Kyrgyzstan, Russia, Tajikistan

Commonwealth of Independent States (CIS)

<http://www.cis.minsk.by>

Armenia, Azerbaijan, Belarus, Georgia, Kazakhstan, Kyrgyzstan, Moldova, Russia, Tajikistan, Turkmenistan*, Ukraine, Uzbekistan

* Turkmenistan announced in 2005 that it will become an associate member of the CIS.

Commonwealth of Nations

<http://www.thecommonwealth.org>

Antigua and Barbuda, Australia, Bahamas, Bangladesh, Barbados, Belize, Botswana, Brunei Darussalam, Cameroon, Canada, Cyprus, Dominica, Fiji, Gambia, Ghana, Grenada, Guyana, India, Jamaica, Kenya, Kiribati, Lesotho, Malawi, Malaysia, Maldives, Malta, Mauritius, Mozambique, Namibia, Nauru, New Zealand, Nigeria, Pakistan, Papua New Guinea, Saint Kitts and Nevis, Saint Lucia, Saint Vincent and the Grenadines, Samoa, Seychelles, Sierra Leone, Singapore, Solomon Islands, South Africa, Sri Lanka, Swaziland, Tanzania, Tonga, Trinidad and Tobago, Tuvalu, Uganda, UK, Vanuatu, Zambia

Conference on Interaction and Confidence-building Measures in Asia (CICA)

<http://www.kazakhstanembassy.org.uk/cgi-bin/index/128>

Afghanistan, Azerbaijan, China, Egypt, India, Iran, Israel, Kazakhstan, Kyrgyzstan, Mongolia, Pakistan, Palestine, Russia, Tajikistan, Thailand, Turkey, Uzbekistan

Council for Security Cooperation in the Asia Pacific (CSCAP)

<http://www.cscap.org>

Member committees: Australia, Brunei Darussalam, Cambodia, Canada, China, CSCAP Europe, India, Indonesia, Japan, Korea (North), Korea (South), Malaysia, Mongolia, New Zealand, Papua New Guinea, Philippines, Russia, Singapore, Thailand, USA, Viet Nam

Council of Europe

<http://www.coe.int>

Albania, Andorra, Armenia, Austria, Azerbaijan, Belgium, Bosnia and Herzegovina, Bulgaria, Croatia, Cyprus, Czech Republic, Denmark, Estonia, Finland, France, Georgia, Germany, Greece, Hungary, Iceland, Ireland, Italy, Latvia, Liechtenstein, Lithuania, Luxembourg, Macedonia (Former Yugoslav Republic of), Malta, Moldova, Monaco, Netherlands, Norway, Poland, Portugal, Romania, Russia, San Marino, Serbia and Montenegro, Slovakia, Slovenia, Spain, Sweden, Switzerland, Turkey, UK, Ukraine

Council of the Baltic Sea States (CBSS)

<http://www.cbss.st>

Denmark, Estonia, European Commission, Finland, Germany, Iceland, Latvia, Lithuania, Norway, Poland, Russia, Sweden

Economic Community of West African States (ECOWAS)

<http://www.ecowas.int>

Benin, Burkina Faso, Cape Verde, Côte d'Ivoire, Gambia, Ghana, Guinea, Guinea-Bissau, Liberia, Mali, Niger, Nigeria, Senegal, Sierra Leone, Togo

European Union (EU)

<http://europa.eu.int>

Austria, Belgium, Cyprus, Czech Republic, Denmark, Estonia, Finland, France, Germany, Greece, Hungary, Ireland, Italy, Latvia, Lithuania, Luxembourg, Malta, Netherlands, Poland, Portugal, Slovakia, Slovenia, Spain, Sweden, UK

Group of Eight (G8)
<http://www.g8.utoronto.ca>
Canada, France, Germany, Italy, Japan, Russia, UK, USA

Gulf Cooperation Council (GCC)
<http://www.gcc-sg.org>
Bahrain, Kuwait, Oman, Qatar, Saudi Arabia, United Arab Emirates

Hague Code of Conduct against Ballistic Missile Proliferation (HCOC)
<http://www.bmaa.gv.at/view.php3?f_id=54&LNG=en&version=>

Afghanistan, Albania, Andorra, Argentina, Armenia, Australia, Austria, Azerbaijan, Belarus, Belgium, Benin, Bosnia and Herzegovina, Bulgaria, Burkina Faso, Burundi, Cambodia, Cameroon, Canada, Cape Verde, Chad, Chile, Colombia, Comoros, Cook Islands, Costa Rica, Croatia, Cyprus, Czech Republic, Denmark, Ecuador, El Salvador, Eritrea, Estonia, Fiji, Finland, France, Gabon, Gambia, Georgia, Germany, Ghana, Greece, Guatemala, Guinea, Guinea-Bissau, Guyana, Haiti, Holy See, Honduras, Hungary, Iceland, Ireland, Italy, Japan, Jordan, Kazakhstan, Kenya, Kiribati, Korea (South), Latvia, Liberia, Libya, Liechtenstein, Lithuania, Luxembourg, Macedonia (Former Yugoslav Republic of), Madagascar, Malawi, Mali, Malta, Marshall Islands, Mauritania, Micronesia, Moldova, Monaco, Mongolia Morocco, Mozambique, Netherlands, New Zealand, Nicaragua, Niger, Nigeria, Norway, Palau, Panama, Papua New Guinea, Paraguay, Peru, Philippines, Poland, Portugal, Romania, Russia, Rwanda, Senegal, Serbia and Montenegro, Seychelles, Sierra Leone, Slovakia, Slovenia, South Africa, Spain, Sudan, Suriname, Sweden, Switzerland, Tajikistan, Tanzania, Timor-Leste, Tonga, Tunisia, Turkey, Turkmenistan, Tuvalu, Uganda, UK, Ukraine, Uruguay, USA, Uzbekistan, Vanuatu, Venezuela, Zambia

Intergovernmental Authority on Development (IGAD)
<http://www.igad.org>
Djibouti, Eritrea, Ethiopia, Kenya, Somalia, Sudan, Uganda

Missile Technology Control Regime (MTCR)
<http://www.mtcr.info>
Argentina, Australia, Austria, Belgium, Brazil, Bulgaria, Canada, Czech Republic, Denmark, Finland, France, Germany, Greece, Hungary, Iceland, Ireland, Italy, Japan, Korea (South), Luxembourg, Netherlands, New Zealand, Norway, Poland, Portugal, Russia, South Africa, Spain, Sweden, Switzerland, Turkey, UK, Ukraine, USA

Non-Aligned Movement (NAM)
<http://www.e-nam.org.my/main.php?pg=2>
Afghanistan, Algeria, Angola, Bahamas, Bahrain, Bangladesh, Barbados, Belarus, Belize, Benin, Bhutan, Bolivia, Botswana, Brunei Darussalam, Burkina Faso, Burundi, Cambodia, Cameroon, Cape Verde, Central African Republic, Chad, Chile, Colombia, Comoros, Congo (Democratic Republic of the), Congo (Republic of the), Côte d'Ivoire, Cuba, Djibouti, Dominican Republic, Ecuador, Egypt, Equatorial Guinea, Eritrea, Ethiopia, Gabon, Gambia, Ghana, Grenada, Guatemala, Guinea, Guinea-Bissau, Guyana, Honduras, India, Indonesia, Iran, Iraq, Jamaica, Jordan, Kenya, Korea (North), Kuwait, Laos, Lebanon, Lesotho, Liberia, Libya, Madagascar, Malawi, Malaysia, Maldives, Mali, Mauritania, Mauritius, Mongolia, Morocco, Mozambique, Myanmar (Burma), Namibia, Nepal, Nicaragua, Niger, Nigeria, Oman, Pakistan, Palestine Liberation Organization, Panama, Papua New Guinea, Peru, Philippines, Qatar, Rwanda, Saint Lucia, Saint Vincent and the Grenadines, Sao Tome and Principe, Saudi Arabia, Senegal, Seychelles, Sierra Leone, Singapore, Somalia, South Africa, Sri Lanka, Sudan, Suriname, Swaziland, Syria, Tanzania, Thailand, Timor-Leste, Togo, Trinidad and Tobago, Tunisia, Turkmenistan, Uganda, United Arab Emirates, Uzbeistan, Vanuatu, Venezuela, Viet Nam, Yemen, Zambia, Zimbabwe

North Atlantic Treaty Organization (NATO)
<http://www.nato.int>

Belgium, Bulgaria, Canada, Czech Republic, Denmark, Estonia, France*, Germany, Greece, Hungary, Iceland, Italy, Latvia, Lithuania, Luxembourg, Netherlands, Norway, Poland, Portugal, Romania, Slovakia, Slovenia, Spain, Turkey, UK, USA

* France is not in the integrated military structures of NATO.

Euro-Atlantic Partnership Council (EAPC)
<http://www.nato.int/issues/eapc>

The NATO member states plus Albania, Armenia, Austria, Azerbaijan, Belarus, Croatia, Finland, Georgia, Ireland, Kazakhstan, Kyrgyzstan, Macedonia (Former Yugoslav Republic of), Moldova, Russia, Sweden, Switzerland, Tajikistan, Turkmenistan, Ukraine, Uzbekistan

Nuclear Suppliers Group (NSG)
<http://www.nuclearsuppliersgroup.org>

Argentina, Australia, Austria, Belarus, Belgium, Brazil, Bulgaria, Canada, China, Croatia, Cyprus, Czech Republic, Denmark, Estonia, Finland, France, Germany, Greece, Hungary, Ireland, Italy, Japan, Kazakhstan, Korea (South), Latvia, Lithuania, Luxembourg, Malta, Netherlands, New Zealand, Norway, Poland, Portugal, Romania, Russia, Slovakia, Slovenia, South Africa, Spain, Sweden, Switzerland, Turkey, UK, Ukraine, USA

Organisation for Economic Co-operation and Development (OECD)
<http://www.oecd.org>

Australia, Austria, Belgium, Canada, Czech Republic, Denmark, Finland, France, Germany, Greece, Hungary, Iceland, Ireland, Italy, Japan, Korea (South), Luxembourg, Mexico, Netherlands, New Zealand, Norway, Poland, Portugal, Slovakia, Spain, Sweden, Switzerland, Turkey, UK, USA

Organization for Security and Co-operation in Europe (OSCE)
<http://www.osce.org>

Albania, Andorra, Armenia, Austria, Azerbaijan, Belarus, Belgium, Bosnia and Herzegovina, Bulgaria, Canada, Croatia, Cyprus, Czech Republic, Denmark, Estonia, Finland, France, Georgia, Germany, Greece, Holy See, Hungary, Iceland, Ireland, Italy, Kazakhstan, Kyrgyzstan, Latvia, Liechtenstein, Lithuania, Luxembourg, Macedonia (Former Yugoslav Republic of), Malta, Moldova, Monaco, Netherlands, Norway, Poland, Portugal, Romania, Russia, San Marino, Serbia and Montenegro, Slovakia, Slovenia, Spain, Sweden, Switzerland, Tajikistan, Turkey, Turkmenistan, UK, Ukraine, USA, Uzbekistan

Organization of American States (OAS)
<http://www.oas.org>

Antigua and Barbuda, Argentina, Bahamas, Barbados, Belize, Bolivia, Brazil, Canada, Chile, Colombia, Costa Rica, Cuba*, Dominica, Dominican Republic, Ecuador, El Salvador, Grenada, Guatemala, Guyana, Haiti, Honduras, Jamaica, Mexico, Nicaragua, Panama, Paraguay, Peru, Saint Kitts and Nevis, Saint Lucia, Saint Vincent and the Grenadines, Suriname, Trinidad and Tobago, Uruguay, USA, Venezuela

* Cuba has been excluded from participation in the OAS since 1962.

Organization of the Black Sea Economic Cooperation (BSEC)
<http://www.bsec-organization.org>

Albania, Armenia, Azerbaijan, Bulgaria, Georgia, Greece, Moldova, Romania, Russia, Serbia and Montenegro, Turkey, Ukraine

Organization of the Islamic Conference (OIC)
<http://www.oic-oci.org>

Afghanistan, Albania, Algeria, Azerbaijan, Bahrain, Bangladesh, Benin, Brunei Darussalam, Burkina Faso, Cameroon, Chad, Comoros, Côte d'Ivoire, Djibouti, Egypt, Gabon, Gambia, Guinea, Guinea-Bissau, Guyana, Indonesia, Iran, Iraq, Jordan, Kazakhstan, Kuwait, Kyrgyzstan, Lebanon, Libya, Malaysia, Maldives, Mali, Mauritania, Morocco, Mozambique, Niger, Nigeria, Oman, Pakistan, Palestine, Qatar, Saudi Arabia, Senegal, Sierra Leone, Somalia, Sudan, Suriname, Syria, Tajikistan, Togo, Tunisia, Turkey, Turkmenistan, Uganda, United Arab Emirates, Uzbekistan, Yemen

Pacific Islands Forum
<http://www.forumsec.org.fj>

Australia, Cook Islands, Fiji, Kiribati, Marshall Islands, Micronesia, Nauru, New Zealand, Niue, Palau, Papua New Guinea, Samoa, Solomon Islands, Tonga, Tuvalu, Vanuatu

Shanghai Cooperation Organization (SCO)
<http://www.sectsco.org>

China, Kazakhstan, Kyrgyzstan, Russia, Tajikistan, Uzbekistan

South Asian Association for Regional Co-operation (SAARC)
<http://www.saarc-sec.org>

Afghanistan, Bangladesh, Bhutan, India, Maldives, Nepal, Pakistan, Sri Lanka

Southeast European Cooperative Initiative (SECI)
<http://www.secinet.info>

Albania, Bosnia and Herzegovina, Bulgaria, Croatia, Greece, Hungary, Macedonia (Former Yugoslav Republic of), Moldova, Romania, Slovenia, Turkey, Serbia and Montenegro

Southern African Development Community (SADC)
<http://www.sadc.int>

Angola, Botswana, Congo (Democratic Republic of the), Lesotho, Madagascar, Malawi, Mauritius, Mozambique, Namibia, South Africa, Swaziland, Tanzania, Zambia, Zimbabwe

Southern Common Market (Mercado Común del Sur, MERCOSUR)
<http://www.mercosur.org.uy>

Argentina, Brazil, Paraguay, Uruguay

Stability Pact for South Eastern Europe
<http://www.stabilitypact.org>

Country partners: Albania, Austria, Belgium, Bosnia and Herzegovina, Bulgaria, Canada, Croatia, Cyprus, Czech Republic, Denmark, Estonia, Finland, France, Germany, Greece, Hungary, Ireland, Italy, Japan, Latvia, Lithuania, Luxembourg, Macedonia (Former Yugoslav Republic of), Malta, Moldova, Netherlands, Norway, Poland, Portugal, Romania, Russia, Serbia and Montenegro, Slovakia, Slovenia, Spain, Sweden, Switzerland, Turkey, UK, USA

Other partners: Central European Initiative, Council of Europe, (Council of Europe Development Bank), European Bank for Reconstruction and Development, European Investment Bank, European Union (Council of the European Union, European Agency for Reconstruction, European Commission, European Parliament, Office for South Eastern Europe), International Finance Corporation, International Monetary Fund, International Organization for Migration, North Atlantic Treaty Organization, Office of the High Representative in Bosnia and Herzegovina, Organisation for Economic Co-operation and Development, Organization for Security and Co-operation in Europe, Organization of the Black Sea Economic Cooperation, Southeast European Cooperative Initiative, South-East European Cooperation Process, United Nations (UN Development Programme, UN High Commissioner for Refugees, UN Mission in Kosovo), World Bank

Visegrad Group (V4)
<http://www.visegradgroup.org>

Czech Republic, Hungary, Poland, Slovakia

Wassenaar Arrangement (WA)
<http://www.wassenaar.org>

Argentina, Australia, Austria, Belgium, Bulgaria, Canada, Croatia, Czech Republic, Denmark, Estonia, Finland, France, Germany, Greece, Hungary, Ireland, Italy, Japan, Korea (South), Latvia, Lithuania, Luxembourg, Malta, Netherlands, New Zealand, Norway, Poland, Portugal, Romania, Russia, Slovakia, Slovenia, South Africa, Spain, Sweden, Switzerland, Turkey, UK, Ukraine, USA

Western European Union (WEU)
<http://www.weu.int>

Belgium, France, Germany, Greece, Italy, Luxembourg, Netherlands, Portugal, Spain, UK

Western European Armaments Organisation (WEAO)
Austria, Belgium, Czech Republic, Denmark, Finland, France, Germany, Greece, Hungary, Italy, Luxembourg, Netherlands, Norway, Poland, Portugal, Spain, Sweden, Turkey, UK

Zangger Committee
<http://www.zanggercommittee.org/Zangger/default.htm>

Argentina, Australia, Austria, Belgium, Bulgaria, Canada, China, Czech Republic, Denmark, European Commission, Finland, France, Germany, Greece, Hungary, Ireland, Italy, Japan, Korea (South), Luxembourg, Netherlands, Norway, Poland, Portugal, Romania, Russia, Slovakia, Slovenia, South Africa, Spain, Sweden, Switzerland, Turkey, UK, Ukraine, USA

Conventions

. .	Data not available or not applicable
–	Nil or a negligible figure
( )	Uncertain data
b.	Billion (thousand million)
kg	Kilogram
km	Kilometre (1000 metres)
kt	Kiloton (1000 tonnes)
m.	Million
Mt	Megaton (1 million tonnes)
th.	Thousand
tr.	Trillion (million million)
$	US dollars, unless otherwise indicated
€	Euros

Introduction

The world of security and peace research in a 40-year perspective

ALYSON J. K. BAILES

I. Introduction

The first SIPRI Yearbook was published in 1969 under the leadership of SIPRI's first Director, Robert Neild.[1] It described a world dominated by the East–West strategic confrontation of the cold war, in which few countries—Sweden being one of them—could avoid becoming militarily aligned with one bloc or the other, and few observers—SIPRI itself aspiring to be one—were in a position to look impartially at the behaviour of both blocs. The strategic temperature in 1969 was hardly at its warmest: only two years earlier the Harmel Report had proposed that the strength of the North Atlantic Treaty Organization (NATO) should be paired with efforts to reach out to the other side in détente,[2] but the brutal realities were underlined in 1968 by the Soviet-led military invasion that crushed a democratic movement in Czechoslovakia. When SIPRI's analysts wrote about developments in weaponry and military technology, therefore, it was natural that they should see the East–West rivalry between the Soviet Union and the United States and between the Warsaw Treaty Organization (Warsaw Pact) and NATO as the main driver of the arms race and the most dangerous context in which weaponry might be used. It is to their credit that, nevertheless, they devoted great attention to conflicts and arms races elsewhere in the world that lacked any direct connection with cold war politics. In doing so and in seeking to document military expenditure in all the world's countries and regions, the drafters of the first Yearbook set targets of comprehensiveness and balance that their successors have always kept in sight, while never finding them simple to achieve.

The present Yearbook is SIPRI's 36th and appears 40 years after the Institute was founded. It presents a natural opportunity to review what has changed and what has not over the past four decades of global security development. While many specific perspectives of change are taken up in subsequent chapters, this introduction is limited to four main themes. Section II looks at the

---

[1] *SIPRI Yearbook of World Armaments and Disarmament 1968/69* (Almqvist & Wiksell: Stockholm, 1969).

[2] NATO, 'The future tasks of the Alliance: report of the Council', Ministerial Communiqué, North Atlantic Council, Brussels, 13–14 Dec. 1967, URL <http://www.nato.int/docu/comm/49-95/c671213b. htm>. The report was written by a study group headed by Pierre Harmel, Belgian Foreign Minister; the full text of the report is available at URL <http://www.nato.int/archives/harmel/harmel.htm>.

transition from an East–West strategic polarity to a global system in which several other kinds of polarity or organizing principles have been mooted, but none has (yet) gained a clear ascendancy. Section III deals with changes in the kind of objects, events, processes and actors that are regarded as important for security analysis and influential—for good or ill—in security developments. Section IV discusses the changing evaluation of, and approaches to, arms control and disarmament and expands on the role of various institutions in security building more generally. Section V closes by highlighting some concerns reflected in the first SIPRI Yearbook that are still all too present today and by underlining the importance of data-based security research and transparency.

II. From East–West confrontation to what?

It became something of a truism in the 1990s, but is none the less true for that, that the bipolar strategic scene of cold war times had some convenient and even comforting features for policy makers. Each side in the confrontation found it easy to identify the primary source of threat and relatively easy to quantify it. Distinctions between friend and foe were for the most part clear, and the peccadilloes of some friends could be overlooked in view of their strategic value. While the obligations of friendship were onerous, demanding from the West's larger powers a constant vigilance against Communist encroachments, no compunction was felt about the welfare of a large category of states 'on the other side'. At the same time, arms control and disarmament processes and other rule-based frameworks that reached across bloc divisions played a clear and widely valued role in limiting both the existential risks and the economic costs of confrontation.

New geo-strategic models

Since the collapse of the two-bloc system in 1989, many thinkers and policy makers have been tempted to seek a 'quick fix' for describing the new strategic environment in terms of equally well-defined camps. Roughly speaking, the formulas proposed for this can be divided into those that still recognize something like geo-strategic 'blocs' and those that use less traditional categories. Among theories of the former type, the notion of East–West tensions being overtaken by North–South ones—manifesting themselves more in the realm of economics and human security than through military relations—has been persistent because it has real descriptive value. There is no precise dividing line between the North and the South,[3] but it is broadly true that the

---

[3] On this point and on the North–South dimension of contemporary security problems in general see Bailes, A. J. K., 'Global security governance: a world of change and challenge', *SIPRI Yearbook 2005: Armaments, Disarmament and International Security* (Oxford University Press: Oxford, 2005), pp. 1–27.

great majority of armed conflicts now occur in Southern locations[4] and that both the levels and the prime causes of mortality are different there from those prevailing among powers in the North, including China and Russia. In recent years there have been growing signs of deliberate South–South cooperation, both in defending developing countries' characteristic commercial and economic interests[5] and in the pattern of arms sales and related technology transfers.[6] Adopting a North–South diagnostic, however, can only lead to a recognition of how different today's security conditions are from those of the East–West divide. Even in the sphere of trade and economics, North and South are far less opposed and more interdependent in their interests than the Eastern and Western blocs ever were. They do not view or treat each other as enemies in any moral or conceptual sense;[7] on the contrary, the only politically correct discourse in the North is about 'aiding' the South in terms of sustainable development, peace-building and so on. Moreover, the neatness of the dichotomy is rapidly being blurred by the rise in economic and military strength of powers like China and India, which show many parallels of behaviour even though the former is considered to be in the North and the latter in the South. Of course, some analysts—especially in the USA—have persistently attempted to position China as the West's strategic rival of the future, taking the place of the Soviet Union.

Also useful for capturing at least a part of the new landscape is the idea of West–West tensions. It is easy to see why these might become more overt and influential than in cold war times. As the discipline imposed by facing a shared geo-strategic threat has weakened, the West itself has become much larger and more diverse. Successive enlargements of the memberships of NATO and the European Union (EU) have brought the number of states integrated into one or both of these institutions from 17 in 1990 to 32 today, to which may be added several applicant countries that are already more or less fixed in a Western alignment. Democratic countries outside the Euro-Atlantic area that have a security partnership with one or more NATO powers (usually the USA) have also been moving into more open and active strategic roles—two examples being the part played by Australia in the Iraq conflict and the ongoing debate about a higher defence profile for Japan.[8] When security views and interests diverge within this extended democratic family, the reper-

---

[4] Of the 17 major armed conflicts in 2005, 15 took place in Africa, South and South-East Asia, the Middle East and South America. See appendix 2A in this volume.

[5] E.g., Brazil's acted as a self-appointed spokesman for the South during the World Trade Organization's Doha round of negotiations in 2004–2005. Two formal 'South Summits' have been held, resulting most recently in the Doha Declaration and Plan of Action and the New Asian–African Strategic Partnership. Second South Summit, 'Doha Declaration' and 'Doha Plan of Action', Doha, Qatar, 12–16 June 2005, URL <http://www.g77.org/southsummit2/>; and Asian–African Summit 2005, 'Declaration on the New Asian–African Strategic Partnership', Bandung, Indonesia, 24 Apr. 2005, URL <http://www.asianafricansummit2005.org/>.

[6] See chapters 10 and 13 in this volume.

[7] At least, enemies are not defined on the ground of geographical location or wealth alone. The idea of opposition between 'civilizations' is given separate treatment below.

[8] Australia contributed 2000 troops to the initial US-led operation in Iraq in Mar. 2003 and has also played a prominent part in regional peace interventions, e.g., in East Timor and the Solomon Islands.

cussions can be truly global. West–West dynamics determine which major cross-regional interventions will be carried out and who will volunteer or be asked to join them. Western factions have touted for support among other countries in a manner sometimes all too reminiscent of the former East–West competition.[9] Even the conceptual currency of West–West debates strongly affects the language in which other actors are permitted, or at least expected, to express their security concerns. West-based, and often distinctly top-down, perspectives are betrayed by the recent move to classify terrorism as an 'asymmetric' threat; the argument over 'pre-emption' or 'extended self-defence' as the criterion for decisions on military intervention in place of internationally sanctioned guidelines; and even the prevailing discourse about 'weak states' and 'human security'.

Even so, it would be verging on the absurd to accept a West–West strategic dynamic as today's equivalent to the blocs of the cold war. Divergences within NATO have been powerful drivers of policy ever since SIPRI began to study them, and it is too early to conclude that they have undergone a decisive change of quality as well as quantity since 1990. Even leaving aside the funda-mental interests and beliefs still shared by the whole West, groups of wealthy democratic countries do not behave in the traditional style of strategic adver-saries: forming fixed alignments to arm against, to subvert and to prepare or incite military action against each other.[10] Up to now at least, the most extreme manifestations of disagreement in US–European or intra-European relations have involved abstention from proposed joint actions, frustrating the joint adoption of new policies and initiatives (e.g., on climate change) or bringing cases peacefully before the relevant international tribunals (such as the World Trade Organization). Moreover, and despite what is said above about the wide reach of West-centric influences, what is going on in the rest of the world patently does not reduce itself to transactions between groups of US or Euro-pean hangers-on. Some Europeans talk about 'multipolarity' as a preferred state of affairs precisely because they recognize the existence of other power bases outside the Euro-Atlantic area that may, at least indirectly, mitigate the consequences for Europe of an otherwise highly asymmetric US–European balance.

This leads on to perhaps the most fertile new geo-strategic vision since Francis Fukuyama's thesis of the post-cold war 'end of history':[11] the one that focuses on the role of the USA as a single superpower vis-à-vis all other countries.[12] Reflecting on the singularity of the USA's position helps to

---

[9] E.g., during the Iraq crisis there was lobbying by pro- and anti-US camps for votes on a possible UN Security Council resolution legitimizing the USA's wish to invade Iraq, leading to the temporary anti-US bloc formed by France and Germany with Russia.

[10] The pattern of an alignment of the UK, Italy, the rest of so-called 'new Europe' and Australia in support of the USA, with France and Germany and now Spain on the other side, has seemed stable since 2001 but is neither self-explanatory nor necessarily permanent. The UK's policies on trade, environment and European defence tend to cut across it in any case.

[11] Fukuyama, F., *The End of History and the Last Man* (Free Press: New York, N.Y., 1992).

[12] The USA's military expenditure, $507 billion in 2005, accounts for 48% of all global spending, while no other country accounts for more than 5%. See chapter 8 in this volume. The USA is also the

explain that country's own evolving policies and also to understand why the Western alliance can never again be a monolith and why the USA's allies sometimes share with non-allies, or even opponents, worries about the super-power's behaviour. Analysts of US reactions have raised important questions about the effectiveness and durability of 'hard' power (i.e., military strength and coercion) compared with 'soft' power (i.e., persuasion and influence); about the merits of unilateral action vis-à-vis institutionalized alliances and global norms; and about the implications of pre-emptive action vis-à-vis a more realist and reactive strategic posture.[13] Considered as general explanations of post-cold war evolution, however, these analyses—together with the obverse view that ascribes all the world's ills to a sole 'rogue superpower'—hold traps for the unwary. Not only do they generally overstate the USA's absolute and relative strength (*inter alia* by undervaluing the constraints on the use of coercive power),[14] but the USA-centric approach more generally risks overlooking security processes and dynamics in which the USA is not engaged, and underplaying the importance of types of power and influence that are less relevant or attractive for Washington. The actual or potential US empire postulated in several of these works is no more omnipresent than the European 19th century empires were, and the onus of proof is on those who wish to claim that it will be more lasting. That said, the issue of US power and of how to relate to it is as nearly omnipresent as makes no difference in today's security discourse. An explanation of modern strategic reality that incorporated not just US actions but also the reasons and ways that others decide to act without the USA, and how they react to the USA's decision not to engage in a given region or process, could start to amass considerable descriptive power.

Models with functionally defined 'opponents'

A community that cannot define its own antithesis in traditional geo-strategic terms readily turns to a more generic, abstract or functional, definition of 'the other'. In the cold war many policies treated Communism as the adversary, rather than, or in addition to, the specifically Communist countries. A subtlety of such visions is that they admit the possibility of an 'enemy within'; that is, of elements integral to the given community that may be corrupted by the

single largest national economy, with a gross domestic product in 2004 of $11 734 billion. International Monetary Fund, *International Financial Statistics* Online Service.

[13] See, e.g., Hassner, P., 'The United States: the empire of force or the force of empire?', Chaillot Paper no. 54, EU Institute of Security Studies, Paris, Sep. 2002, URL <http://www.iss-eu.org/chaillot/chai54e.html>; Eland, I., 'The empire strikes out: the "new imperialism" and its fatal flaws', Policy Analysis no. 459, Cato Institute, Washington, DC, 26 Nov. 2002, URL <http://www.cato.org/pub_display.php?pub_id=1318>; Coker. C., 'Empires in conflict: the growing rift between Europe and the United States', Whitehall Paper no. 58, Royal United Services Institute, London, May 2003; and Garrison, J., *America as Empire: Global Leader or Rogue Power?* (Berrett-Koehler: San Francisco, Calif., 2004).

[14] On the question of limitations to traditional state power and to its exercise through military force see Bailes (note 3), pp. 2–13.

hostile principle and work for it in ways more insidious than conventional spies.

There have been many models based on this kind of analysis since the end of the cold war. With the passing of the 1990s, when the strong focus on local conflicts—each with its own rights and wrongs—tended to push more philosophical visions into the background, the early 21st century has arguably seen a renascence of Manichaean thinking. Samuel P. Huntington's 'clash of civilizations' was an early formulation that hinted at what characterizes many of the new models.[15] While Communism was practised by people many of whom looked like Westerners and had a comparable material civilization, the new 'other' is defined in terms of more fundamental human differences—of ethnicity, belief and general way of life. The 'enemy' is not a particular country or alliance, but Islam, immigration or international terrorism; or from the other side, the infidel, materialistic tyranny of the West. The ground has, arguably, been prepared for such concepts to come to the fore with the fading of the North's (and thus of Christendom's) main internal conflicts; the weakening of what control colonialism and extended East–West competition ever exercised over the behaviour of states in the South; the cultural impact of globalization in non-Western societies (added to their own divides and dysfunctions); and the increasingly typical human experience of living in (perhaps increasingly tense) multicultural communities.[16] All moral objections aside, however, the acceptance of any such ethnically, confessionally or culturally defined duality as the successor to cold war bipolarity creates far more problems for strategy makers than it could solve. In the cold war it was possible to sympathize with fellow human beings living under an imposed Communist system. Under the new approach the individuals themselves must be seen as the problem, even when living in a superficially friendly state (such as the Arab monarchies) and perhaps most of all when based within Western societies. No known military formula could eliminate a 'threat' defined in such terms, and the use of other possible forms of coercion—conversion, suppression, neo-imperialistic occupation and self-isolation—is much hampered by the economic interdependence (mainly but not only because of oil) between the Western and Islamic worlds. It is no wonder that writers who adopt this line of analysis deal more often in the currency of pessimistic prophecy than of strategic prescription.

What has tended to happen in practice is that those setting out to combat new, functionally defined adversaries have fallen back into techniques designed for handling old, geo-strategic ones. The USA's declaration in 2001, following the brutal al-Qaeda attacks on its cities, of a global *war* on terrorism is the classic case in point. True, policy makers in the USA and like-minded countries have not simplistically equated the new 'super-terrorism' with Islam or with specific ethnic groups. They deplore it also as a general aberration of

---

[15] Huntington, S. P., *The Clash of Civilisations and the Remaking of the World Order* (Simon & Schuster: New York, N.Y., 1996).

[16] See also appendix 2C in this volume.

behaviour, whether defined in military strategic terms as a use of asymmetric techniques (by a weaker actor against a stronger target), or in moral and legal terms as the unacceptable use of indiscriminate force against non-combatants.[17] Nevertheless, US policy has repeatedly shown a tendency to concretize and even personalize terrorism as a unitary phenomenon with a limited, identifiable and—given the proper security tools—destructible set of sources. Osama bin Laden and a succession of extremist figures in Iraq have become the new Fidel Castros, Ho Chi Minhs or Ayatollah Khomeinis.[18] Engagement with terrorism plus the additional generic evil of the proliferation of weapons of mass destruction (WMD) has, further, become the typical way for the USA to characterize 'rogue states' and their leaders, as in the cases of Iran and North Korea. According to the US National Security Strategy of 2002, the threat to world peace and to the USA's own interests from such regimes may justify the pre-emptive use of force against them, even without an international legal mandate.[19] It is here that the resemblance to cold war threats starts to break down because the East–West system of strategic deterrence would not have allowed such action by the USA against its primary adversaries of the time. The US-led action against Iraq in 2003 reflected not just the new intimacy of the outrages that struck the US population two years before but also the new permissiveness of the environment that left the USA, in practice, as free to strike out at its foes as al-Qaeda had been to strike at New York and Washington.

Problems arising from the USA's actions against its new *Feindbilder* ('enemy images') have been well documented and are further addressed in this volume.[20] Apart from anything else, as soon as the idea of terrorists and pro-liferators as the adversaries in a new global contest is matched against the actual events of the past five years, it becomes clear that neither the USA nor any other state has been able to use such yardsticks consistently. Countries in de facto possession of WMD—India, Israel and Pakistan, at least one of which has also condoned terrorist action against its adversaries—have continued to enjoy the USA's partnership and have even received some new favours.[21] The

---

[17] On the problems of defining terrorism see Simpson, G., 'Terrorism and the law: past and present international approaches', *SIPRI Yearbook 2003: Armaments, Disarmament and International Security* (Oxford University Press: Oxford, 2003), pp. 23–31. The UN World Summit of Sep. 2005 could not agree on a new, all-purpose definition proposed by the Secretary-General on the basis of a high-level panel's report in 2004. United Nations, 'A more secure world: our shared responsibility', Report of the High-level Panel on Threats, Challenges and Change, UN documents A/59/565, 4 Dec. 2004, and A/59/565/Corr.1, 6 Dec. 2004, URL <http://www.un.org/ga/59/documentation/list5.html>; and United Nations, '2005 World Summit outcome', UN General Assembly document A/RES/60/1, 24 Oct. 2005, URL <http://www.un.org/summit2005/documents.html>.

[18] Compare also the way in which Farad Aideed was branded as the enemy in the ultimately unsuccessful 1993–94 US intervention in Somalia. Findlay, T., SIPRI, *The Use of Force in UN Peace Operations* (Oxford University Press: Oxford, 2002), pp. 166–218.

[19] The White House, 'The National Security Strategy of the United States of America', Washington, DC, Sep. 2002, URL <http://www.whitehouse.gov/nsc/nss.html>.

[20] See chapters 2 and 8 in this volume.

[21] The present administration of US President George W. Bush has recently agreed on closer (civil) nuclear cooperation with India—see appendix 13B in this volume; has been perceived as leaning

USA's greatest military effort was made against a regime—that of Iraq—that in retrospect has been more or less cleared of both terrorist and (recent) WMD offences. US military aid has, indeed, been increasingly directed towards governments fighting terrorism, but it has also been withheld from some staunch anti-terrorist allies because they would not cooperate over the unrelated issue of the International Criminal Court.[22] Resort to forceful methods has also been inconsistent, with one significant anti-terrorist intervention (Afghanistan) and one supposedly WMD-related intervention (Iraq) contrasting with two proliferation cases that have thus far been tackled by non-military means (Iran and North Korea) and one that involved a peaceful buyout (Libya).[23]

To be sure, such patterns of variation can be traced in the pursuit of almost any strategic principle, usually as a function of limited resources, lessons learned and a preference for lower-risk targets. Beyond this, however, it is clear that, in order to judge the acceptability of various partners and the relative degrees of threat from various foes, the USA and its partners have had to use a wider set of criteria than those related to terrorism and WMD. Terrorism and proliferation are not at the origin of all, or even a majority of, current security disorders. They are absent from many significant conflicts, including those in the Balkans and two where the USA has intervened since 2001—Haiti and Liberia. Where they are present, observations both of their course and of the result of efforts to stop them strongly suggest that they are symptoms of other things that are wrong in security and governance, rather than the primary ills to be cured. In sum, the US-defined 'new threats' agenda that represents perhaps the most sustained effort since the cold war to define a global adversary in functional terms is, after a few years, already looking inadequate both as a philosophy and as a practical guide. States need to be judged on the totality of their security-related behaviour as much as on factors of identity, belief and ostensible goals.

In the inaugural speech of his second term in office, in January 2005, US President George W. Bush brought discourse closer to reality in US policy by citing a larger number of principles on which the USA would henceforth judge other countries.[24] Particularly striking was the emphasis that he placed (and other US speakers have since placed) on democracy as a good, also in security terms, and on its absence as one trigger for corrective action. Democracy is, indeed, one of the more logically attractive functional principles for judging the contemporary global scene. It was a major part of what the Western powers stood for during the cold war and one of the criteria (unfortunately, not

towards Israel on the issue of how to proceed towards peace with the Palestinians; and has tightened its cooperation with Pakistan against terrorism.

[22] Wiharta, S., 'Post-conflict justice: developments in international courts', *SIPRI Yearbook 2004: Armaments, Disarmament and International Security* (Oxford University Press: Oxford, 2004), pp. 197–98.

[23] Hart, J. and Kile, S. N., 'Libya's renunciation of nuclear, biological and chemical weapons and ballistic missiles', *SIPRI Yearbook 2005* (note 3), pp. 629–48.

[24] The White House, 'President sworn-in to second term', Press release, Washington, DC, 20 Jan. 2005, URL <http://www.whitehouse.gov/news/releases/2005/01/>.

consistently applied) by which they chose their partners. Since 1990 progress in democracy has been one of the conditions for joining NATO and the EU and has helped to stabilize relations also between these organizations and their neighbours. It has allowed lasting structures of regional cooperation, with clear security benefit, to be built in other parts of the world. Lack of functioning democracy is a frequent factor in conflict generation, and one core aim of modern peace-building is to correct it. Last but not least, it is possible to define democratic norms in terms that are almost wholly culturally neutral, so that the elevation of this principle need not necessarily be linked with West-centric thinking or the more visceral type of reaction to 'the other'.

As commentators on the new US policy have noted, however, there are two levels of difficulty about making democracy the touchstone of judgement and policy in the sphere of security as such.[25] First, it does not correlate closely enough with the absence or solution of other important strategic problems. Democracies are liable to be infected, as well as targeted, by terrorism; they have both aided WMD proliferation and been proliferators themselves; they may rarely go to war with conventional weapons with their neighbours but they can be involved in all other kinds of external and internal turbulence, including civil wars. Democracy, notoriously, cannot be successfully imposed without local ownership, but when local forces are given free play the results may not be to Western tastes.[26] In sum, although the spread of democracy correlates well in the longer term with the chance of more orderly and peaceful international relations, in the short term the qualities of democracy on the one hand and of order, stability and avoidance of conflict on the other hand will by no means coincide everywhere. The second layer of the problem is that, if democracy means anything, then its principles of pluralism, fairness and equality under the law should prevail in relations among states (and in transnational contacts between individuals) as much as inside national systems. This is not an objection to the international use of force as such, since the notion of a 'just war' can be linked philosophically to the right and need to punish wrongdoing within societies. Nor does it mean subordinating democratic goals to considerations of order and risk avoidance: change in the direction of more democracy is as inherently risky as all change but none the less legitimate for that. It does mean, however, that for any single country to decree what democracy is, and to claim a special right to reward and punish other countries accordingly, is something of a contradiction in terms. If a powerful state, while promoting democracy, claims a right to disregard rules and norms that the international community has democratically adopted then

[25] E.g., Hobson, C., 'A forward strategy of freedom in the Middle East: US democracy promotion and the "war on terror"', *Australian Journal of International Affairs*, vol. 59, no. 1 (Mar. 2005), pp. 39–53; Monten, J., 'The roots of the Bush doctrine: power, nationalism and democracy promotion in U.S. strategy', *International Security*, vol. 29, no. 4 (spring 2005), pp. 112–56; and Eizenstat. S., Porter, J. E. and Weinstein, J., 'Rebuilding weak states', *Foreign Affairs*, vol. 84, no. 1 (Jan./Feb. 2005), pp. 134–46.

[26] Thus, post-colonial states often took an anti-Western stance in the first period of their independence, and observers have warned that more democratic forms of government in Arab countries could bring extreme Islamist elements (and even movements with a terrorist background) to power.

the democratic cause itself risks being discredited and its rhetoric being seen by many as just a gloss on the bad old style of strategic power play.

All the bipolar methods of analysis surveyed above, whether geo-strategic terms or functional terms based on some combination of behaviour and identity are used, fall at the first hurdle of failing to capture the full complexity of global security today. None can convincingly describe, let alone prescribe policies towards, all the different regional security dynamics (competitive or cooperative) that now account for so many significant trends in armament and military spending, for the origins of so many conflicts, and also for so many conflicts that have been prevented or resolved. None of the models is completely useless, but the successful modelling of reality calls for a combination of all of them and more. Whether or not the post-cold war world can be described as multipolar, it is certainly multidimensional. In section III, the changed security landscape is described in terms that relate to process: tracking changes in the kind of issues that are thought to belong to the security agenda and in the kinds of actors, instruments and actions that are seen as problematic or appropriate.

III. From armed blocs to multifunctional, 'human' and active security

When the SIPRI Yearbooks were given the sub-title 'World Armaments and Disarmament', and later 'Armaments, Disarmament and International Security', no explanation was needed for why these were matters for concern.[27] In the cold war, with its constant fear of an East–West nuclear conflagration—which might also have been triggered by fighting elsewhere—higher levels of arms anywhere in the world were a danger sign, and anything that would reduce them could be expected to improve security. The slogans of cold war peace movements were almost always about getting rid of some specific weapons[28] or ending some specific conflict, such as that in Viet Nam. Today, protests against the US-led operations in Iraq have inherited part of this approach, but what has become of the arms-directed campaigns? Those that used to target the most destructive—nuclear—weapons have been largely dormant or sidelined since the agitation against French nuclear testing in 1995. The campaigns mustering the largest public support in the past decade have been about weapons, such as anti-personnel mines and small arms, that are abhorrent for the way they affect human beings rather than frightening for the way they promote and escalate conflict.[29] Much energy has been poured into causes with no (or only marginal) military connections, such as ecological and

---

[27] The original subtitle was used up to the 1993 edition and the new title from the 1995 edition onwards.

[28] There were, of course, variations such as the nuclear freeze movement of the early 1980s in the USA.

[29] Direct links even between the flow of small arms and the spread or intensity of intra-state conflicts have been very difficult to demonstrate. See Wezeman, P. D., 'Conflicts and transfers of small arms', SIPRI, Stockholm, Mar. 2003, URL <http://www.sipri.org/contents/armstrad/smarm.html>.

environmental protests—including those against civil nuclear energy; warnings against other forms of technology development such as genetic modification and nanotechnology; and the general anti-globalization movement. While section II above detects no clear answer to who the new 'enemy' is, the question of what people are afraid of—and hence, what kind of security they seek—has no easy answer nowadays either.

At the cost of over-simplification, and bearing in mind the enormous variety of perspectives among different regions and communities, three processes of change may be seen as feeding today's conceptions of danger and security: (*a*) diversification of the security agenda, (*b*) diversity of actors and (*c*) the preference for solutions involving action rather than restraint.

Diversification of the security agenda

The diversification of the security agenda is the functional widening of the concepts of danger and security to cover much more than the traditional business of defence, a process that in its turn has two major aspects. First, the forms of violence that constitute the focus of security policy have broadened and shifted from war between states to cover not just other varieties of 'conflict'—intra-state conflicts[30] and transnational opponents such as terrorists—but also internal lawlessness and criminality, and for some analysts even interpersonal violence. Apart from hurting people, what all these have in common is that they threaten the monopoly of force, and hence the authority and integrity, of the traditional state structure. The security goal of a national government is accordingly increasingly defined as protection of its people and their rights against the whole range of such disorders, with no firm dividing lines between 'external' and 'internal' security. The international community is similarly concerned not just with stopping existing conflicts but also with making 'weak' states strong enough to block both internal outbreaks and external incursions of violence in the future. The growing appreciation of the importance of internal security can be tracked as much in the latest thinking on the goals of international intervention, and the priorities for peace-building in the affected state, as it can in the attention being given by stronger states to their own 'homeland security' or the equivalent.[31]

The second part of this trend involves acknowledging the security importance of phenomena that do not involve any kind of human conflict and perhaps have no human perpetrator at all. Forty per cent of the world's population live on less than $2 per day and 1 billion live in abject poverty on less than $1 a day.[32] By 2005, 40.3 million individuals worldwide were infected with

---

[30] Of the 17 major armed conflicts listed in appendix 2A of this volume, none is classified as inter-state; all reflect some combination of disputes over territory or control of government within countries.

[31] Dwan, R. and Wiharta, S., 'Multilateral peace missions: the challenges of peace-building', *SIPRI Yearbook 2005* (note 3), pp. 139–98.

[32] Moreover, 18 countries with populations totalling 460 million people are now rated lower on the Human Development Index than in 1990, and progress towards the UN's Millennium Goals agreed in 2000 is lagging so much that, without improvement, there will be 4.4 million 'avoidable' child deaths in

HIV/AIDS and there were more than 3 million deaths caused by AIDS in that year.[33] Forecasts of deaths in the next great influenza pandemic have also ranged in the millions, depending on assumptions. A further set of risks involving mass mortality are typified by the tsunami of 26 December 2004, which cost at least 275 000 lives, the severe earthquake of October 2005 in Kashmir and the (apparently) partly irreversible damage that hurricanes Katrina and Rita inflicted in the autumn of 2005 on the USA. Other disorders of climate and the environment that can afflict human beings, and the animals and crops on which they rely, range from one-off events like volcanic eruptions, droughts and floods to large-scale processes of global warming, desertification and attrition of natural resources. All these non-military risks have grown in prominence for rich countries with the relative easing of traditional threats and for poor countries with the sheer scale of damage they can cause to fragile societies. They are, moreover, increasingly seen to be interlinked with the armed conflict agenda, inasmuch as the tensions they cause can trigger or prolong conflict and because conflict itself makes populations more vulnerable to them. Traditional military forces and skills (but fewer kinds of specifically military equipment) can be used to cope with many of these types of disaster, as well as with some of the internal security tasks mentioned above. The larger question remains whether some or all of the money spent on traditional defence would save more lives if transferred to combating non-military scourges that are the common enemies of mankind.[34] The modern successor to the debates of the cold war period on disarmament and development is the notion of a broader concept of 'human security'—including also rights and freedoms which are important for the quality of life—to which the narrow considerations of defence should be subordinate and which the military resources deemed worth retaining should be better tailored to serve.[35]

Diversity of actors

During the cold war, as in much of previous history, threat and risk analysis remained focused on transactions involving traditional nation states and the alliances that they led; this is often called the Westphalian model. Since 1990 the analysis of both security problems and their solutions has given growing attention to other kinds of actors that operate below the national level—insur-

---

2015. United Nations Development Programme (UNDP), *Human Development Report 2005* (UNDP: New York, N.Y., 2005), URL <http://hdr.undp.org/reports/global/2005/>.

[33] Joint United Nations Programme on HIV/AIDS (UNAIDS) and World Health Organization, *AIDS Epidemic Update: Special Report on HIV Prevention* (UNAIDS: Geneva, Dec. 2005), URL <http://www.unaids.org/epi/2005/>.

[34] Sköns, E., 'Financing security in a global context', *SIPRI Yearbook 2005* (note 3), pp. 285–306.

[35] On the concept of human security see Study Group on Europe's Security Capabilities, 'A human security doctrine for Europe', London School of Economics, Centre for the Study of Global Governance, London, Sep. 2004, URL <http://www.lse.ac.uk/Depts/global/Publications/HumanSecurityDoctrine. pdf>; and University of British Columbia, Human Security Centre, *Human Security Report 2005: War and Peace in the 21st Century* (Oxford University Press: New York, N.Y., 2005) URL <http://www.humansecurityreport.info>.

gent movements, ethnic and regional communities and so on—to those above it—multinational companies and multilateral institutions—or to those in some kind of 'transnational' dimension—for instance, terrorist and criminal networks. The broad trends of globalization, democratization and, in the economic sphere, privatization have created new space for all these types of actor to exercise power, but the relative heightening of their security role can also be tied to two other trends mentioned above. Greater focus on intra-state and trans-state forms of conflict brings other participants in armed violence into the arena that used to be monopolized by battling states or by their direct proxies. When the agenda is widened to include other internal and 'human' dimensions of security, the people who are engaged both as victims and as providers in these dimensions—from policemen to doctors, seismologists and people who repair electricity cables or combat cyber-crime—have to be counted as security actors. Aside from public employees and members of civic society, corporate enterprises and employees are also active in practically every one of these fields, not excluding (at the traditional end of the spectrum) the provision of combat services.[36]

The introduction to *SIPRI Yearbook 2005* discussed the ways in which such non-state actors can exercise power and influence in the security field.[37] Most commentators have focused on the problems posed for states, and for multilateral organizations, by these actors when they play negative roles: and these problems are indeed serious. Very few of the groups and individuals involved can be deterred, and not many more can be negotiated with, in the style of Westphalian diplomacy. Traditional military intelligence is not adapted to anticipating and tracking their activities and—as the past few years have abundantly shown—traditional military resources do not perform well in eliminating them. When it comes to risks like disease, aberrations of nature and infrastructure problems not attributable to human intent, techniques for risk analysis and early warning are at best scattered among different expert communities and unevenly developed around the world, and at worst may simply be undeveloped. The sheer variety of types of risk to be assessed and prioritized poses enormous problems in itself for policy development and resource allocation.

A question that follows from this, but which has yet to be fully explored, is how to mobilize the positive potential of new actors within the security community. One challenge that has already been singled out is how to coordinate all the different groups whose skills may be needed to tackle a complex domestic emergency or to carry out a successful conflict intervention and peace-building operation.[38] A more generic problem is that non-military actors are by definition not subject to military discipline or even—if in the private

---

[36] Bailes, A. J. K. and Frommelt, I. (eds), SIPRI, *Business and Security: Public–Private Sector Relationships in a New Security Environment* (Oxford University Press: Oxford, 2004); and Holmqvist, C., *Private Security Companies: The Case for Regulation*, SIPRI Policy Paper no. 9 (SIPRI: Stockholm, Jan. 2005), URL <http://www.sipri.org/>.

[37] Bailes (note 3).

[38] On peace-building see Dwan and Wiharta (note 31); and chapter 3 in this volume.

sector—to the obligations of public service. They do not have the equivalent of the armed forces' trained reserves and of much larger mobilization capacities. They do not come free of charge, aside from citizens' voluntary associations. A government or institution trying to activate mixed military and civilian, public and private sector teams for a single security cause thus has to operate in multiple modes and under multiple rules. Another complicating factor is that almost every state in the world has options for drawing upon resources at levels other than the purely national: they can turn to (more or less integrated) regional communities of fellow states, to the universal community of the UN and its agencies or to ad hoc groups of countries (and private sector entities). The horizontal issue of overlapping competences between different organizations is returned to below, but the point to note here is the growing vertical range of different types of actors with which a modern government can choose to work. Finding the right level or combination of levels for tackling a given defensive need or active task—or, to use EU parlance, the art of subsidiarity in the security field—is a skill that many are still only slowly and haltingly acquiring.

The preference for solutions involving action rather than restraint

As noted in the introduction to *SIPRI Yearbook 2003*, a further change in security behaviour since cold war times has been the greater resort—perhaps above all by strong democratic states—to active methods for building a state's preferred security environment.[39] The most obvious indication of this is the rising number of outside interventions in regional conflicts and against 'rogue states' since 1990.[40] Explanations for this part of the phenomenon include: (*a*) the disappearance of the risk of East–West escalation, (*b*) surplus capacity for 'exporting' security from regions freed from cold war threats, (*c*) more cooperative and active security communities in other regions, (*d*) wider understanding and concern about the implications of any conflict, anywhere, for the world community, and (*e*) doctrines (notably but not only in the USA) providing new rationales to intervene in the context of extended self-defence. There are, however, other forces at work in the new environment that have further weakened the notion of security being based on 'restraint' or on 'avoidance' or (in military technical terms) on a minimal capacity for self-defence. One force that most people would consider to be positive is the falling of cold war barriers to positive military cooperation between former adversaries, including potentially transformational elements like assistance in modernization and reform, as well as collaboration in training and joint missions abroad. This has been going on between East and West in the Euro-Atlantic space under NATO's Euro-Atlantic Partnership and in the framework

---

[39] Bailes, A. J. K., 'Trends and challenges in international security', *SIPRI Yearbook 2003* (note 17), pp. 1–22.

[40] SIPRI counted a total of 34 multilateral peace missions in 1993, of which 20 were led by the UN; in 2005 the total figure was 58, of which 21 were UN-led. See chapter 3 in this volume.

of the Organization for Security and Co-operation in Europe (OSCE);[41] it is also an increasing trend among groups of states emerging from conflict and tension in Africa and Latin America, incipiently in South-East Asia, and in the Shanghai Cooperation Organization made up of China, Russia and four Central Asian states.[42]

A less obvious point is that the functional widening of the security agenda also draws security policy thinking into areas where efforts to avoid risk by eschewing provocation are as meaningless as traditional deterrence would be. Some kind of material defensive measures can be taken against most 'new threats', from terrorism to violent weather, but it is not possible to negotiate disengagement or disarmament deals or confidence-building measures with them. The only kind of active policy that makes sense in these dimensions is one aimed at ejection and suppression of the threatening element—ideally, before it can manifest its threat. The language of crime prevention or disease prevention or accident prevention is just as natural—and for most people as unproblematic—as the ambition of conflict prevention has become in recent years. The step to pre-emption of threats manifesting themselves in more traditional, armed, terms may then strike certain thinkers as a short one, even if it has strategic and moral consequences of a quite different order.

An active, interventionist security policy needs resources; and, as long as the challenges being tackled include some that involve armed violence, the resources in demand will include military ones. The increasingly wide array of international organizations now offering themselves for the execution of peace missions—NATO, the EU, the African Union (AU), the Association of Southeast Asian Nations (ASEAN) and other regional or sub-regional groups—all exhort their members to build up their intervention capabilities as a matter of long-term policy. Increasingly often, following repair efforts in a post-conflict region, the recovering states are encouraged to seal their new respectability by contributing in their turn to cooperative peace missions. The higher levels of armaments (at least, of the varieties needed for long-range missions) that this implies for the given region are no longer seen as problematic when former adversaries are pooling their resources for good works elsewhere. Countries providing support against terrorism or in efforts to stop the proliferation of WMD may also be rewarded with arms sales and the transfer of relevant technologies. In short, far from military abstemiousness being seen as a virtue, the virtuous state today is both expected to rearm itself for the active, collaborative export of security and offered chances to improve its arsenal precisely as a reward for its virtue. Alongside these essentially Western-inspired processes, meanwhile, some states of other regions continue to pile up arms for older reasons of regional balance or competition; and at least one—the USA—does likewise to retain its global superiority over both geographical and functional menaces.

---

[41] Cottey, A. and Forster, A., *Reshaping Defence: New Roles for Military Cooperation and Assistance*, Adelphi Paper no. 365 (Routledge: London, May 2004).
[42] See the glossary in this volume.

This analysis should not be pushed too far: it leaves out the economic reasons that can (and do) drive states to reduce rather than increase their military efforts;[43] and it should give credit for the qualitative shift in armouries (away from the items best suited for attacking neighbours) that the new 'expeditionary' emphasis should logically bring. This wider view of what might be called pro-armament pressures is, however, useful in highlighting that the USA's conspicuous military consumption is only the most extreme example of a much wider trend. Everywhere else in the world today, the policies of leading regional powers typically do not stigmatize armaments and military methods as such but rather aim to reserve them for the 'right' users and purposes. The notion that it is the user, rather than the weapon, that is good or bad goes a very long way to explain how non-proliferation has taken the place of disarmament in the security policy thinking of the world's dominant powers—and why the latter seem less willing than ever to trade their own weapons as the price for non-proliferation solutions (as the original logic of the 1968 Non-Proliferation Treaty implied). It lies behind the evolution in many export control groupings away from restrictions expressed as permanent prohibitions on certain recipients (as with the strategic adversaries of the cold war) to ones based on types of recipient or various generic consequences of transfer.[44] It could help explain why, since the 1987 Intermediate-range Nuclear Forces Treaty and the 1993 Chemical Weapons Convention, it has not proved possible to agree blanket bans on any further items of weaponry except those that are only of marginal interest for the new interventionist agenda (e.g., landmines and blinding lasers).[45] As for the question of the right purposes for which, and conditions under which, armed force may be used outside the narrowest reading of self-defence, this has been at the very heart of the post-2001 debates between the USA, its NATO allies and the rest of the world. It was disappointing, if hardly surprising, that the UN World Summit of September 2005 failed to agree on a full set of proposals—formulated in the report of the High-level Panel on Threats, Challenges and Change in December 2004—that would have clarified the restraints on, as well as the goals of, intentionally legitimated intervention.[46] Even had it done so, recent years have underlined the weakness of such purely normative restraints, in modern conditions, on a state that possesses means, motive and opportunity for military action and anticipates (rightly or wrongly) little backlash against itself.

An environment shaped by these trends is, clearly, not going to be a particularly favourable one for the processes of arms control and disarmament that have held so much of SIPRI's attention since the Institute's establishment.

---

[43] Thus, e.g., Western Europe's aggregate military spending stayed constant at 2.0% of GDP in 2000–2003 despite both NATO and EU demands for greater performance. Sköns, E. et al., 'Military expenditure', *SIPRI Yearbook 2005* (note 3), p. 316.

[44] See chapter 12 in this volume.

[45] Even so, the USA has declined to sign the 1997 Anti-Personnel Mines Convention. See annex A in this volume.

[46] United Nations, 'A more secure world' (note 17); and United Nations, '2005 World Summit outcome' (note 17).

How these processes have fared, against the broader background of developments in institutionalized security work, is the subject of the next section.

IV. From arms control treaties to security building—with or without a rule book

At first glance, what is striking when comparing the early 21st century's institutional landscape with that of the 1960s is how little has changed. The United
Nations and the international financial institutions remain the most universal,
or universally active, frameworks. Of Europe's post-cold war creations,
NATO and the European Union have survived several metamorphoses and
emerged with more members and more competences each time. For 10 former
Communist states, one or both of these institutions now provides the integrated multilateral framework that the Warsaw Pact and the Council for
Mutual Economic Assistance (COMECON) used to attempt to provide.[47] The
OSCE, successor to the Conference on Security and Co-operation in Europe
(CSCE), created in 1975, still exists to link the members of the West-based
integrated groupings with their non-member neighbours as far as the eastern
bounds of the former Soviet Union;[48] and so, with a more limited membership
and remit, does the Council of Europe. Where changes have taken place, their
balance has run more towards institutionalization than de-institutionalization.
The Western European Union (WEU) was reduced to an inactive skeleton
when the EU took over responsibility for European-led military operations in
2000; and the Collective Security Treaty Organization (CSTO), linking Russia
with its more compliant post-Soviet neighbours, remains a shadowy and
under-performing successor to the Warsaw Pact.[49] Elsewhere, however, the
de-colonization process and gradual pacification of post-colonial conflicts
have allowed the rise of many new regional and sub-regional groupings that
contribute indirectly or directly to security. There is an obvious coincidence
between the regions that have not so far found such a cooperative formula and
those where the most security dangers remain: the greater Middle East, South
Asia and East Asia.

Considered in relation to armaments, disarmament and other security processes, however, the cold war pattern of institutional role play has become
blurred in at least two respects: (*a*) in the divide between organizations with
and without a security role, and (*b*) in the relationship between security and
disarmament.

---

[47] On the post-cold war development of regional security processes see chapter 4 in this volume.

[48] For questions raised over the future utility of the OSCE see Dunay, P., 'The Organization for
Security and Co-operation in Europe: constant adaptation but enduring problems', *SIPRI Yearbook 2005*
(note 3), pp. 76–82; and chapter 1 in this volume.

[49] On the WEU and the CSTO see the glossary in this volume.

The move towards multifunctionalism

There used to be a clear divide between organizations that engaged in defence and other security-related activity and those that did not. NATO was a military entity and the European Communities (the EU's predecessor) a civilian, political and economic one. The same role division characterized these bodies' Eastern equivalents, the Warsaw Pact and COMECON. So long as the NATO-style Central Treaty Organization (CENTO) and South-East Asian Treaty Organization (SEATO) were operational, they also played a purely military role for their respective regions.[50] At world level, the security responsibilities held by the UN and more particularly by the Security Council were doubly demarcated from the economic competences of the World Trade Organization, the World Bank and the International Monetary Fund on the one hand and from the functional, humanitarian focuses of the UN agencies on the other. The contrary trend towards multiple competences can perhaps be detected in the 1970s with the conception of the CSCE as having three complementary 'baskets'—military security, the economy and the human dimension. It became a feature also of the Group of Seven industrialized nations (the G7, now the G8 with the addition of Russia), which started as an economic policy-coordinating group, but from the time of the 1983 Williamsburg Summit onwards started adopting positions on strategic issues such as nuclear policy. Today, the G8's agenda has shifted so far towards security topics that Germany was reported to have protested before the 2005 Gleneagles Summit about the lack of any serious economic focus in the principals' draft agenda.[51]

Since the end of the cold war, the model represented by the G7/8—the 'securitizing' of an originally economic, or other civil, forum—has become one affecting many different regions and institutions. The EU is the classic case: it waited 10 years after the fall of the Berlin Wall (until the Helsinki decisions of December 1999[52]) to claim its first specific military competence, but it had been dealing with elements of regional and global security governance, and internal and 'human' security for long before then. In Asia, ASEAN and the Asia–Pacific Economic Cooperation developed explicit policies against terrorism and proliferation after 2001 and by 2005 ASEAN was offering itself as a provider of peacekeeping forces in the Aceh province of Indonesia. When the Organization of African Unity converted itself into the AU in 2001–2002,[53] it seemed natural that the new organization should adopt a man-

---

[50] CENTO was established in 1955 by Iran, Iraq, Pakistan, Turkey and the UK; the USA joined in 1958, but Iraq withdrew in 1959 and Iran in 1979, effectively dissolving the pact. SEATO was established in 1954 and dissolved in 1977; its members were Australia, France, New Zealand, Pakistan, the Philippines, Thailand, the UK and the USA.

[51] Williamson, H. and Blitz, J., 'Berlin pushes for focus on the world economy', *Financial Times*, 5 July 2005, p. 2.

[52] Council of the European Union, 'Presidency conclusions', Helsinki European Council, 11–12 Dec. 1999, URL <http://europa.eu.int/council/off/conclu/dec99/dec99_en.htm>. This included the establishment of the European Security and Defence Policy.

[53] The AU's Constitutive Act entered into force on 26 May 2001, but its inaugural event was a summit meeting held at Durban on 9–10 July 2002.

date that seamlessly combines considerations of conflict management and security building with economic development and good governance.[54] Even purely economic organizations have been building up policies to counter economic abuses that are also security ones, examples being the Financial Action Task Force of the Organisation for Economic Co-operation and Development, which targets money laundering for terrorism and crime, and the recent International Maritime Organization initiative to tighten harbour and container security against WMD trafficking, among other things.[55]

Mirroring this, there have of course been extensions in the competence of formerly defence-focused institutions, such as NATO's progression between 1990 and 2002 from the territorial defence of a specified area to readiness for peace missions (or in theory, operations for extended self-defence) anywhere around the world. The focus of the UN itself has evolved, and is still evolving, towards more integrated multidimensional approaches to human welfare, long-lasting conflict resolution and peace-building. The UN's Millennium Goals dating from 2000 focus on 'human security', with little or no direct reference to conflict or other traditional security processes, such as the arms trade.[56] The Global Compact that was developed in 1999–2000 to enlist private-sector support for UN goals deliberately left military matters aside.[57] By the time of the major UN self-review in 2004–2005, however, the proposals of the High-level Panel on Threats, Challenges and Change and those recommended to governments by the UN Secretary-General in his report 'In larger freedom'[58] drew the connections much more tightly between conflict, armament issues, development, democracy and other factors in human well-being—and with the changes needed in the machinery of the UN itself to deal with the interlocking of all these tasks.

The World Summit outcome document that was adopted in the General Assembly on 20 September 2005, after difficult negotiations, was true to these antecedents at least in that it freely combined development-related, security-related and human rights aspirations.[59] Its chief weaknesses were the truncated (only 8 pages out of 40) and generally toothless nature of its security section—lacking in particular anything on arms control, disarmament and non-proliferation—and its failure either to accept the rationale for major systemic reform at the UN or to explain why it could be dispensed with. Its strong points could all be linked conceptually with the breaking down of inter-

---

[54] A similar mixing of functions is seen in African sub-regional groups such as the Economic Community of West African States (ECOWAS). Adisa, J., 'The African Union: the vision, programmes, policies and challenges', *SIPRI Yearbook 2003* (note 17), pp. 79–85; and Williams, R., 'National defence reform and the African Union', *SIPRI Yearbook 2004* (note 22), pp. 231–49.

[55] On institutions with security-relevant activities see appendices 1 and 2 of eds Bailes and Frommelt (note 36).

[56] United Nations, 'United Nations Millennium Declaration', UN General Assembly document A/RES/55/2, 18 Sep. 2000, URL <http://www.un.org/millenniumgoals/>.

[57] See the website of the United Nations Global Compact, URL <http://www.unglobalcompact.org/>.

[58] United Nations, 'In larger freedom: towards development, security and human rights for all', Report of the Secretary-General, UN document A/59/2005, 21 Mar. 2005, URL <http://www.un.org/largerfreedom/>.

[59] United Nations (note 17).

dimensional barriers: making a state's responsibility to protect its own people a formal matter of international concern; creating a UN peace-building commission to attempt a coordinated, complex approach to all aspects of reconstruction; clarifying several connections between security processes and the protection of individual and gender rights and so on. In terms of the various power models discussed in section II above, it may be noted that constructive new solutions were found in this document where both West–West and North–South interests could be more or less speedily reconciled. Although many commentators adopted the USA-versus-everybody diagnosis in blaming the USA for the loss of the remaining proposals, the negotiating reality was rather that of an unholy alliance between the USA and other countries that are resistant to the increased intrusiveness of international norms (see below).

To return to the phenomenon of institutional 'mission creep' into security, two trends mentioned above are relevant here: (*a*) the increasingly multi-functional understanding of the demands of conflict analysis and resolution and of peace-building; and (*b*) the extension of security agendas towards fields where economic, social and other functional processes (and competences) prevail. The evolution of originally economic regional organizations has also been driven by integration dynamics, which push constantly towards new spheres of cooperation,[60] and by the interest in regional self-sufficiency or at least self-expression, which makes local cooperation attractive as an alternative to—or an efficiency booster for—broader affiliations in the UN or with the USA. It is easier in this light to grasp why the overlapping competences have not been fully symmetrical between former military and non-military institutions. NATO has, indeed, moved into new kinds of security building: but not into economic or functional security operations, hardly even into internal security, and only in limited and experimental fashion (notably in Afghanistan) into hands-on democracy building. The non-military security contributions that are most in demand today require the application of substantial, jointly owned or controlled, resources and often—notably where non-state offenders and contributors must be 'captured'—the exercise of some kind of regulatory competence designed for binding effects both between and within states. The EU has both these things, but NATO has neither, and even its best friends have not suggested that it should acquire, for example, a large aid budget or the power to apply economic sanctions or adopt binding anti-terrorist laws for its members.[61] Of course, there is no objective reason why all institutions should seek all competences, and no shame for an institution that tries, rather, to maximize efficiency in a limited but vital field. Experience since 1990 suggests that overlapping competences merely deepen the prob-

---

[60] Specific explanations for why this pressure should lead to cooperation in defence and security as such could include (*a*) the interest in defending collective assets and interests acquired through economic cooperation and (*b*) the increasingly open frontier between technological and industrial cooperation in the non-military and the military sectors respectively.

[61] The OSCE has the same deficiencies but also lacks any power of global action—hence, perhaps, the current anxieties about its future. Dunay (note 48).

lems of role sharing and collaboration between institutions, as discussed below.

Disarmament and its relationship with other security work

The second way in which institutional roles have become blurred since the classic cold war period relates more particularly to arms control and disarmament. These used to be processes with their own discrete framework and forms. The UN had its Committee (now Conference) on Disarmament, in Geneva, that either negotiated global measures itself or 'spun off' separate negotiating processes for new conventions. NATO, since the time of the Harmel Report,[62] sought arms control agreements with its rival bloc as part of a separately defined, 'détente' wing of its policy (the first wing being deterrence through strong defence). When NATO and the Warsaw Pact agreed to talk about conventional arms cuts they did so in a tailor-made forum with its own rules: first the Mutual and Balanced Force Reductions (MBFR) negotiations, then the Conventional Armed Forces in Europe (CFE) negotiations, which were linked to, but kept formally separate from, the CSCE framework. The Soviet Union and the USA negotiated directly on their strategic nuclear forces, while keeping their allies informed. Characteristic of all these processes were that: (*a*) the agreements sought were framed as treaties, conventions or in some other legally binding form; (*b*) resulting cuts were to be executed by the state owning the weapons, with no outside help; but (*c*) monitoring and verification of the required cuts and constraints were normally provided for through a purpose-built mechanism or agency, as typified by the Organisation for the Prohibition of Chemical Weapons (OPCW) for the 1993 Chemical Weapons Convention or the role that the International Atomic Energy Agency was called upon to play in relation to the Non-Proliferation Treaty. It was thus natural to see arms control and disarmament as a distinct 'business' that worked along different tracks from—if not always in contradiction to—the provision of defence and building of security by active, voluntary and collaborative means. It was certainly handled by distinct departments (usually in foreign ministries) within most national administrations.

This disarmament model did not end with the cold war. It extended well into the mid-1990s with the Russian–US Strategic Arms Reduction Treaties of 1991 and 1993 (START I and II), the 1990 CFE Treaty and its 1999 Adaptation Agreement, the 1992 Open Skies Treaty, the 1993 Chemical Weapons Convention and the 1996 Comprehensive Test-Ban Treaty (CTBT, also with its own follow-up organ).[63] This flowering of arms control after the fall of the Warsaw Pact and Soviet Union, when the worst of the danger might have seemed to be past, did not strike anyone as contradictory at the time. It could be rationalized as putting a seal on the gains of strategic relaxation and limiting risks within the still unsettled and evolving East–West relationship.

---

[62] NATO (note 2).
[63] On these agreements see annex A in this volume.

Equally to the point, it coincided with a period of large voluntary force reductions (and scrapping of plans for increases) by all those most involved in the cold war. At such a time, negotiated reductions did not have to be punitive—as shown by the fact that some countries cut more deeply than they were obliged to—but they could offer some assurance that the other side was acting in parallel and could be called to account if it switched course. For all this, in retrospect, the post-cold war crop of agreements looks not so much like a new start as like the beginning of the end for traditional arms control. Three of its main products—START II, the CTBT and the CFE Adaptation Agreement— have not entered into force. An important earlier agreement, the Soviet–US 1972 Treaty on the Limitation of Anti-Ballistic Missile Systems, ceased to have force in 2002 when the USA abrogated it in order to proceed with its ballistic missile defence programme. True, Russia and the USA did agree in 2002 on a new Treaty on Strategic Offensive Reductions (SORT), but—at US insistence—this was of a much more 'political' nature than its predecessors, with no intrusive verification arrangements and no requirement to take systems permanently out of use.[64]

Taken together with the pressures discussed in section III for quantitative and qualitative arms increases, do these setbacks signal that disarmament— even in the regions that profited most from the end of the cold war—has come to a halt? The answer, of course, depends on what is meant by 'disarmament'. What might be called the 'legislative' approach to arms control and disarmament—quantified and verifiable reductions prescribed by treaty—has certainly suffered serious, and in many cases deliberate, reverses. During the two terms of President Bush, the USA has chastised the old methods for being both too weak and too strong: weak towards the 'bad guys'—who can resile from or choose not to join key treaties and are not effectively enough detected or punished when they offend—and too strong in holding back well-intentioned states that seek the means to defend themselves and export security to others. The growing crisis of faith in recent years among the traditional arms control and disarmament community would not have been so serious if these charges did not, in fact, carry some weight. It is true that treaties as vital as the NPT do not have as parties all the states that are vital for their purpose. Legal instruments of the traditional kind are neither capable of enforcing themselves nor backed in practice by guaranteed enforcement assistance from elsewhere. The treaty method in general has a certain rigidity and sterility, lacking in positive cooperative features and in evolutive potential, that tends to dim its attraction alongside more active modern approaches to security. It would by no means be impossible to reinvent 'legislative' disarmament in a way that overcomes these reproaches—the new universal rules on WMD trafficking contained in UN Security Council Resolution 1540 were an inter-

---

[64] Kile, S. N., 'Nuclear arms control, non-proliferation and ballistic missile defence', *SIPRI Yearbook 2003* (note 17), pp. 604–605.

esting attempt[65]—but it has to be said that no state has yet succeeded in, or even devoted national capital to, this task.

Nevertheless, reductions in forces, weapons and military spending have never completely ended. The end-goals of arms control and non-proliferation have been pursued in several other ways besides the treaty method, even (or especially) in the 15 years since the cold war. Very roughly, the processes involved can be divided into five: (a) unilateral steps, (b) coercive measures, (c) constraints on use rather than numbers, (d) interventions elsewhere in the arms cycle and (e) package approaches.

As noted above, a large part of the reductions in both WMD and conventional weapons made by former cold war antagonists since 1990 have been of type a, that is, wholly voluntary or exceeding treaty obligations. There has also been at least one case of parallel unilateral measures, in the package on short-range ('tactical') nuclear forces announced by Russia and the USA in 1991.[66] Ironically, given that 'unilateral' disarmament was such an ardent wish of the cold war peace movements, it is clear today that such voluntary measures have serious limits in what they can contribute to security. They are not verifiable or—sometimes—even clearly measurable: they can be reversed at any time and they do not prevent the acquisition of different systems that add new qualitative, or even quantitative, capacities. The present US administration's explicit preference for such methods is now often criticized by pro-disarmament lobbies.[67]

The most dramatic cases of type b, enforced disarmament, are those carried out through military action, such as the US-led invasion of Iraq in 2003, but other variants are less immediately controversial. It is now almost routine for the international community to promote disarmament, demobilization and reintegration measures as part of the peace-building process after intervention in an intra-state conflict. Part of the 1995 Dayton Agreement called for enforced, internationally monitored force reductions by the combatants within the former Yugoslavia, and the process was completed smoothly on schedule.[68] The measures to deprive Iraq of its WMD capabilities that were ordered by the UN in 1991, overseen by the UN Special Commission on Iraq (UNSCOM) and later reviewed by the UN Monitoring, Verification and Inspection Commission (UNMOVIC), turn out in retrospect to have been

---

[65] Anthony, I., 'Arms control and non-proliferation: the role of international organizations', *SIPRI Yearbook 2005* (note 3), pp. 539–47.

[66] Fieldhouse, R., 'Nuclear weapon developments and unilateral reduction initiatives', *SIPRI Yearbook 1992: World Armaments and Disarmament* (Oxford University Press: Oxford, 1992), pp. 66–92.

[67] The US permanent representative to the OSCE stated there in Sep. 2005 that: 'We are against negotiating new traditional style arms control/[confidence- and security-building measures], although we MAY be willing to consider specific proposals if there is a clear security need to be addressed.' United States Mission to the OSCE, 'Statement by U.S. Permanent Representative Ambassador Julie Finley', Vienna, 13 Sep. 2005, URL <http://osce.usmission.gov/>.

[68] The General Framework Agreement for Peace in Bosnia and Herzegovina (Dayton Agreement) was signed on 14 Dec. 1995; the text is available at URL <http://www.oscebih.org/overview/gfap/eng/>. Annex 1b covers regional stabilization. Lachowski, Z., *Confidence- and Security-Building Measures in the New Europe*, SIPRI Research Report no. 18 (Oxford University Press: Oxford, 2004); and Lachowski, Z. and Dunay, P., 'Conventional arms control', *SIPRI Yearbook 2005* (note 3), pp. 662–63.

remarkably effective.[69] The obvious pitfall with such measures—as shown by Europe's own earlier experience—is that they will not stop the targeted countries and communities from trying to rearm as soon as they can, unless there is a larger national or regional transformation that removes both opportunity and reason to do so. Lasting effects are more likely if the state concerned commits itself voluntarily to all the relevant local and global arms control regimes.[70]

Measures of type *c*, non-quantitative restrictions, can be of several kinds but most commonly involve either confidence- and security-building measures (CSBMs, which address force deployments and activities plus transparency and accident control) or limitations on the contexts in which a given type of armament can be used—usually for humanitarian purposes.[71] CSBMs have more typically developed in bilateral or limited regional contexts, notably in Europe but also in Latin America and on the China–Russia border. They do not place any constraint on the numbers or types of weapons held or on force levels, and this is both their weakness and their potential strength in the kind of security environment prevailing today. In a few cases they may pave the way to actual disarmament; more often, they have eased and controlled the type of transition described above from an adversarial arms build-up to the pooling and collaborative use of military resources within a given area. Where conditions continue to be tense, CSBMs may at the least reduce risks of surprise attack or of an accidental slide into conflict (as between NATO and the Warsaw Pact in the cold war, or India and Pakistan today). Generic humanitarian restrictions on weapon use can, in turn, reduce the damage done by conflict when it does occur. Many further applications and developments of these methods might be imagined, especially in regional contexts and as part of 'package' approaches (see below).

As documented by SIPRI, measures of type *d* that focus elsewhere than on the size of existing arsenals have been in growing vogue since the end of the cold war.[72] They include technology controls and export controls, designed to stop new destructive techniques being developed at all or, when developed, being disseminated to certain categories of users; and measures at the other end of the arms cycle, designed to ensure that weapons taken out of use (for whatever purpose) are brought under safe control, guarded and preferably destroyed. The latter method of 'disarmament assistance' has thus far been

---

[69] UNSCOM was established by UN Security Council Resolution 687 of 3 Apr. 1991 and was active until Dec. 1998. UNMOVIC was tasked by UN Security Council resolutions 1284 and 1441 of 17 Dec. 1999 and 8 Nov. 2002, respectively, and was active in 1999–2003. For assessments of the Iraqi case see Kile, S. N., 'Nuclear arms control and non-proliferation' and Guthrie, R., Hart, J. and Kuhlau, F., 'Chemical and biological warfare developments and arms control', *SIPRI Yearbook 2005* (note 3), pp. 566–68, 616–21.

[70] This process has so far been conspicuously absent in the case of Iraq. On chemical-related issues see Zanders, J. P., Hart, J., Kuhlau, F. and Guthrie, R., *Non-Compliance with the Chemical Weapons Convention: Lessons from and for Iraq*, SIPRI Policy Paper no. 5 (SIPRI: Stockholm, Oct. 2003), URL <http://www.sipri.org/>.

[71] On CSBMs see Lachowski (note 68).

[72] See, e.g., Anthony, I., 'Arms control in the new security environment', *SIPRI Yearbook 2003* (note 17), pp. 563–76,

applied predominantly to ex-Soviet WMD[73] and to stockpiles of smaller items like landmines, small arms and ammunition.[74] Both approaches have drawn special interest in recent years because of their relevance to threats of non-state origin. Effective export controls can help keep the means of destruction out of terrorist hands and out of the private marketplace; assisted disarmament—which can be applied just as much to voluntary cuts as internationally agreed ones—reduces risks of terrorist or criminal theft, as well as the possible onward sale of the objects to unreliable users. Whether acknowledged to be part of arms control or not, such measures have their own limitations. Export controls have been criticized as inherently discriminatory and non-transparent, and their effectiveness is not easy to prove.[75] There is no obvious downside to disarmament assistance, but questions can be asked about the transparency of its methods and results and whether the resources devoted to it are being optimally used. Nevertheless, both types of measure have earned their place in the modern policy armoury and can be expected to develop further in coming years.

In processes of type *e*, arms control and disarmament 'packages' can be put together at several levels. The simplest kind of packaging is to combine several measures within the (expanded) range of arms control, for example, to supplement a reductions agreement by disarmament assistance and confidence-building measures. Other packages extend beyond the arms control field and perhaps even beyond the security field proper. Since all techniques required for WMD development stem from or are closely related to technologies that also have legitimate civilian uses, the barrier to WMD proliferation needs to be guarded through a combination of measures on both sides of the civil–military divide—by monitoring and disciplining civil nuclear activities (e.g., by international control of the nuclear fuel cycle[76]) or by safety and security controls in the chemical and biotechnology industries,[77] as well as by cracking down on the corresponding weaponized versions. The most diverse packages are typically put together ad hoc to stop a given state from developing dangerous capacities or to make it give up existing ones, using an array of sticks and carrots from the political, economic and technical as well as security spheres. In practice, even the classic cold war disarmament agreements had diverse strategic, political and economic drivers behind them; and the greater readiness to acknowledge and use such methods today matches the general

---

[73] This has been done in the framework of what used to be the USA's national 'Nunn–Lugar' programme, which became the Cooperative Threat Reduction programme and is now the Global Partnership programme of the G8. Anthony, I. and Fedchenko, V., 'International non-proliferation and disarmament assistance', *SIPRI Yearbook 2005* (note 3), pp. 675–98.

[74] On these programmes, and gaps left by them, in the Euro-Atlantic space see Bailes, A. J. K., Anthony, I. and Melnyk, O., *Relics of Cold War: Europe's Challenge, Ukraine's Experience*, SIPRI Policy Paper no. 6 (SIPRI: Stockholm, Nov. 2003), URL <http://www.sipri.org/>.

[75] For a developing-country ('demand-side') critique of export controls see Mallik, A., *Technology and Security in the 21st Century: A Demand-Side Perspective*, SIPRI Research Report no. 20 (Oxford University Press: Oxford, 2004).

[76] See appendix 13C in this volume.

[77] See appendix 14A in this volume.

acceptance of multifunctional approaches to security. The buying-out of Libya's WMD potential in 2004 was a classic example,[78] and the ongoing efforts to resolve the North Korean and Iranian WMD challenges also aim to combine economic or political incentives with strategic disincentives. In such cases, weapons-related inspections and controls may still be vital ingredients, but more as tools for the implementation of an eventual bargain than as the levers to achieve it.

Here, however, it is necessary to return to the question of who has the ability, and is authorized, to put such packages together. It is clear that arms control agencies of the classic, OPCW type cannot do it on their own. Equally, packages are unlikely to do the job demonstrably and to hold fast for long unless they can be anchored in clear definitions of goals and standards, such as those provided by treaties, and serviced by the impartial monitoring and inspection capacities of the corresponding agencies. On this view, recent evolution has not so much superseded the traditional instruments as highlighted their limitations and their dependence on other types of input by other internal actors—organizations, individual states or both. The range of such 'add-ons' required for effective solutions is very wide indeed because it includes not just the tools relevant to meet an arms control or non-proliferation end—from military 'sticks' to economic and financial 'carrots'—but also all the other contributions needed to convert the dysfunctional security situation that lies behind all weapons offences to a stable and cooperative one: in a state, for a state or for an entire region.

Linking this perception with what is said above about the evolution of security institutions, three further thoughts emerge. The first is that institutions with resources to bestow, and with rule-making competences, are at an advantage also in the specific realm of arms control and in promoting durable non-proliferation solutions. The EU has a comprehensive anti-WMD strategy that can include among its instruments the refinement of regulatory systems within the Union and globally, the transfer of funds notably for disarmament assistance, the control of European exports, and the construction of ad hoc carrot-and-stick packages for cases like Iran—while NATO has far fewer tools with which to pursue its similar goals.[79] Second, in most problem cases, several different institutions with differing competences will need to collaborate for good package solutions. Third, joining a strongly integrated institution such as NATO, the EU or (increasingly) ASEAN can itself do much to guarantee virtuous behaviour on the part of the acceding state. The new member may, indeed, be required to upgrade some of its conventional forces for collective interventions, but it will have neither motive nor opportunity to develop types

---

[78] Hart and Kile (note 23).

[79] Council of the European Union, 'EU Strategy against Proliferation of Weapons of Mass Destruction', European Council, Brussels, Dec. 2003, URL <http://ue.eu.int/cms3_fo/showPage.asp?id=718>. NATO has its own WMD Centre following a decision at the 1999 Washington Summit, but this has a relatively limited remit to promote consultation between NATO members; improved performance in areas such as the protection of armed forces in environments with nuclear, biological or chemical contamination; and civil emergency planning. In principle it also prepares joint NATO inputs to international negotiations, but European–US differences on many of the specific issues have hampered this.

of weapons of which the given institution disapproves, and it must expect (direct or indirect) sanctions within the organization if it uses its capacities in prohibited ways.

These five kinds of input to arms control and to general security building—with the important exception of making internationally binding rules—can all, however, also be provided by individual states. In criticizing the treaty method, the current US administration was also expressing a positive preference for freedom to act nationally, alone or with self-picked partners, to tackle threats arising in the armaments field as much as in any other. National action does offer prima facie advantages of speed and flexibility, while a country as powerful as the USA can bring resources to bear (at least initially) that exceed those centrally controlled by any known institution. However, even a little reflection on the lessons of Iraq will show that the longer-term effectiveness and ultimate security impact of such national initiatives are questionable. Their lack of legitimacy in others' eyes, notably the eyes of the populations being acted upon, is an obvious problem when the interveners claim to be upholding generally valid norms (including those of arms control and non-proliferation). A country acting alone is also more prone than a multinational grouping—where internal doubts and differences must be argued out—to act on incomplete information, to misjudge the information that it has, to misread the situation in the target area (also because of subjective likes and dislikes) and to take excessive risks. Even the greatest state's resources will sooner or later buckle under the burden of all the different inputs needed and of sustaining them over time. These practical points reinforce the arguments in section II about how hard it is for any nation to observe and be seen to observe consistent principles of what is 'good' and 'bad' for international security, so long as it insists on being its own judge and executioner.

The world's multilateral security institutions—for their part—seem to be spending less time now on demarcation squabbles than they did during the 1990s, and more on learning better and more varied ways to combine their forces. Some competition as well as confusion between them will probably always remain and need not always be condemned. Self-assertion by an organization can reflect positive factors like *esprit de corps*, internal cohesion and ambition. In an environment that constantly creates new demands, institutions' jostling for a new pecking order can be a way of testing their respective success in adaptation—and hence, their fitness to survive. Nevertheless, the bottom line of this analysis is that all multinational institutions have more in common with each other than they do with purely national, unregulated actions in pursuit of the same goals. The dichotomy between using and not using, respecting and not respecting, institutions is one of the most profound in the whole field of security. De-institutionalization is a threat that would need to be taken extremely seriously, even if the world has not yet approached as close to it in the early 21st century as some believe (or hope) it has. It could come as much from the erosion of confidence within institutions—resulting in poorer-quality outputs, but also the shunning of new tasks—as from attacks on them, or the successful flouting of their rules, from outside. The struggle to ensure that 'the best' do not lose 'all conviction' has become a particularly open one in the EU since the crisis of the constitutional referendums in 2005. It will be fought from now on in the UN, as actors of good will strive to build on and maximize the advances in the 2005 World Summit outcome (and find new ways to fill its gaps), while other actors try to second-guess even what was agreed. To get the most balanced and complete assessment of how institutionalization is faring, however, requires a much fuller survey than research has yet provided of multilateral developments (including relations with global institutions) in all the world's regions as well.

V. Conclusions

In historical terms, 40 years is a brief period of time, representing little more than one generation. It is no wonder that the speed of change in security affairs since 1966 has been uneven and its directions sometimes incoherent. Full credit should be given to some major, positive transformations that the period has witnessed, even if they merely opened the door to new challenges. Alongside the end of the cold war and the peaceful unification of Germany and Europe, examples could include the end of apartheid in South Africa, the end of Communist insurgency in South-East Asia (sealed through the enlargement of ASEAN) and the strategic de-polarization of Central America. A further set of problems have evolved in directions that greatly reduce the risks of major conflict, even if they still have to be seen as problematic: Russia's relations with other Euro-Atlantic powers, the political geography of West and Central Asia, and arguably (although there are more pessimistic schools of thought on this) the strategic role of China.

In depressingly many cases, however, 40 years cannot be said to have made things any better and may even have made them worse. *SIPRI Yearbook 2005* highlighted the problems of longevity and recidivism in the field of conflict:[80] in 2005 also, of 17 armed conflicts defined as 'major', 15 were at least 10 years old and 3 had lasted for 40 years or more.[81] The conflict between Israel, its neighbours and the Palestinians is the most obvious example of such a stubborn case; but the tension between India and Pakistan has also been virtually unremitting since Pakistan was created, and there are states in Africa that have hardly known a year of peace since independence. In very broad terms, what seems to characterize these chronic cases is the zero-sum nature of views and interests within the cycle of conflict, combined with a set of factors that make external intervention ineffective or counterproductive (or, perhaps, deter it altogether). There are other, internal conflicts that do not come above the statistical horizon used in the Yearbook but have persisted for decades or even centuries within some of the world's most advanced democracies: notably Northern Ireland and the Basque issue. There are countries—Cuba and North

---

[80] Dwan, R. and Holmqvist, C., 'Major armed conflicts', *SIPRI Yearbook 2005* (note 3), pp. 83–120.

[81] See appendix 2A in this volume.

Korea—that have clung to the most unregenerate form of Communism, and others that remain gripped by personal dictatorships. The whole Arab region is deeply fissured by internal governance problems and dysfunctional interstate relationships.[82] One loose but still suggestive connection that many of these state-related challenges have in common is a seminal period around the end of World War I, which links them to the first stage of dismantlement of the pre-modern empires.[83] Given that causation, it would have been too much to expect that the end of the cold war (even when combined with the completion of decolonization) would of itself have done much to help with the full range of these problems. As argued in section II, it has made certain kinds of outside interference easier, but almost certainly not the right ones.

The balance sheet of problems solved and unsolved looks, if anything, even gloomier in the functional dimensions of security. US military spending now exceeds its highest cold war levels[84] and the global arms trade was worth $44–53 billion in 2004.[85] Development and human welfare continue to suffer both from conflict and from resources tied up in military assets that are never actively used. It is shaming to reflect on the tenacity of such phenomena as torture, use of child soldiers, rape as a tool of war and human trafficking in conditions close to slavery. Some of the basic riddles about how to move towards the elimination of weapons of mass destruction, and how to live safely with them in the meantime, are as far from solution as ever, and not just because of the proliferators. It is sad to note, for instance, that a fissile material cut-off treaty was being discussed at the time that the earliest SIPRI Year-books were written and is still stuck on the drawing board, despite new concerns about both state and non-state misuse of nuclear capacities that should have redoubled its value. A full stop to nuclear testing has also been discussed ever since the 1960s but now seems blocked on the threshold of the CTBT's entry into force.

One thing that has not changed is the importance of reliable and impartial information: on the statistics of security, the processes, the roles played by different actors and the known or foreseeable consequences of different choices. SIPRI was established as an independent authority partly because the data available from other sources on these topics were so often incomplete and tendentious in the 1960s: and they still are. The problem is actually greater now that so many different dimensions of security-related activity, and so many actors, have to be monitored for the sake of completeness. Good data also need a fourth dimension, of time, to chart all the stages of a given process—not just crisis intervention but follow-up; and not just the production of

[82] Hollis, R., 'The greater Middle East', *SIPRI Yearbook 2005* (note 3), pp. 223–50.

[83] It is fashionable to connect a group of the recently most salient problems with the dismemberment of the Ottoman Empire around the time of World War I, but other cases could just as well be tied to the withdrawal of empire in the early 20th century in East Asia and the Americas.

[84] US military spending during the cold war peaked in 1986 at $472 billion. In 2005 spending reached $478 billion. Figures in constant 2003 prices from the SIPRI Military Expenditure Database. See also chapter 8 in this volume.

[85] This rough estimate of the financial value of the arms trade is arrived at by adding data released by supplier governments. See chapter 10 in this volume.

weapons but where they go, how they are used and whether they are destroyed. Bits of these stories are covered by measures of different kinds that aim at or incidentally produce transparency, including export controls, verification and monitoring, and assisted destruction schemes. There still remain serious gaps in the chain, and great inequalities in coverage from place to place and user to user, and problems of incompatibility in the techniques used and in their findings.[86] These problems not only hamper governments and organizations that are seeking in good will to analyse the security effects of all these transactions and to redress the negative ones. They are also an obstacle to popular understanding; to proper debate within states on choices affecting the defence and security sectors; to the exercise of democratic control at all levels by representative institutions:[87] and to informed reporting and campaigning by the concerned non-governmental organizations and civil society movements.

SIPRI's goal has been, from the start, to produce and disseminate the 'cleanest' possible information on key security transactions, on all states and to all the audiences that it can reach. The task is anything but simple or routine. The targets and sources for information gathering change, technologies change, new audiences enter the picture and existing audiences have new needs. SIPRI is, moreover, far from alone in this field of research and must stay alert to the possibilities of synergy, partnership and division of labour with others. Increasing the range of actors in security processes that produce, exchange and disseminate their own good data is desirable, not just for the sake of transparency itself and for democracy, but because of its potential to foster confidence and active security cooperation. In today's uncertain and complex world, the formulation of goals for security-related action cannot stop at the idea of doing good, and doing it in the right ways. To show, and to convince world opinion, that any given security move is good is perhaps the toughest demand of all, given all the confusions and disagreements about both challenges and remedies that are explored in this introduction. Unless that challenge is also confronted and met, there can be little hope that security in the next 40 years will show even as many elements of progress as SIPRI's first 40 years have done.

---

[86] See chapter 6 in this volume.
[87] See chapter 5 in this volume.

Part I. Security and conflicts, 2005

Chapter 1. Euro-Atlantic security and institutions

Chapter 2. Major armed conflicts

Chapter 3. Peace-building: the new international focus on Africa

Chapter 4. Regional security cooperation in the early 21st century

Chapter 5. National governance of nuclear weapons: opportunities and constraints

1. Euro-Atlantic security and institutions

PÁL DUNAY and ZDZISLAW LACHOWSKI

I. Introduction

Pragmatism dominated Euro-Atlantic relations in 2005. Beyond the still basic-ally unsolved rift over Iraq, the United States and the European countries that are members of the European Union (EU) or the North Atlantic Treaty Organ-ization (NATO) have recognized their roles in global affairs as complemen-tary and cooperative rather than divergent and confrontational. In some cases, the flow of Euro-Atlantic cooperation has reverted to international institutions such as NATO, the Organization for Security and Co-operation in Europe (OSCE) and the United Nations (UN). In other cases, bilateral channels have been used for rapprochement, but much less is now heard from the USA about the value of ad hoc coalitions. The EU's Constitutional Treaty setback in 2005 raised questions about the EU's ambition to be a more effective security actor in world affairs, while NATO strove to underline its relevance by embarking on new kinds of missions.

Relations between Russia and other post-Soviet states on the one hand and the West on the other have not taken any decisive turn. The recognition of Russia's importance in Eurasia beyond its post-Soviet sphere of influence, including Iran, Korea and the Middle East, continued to underpin efforts for strategic cooperation. Several Western actors, however, voiced their concerns more clearly than earlier regarding Russia's domestic political course.

Pragmatism has also prevailed in the policies of the West towards the Western Balkans. Alongside the continued peacekeeping and peace-building effort, attention has switched to how those entities that have not arrived at a final settled status (Kosovo, Serbia and Montenegro) may reach one without destabilizing the region.

Section II of this chapter discusses the development of US policies. Sec-tion III offers a brief overview of inter-institutional relations in the Euro-Atlantic region. Section IV analyses EU developments. Section V reviews developments in NATO, and section VI briefly addresses the results of the OSCE reform process. Section VII examines developments in the former Soviet area, and section VIII presents the conclusions. Current issues in the Western Balkans are examined in more detail in appendix 1A.

II. The policies of the United States

The USA started 2005 with a 'new' administration following the re-election of President George W. Bush in November 2004. The president emphasized one policy theme in two early, major speeches. In his inauguration speech Bush said: 'All who live in tyranny and hopelessness can know: the United States will not ignore your oppression, or excuse your oppressors. When you stand for your liberty, we will stand with you. Democratic reformers facing repression, prison, or exile can know: America sees you for who you are: the future leaders of your free country'.[1] Two weeks later in his State of the Union Address the president stated:

The United States has no right, no desire, and no intention to impose our form of government on anyone else. That is one of the main differences between us and our enemies . . . Our aim is to build and preserve a community of free and independent nations, with governments that answer to their citizens, and reflect their own cultures. And because democracies respect their own people and their neighbours, the advance of freedom will lead to peace.[2]

Without dwelling on the possible inconsistencies, it is important to note the missionary zeal for the global spread of democracy that underlies the agenda of the USA under the current leadership and that follows historical and more recent precedents. The difference is apparently not in the zeal but in the means used to achieve the spread of democracy.

The Bush Administration's vision, however, is increasingly encountering practical barriers that curtail its freedom of action. Bogged down in Iraq and burdened by a still-rising budget deficit, US leaders have found their policies and allocation of resources coming under sharper domestic scrutiny, especially following the suffering caused in August 2005 by Hurricane Katrina.[3] The debate on US security policy has thus moved from the international to the domestic scene, while the USA's relations with other Western partners have improved in the absence of any new source of disagreement to match Iraq. The USA continues to approach the challenges of Iran and the Democratic People's Republic of Korea (North Korea)[4] in a diplomatic style that allows for European synergy, while the EU has pulled back from confrontation on issues like the possible lifting of its arms embargo on China.

While the US Administration modified its actions under the pressure of circumstances, some analysts have started to reassess the merits of Bush's strategy in the light of the long-term interests of the USA. One political analyst has argued that the key question for the USA 'is how multilateralism *should* be

---

[1] The White House, 'President sworn-in to second term', News release, Washington, DC, 20 Jan. 2005, URL <http://www.whitehouse.gov/news/releases/2005/01/20050120-1.html>. p. 2.

[2] The White House, 'State of the Union Address', News release, Washington, DC, 2 Feb. 2005, URL <http://www.whitehouse.gov/news/releases/2005/02/20050202-11.html>, p. 5.

[3] Senator Joseph R. Biden, a leading Democrat, recognized that the 'administration is beginning to realize it's not enough to be strong. We also have to be smart, that we can't secure America's interest solely with force, acting alone. I hope [Condoleezza Rice] completes the turn from ideology to reality'. Quoted in Wright, R. and Kessler, G., 'At State Rice takes control of diplomacy', *Washington Post*, 31 July 2005, p. A01.

[4] See chapter 13 in this volume.

defined and whether it can be reshaped to serve U.S. interests'.[5] Other analysts have noted signs, thus far inconclusive, that at least some of the world's major powers have started 'soft rebalancing' in order to constrain the power and the threatening behaviour of the USA.[6] Warnings have been issued concerning the current low standing of the USA in world opinion,[7] and attention has been called to the importance of US leadership being accepted willingly.[8] In some cases, it has become clear that extreme unilateral action by the USA also does not enjoy full acceptance among the members of the Bush Administration.[9]

The main items on the US security agenda in 2005 were the repercussions of the Iraq conflict, the continuing fight against terrorism, homeland security, problems of US intelligence and defence reform.

The Iraq conflict

The coalition presence in Iraq continued, but the number of states participating militarily alongside the USA continued to decline as more states decided to withdraw or reduce their forces or reassign them to less dangerous tasks.[10] This reflected not only the risks associated with a field presence in Iraq, but also the repercussions in the domestic political life of participating states. Iraq played a role in the change of government in Spain in 2004, contributed to the weakening of government legitimacy in the United Kingdom[11] and reappeared as an issue on the pre-election agenda of some other large European states, like Germany and Italy.[12] The fact that far more governments have been

[5] van Oudenaren, J., 'Containing Europe', *National Interest*, no. 80 (summer 2005), p. 60. Emphasis in the original.

[6] Pape, R. A., 'Soft balancing against the United States', *International Security*, vol. 30, no. 1 (summer 2005), pp. 7–45; and Paul, T. V., 'Soft balancing in the age of U.S. primacy', *International Security*, vol. 30, no. 1 (summer 2005), pp. 46–71.

[7] See Public Agenda, 'Public Agenda Confidence in U.S. Foreign Policy Index', 2005, URL <http://www.publicagenda.org>.

[8] Walt, S. M., *Taming American Power: The Global Response to U.S. Primacy* (W.W. Norton: New York, N.Y., 2005).

[9] E.g., Secretary of State Condoleeza Rice found it difficult to speak for the policies represented by Vice President Dick Cheney regarding certain interrogation practices used on terrorists and secret prisons beyond the borders of the USA. In a major pronouncement on these matters Rice clearly distanced herself from the practice of torturing alleged terrorists, although she remained mute on secret prisons. US Department of State, Secretary Condoleezza Rice, 'Remarks upon her departure for Europe', 5 Dec. 2005, URL <http://www.state.gov/secretary/rm/2005/57602.htm>, p. 2.

[10] Ukraine decided to withdraw its troops from Iraq by the end of 2005. 'Yushchenko signs order for Iraq troop withdrawal', *Kyiv Post*, 22 Mar. 2005, URL <http://www.kyivpost.com/bn/22490>. The withdrawal was implemented by late Dec. 2005. 'Ukraine completes troop withdrawal from Iraq', *Moscow News*, 27 Dec. 2005, URL <http://www.mosnews.com/news/2005/12/27/ukriraqexit.shtml>.

[11] Serfaty, S., *The Vital Partnership—Power and Order: America and Europe Beyond Iraq* (Rowman & Littlefield: Lanham, Md., 2005), p. 3.

[12] The Italian Government has revised its position on withdrawing its troops from Iraq a number of times as the result *inter alia* of disagreements with the USA regarding the activity of US intelligence operatives on Italian soil and an accident in which the international operations chief of Italy's military intelligence was killed. Vinci, A., 'Italy seeks Americans over abduction', CNN.com, 24 June 2005, URL <http://edition.cnn.com/2005/WORLD/europe/06/24/italy.arrests/>; and Hooper, J., 'Italian hostage accuses US of trying to kill her as thousands mourn her rescuer', Guardian Unlimited, 7 Mar. 2005, URL <http://www.guardian.co.uk/Iraq/Story/0,2763,1432040,00.html>. In Poland, the presidential and

weakened than strengthened by their contribution to the military operation in Iraq further undermines the standing and legitimacy of the coalition. Meanwhile, the more conclusive evidence now available that Saddam Hussein possessed neither weapons of mass destruction (WMD) nor terrorist links at the time of the invasion has left little hope of reconciling the US assessment of the crisis with that of its opponents.[13]

If the presence of terrorists in Saddam Hussein's Iraq could not be substantiated, the situation has changed since the occupation in 2003.[14] Although approximately 95 per cent of the individuals who fight in Iraq against the occupation (and against other Iraqis) are Iraqi nationals there are a significant number of international operatives using terrorist methods in Iraq.[15] The fact that Iraq now has a terrorist problem aggravates prospects for a favourable outcome once the withdrawal of occupation forces is contemplated.

In 2005 the Iraq controversy also took centre stage in the domestic politics of the USA, leading some reporters to conclude that 'Iraq is now a cloud over everything'.[16] The bipartisan consensus that surrounded the launch of the war on Iraq in the Congress has evaporated.[17] The reasons for this include the fact that the case made for the initiation of the war could not be substantiated, the mounting US casualties (more than 2000 deaths since April 2003[18]) and the growing objections from various US constituencies to administration activities associated with the occupation and the fight against terrorism more broadly.

As the USA prepares for mid-term elections in 2006 against this background, the Department of Defense (DOD) has begun to consider scenarios for reducing the US military presence in Iraq.[19] Withdrawal from Iraq is partly dependent on domestic political developments there and partly on the ability of newly trained Iraqi forces to take responsibility for the security of the coun-

parliamentary election campaigns were not affected by debate about the country's commitment to the Iraqi operation.

[13] This problem was well illustrated by the brief, joint EU–US statement on Iraq issued during the Feb. 2005 visit to Brussels of President Bush: 'The United States and Europe stand together in support of the Iraqi people and the new Iraqi government . . . [S]hould the new Iraqi government request it, the United States and the European Union are prepared to co-host an international conference to provide a forum to encourage and coordinate international support to Iraq'. The White House, 'Joint Statement by the United States and the European Union on Iraq', News release, Washington, DC, 22 Feb. 2005, URL <http://www.whitehouse.gov/news/releases/2005/02/print/20050222-9.html>.

[14] It is inaccurate to speak about 'occupation' today because this phase formally came to an end on 28 June 2004 with the handing over of power to the Iraqi authorities. In the light of the perception of a part of Iraq's population it may still be accurate to use that word in a political sense, however.

[15] Cordesman, A. H., 'Iraq and foreign volunteers', Working Draft, 18 Nov. 2005, URL <http://www.csis.org>, p. 2. The number of foreign militants totals approximately 3000. Of these, 80% are from Arab states (Algeria, Syria, Yemen, Egypt and Saudi Arabia, in that order); 15% are from the Sudan; and 5% are from other countries. For more details see chapter 2 in this volume.

[16] Weisman, J. and Babington, C., 'Iraq war debate eclipses all other issues', Washington Post, 20 Nov. 2005, p. A01.

[17] 'Without a war on terrorism and people feeling a real threat, it would be like Vietnam' concludes the director of the Pew Research Center. Quoted in Balz, D., '"Lessons of Sept. 11" again take center stage', Washington Post, 29 June 2005, p. A01.

[18] The military of the USA suffered 2108 casualties between Mar. 2003 and Nov. 2005. See Iraq Coalition Casualty Count, URL <http://icasualties.org/oif>.

[19] Graham, B. and Wright, R., '3 brigades may be cut in Iraq early in 2006: some U.S. troops would stay "on call" in Kuwait', Washington Post, 23 Nov. 2005, p. A01.

try. Given the ever clearer risk of sliding into a civil war, the dilemma has no perfect solution. The opinion is widely shared in the US strategic community that '[a] precipitous pullout ... would be destabilizing'.[20] Such a pullout would be destabilizing for Iraq, for the region and for the prestige of the USA. Members of the Bush Administration have emphasized that 'an immediate withdrawal would be "a terrible thing for our country and for the safety of our people"'.[21] The Secretary of State has stated that: '[W]e want the Iraqi forces to be able to hold territory against the terrorists. We don't want the terrorists to be able to control large parts of Iraq or even important cities of Iraq'.[22] Uncertainty thus prevails over the likely speed and phasing of reductions and withdrawal, and further policy adjustments are more likely than not: some observers already conclude that 'conditions for U.S. withdrawal no longer include a defeated insurgency'.[23] During his pre-Christmas 2005 visit to Iraq, Secretary of Defense Donald Rumsfeld announced that the number of US combat brigades in Iraq would be reduced from 17 to 15—a total cut of 7000 troops.[24]

Finally, it may be noted that the more the USA does pull back from Iraq, the more the challenge there will become one for other (Middle Eastern and European) nations and institutions. Even if displaced from its centrality of the past few years, the Iraq problem will long haunt the transatlantic agenda.

Fighting terrorism and homeland security

No successful terrorist attack has been conducted in the USA since 11 September 2001. Terrorist groups and particularly al-Qaeda have found their targets elsewhere: in Spain and Turkey in 2004, and in Egypt, Jordan and the UK in 2005. The reasons for this are not fully clear,[25] although intelligence efforts and the heavy focus on homeland security since September 2001 are certainly among them. Whether or not Congressman Duncan Hunter is correct in his view that: 'Four years have expired without a second attack on our homeland because we've aggressively projected America's fighting forces in the theatres in Afghanistan and Iraq',[26] the USA can be rightly proud of this achievement.

The Department of Homeland Security (DHS), which was established after the terrorist attacks to unite the efforts of various agencies, focused heavily at

---

[20] Graham and Wright (note 19), p. A01.

[21] 'Rumsfeld rejects Iraq withdrawal', BBC News Online, 20 Nov. 2005, URL <http://news.bbc.co.uk/1/4455146.stm>.

[22] US Department of State, 'Secretary Condoleezza Rice, Interview on Fox News with Jim Angle', 22 Nov. 2005, URL <http://www.state.gov/secretary/rm/2005/57284.htm>.

[23] Hirsch, M. and Barry, J., 'Drawing down Iraq', *Newsweek*, 8 Aug. 2005, p. 29.

[24] MacDonald, N., 'Iraqi elections prompt US to cut troops numbers by 7,000', *Financial Times*, 24 Dec. 2005, URL <http://news.ft.com/>, p. 5.

[25] President Bush said 'the United States and its partners have disrupted at least ten serious al Qaeda terrorist plots since September the 11th'. The White House, 'President discusses war on terror at National Endowment for Democracy', News release, Washington, DC, 6 Oct. 2005, URL <http://www.whitehouse.gov/news/releases/2005/10/20051006-3.html>, p. 4.

[26] House Armed Services Committee Chairman Duncan Hunter as quoted in Babington, C., 'Hawkish Democrat joins call for pullout: GOP assails Murtha's demand to leave Iraq', *Washington Post*, 18 Nov. 2005, p. A01.

first on countering terrorism, but it has lately come under pressure to re-evaluate its role. Influential think tanks have recommended that the DHS 'must now also embrace the international dimensions of security, especially given the globally interconnected networks of our global society'.[27] The DHS's lacklustre performance was blamed for some of the failures of response to Hurricane Katrina, insofar as the DHS seemed to have no well-elaborated plan for evacuating a major US city.[28] The total breakdown of the Federal Emergency Management Agency (FEMA), including its incapacity to communicate under crisis conditions, generally demonstrated its ineptitude to address such a problem. Following the terrorist attacks in London in July 2005, the DHS also came under fire for overemphasizing air safety while not paying enough attention to public ground transportation. In face of these shortcomings, the DHS's agenda has been revised to focus also on overall preparedness, particularly for catastrophic events; better transport security systems for people and cargo; strengthening border security and interior enforcement; and reform of immigration processes. It has also introduced some organizational measures to improve performance.[29]

Measures to protect the USA continued to aim at increasing security without endangering US business and other interests. Most countries in the USA's Visa Waiver Program (VWP), including several EU members, have met the deadline to produce passports with digital photographs after 26 October 2005. Passports issued after that date and used for visa-free travel must include a biometric identifier.[30] In implementation of a Canadian–US programme dating back to December 2001, the 6000-kilometre border of the two countries—the longest unprotected border in the world—has become more tightly controlled against possible terrorist infiltration. On the southern border of the USA, where monitoring has been well established, the focus has stayed on the apprehension of illegal aliens and the prevention of smuggling of various kinds. Recent efforts have sped up the repatriation of illegal aliens and thus eased the burden on detention facilities.[31]

The funding of the DHS has modestly increased: for financial year 2006 it is $40.8 billion.[32] Despite some criticism, as mentioned above, popular support continues for improved homeland security and as a result 'DHS spending may be easier to sell . . . than defence expenditures'.[33]

---

[27] Carafano, J. J. and Heyman, D., *DHS 2.0: Rethinking the Department of Homeland Security*, Heritage Special Report (Heritage Foundation and CSIS: Washington, DC, 13 Dec. 2004), p. 7

[28] Robinson, E., 'It's your failure, too, Mr. Bush', *Washington Post*, 6 Sep. 2005, p. A25.

[29] US Department of Homeland Security (DHS), 'DHS organization: the DHS transition', URL <http://www.dhs.gov/dhspublic/display?theme=10>.

[30] US Department of Homeland Security, 'Majority of VWP countries to meet digital photo deadline', 26 Oct. 2005, URL <http://www.dhs.gov/dhspublic/display?theme=43&content=4907&>.

[31] Nunez-Neto, B., 'Border security: the role of the U.S. border patrol', Congressional Research Service Report, 10 May 2005, p. 10. According to the report, 97% of illegal aliens are apprehended at the southern border of the USA.

[32] This means an increase of $1.8 billion from 2005, a nominal rise of 5.8% and similar to the increase from 2003 to 2004.

[33] Tigner, B., 'Trans-Atlantic rift?: Europeans fear homeland security trade war with U.S.', *Defense News*, 13 June 2005, p. 48.

Intelligence

Since the terrorist attacks of September 2001 the critical role of intelligence for national security has been widely recognized and not only by experts. The intelligence services of the USA and those of many other countries have been struggling with the unusually severe challenge presented by recent events. The view is now current that the failure 'to find Iraqi WMD exposed the limits of US intelligence capabilities',[34] and most observers see part of the problem in the way that the autonomy of intelligence analysis was curtailed.[35] The US Administration's earlier efforts to address the issue continued in 2005,[36] and some intelligence problems have gained in prominence.

In October 2005 the Director of National Intelligence[37] issued the National Intelligence Strategy,[38] which is designed to complement the 2002 National Security Strategy and the 2004 Intelligence Reform and Terrorism Prevention Act.[39] It calls for integrating the domestic and foreign dimensions of intelligence in order to leave no gaps in the understanding of threats to national security; bringing more depth and accuracy to intelligence analysis; and ensuring that intelligence resources generate results both now and in future.[40] The strategy links intelligence to more general external aims and asks the intelligence community to forge relationships with new and incipient democracies to help them strengthen the rule of law and ward off threats, thereby providing policy makers with an enhanced analytical framework for identifying both security threats and opportunities for promoting democracy as well as warning of state failure.[41] The analytical language of the intelligence strategy comes close to the concepts of the EU's Security Strategy,[42] although a key difference is the US document's proactive stance towards changing the status quo.

[34] Fukuyama, F., 'The Bush doctrine, before and after', *Financial Times*, 11 Oct. 2005, p. 15.

[35] Jehl, D., 'Report warned in 2002 that Iraq data was false', *International Herald Tribune*, 7 Nov. 2005, p. 7.

[36] For more details see Dunay, P. and Lachowski, Z., 'Euro-Atlantic security and institutions', *SIPRI Yearbook 2005: Armaments, Disarmament and International Security* (Oxford University Press: Oxford, 2005), pp. 51–52.

[37] The establishment in 2004 of the Office of the Director of National Intelligence (ODNI) was the second major reorganization of the federal administration by the Bush Administration, following the establishment of the DHS in 2002. See the ODNI website at URL <http://www.odni.gov/>.

[38] US Office of the Director of National Intelligence, 'The National Intelligence Strategy of the United States of America: transformation through integration and innovation', Oct. 2005, URL <http://www.odni.gov/press_releases/20051025_release.htm>, p. 1.

[39] The White House, 'The National Security Strategy of the United States of America', Washington, DC, Sep. 2002, URL <http://www.whitehouse.gov/nsc/nss.pdf>; and US Congress, *Intelligence Reform and Terrorism Prevention Act of 2004*, 108th Congress 2nd session, House of Representatives, Report 108-796 (US Government Printing Office: Washington, DC, 2004), URL <http://www.gpoaccess.gov/serialset/creports/intel_reform.html>.

[40] US Office of the Director of National Intelligence (note 38). The integration of domestic and foreign dimensions may raise certain human rights concerns when implemented. It blurs the line between the two and—as has been demonstrated in several instances in various countries, including the USA—may jeopardize judicial control over the curtailment of the constitutional rights of citizens.

[41] US Office of the Director of National Intelligence (note 38), p. 8.

[42] Council of the European Union, 'A secure Europe in a better world: European Security Strategy', Brussels, 12 Dec. 2003, URL <http://ue.eu.int/uedocs/cms_data/docs/2004/4/29/European%20Security%20Strategy.pdf>.

The structural role of the Director of National Intelligence is twofold: to ensure that the intelligence agencies work as a single enterprise; and to serve as the president's principal intelligence adviser.[43] A central aim of intelligence reform has been to reduce political influence over intelligence, and it is open to question how combining these two functions helps to achieve it. The view was widespread that too much emphasis on technical means and too little on human intelligence and analytical capacity contributed to the failure of intelligence before September 2001. The USA has thus established a new agency, the National Clandestine Service (NCS), to serve 'as the national authority for the integration, coordination, deconfliction, and evaluation of human intelligence operations across the entire intelligence Community'.[44] The NCS is tasked to help build an intelligence community that is 'more unified, coordinated and effective': it remains to be seen how this will work in practice.

The intelligence services also faced new specific challenges in 2005. The problems of retention of personnel at the Central Intelligence Agency (CIA), the allegations of major violations of human rights and the leaking of the identity of a CIA operative[45] for political reasons have been indications of trouble. The creation of the post of Director of National Intelligence has reduced the centrality of the CIA in intelligence coordination without necessarily freeing it from the kind of political pressure it suffered before the 2003 Iraq War.

The Department of Defense has continued its efforts to become a more central player in intelligence than in the past.[46] It now aims to expand the Counterintelligence Field Activity (CIFA), an agency established in 2002, and to gain access to information about US citizens that is 'deemed to be related to foreign intelligence'.[47] The blurring of the line between foreign and domestic intelligence and the wider sharing of domestic information within the national administration of the USA is a disturbing sign.

The CIA has been accused of acting in ways that go beyond its traditional function: notably, of conducting abusive interrogations during the insurgency in Iraq. In 2005 it was also reported that the CIA maintained secret facilities in various parts of the world where al-Qaeda operatives were held and interrogated, and that European (including EU) states could have been implicated in

---

[43] The White House, 'President congratulates America's first Director and Deputy Director of National Intelligence', News release, Washington, DC, 18 May 2005, URL <http://www.whitehouse.gov/news/releases/2005/05/20050518.html>.

[44] US Office of the Director of National Intelligence, 'Establishment of the National Clandestine Service (NCS)', ODNI News release no. 3-05, 13 Oct. 2005, URL <http://www.dni.gov/press_releases/20051013_release.htm>.

[45] The reference is to Valerie Plame whose identity as a CIA operative was allegedly leaked by 'senior administration officials' following criticism by her spouse, Ambassador Joseph Wilson, of the Bush Administration's case on Iraqi WMD. According to the Intelligence Identities and Protection Act, the unauthorized identification of a CIA operative is a criminal act punishable by up to 10 years in federal prison. The then chief of staff of Vice President Dick Cheney has acknowledged being the source of the leak.

[46] For details see Dunay and Lachowski (note 36), p. 52.

[47] Pincus, W., 'Pentagon expanding its domestic surveillance activity', *Washington Post*, 27 Nov. 2005, p. A06.

this or in the transit of prisoners.[48] The Bush Administration's efforts to quash this scandal have been invalidated by its continuing efforts at the same time to exempt the CIA from congressional legislation that would ban cruel and degrading treatment of any prisoner in US custody.[49] These events have shown major potential to interfere with the USA's external image and relations as well as with the administration's standing at home and could complicate some European states' cooperation with and reliance on US intelligence in future.

Defence reform

As the world's leading military power, the USA has a unique challenge in defence reform since it cannot measure its military performance and development plans against a challenger of the same standing. It enjoys a larger degree of autonomy than any other state to decide what direction its armed forces should take in the long run.

In 2005 the USA issued two documents implementing its 2002 National Security Strategy—the National Military Strategy and the National Defense Strategy (NDS). The NDS separates the emerging challenges the USA faces into traditional, irregular, catastrophic and disruptive types. It concludes that the scope for traditional challenges from states employing regular military capabilities are drastically reduced owing to the USA's superiority in traditional domains and the enormous cost of rivalling it. However, irregular methods (e.g., terrorism and insurgency), perhaps combined with the acquisition of WMD, could seriously challenge the security interests of the USA. Advances in biotechnology, cyber operations, space or directed-energy weapons could also lead to serious threats.[50] The NDS states that the key aims for defence transformation are to: (a) strengthen intelligence; (b) protect critical bases of operation and the USA as the premier base;[51] (c) operate from the 'global commons' (i.e., the high seas and outer space); (d) project and sustain forces in distant environments; (e) deny enemies sanctuary; (f) conduct network-centric operations; (g) improve 'proficiency against irregular challenges'; and (h) increase the capabilities of partners—international and domestic.[52]

---

[48] Priest, D., 'CIA holds terror suspects in secret prisons', *Washington Post*, 2 Nov. 2005, p. A01.

[49] Human Rights Watch, 'U.S.: landmark torture ban undercut, Congress would allow evidence obtained by torture', 16 Dec. 2005, URL <http://www.hrw.org/english/docs/2005/12/16/usdom12311.htm>.

[50] US Department of Defense, 'The National Defense Strategy of The United States of America', Washington, DC, Mar. 2005, URL <http://globalsecurity.org/military/library/policy/dod/nds-usa_mar2005.htm>, pp. 2–3; and US Joint Chiefs of Staff, 'The National Military Strategy of the United States of America: a strategy for today, a vision for tomorrow', Washington, DC, 2004, URL <http://www.defenselink.mil/news/Mar2005/d20050318nms.pdf>.

[51] Compare this to other current pressures for the DOD to 'provide greater support to domestic security'. Carafano and Heyman (note 27), p. 7.

[52] US Department of Defense (note 50), pp. 12–15.

Some elements of rethinking are reflected in the NDS's statement that '[G]etting transformation right is second only to success on the battlefield'.[53] Surveying recent experience, particularly from the wars in Afghanistan and Iraq, it warns that: '[O]veremphasis on airpower, precision engagement, and information superiority at the expense of an ability to seize and hold ground will pose grave risks for decisionmakers if allowed to crowd out, rather than complement, other critical capabilities. . . . [A]irpower has constraints. It lacks staying power'.[54] This realization of the need to have more troops to seize and hold territory is reflected in a plan to increase the size of the operational army by 40 000 troops, from 315 000 to 355 000, in 2007.[55] The current level of field commitment of the US Armed Forces is heavily influenced by the massive commitment in Iraq—approximately 160 000 troops during the Iraqi elections in January 2005.[56] Assuming an eventual drawdown in that theatre, however, it is interesting to speculate about the future missions of the army.

The year 2005 saw the fifth round (since 1988) of US base realignment and closures (BRAC), a highly sensitive matter both at home and abroad. Due to the planned major withdrawals of US troops from bases overseas (some 60 000–70 000 soldiers worldwide over the next 10 years), the BRAC round that became law on 8 November 2005 envisages 22 major base closures at home, rather than the 33 earlier expected.[57]

III. Euro-Atlantic inter-institutional relations

The 60-year history of Euro-Atlantic relations since World War II has abounded not only in successes but also in stalemates, crises and tensions, and the end of NATO has often been—prematurely—announced. The cold war paradigms of US dominance, the primacy of NATO and European political deference are gone, and during the last decade and a half a new 'correlation of forces' has evolved. Although the events of September 2001 resulted briefly in acts of allied solidarity and collaboration, they could no longer hide the widening cracks in transatlantic relations. The crisis in 2003 over the Iraq War can now be viewed as a catalyst in the process of Europe's security maturation and emancipation. Almost two years later, in 2005, there was a continued thaw in West–West relations, but it was based more on considerations of utility and practical interest than on deep-seated philosophical reconciliation. Europe has been forced to recognize its vulnerability to threats springing from Islamic

[53] Hooker, R. D., McMaster, H. R. and Grey, D., 'Getting transformation right', *Joint Forces Quarterly*, no. 38 (4th quarter 2005), p. 20. See also US Department of Defense (note 50).

[54] Hooker, McMaster and Grey (note 53), p. 23.

[55] Carafano, J. J., Kochems, A. and Gentile, D., 'The army's future: a view from the top', Heritage Foundation Web Memo, URL <http://www.heritage.org/Research/NationalSecurity/wm906.cfm?re>, p. 1.

[56] NBC News, 'Meet the Press with Tim Russert: transcript for June 26', 26 June 2005, URL <http://www.msnbc.msn.com/id/8332675>, p. 4.

[57] US Department of Defense, Miles, D., American Forces Press Service, 'BRAC deadline expires; DoD to begin closures, realignments', 9 Nov. 2005, URL <http://www.defenselink.mil/news/Nov2005/20051109_3280.html>, p. 7.

fundamentalism, terrorism and the greater Middle East, especially after the bombings in Madrid in March 2004 and in London in July 2005. The USA is learning how hard it is for any nation, or even institution, to meet the full repercussions of such challenges alone. In purely practical terms, traditional forums and mechanisms now appear more workable than ad hoc arrangements with hand-picked allies; and the USA's post-September 2001 enthusiasm for coalitions of the willing seems to have been quietly laid to rest.

In 2005 there was a further shift in the EU–NATO–US triangle towards a more active EU–US dialogue, signifying US recognition of the growing role played by the EU in security matters and perhaps NATO's waning salience in policy making.[58] German Chancellor Gerhard Schröder was widely criticized in early 2005 for suggesting that a high-level panel should consider ways for the USA to deal more directly with the EU because the relationship 'in its current form does justice neither to the Union's growing importance, nor to the new demands on trans-Atlantic cooperation'.[59] Nonetheless, several events bore out his underlying thought: when President Bush embarked on reconciliation with Europe in February 2005 while paying a visit to the NATO summit meeting, he also, very unusually, went to the EU headquarters. In turn, following the blockage of the EU's Constitutional Treaty in mid-2005 (discussed below), the EU hastened to reassure the USA that it would not stop playing a strong and helpful role on security issues such as with Iran, Iraq and the Middle East.[60] These political trends, however, still need to be reflected in regular institutionalized practices and strengthened with concrete steps.[61]

Despite their membership overlap, the 'strategic partnership' between the EU and NATO has failed to make much progress beyond operational collaboration on the ground. The fault lies partly in specific political and procedural blockages and also in the temptation for both organizations to vie for influence and a security role internationally.[62] The USA is still wary about the EU's defence incarnation, while any success for the EU's more proactive crisis diplomacy risks undermining NATO's attempts to recover its position as the forum for debating key transatlantic issues. The EU has practically taken over

---

[58] Grant, C. and Leonard, M., 'What new transatlantic institutions?', *Centre for European Reform Bulletin*, no. 4441 (Apr./May 2005). On the challenge of building stronger European defence capabilities see Center for Strategic and International Studies (CSIS), *European Defense Integration: Bridging the Gap Between Strategy and Capabilities* (CSIS: Washington, DC, Oct. 2005).

[59] German Federal Chancellor Gerhard Schröder, Speech delivered at the 41st Munich Conference on Security Policy', Munich, 12 Feb. 2005, URL <http://www.securityconference.de/konferenzen/rede.php?menu_2005=&menu_2004=&menu_konferenzen=&sprache=en&id=143&>.

[60] Alden, E., Dinmore, G. and Daniel, C., 'EU leaders reassure Bush on Europe's world role', *Financial Times*, 21 June 2005.

[61] General Klaus Naumann, former Chairman of the NATO Military Committee, called for the creation of a NATO–EU–US steering committee at the highest level to meet in times of serious crises to decide on task-sharing. He was also concerned that if NATO failed to transform it would lose its identity and disappear from the 'radar screen of public opinion'. Gen. Klaus Naumann, former Chairman of the NATO Military Committee, 'NATO: does it have a future?', Speech at the 1st SHAPE Lecture Series, Brussels, 10 May 2005, URL <http://www.shape.nato.int/shape/opinions/2005/s050510a.htm>.

[62] Dempsey, J., 'For EU and NATO, a race for influence', *International Herald Tribune*, 18 Feb. 2005. The failure of the EU constitutional referendum at least temporarily exacerbated the problem since many in EU circles feared NATO would 'take advantage'.

from NATO in European peace missions, but no clear division of labour exists at the global and functional level (the EU now claims also to pursue 'joint disarmament' and anti-terrorist operations). A majority is stabilizing within the EU for endowing it with a broader spectrum of security options (aside from purely military ones), more autonomy from the USA and wider political leeway (*inter alia* in the choice of partners when dealing with future crises).

Other Europe-related security institutions have also faced growing challenges. The OSCE, once perceived as a linchpin of Euro-Atlantic security, remains in a lingering crisis. With the Commonwealth of Independent States (CIS) facing progressive erosion, the other Russia-dominated organization, the Collective Security Treaty Organization (CSTO), is grappling with internal tensions while trying, so far unsuccessfully, to acquire equal status with and full recognition from NATO.[63] The EU and NATO still prefer to cooperate with CSTO members on an individual and differentiated basis.

IV. The European Union

The Constitutional Treaty crisis

In 2005 the European 'grand design' enshrined in the Constitutional Treaty—being 'united ever more closely, to forge a common destiny'[64]—was dealt a hard blow. The popular rejection of the treaty in two referendums, in France on 29 May and the Netherlands on 1 June, confounded the hopes of those who had counted on it to make Europe more effective and streamlined, more democratic and accountable and closer to the citizen. The EU declared a face-saving 'period of reflection', but the Constitutional Treaty's main weakness now seems its virtual irrelevance to more profound European ills. These include the poor performance by and unpopularity of many governments; the destructive practice of putting the blame for member governments' faults on the EU; the gap between the people and the political elites (the 'democratic deficit' or 'enlightened despotism'[65]); different expectations among both the governments and the public regarding the models of development ('social' versus 'liberal' Europe); the conspicuous difference between the old members and the newcomers with regard to integration and enlargement; the difficulties in digesting the recent 'big bang' enlargement of the EU (especially the fear of competition from the new members, as epitomized by the 'Polish plumber'); the reluctance to lay Europe more open to globalization and cultural pressures (the market expansion of China and India as well as the question of member-

---

[63] Similar hints have been dropped by Russian officials regarding the Shanghai Cooperation Organization.

[64] Preamble to the Treaty establishing a Constitution for Europe. The text is at URL <http://europa.eu.int/constitution/index_en.htm>.

[65] Ana Palacio, Head of the Spanish Parliament's Joint Committee on European Affairs, used the phrase 'everything for the people but without the people'. 'Discussions on the EU's future', *International Herald Tribune*, 16 June 2005, URL <http://www.iht.com/articles/2005/06/15/news/voices.php>.

ship for Turkey); and the associated 'neo-nationalism' reflected in the behaviour of both populist rebels and some elites.

All this left Europe uncertain about its future, scope, purpose and course. Many observers believe that any renewal of meaningful debate on the future of the EU will have to wait until mid-2007, following the French presidential elections.[66] The external repercussions of the constitutional crisis are more difficult to read. The blockage of plans for a 'Union minister for foreign affairs', an EU external action service and a longer presidency of the European Council will certainly hamper the effort to make the EU's external activities more effective and efficient. On the other hand, as reflected below, many of the draft Constitutional Treaty's original provisions relating to EU defence and security matters had already been implemented before the Dutch and French referendums, thus effectively insulating them from the constitutional crisis.

Enlargement

The same insulation cannot be said to have occurred for the EU's geographical expansion: 'enlargement fatigue' emphatically caught up with the pre-2004 EU members in 2005.[67] The mixed assessments of 2004's expansion in membership, xenophobia and fear of dilution of the European project (by 'Croatian electricians and Turkish carpenters'[68]) played a significant role in the Dutch and French referendums. The effect was to complicate the prospects even for the next potential entrants in the wider Balkans region and Turkey.[69]

On the Western Balkans, the majority view of European elites remained that the only hope of lasting peace was to hold out the lure of 'a new European dawn'.[70] In March *Croatia* failed to win the go-ahead for EU accession negotiations because it had not handed over a senior war crimes suspect, General Ante Gotovina, to the International Criminal Tribunal for the Former Yugoslavia (ICTY). Not until 3 October did Croatia receive a more favourable assessment, opening the way for it to be given a starting date for accession talks (as demanded by Austria in particular) in parallel with those with Turkey.[71] The other Western Balkan candidates—Albania, Bosnia and Herzegovina (BiH), the Former Yugoslav Republic of Macedonia (FYROM), and

---

[66] Williamson, H. and Parker, G., 'Germany will try to revive European constitution', *Financial Times*, 23 Nov. 2005.

[67] Bowley, G., 'Defining the enlarged EU', *International Herald Tribune*, 9 Mar. 2005.

[68] Stephens, P., 'Turkey cannot be wished away', *Financial Times*, 1 Sep. 2005.

[69] For more on the Western Balkans see appendix 1A.

[70] Jansson, E., 'Brussels sees a "new European dawn" for Balkans', *Financial Times*, 4 Oct. 2005. 'The future of the Western Balkans lies in the EU', asserted the European Commission. Commission of the European Communities, 'Communication from the Commission: 2005 enlargement strategy paper', Brussels, 9 Nov. 2005, document COM (2005) 561, URL <http://europa.eu.int/comm/enlargement/croatia/key_documents.htm#elarg_pck_2005>, pp. 20–21.

[71] Commission of the European Communities (note 70), pp. 20–21. Carla Del Ponte, ICTY chief prosecutor, confirmed that Croatia was 'cooperating fully' in catching Gotovina. He was arrested on Spain's Canary Islands on 7 Dec. 2005.

Serbia and Montenegro—have yet to meet political and economic entry criteria, although some early procedural hurdles were surmounted in 2005.[72]

Negotiations with *Bulgaria* and *Romania* were successfully concluded in December 2004 and their treaties of accession were signed on 25 April 2005, with the aim of full entry in January 2007. Shortly after, however, the European Commission called for 'vigorous steps' to be taken in the fight against corruption and in the reform of the justice system and the public administration to remedy remaining lapses from EU standards in both countries. A monitoring report by the Commission in the spring of 2006 may recommend that the European Council postpone the accession of Bulgaria or Romania by a year if there is a serious risk of either state being unable to meet the requirements of membership by January 2007.[73]

The run-up to the October deadline (set by the EU in December 2004) for a decision on whether *Turkey* could join turned out to be difficult and complicated. In formal terms the difficult points were the apparent slowing of Turkish internal reform (regarding, e.g., the legal and judiciary system, religious and democratic freedoms, the rule of law, human rights and the protection of minorities) and Turkey's refusal to recognize the Republic of Cyprus (now an EU member) without a comprehensive deal to end the long-standing division of the island.[74] At the political level, opinion remained particularly hostile to Turkish entry in Germany (whose future chancellor, Angela Merkel, suggested instead a 'privileged partnership'), Austria, Denmark, France and the Netherlands. Motives included fear of the entry of a large, relatively poor Muslim country into the predominantly Christian, wealthy EU; and the risks of Europe's future entanglement in the volatile Middle East region.[75] The endgame before the October decision was particularly protracted, with the Cyprus issue,[76] the possibility of an alternative to full Turkish membership and Austria's greater attachment to Croatia all coming to the fore again. Ultimately, however, the proposal to open membership talks was duly made by the EU and accepted by Turkey. Few observers expected the coming nego-

---

[72] In mid-Dec. the European Council gave the FYROM formal candidate country status. The EU foreign ministers decided in early Oct. to open Stabilization and Association Agreement (SAA) talks with Serbia and Montenegro after the latter promised to capture war crimes suspects. On 25 Nov. SAA talks were also opened with Bosnia and Herzegovina. See also appendix 1A.

[73] European Commission, 'Enlargement Package 2005, summary paper: Communication from the Commission: comprehensive monitoring report on the state of preparedness for EU membership of Bulgaria and Romania', Brussels, 25 Oct. 2005, document COM (2005) 534, URL <http://europa.eu.int/comm/enlargement/bulgaria/key_documents.htm#elarg_pck_2005>.

[74] On 29 July 2005 Turkey signed a protocol extending its customs union to the 10 new EU members but issued a unilateral declaration stating that the signature did not amount to formal recognition of the Republic of Cyprus. The EU has indicated that the declaration does not affect Turkey's obligations under the protocol.

[75] According to an EU diplomat, EU leaders have never had a serious debate about the strategic implications of Europe's relationship with Turkey. Stephens (note 68).

[76] Turkey refused to allow Cypriot and other ships embarking from Greek Cypriot ports to use its ports. It continues to block Cyprus' membership of certain international organizations and arrangements. It has also been unable, despite good relations with Greece, to reach a compromise over the outstanding Greek–Turkish territorial dispute.

tiations to take less than 10 to 15 years, and all the (substantially unsolved) issues mentioned above and more will doubtless complicate their course.[77]

The European Neighbourhood Policy

The EU's European Neighbourhood Policy (ENP), launched in 2004 to create a 'ring of friends' around the EU,[78] now covers 15 states of the former Soviet area, the southern Mediterranean and the Middle East (including the Palestinian Authority) but not Russia. It is based on a two-tier structure: country reports give a factual analysis of political, economic and institutional reforms, identifying priority areas for bilateral Action Plans. The latter normally cover political, economic and regulatory reforms and cooperation in the fields of freedom, security and justice. Seven Action Plans were agreed in December 2004,[79] and five country reports were presented in March 2005[80] with the hope of Action Plans following shortly. From 2007, EU association programmes with the Mediterranean countries and the partnership and cooperation agreements signed with states in the former Soviet area will be transformed into neighbourhood agreements. The regulatory framework will thus be unified.

The 'ENP aims to support long-term domestic reform, regional cooperation and peace-building in the proximity of the EU by providing new incentives to the neighbours'.[81] The questions relating to it include the sometimes greater influence in these regions of other major players of world politics and doubts about the EU's concrete tools of leverage and conditionality. Apart from the appeal of the EU model, 'carrots' such as trade liberalization, greater access to the Single Market and visa liberalization may have some impact on all partners. The 'incentive-based structure' of the ENP masks, however, a more general weakness: the EU's lack of strategy with regard to those countries that are not willing to comply or cooperate. It may suffice to contrast the case of Belarus with those of Georgia and Ukraine to demonstrate this point. The latter cases also underline that the EU's strongest potential carrot is one it is still far from ready to use: namely, the prospect of membership.[82] The EU has made it clear that 'the near-neighbours like Ukraine, Moldova and Georgia would be well advised not to apply for European Union membership now, because they would be rebuffed'.[83] The EU's present 25 members clearly have

[77] See Bekdil, B. E. and Enginsoy, U., 'Turk threat perception poses EU challenge', *Defense News*, 24 Oct. 2005, p. 16.

[78] See Dunay and Lachowski (note 36), p. 61.

[79] The Action Plans were for Israel, Jordan, Moldova, Morocco, the Palestinian Authority, Tunisia and Ukraine.

[80] The country reports addressed Armenia, Azerbaijan, Egypt, Georgia and Lebanon.

[81] Tocci, N., 'Does the ENP respond to the EU's post-enlargement challenges', *International Spectator*, vol. 40, no. 1 (Jan.–Mar. 2005), p. 25.

[82] The President of Ukraine clearly stated his hope 'that at the end of the Action Plan, in 2007, we will be in the position to begin EU membership negotiations'. Yushchenko, V., 'Ukraine's future is in the EU', Address by President of Ukraine, European Parliament, 23 Feb. 2005, URL <http://europa-eu-un.org/articles/en/article_4382_en.htm>.

[83] EU External Relations Commissioner Benita Ferrero-Waldner is mentioned as the source. See O'Rourke, B., 'EU: Brussels says no point in near neighbors seeking to join Union now', Radio Free

different views on any further eastern expansion, with Poland and other new members the most positive. It remains a serious policy test for the EU whether and how it can find a way 'to act beyond the dichotomy of accession/non-accession, drawing on a range of tools to promote its interests'.[84]

European security and defence

The EU constitutional crisis did not directly hamper the EU's security-related plans and may even have created new pressure for their success. The EU has been raising its profile in many conflict-afflicted areas *inter alia* by appointing special representatives to such places as Afghanistan, the African Great Lakes region, BiH, Central Asia, FYROM, Kosovo, the Middle East, Moldova, the South Caucasus and Sudan.[85] The December 2005 European Council agreed a new EU Strategy for Africa, which aims at a long-term and wide-ranging African training programme.[86]

Crisis management remains the central, steadily evolving operational tool of the European Security and Defence Policy (ESDP), and it is growing in both geographical range and diversity. After the end of three previous operations, in 2005 the EU carried out 11 crisis-management operations and missions, most of them civilian.[87]

Following the May 2005 bloodshed in Andijon, Uzbekistan, the EU foreign ministers decided in June to appoint an EU Special Representative for Central Asia with the aim of being more actively involved in the region. In October, after President Islam Karimov's refusal to allow an independent international investigation, the EU imposed a one-year package of sanctions on Uzbekistan, including an embargo on exports of arms, military equipment and other equipment that might be used for domestic repression.[88] In November the EU foreign ministers warned Belarus to respect human rights and civil liberties or face further 'restrictive measures' against the responsible individuals in the event of failure to uphold international standards.[89] In the Azerbaijan–Armenia

---

Europe/Radio Liberty, 4 May 2005, URL <http://www.rferl.org/featuresarticle/2005/05/089016eb-1789-4b6a-91c8-4bb63366501a.html>.

[84] Lynch, D., 'The security dimension of the European Neighbourhood Policy', *International Spectator*, vol. 40, no. 1 (Jan.–Mar. 2005), p. 34.

[85] EU Special Representatives (EUSRs) provide the EU with a visible and practical presence ('voice' and 'face') in troubled countries and regions. Council of the European Union, 'EU Special Representatives', Fact sheet, June 2005, URL <http://ue.eu.int/cms3_fo/showpage.asp?id=263&lang=en&mode=g>. In 2005 EUSRs were appointed for the first time for Central Asia, Moldova and Sudan.

[86] Council of the European Union, 'The EU and Africa: towards a strategic partnership', Brussels, 19 Dec. 2005, document 15961/05, URL < http://ue.eu.int/cms3_fo/showpage.asp?lang=EN>.

[87] For a list of the EU crisis-management missions in 2005 see chapter 3 in this volume.

[88] The sanctions took effect on 14 Nov. 2005. 'Council Common Position 2005/792/CFSP concerning restrictive measures against Uzbekistan', 14 Nov. 2005, *Official Journal of the European Union*, L 299 (16 Nov. 2005), URL <http://europa.eu.int/eur-lex/lex/LexUriServ/site/en/oj/2005/l_299/l_29920051116en00720079.pdf>, p. 72.

[89] British Presidency of the EU, 'GAERC Conclusions 7 November 2005: External Relations', URL <http://www.eu2005.gov.uk/>.

conflict over Nagorno-Karabakh, at the end of 2005 the EU offered its mediation because both countries have shown progress in peace discussions.[90]

Military capabilities

In 2005 the EU held three autonomous (without using NATO resources) military crisis-management exercises: in April to study cooperation with the UN (EST 05) in such operations; in September–October to rapidly deploy a civil–military mission in response to a sub-Saharan ethnic conflict; and in November–December to test the military planning of an operation (MILEX 05). The EU's civil–military planning cell in the EU Military Staff began its work in the spring of 2005 and is expected to be able to have an operations centre up and running by June 2006.[91]

As in previous years, the issue of inadequate military capabilities continued to dog the ESDP,[92] and 2005 brought no significant improvement in meeting current capabilities requirements (the Headline Goal 2010).[93] The mid-year report on capabilities acknowledged slow progress, noting improvements in only four sectors (deployable laboratories, seaport of disembarkation units, operations headquarters and mechanized infantry battalions). At the end of 2005, the next half-year report recorded no new headway. The main hope for new impetus in capability work rests with the developing role of the European Defence Agency (EDA), which should work with the EU Military Committee to address capabilities shortfalls, assisted by the EU Military Staff and in close coordination with the Political and Security Committee.[94]

The EDA became operational at the start of January 2005, with the objectives of improving European defence capabilities, bringing about more efficient management of multinational arms cooperation, developing and integrating Europe's defence markets, and coordinating research and development. In 2005 the EDA focused on four selected 'flagship' projects.[95] The first

[90] Council of the European Union, 'Summary of remarks by Javier Solana, EU High Representative for the CFSP, at press briefing with foreign ministers of Armenia, Azerbaijan and Georgia following political dialogue meetings', document S411/05, Brussels, 13 Dec. 2005, URL <http://ue.eu.int/cms3_ applications/applications/solana/list.asp?cmsid=358&BID=107&lang=EN>.

[91] Council of the European Union, 'Opening address by Javier Solana, Secretary General of the Council/High Representative for the CFSP, UK Presidency seminar on civil–military relations', London, 17 Oct. 2005, URL <http://ue.eu.int/cms3_applications/applications/solana/list.asp?cmsid=358&BID= 107&lang=EN>.

[92] Among the EU countries, France, Greece, Italy, Poland, Portugal and the UK reached in 2004 the objective of devoting 2% or more of gross domestic product to defence spending. *Atlantic News*, no. 3727 (22 Nov. 2005), p. 2. For discussion of the challenge of building stronger European defence capabilities see Center for Strategic and International Studies (note 58).

[93] For details of the Headline Goal 2010 see Dunay and Lachowski (note 36), p. 65.

[94] 'EU Capabilities Improvement Chart I/2005', *Atlantic News*, no. 3680 (24 May 2005), pp. 6–12; and 'EU Capabilities Improvement Chart II/2005', *Atlantic News*, no. 3727 (22 Nov. 2005), pp. 5–13. In May 2005, 11 ECAP project groups migrated in whole or in part to the more integrated process coordinated by the EDA. In Dec. 2005 it was announced that the EDA had begun to draw up a Long Term Vision for the ESDP (up to 2025). On the EDA see Dunay and Lachowski (note 36), pp. 65–66.

[95] European Defence Agency, 'EU governments agree voluntary code for crossborder competition in defence equipment market', ESDP news, Brussels, 21 Nov. 2005, URL <http://ue.eu.int/cms3_fo/show Page.asp?id=978&lang=EN&mode=g>.

was a voluntary, non-binding intergovernmental regime for the intra-European arms trade—the €30 billion-a-year European Defence Equipment Market (EDEM)—which was launched on 21 November. EDEM is based on the 2005 Code of Conduct on Defence Procurement,[96] which aims to promote competition by improving transparency of tenders for contracts of €1 million or more. Its implementation by individual countries will be scrutinized by the EDA. The new rules will not cover nuclear weapons, chemical, bacteriological and radiological goods and services, or cases of pressing urgency and national security.

Two other EDA projects sought to identify 'communities of interest' among participating member states (PMS) for the future development of unmanned air vehicles (UAVs) and armoured fighting vehicles, and in December a contract for a UAV technology study was signed. The EDA's fourth priority in 2005 was to start analysing the state of European C^3 (command, control and communications) development between PMS, military headquarters, industry and other actors. Eight other initiatives were explored to varying degrees of advancement.[97] The agenda for 2006 will focus on military capabilities in C^3 (especially software-defined radio), air-to-air refuelling and strategic transport.[98] The main challenge for European defence cooperation remains financing and the political will of the PMS. The EU's defence endeavour is still undermined by austere military budgets and continuing national preferences.[99]

The concept of battle groups is part of the EU's rapid response capacity.[100] In 2005 the number of battle groups rose from the originally planned 13 to 18 battle groups involving 26 nations. According to the agreement reached at the Battlegroup Coordination Conference on 8 November, from January 2007 the EU will have the full operational capability to undertake two concurrent battle group-size operations. The outstanding issues include aspects of strategic movement and transportation, logistics, and health and medical support. How to make the EU's battle groups and the NATO Response Force (NRF) mutually reinforcing remained a matter for discussion.[101]

---

[96] European Defence Agency, 'The Code of Conduct on Defence Procurement of the EU Member States Participating in the European Defence Agency', Brussels, 21 Nov. 2005, URL <http://www.eda.eu.int/>.

[97] See the EDA website at URL <http://www.eda.eu.int/>; and European Defence Agency (note 95). In Oct. 13 EU member states committed themselves to work together, in an EDA-supported ad hoc group, to develop more actively capabilities in the field of air-to-air refuelling (tanker aircraft)—one of the main shortfalls in the implementation of the European Capabilities Action Plan.

[98] European Defence Agency, 'EDA urged to focus on communications and transport capabilities for rapid response', Brussels, 24 Jan. 2006, URL <http://www.eda.eu.int/news/2006-01-24-0.htm>. In Jan. 2006 France and the UK decided to jointly examine lightweight radar technology on small platforms, such as UAVs and missiles.

[99] The EU failed to agree on a 3-year budgetary framework for the EDA and deferred the decision by 1 year, until autumn 2006.

[100] For details of the battle groups see Dunay and Lachowski (note 36), p. 66.

[101] Council of the European Union, 2691st Council meeting, General Affairs and External Relations, Press release, Brussels, 21–22 Nov. 2005, URL <http://ue.eu.int/cms3_applications/Applications/newsRoom/loadBook.asp?target=2005&bid=71&lang=1&cmsId=349>.

V. The North Atlantic Treaty Organization

In 2005 developments both within NATO and in its out-of-area engagements and activities boosted the alliance's self-confidence.[102] In February President Bush reconfirmed that NATO remains the 'cornerstone' of transatlantic relations and promised to beef up its role as a policy forum *inter alia* by more frequent and deeper contacts between senior European and US officials.[103]

Since the 2002 Prague summit meeting NATO has moved steadily away from the static 'area' defence of Europe to focus on out-of-area expeditionary missions.[104] While maintaining its collective defence obligation, NATO today is focused on its 'non-Article 5' missions.[105] It has a standing presence in the Balkans (military headquarters in BiH, assistance in Bosnia's defence reform and the 16 000-strong Kosovo Force); in Afghanistan (the 12 000-strong International Security Assistance Force, ISAF); in the Mediterranean (Operation Active Endeavour naval monitoring and surveillance); and in Iraq (military training). In 2005 NATO was temporarily engaged in Africa (Darfur, Sudan) and Pakistan, and in a relief mission in the USA.[106] Such tasks were previously *terra incognita* for NATO (i.e., non-military state-building tasks, indirect peacekeeping support and humanitarian relief using military resources).

NATO remains best fitted for pursuing 'hard security' in the Euro-Atlantic area in both bilateral (e.g., relations with Russia and Ukraine and the Partnership for Peace) and multilateral formats (the Euro-Atlantic Partnership Council). At the same time it is vulnerable to the vicissitudes of US policy, which in future could sidestep NATO for unilateral action or coalitions of the willing, and to the legal requirement for full intra-alliance consensus.

Many unanswered questions remain about NATO's future and about its priorities in terms of core tasks, military transformation and combating terrorism.

---

[102] NATO Secretary General Jaap de Hoop Scheffer stated proudly that '[T]his is an Alliance that is very much in business. That's why . . . there simply is no fundamental debate any more about NATO's relevance'. North Atlantic Treaty Organization (NATO), 'Keeping NATO relevant: a shareholders report', Speech by NATO Secretary General at the NATO Parliamentary Assembly annual session, Copenhagen, 15 Nov. 2005, URL <http://www.nato.int/docu/speech/2005/s051115a.htm>. In previous years some decline was noted in the quality of the US personnel sent to NATO's Brussels headquarters. Everts, S. et al., *A European Way of War* (Centre for European Reform: London, May 2004), URL <http://www.cer.org.uk/defence/>, p. 62.

[103] North Atlantic Treaty Organization (NATO), 'Opening statement by US President George W. Bush at the press conference following the meeting of the North Atlantic Council at the level of Heads of State and Government', Brussels, NATO speeches, 22 Feb. 2005, URL <http://www.nato.int/docu/speech/2005/s050222j.htm>. Under Secretary of State Nicholas Burns stated: 'The US wants to use NATO more, and more effectively, as the principal Trans-Atlantic forum for strategic discussions on the most vital issues of the day'. US Department of State, International Information Programs, 'Under Secretary of State Burns outlines trans-Atlantic agenda', 11 Apr. 2005, URL <http://usinfo.state.gov/mena/Archive/2005/Apr/08-637379.html>.

[104] This de facto development has not entirely stilled objections from some nations. E.g., France, opposed the plan to conduct the NRF's first exercise in 2006 in continental Africa, but it eventually agreed to a 'depoliticized compromise' with Cape Verde as the location for the exercise. 'NATO picks Cape Verde for staging maneuvers', *International Herald Tribune*, 13 Apr. 2005, p. 3.

[105] Article 5 of the 1949 North Atlantic Treaty (Washington Treaty) defines the members' commitment to respond to an armed attack against any party to the treaty.

[106] In 2005 cautious steps were also taken to establish a dialogue with the parties to the Israeli–Palestinian conflict.

NATO is still striving to 'cut across the full spectrum of missions and operations', to secure increases in national defence budgets, to keep its end up vis-à-vis the EU in the operational field and to address more boldly the West's 'strategic choice' in combating terrorism.[107]

Out-of-area missions

Afghanistan remains the key priority for NATO's external operations. Since 2003 it has exercised command of the International Security Assistance Force and assisted in state-building efforts through small civil–military Provincial Reconstruction Teams (PRTs) that were set up in the areas under ISAF control. The NATO force has operated as a stabilizing presence in Kabul and in the northern (October 2004) and western (summer 2005) parts of the country. In mid-September 2005 the 9000-strong ISAF, with troops from 26 NATO member states and 10 partner countries, completed its expansion into the western provinces, and preparations started for the third phase of expansion (most likely in May 2006) to the southern sector of Afghanistan. This will require a reinforcement of up to 16 000 troops, a new operations plan and new rules of engagement designed for this militant part of the country. In the meantime, 2000 additional NATO troops were sent as reinforcements for the Afghan legislative and provincial election period in September. In October the UN extended the ISAF mandate for another year.

A larger political issue for NATO is whether its role in Afghanistan will remain limited to 'security assistance', peacekeeping and reconstruction or should formally extend to counter-insurgency.[108] The plan for NATO to eventually take command of all forces in all parts of Afghanistan is already demanding greater coordination between ISAF and the US-led Operation Enduring Freedom (OEF).[109] As in 2004, the idea of a merger between the two forces continued to meet strong objections in 2005 from France and other states, although possible 'synergy' between the two operations was not ruled out.[110] In November the operations plan for ISAF's 'phase 3', including the implications for cooperation with the OEF, was finalized by the NATO Military Com-

---

[107] North Atlantic Treaty Organization (note 103).

[108] British expert Mark Joyce noted that: 'By sheer force of operational momentum, and in spite of internal political misgivings, European forces under a NATO flag may soon find themselves operating at the sharp end of the American "war on terrorism"'. Joyce, M., 'NATO's incremental transformation', *International Herald Tribune*, 8 Oct. 2005, URL <http://iht.com/articles/2005/10/07/opinion/edjoyce. php>.

[109] In this context, there is concern that the expansion of ISAF may lead to a drop in OEF military involvement, especially that of the USA. Moreover, Afghan officials are not sure about ISAF's ability to confront the restive armed opposition and terrorists, which are active in southern Afghanistan. Tarzi, A., 'Afghanistan: NATO prepares to move into most restive provinces', Radio Free Europe/Radio Liberty, 12 Dec. 2005, URL <http://www.rferl.org/featuresarticle/2005/12/555dd2f4-e303-4a6f-b635-146a304de 707.html>.

[110] According to *Le Monde*, a general ISAF command for the whole of Afghanistan would be created. The general in command of the ISAF would be seconded by 3 deputies, who would be responsible for stabilization, air operations and security, respectively. Zecchini, L., 'Il n'y aura pas de "fusion" des opérations militaires en Afghanistan' [There will be no 'merger' of military operations in Afghanistan], *Le Monde*, 19 Oct. 2005.

mittee to be presented to the North Atlantic Council in December. In military terms, ISAF is now mandated additionally to conduct 'stability and security operations' in coordination with Afghan national security forces and to provide support to Afghan government efforts to 'disarm illegally armed groups'.[111] The NATO members promised to earmark an additional 6000 troops for Afghanistan in early 2006. It is assumed that NATO's mission in Afghanistan should take six or seven more years.[112]

The division over *Iraq* continued in 2005, with France, Germany and several other states still opposing a NATO military role there. In February the NATO states declared that they had collected sufficient funds for the security-force training mission in Baghdad and in September the military academy at Ar-Rustamiya was inaugurated with the aim of training some 900 Iraqi medium-rank and senior officers per year.[113] Some NATO states that are unwilling to send personnel to Baghdad are financing the training of Iraqi military personnel outside the country, and NATO states also donated €100 million worth of arms and equipment to the Iraqi Armed Forces.

New missions

On 26 April 2005 the African Union (AU) asked NATO to consider the possibility of providing purely logistical support to its operation in *Darfur, Sudan*, in an attempt to halt the continuing violence in the region. NATO agreed in May–June 2005 to help the AU expand its peacekeeping mission, thus launching the first-ever NATO involvement in Africa. Both NATO and the EU were asked for support and coordinated their efforts under AU control.[114] The coordination of NATO's airlift was done from Europe, while also working with the UN, non-governmental organizations (NGOs) and individual nations. NATO started to airlift African peacekeepers into Darfur in early July; it also trained AU troops in command and control and operational planning, running a multinational military headquarters and managing intelligence. In September NATO decided to offer similar logistical support, up to 31 March 2006, for troop rotations to the AU Mission in Sudan (AMIS) forces and further training to improve the skills of the AU officers.

Three days after the earthquake in *Pakistan* and *India* on 8 October, NATO decided to assist relief efforts by sending emergency supplies to northern Pakistan together with a battalion of engineers, mobile international medical units from the NATO Response Force, a deployable headquarters and

---

[111] North Atlantic Treaty Organization (NATO), 'Final communiqué, Ministerial meeting of the North Atlantic Council', Press release (2005)158, Brussels, 8 Dec. 2005, URL <http://www.nato.int/docu/pr/2005/p05-158e.htm>. It is not clear whether ISAF is authorized to use force if such an approach is adopted by the Kabul authorities.

[112] In Nov. Uzbekistan closed its territory and airspace to NATO forces, thus making it more difficult for the allied troops to conduct operations in Afghanistan.

[113] In 2005 *c.* 700 officers are estimated to have trained in Iraq, and several hundred officers trained at NATO facilities in Europe.

[114] Some NATO/EU countries—France, Germany, Spain and others—decided to place themselves under EU leadership.

specialist equipment.[115] In addition, water purification plants (from Lithuania) and over 40 helicopters were sent, and a field hospital was set up in November. The strategic airlift involved was unique in NATO's history. Supplies donated by NATO members and partners as well as the UN High Commissioner for Refugees were dispatched via two airlifts, from Germany and Turkey. During the first month after the earthquake some 1600 tonnes of relief supplies were transported to the disaster area by more than 100 flights, and 18 camps for more than 200 000 people were built in the affected areas. NATO troops were scheduled to remain in Pakistan until the end of January.

Enlargement

Like the EU, NATO has also been affected by 'enlargement fatigue' in the wake of its 2004 membership expansion. Following the fifth, and largest, round of NATO enlargement in March 2004, three Balkan countries— Albania, Croatia and FYROM—are now participants in NATO's Membership Action Plan (MAP), which is a route to possible future membership. In September 2005, however, a senior US official stated that the three Balkan candidates are 'not yet ready' for membership. The issue of further enlargement will reportedly be addressed at a summit meeting in 2008 at the earliest.[116] Meanwhile, Ukraine's hope of joining NATO by 2008 dwindled when NATO indicated that, while it was willing to help Ukraine carry out necessary reforms, the main responsibility for Ukraine's eligibility rested on the 'shoulders of the Ukrainian leadership'.[117]

Transformation

Together with the Allied Command for Transformation in Norfolk, Virginia, the catalyst for the transformation process launched at the 2002 Prague NATO summit meeting is the expeditionary NATO Response Force. The now 17 000-strong force is designed to spearhead interventions in crises worldwide and is scheduled to become fully operational in October 2006. The natural disasters in the USA (Hurricane Katrina) and in Pakistan (the earthquake) presented opportunities to test the NRF in crisis-response mode.[118]

Debate in NATO has shifted focus from the NRF's basic organization to the questions of its aim, function and role and how it relates to other force frameworks (e.g., the EU's European Rapid Reaction Force or battle groups). As NATO officials and military officers never tire of repeating, success depends

---

[115] Earlier in 2005 Jaap de Hoop de Scheffer commented that if the Dec. 2004 Asian tsunami had happened closer to NATO's area, the NRF almost certainly would have been deployed to help.

[116] *Atlantic News*, no. 3671, 23 Apr. 2005, p. 1; and *Atlantic News*, no. 3706, 13 Sep. 2005, p. 3.

[117] *Atlantic News*, no. 3691, 28 June 2005, p. 1. In Apr. 2005 Ukraine entered an Intensified Dialogue on Membership, commonly viewed as the precursor to being invited to enter the MAP process.

[118] In previous deployments the NRF provided assistance to the 2004 Athens Olympic Games and the 2004 presidential elections in Afghanistan.

on capabilities,[119] but formal steps must wait until the 'transformation' summit meeting scheduled for November 2006 in Riga.

In March 2005 NATO announced that it had reached a key milestone in its plans to field a theatre missile defence programme by adopting the Charter for the Active Layered Theatre Ballistic Missile Defence. The programme aims at integrating the various missile defence systems (such as Patriot or the medium-extended air defence system, MEADS) 'into a coherent, deployable defensive network'. It will reach its initial operational capability in 2010.[120]

VI. The Organization for Security and Co-operation in Europe

Following the decisions of the OSCE Ministerial Council of December 2004[121] the emphasis in OSCE circles has remained on internal issues, including the call for reform. The programme of the Chairman-in-Office (CIO), Slovenia, could be summarized as 'the triple R agenda: Revitalize, Reform and Rebalance'.[122] The formal vehicle for the reform debate was the report of the panel of eminent persons submitted to the CIO in June 2005, followed by consultations among the participating states. The report contained more than 70 proposals to improve the OSCE's effectiveness,[123] but most were relatively non-radical, practical and focused on management and institutional matters. Once the high-level consultations started among the OSCE participating states it was clear that only a modest set of proposals could count on consensus.

The theme of 'rebalancing' reflected a continuing major disagreement as to the OSCE's future between the USA and Russia. The EU, partly owing to some disagreement among its member states, did not take a high profile in this debate.[124] The USA would like to continue the OSCE's heavy emphasis on the human dimension, including the monitoring of elections and the immediate release of the preliminary results,[125] but to concentrate OSCE efforts on the

---

[119] On the table are the pressing matters of acquiring an airborne warning and control system (AWACS) surveillance aircraft, strategic transport and tactical helicopters. The call for joint funding has received a cool response from some member states. *Atlantic News*, no. 3707, 15 Sep. 2005, p. 1.

[120] 'NATO to deploy missile defence system by 2010', *Jane's Defence Weekly*, 23 Mar. 2005, p. 5.

[121] See Dunay, P., 'The Organization for Security and Co-operation in Europe: constant adaptation but enduring problems', *SIPRI Yearbook 2005* (note 36), pp. 76–82.

[122] Organization for Security and Co-operation in Europe (OSCE), 'Address by H.E. Dimitrij Rupel, Ph.D., Chairman-in-Office of the OSCE, at the Permanent Council', OSCE document CIO.GAL/2/05, 13 Jan. 2005, URL <http://www.osce.si/docs/2005-01-13-govor-cio-na-zasedanju-pc-eng.pdf>, p. 1.

[123] Organization for Security and Co-operation in Europe (OSCE), 'Common purpose: towards a more effective OSCE', 27 June 2005. NGO reports include Zellner, W., *Managing Change in Europe: Evaluating the OSCE and Its Future Role, Competencies, Capabilities, and Missions*, CORE Working Paper 13 (Centre for OSCE Research: Hamburg, 2005); and OSCE Parliamentary Assembly and the Swiss Foundation for World Affairs, 'Report: Colloquium on "The Future of the OSCE"', Washington, DC, 5–6 June 2005. OSCE publications are available at URL <http://www.osce.org>.

[124] It was noteworthy that following the EU statement at the high-level consultations, several EU member states—e.g., Austria and Poland—deemed it necessary to make national statements. British Presidency of the Council of the European Union, 'EU Statement for High Level OSCE Consultations in Vienna', PC.DEL/865/05, 13 Sep. 2005.

[125] Such preliminary assessments have been instrumental in depriving of legitimacy the winners of various recent elections that were not 'free and fair'.

former Soviet area and to a somewhat lesser extent on the Western Balkans.[126] The position of Russia and some other former Soviet countries is diametrically opposite: they want to 'rebalance' the OSCE not geographically but function-ally and in a way reminiscent of its cold war role, when the West did not in practice intrude into the politics of the Soviet zone of influence. Their view is that less attention should be paid to the human dimension, more to politico-military cooperation; the focus should be on the entire OSCE area; and elec-tion monitoring should not be used as a vehicle of regime change.[127]

In the light of the high-level consultations it was not surprising that the OSCE Ministerial Council of December 2005 was unable to achieve a major breakthrough. The 19 decisions passed could not hide the fact that on political reform the parties agreed to differ. Some institutional changes that were agreed—like turning the OSCE into a career-based organization and granting immunity to OSCE missions and observers—should at least improve the pro-fessionalism of OSCE performance.

VII. 'Normalizing' interstate relations in the post-Soviet area

No more high-profile regime changes, like those in Georgia and Ukraine in 2003–2004, occurred in the area of the former Soviet Union in 2005. Instead, different national policies and practices were consolidated, resulting in a more normal international disposition in the region. Although states that made different domestic choices held strong views about each other, the impact of their antagonisms seemed to be somewhat reduced.

Russia

Russia remains the central player in the post-Soviet space, and it sets the standard (for good or ill) for domestic transformations in the region. Russia, however, has been increasingly facing an image problem. Western anxiety was raised by decisions like the sentencing of Mikhail Khodorkovsky, the former head of oil giant Yukos, and the proposals for de facto banning of for-eign (and foreign-funded) NGOs pursuing political activity.[128] Russia, in turn, has been anxious about the shifting of the power balance in the world and con-cerned to curtail the USA's freedom of action. In a pattern seen before, Russia has played up its policy contacts with other major actors such as China and

---

[126] US Mission to the OSCE, Under Secretary for Political Affairs R. Nicholas Burns, 'Intervention at the Thirteenth OSCE Ministerial Council', Ljubljana, 5 Dec. 2005, URL <http://osce.usmission.gov/mc/ljubljana.html>.

[127] Transcript of Remarks by Russian Minister of Foreign Affairs Sergei Lavrov, 13th Meeting of the OSCE Ministerial Council, Ljubljana, 5 Dec. 2005, URL <http://www.mid.ru/>, p. 2.

[128] Myers, S. L., 'Russians seek to put restrictions on NGOs', *International Herald Tribune*, 24 Nov. 2005, p. 6; and Veretennikova, K., 'Byudzhetnaya demokratiya: grazhdanskoye obshchestvo budet sozdavat'sya za kazennyi schot [Budgetary democracy: civil society will be organized on the account of the treasury]', *Vremya novostey*, 18 Nov. 2005, URL <http://www.vremya.ru/print/139353.html>.

India.[129] Russia also remains a significant and perhaps key player in such high-profile issues as nuclear proliferation in Iran and North Korea.[130] Most obviously, Russia's continuing role in the former Soviet area makes it hard to imagine any of the region's frozen or pending conflicts being resolved without either involving Russia or facing its abstention.

A gradually unifying Europe presents a dilemma for Russia, while Russia also presents a dilemma for the EU.[131] Since 2003 the two sides have been working on an agreement to create four 'common spaces'. It appears that the practical provisions will be diluted and offer no real advance on the Partnership and Cooperation Agreement that expires in 2007.[132] Russia has not achieved objectives such as visa-free travel for its citizens or a special status in the ESDP, and it has expressed displeasure that some 'new EU members . . . have tried to introduce some confrontational tones into the dialogue between Russia and the EU'.[133] Russia suffers from the asymmetry whereby nearly half of its foreign trade is conducted with the EU, but Russia accounts for only 7.6 per cent of the EU's aggregate import and 4.4 per cent of its aggregate export.[134] On the other side, the EU objects to Russia's backtracking on democracy and its support to dictatorial post-Soviet regimes, and the EU perceives that Russia has not made up its mind whether the USA or the EU is its main partner in the long run.[135] In a dialogue overshadowed by the EU's constitutional woes,[136] both sides have had to settle for minor advances like the agreements that were initialled on 12 October 2005 on visa facilitation and readmission: the former more important for Russia, the latter for the EU.[137]

While in past years most criticism of Russia's record on democracy and human rights came from NGOs, in 2005 President Bush noted that: 'Democracies have certain things in common. They have a rule of law and protection of minorities, a free press and a viable political opposition'.[138] Other Western

---

[129] This idea dates back to the mid-1990s when Foreign Minister Yevgeny Primakov advocated a Chinese–Indian–Russian 'strategic' entente.

[130] See chapter 13 in this volume.

[131] As a Polish newspaper stated: 'Russia too weak to subordinate to Europe, too strong to become a normal European power', *Polish News Bulletin*, 28 July 2005.

[132] Karaganov, S., 'Russia's European strategy: a new start', *Russia in Global Affairs*, no. 3 (July–Sep. 2005), URL <http://eng.globalaffairs.ru/region-snt/numbers/12/941.html>, pp. 72–85.

[133] Latyshev, A., 'Russia and Europe need each other: interview with Sergei Yastrzhembsky', *Russia Journal*, vol. 25, no. 102 (Nov. 2005), p. 36.

[134] Karaganov (note 132).

[135] See Skorov, G., 'Rossiya–Evrosoyuz: voprosy strategicheskogo partnerstva' [Russia–EU: the questions of strategic partnership], *Mirovaya ekonomika i mezhdunarodnye otnosheniya*, no. 3 (2005), pp. 79–84.

[136] 'Russia and the EU's constitutional crisis', *CEPS Neighbourhood Watch*, issue 5 (June 2005), pp. 11–14.

[137] European Commission, 'EU–Russia relations: next steps towards visa facilitation and readmission agreement', URL <http://europa.eu.int/comm/external_relations/russia/intro/ip05_1263.htm>. Visa application for Russian citizens will be decided faster for smaller fees and will require less documentation. The application of the rule on the readmission of citizens of third countries who cross the Russian Federation and enter EU territory will start after a transition period of 3 years following entry into force.

[138] The White House, 'President and President Putin discuss strong U.S.–Russian partnership', News release, Bratislava, 24 Feb. 2005, URL <http://www.whitehouse.gov/news/releases/2005/02/20050224-9.html>. In the assessment of Freedom House, Russia's political rights rating in 2005 declined from 5 to

leaders have been less articulate, but democracy and human rights have returned to the agenda between Russia and the West.

At the same time, Russia's windfall oil profits in 2005 made it feel at least temporarily less reliant on outsiders[139] and reawoke visions of an influential but separate Russian pole of power. This may help explain some attempts by Russia to flex its muscles vis-à-vis some new members of the EU and NATO, as well as its tough and essentially zero-sum policy in the post-Soviet space. States that do not align with the West and accept the integrity of the post-Soviet space can count on Russian support irrespective of the nature of their regimes. Those who 'go West' and leave the Russian camp cannot. States ready to 'return' to Russia may attract especially vigorous Russian support, as the cases of Azerbaijan and Uzbekistan have demonstrated recently. For the non-compliant, President Vladimir Putin has again shown a preference to apply economic levers, including manipulation of the price and conditions for energy (a form of blackmail that Ukraine suffered especially in late 2005 and early 2006).[140] Russia also made similar attempts with Moldova and Bulgaria. The choice of such tactics reflects *inter alia* Russia's reduced military presence in the neighbourhood owing to shrinking conventional capabilities and may imply a historic and irreversible change.[141]

On the domestic security agenda, the smouldering conflict in Chechnya is the most acute. Russia may have tightened its control in the province, but horizontal escalation threatens the North Caucasian neighbourhood.[142] Russian special forces coped adequately, however, with the October 2005 terrorist attack in Nalchik, Kabardino-Balkaria, which—unlike the Beslan tragedy of September 2004—did not divide Russian society. From the end of 2005, only volunteer troops of the Interior Ministry will stay in Chechnya and that should make it politically easier to sustain the operation.[143] The November 2005 parliamentary elections in Chechnya have demonstrated slow, inconclusive reconciliation. It is certain that the local population feels exhausted by the conflict.

6, and its status from 'partly free' to 'not free' because of the virtual elimination of influential political opposition parties in the country and the further concentration of executive power. Freedom House, 'Russia: legislating repression of civil society', URL <http://www.freedomhouse.org/>.

[139] Russia's international reserves increased by *c.* $40 billion between the end of 2004 and the end of Oct. 2005 and have reached nearly $165 billion. Central Bank of the Russian Federation, 'International reserves assets of the Russian Federation in 2005', URL <http://www.cbr.ru/eng/statistics/credit_statistics/print.asp?file=inter_res_05_e.htm>.

[140] FT reporters, 'Russians agree deal on supply of gas to Ukraine', *Financial Times*, 5 Jan. 2006, p. 1; Buckley, N. and Warner, T., 'Moscow and Kiev can both claim "victory"', *Financial Times*, 5 Jan. 2006, p. 4; and Buckley, N. and Warner, T., 'Kiev turmoil raises more doubts over gas deal', *Financial Times*, 12 Jan. 2006, p. 3.

[141] Mukhin, V., 'Sila kak instrument vneshnepoliticheskogo vliyaniya' [Force as the instrument of influence in foreign policy], *Nezavisimaya gazeta, Dipkur'er*, 10 Oct. 2005, p. 2.

[142] See chapter 2 in this volume.

[143] 'Russian brigade in Chechnya to become all-volunteer force by year-end 2005', Agenstvo Voyennykh Novostey, 26 Oct. 2005, URL <http://dlib.eastview.com/sources/article.jsp?id=8483147>.

Ukraine and the Caucasus

Ukraine's new regime continues its pro-Western political course, but the high hopes of early 2005 have given way to more realistic assessments. Integration with Western Europe is a long-term project,[144] and Ukraine cannot move towards the West without looking to the East—the practical imperative to cooperate with Russia and other neighbours has not changed. Recognizing that EU accession will not be realized soon, Ukraine intends to develop relations with the single economic space under the assumption that it will not become more than a trade zone.[145] Not all aspects of Western integration have majority support inside Ukraine: NATO accession remains an especially divisive issue.

Externally, Ukraine has made efforts to play an active role in the region *inter alia* through an alignment with *Georgia*. The cooperation of the two 'reform' countries has contributed to revitalizing the GUAM (Georgia, Ukraine, Azerbaijan and Moldova) grouping of countries and to efforts to resolve the Trans-Dniester deadlock.[146]

The achievements of the Georgian leadership two years after the 2003 'Rose Revolution' remain mixed. There are impressive results in the domestic transformation process, ranging from the fight against corruption to infrastructure development,[147] but Georgia's poor ranking on Transparency International's Corruption Perception Index may show the limits of top–down efforts.[148] Reports also note the violation of some democratic principles, the bias of the mass media, the inadequate functioning of the judiciary and abuse of power by members of the elite.[149] A further unanswered question is how much of the new regime's success is self-maintaining and how much is because of the attention, support and financing of the world at large.[150]

The new Georgian regime has made undoubted progress, however, on issues of territorial integrity. In 2004 it solved the problem presented by Adjaria, one

---

[144] Ukraine hopes to be ready to join NATO by 2008, a view NATO does not share. EU integration will certainly take much longer. Agentstvo Voyennykh Novostey (Moscow), 'Defense Minister: Ukraine will be ready to join NATO by 2008', URL <http://dlib.eastview.com/sources/article.jsp?id=8468767>.

[145] Inter TV (Kiev), 'Ukrainian security chief says possible to cooperate with Russia, EU', BBC Monitoring Kiev Unit, 10 June 2005. The framework agreement establishing a 'single economic space' for Belarus, Kazakhstan, Russia and Ukraine, was signed at the CIS Summit in Sep. 2003. It aims to accelerate the economic and political integration of those countries.

[146] Popescu, N., EU Institute for Security Studies, 'The EU in Moldova: settling conflicts in the neighbourhood', Occasional Paper no. 60, Oct. 2005, URL <http://www.iss-eu.org/>, particularly pp. 26–28.

[147] These are presented in the not entirely unbiased report by Leonard, M. and Grant, C., 'Georgia and the EU: can Europe's Neighbourhood Policy deliver?', Centre for European Reform Policy Brief, Sep. 2005, URL <http://www.cer.org.uk/pdf/policybrief_georgia_sept05.pdf>.

[148] Georgia is ranked 130th equal on the Transparency International Corruption Perception Index 2005, which measures the performance of 159 countries. URL <http://www.transparency.org>.

[149] It is sometimes hard to judge whether the over-representation of the government in the media simply reflects the president's popularity or whether it is manipulation by the victors of the 'Rose Revolution'. Compare 'Is Georgia heading for a new revolution?', Radio Free Europe/Radio Liberty, *Caucasus Report*, vol. 8, no. 31 (10 Sep. 2005), URL <http://www.rferl.org/reports/caucasus-report/2005/09/31-100905.asp>; and Leonard and Grant (note 147).

[150] On the role of external financing see Leonard and Grant (note 147), p. 3.

of three separatist entities on Georgian territory. In 2005 Georgia concluded an agreement on the withdrawal of Russian forces from its territory and the closure of Russian military bases by 2008.[151] It restarted the effort to reach settlement on South Ossetia with an offer of extensive autonomy that is not easy for South Ossetia or Russia to reject outright,[152] and a stage-by-stage implementation plan for the settlement has been presented.[153] Further progress on this issue would demonstrate that President Mikheil Saakashvili's pro-gramme to re-establish Georgia's territorial integrity is on the way to full implementation, despite the continuation of the conflict over Abkhazia.

Azerbaijan held parliamentary elections on 6 November 2005. President Ilham Aliyev did not have as tight a grip on power as his father, former Presi-dent Heydar Aliyev, and it was thought that attempts to manipulate election results might unleash a scenario familiar from Georgia and Ukraine. However, although the OSCE and the Council of Europe concluded that the parlia-mentary elections 'did not meet a number of OSCE commitments and Council of Europe standards and commitments for democratic elections',[154] the sequel was different from that in Georgia and Ukraine. The Azerbaijani authorities acted resolutely against the demonstrators, the opposition was less organized and lacked a charismatic leader, and external support was limited (perhaps owing to Azerbaijan's strategic oil reserves and the importance of the newly opened Baku–Ceyhan pipeline).[155] Russia also provided effective 'pre-election support' to Aliyev, helping him to prevent a possible coup d'état two weeks before the elections.[156] Although his regime may not regain full control, it has shown that the 'colour revolution' method applied elsewhere can be blocked.

There were signs in 2005 that the frozen Nagorno-Karabakh conflict could be resolved with external encouragement.[157] The opportunity is important to seize because Azerbaijan has been determined to turn its economic superiority into military advantage,[158] which may reduce the long-term chances of peace.

---

[151] For details see chapter 15 in this volume.

[152] 'Georgian president addresses South Ossetia conference on autonomy issues', Georgian TV1, 10 July 2005.

[153] Prime Minister Zurab Nogaideli, Speech at the meeting of the OSCE Permanent Council, 27 Oct. 2005. The speech is summarized in Socor, V., 'Georgia's action plan on South Ossetia: a test for the international community', *Eurasia Daily Monitor*, vol. 2, issue 219 (23 Nov. 2005), URL <http://www.jamestown.org/publications>.

[154] Organization for Security and Co-operation in Europe (OSCE), International Election Observation Mission, 'Parliamentary election, Republic of Azerbaijan—6 November 2005: statement of preliminary findings and conclusions', URL <http://www.osce.org/odihr-elections/15649.html>.

[155] Sultanova, A., Associated Press, 'Officials inaugurate pipeline to ship Caspian Sea oil to Mediter-ranean', 25 May 2005, URL <http://www.armeniandiaspora.com/archive/30451.html>.

[156] Mandeville, L., 'Moscou veut tuer dans l'oeuf la révolution de Bakou' [Moscow wants to nip the revolution in Baku in the bud], *Le Figaro*, 14 Nov. 2005, p. 4 ; and 'Poutine reprend la main en Azerbaidjan' [Putin retakes the initiative in Azerbaijan], *Le Figaro*, 14 Nov. 2005, p. 1.

[157] International Crisis Group, 'Nagorno-Karabakh: a plan for peace', Europe report no. 167, 11 Oct. 2005, URL <http://www.crisisgroup.org/home/index.cfm?id=3740&l=1>.

[158] See International Crisis Group (note 157).

Central Asia

Central Asia's general immunity from conflicts, after the end of the war in Tajikistan, ended in 2005. Kyrgyzstan experienced a regime change, while the demonstrations in Andijon, Uzbekistan, and the leadership's reaction to them had far-reaching implications.

The February 2005 elections to *Kyrgyzstan*'s parliament 'fell short of OSCE commitments and other international standards in several important areas'.[159] Demonstrations followed and led to the resignation of President Askar Akayev, who had presided over one of the more democratic regimes in Central Asia, although marred by nepotism and corruption. The presidential elections of July 2005 brought the Kyrgyz revolution to an 'anti-climactic' end under which the assessment of change remains inconclusive.[160] The USA has persuaded the new Kyrgyz leadership to prolong the availability of the Manas airbase for the military operation in Afghanistan—all the more important in the light of US setbacks in Uzbekistan.[161]

Uzbekistan's size and location make it a key actor in Central Asia. At Andijon on 12–13 May, probably due to the overreaction of security forces, hundreds of local demonstrators, and perhaps as many as 1000, were shot.[162] The regime sought to blame Islamic militants and, later, 'an attempt by political circles in the west to dominate the region to get access to raw materials and to serve their strategic interests'.[163] The Western outrage in the aftermath of these events pushed Uzbekistan's president into Russia's embrace, at least for the time being.[164] Not long after the Andijon incident, an extremely critical assessment of the presence of foreign troops in Uzbekistan was published,[165] and three weeks later the government requested the USA to vacate the Karshi-Khanabad airbase and withdraw its military units from Uzbekistan by the end of 2005. In November 2005 Uzbekistan informed 'European members of NATO they will not be able to use its airspace or territory for operations linked to peacekeeping in neighbouring Afghanistan'.[166] Uzbekistan, however,

---

[159] Office for Democratic Institutions and Human Rights, 'The Kyrgyz Republic: parliamentary elections, 27 February and 13 March 2005', OSCE/ODIHR Election Observation Mission Final Report, Warsaw, 20 May 2005, URL <http://www.osce.org/odihr/>, p. 4.

[160] Socor, V., 'Anticlimactic end to Kyrgyz revolution', *Eurasia Daily Monitor*, vol. 2, no. 162 (18 Aug. 2005).

[161] Kyrgyzstan has been keen to use its improved negotiating position over Manas to secure better payments for landing and take-off. Under the Akayev regime the USA paid $7000 for one take-off or landing. US embassy official in Bishkek, Communication with the authors, 12 Jan. 2005.

[162] See Blank, S., 'The future of Uzbekistan after Andijan', *Terrorism Monitor*, vol. 3, no. 11 (2 June 2005), URL <http://jamestown.org/terrorism/news/uploads/ter_003_011.pdf>.

[163] Press Service of the President of Uzbekistan, 'Problems of security in Central Asia', 22 Oct. 2005, URL <http://www.press-service.uz/en/gsection.scm?groupId=5203&content>.

[164] Press Service of the President of Uzbekistan, 'President's visit to Russia', 30 June 2005, URL <http://www.press-service.uz/en/gsection.scm?groupId=5203&content>.

[165] Press Service of the President of Uzbekistan, 'Uzbek Foreign Ministry statement on presence of foreign troops in SCO countries', 8 July 2005, URL <http://www.press-service.uz/en/gsection.scm?groupId=5203&contentId=11060>.

[166] Reuters Alertnet, 'Uzbekistan to ban some NATO overflights—alliance', 24 Nov. 2005, URL <http://www.craigmurray.co.uk/archives/2005/11/uzbekistan_to_b.html>. Carstens, P., 'Mit Unterstützung Europas: Die Bundeswehr darf "auf lange Zeit" in Uzbekistan bleiben' [With Europe's support:

permitted Germany to continue to operate from the Termez airbase 'for a long time' and to develop it further. These events illustrated not only the Russian calculus regarding support for oppressive rulers—especially when it is possible to inflict a strategic reverse on the USA—but also the differentiated trends that are widening gaps between former Soviet neighbours. After the Andijon incident, Uzbek refugees fled to neighbouring Kyrgyzstan and some were evacuated from there to Romania despite Uzbekistan's protests.

VIII. Conclusions

Transatlantic relations eased further in 2005 despite unresolved differences over Iraq. Western democracies have been reminded of their shared interests and common objectives. The USA has gradually normalized relations and coordinated its policy more closely with its European partners. How the currently more pro-US 'new Europe' will affect the longer-term transatlantic and intra-European balances remains to be seen. The USA's pragmatism in its dealings with European nations and institutions seems to owe less to a philosophical reassessment than to specific blockages in Iraq and on the domestic front. The Bush Administration's taste for using force unilaterally seems unchanged, but the Iraqi stalemate prevents it from going beyond occasional hints of further 'pre-emptive' use of force. The present posture of the USA could thus be characterized as self-restrained, 'coordinated' unilateralism.

In the institutional dimension of Euro-Atlantic relations, the rivalry between the main actors—the EU and NATO—is entering a new phase as their geographical and functional agendas increasingly overlap. The 2005 crisis in the EU has had a muted, apparently non-fatal, impact on the implementation of its ambitious security agenda for the coming years. NATO, entangled in the competing visions and interests of its members, still lacks a clear strategic mission for the future. Both organizations have evidently lost their enlargement momentum for years to come. Other European security-related bodies are even more burdened with internal troubles and dwindling legitimacy.

In the former Soviet area there is an increasingly clear and sharp divide between countries that have embarked on democratization and those that strive to maintain authoritarian rule. The international impact of these divergent political courses is heightened by populist pronouncements, megaphone diplomacy and symbolic demonstrations from both the reform countries and others. The resulting bad chemistry could complicate the resolution of pending conflicts. Central Asia, thus far much less scarred by conflicts than the Caucasus, could be more vulnerable to instability as a result of the push for regime change. The strategic implications of a major breakdown in any larger Central Asian state, given the acute interest of the USA and Russia as well as China in the region, are difficult to compute.

the Bundeswehr needs to remain in Uzbekistan 'for a long time'], *Frankfurter Allgemeine Zeitung*, 16 Dec. 2005, p. 12.

Appendix 1A. Status and statehood in the Western Balkans

PÁL DUNAY

I. Introduction

The Western Balkans region has experienced turbulent times since the end of the cold war.[1] The massive violence that followed the break-up of the multi-ethnic Socialist Federal Republic of Yugoslavia (FRY) has now ended and the risks of its recurring have diminished significantly. Not all the consequences of the violent break-up of Yugoslavia have been successfully accommodated, however. Europe's security is affected in various ways by the outcomes of earlier wars between and within the successor republics, of international interventions, and of other internal tensions (notably, in the Former Yugoslav Republic of Macedonia, FYROM). The ultimate statuses of Kosovo and, to a different extent, Montenegro, are unclear. In the case of Kosovo the question is whether the entity will gain independent statehood, whereas in the case of Montenegro it concerns the framework in which state sovereignty will be realized. Meanwhile, a massive international presence—by the United Nations (UN), the European Union (EU), the North Atlantic Treaty Organization (NATO) and the Organization for Security and Co-operation in Europe (OSCE)—remains in the area, carrying out some direct administration functions as well as 'peace-building' (including programmes for economic and social development).[2] This in itself shows how far the area remains from any kind of normalization.

There is a certain rhythm in the evolution of the history of the former Yugoslavia, with major events and course corrections every five to six years. One such major event came when, in parallel with the end of the cold war, Serbian President Slobodan Milosevic eliminated the autonomous status of Kosovo (and that of Vojvodina) in 1989. The wars of liberation, which began in 1991, ended in 1995 with the General Framework Agreement for Peace in Bosnia and Herzegovina (Dayton Agreement),[3] which guaranteed not only the de jure but also the de facto independence of Bosnia and Herzegovina (BiH). Between 1999 and 2001 a further set of unsolved problems spilled over. As well as Serbia's loss of control over Kosovo following the NATO military operation of March–June 1999, three major leaders of post-Yugoslav history left power before the end of 2001: presidents Franjo Tudjman of Croatia, Alija

---

[1] 'The Western Balkans' is the term which the European Union (EU) has used since 1999 to refer to those countries of South-Eastern Europe which are not yet EU members and have not yet received a specific commitment or date for future membership, but which enjoy a credible prospect of membership once political stability in the countries is restored. The region consists of Albania and 4 successor states of the former Yugoslavia—Bosnia and Herzegovina, Croatia, the Former Yugoslav Republic of Macedonia, and Serbia and Montenegro, including the international protectorate of Kosovo, a province of the Republic of Serbia. Slovenia is not included, as it has joined the EU (May 2004) and the North Atlantic Treaty Organization (Mar. 2004).

[2] On peace missions in the region see appendix 3A in this volume.

[3] General Framework Agreement for Peace in Bosnia and Herzegovina (Dayton Agreement), Dayton, Ohio, 14 Dec. 1995, Annex 1-B, Regional Stabilization, URL <http://www.oscebih.org/overview/gfap/eng/>.

Figure 1A.1. Map of the Western Balkans

Izetbegovic of BiH, and Slobodan Milosevic of the FRY. The chances of lasting peace in the Western Balkans, and of the region's eventual full incorporation in European institutions, were improved overall by this round of events; but a further consequential set of policy challenges and choices faces the international community in 2006.[4]

Decisions about new statuses for the territories of the former Yugoslavia need to have, among other things, a viable economic basis. At present it is hard to speak of economic progress except in Croatia and Slovenia. Economic recovery has not been adequate to compensate for the losses caused by war, turbulence and oppression in the 1990s. High unemployment,[5] insufficient investment and large 'grey' and 'black' economies contribute to the persistence of problems. Per capita gross domestic product in Serbia and Montenegro was about €2240 in 2003, whereas in Kosovo it was barely €1000.[6] Levels of corruption continue to be high: BiH is ranked 88th and

---

[4] See also chapter 1.

[5] The data are most dramatic in Kosovo: according to official data, unemployment continues to run at 50% in general and at 70% among people under 25 (half the population). Pond, E., 'Kosovo and Serbia after the French *non*', *Washington Quarterly*, vol. 28, no. 4 (autumn 2005), p. 29. It is difficult, however, to take account of work done in the 'grey' and 'black' sectors.

[6] For data on Serbia and Montenegro see European Commission, 'Serbia and Montenegro: 2005 Progress Report', Brussels, 9 Nov. 2005, SEC (2005) 1428, [COM (2005) 561 final], URL <http://europa. eu.int/comm/enlargement/report_2005/index.htm#pcc>, p. 60. For data on Kosovo see Commission of the European Communities, 'Communication from the Commission: a European future for Kosovo',

Serbia and Montenegro is 97th on Transparency International's Corruption Perceptions Index for 2005.[7] Such an economic situation does not provide a favourable
environment in which to reconcile old grievances.

The year 2006 should help to shape the future for three remaining problematic parts
of the region. First, negotiations have taken place about the final status of Kosovo
(with a green light from the UN Security Council[8]) since early 2006. Second, Montenegro will hold a referendum in the spring of 2006 on whether or not to maintain the
Serbian–Montenegrin federal state.[9] Third, parliamentary elections in late 2006 in
BiH should provide evidence about the direction that state is taking and, in particular,
whether it is necessary to move beyond or modify the Dayton Agreement as a framework for further progress. Although these three events are only loosely interrelated,
their outcome taken together will help shape the Western Balkans for the future.

II. Pending status and statehood issues

Kosovo

When the NATO military operation ended in June 1999 the UN Security Council
passed Resolution 1244.[10] It did not address the final status of Kosovo but had the
following key elements: (*a*) a reaffirmation of the sovereignty and territorial integrity
of the FRY and the other states of the region; (*b*) a reference to the 1999 Interim
Agreement for Peace and Self-Government in Kosovo, known as the Rambouillet
Accord,[11] which had been signed by the Kosovan side although not by Belgrade; and
(*c*) a statement that the international presence had the aim *inter alia* to 'determine
Kosovo's future status'.[12] Some analysts see this text as a typical case of constructive
ambiguity,[13] but it can also be read as a product of realism since it would have been
impossible for members of the Security Council to agree on Kosovo's status at the
time. The reference to the territorial integrity of the FRY aimed to reassure Belgrade
that it had not lost Kosovo by default, while applying the same principle to other
states of the region hinted that changes in Kosovo would not mean any wider redraw-

---

Brussels, 20 Apr. 2005, [COM (2005) 156 final], URL <http://www.eu.int/comm/enlargement/docs/
pdf/COMM_PDF_COM_2005_0156_F_EN_ACTE.pdf>, p. 4.

[7] The Transparency International Corruption Perceptions Index 2005 ranked 159 states in 2005.
Except for Palestine, it does not measure the performance of quasi-independent territories, such as
Kosovo. See the Transparency International website, URL <http://www.transparency.org/>.

[8] UN Security Council, 'Statement by the President of the Security Council', UN document
S/PRST/2005/51, 24 Oct. 2005. The statement contained the approval to start negotiations on the future
status of Kosovo. For background see UN Security Council, 'Security Council presidential statement
offers full support for start of political process to determine Kosovo's future status', 24 Oct. 2005, URL
<http://un.org/News/Press/docs/2005/sc8533.doc.htm>.

[9] International Crisis Group, 'Montenegro's independence drive', Europe report no. 169, 7 Dec. 2005,
URL <http://www.crisisgroup.org>, p. 1.

[10] UN Security Council Resolution 1244, 10 June 1999.

[11] US Institute of Peace, Peace agreements digital collection: Kosovo, Interim Agreement for Peace
and Self-Government in Kosovo, Rambouillet, France, 23 Feb. 1999, URL <http://www.usip.org/library/
pa/kosovo/kosovo_rambtoc.html>.

[12] UN Security Council Resolution 1244 (note 10), preamble, points 11 a., e.

[13] The ambiguity lies *inter alia* in juxtaposing reference to the territorial integrity of the FRY with a
reference to the Rambouillet Accord, hinting that 'independence was not ruled out'. Batt, J., *The
Question of Serbia*, Chaillot Paper no. 81 (EU Institute for Security Studies: Paris, Aug. 2005), URL
<http://www.iss-eu.org/>, p. 35.

ing of boundaries. Although the Dayton Agreement of 1995 did not redraw international borders, it secured the recognition of the independence of BiH by the FRY and gave legal recognition to the entities of BiH whose borders were the product of war. Moreover, Resolution 1244 means that no other state (*vide* Albania) should think of using Kosovo's open status to extend its own sovereign territory. At the same time, the leaving open of the future status (plus the international presence) has reassured the Kosovan Albanian community that they would not return to de facto Serbian rule.

Stability versus status

Since 1999 Kosovo has been run by the UN Interim Administration in Kosovo (UNMIK) and security has been provided by NATO's Kosovo Force (KFOR)—with no remaining organic link with Belgrade, except for the northern parts of Kosovo with a majority Serb population. Those who shaped the 1999 settlement expected time to have a major 'healing effect'. The population of Serbia would get used to the de facto secession of Kosovo, and the two ethnic communities in Kosovo would be reconciled with the help of new economic prosperity.

Against this background the UN administration developed a policy of '[meeting] standards before status'. Progress was supposed to be made on, notably, functioning democratic institutions, the rule of law, freedom of movement, refugee returns and reintegration, the economy, property rights, dialogue with Belgrade, and the role of the Kosovo Protection Corps (for internal order) before the final status issue could be put on the table. The assumptions on which this approach was based have proved partly unsound, however, in that non-status-linked progress has proved inadequate; has not had the desired effect; and, in some cases, has been blocked by the lack of clarity over status. For example, the separation of ethnic Serbs and Albanians could have contributed to accommodation of the two ethnic groups. However, the de facto separation of Kosovo from Serbia did not produce reconciliation and had an adverse bearing on cooperation and coexistence—as the outbreak of violence in March 2004 and some less visible subsequent events have shown. The lack of economic prosperity combined with the Kosovo–Serbia divide, including the closure of the Kosovo–Serbia border, did not provide healthy ground for coexistence between the ethnic communities. Meanwhile, the absence of a clear final status and uncertainty over Kosovo's future degree of sovereignty have precluded the clarity and predictability regarding the local legal framework that is an essential precondition of any lasting, large-scale business interest, particularly of foreign direct investment. This uncertainty also makes it difficult to address property rights: another factor that obstructs economic development and especially privatization. The standards before status policy has not, however, been entirely without merit. It has put pressure on Kosovo's political class to make efforts to respect certain standards, while the UN has gradually transferred some responsibility to it for managing the affairs of the territory.

A long-awaited report presented in October 2005 by the Special Envoy of the UN Secretary-General, Ambassador Kai Eide, concluded that the aims of the UN's policy had been only partly met.[14] The Serbian Government's Council for Kosovo made a similar point more forthrightly, estimating that 'standards are far from being met in the province, especially regarding the non-Albanian communities' basic rights and

---

[14] See, e.g., Eide, K., 'A comprehensive review of the situation in Kosovo', reproduced in UN Security Council, Letter dated 7 October 2005 from the Secretary-General addressed to the President of the Security Council, UN document S/2005/635, 7 Oct. 2005.

the creation of a multi-ethnic society'.[15] In the face of these realities, international policy makers had to consider whether to make greater efforts for full compliance with the standards, or effectively give up on the concept—and what that would mean for the final status.

By the end of 2005 the view was gaining ground in international circles that a rigid interpretation of the standards before status policy would not produce the desired goal of a well-governed, self-sufficient and stable Kosovo. As one senior US official put it, 'we are effectively moving to an approach of "standards with status"—recognizing that only with a resolution of the status question will we bring the kind of stability to Kosovo necessary for the building of the kind of advanced democratic and market-oriented institutions that the standards process has sought to achieve'.[16] This realignment of Western policy opened the way for agreement that talks on the future status of Kosovo could begin, with standards only partially met.[17]

During the months before the opening of these talks, the parties made efforts to consolidate their pre-negotiating positions by addressing a number of different audiences. Both the Serbian leadership[18] and the political establishment of Kosovo have addressed themselves to the states and institutions that will have a decisive say in any accord on the final status. At the same time, they have been sending messages to each other and to their respective electorates. Although the messages to the three constituencies have overlapping elements, they are not identical. Communication between Belgrade and Pristina and with the domestic audiences can be summarized as signalling resolve not to shift from their fundamental positions of, respectively, 'no surrender of Serbian sovereignty' and 'independence'. Messages to the international community have been crafted more carefully. Each party, despite clearly expressed positions, seeks some degree of flexibility in order to bridge the difference during the talks. One example may lie in the ways each side currently defines what is 'acceptable' domestically: Belgrade arguing that any solution unacceptable to Serbia would radicalize its own population and perhaps destabilize the state. In reality, however, increasingly broad strata of the Serbian population seem not to have strongly negative feelings on an independent Kosovo state, although the issue of how it would treat its Serbian minority is far more sensitive. It is thus open to debate when and under what conditions Serbian politics would be able to recognize that 'Kosovo is lost'. However, no Serbian politician would like to have his name associated with the loss. Various

[15] 'Serbian Government's Council for Kosovo: standards far from being met in the province', *V.I.P. Daily News Report*, no. 3133 (1 Aug. 2005), p. 1.

[16] US Department of State, Burns, R. N., Under Secretary of State for Political Affairs, 'Ten years after Dayton: winning the peace in the Balkans', Address at the Woodrow Wilson Center, Washington, DC, 19 May 2005, URL <http://www.state.gov/p/us/rm/2005/46548.htm>. The EU, in turn, refers to 'status with standards'. See 'Summary note on the joint report by Javier Solana, EU High Representative for the CFSP, and Olli Rehn, EU Commissioner for Enlargement, on the future EU Role and Contribution in Kosovo', Information for journalists, S412/05, Brussels, 9 Dec. 2005, URL <http://ue.eu.int/ueDocs/cms_Data/docs/pressdata/EN/reports/87565.pdf>, p. 1.

[17] Consultations have begun with the parties as well as in the capitals of some Contact Group countries (France, Germany, Italy, Russia, the United Kingdom, the United States and the EU). This stage of 'shuttle diplomacy' will be followed by the drafting of an agreement that will then be discussed with the Serbian and Kosovan Albanian negotiating teams in the spring of 2006 at the earliest. The formal opening of the talks has been delayed so that the two parties do not state their positions publicly and thus 'tie their own hands'. See Judah, T., 'Kosovo's moment of truth', *Survival*, vol. 47, no. 4 (winter 2005–2006), p. 79.

[18] The leadership of Montenegro has declared itself disinterested in the Kosovo talks and their outcome. This is understandable in light of the referendum to be held about the future relationship of Serbia and Montenegro.

analysts have drawn the same conclusion: 'If the Contact Group pushes for independence, it could face a Serb walk-out and will then have to decide whether to impose a settlement. Such a scenario might even suit . . . the Serb prime minister. He will be able to claim he fought as hard as he could then retreated without surrendering.'[19] Meanwhile, Kosovo naturally argues that depriving it of its right to self-determination (and hence, independent statehood) would risk a breakdown of order in Kosovo itself.

On paper there is an unbridgeable gap between the opening bids. The Serbian side argues *inter alia* that Security Council Resolution 1244 is based on territorial integrity: since Kosovo has never attained independent statehood, the only answer is to restore the sovereignty of the successor state to Yugoslavia (Serbia and Montenegro).[20] This position offers no more than some type of *sui generis* solution for Kosovo that might offer 'more than autonomy'. Kosovan Albanian politicians for their part argue that such a solution is unacceptable, because they view Kosovo as having a moral claim to independence in the light of its population's suffering at Serbian hands. The autonomy Kosovo once enjoyed under Yugoslavia's 1974 constitution is, for them, no solution: Kosovo lived 'under the control of Belgrade much too long' and its case is similar to that of 'the oppressed people of Iraq and Afghanistan after their liberation'.[21] At bottom, the Kosovan Albanian case, as presented, is grounded in the right to self-determination, which implies nothing less than the right to independent statehood. Kosovan Albanian politicians are reluctant even to discuss solutions involving decentralization within Serbia, fearing that Kosovo might inadvertently lose the chance of full independence.

The international community—notably, the Contact Group of France, Germany, Italy, Russia, the United Kingdom, the United States and the EU—has considered various options. Some have been excluded *expressis verbis*: (*a*) returning Kosovo to Serbian dominance, (*b*) permitting a union with Albania, or (*c*) partitioning Kosovo.[22] It is clear that the return to Serbian dominance is neither feasible nor desirable. An eventual union with Albania, a step towards a greater Albania, would have major regional repercussions unacceptable to most parties. Allowing Kosovo to unite with any other neighbouring Albanian-inhabited territory (e.g., parts of Macedonia and southern Serbia) has also been excluded. Partition, apart from local objections, might have dangerous domino effects leading to border revisions elsewhere in the Western Balkans. These three considerations combined mean that all internationally acceptable solutions assume the territorial integrity of Kosovo.

Defining what the final status of Kosovo should not be leaves the question of what options are left. Currently, independent statehood as well as a *sui generis* status short of it remain equally possible. Responsible officials have denied 'that the international community has a solution which has already been established and written and should just be implemented. There is no such thing. Furthermore, a solution is to be found at

[19] Wagstyl, S., 'Struggling towards stability: why Kosovo may hold the key to the Balkans' future', *Financial Times*, 20 Feb. 2006, p. 11.

[20] This is why there are forces in Kosovo which argue that first the entity should practice its right to self-determination (gain independent statehood) and only then negotiate bilaterally with Belgrade. Judah (note 17), pp. 81–82.

[21] Thaci, H., 'My people deserve their independence', *International Herald Tribune*, 26–27 Nov. 2005, p. 4.

[22] Rasmussen, N. A., Danish Institute for International Affairs (DIIS), 'Kosovo independence—de jure versus de facto', DIIS report 2005:14, Oct. 2005, URL <http://www.diis.dk/sw15761.asp>, p. 13. Other sources add a 4th 'no' for immediate full sovereignty for Kosovo. See Pond (note 5), p. 23.

the end of a long and hopefully constructive negotiation process.'[23] Bearing in mind the distance between the starting positions of the parties, the negotiation process now beginning is unlikely to be particularly constructive or amicable and the aim of concluding the talks in less than a year appears ambitious.[24]

The issue of minority rights

Establishing the final status of Kosovo should contribute to stability in the Western Balkans, but it will require the regulation of a broad range of issues. If partition is indeed off the agenda, respect for minority rights becomes a central issue. It is probably the major issue to be settled at the negotiations on future status, irrespective of whether Kosovo becomes a sovereign entity de jure or only de facto. The legal framework will be quite different in the two cases, however. If Kosovo attains independent statehood it will have a state's responsibility for guaranteeing minority rights, whereas if it acquires a status short of independent statehood it will not have such responsibility—a paradoxical situation from the viewpoint of Serbian concerns. Regardless of the outcome, it is the assumption of the international community that some form of international presence will continue in Kosovo, with particular responsibility for minority rights.

There are no reliable data available on the ethnic composition of Kosovo,[25] but it is certain that it has changed gradually. According to the census of 1981 less than 80 per cent of the population of Kosovo was Albanian; now it is close to 90 per cent. According to estimates, 7 per cent of the population was Serbian in 2003.[26] Experts have estimated the current size of the ethnic Serb population of Kosovo as approximately 70 000, equivalent to 3.5 per cent of the population.

The record in Kosovo since 1999 regarding respect for minority rights, particularly that of the Serbian minority, has been uneven at best. It can be argued that a 'multi-ethnic Kosovo does not exist except in the bureaucratic assessments of the international community'.[27] In the forthcoming talks, the Kosovan authorities can be expected to make promises about respect for human rights, including minority rights: but it is another question how sincere and how enforceable such pledges will be. As things stand, a continued international presence in Kosovo and a role in enforcement appear to be the only way to guarantee minority rights.[28] The dilemma is that accepting a continued international responsibility in this sphere (perhaps also in a status settlement) does nothing to promote better behaviour by the Kosovan authorities. On the

[23] An interview with the German Ambassador to Serbia and Montenegro, Andreas Zobel, in the daily *Dnevnik* (Novi Sad) is cited in Serbian and Montenegrin Ministry of Foreign Affairs, Daily survey, Belgrade, 15 Apr. 2005, URL <http://www.mfa.gov.yu/Bilteni/Engleski/b250405_e.html#N16>.

[24] Various estimates have been made, usually mentioning a 6–12 month period of negotiations. Some analysts predict even more protracted talks. See *V.I.P. Daily News Report*, no. 3215 (23 Nov. 2005), p. 1. The first round of talks between representatives of Belgrade and Pristina started on 20 Feb. 2006. See 'Kosovo talks start in "polite" tone, no rapprochement of stands', *V.I.P. Daily News Report*, no. 3277 (21 Feb. 2006), p. 1.

[25] It is partly for this reason that the Albanian population of Kosovo boycotted the census in 1991. The next census is scheduled for 2006.

[26] European Centre for Minority Issues, 'Statistics', URL <http://www.ecmi.de/emap/download/KosovoStatisticsFinalOne.pdf>.

[27] International Commission on the Balkans, *The Balkans in Europe's Future* (Centre for Liberal Strategies: Sofia, 2005), URL <http://www.balkan-commission.org>, p. 14.

[28] It has been suggested that a centralized international power should be established in Kosovo temporarily similar to that which existed in BiH under Lord Ashdown, who represented the EU and the UN.

other hand, the kind of decentralization solutions proposed by Serbia would not help with this aspect either, and it is hard to see how protection of the Serbian minority by Belgrade could work. At present, the Serbian side maintains that 'autonomy for Serbs in Kosovo must be secured within the framework of Kosovo's political autonomy'.[29]

The riddle of rights for the Serbian minority might be simplified by one other factor: the role of reciprocity. There is not only a Serbian minority in Kosovo but also an Albanian minority in the south of Serbia, in the area of Presevo. If Kosovo gains independence and, with it, state responsibility to enforce minority rights, any possible mistreatment of the ethnic Serbs in Kosovo could have obvious repercussions for the treatment of the Albanian minority in Serbia. This creates an element of interdependence, but may also add to the volatility of the situation.

The allure of a 'return to Europe'

The process of the status talks, and any subsequent period of phasing-in,[30] will provide an opportunity for external powers to observe how the authorities of Kosovo can 'grow into' their future responsibilities. The future rulers in Kosovo will need to reassure the international community that any given final status does not result in a weak entity that risks spreading instability beyond its borders and fostering transnational threats. At the same time, it should be noted that the talks are not traditional bilateral negotiations. The UN's appointed mediator, Martti Ahtisaari, the former President of Finland, will be working for compromise, while many powerful external actors are in a position to offer practical inputs. Such 'sticks and carrots' may include contributions to prosperity and welfare in both Serbia and Kosovo, but the largest single inducement is widely perceived as being the opening of the way for both entities to join the EU and NATO. It is necessary to note, however, that the failure to bring the EU Constitutional Treaty into force and the EU budget for 2007–2013 make any EU promise of future membership less credible than before.[31] In practical terms, the road to membership would lie first through joining NATO's Partnership for Peace (PFP), and the prospect of some status with the EU that would go beyond the current option of a Stabilization and Association Agreement.[32] If members of the Contact Group would like to achieve reconciliation between Serbia and Kosovo, they (and some of the international organizations where they play a key role) will have to make some sacrifices.[33]

[29] 'Serbian Parliament endorses resolution for Kosovo talks', *V.I.P. Daily News Report*, no. 3214 (22 Nov. 2005), p. 1.

[30] As in similar cases, there have been 'trial balloons' to test the reactions of the parties. Slovenian President Janez Drnovsek put forward a plan whereby the international community would hand over all prerogatives to the authorities in Kosovo over an 18-month period, during which general and presidential elections would be held. Kosovo would gain international recognition in 5 years, if the international community determined that fundamental democratic standards were being respected. Serbian and Montenegrin Ministry of Foreign Affairs, Daily survey, Belgrade, URL <http://www.mfa.gov.yu/Bilteni/Engleski/b211005_e.html>. The Serbian authorities reacted strongly to this 'implied independence plan' for Kosovo and cancelled the visit of the Slovenian president to Belgrade.

[31] See Peel, Q., 'Address the constitution or abandon expansion', *Financial Times*, 19 Jan. 2006, p. 13. There are those who continue to argue, like Italy's Foreign Minister, that 'the carrot is EU membership'. See Fini, G., 'Kosovo and the Balkans: the carrot is EU membership', *International Herald Tribune*, 17 Jan. 2006, p. 7.

[32] Bildt, C., 'Europe's third chance to get it right in the Balkans may be its last', *Europe's World*, autumn 2005, URL <http://www.europesworld.org/>, p. 112.

[33] Further concretizing any entity's accession prospects is not a painless option for EU governments at a time when their publics are showing clear 'enlargement fatigue'. See section IV of chapter 1.

In this situation the international institutions have two types of means at their disposal: socialization and conditionality. Whereas the EU has relied more on the former vis-à-vis both Kosovo and Serbia and Montenegro, NATO has taken a more 'conditional' approach in its institutional relations with Serbia and Montenegro, insisting primarily on full cooperation with the International Criminal Tribunal for the former Yugoslavia (ICTY). It remains to be seen whether the NATO policy can be sustained without endangering the hopes of Serbian accommodation to an adequate final status for Kosovo. The EU has demonstrated significant commitment to the Western Balkans, both in declared policy and in the carrying out of projects. The EU–Western Balkans Summit of June 2003 went furthest, declaring that the 'future of the Balkans is within the European Union'.[34] It is widely advocated that the EU upgrade its commitment both in terms of political attention, for example by convening a Western Balkans summit in 2006,[35] and by the allocation of resources to back up its goals for the region. It remains to be seen, however, whether the EU is in a position to demonstrate sufficient determination for such purposes amid the lingering consequences of its failure to bring the EU Constitution into force.

Conversely, if policies short of guaranteed membership are to be adopted towards the Western Balkans, the EU will need to be extremely innovative in order to have any chance of securing long-term influence at an affordable 'price'. While the EU is contemplating various options, the official policy on membership remains unchanged and is underlined by the opening of EU accession negotiations with Croatia, the advancement of FYROM to candidate status and the opening of talks on Stabilization and Association Agreements with BiH and Serbia and Montenegro. It is particularly important that borders become more open and provide more for inclusion than exclusion. In principle—for Kosovo and the Western Balkans generally—divisions might gradually be eased if national separation could be reduced for purposes of human contacts, education and the movement of labour. Without such changes at the grass roots, increased external commitment to the development of Kosovo may fail to bring the switch in attitudes of the population and the political establishment that is needed to break out of the current situation. The need for such deep-reaching transformation, added to the concerns already mentioned that a hastily emancipated Kosovo could become a 'Colombia in Europe . . . an El Dorado for organised crime',[36] reinforces the logic of planning for a carefully managed transition phase before full statehood is attained. During this period Kosovo would have to be helped to develop structures to carry out basic state functions, including public safety, justice and social services. Some of the necessary steps have been under way for some time, but an agreement on final status would add a perhaps decisive impetus and clear end goal. Although it would be the easy way out to conclude that it is better to focus on 'future status' rather than on 'final status' when any further step is considered, the latter has to be borne in mind. The evolution of the issue is being followed closely not only by the direct stakeholders, but also by countries that have similar problems related to conflicts where the emergence of statehood may provide a solution. To quote the

---

[34] 'EU–Western Balkans Summit Declaration', 10229/03 (Presse 163), Thessaloniki, 21 June 2003, URL <www.mfa.gr/english/foreign_policy/eu/EU-WBalkans_en.pdf>, p. 2.

[35] International Commission on the Balkans (note 27), p. 36.

[35] According to the Commission the summit meeting should present a 'Balkan audit' in order to get a clear idea about the commitment of the EU to the Western Balkans.

[36] International Crisis Group, 'Kosovo: toward final status', Europe report no. 161, 24 Jan. 2005, URL <http://www.crisisgroup.org>, p. 8.

Foreign Minister of Azerbaijan in December 2005: 'Next year is expected to be a decisive one in the process of the settlement of the Kosovo conflict. It is a firm and unequivocal position of the Republic of Azerbaijan that this process should be carried out in full accordance with the UN Security Council resolution 1244 and on the basis of the Helsinki Final Act, and regardless [of] its outcome it must not establish any precedent whatsoever'.[37]

Montenegro

Montenegro is the last republic of the former Yugoslavia whose statehood remains formally, if loosely, associated with Serbia. The relationship is based on shaky foundations, however. According to the Constitutional Charter of the State Union of Serbia and Montenegro negotiated with EU assistance in 2003: 'Upon the expiry of a 3-year period, member states shall have the right to initiate the proceedings for the change in its state status or for breaking away from the state union of Serbia and Montenegro . . . The decision on breaking away from the state union . . . shall be taken following a referendum'. Each republic has the right to such a referendum.[38] According to the Constitutional Charter the two constituent entities of the state union are equal in other respects, too, although some of the related provisions have been systematically violated.[39]

Unlike the issue of the future status of Kosovo, the issue of Montenegro was not prominent until late 2005. During the Milosevic era Montenegro regularly received encouragement primarily from the USA to seek independence as a means to weaken the position of Belgrade and distract its leadership's attention from its other demands. Since the autumn 2000 revolution in Belgrade, however, the position of the world at large is far more ambiguous. Complications include the fact that ethnicity has been the foundation of statehood in the Western Balkans since the break-up of the former Yugoslavia, and it would be difficult to contend that there is a separate Montenegrin ethnic identity.[40] Second, Montenegro has been criticized for weakness in fighting trans-boundary criminality, and there is little reason to hope that it would deal better with this on its own. This may be a major reason for the EU's hesitation on the independence of Montenegro. Finally, there are doubts as to the economic viability of Montenegro, a country of 700 000 people.

Montenegro's referendum on independence will be held on 21 May 2006.[41] The biggest opposition party in Montenegro has opposed a referendum,[42] and the outcome is unpredictable. It is also not clear whether the de facto dissolution of the State Union of Serbia and Montenegro and thus de facto independence of the two constitu-

[37] Organization for Security and Co-operation in Europe (OSCE), 'Address by H. E. Dr Elmar Mammadyarov, Minister of Foreign Affairs of the Republic of Azerbaijan, at the 13th meeting of the OSCE Ministerial Council', OSCE document MC.DEL/18/05, 5 Dec. 2005, p. 2.

[38] The Consitutional Charter of the State Union of Serbia and Montenegro, adopted in Feb. 2003, Art. 60. It is available in English and Serbian at URL <http://www.mfa.gov.yu/Facts/const_scg.pdf>.

[39] It suffices to note that the 'candidates for the Minister of Foreign Affairs and the Minister of Defence [in Belgrade] shall be from different member states' according to the Constitutional Charter of the State Union of Serbia and Montenegro, Art. 35. This rule has not been put into practice.

[40] See International Crisis Group (note 9), pp. 12–14.

[41] 'Montenegro referendum to take place on May 21, local elections in fall', *V.I.P. Daily News Report*, no. 3283 (1 Mar. 2006), p. 1.

[42] 'EU Ministerial Council urges against unilateral actions in Montenegro', *V.I.P. Daily News Report*, no. 3235 (21 Dec. 2005), p. 1.

ent entities must entail their de jure independence from each other (it would certainly leave practical issues like a custom union and other economic links outstanding). Nevertheless, the Prime Minister of Montenegro has 'announced his withdrawal from politics if the project of independence is not backed by the majority of the citizens'.[43]

If the rule is observed that any referendum has to have a minimum of 50 per cent plus 1 of the votes cast (although some analysts advocate a weighted majority), the popular vote may well be inconclusive. The Montenegrin Government opposes this approach because opinion polls have indicated that it would be extremely difficult to achieve such a majority. If, despite expectations, the vote favours independence, it might still fail to obtain the endorsement by two-thirds of the parliament that is necessary according to some interpretations of the Montenegrin Constitution.[44]

Those international actors most concerned in the issue are giving mixed signals. Both EU member states and the USA emphasize that they would back 'any decision the people of Montenegro should reach in a democratic referendum'. It has also been emphasized, however, that 'both Montenegro and Serbia would fare better if they remained close'.[45] According to the British ambassador to Serbia and Montenegro, 'the general assessment of EU officials was that Serbia and Montenegro would continue drawing closer to EU membership faster and more successfully if they would remain together in the same union'.[46] Cooperation between the EU and Serbia and Montenegro is held back by the limited cooperation of Serbia with the ICTY, which Montenegro cannot influence. Montenegro thus may conclude that its advancement towards EU membership would be accelerated were it to seek independence.

The security implications of an eventual separation of Serbia and Montenegro are twofold. It may compound the perception of the Serbian population that their country has been punished unjustly. This may generate some adverse political reactions, particularly if no satisfactory compromise is found in the talks on the final status of Kosovo. A further concern is that the transnational risks especially of organized crime and corruption may not be managed adequately by an independent Montenegro, although current performance by the 'state union' is not inspiring either. Generally, criminal structures seem to have cooperated more effectively than states in the Western Balkans.

Bosnia and Herzegovina

In contrast to Kosovo and Montenegro, the statehood of Bosnia and Herzegovina was reaffirmed in the 1995 Dayton Agreement—but with provision for significant autonomy to its constituent entities. During the 10 years that have passed since the signing of the peace arrangement, some steps have been taken to strengthen the central state authorities. They have included symbolic measures, like the standardization of licence

---

[43] Serbian and Montenegrin Ministry of Foreign Affairs, 'Montenegro—referendum in spring of 2006, Vujanovic', Daily survey, Belgrade, 15 Apr. 2005, URL <http://www.mfa.gov.yu/Bilteni/Engleski/b250405_e.html#N16>.

[44] International Crisis Group (note 9), p. 13.

[45] Serbian and Montenegrin Ministry of Foreign Affairs (note 43) cites US Ambassador to Serbia and Montenegro, Michael Polt.

[46] See 'Gowan: partitioning of Kosovo would be a mistake', *V.I.P. Daily News Report*, no. 3245 (6 Jan. 2006), p. 2. It is open to question, however, what time frame for EU membership would motivate local politicians and electorates to act in accordance with external expectations.

plates, and measures of major import such as the unification of the intelligence services and the armed forces.[47]

On the other hand, it is widely recognized that the Dayton Agreement and the subsequent constitutional arrangements have 'cemented divisions' and made further progress difficult. The US foreign policy establishment, in particular, seems unified in thinking that Bosnia should be heading towards more state unity. This requires that the ethnically Serbian entity, the Republika Srpska, should recognize 'once and for all that it is part of a single country'.[48] 'Bosnia's leaders and citizens need to break down the last political and ethnic divisions that have persisted since the end of the war ... it is time for constitutional reform ... to create a single presidency from the three men who hold the office now, a strong Prime Minister and a more effective Parliament'.[49] The position of the USA is straightforward and understandable in the light of the potential broader implications for the Western Balkans. The EU has been less demanding and has expressed the view that it has no blueprint for constitutional reform and will satisfy itself with the agreement achieved by the parties.[50] When specifically asked about a revision of the borders of BiH in favour of Serbia, UN mediator Ahtisaari has expressed the view that: 'The answer to this is quite simple: the one who does not hold to the rules of the game should forget about his own objectives.'[51]

Various objectives have been mooted for a new phase of change. Among them is to improve the stability of Bosnia and Herzegovina in the interests of its population and to make it less dependent on external forces to provide that stability (the unusually strong powers wielded by Lord Ashdown while UN High Representative and the EU High Representative in BiH have been one focus for questioning here). The pace of consolidation of the central state structures has become linked with concerns that Serbia might consider seeking compensation at the expense of BiH (i.e., through change in the current status of the Republika Srpska) for its possible impending 'losses' in Kosovo and Montenegro. Such worries, even if not always prominent, are kept alive by the perception that 'the Serb republic remains a Serb citadel and joint, central institutions do not function'.[52] Those who are working to prevent any further slide towards partition are also concerned that human rights, including minority rights, should be respected. While these last issues—as well as the potential role of leverage linked with the prospects of EU and NATO accession—recall what has been said about Kosovo, the key difference is that the statehood of BiH was 'settled' in the Dayton Agreement and certain elements of a unified statehood have existed there since the mid-1990s. This not only gives a practical basis to build on, but also means that the international community is more solidly biased towards the defence (or, more

[47] On this and other challenges of security governance in the Western Balkans states see Caparini, M., 'Security sector reform in the Western Balkans', *SIPRI Yearbook 2004: Armaments, Disarmament and International Security* (Oxford University Press: Oxford, 2004), pp. 251–82.

[48] Richard Holbrooke is cited in Knowlton, B., 'Bosnians reach deal to modify charter: the leaders agree to press for stronger national government', *International Herald Tribune*, 23 Nov. 2005, p. 8.

[49] US Department of State, Burns, R. N., 'Bosnia ten years later: successes and challenges', Address at the United States Institute of Peace, Washington, DC, 21 Nov. 2005, URL <http://www.state.gov/p/us/rm/2005/57189.htm>.

[50] European Union @ United Nations, 'Speech by Commissioner Rehn—from peace-building to statebuilding', Geneva, 20 Oct. 2005, URL <http://europa-eu-un.org/articles/en/article_5172_en.htm>.

[51] Interview with Martti Ahtisaari about the future status of Kosovo, reported in Ertel, M. and Kraske, M., 'Es Wird keine Teilung geben' [There will be no division], *Der Spiegel*, 20 Feb. 2006, p. 114 (author's translation).

[52] Joseph, E. P., 'Back to the Balkans', *Foreign Affairs*, vol. 84, no. 1 (Jan./Feb. 2005), p. 121.

correctly, active consolidation) of the status quo. The difficult question, as already indicated, is what mix of direct international aid and 'localization' policies—and of faithfulness and flexibility regarding the terms of the Dayton Agreement—might offer the best hope of a stable and self-sustaining BiH for the future.

The Former Yugoslav Republic of Macedonia

The impact of the changing status of Kosovo on FYROM is infrequently mentioned nowadays, although the Albanian ethnic component in the Macedonian state provides a link. The assumption is that the 2001 Ohrid Framework Agreement[53] has resulted in adequate political reconciliation to allow the country's affairs to be managed without open talk of partition. This optimism is somewhat surprising given the findings of a recent opinion poll that 76 per cent of Macedonian respondents 'rather agreed' with the view that 'there are still military conflicts to come' in their country.[54] The disparity between public pronouncements and concerns expressed behind closed doors is apparent. Although some dissatisfaction is noticeable with respect to the implementation of the Ohrid Agreement,[55] it seems 'stability for democracy' works. When the spectre of an eventual internal division of Macedonia along ethnic lines is raised by local politicians, it is mentioned in a passing manner in the hope that the coexistence of three factors will help avoid it: (a) the reluctance of the population of Macedonia to use violence to change the status quo; (b) the declared success of the implementation of the Ohrid Agreement; and (c) the advancement of the integration of the country into the EU.[56]

It is interesting that the EU has qualified FYROM as a candidate country and at the same time has upgraded its commitment to contribute to the development of FYROM's state capacity in policing, including border police, public peace and order and accountability, the fight against corruption and organized crime. The EU police advisory team (EUPAT) was initially established for six months, starting its activity in mid-December 2005.[57]

III. Conclusions

The Western Balkans region is currently speeding up its movement towards lasting solutions of several pending problems of statehood and status. The interrelated nature of the various outstanding issues makes it logical to address them at about the same

---

[53] See Association for Democratic Initiatives, 'Framework Agreement', 13 Aug. 2001 URL <http://www.adi.org.mk/frameworkagreement.html>; and Caparini (note 47), pp. 270, 272, 281.

[54] Based on a comparative survey in the Western Balkans, published in Apr. 2005, the population of every other country and entity in the region assessed the likelihood of military conflict as much less. International Commission on the Balkans (note 27), p. 46.

[55] *Inter alia* the International Crisis Group reports on the severe shortcomings of police and judicial reform. International Crisis Group, 'Macedonia: wobbling toward Europe', Europe briefing no. 41, 12 Jan. 2006, URL <http://www.crisisgroup.org>.

[56] As the European Council concluded, 'the European Council decides to grant candidate country status to the former Yugoslav Republic of Macedonia'. Council of the European Union, 'Presidency Conclusions', Brussels European Council, 15–16 Dec. 2005, URL <http://ue.eu.int/ueDocs/cms_Data/docs/pressData/en/ec/87642.pdf>, point 24.

[57] Council of the European Union, 'Council establishes an EU police advisory team in the former Yugoslav Republic of Macedonia', 14912/05 (Presse 313), Brussels, 24 Nov. 2005, URL <http://ue.eu.int/ueDocs/cms_Data/docs/pressdata/en/misc/87118.pdf>.

time, although to solve them all in such a time span is a tall order. What is clear is that, without such efforts, there could be entrenchment of the stalemate that has so far failed to bring either consolidated statehood, or the prosperity so badly needed, to the territories concerned. Each entity affected by the forthcoming changes poses its own dilemmas, and no option can be seen as unambiguously positive and without risk. The dynamic of events may result in a critical realignment of forces in the region. The four challenges mentioned above—Kosovo's status, Montenegro's referendum, the parliamentary elections in Bosnia and Herzegovina, and the stability of FYROM—are all linked in some sense with Serbia's role and status. This is not least because, if BiH consolidates its statehood on its current territory and if Montenegro chooses independence and Kosovo also gains it, Serbia will become a considerably smaller and less central player in the Western Balkans than before. Serbian influence has shrunk significantly since the early 1990s, and the question now is whether it can accept this reality and learn to make its influence felt in a different fashion. In addition, if Albanian-populated areas, such as Kosovo and a part of FYROM, associate themselves with the state of Albania in the long run, the Western Balkans may acquire a bipolar structure where both Albania and Serbia will appear to carry the potential to compete for regional hegemony. The absence of EU membership prospects for the two states in the medium term may not be conducive to stability in the Western Balkans.

The members of the Contact Group and the main Euro-Atlantic institutions are well aware of the intricate interrelationship of the issues. The USA seems to be the external actor pushing hardest both for rearrangement of elements of the Western Balkans puzzle and for measures to contain and mitigate the possible adverse consequences. This is obvious in its recent policies on Montenegro and on Bosnia and Herzegovina. Paradoxically, however, both the strongest long-term levers available to move local actors—and the ultimate bill to be paid for bringing these nations into the European mainstream—belong to the EU rather than to the USA (or even to NATO).

Currently, Kosovo is driving events. Political reality offers a fairly clear idea of the final status it will acquire. Its likely progress towards statehood will demonstrate the continuation of the post-cold war process of state creation in the Balkans, based crucially on ethnic composition. The practical implications are more troubling. It is not clear how the transition towards statehood for Kosovo could be regulated and implemented, how the acquiescence of Serbia could be guaranteed and what the EU, NATO and their members are ready to offer to accommodate Serbia and the Kosovo entity in the process. While the immediate concern must be to prevent instability in the transition process, Europe's longer-term security will rest more on the success or lack of it in creating properly functioning states (and economies) in the region.

2. Major armed conflicts

CAROLINE HOLMQVIST*

I. Introduction: changes in conflicts

Analysis of armed conflict has been a standing feature of the SIPRI Yearbook since the publication of the first edition, in 1969. Even a cursory glance at the conflicts of the past four decades reveals significant changes in both the dynamics and conceptualization of conflicts. Notably, the geopolitical framework has evolved, and attempts have been made to adjust international laws and norms in the light of the increasing prominence of non-state over state actors in conflict.[1]

While the bipolar structure of the international system during the cold war was sometimes characterized as a 'long peace' between the Soviet Union and the United States, it had a decidedly non-peaceful impact internationally, as the conflicts in Angola, Korea and Viet Nam testified.[2] The convergence of motives of ideology and power politics resonated with a second main theme of conflicts during the 1960s: national self-determination.[3] Wars of liberation in Africa, Asia and Latin America frequently assumed the shape of proxy conflicts, with one or other of the superpowers seeking to expand and consolidate its sphere of influence. While the end of the cold war brought optimism about a new potential for peaceful resolution of conflict in the absence of the superpower stand-off, distinct new conflict themes have emerged.[4]

During the 1990s much attention was devoted to the rise of 'ethnic' conflicts (e.g., those in the former Soviet republics, the Balkans and Rwanda) as well as to conflicts featuring state weakness and competition for the control of natural resources.[5] Although the issue of statehood remained a central concern,

---

[1] For a comprehensive analysis of the changing dynamics of international security politics over the past 40 years see the Introduction in this volume.

[2] Gaddis, J. L., *The Long Peace: Inquiries into the History of the Cold War* (Oxford University Press: New York, N.Y., 1987).

[3] The passing of the United Nations General Assembly Declaration on the Granting of Independence to Colonial Countries and Peoples was a significant landmark in this respect. UN General Assembly Resolution 1541, 14 Dec. 1960. This and other General Assembly resolutions are available at URL <http://www.un.org/documents/resga.htm>.

[4] Ignatieff, M., *The Warriors Honour: Ethnic War and the Modern Conscience* (Metropolitan Books: New York, N.Y., 1997). The Human Security Report argues that the incidence of conflict has decreased over the past decade and a half. University of British Columbia, Human Security Centre, *The Human Security Report 2005: War and Peace in the 21st Century* (Oxford University Press: New York, N.Y., 2005), URL <http://www.humansecurityreport.info/>, pp. 68–70.

[5] See, e.g., Bowen, J. R., 'The myth of global ethnic conflict', *Journal of Democracy*, vol. 7, no. 4 (Oct. 1996); Brown, M. E., 'Causes and implications of ethnic conflict', eds M. Guibernau and J. Rex,

* SIPRI interns Sara Lindberg and Haruko Matsuoka assisted the author in the preparation of this chapter.

'ethnic' and resource wars appeared to shift the emphasis from national self-determination to the issue of 'good' or equitable governance.[6] However, the international transition from bi- to multi-polarity did not quite deliver on the initial post-cold war expectations of international cooperation in dealing with violent conflict. The broad international consensus that developed around the first Gulf War, in 1991, failed tragically to translate into collective action in the face of the impending genocide in Rwanda in 1994. By the time of the intervention in Kosovo in 1999, a deadlock in the United Nations (UN) Security Council led the North Atlantic Treaty Organization (NATO) to intervene without UN sanction.[7]

Significant change has also occurred with regard to international norms governing the use of force. Forty years ago it was difficult to hold non-state actors accountable under the international norms and laws of war—most importantly, international humanitarian law and human rights law. The addition in 1977 of Protocol II to the 1949 Geneva Conventions represents the most significant attempt to confront the inherent state bias in the provisions of international law, imposing on non-state armed actors the same obligations regarding conduct in war as had previously been defined for states—thus altering the legal personality and standing of non-state actors in international law.[8] It was only in the 1980s and 1990s that leading organizations advocating respect for human rights, such as Amnesty International and Human Rights Watch, altered their definitions of human rights abuses to include acts committed by non-state actors.[9] Although the broadening of the human rights framework is a considerable achievement, the international community's capacity to hold armed non-state actors accountable for breaches of international humanitarian law remains limited.[10]

The Ethnicity Reader (Polity Press: Cambridge, 1997), pp. 80–100; and Campbell, D., 'Apartheid cartography: identity, territory and co-existence in Bosnia', Corner House briefing no. 22, Jan. 2001, URL <http://www.thecornerhouse.org.uk/item.shtml?x=51981>. On 'resource wars' see Berdal, M. and Malone, D. (eds), *Economic Agendas in Civil Wars* (Lynne Rienner: Boulder, Colo., 2000); and Ballentine, K. and Sherman, J., *The Political Economy of Armed Conflict: Beyond Greed and Grievance* (Lynne Rienner: Boulder, Colo., 2003).

[6] Certain conflicts seemed to escape the notion of statehood entirely, however—notably recent conflicts featuring religious aims. On religiously motivated violence see appendix 2C.

[7] For the debate on military 'humanitarian' intervention see, e.g., Wheeler, N., *Saving Strangers: Humanitarian Intervention in International Society* (Oxford University Press: Oxford, 2000); and Chandler, D., *From Kosovo to Kabul: Human Rights and International Intervention* (Pluto Press: London, 2002).

[8] The Protocol Additional to the Geneva Conventions of 12 August 1949, and Relating to the Protection of Victims of Non-International Armed Conflicts (Protocol II) was opened for signature on 12 Dec. 1977 and entered into force on 7 Dec. 1978; for the text see URL <http://www.unhchr.ch/html/menu3/b/94.htm> and for the parties to Protocol II see annex A in this volume.

[9] Previously, it was argued that, because states are responsible for upholding human rights on their territory, states are by definition the only abusers of human rights. For further discussion see, e.g., Menkhaus, K., 'Warlords and landlords: non-state actors and humanitarian norms in Somalia', Paper presented at the conference on Curbing Human Rights Violations by Non-State Armed Groups, Armed Groups Project, Vancouver, Canada, 13–15 Nov. 2003, URL <http://www.armedgroups.org/>.

[10] Sriram, C. L., 'Achieving accountability for armed non-state groups: the use of domestic mechanisms for international crimes', Paper presented at the conference on Curbing Human Rights Violations by Non-State Armed Groups (note 9); and Holmqvist, C., 'Engaging armed non-state actors in post-

Discussions in the late 1990s on the emergence of 'new wars' coincided with the analysis of 'new security threats'—threats or risks that were non- or supranational and non-military in nature.[11] In effect, the global discourse on security shifted from geopolitics in the traditional sense to normative (with the spread of the human rights culture and human security agenda) and functional concerns. However, the 'new' functional threats of international terrorism, organized crime, state failure, trafficking in humans and illegal substances, environmental hazards, disease and uncontrolled migration could not be neatly separated from conflicts; and both debates brought to the forefront the role of non-state actors, frequently with transnational links.[12] *The Human Security Report 2005* reinvigorated discussion about the relevance of the traditional focus on state actors in conflicts: in addition to measuring battle-related deaths in conflicts between the government of a state and one or more opposition groups, it recorded the categories of 'non-state conflict' and 'one-sided violence', highlighting the increasing significance of the activity of non-state actors.[13] The fact that non-state conflicts—conflicts involving the use of armed force between two organized groups, neither of which is the government of a state—were found to outnumber those involving state parties in 2002 and 2003 (the only years for which data are available) indicates that the international community needs to find more effective ways of addressing non-state actors.[14]

Section II of this chapter discusses two conflicts that have outlived (or reflected) global changes over the past few decades: the conflict in Israel (Palestine) and that in India (Kashmir). Section III focuses on non-state actors in conflict and elaborates on three themes that have been associated with their increased role in contemporary conflicts.[15] It includes synopses of selected conflicts that were prominent in 2005 and which illustrate some of the key

conflict settings', eds A. Bryden and H. Hänggi, Geneva Centre for the Democratic Control of Armed Forces (DCAF), *Security Governance in Post-Conflict Peacebuilding* (Lit Verlag: Hamburg, 2005).

[11] See, e.g., Kaldor, M., *New and Old Wars: Organised Violence in a Global Era* (Polity Press: Cambridge, 1999); and Duffield, M., *Global Governance and the New Wars: The Merging of Development and Security* (Zed Books: London, 2001).

[12] See, e.g., 'A secure Europe in a better world: European Security Strategy', European Council, Brussels, 12 Dec. 2003, URL <http://www.iss-eu.org/solana/solanae.pdf>; United Nations, 'A more secure world: our shared responsibility', Report of the High-level Panel on Threats, Challenges and Change, UN documents, A/59/565, 4 Dec. 2004, and A/59/565/Corr.1, 6 Dec. 2004, URL <http://www.un.org/ga/59/documentation/list5.html>; and United Nations, 'In larger freedom: towards development, security and human rights for all', Report of the Secretary-General, UN documents A/59/2005, 21 Mar. 2005, A/59/2005/Add.1, 23 May 2005, A/59/2005/Add.2, 23 May 2005, and A/59/2005/Add.3, 26 May 2005, URL <http://www.un.org/largerfreedom/>.

[13] University of British Columbia, Human Security Centre (note 4), parts I, II and V.

[14] University of British Columbia, Human Security Centre (note 4), p. 63.

[15] The conflict chapters in *SIPRI Yearbooks 2004* and *2005* focused on intra-state conflict—examining the often protracted nature of such conflicts, their often internationalized nature and specific features of contemporary intra-state conflict. Dwan, R. and Gustavsson, M., 'Major armed conflicts', *SIPRI Yearbook 2004: Armaments, Disarmament and International Security* (Oxford University Press: Oxford, 2004), pp. 97–113; and Dwan, R. and Holmqvist, C., 'Major armed conflicts', *SIPRI Yearbook 2005: Armaments, Disarmament and International Security* (Oxford University Press: Oxford, 2005), pp. 83–110.

dimensions of the involvement of non-state actors in conflict today.[16] Section IV looks exclusively at Iraq, which perhaps most clearly reflects the complexity of conflicts involving high levels of violence by non-state actors. Section V concludes with lessons for conflict management. Appendix 2A presents the findings of the Uppsala Conflict Data Program (UCDP), and appendix 2B provides definitions, sources and methods for the UCDP data. Appendix 2C outlines the current discussion of Islamist violence and terrorist incidents.

II. Enduring conflicts

Important features of conflict have remained constant over the past four decades despite far-reaching changes in the nature of the actors involved and the normative frameworks evoked. Numerous conflicts take place in the same location today as in the 1960s: for example, the Democratic Republic of the Congo (DRC), India (Kashmir), Israel (Palestine) and Colombia. The flare-up of loyalist violence in Northern Ireland in September 2005 and the unresolved issue of Basque separatism in Spain are other reminders of the persistence of low-intensity conflict.[17] The conflicts in India (Kashmir) and Israel (Palestine) in particular demonstrate how shifting perceptions of conflict—from decolonization and superpower dominance to the current preoccupation with international terrorism—have influenced international attitudes and engagement, or the lack thereof, in certain conflicts. Despite the continuity in the insurgent groups' ultimate objectives in both conflicts (control over disputed territory and sovereign statehood), both cases also illustrate a changing trajectory of conflict owing to the particularities of contemporary non-state actor activity.

Israel–Palestinians

The conflict between the Israeli Government, the Palestinian Authority (PA) and various Palestinian groups stands out as one of the world's most intractable conflicts. Originating in the war of 1948–49, the current phase of the conflict began in September 2000 with the collapse of the Oslo Peace Process and the beginning of the second intifada.[18] The election of Mahmoud Abbas (also known as Abu Mazen), a moderate who is viewed positively by the United States, as President of the PA on 9 January 2005 raised hopes for a reinvigoration of the peace process.[19] The first top-level meeting in four years between Israeli and Palestinian leaders took place at Sharm el-Sheikh, Egypt,

---

[16] It should be noted that this is a selection: the themes discussed here overlap and the same conflict may illustrate several different themes. Similarly, more than 1 conflict may suitably illustrate the same theme.

[17] 'Loyalist violence erupts in city', BBC News Online, 16 Sep. 2005, URL <http://news.bbc.co.uk/1/4249760.stm>.

[18] The Oslo Peace Accords were signed in Washington, DC, on 13 Sep. 1993 by Yasser Arafat for the Palestinian Liberation Organization and Shimon Peres for the Government of Israel.

[19] 'Palestine's election: from the circus ring to the tightrope', The Economist, 8 Jan. 2005, pp. 39–40.

on 8 February and, although both leaders stopped short of using the term 'ceasefire', coordinated declarations from the two leaders offered prospects of a temporary truce.[20]

The challenges faced by President Abbas in reining in militant elements of the Palestinian uprising were underscored by the 25 February suicide bombing outside a Tel Aviv nightclub. Officials of the Islamic Jihad organization in the West Bank and Damascus, Syria, later claimed responsibility for the bombings.[21] The PA made several arrests in the aftermath of the bombings.[22] Another suicide bomb attack in the coastal town of Netanya, on 12 July, also claimed by Islamic Jihad, killed three people and caused the Israeli army to again seal off the West Bank and the Gaza Strip, following four months of relative calm.[23] Repeated instances of Israeli use of force against Palestinian civilians continued to stir unrest in the occupied territories.[24]

Great hope was pinned on the high-level meeting of representatives of the 'Quartet' (Russia, the USA, the European Union and the United Nations), President Abbas, and a number of other states and organizations that was organized by the British Prime Minister, Tony Blair, in London on 1 March. Although the participants made a commitment to support Palestinian plans for capacity building in the areas of governance, security and economic development, the meeting failed to have a tangible impact on the peace process because Israel did not attend it. The USA later pledged $50 million in direct aid to the PA during 2005.[25]

Under the disengagement plan of the Israeli Prime Minister, Ariel Sharon, withdrawal from the occupied territories in the Gaza Strip began in July amid

---

[20] Erlander, S., 'Urging new path, Sharon and Abbas declare truce', *New York Times*, 9 Feb. 2005, p. 1.

[21] 'Militants claim Tel Aviv bombing', BBC News Online, 26 Feb. 2005, URL <http://news.bbc. co.uk/1/4301249.stm>. The al-Aqsa Martyrs' Brigades, a splintered multitude of militias, are responsible for nearly as many attacks as Hamas. According to Israeli intelligence, some four-fifths of al-Aqsa attacks are now sponsored by Hizbullah. See 'Palestine's election: from the circus ring to the tightrope', *The Economist*, 8 Jan. 2005, pp. 39–40.

[22] Rapaport, A., 'Palestinians carry our real arrests', *Tel Aviv Ma'ariv*, 3 Mar. 2005, Translation from Hebrew, World News Connection, National Technical Information Service (NTIS), US Department of Commerce.

[23] Myre, G. and Erlanger, S., 'Israel seals West Bank and Gaza to suppress violence', *New York Times*, 14 July 2005; and 'Bomber strikes Israeli coast town', BBC News Online, 12 July 2005, URL <http://news.bbc.co.uk/2/4676257.stm>.

[24] Morris, H., 'Mideast violence flares up ahead of US summit', *Financial Times*, 10 Apr. 2005; Middle East News Agency (MENA), 'Egypt: minister condemns Israel's use of live ammunition against Palestinians', 5 May 2005, World News Connection, NTIS, US Department of Commerce; and 'Five Palestinians wounded by Israeli gunfire in Yattah, Al-Zahiriyah stormed', *Ramallah Voice of Palestine*, 8 May 2005, Translation from Arabic, World News Connection, NTIS, US Department of Commerce.

[25] Those attending the London meeting reached agreement on their support for several concrete efforts on the part of the PA regarding the issue of security, including the strengthening of the National Security Council and the appointment of a National Chief of Police. British Foreign and Commonwealth Office, 'Conclusions of the London meeting on supporting the Palestinian Authority', 1 Mar. 2005, URL <http://www.fco.gov.uk/>; and 'Bush pledges $50 million to Palestinian Authority', CNN News, 26 May 2005, URL <http:// www.cnn.com/2005/WORLD/meast/05/26/abbas.bush/index.html>.

widespread protest from hard-line Israeli settlers.[26] On 15 August 2005 the main crossing point was sealed off and the remaining settlers were forcibly evicted. Thousands of PA security forces were deployed to prevent militant attacks during the Israeli pull-out. In addition, some 10 000 Israeli troops were required to clear out two of the West Bank settlements, where withdrawal attracted fierce resistance from radical Zionists from across Israel and abroad.[27] Violence rose again in mid-October: responsibility for the killing of three Israelis outside Gush Etzion, a northern West Bank town, was claimed by the al-Aqsa Martyrs Brigades, and Israeli forces launched missile attacks on the Gaza Strip, killing eight Palestinians.[28] Attacks by Hezbollah on northern Israel and the Golan Heights led to repeated clashes between Israeli and Hezbollah fighters on the Lebanese border. Such events, together with air strikes in Lebanon at the end of November, indicated the continued regional, and indeed global, repercussions of the Israeli–Palestinian conflict.[29]

At the end of the year there were more positive signs of the Palestinian prospects for statehood. Great symbolic value was attached to the formal establishment of Palestinian control of the Gaza Strip's border crossing with Egypt at Rafah on 25 November: Israel has controlled the perimeter of Gaza since the 1967 Six-Day War, and crossing the border into or out of Gaza has been notoriously difficult.[30] Nevertheless, prospects for a comprehensive settlement of the conflict (envisaged to be completed by 2005 under the 2003 'roadmap to peace'[31]) still seemed remote at the end of the year. President Abbas maintained the same minimum conditions for peace as his predecessor, Yasser Arafat: Israeli withdrawal from all of the West Bank and the Gaza Strip; designation of East Jerusalem as the capital of a Palestinian state; and a negotiated right of return for Palestinian refugees.[32] In December, the success of Hamas in municipal elections led to Israeli apprehension regarding the

---

[26] 'Israeli Cabinet approves disengagement plan', BBC News Online, 20 Feb. 2005, URL <http://news.bbc.co.uk/1/4281039.stm>.

[27] Devi, S., 'Israel begins process of Gaza withdrawal', Financial Times, 14 Aug. 2005; and Plushnick, R., 'Israeli troops and extremists face off in West Bank', New York Times, 23 Aug. 2005.

[28] 'Three Israelis killed in W Bank', BBC News Online, 16 Oct. 2005, URL <http://news.bbc.co.uk/1/4347518.stm>; and 'Eight killed in Gaza air strike', BBC News Online, 28 Oct. 2005, URL <http://news.bbc.co.uk/1/4383556.stm>.

[29] Fattah, H. M., 'Israeli troops and Hebollah clash again near the border', New York Times, 23 Nov. 2005.

[30] Weisman, S. R., 'For Rice, a risky dive into the Mideast storm', New York Times, 16 Nov. 2005; and Myre, G., 'Palestinians taking control over a Gaza border crossing', New York Times, 26 Nov. 2005. On the EU monitoring mission sent to Rafah at the end of the year see appendix 3A in this volume.

[31] For details of the Quartet-brokered 'roadmap' see United Nations, Annex to Letter dated 7 May from the Secretary-General addressed to the President of the Security Council, 'A performance-based roadmap to a permanent two-state solution to the Israeli–Palestinian conflict', UN document S/2003/529, 7 May 2003.

[32] Asser, M., 'Analysis: chinks of light in Mid-East', BBC News Online, 14 Jan. 2005, URL <http://news.bbc.co.uk/1/4161769.stm>. The second summit meeting of President Abbas and Prime Minister Sharon, on 21 June, failed to make substantive progress. 'There you don't go again', The Economist, 25 June 2005, p. 47.

Palestinian parliamentary elections scheduled for January 2006.[33] Speculations about future political realignment also on the Israeli side started when Sharon left the Likud Party and then had serious health problems. Although classic issues of political leadership were central to the conflict at the close of 2005, the Israeli–Palestinian conflict demonstrated that protracted conflicts can also assume new characteristics and patterns, often related to the activity of non-state actors.

India–Pakistan

The Indian and Pakistani governments have vied for control over the territory of Kashmir since 1947. A Line of Control (LOC) divides Kashmir into two main parts administered by India and Pakistan, with a smaller area under Chinese control.[34] Subsequently, rivalry between the two nuclear weapon powers India and Pakistan has been complicated by the territorial insurgency in Kashmir, and the conflict is estimated to have cost around 45 000 lives.[35] The Composite Dialogue, initiated in early 2004, continued to offer prospects of tangible improvement in Indo-Pakistani relations in 2005, although tensions mounted temporarily in January with mutual accusations of violations of the LOC.[36] Several confidence-building measures were undertaken during the year; for instance, bus services were started between Pakistan- and India-controlled Kashmir.[37] Moreover, the two governments made a commitment to increase trade and facilitate transit across the frontier, and deals were struck on security cooperation.[38] The devastating earthquake that struck Kashmir on 8 October and the resulting humanitarian catastrophe—in which over 74 000 people were killed and 3 million made homeless in the Kashmir region—prompted both sides to make conciliatory gestures. However, it was not until a month after the earthquake that the LOC was opened to allow

[33] 'Hamas wins in West Bank elections', BBC News Online, 16 Dec. 2005, URL <http://news.bbc.co.uk/1/4534224.stm>.

[34] Since 1947 there have been 3 periods of armed conflict between the 2 states for control of Kashmir: 1947–49, 1965 and 1999. Most recently, the transfer of Pakistani militant groups to Kashmir in May 1999 precipitated the so-called 'Kargil war'.

[35] Reuters, 'Kashmir insurgency keeps rhythm with peace talks', 30 Aug. 2005, URL <http://www.jammu-kashmir.com/archives/archives2005/kashmir20050830c.html>.

[36] Kemp, D., 'Pakistan accuses India of violating ceasefire in Kashmir', Agence France-Presse (Hong Kong), 24 Jan. 2005, World News Connection, NTIS, US Department of Commerce. No battle-related deaths were recorded for the conflict between India and Pakistan in 2004. For a brief discussion of the peace process in 2004 see Dwan and Holmqvist (note 15), p. 84.

[37] Luce, E., 'Hope high for bus travel breakthrough in Kashmir', Financial Times, 15 Feb. 2005; and Luce, E., 'Signs of hope emerge as Islamabad starts to see dividends of peace with New Delhi', Financial Times, 23 Feb. 2005.

[38] Johnson, J., 'India and Pakistan agree steps to create "soft border"', Financial Times, 17 Apr. 2005; Kumar, H., 'India and Pakistan agree to ease risk of conflict', New York Times, 9 Aug. 2005; and 'S Asia rivals sign security deals', BBC News Online, 3 Oct. 2005, URL <http://news.bbc.co.uk/1/4302144.stm>.

transit for relief agencies.[39] India continued in 2005 to accuse Pakistan of supporting extremist groups in Kashmir, and allegations of Islamabad's support for infiltrations across the LOC were often followed by retaliations by Indian troops against members of Kashmiri militant groups.[40]

Developments in interstate relations provided only a partial picture of the developments in Kashmir in 2005. The emergence of new armed groups in the region and the purported links between Kashmiri extremist groups and international Islamist networks, accompanied by a shift in emphasis from secular nationalism to Islamist goals, was testimony to the fluidity of the insurgency.[41] Thus the Lashkar-e-Toiba group, the first in Kashmir to espouse jihadist aims in 1999, has officially ceased to exist but is believed to have broken up into several smaller groups with similar aims, one of which (the Inqilabi) claimed responsibility for the major bomb attacks in New Delhi on 29 October, which killed 59 and injured 210 people.[42] Local elections were held for the first time in the Indian state of Jammu and Kashmir in the beginning of the year but separatists' calls for a boycott of the elections and violence led to low voter turnout, and on 24 February militants stormed government buildings in Srinagar.[43] There was a rise in violence in the summer months.[44] Despite the announcement in the autumn of a ceasefire by the United Jihad Council, an umbrella body of Kashmiri separatists, this did not result in any lasting renunciation of insurgent violence.[45]

[39] Khan, A. A., 'Analysis: opening up Kashmir', BBC News Online, 19 Oct. 2005, URL <http://news.bbc.co.uk/1/ 4357006.stm>; 'Aftershocks and afterthoughts in Kashmir', *The Economist*, 22 Oct. 2005, p. 61; and Watson, P. and Glionna, J. M., 'Familiar gloom replaces hope for an open Kashmir border', *Los Angeles Times*, 8 Nov. 2005, p. 5.

[40] E.g., Agence France-Presse, 'Indian troops kill four rebel infiltrators along Kashmiri border', 7 Jan. 2005. For a detailed examination of the complex relationship between the Government of Pakistan and various Kashmiri groups see Khan, A. U., *The Terrorist Threat and the Policy Response in Pakistan*, SIPRI Policy Paper no. 11 (SIPRI: Stockholm, Sep. 2005), URL <http://www.sipri.org>.

[41] The pro-independence Jammu-Kashmir Liberation Front (JKLF), previously at the forefront of the insurgency, is perceived as less active, while more religiously motivated groups—such as the Save Kashmir Movement (SKM), Hizbul Mujahideen, Farzandan-e-Milat and al-Badr—have increasingly taken centre stage. 'Who are the Kashmiri insurgents?', BBC News Online, 6 Apr. 2005, URL <http://news.bbc.co.uk/1/4416771.stm>. See also Council on Foreign Relations, Questions & answers website, 'Kashmir militant extremists', URL <http://cfrterrorism.org/groups/harakat.html>.

[42] 'Delhi bomb probes make headway', BBC News Online 30 Oct. 2005, URL <http://news. bbc.co.uk/1/4390464.stm>; and 'Profile: Lashkar-e-Toiba', BBC News Online, 31 Oct. 2005, URL <http://news.bbc.co.uk/2/3181925.stm>.

[43] Agence France-Presse, '26 hurt in Muslim rebel grenade attack ahead of Indian Kashmir poll', 27 Jan. 2005, World News Connection, NTIS, US Department of Commerce; Wani, I., 'Voters in revolt-hit Kashmir defy threats to take part in polls', Agence France-Presse, 5 Feb. 2005, World News Connection, NTIS, US Department of Commerce; and Agence France-Presse, 'Indian troops shoot dead 4 Islamic rebels in Kashmir', 26 Feb. 2005, World News Connection, NTIS, US Department of Commerce.

[44] Sengupta, S., 'Warming fades for India and Pakistan', *International Herald Tribune*, 29 July 2005.

[45] 'Kashmir minister killed in attack', BBC News Online, 18 Oct. 2005, URL <http://news. bbc.co.uk/1/4351950.stm>.

III. Non-state actors in conflict

Non-state actors in conflict have received considerable attention in recent years, highlighting the challenges of even defining or reliably identifying, let alone dealing with, these actors. At the same time, it has become increasingly difficult to adequately define 'state actors', *inter alia* because of the extensive use of private companies to carry out functions traditionally associated with the state in the context of armed conflict.[46] In broad terms, however, 'armed non-state actors' can be said to include rebel opposition groups and other groups not under state control (militias, warlords, vigilantes, and so on) that use armed force for a variety of purposes, often 'shadowing' the equivalent functions of the state.[47] This definition does not view 'terrorist groups' as necessarily distinct from other armed non-state actors: armed groups have used terrorist tactics throughout history.[48] Three key themes that emerge from a focus on armed non-state actors in conflict are discussed below: (*a*) the frequent irregularity or fluidity of non-state actors and the challenges this poses for the management and resolution of conflicts; (*b*) the scope for state actors to deny the existence of 'conflict' (traditionally understood as physical confrontation between two parties with a stated incompatibility[49]) when faced with non-state opposition; and (*c*) the artificiality of distinct 'conflict', 'post-conflict' and 'peace' phases given the frequent presence and activity of armed non-state actors throughout.

The fluidity of non-state actors

Armed non-state groups vary considerably in their degree of organization and cohesiveness. They are liable to splinter into different factions, to re-form under new command or resurface as yet more loosely bound entities, and to be

[46] For a detailed account see Holmqvist, C., *Private Security Companies: The Case for Regulation*, SIPRI Policy Paper no. 9 (SIPRI: Stockholm, Jan. 2005), URL <http://www.sipri.org>.

[47] The definition used here draws on David Petrasak's definition: 'groups that are armed and use force to achieve their objectives and are not under state control'. See Petrasak, D., *Ends and Means: Human Rights Approaches to Armed Groups* (International Council on Human Rights Policy: Geneva, Sep. 2000). The International Institute for Strategic Studies (IISS) defines 'non-state actors' as 'an organized and armed opposition group with a recognized political goal, acting independently from state or government. . . . The definition covers groups variously described as guerrillas, militia forces, para-military or self-defence groups'. IISS, *The Military Balance 2005/2006* (Routledge: London, 2005), p. 421. There is also considerable contention over terminology used in the literature: 'irregular armed forces'—see Davis, D. E. and Pereira, A. W. (eds), *Irregular Armed Forces and Their Role in State Formation* (Cambridge University Press: Cambridge, 2003); 'armed groups'—the Armed Groups Project of Pablo Policzer and David Capie, URL <http://www.armedgroups.org>; and 'armed groups as non-state actors'—Bruederlein, C., *The Role of Non-State Actors in Building Human Security: The Case of Armed Groups in Intra-State Wars* (Human Security Network: Geneva, 2000), URL <http://www.humansecuritynetwork.org/docs/report_may2000_2-e.php>.

[48] For more detail see Policzer, P., 'Neither terrorists nor freedom fighters', Paper presented at the International Studies Association Conference, Honolulu, Hawaii, 3–5 Mar. 2005, URL <http://www.armedgroups.org/content/view/20/43/>; and appendix 2C.

[49] For the definitions and methodology used by the UCDP see appendix 2B.

backed up by international networks.[50] The presence of several irregular armed groups may lead to a fragmentation of violence, thereby drawing in civilians as both targets and perpetrators. The arming of civilians has occurred in various places: for example, in Colombia, in *soldados campesinos* (peasant soldiers) have been trained and armed by the central government. In Nigeria, the Bakassi Boys have periodically been sponsored by state authorities and have even been given official status as the Anambra State Vigilante Services, despite documented abuses of human rights.[51] Conflicts featuring irregular non-state actors are particularly prone to a blurring of the distinction between combatants and non-combatants.

Demographic patterns (both national and regional) provide part of the explanation for the fluidity in the composition of armed non-state actors. In particular, large populations of unemployed and marginalized youth provide recruitment pools for armed groups, as the West African cases of Côte d'Ivoire, Liberia and Sierra Leone illustrate.[52] Abducted children are forced to carry out much of the insurgency waged by the Lord's Resistance Army (LRA) in Uganda.[53] Similarly, disenfranchised refugee populations may be tempted to join armed groups, such as the refugees in Guinea's Région Forestière or refugees from Myanmar in northern Thailand.[54] In other cases, the fluidity of non-state actors may result from direct state policies: for instance, the USA has raised and funded local 'irregular brigades' in Iraq to stem the insurgency there.[55]

---

[50] 'Fluidity' as used here is in part derived from the concept of 'liquidity' used by sociologist Zygmunt Bauman to argue that social relationships in the post-modern world are more brittle and transient than in previous eras. Bauman, Z., *Liquid Modernity* (Polity Press: Cambridge, 2000). The concept of liquidity has been used in writings on international security; see, e.g., Coker, C., 'NATO's unbearable lightness of being', *RUSI Journal*, vol. 149, no. 3 (June 2004).

[51] Human Rights Watch (HRW)/Centre for Law Enforcement Education in Nigeria (CLEEN), 'The Bakassi Boys: the legitimization of murder and torture', *Human Rights Watch*, vol. 14, no. 5 (May 2002); and HRW, 'Rivers and blood: guns, oil and power in Nigeria's river states', HRW Briefing Paper, Feb. 2005. See also Ero, C., Vigilantes, civil defence forces and militia groups: the other side of the privatization of security in Africa', *Conflict Trends*, vol. 1 (2000), pp. 25–29.

[52] Research in 2005 showed significant re-recruitment of 'demobilized' ex-fighters across the sub-region of West Africa. Human Rights Watch, 'Youth, poverty and blood: the lethal legacy of Africa's regional warriors', *Human Rights Watch*, vol. 17, no. 5 (13 Apr. 2005). For a discussions of the relationship between youth, underemployment and conflict see Picciotto, R., Olonisakin, F. and Clarke, M., *Global Development and Human Security: Towards a Policy Agenda* (forthcoming 2006), pp. 152–53.

[53] It is estimated that the LRA has abducted a total of 25 000 children since 1986. Amnesty International (AI), 'Uganda: child "night commuters" fear abduction', Public statement, 22 Nov. 2005, AI Index: AFR 59/016/2005, URL <http://www.amnestyusa.org/child_soldiers/document.do?id=ENGAFR 590162005>.

[54] Integrated Regional Information Network (IRIN) Web special, 'Guinea: living on the edge', IRINnews.org, Jan. 2005, URL <http://www.irinnews.org/webspecials/guinea/default.asp>; and Milner, J. and Loescher, G., International Institute for Strategic Studies, *Protracted Refugee Situations: Domestic and International Security Implications*, Adelphi Paper no. 375 (Oxford University Press: Oxford, 2005), pp. 56–61.

[55] 'Middle East and North Africa: Iraq', IISS (note 47), pp. 173–74. For more detail on Iraq see section IV below.

Several conflicts in 2005 demonstrated how the irregularity of armed non-state actors may cause conflicts to assume the characteristics of an insurgency. Mounting tension and periodic violence perpetrated by loosely organized groups in southern Thailand constitute one such example: the insurgency, which began in early 2004, worsened considerably in mid-2005.[56] From the perspective of conflict management and resolution, groups with a fluid or irregular structure are particularly difficult to negotiate a peace with—in part because it is difficult to discern the dominant party and the leadership may be unclear (as in Somalia). Much of the attention devoted to 'lessons of counter-insurgency' in 2005 focused on the US strategy in Iraq (see section IV), but the problem of dealing with a fluid opposition was not unique to that setting.[57] Similar developments in Kashmir showed that dealing with irregular non-state actors complicated conflict resolution efforts. In 2005 the efforts to manage the conflict in Darfur, Sudan, were notably complicated by a lack of cohesiveness on the part of the non-state actors.

Sudan

The Comprehensive Peace Agreement (CPA), signed on 9 January 2005, formally ended Sudan's long-standing conflict in the south between the National Islamic Front (NIF) Government of Sudan and the Sudan People's Liberation Movement/Army (SPLM/A). It provided for a sharing of revenues from natural resources and partial autonomy for the south.[58] A new Government of National Unity was sworn in on 9 July, with SPLM/A leader John Garang as vice-president and the former rebels receiving 28 per cent of the positions in the national transitional administration.[59] The death of Garang on 31 July and the ensuing riots and violence in Khartoum and several southern towns, killing at least 130 people, raised serious concerns over the fate of the peace process.[60] Despite the quick identification of a successor to Garang—Salva Kiir Mayardit—progress on implementation of the CPA and democratic reform were lagging. Moreover, local populations in the south were still affected by

---

[56] International Crisis Group (ICG), 'Southern Thailand: insurgency, not jihad', Asia Report no. 98, 18 May 2005, URL <http://www.crisisgroup.org/home/index.cfm?id=3436&l=1>.

[57] See, e.g., IISS (note 47); and Ucko, D., 'US counterinsurgency in the information age', *Jane's Intelligence Review*, 1 Dec. 2005.

[58] Agence France-Presse (World Service) in English, 'Sudan, southern rebels sign peace accord ending Africa's longest conflict', 9 Jan. 2005; and Lacey, M., 'Pact ends one of Sudan's civil wars; but in Darfur region conflict continues', *International Herald Tribune*, 10 Jan. 2005.

[59] England, A., 'Ex-rebel leader Garang sworn in as Sudan's vice-president', *Financial Times*, 11 July 2005.

[60] In Khartoum 84 people were killed after thousands of southern Sudanese clashed with police; similar unrest was reported in Juba and other southern towns in government-controlled areas. England, A., 'Khartoum suffers third day of ethnic violence', *Financial Times*, 4 Aug. 2005; and Integrated Regional Information Network for the Horn of Africa (IRIN-HOA), 'Leaders call for calm as death toll rises to 130', IRIN-HOA Weekly Round-up 288, 30 July–5 Aug. 2005.

violence during the year, often at the hands of the South Sudan Defence Forces (SSDF), a band of government-aligned militias.[61]

The conflict in Darfur between the Government of Sudan and several rebel groups has killed at least 200 000 people and displaced over 2 million since 2003. In 2005 it remained a grave threat both to the lives of local populations and to regional security, particularly because of criminal activities and clashes across the border with Chad.[62] Extreme violence against civilians continued and led to further displacements during the year.[63] Moreover, members of the African Union Mission in Sudan (AMIS) were repeatedly targeted, together with humanitarian agencies and aid workers.[64] While the Sudan Liberation Movement/Army (SLM/A) and the Justice and Equality Movement (JEM) remained the main groups opposing the government, several other factions, such as the National Movement for Reform and Development (NMRD), which emerged as a breakaway group from the JEM in 2004, continued to operate in the region. The proxy use of the Janjaweed militias by Khartoum in attacks on civilians in the region continued, in violation of the ceasefire agreements reached in April 2004.[65]

Efforts to instigate a comprehensive peace process, led by the African Union (AU), were compromised by the irregularity of the Darfurian groups and the corresponding failure to identify adequate and able representation from the rebel side.[66] On 5 July the government, the SLM/A and the JEM signed the Declaration of Principles for the Resolution of the Sudanese Conflict in Darfur, which stated the need for a negotiated settlement but failed to spell out all the details.[67] Statements by rebel leaders indicated their scepticism about the process, and the peace talks in Abuja, Nigeria, backed by the AU, did not resume until 15 September. The failure of one faction of the SLM/A to participate derailed the process from the outset and the talks were largely ineffective, lending to an increase in violence.[68] On 20 September, 500 SLM/A

[61] IRIN-HOA, 'Awaiting peace in the southern region', IRIN-HOA Weekly Round-up 233, 5–11 Mar. 2005; and ICG, 'The Khartoum–SPLM agreement: Sudan's uncertain peace', ICG Africa Report no. 96, 25 July 2005, URL <http://www.crisisgroup.org/home/index.cfm?action=login&ref_id=3582>, p. 3.

[62] United Nations, Monthly report of the Secretary-General on Darfur, UN document S/2005/719, 16 Nov. 2005, para. 7; and 'Chad accuses Sudan after clashes', BBC News Online, 19 Dec. 2005, URL <http://news.bbc.co.uk/1/4540192.stm>.

[63] For more detail see IRIN-HOA, 'Violence in Darfur still prevalent—MSF (Médecins Sans Frontières)', IRIN-HOA Weekly Round-up 288, 30 July–5 Aug. 2005; and United Nations (note 62).

[64] IRIN-HOA, 'Darfur situation deteriorating—UNHCR', IRIN-HOA Weekly Round-up 300, 22–28 Oct. 2005; and United Nations (note 62), para. 15.

[65] McDoom, O., 'Sudan accused of aiding in latest Darfur violence', Washington Post, 2 Oct. 2005.

[66] ICG, 'Unifying Darfur's rebels: a prerequisite for peace', Africa Briefing no. 32, Nairobi and Brussels, 6 Oct. 2005.

[67] Declaration of Principles for the Resolution of the Sudanese Conflict in Darfur, 5 July 2005, URL <http://www.sudantribune.com/IMG/pdf/DOP_Darfur.pdf>. See also IRIN-HOA, 'SLA rebels sceptical about peace in Darfur', IRIN-HOA Weekly Round-up 288, 30 July–5 Aug. 2005.

[68] IRIN-HOA, 'SLA rebels sceptical about peace in Darfur', IRIN-HOA Weekly Round-up 288, 30 July–5 Aug. 2005; Agence France-Presse (Paris), 'Sudan rebels say no to talks with government in Abuja', 14 Sep. 2005, World News Connection, NTIS, US Department of Commerce; and Wadhams, N.,

fighters launched attacks and seized the town of Sheiria in southern Darfur; military officials blamed the SLM/A faction that had been absent from the Abuja talks, and a pro-government militia simultaneously attacked rebel strongholds in the Marra mountains, killing at least 40 people.[69] Mutual accusations followed between the SLM/A delegation and government representatives that each side was purposely letting violence derail the talks, and the conflict in September reached an intensity not seen since January 2005.[70] Leadership struggles within the SLM/A delayed the talks until 29 November,[71] when the SLM/A was finally able to participate as a single party. However, no decisive agreement was reached.[72] Moreover, despite their agreement to resume the talks, and reaffirmation of the existing ceasefire agreement, the NMRD rebels did not attend the Abuja talks.[73] However, the NMRD continued to threaten local populations during the year and was involved in heavy clashes with government forces in the northern Jebel Moon region in April.[74] At the end of 2005, an intra-Darfur dialogue to consolidate the irregular armed groups appeared to be a precondition for negotiations and a relaunch of the peace process, along with an end to the 'scorched earth' policy of the government reflected in its use of the Janjaweed militia, which continued to inflict immense suffering on the civilian population.[75]

Disputing the existence of conflict

Among the conflicts involving non-state actors, some stand out as having little or no foreign involvement, often because governments portray such conflicts as an 'internal affair'. Violence by non-state actors is particularly likely to cause a blurring of the distinction between conflict and crime or between conflict and terrorism; defining or labelling an armed group as 'terrorist' or 'criminal' may prove to be an effective way of denying that group a role as a polit-

'Top U.N. envoy for Sudan says violence on the rise in Darfur', Associated Press (New York), 22 Sep. 2005.

[69] 'Sudan's rebels seize Darfur town', BBC News Online, 20 Sep. 2005, URL <http://news.bbc.co.uk/1/4263926.stm>.

[70] United Nations, Monthly report of the Secretary-General on Darfur, UN document S/2005/650, 14 Oct. 2005, para. 2.

[71] Abdul Wahid, the Chairman, and Mini Minavi, the Secretary-General, of the group were the main competitors for leadership of the SLM/A. 'Rebels dispute delay peace talks', Reuters, 18 Nov. 2005.

[72] 'Darfur rebels "united" for talks', BBC News Online, 29 Nov. 2005, URL <http://news.bbc.co.uk/1/4480748.stm>.

[73] A ceasefire agreement was signed between the Government and the NMRD in Chad, December 2004. Khan, A., 'Sudanese Darfur rebel group abandons ceasefire', *Epoch Times*, 14 Sep. 2005, URL <http://english.epochtimes.com/news/5-9-14/32318.html>.

[74] USAID, 'Darfur—Humanitarian emergency: Fact sheet no. 31, fiscal year (FY) 2005', 29 Apr. 2005; and United Nations, Monthly report of the Secretary-General on Darfur, UN document S/2005/240, 12 Apr. 2005.

[75] United Nations (note 62), para. 32. On the government's policy towards Darfur see de Waal, A., *Famine that Kills: Darfur, Sudan* (Oxford University Press: Oxford, 2005).

ical agent.[76] The rejection of classic or traditional conflict management measures (negotiation and mediation) in favour of 'law enforcement' mechanisms is a tendency in the conflicts dominated by non-state actors. In such cases, international aid for border control to stem the movement of armed groups between states, the provision of military aid and training to foreign state forces, or interstate police and intelligence cooperation may amount to international engagement to mitigate the effects of conflict, rather than efforts directed at the root causes of conflict. The revival of the 'responsibility to protect' agenda (stipulating the responsibility of the international community to intervene, even militarily, to protect the lives of civilians in the face of impeding genocide or other large-scale crisis), and its inclusion in both the 2004 report of the UN High-level Panel on Threats, Challenges and Change and the 2005 UN World Summit outcome document, should in principle signal greater international willingness to combat widespread and serious harm to civilian lives, although to what extent this will materialize remains to be seen.[77]

However, international engagement in conflicts in 2005 was still to a large extent contingent on securing cooperation from the government in question. A case in point is the conflict in Colombia, where President Álvaro Uribe Vélez continued to refer only to a domestic problem of 'narco-terrorism'; he also banned contact with the armed groups unless expressly sanctioned by the government and even explicitly forbade the use of the term 'conflict' by Colombian diplomats.[78] The conflict between the Russian Government and Chechen separatists makes the point even more explicit, illustrating the scope for governments to deny the existence of 'legitimate' conflict when faced by non-state opposition and the impact of that denial on the international community's capacity (or willingness) to engage in conflict management or resolution efforts.[79]

Russia (Chechnya)

The second conflict between the Russian Government and Chechen separatists, which began in 1999, continued to pose a growing threat to the wider North Caucasus region in 2005. Russian President Vladimir Putin has gone to

[76] See *Third World Quarterly, Special Issue: The Politics of Naming—Rebels, Terrorists, Criminals, Bandits and Subversives*, vol. 25, no. 1 (2005), especially Bhatia, M. V., 'Fighting words: naming terrorists, rebels and other violent actors', pp. 5–22.

[77] International Commission on Intervention and State Sovereignty (ICISS), *The Responsibility to Protect: Report of the International Commission on Intervention and State Sovereignty* (International Development Research Centre (IDRC): Ottawa, Dec. 2001), URL <http://www.iciss.ca/report-en.asp>. For more on the High-level Panel report (note 12) and the UN World Summit (the documents are available at URL <http://www.un.org/summit2005/>) see the Introduction and chapter 3 in this volume. See also United Nations, Report of the Secretary-General on the protection of civilians in armed conflict, UN document S/2005/740, 28 Nov. 2005.

[78] 'Highlights: Colombia military/guerrilla/paramilitary activities 10–13 Jun 05', Translation from Spanish, World News Connection, NTIS, US Department of Commerce.

[79] Myers, S. L., 'Russians seek to put restrictions on NGOs', *New York Times*, 24 Nov. 2005.

great lengths to portray the problems in the region—including instability and insurgent attacks in the republics of Dagestan, Ingushetia, Kabardino-Balkaria and North Ossetia—as an internal concern for the Russian Federation of 'organized crime' or 'terrorism' rather than politically motivated 'conflict'.[80] Meanwhile, the toll of the conflict on civilian populations in Chechnya has been significant: one human rights organization estimates that there had been 3000–5000 'enforced disappearances' in the country in the five-year period 2000–2004, and total casualties are estimated at 80 000–100 000 people, including civilians, Russian forces and Chechen fighters.[81] Abductions (often of young men and relatives of rebel fighters), frequently at the hands of Russian forces, were still carried out with impunity in 2005.[82]

The Russian Government's policy of 'Chechenization' (ironically also referred to as 'normalization') derives from its consistent denial of the continued existence of conflict.[83] The main tenet of this policy has been to shift the task of fighting the insurgents to local forces, mainly the 'Kadyrovtsy' forces under the command of Ramzan Kadyrov, Deputy Prime Minister of Chechnya (and son of the pro-Moscow President Akhmad Kadyrov, who was killed in rebel attacks in 2004). The Kadyrovtsy carried out numerous search ('clean-up') operations in 2005, also outside the Chechen republic, resulting in, for example, the capture of Chechen fighters in the Ingush town of Nazran in January.[84] The Russian authorities accepted the activities of the Kadyrovtsy; indeed, some argue that they have endorsed them by giving the Hero of Russia award to Ramzan Kadyrov in December 2004.[85] Perhaps the starkest, and most alarming, indication that Moscow eschewed any political solution to the conflict was the killing of rebel leader and former Chechen President Aslan Maskhadov on 8 March by Russian forces, despite the fact that Mashkadov had publicly distanced himself from the use of terrorist tactics and had declared a unilateral ceasefire in February.[86] In mid-April Russian Special

[80] For more detail see Russell, J., 'Terrorists, bandits, spooks and thieves: Russian demonisation of the Chechens before and since 9/11', *Third World Quarterly Special Issue* (note 76), pp. 101–17; and Galeotti, M., 'Conflict in Dagestan is reaching "critical level"', *Jane's Intelligence Review*, vol. 17, no. 9 (Sep. 2005), pp. 46–47.

[81] Memorial, 'Chechnya 2004: abductions and "disappearances" of people', 7 Feb. 2005, URL <http://www.memo.ru/hr/hotpoints/caucas1/msg/2005/02/m31404.htm> (in Russian); and Hill, F., Lieven, A. and de Waal, T., 'A spreading danger: time for a new policy toward Chechnya', Carnegie Endowment for Peace, Policy brief no. 35, Mar. 2005, p. 5. On the effects on civilian populations see HRW, 'Worse than a war: "disappearances" in Chechnya—a crime against humanity', HRW Briefing paper, Mar. 2005, URL <http://hrw.org/backgrounder/eca/chechnya0305/>.

[82] HRW (note 81), p. 16.

[83] 'Putin's heroes', *The Economist*, 3 Dec. 2005, pp. 27–28. Addressing journalists in Schleswig, Germany, in Dec. 2004, Putin stated: 'There has been no more war in Chechnya for three years. It's over'. 'Putin signals Chechnya initiative', BBC News Online, 21 Dec. 2004, URL <http://news.bbc.co.uk/1/4115279.stm>.

[84] Dudayev, U., 'Chechnya: new year, new brutality', IWPR Caucasus Reporting Service (Institute for War & Peace Reporting), no. 269 (12 Jan. 2005).

[85] Hill, F., 'Now let the Chechens select their leaders: Chechnya after Maskhadov', *International Herald Tribune*, 12 Mar. 2005; and Hill, Lieven and de Waal (note 81).

[86] 'Russian MPs hail Mashkadov death', BBC News Online, 9 Mar. 2005, URL <http://news.bbc.co.uk/1/4333067.stm>; Aliev, T., 'Chechnya shocked by Maskhadov killing', Institute for War & Peace

Forces suffered their greatest casualties since the Beslan siege of 2004, in a shoot-out with rebels in Grozny, Chechnya.[87]

Meanwhile, Russian (and Russian-backed) forces were unable to stem the spread of the insurgency across the region and in 2005 made several violent raids in Nalchik, Dagestan, in search of members of the Yarmuk rebel group. Rebels for the first time launched attacks on the town of Nalchik in southern Kabardino-Balkaria in October, resulting in at least 60 deaths.[88]

In its insistence on denying the existence of conflict, the Russian Government's policy appears to be counterproductive, resulting rather in the promotion of radicalism. First, Abdul-Khalim Saidulaev succeeded Maskhadov as leader of the Chechen rebels in March and soon emerged as more radical than his predecessor by announcing the creation of a 'Caucasian front' to counter Russian influence.[89] Shamil Basayev (who was previously linked to the Beslan hostage taking in 2004 and Moscow theatre siege in 2002, and was routinely condemned by Maskhadov) was made second in line in the Chechen rebel leadership in August.[90] Moreover, the persecution of Muslims in the Russian Federation (including the closing of mosques) has only served to fuel confessional elements of the conflict, thereby pushing Chechen separatists closer to international jihadist networks.[91] Third, the Russian policy on Chechnya has precluded effective engagement on the part of the international community with the conflict in Chechnya and the wider North Caucasus. In a typical instance, a meeting held at the European Parliament in March 2005 was unproductive because the rebels were not represented there.[92]

Attempts at Chechen reform and 'democracy' were halting; the parliamentary elections held on 27 November, awarding a 61 per cent majority to the Kremlin-backed United Russia Party, were widely criticized as fraudulent and seen as concentrating effective power in the hands of Ramzan Kadyrov.[93] The refusal to engage in dialogue with the Chechen rebels was not confined to

Reporting, 9 Mar. 2005, URL <http://iwpr.gn.apc.org/?s=f&o=239824&apc_state=henicrs2005>; and 'Chechnya: cease-fire holding, but little chance of negotiations seen', Radio Free Europe/Radio Liberty (RFE/RL), vol. 9, no. 24 (7 Feb. 2005).

[87] 'Russian forces accused of torture', BBC News Online, 18 Nov. 2005, URL <http://news.bbc.co. uk/1/4450186.stm>; and 'Rebels and Spetsnaz shoot it out in Grozny', Chechnya Weekly, vol. 11, no. 5 (20 Apr. 2005).

[88] Another Dagestani militant group, Sharia Jamaat, was found to be linked to Chechen separatists. Tumelty, P., 'Chechnya and the insurgency in Dagestan', Chechnya Weekly, vol. 6, no. 18 (11 May 2005); and Reuters, 'Chechen rebel Basayev said he directed town raid', 17 Oct. 2005.

[89] Dudayev, U., 'Chechen rebels declare new front', IWPR Caucasus Reporting Service no. 289 (2 June 2005), URL <http://iwpr.gn.apc.org/?s=f&o=243909&apc_state=henicrs200506>.

[90] Buckley, N. and Ostrovsky, A., 'Chechen rebels vow to fight on after leader's death', Financial Times, 8 Mar. 2005; and 'Profile: Chechen rebel's new boss', BBC News Online, 10 Mar. 2005, URL <http://news.bbc.co.uk/1/4336445.stm>.

[91] Wilhelmsen, J., 'Between a rock and a hard place: the Islamisation of the Chechen separatist movement', Europe–Asia Studies, vol. 57, no. 1 (Jan. 2005), pp. 35–59.

[92] Aliev, T., 'Chechnya: not all around the table', IWPR Caucasus Reporting Service, no. 297 (25 Mar. 2005), URL <http://www.iwpr.net/index.php?apc_state=hen&s=o&o=archive/cau/cau_ 200503_279_2_eng.txt>.

[93] 'Mixed press on Chechnya election', BBC News Online, 28 Nov. 2005, URL <http://news.bbc.co. uk/1/4477832.stm>.

Moscow but extended to the Chechen government under President Alu Alkhanov.[94] Ultimately, progress in Chechnya and the wider Caucasus will only come about if the devastating socio-economic situation in the region is effectively addressed and basic state structures are established.[95] Russia's neglect in this respect has allowed the insurgency to recruit from an ever-growing pool of discontented and marginalized people. To further complicate developments, there were indications in 2005 that Russia's reliance on the Kadyrovtsy posed a threat not only to local populations but also to the central government, as the private forces appeared increasingly unruly and at times clashed with Russian federal troops as well as Chechen police. The increased autonomy and licence of the Kadyrovtsy led some analysts to speculate about the development of 'another war' in the region.[96]

Violent peace?

The assumption that there are discrete 'conflict' and 'post-conflict' phases, which still informs most conflict prevention, management and peace-building efforts, often proves to be misleading. Instead, situations on the ground may more closely resemble a war–peace continuum, where armed non-state actors continue to commit acts of violence and exert pressure on local communities irrespective of a formal ending of conflict.[97] In various 'post-conflict' circumstances, violence continues unabated even after peace agreements are signed or demobilization, disarmament and reintegration processes have started, including the incorporation of groups into transitional government— sometimes owing to the formation of new warring parties (breakaway factions and changing allegiances) and in other cases to various groups being left outside the formal peace process (e.g., the Palipehutu-FNL in Burundi[98]). It is increasingly recognized that peace-building is simultaneously post-conflict reconstruction and conflict prevention: the failure to instigate successful peace-building means the re-eruption of conflict, and 'getting out of the "conflict cycle" at the right time' remains a key challenge.[99] Afghanistan and Haiti are both cases that continued to be affected by violence in 2005 despite extensive efforts by the international community. Similarly, the formation of

[94] Interfax (Grozny), 'Alkhanov will have no contact with wanted separatists', 1 Dec. 2005.

[95] Hill, F., 'Now let the Chechens select their leaders: Chechnya after Maskhadov', *International Herald Tribune*, 12 Mar. 2005.

[96] 'Putin's heroes' (note 83).

[97] Keen, D., 'War and peace: what's the difference?', *International Peacekeeping*, vol. 7, no. 4 (2000), pp. 1–22.

[98] The full name of the group is the Parti pour la libération du peuple Hutu–Forces nationales de libération, or the Party for the Liberation of the Hutu People–National Liberation Forces.

[99] Evans, G., 'Peacebuilding: six golden rules for policy makers', Keynote address to UN Office in Geneva (UNOG)/Geneva Centre for the Democratic Control of Armed Forces (DCAF) seminar on Security and Peacebuilding: The Role of the United Nations, Geneva, 27 Oct. 2005, URL <http:// www.crisisgroup.org/home/index.cfm?id=3771&l=1>. See also World Bank, *Breaking the Conflict Trap: Civil War and Development Policy* (Oxford University Press: New York, N.Y., 2003); and Berdal, M., 'Beyond greed and grievance—and not too soon', *Review of International Studies*, vol. 31 (2005), pp. 687–98.

local vigilante groups in Liberia illustrates a situation of continuing insecurity and violence despite a formal 'peace'.[100] In Côte d'Ivoire, both the rebels and the government appeared to accept a stalemate after the division of the country into a rebel-held north and a government-controlled south in 2002, as this allowed them to exercise control over their respective territories. Meanwhile, periodic violence continued to affect the country throughout 2005.[101]

Developments in the Horn of Africa highlighted the danger of latent inter-state conflict as tensions mounted anew between Eritrea and Ethiopia in November.[102] The role of neighbouring states was also called into question as the murder of the former Lebanese Prime Minister, Rafik Hariri, on 14 February sparked political turmoil—in this case Syria was accused of involvement and tensions mounted between the two states.[103]

High rates of communal violence and crime constitute another indicator that societies which are not recognized as being at war may nonetheless be living in conditions that are far from peaceful, as illustrated by the cases of Brazil and Nigeria, each in their own way.[104] The Democratic Republic of the Congo stands out as a case where numerous peace agreements have been signed but violence at the hands of non-state actors continues—also with a significant regional dimension. Moreover, developments in the DRC show how failure on the part of the international community to directly address armed non-state actors, other than through formal negotiating procedures, remains a significant challenge to effective conflict management and the protection of civilian populations.

The Democratic Republic of the Congo

The conflict between the DRC Government and various rebel groups formally ended with the signing of the Global and Inclusive Agreement on Transition in

---

[100] United Nations, Eighth progress report of the Secretary-General on the United Nations Mission in Liberia, UN document S/2005/560, 1 Sep. 2005.

[101] Washington, J. M., 'Analysis: Ivory Coast's missing peace', AMPMlist: Aspects of Conflict in the 3rd World, 8 Apr. 2005; 'A perilous peace deal'. *The Economist*, 16 Apr. 2005, p. 37; Integrated Regional Information Network for West Africa (IRIN-WA), 'Fresh ethnic violence in volatile West kills at least 41', IRIN-WA Weekly Round-up 279, 28 May–3 June 2005, 1 June 2005; and 'Ivorian rebels refuse to disarm', BBC News Online, 1 Aug. 2005, URL <http://news.bbc.co.uk/1/4733879.stm>.

[102] 'New war fears in Horn of Africa', BBC News Online, 3 Nov. 2005, URL <http://news.bbc.co.uk/1/4401782.stm>.

[103] Uscher, S., 'Arab media outrage at Hariri killing', BBC News Online, 14 Feb. 2005, URL <http://news.bbc.co.uk/1/4266053.stm>. The UN inquiry into Hariri's death had not reached any conclusion by the end of 2005. 'UN extends Hariri killing inquiry', BBC News Online, 16 Dec. 2005, URL <http://news.bbc.co.uk/1/4533614.stm>.

[104] HRW, *World Report 2005: Events of 2004* (HRW: New York, N.Y., Jan. 2005), URL <http://hrw.org/wr2k5/wr2005.pdf>, p. 144; and United Nations Human Settlement Programme, 'State of the world's cities 2004/5', URL <http://www.unhabitat.org/mediacentre/sowckit.asp>. The activities of criminal gangs such as Mara 18 (M18) and Mara Salvatrucha, primarily in El Salvador, Honduras and Guatemala, have been described as a 'war without fronts'. Arana, A., 'How the street gangs took Central America', *Foreign Affairs*, vol. 84, no. 3 (2005); and Rosas, M. C., 'Latin America and the Caribbean: security and defence in the post-cold war era', *SIPRI Yearbook 2005* (note 15), p. 255, especially note 23.

December 2002.[105] The agreement was subsequently endorsed by all parties in connection with the approval of a two-year transitional constitution and the establishment of a transitional power-sharing government under President Joseph Kabila in July 2003. Despite this, the DRC continued to be plagued by violence in 2005 and peace remained elusive. Although a draft constitution was adopted by the National Assembly on 13 May, the national elections that were scheduled for June 2005 were postponed until March 2006.[106] Mass protests greeted the postponement, and government forces responded by firing at demonstrators.[107]

The Congolese transitional government forces—the Forces armées de la République Démocratique du Congo (FARDC), or the Armed Forces of the Democratic Republic of the Congo—and the UN Organization Mission in the Democratic Republic of the Congo (MONUC) continued to face attacks from various armed groups, primarily in the country's eastern regions of Ituri, North and South Kivu, and the Katanga provinces.[108] Insecurity was exacerbated as several parties in the transitional authority relied on the support of militias for influence in lieu of a political base.[109] Fighting between the Rassemblement congolais pour la démocratie (RCD, or the Congolese Rally for Democracy)-Goma and government forces was intense in North Kivu in the beginning of the year, and in March fighting between government forces and the Mayi-Mayi militia forced over 5000 people to flee.[110] Facing opposition from at least five militias in Ituri province, MONUC forces suffered repeated attacks in January, and on 25 February responded by storming a stronghold of the rebel Front des nationalistes intégrationnistes (FNI, or the Nationalist Integrationist Front), killing 50–60 members of the militia in the worst fighting the UN has experienced in the DRC since the 1960s.[111]

The presence of Rwandan rebels, organized under the Forces démocratiques de libération du Rwanda (FDLR, or the Democratic Liberation Forces of Rwanda), in eastern DRC continued to constitute a security threat and raise concerns about a re-engagement of Rwanda in Congolese affairs and further

---

[105] The Global and Inclusive Agreement on Transition in the Democratic Republic of the Congo, signed on 16 Dec. 2002, URL <http://www.reliefweb.int/library/documents/2002/gov-cod-16dec-02.pdf>. The agreement was signed by the Government of the DRC, the Congolese Rally for Democracy (RCD), the Movement for the Liberation of the Congo (MLC), the political opposition, civil society, the Congolese Rally for Democracy/Liberation Movement (RDC/ML), the Congolese Rally for Democracy/National (RCD/N) and the Mayi-Mayi.

[106] Opposition leaders inferred that the decision to postpone the elections was a convenient stalling manoeuvre by the transitional authority. 'Peace is pricey', *Africa Confidential*, vol. 46, no. 3 (4 Feb. 2005), p. 3.

[107] United Nations, Eighteenth report of the Secretary-General on the United Nations Organization Mission in the Democratic Republic of the Congo, UN document S/2005/506, 2 Aug. 2005.

[108] On MONUC's mandate and size see chapter 3 in this volume.

[109] Traub, J., 'The Congo case', *New York Times*, 3 July 2005.

[110] Integrated Regional Information Network for Central and Eastern Africa (IRIN-CEA), 'DRC: EU suspends projects in North Kivu', IRIN-CEA Weekly Round-up 268, 26 Feb.–4 Mar. 2005, 1 Mar. 2005; and IRIN-CEA, 'DRC: thousands displaced after Mayi-Mayi clashes with Congolese troops', IRIN-CEA Weekly Round-up 273, 2–8 Apr. 2005, 7 Apr. 2005.

[111] 'The UN gets tougher', *The Economist*, 12 Mar. 2005, p. 44.

regional repercussions.[112] The Tripartite Agreement, signed between the DRC, Rwanda and Uganda on 21 April 2005, did not prevent violence:[113] 18 civilians were killed and 50 taken hostage after an attack by the 'Rastas', another armed group dominated by Rwandans, on 23 May, and FDLR attacks on Kigalama village, South Kivu, caused a further 5000 villagers to flee in late July.[114]

By the end of 2005 little substantial progress had been made on governance or effective post-conflict peace-building in eastern DRC. Apart from the direct physical security needs of civilian populations, the painstaking integration of rebel fighters into the FARDC exposed problems of corruption and impunity outside and within the state security apparatus.[115] The relationship of local populations with both international forces and the FARDC remained problematic and subject to abuse by all parties. The burning alive of 39 villagers by Rwandan militia in South Kivu on 9 July, purportedly as a punishment for local support of UN forces, was a gruesome example.[116] Despite progress made on demobilization of some rebel groups in eastern DRC, resulting in the official neutralization of the Forces armées du peuple Congolais (FAPC, or the People's Armed Forces of Congo) and the Union of Congolese Patriots under Floribert Kisembo (UPC-K) by August, significant problems remained with reintegration of former combatants.[117] The presence of a large number of unemployed former rebels and several remaining militia groups—the Union des patriotes congolais (Union of Congolese Patriots) under Thomas Lubanga (UPC-L), the FNI and the Forces de résistance patriotiques en Ituri (FRPI, or the Patriotic Resistance Forces in Ituri)— constituted a volatile mix in the eastern provinces. With the limited effect of the UN arms embargo on militia violence, the situation for large segments of the Congolese population in 2005 resembled war more than transition to a stable peace.

IV. Iraq

In *SIPRI Yearbook 2005* the chapter on major armed conflicts noted how the situation in Iraq resembled a reversal of the classic spillover from intra-state to interstate conflict, as the international intervention had sowed the seeds of a

---

[112] ICG, 'The Congo: solving the FDLR problem once and for all', Africa Briefing no. 25, Nairobi and Brussels, 12 May 2005.

[113] A UN report in May recorded over 1700 instances of abuse of civilians by the FDLR and other Rwandan militias in Walungu, South Kivu, alone in the preceding year. United Nations (note 107); and IRIN-CEA, 'DRC: Rwandan rebels abuse Congolese civilians—UN report', IRIN-CEA Weekly Round-up 279, 14–20 May 2005, 19 May 2005.

[114] IRIN-CEA, 'DRC: latest killings in South Kivu part of long-standing abuse', IRIN-CEA Weekly Round-up 280, 21–27 May 2005; and IRIN-CEA, 'DRC: Thousands flee latest attack in South Kivu', IRIN-CEA Weekly Round-up 289, 23–29 July 2005, 25 July 2005.

[115] ICG, 'A Congo action plan', Africa Briefing no. 34, Nairobi and Brussels, 19 Oct. 2005.

[116] 'Rwandan rebels burn 39 villagers alive in Congo', *New York Times*, 11 July 2005.

[117] The UPC was originally formed by Lubanga in 2001, but a faction led by Kisembo had split off. United Nations (note 107).

civil war; indeed, the country continued to move in that direction in 2005. From the restoration of sovereignty on 28 June 2004 and throughout 2005 the US-led Multinational Force (MNF) in Iraq participated in the conflict on the side of the Iraqi Government, against various insurgent groups. While significant milestones were passed with respect to the political development of the country, violence continued unabated. The conflict in 2005 demonstrated to the extreme the difficulties of analysing and responding to non-state violence. Armed groups were irregular or fluid in structure, high crime rates complicated the distinction between conflict and crime, and the use of terrorist tactics, as well as links to international terrorist networks, to a great extent shaped perceptions of the insurgency and unfolding civil war.[118] On 9 November 2005 the UN Security Council unanimously agreed to a one-year renewal (until 31 December 2006) of the UN mandate for the MNF under UN Security Council Resolution 1637, albeit with a stipulated revision of terms in June 2006 and earlier termination of MNF presence if expressly demanded by the Iraqi Government.[119]

Political developments

The year 2005 was one of major political restructuring for the country, jump-started by the elections of 30 January. The results of the election—in which the United Iraqi Alliance (UIA), a multi-party, Shia-dominated group, took a 48 per cent majority and the Democratic Patriotic Alliance of Kurdistan came second, with 25.7 per cent of the votes—were perceived in many quarters as embodying a process that disadvantaged the Sunni minority in the country.[120] Several Sunni parties, such as the Iraqi Islamic Party (IIP), boycotted the elections, in part out of a fear of violent reprisals.[121] The creation of the UIA was largely the initiative of Iranian-born Grand Ayatollah Sayyid Hussein Ali al-Sistani, the most respected Shiite religious leader in Iraq. With a high proportion of politically unaffiliated candidates, the UIA coalition looked fragile from the outset.[122] After protracted negotiations, the new 275-member

---

[118] For attempts to list insurgent groups and trends see 'Who are the insurgents in Iraq?', BBC News Online, 27 Sep. 2005, URL <http://news.bbc.co.uk/1/4268904.stm>; United States Institute of Peace (USIP), *Who Are the Insurgents? Sunni Arab Rebels in Iraq*, USIP Special Report no. 134 (Apr. 2005); and Cordesman, A. H., 'Iraq's evolving insurgency', Center for Strategic and International Studies (CSIS), Washington, DC, CSIS, Working draft, revised 9 Dec. 2005, URL <http://www.csis.org/media/csis/pubs/051209_iraqiinsurg.pdf>.

[119] UN Security Council Resolution 1637, 9 Nov. 2005.

[120] Kapiszewski, A., 'The Iraqi elections and their consequences: power-sharing, a key to the country's political future', ed W. Posch, Institute for Security Studies (ISS), *Looking into Iraq*, Chaillot Paper no. 79 (ISS: Paris, July 2005), pp. 13–25. Interim Prime Minister Iyad Allawi's secular list received 14.5% of the votes.

[121] Among others, the influential (Sunni) Muslim Scholars Board called for a boycott of the elections and various insurgent groups threatened voters. As a result, voter turnout in Sunni provinces ranged from c. 29% in Salaheddin to barely 2% in Anbar. 'Shia delight and Sunni gloom', *The Economist*, 19 Feb. 2005, pp. 38–39.

[122] Filkins, D., 'Elections over, Iraqi Shiites confront internal rivals', *New York Times*, 1 Feb. 2005.

Transitional National Assembly finally convened on 16 March. The Iraqi Transitional Government (ITG) was formed on 28 April, under the leadership of President Jalal Talabani (leader of the Patriotic Union of Kurdistan, PUK) and Prime Minister Ibrahim al-Jafari (from the Shia Islamist Dawaa Party).[123] The main task of the ITG was the drafting of a permanent constitution, to pave the way for new national elections in December 2005.

Iraq's ethnic and religious composition (broadly divided into approximately 20 per cent Sunni Arab, 60 per cent Shia Arab and 20 per cent Kurdish) featured as a baseline for discussion of the country's political future.[124] While the tripartite categorization of the Iraqi population into distinct communities is itself flawed (groups are rarely homogenous and in many areas coexist), the increasing politicization of ethnic or sectarian identity during the year created a dangerously self-perpetuating logic: 'it appears that tripartite Iraq has become a political reality and the very framework in which political discourse takes place in today's Iraq'.[125]

Initially, the constitution drafting process was hampered by a lack of representation from the constituencies that did not participate in the January elections. Overtures were made by both the USA and Al-Sistani's UIA to ensure the inclusion of Sunni representatives, but belatedly.[126] The final draft of the constitution, approved by the parliament on 28 August, was widely portrayed as a flawed document. Analysts warned that ambiguities contained in the text created the risk of postponing the settlement of several key issues.[127] Most notably, the constitution was inconclusive on the prospects for a federal structure for the country—a sticking point for many Sunni Arab politicians who feared that greater autonomy for the Kurdish north and the Shia south (potentially under Iranian influence) would divide the country and

---

[123] 'The haggling continues', *The Economist*, 12 Mar. 2005, p. 42; and Worth, R. E., 'Shiite leader named Iraqi premier to end two months of wrangling', *New York Times*, 8 Apr. 2005.

[124] 'Hopeful turning point, or descent into chaos?', *The Economist*, 29 Jan. 2005, pp. 21–23.

[125] Posch, W., 'A majority ignored: the Arabs in Iraq', ed. Posch (note 120), p. 26. The policies of the occupying powers have been blamed for aggravating this process by assigning posts in, e.g., the Iraqi Governing Council on the basis of ethnic identity, and the effective delegation of authority to the Kurds in the north. For more detail see Dodge, T., *Iraq's Future*, IISS Adelphi Paper no. 372 (Oxford University Press: Oxford, 2005). Kurdish aspirations for autonomy/independence are not new, of course. On this issue see, e.g., 'The temptation to break free', *The Economist*, 22 Jan. 2005, pp. 39–40; and Leezenberg, M., 'Iraqi Kurdistan: contours of a post-civil war society', *Third World Quarterly, Special Issue: Reconstructing Post-Saddam Iraq*, vol. 26, no. 4–5 (2005).

[126] Only 2 of the initial 55 members of the Constitution Drafting Committee were Sunni Arabs. By 5 July, 15 Sunni Arab representatives were added to the 55-member committee. United Nations, Report of the Secretary-General pursuant to paragraph 30 of Resolution 1546 (2004), UN document S/2005/585, 7 Sep. 2005, p. 2; and ICG, 'Unmaking Iraq: a constitutional process gone awry', Middle East Briefing no. 19, Amman and Brussels, 26 Sep. 2005, p. 2.

[127] 'Text of the draft Iraqi Constitution', Translated from Arabic by Associated Press, full text available at URL <http://news.bbc.co.uk/1/shared/bsp/hi/pdfs/24_08_05_constit.pdf>. See also ICG (note 126); and 'Politics in Iraq: the constitution and beyond', Transcript of Saban Center Policy Luncheon, Brookings Institution, Washington, DC, 29 Sep. 2005, URL <http://www.brookings.edu/fp/saban/events/20050929.htm>.

compromise their share of oil revenues in these regions.[128] Further Sunni Arab opposition derived from provisions hinting at the exclusion of former Baath Party officials from public office.

The politicized nature of the constitution-drafting process was established from the outset. The scramble to ensure Sunni Arab participation at the beginning, but their marginalization in the final stages, meant that the process further entrenched ethnic–sectarian identities and, as a result, played into the hands of elements of the insurgency.[129] The constitution was not only opposed by Sunnis, however, and an estimated 100 000 supporters of the Shia cleric Moqtada al-Sadr (instrumental in triggering the Shia uprising in 2004) rallied in protest on 14 October 2005.[130] As expected, the fate of the constitution in the referendum of 15 October was determined by reactions in Sunni-dominated provinces: the constitution was passed with only a razor-fine margin as Sunni Arab opponents failed to mobilize enough voters.[131] Ironically, the constitution-drafting process became 'a new stake in the political battle rather than an instrument to resolve it'.[132]

Political developments in Iraq throughout the year were accompanied, and marred, by unabated violence. A surge in attacks preceded the January elections to the national assembly, and on the day of the elections suicide bombings and mortar attacks killed at least 30, mainly in Baghdad.[133] In the worst single attack since the invasion in 2003, a suicide attack on 28 February in Hillah, a Shia town 100 km south of Baghdad, killed over 125 civilians, police and National Guard volunteers and wounded more than 140. The attack (claimed on an Islamist website by a group calling itself Jama'at al-Tawhid Wa al-Jihad, or the al-Qaeda Organization for Holy War in Iraq) was followed by mass protests in the city, where demonstrators expressed outrage at local police and security forces for failing to prevent the attack.[134]

Yet another surge in violence followed the announcement of the members of the Transitional Government: from 28 April to 6 May, 10 major suicide bombings and 35 major attacks killed over 270 people.[135] The constitution-drafting process was also directly affected by violence: the killing of three of

---

[128] 'Deadlock over Iraq constitution', BBC News Online, 15 Aug. 2005, URL <http://news.bbc.co.uk/1/4150160.stm>; and 'Iraq's Sunnis reject constitution', BBC News Online, 28 Aug. 2005, URL <http://news.bbc.co.uk/1/4192122.stm>.

[129] ICG (note 126), p. 5.

[130] On the Shia uprising and its consequences see Dwan and Holmqvist (note 15), pp. 113–16.

[131] The constitution was rejected in the provinces of Anbar and Salahuddin by the two-thirds margin required for a veto (but in Nineveh by only 55%). Anderson, J. W., 'Sunnis failed to defeat Iraq constitution', *Washington Post*, 26 Oct. 2005.

[132] ICG (note 126), p. 1; and Thier, A., 'Iraq's rush to failure', *New York Times,* 14 July 2005.

[133] 'Iraq votes as attacks hit Baghdad', BBC News Online, 30 Jan. 2005, URL <http://news.bbc.co.uk/1/4219569.stm>.

[134] United Nations, Report of the Secretary-General pursuant to paragraph 30 of Resolution 1546 (2004), UN document S/2005/141, 7 Mar. 2005, p. 3; and 'Iraqi town protests at bomb blast', BBC News Online, 1 Mar. 2005, URL <http://news.bbc.co.uk/1/4308529.stm>.

[135] United Nations, Report of the Secretary-General pursuant to paragraph 30 of Resolution 1546 (2004), UN document S/2005/373, 7 June 2005, p. 3.

the Sunni Arab representatives on the Constitutional Committee on 19 July led to a one-week boycott of the committee's work by the Sunni Arab delegates.[136] In the final days of the negotiations on the draft text tension mounted and, following a suicide attack on police forces in Baghdad, fierce gunfighting broke out in the city. Violence again followed the referendum on the constitution on 15 October as US forces clashed with insurgents in the town of Rutba in Anbar Province and across central and western Iraq.[137] Meanwhile, there were indications that Shia groups around Basra interpreted the draft constitution as further consolidating their hold on the southern part of the country. Lethal roadside bombings and other attacks in mid-October pushed British troops further into retreat from the centre to the outskirts of the city.[138]

Patterns of the insurgency

Several factors complicated analysis of the Iraqi insurgency in 2005. First, there was little reliable information on the size or composition of the insurgency. Estimates varied between 20 000 (the figure most frequently cited by US officials) and over 60 000 individuals, and attempts to draw up comprehensive lists showed significant variation.[139] Many of the insurgents appeared to be 'part-timers', not formally associated with any one group; and civilians (both unemployed and criminal elements) were frequently co-opted.[140] Evidence suggested that insurgent groups paid civilians to plant improvised explosive devices and offered bounties for the killing of government officials. Analysis of hostage-taking and kidnapping incidents indicated a three-tier structure where abductions were frequently carried out by hired 'foot soldiers', paid by organized criminal groups, which in turn acted as 'contractors' for insurgent groups.[141] Suicide bombers were recruited from various constituencies, and the rate of attacks stood at a devastating average of 50 per month throughout 2005.[142]

---

[136] 'Iraqi constitution-writer killed', BBC News Online, 19 July 2005, URL <http://news.bbc. co.uk/1/4696869.stm>; United Nations, Report of the Secretary-General pursuant to paragraph 30 of Resolution 1546 (2004), UN document S/2005/585, 7 Sep. 2005, p. 2; and Wong, E., 'Sunnis boycott panel drafting charter for Iraq', New York Times, 21 July 2005.

[137] 'Gunfights erupt in Iraqi capital', BBC News Online, 24 Aug. 2005, URL <http://news.bbc.co.uk/ 1/4180672.stm>; and Wong, E., 'Iraqis begin audit of heavy "yes" vote; may take three days', New York Times, 19 Oct. 2005.

[138] Wood, P., 'Shia militants gaining strength in Basra', BBC News Online, 10 Oct. 2005, URL <http://news.bbc.co.uk/1/4347636.stm>.

[139] See, e.g., Cordesman, A. H., 'New patterns in the Iraqi insurgency: the war for a civil war in Iraq', CSIS Working draft, revised 27 Sep. 2005, p. 2; and IISS (note 47), pp. 425–26.

[140] Giustozzi, A., 'Conflicting intelligence clouds assessment of Iraqi insurgency', Jane's Homeland Security and Resilience Monitor, vol. 4, no. 3 (Apr. 2005), pp. 14–16.

[141] Krepinevich, A. F., Jr, 'How to win in Iraq', Foreign Affairs, vol. 84, no. 5 (Sep./Oct. 2005), p. 103; Aaron, C., 'Kidnappings endanger foreign reconstruction in Iraq', Jane's Intelligence Review, Mar. 2005, p. 9; and Carroll, J., 'Iraq's rising industry: domestic kidnapping', Christian Science Monitor, 22 Apr. 2005, URL <http://www.csmonitor.com/2005/0422/p06s01-woiq.html>.

[142] Wong, E., 'Suicide bombing in Iraq kills 30 and wounds dozens', New York Times, 25 Nov. 2005.

Second, difficulties encountered in determining the identity of and in categorizing insurgent groups in Iraq obscured clear analysis of their motives. High rates of both petty and spectacular violent crime complicated the distinction between politically and criminally motivated violence.[143] Attempts to map the insurgency coalesced around the identification of three broad groups: Islamist (radical/Jihadi/Salafist/Wahhabi), Sunni Arab/nationalist (including ex-Baathist elements, as well as the Islamic Army of Iraq and Ansar al-Sunnah groups) and Shia (the most well-known being the Moqtada al-Sadr's Mahdi Army and the Badr Brigade).[144] Most analysts found the majority of insurgents to be Sunni Arab (one source estimated that close to 90 per cent of the attacks were perpetrated by Sunni Arab groups), while other sources suggested that a better characterization might be opposition groups operating in traditionally Sunni areas, or insurgents derived from formerly powerful groups, disenfranchised by the collapse of the complex structures of power and possession under the Baathist regime, which included networks defined in terms of tribe and clan.[145]

Third, deconstructing an insurgency that was predominantly opposed to the US-led MNF and anti-government was complicated by the maintenance of militias by several groups that supported the government. Although Iraqi officials periodically suggested that reliance on local militias was necessary to ensure 'security' on a local basis, the continued existence of such militias indicated a fragmentation of authority and further proliferation of non-state actors in Iraq's complex security landscape.[146] Most prominent among the militias were the Peshmerga, controlled by the Kurdish Democratic Party (KDP) and the PUK, and the Badr Brigade, backed by the (Shiite) Supreme Council for the Islamic Revolution in Iraq (SCIRI), a member of the UIA.[147] Inter-militia violence, such as the clashes that took place between al-Sadr's Mahdi Army and the Badr Brigade (both Shia militias) across the south in August, indicated that there were divisions in Iraq beyond the opposition to the MNF or ethnic–sectarian divides related to local competitions for power.[148]

[143] Prior to the invasion in 2003 Saddam Hussein released 38 000 inmates from prison, setting the scene for widespread criminality. Perito, R. M., 'The Coalition Provisional Authority's experience with public security in Iraq', USIP Special Report no. 137, Apr. 2005, URL <http://www.usip.org/pubs/specialreports/sr137.html>, p. 7.

[144] ed. Posch (note 120), pp. 107–13; USIP (note 143); Cordesman (note 118); and HRW, 'A face and a name: civilian victims of insurgent groups in Iraq', Human Rights Watch, vol. 17, no. 9 (Oct. 2005).

[145] HRW (note 144), p. 8; and Haugh, T., 'Analysis of Sunni-based opposition in Iraq', Strategic Insights, vol. 4, no. 5 (May 2005), URL <http://www.ccc.nps.navy.mil/si/2005/May/haughSunni May05.asp>. Nevertheless, some analysts argue that the satisfying of Sunni grievances would neutralize a large share of insurgent groups. ed. Posch (note 120), pp. 25–44.

[146] Jalal Talabani, President of the Iraqi Transitional Government, floated the idea of using 'grassroots militias' to ensure security on a local basis. Muir, J., 'Iraq ministers facing uphill task', BBC News Online, 8 May 2005, URL <http://news.bbc.co.uk/2/4527913.stm>.

[147] Mite, V., 'Iraq: doubts raised about militias' ability to restore law and order', Radio Free Europe/Radio Liberty (RFE/RL), 21 Apr. 2005.

[148] 'Violence flares among Iraq Shias', BBC News Online, 24 Aug. 2005, URL <http://news.bbc.co.uk/1/4182230.stm>; and Spiegel, P., 'Rivalry between Badr and Sadr militias worries UK forces', Financial Times, 14 Dec. 2005.

Fourth, the proportion of jihadist elements in the insurgency, and the extent to which they maintained links with international terrorist networks (or were externally directed) remained under question. International dimensions of the Iraqi conflict were clear, given that the porous border with Syria functioned as a transit route for insurgent recruits as well as weaponry and ammunition; Shia militias in the south were allegedly provided with Iranian (and by some accounts Hezbollah) materiel support and training; and sources in Jordan stood accused of financing parts of the insurgency.[149] Several US offensives deployed to seal the Syrian border indicated the emphasis placed by the US military on the insurgency's external links.[150]

Frequent reference to 'international terrorism' and 'foreign jihadists' in the international media notwithstanding, in the spring of 2005 coalition officials reported that more than 95 per cent of the insurgents who had been killed or captured were Iraqi, and in November both Iraqi and US officials estimated that the proportion of fighters with Iraqi citizenship was close to 95 per cent.[151] Domestically, most analysts judge the extremist/jihadist element of the Sunni Arab insurgency, often 'neo-Salafi' groups, to be 5–10 per cent of the insurgency, yielding (depending on which figure is taken as the total) anywhere between 1500 and 6000 members.[152] Most ominously, the al-Qaeda Organization in Mesopotamia under the Jordanian Abu Musab al-Zarqawi was responsible for several high-profile attacks in 2005.[153] Devastating triple bomb attacks on three hotels in Amman, Jordan, on 8 November—killing over 50 people and wounding over 100—underscored the threat that the organization posed not just in Iraq (where al-Zarqawi propagated sectarian violence against Shiite religious targets) but also for wider regional and international security.[154] A rocket attack on two US warships in Aqaba, Jordan, in August 2005 also appeared to have been directed by an unidentified insurgent group within Iraq.[155]

---

[149] 'The south is a mess too', *The Economist*, 24 Sep. 2005, p. 49; Fattah, H. M., 'Syrians clash with fighters linked to the Iraqi insurgency', *New York Times,* 5 July 2005; and Oppel, R. A., 'Iraq accuses Jordan of allowing financing of insurgency', *New York Times,* 22 Aug. 2005. For closer analysis of the role of Iran see ICG, 'Iran in Iraq: how much influence?', Middle East Report no. 38, Amman and Brussels, 21 Mar. 2005.

[150] Oppel, R. A., '100 rebels killed in US offensive in western Iraq', *New York Times,* 10 May 2005; Semple, K., 'Five marines dead and 11 hurt in an ambush by insurgents', *New York Times,* 17 Nov. 2005; and '"New militant threat" from Iraq', BBC News Online, 23 June 2005, URL <http://news.bbc.co.uk/2/4122040.stm>.

[151] HRW (note 144), p. 7. Of the foreign insurgents, over half were estimated to be of Saudi origin. Cordesman, A. H., *Iraq and Foreign Volunteers*, CSIS Report, 17 Nov. 2005, URL <http://www.csis.org/index.php>, p. 2.

[152] Cordesman (note 139).

[153] E.g., the organization claimed the responsibility for the deadliest attack on the capital's main police academy in Baghdad on 6 Dec., killing at least 36 police officers and wounding 72 other people. Wong, E., 'Suicide bombers kill 36 officers at Iraqi academy', *New York Times,* 7 Dec. 2005; and Cordesman (note 118), pp. 28, 50–56.

[154] '"Al-qaeda" claims Jordan attacks', 10 Nov. 2005, BBC News Online, URL <http://news.bbc.co.uk/1/4423714.stm>; and Jehl, D., 'Iraq-based jihad appears to seek broader horizons', *New York Times,* 11 Nov. 2005.

[155] Fattah, H. M., 'Jordan arrests key suspect in rocket attack', *New York Times,* 23 Aug. 2005.

In terms of tactics, the insurgent forces appeared to retain the initiative over the MNF and Iraqi Security Forces (ISF) and continued to exploit the strategic vulnerabilities of the new regime. The ISF stood out as key targets of the violence: in a striking example over 60 people were killed in a single suicide bombing attack (carried out by a member of the Ansar al-Sunna group) on a police recruitment centre in the Kurdish city of Irbil, in northern Iraq, on 4 May. Between May and October the ISF lost more personnel than in any previous comparable period, averaging 69 fatalities per week.[156] By June over 2600 Iraqi security personnel had been killed since the overthrow of Saddam Hussein, more than coalition military and non-military casualties combined.[157] Targeted assassinations of Iraqi officials further destabilized the political landscape, and a surge in attacks, on occasion lethal, on foreign diplomats in Iraq caused embarrassment for the transition regime internationally.[158]

Most extreme, however, was the extent of civilian casualties caused by insurgent attacks. Suicide attacks perpetrated against civilians queuing outside a hospital in Mahmudiya in the Euphrates River valley south of Baghdad on 25 November, killing over 30, were indicative of the indiscriminate nature of the violence.[159] The Iraq Body Count in mid-December estimated the number of civilians killed since March 2003 at 30 989.[160] In terms of location, the Euphrates River valley south of Baghdad continued to be an epicentre of violence in 2005 (frequently referred to as the Triangle of Death), combining bandit ambushes with sectarian struggle for control of the towns and of the major arteries leading south from the capital to the Shiite holy cities of Najaf and Karbala.[161] Baghdad, Mosul and the western province of Al-Anbar were worst affected by the violence, but the northern Kurdish provinces also faced serious unrest. A series of attacks in the centre and north of the country in the last week of October and the first week of November in Baghdad, Tikrit and the town of Hawija, near Kirkuk, left close to 400 Iraqis dead.[162]

The prospects at the end of 2005

By the end of 2005, the British and US administrations had not found a way to contend with the MNF's paradoxical role in Iraq: while the MNF presence

---

[156] 'Seven days of violence', *Washington Post*, 8 May 2005; and Bensahel, N., 'Gauging counter-insurgency', *Baltimore Sun*, 9 Aug. 2005.

[157] Lins de Albuquerque, A. and O'Hanlon, M., 'Protecting Iraqi security forces', *Washington Times*, 18 July 2005; and 'Militants massacre 21 Iraq police', BBC News Online, 7 Nov. 2005, URL <http://news.bbc.co.uk/1/3989671.stm>.

[158] The Egyptian ambassador to Iraq, Ihab el-Sherif, was killed on 8 July, and diplomats from Pakistan and Bahrain were targeted. Burns, J. F., 'Iraq asks Muslim states for support after envoy's killing', *New York Times*, 9 July 2005.

[159] Wong (note 142).

[160] 'Iraq Body Count', URL <http://www.iraqbodycount.org>, 20 Dec. 2005. For a breakdown of the violence directed against civilians in Iraq see HRW (note 144).

[161] Wong (note 142).

[162] Hardy, R., 'Analysis: surge in Iraq violence', BBC News Online, 5 Nov. 2005, URL <http://news.bbc.co.uk/2/4537065.stm>.

provided a key recruiting incentive for the insurgency, its departure amid highly insecure conditions would be widely regarded as an abdication of responsibility.[163] Meanwhile, US opinion polls in June recorded the lowest level of support since the invasion in 2003: more than half the number of respondents believed that the war in Iraq had not contributed to US security and 56 per cent that it had not been worth going to war in the first place. At the end of the year domestic pressure was propelled further by the symbolic impact of total US troop casualties passing the 2000 mark.[164] Moreover, much of the analysis in 2005 noted the poor historical record of external parties in defeating insurgencies.[165] As the insurgency gained ground anew in Fallujah (seen as a 'successful' operation after US forces retook the city from insurgent control in November 2004) it was clear that a lack of local support and inadequate economic reconstruction made consolidation of temporary gains against the insurgents difficult.[166]

Progressive handing over of security operations to the ISF was widely regarded as the solution to the coalition's deepening embroilment in Iraq.[167] About 75 000 local police officers had been trained and deployed by the end of 2005, about half the estimated requirement of 135 000. Although another 7300 are currently in training, the training of local police is lagging. In the meantime, 99 000 Iraqi soldiers have been trained and equipped, out of a total target of 160 000.[168] US and Iraqi security forces launched several joint offensives in the year, with mixed results. At the end of February a major counterinsurgency operation was conducted in Anbar Province on the border with Syria, but strong concerns were raised over the political and humanitarian impact of the operation.[169] In June ISF units were left in charge of small parts of Baghdad and Mosul, and further joint operations were conducted in the northern town of Tal Afar. Because the Iraqi forces were hampered by the attacks and lacked both training and equipment US officials doubted their

[163] Anti-US sentiments ran high amongst Shia and Sunni groups alike. Negus, S. and Waldmeir, P., 'Sadr followers plan campaign to oust US', *Financial Times*, 11 Apr. 2005, p. 8; and Byman, D., 'Five bad options for Iraq', *Survival*, vol. 47, no. 1 (spring 2005), p. 10.

[164] 'That not-winning feeling', *The Economist*, 18 June 2005, pp. 39–40; and Brookings Institution, 'Iraq Index: Tracking Variables of Reconstruction and Security in Post-Saddam Iraq', updated 28 Nov. 2005, URL <http://www.brookings.edu/iraqindex>, pp. 5, 7–8. On arms transfers to Iraq see chapter 10 in this volume.

[165] Conetta, C., *Vicious Circle: The Dynamics of Occupation and Resistance in Iraq*, Research Monograph (Commonwealth Project on Defence Alternatives: Cambridge, Mass., 18 May 2005), URL <http://www.comw.org/pda/0505rm10exsum.html>.

[166] Testimony by Kenneth M. Pollack, Senior Fellow and Director of Research, Saban Centre for Middle East Policy, Brookings Institution, before the Senate Foreign Relations Committee on Iraq's Security, 18 July 2005, URL <http://www.brook.edu/views/testimony/pollack/20050718.htm>.

[167] Schmitt, E., 'Iraqis not ready to fight rebels on own, US says', *New York Times*, 21 July 2005. Training of Iraqi police was in part outsourced to the US private security company DynCorp in 2003. On the private security industry in Iraq see Holmqvist (note 46), especially chapter 3.

[168] Filkins, D., 'General says militias split loyalties of Iraqi Security Forces', *New York Times*, 3 Dec. 2005, p. 12.

[169] United Nations, Report of the Secretary-General pursuant to paragraph 30 of Resolution 1546 (2004), UN document S/2005/141, 7 Mar. 2005, p. 3.

capacity to take over operations; and major changes in the US strategy were considered in order to make better use of local forces.[170]

More disturbing than the deficit in effectiveness was the failure of both ISF and MNF forces to uphold democratic standards. The detention of nearly 20 000 people without due process was identified in several reports of the UN Secretary-General as one of the major human rights challenges in the country, and repeated accusations of excessive use of force deeply tarnished the standing of both Iraqi and US security forces.[171] Charges of sectarian violence directed against Sunni communities by the mainly Shia ISF mounted during 2005. In November pictures of Sunni Arab prisoners who had suffered torture at a Ministry of Interior centre for detainees were leaked to the international press.[172] Sectarian abductions and executions by the ISF were substantiated also by human rights organizations, and allegations that insurgents were infiltrating Iraq's new police force continued to raise serious concerns about the credentials of the new Iraqi forces.[173]

The failure of the MNF to promote effective and accountable behaviour on the part of the ISF led some analysts to conclude that the effort to build up security forces was linked more to the USA's wish to exit than to a nuanced understanding of the population's security needs or of governance networks.[174] Despite sporadic assertions of insurgent groups expressing their willingness to join the political process, the credibility of such contacts was doubted and any wider renouncing of violent means seemed remote at the end of 2005.[175] A visit to Iraq in October by the Secretary-General of the Arab League, Amre Moussa, led to the holding of a conference on Iraqi 'national reconciliation' in Cairo, Egypt, in November, and seemed to offer prospects of a new kind of external engagement with the situation in Iraq.[176] Encouragingly, parliament-

[170] 'Heroes wanted', *The Economist*, 18 June 2005, p. 23; and Schmitt, E., 'Iraqis not ready to fight rebels on own, US says', *New York Times*, 21 July 2005.

[171] United Nations, Report of the Secretary-General pursuant to paragraph 30 of Resolution 1546, UN document S/2005/373, 7 June 2005, p. 13; United Nations, Report of the Secretary-General pursuant to paragraph 30 of Resolution 1546, UN document S/2005/585, 7 Sep. 2005, p. 11; and HRW (note 144).

[172] Muir, J., 'Abuse reports fuel Iraqi tensions', BBC News Online, 16 Nov. 2005, URL <http://news.bbc.co.uk/1/4443126.stm>; and 'New "torturee" jail found in Iraq', BBC News Online, 12 Dec. 2005, URL <http://news.bbc.co.uk/2/4520714.stm>.

[173] One Sunni group taking testimony from families in Baghdad stated that it had documented over 700 deaths or disappearances of Sunni civilians in the preceding 4 months. Filkins, D., 'Sunnis accuse Iraqi military of kidnappings and slayings', *New York Times*, 29 Nov. 2005; Carroll, J., 'Old brutality among new Iraqi forces', *Christian Science Monitor*, 4 May 2005, URL <http://www.csmonitor.com/2005/0504/p01s04-woiq.html>; and 'Insurgents "joining Iraqi police"', BBC News Online, 26 July 2005, URL <http://news.bbc.co.uk/2/4716531.stm>.

[174] Hills, A., 'Something old, something new: security governance in Iraq', *Conflict, Security and Development*, vol. 5, no. 2 (Aug. 2005), pp. 183–84, 196.

[175] Wong, E., 'Iraqi aide says rebel groups offer feelers', *New York Times*, 26 Nov. 2005.

[176] 'Arab League chief satisfied with visit to Iraq', Arabic News Online, 25 Oct. 2005, URL <http://www.arabicnews.com/ansub/Daily/Day/051025/2005102505.html>; Janabi, A., 'Cairo conference fuels resentment', Arabic News.com, 15 Nov. 2005, URL <http://www.arabicnews.com/ansub/Daily/Day/051025/2005102505.html>; and Cordesman, A. H., *The Arab Role in Iraq: A Strategy for Action*, CSIS Report, 6 Oct. 2005, URL <http://www.csis.org/>.

ary elections were held in Iraq on schedule on 15 December, under relatively calm conditions. The results were inconclusive at the end of the year, however, especially as regards the future role of Sunni constituencies.[177]

Despite the passing of several political milestones for Iraq during the year, relentless violence indicated that the Iraqi Transitional Government, the multinational forces and the international community more broadly were hopelessly ill equipped to avert the country's decent into civil war. Dealing with the activity of non-state actors was at the heart of the challenges faced; the failure to understand either the motivations or the composition of the insurgency, let alone identify reliable entry points for political dialogue, continued to cast a shadow over Iraq at the end of 2005.

V. Conclusions: dealing with non-state actors in conflict

The brief retrospect at the beginning of this chapter noted some significant changes in conflict patterns and dynamics over the past four decades. Forty years ago states were treated as the key actors in both conflicts and international security relations more broadly, and it was largely taken for granted that self-determination was the goal of any rebel movement. Subsequently, the increasingly significant role of non-state actors in conflict, together with the emergence of non-traditional or 'new' security threats, has significantly altered the dynamics of and international responses to conflicts around the world.[178] In addition, the growth of the human rights culture and the emphasis on individual and multidimensional, or human, security have shifted the traditional concern from physical and national security to promoting greater efforts to deal with threats to the lives of civilian populations, regardless of whether those threats originate from state or non-state actors.

Nevertheless, the instruments that are available to deal with non-state threats and actors are still to a large extent wielded by states. Events in 2005 demonstrated the extent to which the United Nations—the most important international organization in terms of addressing threats to peace and security—still battles with the tension between individual state interest and institutional development in response to changed international circumstances.[179] In particular, the UN is limited in its capacity to directly address armed non-state actors in conflict, in large part owing to the risks of being seen to confer undue legitimacy on armed opposition groups or antagonize the government in question. In other words, the UN needs to 'solve the rebel problem'. The particular characteristics of non-state actors' activity that are highlighted in this chapter—the fluidity of armed groups, the portrayal of conflict as a domestic

---

[177] 'The wrong lot won, dammit', *The Economist*, 5 Jan. 2006.

[178] For a comprehensive account of the relationship between the emergence of new threats and the proliferation of non-state actors see Krahmann, E. (ed.), *New Threats and New Actors in International Security* (Palgrave Macmillan: New York, N.Y., 2005).

[179] The Sep. 2005 UN World Summit was, of course, the central event in this respect. See chapter 3 in this volume.

problem of criminality or terrorism activity, and the continued activity of armed groups after the formal ending of conflict—help to explain why efforts to address armed groups are so notoriously difficult.

Another much-debated dimension of the contemporary political climate is the growth and proliferation of civil society organizations engaged in conflict management and peace-building.[180] In part this is a natural outgrowth of the established role of civil society (notably, non-governmental organizations) in humanitarian aid and development activity more broadly, as the inseparability of security and development is increasingly recognized.[181] Some analysts suggest that non-state conflict managers and peace-builders may in fact be better suited to addressing armed groups, and non-state threats more generally, than state (or inter-governmental) actors.[182] In particular, non-governmental organizations are emerging as willing and able to engage directly with armed groups, for example, through 'sensitization' programmes and broader pro-motion of human rights, precisely because they do not face the same political obstacles as states do.[183] While states are increasingly recognizing the need to cooperate to address (transnational) non-state threats, cooperation between state-led and civil society efforts is still inadequate. The newly established UN Peacebuilding Commission could provide a forum to address this gap and improve the integration of official and non-official efforts: in this case, it is important to investigate preventive action, including early mediation.

The conflict in Iraq has been at the centre of international debates on con-flict since the much-contested US-led invasion in 2003. Developments in 2005 indicated that the conflict will continue to resonate internationally and, despite its unique origins, have implications for broader conceptions of conflict and conflict management. In particular, the conflict in Iraq brought to the forefront the problems associated with a diversity of non-state groups in conflict. The question whether viable political entities will emerge out of the insurgency, or whether the conflict will spread in the region or internationally because of the activity of non-state actors, will undoubtedly feed into debates about conflict, security and transnational threats for the foreseeable future.

---

[180] For an account of the role of NGOs in peace-building see Gerstbauer, L. C., 'New conflict man-agers: peacebuilding NGOs and state agendas', ed. Krahmann (note 178), pp. 23–45.

[181] See, e.g., International Peace Academy, 'The security–development nexus: conflict, peace and development in the 21st century', Programme description, Mar. 2004, URL <http://www.ipacademy.org/Programs/Programs.htm>; and British Department for International Trade and Development (DFID), *Fighting Poverty to Build a Safer World: A Strategy for Security and Development* (DFID: London, Mar. 2005), URL <http://www.dfid.gov.uk/pubs/files/securityforall.pdf>.

[182] Krahmann (note 178), pp. 199–213.

[183] The International Committee of the Red Cross (ICRC) occupies a unique position in its work to raise awareness of, and increase respect for, international humanitarian law and human rights standards among armed groups by virtue of its permanent mandate under international law and its recognized policy of impartiality, independence and neutrality. On the ICRC see URL <http://www.icrc.org/>.

Appendix 2A. Patterns of major armed conflicts, 1990–2005

LOTTA HARBOM and PETER WALLENSTEEN*

I. Global patterns

In 2005, 17 major armed conflicts were active in 16 locations throughout the world. The number of major armed conflicts has declined steadily since 1999, and the figure for 2005 is the lowest for the entire post-cold war period 1990–2005. The annual number of conflicts was substantially higher in the first half of the 1990s, ranging from 27 to 31, with 1991 the peak year.

No interstate conflict was recorded for 2005, but a low number of interstate conflicts is not a new phenomenon. In the 16-year period 1990–2005, only four of the 57 active conflicts were fought between states: Eritrea–Ethiopia (1998–2000); India–Pakistan (1990–92 and 1996–2003); Iraq–Kuwait (1991); and Iraq versus the USA and its allies (2003). The remaining 53 conflicts in the period were fought within states and concerned either control over government (30 conflicts) or control over territory (23 conflicts). The conflicts over government outnumbered the conflicts over territory in all years of the post-cold war period apart from 1993.

In 2005 external states contributed troops to the side of the government in three internal conflicts: the conflict between the Government of Afghanistan and the Taliban; the conflict between the Iraqi Government and numerous Iraqi insurgent groups; and the conflict between the Government of the USA and al-Qaeda.[1] The USA was also a major actor in the first two of these conflicts, making it the state that was most frequently involved in major armed conflicts in 2005.

II. Regional patterns

In 2005 Asia was the region with the highest number of conflicts, with seven active major armed conflicts. There were three conflicts in each of the three regions Africa, the Americas and the Middle East, and one in Europe. The regional distribution of major armed conflicts and locations over the period 1990–2005 is shown in tables 2A.1 and 2A.2, respectively. Figure 2A.1 displays the regional distribution and total number of conflicts for each year in this period.

---

[1] For information on the states contributing troops in these conflicts see table 2A.3. For background to the conflict between the USA and al-Qaeda and the complex issues affecting its coding in the database see Eriksson, M., Sollenberg, M. and Wallensteen, P., 'Patterns of major armed conflicts, 1990–2001', *SIPRI Yearbook 2002: Armaments, Disarmament and International Security* (Oxford University Press: Oxford, 2002), pp. 67–68.

* Uppsala Conflict Data Program (UCDP), Department of Peace and Conflict Research, Uppsala University. For table 2A.3, Johan Brosche was responsible for the conflict locations Russia and Sudan; Kristine Eck for India and Nepal; Hanne Fjelde for Afghanistan; Erika Forsberg for the Philippines; Helena Grusell for Colombia and Peru; Joop de Haan for Turkey; Lotta Harbom for Sri Lanka and Uganda; Stina Högbladh for Burundi; and Joakim Kreutz for Iraq, Israel and Myanmar.

Throughout the post-cold war period, *Africa* was one of the main arenas for major armed conflict. From 1990, 19 conflicts were fought in 17 locations in this region, only one of which was an interstate conflict—that between Eritrea and Ethiopia.[2] After 2000 there was a constant decline in the number of conflicts in Africa; in 2005 only three were recorded—the lowest figure for the region in the post-cold war period. The peak years were 1998 and 1999: 11 conflicts were active in Africa in both these years. The vast majority (15) of the 18 intra-state conflicts in Africa in the period 1990–2005 concerned governmental power.

The Americas (including North, Central and South America as well as the Caribbean) accounted for six major armed conflicts in the period 1990–2005.[3] The number of conflicts in the region has decreased steadily from a peak in the first year of the period, when there were five active conflicts, until 1997–2000, when only two conflicts were registered. Since 2001 the same three conflicts have been active each year. Two of these, Colombia and Peru, were registered for each year in the entire period since 1990.[4] All the region's conflicts were intra-state conflicts fought over governmental power.

Asia was the scene of 15 major armed conflicts in the period 1990–2005.[5] While Africa had the highest total number of conflicts in the period, the annual totals were higher in Asia (see figure 2A.1). Over the seven-year period 1990–96 the number of conflicts in Asia fluctuated between 9 and 12, but since 1997 the number has slowly declined, reaching the lowest level in 2004, with six conflicts. In 2005 the number increased by one—the conflict between the Government of Afghanistan and the Taliban. Four of the Asian conflicts recorded for 2005—India (Kashmir), Myanmar (Karen), Sri Lanka (Eelam) and the Philippines—were active in all 16 years of the period. One conflict in the region, between India and Pakistan, was fought between states. Of the 14 intra-state conflicts in Asia, only six concerned governmental power, with the remaining eight concerning territory.

Europe accounted for seven major armed conflicts in the post-cold war period.[6] Apart from the two years 1993 and 1994, Europe has been the region that annually experienced the lowest number of major armed conflicts.[7] After an increase between 1990 (zero) and 1993–94 (four in each of the two years), brought about mainly by the

---

[2] The 19 major armed conflicts recorded for Africa for the period 1990–2005 were Algeria, Angola, Burundi, Chad, the Democratic Republic of the Congo (formerly Zaire), the Republic of Congo, Ethiopia, Ethiopia (Eritrea), Eritrea–Ethiopia, Guinea-Bissau, Liberia, Morocco (Western Sahara), Mozambique, Rwanda, Sierra Leone, Somalia, Sudan, Sudan (Southern Sudan) and Uganda. Note that in this appendix, when only the name of a country is given, this indicates that the conflict is over government. When the conflict is over territory, the name of the contested territory appears in parentheses after the country name.

[3] The 6 major armed conflicts recorded for the Americas in 1990–2005 were Colombia, El Salvador, Guatemala, Nicaragua, Peru and the USA (the conflict between the US Government and al-Qaeda).

[4] The third conflict in this category was that fought between the USA and al-Qaeda.

[5] The 15 major armed conflicts recorded for Asia in 1990–2005 were Afghanistan, Cambodia, India (Kashmir), India (Punjab), India–Pakistan, Indonesia (East Timor), Myanmar (Kachin), Myanmar (Karen), Myanmar (Shan), Nepal, the Philippines, the Philippines (Mindanao), Sri Lanka, Sri Lanka (Eelam) and Tajikistan.

[6] The 7 major armed conflicts in Europe in 1990–2005 were Azerbaijan (Nagorno-Karabakh), Bosnia and Herzegovina (Herceg-Bosna), Bosnia and Herzegovina (Republika Srpska), Georgia (Abkhazia), Russia (Chechnya), the Socialist Federal Republic of Yugoslavia (Croatia) and the Federal Republic of Yugoslavia (Kosovo).

[7] In 1999 the Americas matched this level.

Table 2A.1. Regional distribution, number and types of armed conflicts, 1990–2005

Region	1990 G	1990 T	1991 G	1991 T	1992 G	1992 T	1993 G	1993 T	1994 G	1994 T	1995 G	1995 T	1996 G	1996 T	1997 G	1997 T	1998 G	1998 T	1999 G	1999 T	2000 G	2000 T	2001 G	2001 T	2002 G	2002 T	2003 G	2003 T	2004 G	2004 T	2005 G	2005 T
Africa	6	3	7	3	5	1	5	1	6	1	5	1	3	1	4	1	9	2	9	2	7	2	7	1	6	1	5	1	5	1	3	0
Americas	5	0	4	0	3	0	3	0	3	0	3	0	3	0	2	0	2	0	2	0	2	0	3	0	3	0	3	0	3	0	3	0
Asia	4	8	3	7	4	7	4	6	4	5	4	6	4	5	3	5	3	5	2	5	2	5	2	5	2	5	2	5	2	4	3	4
Europe	0	0	0	1	0	2	0	4	0	4	0	2	0	1	0	0	0	1	0	2	0	1	0	1	0	1	0	1	0	1	0	1
Middle East	1	3	3	3	2	3	2	4	2	4	2	4	2	4	2	2	2	2	1	2	2	2	1	2	0	2	1	2	1	2	1	2
Total G&T	**16**	**14**	**17**	**14**	**14**	**13**	**14**	**15**	**15**	**14**	**14**	**13**	**12**	**11**	**11**	**8**	**16**	**10**	**14**	**11**	**13**	**10**	**13**	**9**	**11**	**9**	**11**	**9**	**11**	**8**	**10**	**7**
Total	**30**		**31**		**27**		**29**		**29**		**27**		**23**		**19**		**26**		**25**		**23**		**22**		**20**		**20**		**19**		**17**	

G = Government and T = Territory, the two types of incompatibility.

Table 2A.2. Regional distribution of locations with at least one major armed conflict, 1990–2005

Region	1990	1991	1992	1993	1994	1995	1996	1997	1998	1999	2000	2001	2002	2003	2004	2005
Africa	8	9	6	6	7	6	4	5	11	11	9	8	7	5	5	3
America	5	4	3	3	3	3	3	2	2	2	2	3	3	3	3	3
Asia	8	8	9	8	8	8	9	8	8	7	6	6	6	6	5	6
Europe	0	1	2	3	3	2	1	0	1	2	1	1	1	1	1	1
Middle East	4	4	4	4	5	4	4	4	4	3	4	3	2	3	3	3
Total	**25**	**26**	**24**	**24**	**26**	**23**	**21**	**19**	**26**	**25**	**22**	**21**	**19**	**18**	**17**	**16**

Source: Uppsala Conflict Data Program.

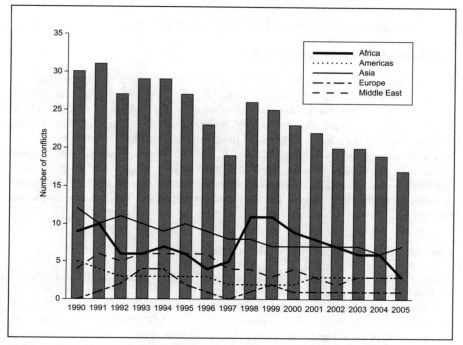

Figure 2A.1. Regional distribution and total number of major armed conflicts, 1990–2005

conflicts in the Balkans, the number again dropped to zero in 1997. Since 2000, the only active conflict in Europe has been that between the Government of Russia and the Republic of Chechnya. The seven conflicts fought in Europe over the 16-year period have all been intra-state conflicts. In contrast to the situation in other regions, they were all fought over territory.

For *the Middle East*, a total of 10 major armed conflicts were registered for the period 1990–2005.[8] The lowest number was recorded for 2002, when two conflicts were active. The number then increased to three in 2003 and remained at that level in 2005. Only one conflict was active in all years of the period, that between the Government of Israel and Palestinian groups. However, it is worth noting that the protracted conflict in Turkey (Kurdistan) has been registered for all years of the period since 1992. There have been two interstate conflicts in the region: that between Iraq and Kuwait, and that between Iraq and the US-led coalition. Eight of the major armed conflicts were intra-state: three of these conflicts were fought over governmental power and five over territory.

[8] The 10 major armed conflicts in the Middle East in 1990–2005 were Iran; Iran (Kurdistan); Iraq; Iraq (Kurdistan); Iraq–Kuwait; Iraq–USA, UK and Australia; Israel (Palestine); Lebanon; Turkey (Kurdistan); and Yemen.

III. Changes in the table of conflicts for 2005

Conflicts added to the table in 2005

One conflict was added to the table for 2005: that between the Government of Afghanistan and the Taliban. A major armed conflict was last recorded in Afghanistan in 2001, when the United Islamic Front for the Salvation of Afghanistan (UIFSA, commonly referred to as the Northern Alliance) toppled the Taliban government with the support of a US-led multinational coalition. By 2003 the Taliban was able to regroup and reorganize, and it took up arms against the new Afghan regime. In 2005 the conflict escalated markedly and resulted in more than 1000 battle-related deaths. What was initially widely believed to be temporary violence related to the run-up to the September elections is now viewed as an escalation of the conflict.

Conflicts removed from the table in 2005

Three conflicts were removed from the table for 2005: those in Rwanda, Sudan (Southern Sudan) and Algeria.

There was no fighting between the Government of Rwanda and the Hutu rebel group Forces démocratiques de libération du Rwanda (FDLR, or the Democratic Liberation Forces of Rwanda) in 2005. In March the FDLR, which is based on Congolese territory, declared that it was willing to cease military action against Rwanda and return home. The group now aims to establish itself as a political party, which the Government of Rwanda opposes. No deal on repatriation was reached during the year, and FDLR forces remain on Congolese territory.

The protracted conflict between the Government of Sudan and the Sudan People's Liberation Movement/Army (SPLM/A), ongoing since 1983, came to a halt with the signing on 9 January 2005 of the Comprehensive Peace Agreement.[9] The death of SPLM Chairman John Garang only weeks after he had been sworn in as First Vice-President on 9 July was a great blow to the peace process. However, no fighting took place between Sudanese government forces and former SPLM/A rebels. Salva Kiir Mayardit, deputy leader of the SPLM/A, was elected as Garang's successor and took up the position as Sudan's First Vice-President and President of Southern Sudan. In December an important milestone in the implementation of the peace agreement was reached, when a new constitution for Southern Sudan was signed.

In Algeria, the long-running conflict between the government and Groupe islamique armé (GIA, or the Armed Islamic Group) seemed to be over by early 2005. In late 2004 GIA leader Nourredine Boudiafi was captured by the Algerian authorities and in January 2005 the Algerian Interior Ministry declared that this, coupled with the death of another GIA leader in July 2004, had led to the 'almost

---

[9] For the Comprehensive Peace Agreement see the website of the United States Institute of Peace at URL <http://www.usip.org/library/pa/sudan/cpa01092005/cpa_toc.html>.

total collapse' of the rebel movement.[10] In line with this, no casualties were reported for this conflict in 2005.[11]

Changes in intensity of conflict

Four of the 17 major armed conflicts that were active in 2005 showed an increase in intensity compared to 2004.[12] In two of these conflicts—Myanmar (Karen) and Sri Lanka (Eelam)—the battle-related deaths increased by more than 50 per cent.

The conflict between the Government of Myanmar and the Karen National Union (KNU) increased in intensity after a year of only sporadic ceasefire violations in 2004. In 2005, following a reshuffle within the ruling junta, negotiations between the parties became increasingly difficult and subsequently broke down. However, it should be noted that, while the violence escalated greatly in relative terms, the conflict is still one of the least intensive of the conflicts in 2005.

In the wake of the December 2004 tsunami in South-East Asia, there were cautious hopes that the disaster might bring the parties in the Sri Lankan conflict closer together. However, the optimism was quickly dampened as the government and the Liberation Tigers of Tamil Eelam (LTTE) failed to come to an agreement on distribution of the humanitarian aid that flowed into the country. No talks on substantial conflict issues were held during the year. Instead, there was a marked escalation of violence between the parties in 2005. In November, the former Prime Minister, Mahinda Rajapakse, won the Sri Lankan presidential elections and the positions of the parties seemed to be far apart. By late December the Norwegian-led truce monitoring mission warned that war might not be far away.

Nine conflicts exhibited a decrease in intensity in 2005 compared to 2004: Israel, Uganda, Sudan, USA–al-Qaeda, Burundi, Iraq, Nepal, Philippines and Russia (Chechnya)—the first four by more than 50 per cent.

In Israel, the parties agreed to a ceasefire in February 2005. Even though there were numerous breaches of the truce, it led to a marked decrease in violence. In Uganda, the protracted conflict between the government and the Lord's Resistance Army (LRA) continued in 2005, albeit on a much lower scale than the previous year. In the last two months of 2004 a process was initiated to lead to peace talks, and by the end of the year there were high hopes that a formal ceasefire agreement would be signed. However, at the last minute the consultations broke down, and both parties resumed armed operations in 2005. The process suffered another setback in February, when the LRA's chief negotiator, Sam Kolo, surrendered to the Ugandan Army. The rebels continue to be based in Sudan, but they are coming under increased pressure as a consequence of the peace agreement for Southern Sudan. In Sudan's Darfur region, the conflict between the government and two rebel groups—the Sudan Liberation Movement/Army (SLM/A) and the Justice and Equality Movement (JEM)—con-

[10] Agence France-Presse, 'Algeria's deadliest armed group virtually wiped out', 4 Jan. 2005.

[11] It should be noted that the situation in Algeria was far from stable in 2005, with numerous deaths in the fighting between Algerian forces and the rebel Group Salafite pour la prédication et le combat (GSPC, or Salafiste Group for Preaching and Combat). However, since the fighting between the GSPC and the government never reached the threshold of 1000 battle-related deaths in any calendar year, this conflict is not defined as a major armed conflict and is therefore not included here.

[12] The 4 higher-intensity conflicts are Colombia, Myanmar (Karen), Sri Lanka (Eelam) and Turkey (Kurdistan).

tinued, but on a lower scale. However, there was a significant increase in warlordism and banditry in the region, and the population continued to suffer. Very little fighting occurred in the conflict between the USA and al-Qaeda. The few incidents that did take place were reported mainly from the Pakistani region Waziristan, a tribal area on the border with Afghanistan.

Three conflicts showed no change in intensity from 2004: the conflict between the Government of Peru and Sendero Luminoso (Shining Path); between the Government of the Philippines and the Moro Islamic Liberation Front (MILF); and between the Government of India and Kashmiri insurgents.

In 5 of the 17 active major armed conflicts in 2005 there were more than 1000 battle-related deaths: Afghanistan, Colombia, India (Kashmir), Iraq and Nepal.

In Colombia, both the Fuerzas Armadas Revolucionarias de Colombia (FARC, or the Revolutionary Armed Forces of Colombia) and the Ejército de Liberación Nationale (ELN, or National Liberation Army) continued their armed struggle against the government. FARC refused to negotiate and there was a slight escalation of violence. The ELN, on the other hand, was engaged in a tentative process that may lead to substantive talks in 2006. The conflict between the Government of India and Kashmiri insurgents continued unabated in 2005. This was the seventh consecutive year in which the Kashmir conflict resulted in more than 1000 battle-related deaths. Despite a slight de-escalation of the violence in Iraq, the conflict reached a level well above 1000 battle-related deaths: it was the most deadly conflict in 2005, and attacks continued on a daily basis. In Nepal, fighting continued between the government forces and the Communist Party of Nepal–Maoist (CPN-M). However, in September the rebels declared a three-month unilateral ceasefire, which they subsequently extended. Thus, there was a marked de-escalation of the conflict during the last four months of the year.

Table 2A.3. Conflict locations with at least one major armed conflict in 2005

Location	Incompat-ibility[a]	Yr formed/ yr stated/ yr joined/ yr entered[b]	Warring parties[c]	Total deaths[d] (incl. 2005)	Deaths in 2005[e]	Change from 2004[f]
Africa						
Burundi	Govt	1991/ 1991/1991/ ..	Govt of Burundi vs Palipehutu–FNL	>7 100	<300	–

Palipehutu–FNL: Parti pour la libération du peuple Hutu–Forces nationales de libération (Party for the Liberation of the Hutu People–National Liberation Forces)

Sudan	Govt	2003/ 2003/2003/ 2003	Govt of Sudan vs SLM/A vs JEM	>5 700	<500	– –

SLM/A: Sudan Liberation Movement/Army
JEM: Justice and Equality Movement

Uganda	Govt	1987/ 1987/1988/ 1991	Govt of Uganda vs LRA*	<9 400	>700	– –

LRA: Lord's Resistance Army
* Note that in the early years of its existence the LRA used a number of different names, principally the Ugandan Christian Democratic Army (UCDA).

Americas						
Colombia	Govt	1964/ 1966/1966/ .. 1964/1965/ ..	Govt of Colombia vs FARC vs ELN	>42 000*	>1 200	+

FARC: Fuerzas Armadas Revolucionarias de Colombia (Revolutionary Armed Forces of Colombia)
ELN: Ejército de Liberación Nationale (National Liberation Army)
* This figure includes deaths involving other parties than those listed above in the fighting since 1964, although a vast majority of the deaths can be attributed to FARC and, to a lesser extent, the ELN.

Peru	Govt	1980/ 1980/1980/ 1981	Govt of Peru vs Sendero Luminoso	>28 000	<25	0

Sendero Luminoso: Shining Path

Location	Incompat- ibility[a]	Yr formed/ yr stated/ yr joined/ yr entered[b]	Warring parties[c]	Total deaths[d] (incl. 2005)	Deaths in 2005[e]	Change from 2004[f]
USA	Govt	2001/ 2001/2001/ 2001	Govt of USA, Multinational coalition* vs al-Qaeda	>3 700	<25	– –

* Note that reliable information regarding which states contributed troops to the multinational coalition is sensitive and hard to find. Thus, this list should be seen as preliminary. In 2005, the following countries contributed combat troops to the multinational coalition: Belgium, Canada, Croatia, Denmark, Estonia, France, Italy, the Netherlands, Norway, Poland, Romania, Slovakia, Spain and the UK. For background and the origins of this intra-state conflict see *SIPRI Yearbook 2002*, pages 67–68.

Asia

Location	Incompat- ibility[a]	Yr formed/ yr stated/ yr joined/ yr entered[b]	Warring parties[c]	Total deaths[d] (incl. 2005)	Deaths in 2005[e]	Change from 2004[f]
Afghanistan	Govt	1990/ 1994/1994/ 2005	Govt of Afghanistan, Multinational coalition* vs Taliban	. .	<1 300	n.a.

* Note that reliable information regarding which states contributed troops to the multinational coalition is sensitive and hard to find. Thus, this list should be seen as preliminary. In 2005, the following countries contributed combat troops to the multinational coalition: Belgium, Canada, Croatia, Denmark, Estonia, France, Italy, the Netherlands, Norway, Poland, Romania, Slovakia, Spain and the UK.

Location	Incompat- ibility[a]	Yr formed/ yr stated/ yr joined/ yr entered[b]	Warring parties[c]	Total deaths[d] (incl. 2005)	Deaths in 2005[e]	Change from 2004[f]
India	Terr.	1977/ 1977/1984/ 1990	Govt of India vs Kashmir insurgents	>28 000	<1 100	0
Myanmar	Terr.	1948/ 1948/1948/ 1948	Govt of Myanmar vs KNU	>20 000	25–100	+ +

KNU: Karen National Union

Location	Incompat- ibility[a]	Yr formed/ yr stated/ yr joined/ yr entered[b]	Warring parties[c]	Total deaths[d] (incl. 2005)	Deaths in 2005[e]	Change from 2004[f]
Nepal	Govt	1996/ 1996/1996/ 2002	Govt of Nepal vs CPN-M	<7 800	<1 400	–

CPN-M: Communist Party of Nepal–Maoist

Location	Incompat-ibility[a]	Yr formed/ yr stated/ yr joined/ yr entered[b]	Warring parties[c]	Total deaths[d] (incl. 2005)	Deaths in 2005[e]	Change from 2004[f]
Philippines	Govt	1968/ 1968/1969/ 1982	Govt of the Philippines vs CPP*	20 000– 27 000	>200	–
	Terr.	1968/ 1981/1986/ 2000	vs MILF	>37 500	25–100	0

CPP: Communist Party of the Philippines
MILF: Moro Islamic Liberation Front
* Note that the CPP was previously listed as the New People's Army (NPA), the name of the armed wing of the CPP.

| Sri Lanka | Terr. | 1976 1976/1975/ 1989 | Govt of Sri Lanka vs LTTE | 60 000 | 25–100 | + + |

LTTE: Liberation Tigers of Tamil Eelam

Europe

| Russia | Terr. | 1991/ 1991/1991/ 1995 | Govt of Russia vs Republic of Chechnya | 40 000– 70 000 | <700 | – |

Middle East

| Iraq | Govt | 2003/ 2003/2003/ 2004 | Govt of Iraq, Multinational coalition* vs Iraqi insurgents** | >13 100 | >5 500 | – |

* The US-led multinational coalition in Iraq included combat troops from Albania, Armenia, Australia, Azerbaijan, Bosnia and Herzegovina, Bulgaria, the Czech Republic, Denmark, El Salvador, Estonia, Georgia, Italy, Japan, Kazakhstan, South Korea, Latvia, Lithuania, Macedonia (Former Yugoslav Republic of), Moldova, Mongolia, Netherlands, Norway, Poland, Portugal, Romania, Slovakia, the UK, Ukraine and the USA.
** These included, e.g., the Tanzim Qa'idat al-Jihad fi Bilad al-Rafidayn (Organization of Jihad's Base in the Country of the Two Rivers), the Jaish Ansar Al-Sunna (Army of Ansar Al-Sunna), and Al Jaysh al-Islami fi Iraq (Islamic Army of Iraq).

| Israel | Terr. | 1964/ 1964/1964/ .. | Govt of Israel vs Palestinian organizations* | <14 300 | <200 | – – |

* These included Fatah (Movement for the National Liberation of Palestine), Hamas (Islamic Resistance Movement), Palestinian Islamic Jihad and the Popular Front for the Liberation of Palestine.

Location	Incompat- ibility[a]	Yr formed/ yr stated/ yr joined/ yr entered[b]	Warring parties[c]	Total deaths[d] (incl. 2005)	Deaths in 2005[e]	Change from 2004[f]
Turkey	Terr.	1974/ 1974/1984/ 1992	Govt of Turkey vs PKK*	<30 100	<200	+

PKK: Partiya Karkeren Kurdistan: Kurdistan Worker's Party
* Note that PKK has changed names three times in as many years. In 2002 PKK changed its name to Kadek (Kurdish Freedom and Democracy Congress). In November 2003, the name was changed to the Conference of the People's Congress of Kurdistan (KONGRA-GEL). Finally, in April 2005, the group reverted back to its old name, the PKK.

Note that, although some countries are also the location of minor armed conflicts, the table lists only the major armed conflicts in those countries. For the definitions, methods and sources used see appendix 2B.

The conflicts in table 2A.3 are listed by location, in alphabetical order, within 5 geographical regions: Africa—excluding Egypt; the Americas—including North, Central and South America and the Caribbean; Asia—including Oceania, Australia and New Zealand; Europe—including the Caucasus; and the Middle East—Egypt, Iran, Iraq, Israel, Jordan, Kuwait, Lebanon, Syria, Turkey and the states of the Arabian peninsula.

[a] The stated general incompatible positions—'Govt' and 'Terr.'—refer to contested incompatibilities concerning *government* (type of political system or a change of central government or its composition) and *territory* (control of territory, secession or autonomy), respectively. Each location may have 1 or more incompatibilities over territory, if the disputed territories are different entities. There can be only 1 incompatibility over government in each location as, by definition, there can be only 1 government in each location.

[b] 'Year formed' is the year in which the original party in a major armed conflict—in conflicts where several parties have fought over the same incompatibility—first stated the incompatibility. 'Year stated' is the year in which *the active group* stated its incompatibility. 'Year joined' is the year in which the use of armed force began in the conflict between the active warring parties. 'Year entered' is the year in which the fighting between the government and the warring party for the first time reached the threshold of 1000 battle-related deaths in a single calendar year and was therefore entered in the database. In connection with the major data revision carried out by the UCDP (see appendix 2B, *SIPRI Yearbook 2005*), it became evident that the years listed in the tables for the early and mid-1990s sometimes referred to the start of the entire conflict and sometimes referred to the year in which the active group had stated its incompatibility. Although these years are often the same, there are also instances in which they are not. Therefore, in order to code this variable more stringently, 'Year formed' now refers to the start of the armed conflict itself, while the other 3 years listed in the table ('Year stated', 'Year joined' and 'Year entered') refer to the active warring party.

[c] An opposition organization is any non-governmental group which has publicly announced a name for the group as well as its political goals and has used armed force to achieve its goals. Only those parties and alliances that were active during 2005 are listed in this column. Alliances are indicated by a comma between the names of warring parties.

[d] The figures for total battle-related deaths refer to those deaths caused by the warring parties which can be directly connected to the incompatibility since the start of the conflict. This

figure thus relates to the 'Year formed' variable. In the instance of intra-state conflicts, it should be noted that the figures include only battle-related deaths that can be attributed to fighting between the government and parties which were at some point listed in the table (i.e., groups that have crossed the threshold of 1000 battle-related deaths in a year). Information that covers a calendar year is necessarily more tentative for the last months of the year. Experience has also shown that the reliability of figures improves over time; they are therefore revised each year.

e Numbers over 100 are as far as possible rounded to the nearest hundred. Thus, figures ranging between 101 and 150 are presented as >100, while figures ranging between 151 and 199 are presented as <200. Figures between 1 and 24 are presented as <25, while those between 25 and 100 are presented as 25–100.

f The 'change from 2004' is measured as the increase or decrease in the number of battle-related deaths in 2005 compared with the number of battle-related deaths in 2004. Although the symbols are based on data that cannot be considered totally reliable, they represent the following changes:

+ +   increase in battle deaths of >50%

+   increase in battle deaths of >10–50%

0   stable rate of battle deaths ($\pm$10%)

−   decrease in battle deaths of >10–50%

− −   decrease in battle deaths of >50%

n.a.   not applicable, since the major armed conflict was not recorded for 2004.

Appendix 2B. Definitions, sources and methods for the conflict data

UPPSALA CONFLICT DATA PROGRAM

This appendix clarifies the definitions and methods used in the compilation of data on major armed conflicts, and explains the treatment of the sources consulted. The armed conflict records presented in appendix 2A are compiled by the Uppsala Conflict Data Program (UCDP) of the Department of Peace and Conflict Research, Uppsala University.[1]

I. Definitions

The UCDP defines a major armed conflict as a contested incompatibility concerning government or territory over which the use of armed force between the military forces of two parties, of which at least one is the government of a state, has resulted in at least 1000 battle-related deaths in a single calendar year.[2] The separate elements are defined as follows:

1. *Incompatibility that concerns government or territory*. This refers to the stated generally incompatible positions of the parties to the conflict. An *incompatibility that concerns government* refers to incompatible positions regarding the state's type of political system or the composition of the government. It may also involve an aim to replace the current government. An *incompatibility that concerns territory* refers to incompatible positions regarding the status of a territory and may involve demands for secession or autonomy (intra-state conflict) or aims to change the state in control of a certain territory (interstate conflict).

2. *Use of armed force*. This refers to the use of armed force by the military forces of the parties to the conflict in order to promote the parties' general position in the conflict. Arms are defined as any material means of combat, including anything from manufactured weapons to sticks, stones, fire, water, and so on.

3. *Party*. This refers to the government of a state or an opposition organization or alliance of opposition organizations. The *government of a state* is the party which is generally regarded as being in central control, even by those organizations seeking to seize power. If this criterion is not applicable, the party controlling the capital of the state is regarded as the government. In most cases these two criteria coincide. An *opposition organization* is any non-governmental group which has announced a name for the group as well as its political goals and which has used armed force to achieve them. It should be noted that opposition organizations operating from bases in neighbouring states are listed as parties to the conflict in the location (country) where the

---

[1] See the UCDP Internet site at URL <http://www.pcr.uu.se/research/ucdp>.

[2] This definition of major armed conflicts differs slightly from that used by the UCDP in *SIPRI Year-books 1988–1999* (Oxford University Press: Oxford, 1988–99). The requirement that a conflict must cause at least 1000 battle-related deaths in a single year, rather than over the entire course of the conflict, ensures that only conflicts which reach a high level of intensity, as measured by the number of battle-related deaths, are included. Tables 2A.1 and 2A.2 have been retroactively revised accordingly.

government is challenged. Apart from these primary parties to the conflict, one other type of actor may be included in the table: a state or a multinational organization that supports one of the primary parties with regular troops. In order to be listed in the table, this secondary party must share the position of one of the warring parties. In contrast, a traditional peacekeeping operation is not considered to be a party to the conflict but is rather seen as an impartial part of a consensual peace process.

4. *State.* A state is an internationally recognized sovereign government controlling a specific territory or an internationally non-recognized government controlling a specific territory whose sovereignty is not disputed by an internationally recognized sovereign state which previously controlled the territory in question.

5. *Battle-related deaths.* This refers to the deaths caused by the warring parties that can be directly related to combat over the contested incompatibility. Once a conflict has reached the threshold of 1000 battle-related deaths in a year, it continues to appear in the annual table of major armed conflicts until the contested incompatibility has been resolved or until there is no recorded use of armed force resulting in at least one battle-related death between the same parties and concerning the same incompatibility during a year. The same conflict may reappear in subsequent years if there is renewed use of armed force between the same warring parties, resulting in at least one battle-related death and concerning the same incompatibility. The focus is thus not on political violence per se but on incompatibilities that are contested by the use of armed force. Thus, the UCDP registers one major type of political violence—battle-related deaths—which serves as a measure of the magnitude of a conflict. Other types of political violence are excluded: for example, the unilateral use of armed force (e.g., massacres); unorganized or spontaneous public violence (e.g., communal violence); and violence that is not directed at the state (e.g., rebel groups fighting each other) These categories of political violence are thus expressions of phenomena that are distinct from armed conflict as defined here.

II. Sources

The data presented in appendix 2A are based on information taken from a wide selection of publicly available sources, printed as well as electronic. The sources include news agencies, newspapers, academic journals, research reports, and documents from international and multinational organizations and non-governmental organizations (NGOs). In order to collect information on the aims and goals of the parties to the conflict, documents of the warring parties (governments and opposition organizations) and, for example, the Internet sites of rebel groups are often consulted.

Independent news sources, carefully selected over a number of years, constitute the basis of the data collection. The Factiva news database (previously known as the Reuters Business Briefing) is indispensable for the collection of general news reports. It contains 8000 sources in 22 languages from 118 countries and thus provides sources from all three crucial levels of the news media: international (e.g., Reuters and Agence France-Presse), regional and local. However, it is worth noting that the availability of the regional and national news sources varies. This means that for some countries several sources are consulted, whereas for other countries and regions only a few high-quality region- or country-specific sources are used. Since 2003, more efficient automated software has been used when extracting sources, serving *inter alia* to enhance the comparability of the material.

The UCDP regularly scrutinizes and revises the selection and combination of sources in order to maintain a high level of reliability and comparability between regions and countries. One important priority is to arrive at a balanced combination of sources of different origin with a view to avoiding bias. The reliability of the sources is judged using the expertise within the UCDP together with advice from a global network of experts (academics and policy makers). Both the independence of the source and the transparency of its origins are crucial. The latter is important because most sources are secondary, which means that the primary source also needs to be analysed in order to establish the reliability of a report. Each source is judged in relation to the context in which it is published. The potential interest of either the primary or secondary source to misrepresent an event is taken into account, as are the general climate and extent of media censorship. Reports from NGOs and international organizations are particularly useful in this context, to complement media reporting and facilitate cross-checking.The criterion that a source should be independent does not, of course, apply to those sources that are consulted precisely because they *are* biased, such as government documents or rebel groups' Internet sites. The UCDP is aware of the high level of scrutiny required and makes great effort to ensure the authenticity of the material used.

III. Methods

The data on major armed conflicts are compiled by calendar year. They include data on conflict location, type of incompatibility, onset of the armed conflict, warring parties, total number of battle-related deaths, number of battle-related deaths in a given year and change in battle-related deaths from the previous year.[3]

The data on battle-related deaths are given the most attention in the process of coding for the conflict database. Information on, for example, the date, news source, primary source, location and death toll is recorded for every event. Ideally, these individual events and figures are corroborated by two or more independent sources. The figures are then aggregated for the entire year of each conflict. The aggregated figures are compared to total figures given in official documents, in special reports or in the news media. Regional experts, such as researchers, diplomats and journalists, are often consulted during the data collection process. Their role is mainly to clarify the contexts in which the events occur, thus facilitating proper interpretation of the reporting in published sources.

Because very little precise information is publicly available on death figures in armed conflicts, the numbers presented by the UCDP are best viewed as estimates. Rather than always providing exact numbers, ranges are sometimes given. The UCDP is generally conservative when estimating the number of battle-related deaths. Experience shows that, as more in-depth information on an armed conflict becomes available, the conservative, event-based estimates often prove more correct than others widely cited in the news media. If no figures are available or if the numbers given are unreliable, the UCDP does not provide a figure. Figures are revised retroactively each year as new information becomes available.

---

[3] See also the notes for table 2A.3 in appendix 2A.

Appendix 2C. Islam, conflict and terrorism

NEIL J. MELVIN

I. Introduction

In 2005 suicide bomber attacks carried out by individuals with links to Islamist groups in Bangladesh, Jordan and the United Kingdom, as well as the ongoing conflict in Iraq and violence linked to Islamists in Thailand, Uzbekistan and other locations, underlined the continuing threat posed by such groups to security around the globe. With an estimated 18 000 al-Qaeda-trained operatives currently at large in the world, the threat posed by violent Islamist groups appeared as potent during the year as it did immediately after the 11 September 2001 attacks on the United States.[1] Indeed, data collected by the US Department of State indicate that, despite the launch of the 'global war on terrorism' to stop such groups, the incidents of international terrorism had reached at least 655 significant attacks per year by 2004, up from 175 in 2003.[2]

Reflecting the centrality of Islamist terrorism on the contemporary security agenda of the international community, considerable effort has been made to understand the nature of this phenomenon. This appendix outlines the major contours of the debate on the character of Islamist terrorism that have emerged as a result of these efforts. The findings of recent research highlight the diversity of groups and ideas that constitute the Islamist movement today as well as the complex relationship of the movement to Islam, Muslim societies and the international community. The findings also point to a range of factors that have contributed to the emergence of Islamist violence, including terrorism, and draws attention to the dynamism within the Islamist movement.

Research on the emergence and spread of Islamist extremism challenges conventional understandings of the sources of violence within Muslim communities and calls into questions key aspects of current approaches to combating violent Islamist organizations, notably the emphasis on counter-terrorism as the primary means to defeat such groups. Indeed, such research suggests that in some instances the US-led war on terrorism may have served to strengthen the threat of Islamist violence and to have facilitated the employment of harsh and counterproductive policies in areas such as Chechnya, southern Thailand, Uzbekistan and Xinjiang. Instead, these findings suggest that security policy with respect to the Islamist challenge is likely to be more effective if it is based on the integration of a variety of elements—including development, counter-terrorism and conflict prevention policies—in frameworks tailored to address the emergence and development of Islamist violence in specific contexts.

Section II notes the significance for the post-cold war world of conflict related to religion. The emergence of extremist violence linked to Islam is considered with respect to the events of 11 September 2001. Section III explores the main charac-

---

[1] International Institute for Strategic Studies (IISS), *The Military Balance 2004–2005* (Oxford University Press: Oxford, 2004), p. 378.

[2] Glasser, S. B., 'U.S. figures show sharp global rise in terrorism: State Dept. will not put data in report', *Washington Post*, 27 Apr. 2005.

teristics of Islamist terrorism with particular reference to the methods employed by those engaged in violence. It describes the relationship of Islamist violence to Islam and conflict linked to the Muslim world and outlines the principal explanations put forward as to why elements within the Islamist movement have turned to extreme violence. Section IV notes recent developments in the Islamist movement, especially in response to the war on terrorism. The evolving policy response of the international community to the challenge of Islamist violence is considered in the light of evidence of the shortcomings of the initial approach to the issue. The appendix concludes with a discussion of likely future policy directions for more effectively meeting the challenge of Islamist violence.

II. Religion, conflict and terrorism

Recent years have seen important changes in the extent and nature of conflict around the globe, notably as a result of the end of the two-bloc confrontation in the international system. Research data indicate that with the conclusion of the cold war there has been a marked decline in violent conflict,[3] particularly conflict between states. At the same time, while conflict as a whole has decreased, its character has undergone an important shift. Increasingly, it is non-state actors that are involved in conflict.[4] One of the most important sources of conflict has been identified as violence carried out on the basis of culture, ethnicity and religion, although—as the cases of Rwanda, Timor-Leste and the former Yugoslavia highlight—state-based actors continue to have central roles in conflict.[5]

The move away from state-focused conflicts deriving from political and economic disputes towards a more complex type of conflict involving both state and non-state actors—the latter defined, in large part, by different identities—was viewed by some as the onset of conflict between civilizations.[6] Such views have appeared to gain credence with an intensification of new forms of violent extremism, including terrorism.

The changing character of conflict in the world and the threat that this poses have stimulated a broad debate about the security challenges facing both the international community and particular states. In this context, the issue of religion and conflict has received increased attention.[7] Conflict in Afghanistan, Kashmir, Sri Lanka and a number of states in the Middle East, coupled with the rise of religious extremism, has reinforced the view that there is a close and strengthening linkage between religion and conflict.

Religious conflict is not, of course, exclusive to the present day but has existed in various forms for much of known history.[8] Indeed, it has been suggested that violence

[3] University of British Columbia, Human Security Centre, *The Human Security Report 2005: War and Peace in the 21st Century* (Oxford University Press: Oxford, 2005), URL <http://www.human securityreport.info/>.

[4] On non-state actors in conflict see chapter 2 in this volume.

[5] Kaldor, M., *New and Old Wars: Organized Violence in a Global Era* (Polity: Oxford, 2004); and Brubaker, R., *Ethnicity Without Groups* (Harvard University Press: Cambridge, Mass., 2004), pp. 11–18.

[6] See, e.g., Huntington, S. P., *The Clash of Civilizations and the Remaking of the World Order* (Simon & Schuster: London, 1998).

[7] Reychler, L., 'Religion and conflict', *International Journal of Peace Studies*, vol. 2, no. 1 (Jan. 1997), URL <http://www.gmu.edu/academic/ijps/vol2_1/Reyschler.htm>.

[8] Ranstorp, M., 'Terrorism in the name of religion', *Journal of International Affairs*, vol. 50, no. 1 (summer 1996), pp. 41–62.

is an integral part of religion.[9] Even at the height of the cold war and in the post-World War II period of national liberation conflicts, religious conflicts continued to flare. According to one scholar's estimates, throughout the 46-year period 1950–96 religious conflicts constituted 33–47 per cent of all conflicts.[10] Since the end of the cold war, the number of religious conflicts has increased relative to other types of conflict.[11] Moreover, the salience of religion as a factor in conflict has been strengthened by what many see as the emergence in recent decades of a new type of religious-based violence—'cosmic war'.[12] As part of this development, religion has been used as a justification not only for violence but also for terrorism.[13] Within this new environment for conflict, adherents of all the world's major religions—Buddhism, Christianity, Hinduism, Islam, Judaism and Sikhism—have been linked to extremist violence.[14]

The religious terrorism that has emerged, particularly during the 1990s, as part of a 'fourth wave of terrorism' is viewed as being distinct from other forms of terrorism, notably the politically inspired terrorism of the 1970s and 1980s.[15] Religious terrorism tends to 'be more lethal than secular terrorism because of the radically different value systems, mechanisms of legitimization and justification, concepts of morality, and Manichean worldviews that directly affect the "holy terrorists" motivation'.[16] From this view, religion functions as a legitimizing force, specifically sanctioning wide-scale, and often extreme, violence against an almost open-ended category of opponents—since there is little distinction between military combatants and civilians—and having a tendency to 'satanize' enemies. As such, those who practice violence in the name of religion are seen as less prone to compromise or co-option.

While followers of a wide variety of religions have been linked to violent conflict and terrorism, in recent years radical Islamists have been particularly associated with this phenomenon. Indeed, following the attacks by Islamists of 11 September 2001 in the USA, and subsequent attacks in Madrid, Bali and London as well as the use of terrorist methods by groups such as Hamas, Hezbollah and al-Qaeda in the Middle East—notably with respect to the Israel–Palestinian conflict and in the context of the

[9] Juergensmeyer, M., 'Sacrifice and cosmic war', *Terrorism and Political Violence*, vol. 3, no. 3 (1991), pp. 101–17; and Zitrin, S., 'Millenarianism and violence', *Journal of Conflict Studies*, vol. 12, no. 2 (1998), pp. 110–15.

[10] Fox, J., 'Religion and state failure: an examination of the extent and magnitude of religious conflict from 1950 to 1996', *International Political Science Review*, vol. 25, no. 1 (2004), pp. 55, 64.

[11] Fox notes: 'One factor that seems to have influenced the rise of nonreligious conflict is the cold war. During the cold war, nonreligious conflicts became more common than religious conflicts for conflict types but after the cold war all conflict dropped, with nonreligious conflicts dropping more than religious conflicts. If this trend continues, religious conflict will be a common as other types of conflicts'. Fox (note 10), p. 70.

[12] Juergensmeyer, M., *Terror in the Mind of God: The Global Rise of Religious Violence* (University of California Press: Berkeley, Calif., 2001).

[13] Drake, C. J. M., 'The role of ideology in terrorists' target selection', *Terrorism and Political Violence*, vol. 10, no. 2 (1998), pp. 53–85.

[14] Shah, S. A. A., 'Religious terrorism in other faiths', *Strategic Studies*, vol. 25, no. 2 (summer 2005), pp. 126–41.

[15] Rapoport, D. C., 'The four waves of modern terrorism', eds A. Cronin and J. Ludes, *Attacking Terrorism: Elements of a Grand Strategy* (Georgetown University Press: Washington, DC, 2004), pp. 46–73.

[16] Hoffman, B., *Holy Terror: Implications of Terrorism Motivated by a Religious Imperative*, RAND Paper P-7834 (RAND: Santa Monica, Calif., 1993).

civil war in Iraq—Islamist groups have been viewed by many as playing the defining role in contemporary terrorism.

In assigning pre-eminence to Islamist groups, observers have sought to draw a distinction between the practices of such groups and other forms of terrorism.[17] The Islamist terrorism that has emerged in recent years is identified as enigmatic in character and as lacking clear political goals and demands. For Islamists, it appears to be the changes brought about by Western modernity per se and secular globalization that they oppose, rather than some distinct set of political, social or economic practices.

On the basis of this understanding, initial accounts of the new Islamist groups, principally al-Qaeda, drew a vivid picture of the organizations engaged in terrorism. Motivated by religious zeal, supported by wealthy individuals (primarily in Saudi Arabia) and composed of individuals skilled in the use of modern technology (the mass media and the Internet), as well as able to employ highly effective tactics (suicide bombing) to conduct their campaign of terror, these organizations were viewed as being especially difficult to combat. These characteristics enabled the Islamist terrorist groups to extend their reach from bases in Afghanistan and other failing states beyond terrorism's previous main operational theatres in Europe and the Middle East to inflict mass and indiscriminate violence in a wide variety of locations.

Having provided the dominant paradigm for understanding contemporary terrorism, Islamist groups have become the primary target for counter-terrorist and military strategies and operations. Reflecting the understanding of the goals, organization and nature of Islamist groups outlined above, the principal means that have been used to counter the threat of radical Islamists have been to challenge and eliminate the men of violence—the so-called 'capture/kill' policy; to impede and break up the jihadi organizations[18] engaged in terrorism through a variety of security measures (anti-money laundering initiatives, surveillance and heightened security); and to undermine or overthrow the authorities in states that are seen to support Islamist international terrorism.

III. Islamist violence and its context

The methods of Islamist terrorism

As a result of the dramatic impact of Islamist terrorism on Western societies through high-profile attacks, the methods used by Islamist terrorist groups have attracted special scrutiny. Their methods, as much as their motivation and aims, have been seen as setting these groups apart from other terrorist movements. Two particular elements have been closely associated with Islamist terrorism: the use of the modern media and suicide bombing.

Writers on religious extremism have highlighted the essentially symbolic rather than strategic character of violence for terrorist organizations.[19] In this context, the

---

[17] Hoffman, B., 'Testimony: Lessons of 9/11, Joint Inquiry Staff Request, Submitted for the Committee Record to the United States Joint September 11, 2001 Inquiry Staff of the House and Senate Select Committees on Intelligence on October 8, 2002', RAND, Santa Monica, Calif., 2002, URL <http://www.rand.org/pubs/testimonies/2005/CT201.pdf>.

[18] These are militant Islamist groups who believe that they are engaged in a holyt war that justifies the use of extreme violence.

[19] Juergensmeyer (note 12).

location and time of a violent act take on a special resonance. Such acts are designed not to defeat an enemy but to demonstrate its weakness and to mobilize further support. In order to achieve this aim, terrorism needs an audience, principally someone to terrify. In addition, Islamist terrorists appear to launch attacks with the aim of provoking violent reactions or crackdowns, in part through widespread media coverage, which can strengthen popular support for an organization and aid recruitment.[20] In this sense, there appears to be a strong relationship between the emergence of the modern mass media and the development of religious terrorism. The symbolic dimension of many acts of terrorism inspired by religion has found a global audience that can be reached quickly and directly.[21] Some have argued that there is a symbiotic relationship between terrorism and the modern mass media.[22]

Islamist terrorist groups, more than other groups, have understood and manipulated the global media. Al-Qaeda and the wider jihadi movement are relevant as long as they can stay in the news, and dramatic instances of violence have proved to be the best way to achieve this. The emergence of Arab television stations has been a factor in raising the profile of such groups, although jihadi leaders have expressed frustration that their message is not conveyed as they would wish through these stations.[23] The Internet has also been a vital tool that terrorists have been able to utilize:[24] there is considerable evidence that Islamist groups have made extensive use of the Internet for propaganda and organizational purposes and that it has also served as a medium for building a community of like-minded activists.[25] In the five years after 2000 the number of jihadi websites was reported to have increased from fewer than 20 to more than 4000.[26]

The expansion of the global financial system has provided new opportunities to channel resources quickly and confidentially to terrorist cells.[27] At the same time, the ability to move rapidly from one location to another throughout the world and to communicate quickly have together been additional elements in developing and sustaining international Islamist terrorist networks.

Perhaps more than any other aspect of Islamist terrorism, the suicide bomber has come to define to the outside world the movement—combining, in a devastating act, fanaticism with an almost unstoppable threat. The popular image of suicide terrorists has been one of lonely, poor, unemployed young people with no real prospects, who feel that they are desperate and who find comfort among extremists advocating a medieval-style religious fervour. However, recent studies have highlighted the com-

[20] Schiffauer, W., 'Production of fundamentalism: on the dynamics of producing the radically different', eds H. de Vries and S. Weber, *Religion and Media* (Stanford University Press: Stanford, Calif., 2001), pp. 435–55.

[21] Schmid, A. P., 'Frameworks for conceptualising terrorism', *Terrorism and Political Violence*, vol. 16, no. 2 (summer 2004), p. 207.

[22] See, e.g., Wilkinson, P., 'The media and terrorism: a reassessment', *Terrorism and Political Violence*, vol. 9, no. 2 (summer 1997), pp. 51–64.

[23] Miles, H., *Al-Jazeera: How Arab TV News Challenged the World* (Abacus: London, 2005).

[24] Weimann, G., *How Modern Terrorism Uses the Internet*, United States Institute for Peace (USIP) Special Report 116 (USIP: Washington, DC, 2004).

[25] Wright, L., 'The terror web: were the Madrid bombings part of a new, far-reaching jihad being plotted on the Internet?', *New Yorker*, 2 Aug. 2004.

[26] Study by Marc Sageman cited in Atran, S., 'The "virtual hand" of jihad', *Terrorism Monitor* (Jamestown Foundation), vol. 3, issue 10 (19 May 2005), URL <http://www.jamestown.org/terrorism/news/article.php?articleid=2369701>.

[27] Haslerud, G. and Tranøy, B. S., Forsvarets Forskningsinstitutt (FFI), *Fighting Terrorist Finance: Issues, Impacts and Challenges*, FFI/Rapport 2005/02100 (Norwegian Defence Research Establishment: Kjeller, 2005).

plexity of the elements that produce suicide bombers. Not only have these studies challenged common perceptions about who becomes a suicide terrorist but they have also shed new light on the nature of the act itself.

Analysis of the sociology of Islamist suicide terrorists suggests that the bombers have come from a diversity of backgrounds but that in recent years there is an increasingly common profile. Those who planned and carried out the September 2001 aircraft hijackings, for example, were mostly highly educated, middle class professionals.[28] Mohamed Atta was an architect; Ayman al-Zawahiri, Osama bin Laden's second in command, was a pediatric surgeon; and Ziad Jarrah, one of the founders of the al-Qaeda Hamburg cell, was a dental student who later turned to aircraft engineering. The new generation of global jihadis is not composed of the urban poor from underdeveloped societies so much as 'the privileged children of an unlikely marriage between Wahhabism and Silicon Valley, which al-Zawahiri visited in the 1990s. They were heirs not only to jihad and the umma but also to the electronic revolution and American-style globalization'.[29] Indeed, many of the suicide bombers appear to have had little religious background.

While religion is not seen per se as being at the heart of suicide bombing, it does appear to reinforce this method of violence by providing incentives through the notion of 'martyrdom'.[30] The heroic death is the ultimate sacrifice, in which 'martyrs' give up their lives for the community, but it is also part of the narrative of good and evil that underpins 'cosmic war'. The creation of heroes is also a means to demonize the enemy.[31]

Work on the motivation of Palestinian bombers has suggested that the construction of new interpretations of sacrifice/martyrdom by jihadi groups (al-Qaeda, Hamas, Hezbollah and others) in loose connection with traditional Islamic theology has been vital to the development of such acts. At the same time, the local community's support for these ideas as part of a national–religious struggle to establish a Palestinian nation state has been a necessary condition for suicide bombers to operate.[32] In this sense, religion and nationalism combine and give suicide bombing a distinctly political character.

Other research has also questioned accounts that identify suicide bombing as being motivated primarily by a religious impulse. Instead, it has been suggested that suicide bombing is a highly effective tactical weapon designed to achieve strategic political aims. It was, in fact, in the context of the conflict in Sri Lanka that suicide bombing became most developed during the 1990s, rather than in connection with the activities of Islamist groups. The factor that emerges as the principal objective for suicide bombing, according to this account, is an effort to compel foreign powers to with-

---

[28] McDermott, T., *Perfect Soldiers: The Hijackers: Who They Were, Why They Did It* (Politicos: London, 2005).

[29] Kepel, G., *The War for Muslim Minds: Islam and the West* (Harvard University Press: Cambridge, Mass., 2004). Umma refers, literally, to the community of believers and thus the whole Islamic world.

[30] Oliver, A. M. and Steinberg, R. F., *The Road to Martyr's Square: A Journey into the World of the Suicide Bomber* (Oxford University Press: Oxford, 2005).

[31] Juergensmeyer (note 12), pp. 164–84.

[32] Strenski, I., 'Sacrifice, gift and the social logic of muslim "human bombers"', *Terrorism and Political Violence*, vol. 15, no. 3 (autumn 2003), pp. 1–34.

draw military forces from the occupation of territory that the bombers view as their homeland.[33]

The dramatic upsurge of suicide attacks in recent years has, however, led some to question the idea that suicide terrorism is always the product of organized campaigns aimed at achieving clear political goals, such as national liberation. While political motivation may have informed suicide terrorism in Chechnya and the West Bank, this does not appear to be the case for many of the recent attacks.[34] Studies based on interviews of would-be suicide bombers suggest that at the root of the actions by persons engaged in religious-based suicide bombing is a sense of humiliation in their own lives or a close identification with others who have faced humiliation.[35] Furthermore, these accounts suggest that in order to understand how terrorist networks cohere to act on the sense of humiliation it is necessary to pay close attention to the psychology of small groups and the role of values, for it is these together that can furnish the means to override rational self-interest to produce extreme violence in ordinary people.[36]

The idea that the nature of suicide terrorism may be changing is reinforced by analysis of the bombings that have been carried out following the launch of the US-led war on terrorism. Research suggests that 81 per cent of the suicide attacks that have occurred since 1968 have taken place after the terrorist attacks of September 2001. Moreover, 31 of the 35 groups held responsible for recent attacks are Islamist militants.[37] The motivation of the jihadis that emerges from such work is not the desire to achieve a specified political goal but to oppose a perceived global evil—usually the West.

Work on this new generation of jihadi terrorists—those who have targeted the USA and the West, rather than those involved in the nationalist struggles of Chechnya, Kashmir or Palestine—has provided a more detailed profile of suicide terrorists.[38] Groups like al-Qaeda appear in this account as a network of self-selected individuals who are technically skilled and in many cases multilingual. Most are from middle class backgrounds and are university educated; they are geographically and upwardly mobile. The average age of suicide bombers is 26 years, most of them are married, and many have children. The bombers usually only became religious after they had joined a jihadi organization. Because they were the best and the brightest, they were sent abroad to study. More than 80 per cent of known jihadis live in diaspora communities, often marginalized from the host society, and in hard-to-penetrate social networks that consist of about 70 per cent friends and 20 per cent family. Seeking a sense of community, many of these small groups bond as they surf on jihadi websites to find direction and purpose. This is very different from the usual terrorist of the past, someone from one country, living in that country and targeting that country's government.[39]

[33] Pape, R. A., *Dying to Win: The Strategic Logic of Suicide Terrorism* (Random House: New York, N.Y., 2005); and Gambetta, D. (ed.), *Making Sense of Suicide Missions* (Oxford University Press: Oxford, 2005).

[34] Atran, S. and Stern, J., 'Small groups find fatal purpose through the web', *Nature*, vol. 437, no. 7059 (29 Sep. 2005), p. 620.

[35] Stern, J., *Terror in the Name of God* (Harper Collins: New York, N.Y., 2003)

[36] Atran and Stern (note 34).

[37] Research by Bruce Hoffman, of the RAND Center for Terrorism Risk Management Policy in Washington, DC, cited in Atran and Stern (note 34).

[38] Sageman, M., *Understanding Terror Networks* (University of Pennsylvania Press: Philadelphia, Pa., 2004).

[39] Sageman (note 38).

The sources of Islamist jihad

The emergence of radical Islamist groups as the principal source of international terrorism has promoted considerable debate about the challenge of countering these terrorist groups. A key question concerns the factors that have promoted the emergence and expansion of such groups. One influential interpretation has highlighted a profound and deep-seated crisis within Islam as the ultimate source of the problems in Muslim society that have produced terrorism.[40] In this view, it is the failure of Islam to come to terms with modernity and a backlash against change focused on a revival of tradition that have driven the emergence of fundamentalist politics (the Iranian Revolution) and later neo-fundamental jihadi groups. In this theory it is therefore the opposition to modernity within Muslim communities that stands in the way of democratization in the Arab states of the Middle East, rather than more specific political factors such as the Israel–Palestine conflict.[41]

Those who argue that Muslims have, in fact, been held back by key elements within their own societies—the military and corrupt elites, usually in collusion with the West—provide a contrasting view. The rise of Islamist radicalism occurs, from this perspective, because Muslims live in societies that are repressive and exclusionary and in which political participation is prevented. In this environment, it is argued, the only effective means to achieve political change is through violence and militancy.[42] Furthermore, it is noted that in many contexts, notably where Muslims form minorities, it is secular and non-Muslim governments and majority non-Muslim populations that appear to have instigated violence against Muslim communities.

Explanations of Islamist militancy that focus on a process of deep-seated reaction within the Muslim world—either as a result of internal or external reasons—have been challenged by scholarship based on the study of jihadi groups and on the actual practice of Islam in various contemporary contexts, including Muslim communities outside the Middle East. In contrast to the image of al-Qaeda that was often presented following the September 2001 attacks on the USA—as an Islamist front united in armed struggle or jihad at the vanguard of Muslim discontent with the (Christian) West—these studies paint a rather different picture. Al-Qaeda emerges instead as a minority group within the jihadist movement, with its strategies criticized and opposed by religious nationalists among the jihadis, who prefer to concentrate on changing the Muslim world rather than launching a global fight.[43]

Other writers have questioned the view that the Islamist groups represented by al-Qaeda and other radical factions constitute a unique form of terrorism. Instead, they note that such groups share much in common with other global movements, such as environmentalists and anti-globalization protesters.[44] The similarities include a decentralized organization and an emphasis on ethical rather than properly political

[40] Lewis, B., *The Crisis of Islam: Holy War and Unholy Terror* (Weidenfeld & Nicolson: London, 2003).

[41] Lewis, B., *What Went Wrong? Western Impact and Middle Eastern Response* (Oxford University Press: Oxford, 2002).

[42] Hafez, M. M., *Why Muslims Rebel: Repression and Resistance in the Islamic World* (Lynne Reiner: Boulder, Colo., 2003).

[43] Gerges, F. A., *The Far Enemy: Why Jihad Went Global* (Cambridge University Press: Cambridge, 2005).

[44] Devji, F., *Landscapes of the Jihad: Militancy, Morality and Modernity* (C. Hurst & Co: London, 2005).

action. Such an analysis of the new jihadi groups locates them squarely within the transformation of political thought after the cold war. The ideas that have emerged associated with the jihadi organizations are neither dogmatic in a traditional sense nor comprehensive in the sense of modern ideologies (fascism or communism); they are concerned neither with correct doctrinal practice in the present nor with some revolutionary utopia of the future. Instead, current jihadi theology is fragmented, disparate and individualistic. The jihadi movement thus emerges from the breakdown of authority in the Muslim world, both traditional religious and secular modern forms, and the failure of Islamic fundamentalism to take hold beyond Iran.[45]

Indeed, from such a perspective the source of conflict for Islamist groups is not situated in the traditional culture and beliefs of Muslim societies but rather in the decoupling of religion from culture (in the sense of the specific forms of Islam practised in various locations around the globe). The jihadi movement, in this interpretation, becomes not an expression of traditional religion—a protest of original cultures under threat or a 'clash of civilizations'—but a reflection of these cultures' disappearance. Thus, the rise and spread of jihadi networks is not a reaction to the West derived from tradition but rather a symptom of Islam being transformed by Westernization and globalization.[46]

A vital element of the sociology of modern Islam that underpins this change is a movement of political activity and theological innovation away from the Muslim communities rooted in the traditional cultures of the Middle East and Central Asia to the newly self-conscious Muslim communities in the West, particularly in Europe. The origins of this movement are diverse. A key development was the rise of Islamist mobilization, usually of a peaceful character, especially in British India as a response to colonial rule and the growth of the Muslim Brotherhood in Egypt, Iraq, Palestine and Syria in the first half of the 20th century. The subsequent emergence of splits in the Islamist movement and the scattering of splinter groups across the Middle East and Asia promoted an increased pluralism of theological views within Muslim communities. The migration in recent decades of substantial numbers of Muslims from their traditional homelands to Europe and the USA has also served to challenge long-standing structures of authority rooted in traditional religious practices.

The spread of Islam around the globe has, in particular, blurred the connection between Islam, a specific society and a territory. One-third of the world's Muslims now live as members of a minority. At the heart of this development is, on the one hand, the voluntary settlement of Muslims in Western societies and, on the other, the pervasiveness and influence of Western cultural models and social norms within these immigrant communities. Research on these communities suggests that the 'neofundamentalism' that informs the jihadi movement has been gaining ground among a rootless Muslim youth—particularly among the second- and third-generation migrants in the West—and this phenomenon is feeding new forms of radicalism, ranging from support for al-Qaeda to the outright rejection of integration into Western society.

In this context Islamic revival, or 're-Islamization', thus results from the efforts of Westernized Muslims to assert their identity in a non-Muslim context. As a result, a schism exists between many of the mainstream Islamist movements in the Muslim world—including Hamas in Palestine and Hezbollah in Lebanon—with a focus on

---

[45] Roy, O., *The Failure of Political Islam* (Harvard University Press: Cambridge, Mass., 1994).

[46] Roy, O., *Globalised Islam: The Search for a New Ummah* (Columbia University Press: New York, N.Y., 2004).

national struggles and the uprooted militants who strive to establish an imaginary umma that is not embedded in any particular society or territory, whether by violent means, like al-Qaeda, or peacefully, like Hizb-ut Tahrir.[47] Indeed, the contradictions between the aims of global jihadi groups and the more nationalist insurgency in Iraq have been identified as a principal obstacle to the formation of a single, coordinated movement to challenge the US-led occupation.[48]

The picture of the contemporary Muslim world has been further clouded by analysis of the Islamist movements in different countries. Such work has highlighted the diversity of factors that have promoted the rise of Islamist politics and the turn to violence. In Pakistan, for example, the role of the state as an agent promoting radical Islam has been identified as a key factor behind the emergence of Islamist groups.[49] Elsewhere, the intersection of local conditions with domestic Islamist groupings, often linked to the global jihadi network, has fostered new and diverse forms of radicalism.[50] At the same time, such research has in many cases, for example in Africa, highlighted the constraints on radicalization and the challenges involved in governing nation states on the basis of political Islam.[51]

Thus, rather than a static vision of Islamic society which informs many previous accounts of the relationship between Islam and Western society, a significant number of recent studies offer a picture of a dynamic and diverse Muslim world—a world undergoing a turbulent transformation in which tradition is being challenged. This transformation is taking place in a variety of geographical locations and involves different issues and actors. At its heart is a struggle over the interpretation of Islam in the light of theological innovations, such as Wahhabism and Salafism.[52] Within this struggle, relations to the West and to characterizations of the nature of Western society have become a key issue and violence a means of enforcing and highlighting new thinking.

IV. New developments and responses

The changing nature of Islamist terrorism

The West's increased understanding since 11 September 2001 of the complexity and dynamism that characterize the Muslim world has also brought an awareness that one of the principal challenges for countering international terrorism stemming from

---

[47] Hizb-ut Tahrir seeks to replace what it characterizes as the Judeo-Christian-dominated nation state system with a borderless umma ruled by a new Caliph. Despite the organization's avowed opposition to violence, the radical nature of its ideas and the practice of indoctrination of recruits has led some, including governments in Europe and Central Asia, to ban the organization. Baran, Z., 'Fighting the war of ideas', *Foreign Affairs*, Nov./Dec. 2005, pp. 68–78.

[48] Ulph, S., 'Al-Zarqawi's group under pressure and seeking allies', *Terrorism Focus* (Jamestown Foundation), vol. 3, issue 2 (18 Jan. 2006), URL <http://jamestown.org/terrorism/news/article.php?articleid=2369867>.

[49] Khan, A. U., *The Terrorist Threat and the Policy Response in Pakistan*, SIPRI Policy Paper no. 11 (Sep. 2005), URL <http://www.sipri.org>.

[50] See the reports on Islamist movements in a wide variety of countries on the website of the International Crisis Group, URL <http://www.icg.org>.

[51] De Waal, A. (ed.), *Islamism and Its Enemies in the Horn of Africa* (Indiana University Press: Bloomington, Ind., 2004).

[52] Stanley, T., 'Understanding the origins of Wahhabism and Salafism', *Terrorism Monitor* (Jamestown Foundation), vol. 3, issue 14 (15 July 2005), URL <http://jamestown.org/terrorism/news/article.php?articleid=2369746>.

Islamist groups is the evolving character of the Islamist movement itself. A particular stimulus for recent change has come as a consequence of the 'global war on terrorism'. As a result of concerted international action against al-Qaeda and affiliated groups, the original terrorist organizations have been broken up and their leaders killed, arrested or forced into hiding. The jihadi movement has not, however, disappeared but has changed to become a 'networked transnational constituency rather than the monolithic, international terrorist organization with an identifiable command and control apparatus that it once was'.[53]

Analysts now characterize the movement as divided into four distinct but not mutually exclusive dimensions including a range of affiliates, associates, local groups and a network that works in support of al-Qaeda. Affiliates include Abu Sayyaf, Jemmah Islamiyah, Ansr Al Islam and Jamaat Yarmuk in the North Caucasus, although there is considerable doubt about the degree to which al-Qaeda and its 'affiliates' constitute genuine organizations rather than loose collections of like-minded individuals. The Islamist movement has thus transformed into a diffuse and amorphous ideological movement that may have become essentially leaderless.[54] Indeed, as a result of these changes some have argued that the threat of Islamist terrorism is greater today than before September 2001, with fragments of al-Qaeda dispersed in locations including Kashmir, the southern Philippines and Yemen.[55]

As well as transforming the organizational character of the jihadi movement, many of the measures undertaken in the name of the global war on terrorism also appear to have assisted in shifting thinking within radical Islamist circles, reinforcing the arguments of those who believe that the violent struggle should not be focused on particular countries but on the real enemy: the Western world and its influences.[56] This change has fostered an intensification of contacts between local, regional and international terrorist networks. The invasion of Iraq, and to a lesser extent the intervention in Afghanistan, appears to have done much to promote a strengthened resolve among jihadi activists around the globe. These interventions have especially fostered political solidarity between groups located in long-standing areas of Muslim settlement and the new migrant Muslim communities in Europe, as indicated in video testimony that has appeared on jihadi websites—notably the statements by al-Zawahiri and Mohammad Sidique Khan, one of the London bombers. Indeed, there is evidence that the invasion of Iraq and the subsequent civil war have become a recruiting vehicle for militant organizations.[57]

Evolving responses to the Islamist challenge

The complex relationship of the Islamist movement to Islam as well as to specific Muslim communities around the globe, coupled with the increasingly decentralized structure of jihadi groups, raises major questions about the most appropriate way to

---

[53] Hoffman, B., 'Does our counter-terrorism strategy match the threat?', Testimony presented before the House International Relations Committee, Subcommittee on International Terrorism and Nonproliferation, 29 Sep. 2005, RAND, Santa Monica, Calif., 2005, URL <http://www.rand.org/pubs/testimonies/2005/RAND_CT250-1.pdf>.

[54] Bokhari, F., 'Al-Qaeda leader "has lost control of militants"', *Financial Times*, 13 Dec. 2005, p. 4.

[55] Knowlton, B., 'Greater-than-ever risk of terror is seen by U.S.', *International Herald Tribune*, 3 Feb. 2006.

[56] Mattera, O., 'Jihad, from localism to globalism', *CeMiSS Quarterly*, summer 2005, pp. 9–21.

[57] Jehl, D., 'Iraq may be prime place for training militants, CIA report concludes', *New York Times*, 22 June 2005. On Iraq see also chapters 1 and 2 in this volume.

combat this form of terrorism. Growing recognition of the difficulties involved in countering Islamist terrorism has led some to conclude that 'it cannot be destroyed or defeated in a single tactical, military engagement or series of engagements'.[58] The criticism of the initial approach to countering the rise of Islamist groups and the shortcomings that have been identified in key policies have not gone unnoticed in policy circles. Increased awareness of the nature of the challenge has also promoted discussion about the appropriate approach to counter-terrorism and to combating the rise of violent extremism within Muslim communities.

From the outset of the intensification of measures against Islamist terrorist groups after September 2001, distinct approaches have been employed by, for example, the USA and Europe, perhaps reflecting their different strategic cultures.[59] The USA has tended to employ a 'national security' approach to the terrorist threat and has emphasized unilateralism. In contrast, Europe, based on its past experience of terrorism, has adopted a regulatory style pursued through multilateralism—although Europe, too, has been characterized by differences over counter-terrorism.[60] These divergences in approach, with potentially major implications for the future of the transatlantic relationship, have appeared to be mitigated by a revised US approach to counter-terrorism that emerged in 2005. In the latter, the US Administration recognized that the war on terrorism is not to be viewed as an exclusively military endeavour but also involves fundamental and parallel political, social, economic and ideological activities. As such, it is a struggle with violent extremism that constitutes the principal task for the USA rather than a war on terrorism.[61] This new view of the threats posed by Islamist groups has led analysts in the USA to argue that what is required is not just cooperation but also collaboration to counter the decentralized extremist groups.[62]

Such changes have raised important questions about the utility of the concept of terrorism as a primary means to understand the security challenge posed by Islamist groups and by which to organize the appropriate response. Historically, providing a definition of terrorism has been controversial and, as a result, elusive. In recent years a growing consensus has emerged around the idea that it is methods rather than aims and identities that should provide the means to define terrorism.[63] Such an interpretation has found support from the majority of states and it was this approach that informed United Nations Security Council Resolution 1617, which sought to define terrorist methods.[64] This non-political definition of terrorism appears to have won endorsement from some states, at least in part because it assisted them in their struggles with violent challenges to their authority without engaging with the complex issue of the contexts, including state policies, that help to bring forth such

[58] Hoffman (note 53).

[59] Rees, W. and Aldrich, R. J., 'Contending cultures of counterterrorism: transatlantic divergence or convergence?', *International Affairs*, vol. 81, issue 5 (Oct. 2005), pp. 905–23.

[60] Keohane, D., *The EU and Counter-terrorism* (Centre for European Reform: London, May 2005).

[61] Schmidt. E. and Shanker, T., 'Washington recasts terror as "struggle"', *International Herald Tribune*, 27 July 2005; and Shanker, T., 'U.S. crafts a precise strategy to halt terror', *International Herald Tribune*, 5 Feb. 2006.

[62] Gunaratna, R., 'Responding to the post 9/11 structural and operational challenges of global jihad', *Connections*, vol. 4, issue 1 (spring 2005), pp. 9–42, URL <http://www.isn.ethz.ch/pubs/ph/details.cfm?id=10676>; and US Department of Defense, *Quadrennial Defense Review Report*, 6 Feb. 2006, URL <http://www.defenselink.mil/qdr/report/Report20060203.pdf>, pp. 87–91.

[63] Schmid (note 21), pp. 197–221.

[64] UN Security Council Resolution 1617, 29 July 2005.

violence, including terrorism.[65] Indeed, it has been suggested that in certain cases the popular political support that can result from the engagement of authorities in combating 'terrorists' has been a leading incentive for waging such conflicts.[66] The September 2005 UN World Summit was unable to agree on a definition of terrorism—despite the call of the UN High-level Panel on Threats, Challenges and Change—in part because of the concern of some states that their actions might be considered as state terrorism within the terms of such a definition.[67]

A focus on methods of terrorism has also won support from those who have stressed counter-terrorism, and the gamut of technical approaches associated with this approach, as the principal means by which to counter Islamist groups. In 2005, however, broad debates emerged both in the UK (with respect to the Terrorism Bill 2005) and the USA (in the light of revelations about the far-reaching measures taken by the US Government in the name of the war on terrorism) about the threat to civil liberties embodied in policies developed to counter the challenge of terrorism.[68] Growing concern about the narrow focus on counter-terrorism approaches to contemporary security threats has led some to conclude that the war on terrorism may be 'a good cause' but the 'wrong concept'.[69]

Despite the paradigm shift beyond military and counter-terrorism approaches to Islamist violence that was visible in 2005, the changes in policy remain relatively modest. Most significantly, there appears to be little elaborated thinking about alternatives to the former security approaches beyond a broad commitment to democratization as a means to stabilize societies that have been identified as sources of Islamist terrorism.[70] Here, too, however, recent research has raised questions about the utility of such an approach. Such work has noted that 'the data available do not show a strong relationship between democracy and an absence of or a reduction in terrorism'.[71] Indeed, genuine democracy in a number of countries with majority Muslim populations, notably in the Middle East, could be expected to give rise to powerful Islamist political movements or even governments. Such suggestions appeared to be confirmed by the strong showing of the Muslim Brotherhood in Egypt in elections in 2005 and the victory of Hamas in Palestinian elections in 2006.

While democratization might help to marginalize Islamic neo-fundamentalists and to discredit violence as a political tool, it cannot be expected to dispel, at least in the short term, the sense of economic and cultural alienation and humiliation that appears

[65] Human Rights Watch, 'In the name of counter-terrorism: human rights abuses worldwide', URL <http://hrw.rg/un/chr59/counter-terrorism-bck4.htm>.

[66] Baev, P. K., 'Putin's counter-terrorism: the parameters of a strategic dead-end?', *Small Wars and Insurgencies*, vol. 17, no. 1 (Mar. 2006), pp. 1–21.

[67] Lynch, C., 'Bolton voices opposition to U.N. proposals', *Washington Post*, 1 Sep. 2005. For the documents of the World Summit, held on 14–16 Sep. 2005 at the UN General Assembly, see URL <http://www.un.org/summit2005/>; and for the report of the High-level Panel see United Nations, 'A more secure world: our shared responsibility', Report of the High-level Panel on Threats, Challenges and Change, UN documents A/59/565, 4 Dec. 2004, and A/59/565/Corr.1, 6 Dec. 2004, URL <http://www.un.org/ga/documentation/list5.html>.

[68] Press Association, 'Terror plans thrown out by Lords', *The Guardian*, 18 Jan. 2006, URL <http://www.guardian.co.uk/terrorism/story/0,,1689069,00.html>; and the Amnesty International USA website, URL <http://www.amnestyusa.org/waronterror/index.do>.

[69] Andréani, G., '"The war on terror": good cause, wrong concept', *Survival*, vol. 46, no. 4 (winter 2004/2005), pp. 31–50.

[70] Dalacoura, K., 'US democracy promotion in the Arab Middle East since 11 September 2001: a critique', *International Affairs*, vol. 81, no. 5 (2005), pp. 963–79.

[71] Gregory Gause III, F., 'Can democracy stop terrorism?', *Foreign Affairs*, vol. 84, no. 5 (Sep./Oct. 2005), p. 62.

to motivate key sections of the movement. In this context, certain groups are likely to be impervious to efforts at political and socio-economic accommodation and to remain implacably wedded to the concept of violent jihad. Further democracy, with its focus on the concerns of nation states, would not automatically draw Islamist radicals into the political process. Groups such as al-Qaeda have tended not to concern themselves overly with nationalist causes, especially the Palestinian uprising, even if there is a strong Islamic element in them, and they have been disinclined to work towards the establishment of an Islamic nation state. Instead, the focus has been on the global jihad.

V. Conclusions: new approaches to Islamist violence

The research reviewed above highlights that the Islamist terrorist movement that has developed in recent decades has done so against the background of an increase in religious violence and the emergence of new forms of terrorism around the globe. At the same time, much of this work challenges, explicitly and implicitly, the notion of a growing conflict between civilizations and the suggestion that religious, non-state actors have come largely to determine the character of contemporary conflict. Instead, recent studies point to the greater complexity of conflict, within which different types of violence—including terrorism—are carried out by a variety of actors and with a range of motivations. As such, Islamist violence seems at least related to other types of conflict.

In terms of organization and methods, the Islamist movement, particularly in its early incarnation, appears to be similar in many respects to a number of religious- and non-religious-based terrorist organizations that have emerged over the past two decades. In this sense, the rise of Islamist terrorism can only be understood in the context of the interrelated social, political and economic dynamics that are shaping the world. This is not to downgrade the role of particular leaders and organizations within the jihadi movement or their actions to develop the movement and to focus it on certain issues. Rather, it is to note that the emergence of such organizations and their ability to operate have been contingent upon and contributed to the ongoing process of change that is affecting traditional Muslim communities and the new Muslim minority communities that have developed as a result of large-scale emigration, especially to Western Europe.

While research on Islamist terrorism has underlined that the phenomenon needs to be understood in a broad context, its prominence as an issue for the international community suggests that it does, nevertheless, possess distinct characteristics, even if these are essentially ones of degree rather than quality. Given this, a key issue becomes the precise nature of the linkage between Islamist groups, Islam and the diverse Muslim communities around the world. The picture that emerges from the studies that have been undertaken on this issue is a complex one. Islamist terrorist groups are generally characterized by relatively weak links to formal Islam and to the traditional institutions of Islam. While jihadi groups profess to be engaged in a holy war on behalf of their faith, this is a self-proclaimed war in which traditional Islam is as much the target as is the West. Moreover, a number of other factors, notably the bonds of kinship and the psychology of small groups, appear to play at least as important a role as religious conviction in maintaining group identity and cohesiveness.

At the same time, groups such as al-Qaeda are an intrinsic part of the struggle to define Islam in the modern world, and many of their actions, such as suicide bombings, only make sense when viewed through the lens of religious conventions, old or new. Furthermore, although suicide bombers appear most often to have weak links to formal Islam, those undertaking bombing missions seem to understand their actions in terms of religion—as martyrdom. This sense is reinforced in some contexts, particularly the struggle over the state of Palestine, where significant parts of the local community support these actions and express that support in religious and quasi-religious forms.

The relationship of Islamist terrorist groups to Islam is further complicated by the diversity within the Muslim world, which makes straightforward generalizations difficult. The Muslim world is fractured by various fault lines, including between Shia and Sunni, between Arab and non-Arab, as well as socio-culturally in terms of *inter alia* ethnic, tribal and clan divisions.[72] In a number of contexts, such as the North Caucasus, southern Thailand and Palestine, religious motivations for violence are interwoven, even fused, with separatist aspirations and long-standing ethno-national conflicts involving Muslim communities.

Five years after the attacks on the USA that led to the launch of the 'global war on terrorism', understanding of the factors that have produced Islamist terrorism has advanced considerably. At the same time, this increased understanding has brought with it a growing realization that the phenomenon itself is complex, consisting of economic, social, cultural, demographic and political elements. Furthermore, the rise of Islamist violence has occurred in diverse forms in a variety of locations and continues to undergo transformation. Reflecting this better understanding, concern has mounted that a number of the key initiatives that have been launched in response to Islamist terrorist attacks have in fact been counter-productive, provoking a strengthening of the global jihadi movement. Together, these developments suggest that further change can be expected in international policies in respect to this issue.

The dominance in recent years of approaches to Islamist violence based primarily on counter-terrorism appears likely to weaken as increased efforts are made to fashion comprehensive policies that take into account the range of factors affecting the emergence and spread of extremist groups. Such initiatives will need to combine developmental, diplomatic, and political and counter-terrorism approaches within an integrated framework of measures if they are to be effective.[73] As recent research underlines, however, such approaches are only likely to succeed if they are employed in the context of a strategy that takes careful account of the diversity of outlooks within political Islamism and in different locations. In this regard it will be important to ensure that the appropriate balance of policies is employed in long-standing conflict environments involving Muslim communities in ethno-national struggles— for example, the North Caucasus, the Philippines, Somalia and southern Thailand—in order to prevent them from emerging as incubators for new Islamist extremist movements.[74]

[72] Rabasa, A. et al., *The Muslim World After 9/11* (RAND: Santa Monica, Calif., 2004).

[73] The Danish Government has been thinking along these lines with respect to its overseas aid programme. Danish Ministry of Foreign Affairs, 'Principles governing Danish development assistance for the fight against the new terrorism', 4 July 2005, URL <http://www.um.dk/en/menu/Development Policy/DanishDevelopmentPolicy/FightagainsttheNewTerrorism/>.

[74] International Crisis Group (ICG), *Somalia's Islamists*, Africa Report no. 100 (12 Dec. 2005); and ICG, *Philippines Terrorism: The Role of Militant Islamic Converts*, Asia Report no. 110 (19 Dec. 2005).

A particular area for future attention is likely to be the question of recruitment and the motivations and methods that provide the Islamist movement with a steady flow of new members from a wide variety of countries around the world. While spiritual, financial, and emotional factors have been identified as vital elements for recruitment, evidence suggests that political issues also play a role. In part, the source of such recruits appears to lie in the frustrations born from the failure of the authoritarian political regimes in the Middle East, the weaknesses of the nation state-building approach of the post-colonial era in many parts of the globe, as well as reactions to the economic and political policies pursued by the West in respect to these regions.[75]

Key elements of the 'global war on terrorism' now appear to be further strengthening recruitment. This suggests that if the flow of volunteers to violent Islamist groups is to be challenged effectively, some basic aspects of Western policy will have to be resolved, notably the occupation of Iraq. Failure to secure a lasting peace between Israel and the Palestinians is also likely to stand in the way of efforts to challenge the growth of violent Islamist groups.

At the same time, the internal dynamics of Muslim society emerge as a key factor in both promoting and preventing extremist violence in different contexts and at different times. The events of 2005 also highlighted the increasingly transnational character of Islamist terrorism and the growing significance of the Muslim communities of Europe.[76] For this reason, new approaches to preventing Islamist violence in Africa, Asia and the Middle East are only likely to achieve success if they are coupled with renewed efforts to promote social integration within Western societies.

---

[75] Fuller, G. E., *The Future of Political Islam* (Palgrave Macmillan: London, 2004).

[76] Sendagorta, F., 'Jihad in Europe: the wider context', *Survival*, vol. 47, no. 3 (autumn 2005), pp. 63–72.

3. Peace-building: the new international focus on Africa

SHARON WIHARTA

I. Introduction

Since the end of the cold war the international security agenda has undergone a transformation: it has been broadened and redefined to include a host of new issues ranging from ethnic strife, environmental degradation and transnational organized crime to diseases such as AIDS. The new concept of security is based on a comprehensive understanding of this type of threat and is oriented towards 'human security'.[1] The nature of the new security threats is characterized by their inter-connectedness and their propensity to 'cross borders', making them shared threats. In the light of this normative change Africa is experiencing a geopolitical renaissance: its peace and security concerns have become greater global concerns. This has been attributed partly to the 'global war on terrorism'[2] but also to the fact that certain sub-regions of Africa, mainly West Africa, are becoming significant world providers of oil and gas.

It is against this background that post-conflict peace-building, and in particular the peace missions conducted in Africa, featured prominently on the international peace and security agenda in 2005. *The Human Security Report 2005* showed a strong correlation between the recent sharp decline in armed conflicts and the rise in international engagement, especially in the deployment of peace missions.[3] In the light of the growing recognition of the critical role of peace missions in rebuilding war-affected countries, the international community sought in 2005 to build on recent successes and elaborate comprehensive policies for peace-building. Africa was a particular area of attention and is therefore the central theme of this chapter.

Section II of this chapter examines recent initiatives in the field of global peace-building and human security, in particular the establishment of the United Nations (UN) Peacebuilding Commission. Section III reviews the successes and failures of multilateral peace missions that operated in Africa in 2005 and discusses possible future developments. Section IV presents the con-

[1] On the new security agenda see also chapter 7 in this volume.

[2] Klingebiel, S., 'Africa's new peace and security architecture: converging the roles of external actors and African interests', *African Security Review*, vol. 14, no. 2 (2005), pp. 35–44. E.g., international efforts have been made to stamp out Islamist fundamentalist organizations in Sudan and in other parts of the Horn of Africa.

[3] University of British Columbia, Human Security Centre, *The Human Security Report 2005: War and Peace in the 21st Century* (Oxford University Press: New York, N.Y., 2005), URL <http://www.humansecurityreport.info/>.

clusions. Appendix 3A contains a table with extensive data on the multilateral peace missions that were ongoing or terminated in 2005.

II. Peace-building and human security

The release in early 2005 of major reports by the UN Millennium Project and the British-led Commission for Africa moved the African continent into the focus of international policy discourse and prompted various intergovernmental bodies, such as the UN, the European Union (EU) and the Group of Eight (G8) leading industrialized nations, to re-examine and strengthen their support of Africa's development efforts. Both reports drew attention to the fact that Africa is currently the region that is the farthest from attaining any of the goals set in the Millennium Declaration for 2015 and that 'Sub-Saharan Africa is poorer now than it was 10 years ago'.[4] The Millennium Development Goals (MDGs) list a range of collective actions aimed at eradicating extreme poverty by addressing hunger, disease, lack of adequate shelter and social exclusion—while concomitantly promoting basic human rights, gender equality, education and environmental sustainability, as well as devoting special attention to Africa. The 2000 Millennium Declaration paved the way for an individual rights-based approach to security and development issues and for an emerging consensus that security, development and human rights reinforce each other. Africa has provided pointed illustrations of the negative impact of weak governance and conflict on economic development, as in Liberia, Côte d'Ivoire and Zimbabwe, and also of how strong the turnaround can be when governance improves and conflict is resolved, as in Mali and Mozambique. At the same time there is growing political will in Africa at the national, sub-regional and regional levels to tackle the challenges facing the continent. Consequently, increasing stability, strengthening the continent's own capacity and improving state governance are priority tasks, but none of them can be mastered without external engagement. With only a decade left in which to achieve the Millennium Goals, 2005 represented a critical point for a renewal of the global commitment to Africa.

The United Nations Peacebuilding Commission

The UN High-level Panel on Threats, Challenges and Change recommended in 2004 that a new UN organ be created to address post-conflict peace-building. This proposal was endorsed in September 2005 by the UN World Summit, and in December the Security Council and the General Assembly

---

[4] The final report of the UN Millennium Project, *Investing in Development: A Practical Plan to Achieve the Millennium Development Goals*, and details of each of the 8 Millennium Development Goals and global efforts to achieve them are available at URL <http://www.unmillenniumproject.org>. The report of the Commission for Africa, *Our Common Interest: Report of the Commission for Africa*, is available at URL <http://www.commissionforafrica.org/>. See also Council of the European Union, 'A secure Europe in a better world: European Security Strategy', Brussels, 12 Dec. 2003, URL <http://ue.eu.int/cms3_fo/showPage.ASP?id=266>.

adopted concurrent resolutions on establishing the Peacebuilding Commission.[5] The creation of the Commission was the first tangible achievement of the World Summit, where world leaders gathered to take up *inter alia* proposals for reform of the UN.[6] The Commission is intended to fill the institutional gap between peacekeeping and development activities and further strengthen the UN's capacity for peace-building 'in the widest sense'. On a practical level, it is an attempt to simplify the UN's increasingly convoluted programming procedures. The lack of coordination and complementarity between actors has prevented otherwise sound peace-building strategies from being converted into concrete, sustained achievements.

The three main purposes of the Peacebuilding Commission are: (*a*) to serve as a central node to bring together different international actors, marshal resources, and propose integrated strategies and overall priorities for post-conflict peace-building in general terms and in specific country situations, thus enhancing inter-institutional coordination; (*b*) to focus attention on the reconstruction and institution-building efforts necessary for the functioning of a state; and (*c*) to develop expertise and best practices, with a view above all to ensuring predictable and sustained financing as well as sustained international attention to peace-building activities.[7] The decision not to include conflict prevention in the Commission's purview was seen by many as a realistic compromise because it is too vast and complex an agenda for any one UN body to undertake.[8] The core of the Commission's work is envisaged to be its country-specific activities, notably in the period when countries move from transitional recovery towards development. The Peacebuilding Commission is expected to report on its activities initially to the Security Council and then to the Economic and Social Council (ECOSOC). Acknowledging the need to anchor peace-building efforts in local context and dynamics, the Commission is expected to promote the principle of local ownership where the primacy of local stakeholders is recognized.[9]

The consensus-based Commission will have a 31-member standing Organizational Committee that is responsible for its procedures and organizational matters. Seven of the Committee members will come from the Security Council, including the five permanent members; seven from among the 54 members of ECOSOC; five from the top 10 providers of assessed contributions to UN budgets and of voluntary contributions to UN funds, programmes and agen-

---

[5] UN Security Council Resolution 1645, 20 Dec. 2005, URL <http://www.un.org/documents/scres. htm>; and UN General Assembly Resolution A/RES/60/180, 30 Dec. 2005, URL <http://www.un.org/ documents/resga.htm>. See also United Nations, 'A more secure world: our shared responsibility', Report of the High-level Panel on Threats, Challenges and Change, UN documents A/59/565, 4 Dec. 2004, and A/59/565/Corr.1, 6 Dec. 2004, URL <http://www.un.org/ga/documentation/list5.html>.

[6] On the summit meeeting, held on 14–16 Sep. 2005 at the UN General Assembly, and for the summit documents see URL <http://www.un.org/summit2005/>.

[7] These purposes are listed in UN Security Council Resolution 1645 (note 5), para. 2(a)–(c).

[8] UN General Assembly, 'In larger freedom: towards development, security and human rights for all', Report of the Secretary-General, Addendum: Peacebuilding Commission, UN document A/59/2005/ Add. 2, 23 May 2005.

[9] On local ownership see Hansen, A. S. and Wiharta, S., *Transition to Order after Conflict* (Folke Bernadotte Academy Publications: Stockholm, 2006).

cies; five from the top 10 contributors of military personnel and civilian police to UN peace missions; and seven elected by the General Assembly to ensure geographical balance.[10] When the Commission meets to consider a country-specific situation, it will be enlarged with additional representatives from the national or transitional authorities in question, key UN bodies, international financial institutions and regional organizations. Non-permanent membership of the Organizational Committee is limited to a renewable two-year term and, to avoid double representation, member states may be selected from only one category at any one time. It is uncertain whether the leadership of the Committee will be provided by a senior UN official, as previously suggested by the Secretary-General, or by one of the elected members. The size of the Organizational Committee is twice as large as the Secretary-General originally envisaged, and its complex make-up raises the question whether it will be able to carry out its functions effectively or will become bogged down in the UN's unwieldy bureaucracy.[11] There is also concern that the powers of the Peace-building Commission, which are only advisory in nature, may render the body toothless.

In order to aid the work of the Commission, a small unit was created within the UN Secretariat using existing resources. The main tasks of this Peacebuilding Support Office (PSO) are: (a) to gather and analyse information from the Commission members on their peace-building activities and the availability of financial resources; (b) to contribute to the planning process for peace-building operations; and (c) to conduct best practices analysis and develop policy guidance.[12] However, given the PSO's potentially limited size (approximately 20 staff members) and the fact that the UN Secretariat is per-ennially under-resourced, there is a danger that the PSO will suffer the same fate as most UN departments and barely fulfil the Commission's basic organi-zational and monitoring needs, let alone perform its analytical and policy-forming tasks.[13]

In support of the Peacebuilding Commission, a standing Peacebuilding Fund, financed by voluntary contributions and designed to accelerate the release of funds for the launch of peace-building activities, was established. This step reflects the realization that the implementation of peace-building programmes has in the past often suffered from a lack of resources. It would be more useful for the promotion of sustainable recovery of a post-conflict country if the Fund financed longer-term programmes and activities instead of only quick-impact projects. Ideally, the Fund should also have more resources at its disposal than the proposed level of $250 million.[14] This issue should be

---

[10] In spite of this, strong concerns have been voiced by developing countries that the Commission's composition will still reflect a West European/North American bias.

[11] UN General Assembly (note 8).

[12] UN General Assembly (note 8).

[13] Ponzio, R., *The Creation and Functioning of the UN Peacebuilding Commission*, Saferworld Brief-ing (Saferworld: London, Nov. 2005).

[14] UN General Assembly (note 8).

revisited when the size, the scope of activities to be covered and the manner in which the Fund is to be used are discussed.

The Peacebuilding Commission, the Peacebuilding Support Office and the Peacebuilding Fund are all expected to be operational by mid-2006.[15]

Towards a coherent strategy for Africa

Other multilateral organizations undertook parallel efforts in 2005 to review the Millennium Development Goals. Africa benefited from the happy coincidence that the United Kingdom—a traditionally important actor in Africa—both chaired the 2005 G8 Summit and held the EU Presidency in the last six months of 2005, contributing to putting the continent's security and development needs firmly on the agendas of the Western world. The G8 and the EU collectively represent the largest aid donors, and their development policies have a profound effect on Africa's socio-economic growth. Both organizations have taken a comprehensive approach and share a similar perspective that a wide range of political, economic and social tools exist to address underdevelopment in sub-Saharan Africa. The policy documents of the Commission for Africa and the EU emphasize an equal partnership between Africa and the developed world. For instance, in order to move the principle of ownership from rhetorical expression to practical policy, the EU has indicated that support for budgets (direct contributions to a partner government's budget for sectoral policies) is to be the main form of aid delivery.[16]

Under the coordination of the British Prime Minister, Tony Blair, the Commission for Africa was set up in 2005 to identify the global trends that influence Africa's development and to propose effective policies to tackle the continent's problems.[17] The Commission's findings were presented in March 2005, ahead of the July Gleneagles G8 Summit. The Commission's recommendations included a 100 per cent debt cancellation for the poorest countries, the doubling of official development aid (ODA) for Africa to $25 billion a year by 2010, improved governance of African nations through increasing transparency and stamping out corruption, and further strengthening of key institutions of the African Union (AU) and the New Partnership for Africa's Development (NEPAD).[18] These Commission proposals are aimed at accelerating Africa's progress towards the Millennium Goals. An important element of the recommendations is the focus on promoting African ownership of initiatives and steps to build on Africa's own development efforts. The African Peer Review Mechanism and NEPAD are key instruments: NEPAD

[15] United Nations, Daily press briefing by the offices of the spokesman for the Secretary-General and the spokesperson for the General Assembly President, 2 Feb. 2006.

[16] Commission for Africa (note 4).

[17] The Commissioners included British, other European, US and African experts and dignitaries.

[18] Commission for Africa (note 4); and 'Africa Commission report: analysis,' BBC News Online, 11 Mar. 2005, URL <http://news.bbc.co.uk/1/4337853.stm>. On the AU and NEPAD see, e.g., Adisa, J., 'The African Union: the vision, programmes, policies and challenges', *SIPRI Yearbook 2003: Armaments, Disarmament and International Security* (Oxford University Press: Oxford, 2003), pp. 79–85.

has been endorsed by virtually all international agencies and bilateral donors as the general framework around which the international community should structure its development efforts in Africa.

In July 2005 the G8 Gleneagles Summit adopted many of the proposals advanced by the Commission for Africa. In areas relating to Africa's peace and security structure, the G8 leaders reiterated their previous commitments to support the AU's efforts to build its own peacekeeping forces. To many observers, however, the only concrete commitment made by the G8 was the 100 per cent relief of all debts of eligible heavily indebted poor countries to the International Monetary Fund and other international financial institutions, and the increased financing commitments.[19] The United States pledged to double its aid contribution over the period 2004–10 and created the Millennium Challenge Account with the aim of providing up to $5 billion a year. Similarly, each of the EU member states pledged to give 0.7 per cent of its gross national income in ODA by 2015 with an interim collective target of 0.56 per cent by 2010. Furthermore, it was agreed that the EU will double its ODA between 2004 and 2010, from €34.5 billion to €67 billion, of which half will go to Africa.[20] This was seen by some analysts as a catalytic step and built on lessons learned from the recent experience of Burundi, the Democratic Republic of the Congo (DRC), Iraq and Liberia, which highlighted that debt is often a major issue for countries emerging from conflict.[21] In addition, empirical research shows that increased and targeted aid reduces the risk of recurring conflicts.[22]

The European Commission presented the EU Strategy for Africa in October with a view to reviewing and updating the EU's existing policies and giving the EU a comprehensive, integrated, long-term framework for its relations with Africa.[23] The aim of the Strategy is to strengthen the EU's contribution to reducing poverty and enabling the achievement of the UN's Millennium Development Goals in Africa over the period 2005–15, together with African partners, and to ensure that EU policies are in line with Africa's needs and priorities. It is also aimed at enhancing the EU's political dialogue and broader relationship with Africa and its institutions. For instance, the Strategy highlighted how current relief, rehabilitation and development efforts can be

---

[19] 'Africa: G8 Gleneagles 2005', URL <http://www.g8.gov.uk>.

[20] Group of Eight (G8), 'Financing commitments (as submitted by individual G8 members)', Gleneagles Communiqué, Annex II, 6–8 July 2005, URL <http://www.g8.gov.uk>.

[21] Dwan, R. and Wiharta, S., 'Multilateral peace missions: challenges of peace-building', *SIPRI Yearbook 2005: Armaments, Disarmament and International Security* (Oxford University Press: Oxford, 2005), pp. 158–61.

[22] Collier, P. and Hoeffler, A., 'Aid, policy and growth in post-conflict countries', World Bank Policy Research Working Paper no. 2902, Oct. 2002, URL <http://www-wds.worldbank.org/servlet/WDS ContentServer/WDSP/IB/2002/11/01/000094946_02101904245026/Rendered/PDF/multi0page.pdf>.

[23] The document was adopted by the European Council in Dec. 2005. European Union, 'EU Strategy for Africa: towards a Euro-African Pact to accelerate Africa's development', Communication from the Commission of the European Communities to the Council, the European Parliament and the European Economic and Social Committee, EU document COM(2005) 489 final, Brussels, 12 Oct. 2005, URL <http://europa.eu.int/comm/development/body/communications/docs/eu_strategy_for_africa_12_10_200 5_en.pdf>.

streamlined by using the EU's newly created financing mechanism, the stability instrument.[24] However, the result may be that the EU will have enhanced the flexibility of its financing instruments without necessarily guaranteeing the resources for real growth in security–development activities.[25] The Strategy did not spell out many new initiatives as such, but rather focused on how the EU could utilize existing instruments more effectively, and it highlighted concrete measures for specific countries.

While the dedication of entire summit meetings to issues concerning Africa has contributed political momentum, this will not translate into action if the political and financial commitments are not backed up by actual budget allocations.

III. Peace-building in practice in Africa

In 2005, with over 65 000 personnel deployed in 14 peace missions, Africa was the region with the highest concentration of large, multi-dimensional, costly peace operations (see table 3.1 and figure 3.1).[26] This level of engagement by external actors reflects the ebbing of concerns that they might become embroiled in disasters such as those in Mogadishu or Kigali.[27] Over the past decade the UN has intensified its engagement in Africa and, by December 2005, 75 per cent of UN resources, both personnel and peacekeeping budgets, were devoted to Africa.[28] Nearly half the number of deployed UN peacekeeping personnel are African, a reflection of the 'African solutions for African problems' renaissance. Since 2004 the UN has deployed nine missions in Africa—the highest number recorded since 1991 and the highest for any region.[29] Several of the nine UN missions that were under way in 2005 took place in neighbouring countries—for example, those in Côte d'Ivoire, Liberia and Sierra Leone; and those in Burundi, the DRC and Sudan. Based on this operational reality and on the regional nature of conflicts across the

[24] On the stability instrument see Dewaele, A. and Gourlay, C., 'The stability instrument: defining the Commission's role in crisis response', ISIS Briefing, International Security Information Service, Europe (ISIS Europe), Brussels, 27 June 2005.

[25] Funding for the EU's external actions falls under Heading 4 of the 2007–13 budget cycle. The European Development Fund remains in the intergovernmental framework and is set at €22.7 million for 2008–13. European Union, 'Financial perspective 2007–2013', European Council document no. 15915/05, Brussels, 19 Dec. 2005, URL <http://ue.eu.int/ueDocs/cms_Data/docs/pressData/en/misc/87677.pdf>.

[26] These figures are as of 31 Dec. 2005.

[27] This refers to incidents in Somalia in 1993 and in Rwanda in 1994, when UN peacekeepers in the UN Operation in Somalia and the UN Assistance Mission for Rwanda, respectively, were attacked and drawn into violent confrontations.

[28] Heldt, B. and Wallensteen, P., *Peacekeeping Operations: Global Patterns of Intervention and Success, 1948–2004* (Folke Bernadotte Academy Publications: Stockholm, 2005), p. 21; and United Nations, 'Security Council calls for regional approach in West Africa to address such cross-border issues as child soldiers, mercenaries, small arms', Press release, UN document SC/8037, 25 Mar. 2004.

[29] For an in-depth statistical analysis of peace operations in Africa see Heldt, B., *Patterns of Peacekeeping in Africa* (Folke Bernadotte Academy Publications: Stockholm, forthcoming 2006).

Table 3.1. Number of peace missions in Africa, 1991–2005

Led by	1991	1992	1993	1994	1995	1996	1997	1998	1999	2000	2001	2002	2003	2004	2005
United Nations[a]	1	1	2	8	7	4	4	4	6	5	4	5	6	9	9
Regional organizations	1	1	2	2	2	2	4	5	6	5	3	3	5	5	4
Ad hoc coalitions	–	–	–	1	–	–	1	2	1	1	1	1	1	1	1
Total	**2**	**2**	**4**	**11**	**9**	**6**	**9**	**11**	**13**	**11**	**8**	**9**	**12**	**15**	**14**

[a] UN peace operations are those administered by the UN Department of Peacekeeping Operations or the UN Department of Political Affairs.

Source: SIPRI Peacekeeping Missions Database.

continent, a broad consensus has emerged in the peace-building community on the need for regional approaches.[30] Such approaches would address linkages in regional conflict, prevent conflicts from spreading across borders, and promote sustainable regional economic and social development.

UN peace missions in West Africa

The year 2005 marked the successful completion of the long-standing UN Assistance Mission in Sierra Leone (UNAMSIL). The UN Mission in Liberia (UNMIL) also made salient progress in assisting the National Transitional Government of Liberia (NTGL) to implement the transition priorities set out in the 2003 Comprehensive Peace Agreement,[31] but such results were less apparent in the case of the UN Operation in Côte d'Ivoire (UNOCI). The year also marked the deepening of cooperation between these three missions in terms of joint cross-border patrolling to prevent the illicit movement of small arms, human trafficking, and smuggling of and illegal trade in natural resources; and logistical support and information sharing.[32] UNMIL was also uniquely mandated to assume responsibility for providing security for the Special Court for Sierra Leone, and it was given arrest and detention powers with respect to former Liberian President Charles Taylor.[33]

---

[30] United Nations (note 28).

[31] The Comprehensive Peace Agreement between the Government of Liberia, the Liberians United for Reconciliation and Democracy (LURD), the Movement for Democracy in Liberia (MODEL) and Political Parties was signed on 18 Aug. 2003; for the agreement see URL <http://www.usip.org/library/pa/liberia/liberia_08182003_cpa.html>.

[32] United Nations, Ninth progress report of the Secretary-General on the United Nations Mission in Liberia, UN document S/2005/764, 7 Dec. 2005, paras 26–29.

[33] UN Security Council Resolution 1638, 11 Nov. 2005.

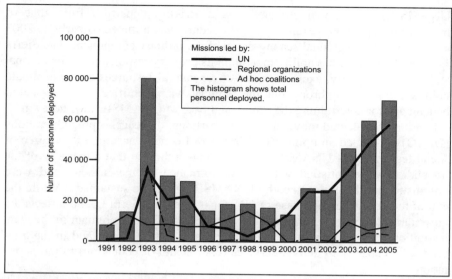

Figure 3.1. Number of personnel deployed in peace missions in Africa led by the United Nations, regional organizations and ad hoc coalitions, 1991–2005

Sierra Leone

At the end of its six-year mandate in 2005, UNAMSIL had accomplished several key elements of its mandate: the mission had disarmed, demobilized and reintegrated more than 72 000 former combatants; assisted in restoring government authority throughout the country; organized both national and local elections; assisted in the rebuilding of the security forces; and repatriated nearly 300 000 refugees.[34] UNAMSIL is heralded as one of the UN's successes, not least because of its remarkable recovery from a near collapse in 2000 after the kidnapping of 500 peacekeepers by rebels of the Revolutionary United Front (RUF).[35]

UNAMSIL was also credited with breaking new ground in a number of areas. It was the first UN mission to employ the integrated mission concept (in which humanitarian aid and development agencies are subsumed in the peace-keeping mission), to 're-hat' a parallel regional peacekeeping force to take over the running of a mission,[36] and to enter into an 'over-the horizon' (rapid reaction reinforcement) arrangement with a bilateral troop contributor.

[34] United Nations, Twenty-fifth report of the Secretary-General on the United Nations Mission in Sierra Leone, UN document S/2005/273, 26 Apr. 2005; and Integrated Regional Information Network for West Africa (IRIN-WA), 'Disarmament and rehabilitation completed after five years', IRIN-WA Weekly Round-up 213, 31 Jan.–6 Feb. 2004.

[35] Reno, W., 'War and the failure of peacekeeping in Sierra Leone', *SIPRI Yearbook 2001: Armaments, Disarmament and International Security* (Oxford University Press: Oxford, 2001), pp. 149–61.

[36] UNAMSIL absorbed the personnel of the Economic Community of West African States Monitoring Group (ECOMOG) in Sierra Leone. United Nations, Presidential Statement, UN document S/PRST/2005/63, 20 Dec. 2005. At the same time, in the former Yugoslavia the UN Protection Force was re-hatted as the NATO-led Implementation Force.

UNAMSIL's drawdown strategy was a striking departure from that of previous missions. For example, the procedure was initiated as early as 2003 and consisted of a gradual scaling down of the military component. The Sierra Leonean Government's ability to assume its primary responsibility for internal and external security, exercise control over natural resources and consolidate civil administration throughout the country was identified as an essential benchmark for determining the timing and pace of UNAMSIL's withdrawal.[37]

In an unprecedented move, the UN Department of Peacekeeping Operations (DPKO) conducted an opinion poll in Sierra Leone to ascertain the degree of social legitimacy of UNAMSIL. The findings indicated that a majority of the population were satisfied with the performance of the mission and were optimistic that the gains made by UNAMSIL would be sustained.[38] While the end of the peacekeeping phase of UN engagement in Sierra Leone reflects the now stable security environment, considerable weaknesses remain in the state institutions, particularly those belonging to the justice sector, and in the government's capacity to deliver services (e.g., health or education) to the population.

A smaller UN presence—the United Nations Integrated Office in Sierra Leone (UNIOSIL)—was established with a strong peace-building mandate to address the shift to 'soft' issues, such as corruption and youth unemployment.[39] One of the central functions of UNIOSIL is to support the government's efforts to implement the country's MDG-based poverty-reduction strategy by coordinating donor support in key areas such as the capacity building of state institutions (including transparency and anti-corruption measures), human rights and the rule of law.[40] In November the Consultative Group for Sierra Leone pledged a total of $800 million for implementation of the strategy over the three-year period 2005–2007.[41]

Liberia

The monumental task of preparing for Liberia's first presidential and parliamentary elections since the end of the 14-year conflict consumed UNMIL's attention for most of 2005. More than 1 million Liberians went to the polls in October and about 800 000 in the November run-off elections, in which Ellen Johnson-Sirleaf was elected president—Africa's first elected

---

[37] United Nations, Fifteenth report of the Secretary-General on the United Nations Mission in Sierra Leone, UN document S/2002/987, 5 Sep. 2002.

[38] Krasno, J., 'Public opinion survey of UNAMSIL's work in Sierra Leone', External study for the Best Practices Unit, UN Department of Peacekeeping Operations, July 2005, URL <http://www.un.org/Depts/dpko/lessons/>.

[39] UNIOSIL was established in Aug. 2005 but was not deployed until 1 Jan. 2006. United Nations Security Council Resolution 1620, 31 Aug. 2005.

[40] United Nations, Twenty-third report of the Secretary-General on the United Nations Mission in Sierra Leone, UN document S/2005/273, Apr. 2005.

[41] World Bank, 'Donors pledge $800m to fast-track poverty reduction in Sierra Leone', News release no. 2006/177/AFR, 30 Nov. 2005, URL <http://web.worldbank.org/>.

female head of state.[42] These pivotal elections furthered Liberia's transition from a near-failed state that was a source of regional instability to a more democratic state that will be governed by the rule of law.[43] UNMIL's role was to provide security, assist in the establishment of electoral offices throughout Liberia, and provide public information and voter education training. Persistent allegations that former President Charles Taylor was trying to disrupt Liberian politics and threats of possible large-scale violence cast a shadow over the process, but UNMIL's substantial presence of 15 000 troops and the 1800-strong, newly trained Liberian National Police proved to be effective deterrents.[44]

The restructuring of the Armed Forces of Liberia (AFL) made little headway in 2005. Although phase I, which consisted of demobilizing the 9000 irregular armed forces personnel, was completed, disagreement between international donors resulted in funding shortfalls, affecting the demobilization of the 4000 AFL personnel due in phase II.[45] The delay in the demobilization process coupled with the refusal of squatters to vacate Camp Schiefflin, the site of the new AFL barracks, contributed to postponing the recruitment and training of the new AFL.[46] The core of security sector reform in Liberia is driven by the twin imperatives of enhancing operational efficiency and strengthening democratic governance. The reform process in Liberia has, to date, focused almost exclusively on the efficiency aspect; for it to be sustainable, efforts to improve democratic oversight of the security functions need to be strengthened.[47]

Economic governance was a central issue for peace-building in Liberia in 2005. In May, international partners, led by the European Commission and the World Bank, proposed an initiative for Liberia aimed at tackling public service corruption and at ensuring the proper management and accountability of Liberia's public revenue streams. The plan provided for international control for a period of three years through the appointment of international experts with co-signature authority in the Central Bank and the finance and other key ministries.[48] Objecting to the plan as eroding Liberia's sovereignty and as being tantamount to international trusteeship, in July the NTGL

---

[42] 'Iron lady named Liberian leader', BBC News Online, 23 Nov. 2005, URL <http://news.bbc.co.uk/2/4462032.stm>.

[43] Human Rights Watch, 'Liberia at a crossroads: human rights challenges for the new government', Human Rights Watch Briefing Paper, 30 Sep. 2005, URL <http://hrw.org/backgrounder/africa/Liberia0905>.

[44] International Crisis Group (ICG), 'Liberia's elections: necessary but not sufficient', Africa Report no. 98, 7 Sep. 2005; and United Nations, Eighth progress report of the Secretary-General on the United Nations Mission in Liberia, UN document S/2005/560, 1 Sep. 2005, para. 30.

[45] UNMIL staff, Interview with the author, 15 Nov. 2005.

[46] DynCorp representative, Interview with the author, 16 Nov. 2005; and IRIN-WA, 'Soldiers refuse to quit camp needed for new army', IRIN-WA Weekly Round-up 311, 31 Dec.–6 Jan. 2006.

[47] Ebo, A., *The Challenges and Opportunities of Security Sector Reform in Post-Conflict Liberia*, Geneva Centre for the Democratic Control of Armed Forces (DCAF) Occasional Paper no. 9 (DCAF: Geneva, Dec. 2005).

[48] New York University, Center on International Cooperation (CIC), *Annual Review of Global Peacekeeping Operations* (Lynne Reinner: Boulder, Colo., Feb. 2006), pp. 54–61.

presented its own proposal, the Governance and Economic Management Assistance Programme (GEMAP).[49] A compromise plan, which retained the key co-signatory element of the international plan, was hammered out and, after much political pressure, the NTGL finally signed the agreement in September.[50] GEMAP remains a controversial issue, but the newly installed government has indicated that it will accept the terms of the plan and work with the international community towards its implementation.[51]

At the end of the year cautious optimism prevailed regarding Liberia. Given the relatively stable security environment, a drawdown of at least the military component of UNMIL is planned for 2006, and a concurrent augmentation of the civilian component is planned to secure the gains made thus far. The reshaping of UNMIL's deployment is expected to draw on lessons from the Sierra Leonean model of gradual downsizing tied to specific benchmarks.[52]

Côte d'Ivoire

In 2005 the impasse in the battle over the eligibility of the presidential candidates in Côte d'Ivoire brought the peace process there to a grinding halt and has resulted in a nearly three-year 'no peace, no war' stalemate. Fresh violence was prompted by the failure to hold elections in October owing to the intransigence of the factions on issues relating to citizenship, voting rights and land ownership and also because of the subsequent decision by the AU to extend the term of the transitional president, Laurent Gbagbo, by a year.[53] The stalled implementation of the 2004 Accra III Agreement not only hampered the ability of UN Operation in Côte d'Ivoire to carry out its mandated tasks but also threatened the already fragile stability in the region.[54] By the end of the year, the severity of the situation led UN Secretary-General Kofi Annan to call for a sharp increase in the number of UNOCI troops in order to allow the mission to 'react robustly' if necessary.[55] Alternatively, the Security Council

[49] On GEMAP see URL <http://www.worldbank.org/liberia>.

[50] Mahtani, D., 'Liberians seek nation-building president: despite international help the winner of the West African election will face a daunting task', *Financial Times*, 4 Oct. 2005, p. 10.

[51] President Johnson-Sirleaf pointed out that her administration will put in place its own oversight programme so that the GEMAP plan would not need to be renewed beyond its initial timeframe. Johnson-Sirleaf, E., Inaugural address, Monrovia, 17 Jan. 2006, URL <http://allafrica.com/stories/200601170106.html>.

[52] United Nations, Ninth progress report of the Secretary-General on the United Nations Mission in Liberia, UN document S/2005/767, 7 Dec. 2005, para. 87.

[53] On other causes of the breakdown of the peace process see IRIN-WA, 'Banny sworn in as new prime minister', IRIN-WA Weekly Round-up 307, 3–9 Dec. 2005; and 'A perilous peace deal', *The Economist*, 16 Apr. 2005, p. 37.

[54] United Nations, Report of the Secretary-General on inter-mission cooperation and possible cross-border operations between United Nations Mission in Sierra Leone, the United Nations Mission in Liberia and the United Nations Operation in Côte d'Ivoire, UN document S/2005/135, 2 Mar. 2005; and 'Nervy neighbours', *Africa Confidential*, vol. 47, no. 7 (1 Apr. 2005), p. 3. The Accra III Agreement was signed on 30 July 2004; it consolidated implementation of the peace process agreed in the 2003 Linas-Marcoussis Agreement. For the Acra III Agreement see URL <http://www.issafrica.org/AF/profiles/cotedivoire/research.htm#pax>.

[55] IRIN-WA, 'Annan wants more peacekeepers on ground', IRIN-WA Weekly Round-up 311, 31 Dec.–6 Jan. 2006.

may consider redeploying troops from UNMIL to UNOCI, as allowed by Resolution 1609 'within the authorized personnel ceiling', but this could run into various financial, procedural and political obstacles.[56]

AU and UN missions in Sudan

After a series of intensive negotiations that lasted for two and half years, the Comprehensive Peace Agreement (CPA), signed in January 2005 between the Government of Sudan and the Sudan's People's Liberation Movement/Army (SPLM/A), brought to an end one of Africa's longest-running wars.[57] A major new UN peace operation, the UN Mission in Sudan (UNMIS), was established in March 2005 to support implementation of the agreement.

Notwithstanding a long lead time, the deployment of the UN Advance Mission in Sudan (UNAMIS) in 2004 and participation by the DPKO in the political negotiations of the CPA, UNMIS faced difficulties throughout 2005 in building up the mission.[58] By the end of the year UNMIS was operating at only a third of its authorized capacity. Military and civilian elements were deployed in the south to monitor the security elements of the CPA and in support of the fledgling Government of Southern Sudan. Meanwhile, implementation of the CPA made slow but steady headway in 2005. The establishment of state institutions in Southern Sudan, however, proved to be a major challenge, partly because of a lack of resources. Capacity building in policing, the rule of law and human rights was initiated through various training programmes. The facilitation of the return of internally displaced persons (IDPs) showed more tangible dividends—500 000 persons have returned home.[59] The mandate of UNMIS allows for a robust approach to protecting civilians in areas where it is deployed. However, its ability to do more than deal with minor disturbances in its immediate vicinity is questionable. Even when the mission reaches full strength, it will have neither the mandate nor the capacity to deal with a major breakdown in security in Sudan. The slow progress in Southern Sudan has led many Sudanese to feel that the peace dividend is small.[60]

The continued worsening of the conflict in Darfur led to the deployment of the African Union's second-ever peace operation.[61] The African Union Mission in Sudan (AMIS) was originally deployed in Darfur in June 2004,

[56] United Nations, 'January 2006: Côte d'Ivoire (UNOCI)', Security Council Report, 22 Dec. 2005, URL <http://www.securitycouncilreport.org/site/c.glKWLeMTIsG/b.1313229/k.C896/January_2006br Cte_dIvoire_UNOCI.htm>; and UN Security Council Resolution 1609, 24 June 2005.

[57] On the conflict in Sudan see chapter 2 in this volume.

[58] New York University (note 48), pp. 34–41.

[59] United Nations, Report of the Secretary-General on the Sudan, UN document S/2005/821, 21 Dec. 2005.

[60] 'Little cheer from Sudan peace', BBC News Online, 9 Jan. 2006, URL <http://news.bbc.co.uk/2/4594242.stm>.

[61] The AU was the lead mediator in negotiating a series of agreements for resolution of the conflict in Darfur. They include the 2004 N'djamena Agreement, Addis Ababa Agreement and Abuja Protocols. On these agreements see URL <http://www.unsudanig.org/emergencies/darfur/index.htm>.

with only 60 unarmed observers and a protection force of 300 soldiers mandated to monitor both parties' compliance with the agreement.[62] The option of establishing a joint UN–AU protection force was considered at the time, but it was dropped because of the AU's determination to succeed in Darfur and because the Sudanese Government opposed the deployment of non-African troops.[63] The decision to rely on AU monitors, peacekeepers and police had broad support: African leaders viewed it as an opportunity to establish the AU's credentials as the primary political–military institution in Africa.

As events on the ground unfolded, it quickly became evident that AMIS was woefully inadequate and that it was necessary to significantly 'scale up' the mission in order to make an impact on the security and humanitarian situation in Darfur.[64] Thus, in the wake of heightened media and political pressure, in October 2004 the AU Peace and Security Council authorized the enhancement of the mission's strength to just over 3000 personnel and gave it a more robust mandate.[65]

The fundamental objective of AMIS in 2005 was to overcome its own persistent deployment and operational challenges. Following an AU-led Assessment Mission in March 2005, AMIS was again expanded, to a force of 6171 military personnel and 1586 civilian police.[66] At the same time it was acknowledged that it could not be made larger without a corresponding increase in its capacity to equip, transport and finance the large number of troops required. Accordingly, the EU and the North Atlantic Treaty Organization (NATO) agreed to provide AMIS with strategic airlift, in-mission training in areas of command and control and operational planning, as well as financial and material support.[67] The mission finally reached full strength at the end of October. Its new tasks included helping to create 'a secure environment for the delivery of humanitarian relief; the return of IDPs and refugees to their homes'; protection of civilians 'under imminent threat and in the immediate vicinity' within the limits of its resources and capabilities; and proactive deployment to areas where trouble was expected 'in order to deter armed groups from committing hostile acts against the population', not just in response to reports of violations.[68] However, since the creation of AMIS, there

---

[62] AMIS was established by the Agreement with the Sudanese Parties on the Modalities for the Establishment of the Ceasefire Commission and the Deployment of Observers in the Darfur on 28 May 2004 as an observer mission and was endorsed by UN Security Council Resolution 1556, 30 July 2004.

[63] New York University (note 48).

[64] O'Neill, W. G. and Cassis, V., *Protecting Two Million Internally Displaced: The Successes and Shortcomings of the African Union in Darfur*, Brookings–Bern Project on Internal Displacement, Occasional Paper (Brookings Institution, Washington, DC, and University of Bern, Bern, Switzerland, Nov. 2005), URL <http://www.brookings.edu/fp/projects/idp/200511au_darfur.htm>.

[65] African Union, Report of the Chairperson of the Commission on the Situation in Darfur, the Sudan, AU document PSC/PR/2(XVII), 20 Oct. 2004.

[66] United Nations, Report of the Secretary-General on United Nations Assistance to the African Union Mission in the Sudan, UN document S/2005/285, 3 May 2005.

[67] European Union, 'Factsheet: Darfur–consolidated EU package in support of AMIS II', URL <http://ue.eu.int/newsroom>; and NATO, 'NATO diversifies aid to African Union', 11 Aug. 2005, URL <http://www.nato.int/shape/news/2005/08/050811a.htm>.

[68] African Union, Communiqué of the 17th meeting of the Peace and Security Council, AU document PSC/PR/Comm.(XVII), 20 Oct. 2004.

have been 170 reported violations of the 2004 N'djamena Agreement and over 700 deaths.[69]

At the end of 2005, UN Secretary-General Annan declared Darfur to be in a state of anarchy.[70] Equipment shortages, combined with intelligence and communications problems, were still sapping the operational efficiency of AMIS and prevented it from carrying out its duties. The mission itself was a target of repeated attacks in 2005. There were also reports that the government had painted its military vehicles in the white colours of the AU's ceasefire monitors during attacks in North Darfur.[71] While the international community continues to work for local consent to its activities in Darfur, the collapse of the situation in the autumn of 2005 suggested that this may be a vain hope. Events towards the end of the year raised questions about the peacekeepers' capacity to respond to widespread and systematic violence and the intertwined challenges facing UNMIS and AMIS were plentiful. They included constant delays by the ruling National Congress Party to comply with the 'sharing' principles embodied in the CPA, the problem of how to deal with marginalized opposition groups throughout Sudan, and the slow build-up of state institutions in the South.

The AU experiment in Darfur became in 2005 a critical test of Africa's ability to assume responsibility for regional crises. If it succeeds, this could substantially enhance the international community's ability to halt future human rights catastrophes in Africa. The challenge posed by the multiple conflicts in Sudan is a test of the ability of the UN, the AU and a host of other organizations to work cohesively to assist a fragile and lengthy peace process. The AU's fundamental vulnerability remained its dependence on external financial support. For instance, despite initial promises of support, the USA decided to withdraw the $50 million it had pledged to AMIS.[72] Meanwhile, on the ground the AU's valiant efforts to halt the violence have not succeeded. The AU seems ready to integrate AMIS into the existing UNMIS or into a separate UN mission.[73] This option would ensure that the mission had more reliable sources of funding and better-equipped and -trained personnel.

EU and UN missions in the Democratic Republic of the Congo

EU engagement in the DRC is not new: the EU launched its first out-of-area military mission, Operation Artemis, in 2003 to assist the UN Operation in the DRC (MONUC) to clamp down on insurgent attacks in Ituri. Since then, the

[69] Appiah-Mensah, S., 'AU's critical assignment in Darfur', *African Security Review*, vol. 14, no. 2 (2005), pp. 7–21.

[70] 'It'll do what it can get away with', *The Economist*, 3 Dec. 2005, pp. 22–24.

[71] Mitchell, A., 'Sudan troops disguising as peacekeepers in Darfur, AU report says', *Arab News*, 13 Jan. 2006, URL <http://www.arabnews.com/?page=4&section=0&article=76176&d=13&m=1&y=2006>.

[72] LaFranchi, H., 'Sudan falters as US House rethinks aid', *Christian Science Monitor*, 14 Nov. 2005, URL <http://www.csmonitor.com/2005/1114/p02s02-usfp.html>.

[73] Turner, M. and England, A., 'UN looks out of Africa for help in ending Sudan's cycle of violence', *Financial Times*, 18 Jan. 2006, p. 3.

EU has redoubled its efforts to help bring stability to the DRC with two civilian crisis management missions in 2005—the EU Police Mission in Kinshasa (EUPOL Kinshasa) and the EU Advisory and Assistance Mission for DRC Security Reform (EUSEC DR Congo). Both missions were launched to provide assistance in security sector reform, particularly in the formation of an integrated DRC national police force. The EU's past experience in capacity building in the Balkans makes it well placed to lead such missions.

EUPOL Kinshasa, a civilian police mission consisting of 30 police officers, was established in April 2005 to assist the DRC Government in its efforts to consolidate internal security, complementing the previously launched Integrated Police Unit (IPU) in Kinshasa.[74] EUPOL Kinshasa is mandated to monitor, mentor and advise the IPU once IPU personnel have been trained and become operational under a Congolese chain of command. The purpose of the mission is to ensure that the unit acts in accordance with its training and with best international practices. EUPOL Kinshasa operates in the framework of UN–EU cooperation in crisis management, and so far this has functioned relatively smoothly. The main criticism of the mission (perhaps directed more at the institutional level than at the mission itself) is its size—EUPOL Kinshasa is considerably smaller than both the EU Police Mission in Bosnia and Herzegovina and the EU Police Mission in the Former Yugoslav Republic of Macedonia.

The subsequent launch of EUSEC DR Congo, a mission for security reform, is intended to further strengthen EUPOL's implementation, with the aim of contributing to a successful integration of the Forces armées de la République Démocratique du Congo (FARDC, or Armed Forces of the Democratic Republic of the Congo). Following the model of the EU's mission in Georgia, where civilian experts were embedded in relevant ministeries, EUSEC DR Congo will comprise eight EU advisers assigned to posts in the DRC's newly integrated military structure, the army general staff, the National Committee for Disarmament, Demobilization and Reintegration, the Joint Operational Committee and the Ministry of Defence.

While the EU has focused its efforts on institutional capacity building in the security sector, the UN concentrates its efforts on bringing stability to the eastern part of the DRC. In 2005 the strength of MONUC was almost doubled, from 10 800 to 17 500 personnel, and its mandate was expanded, in terms of both the tasks it was to accomplish and its ability to use force to accomplish them. Following brutal attacks on several UN peacekeepers, a three-phase military campaign plan—carried out in conjunction with troops from the FARDC—orchestrated to gain control of territories occupied by rebel forces, starting with the province of Ituri and followed by the North and South Kivu provinces.[75] In an innovative step to improve command and control of forces

---

[74] European Union, Council Joint Action 2004/847/CFSP, 9 Dec. 2004; and European Union, Council Joint Action 2004/494/CFSP, 17 May 2004.

[75] United Nations, Nineteenth report of the Secretary-General on the United Nations Organization Mission in the Democratic Republic of the Congo, UN document S/20025/603, 26 Sep. 2005; 'Rwandan rebels burn 39 villages alive in Congo', *New York Times* (Internet edn), 11 July 2005, URL <http://

operating in a demanding environment, the mission created a Divisional Head-quarters, located in Kisangani. It is responsible for tactical operations against the militia groups and foreign armed combatants in Ituri and the Kivu provinces. Repeating the model employed in West Africa, MONUC also collaborated with the UN Mission in Burundi to prevent cross-border infiltration of combatants. MONUC's increasingly robust posture from 2003 onward reflects the UN's determination to bring the DRC peace process to a successful conclusion, which is not possible without the creation of a secure environment for the holding of credible elections.

Despite the increasingly militarized nature of the mission, MONUC has taken on a widening range of tasks related to the DRC's political, economic and social transition. A successful programme of voter registration was also undertaken throughout the country, in anticipation of a constitutional referendum at the end of the year and elections scheduled for June 2006.[76]

The year 2005 ended on a mixed note for peace operations in the DRC. The security situation in eastern DRC remained perilous, while attempts to integrate the FARDC and police have produced marginal results.

The way forward for African capacities in peace operations

International efforts to boost African capacities to conduct peace operations intensified in 2005.[77] They include the G8's commitment to assist the AU in building a peacekeeping force, the African Standby Force (ASF), to consist of five regional brigades (West, South, East, Central and North) and a total of nearly 25 000 personnel by 2010, as part of the AU's Common African Defence and Security Policy. The G8 is also committed to supporting international training programmes across Africa and the EU's Africa Peace Facility.[78] The G8 Africa Action Plan, adopted at its 2002 Summit, set out a detailed list of AU priority areas which the G8 is committed to support, focusing on human rights and political governance as well as on economic issues.[79] The Africa Action Plan also generally mentioned the promotion of

nytimes.com/reuters/international-congo-democractic-killings.html>; and Agence France-Presse, 'DRC: UN peacekeepers dismantle 5 militia camps in Ituri region', 18 Apr. 2005, World News Connection, National Technical Information Service (NTIS), US Department of Commerce.

[76] United Nations, Special report of the Secretary-General on election in the Democratic Republic of the Congo, UN document S/20025/320, 26 May 2005, pp. 2–3.

[77] On regional peacekeeping efforts see Dwan, R. and Wiharta, S., 'Multilateral peace missions', SIPRI Yearbook 2004: Armaments, Disarmament and International Security (Oxford University Press: Oxford, 2004), pp. 155–61.

[78] African Union, Policy Framework for the Establishment of the African Standby Force and the Military Staff Committee, Addis Ababa, 12–14 May 2003; IRIN, 'Focus on the African Union summit', 5 July 2003; African Union, 'Solemn Declaration on a Common African Defence and Security Policy', 28 Feb. 2004, URL <http://www.afrrica-union.org/News_Events/2ND%20EX%20ASSEMBLY/Declaration%20on%20a%20Comm.Af%20Def%20Sec.pdf>; and Group of Eight (G8), 'G8 Factsheet: Peace and security in Africa today', URL <http://www.g8.gov.uk/servlet/Front?pagename=OpenMarket/Xcelerate/ShowPage&c=Page&cid=1119518704554>. This decision is congruent with the commitments of the Kananaskis (2002) and Evian (2003) G8 summits.

[79] The G8 Africa Action Plan was released at Kananaskis, Canada, on 27 June 2002. See URL <http://www.g8.gc.ca/2002Kananaskis/afraction-en.asp>.

peace and security, but its only specific, time-limited commitment was 'to deliver a joint plan, by 2003, for the development of African capability to undertake peace support operations, including at the regional level'. A report on the progress in implementing the Action Plan was duly presented to the 2003 and 2004 G8 summits. In 2004 the G8 members committed themselves to train 'and, where appropriate, equip' 75 000 troops worldwide by 2010.[80] However, although the reports read as if much has been achieved, in practice there have been more words than action or financial support. The plan for the promised development of African capacity in peace support operations itself acknowledged freely that 'it will take time and considerable resources to create, and establish the conditions to sustain, the complete range of capabilities needed to fully undertake complex peace support operations and their related activities'.[81]

Over the past decade, regional security arrangements have been given the licence and some means to develop their own capacity. The recent AU initiatives are the latest in this evolutionary process. However, because of resource limitations, African security arrangements, including the most recent AU initiatives, can hardly be seen as self-sufficient. For example, the ASF will have half the number of personnel that the UN has deployed on the continent—and the demand for deployments is on the rise. AU members currently contribute nearly half (43 per cent) of the number of troops deployed in UN operations in Africa. Given the need for troop rotation and the likelihood that the brigades will be composed at least partially of already deployed troops, the implications are clear: a large gap would have to be filled before AU member states can assume primary operational responsibility for peace operations on the continent. Success of the ASF and of African security organizations in general in carrying out peace operations hinges on the capacity to plan and develop missions quickly, on the establishment of rosters of mission leadership, on having the necessary military, police and civilian experts for mission start-up, and on the development of a logistics base. All these are critical elements which so far have been given too little attention.[82]

IV. Conclusions

The missions surveyed in this chapter demonstrated the austere realities of peace-building in Africa in 2005 and the problems that will continue to challenge peace operations in 2006. At the close of 2005, the MONUC, UNMIL, UNMIS and UNOCI missions placed a severe strain on the UN. If calls for the UN to take over AMIS are heeded, then certainly the DPKO and the newly created Peacebuilding Commission are likely to become over-

[80] G8, 'Sea Island Summit 2004: G8 Action Plan for Expanding Global Capacity for Peace Support Operations', URL <http://www.g8.utoronto.ca/summit/2004seaisland/peace.html>.

[81] Nowrojee, B., 'Africa on its own: regional intervention and human rights', *Human Rights Watch World Report 2004*, URL <http://www.hrw.org>.

[82] Neethling, T., 'Realizing the African Standby Force as a pan-African ideal: progress, prospects and challenges', *Journal of Military and Strategic Studies*, vol. 8, no. 1 (fall 2005).

burdened quickly. The success of UNAMSIL is attributed to the long-term commitment of the international community and serves as a reminder that peace-building is a long process. The efforts described in this chapter have the aim of boosting the capacity for peace operations in Africa—to enhance the ability of regional actors and organizations in Africa, of external countries and of the UN system to respond more quickly, consistently and effectively in order to halt violent and destabilizing conflicts on the continent. Africa's wider security architecture may have been put in place, but considerable operational challenges remain. The AU's recent experience in Darfur highlights one of the stark realities of African peacekeeping: the level of activity and success was not limited by political will or the availability of troops, but by financial constraints, lack of technical know-how and appropriate transport mechanisms. The poor showing of the AU in Darfur underlines that its capacity to launch complex peace operations in a sustainable manner remains embryonic. This provides a strong argument for the international community to seriously consider the recommendations of the UN High-level Panel on Threats, Challenges and Change that the UN should provide equipment for regional operations and that such operations, when appropriate, should be financed from the UN peacekeeping budget.

Appendix 3A. Multilateral peace missions in 2005

SHARON WIHARTA*

I. The evolution in peace operations

The notion and practice of peacekeeping have undergone significant change over the past 40 years. During the cold war, peace operations were mandated to perform such discrete functions as the monitoring of ceasefires, interpositioning between the parties to conflicts and maintaining buffer zones. These are often referred to as 'traditional' peacekeeping missions or 'Chapter VI operations'.[1] Peacekeeping has evolved and expanded since the first deployment of a United Nations (UN) mission, to monitor the armistice between Egypt, Israel, Lebanon and Syria in 1948. Besides the sheer number of operations deployed today—only 40 peace operations in all were deployed between 1948 and 1989—the present landscape is marked by increasingly costly and complex operations, with various functions and conducted by a multitude of actors. The mandates of peace operations have expanded beyond traditional peacekeeping tasks to peace-building, including the holding of elections, the provision of humanitarian support and reform of the security sector. At the other end of the spectrum, they have in some cases been strengthened with Chapter VII powers, thereby enabling them to legitimately 'take all necessary measures to fulfil their mandates' or to carry out what is more commonly termed as 'peace enforcement'.[2] The size of peace missions has also been expanded correspondingly—missions launched after the end of the cold war typically have at least several thousand personnel.

II. Global and regional trends in 2005

A total of 58 multilateral peace missions were conducted in 2005, deploying 289 500 military[3] and 17 500 civilian personnel. Eight new multilateral peace missions were launched in 2005, six of which were civilian missions deployed by the

---

[1] Diehl, P. F., *International Peacekeeping: With a New Epilogue on Somalia, Bosnia, and Cambodia* (Johns Hopkins University Press: Baltimore, Md., 1995). Chapter VI of the UN Charter vest authority in the Security Council for the settlement of disputes in a peaceful manner.

[2] See, e.g., Goulding, M., *Peacemonger* (John Murray Publishers: London, 2002); Findlay, T., SIPRI, *The Use of Force in UN Peace Operations* (Oxford University Press: Oxford, 2002); Nassrine, A. and Chang, L. (eds), *United Nations as Peacekeeper and Nation-builder: Continuity and Change—What Lies Ahead?*, Report of the 2005 Hiroshima Conference organized by the United Nations Institute for Training and Research (UNITAR) and the Institute of Policy Studies of Singapore (IPS) (Martinus Nijhoff: Leiden/Boston, 2005). Chapter VII of the UN Charter authorizes the Security Council to use enforcement powers, including the use of force, to maintain or restore international peace and security in situations where the Security Council has determined the existence of a threat to the peace, breach of the peace or act of transgression.

[3] Of this number, 183 000 soldiers (or 63%) were deployed to the Multinational Force in Iraq.

* SIPRI interns Sara Lindberg and Haruko Matsuoka assisted in the preparation of this appendix.

European Union (EU) while the remaining two are the UN Mission in Sudan (UNMIS) and the UN Office in Timor-Leste (UNOTIL). Five missions were closed in 2005—the UN Mission in Sierra Leone (UNAMSIL), the UN Mission of Support in East Timor (UNMISET), the UN Advance Mission in Sudan (UNAMIS), the EU Police Mission in the Former Yugoslav Republic of Macedonia (EUPOL PROXIMA) and the EU Rule of Law Mission in Georgia (EUJUST THEMIS). UNAMSIL, UNMISET and EUPOL PROXIMA were each succeeded by smaller, follow-on missions to further institution- and capacity-building efforts and to maintain a residual presence in the countries involved. These missions testify to the international community's recognition that continued engagement is required to ensure the sustainability of peace processes.

Since 1998, owing to a surge in the global demand for peacekeeping and notwithstanding the primacy of the UN in conflict management and resolution, the engagement of regional organizations and UN-sanctioned non-standing coalitions of states has consistently been more pronounced than that of the UN. This recent trend continued in 2005. A total of 37 such missions were conducted during the year, equalling the peak reached in 1999. Table 3A.1 shows opposite trends in the roles of regional organizations and ad hoc coalitions. The number of peace missions carried out by standing regional organizations has steadily risen since 2002 and in 2005 reached the highest level since the end of the cold war. Moreover, beginning with the takeover in 2003 by the North Atlantic Treaty Organization (NATO) of the International Security Assistance Force (ISAF) in Afghanistan, there has been a growing willingness on the part of regional organizations to launch out-of-area operations. However, the number of ad hoc coalition operations stayed constant over the four-year period 1999–2002 and has been on the decline since 2003. Given the current international political context, and the enormity of the resource and financial burdens on the lead nations, it is unlikely that sizeable peace missions will be launched by coalitions of the willing in the foreseeable future.

The year 2005 was a significant one for civilian missions under the EU's European Security and Defence Policy (ESDP). The number of peace missions burgeoned—the EU carried out 11 peace missions, twice as many in the previous year. The total of six new missions deployed by the EU in 2005—three times as many as the number initiated in 2004—was the highest number of new missions initiated in a single year by any regional organization. The EU launched, in succession, the EU Police Mission in Kinshasa in the Democratic Republic of the Congo (EUPOL Kinshasa); the EU Integrated Rule of Law Mission for Iraq (EUJUST LEX), the first EU mission in the Middle East; the EU Advisory and Assistance Mission for DRC Security Reform (EUSEC DR Congo); the Aceh Monitoring Mission (AMM), the first EU mission in Asia; the EU Police Advisory Team in the Former Yugoslav Republic of Macedonia (EUPAT); and the EU Border Assistance Mission for the Rafah Crossing Point (EU BAM Rafah) in the Palestinian Territories on the Israeli–Egyptian border.

The most notable development in the EU's peacekeeping efforts is that a majority of the new missions are out-of-area operations: the EU is engaged in four non-European regions. The intensity and the geographic diversity of the missions represent a new stage in Europe's involvement in peace missions and are testimonies

Table 3A.1. Number of peace missions conducted by the United Nations, regional organizations and non-standing coalitions worldwide, 1996–2005

	1996	1997	1998	1999	2000	2001	2002	2003	2004	2005
UN peace missions (DPKO- and DPA-administered)	24	23	21	24	22	18	20	18	21	21
Peace missions conducted or led by regional organizations or alliances	18	22	26	30	25	26	21	26	29	31
Peace missions led by non-standing coalitions	4	7	8	7	7	7	7	8	7	6
Total	**46**	**52**	**55**	**61**	**54**	**51**	**48**	**52**	**57**	**58**

DPKO = UN Department of Peacekeeping Operations; DPA = UN Department of Political Affairs.
Source: SIPRI Peacekeeping Missions Database.

to the EU's deepening commitment to be a global security actor.[4] The AMM also represents the first joint operation between two regional organizations—the EU and the Association of South East Asian Nations (ASEAN). It is still early days to draw any conclusions about the EU BAM Rafah mission, but the apparent success of the AMM, at least in the disarmament and demobilization process, has led to calls for the mission to be extended beyond March 2006 and for its mandate to be expanded.[5]

The various EU civilian missions initiated in 2005 illustrate that the EU is the most forward-looking institution with respect to building its civilian crisis management capacity and has achieved some success on this front. However, it remains to be seen if the General Secretariat of the Council of the EU will cope with planning and running multiple peace missions. The biggest challenge faced by both the UN and regional actors in peacekeeping in 2005 was that of resource constraints. This was cogently demonstrated in Africa where missions for a multitude of reasons had difficulties in reaching the authorized (and necessary) staffing level needed to carry out their duties effectively. NATO's extensive commitment in Kosovo and its growing role in Afghanistan will probably prevent it from increasing its presence elsewhere.[6] The challenge of fielding well-trained and -equipped soldiers and civilians with appropriate expertise will remain a central concern in 2006.

Table 3A.2 shows the breakdown of missions that were conducted in 2005 by type of mission and by the world region in which they were conducted.

---

[4] This has been articulated in policy documents of the EU. Council of the European Union, 'A secure Europe in a better world: European Security Strategy', Brussels, 12 Dec. 2003, URL <http://ue. eu.int/cms3_fo/showPage.ASP?id=266>.

[5] 'AMM hails plan to deploy TNI to help rebuild Aceh', *Jakarta Post*, 12 Dec. 2005.

[6] The troop strength of ISAF is expected to increase in 2006.

Table 3A.2. Number of peace missions conducted by the United Nations, regional organizations and non-standing coalitions, by region, 2005

	Africa	Americas	Asia	Europe	Middle East	**World total**
UN peace missions (DPKO- and DPA- administered)	9	1	4	3	4	21
Peace missions conducted or led by regional organizations or alliances	4	2	4	18	3	31
Peace missions led by non-standing coalitions	1	–	2	–	3	6
Total	**14**	**3**	**10**	**21**	**10**	**58**

DPKO = UN Department of Peacekeeping Operations; DPA = UN Department of Political Affairs.

Source: SIPRI Peacekeeping Missions Database.

III. Table of multilateral peace missions

Table 3A.3 contains more data than were included in the tables of multilateral peace missions that appeared in previous editions of the SIPRI Yearbook. First, the table lists the troop-contributing countries by type of personnel (troop, military observer, civilian police or civilian staff). Second, data on mission strength also include approved numbers in order to show whether a mission is deployed at full strength. Finally, the data on fatalities for the reporting year are broken down in the table by cause of death.

Table 3A.3 presents extensive data on the 58 multilateral peace missions that were ongoing or terminated in 2005. The table lists only those operations that were conducted under the authority of the UN and operations conducted by regional organizations or by ad hoc coalitions of states that were sanctioned by the UN or authorized by a UN Security Council resolution, with the stated intention to: (*a*) serve as an instrument to facilitate the implementation of peace agreements already in place, (*b*) support a peace process, or (*c*) assist conflict prevention and/or peace-building efforts.

SIPRI uses the UN Department of Peacekeeping Operations (DPKO) description of peacekeeping as a mechanism to assist conflict-ridden countries to create conditions for sustainable peace—this may include monitoring and observing ceasefire agreements; serving as confidence-building measures; protecting the delivery of humanitarian assistance; assisting with the demobilization and reintegration process; strengthening institutional capacities in the areas of judiciary and the rule of law (including penal institutions), policing, and human rights; electoral support; and economic and social development. The table thus covers a broad range of peace missions to reflect the growing complexity of mandates of peace operations and the potential for operations to change over the course of their mandate. The table does not include good offices, fact-finding or electoral assistance missions, nor does it include peace missions comprising non-resident individuals or teams of negotiators or operations not sanctioned by the UN.[7]

The missions are grouped by organization and listed chronologically within these groups. The first group, covering UN operations, is divided into two sections: 17 operations run by the UN DPKO; and 4 operations that are defined as special political missions and peace-building missions. The next eight groups cover operations conducted or led by regional organizations or alliances: 1 by the African Union; 1 by the Economic and Monetary Community of Central African States (CEMAC, Communauté Economique et Monétaire d'Afrique Centrale), 3 by the Commonwealth of Independent States (CIS), including 1 mission carried out by Russia under bilateral arrangements; 11 by the EU; 3 by NATO; 2 by the Organization of American States (OAS); and 10 by the Organization for Security and Co-operation in Europe (OSCE). The final group lists 6 operations led by ad hoc coalitions of states that were sanctioned by the UN.

Missions which were initiated in 2005 and new states joining an existing mission appear in bold text; operations and individual state participation which ended in 2005 are shown in italics; and designated lead states (those that either have operational control or contribute the most personnel) are underlined.

Legal instruments underlying the establishment of an operation—UN Security Council resolutions or formal decisions by regional organizations—and the start dates for the operations (by which SIPRI refers to dates of first deployments) are cited in the first column.

Approved personnel numbers, particularly for UN operations, refer to the most recently authorized staffing level. National breakdowns of personnel numbers and the number of local support staff are not included in the figures presented in the table but, where available, are given in the notes below the table.

Mission fatalities are recorded as a total from the beginning of the mission until the last reported date for 2005 and as a total for 2005. Fatality numbers for the reporting year are broken down by cause of death: accidental, hostile acts and illness.

Unless otherwise stated, all figures are as of 31 December 2005 or as of the date on which the mission closed.

Budget figures are given in millions of US dollars. Starting this year, conversions from budgets set in other currencies are based on the aggregated market exchange rates for 2005 of the International Monetary Fund (IMF).[8] Budget figures presented for UN operations refer to core operational costs, which among other things include the cost of deploying personnel, per diems for deployed personnel and direct non-field support costs (e.g., requirements for the support account for peacekeeping operations and the UN logistics base in Brindisi). The cost of UN peacekeeping missions is shared by all UN member states through a specially derived scale of assessed contributions that takes no account of their participation in the peacekeeping operations. Political and peace-building missions are funded through regular budget assessments. UN peacekeeping budgets do not cover programmatic costs, such as

---

[7] E.g., in its capacity as a mediator in the conflict in the Philippines, Malaysia has led a team of observers to monitor the ceasefire between the Philippine Government and the Moro Islamic Liberation Front.

[8] This follows the methodology employed by the SIPRI Military Expenditure Project in its data analysis. In previous years, figures as of 31 Dec. were used in the peace missions table. The change to using the IMF's aggregated market exchange rates limits the inconsistency of the budget data owing to fluctuating currency exchange rates.

those for disarmament, demobilization and reintegration, which are financed by voluntary contributions.

In contrast, budget figures for operations conducted by regional organizations such as the EU and NATO refer only to common costs. This includes mainly the running costs of EU and NATO headquarters (the costs of civilian personnel and operations and maintenance) and investments in the infrastructure necessary to support the operation. The costs of deploying personnel are borne by the states which send personnel and do not appear in the budget figures given here. Most EU missions are financed in one of two ways, depending on whether they are civilian or military missions. Civilian missions are funded through the Community Budget, while military missions or missions with military components are funded through the Athena mechanism, to which only the participating member states contribute.[9] In missions by other organizations, such as the OAS Mission in Haiti and in general the ad hoc missions, budget figures for missions may include programme implementation. For these reasons, budget figures presented in this table are best viewed as estimates and the budgets for different missions should not be compared.

Data on multilateral peace missions are obtained from the following categories of open source: (a) official information provided by the secretariat of the organization; (b) information from the mission on the ground, either in official publications or in responses to annual SIPRI questionnaires; and (c) information from national governments contributing to the mission in question. These primary sources are supplemented with a wide selection of publicly available secondary sources consisting of specialist journals; research reports; news agencies; and international, regional and local newspapers. The sources are given in the notes.

[9] The Athena mechanism is a financial and administrative instrument that provides for the administration of costs that are defined as common costs. European Union, Council Joint Action 2004/197/CFSP, 23 Feb. 2004, establishing a mechanism to administer the financing of the common costs of European Union operations having military or defence implications.

Table 3A.3. Multilateral peace missions, 2005

Acronym/ (Legal instrument)/ Start date	Name/ (Location)	Countries contributing troops, military observers (Mil. Obs), civilian police (Civ. Pol.) or civilian staff (Civ. Staff) in 2005	Troops/ Military observers/ Civilian police/ Civilian staff		Total deaths to date/in 2005/ (owing to hostilities, accidents, illness)[1]	Cost ($ m.): 2005/ Unpaid
			Approved	Actual		
UN (17 operations)		108 countries participated in 2005[2]	73 591 3 145 8 925 8 421	61 284 2 626 7 025 4 850[3]	1 010 196	5 030.0 1 990.0[4]
UNTSO (SCR 50)[5] June 1948	UN Truce Supervision Organization (Egypt, Israel, Lebanon, Syria)	Mil. Obs: Argentina, Australia, Austria, Belgium, Canada, Chile, China, Denmark, Estonia, Finland, France, Ireland, Italy, Nepal, Netherlands, New Zealand, Norway, Russia, Slovakia, Slovenia, Sweden, Switzerland, USA	– 150 – 123[6]	– 150 – 104[7]	44 5 (1, –, 3)	29.0 –
UNMOGIP (SCR 91)[8] Jan. 1949	UN Military Observer Group in India and Pakistan (India, Pakistan: Kashmir)	Mil. Obs: Belgium, Chile, Croatia, Denmark, Finland, Italy, Korea (South), Sweden, Uruguay	– 45 – 24[9]	– 42 – 22[10]	11 2 (–, –, 1)	8.4 –
UNFICYP (SCR 186)[11] Mar. 1964	UN Peacekeeping Force in Cyprus (Cyprus)	Troops: Argentina, Austria, Canada, Croatia, Finland, Hungary, Ireland, Korea (South), Slovakia, UK, Uruguay CIV. POL.: Argentina, Australia, Bosnia and Herzegovina, Croatia, El Salvador, India, Ireland, Italy, Netherlands	860 – 69[12] –	840 – 69 37[13]	175 2 (–, 1, 2)	46.5 19.9[14]
UNDOF (SCR 350)[15] June 1974	UN Disengagement Observer Force (Syria: Golan Heights)	Troops: Austria, Canada, Japan, Nepal, Poland, Slovakia	1 047 – – 40[16]	1 047 – – 37[17]	42 2 (1, –, –)	43.7 22.7[18]

Mission (SCR)	Location	Start	Personnel / Contributing countries				
UNIFIL (SCR 425 & 426)[19]	UN Interim Force in Lebanon (Lebanon)	Mar. 1978	TROOPS: France, Ghana, India, Ireland, Italy, Poland, Ukraine	2 000	1 989	256	99.2
				–	–	6	
				124[20]	100[21]	(1, –, 3)	72.6[22]
MINURSO (SCR 690)[23]	UN Mission for the Referendum in Western Sahara (Western Sahara)	Sep. 1991	TROOPS: **Denmark**, Ghana, Korea (South)	27	31	14	48.0
			MIL. OBS: Argentina, Austria, Bangladesh, China, Croatia, Egypt, El Salvador, France, Ghana, Greece, Guinea, Honduras, Hungary, Ireland, Italy, Kenya, Malaysia, Mongolia, Nigeria, Pakistan, Poland, Russia, Sri Lanka, Uruguay	203	195	4	51.8[26]
			CIV. POL.: Egypt, El Salvador	6[24]	6	(–, 2, 1)	
				–	120[25]		
UNOMIG (SCR 849 & 858)[27]	UN Observer Mission to Georgia (Georgia: Abkhazia)	Aug. 1993	MIL. OBS: Albania, Austria, Bangladesh, **Croatia**, Czech Rep., Denmark, Egypt, France, Germany, Greece, Hungary, Indonesia, Jordan, Korea (South), Pakistan, Poland, **Romania**, Russia, Sweden, Switzerland, Turkey, UK, Ukraine, Uruguay, USA	136	–	10	36.4
			CIV. POL.: Germany, Hungary, **India**, Poland, Russia, Switzerland	20[28]	122	3	13.7[30]
				–	11	(1, –, 1)	
					107[29]		
UNMIK (SCR 1244)[31]	UN Interim Administration Mission in Kosovo (Serbia and Montenegro: Kosovo)	June 1999	MIL. OBS: Argentina, Bangladesh, *Belgium*, Bolivia, Bulgaria, Chile, Czech Rep., Denmark, Finland, Hungary, Ireland, Italy, Jordan, Kenya, Malawi, Malaysia, Nepal, New Zealand, Norway, Pakistan, Poland, Portugal, Romania, Russia, Spain, UK, Ukraine, Zambia	38	–	42	252.6
			CIV. POL.: Argentina, Austria, Bangladesh, Brazil, Bulgaria, *Cameroon*, China, **Croatia**, Czech Rep., Denmark, Egypt, Fiji, Finland, France, Germany, Ghana, Greece, Hungary, India, Italy, Jordan, Kenya, Kyrgyzstan, Lithuania, Malawi, Malaysia, Nepal, Netherlands, Nigeria, Norway, Pakistan, Philippines, Poland, Portugal, Romania, Russia, Slovenia, Spain, Sweden, Switzerland, **Timor-Leste**, *Tunisia*, Turkey, UK, Ukraine, USA, Zambia, Zimbabwe	3 055	36	13	132.4[34]
				910[32]	2 188	(5, 1, 9)	
					623[33]		

Acronym/ (Legal instrument/ Start date)	Name/ (Location)	Countries contributing troops, military observers (MIL. OBS), civilian police (CIV. POL.) or civilian staff (CIV. STAFF) in 2005	Troops/ Military observers/ Civilian police/ Civilian staff		Total deaths to date/in 2005 (owing to hostilities, accidents, illness)[1]	Cost ($ m.): 2005/ Unpaid
			Approved	Actual		
UNAMSIL (SCR 1270)[35] Nov. 1999	UN Mission in Sierra Leone (Sierra Leone)	TROOPS: *Bangladesh, Germany, Ghana, Jordan, Kenya, Nepal, Nigeria, Pakistan, Sweden, UK*	3 250	944	188	113.2
			141	69	29	94.5[38]
		MIL. OBS: *Bangladesh, Bolivia, China, Croatia, Egypt, Gambia, Ghana, Guinea, Indonesia, Jordan, Kenya, Kyrgyzstan, Malaysia, Nepal, Nigeria, Pakistan, Russia, Slovakia, Tanzania, UK, Ukraine, Uruguay, Zambia*	80[36]	30	(6, 7, 25)	
			–	216[37]		
		CIV. POL.: *Germany, Ghana, India, Jordan, Kenya, Malaysia, Namibia, Nepal, Nigeria, Pakistan, Sweden, Turkey, Zambia, Zimbabwe*				
MONUC (SCR 1279)[39] Nov. 1999	UN Organization Mission in the Democratic Republic of the Congo (Democratic Republic of the Congo)	TROOPS: Bangladesh, Belgium, Benin, Bolivia, *Cameroon, Canada, China, Czech Rep., Egypt, France, Ghana,* **Guatemala**, India, Indonesia, Ireland, Jordan, Kenya, **Malawi**, *Malaysia, Mali,* Morocco, Nepal, **Netherlands**, *Niger, Nigeria,* Pakistan, *Russia,* **Senegal, Serbia and Montenegro**, South Africa, *Sweden, Switzerland, Tunisia,* **UK**, *Ukraine,* Uruguay, *Zambia*	16 240	15 051	75	1 153.8
			760	724	31	292.9[42]
		MIL. OBS: Algeria, Bangladesh, **Belgium**, Benin, Bolivia, Bosnia and Herzegovina, Burkina Faso, Cameroon, **Canada**, China, Czech Rep., Denmark, Egypt, France, Ghana, **Guatemala**, India, Indonesia, Ireland, Jordan, Kenya, Malawi, Malaysia, Mali, Mongolia, Morocco, Mozambique, Nepal, **Netherlands**, Niger, Nigeria, Pakistan, Paraguay, Peru, Poland, Romania, Russia, Senegal, South Africa, Spain, Sri Lanka, Sweden, **Switzerland**, Tunisia, **UK**, Ukraine, Uruguay, Zambia	966[40]	786	(12, 4, 19)	
			–	828[41]		
		CIV. POL.: Argentina, **Bangladesh**, Benin, Burkina Faso, Cameroon, **Central African Republic**, Chad, Côte d'Ivoire, **Egypt**, France, Guinea, **India**, Jordan, **Madagascar**, Mali, *Morocco,* Niger, Nigeria, *Portugal,* Romania, Russia, *Senegal,* Sweden, *Switzerland,* Turkey, **Vanuatu, Yemen**				

UNMEE (SCR 1312)[43] — UN Mission in Ethiopia and Eritrea (Eritrea, Ethiopia) — July 2000	TROOPS: *Australia*, Austria, Bangladesh, Bulgaria, *Finland*, France, Gambia, Ghana, India, *Italy*, Jordan, Kenya, Malaysia, Namibia, Nigeria, *South Africa*, Spain, Tanzania, Tunisia, Uruguay, Zambia	4 200	3 132	13	186.0
	MIL. OBS: Algeria, Austria, Bangladesh, Bosnia and Herzegovina, Bulgaria, China, Croatia, Czech Rep., Denmark, Finland, Gambia, Germany, Ghana, Greece, **Guatemala**, India, **Iran**, Jordan, Kenya, Malaysia, Namibia, Nepal, Nigeria, Norway, Paraguay, Peru, Poland, Romania, Russia, South Africa, Spain, Sweden, Switzerland, Tanzania, Tunisia, Ukraine, Uruguay, USA, Zambia	230[44]	205	5	48.1[46]
		–	–	(–, –, 5)	
		–	191[45]		
UNMISET (SCR 1410)[47] — UN Mission of Support in East Timor (Timor-Leste) — May 2002	TROOPS: *Australia, Bangladesh, Bolivia, Brazil, Denmark, Fiji, Jordan, Malaysia, Mozambique, Nepal, New Zealand, Pakistan, Philippines, Portugal, Russia, Sweden*	477	428	25	85.2
	MIL. OBS: Australia, Bangladesh, Bolivia, Brazil, Denmark, Jordan, Malaysia, Mozambique, Nepal, New Zealand, Pakistan, Philippines, Portugal, Russia, Sweden	42	41	12	66.4[50]
	CIV. POL..: Australia, Bangladesh, Bosnia and Herzegovina, Brazil, China, Croatia, Ghana, Jordan, Malaysia, Nepal, Norway, Pakistan, Philippines, Portugal, Russia, Samoa, Spain, Sri Lanka, Sweden, Turkey, Ukraine, USA, Zambia, Zimbabwe	157	134	(–, 3, 10)	
		950[48]	264[49]		

Acronym/ (Legal instrument)/ Start date	Name/ (Location)	Countries contributing troops, military observers (MIL. OBS), civilian police (CIV. POL.) or civilian staff (CIV. STAFF) in 2005	Troops/ Military observers/ Civilian police/ Civilian staff		Total deaths to date/in 2005 (owing to hostilities, accidents, illness)[1]	Cost ($ m.): 2005/ Unpaid
			Approved	Actual		
UNMIL (SCR 1509)[51] Nov. 2003	UN Mission in Liberia (Liberia)	TROOPS: Bangladesh, Benin, Bolivia, Brazil, China, Croatia, Ecuador, Ethiopia, Finland, France, Germany, Ghana, Ireland, Jordan, Kenya, Korea (South), Malawi, Mali, Moldova, Namibia, Nepal, Nigeria, Pakistan, Paraguay, Peru, Philippines, Senegal, South Africa, Sweden, Togo, UK, Ukraine, USA MIL. OBS: Bangladesh, Benin, Bolivia, Bulgaria, China, Czech Rep., Denmark, Ecuador, Egypt, El Salvador, Ethiopia, Gambia, Ghana, Indonesia, Jordan, Kenya, Korea (South), Kyrgyzstan, Malaysia, Mali, Moldova, Namibia, Nepal, Niger, Nigeria, Pakistan, Paraguay, Peru, Philippines, Poland, Romania, Russia, Senegal, Serbia and Montenegro, Togo, Ukraine, USA, Zambia CIV. POL.: Argentina, Bangladesh, Bosnia and Herzegovina, China, Czech Rep, El Salvador, Fiji, Gambia, Germany, Ghana, Jamaica, Jordan, Kenya, Kyrgyzstan, Malawi, Namibia, Nepal, Niger, Nigeria, Norway, Pakistan, Philippines, Poland, Portugal, Russia, Samoa, Senegal, Serbia and Montenegro, Sri Lanka, Sweden, Turkey, Uganda, Ukraine, Uruguay, USA, Yemen, Zambia, Zimbabwe	15 250 250 1 115[52] –	14 656 193 1 008 552[53]	67 39 (–, 8, 28)	760.6 3.2[54]
UNOCI (SCR 1528)[55] Apr. 2004	UN Operation in Côte d'Ivoire (Côte d'Ivoire)	TROOPS: Bangladesh, Benin, Brazil, Burkina Faso, France, Gambia, Ghana, India, Jordan, Kenya, Morocco, Niger, Pakistan, Paraguay, Philippines, Senegal, Togo, Tunisia, Uganda, Uruguay MIL. OBS: Bangladesh, Benin, Bolivia, Brazil, Chad, China, Congo (Rep. of), Croatia, Dominican Republic, Ecuador, El Salvador, France, Gambia, Ghana, Guatemala, Guinea, India, Ireland, Jordan, Kenya, Moldova, Morocco, Namibia, Nepal, Niger, Nigeria, Pakistan,	7 090 200 725 964[56]	6 701 195 674 358[57]	14 14 (1, 3, 7)	438.2 109.6[58]

Paraguay, Peru, Philippines, Poland, Romania, Russia, Senegal, Serbia and Montenegro, Togo, Tunisia, **Uganda**, Uruguay, Yemen, Zambia

CIV. POL.: *Argentina*, Bangladesh, Benin, Cameroon, Canada, **Central African Republic**, Chad, Djibouti, El Salvador, France, Ghana, **India**, **Jordan**, Lebanon, **Madagascar**, Niger, Nigeria, **Philippines**, *Portugal*, Senegal, *Sri Lanka*, Togo, Turkey, Uruguay, **Vanuatu**, **Yemen**

Operation	Location (Start date)	Countries contributing personnel				
ONUB (SCR 1545)[59] June 2004	UN Operation in Burundi (Burundi)	**TROOPS:** **Algeria**, **Belgium**, Burkina Faso, Ethiopia, **Guatemala**, India, Jordan, Kenya, Mali, Mozambique, Nepal, *Netherlands*, Nigeria, Pakistan, Russia, Senegal, South Africa, *Spain*, Thailand, Togo, **Tunisia** MIL. OBS: **Algeria**, Bangladesh, Belgium, Benin, Bolivia, Burkina Faso, Chad, China, Egypt, Ethiopia, *Gabon*, Gambia, Ghana, Guatemala, Guinea, India, Jordan, Kenya, Korea (South), **Kyrgyzstan**, Malawi, Malaysia, Mali, Mozambique, Namibia, Nepal, Niger, Nigeria, Pakistan, Paraguay, Peru, Philippines, Portugal, Romania, Russia, Senegal, Serbia and Montenegro, South Africa, Sri Lanka, Thailand, Togo, Tunisia, Uruguay, Yemen, Zambia CIV. POL.: Benin, Burkina Faso, Cameroon, Chad, *Côte d'Ivoire*, Guinea, Madagascar, Mali, Niger, Nigeria, *Senegal*, *Turkey*	5 650 / 200 / 120 / –	5 170 / 187 / 82 / 316[60]	20 / 15 / (–, 9, 5)	307.7 / 112.2[61]
MINUSTAH (SCR 1542)[62] June 2004	UN Stabilization Mission in Haiti (Haiti)	TROOPS: Argentina, *Benin*, Bolivia, Brazil, Canada, Chile, Croatia, Ecuador, France, Guatemala, Jordan, **Malaysia**, Morocco, Nepal, Paraguay, Peru, Philippines, Spain, Sri Lanka, Uruguay, USA, **Yemen** CIV. POL.: *Argentina*, Benin, Bosnia and Herzegovina, Brazil, Burkina Faso, Cameroon, Canada, Chad, Chile, China, Egypt, El Salvador, France, Ghana, Guinea, Jordan, Mali, *Mauritius*, Nepal, Niger, Nigeria, Pakistan, Philippines, *Portugal*, Romania, **Russia**, Senegal, Sierra Leone, Spain, *Sri Lanka*, Togo, Turkey, Uruguay, USA, **Vanuatu**, **Yemen**, Zambia	7 500 / – / 1 897 / 1 543[63]	7 286 / – / 1 748 / 449[64]	13 / 13 / (6, 3, 2)	541.3 / 331.7[65]

Acronym/ (Legal instrument)/ Start date	Name/ (Location)	Countries contributing troops, military observers (MIL. OBS), civilian police (CIV. POL.) or civilian staff (CIV. STAFF) in 2005	Troops/ Military observers/ Civilian police/ Civilian staff		Total deaths to date/in 2005 (owing to hostilities, accidents, illness)[1]	Cost ($ m.): 2005/ Unpaid
			Approved	Actual		
UNMIS (SCR 1590) Mar. 2005	UN Mission in Sudan (Sudan)	TROOPS: Australia, Austria, Bangladesh, Canada, China, Croatia, Denmark, Egypt, Finland, Germany, Greece, India, Jordan, Kenya, Malaysia, Nepal, New Zealand, Norway, Pakistan, Rwanda, Switzerland, Turkey, UK, Zambia	10 000 750 715 3 743	4 009 467 289 526[66]	1 1 (–, 1, –)	969.5 192.6[67]
		MIL. OBS: Australia, Bangladesh, Belgium, Benin, Bolivia, Brazil, Cambodia, Canada, China, Ecuador, Egypt, El Salvador, Fiji, Gabon, Germany, Greece, Guatemala, Guinea, India, Indonesia, Italy, Jordan, Kenya, Korea (South), Kyrgyzstan, Malawi, Malaysia, Moldova, Mongolia, Mozambique, Namibia, Nepal, New Zealand, Nigeria, Norway, Pakistan, Paraguay, Peru, Philippines, Poland, Romania, Russia, Rwanda, Sri Lanka, Sweden, Tanzania, Uganda, Ukraine, Yemen, Zambia, Zimbabwe				
		CIV. POL.: Argentina, Bangladesh, Brazil, China, El Salvador, Fiji, Finland, Ghana, India, Jamaica, Jordan, Kenya, Malaysia, Namibia, Nepal, Nigeria, Norway, Pakistan, Philippines, Russia, Samoa, Sri Lanka, Sweden, Tanzania, Turkey, Uganda, Ukraine, USA, Zambia, Zimbabwe				
UN special political and peace-building missions[68] (4 operations)			15 25 60 399	19 35 69 1 017	21 6	221.9[69] –
UNAMA (SCR 1401)[70] Mar. 2002	UN Assistance Mission in Afghanistan (Afghanistan)	MIL. OBS: Australia, Austria, Bangladesh, Canada, Denmark, Germany, Korea (South), New Zealand, Poland, Romania, Sweden, Uruguay	– – – –	– 11 7 187[71]	4 4 (–, 1, 3)	63.6 –
		CIV. POL.: Canada, China, Denmark, Jordan, Nepal, Nigeria, Norway, Philippines, Sweden				

CIV. STAFF: Australia, Austria, Bangladesh, Belarus, Belgium, Bosnia and Herzegovina, Brazil, Burundi, Canada, China, Croatia, El Salvador, Ethiopia, Fiji, Finland, France, Germany, Ghana, Guatemala, Honduras, Hungary, India, Iran, Iraq, Ireland, Italy, Jamaica, Japan, Jordan, Kenya, Korea (South), Kyrgystan, Liberia, Macedonia, Malaysia, Myanmar, Netherlands, New Zealand, Pakistan, Peru, Philippines, Poland, Portugal, Romania, Russia, Rwanda, Sierra Leone, South Africa, Spain, Sri Lanka, Sudan, Sweden, Switzerland, Syria, Tajikistan, Thailand, Trinidad and Tobago, Tunisia, UK, Ukraine, _USA_, Uzbekistan, Zimbabwe

UNAMI (SCR 1500)[72] Aug. 2003	UN Assistance Mission for Iraq (Iraq)	–	–	–	4	17	99.8
		–	–	–	–	2	–
		344	227[73]			(–, –, 2)	

CIV. STAFF: **Afghanistan, Australia, Austria, Australia, Bangladesh, Barbados, Belgium, Bosnia and Herzegovina, Brazil, Canada, Congo (Dem. Rep. of), Croatia, Czech Rep, Denmark, Ecquador, Egypt, Estonia, Ethiopia, Fiji, Finland, France, Germany, Ghana, Greece, India, Ireland, Italy, Jamaica, Japan, Jordan, Kenya,** _Kuwait,_ **Lebanon, Macedonia, Malta, Morocco, Myanmar, Netherlands, New Zealand, Nigeria, Pakistan, Peru, Philippines, Portugal, Russia, Spain, Sri Lanka, Sudan, Sweden, Syria, Tajikistan, Thailand, Trinidad and Tobago, Uganda, UK, Uruguay, USA**

UNAMIS (SCR 1547)[74] June 2004	UN Advance Mission in Sudan (Sudan)	–	25[75]	–	–	–	36.6
				24		–	
				6			
				164			

CIV. STAFF: _Albania, Australia, Austria, Bangladesh, Belarus, Bhutan, Canada, Central African Republic, Croatia, Denmark, Egypt, Eritrea, Ethiopia, Fiji, France, Germany, Ghana, India, Iraq, Ireland, Jamaica, Japan, Jordan, Kenya, Lebanon, Malaysia, Morocco, Nepal, Netherlands, New Zealand, Nigeria, Norway, Pakistan, Palestinian Territory, Philippines, Poland, Romania, Russia, Rwanda, Serbia and Montenegro, Sierra Leone, Somalia, South Africa, Spain, Sri Lanka, Sweden, Tajikistan, Tanzania, Thailand, Trinidad and Tobago, Tunisia, Turkey, Uganda, UK, USA, Zimbabwe_

Acronym/ (Legal instrument/ Authorization date)/ Start date	Name/ (Location)	Countries contributing troops, military observers (MIL. OBS), civilian police (CIV. POL.) or civilian staff (CIV. STAFF) in 2005	Troops/ Military observers/ Civilian police/ Civilian staff		Total deaths to date/in 2005 (owing to hostilities, accidents, illness)[1]		Cost ($ m.): 2005/ Unpaid
			Approved	Actual			
UNOTIL (SCR 1599)[76] May 2005	UN Office in Timor-Leste (Timor-Leste)	TROOPS: **Australia, Bangladesh, Brazil, Malaysia, New Zealand, Pakistan, Philippines, Portugal** CIV. POL.: **Australia, Bangladesh, Brazil, China, Croatia, Jordan, Malaysia, Pakistan, Palau, Philippines, Portugal, Russia, Samoa, Spain, Sri Lanka, Turkey, USA** CIV. STAFF: **Angola, Australia, Austria, Bangladesh, Belgium, Bosnia and Herzegovina, Brazil, Cambodia, Canada, Cape Verde, Chile, Colombia, Croatia, Ethiopia, Fiji, Finland, France, Germany, Guatemala, Guinea, Honduras, India, Indonesia, Ireland, Italy, Jamaica, Japan, Kenya, Liberia, Malaysia, Mozambique, Nepal, Netherlands, New Zealand, Pakistan, Philippines, Poland, Portugal, Sierra Leone, Singapore, Spain, Sri Lanka, St Vincent and the Grenadines, Switzerland, Thailand, Uganda, UK, USA, Zambia, Zimbabwe**	15 – 60 55	15 – 56 439	– –		21.9 –
AU (1 operation)		**(27 countries participated in 2005)**	**6 171 450 1 560 –**	**5 645 650 1 320 –**	**8 8**		**52.4 –**
AMIS (AU, 28 May 2004)[77] June 2004	African Union Mission in Sudan[78] (Sudan: Darfur)	TROOPS: Chad, Gambia, Nigeria, Rwanda, Senegal, South Africa MIL. OBS: Algeria, Benin, Botswana, Burkina Faso, Cameroon, Chad, Congo (Rep. of), Egypt, Gabon, Gambia, Ghana, Kenya, Lesotho, Libya, Madagascar, Malawi, Mali, Mauritania, Mozambique, Namibia, Nigeria, Rwanda, Senegal, South Africa, Togo, Zambia	6 171 450 1 560[79] –	5 645 650 1 320 –	8 8 (2, 1, 5)		52.4[80] ..

CIV. POL.: Botswana, Cameroon, Egypt, Gambia, Ghana, Kenya, Madagascar, Mali, Mauritania, Nigeria, Rwanda, Senegal, South Africa, Uganda, Zambia

Operation / start	Name / legal basis	(Location) / end date	Participating countries				
CEMAC (1 operation)			**(3 countries participated in 2005)**	–	380	6	6.2
				–	–	–	–
FOMUC (Libreville Summit, 2 Oct. 2002)[81]	CEMAC Multinational Force in the Central African Republic[82]	(Central African Republic) Dec. 2002	TROOPS: Chad, Congo (Rep. of), Gabon	–	380	6	6.2
				–	–	–	–
CIS (3 operations)			**(3 countries participated in 2005)**	1 500	4 031	(144)	–
				–	40	–	–
–(Bilateral, 21 July 1992)[83]	Joint Control Commission Peacekeeping Force[84]	(Moldova: Trans-Dniester) July 1992	TROOPS: Moldova, Russia, (Trans-Dniester)	1 500[85]	1 120	(32)[86]	–
				–	–	–	–
–(Bilateral, 24 June 1992)[87]	South Ossetia Joint Force[88]	(Georgia: South Ossetia) July 1992	TROOPS: Georgia, Russia	–	586	19	..
				–	40	–	–

Acronym/ (Legal instrument/ Authorization date)/ Start date	Name/ (Location)	Countries contributing troops, military observers (Mil. Obs), civilian police (Civ. Pol.) or civilian staff (Civ. Staff) in 2005	Troops/ Military observers/ Civilian police/ Civilian staff		Total deaths to date/in 2005 (owing to hostilities, accidents, illness)[1]	Cost ($ m.): 2005/ Unpaid
			Approved	Actual		
– (CIS, 15 Oct, 1994[89] June 1994	CIS Peacekeeping Forces in Georgia[90] (Georgia: Abkhazia)	TROOPS: Russia	– – – –	2 325 – – –	125 –	.. ..
EU (11 operations)	(44 countries participated in 2005)		7 000 – 557 510[91]	6 270 – 534 500	16 2	179.0 –
EUMM (Brioni Agreement)[92] July 1991	EU Monitoring Mission[93] (Western Balkans)[94]	Civ. Staff: Austria, Belgium, Denmark, Finland, France, Germany, Greece, Ireland, Italy, Netherlands, Norway, Slovakia, Spain, Sweden, UK	– – – 100	– – – 90[95]	11 –	5.4
EUPM (Joint Action 2002/210/ CFSP)[96] Jan. 2003	EU Police Mission in Bosnia and Herzegovina[97] (Bosnia and Herzegovina)	Civ. Pol.: Austria, Belgium, Bulgaria, Canada, Cyprus, Czech Rep., Denmark, Estonia, Finland, France, Germany, Greece, Hungary, Iceland, Ireland, Italy, Latvia, Lithuania, Luxembourg, Malta, Netherlands, Norway, Poland, Portugal, Romania, Russia, Slovakia, Slovenia, Spain, Sweden, Switzerland, Turkey, UK, Ukraine Civ. Staff: Austria, Belgium, Bulgaria, Finland, France, Germany, Ireland, Italy, Netherlands, Norway, Portugal, Spain, Turkey, UK, Ukraine	– – 367 53	– – 367 53	3 –	22.3 –

Mission / legal basis / date	Contributing states				Cost
EUPOL PROXIMA (EU Police Mission in the Former Yugoslav Republic of Macedonia[99]) (Joint Action 2003/681/CFSP[98]) Dec. 2003	_CIV. POL.: Austria, Belgium, Cyprus, Czech Rep., Denmark, **Estonia**, Finland, France, Germany, Greece, Hungary, Ireland, Italy, Latvia, Lithuania, Luxembourg, Netherlands, Norway, Poland, Portugal, Slovakia, **Slovenia**, Spain, Sweden, Switzerland, Turkey, UK, Ukraine_ _CIV. STAFF: Finland, France, Germany, Greece, Ireland, Italy, Netherlands, Spain, UK_	140 28	128 28	— —	14.0 —
EUJUST THEMIS (EU Rule of Law Mission in Georgia[101]) (Joint Action 2004/523/CFSP[100]) July 2004	_CIV. STAFF: Denmark, France, Germany, Greece, Italy, Latvia, Lithuania, Netherlands, Poland, Spain, Sweden_	12	12[102]	— —	2.6[103] —
EUFOR ALTHEA (EU Military Operation in Bosnia and Herzegovina[105]) (Joint Action 2004/570/CFSP[104]) Dec. 2004	TROOPS: Albania, Argentina, Austria, Belgium, Bulgaria, Canada, Chile, Czech Rep., Estonia, Finland, France, Germany, Greece, Hungary, Ireland, Italy, Latvia, Lithuania, Luxembourg, Morocco, Netherlands, New Zealand, Norway, Poland, Portugal, Romania, Slovakia, Slovenia, Spain, Sweden, Switzerland, Turkey, UK	7 000	6 270	2 2 (–, 1, –)	91.3 —
EUPOL Kinshasa (EU Police Mission in Kinshasa (DRC)[108]) (Joint Action 2004/847/CFSP[106]) Apr. 2005[107]	CIV. POL.: **Belgium**, **Canada**, **France**, **Italy**, **Netherlands**, **Portugal**, Sweden, Turkey	30	19 9	— —	5.5 —

Acronym/ (Legal instrument/ Authorization date)/ Start date	Name/ (Location)	Countries contributing troops, military observers (MIL. OBS), civilian police (CIV. POL.) or civilian staff (CIV. STAFF) in 2005	Troops/ Military observers/ Civilian police/ Civilian staff		Total deaths to date/in 2005 (owing to hostilities, accidents, illness)[1]		Cost ($ m.): 2005/ Unpaid
			Approved	Actual			
EUJUST LEX (Joint Action 2005/190/ CFSP)[109] **July 2005**	**EU Integrated Rule of Law Mission for Iraq[110]** **(Iraq)**	CIV. STAFF: **Belgium, France, Germany, Spain**	– – – –	– – – **21**	–	–	**12.7** –
EUSEC DR Congo (Joint Action 2005/355/ CFSP)[111] **July 2005**	**EU Advisory and Assistance Mission for DRC Security Reform[112]** **(Democratic Republic of the Congo)**	CIV. STAFF: **Belgium, France, Hungary, Portugal, UK**	– – – **8**	– – – **8**	–	–	**2.0** –
AMM (Joint Action 2005/643/ CFSP)[113] **Aug. 2005**	**EU Aceh Monitoring Mission[114]** **(Indonesia: Aceh)**	CIV. STAFF: **Austria, Belgium, Brunei Darussalam, Denmark, Finland, France, Germany, Ireland, Italy, Lithuania, Malaysia, Netherlands, Norway, Philippines, Singapore, Spain, Sweden, Switzerland, Thailand, UK**	– – – **229**	– – – **216[115]**	–	–	**19.1** –

Mission (legal instrument / start date / location)	Countries contributing	Troops (approved / actual)	Civ. pol. / staff (approved / actual)	Deaths to date (in 2005)	Cost ($ m.)
EU BAM Rafah (Joint Action 2005/889/CFSP)[116] Nov. 2005 **EU Border Assistance Mission for the Rafah Crossing Point[117]** (Rafah Crossing Point at the Egyptian–Israeli border)	CIV. STAFF: **Austria, Denmark, Finland, France, Germany, Italy, Luxembourg, Portugal, Romania, Spain, Sweden, UK**	– / –	70 / 53	–	2.2 / –
EUPAT (Joint Action 2005/826/CFSP)[118] Dec. 2005 **EU Police Advisory Team in the former Yugoslav Republic of Macedonia[119]** (Former Yugoslav Republic of Macedonia)	CIV. POL.: Austria, Belgium, Cyprus, Denmark, Finland, France, Germany, Hungary, Italy, Latvia, Slovakia, Slovenia, Spain, Sweden, UK CIV. STAFF: France, Germany, Italy, UK	20 / 10 20 / 10		–	1.9 / –
NATO and NATO-led (3 operations)	(40 countries participated in 2005)	26 300 / 26 263 – / – – / – – / –		181 26	127.0[120] –
KFOR (SCR 1244)[121] June 1999 NATO Kosovo Force[122] (Serbia and Montenegro: Kosovo)	TROOPS: Argentina, Armenia, Austria, Azerbaijan, Belgium, Bulgaria, Canada, Czech Rep., Denmark, Estonia, Finland, France, Georgia, Germany, Greece, Hungary, Ireland, Italy, Latvia, Lithuania, Luxembourg, Morocco, Norway, Poland, Romania, Slovakia, Slovenia, Spain, Sweden, Switzerland, Turkey, UK, Ukraine, USA	17 000 / 17 174[123] – / – – / –		71 (–, …, –)	31.6 –
ISAF (SCR 1386)[124] Dec. 2001 International Security Assistance Force[125] (Afghanistan)	TROOPS: Albania, Austria, Azerbaijan, Belgium, Bulgaria, Canada, Croatia, Czech Rep., Denmark, Estonia, Finland, France, Germany, Greece, Hungary, Iceland, Ireland, Italy, Latvia, Lithuania, Luxembourg, Netherlands, New Zealand, Norway, Poland, Portugal, Romania, Slovakia, Slovenia, Spain, Sweden, Switzerland, Turkey, UK, USA	9 000 / 8 934 – / – – / –		110 26 (5, 17, –)	83.1 –

Acronym/ (Legal instrument/ Authorization date)/ Start date	Name/ (Location)	Countries contributing troops, military observers (MIL. OBS), civilian police (CIV. POL.) or civilian staff (CIV. STAFF) in 2005	Troops/ Military observers/ Civilian police/ Civilian staff		Total deaths to date/in 2005 (owing to hostilities, accidents, illness)[1]	Cost ($ m.): 2005/ Unpaid
			Approved	Actual		
NTM-I (SCR 1546)[126] Aug. 2004	NATO Training Mission in Iraq[127] (Iraq)	TROOPS: Belgium, Bulgaria, Canada, Czech Rep., Denmark, Estonia, Germany, Greece, Hungary, Iceland, Italy, Latvia, Lithuania, Luxembourg, Netherlands, Norway, Poland, Portugal, Romania, Slovakia, Slovenia, Spain, Turkey, UK, USA	300	155	– –	12.4 –
OAS (2 operations)		(14 countries participated in 2005)	– 6 22	– 6 34	1 1	18.2 –
MAPP/OEA (CP/RES. 859)[128] Feb. 2004	Mission to Support the Peace Process in Colombia[129] (Colombia)	CIV. STAFF: Argentina, Costa Rica, Guatemala, Nicaragua, Norway, Peru, Sweden, Uruguay	–	10[130]	– –	3.2[131] –
– (CP/RES. 806)[132] June 2004	OAS Special Mission for Strengthening Democracy in Haiti[133] (Haiti)	CIV. STAFF: **Argentina**, Canada, Colombia, Dominica, **Ecuador**, Grenada, **Guatemala**, Mexico, **Peru**	– 6 22	6 24[134]	1 1 (–, –, 1)	15.0 –
OSCE (10 operations)		(46 countries participated in 2005)	– – –	– – –	3 –	131.5[135] –
			424	762		

Establishment	Mission (location)	Civilian staff					
–(CSO 18 Sep. 1992)[136] Sep. 1992	OSCE Spillover Mission to Skopje[137] (Former Yugoslav Republic of Macedonia: FYROM)	CIV. STAFF: Austria, Azerbaijan, Belarus, Bosnia and Herzegovina, Croatia, Estonia, Finland, France, Georgia, Germany, Hungary, Ireland, Italy, Japan, Netherlands, Norway, Poland, Portugal, Romania, Russia, Slovenia, Spain, Sweden, Switzerland, Tajikistan, Turkey, UK, Ukraine, USA	210[138]	–	104	–	–	14.3	–
–(CSO 6 Nov. 1992)[139] Dec. 1992	OSCE Mission to Georgia[140] (Georgia)	CIV. STAFF: Armenia, Austria, Azerbaijan, Belarus, Belgium, Bosnia and Herzegovina, Bulgaria, Canada, Croatia, Czech Rep., Estonia, Finland, France, Germany, Greece, Hungary, Ireland, Italy, Latvia, Lithuania, Macedonia (Former Yugoslav Republic of, FYROM), Moldova, Netherlands, Norway, Poland, Romania, Russia, Slovakia, Sweden, Switzerland, Turkey, UK, Ukraine, USA	78[141]	71	–	–	16.4	–
–(CSO 4 Feb. 1993)[142] Apr. 1993	OSCE Mission to Moldova[143] (Moldova)	CIV. STAFF: Belarus, France, Germany, Norway, Poland, Slovakia, UK, USA	10[144]	11[145]	–	–	1.9	–
–(Rome Ministerial Council Decision, no. 4.1 on 1 Dec. 1993)[146] Feb. 1994	OSCE Centre in Dushanbe[147] (Tajikistan)	CIV. STAFF: Belarus, Bulgaria, France, Hungary, Italy, Latvia, Lithuania, Netherlands, Norway, Romania, Russia, Sweden, USA	16[148]	17[149]	–	–	5.1	–

Acronym/ (Legal instrument/ Authorization date/ Start date	Name/ (Location)	Countries contributing troops, military observers (MIL. OBS), civilian police (CIV. POL.) or civilian staff (CIV. STAFF) in 2005	Troops/ Military observers/ Civilian police/ Civilian staff		Total deaths to date/in 2005 (owing to hostilities, accidents, illness)[1]	Cost ($ m.): 2005/ Unpaid
			Approved	Actual		
–(10 Aug. 1995)[150] Aug. 1995	Personal Representative of the Chairman-in-Office on the Conflict Dealt with by the OSCE Minsk Conference[151] (Azerbaijan: Nagorno-Karabakh)	CIV. STAFF: Czech Rep., **Finland**, Hungary, Poland, UK, Ukraine	– – 6	– – 6	– –	1.3 –
–(Ministerial Council, 8 Dec. 1995)[152] Dec. 1995	OSCE Mission to Bosnia and Herzegovina[153] (Bosnia and Herzegovina)	CIV. STAFF: Albania, *Armenia*, Austria, Azerbaijan, Belgium, Bulgaria, Canada, Czech Rep., *Denmark*, **Finland**, France, Georgia, Germany, Hungary, Ireland, *Italy*, **Japan**, *Kyrgyzstan*, Latvia, Lithuania, Moldova, Netherlands, Norway, **Portugal**, *Romania*, Russia, **Slovenia**, Spain, Sweden, Switzerland, **Tajikistan**, Turkey, UK, USA	– – 37[154]	– – 127	– –	21.3 –
–(PC/DEC 112, 18 Apr. 1996)[155] July 1996	OSCE Mission to Croatia[156] (Croatia)	CIV. STAFF: *Armenia*, Austria, *Belarus*, *Belgium*, Bulgaria, *Canada*, Czech Rep., *Denmark*, **Estonia**, Finland, France, Georgia, Germany, Greece, *Ireland*, Italy, *Japan*, *Kyrgyzstan*, *Latvia*, **Lithuania**, Moldova, Netherlands, *Norway*, Poland, Romania, *Russia*, Slovakia, Spain, Sweden, UK, *Ukraine*, USA, **Uzbekistan**	– – 67[157]	– – 51	– –	11.6 –
–(PC/DEC 160, 27 Mar. 1997)[158] Apr. 1997	OSCE Presence in Albania[159] (Albania)	CIV. STAFF: Austria, Belarus, Bulgaria, *Canada*, *Croatia*, Czech Rep., Finland, France, Germany, *Hungary*, Ireland, *Italy*, *Japan*, **Latvia**, *Moldova*, **Netherlands**, *Romania*, Spain, Sweden, UK, USA	– – –	– – 27	– –	4.7 –

Acronym (legal basis) / Start date	Name, Location	Contributing countries	Approved	Actual	Deaths	Cost ($ m.)
OMIK (PC.DEC 305, 1 July 1999)[160] July 1999	OSCE Mission in Kosovo[161] (Serbia and Montenegro: Kosovo)	CIV. STAFF: Albania, Armenia, Austria, Azerbaijan, *Belarus*, Belgium, Bosnia and Herzegovina, Bulgaria, Canada, *Croatia*, Czech Rep., Denmark, Estonia, Finland, France, Georgia, Germany, Greece, Hungary, *Iceland*, Ireland, Italy, *Japan, Kyrgyzstan, Latvia, Lithuania, Macedonia,* Moldova, Netherlands, Norway, Poland, Portugal, Romania, Russia, *Slovakia,* Slovenia, Spain, Sweden, *Switzerland,* Tajikistan, Turkey, <u>UK,</u> *Ukraine,* <u>USA,</u> Uzbekistan	–	284	3	42.8
OMiSaM (PC.DEC 401, 11 Jan. 2001)[162] Mar. 2001	OSCE Mission to Serbia and Montenegro[163] (Serbia and Montenegro)	CIV. STAFF: *Austria,* Belgium, Bosnia and Herzegovina, Bulgaria, Canada, Estonia, **Finland,** France, Germany, Greece, Ireland, Italy, *Kyrgyzstan,* Latvia, *Liechtenstein,* **Moldova,** Netherlands, Norway, Portugal, **Romania,** *Slovakia,* Sweden, Turkey, UK, <u>USA</u>	–[164]	64	–	12.1
Ad hoc coalitions (6 operations)	**(55 countries participated in 2005)**		187 000 2 000 – 195	187 086 1 695 1 377 175	2 459 904	68 362.8
NNSC (Armistice Agreement)[165] July 1953	Neutral Nations Supervisory Commission[166] (North Korea/South Korea)	MIL. OBS: Sweden, Switzerland	–	9	–	2.3
MFO (Protocol to Treaty of Peace)[167] Apr. 1982	Multinational Force and Observers[168] (Egypt: Sinai)	MIL. OBS: Australia, Canada, Colombia, Fiji, France, Hungary, Italy, New Zealand, Norway, Uruguay, <u>USA</u> CIV. STAFF: USA	2 000 15[169]	1 686 15	49 1 (–, –, 1)	51.0
TIPH 2 (Hebron Protocol)[170] Jan. 1997	Temporary International Presence in Hebron[171] (Hebron)	TROOPS: Turkey CIV. POL.: Denmark, Italy, <u>Norway</u> CIV. STAFF: Denmark, Italy, <u>Norway,</u> Sweden, Switzerland, Turkey	180[172]	6 26 40	2	2.0

Acronym/ (Legal instrument/ Authorization date)/ Start date	Name/ (Location)	Countries contributing troops, military observers (MIL. OBS), civilian police (CIV. POL.) or civilian staff (CIV. STAFF) in 2005	Troops/ Military observers/ Civilian police/ Civilian staff		Total deaths to date/in 2005 (owing to hostilities, accidents, illness)[1]	Cost ($ m.): 2005/ Unpaid
			Approved	Actual		
-(SCR 1464)[173] Feb. 2003	Operation Licorne[174] (Côte d'Ivoire)	TROOPS: France	4 000	4 000	20[175] 8	350.4[176] –
			–	–		
			–	–		
			–	–		
RAMSI (Biketawa Declaration)[177] July 2003	Regional Assistance Mission in the Solomon Islands[178] (Solomon Islands)	TROOPS: Australia, Fiji, Papua New Guinea, New Zealand, Tonga CIV. POL.: Australia, Cook Islands, Fiji, Kiribati, Papua New Guinea, Nauru, New Zealand, Samoa, Tonga, Tuvalu, Vanuatu	–	80	2 2 (1, 1, –)	157.0[180] –
			–	–		
			–	300[179]		
			–	120[179]		
MNF-I (SCR 1511)[181] Nov. 2003	Multinational Force in Iraq[182] (Iraq)	TROOPS: Albania, Armenia, Australia, Azerbaijan, Bosnia and Herzegovina, *Bulgaria*, Czech Rep., Denmark, El Salvador, Estonia, Georgia, Italy, Japan, Kazakhstan, Korea (South), Latvia, Lithuania, Macedonia (Former Yugoslav Republic of, FYROM), Moldova, Mongolia, Netherlands, *Norway*, Poland, Portugal, Romania, Singapore, Slovakia, UK, *Ukraine*, USA CIV. POL.: Australia, Austria, Belgium, Canada, Croatia, Czech Rep., Estonia, Finland, *Hungary*, Jordan, Singapore, Slovakia, Slovenia, Sweden, UK, USA	–	183 000[183]	2 387 895 (707, 140, 29)[185]	67 800.8[186] –
			–	1 051[184]		
			–	–		

Notes: A/RES = UN General Assembly Resolution; CPA = Coalition Provisional Authority; CSO = OSCE Committee of Senior Officials (now the Senior Council); DDR = disarmament, demobilization and reintegration; DMZ = Demilitarized Zone; DPA = UN Department of Political Affairs; DPKO = UN Department of Peacekeeping Operations; FY = financial year; GA = UN General Assembly; MC = Ministerial Council; MOU = Memorandum of Understanding; NAC = North Atlantic Council; PC = OSCE Permanent Council; PC.DEC = OSCE Permanent Council Decision; SC = UN Security Council; SCR = UN Security Council Resolution; UNVs = UN Volunteers.

[1] The breakdown according to cause of death gives deaths classified in 2005. This may include deaths in the preceding year whose cause was previously unknown. Some deaths in 2005 have not yet been classified. Consequently, subtotals for deaths owing to hostilities, accidents and illness may not add up to the total number of deaths in 2005. Data on fatality numbers for all DPKO missions were obtained from UN, DPKO, 'Fatalities by mission and incident type—as of December 29 2005', URL <http://www.un.org/Depts/dpko/fatalities/fatal2.htm>.

[2] For UN operations, the underlined country represents the country with the largest number of personnel deployed to the field. Data on countries participating in UN operations were obtained from United Nations, DPKO, 'UN mission's contributions by country', 31 Dec. 2005, URL <http://www.un.org/Depts/dpko/dpko/contributors/2005/dec2005_5.pdf>.

[3] Total for the 17 operations listed in the table. Data on the number of personnel for all DPKO missions were obtained from UN, DPKO, 'Missions summary of military and police', 31 Dec. 2005, URL <http://www.un.org/Depts/dpko/dpko/contributors/2005/dec2005_4.pdf>.

[4] Total for the costs of the 17 operations listed in the table. UNTSO and UNMOGIP are funded through the UN's regular budget and consequently should not suffer arrears. Data on budgets for all 17 operations were obtained from UN, DPKO, 'Background note on peacekeeping operations', 31 Dec. 2005, URL <http://www.un.org/Depts/dpko/dpko/bnote.htm>.

[5] UNTSO was established in May 1948 to assist the Mediator and the Truce Commission in supervising the observance of the truce in Palestine after the 1948 Arab–Israeli War. The mandate was maintained during 2005.

[6] UN, Proposed programme budget for the biennium 2006–2007, UN document A/60/6 (section 5), 2 May 2005, p. 29.

[7] The mission is supported by 119 locally recruited staff members.

[8] UNMOGIP was established by SCR 91 (30 Mar. 1951) to replace the UN Commission for India and Pakistan. Its task is to supervise the ceasefire in Kashmir under the 1949 Karachi Agreement. A positive decision by the SC is required to terminate the mission.

[9] UN (note 6), p. 26.

[10] The mission is supported by 47 locally recruited staff members.

[11] UNFICYP was established by SCR 186 (4 Mar. 1964) to prevent fighting between the Greek Cypriot and Turkish Cypriot communities and to contribute to the maintenance and restoration of law and order. Since 1974 UNFICYP's mandate has included monitoring the ceasefire and maintaining a buffer zone between the 2 sides.

[12] SCR 1486 (11 June 2003) authorized the increase in the number of Civ. Pol. and SCR 1568 (22 Oct. 2004) reduced the authorized force level by 30% to 860 military personnel (including Mil. Obs).

[13] The mission is supported by 110 locally recruited staff members.

[14] Budget includes a voluntary contribution amounting to one-third of the total cost from the Government of Cyprus and $6.5 million from the Government of Greece. Unpaid costs as of 31 Oct. 2005. UN, Report of the Secretary-General on the United Nations Operation in Cyprus, UN document S/2005/743, 29 Nov. 2005, para. 32.

[15] UNDOF was established after the 1973 October War under the Agreement on Disengagement and SCR 350 (31 May 1974), to maintain the ceasefire between Israel and Syria and to supervise the disengagement of Israeli and Syrian forces. The mandate was extended until 30 June 2006 by SCR 1648 (21 Dec. 2005).

[16] UN, Performance report on the budget of the United Nations Disengagement Observer Force for the period from 1 July 2003 to 30 June 2004: Report of the Secretary-General, UN document A/59/625, 20 Dec. 2004.

[17] The mission is supported by 105 locally recruited staff members.

[18] As of 28 Nov. 2005. UN, Report of the Secretary-General on the United Nations Disengagement Observer Force, UN document S/2005/767, 7 Dec. 2005, para. 9.

[19] UNIFIL was established by SCR 425 and 426 (19 Mar. 1978) to confirm the withdrawal of Israeli forces from southern Lebanon and to assist the Government of Lebanon in ensuring the return of its effective authority in the area. The mandate was renewed until 31 July 2006 by SCR 1655 (31 Jan. 2006).

[20] UN (note 16).

21 The mission is supported by 297 locally recruited staff members.

22 As of 30 Nov. 2005. UN, Report of the Secretary-General on the United Nations Interim Force in Lebanon, UN document S/2006/26, 18 Jan. 2006, para. 30.

23 MINURSO was established by SCR 690 (29 Apr. 1991) to monitor the ceasefire between the Frente Polisiario and the Moroccan Government, verify the reduction of Moroccan troops in Western Sahara, and organize a free and fair referendum. The mandate was renewed until 30 Apr. 2006 by SCR 1634 (28 Oct. 2005).

24 UN, Report of the Secretary-General on the situation concerning Western Sahara, UN document S/2005/254, 19 Apr. 2005, para. 3.

25 The mission is supported by 96 locally recruited staff members.

26 As of 31 Aug. 2005. UN, Report of the Secretary-General on the situation concerning Western Sahara, UN document S/2005/648, 13 Oct. 2005, para. 23.

27 UNOMIG was established by SCR 849 (9 July 1993) and SCR 858 (24 Aug. 1993). The mission's original mandate—to verify the ceasefire between the Georgian Government and the Abkhaz authorities—was invalidated by resumed fighting in Abkhazia in Sep. 1993, and UNOMIG was given an interim mandate to maintain contacts with both sides to the conflict and with Russian military contingents as well as to monitor and report on the situation. Following the signing of the 1994 Agreement on a Ceasefire and Separation of Forces, UNOMIG's mandate was expanded to include monitoring and verification of the implementation of the agreement of SCR 937 (27 July 1994). The present mandate was renewed until 31 Mar. 2006 by SCR 1656 (31 Jan. 2006).

28 SCR 937 (21 July 1994) authorized the increase in the number of Mil. Obs and SCR 1494 (30 July 2003) authorized the addition of a Civ. Pol. component of up to 20 officers.

29 The mission is supported by 187 locally recruited staff members and 2 UNVs.

30 As of 30 Nov. 2005. UN, Report of the Secretary-General on the situation in Abkhazia, Georgia, UN document S/2006/19, 13 Jan. 2006, para. 40.

31 UNMIK was established by SCR 1244 (10 June 1999). Its main tasks are: to promote the establishment of substantial autonomy and self-government in Kosovo; to perform civilian administrative functions; to maintain law and order; to promote human rights; and to ensure the safe return of all refugees and displaced persons. A positive decision by the SC is required to terminate the mission.

32 UN, Report of the Secretary-General on the budget for the United Nations Interim Administration Mission in Kosovo from 1 July 2005 to 30 June 2006, UN document A/59/633, 18 Dec. 2004, p.3.

33 The mission is supported by 2289 locally recruited staff members and 202 UNVs.

34 Sum outstanding as of 28 Feb. 2005. UN, Financing of the United Nations Interim Administration Mission in Kosovo: Report of the Fifth Committee, UN document A/59/772, 8 Apr. 2005.

35 UNAMSIL was established by SCR 1270 (22 Oct. 1999) following the signing of the Lomé Peace Agreement between the Sierra Leone Government and the Revolutionary United Front (RUF) on 7 July 1999. SCR 1346 (30 Mar. 2001) revised the mission's mandate to that of assisting the Sierra Leone Government's efforts to extend its authority, to restore law and order in the country, to promote the resumption of DDR activities and to assist in the anticipated elections. The mission was closed in Dec. 2005, to be succeeded by UNIOSIL in Jan. 2006.

36 SCR 1537 (30 Mar. 2004) authorized the stated level of the mission's residual presence in preparation for withdrawal in Dec. 2005.

37 The mission is supported by 369 locally recruited staff members and 83 UNVs.

38 As of 30 Apr. 2005. UN, Twenty-fifth report of the Secretary-General on the United Nations Mission in Sierra Leone Addendum, UN document S/2005/273/Add.1, 21 June 2005, para. 3.

39 MONUC was established by SCR 1279 (30 Nov. 1999). SCR 1291 (24 Feb. 2000) mandated MONUC to monitor the implementation of the Ceasefire Agreement, to supervise and verify the disengagement of forces, to monitor human rights violations and to facilitate the provision of humanitarian assistance. SCR 1493 (28 July 2003) revised the mandate to a Chapter VII mandate, authorizing the mission to use 'all necessary means' to fulfil its tasks. In 2004 SCR 1565 (1 Oct. 2004) revised the mission's mandate to deploy and maintain a presence in key areas of potential volatility, to cooperate with ONUB to monitor and prevent the movement of combatants and arms across shared borders,

to ensure the protection of civilians and UN staff and facilities, to facilitate the DDR process and to assist in the successful completion of the electoral process. SCR 1635 (28 Oct. 2005) extended MONUC's mandate to Sep. 2006.

40 SCR 1565 (1 Oct. 2004) authorized the expansion of military personnel to 16 700 and SCR 1621 (6 Sep. 2005) authorized the increase in Civ. Pol. personnel. A temporary increase of 300 personnel to MONUC's military strength was authorized by SCR 1635 (28 Oct. 2005) in preparation for the upcoming elections.

41 The mission is supported by 1 388 locally recruited staff members and 491 UNVs.

42 Sum outstanding as of 15 Nov. 2005. UN, Twentieth report of the Secretary-General on the United Nations Organization Mission in the Democratic Republic of the Congo, UN document S/2005/832, 28 Dec. 2005, para. 69.

43 UNMEE was established by SCR 1312 (31 July 2000). The mission was mandated to prepare a mechanism for verifying the cessation of hostilities, the establishment of the Military Co-ordination Commission provided for in the ceasefire agreement, and a peacekeeping deployment. The mission was expanded in Sep. 2000 and tasked to monitor the ceasefire, repatriate Ethiopian troops and monitor the positions of Ethiopian and Eritrean troops outside a 25-km temporary security zone, to chair the Military Co-ordination Commission of the UN and the AU, and to assist in mine clearance. Delays in the demarcation process continue to necessitate the prolongation of the mandate.

44 SCR 1320 (15 Sep 2000) authorized the expansion of the mission's troop level, and SCR 1622 (13 Sep 2005) authorized the reconfiguration of the troop deployment and increased the number of Mil. Obs to 230.

45 The mission is supported by 228 locally recruited staff members and 75 UNVs.

46 As of 31 July 2005. UN, Report of the Secretary-General on Ethiopia and Eritrea, UN document S/2005/553, 30 Aug. 2005, para. 36.

47 UNMISET was established by SCR 1410 (17 May 2002) as a follow-up mission to UNTAET. The tasks were to provide assistance to the administrative structures of the Timorese Government, to provide interim law enforcement while assisting in the development of a new law enforcement agency, and to contribute to the overall security of Timor-Leste. The mission was succeeded by UNOTIL in Apr. 2005.

48 SCR 1543 (14 May 2004) reduced the size of the mission in preparation for its closure.

49 The mission is supported by 523 locally recruited staff members and 100 UNVs.

50 UN, End of mandate report of the Secretary-General on the United Nations Mission of Support in East Timor, UN document, S/2005/310, 12 May 2005.

51 UNMIL was established by SCR 1509 (19 Sep. 2003) with UN Charter Chapter VII powers. The mission is mandated to support the implementation of the ceasefire agreement and the peace process; assist the government's efforts in national security reform, including national police training and the formation of a new, restructured military; support humanitarian and human rights activities; and protect UN staff, facilities and civilians. In carrying out its mandate, the mission cooperates with UNAMSIL and UNOCI.

52 SCR 1626 (19 Sep. 2005) authorized the increase in troop level in preparation for national elections held in Liberia.

53 The mission is supported by 828 locally recruited staff members and 286 UNVs.

54 As of 30 June 2005. UN, Eighth progress report of the Secretary-General on the United Nations Mission in Liberia, UN document S/2005/560, 1 Sep. 2005, para. 96.

55 UNOCI was established by SCR 1528 (27 Feb. 2004) with UN Charter Chapter VII powers, as a follow-up mission to MINUCI. The mission is mandated to monitor the ceasefire agreement and to prevent the movement of combatants and arms across shared borders with Liberia and Sierra Leone; to assist the interim Government of National Reconciliation in implementing DDR programmes, restoring state authority and holding elections; and facilitate the provision of humanitarian assistance. In carrying out its mandate, the mission cooperates with UNAMSIL, UNMIL and the French Licorne forces in Côte d'Ivoire.

56 SCR 1609 (24 June 2005) authorized the expansion of the mission to address the deteriorating situation in the country.

57 The mission is supported by 424 locally recruited staff members and 205 UNVs.

58 As of 30 Nov. 2005. UN, Seventh progress report of the Secretary-General on the United Nations Operation in Côte d'Ivoire, UN document S/2006/2, 3 Jan. 2006, para. 72.

[59] ONUB was established by SCR 1545 (21 May 2004) with UN Charter VII powers. The mission is mandated to ensure the respect of the ceasefire agreement; to promote the re-establishment of confidence among the Burundian forces through a comprehensive DDR programme; to assist in the successful completion of the electoral process; and to protect UN staff, facilities and civilians. In carrying out its mandate, ONUB cooperates with MONUC.

[60] The mission is supported by 388 locally recruited staff members and 146 UNVs.

[61] As of 30 Sep. 2005. UN, Fifth report of the Secretary-General on the United Nations Operation in Burundi, UN document S/2005/728, 21 Nov. 2005, para. 66.

[62] MINUSTAH was established by SCR 1542 (30 Apr. 2004) with UN Charter Chapter VII powers. The mission is tasked to establish a secure and stable environment to ensure that the peace process is carried forward; assist the government's efforts in national security reform, including a comprehensive DDR programme, national police training and the restoration and maintenance of the rule of law; support humanitarian and human rights activities; and protect UN staff, facilities and civilians.

[63] SCR 1608 (22 June 2005) expanded the size of the mission to address the worsening security situation in Haiti.

[64] The mission is supported by 512 locally recruited staff members and 171 UNVs.

[65] As of 31 July 2005. UN, Report of the Secretary-General on the United Nations Stabilization Mission in Haiti, UN document S/2005/631, 6 Oct. 2005, para. 58.

[66] The mission is supported by 512 locally recruited staff members and 171 UNVs.

[67] As of 30 Nov. 2005. United Nations, Report of the Secretary-General on the Sudan, UN document S/2005/821, 21 Dec. 2005, para. 77.

[68] These are UN peace operations not deployed under Chapter VI or VII of the UN Charter but which are directed and administered by the DPKO, with the exception of UNAMI, which is administered by DPA. Civilian staff are not seconded by their governments.

[69] Budget information for missions in this category was obtained from Sang, S., Peace and Security Section, Department of Public Information, United Nations, email to author, 16 Jan. 2006; and UN, Special political missions: estimates in respect of matters of which the GA and/or SC is seized: Timor Leste, UN document, A/RES/60/244, 23 Dec. 2005.

[70] UNAMA was established by SCR 1401 (28 Mar. 2002). The mission is mandated to promote national reconciliation; to fulfil the tasks and responsibilities entrusted to the UN in the 2001 Bonn Agreement, including those related to human rights, the rule of law and gender issues; and to manage all UN humanitarian, relief, recovery and reconstruction activities in Afghanistan in coordination with the Afghan Transitional Authority. In carrying out its mandate, UNAMA cooperates with ISAF.

[71] The mission is supported by 749 locally recruited staff and 42 UNVs.

[72] UNAMI was established by SCR 1500 (July 2003) to support the efforts of the UN Secretary-General's Special Representative to fulfil his mandate to coordinate the UN's humanitarian and reconstruction efforts, promote the safe return of refugees and IDPs, and facilitate international efforts to help rebuild the local institutional capacities, as provided for by SCR 1483 (22 May 2003). In carrying out its mandate, UNAMI cooperates with MNF-I. The current mandate was extended till 10 Aug. 2006 by SCR 1619 (11 Aug. 1005).

[73] These are military advisers. The mission is also supported by 281 locally recruited staff members and 36 UNVs.

[74] UNAMIS was established by SCR 1547 (11 June 2004) to monitor the ceasefire agreement of 25 Sep. 2003 in cooperation with AMIS, and to plan and prepare for the establishment of a full-fledged peace operation. With the signing of the Comprehensive Peace Agreement of 9 Jan. 2005, UNAMIS was replaced by UNMIS in Mar. 2005.

[75] SCR 1547 (11 June 2004), which authorized the mission's strength, did not specify the number of Civ. Pol. or civilian staff.

[76] UNOTIL was established as a follow-on special political mission to UNMISET by SCR 1599 (28 Apr. 2005). UNOTIL is mandated to support the capacity development of state institutions, including the National Police (PNTL) and Border Patrol Unit; and provide training in the area of human rights.

[77] AMIS was initially established by the Agreement with the Sudanese Parties on the Modalities for the Establishment of the Ceasefire Commission and the Deployment of Observers in the Darfur on 28 May 2004 as an observer mission and was endorsed by SCR 1556 (30 July 2004) with UN Charter Chapter VII powers. The mandate was expanded pursuant to a decision adopted at the 17th Meeting of the Africa Union's Peace and Security Council. The mission is currently mandated to monitor the N'Djamena ceasefire

agreement, assist in confidence building between the parties and contribute to a secure environment in Darfur. AU, Communiqué of the 17th meeting of the Peace and Security Council, AU document PSC/PR/Comm. (XVII), 20 Oct. 2004.

[78] In 2005, AMIS underwent 2 phases of expansion (May and June–Aug.) to deploy to full strength. Additional contributors of Mil. obs. are non-specified states listed as EU/US, the Government of Sudan (GOS), the Justice and Equality Movement (JEM), and the Sudan Liberation Movement/Army (SLM/A). EU/US also contributes Civ. Pol. Mtimkulu, B., Head of Peace Support Operations, African Union Secretariat, email to author, 12 Oct. 2005.

[79] 28th Meeting of the Peace and Security Council. AU document PSC/PR/Comm.(XXVIII), 28 Apr. 2005, p. 2.

[80] Official data are not available for 2005. This figure represents estimated cash requirements for 1 July 2005–30 June 2006 at a projected personnel level of 7936. In-kind pledges amount to $213 million. The AU has identified an unspecified funding gap for AMIS for 2005. In Aug. the UNSG reported a funding shortfall of at least $4.6 million. ICG, 'The EU/AU partnership in Darfur: not yet a winning combination', Crisis Group Report, no. 99, 25 Oct. 2005; and UN, Monthly Report of the Secretary-General on Darfur, UN document S/2005/523, 11 Aug. 2005.

[81] The CEMAC Multinational Force was established on 2 Oct. 2002 by decision of the Libreville Summit to secure the border between Chad and the CAR and to guarantee the safety of former President Patassé. Following the 15 Mar. 2003 coup, CEMAC decided at the 21 Mar. 2003 Libreville Summit to amend the mission's mandate to contribute to the overall security environment, to assist in the restructuring of CAR's armed forces and to support the transition process. Communiqué Final du Sommet des Chefs d'État et de Délégation de la Communauté Économique et Monétaire de l'Afrique Centrale, Libreville, 2 Oct. 2002; and 3rd Ordinary Session of the Executive Council, African Union, 4–8 July 2003.

[82] FOMUC is supported and co-located with a detachment of approximately 220 French soldiers. 39 locally recruited staff members provide administrative support. Bibaye Itandas, A. R., Commander, CEMAC Multinational Force, fax to author, 5 Oct. 2005.

[83] Agreement on the Principles Governing the Peaceful Settlement of the Armed Conflict in the Trans-Dniester region, signed in Moscow on 21 July 1992 by the presidents of Moldova and Russia. A Monitoring Commission with representatives of Russia, Moldova and Trans-Dniester was established to coordinate the activities of the joint peacekeeping contingent.

[84] The participation of parties to a conflict in peace operations is typically not included in the table; however, the substantial involvement of the parties to the conflict in this operation is a distinctive feature of CIS operations and of the peace agreement that is the basis for the establishment of the operation. Russia, Moldova and Trans-Dniester contributed 340, 400 and 380 military personnel, respectively. Barbin, V., Minister-Counsellor of the Embassy of Russia in Stockholm, email to author, 26 Sep. 2005; and Galbur, A., Director, DMC, Ministry of Foreign Affairs, Moldova, email to author, 11 Oct. 2005.

[85] The authorized size of each contingent is c. 500 military personnel.

[86] This figure is the total of Russian and Moldovan fatalities only. Causes of deaths were accidents and illnesses.

[87] Agreement on the Principles Governing the Peaceful Settlement of the Conflict in South Ossetia, signed in Dagomys, on 24 June 1992, by Georgia and Russia. A joint Monitoring Commission with representatives of Russia, Georgia, and North and South Ossetia was established to oversee the implementation of the agreement.

[88] The participation of parties to a conflict in peace operations is typically not included in the table; however, the substantial involvement of the parties to the conflict in this operation is a distinctive feature of CIS operations and of the peace agreement that is the basis for the establishment of the operation. The official name of the Ossetian battalion is the Battalion of North Ossetian/Alania. Barbin (note 84).

[89] Georgian–Abkhazian Agreement on a Cease-fire and Separation of Forces, signed in Moscow on 14 May 1994. The operation's mandate was approved by heads of states members of the CIS Council of Collective Security, 21 Oct. 1994, and endorsed by the UN through SCR 937 (21 July 1994). The period of the mission's mandate was extended indefinitely from Jan. 2004. Moscow ITAR-TASS, 17 Dec. 2003, in 'Russia peacekeepers begin planned rotation in Georgia–Abkhazia conflict zone', Foreign Broadcasting Information Service (FBIS), Daily Report-Soviet Union (FBIS-SOV), FBIS-SOV-3003-1217, 18 Dec. 2003.

[90] Other CIS states may participate in the mission. Moscow ITAR-TASS, 25 Dec. 2003, in 'Russian defence minister rules out use of force in Georgia-Abkhaz conflict', FBIS-SOV-2003-1225, 2 Jan. 2004. Barbin (note 84).

[91] EU Council Joint Actions do not provide specific authorized personnel numbers; rather, they only request that staff levels are consistent with the objectives and structures of each missions. The numbers listed below are those that have been agreed by the EU.

[92] The mission was established by the Brioni Agreement, signed on 7 July 1991 at Brioni, Croatia, by representatives of the European Community (EC) and the 6 republics of the former Yugoslavia. MOUs were signed with the governments of Albania in 1997 and Croatia in 1998. The ECMM became the EUMM upon becoming an instrument of the EU's Common Foreign and Security Policy (CFSP), and was mandated to monitor political and security developments, borders, inter-ethnic issues and refugee returns; to contribute to the early-warning mechanism of the European Council; and to contribute to confidence building and stabilization in the region. Council Joint Action of 22 Dec. 2000 on the European Union Monitoring Mission, EU document 2000/811/CFSP, 23 Dec. 2000, Introduction, para. 6 and Article 1, para. 2. In 2005, Council Joint Action 2005/807/CFSP (21 Nov. 2005) amended the mission's geographical mandate to focus on Kosovo and Serbia and Montenegro.

[93] Backman, T., Chief of Personnel EUMM HQ Sarajevo, email to author, 27 Sep. 2005.

[94] The EUMM operates in Albania and in Bosnia and Herzegovina, Croatia, FYROM, Serbia and Montenegro, Kosovo and Presovo.

[95] Mission is supported by 74 locally contracted staff and around 40 temporary/replacement employees.

[96] The EUPM was established by Council Joint Action 2002/210/CFSP of 11 Mar. 2002 to ensure sustainable policing arrangements under BiH ownership in accordance with European and international standards. The mission is tasked to monitor, mentor and inspect local police management.

[97] As of 20 Sep. 2005. 321 of the 367 Civ. Pol. deployed are seconded by their respective EU member states, and 45 of the 53 civilian staff are from EU member states. Ilaria, Z., Senior Spokesperson EUPM, email to author, 22 Sep. 2005; and Kis, A., EU Council Secretariat, DG(E), Directorate IX–Civilian crisis management and coordination, Police Unit, telephone conversation with author, 18 Oct. 2005.

[98] EUPOL PROXIMA was established by Council Joint Action 2003/681/CFSP of 29 Sep. 2003 to support the development of professional police service in FYROM in accordance with European policing standards. In carrying out its activities, the mission cooperated with the OSCE Spillover Mission to Skopje. The mission closed on 15 Dec. 2005 and was succeeded by EUPAT.

[99] As of 31 Aug. 2005. Magnaguagno, L., Press and Public Information Officer, EUPOL PROXIMA, email to author, 31 Aug. 2005.

[100] EUJUST THEMIS was established by Council Joint Action 2004/523/CFSP of 28 June 2004 to assist the Georgian Government in developing a coordinated strategy for reform of the criminal justice sector. The mission closed on 14 July 2005.

[101] Paesen, S., EU Council Secretariat, DG E, Directorate IX, telephone conversation with author, 22 Sep. 2005.

[102] The mission was supported by 16 local staff. Two rule-of-law experts will remain for an additional 6 months beyond the mission's closure under EUSR to assist the Georgians in the implementation of reform strategies.

[103] Budget was allocated for the mission's mandated period, 15 July 2004–15 July 2005.

[104] EUFOR ALTHEA was established by Council Joint Action 2004/570/CFSP of 12 July 2004, and was endorsed and given Chapter VII Powers by UN Security Council Resolution 1551 (9 July 2004). The mission is a follow-up mission to NATO's SFOR and is mandated to maintain a secure environment for the implementation of the 1995 Dayton Agreement, to assist in the strengthening of local capacity, and to support Bosnia and Herzegovina's progress towards EU integration.

[105] The contingents are grouped into 3 task forces—MNTF North (Tuzla), MNTF Southeast (Mostar) and MNTF Northwest (Banja Luka)—for which Finland, France and the UK are the framework nations. As of 11 Nov. 2005, EU nations contribute 5502 troops and non-EU states contribute 768 troops. EUFOR website, URL <http://www.euforbih.org/organisation/050810_strength.htm>.

[106] EUPOL Kinshasa was established by Council Joint Action 2004/847/CFSP of 9 Dec. 2004 as a follow-on mission to the Integrated Police Unit (IPU) and is mandated to monitor, mentor and advise the Congolese police force.

[107] After having been pre-deployed 3 Feb. 2005, the mission was officially launched 12 Apr. 2005. Bianchi, S., Principal Administrator, Directorate-General DG(E), Directorate IX, Police Unit, email to author, 22 Sep. 2005.

[108] Bianchi (note 107).

[109] EUJUST LEX was established by Council Joint Action 2005/190/CFSP of 7 Mar. 2005 as an integrated civilian mission to strengthen Iraq's criminal justice system through training of police officers and magistrates. The mission will serve as a complement to current UN and NATO operations in Iraq and work in accordance with SCR 1546 (8 June 2004).

[110] Training is hosted by 10 member states while 10 other states are providing training and other support. Those countries that have been unwilling to offer personnel for NTM-I are anticipated to host the training. Training is conducted mainly in undisclosed locations in EU countries. White, S., Head of Mission, EUJUST LEX, email to author, 31 Aug. 2005.

[111] EUSEC DR Congo was established by Council Joint Action 2005/355/CFSP of 2 May 2005 as a follow-up and complement to EUPOL Kinshasa. The mission is mandated to advise and assist the Congolese authorities in security issues, ensuring that policies are congruent with international humanitarian law, the standards of democratic governance and the principles of the rule of law. In carrying out its activities, EUSEC operates in close coordination with EUPOL Kinshasa and MONUC.

[112] Déjoué, G., EU Council Secretariat, Directorate-General E DG(E), External Economic Relations, Common Foreign and Security Policy, Directorate VIII–Defence aspects: exercises, email to author, 26 Aug. 2005.

[113] The AMM was established by Council Joint Action 2005/643/CFSP of 9 Sep. 2005 to monitor implementation of the peace agreement set out in the MOU signed by the Government of Indonesia (GoI) and the Free Aceh Movement (GAM) on 15 Aug. 2005. The mission's mandated tasks include monitoring the ceasefire; the DDR of GAM fighters; assisting in the withdrawal of Indonesian military and police forces; and monitoring the human rights situation.

[114] Hueso, V., EU Council Secretariat, email to author, 28 Sep. 2005.

[115] Of this total, 124 are from EU member states as well as Norway and Switzerland and 92 are from the 5 participating ASEAN countries. The mission is also supported by 77 locally recruited staff members.

[116] EU BAM Rafah was established pursuant to Council Joint Action 2005/889/CFSP of 12 Dec. 2005 and on the basis of the Agreement on Movement and Access reached between Israel and the Palestinian Authority (PA) on 15 Nov. 2005. The mission is mandated to support the PA's efforts in capacity building.

[117] Bruzzesse del Pozzo, F., EU Council Secretariat, Directorate-General DG(E), Directorate IX, Police Unit, email to author, 26 Jan. 2006.

[118] EUPAT was established by Council Joint Action 2005/826/CFSP of 24 Nov. 2005 as a follow-up mission to EUPOL PROXIMA. The mission is mandated to monitor the country's police in the field of border control, public peace and order and accountability, the fight against corruption and organized crime. EUPAT activities will focus on middle and senior levels of management.

[119] Magnaguagno, L., EUPAT, email to author, 19 Jan. 2006.

[120] Data on budgets for NATO-led missions received from Day, J., Military Budget Committee Section, NATO, email to author, 6 Oct. 2005.

[121] KFOR received its mandate from the SC on 10 June 1999. Its tasks include deterring renewed hostilities, establishing a secure environment, supporting UNMIK and monitoring borders. SCR 1244 (10 June 1999).

[122] Along with KFOR Headquarters in Pristina, KFOR contingents are grouped in 5 task forces: MNTF Centre located in Lipljan is led by Finland; MNTF North located in Novo Selo is led by France; MNB Southwest located in Prizren is led by Germany; MNB East located in Urosevac is led by USA; and MN Specialized Unit (MSU) located in Pristina is led by Italy. The MSU is a police force with military status that is among other things, mandated to maintain a secure environment, patrol and perform law enforcement duties. Dehaes, K., Public Information Office of the International Military Staff of NATO HQ, phone conversation with author, 12 Oct. 2005; and KFOR website, URL <http://www.nato.int/kfor/kfor/structure.htm>.

[123] NATO member states contributed a total of 14 310 personnel and Partnership for Peace countries contributed 2864.

[124] On 20 Dec. 2001 the SC, acting under UN Charter Chapter VII, authorized a multinational force to help the Afghan Interim Authority maintain security, as envisaged in Annex I of the 2001 Bonn Agreement. UN document SC/7248, 20 Dec. 2001. In Aug. 2003 NATO took on the command and coordination of the mission, with the Allied Joint Force Command Brunssum in charge of overall operations. In 2004 ISAF expanded its area of operations beyond Kabul to include 9 other provinces. The current mandate was extended until 12 Oct. 2006 by SCR 1623 (13 Sep. 2005).

[125] As of 23 Jan. 2006. France and Germany are the designated lead nations for the Kabul Multinational Brigade (KMNB). Germany, Italy and Canada are the 3 principal contributors and account for half the number of mission troops. Szabo, Z., SHAPE PIO, email to author, 24 Jan. 2006.

[126] The mission was established under the authority of SCR 1546 (8 June 2004), which requests member states and other international organizations to assist the Iraqi Government's efforts in building the capacity of Iraq's security forces. The NAC agreed on 30 July 2004 to the establishment of NATO Training Implementation Mission (NTIM-I). On 16 Dec. 2004, the NAC, decided to transform the training implementation mission into a full-fledged training mission to support the build-up of the Iraqi Security Forces in Iraq.

[127] Training is also conducted in undisclosed locations outside Iraq. Veltri, F., Deputy Chief Public Information Officer, JFC Naples, NATO, email to author, 12 Oct. 2005.

[128] Misión de Apoyo al Proceso de Paz (MAPP/OEA) was established by OAS Permanent Council decision CP/RES. 859 (1397/04) on 6 Feb. 2004 in support of the efforts of the Colombian Government to engage in a political dialogue with the ELN. The mission is tasked to facilitate the DDR process.

[129] Perez de Vargas, C., Head of Mission, Mission to Support the Peace Process in Columbia, email to author, 17 Jan. 2006.

[130] The mission is supported by 11 national professionals and 28 administrative staff members.

[131] Budget for the mission is financed by contributions from Ireland, the Netherlands, Sweden and the International Organization for Migration.

[132] The mission was established by OAS Permanent Council decision CP/RES. 806 (1303/02) on 16 Jan. 2002 to contribute to the resolution of the political crisis by *inter alia* assisting the Government of Haiti to strengthen its democratic processes and institutions. In June 2004, the OAS General Assembly, through A/RES. 2058 (XXXIV-O/04) amended the mandate to include: assistance in the holding of elections, promoting and protecting human rights, and in the professionalization of the Haitian National Police. In carrying out its mandate, the mission cooperates with MINUSTAH and CARICOM.

[133] Brunet, L., OAS Special Mission to Haiti, email to author, 14 Sep. 2005.

[134] The mission is supported by 50 locally employed staff members.

[135] Data on budgets for all OSCE missions obtained from the OSCE Unified Budget for 2005, adopted at the 555th Plenary Meeting of the Permanent Council, PC.DEC/672, 12 May. 2005.

[136] Decision to establish the mission taken at 16th Committee of Senior Officials (CSO) meeting, *Journal*, no. 3 (18 Sep. 1992), Annex 1. The mission was authorized by the FYROM Government through Articles of Understanding agreed by an exchange of letters on 7 Nov. 1992. The mission's tasks include assessing the level of stability and the possibility of conflict and unrest.

[137] Broughton, S., Public Information Officer, OSCE Spillover Monitor to Skopje, email to author, 6 Sep. 2005.

[138] OSCE, PC.DEC/439, 28 Sep. 2001.

[139] Decision to establish the mission taken at the 17th CSO meeting, *Journal*, no. 2 (6 Nov. 1992), Annex 2. The mission was authorized by the Government of Georgia through an MOU of 23 Jan. 1993 and by South Ossetia's leaders through an exchange of letters on 1 Mar. 1993. Initially, the objective of the mission was to promote negotiations between the conflicting parties. The mandate was expanded on 29 Mar. 1994 to include monitoring of the Joint Peacekeeping Forces in South Ossetia. In Dec. 1999 this was expanded to include the monitoring of Georgia's borders with Ingushetia. OSCE, PC.DEC/450, 13 Dec. 2001. In Nov. 2002 the mandate was again expanded to observe and report on cross-border movement between Georgia and the Dagestan Republic of the Russian Federation. OSCE, PC.DEC/522, 19 Dec. 2002.

[140] Okropiridze, I., Personnel Department, OSCE Mission to Georgia, email to author, 7 Sep. 2005.

[141] OSCE, PC.DEC/628, 6 Aug. 2004.

[142] Decision to establish the mission taken at the 19th CSO meeting, *Journal*, no. 3 (4 Feb. 1993), Annex 3. Authorized by the Government of Moldova through MOU, 7 May 1993. The mission's tasks include assisting the parties in pursuing negotiations on a lasting political settlement to the conflict as well as gathering and providing information on the situation.

[143] Neukirch, C., Press and Public Affairs Officer, OSCE Mission to Moldova, email to author, 16 Dec. 2005.

[144] OSCE, PC.DEC/469, 11 Apr. 2002.

[145] The mission is currently also supported by an arms control consultant and an officer seconded temporarily to the Mission's Program Management Cell (PMC) by the US Armed Forces.

[146] The OSCE Centre in Dushanbe was established by a decision taken at the 4th meeting of the Ministerial Council, Rome (CSCE/4-C/Dec. 1), Decision I.4, 1 Dec. 1993. No bilateral MOU was signed. The tasks of the mission include facilitating dialogue, promoting human rights and informing the OSCE about further developments. This was expanded in 2002 to include an economic and envionmental dimension.

[147] Formerly the OSCE Mission to Tajikistan. In Oct. 2002 a decision was taken to change the name of the mission to reflect the change of focus of its activities. Benigni, E., Political and Media Officer, OSCE Centre in Dushanbe, email to author, 26 Jan. 2006.

[148] OSCE, PC.DEC/469, 11 Apr. 2002.

[149] The mission is supported by 70 locally recruited staff members.

[150] In Aug. 1995 the OSCE Chairman-in-Office (CIO) appointed a Personal Representative (PR) on the Conflict Dealt with by the OSCE Minsk Conference, which seeks a peaceful settlement of the Nagorno-Karabakh conflict. The PR's mandate consists of assisting the Minsk Group in planning possible peacekeeping operations, assisting the parties in confidence-building measures and in humanitarian matters, and monitoring the ceasefire between the parties. OSCE, Annual Report 2000 on OSCE Activities (1 Nov. 1999–31 Oct. 2000), 24 Nov. 2000.

[151] Schrooten, S., Mission Programme Section, Conflict Prevention Center, OSCE Secretariat, email to author, 30 Jan. 2006.

[152] Decision to establish the mission taken at 5th meeting, Ministerial Council, Budapest, 8 Dec. 1995 (MC(5). DEC/1) in accordance with Annex 6 of the 1995 Dayton Agreement. The tasks of the mission include assisting the parties in regional stabilization measures and democracy building.

[153] Soldo, M., Personal Assistant to the Chief of Staff and Planning, OSCE Mission to Bosnia and Herzegovina, email to author, 26 Aug. 2005.

[154] OSCE, PC.DEC/451, 21 Dec. 2001.

[155] The decision to establish the mission was taken by the PC on 18 Apr. 1996 (PC.DEC/112). Adjustments to the mandate were made by the PC on 26 June 1997 (PC.DEC/176) and 25 June 1998 (C/DEC/239). The mission's tasks include assisting and monitoring the return of refugees and displaced persons as well as the protection of national minorities.

[156] Cesarino, A., Spokesperson, Media and Public Affairs Unit, OSCE Mission to Croatia, email to author, 29 Aug. 2005.

[157] OSCE, PC.DEC/514, 12 Dec. 2002.

[158] The decision to establish the mission was taken at the 108th meeting of the PC in 27 Mar. 1997 (OSCE, PC/DEC/160). The current mandate was set on 11 Dec. 1997 (PC.DEC/206).

[159] Ackerman, A., Mission Programme Officer, Conflict Prevention Centre, OSCE Secretariat, email to author, 24 Jan. 2006.

[160] On 1 July 1999 the PC established the OSCE Mission in Kosovo to replace the transitional OSCE Kosovo Task Force, which had been established on 8 June 1999 (PC.DEC/296). The tasks of the OSCE Mission to Kosovo include training police, judicial personnel and civil administrators, and monitoring and promoting human rights. The mission is a component (Pillar III) of UNMIK.

[161] Cycmanick, C., Information Officer, OSCE Mission in Kosovo, email to author, 10 Oct. 2005.

[162] On 11 Jan. 2001 the PC established the OSCE Mission in the Federal Republic of Yugoslavia with an initial mandate of 1 year. Its mandate is to provide expert assistance to the authorities of Serbia and Montenegro and civil society groups in the areas of democratization and human and minority rights, assist with the restructuring and training of law enforcement agencies and the judiciary, provide media support and facilitate the return of refugees. OSCE, PC.DEC/401, 11 Jan. 2001. On 15 Nov. 2001 the PC directed the mission to open an office in Podgorica, Montenegro. OSCE, PC.DEC/444, 15 Nov. 2001.

[163] Formerly the OSCE Mission to the Federal Republic of Yugoslavia. In Feb. 2003, a decision (PC.DEC/533) was taken to change the name of the country, following the adoption of the Constitutional Charter of the State Union of Serbia and Montenegro. Eick, M., Spokesperson, OSCE Mission to Serbia and Montenegro, email to author, 12 Oct. 2005.

[164] An MOU regarding the modalities of the Mission including the appropriate number of international staff was signed with the Government of the Federal Republic of Yugoslavia on 16 Mar. 2001.

[165] Agreement concerning a military armistice in Korea, signed at Panmunjom on 27 July 1953 by the Commander-in-Chief, UN Command; the Supreme Commander of the Korean People's Army; and the Commander of the Chinese People's Volunteers. Entered into force on 27 July 1953.

[166] Baumgartner, A., Chief Public Information Officer, Embassy of Switzerland in Stockholm, email to author, 26 Jan. 2006; and Lindström, K., Deputy Director, Head of East Asia Group, Division for Asia and the Pacific, Ministry for Foreign Affairs, Sweden, email to author, 27 Jan. 2006.

[167] The Multinational Force and Observers (MFO) was established on 3 Aug. 1981 by the Protocol to the Treaty of Peace between Egypt and Israel, signed on 26 Mar. 1979. Deployment began on 20 Mar. 1982 following the withdrawal of Israeli forces from Sinai but was nonetheless not operational until 25 Apr. 1982, the same day that Israel was to return the Sinai to Egyptian sovereignty.

[168] MFO, Director General's Report delivered to the Trilateral Meeting, Rome, 11 Oct. 2004, p. 5, URL <http://www.mfo.org/files/Trilat_2004_report.pdf>.

[169] A large part of the MFO's basic duties is performed by the Civilian Observer Unit (COU). The COU has its origins in the US Sinai Field Mission (SFM) which came into existence with the Sinai II Agreement of 1975. The SFM ceased operations in 1982 and most of its members transferred to the COU. The present COU contains 15 members, all of whom are US nationals. Protocol to the Treaty of Peace, Protocol Establishing the Multilateral Force and Observers, 3 Aug. 1981, p. 7.

[170] The mission receives its authority from the Protocol Concerning the Redeployment in Hebron, 15 Jan. 1997, and the Agreement on the Temporary International Presence in Hebron, 21 Jan. 1997. The mandate of the mission is to provide by its presence a secure and stable environment. The mandate is renewed every 3 months pending approval from both the Palestinian and Israeli parties.

[171] Forselv, G., Senior Press and Information Officer, TIPH, email to author, 23 Aug. 2005.

[172] Agreement on Temporary International Presence in City of Hebron, 21 Jan. 1997, URL <http://www.tiph.org/documents/Agreement.asp>.

[173] The SC initially authorized, under Chapter VII and in accordance with Chapter VIII, the deployment of French troops alongside ECOMICI to contribute to a secure environment and allow for the implementation of the Linas-Marcoussis Agreement. SCR 1464 (4 Feb. 2003). The mission receives its current authorization through SCR 1528 (27 Feb. 2004). Licorne forces work in close cooperation with UNOCI.

[174] Lyet, F. Defence Attaché, Embassy of France in Stockholm, fax to author, 17 Oct. 2005.

[175] Thus far, there have been 12 casualties resulting from hostile action, 7 accidental deaths, and 1 death caused by illness. The breakdown for 2005 was not available.

[176] This sum is referred to as 'surcôut' budget, a figure accounting for real expenses as well as anticipated and inevitable expenses.

[177] The Regional Assistance Mission was established in the framework of the 2000 Biketawa Declaration in which members of the Pacific Islands Forum agree to a collective response to crises usually on the request of the host government. 31st Pacific Islands Forum Comuniqué 2000, Tarawa, Kiribati, 23–30 Oct. 2000. The mission is mandated to assist the Solomon Islands Government in restoring law and order and in building up the capacity of the police force.

[178] McCaffrey, N., Policy Adviser, Office of the Special Coordinator, RAMSI, email to author, 11 Oct. 2005.

[179] This figure includes 20 lawyers and legal advisers, 30 advisers for prisons, up to 60 advisers for the nation-building and development components of the operation, and 17 advisers and in-line personnel for the Ministry of Finance.

[180] This figure covers both RAMSI activities and Australia's overseas development aid to Solomon Islands.

[181] The Multinational Force in Iraq was authorized by SCR 1511 (16 Oct. 2003) to contribute to the maintenance of security and stability in Iraq, including for the purpose of ensuring the necessary conditions for the implementation of UNAMI's mandated tasks. The mandate of the MNF was reaffirmed by SCR 1546 (8 June 2004) following the dissolution of the Coalition Provisional Authority and the subsequent transfer of sovereignty to the Interim Government of Iraq.

[182] The territory of Iraq is divided into 6 major areas of responsibility and is covered by the following units: MNF Northwest MND Baghdad, MND North Central, MNF West (for which the USA is the lead nation). MND Central South and MND Southeast are maintained by Poland and the UK, respectively. 'Multi-National Force–Iraq Major Units', URL <http://www.mnf-iraq.com/oif.htm>, 5 Oct. 2005; O'Hanlon, M. E. and Kamp, N., Brookings Institution, Saban Center for Middle East Policy, 'Iraq Index: Tracking reconstruction and security in post-Saddam Iraq', 5 Jan. 2006, URL <http://www.brookings.edu/iraqindex>; Bertucci, A., Public Affairs officer, Civilian Police Assistance Training Team, email to author, 5 Oct. 2005; Iraq Weekly Status Report, URL <http://www.state.gov/p/nea/rls/rpt/iraqstatus/>, 14 Sep. 2005; and Iraq Coalition Casualty Count, URL <http://icasualties.org/oif/>.

[183] The USA contributed 160 000 soldiers; the UK, 8000; South Korea, 3600; Italy, 3000; Poland, 1700; and the remaining 6700 soldiers by the rest of the coalition. Of this total, 372 British and US military personnel are assigned to provide support to the Civilian Police Assistance Training Team.

[184] This figure includes the 291 training officers operating out of the Jordanian facility.

[185] As of 4 Jan. 2006. This figure includes 20 deaths owing to unspecified causes. 841 of the 895 fatalities were US soldiers, 26 were British soldiers and the remaining 28 were from other countries.

[186] This figure is the sum of British and US contributions; contributing countries bear the cost for their personnel. The US contribution for FY 2005 (1 Oct. 2004–30 Sep. 2005) is $66.2 billion, which includes the $25 billion emergency reserve fund, approved by Congress in Aug. 2004, to be appropriated in early 2005. The British contribution for the period 1 Oct. 2004–30 Sep. 2005 is estimated to be £910 million. This figure is calculated based on figures for FYs 2004/2005 and 2005/2006 and on the assumption of an even rate of expenditure throughout the financial year. Hough, J., Directorate of Performance and Analysis, British Ministry of Defence, email to author, 4 Oct. 2005.

4. Regional security cooperation in the early 21st century

ALYSON J. K. BAILES and ANDREW COTTEY

I. Introduction

Since 1945, especially since the 1990s, regionalism and regional cooperation have been growing features of world politics. In the decades after World War II, the cold war and decolonization resulted in the establishment of multilateral regional organizations across the world, including the North Atlantic Treaty Organization (NATO), the predecessors of what is today the European Union (EU), the Organization of American States (OAS), the Organization of African Unity (OAU, the predecessor of the African Union, AU), the Arab League and the Association of South East Asian Nations (ASEAN). (A list of these and other regional organizations is presented in table 4.1.) In the 1990s the end of the cold war and the advance of globalization triggered the so-called new regionalism, with the establishment of a number of regional cooperation frameworks, such as the North American Free Trade Agreement (NAFTA) and the Asia–Pacific Economic Cooperation (APEC) process, as well as efforts to rejuvenate and strengthen existing regional institutions and the creation of several sub-regional ones in Europe and Africa.

Security cooperation has been an important part of this wider phenomenon. Some institutions, such as NATO, the Organization for Security and Co-operation in Europe (OSCE) and the ASEAN Regional Forum (ARF), are explicitly and primarily security organizations. Most of the general-purpose regional organizations—such as the Arab League, the AU and the OAS—have significant security dimensions, as do a number of other smaller regional (or sub-regional) groups—such as the Southern African Development Community (SADC) and the Economic Community of West African States (ECOWAS). Many regional and sub-regional organizations bridge the gap between traditional definitions of security and wider concepts of security involving democracy, human rights, and economic and environmental issues. Although many regional institutions are primarily economic and have no explicit or direct security role, even these are often implicitly designed to promote stability, conflict avoidance and the collective viability of their communities—important factors for security—by encouraging integration among their members. This was most obvious in the early development of European integration but is arguably also the case today in institutions such as APEC and the Mercado Común del Sur (MERCOSUR, the Southern Common Market).

Despite this trend towards regional security cooperation, there has been surprisingly little theoretically informed comparative analysis of the phenom-

Table 4.1. Regional organizations and groups with security functions

Organization	Year founded	Number of members	Website URL
Africa			
African Union (AU)	2001	53[a]	www.africa-union.org
Common Market for Eastern and Southern Africa (COMESA)	1994	20	www.comesa.int
Community of Sahel-Saharan States (CEN-SAD)	1998	23	www.cen-sad.org
East African Community (EAC)	1999	3	www.eac.int
Economic and Monetary Community of Central Africa (CEMAC)	1998	6	www.cemac.cf
Economic Community of West African States (ECOWAS)	1975	15[a]	www.ecowas.int
Intergovernmental Authority on Development (IGAD)	1996	7[a]	www.igad.org
Mano River Union	1973	3	–
Southern African Development Community (SADC)	1992	14[a]	www.sadc.int
Americas			
Andean Community of Nations (Andean Pact)	1969	5[a]	www.comunidadandina.org
Caribbean Community (CARICOM)	1973	15	www.caricom.org
Central American Integration System (SICA)	1991	7	www.sgsica.org
Latin American Integration Association (LAIA)	1980	12	www.aladi.org
MERCOSUR (Southern Common Market)	1991	4	www.mercosur.int
North American Free Trade Agreement (NAFTA)	1994	3	www.nafta-sec-alena.org
Organization of American States (OAS)	1948	35[a]	www.oas.org
Rio Group	1987	19	–
Asia			
Australia, New Zealand, United States (ANZUS) Security Treaty	1951	3	–
Asia–Pacific Economic Cooperation (APEC)	1989	21	www.apec.org
Association of South East Asian Nations (ASEAN):	1967	10[a]	www.aseansec.org
ASEAN Regional Forum (ARF)	1994	25[a]	www.aseanregionalforum.org
ASEAN Plus Three (APT)	1997	13[a]	www.aseansec.org/16580.htm
Conference on Interaction and Confidence-building measures in Asia (CICA)	1992	17[a]	www.kazakhstanembassy.org. uk/cgi-bin/index/128

Organization	Year founded	Number of members	Website URL
Economic Cooperation Organization (ECO)	1985	10	www.ecosecretariat.org
Pacific Community	1947	26	www.spc.org.nc
Pacific Islands Forum	1971	16[a]	www.forumsec.org.fj
Shanghai Cooperation Organization (SCO)	2001	6[a]	www.sectsco.org
South Asian Association for Regional Co-operation (SAARC)	1985	8[a]	www.saarc-sec.org
Europe and Euro-Atlantic			
Arctic Council	1996	8	www.arctic-council.org
Baltic Council	1993	3	–
Barents Euro-Arctic Council (BEAC)	1993	7	www.beac.st
Organization of the Black Sea Economic Cooperation (BSEC)	1992	12[a]	www.bsec-organization.org
Central European Initiative (CEI)	1989	17[a]	www.ceinet.org
Collective Security Treaty Organization (CSTO)	2003	6[a]	–
Commonwealth of Independent States (CIS)	1991	11[a]	www.cis.minsk.by
Council of the Baltic Sea States (CBSS)	1992	12[a]	www.cbss.st
Council of Europe	1949	46[a]	www.coe.int
European Union (EU)	1951	25[a]	europa.eu.int
North Atlantic Treaty Organization:	1949	26[a]	www.nato.int
Euro-Atlantic Partnership Council (EAPC)	1997	46[a]	www.nato.int/issues/eapc/
Nordic Council	1952	5	www.norden.org
Organization for Security and Co-operation in Europe:	1973	55[a]	www.osce.org
Stability Pact for South Eastern Europe	1999	40[a]	www.stabilitypact.org
Southeast European Cooperative Initiative (SECI)	1996	12[a]	www.secinet.info
Visegrad Group (V4)	1991	4[a]	www.visegradgroup.org
Western European Union (WEU)	1954	10[a]	www.weu.int
Middle East			
Arab League	1945	22[a]	www.arableagueonline.org
Arab Maghreb Union	1989	5	www.maghrebarabe.org
Council of Arab Economic Unity	1964	10	www.caeu.org.eg
Gulf Cooperation Council (GCC)	1981	6[a]	www.gcc-sg.org
Organization of the Islamic Conference (OIC)	1971	57[a]	www.oic-oci.org

[a] Lists of members and further details of these organizations are given in the glossary in this volume.

enon. There is a growing body of literature on the general phenomenon of regionalism in world politics, particularly the 'new regionalism' that has emerged since the 1990s.[1] However, this literature has primarily an international political economy perspective, reflecting not only the fact that many of the new regional institutions are economic in nature but also an assumption that economic factors are the main drivers behind the new regionalism. This chapter addresses the gap in the literature by providing a generic framework for analysing regional security cooperation as an aspect of global, interstate and (where appropriate) intra-state security governance in the conditions of the first decade of the 21st century.[2]

Section II of this chapter addresses the issue of what defines a region, while section III reviews conceptual models of regional security cooperation, drawing on recent and contemporary history. Section IV examines emerging patterns of regional security cooperation since the 1990s, offering a new categorization of the direct and indirect security functions that regional organizations and cooperation processes fulfil. Section V discusses, and advocates further research on, the dos and don'ts for making regional cooperation benign yet effective in security terms and the conditions that promote or obstruct it in particular regions. The conclusions are presented in section VI.

II. Regions, regionalism and security

Both 'region' and 'security' are widely used but vague and contested terms. In world politics the term region has become most closely associated with the different continents of the world: Africa, the Americas, Asia, Oceania and Europe. Subcontinents (e.g., South Asia) and the areas surrounding seas (e.g., the Baltic and the Caspian seas) are sometimes also referred to as regions. An additional distinction may be drawn between regions and sub-regions, with the latter understood as geographically distinct sub-areas of continents, although the two terms are often used interchangeably and the difference between them is sometimes blurred.

Geography alone, however, does not define regions in world politics.[3] Regions are political and imagined constructs just as nations are: they are shaped both by local countries' concepts of identity and connections and by

---

[1] Hurrell, A., 'Explaining the resurgence of regionalism in world politics', *Review of International Studies*, vol. 21, no. 4 (Oct. 1995), pp. 331–58; Fawcett, L. and Hurrell, A. (eds), *Regionalism in World Politics: Regional Organization and International Order* (Oxford University Press: New York, N.Y., 1995); and Mattli, W., *The Logic of Regional Integration: Europe and Beyond* (Cambridge University Press: Cambridge, 1999).

[2] Chapters reviewing security conditions in individual regions have appeared in several recent editions of the SIPRI Yearbook. E.g., Hollis, R., 'The greater Middle East' and Rosas, M. C., 'Latin America and the Caribbean: security and defence in the post-cold war era', *SIPRI Yearbook 2005: Armaments, Disarmament and International Security* (Oxford University Press: Oxford, 2005), pp. 223–50 and 251–82.

[3] Russett, B. M., *International Regions and the International System* (Rand MacNally: Chicago, Ill., 1967); Cantori, L. J. and Speigel, S. L., *The International Politics of Regions: A Comparative Approach* (Prentice Hall: Englewood Cliffs, N.J., 1970); and Buzan, B. and Wæver, O., *Regions and Powers: The Structure of International Security* (Cambridge University Press: Cambridge, 2003).

the way outsiders view and react to them—*vide* the use of the names Near East and Far East at a time when Eurocentric imperialist visions were dominant. The recognition or willed construction of regional and sub-regional systems, interstate groupings and organizations is similarly driven by historical and cultural factors and by a range of subjective perceptions and preferences as much as by any objective logic. Regions can be 'made' as part of a conscious policy programme, as happened with European integration in the 1950s, and as some observers see happening now in regions like Latin America and East Asia in an effort to balance potential US hegemony.[4] A similar interplay of motives determines the definition and the aspects of security that a given set of countries will select for their activities. All these explanations are needed to understand why real-life regional ventures sometimes leave out countries that seem geographically to belong to the region or take in additional countries; why several security-related groups with different memberships and agendas can coexist on the same territory; why sub-regional groups form in some regions but not others and often lack an obvious geographical basis; and why a region as defined in security terms may not have the same boundaries as it does for economic, climatic, cultural or other purposes. This chapter's subject of study is necessarily those regions and sub-regions that governments have created and deemed to exist and which can directly or indirectly shape security-related policy.

III. Conceptualizing regional security cooperation

How can regional security cooperation be conceptualized and understood? At least four models of regional security cooperation have prima facie relevance for the 21st century: alliances, collective security, security regimes and security communities.

Alliances are one of the oldest forms of international cooperation, designed for both defence and attack (typically by military means) against a common external, or even internal, threat or opponent. They use cooperation as a means to an end rather than a good in itself, and an alliance's membership necessarily excludes the enemy. These relatively zero-sum characteristics are matched by the often negative practical impacts of the alliance method on international security: even a purely defensive alliance may heighten its members' threat consciousness more than it eases it, may exacerbate tensions and entrench dividing lines, and may take part in competitive arms acquisition. Alliances that turn on internal enemies (whether aberrant states or religious or ethnic groups) can also radicalize the latter and encourage them to seek external backers. On the other hand, an alliance should at least reduce the likelihood of war between its members by promoting confidence, encouraging dispute avoidance and resolution, and perhaps triggering cooperation in other non-

---

[4] The USA was deliberately not invited to the new East Asian Summit meeting in Dec. 2005. McGregor, R., Mallet, V. and Burton, J., 'A new sphere of influence: how trade clout is winning China allies yet stoking distrust', *Financial Times*, 9 Dec. 2005, p. 11.

security areas. Both ASEAN and NATO may be seen as examples of this type of dynamic. Despite the ending of the classic East–West confrontation in 1989–90, NATO and (albeit much less intensely) a number of other groupings continue to fulfil at least some of the roles associated with alliances.

The concept of *collective security* emerged in the 20th century in response to the ambivalent effects of older-style balance-of-power politics and alliances. First attempted in the framework of the League of Nations and again in the United Nations (UN), a collective security system aims to prevent or contain war by assuring a response to any act of aggression or threat to peace among its members. To work as intended, any such system must include all states in a region or the world, and it directs its attention inwardly at their actions. Apart from the global UN, some larger regional entities—such as the AU, the OAS and the OSCE—may be viewed as institutions that explicitly or implicitly aim at, and at least partially produce, collective security.[5] Notoriously, however, no such system has ever been made to work perfectly because of the evident problem—which is more difficult the larger the membership—of arriving at a common judgement and common will to act against offenders. Experience shows that the approach works well when there is consensus among the major powers but fails when faced with the largest dangers, including when the major powers come into conflict. The lessons here may indicate some limiting factors for the security aspirations of regional groups as well.

A third type of regional security cooperation is a *security regime*.[6] Regimes are a common phenomenon in such non-security dimensions of international relations as the regulation of international trade and transport. They define norms—of a cooperative and generally positive nature—for states' behaviour and often provide ways to implement, support and verify these norms. A security-related regime may cover broad prescripts for behaviour such as the non-use of force and respect for existing international borders, or may more concretely regulate certain types and uses of weapons or activities like military movements and transparency. Several regional constructs, notably the OSCE and some Latin American initiatives, may be understood as security regimes, as may regional arms control measures such as nuclear weapon-free zones or the 1990 Conventional Armed Forces in Europe (CFE) Treaty.[7] The value of all such constructs depends on how well their norms are respected, and there is much debate on what features—in terms of internal power patterns, institutionalization, incentives and penalties—are needed to ensure observance. It should be noted that regimes with functional security goals may not need, or lend themselves to, a geographically contiguous membership. Indeed, some

---

[5] For details see the subsection on 'Security dialogue and conflict management' in section IV below.

[6] Jervis, R., 'Security regimes', *International Organization*, vol. 36, no. 2 (spring 1982), pp. 357–78.

[7] On the 1990 CFE Treaty, and 1999 Adaptation Agreement, which has not yet entered into force, see Lachowski, Z., *The Adapted CFE Treaty and the Admission of the Baltic States to NATO*, SIPRI Policy Paper no. 1 (SIPRI: Stockholm, 2002), URL <http://www.sipri.org/>. For the latest CFE developments see chapter 15 in this volume.

would argue that using limited groups to handle tasks like export control has zero-sum overtones and that certain regimes work best when fully global.[8]

A *security community* has been defined as a group of states among which there is a 'real assurance that the members of that community will not fight each other physically, but will settle their disputes in some other way'.[9] The concept was developed by Karl Deutsch in the late 1950s to reflect the particularly far-reaching goals of post-World War II European integration, which in turn placed Europe in a larger security community of the world's industrialized democracies. A security community implies more intense, sustained and comprehensive interaction than any of the above models. Starting by removing the risk of conflict within the group, it can develop strengths that are greater than the sum of its parts for security tasks going well beyond the prevention of specific ills. Ambitions to build such communities have recently been displayed also in several non-European regions, but the nature and effects of regional integration in the security domain remain poorly understood. The EU experiment has eliminated conflict between but not within its states (*vide* Northern Ireland and the Basque region). The tendency of security communities to weaken internal frontiers potentially means that they can be more quickly affected by 'transnational' threats (e.g., terrorism, criminal traffic and disease). Their open-ended agendas tend to lead them to confront new security challenges as soon as old ones are settled and, in particular, to feel an impulse to start 'exporting' their surplus of security to others, notably in the form of peace missions (on which more below).

These four models can help in understanding the nature of, prospects for and limitations of particular forms of regional security cooperation; but they use a language that is rare today in the actual public discourse or decision making of the regions concerned. They also suffer from being relatively static, revealing little about why regional groups change their membership or agenda and why they may mutate from one form to another.[10] Various alternative ways of categorizing regional structures could be mooted, for example in terms of their institutional or governance characteristics (i.e., their degree of institutionalization, the nature of any fixed decision-making procedures, their collective organs and funds, the depth of involvement of non-state and local actors, and so on). This would not, however, directly lead to judgements on security utility since experience shows that different institutional forms can be appropriate for different types of security task in different environments. For instance, when several security institutions exist in the same region, this could be because states prefer to address various aspects of security in a variety of procedural styles. The most straightforward way to approach a new understanding of regional groups is through the functions they perform in terms of security as such.

---

[8] See chapter 16 in this volume.

[9] Deutsch, K. W. et al., *Political Community and the North Atlantic Area: International Organization in the Light of Historical Experience* (Greenwood Press: New York, N.Y., 1969), p. 5.

[10] On institutional change and 'drift' see the Introduction to this volume.

IV. New patterns of regional security cooperation

This section examines the emerging patterns and functions of regional security cooperation as they have evolved since the 1990s. It proposes a four-way (but not exhaustive) generic framework for understanding contemporary regional security cooperation: security dialogue and conflict management, new forms of military cooperation, democracy and human rights, and economic integration and the wider non-military security agenda. Since the section looks for evidence of regional contributions wherever they can be found, it may seem to present an over-positive balance, but this has been done consciously in order to offset a more usual analytical tendency (both within and outside the most integrated regions) to see the glass as half empty. It can also be argued that some achievements of regional cooperation are ignored because of the difficulty of proving a negative (e.g., that conflicts would have been worse otherwise).

Security dialogue and conflict management

At the most basic level, regional security institutions serve as frameworks for communication and dialogue among their members. Regular meetings of heads of state or government, ministers and lower-level officials, and the military arguably help to build trust between states, avoid miscommunication, resolve disagreements and develop a sense of common interests and identity. The EU and its predecessors have done much to overcome historic patterns of enmity between the countries of Western Europe, especially France and Germany; and founding of MERCOSUR in Latin America in 1991 has had a similar role in reinforcing the rapprochement between Argentina and Brazil that has existed since the 1980s. Analysis of the cause–effect cycle between institutions and changed relationships is, however, disputed and problematic: it may be argued that the conflict resolution is as much a facilitating factor as a consequence of regional cooperation.[11]

Since the 1990s there have been significant efforts to extend (geographically) the pacifying effect of long-standing regional security frameworks, in particular in Europe and Asia. In Europe, the enlargement of the EU and NATO has been based in significant part on the view that their success in contributing to the emergence of a security community in Western Europe can now be extended to Central and Eastern Europe. The EU and NATO are now seen as doing for Germany and Poland or Hungary and Romania, among others, what they did for Franco-German rapprochement in the 1950s and 1960s (and in avoiding open war between Greece and Turkey). During the 1990s the EU and NATO made accession conditional in effect on candidates' resolving conflicts with neighbouring states, thus encouraging governments throughout Central and Eastern Europe to conclude treaties reaffirming exist-

[11] Haftendorn, H., Keohane, R. O. and Wallander, C. A., *Imperfect Unions: Security Institutions over Time and Space* (Oxford University Press: Oxford, 1999).

ing borders and guaranteeing ethnic minority rights and to establish new forms of cooperation such as joint peacekeeping forces and cross-border economic zones. Following the 2004 'big bang' enlargements of the EU and NATO, the two institutions now face the perhaps even more difficult challenge of extending their integrative model to the Western Balkans.[12] In the 1990s ASEAN followed a somewhat similar enlargement process: between 1995 and 1999 taking in Cambodia, Laos, Viet Nam and, controversially, Myanmar. As part of this enlargement process, all four countries signed ASEAN's 1976 Treaty of Amity and Cooperation in Southeast Asia, which commits signatories to prevent disputes from arising and to renounce the threat or use of force to resolve disagreements.[13] Parallel to this, the ASEAN Regional Forum was established in 1994 as a means of promoting dialogue with ASEAN's neighbours in the wider Asia–Pacific region. Since then the ARF has become an established feature of the region's international politics.[14] Most recently, China signed the Treaty of Amity and Cooperation in 2003—an arguably important achievement for ASEAN and the ARF given unresolved disputes between China and ASEAN members over the South China Sea.[15]

A number of regional organizations have developed more explicit and formal mechanisms for the prevention, management and resolution of conflicts among their members. Since the end of the cold war, for example, the OSCE has developed semi-permanent missions and the use of special envoys in areas of actual or potential conflict and has used the OSCE High Commissioner on National Minorities to help prevent and resolve conflicts relating to ethnic minorities. Similarly, the African Union has established new mechanisms for conflict management: the AU Commission includes a Commissioner for Peace and Security, a Peace and Security Directorate (incorporating a Conflict Management Centre) and an Early Warning System, and is supported by a Panel of the Wise (composed of five 'highly respected African personalities') tasked to provide advice and support.[16] Since it was established in 2002, the AU has engaged in a number of political mediation missions for internal conflicts in member states (in the Comoros, Côte d'Ivoire, Madagascar, Somalia and Sudan). The OAS has its own Office for the Prevention

---

[12] On recent and future developments in the Western Balkans see appendix 1A in this volume.

[13] The text of the Treaty of Amity and Cooperation in Southeast Asia is available at URL <http://www.aseansec.org/1217.htm>.

[14] Khong Y. F., 'The ASEAN Regional Forum: still thriving after all these years', Institute for Defence and Strategic Studies (IDSS) Commentaries no. 46/2005, IDSS, Singapore, 27 July 2005, URL <http://www.ntu.edu.sg/IDSS/publications/commenatries.html>.

[15] Between the late 1960s and the early 1990s the OAS expanded by accepting a number of Caribbean countries and Canada; its 35 members (of which, Cuba is suspended from participation) now include all independent states of the Americas. Organization of American States, 'The OAS and the inter-American system', 2005, URL <http://www.oas.org/documents/eng/oasinbrief.asp>.

[16] Protocol relating to the Establishment of the Peace and Security Council of the African Union, Assembly of the African Union, First Ordinary Session, Durban, 9 July 2002, URL <http://www.au2002.gov.za/docs/summit_council/secprot.htm>. See also Williams, R., 'National defence reform and the African Union', *SIPRI Yearbook 2004: Armaments, Disarmament and International Security* (Oxford University Press: Oxford, 2004), pp. 231–50.

and Resolution of Conflicts for the design and implementation of conflict prevention and resolution mechanisms.[17]

The EU's Common Foreign and Security Policy (CFSP) is the most developed example of a regional construct that goes beyond internal peace goals to use collective modes of action externally, designed *inter alia* to help avoid and manage conflicts beyond the EU's borders. While the EU has had its well-known failures and setbacks, including those in the conflicts in the former Yugoslavia on its own doorstep in the 1990s, the trend has been for a steadily growing ambition, reach and diversity of the CFSP and, since 2000, its military instrument, the European Security and Defence Policy (ESDP). Other institutions, such as ASEAN and MERCOSUR, include elements of common policies towards their wider regions, an example being ASEAN's leadership role in the ARF and its dialogue with large neighbours like China. However, none has gone as far as the EU in attempting to develop a wider common foreign and security policy. For the moment, the strongest dynamics in regions other than Europe seem to run either towards the better projection of shared regional interests in world economic and functional negotiations (e.g., talks in the World Trade Organization) or towards fending off unwanted external security influences by gaining better control of the region's own internal weaknesses.

New forms of military cooperation

Regionally based military cooperation has historically focused on either cooperation driven by and directed against (perceived) external enemies or efforts to contain the risks of such confrontation through regional arms control agreements and military confidence- and security-building measures (CSBMs). The best-developed set of CSBMs are those concluded in the frameworks of the OSCE and its predecessor, the Conference on Security and Co-operation in Europe (CSCE), since the 1970s,[18] the CFE Treaty, and the nuclear weapon-free zones agreed in various regions of the world. More recently, China, Russia, Kazakhstan, Kyrgyzstan, Tajikistan and Uzbekistan have concluded a set of agreements limiting their deployment of military forces in mutual frontier zones.[19] Other regional organizations, such as the OAS, have engaged in more limited discussions on arms control, CSBMs and military transparency. Overall, however, regional arms control and CSBMs are far from having been explored to their full potential.[20]

---

[17] Organization of American States, Department of Democratic and Political Affairs, Office for the Prevention and Resolution of Conflicts, 'Work plan 2005', Washington, DC, 2005, URL <http://www.ddpa.oas.org/oprc/work_plan.htm>.

[18] Lachowski, Z., *Confidence- and Security-Building Measures in the New Europe*, SIPRI Research Report no. 18 (Oxford University Press: Oxford, 2004).

[19] Trofimov, D., 'Arms control in Central Asia', A. J. K. Bailes et al., *Armament and Disarmament in the Caucasus and Central Asia*, SIPRI Policy Paper no. 3 (SIPRI: Stockholm, July 2003), URL <http://www.sipri.org/>, pp. 46–56.

[20] See chapter 15 in this volume.

Since the early 1990s new patterns and forms of regional military cooperation have begun to emerge in most parts of the world. Primary examples include NATO's Partnership for Peace (PFP), the EU's ESDP and the AU's Common African Defence and Security Policy (CADSP). These ventures are generally inclusive rather than exclusive, seeking to engage most or all states in a region rather than being directed against particular states. They are process-oriented and open-ended, emphasizing active military dialogue and cooperation in contrast to the traditional arms control methods of abstinence and formal constraints. They have the flexibility to address a range of practical military challenges such as reforming armed forces, peacekeeping and support for humanitarian relief work. Their methods can be characterized as 'defence diplomacy': multilateral and bilateral dialogue among defence ministries and armed forces aiming to foster confidence and transparency, as well as helping partners with concrete challenges such as downsizing armed forces and establishing democratic, civilian control of militaries.[21] The archetypal example, NATO's PFP (established in 1994), has at the same time been the central vehicle for helping to prepare applicant states for NATO membership. Similar, although less extensive and developed, cooperation frameworks have emerged in other regions. Since the mid-1990s defence ministers from the Americas have met biennially to discuss common challenges, although this forum has not resulted in much grassroots military cooperation. In the Asia–Pacific region, bilateral military ties (notably with the USA) remain strong, but states were until quite recently reluctant to engage in region-wide defence dialogue or cooperation. The Shangri-La Dialogue, established by the non-governmental International Institute for Strategic Studies (IISS) in 2002, was the first framework that brought together defence ministers and senior military leaders from across Asia and the Pacific.[22] Since then, the ARF has begun, albeit cautiously, to develop limited military dialogue and cooperation.[23]

Humanitarian assistance, peacekeeping and, more controversially, peace enforcement have been a key functional focus of much of the new regional military cooperation.[24] As documented in the SIPRI Yearbook, both NATO and the EU (through the ESDP) have evolved since the cold war into providers of a variety of types of crisis intervention worldwide. They both have mechanisms to allow non-members to join in the coalitions of member states set up for each operation.[25] Peacekeeping has also been undertaken by African sub-regional groups, in particular ECOWAS, and was defined from the start as a core role of the AU. In a significant break with the OAU's previous emphasis

[21] Cottey, A. and Forster, A., *Reshaping Defence Diplomacy: New Roles for Military Cooperation and Assistance*, Adelphi Paper no. 365 (Oxford University Press: Oxford, 2004).

[22] On the Shangri-La Dialogue see the IISS website, URL <http://www.iiss.org/shangri-la.php>.

[23] An example was the ARF's Sep. 2005 workshop on Civil–Military Operations in Disaster Response. ASEAN Regional Forum, '21 nations attend ASEAN workshop on disaster', News release, 13 Sep. 2005, URL <http://www.aseanregionalforum.org/Default.aspx?tabid=50>.

[24] Cottey, A. and Bikin-kita, T., 'The military and humanitarianism: emerging patterns of intervention and engagement', Overseas Development Institute (ODI), Humanitarian Policy Group, *Monitoring Trends 2004–2005: Resetting the Rules of Engagement* (ODI: London, 2006), pp. 21–38.

[25] See chapters 1 and 3 in this volume.

on state sovereignty, the AU's Constitutive Act establishes 'the right of the Union to intervene in a Member State . . . in respect of grave circumstances, namely: war crimes, genocide and crimes against humanity'.[26] A key goal of the AU's CADSP is the establishment of an African Standby Force of 20 000 military, police and civilian personnel, based on five brigades to be provided by each of the continent's five sub-regions.[27] The AU undertook its first peacekeeping missions in Burundi in 2003–2004 (where an AU mission preceded the deployment of a larger UN force) and in the Darfur region of Sudan from 2004. These experiences have highlighted the AU's capacity problems (also in the non-military dimensions) and strong dependence on outside support.[28] There have also been steps towards regional cooperation in peacekeeping in other areas of the world, although thus far these are less developed: for instance, the UN Stabilization Mission in Haiti has since 2004 been viewed as a model for a regionally led UN peacekeeping operation, with Latin American states providing the majority of forces under Brazilian leadership. In Central America, common problems with drug trafficking, criminal gangs and natural disasters led in mid-2005 to a proposal from the presidents of El Salvador, Guatemala, Honduras and Nicaragua to establish a regional military force—although critics argue that this risks turning into an overly militarized and US-dominated approach to these challenges.[29]

Democracy and human rights

Democracy and human rights have increasingly come to be viewed as part of the security agenda. There is evidence (although it is not uncontested) to support the hypothesis that war is rare, perhaps even non-existent, between democracies—even though transitional, 'democratizing' states may, at least in some circumstances, be more prone to involvement in international and civil wars.[30] Democracies are also less prone than authoritarian regimes to engage in genocide or other forms of mass violence against their own citizens.[31] These links between governance and security are gaining in significance with the wider acceptance of definitions of human security, which see human rights

---

[26] Constitutive Act of the African Union, signed on 11 July 2000, URL <http://www.africa-union.org/About_AU/Constitutive_Act.htm>, Article 4(h).

[27] Protocol relating to the Establishment of the Peace and Security Council of the African Union (note 16), Article 13.

[28] On peacekeeping and peace-building missions in Africa see chapter 3 in this volume.

[29] Kraul, C. and Renderos, A., 'Central America's crime wave spurs plan for a regional force', *Los Angeles Times*, 16 Aug. 2005, URL <http://www.americas.org/item_21317>; and 'Stan's deadly blow', *The Economist*, 15 Oct. 2005, p. 59.

[30] Russett, B., *Grasping the Democratic Peace: Principles for a Post-Cold War World* (Princeton University Press: Princeton, N.J., 1993); and Brown, M. E., Lynn-Jones, S. M. and Miller, S. E. (eds), *Debating the Democratic Peace* (MIT Press: Cambridge, Mass., 1996).

[31] Rummel, R. J., 'Power, genocide and mass murder', *Journal of Peace Research*, vol. 31, no. 1 (Jan. 1994), pp. 1–10.

abuses as major threats to the latter.[32] Furthermore, the dramatic global extension of democracy to many previously authoritarian states since the 1970s has given credibility to the idea of a global community of democracies, within which regional organizations may play a natural role in promoting and protecting good governance and human rights among states with comparable cultures and histories.

The longest history of regional organizations designed to support democracy and human rights is in Europe. The central mission of the Council of Europe is to support democracy and human rights. Through its Committee of Ministers, Parliamentary Assembly, European Court of Human Rights and various legally binding conventions (most prominently the 1950 European Convention on Human Rights[33]), the Council of Europe plays an important role in setting standards for human rights and democracy for its members, monitoring whether member states are living up to those standards and putting political pressure on states that may have breached them. Since it started in the 1950s, the European integration process that evolved into today's EU has also made democracy a prerequisite for membership. The creation of NATO had explicit democratizing motives vis-à-vis states like Germany and Italy, although the exigencies of the cold war made the alliance willing to tolerate authoritarian regimes in Greece, Portugal and Turkey at various times. In the 1970s, human rights were included as one of the three 'baskets' of issues addressed by the CSCE, alongside military CSBMs and scientific and technological cooperation.

Since the end of the cold war, all these European organizations have directed considerable effort to promoting democracy and human rights beyond their own borders. The Council of Europe, the EU and NATO have extended their membership to include Central and East European and Mediterranean states. The EU and NATO actively supported both acceding and other neighbour states in transforming post-communist political and bureaucratic structures. The leverage of the EU and NATO has arguably played a central role in underpinning democratic consolidation as well as peace in the territory from the Baltic Sea to the Black Sea. Both organizations now face the even more daunting task of extending this model to the post-conflict Western Balkans, where the legacy of the wars of the 1990s poses major challenges for democratization.[34] The Council of Europe and the CSCE/OSCE have also played important roles in promoting democracy and human rights in Central and Eastern Europe and the former Soviet Union by establishing basic normative standards in this area, monitoring elections and providing advice and technical

---

[32] E.g., University of British Columbia, Human Security Centre, *Human Security Report 2005: War and Peace in the 21st Century* (Oxford University Press: New York, N.Y., 2005), URL <http://www.humansecurityreport.info/>.

[33] The Convention for the Protection of Human Rights and Fundamental Freedoms was opened for signature by the member states of the Council of Europe on 4 Nov. 1950 and entered into force on 3 Sep. 1953. The text of the convention is available at URL <http://conventions.coe.int/>.

[34] See appendix 1A in this volume.

assistance to states.[35] Developments since the 1990s have also highlighted the limits of these regional organizations, with states such as Belarus and Uzbekistan (both members of the OSCE, but neither a member of the Council of Europe) still violating basic democratic and human rights norms and ignoring criticisms from all European sources. Moreover, it is arguable that certain aspects of the Western powers' policy—notably, their insistence on stronger national and group measures against terrorism since the events of 11 September 2001—have encouraged or at least provided fresh excuses for anti-democratic excesses in the field of internal security, both in Europe's neighbouring regions and elsewhere.[36]

In the Americas the democratic transitions which many South and Central American states underwent in the 1980s created new momentum for using the OAS as a means of consolidating democracy across the region. The OAS's 1948 Charter includes the goal of promoting and consolidating democracy,[37] and the separate Inter-American Commission on Human Rights and the Inter-American Court of Human Rights did valuable work, for example, in Peru. However, in practice the prevalence of authoritarian regimes across South and Central America and US willingness to support those regimes as bulwarks against Communism meant that the OAS as such played little role in this area until the 1990s. In 1990 the OAS created its Unit for the Promotion of Democracy to provide advice and technical assistance to member states, and in 1991 it adopted the Santiago Commitment to Democracy and the Renewal of the Inter-American System, reaffirming the OAS's commitment to the 'defense and promotion of representative democracy and human rights' and created procedures for responding to 'sudden or irregular interruption of the democratic political institutional process or of the legitimate exercise of power'.[38] On the basis of the Santiago Commitment, the OAS responded to threats to the democratic regimes in Guatemala, Haiti and Peru in the early and mid-1990s by mobilizing various forms of political and economic pressure against democratic backsliding—with some success in Guatemala and Peru, although it failed to prevent the effective collapse of the Haitian state.[39]

---

[35] The CSCE expanded its members' existing human rights commitments to include democracy and free elections in its 1990 Charter of Paris for a New Europe and has established a number of institutions to promote democracy and human rights, in particular its Office for Democratic Institutions and Human Rights (ODIHR) and, since 1997, its Representative on the Freedom of the Media. Conference on Security and Co-operation in Europe, Charter of Paris for a New Europe, Paris Summit, 21 Nov. 1990, URL <http://www.osce.org/item/16336.html>.

[36] See the Introduction to this volume. For further examples of the tension between anti-terrorist rigour and positive goals in regional security see, e.g., Rosas (note 2); and Dwan, R. and Holmqvist, C., 'Major armed conflicts', *SIPRI Yearbook 2005* (note 2), pp. 83–120.

[37] The Charter of the Organization of American States was signed on 30 Apr. 1948 and came into effect on 13 Dec. 1951. The text is available at URL <http://www.oas.org/juridico/english/charter.html>.

[38] Organization of American States, 'Santiago Commitment to Democracy and the Renewal of the Inter-American System', General Assembly, Santiago, 4 June 1991; and Organization of American States, 'Representative democracy', Resolution 1080, General Assembly, Santiago, 5 June 1991—both available at URL <http://www.ddpa.oas.org/about/documents_related.htm>.

[39] Parish, R. and Peceny, M., 'Kantian liberalism and the collective defense of democracy in Latin America', *Journal of Peace Research*, vol. 39, no. 2 (Mar. 2002), pp. 229–50.

The challenges that the OAS still faces in the domain of democratization are illustrated by Cuba and Venezuela. Cuba is now the only clearly undemocratic state in the Americas and, while still a member of the OAS, has been excluded from participation since 1962. The USA wishes to use the OAS to put further pressure on Cuba, but many South and Central American states—wary of what they view as US neo-imperialism—argue that the best way to encourage liberalization in Cuba is through constructive engagement. As a consequence, the OAS has been unable to agree a common approach towards Cuba. Similarly, many in the USA view Venezuelan President Hugo Chavez's 'Bolivarian revolution' as a dangerously populist threat to democracy and free enterprise. However, Chavez has confirmed the strength of his domestic support (notably in presidential elections of 1998 and 2000 and referendums of 2004), and indications that the USA supported a 2002 coup attempt against Chavez have reinforced perceptions elsewhere in the Americas that the USA may be more interested in defending its economic interests than the cause of democracy.[40] As a consequence, the OAS has also been divided over Venezuela, although the OAS Secretary General has played a role in trying to encourage moderation from both Chavez and his right-wing opponents. These cases highlight tension over the USA's hegemonic role in the region as one factor complicating the OAS's efforts for democracy: another problem is the continuing high degree of economic inequality in South and Central America.

The promotion of democracy and human rights is also viewed as a central role for the more recently established African Union. In contrast to its non-interventionist predecessor, the OAU, the AU's goals as defined by its 2000 Constitutive Act include the promotion of 'democratic principles and institutions, popular participation and good governance' and 'human and peoples' rights'.[41] Governments which 'come to power through unconstitutional means' will be suspended from participation in the AU's activities.[42] The AU Peace and Security Council, a key decision-making body, is mandated to 'institute sanctions whenever an unconstitutional change of Government takes place'.[43] The African Commission on Human and Peoples' Rights can also issue comments and advice (albeit without enforcement capacity) on abuses found in such states as Eritrea, Ethiopia, Uganda and Zimbabwe, and on generic issues such as avoiding damage to human rights through counter-terrorism policy. Against this background, the AU has mobilized political pressure in order to

---

[40] Borger, J. and Bellos, A., 'US "gave the nod" to Venezuelan coup', *The Guardian*, 17 Apr. 2002, URL <http://www.guardian.co.uk/international/story/0,3604,685531,00.html>; Campbell, D., 'American Navy "helped Venezuelan coup"', *The Guardian*, 29 Apr. 2002, URL <http://www.guardian.co.uk/international/story/0,3604,706802,00.html>; and Palast, G., 'Opec chief warned Chavez about coup', *The Guardian*, 13 May 2002, URL <http://www.guardian.co.uk/venezuela/story/0,,858072,00.html>.

[41] Constitutive Act of the African Union (note 26), Article 3.

[42] Constitutive Act of the African Union (note 26), Article 30.

[43] Protocol relating to the Establishment of the Peace and Security Council of the African Union (note 16), Article 7(1)(g).

counter, for example, a coup in Mauritania.[44] The states thus targeted have, however, been small ones, while larger AU members have found ways to escape censure. The AU has been reluctant to criticize the Sudanese Government over human rights abuses in Darfur and has been reticent about what some see as a worrying drift towards authoritarianism in Ethiopia—all the more problematic since the AU's headquarters is in the Ethiopian capital, Addis Ababa. Most prominently, Zimbabwe's increasingly authoritarian leader, President Robert Mugabe, has long been able to portray himself as an African nationalist resisting Western neo-imperialism and thus to escape significant pressure from the AU over his regime's human rights abuses.[45] How far the relatively young AU can extend its role in promoting and protecting democracy and human rights remains to be seen.

In contrast to Africa, the Americas and Europe, the states of Asia and the Middle East remain reluctant to give regional organizations any role in relation to democracy and human rights. ASEAN has been inhibited by the Asian historical and cultural preference for non-interference in neighbours' internal affairs, which in turn is explained partly by concerns about avoiding interstate conflict. Despite democratization in some states (most prominently Indonesia since 1998), ASEAN members still argue that the principle of non-interference has served the region well and should not be abandoned. Moreover, ASEAN's four most recent members—Cambodia, Laos, Myanmar and Viet Nam—all have undemocratic regimes, and some critics see their entry as a strategic mistake that has significantly weakened the organization.[46] Beyond ASEAN, China's Communist regime would presumably resist any efforts to give pan-Asian institutions such as the ARF or APEC any democracy-promoting or human rights functions.

The situation in the Middle East is even starker, with Israel being the region's only democracy (although Iran arguably underwent a partial, albeit limited, democratic transition in the 1990s and some would hope that a democracy may yet emerge from the current chaos in Iraq). So long as their key members remain authoritarian states, it is difficult to conceive of the Arab League or the Gulf Cooperation Council adopting any role in relation to democracy and human rights. Since the 2003 Iraq War, the administration of US

[44] The AU's approach is complicated by the apparent popular welcome for the new military regime. Mauritania will remain suspended from the AU until elections are held. 'Envoys snub ex-Mauritania leader', BBC News Online, 10 Aug. 2005, URL <http://news.bbc.co.uk/2/4137434.stm>.

[45] In Dec. 2005 the AU Commission on Human and Peoples' Rights for the first time criticized the Zimbabwean Government for violating the AU Charter and the UN Declaration on Human Rights, and called on it to repeal several repressive laws, end forced evictions of slum dwellers and allow an AU fact-finding mission to visit the country. Final Communiqué of the 38th Ordinary Session of the African Commission on Human and Peoples' Rights, Banjul, Gambia, 5 Dec. 2005, URL <http://www.achpr.org/english/communiques/communique38_en.htm>. See also Meldrum, A., 'African leaders break silence over Mugabe's human rights abuses', The Guardian, 4 Jan. 2006, URL <http://www.guardian.co.uk/zimbabwe/article/0,,1677460,00.html>.

[46] Henderson, J., Reassessing ASEAN, Adelphi Paper no. 328 (Oxford University Press: Oxford, 1999). In Dec. 2005 ASEAN cautiously took a new approach and 'encouraged' Myanmar to speed up the democratization process. 'Asian group raps Burma on rights', BBC News Online, 12 Dec. 2005, URL <http://news.bbc.co.uk/2/4520040.stm>.

President George W. Bush has made the promotion of democracy one of its key long-term objectives for the Middle East, institutionalizing this through the Middle East Partnership Initiative.[47] However, this remains an essentially external effort, to which Middle Eastern states have at best reluctantly acquiesced. The larger lesson from Asia and the Middle East is that, in the absence of a significant core of democratic states willing to use regional frameworks to promote democracy and human rights, the role of such institutions in this area is likely to remain limited.

Economic integration and the wider security agenda

Many of the new or reinvigorated regional institutions that have emerged since the early 1990s are primarily economic in character. Regional economic cooperation and integration can, however, be regarded as having important security dimensions or implications. Economic cooperation and integration may be driven by the desire to reduce the likelihood of political or military conflict between the states involved: economic interdependence between states, it is argued, increases the costs of using force and creates shared interests.[48] This logic was one of the driving forces behind the early post-World War II process of European integration, and similar dynamics are arguably at work in APEC, ASEAN and MERCOSUR. Much of the economic regionalism of the past two decades can also be seen as a self-protecting response— with security overtones—to economic globalization: by working together in regional groups, states can help to protect markets and industries in their region, increase their competitiveness in the global economy and strengthen their hand in global economic forums (such as the World Trade Organization). Regionalism is thus intimately linked with the wider debate on globalization and neo-liberal economics. Analysts draw a distinction between open and closed economic regionalism, with the first being essentially compatible with the liberalization of trade and finance and the latter representing an alternative model that limits the free flow of trade and finance. This debate can also be translated into terms of 'economic security', which on one view benefits from market-driven economic growth but on the opposite view suffers from the damage done by competition to state solvency, employment, social security safety nets and so on. It can also be argued that the more complex international interdependence and longer supply chains fostered by globalization increase states' vulnerability to security setbacks not just on their own territories but also on those of suppliers and transit states. This is a problem most often 'securitized' in the context of energy supplies, but relevant in several other dimensions as well. While it is beyond the scope of this chapter to address this debate, it is clear that regional institutions are a significant part of the larger question of global economic security.

---

[47] Hollis (note 2), pp. 244–48.

[48] Nye, J. S. and Keohane, R. O., *Power and Interdependence*, 3rd edn (Longman: New York, N.Y., 2001).

Beyond economics, regional organizations have also been one of the main institutional frameworks in which the idea of a wider security agenda—beyond traditional political military security—has been pursued. A number of organizations have explicitly adopted concepts of comprehensive security. This development has probably proceeded furthest in Europe, where the OSCE's common and comprehensive concept of security was developed during the 1990s to incorporate economics and environmental issues alongside traditional political military security concerns and democracy and human rights.[49] A number of European sub-regional groups, such as the Council of the Baltic Sea States and the Black Sea Economic Cooperation, have also adopted broad approaches to security, seeking to respond to cross-border problems such as environmental degradation and pollution and transnational organized crime.[50] Non-European groups have carried cooperation into novel fields that are particularly relevant for their regions, such as the Kimberley Process set up in response to the problem of 'conflict diamonds' in Africa,[51] ASEAN's anti-piracy measures,[52] the proposed new tsunami warning network for the Indian Ocean region and the Asia–Pacific Partnership on Clean Development and Climate, launched in July 2005 under US leadership.[53] Since the September 2001 terrorist attacks on the USA, there has been a parallel trend in all major regional groups to develop common initiatives against non-state threats—most obviously terrorism, but also the illicit trade in weapons of mass destruction (WMD) and associated materials and technologies, crime and drugs trafficking. Such efforts have been boosted by patent threats in the regions themselves, such as the March 2004 Madrid and July 2005 London bombings in Europe or the October 2002 Bali bombings in Asia, but also by the wish to support US endeavours or the global efforts embodied in UN Security Council resolutions 1373 and 1540.[54] The EU, with its legislative powers and central resources, has gone particularly far and fast in elaborating such non-military security policies.[55] New policy frameworks in this field have, however, also been adopted by APEC, ASEAN, the Collective Security

[49] See, notably, the OSCE's Charter for European Security adopted at its Istanbul Summit, 18–19 Nov. 1999, URL <http://www.osce.org/ec/13017.html>.

[50] Cottey, A. (ed.), *Subregional Cooperation in the New Europe: Building Security, Prosperity and Solidarity from the Barents to the Black Sea* (Macmillan: Houndmills, 1999).

[51] For background see Bone, A., 'Conflict diamonds: the De Beers Group and the Kimberley Process', eds A. J. K. Bailes and I. Frommelt, SIPRI, *Business and Security: Public–Private Sector Relationships in a New Security Environment* (Oxford University Press: Oxford, 2004), pp. 129–47.

[52] Raymond, C. Z., 'Piracy in Southeast Asia: new trends, issues and responses', Institute for Defence and Strategic Studies (IDSS) Working Paper no. 89, IDSS, Singapore, Oct. 2005, URL <http://www.ntu.edu.sg/idss/publications/Working_papers.html>.

[53] The White House, 'Fact sheet: President Bush and the Asia–Pacific Partnership on Clean Development and Climate', News release, 27 July 2005, URL <http://www.whitehouse.gov/news/releases/2005/07/>.

[54] UN Security Council Resolution 1371, 28 Sep. 2001, laid down rules for universal application against terrorist financing; Resolution 1540, 28 Apr. 2004, did the same for illicit (including individual) WMD possession and transfer. The texts of the resolutions are available at URL <http://www.un.org/Docs/sc/>.

[55] For EU reactions post-Sep. 2001 see Burgess, N. and Spence, D., 'The European Union: new threats and the problem of coherence', eds Bailes and Frommelt (note 51), pp. 84–101.

Treaty Organization (CSTO), MERCOSUR, the OAS and the Shanghai Cooperation Organization, among others.[56] The nature of the problems being tackled in all these cases is such that, with the best political will, even the strongest states are only starting to devise cooperative methods that can make a meaningful impact on them. Yet systematic international cooperation is the logical response to truly transnational threats and also has the potential to speed up global responses (e.g., to an epidemic or sudden environmental challenge) by reducing the number of 'addresses' involved in coordination. This looks set to be a significant growth area for regional endeavours in the future.

The US dimension

As the world's only superpower, the USA plays a central role in shaping the security dynamics of all regions of the world and is a leading member of many regional security institutions, including NAFTA and the OAS in the Americas, NATO and the OSCE in Europe, and APEC and the ARF in Asia. Indeed, the global character of US power means that it may be seen today as a power of all regions and none. The USA continues to have formal defence and security commitments in Europe, through NATO, and in the Asia–Pacific region, through its commitments notably to Japan and South Korea, its policies on Taiwan and various troop stationing arrangements. The five regional commands of the USA's own forces, covering Europe (and Africa), the broader Middle East, the Asia–Pacific region, South America and North America, all maintain extensive bilateral and multilateral military ties in their regions.[57] In these and other contexts the USA has developed military outreach activities aimed at more inclusive multilateral regional cooperation. It has established a series of regional security studies centres that train military and civilian defence personnel and act as forums for defence dialogue.[58] Similarly, the US regional military commands sponsor region-wide multilateral military exercises in areas such as peacekeeping and humanitarian assistance.

---

[56] Asia–Pacific Economic Cooperation, 'Bangkok Declaration on Partnership for the Future', Bangkok, 21 Oct. 2003, URL <http://www.apecsec.org.sg/content/apec/leaders_declarations/2003.html>; Association of South East Asian Nations, 'ASEAN efforts to counter terrorism', URL <http://www.aseansec.org/14396.htm>; Organization of American States, 'Declaration on Security in the Americas', 28 Oct. 2003, URL <http://www.oas.org/documents/eng/DeclaracionSecurity_102803.asp>; Bromley M. and Perdomo, C., 'CBMs in Latin America and the effect of arms acquisitions by Venezuela', Working Paper no. 41/2005, Real Instituto Elcano de Estudios Internacionales y Estratégicos, Madrdi, Sep. 2005, <http://www.realinstitutoelcano.org/documentos/216.asp>; and African Union. 'Decision on terrorism in Africa', Assembly/AU/Dec.15(II), Maputo, 2003, URL <http://www.africa-union.org/Official_docu ments/Decisions_Declarations/offDecisions_&_Declarations.htm>. On 28 Apr. 2003 the 6 members of the CSTO agreed on a joint rapid reaction force against terrorism and drug trafficking. 'Six CIS countries formalize collective-security bloc', Radio Free Europe/Radio Liberty Newsline, 29 Apr. 2003, URL <http://www.rferl.org/newsline/2003/04/290403.asp>.

[57] The respective command abbreviations are EUCOM, CENTCON, PACOM, SOUTHCOM and NORTHCOM. Priest, D., *The Mission: Waging War and Keeping Peace with America's Military* (W. W. Norton & Company: New York, N.Y., 2003), pp. 61–77

[58] These centres are the George C. Marshall Center for European Security Studies, based near Munich; the Asia–Pacific Center for Security Studies, based in Honolulu; and the Center for Hemispheric Defense Studies, the African Center for Strategic Studies and the Near East Center for Strategic Studies, all based in the National Defense University in Washington, DC.

During the cold war, US support for regional security cooperation was oriented towards supporting allies in the global conflict with Communism. In the 1990s the administration of President Bill Clinton sought to build more inclusive regional institutions: the USA was thus a supporter of NATO's reorientation and the PFP in Europe, of APEC and the ARF in Asia, and of efforts to rejuvenate the OAS in the Americas. Post-September 2001 the administration of President Bush has sought to use regional organizations as one element of its broader war on terrorism, but regional endeavours have also been affected by the more general shift in US foreign policy towards action outside institutional (and sometimes international legal) constraints. As a consequence, the US approach to regional security cooperation has become rather narrowly utilitarian, viewing it as useful in as far as it contributes to specific US goals, especially in the context of the war on terrorism, but certainly not as a goal in itself.

There are, thus, undeniable and growing elements of ambivalence in the US impact on 'regionalizing' endeavours. At least three levels of this problem can be identified, the first lying in the way in which US national demands may skew or unbalance local cooperation agendas both when local groups exert themselves to meet the USA's wishes and when they unite against some feature of US policy. The second problem is that steps taken by the USA to safeguard its own interests and power in a given region often have a de facto polarizing effect, dividing local 'friends' and 'foes' or using some states to balance and encircle others, in a way that (to say the least) complicates local multilateralism.[59] This pattern is clear in the greater Middle East and East Asia but has sometimes also cut across the multilateral nature of the USA's European ties. In early 2003, in the lead-up to the US-led action against Iraq, US Secretary of Defense Donald Rumsfeld drew a distinction between the unhelpful attitudes of 'old Europe' and the helpful attitudes of 'new Europe' that has cast a shadow over the relations between these two groups in the EU and NATO.[60]

The Iraq crisis also fuelled debate in the USA itself about the third level of the issue: are advanced regional structures becoming such an inherent threat to US supremacy in themselves that they should be actively disrupted to avert the spectre of a 'multipolar' world? The clear temptation during President Bush's first term in office was to answer 'Yes' to this question: the USA should not only evade institutionalized constraints on itself in favour of 'coalitions of the willing' but should also try to prevent the rise of multilateral as well as one-state regional competitors. In parallel, against a background of deadlock in the Doha round of world trade talks,[61] US negotiators sought bilateral trade deals

---

[59] There are some signs of China's pursuing a mirror-image strategy by courting those states that face local and global isolation as a result *inter alia* of US disfavour: *vide* recent Chinese oil deals with Iran and Venezuela.

[60] 'Outrage at "old Europe" remarks', BBC New Online, 23 Jan. 2003, URL <http://news.bbc.co.uk/2/2687403.stm>.

[61] On the Doha round of trade talks see the website of the World Trade Organization, URL <http://www.wto.org/>.

with local partners rather than going through regional channels. While such bilateralism may reflect a certain 'default mode' in US thinking, there are signs—as in other fields—of some re-balancing of policy since Bush's re-election in November 2004. The EU's internally generated crisis over its proposed Constitutional Treaty in 2005 made many US policy makers realize how inconvenient a seriously weakened Europe would be at this delicate juncture in world affairs,[62] while the USA now more actively supports regional peacekeeping (by the EU in the Balkans or by African organizations) that frees its own troops for new missions elsewhere. In any event, as the EU showed after the invasion of Iraq in March 2003, US efforts to discourage or to 'divide and rule' regional groups may merely harden the determination of other states to consolidate their regional institutions beyond the point where the USA could do them any serious harm. Where these dynamics will ultimately lead is still an open question and is addressed again in section VI below.

V. The 'quality' of regional cooperation and how to promote it

Not all regional constructions that fit the definitions of this chapter can be judged to have positive aims and effects nor have all well-intentioned ones been successful. Even after the cold war, judgements on whether a given group is intrinsically good or bad—and whether or not it can be trusted with a certain task—remain tinged by politics and partisanship. Policies towards existing organizations and efforts to create new ones should benefit if some more reliable, evidence-based means of evaluation could be devised. As a starting point and to encourage further work, five relevant criteria are suggested here: (a) whether cooperation is coerced and hegemonic; (b) whether it posits a zero-sum relationship with the outside world; (c) whether it is rigid or static; (d) whether it is artificial and superficial; and (e) whether it is efficient in terms of management and resource use.[63]

An example of *coerced and hegemonic* regional cooperation is the Warsaw Treaty Organization (the Warsaw Pact) of cold war times. The model is rare these days, although some would see Russia's successive attempts to build new security groupings in the former Soviet space—making allowance for the greatly changed context—as hegemonic in intention and to a certain extent in style.[64] The leaders of such groups will, of course, do their best to make them look respectable, while complaints from smaller members may be stifled by precisely those power imbalances that allowed them to be corralled in the first place. To judge a given group as abusive, therefore, outside observers must go

---

[62] See chapter 1 in this volume.

[63] The discussion that follows is based on the record of larger regional and sub-regional groupings that have been active since 1945. It is inevitably coloured by the authors' Euro-Atlantic experience but takes account of other regional groupings. A detailed statistical test of the hypotheses offered would demand much more research on the extra-European cases in particular.

[64] Arbatov, A., 'Russian foreign policy thinking in transition', ed. V. Baranovsky, SIPRI, *Russia and Europe: The Emerging Security Agenda* (Oxford University Press: Oxford, 1997), pp. 146–47; and Trenin, D., 'Rossiya i konets Evrazii' [Russia and the end of Eurasia], *Pro et Contra*, vol. 9, no. 1 (28) 2005, URL <http://www.carnegie.ru/en/pubs/procontra/72915.htm>, pp. 11–13.

by what they know of its origin and history, by how far the group's actions seem fairly to reflect its members' interests and how its internal governance works. The single best diagnostic is a lack of *democracy* in the group's working at the interstate level, which often turns out to be coupled with non-democratic and anti-democratic impacts within its constituent states—the invasion of Czechoslovakia by the Soviet Union and its allies in 1968 being a flagrant example.

Such structures may sometimes look more effective than democratic ones in eliminating (overt) conflict among their members and avoiding (overt) outside interference. Since these goals are achieved by coercion, however, the members' 'true' wishes and interests are always liable to break through. In the worst case this leads to conflict among or within former member states (or with neighbours), but in all cases the group's collapse will at least temporarily affect the region's stability and its standing in the international power balance. Coerced and unwilling groupings are also likely to fail in subtle aspects of *efficiency* among other reasons because: their 'command' style of management cannot exploit members' true comparative advantages; hegemons often maintain or worsen inherent tensions between members by divide-and-rule tactics; and lack of democracy makes it harder to deal with dimensions of security where willing support from different actors in society is important. Such groups also have trouble in adjusting to changed environments because of the hegemon's attachment to tried and trusted methods of control.

As argued above, *zero-sum* goals as such are not enough to judge a group negatively. However, even the most justified and democratic groups with an adversarial agenda cannot avoid some inherent hazards. Lasting tension between groups breeds permanent arms races that both burden group members and increase the risk of proliferation to others. Such tension also makes it harder to address the more universal components of threat (*vide* terrorism in the cold war) in a cooperative way. Any lengthy confrontation also tends to draw other players into the game with equally zero-sum roles, as backers and sympathizers, equipment suppliers, or flag-carriers and dependents in other regions. During the cold war, the price of avoiding outright conflict between the blocs in Europe was paid, not least, in a series of 'proxy' wars elsewhere between countries or territories whose precarious state of development made them least able to afford it.

The understanding of these risks was, of course, also at the source of positive inter-bloc measures of détente, including arms control agreements, 'confidence-building' measures and the development of wider frameworks of regional cooperation available to members of both camps.[65] In retrospect, the very dysfunctionality of the East–West confrontation generated some of the strongest and most significant arms control and disarmament measures ever

---

[65] A notable example is the CSCE/OSCE, as discussed above. However, pan-European networks for cooperation in fields like the environment, energy, communications, sports and culture also played their part, and some limited cross-bloc sub-regional cooperation was also initiated before the fall of the Berlin Wall in Nov. 1989 (e.g., the Pentagonale cooperation between Austria, Czechoslovakia, Hungary, Italy and Yugoslavia).

enacted;[66] while the more diffuse global balance and vogue for intervention since 1989 has made it hard to conserve the progress made, let alone go further.[67] In this specific sense, two 'wrongs' (i.e., zero-sum and opposed regional groupings) can make a partial 'right'. Even so, it is clearly better if a group can set constructive goals from the outset and devote all its resources to them, rather than going round by the long way of confrontation with all the concomitant costs and risks. A group at ease with its own members and neighbours will have more security 'surplus' for helping the less fortunate—and is less likely to be mistrusted by the recipients. Without a siege mentality, it can accord its members and their citizens more freedom to apply their diverse capacities. It will work more easily with other international actors to combat security challenges—including the newer and 'softer' ones. Finally, a group based on positive common interests and aspirations may survive longer because positive aims can generally be extended and reformulated for new conditions, while threats are defeated or withdrawn.

The third criterion, the *rigid or static* nature of a regional group, may apply to democratic as well as undemocratic constructions. The key is not how formal the group's governance is, but how smoothly it can be adapted to external change and to internal drivers such as a larger membership, the demands for involvement by new internal constituencies or the exhaustion of earlier (and simpler) agendas. A group that cannot adjust risks being sidelined or hollowed out while its members (or at least the more powerful ones) look for satisfaction elsewhere. The death or mothballing of an institution is not necessarily bad for security if members can move on to higher things, including action in more effective frameworks.[68] More worrying are cases of 'de-institutionalization', where actors step out of regional frameworks for security action of their own choosing, as the USA did by creating non-UN, non-NATO coalitions for its interventions in Afghanistan and Iraq. These cases highlight, however, that it is hard to defend and reassert the institutionalized approach unless it can be shown to satisfy the needs even of those members (the strongest) which have the most alternatives. This requires delicate calculation, since giving too much ground to the most rule-averse parties may compromise the group's normative authority as seen by other members or the wider cause of security. Worst of all is the case where the group and its principles maintain a formal existence—and thus risk being ascribed some of the blame—while their members increasingly take actions without peer discipline or support.

This leads to the fourth set of indicators: *artificiality and superficiality*. These characterize structures that are set up to distract attention from the region's true security problems, to make the region look good to other regions,

---

[66] Examples are the treaties between the Soviet Union and the USA on strategic nuclear arms reductions (SALT and START) and the agreement to ban a whole category of intermediate-range nuclear weapons. For details of treaties see annex A in this volume.

[67] See the Introduction and chapter 15 in this volume.

[68] An example is the fate of the Western European Union when the EU took over European-led crisis management missions.

or to glorify the country or countries taking the initiative (*vide* the series of competitive group-forming attempts during the post-cold war period in Central Asia[69]). Alternatively, artificiality and superficiality may set in during a group's declining days as members turn up to its meetings only out of habit, sending representatives of a declining level of rank. A group should not be hastily labelled as superficial, however, just because it lacks stable bureaucratic forms and resources or addresses only a small and non-vital part of the region's security agenda. Such creations can be the first seeds of greater things and it makes sense to keep them 'light' as long as confidence needs to be built up and participants are learning to understand each other's priorities. More reliable danger signs are: (*a*) a patently uneven level of enthusiasm among the participants, (*b*) a rapid decline in activities, (*c*) a duplication or multiplication of groups without complementarity, (*d*) a failure to engage meaningfully with outside actors who are relevant for the given agenda, and (*e*) widespread behaviour by the members that conflicts with the apparent aims and rules of the grouping. Even in such apparently hopeless cases, it is hard to say that security will actually be harmed by the nominal existence of such groups. 'Rhetorical regionalism' of this kind acknowledges that other actors and the world in general see cooperation as valuable. The greater risk of misjudgement may come when artificial groups appear just good enough to confuse—and create a sense of false security about—the real internal and external challenges of the region.

Efficiency in management and resource use must be a relative measure, since the right amount of effort for a regional endeavour relates to the prospective gains and to how much the region can afford (or can get from others)—and it will consequently vary over time. An input–output balance must take account not just of visible cash flows and support in kind (e.g., buildings, the staffing of secretariats, or the loan of troops and other assets for operations), but also of 'process costs', including attendance at group activities and the time spent on group affairs in national administrations. On the other side of the balance are potentially large process benefits in terms of intra-group trust, understanding and solidarity, as well as the tangibles (e.g., greater negotiating power) and intangibles (e.g., standing and influence) of interaction with the outside world. Overall, a dysfunctional group can be one that either contributes too much in relation to what it gets out or one that contributes too little to achieve critical mass for its stated ends. The final balance must also take account of whether the group looks effective—to outsiders and to its own citizens and paymasters. Contradictions arise when a method of working that is acceptable and even appropriate internally makes no sense to outsiders whom it is important to impress, as often happens between the EU and the USA. In such cases the group may need to think about using double languages or messages, although preferably not double standards.

---

[69] Allison, R., 'Regionalism, regional structures and security management in Central Asia', *International Affairs*, vol. 80, no. 3 (May 2004), pp. 469–73.

The regional environment: facilitating and complicating factors

What has made security cooperation flourish in some regions or sub-regions and not in others? Finding the answers could be important for those seeking to fill the existing gaps in cooperation, but there is no simple formula. A few relevant factors are discussed here to show how complex their effects may actually be.

1. *State size and balance of power.* In East and South Asia the disproportionate size of China and India, respectively, presents a patent challenge for security-related cooperation, and the Soviet Union certainly exercised an unhealthy dominance in the Warsaw Pact. In NATO, however, the USA's strength and leadership is generally seen as having made and kept the alliance viable;[70] and history shows several cases of the alternative scenario where the presence of one or more large states encourages others to join together in order to balance it or them.[71] The most that can safely be said is that groups encompassing giant members will find it hard to be highly integrative and intrusive because the large state will not accept dictation on its own territory and the others will be wary of simply accepting that state's model.

2. *Intra-region relations.* Cooperation ought to be easiest when there is the least tension and the maximum of common security interests among neighbours or, alternatively, when a region is neatly divided into blocs (as in Europe in the cold war). The greater Middle East is a good example of the opposite situation, since cooperation is obstructed there not just by the fierceness but also by the complexity of extant rivalries and conflicts.[72] On the other hand, in Western Europe's institution building the presence of four or five larger states (now six with Poland) with contrasting agendas and shifting alignments has been a motive for and driver of, as much as an obstacle to, integration. Rivalries between Argentina and Brazil or Brazil and Mexico have not, so far, thrown off course Latin America's slow and complicated progress towards an institutionalized security regime.[73] Sometimes relations between neighbours are simply not problematic enough to justify formal security solutions (the Nordic region is a case in point). Another important variable is the behaviour of large outside players. As noted above, if the deliberate or intrinsic effect of their actions is to 'divide and rule', a solid regional structure will either fail to emerge or be of a bipolar kind (like the Middle East in the earlier stages of Arab–Israeli confrontation).[74]

---

[70] Of Africa's 3 most active sub-regional groups, 2—SADC and ECOWAS—contain a disproportionately powerful state—South Africa and Nigeria, respectively.

[71] Part of the logic of ASEAN can be read in this way, especially vis-à-vis China.

[72] Hollis (note 2).

[73] Rosas (note 2).

[74] Since 2001 Europe has oscillated between being divided in pro- and anti-USA camps and pulling itself together in order to engage more effectively with, or offer an alternative to, the USA. The odds in this case are tilted towards the latter model, *inter alia* since the USA has more often than not encouraged European integration.

3. *History and culture.* There are two, contrasting ways in which shared histories have boosted modern regional cooperation. The past existence of supranational structures and authorities (such as empires and earlier forms of alliance) in the region creates habits, and experience, that can at least shorten the path to new agreements.[75] Such traditions are sometimes deliberately invoked to give newly (re)created regions legitimacy, as when Norway in 1993 referred to medieval 'Pomor' cooperation when launching the Barents Euro-Arctic Council.[76] Sometimes, a voluntary local grouping arises to replace and contrast with an externally imposed multilateral framework after the latter's withdrawal (e.g., Central European cooperation after the dissolution of the Warsaw Pact and the Council for Mutual Economic Assistance, COMECON). Conversely, a region that has suffered disastrous internal conflict can be driven to new forms of multilateral governance in a 'never again' spirit, as with Europe's European Communities and the Western European Union after World War II. In such cases the new collective identity provides new legitimacy, especially for the losers of the previous conflict. History seems to be an impediment when it offers only models of division or of completely discredited multilateral experiments and where reconciliation after previous wars has not been complete and 'leftover' claims or border disputes stymie the building of regional structures from the outset.[77]

The issue of political and cultural compatibility among neighbours is even more complex. Political and cultural identities have a subjective component that can change over time, and states that 'reinvent' themselves are likely to take a different view on who their natural neighbours and partners are. As to the impact on institutionalized regional processes, strong cultural resemblances may (as among the Nordic countries) make cooperation so easy that it remains little formalized. The common heritage of Islam has not saved the greater Middle East, or even North Africa, from remaining seriously 'under-regionalized'—and is arguably an obstacle insofar as it offers an alternative transnational frame of reference qualifying the modern state's authority. Successfully integrated regions, including Europe, have arisen in conditions of ethnic, religious, linguistic and behavioural diversity, powered partly by the wish to stop these differences leading to conflict.[78] In sum, while cultural

[75] Europe itself is an example, but it seems more than coincidence that ASEAN, MERCOSUR and the African groups have taken root in regions that were extensively colonized. On the other hand, cultural boundaries established within regions by formerly competing empires (e.g., between the franco-phone and anglophone parts of Africa) have created some specific extra complications, both practical and political, in the building of modern sub-regional groups that cut across these borderlines, such as ECOWAS in West Africa.

[76] Neumann, I. B., 'A region-building approach to northern Europe', *Review of International Studies*, vol. 20, no. 1 (Jan. 1994), pp. 53–74.

[77] The blockage effect is worst when the factors of legitimacy and identity involved for each side in the dispute are too powerful to allow it to be 'compartmentalized' and bypassed (e.g., India and Pakistan over Kashmir, and Russia and Japan over the Northern Territories). The extreme case is when history leaves it uncertain how many states there are in the local regional system (e.g., Taiwan and Palestine).

[78] A high level of integration helps in a practical way by giving ethnic groups similar rights, whichever sovereignty they live under, and allowing full freedom of movement.

compatibility can be a facilitator, cultural diversity need not be a decisive obstacle if: (*a*) strategic interests are strong enough and (*b*) the differences are not defended as political goods in themselves but are mediated by a culture of compromise.[79] Last but not least, states do not have to be democratic to make security groupings work, as seen in the case of historical alliances, the Warsaw Pact or the Shanghai Cooperation Organization (a group of six, at best imperfect democracies). There is, however, much evidence that groups pervaded by democracy can integrate more deeply and survive better, as discussed in the first part of this section.

VI. Conclusions

If nothing else, this chapter shows that 20th and 21st century regional security cooperation is not a transient phenomenon. It is a rich and diverse phenomenon that now involves the great majority of the world's states—albeit some more deeply, sincerely and willingly than others. It is developing forms to cover the widest span of the contemporary security spectrum and is starting to combine security with non-security tools for both strategic and operational purposes. Nevertheless, many observers would still question whether the plethora of meetings, declarations and statements, military contacts, and the bureaucratic work of institutional headquarters and the like brings the proportionate value in terms of enhanced security for states or peoples. Those analysts who focus on the toughest security challenges—terrorism, proliferation, violent conflicts and large-power rivalries—may easily conclude that regional approaches are ineffective or irrelevant. The present authors' view is that such arguments are simplistic and misleading. From a historical perspective, there is a powerful case that some key institutions—ASEAN, the EU, MERCOSUR and NATO in particular—have played an important role in overcoming deep-rooted conflicts between their members and in contributing to peaceful international relations at home and abroad. Since the 1990s these institutions have acquired many eager new members and partners. Over the whole period, there is mounting evidence that these processes—in locations as varied as Central America and Southern Africa, South-East Asia, Central Europe and the Balkans—have contributed to the prevention and resolution of conflicts between and within states and to the consolidation of democracy and the protection of human rights.

Part of the problem in assessing regional security cooperation lies in the choice of benchmarks. It is easy to identify failure and weakness: Europe's inability to deal with the conflicts in the former Yugoslavia at its own backdoor during the 1990s, Africa's failings in responding to the continent's many conflicts or East Asia's inability to halt North Korea's nuclear ambitions, to

---

[79] Experience shows, however, that there are pitfalls in trying to create active security communities over very large areas where the true commonalities in culture as well as governance become too weak to sustain the weight of common standards laid upon them—an issue familiar from the debate over EU and NATO expansion.

cite only the most obvious examples. Yet other approaches to these security challenges—national or unilateral action, ad hoc coalitions of the willing and global action through institutions such as the UN—have proved little more successful. A fairer question would thus be what added value (if any) regional approaches provide compared to the alternatives on offer. In this context, both logic and the evidence suggest that local, inclusive approaches can provide legitimacy, a framework for long-term, self-sustaining efforts and an impact greater than their parts, especially when achieving deeper integrative effects. At the same time, they have the weakness of their strengths: notably, the cumbersome, usually consensus-based character of decision making. Regional security cooperation thus cannot wholly substitute for national action or for decision making via the UN Security Council but can at best powerfully supplement them. Lastly, states are likely to judge the value of regionalism in the light not just of their own size, location and attitudes to others, but also of their security priorities and favoured responses: a state that prefers to deploy military force against terrorism and to strengthen its border defences will not rate highly the civilian and legalistic, transnational and intrusive remedies being explored, for example, in the EU. Cooperative regional approaches have much clearer advantages, however, for tackling other priorities such as long-term peace-building between states, the promotion of democracy and human rights, and transnational challenges such as environmental pollution and organized crime.

How do such 'regions of security' relate to global security governance more broadly? The regionalization–globalization dialectic is a familiar theme in economics but, in the security context, is all too often addressed in polemical terms if at all. Thus, as noted in section IV above, regions that are integrating without the USA can be seen both by participants and the USA as attempts to balance US power or at least to mitigate US interference. As they gain confidence, local groups can and do reach out to others that they regard as following, or want to encourage to follow, their cooperative models—thus spreading the regionalizing 'virus' further.[80] At the same time, states in weaker, more disorganized parts of the world may reasonably worry about the strengths of the larger groups being turned against them: an atmosphere of this kind still bedevils NATO and EU attempts at 'outreach' in the Mediterranean.

In more analytical terms, it may be questioned how the entrenchment of regional clubs fits with the increasingly global nature both of the repercussions of traditional security ills like conflict and of scourges like terrorism and disease. The answers should be positive if regional outputs can be shown to promote rather than interfere with shared global objectives. Where threats arise in a disaggregated way, as with local conflict, local response capacities like those in Africa and Europe reduce the risk of overloading the UN's 'last resort' capacities for intervention. These local capacities allow the UN to be focused

---

[80] Thus, the EU has had dialogue with groups like ASEAN and MERCOSUR and offers collective support for AU peacekeeping policies. There are also informal global networks of security-relevant organizations convened notably by the UN to discuss conflict topics.

where most needed, thus helping to equalize security standards in the longer term.[81] In the case of transnational threats, organized regions can work to maximize their own defences and deliver 'pre-packed' inputs to global endeavours. Both these examples, however, point to the heightened importance of universal standards and frameworks of authority (including UN legitimation for forceful intervention) if the old vision of a 'world of regions' is not to become just a jungle with fewer beasts.

In any case, a world of regions is still a remote prospect, so long as China, India, Russia and, in particular, the USA are players with such limited experience of and commitment to regionalization.[82] The immediate issue is how a heterogeneous world system of individual large states plus regional groups (whose states sometimes do and sometimes do not operate within group disciplines) can be made to work. Part of the answer lies in the existence of forums—not just the UN but also the international financial institutions and the World Trade Organization—where participants can interact on the basis of both national and group positions; and another part lies in the strengthened pressure for global cooperation that threats like terrorism, WMD and many 'softer' security challenges sours. The prospects are complicated, however, by cultural and normative differences among the players—even regarding some of the most basic premises of security—which the experience of living or not living in an integrated region has undoubtedly reinforced. Further objective study of regional security processes might help all concerned to approach the phenomenon more calmly and to focus more on its actual and potential instrumentality. In reality, even lacking such a conceptual framework, the EU and the USA are both struggling with the issue of how to give the greater Middle East, East Asia and South Asia at least some of the benefits of a stable regional system. The analysis above suggests that this is indeed a worthy and urgent cause and that it deserves even more informed thought and effort than it receives at present.

---

[81] Sköns, E., 'Financing security in a global context', *SIPRI Yearbook 2005* (note 2), pp. 285–306.

[82] The USA's involvement in NATO is only a partial exception in the sense that it had no intrusive or culture forming, and very few visible, effects in the USA's own territory. In any case, the USA is busy redesigning NATO in a way that makes its own assets less regionally present in, and committed to, the territory of Europe as such.

5. National governance of nuclear weapons: opportunities and constraints

HANS BORN

I. Introduction[1]

More than 60 years after the dawn of the nuclear age, the governance of nuclear weapons is an issue that is ripe for revisiting. In this chapter the term 'governance' encompasses not only the functions of those who possess the power to make decisions of various kinds regarding nuclear weapons, but also the functions of those who have the practical means and the physical opportunity to execute these decisions. Nuclear weapons continue to hold a prominent place in the security concerns of both nuclear weapon states and non-nuclear weapon states, despite the end of the cold war and the indefinite prolongation of the 1968 Treaty on the Non-proliferation of Nuclear Weapons (Non-Proliferation Treaty, NPT).[2] This chapter focuses in a broader way, and with a governance rather than a security perspective, on the whole spectrum of political oversight and control mechanisms that may apply within and, to some extent, between nuclear weapon states. Drawing on the notions of civilian control and of democratic accountability that have become established in the context of efforts for security sector reform,[3] it examines the roles and requirements not just of the state executive, the military and specialized civilian institutions, but also of parliamentary institutions and civil society at large.

In the calculation of the risks involved for regional and global security, the question of who commands and controls nuclear forces—and what this means for their possible use—is important.[4] Civilian control and democratic account-

---

[1] This chapter draws on the preliminary results of a research project by the Geneva Centre for the Democratic Control of Armed Forces (DCAF), which will conclude in 2007 with the publication of *Governing Nuclear Weapons: Opportunities and Constraints for Democratic Accountability and Civilian Control of Nuclear Weapons*. On the project and DCAF see URL <http://www.dcaf.ch/civnuc/_index.cfm>. See also Born, H., 'Civilian control and democratic accountability of nuclear weapons', eds H. Hänggi and T. Winkler, *Challenges of Security Sector Governance* (LIT Verlag: Münster, 2003). The author wishes to thank DCAF colleagues Heiner Hänggi and Wendy Robinson for their help in preparing this text.

[2] As defined in Article IX of the NPT, only states that manufactured and exploded a nuclear device before 1 Jan. 1967 are recognized as nuclear weapon states. By this definition, China, France, Russia, the United Kingdom and the United States are the nuclear weapon states parties to the treaty. For the signatories and parties to the NPT see annex A in this volume. The full text is available at URL <http://www.iaea.org/Publications/Documents/Treaties/npt.html>.

[3] See Hänggi and Winkler (note 1); and Caparini, M., 'Security sector reform and NATO and EU enlargement', *SIPRI Yearbook 2003: Armaments, Disarmament and International Security* (Oxford University Press: Oxford, 2003), pp. 237–60.

[4] See, e.g., Blair, B., *The Logic of Accidental Nuclear War* (Brookings Institution: Washington, DC, 1993); and Bracken, P., *The Command and Control of Nuclear Forces* (Yale University Press: New Haven, Conn., 1983).

ability of nuclear weapons is a sparsely researched domain. Most of the existing studies have a national focus, usually on the United States, and address executive control,[5] while other studies discuss emerging nuclear weapon states.[6] Robert Dahl and other authors have addressed the interplay and compatibility between democracy and nuclear 'guardianship', including the question of how greater democracy might promote the aims of arms control and disarmament.[7] These studies have highlighted several grounds for concern about the *process* of nuclear weapon development and nuclear policy making, in addition to the evident reasons for worrying about the number of weapons still extant today and the risks of both 'horizontal' and vertical' proliferation.[8] Even in advanced democracies, the balance between secrecy and openness has arguably tilted in a way that largely exempts national decisions on nuclear weapon capabilities from normal democratic controls.[9] Countries with authoritarian governments and hostile neighbours commonly perceive tight central control of nuclear weapon programmes as a requisite for regime survival and regional stability. The different degrees of non-transparency and curtailment of democracy that result point *inter alia* to the scope for 'nuclear learning' about governance solutions between new and older nuclear weapon possessors.[10] At the international level, it has been argued since cold war times that a lack of internal debate and control correlates with greater uncertainty and risk regarding the external behaviour of the state in question. In the current security environment, further arguments could be added about the way in which secretive and undemocratic handling of nuclear decisions may aggravate the scope both for new weapon acquisition and for drift towards greater nuclear dependence in the nuclear weapon states; while differing governance practices and degrees of openness also obstruct progress in regional and global cooperation against dangers (like nuclear terrorism and nuclear smuggling) that are common to all.

[5] Feaver, P., *Guarding the Guardians: Civilian Control of Nuclear Weapons in the United States* (Cornell University Press: Ithaca, N.Y., 1992).

[6] E.g., Lavoy, P., Sagan, S. and Wirtz, J., *Planning the Unthinkable: How New Powers Will Use Nuclear, Biological and Chemical Weapons* (Cornell University Press: Ithaca, N.Y., 2000); and Feaver, P., 'Command and control in emerging nuclear nations', *International Security*, vol. 17, no. 3 (winter 1992/93), pp. 160–87.

[7] Dahl, R., *Controlling Nuclear Weapons: Democracy Versus Guardianship* (Syracuse University Press: Syracuse, N.Y., 1985). See also Sagan, S. and Waltz, K., *The Spread of Nuclear Weapons: A Debate Renewed* (Norton: New York, N.Y., 2003); Müller, H., 'Nuclear disarmament: the case for incrementalism', eds. J. Baylis and R. O'Neill, *Alternative Nuclear Futures: The Role of Nuclear Weapons in the Post-Cold War World* (Oxford University Press: Oxford, 2000), pp. 125–44; and Sagan, S., Center for International Security and Arms Control (CISAC), *Civil–Military Relations and Nuclear Weapons*, CISAC report (Stanford University, CISAC: Stanford, Calif., June 1994).

[8] For information on nuclear forces and planned developments see appendix 13A in this volume; and for a discussion of current proliferation concerns see chapter 13 in this volume.

[9] According to Dahl, the 'crucial choices about nuclear weapon strategy have been made by a very small group of decision makers, including those of the president, have been subject only weakly, if at all, to democratic procedures . . . For all practical purposes, on these matters, no public opinion existed and the democratic process was inoperable'. Dahl (note 7), p. 34.

[10] On 'nuclear learning' processes in nuclear weapon states see Nye, J. S., 'Nuclear learning and US–Soviet security regimes', *International Organisation*, vol. 41 (summer 1987), pp. 378–85; and Gaddis, J. L. et al. (eds), *Cold War Statesmen Confront the Bomb: Nuclear Diplomacy Since 1945* (Oxford University Press: Oxford, 1999).

Section II of this chapter addresses aspects of national governance in the five NPT-defined nuclear weapon states—the USA, Russia, China, France and the United Kingdom—and in three de facto nuclear possessor states—India, Israel and Pakistan.[11] This selection considers states that have widely varying nuclear arsenals (in quantity and quality) as well as different internal systems and historical, cultural and geographical backgrounds. Section III discusses four different indicators of accountability: command and control arrangements, executive control, parliamentary control and the role of the public. It also examines the controls inherent in international instruments and relationships. The conclusions are presented in section IV. Throughout this analysis, it is necessary to recognize the problems placed in the way of comparative research by the culture of confidentiality, and sometimes of deliberate ambiguity and misdirection, that characterizes the field of nuclear weapon decision making.

II. Governance in the states possessing nuclear weapons

The United States[12]

In 1945 the USA became the first state to carry out a nuclear weapon test as well as the first (and still the only) state to use such weapons. From the outset the USA has emphasized the political control of its nuclear assets. In the early 1950s nuclear weapons were stored separately from the delivery vehicles by the Atomic Energy Commission (AEC), not by the military. Under the provisions of the 1946 Atomic Energy Act only the president could authorize the transfer of nuclear weapons to the military (as happened, for example, in 1950, shortly after the Korean War broke out). However, over time attitudes to nuclear weapons became to some extent 'conventionalized', allowing gradual delegation of control, until today the military has physical custodianship over the US nuclear arsenal. Nevertheless, the National Nuclear Security Administration (NNSA), within the Department of Energy (DOE), remains responsible for research, development, production, modernization and dismantling of US nuclear weapons.[13] The employment of nuclear weapons is controlled by a system of permissive action links (PALs) that use an electronic code that can be released to military personnel only on the president's authority. PALs, other safety devices and various elements of physical protection are designed to shield the weapons against accident as well as theft or unauthorized use.

The president is the final authority on nuclear doctrine, development and operational status but relies heavily on a collection of statutory policy advisers, notably the Office of the Secretary of Defense and the Joint Chiefs of Staff. The Department of State and the DOE also have a decision-making role

---

[11] In Feb. 2005 North Korea announced that it possessed operational nuclear weapons. This claim has not been independently confirmed.

[12] This section draws on the contributions of Peter Feaver and Kirstin Thompson Sharp to the DCAF research project on governing nuclear weapons (note 1).

[13] See the NNSA website at URL <http://www.nnsa.doe.gov>.

on nuclear issues, as does the National Security Council. As commander-in-chief of the armed forces, the president also has an operational role; this includes approving targeting policy, setting the alert rate of US nuclear forces and authorizing the release of nuclear weapons to military units. A suitcase (the 'nuclear football') containing nuclear access codes and launch options is close to the president at all times.

Arrangements are in place to safeguard the continuity and power of action of the US Government should an attack occur, and there is little doubt that the president has the right *inter alia* to pre-delegate authority to launch nuclear weapons.[14] Pre-delegation was conceived as a way of using the military chain of command to solve command and control problems in the event of a nuclear attack. It set out a specific set of circumstances under which the president authorized in advance the use of nuclear weapons. The civilian authorities still retained overall control of the process because they specified the circumstances for pre-delegating nuclear launch authority to military commanders. Recently declassified documents at the National Security Archives show that pre-delegation happened under presidents Dwight D. Eisenhower and John F. Kennedy and supposedly continued until the late 1980s.[15] It is unclear to what extent it currently occurs.

To date no documents have been declassified that reveal plans for reconnecting the president or the president's successor with the National Command Authority (NCA) after a pre-delegated nuclear retaliatory strike. In addition, the NCA's devolution of command for authorizing the release of nuclear weapons does not match the line of presidential succession set out in the US Constitution. This presents a potential problem for democratic governance of nuclear weapons in grave or extreme circumstances.

The power of the president as commander-in-chief concerning nuclear weapons is constitutionally limited by the powers of the US Congress. Under the Constitution, the Congress declares war, raises armies and has the power (in this instance only the Senate) to consent to treaty ratification as well as to approve high-level civilian and military appointments. The Congress also controls the federal budget, including defence spending. The power of the purse was recently demonstrated when the Congress denied funding requested by the administration for a programme to develop a new nuclear warhead for the third consecutive year.[16] More generally, the Congress has a constitutional mandate to oversee the executive branch's activities. In order to fulfil this function, the Congress has set up a number of bodies, such as the Congressional Research Service (CRS) and the Congressional Budget Office (CBO), to provide members with independent information and advice. In addition, the Government Accountability Office (GAO) is directly engaged in auditing the

---

[14] Feaver (note 5), p. 48.

[15] Blair (note 4).

[16] The programme was for the robust nuclear earth penetrator (RNEP) warhead. See Norris, R. S. and Kristensen, H. M., 'U.S. nuclear forces 2006', *Bulletin of the Atomic Scientists*, vol. 62, no. 1 (Jan./Feb. 2006), pp. 68–71.

executive branch's implementation of congressionally approved policies and programmes, including in the national security field.

In comparison with some other nuclear weapon states, the USA has a vigorous civil society with the potential for demonstrable impact on the nuclear debate. The 'revolving door' system whereby a new president can place his or her own appointees (often from non-official backgrounds) into even quite modest-level official posts maintains a two-way traffic between officials dealing with nuclear matters and individuals with positions outside of government. Nuclear weapons have become a major issue in some presidential elections: *vide* the alleged 'missile gap' in President Kennedy's 1960 campaign, the play made with President Jimmy Carter's 'softness on defence' by the 1980 campaign of Ronald Reagan and the issue of missile defence in the campaign for the 2000 election. These elements of a strong democratic system, combined with relative openness about US nuclear systems and plans—and the USA's record of cooperative international engagement, notably, with Russia[17]—have made the USA something of a reference point and yardstick for investigations of nuclear governance in other less transparent states.[18] Nevertheless, elements of secrecy within the system, and the centralization of operational power in the hands of the president, pose challenges to democratic governance even in the US case.

Russia[19]

The Russian Federation is the legal successor state to the Soviet Union, which was the second state to test a nuclear weapon, in 1949.[20] Its challenges in nuclear governance reflect not only the difficult and still inchoate course of its democratic transition, but also a strategic setting in which nuclear weapons have come to be seen as one of the last symbols of Russia's status as a superpower. These factors tend to concentrate nuclear decision making in the hands of a tight official circle outside public scrutiny: but, paradoxically, the very relevance of nuclear capability to the nation's general fate and self-image makes it an actively debated topic among experts and the general public.

[17] The USA and the Soviet Union/Russia are the only nuclear weapon states to have concluded formal, reciprocal nuclear arms control agreements, in some cases entailing verified reductions. While the USA has recently moved away from such formal commitments (see chapter 12 in this volume), current cooperative programmes between the USA and Russia for the security and disposition of surplus nuclear weapons and weapon-usable nuclear material have served to increase transparency in their respective arsenals. See Zarimpas, N. (ed.), SIPRI, *Transparency in Nuclear Warheads and Materials: The Political and Technical Dimensions* (Oxford University Press: Oxford, 2003).

[18] Swiss Foundation for World Affairs and the Geneva Centre for the Democratic Control of Armed Forces, Report on the Conference on Governing Nuclear Weapons: Addressing Political Control, Military Prerogatives, and Scientific Lobbies, Johns Hopkins University, Washington, DC, 11 Apr. 2005.

[19] This section draws on the contribution of Alexei G. Arbatov to the DCAF research project on governing nuclear weapons (note 1).

[20] On the status of the Soviet Union's nuclear weapons after its dissolution in Dec. 1991 see Lockwood, D., 'Nuclear arms control', *SIPRI Yearbook 1994* (Oxford University Press: Oxford, 1994), pp. 639–72; and Goldblat, J., SIPRI and International Peace Research Institute, Oslo, *Arms Control: The New Guide to Negotiations and Agreements* (SAGE Publications: London, 2002), p. 90. See also the details of the Treaty on the Reduction and Limitation of Strategic Offensive Arms (START I Treaty) in annex A in this volume.

The Russian president has the formal decision-making power over all major aspects of the nuclear weapon cycle, including the development, production, storage, deployment and use of nuclear weapons. The president takes decisions on funding and the size of the nuclear arsenal. In constitutional terms, the president's authority over military policy is exercised with the support of a Security Council including the prime minister, the defence minister, the foreign minister and the director of the Federal Security Services (Federal'naya Sluzhba Bezopasnosti, FSB). In contrast with the US president, the Russian president does not have the sole authority to use nuclear weapons. The suitcase containing the release codes is under joint control of the president, the defence minister and the chief of the general staff.[21] In practice, another limitation on the president's role as the civilian arbiter of nuclear policy is the lack of well-qualified and independent civilian advice. This problem has been exacerbated by the rise during President Vladimir Putin's term of office of the *siloviki* (military and civilian security and intelligence officials), who now almost monopolize the top posts. This situation has some parallels with the fusion of civilian and military leadership in China and in Pakistan (see below).

The institutional responsibilities and competences of the Russian military in relation to the civilian leadership have been curtailed in recent years. In the past, war planning and nuclear modernization programmes were left largely to the military—within the given budget limits—and arguably led to a needless proliferation of weapon types. The June 2004 amendments to the 1996 law 'On Defence'[22] unequivocally put the general staff under the authority of the civilian defence minister.

The problems related to the physical control of Russia's nuclear forces remain a serious concern, given the fragmentation of the former Soviet system (e.g., five out of eight former Soviet early-warning radars are now outside Russia) and the lack of funds, which has allowed satellite systems and other physical assets to degrade.[23] Concern about the security of Russia's nuclear arsenal, in particular its tactical nuclear weapons, has spurred but not been fully resolved by programmes of international non-proliferation and disarmament assistance to the states of the former Soviet Union.[24] However, the physical security of Russian warheads is generally considered to be adequate. There is no evidence to counter the Russian statements that all Russian warheads have been consolidated at storage sites, and the USA has worked with Russia to upgrade the security of these sites. The current problems with phys-

---

[21] Waller, J., 'Changing the nuclear command', *Insight on the News*, vol. 17, issue 7 (Feb. 2001), p. 14; and Collina, T., 'Nuclear terrorism and warhead control in Russia', *Survival*, vol. 44, no. 2 (spring 2002), p. 75.

[22] Russian Federation Ministry of Defence, Federal Law 'On Defence', no. 61-FZ, 31 May 1996, URL <http://www.mil.ru/articles/article3863.shtml> (in Russian).

[23] E.g., in 1995 the launch of a Norwegian research rocket put Russia's command and control mistakenly on alert status. Sokov, N., *Could Norway Trigger a Nuclear War? Notes on the Russian Command and Control System*, PONARS Policy Memo 24 (Center for Nonproliferation Studies, Monterey Institute: Monterey, Calif. 1997).

[24] Anthony, I. and Fedchenko, V., 'International non-proliferation and disarmament assistance', *SIPRI Yearbook 2005: Armaments, Disarmament and International Security* (Oxford University Press: Oxford, 2005), pp. 675–98; and Russian Federation Ministry of Defence (note 22).

ical security relate to weapon-usable material and the question of whether all weapons were accounted for in the very special circumstances in the former Soviet Union in the early to mid-1990s.

The role of the State Duma (the lower house of the Russian Parliament), is confined to routinely approving the government's decisions. Members of the Duma can examine the annual armaments programme documents, but most of them lack the expertise to independently assess the programme while secrecy laws effectively prevent them from engaging experts. The staff of the Duma's Defence Committee are either former or active military personnel. As a result of all these factors, the Duma has little say in nuclear doctrine and strategy, and its annual debate on the defence budget leads to few if any changes. In comparison, as a result *inter alia* of three decades of arms control negotiations with the USA, a rather large body of nuclear-relevant information is available to non-governmental experts outside parliament and to the media: but they have no channel to influence government decisions and risk being imprisoned if they disclose 'state secrets'.[25] Journalists and scholars are now understandably reluctant to comment on the nuclear topic.

China[26]

China conducted its first nuclear weapon test in 1964, the last of the five NPT-defined nuclear weapon states to do so. Its nuclear decision-making system has been described as one of 'civilian control with Chinese characteristics', but one which is not 'democratically accountable'. Although the Chinese Communist Party (CCP) stays firmly 'in control of the gun', the military possesses a critically important, although not necessarily determinant, role in nuclear weapon affairs.

The way in which the Chinese executive handles nuclear decisions reflects the close symbiosis of the CCP with the military, which goes back to the party's origins. President Hu Jintao, the General Secretary of the CCP, also heads the two top decision-making bodies for defence policy—the Politburo Standing Committee (PBSC) and the Central Military Commission (CMC). All members of the two bodies are party members, meaning that civilian control equates closely with party control. Nuclear weapon decision making is based largely on consensus among the 'collective leadership' in these bodies, and the channels for its execution at the military level are direct and tightly controlled. According to US intelligence officials, 'an unauthorized or accidental launch of . . . Chinese strategic missiles is highly unlikely . . . China keeps its missiles un-fuelled and without warheads mated'.[27] The commander

---

[25] 'Russian gets 15 years for spying', BBC News Online, 7 Apr. 2004, URL <http://news.bbc.co.uk/1/3606649.stm>.

[26] This section draws on the contributions of Bates Gill and Evan Medeiros to the DCAF research project on governing nuclear weapons (note 1).

[27] Briefing by Robert Walpole, US National Intelligence Officer for Strategic and Nuclear Programs, Carnegie Endowment for International Peace, 17 Sep. 1998, URL <http://www.ceip.org/programs/npp/walpole.htm>.

of the Second Artillery Corps, which has responsibility for the nuclear launch units, is a member of the CMC. According to David Shambaugh, the units will not take action—for instance, to 'mate' the warheads with the missiles— without separate orders from both the CMC and the general staff.[28] Only since the 1989 Tiananmen Square uprising has the Chinese leadership reportedly begun to provide for maintaining control of nuclear weapons in the event of a national crisis (e.g., by introducing US-style PALs).[29]

The question is whether this well-established picture could change as China itself changes. The generation of CCP leaders who were military heroes has died out and the civilian leaders must maintain their authority by new means, including bureaucratic bargaining and appointments. China's fast-growing economy combined with its new global ambitions allows for a rapid modernization of its nuclear force structure and posture. However, while in the future China will have the material means for an accelerated nuclear modernization programme, there is no evidence that such a programme has been approved.[30] A larger, more accurate and more mobile arsenal could in turn call for more professional—and, perhaps, delegated—military control. There are reasons to believe that the role of the People's Liberation Army (PLA) in nuclear doctrine, development and procurement could grow as a result of, rather than in spite of, the PLA's growing professionalism and depoliticization.

As for the legislative branch, the constitution formally grants the National People's Congress (NPC) wide constitutional powers that amount to parliamentary supremacy in decision making. In reality, under the dominance of a single party, the NPC has never sought to exercise such a role and merely rubber-stamps executive decisions on matters of high policy. There is no publicly available evidence of legislation or parliamentary debate on the subject of nuclear weapons. As for the public at large, China has neither an informed civil society nor non-governmental organizations (NGOs) capable of offering policy alternatives. Moreover, the media remain under the direction of the CCP. As a result, nuclear affairs in China remain subject to extreme secrecy. This is amplified by the fact that China has never engaged in international disarmament talks and has not participated in joint weapon development and procurement with a democratic country.

France[31]

France carried out its first nuclear weapon test in 1960. France's political system is a 'presidential democracy' that gives strong powers to the president, particularly in foreign affairs and defence policy, including nuclear weapon

---

[28] Shambaugh, D., *Modernizing China's Military: Progress, Problems and Prospects* (University of California Press: Berkeley, Calif., 2003), pp. 166–67.

[29] Coll, S. and Ottaway, D., 'Will the United States, Russia, and China be nuclear partners or rivals in the 21st Century?', *Washington Post*, 11 Apr. 1995.

[30] On China's nuclear modernization programme see appendix 13A in this volume.

[31] This section draws on the contribution of Bruno Tertrais to the DCAF research project on governing nuclear weapons (note 1).

decision making. The president appoints the prime minister, chairs the Council of Ministers and can dissolve the National Assembly. Because of the role that nuclear responsibilities have played in reinforcing this pre-eminence, the French presidential system has been nicknamed the 'nuclear monarchy'.[32]

No French nuclear weapon can be physically moved without political authorization, and the president has to personally approve any change in alert status. Unlike their US counterparts, for instance, the commanders of France's nuclear-armed ballistic missile submarines cannot launch their missiles without a presidential command that combines authorization with an enabling code. No weapon can be physically detonated without both the presidential code and a military code.[33] In exercising nuclear authority, the French president is supported by a small private military staff and by the Defence Council, which includes the prime minister, the minister of defence and the minister of foreign affairs. The military industry and the scientific establishment have no seats on this body. Decisions concerning the use of nuclear weapons would generally involve only three people: the president, the chief of the presidential military staff and the chief of the defence staff. Constitutionally, if the president were unable to exercise these powers, they would devolve to the president of the Senate and then to the government.

According to Article 34 of the Constitution, the French Parliament shall 'determine the fundamental principles of the general organization of national defence'. However, a presidential decree of 1964 excludes parliament from involvement in the president's mandate and power over nuclear weapons.[34] Parliament was not consulted when President Charles de Gaulle started the nuclear programme in 1958. However, the parliament votes on the annual defence budget and on the five-yearly military procurement programmes, which set the budget guidelines for the development and maintenance of the nuclear arsenal. Parliamentary reports on nuclear weapon issues can be critical of government policy, but without material consequences. Nevertheless, they help to provide members of parliament and the general public with authoritative information about nuclear affairs.

Over the years, a roughly two-thirds majority (60–70 per cent) of the French public has continued to support the nuclear weapon programme,[35] but it is hard to assess how informed this attitude may be. Think tanks play a limited role in public debate on nuclear weapons and, although non-proliferation issues are well covered, information on France's own nuclear arsenal seldom appears in the media.

[32] Cohen, S., *La monarchie nucléaire: Les coulisses de la politique étrangère sous la Vielle République* [The nuclear monarchy: what goes on behind foreign policy under the fifth republic] (Hachette: Paris, 1986), pp. 15–32.

[33] Isnard, J., 'Le code d'engagement de la force nucléaire' [The code for launching the nuclear force], *Le Monde*, 20 May 1981.

[34] Décret no. 64-46 du 14 janvier 1964 relatif aux forces aériennes stratégiques [Decree no. 64-46 of 14 January 1964 concerning strategic air forces]. The decree was abrogated and replaced by Décret no. 96-520 du 12 juin 1996 portant détermination des responsabilités concernant les forces nucléaires [Decree no. 96-520 of 12 June 1996 on the allocation of responsibilities pertaining to nuclear forces].

[35] See the 1984 and 1996 opinion polls, cited in Sinnott, R., *European Public Opinion and Security Policy*, Chaillot Paper no. 28 (Institute for Security Studies of the Western European Union: Paris, 1997).

The United Kingdom[36]

The UK has had operational nuclear weapons since 1956 (it conducted its first test of a nuclear weapon in 1952), but it gradually cut back its arsenal after the collapse of the Soviet Union. In 1998 the Labour government announced the results of a Strategic Defence Review that mandated reductions in the size and the operational readiness of the UK's submarine-launched ballistic missile force.[37] The stated purpose of British nuclear weapons continues to be to serve as a 'minimum nuclear deterrent'.[38] Under the 1958 Mutual Defence Agreement between the UK and the USA, the UK maintains independent control over its nuclear forces but is dependent on the USA for weapon technology and maintenance.[39] In addition, US nuclear weapons are based in the UK. In accordance with the policy of the North Atlantic Treaty Organization (NATO), the USA has full custody over these weapons, and it is believed that the USA is committed to consult the UK—time and circumstances permitting—before releasing these weapons for use.

The main decisions on defence policy in the UK, including all aspects of its nuclear weapon programme, are taken by the prime minister and the Cabinet. Peter Hennessey claims that each prime minister, at the start of his or her term, writes a 'beyond the grave' letter instructing the commander of the on-duty nuclear submarine as to what to do should all communications from the UK cease.[40] However, there is no pre-delegation of launch authority to the military. All missiles on British nuclear submarines are de-targeted, and missiles can only be fired by turning multiple keys (held by different officers) on receipt of a command message. Reportedly, these command and control arrangements were reviewed after the events of 11 September 2001, and the deputy prime minister was nominated to be responsible for nuclear-use decisions if the prime minister is unable to act as a consequence of an attack on the UK.[41]

Although the British Parliament 'has the ultimate power to refuse to endorse government expenditure', in practice this power is very rarely, if ever, exercised in relation to defence policy. Parliament 'does not analyse specific programmes in detail and cannot exercise advance control'. Rather, its role remains limited to performing an audit after decisions have been made by the executive, as well as questioning on an ad hoc basis current policy and deci-

---

[36] This section draws on the contributions of John Simpson and Jenny Nielsen to the DCAF research project on governing nuclear weapons (note 1).

[37] British Ministry of Defence (MOD), *Strategic Defence Review* (MOD: London, July 1998), URL <http://www.mod.uk/issues/sdr/deterrence.htm>.

[38] British Ministry of Defence (note 37), para. 60.

[39] Harris, R., 'The state of the special relationship', *Policy Review*, June 2002, URL <http://www.policyreview.org/JUN02/harris.html>. See the text of the Mutual Defence Agreement at URL <http://www.basicint.org/nuclear/1958MDA.htm>.

[40] Hennessey, P., *The Secret State: Whitehall and the Cold War* (Penguin: London, 2003), pp. 208–10.

[41] Hennessey (note 40), pp. 206–208.

sions.[42] The House of Commons Defence Committee has closely overseen the development of the current Trident nuclear weapon system, and various members of parliament have already made clear that they will closely watch the decision required shortly on its possible replacement.[43] In addition, the authority of the Commons Public Accounts Committee to ensure that government expenditure is compliant with both legal and parliamentary stipulations may extend to the nuclear deterrent.

According to public opinion polls, 58 per cent of the respondents believe that the UK should keep its nuclear weapons until the other nuclear weapon states disarm.[44] NGOs both in favour of and opposing nuclear weapons have played a prominent part in mobilizing public interest and debate. For example, during the cold war the Campaign for Nuclear Disarmament influenced mainstream politics via the Labour Party.[45] However, secrecy clauses limit the possibility of an informed debate in the public domain, a particularly important question at a time when the modernization of British nuclear forces is under review. This is partly remedied by the 2000 Freedom of Information Act, although the government may, and does, hold back some nuclear-related documents from disclosure.

At the international level, British policy operates within the constraints of various bilateral and regional alliance structures as well as those of global governance and arms control arrangements. As a member of NATO, the UK's current nuclear posture allows for nuclear first-use, and the Labour Party dropped its opposition to a no-first-use policy after taking over government in 1997.

Israel[46]

Having started its nuclear programme in the mid-1950s, Israel was generally considered by 1970 to have achieved an operational nuclear weapon capability. Since 1986, after the disclosures of Mordechai Vanunu,[47] Israel is believed to have a mature nuclear weapon programme. Estimates of the size of its nuclear arsenal vary, usually ranging from fewer than 100 warheads to 200–300 warheads.[48]

Israel's official policy of neither confirming nor denying possession of nuclear weapons is combined with strict confidentiality measures and insula-

---

[42] McLean, S. (ed.), *How Nuclear Weapons Decisions Are Made* (MacMillan and Oxford Research Group: Basingstoke, 1986), p. 132.

[43] E.g., Portillo, M., 'Does Britain need nuclear missiles? No, scrap them', *The Times*, 19 June 2005; and British House of Commons, 'Oral answers', *Parliamentary Debates (Hansard)*, 6th series, vol. 436, C5 (4 July 2005).

[44] The figures are from opinion polls in 1984 and 1996. See Sinnott (note 35).

[45] Freedman, L., *The Evolution of Nuclear Strategy* (Palgrave MacMillan: London, 2003).

[46] This section draws on the contribution of Avner Cohen to the DCAF research project on governing nuclear weapons (note 1).

[47] Vanunu is an Israeli former nuclear scientist who revealed details of Israel's nuclear weapon programme to *The Sunday Times* in 1986. He was subsequently abducted by the Israeli secret services and taken back to Israel, where he was tried behind closed doors and convicted of treason.

[48] Appendix 13A in this volume contains data on the nuclear weapon arsenal of Israel.

tion of the issue from national politics.[49] In 2004 when the Director General of the International Atomic Energy Agency (IAEA), Mohamed ElBaradei, tried to persuade Israel to start a dialogue about a nuclear weapon-free zone in the Middle East, Prime Minister Ariel Sharon stated publicly that 'our policy of ambiguity on nuclear arms has proved its worth, and it will continue'.[50] In such conditions, hardly anything is known about Israel's command and control system, but it is believed to include a system of PALs to protect against unauthorized use or theft. Israel's nuclear arsenal is subject to a system of tight civilian control by a few officials in the executive and under the direct responsibility of the prime minister. Internal advisory panels of economists, chief scientists, army officers and academics with top security clearance are thought to exist, but information about such panels is not public.

In the first period of Israel's nuclear weapon programme (1955–61), neither the Knesset (parliament) nor the State Comptroller's Office played any oversight or supervisory role. Only in the early 1960s did a group of senior members of parliament take part in approving the budget for the nuclear weapon project. At the end of the 1970s the Defence and Foreign Affairs Committee of the Knesset established a sub-committee dealing with Israel's nuclear capacity. The lack of expertise and opportunities for outside consultation limit what the Knesset can make of its role, but some parliamentarians openly and critically debated Israel's nuclear deterrence policy on 2 February 2000.[51] Financial control over nuclear weapons is exercised by Israel's State Comptroller, whose reports are kept secret. The office of the military censor forbids any media reference to Israel's nuclear arsenal, which poses obvious problems for public accountability and debate.

Israel is not a party to the NPT and has not concluded any facility-specific safeguards agreement with the IAEA. Successive Israeli governments have rejected requests from the IAEA for the country to open for inspection its nuclear facility at Dimona.

India[52]

After testing a 'peaceful nuclear device' (known as the Smiling Buddha) in 1974, India conducted five underground nuclear explosions in May 1998.[53] In August 1999 the Indian National Security Advisory Board released the Draft Nuclear Doctrine (DND). Largely patterned on the doctrines and deployment postures of the nuclear weapon states, the DND stated that 'India shall pursue

---

[49] Cohen, A., *Israel and the Bomb* (Columbia University Press: New York, N.Y., 1998).

[50] 'Sharon sticks to nuclear policy', BBC News Online, 6 July 2004, URL <http://news.bbc.co.uk/2/3869125.stm>. Sharon added that Israel would consider giving up its 'deterrent capability' if its neighbours gave up their weapons of mass destruction and fully implemented a comprehensive regional peace agreement.

[51] Steinberg, G., 'The Knesset's nuclear farce', *Jerusalem Post*, 18 Feb. 2000.

[52] This section draws on the contribution of Waheguru Pal Singh Sidhu to the DCAF research project on governing nuclear weapons (note 1).

[53] See Ferm, R., 'Nuclear explosions, 1945–98', *SIPRI Yearbook 1999: Armaments, Disarmament and International Security* (Oxford University Press: Oxford, 1999), pp. 556–64.

a doctrine of credible minimum nuclear deterrence' based on a policy of no-first-use.[54] There have been no official statements specifying the size of the nuclear stockpile required for 'credible minimum deterrence'.[55] Currently, India is estimated to have approximately 50 nuclear warheads, a number that is likely to grow over the next decade.[56] Most observers believe that India maintains a recessed nuclear posture, in accordance with its no-first-use policy: that is, nuclear warheads are not mated to their delivery vehicles, and some nuclear warheads may be stored in unassembled form.

India's political leaders, the scientific establishment and the military all play a part in the governance of nuclear weapons and depend on cooperation with each other. The scientific establishment holds the nuclear warheads, the military holds the delivery systems and the political authorities exercise general oversight *inter alia* of weapon use. In January 2003 the Indian Government established a two-layered structure called the Nuclear Command Authority (NCA) to manage its nuclear and missile arsenals. The NCA comprises the Executive Council, chaired by the prime minister's national security adviser, and the Political Council, chaired by the prime minister. The Political Council is the only body that can authorize the use of nuclear weapons. In addition, a tri-service Strategic Forces Command (SFC) has been created to oversee the nuclear forces.[57] In the event of a decision by the civilian leadership to use nuclear weapons, they would be released to the SFC for delivery to their targets. The complex system of control may be seen as a barrier against accidental or unauthorized use.

The parliament has debated nuclear weapons a few times since independence in 1947 but has not played a decisive role. The 1974 and 1998 tests were decided by a small circle of decision makers within the executive. The parliament's standing defence committee exercises only perfunctory oversight of India's nuclear arsenal. The costs of the nuclear arsenal are hidden: warheads and delivery systems do not figure as a separate entry in the defence budget. The policy issue of how many nuclear weapons constitute a minimum deterrent has in practice been left to the scientists and the military, who have their own interests to serve. The role played by civil society is small, if any. Public opinion polls showed that the approval ratings for the government and for the weapon tests increased significantly in the days directly after the 1974 and 1998 tests but decreased to normal or even low rates a few months later.[58]

---

[54] Indian Government, Ministry of External Affairs, *Draft Report of National Security Advisory Board on Indian Nuclear Doctrine*, 17 Aug. 1999, URL <http://meaindia.nic.in//disarmament/dm 17Aug99.htm>.

[55] For a critique of the notion of deterrence, especially in a South Asian context, see Bidwai, P. and Vanaik, A., *South Asia on a Short Fuse: Nuclear Politics and the Future of Global Disarmament* (Oxford University Press: New Delhi, 1999).

[56] See appendix 13A in this volume.

[57] Patney, V., 'Nuclear force structures: challenges', ed. V. Raghavan, *Nuclear Weapons and Security* (Delhi Policy Group: Delhi, 2005), pp. 53–55.

[58] Perkovich, G., *India's Nuclear Bomb: The Impact on Global Proliferation* (University of California Press: Berkeley, Calif., 2001), pp. 180, 188, 416 and 439.

Pakistan[59]

Pakistan confirmed its status as a de facto nuclear weapon state in May 1998, when it carried out a series of nuclear explosions a few days after India had done so.[60] In the 1970s President Zulfikar Ali Bhutto created a nuclear management infrastructure of civilian politicians and scientists to develop and control Pakistan's nuclear weapons. However, in February 2000 the military government created a new organization that is responsible for formulating policy and exercising control over the development and employment of Pakistan's strategic nuclear forces—the National Command Authority (NCA). The NCA is currently headed by President Pervez Musharraf. It is a mixed civilian–military body that has three components: the Employment Control Committee, the Development Control Committee and the Strategic Plans Division. The military's representatives are in a majority in all three bodies and hence play a dominant role in the overall formulation of Pakistan's nuclear strategy.

The authority to allow the use of nuclear weapons is vested in the president and the prime minister. According to a senior Pakistani military official, the control of the nuclear arsenal is governed by a 'three-men rule': any decision about the use of nuclear weapons requires the concurrent agreement of three persons, although the third person besides the president and the prime minister is not identified.[61]

With the help of the USA, allegedly Pakistan's nuclear weapons have been equipped with modern PALs and other security devices to protect against unauthorized and accidental use. The USA has shown concern about making Pakistan's nuclear arsenal safer, especially in view of the perceived risk of Islamic extremists overthrowing the present regime. *The Wall Street Journal* has reported that US Department of Defense strategists are 'planning around possible crises like the take-over of a nuclear armed ally, such as Pakistan, by Islamic extremists'.[62] In this instance, military control over the country's nuclear capacity may be seen *faute de mieux* as the norm to be preserved.

Pakistan's parliament was regularly dissolved and dismissed during periods of military rule and has become incapable of providing an effective democratic counterbalance to the military-led executive. Command and control of the nuclear arsenal are mostly based on executive decrees, thus sidelining parliament in the legislative process. The prime minister does remain accountable to parliament, but parliament has so far not debated the development, deployment and employment of the Pakistani nuclear arsenal.

Pakistan has an active civil society, but public debate hardly extends to national security and defence. According to a recent public opinion poll, the

---

[59] This section draws on the contribution of Zafal Iqbar Cheema to the DCAF research project on governing nuclear weapons (note 1).

[60] Ramana, M. V. and Mian, Z., 'The nuclear confrontation in South Asia', *SIPRI Yearbook 2003* (note 3), pp. 195–212. See also Ferm (note 53),

[61] Cotta-Ramusino, P. and Martellini, M., 'Nuclear safety, nuclear stability and nuclear strategy in Pakistan', 2001, URL <http://www.mi.infn.it/~landnet/Doc/pakistan.pdf>, pp. 4–5.

[62] Jaffe, G., 'Rumsfeld's gaze is trained beyond Iraq', *Wall Street Journal*, 9 Dec. 2004, p. 4; and NBC Nightly News, 6 Feb. 2004, URL <http://www.msnbc.msn.com/id/4201930>.

army is considered the most reliable institution in Pakistan to control the nuclear arsenal.[63] The free press is limited, although it is active by the region's standards. Journalists may be intimidated by the intelligence and security forces if they criticize the regime.[64]

III. Layers of accountability for controlling nuclear weapons

Command and control

Command and control systems are the medium by which the use of nuclear weapons can enter into military operations. Of necessity command and control systems involve military knowledge and action, but—despite the prevailing secrecy in this area—it may be stated with some confidence that no country at present places the power of decision on nuclear use completely in military hands. Concern has focused rather on the risk that military 'cultures' and interests may lead to the accidental or deliberate flouting of restraints on nuclear use and that civilian control may be weakened, as it were, from the bottom-up.[65] Political leaders in different states have used a variety of measures to reduce this risk, including separate storage of nuclear warheads from delivery systems (still practised in China and India) or the use of PALs that may only be triggered by civilian leaders. In some cases (e.g., India), elements of control by the scientific–industrial complex form an additional check on military autonomy. Conversely, however, it should be noted that the invariable need for military action to execute both general nuclear policies and ad hoc use can in some cases be a useful safety net against irresponsible political decisions.

Executive control over nuclear weapons

Executive control is a wider concept than 'command and control' since it covers decisions on nuclear policy and strategy, procurement, deployment and resource use as well as determining the country's position on relevant international issues and instruments. In the eight countries studied in this chapter, this function is formally invested in the head of state or government, who in practice leads the executive of the country concerned. The importance of this individual (president or prime minister) is sometimes physically represented by his or her possession of the suitcase containing the nuclear release codes— as in Russia and the USA—and also by the lines of succession established to permit nuclear decision taking should the first individual be unable to act. It is worth noting that the line of devolution of this nuclear authority may be different from the normal constitutional line of succession (as, e.g., in France,

[63] Nizamani, H. K., 'Whose bomb is it anyway? Public opinion and perceptions about nuclear weapons and policy in the post-explosions phase in Pakistan', South Asia Research Network for the Social Sciences and Humanities, 14 June 2003, URL <http://sarn.ssrc.org/publications/>.

[64] Freedom House, 'Freedom in the world—2005', URL <http://www.freedomhouse.org/research/freeworld/2005/Kuwait-PNG.pdf>.

[65] See, e.g., Sagan and Waltz (note 7), p. 47; and Feaver (note 5).

Russia and the USA), where the latter involves persons like the speaker of parliament, who may be ill-placed to play a role in nuclear decision making.

In most cases, the top individual's freedom of action is limited by the existence of multi-person release procedures (normally including one or more military officers) and of formal bodies with advisory and policy-making powers over nuclear matters alone or defence in general. Examples of the latter are the Indian Nuclear Command Authority, the Chinese Central Military Committee and the French Defence Council. What is much harder to determine, especially in the more secretive countries, is how far such constitutional arrangements can guarantee 'civilian' control.

Parliamentary control

The theoretical powers of parliament can range from debate via legislative and budgetary powers to some degree of co-decision. In some cases parliament's role is formally reduced by the existence of presidential or executive decrees determining aspects of nuclear policy and management (e.g., in France, Pakistan and the UK). The strongest combination of legislative, budgetary and debating powers is possessed by the US Congress. The British and French parliaments can hold debates (as is the case in India) and exercise a more generalized budgetary control, while other parliaments (those of China, Israel and probably Pakistan) are not allowed to address nuclear issues at all. However, the place of parliament in policy-forming structures is not defined only by such formal considerations but also by parliamentarians' expertise and attitudes and by the degree to which they act as mouthpieces and stimulants for a broader national debate. To a greater extent even than in the field of defence generally, most parliaments lack access to independent expertise on nuclear matters and in many cases their ability to remedy this is stymied by secrecy laws. Parliaments (e.g., in Russia) may in any case perceive no motive to challenge nuclear weapon policy, depending on their own backgrounds and their assessment of public opinion (see below).

'Public' control

Civil society, including NGOs, independent experts, the media and individuals exercising their political rights, may in principle both pass judgement on official policies and generate new alternatives. In practice, the importance of public control depends on the way in which the given system distributes political power, the degree of civic freedom and the public availability of information on the policy matters in hand. Even well-established democratic systems have a tendency to restrict information on nuclear matters while other systems use secrecy laws to restrain or make a deterrent example of individuals who question the system.[66] Dahl has argued that, as a result, citizens have generally

---

[66] On Russia see 'Russian gets 15 years for spying' (note 25); on Israel see note 47.

abandoned any attempt to affect nuclear matters and are themselves abstaining from, not only being debarred from, any challenging debate.[67]

Nevertheless, civil protest, especially in democratic nuclear weapons states, has occurred on numerous occasions since 1945. For example, there were internationally coordinated civil protests at the end of the 1970s against the deployment of the neutron bomb (an enhanced radiation weapon) and during the early 1980s against NATO's decision to deploy cruise missiles and ballistic missiles in five European NATO states. Not only were political parties (especially centre and left-wing parties) obliged to take these protests seriously, but a new field was created in which independent experts and think tanks covering nuclear matters could find a base and an audience. These influences undoubtedly propelled the effort to find arms control or other cooperative solutions to the issues concerned between East and West.

Research institutes have continued to play a role in shaping thinking on nuclear strategy, especially in the USA where the RAND Corporation, the Brookings Institution and the Carnegie Endowment for International Peace are among the organizations that publish influential reports. Lawrence Freedman points out that the role of independent research institutes is strongest where the 'demarcation line' between government and academics is least strict, notably in the USA.[68]

IV. Conclusions

This analysis shows both that the governance of nuclear weapons entails a combination of many factors and players and that there is a prima facie and widespread democratic deficit in this field. It is often argued that nuclear weapon decision making cannot be subject to democratic due process because of the need for secrecy and the supreme urgency and difficulty of the judgements involved. Not all relevant decisions, however, are taken under acute time pressure or require highly specialized—including military—nuclear weapon knowledge. Especially after the end of the cold war, the contention remains untested and unproven that disclosing the premises of nuclear decision making or strategic thinking would endanger national security. Because nuclear choices have major financial, moral and environmental—and even life-and-death—consequences, decision making in a democratic state should involve and balance all the interests concerned and should guarantee the necessary minimum of democratic accountability.

The analysis also shows that focusing on who is pushing the launch 'button' is an insufficient and oversimplified approach for evaluating nuclear control. Decisions at each phase of the nuclear weapon life cycle, from the decision to acquire nuclear weapons to decisions on use, provide opportunities for substantive and effective civilian oversight and for democratic control as parts of good security sector governance. Parliament can and should play a meaningful

[67] Dahl (note 7), p. 3
[68] Freedman (note 45), p. 492.

role in decisions that require public funding, notably in the procurement phase of nuclear weapon programmes. Civil society, supported by research institutes and NGOs, can play a role in offering their opinions to decision makers in parliament and government, although this seems to happen less frequently than it did during the cold war.

The key findings of the analysis can be summarized in three main points.

1. The governance of nuclear weapons is stronger if all layers of accountability play a substantial role. This is not the case in all the states with nuclear weapons because of both formal and informal features of the political process. National legislatures play a marginal role in most countries either because they do not have the power to control nuclear weapons effectively (China, India, Pakistan and Russia) or because they do not choose to seriously challenge the position of the government (France, Israel and the UK). Only in the USA does legislative debate sometimes take on such an edge as to materially alter government policy. The role of civil society also seems strongest in the USA. These examples illustrate that the willingness of legislators to hold the government accountable is as important as the democratic nature of the country.

2. Transparency is an essential condition for both the internal and external components of good governance of nuclear weapons. Civilians in the executive cannot perform their oversight function in the absence of correct and complete information from military command and control structures. Parliamentary control cannot function if the executive withholds information. Without government information, the public and the media can neither judge the consistency of the government's own actions nor evaluate information gleaned from informal or confidential sources (e.g., whistle-blowers).

3. The USA is a genuine, if imperfect, model for civilian control and democratic accountability of nuclear weapons because of its open society, vigorous press and expert resources as well as a highly elaborate system of checks and balances. Nevertheless, nuclear weapon decision making remains a jealously guarded executive privilege. The US Congress does play a substantial role in budget control and legislation but not in the fields of doctrine, deployment and use of nuclear weapons. This example underlines that, while the general degree of democracy in a national system is vital for good nuclear governance, it is not enough in itself to guarantee the quality and transparency of official process.

In summary, the provision of information about nuclear weapons by states and its widespread dissemination remain crucial elements of democratic governance. The issue is one that extends much further than traditional command and control. Only with better information and better chances to act on it can individual societies decide on their true security needs, rather than leaving such momentous decisions to a small circle of national 'guardians' and other vested interests. The future choice lies between improved democratic civilian control of nuclear weapons or ever-greater opacity, unaccountability and unpredictability.

Part II. Military spending and armaments, 2005

Chapter 6. Transparency in the arms life cycle

Chapter 7. Military expenditure data: a 40-year overview

Chapter 8. Military expenditure

Chapter 9. Arms production

Chapter 10. International arms transfers

Chapter 11. The security dimension of European collective efforts in space

6. Transparency in the arms life cycle

BJÖRN HAGELIN, MARK BROMLEY, JOHN HART,
SHANNON N. KILE, ZDZISLAW LACHOWSKI,
WUYI OMITOOGUN, CATALINA PERDOMO,
EAMON SURRY and SIEMON T. WEZEMAN*

I. Introduction

This chapter considers how transparent, on a global scale, the arms life cycle 'from development to destruction' is. Transparency is basically understood to mean the release of information by those who possess it: in this case primarily governments. However, information may be shared just to aid coordination between different parts of a government or to help cooperation and build confidence between states, thus keeping the information flow within the official sector. This chapter argues that intra- and inter-government openness is not sufficient for transparency in the arms life cycle. What is of interest is transparency that goes beyond the government sector to provide information—and the opportunity to process and analyse it—to representative institutions, the media and the public at large.[1] Such openness is widely and correctly seen as a prerequisite for democratic control and for the accountability of government actions at national and international level.[2] Alternatively, as formulated by an international non-governmental organization (NGO), 'accountability is democracy, transparency is security'.[3]

The value of information for this purpose is not absolute and uniform, but depends on features such as availability (ease of access and timeliness), reliability (confidence in the accuracy and validity of information), comprehensiveness (type, quantity and coverage of information), comparability (over time and between countries) and disaggregation (detail of information).[4] These

---

[1] The owners of the information may provide it voluntarily and actively, or it may be accessible under certain conditions on request (e.g., under 'freedom of information' legislation or the disclosure of company information during legal proceedings). It should be noted that transparency of the national or international arms acquisition process is not the topic for this chapter.

[2] In 2004 the US General Accounting Office, after over 80 years, changed its name to the General Accountability Office as it believes that it is important to 'provide the public with an accurate, fair, and balanced picture of government today'. Walker, D. M., 'GAO answers the question: what's in a name?', *Roll Call*, 19 July 2004, URL <http://www.gao.gov/about/namechange.html>.

[3] Women's International League for Peace and Freedom, *The Model Nuclear Inventory: Accountability is Democracy, Transparency is Security* (Reaching Critical Will: New York, N.Y., 2005), URL <http://www.reachingcriticalwill.org/about/pubs/Inventory.html>.

[4] Bauer, S., 'The Europeanisation of arms export policies and its impact on democratic accountability', Doctoral thesis, Université libre de Bruxelles and Freie Universität, Berlin, May 2003.

* Valuable comments on this chapter were received from SIPRI colleagues and from Michael Brzoska of the Bonn International Center for Conversion.

qualitative criteria are better indicators of the degree of transparency than the mere quantity of information provided, which can result (perhaps deliberately) in overload and make the most important data harder to find.[5]

Information can also take different forms, but this chapter focuses on the availability of quantitative data (figures and statistics) on a global or at least international level. If the information is of good quality in the above senses, this can make possible the tracing of trends over time, international comparison of the scale of national and institutional actions, and the measurement and tracing of resource movements. Thus, military expenditure data measure the national economic burden of the military and can help to track sub-aspects of spending like equipment acquisition. Quantitative data on arms transfers are an indicator of national arms export policies and of national compliance with international arms control agreements, while arms inventories are an indication of military capability. However (and as discussed further below), the provision of 'bare' figures—even when accurate—may tell an incomplete or misleading story. The amount, type and detail of information published at any one time may be seen as the result of a balance between public demands for openness and government demands for secrecy. The relationship between what the authorities supply and what the demanders of information want and need is neither always positive nor linear. For instance, revealing the facts of defence-related actions may not always strengthen international confidence and security,[6] and the data may be supplied in a deliberately skewed and selective way to suit the supplier's purposes.

A partial remedy for the problem of low government transparency is that it is not only governments that control data. There are three generic sources of data: (*a*) national sources, including both government and industry, (*b*) international organizations and (*c*) civil society actors like academics, NGOs (whether academic, purpose-oriented or lobbying) and the media. The study of the arms life cycle needs data from companies as well as governments, particularly given the increasing multinationalization of production. While some international organizations mainly publish data released by governments—sometimes as a result of an international agreement—other organizations also actively collect information from other sources. The value that can be added to 'raw' or unsatisfactory data by researchers, NGOs and investigative journalists should not be underestimated. Systematic research, by collating and analysing information from different open sources, may provide a more accurate picture and will support better judgement of policy than a government's own offerings would permit. Expert processing can also help the wider public to make use of information that is initially harder to retrieve and understand. It was in this spirit that Robert Neild, SIPRI's first director, designed the first SIPRI Yearbook, in 1969, to provide in one place an account of recent trends in world military expenditure, the state of the technological

[5] In some countries, information of the types discussed in this chapter may not even be compiled. This suggests that transparency also depends on the quality of the data's structure and organization.

[6] Florini, A., 'The end of secrecy', eds B. I. Finel and K. M. Lord, *Power and Conflict in the Age of Transparency* (Palgrave: New York, N.Y., 2000), p. 13.

arms race and the success or failure of recent attempts at arms limitation or disarmament.[7]

This chapter covers a broad and multifaceted topic; in doing so, it considers some important quantitative aspects and major data sources without going into great detail. The chapter is organized around four phases of the arms life cycle: military expenditure and arms production including research and development (R&D), discussed in section II; arms transfers, in section III; national arms inventories held and used at any given time, in section IV; and the disposal of arms, in section V. Four questions are addressed. Is quantitative information available? What are its qualitative features? Has there been any notable change in transparency over the years? To what extent can such changes be attributed to policy or demands from the public? Conclusions are given in section VI.

The chapter is a collective SIPRI effort which covers—when relevant and with due regard to their differences—(a) major conventional weapons; (b) nuclear, biological and chemical weapons (weapons of mass destruction, WMD); and (c) small arms and light weapons (SALW). SALW are currently high on the political agenda because of their use in crime and intra-state conflicts as well as the specific control problems compared with major conventional weapons.[8] The contemporary political importance of major conventional weapons comes second after the perceived threat of WMD,[9] although the likelihood of actual use of WMD is probably low.

II. Military expenditure and arms production

There are a number of multilateral arms control agreements that impose voluntary or legal restrictions on states' acquisition of particular types of weapon.[10] As the United Nations (UN) Charter allows countries to acquire weapons for national defence, only a few of these agreements aim for the complete abolition of a class of weapons. Almost all countries therefore allocate financial and other resources to the acquisition of weapons.

[7] Neild, R., 'Preface', *SIPRI Yearbook of World Armaments and Disarmament 1968/69* (Almqvist & Wiksell: Stockholm, 1969), pp. 5–7.

[8] SALW have, along with conflict, serious diseases, terrorism and transnational crime, been considered as one of the the main new international threats. Krahmann, E. (ed.), *New Threats and New Actors in International Security* (Palgrave Macmillan: New York, N.Y., 2005).

[9] It may be symptomatic of today's international threat perceptions that major conventional weapons do not attract more attention and concern as a threat to peace. See United Nations, 'A more secure world: our shared responsibility', Report of the High-level Panel on Threats, Challenges and Change, UN documents A/59/565, 4 Dec. 2004, and A/59/565/Corr.1, 6 Dec. 2004, URL <http://www.un.org/ga/59/documentation/list5.html>; and the discussion about norms and intentions in the introduction to this volume.

[10] See chapter 12 in this volume; and United Nations, Department for Disarmament Affairs, 'Multilateral disarmament and non-proliferation regimes and the role of the United Nations: an evaluation', Occasional Paper no. 8, New York, N.Y., Oct. 2004, URL <http://disarmament.un.org/ddapublications>.

Military expenditure[11]

Military expenditure is the total of financial resources applied by governments to create and maintain the national military (or 'defence') establishment. Two particular issues have recently increased the political importance of and demand for reliable and disaggregated military expenditure data. First, the level of military spending by recipients of development assistance has, since the end of the cold war, become a criterion in economic aid decisions, especially among the donor countries of the Organisation for Economic Co-operation and Development (OECD). Second, the changing character of threats and armed conflict has increased the demand for data on internal security expenditure and the balance between expenditure for internal and external security.[12] However, low reliability and lack of disaggregation of data make it difficult to use the total amounts allocated for, or spent on, the military for either of these purposes. Owing to the secrecy that most governments apply to military matters, large parts of military spending are often hidden in non-military accounts or completely left out of official accounts.

Transparency in government reporting of military expenditure is also complicated by the fact that the UN definition of such expenditure is not always applied in national government accounting. Each country reports according to its own standards and government expenditure data therefore vary with regard to disaggregation and comprehensiveness. Even though most countries, including the major arms producers, publish at least gross figures of their military expenditure, only a few provide disaggregated data. The general lack of such data makes it difficult to assess what a reported figure includes and what it does not. Another difficulty is that expenditure by the arms industry itself for military R&D and arms production is not included in government military expenditure data.

National government sources that provide international data include the Bureau of Verification, Compliance, and Implementation of the US Department of State. It publishes the *World Military Expenditures and Arms Transfers* (WMEAT) reports.[13] Similarly, the Defence Intelligence Organisation (DIO) of the Australian Department of Defence has since 2000 published *Defence Economic Trends in the Asia–Pacific*, an attempt to provide a unified source for defence budgets in the region.[14] One difficulty with both of these sources is that the figures are based partly on intelligence information. This

---

[11] For an overview of the availability and uses made of military expenditure data over the past 40 years see chapter 7 in this volume.

[12] This aspect was, e.g., taken up in United Nations, Economic Commission for Latin America and the Caribbean (ECLAC), *Methodology for the Comparison of Military Expenditures* (ECLAC: Santiago, July 2005), URL <http://www.eclac.cl/cgi-bin/getProd.asp?xml=/publicaciones/xml/9/22549/P22549. xml>. See also Sköns, E., 'Financing security in a global context', *SIPRI Yearbook 2005: Armaments, Disarmament and International Security* (Oxford University Press: Oxford, 2005), pp. 285–306.

[13] US Department of State, *World Military Expenditures and Arms Transfers* website, URL <http://www.state.gov/t/vci/rls/rpt/wmeat/>.

[14] Australian Department of Defence, Defence Intelligence Organisation, Product website, URL <http://www.defence.gov.au/dio/product.html>.

limits the usefulness of the data for other users as their validity cannot be assessed.

National military expenditure data are published by a number of international organizations, such as the UN and the International Monetary Fund (IMF). The IMF publishes government financial statistics, including gross military expenditure, for most countries in the *Government Finance Statistics Yearbook* (GFSY).[15] In 1981 the UN created a reporting system operated by its Department for Disarmament Affairs (DDA). The DDA collects data from questionnaires sent to governments, but the figures thus obtained are not checked against other sources. Moreover, relatively few member states report data to the DDA in spite of attempts to promote engagement through regional workshops and the creation of a simplified reporting system.[16] The incentive for member countries to report their military spending is low and the UN can apply no sanctions if a country does not report. A country participating in this activity may regard it mainly as a way to receive political recognition for being transparent, not necessarily to establish more or better transparency. The national DDA reports are made available to the public, but there is no compilation or analysis of the data.[17]

In order to counter the general lack of transparency, facilitate national and international debate on military expenditure and make available to the public what information is available on national military expenditure, SIPRI collects and presents consistent, systematic and comparable national data.[18] SIPRI includes in its definition of military expenditure spending on personnel, operations and maintenance, procurement including R&D, military construction, and paramilitary forces. One major difference between the IMF data and SIPRI's is that the IMF excludes and SIPRI includes military pensions for retired personnel.[19] It is of conceptual importance for SIPRI to include military pensions as the purpose is to assess the economic burden to society represented by the military, and pensions may constitute a significant part of the resources allocated to the military.[20]

[15] The IMF's military expenditure data set is analysed and corrected by the IMF staff but is only published in an aggregate form.

[16] See appendix 8D in this volume.

[17] One particular problem concerns the method for comparing expenditures; see appendix 8E in this volume.

[18] As a recent SIPRI study has shown, under certain circumstances it is also possible to obtain previously unpublished national expenditure data, although these are still mostly presented only as total military spending. Omitoogun, W., *Military Expenditure Data in Africa: A Survey of Cameroon, Ethiopia, Ghana, Kenya, Nigerian and Uganda*, SIPRI Research Report no. 17 (Oxford University Press: Oxford, 2003). See also Omitoogun, W. and Hutchful, E. (eds), SIPRI, *Budgeting for the Military Sector in Africa: The Processes and Mechanisms of Control* (Oxford University Press: Oxford, 2006).

[19] European Union, Economic Policy Committee, 'The impact of ageing populations on public finances: overview of analysis carried out at EU level and proposals for a future work programme', Brussels, 22 Oct. 2003, URL <http://europa.eu.int/comm/economy_finance/epc/epc_ageing_en.htm>.

[20] Another NGO that publishes military expenditure data is the International Institute for Strategic Studies (IISS) in its annual publication *The Military Balance*. Although the IISS data have good global coverage, there is no transparency with regard to the sources used and so its data share the reliability problems of the WMEAT and DIO publications. International Institute for Strategic Studies, *The Military Balance* (Brassey's: London, 1992–1994; Oxford University Press: Oxford, 1996–2004; Routledge: Abingdon, 2005–).

Research and development

The earliest phase of arms production is R&D. Most government R&D expenditure is allocated to the development of equipment, performed at the company level. There is large variation among countries as to the availability and scope of government R&D data. More detailed figures are available in the United States than in any other country. The Eurostat Internet-based database reports the gross military R&D expenditure of the European Union (EU) member states, Japan and the USA.[21] Data on R&D expenditure published by the OECD are highly reliable and comparable as they are produced nationally according to common (Frascati) guidelines,[22] but they are only as good as the original national data. Even given the best national data it is often difficult or impossible to find systematic and reliable data on government and company funding of military R&D—arms-producing companies seldom break their R&D spending down into civil and military sub-categories. It is generally not possible to distinguish between basic research, applied research, and development, between R&D for specific types of weapons such as SALW, major conventional weapons or WMD, and between military R&D for national and foreign (cooperation and export) purposes.

SIPRI's military expenditure questionnaire sent to governments covers military R&D, primarily to determine if spending on R&D is part of the national definition of military expenditure.[23] However, governments report R&D data irregularly and use different definitions and so the reliability is problematic. There is no publication that includes a systematic compilation, analysis and comparison of the best military R&D data available. The reliability of government military R&D data has become increasingly complicated by the shift in emphasis towards, first, greater use of science and technology for military purposes in the major arms-producing countries and, second, the internationalization of arms production.[24]

Arms production

Government military expenditure does not define the cost—to governments and companies—of arms production, as noted above. This is instead reflected in the value of military sales from the arms-producing companies. This output is bought by the national armed forces or transferred to other armed forces or foreign organizations (on arms transfers see section III below). The national

---

[21] See the data on outlays on civilian and military R&D on the Eurostat website, URL <http://epp.eurostat.cec.eu.int/pls/portal/url/page/SHARED/PER_RESDEV>.

[22] Organisation for Economic Co-operation and Development (OECD), *Main Science and Technology Indicators*, 2005/1 edn (OECD: Paris, 2005). See also Hartley, K., 'Defence R&D: data issues', *Defence and Peace Economics* (forthcoming 2006).

[23] See appendix 8D in this volume.

[24] See Hagelin, B., 'Science- and technology-based military innovation: the United States and Europe', *SIPRI Yearbook 2004: Armaments, Disarmament and International Security* (Oxford University Press: Oxford, 2004), pp. 300–301.

output is therefore not equal to national procurement, which consists of domestic output bought by the national armed forces plus arms imports.[25] It has become increasingly difficult to draw a clear line between types of equipment and between civil and military production resources—and thus to define the boundaries of the arms industry itself.[26] Not only does the term 'defence equipment', commonly used by producer nations, have a more positive political connotation than 'military equipment', but the two terms can also be used simultaneously to cover partly different types of equipment. In European arms transfers data there also exists a distinction between 'war-fighting' and 'support' equipment. The latter includes civilian equipment that may be used for military purposes: 'dual-use' equipment. As a consequence, the amount of resources going into arms production is difficult to determine.

Conventional weapons

Although several of the major countries producing conventional weapons publish (on a regular or ad hoc basis) some sort of arms production data,[27] the public availability of quantitative, systematic and detailed information about national and company resources devoted to conventional arms production is unsatisfactory. Reliability is difficult to assess, and comparability is difficult to achieve because of the absence of internationally harmonized legal requirements for the national reporting of data on arms production. The comparability of financial data remains a serious and general problem; in addition, a company's military sales are seldom broken down with regard to type of product or destination (whether domestic or foreign). It can even be difficult to compare the data provided by a single government or company across time. All the major arms-producing companies have websites on which they publish information, but the type, quality and quantity of available arms production data vary widely and are generally insufficient for detailed analysis.[28]

[25] NATO, in its annual publication of the military expenditure of its members, includes a percentage share for expenditure on equipment. North Atlantic Treaty Organization (NATO), 'NATO–Russia compendium of financial and economic data relating to defence', Press Release (2005)161, 9 Dec. 2005, URL <http://www.nato.int/docu/pr/pr2005e.htm>.

[26] See the SIPRI Arms Production Project website, sources and methods section, URL <http://www.sipri.org/contents/milap/milex/aprod/siprisources.html>; and chapter 9 in this volume. On the different ways to define the arms industry see Chu, D. S. C. and Waxman, M. C., 'Shaping the structure of the American defense industry', eds G. I. Susman and S. O'Keefe, *The Defense Industry in the Post-Cold War Era* (Pergamon Press: Amsterdam, 1998), pp. 36–39. See also Gummett, P and Reppy, J. (eds), *The Relations between Defence and Civil Technologies*, NATO ASI Series, Series D, Behavioural & Social Sciences vol. 46 (Kluwer: Dordrecht, 1988).

[27] SIPRI, Arms Production Project, 'National data on arms production', URL <http://www.sipri.org/contents/milap/milex/aprod/nat_data.html>.

[28] As an illustration of the data problems, the Small Arms Survey uses a sector-oriented approach as a framework for its production analysis because detailed information is lacking. Small Arms Survey, 'Unpacking production: the small arms industry', *Small Arms Survey 2005: Weapons at War* (Oxford University Press: Oxford, 2005), URL <http://www.smallarmssurvey.org/publications/yb_2005.htm>, pp. 39–65. Attempts in 2004–2005 by the European Commission to establish procedures for opening the European arms market to more and fair competition may lead to some transparency in regional arms acquisitions under the European Defence Agency. Commission of the European Communities, 'Defence procurement', Green Paper, 23 Sep. 2004, URL <http://europa.eu.int/comm/internal_market/public procurement/dpp_en.htm>; and chapter 9 in this volume.

The majority of arms producers are involved in both 'military' and 'civil' activities. A pronounced trend towards privatization in the major producer countries has resulted in arms production moving from the part of the economy controlled by the government to the private sector.[29] The fact that publicly listed companies must disclose general financial data on revenues and profits, for example, to their shareholders results in some public transparency in the form of company reports or filings.[30] However, there are no national or internationally harmonized legal requirements that publicly listed companies should disclose detailed information on their arms production activities.[31] Government-owned arms producers report only to the government or department to which they are attached, and the government may not necessarily convey this information to the public.[32]

In 1989 SIPRI established its Arms Production Project.[33] It maintains a database on arms-producing companies and collects data made available by national governments, industry and other open sources. The project reports financial and employment data for the 100 largest arms-producing companies but does not compile information about the types and numbers of conventional weapons produced.[34] This gap is partly covered by the SIPRI Arms Transfers Database, which includes the licensed manufacture of major weapons. Other institutes, such as the International Institute for Strategic Studies (IISS), report on national arms inventories, and by combining different sources it is possible to assess the types and numbers of indigenously produced major weapons.[35]

As the latest addition to global and systematic arms production studies, the Geneva-based Small Arms Survey has reported annually since 1999 on pro-

---

[29] Sköns, E. and Weidacher, R., 'Arms production', *SIPRI Yearbook 2002: Armaments, Disarmament and International Security* (Oxford University Press: Oxford, 2002), pp. 341–46.

[30] This has become important information for institutions that do not want to invest in arms manufacturing companies. See, e.g., the Campaign Against Arms Trade (CAAT) Clean Investment campaign website, URL <http://www.caat.org.uk/campaigns/clean-investment.php>.

[31] Surry, E., *Transparency in the Arms Industry*, SIPRI Policy Paper no. 12 (SIPRI: Stockholm, Jan. 2006), URL <http://www.sipri.org/>.

[32] The importance of this lack of transparency is serious not only because of the nature of the products: the arms industry is considered to be one of the most corrupt industrial sectors. Transparency International, 'Transparency International releases new Bribe Payers Index', Press release, Berlin, 14 May 2002, URL <http://www.transparency.org/pressreleases_archive/>. The largest companies are also significant economic forces. The total 2003 revenue of the SIPRI Top 100 arms-producing companies was roughly equal to the combined national output of 61 low-income countries. Sköns, E. and Surry, E., 'Arms production', *SIPRI Yearbook 2005* (note 12), pp. 388–89.

[33] See the SIPRI Programme on Military Expenditure and Arms Production website, URL <http://www.sipri.org/contents/milap/>; and chapter 9 in this volume.

[34] See appendix 9A in this volume; and Surry (note 31). Data on employment in military companies do not always separate employment in military and civilian production, as many companies are involved in both activities. While variations in employment may reflect changes in military R&D or production, employment figures by themselves do not reflect the type of military production, its volume or sales. For such figures see, e.g., Bonn International Conversion Center (BICC), *Conversion Survey* (Oxford University Press: Oxford, 1996–98; NOMOS Verlagsgesellschaft: Baden-Baden, 1999–).

[35] The IISS gives numbers of weapons acquired domestically as well as from abroad. International Institute for Strategic Studies, *The Military Balance 2005–2006* (Routledge: Abingdon, 2005), table 16.

duction and other issues related to SALW as defined by the UN.[36] The task is ambitious but difficult as the availability of reliable national data is limited. It was recently concluded that it is impossible even to provide a reliable estimate of the current size of the military SALW industry in Western Europe,[37] a region where transparency in conventional weapons is generally relatively high compared to other parts of the world (see below).

Weapons of mass destruction

Four countries are known to have voluntarily discontinued relatively advanced nuclear weapon development or production processes: Argentina, Brazil, South Africa and Sweden.[38] Such development and production are difficult to verify owing not least to the dual-use or dual-purpose character of many phases of the production, which uses equipment, technology, materials and know-how that can be applied for both civil and military purposes. Very limited information is available about nuclear weapon production facilities— these facilities are not covered by the safeguards system for the civil nuclear industry monitored by the International Atomic Energy Agency (IAEA). Their sensitive nature and the unwillingness of governments to permit inspection are major impediments to progress towards building transparency in global fissile material production and storage. However, the IAEA maintains comprehensive nuclear-related databases.[39]

The level and quality of transparency regarding production and possession of chemical weapons are continuing to grow largely because of the implementation of the 1993 Convention on the Prohibition of the Development, Production, Stockpiling and Use of Chemical Weapons and on their Destruction (Chemical Weapons Convention, CWC). As of March 2006 it had 178 states parties.[40] The CWC has provisions that allow for informal consultation, clarification and fact-finding that have been successfully used to clarify some (but not all) concerns by some of the parties.[41]

There is less transparency in the field of biological weapons and it may be said to be decreasing. This is partly because the 1972 Convention on the Prohibition of the Development, Production and Stockpiling of Bacteriological

[36] In 2004 it was estimated that there were over 1200 companies in *c.* 90 countries producing small arms and light weapons. Small Arms Survey, *Small Arms Survey 2004: Rights at Risk* (Oxford University Press: Oxford, 2004).

[37] Weidacher, R., *Behind a Veil of Secrecy: Military Small Arms and Light Weapons Production in Western Europe*, Small Arms Survey Occasional Paper no. 16 (Small Arms Survey: Geneva, 2005), URL <http://www.smallarmssurvey.org/publications/occasional.htm>, p. 77.

[38] Other countries have ended smaller or less developed nuclear weapon programmes, e.g., South Korea and Taiwan. See appendix 13A in this volume for details of the current holders of nuclear forces.

[39] See the International Atomic Energy Agency website, URL <http://www.iaea.org/>. On nuclear weapon inventories see section IV below.

[40] The declared chemical weapon possessors are Albania, India, South Korea, Libya, Russia and the USA. See annex A in this volume for lists of signatories and parties to the CWC.

[41] Such concerns involved the completeness of declarations to the Organisation for the Prohibition of Chemical Weapons (OPCW), the body that implements the CWC, on past chemical weapon programmes and current activities being carried out by other parties' national defence establishments as part of programmes permitted by the CWC.

(Biological) and Toxin Weapons and on their Destruction (Biological and Toxin Weapons Convention, BTWC) lacks a standing institutional mechanism to implement the convention and to clarify compliance concerns.[42] In addition, a 1992 admission by Russia that the Soviet Union had violated the BTWC has since been publicly contradicted by a number of Russian officials, including individuals within the country's defence establishment.[43] Finally, the potential for misusing the results of advances in scientific and technological research with dual-purpose applications is continuing to grow.

The most difficult question regarding the nature of work carried out by a state's biological defence establishment is whether the work is part of a defensive programme or is offensive. If it is offensive, then it is prohibited by the BTWC.[44] However, most, if not all, research and testing short of large-scale production might be justified on the grounds that it is necessary for the evaluation of possible biological weapon threats. The matter is further complicated by a need to protect intelligence sources and methods, by difficulties associated with how such information can be acted on effectively, including within multilateral frameworks, and by ensuring the effectiveness of international prohibitions against non-state actors (i.e., terrorists).

There are suspected but unconfirmed national producers of all three classes of WMD.[45] A number of NGOs publish information about issues related to the production of all types of WMD—for instance SIPRI—or particular WMD—such as the Nuclear Threat Initiative.[46] They are all severely constrained in their analysis by the transparency problems.

III. Arms transfers

Since the 1960s governments have developed a number of mechanisms for collecting and releasing information on their arms transfers. These mechanisms can be broadly categorized as including either confidential, multinational reporting mechanisms (such as the Wassenaar Arrangement[47]), pub-

---

[42] On the BTWC see annex A in this volume.

[43] 'Statement on 29 January 1992 by B. N. Yeltsin, President of the Russian Federation, on Russia's policy in the field of arms limitations and reduction', Conference on Disarmament document CD/1123, 31 Jan. 1992.

[44] Roffey, R., 'Biological weapons and potential indicators of offensive biological weapon activities', *SIPRI Yearbook 2004* (note 24), pp. 557–71.

[45] On suspected nuclear, biological, chemical and ballistic missile weapon programmes see US Department of State, *Adherence to and Compliance with Arms Control, Nonproliferation and Disarmament Agreements and Commitments* (Department of State: Washington, DC, Aug. 2005), URL <http://www.state.gov/t/vci/rls/rpt/c15720.htm>.

[46] See chapters 13 and 14 in this volume; and the Nuclear Threat Initiative website, URL <http://www.nti.org/>.

[47] The Wassenaar Arrangement was established in July 1996 to promote 'transparency and greater responsibility in transfers of conventional arms and dual-use goods and technologies, thus preventing destabilising accumulations'. It replaced the voluntary Coordinating Committee for Multilateral Export Controls (COCOM), established in the 1950s and directed against Communist states. The participants in the Wassenaar Arrangement exchange information in confidence on the export of 7 categories of major conventional weapon to non-participating states. Anthony, I. and Bauer S., 'Transfer controls and destruction programmes', *SIPRI Yearbook 2004* (note 24), pp. 744–47; and Lewis, J. A., 'Multilateral

licly available multinational reporting mechanisms (such as the UN Register of Conventional Arms, UNROCA) and publicly available, unilateral reporting mechanisms (such as the various annual reports on arms exports that governments now produce). The EU Annual Report on the Code of Conduct on Arms Exports began as a confidential exchange between governments but became public after pressure from the European Parliament, NGOs and the 1999 Finnish EU Presidency.[48]

The motivations behind these mechanisms and the types of data collected and distributed vary considerably. In general, however, reliable, systematic and comparable data on arms exports would make it possible to analyse the implementation of national arms export policies and national compliance with international agreements to prevent the spread of specific weapons and related technologies and components, as well as to assess weapon build-ups.[49] Moreover, like military expenditure figures, data on arms transfers are relevant for making assessments of the impact of arms acquisitions on a recipient country's economy. Under the 1998 EU Code of Conduct, European suppliers are expected to assess the balance between accepting a recipient's legitimate security and self-defence needs and avoiding the diversion of the recipient's human and economic resources.[50]

Missiles—whether cruise, ballistic or anti-ballistic—have become the focus of political concerns because of a change in the nature of armed conflicts, the potential use of missiles as vehicles for WMD, their spread through licensed manufacture as well as deliveries and their potential destabilizing effects.[51] The Missile Technology Control Regime (MTCR), established in 1986, has tried since 1993 to limit the proliferation of any type of missile, unmanned

arms transfer restraint: the limits of cooperation', *Arms Control Today*, vol. 35, no. 9 (Nov. 2005), <http://www.armscontrol.org/act/2005_11/>. See chapter 16 and also the glossary in this volume for a list of participants in the Wassenaar Arrangement.

[48] Bauer, S. and Bromley, M., *The European Union Code of Conduct on Arms Exports: Improving the Annual Report*, SIPRI Policy Paper no. 8 (SIPRI: Stockholm, Nov. 2004), URL <http://www.sipri.org/>, p. 5. It has also been suggested that a change in national arms export policies towards stricter controls and transparency is generally the result of popular demands. Hagelin, B., *Neutrality and Foreign Military Sales* (Westview Press: Boulder, Colo., 1990); and Hagelin, B., *Arm in Arm: Swedish–Australian Military Trade and Cooperation*, Peace Research Centre Monograph no. 15 (Peace Research Centre, Australian National University: Canberra, 1994).

[49] For an overview see Squassoni, S. A., Bowman, S. R. and Behrens, C. E., 'Proliferation control regimes: background and status', Library of Congress, Congressional Research Service, Washington, DC, 10 Feb. 2005; the latest revision is available at URL <http://fpc.state.gov/fpc/42407.htm>.

[50] Council of the European Union, 'User's guide to the EU Code of Conduct on Arms Exports', Brussels, 14 Oct. 2005, URL <http://register.consilium.eu.int/pdf/en/05/st13/st13296.en05.pdf>, pp. 24–28.

[51] Several initiatives have been launched to investigate how best to address the proliferation of ballistic missiles. E.g., in Nov. 2002 over 90 states declared their readiness to subscribe to the Hague Code of Conduct against Ballistic Missile Proliferation. The intention was to address some of the shortcomings of the Missile Technology Control Regime (MTCR) by introducing demand-side policy controls. However, this can only be described as a partial success as several states with missile-development programmes decided not to join the initiative. Ahlström, C., 'Non-proliferation of ballistic missiles: the 2002 Code of Conduct', *SIPRI Yearbook 2003: Armaments, Disarmament and International Security* (Oxford University Press: Oxford, 2003), pp. 749–59; and US Department of State, Bureau of Nonproliferation, 'International Code of Conduct against Ballistic Missile Proliferation', Fact sheet, Washington, DC, 6 Jan. 2004, URL <http://www.state.gov/t/np/rls/fs/27799.htm>. See the glossary in this volume for a list of participants in the Hague Code of Conduct.

aerial vehicles and any items in the MTCR annex intended for the delivery of WMD (the 'catch-all' clause).[52] As many such missiles are 'conventional' weapons, much missile proliferation is covered by data on major conventional weapon transfers and thus states' observance of the MTCR can be monitored.

Major conventional weapons

The transfer of major conventional weapons is an area where more systematic and detailed data have become available from governments and NGOs.[53] The countries that regularly report on their national arms transfers are mainly in North America and Europe. In the USA two government organizations publish national and global data on arms transfers: the Congress publishes an annual report on transfers to developing nations and the Department of State publishes the WMEAT reports.[54] These reports use classified sources that reduce the reliability of the data.[55] In addition, the compilation of long time series is complicated as the data are presented for different periods in subsequent publications. Most EU countries report annually on their arms exports in a standard format, but without a common definition of 'arms exports'. These data are the basis for the public EU Annual Report on the Code of Conduct on Arms Exports.

Among international sources of data on global arms transfers available to the public, the voluntary UNROCA, begun in 1991, is the only official and global register of major arms transfers in the public domain. The EU Annual Report is not global with regard to suppliers since it covers exports from EU members only, but it does include the world's major arms suppliers other than the USA and Russia.[56] These organizations use different definitions and principles for collecting the data, partly because the purposes of the data sets

---

[52] See the Missile Technology Control Regime website, URL <http://www.mtcr.info/english/>; Arvidsson, P., 'Small arms and grenade launchers today and in the future', *Swedish Journal of Military Technology*, no. 1, 2005, pp. 17–21; and Fiorenza, N., 'NATO arms conference to focus on terrorist threats to aircraft', *Defense News*, 14 Mar. 2005, p. 13. See chapter 16 and also the glossary in this volume for a list of participants in the MTCR.

[53] Depending on the research questions, the need for detailed information on arms transfers may vary. Bauer and Bromley (note 48). See also United Nations, Office for Disarmament Affairs, *Study on Ways and Means of Promoting Transparency in International Transfers of Conventional Arms*, Report of the Secretary-General, Study Series 24, UN document A/46/301 (United Nations: New York, N.Y., 1992); Goldring, N. J., 'Moving toward transparency: an evaluation of the United Nations Register of Conventional Arms', British American Security Information Council (BASIC) Research Report no. 93.6, BASIC, London, Oct. 1993; and United Nations, Department of Disarmament Affairs, 'Transparency in armaments: 10th anniversary of the United Nations Register of Conventional Arms', New York, N.Y., 2002, URL <http://disarmament2.un.org/cab/Bk1-TransArms.pdf>.

[54] Grimmett, R. F., 'Conventional arms transfers to developing nations, 1997–2004', Library of Congress, Congressional Research Service, Washington, DC, Aug. 2005 (updated annually); and US Department of State (note 13),

[55] For a positive review of the US arms export system see Schroeder, M., 'Transparency and accountability in arms export systems: the United States as a case study', *Disarmament Forum*, no. 3, 2005, URL <http://www.unidir.org/bdd/fiche-article.php?ref_article=2393>, pp. 29–37.

[56] The combined exports from the 25 current EU member states accounted for 27% of total global exports of major conventional weapons in the period 2001–2005, making the EU the third largest exporter. See chapter 10 in this volume.

differ. The UNROCA was established after the 1991 Gulf War as a confidence-building measure for UN members to avoid destabilizing surprises. The aim of the EU Annual Report is to assist the EU Code of Conduct in its efforts to harmonize the national arms export policies of the EU member states. The increase in publicly available data on arms transfer is, generally, the result of the quality and quantity of national reports produced by EU member states and largely due to pressures exerted by the EU Code of Conduct.

Moreover, the UNROCA is incomplete and inaccurate.[57] The UN's Advisory Board on Disarmament Matters proposed to the UN High-level Panel on Threats, Challenges and Change that, in order to increase transparency, all members should report completely and accurately on all elements of the UNROCA.[58] One problem is political: namely, that detailed and correct data about arms imports for countries with no indigenous arms industry, not least in the Middle East, would reveal their arms inventories. Furthermore, the UN Secretary-General should be, but is not, required to report annually to the General Assembly and Security Council on any inadequacies in the reporting. Similarly, EU reporting could be improved.[59] With regard to the 2001 UN Programme of Action to Prevent, Combat and Eradicate the Illicit Trade in Small Arms and Light Weapons in All its Aspects, one area that has attracted the least amount of financial and technical assistance is transparency.[60]

The SIPRI Arms Transfers Project systematically analyses open information (both official and unofficial) about transfers of major conventional weapons but excluding most SALW. One result is a 'trend-indicator value' that permits comparisons over time and between countries from 1950.[61] The IISS also publishes international arms transfer data. Until 2005 it published financial data on arms exports; from 2005 the information is organized in a fashion similar to SIPRI's Arms Transfers Register but it differs from the SIPRI information.[62] As with other IISS data, it is not possible to assess the data's reliability.

The use, and especially the combination, of arms transfer data from different sources is complicated; the UNROCA gives the number of items transferred, while the US and EU reports calculate a financial value. The SIPRI trend-indicator value should not be compared with any of these figures. SIPRI also estimates a financial value of global arms exports from national reports, a task

[57] Wezeman, S. T., *The Future of the United Nations Register of Conventional Weapons*, SIPRI Policy Paper no. 4 (SIPRI: Stockholm, Aug. 2003), URL <http://www.sipri.org/>.

[58] The reporting request was taken up among the UN High-level Panel's recommendations. United Nations (note 9), Paragraph 97 and Recommendation 16.

[59] See the recommendations in Bauer and Bromley (note 48), pp. 32–33.

[60] Kytömäki, E. and Yankey-Wayne, V., 'Executive summary', *Implementing the United Nations Programme of Action on Small Arms and Light Weapons: Analysis of Reports Submitted by States in 2003* (UN Institute for Disarmament Research: Geneva, 2005), pp. xiii–xxii.

[61] See appendix 10C in this volume; and the SIPRI Arms Transfers Project website, URL <http://www.sipri.org/contents/armstrad/>.

[62] International Institute for Strategic Studies (note 20).

complicated by the lack of a common international definition of 'arms exports'.[63]

Small arms and light weapons

Compared to major weapons, there are many more producers of SALW and there are greater opportunities to hide their transfer. As a consequence, it has been more difficult to compile systematic and reliable data at the global level about SALW transfers, especially since such weapons were not in the past separated from major weapons in national arms transfers reporting. However, as a result of their use in crime, the increase in the number of intra-state conflicts and the specific control problems compared with major conventional weapons, many countries now exchange information on their transfers of SALW. For example, all member states of the Organization for Security and Co-operation in Europe (OSCE) share information on the import and export of SALW to and from other OSCE states under the 2000 Document on Small Arms and Light Weapons.[64] While most member states share such information in confidence, some governments, including the Czech Republic, Germany and Spain, chose to make their reports public.[65]

There is one NGO that has a systematic focus specifically on issues related to SALW: the Small Arms Survey. It acknowledged in 2003 that its most difficult research task involves the documenting of international transfers, mainly owing to lack of data and coverage.[66] No national or global series of data are available for small arms transfers, and understanding of the authorized trade remains partial. All global and most national estimates are highly unreliable. In order to overcome this situation, governments need to regularly report on transfers of small arms, light weapons and major weapons in separate categories.[67]

While the SIPRI Arms Transfers Database includes some UN light weapons categories, the Small Arms Survey makes use of the Norwegian Initiative for Small Arms Transfers (NISAT) to compile information on SALW transfers from the UN Commodity Trade Statistics (UN Comtrade) Database[68] and

---

[63] SIPRI Arms Transfers Project, 'Financial value of arms exports', URL <http://www.sipri.org/contents/armstrad/at_gov_ind_data.html>. See also chapter 10 in this volume.

[64] Organization for Security and Co-operation in Europe, OSCE Document on Small Arms and Light Weapons, FSC.DOC/1/00, 24 Nov. 2000, URL <http://www.osce.org/item/16343.html>.

[65] Hagelin, B. et al., 'International arms transfers', *SIPRI Yearbook 2003* (note 51), pp. 463–64. In 2003 the Wassenaar states agreed to exchange, in confidence, information on transfers of SALW and man-portable air defence systems (MANPADS). Anthony and Bauer (note 47).

[66] Small Arms Survey, *Small Arms Survey 2003: Development Denied* (Oxford University Press: Oxford, 2003), p. 5.

[67] Small Arms Survey (note 28), p. 117. From 2004 the Small Arms Survey has produced the Small Arms Trade Transparency Barometer, which gives points to individual nations according to their official reporting; see URL <http://www.smallarmssurvey.org/barometer/>.

[68] See the UN Commodity Trade Statistics Database website, URL <http://unstats.un.org/unsd/comtrade/>. The data are discussed in Small Arms Survey (note 28), pp. 98–100.

national arms export reports.[69] However, the disaggregation and reliability of customs data in particular is complicated by problems of distinguishing between civil and military goods and between other goods in many of the open customs categories. The ambition of the NISAT database is also to permit an analysis of the illicit trade. However, most states make available very little information on customs seizure of illicit arms.[70] In 2004 a UN report recommended legally binding agreements on the transfers (as well as the marking, tracing and brokering) of SALW.[71]

IV. Arms inventories

As quantitative information seems so precise, it is easily misused. It is not uncommon to see (changes in) a country's military expenditure being cited by governments and others as evidence for the defence capability of that country, of the threat it may present, and even of its intentions. It is particularly tempting to use budget data for such purposes, especially when other criteria of transparency are low.[72] However, such analysis could support worst-case analysis and increase the risk of mis- or disinformation with potentially serious consequences, as recently seen in the case of Iraq. National military strength, or capability, is not a simple function of financial or other material inputs. 'Bean counting', therefore, does not answer crucial questions about military capability.[73]

Capability assessments need to consider, among other things, the potential use (and usefulness) of specific parts or all of the operational inventory, including factors such as the technical level of modernization, deployability, mobility and maintenance, the doctrine according to which the weapons are to be used, and the training and motivation of those handling the equipment.[74]

---

[69] See the Norwegian Initiative on Small Arms Transfers (NISAT) website, URL <http://www.prio. no/nisat/>.

[70] Small Arms Survey (note 28), p. 117.

[71] United Nations (note 9), Recommendation 15.

[72] E.g., the US Government is concerned about an increase in Chinese military capabilities and the parallel lack of transparency of its defence budget. US Department of Defense, 'Annual report on the military power of the People's Republic of China, FY04 report to Congress on PRC military power', Washington, DC, 2005, URL <http://www.defenselink.mil/pubs/d20040528PRC.pdf>; and 'Eyes on China', *Aviation Week & Space Technology*, 5 Sep. 2005, p. 21. See also chaper 8 in this volume.

[73] See, e.g., publications by the former SIPRI Military Technology Project: Arnett, E., 'Iran, threat perception and military confidence-building measures', SIPRI, Stockholm, 1996, URL <http://projects. sipri.org/technology/Iran_CBM.html>; and Arnett, E. (ed.), SIPRI, *Military Capacity and the Risk of War: China, India, Pakistan and Iran* (Oxford University Press: Oxford, 1997). There are several RAND publications on the issue of capability, including Treverton, G. F. and Jones, S. G., *Measuring National Power* (RAND: Santa Monica, Calif., 2005), URL <http://www.rand.org/pubs/conf_proceedings/ CF215/>; and Tellis, A. J. et al., *Measuring National Power in the Postindustrial Age* (RAND: Santa Monica, Calif., 2000), URL <http://www.rand.org/pubs/monograph_reports/MR1110/>.

[74] E.g., in the negotiation of the 1990 Treaty on Conventional Armed Forces in Europe, participants from both sides of the East–West divide, having failed to set more complex parameters for heavy weapons, agreed to a quantitative 'one-for-one' rule in each of the weapon categories. An even more complicated issue was how to define the comparative effectiveness of NATO and Warsaw Treaty Organization soldiers. Eventually, the parties agreed to a politically binding agreement in which each party set a limit on national land personnel. The agreement on personnel strength was signed in 1992 and was

Moreover, not only does military capability vary over time, but it is only relevant to security analysis in relation to the capability of a potential military opponent.[75] It is difficult to make an objective and accurate assessment of 'military balance' or 'the balance of power'. Today, international armed conflicts are fought abroad rather than in defence of national territory, with allies rather than alone, and do not necessarily define a military opponent in a geographical sense.[76] The existence of national forces and stocks of weapons abroad as well as the access to foreign bases complicate not only reliable estimates of the size and deployment of national inventories at a particular time, but also the assessment of operational military capability.[77]

Owing to the problems with quantifying the production and trade of SALW (see above), they are not covered in this section. Nor are chemical and biological weapons since there are no publicly proven stockpiles of biological weapons and since detailed inventories of chemical weapon stockpiles among states parties to the CWC are already known.[78]

Conventional weapons

As illustrated above with regard to imports by nations lacking indigenous production capabilities, most countries closely guard the exact information about their arms inventories. There is no officially confirmed or otherwise verifiable figure for the size of all conventional weapon inventories in the world, although the aim of the UNROCA was to achieve transparency in national holdings of the types of major weapons reported. There are, however, organizations that try to quantify and analyse such information from available information—some of it official information—such as the Bonn International Center for Conversion, the IISS, Jane's publications on weapon systems[79] and

implemented by 1995. The official figures are publicly available. Crawford, D., 'Conventional Armed Forces in Europe (CFE): a review and update of key treaty elements', Arms Control Bureau, US Department of State, Washington, DC, Dec. 2004; and International Institute for Strategic Studies (note 20). Estimates of personnel strength in other countries are published by the US Department of State (note 13), International Institute for Strategic Studies (note 20) and the Bonn International Center for Conversion (note 34).

[75] The particular problem of arms inventories of non-state actors is illustrated by MANPADS, comparably light weapons which in the hands of well-trained users pose a greater risk than some heavier weapons. Bolkcom, C., Feickert, A. and Elias, B., 'Homeland security: protecting airliners from terrorist missiles', Library of Congress, Congressional Research Service, Washington, DC, Nov. 2003; the latest revision is available at URL <http://fpc.state.gov/fpc/38031.htm>.

[76] Zanini, M. and Taw, J. M., *The Army and Multinational Force Compatibility* (RAND: Santa Monica, Calif., 2000), URL <http://www.rand.org/publications/MR/MR1154/>.

[77] Foreign pre-positioning of weapons is mainly relevant for US forces. Harkavy, R. E., 'Thinking about basing', *Naval War College Review*, vol. 58, no. 3 (summer 2005), pp. 26–27; Cooley, A., 'Base politics', *Foreign Affairs*, vol. 84, no. 6 (Nov./Dec 2005), pp. 79–92; Bonn International Center for Conversion, *Conversion Survey 2005: Global Disarmament, Demilitarization and Demobilization* (Nomos Verlagsgesellschaft: Baden-Baden, 2005), pp. 44–46; and Lachowski, Z., *Foreign Military Bases in the Euro-Asian Region*, SIPRI Policy Paper (SIPRI: Stockholm, forthcoming 2006).

[78] Even among suspected, undeclared chemical weapon states, none is believed to possess large stockpiles.

[79] The number of Jane's specialized military equipment publications has increased over time; a list is available at URL <http://catalog.janes.com/catalog/public/index.cfm?fuseaction=home.ProductIndex>.

the Small Arms Survey. The reliability of such figures is in most cases controversial. For instance, the IISS claims that the national equipment holdings are based on the most accurate data available or on best estimates as well as judgements based on the available information.[80]

Europe is an exceptional region in that official transparency of certain categories of major conventional weapon inventories is pursued under arms control agreements reached within the framework of the OSCE, until 1995 known as the Conference on Security and Co-operation in Europe. Both the legally binding 1990 Treaty on Conventional Armed Forces in Europe (CFE Treaty), based on the NATO and Warsaw Treaty Organization alliances at the time, and the politically binding Vienna Document 1999 on Confidence- and Security-Building Measures contribute to public openness and transparency of the arsenals of the European states.[81] The 1999 Agreement on the Adaptation of the CFE Treaty has not yet formally entered into force, but its enhanced transparency procedures are already respected.[82] The historical record of limits and national holdings in five treaty-limited conventional weapons categories—battle tanks, armoured combat vehicles, artillery pieces, combat aircraft and attack helicopters—by 28 countries, including Russian and US holdings in Europe but excluding the neutral European countries, is public information. SIPRI's activity in disseminating this information is an example of how an NGO may act as a 'transparency agent' of an international organization.[83]

Nuclear weapons

Nothing similar to the CFE Treaty's transparency regime has been achieved in other parts of the world or in other weapon categories. Although there has been some progress made since the late 1960s towards greater transparency in nuclear arsenals, there remain large uncertainties about global inventories of nuclear weapons and weapon-usable fissile material.[84] The five states defined

---

[80] International Institute for Strategic Studies (note 35), p. 6.

[81] For a presentation of the history, negotiations and status of the CFE Treaty see the SIPRI Yearbooks 1991–2005; Lachowski, Z., *Confidence- and Security-Building Measures in the New Europe*, SIPRI Research Report no. 18 (Oxford University Press: Oxford, 2004); and Peters, J. E., *CFE and Military Stability in Europe* (RAND: Santa Monica, Calif., 1997), URL <http://www.rand.org/pubs/mono graph_reports/MR911/>. On the Vienna Ducument 1999 see annex A in this volume.

[82] Lachowski, Z., 'Conventional arms control', *SIPRI Yearbook 2000: Armaments, Disarmament and International Security* (Oxford University Press: Oxford, 2000), pp. 599–600.

[83] The CFE weapon ceilings and holdings are available on SIPRI's Facts on International Relations and Security Trends (FIRST) website, URL <http://first.sipri.org/>. SIPRI plays the role of a conduit for OSCE information to the public. The publication of OSCE information and data must not exceed the limits beyond which sensitive information and the security interests of states concerned might be compromised. Thus, e.g., SIPRI does not publish details about the location or deployments of weapons provided under the CFE and Vienna Document regimes. See also Lachowski, Z. and Sjögren, M., 'Conventional arms control', *SIPRI Yearbook 2004* (note 24), p. 714.

[84] The negotiations about a prospective fissile material cut-off treaty remains stalled in the Conference on Disarmament in Geneva in part because of a dispute about the adequacy of verification arrangements. Carlson, J., 'Can a fissile material cut-off treaty be effectively verified?', *Arms Control Today*, vol. 35, no. 1 (Jan./Feb. 2005), pp. 25–29.

as nuclear weapon states by the 1968 NPT—China, France, Russia, the United Kingdom and the USA—publish some official data about their nuclear forces in different national sources. In addition, considerable official information about US nuclear forces has been declassified and made public through the USA's Freedom of Information Act.[85] However, the reliability and comprehensiveness of official information about the force holdings of the five NPT-defined nuclear weapon states varies and is especially limited with respect to China. There is also very little public information available about the nuclear stockpiles of the three de facto nuclear weapon states—India, Israel and Pakistan—and about the numbers and the operational status of their nuclear weapon delivery systems, including ballistic and cruise missiles, artillery and aircraft. Despite the lack of transparency, several NGOs—including SIPRI—compile and publish estimates of nuclear force holdings.[86]

The nuclear arms limitation and reduction treaties concluded during the cold war provided for verification measures that have introduced a limited degree of public transparency into Russian and US deployed strategic nuclear forces.[87] However, there is still no reliable information about the numbers and operational status of Russian and US non-strategic (or 'tactical') nuclear weapons. These weapons remain unregulated by any legally binding arms control agreement. They pose special challenges for arms control accountancy—they are mobile and too small to be monitored by traditional national technical means—and their associated delivery systems can be used to deliver conventional as well as nuclear munitions.[88]

A number of studies have advocated the idea of establishing a comprehensive transparency regime for nuclear warheads and materials in order to complement and strengthen treaties imposing numerical limits on nuclear forces.[89]

[85] See, e.g., documents published by the Nuclear Information Project at URL <http://www.nukestrat.com/>.

[86] See appendix 13A in this volume. Additional information about world nuclear weapon inventories is also available in the Federation of American Scientists Nuclear Forces Guide at URL <http://www.fas.org/nuke/guide/>. The Russian Nuclear Forces Project maintains a comprehensive website devoted to information about Russia's strategic nuclear forces at URL <http://russianforces.org/eng/>. For comprehensive estimates by non-governmental experts of global inventories of highly enriched uranium and plutonium see Albright, D., Berkhout, F. and Walker, W., SIPRI, *Plutonium and Highly Enriched Uranium 1996: World Inventories, Capabilities and Policies* (Oxford University Press: Oxford, 1997).

[87] Under the 1991 Treaty on the Reduction and Limitation of Strategic Offensive Arms (START I Treaty), Russia and the USA exchange classified memoranda of understanding about their deployed strategic nuclear delivery vehicles, and the warheads attributed to them under START I counting rules, every 6 months. Declassified versions of this data are made available to the public. See, e.g., US Department of State, Bureau of Arms Control, 'START aggregate numbers of strategic offensive arms', Washington, DC, 1 Oct. 2005, URL <http://www.state.gov/t/ac/rls/fs/54166.htm>. On START I see annex A in this volume.

[88] Handler, J., 'The September 1991 presidential nuclear initiatives and the elimination, storing and security aspects of TNWs', ed. T. Susiluoto, *Tactical Nuclear Weapons: Time for Control* (UN Institute for Disarmament Research: Geneva, 2002), pp. 107–32.

[89] E.g., Fetter, S. and Feiveson, H. A., 'Verifying deep reductions in nuclear forces', ed. H. A. Feiveson, *The Nuclear Turning Point: A Blueprint for Deep Cuts and De-alerting of Nuclear Weapons* (Brookings Institution Press: Washington, DC, 1999), URL <http://www.brook.edu/press/books/nucturn.htm>. On the political and technical dimensions of creating a nuclear warhead transparency regime see Zarimpas, N. (ed.), SIPRI, *Transparency in Nuclear Warheads and Material: The Political and Technical Dimensions* (Oxford University Press: Oxford, 2003).

This would involve *inter alia* declaring and verifying existing stockpiles of warheads and weapon-usable fissile material, monitoring the dismantling of individual weapons, and verifying the safe and secure disposal of the fissile material that they contained. Attempts by Egypt and some other countries to establish a UN nuclear register and include nuclear weapons in the UNROCA have failed, as have attempts to create a nuclear transparency regime in the Russian–US context.[90]

V. Disposal of arms

Global major weapon inventories (as well as armed forces personnel and employment in arms production) are decreasing owing to military modernization.[91] This modernization might imply that fewer weapons are needed as each weapon becomes more technologically sophisticated and acquires a higher military capability, or that old weapons are exchanged for new weapons. In either case, weapons become surplus. Rather than paying for their storage, countries may destroy them or, in the case of SALW and major conventional weapons, export them.

In addition, weapons are disposed of under the auspices of multinational organizations or agreements. From the 1990s, the disposal of conventional weapons and ammunition inventories in the countries of the former Soviet Union in particular, as well as WMD in some of these and other countries, has been among the most urgent tasks. During the 1990s major conventional weapons in Europe were disposed of under the CFE Treaty.[92] Today, SALW, including landmines, and ammunition are being disposed of under post-conflict arrangements in many regions, often under UN management.[93] The UN has designated 9 July as International Weapons Destruction Day, focusing on illicit small arms around the world.[94] In Europe, SALW and ammunition are disposed of under the auspices of the OSCE and NATO's Partnership for Peace Trust Fund.[95] However, the particular problems of transparency in the

---

[90] In 1994–95 talks were held in the Joint Working Group on Safeguards, Transparency and Irreversibility, a forum launched for negotiations to establish a new arms control regime covering Russian and US stockpiles of nuclear weapons and fissile materials. These talks ended inconclusively.

[91] Bonn International Center for Conversion (note 77), p. 29.

[92] See chapter 15 in this volume.

[93] Small Arms Survey (note 28), pp. 267–301. See also 'Small arms and light weapons', *Compendium of Good Practices on Security Sector Reform* (Global Facilitation Network for Security Sector Reform: Shrivenham, 2005), URL <http://www.gfn-ssr.org/good_practice.cfm>. Anti-personnel landmines are one type of 'small arm' around which the international community is to a large extent united in the need for action. The Convention on the Prohibition of the Use, Stockpiling, Production and Transfer of Anti-Personnel Mines and on their Destruction (APM Convention) was opened for signature on 3 Dec. 1997 and came into force on 1 Mar. 1999; the text of the convention is available at URL <http://www.un.org/millennium/law/xxvi-22.htm>. See also annex A in this volume; and Foreign Affairs Canada, 'Canada's guide to the global ban on mines', SafeLane website, URL <http://www.mines.gc.ca/>.

[94] 'International Weapons Destruction Day', *Federalist Debate*, vol. 18, no. 3 (Nov. 2005), p. 46.

[95] The Partnership for Peace Trust Fund was established in Sep. 2000, originally to assist in the destruction of stockpiled anti-personnel landmines under the APM Convention. In 2005 a new project was created to help Ukraine, this time to destroy stockpiles of surplus munitions, SALW and MANPADS over 12 years. 'Trust Fund project to destroy surplus weapons and ammunition in Ukraine',

production, transfers and inventories of many SALW makes it difficult to know how many of these weapons remain in civilian or military circulation.

Weapons of mass destruction

The ending of the cold war brought dramatic decreases in the size of the US and former Soviet nuclear arsenals. However, only limited public information is available about the numbers of nuclear warheads that have been disassembled and eliminated. There are no treaty-mandated arrangements for monitoring the dismantlement of warheads, since the parties are concerned that this process could reveal sensitive design information. Many arms control advocates have promoted the idea of requiring the irreversible elimination of nuclear warheads as a way of making permanent the treaty-mandated force reductions. The idea has been rejected, primarily because of US objections that it would inhibit the parties' ability to 'reconstitute' their strategic forces in the event of an unexpected change in the security environment.[96]

According to figures provided by the US Department of Energy, during the decade after 1989 the USA removed from service and dismantled about 11 000 nuclear warheads.[97] These included non-strategic nuclear warheads that were deployed by the USA outside its territory.[98] US Department of Defense and Central Intelligence Agency estimates suggest that Russia dismantled slightly more than 1000 warheads per year during the 1990s; that is, more than 10 000 were dismantled over the decade.[99] In addition, the two countries have eliminated several categories of nuclear weapon systems, including intermediate-range land-based missiles, artillery shells and landmines. With the end of the cold war, the UK also significantly reduced its nuclear arsenal. This included the withdrawal from service and elimination of its stockpile of

NATO's Nations and Partners for Peace, vol. 50, no. 1 (2005), p. 118. See also 'NATO achieves demilitarization milestones in Albania, Ukraine', *Jane's International Defence Review*, Jan. 2006, p. 17.

[96] On the Russian–US Strategic Offensive Reductions Treaty (SORT) negotiations see Kile, S. N., 'Nuclear arms control, non-proliferation and ballistic missile defence', *SIPRI Yearbook 2003* (note 51), pp. 600–602. On the SORT itself see annex A in this volume.

[97] Norris, R. S. and Kristensen, H. M., 'Nuclear notebook: U.S. nuclear reductions', *Bulletin of the Atomic Scientists*, vol. 60, no. 5 (Sep./Oct. 2004), pp. 70–71. The USA produced *c.* 70 000 nuclear warheads in 1945–90. At its peak, in 1967, the US operational stockpile held *c.* 32 000 warheads.

[98] In 2005 the USA deployed *c.* 160 aircraft-delivered nuclear bombs in NATO countries in Europe. In 1985 the USA deployed *c.* 6500 weapons, encompassing a number of different types, in Europe. Kile, S. N. and Kristensen, H. M., 'World nuclear forces, 2005', *SIPRI Yearbook 2005* (note 12), pp. 578–602; and Arkin, W. M., 'Nuclear weapons', *World Armaments and Disarmament: SIPRI Yearbook 1986* (Oxford University Press: Oxford, 1986), pp. 37–80.

[99] Kristensen, H. M., 'World nuclear forces', *SIPRI Yearbook 2004* (note 24), p. 633. In addition, a variety of nuclear weapon-related dismantlement and security projects have been undertaken as part of the Russian–US Cooperative Threat Reduction (CTR) programme. The programme was initiated by the US Government in 1991 and since 1993 has evolved to encompass a wide range of nuclear non-proliferation and demilitarization activities across the former Soviet Union in addition to weapon destruction and dismantlement. SIPRI Pilot Project, *Strengthening European Action on WMD Non-proliferation and Disarmament: How Can European Community Instruments Contribute?*, Interim report (SIPRI: Stockholm, Nov. 2005); and Anthony, I., *Reducing Threats at the Source: A European Perspective on Cooperative Threat Reduction*, SIPRI Research Report no. 19 (Oxford University Press: Oxford, 2004).

aircraft-delivered nuclear bombs, which was completed in 1998. Although France has made smaller cuts in its nuclear arsenal, it has removed some categories of nuclear delivery vehicles from service. These include its entire force of land-based ballistic missiles.

No internationally transparent destruction of biological weapons is currently under way. The parties to the BTWC committed themselves to destroy any such stockpiles when they joined the regime in the 1970s and 1980s, but there is no mechanism requiring the parties to submit legally binding annual declarations or for an international body to verify the content of such declarations. Moreover, no state that is not a party to the BTWC is currently willing to publicly acknowledge having an offensive biological weapon programme or stockpiling such weapons.

In contrast, the amount and type of chemical weapons held by states parties to the CWC are well documented. These weapons, including old or abandoned weapons, are currently being verifiably destroyed, and the main results are publicly available. As of November 2005, of approximately 71 373 agent tonnes of declared chemical weapons, about 12 332 agent tonnes had been destroyed; and of approximately 8.7 million declared items, about 2.4 million munitions and containers had been destroyed.[100] As of the same date, 12 states had declared 64 chemical weapon production facilities, of which 37 had been certified as being destroyed and 14 as being converted for purposes not prohibited under the CWC.[101]

The cost of disarmament

The disposal or destruction of weapons (outside of actual combat), as well as cleaning of the production sites, is not without cost.[102] It relates both to 'the remnants of previous wars' and 'the remnants of the present peace' as the destruction of weapon stockpiles and installations is in consequence of them not having been used or not (being allowed to be) used in today's and future wars. The cost of disposal or destruction may be too high for an individual country. The most critical period in the CFE destruction process was 1993–95, when the force reduction took place. The responsibility was with individual states parties, and some nations requested assistance: in 1994 Belarus and Ukraine received approximately $10 million from the US Congressional Peace Project.[103] In 2000, financial problems arose concerning Russian military equipment in Georgia and Moldova and ammunition in Moldova. The OSCE set up a fund for helping Russia with the disposal. Various programmes are ongoing for the elimination of 'the remnants of the war that never was' (the cold war

---

[100] Organisation for the Prohibition of Chemical Weapons, 'Inspection activity', URL <http://www.opcw.org/ib/html/insp_act.html>.

[101] These 12 states are Bosnia and Herzegovina, China, France, India, Iran, Japan, South Korea, Libya, Russia, Serbia and Montenegro, the UK and the USA.

[102] See reports from the UN Institute for Disarmament Research (UNIDIR) Costs of Disarmament project, 1999–2004, URL <http://www.unidir.ch/bdd/fiche-activite.php?ref_activite=3>.

[103] *Arms Control Reporter*, sheet 407.B.507-8, 1994.

legacy)—small arms, excessive ammunition, unexploded ordnance and toxic rocket fuel—in the OSCE area.[104] To assist the former Soviet republics, among others, the OSCE acts as the clearing house, and financial resources are sought from such international bodies as NATO, the EU and the UN Development Programme.[105]

The cost of getting rid of 'remnants of peace' is substantial, but in most cases not prohibitive, especially with US and international support. Should such expenditure be considered 'defence' expenditure, in the same way as military pensions remain a military expenditure even after the individuals have left active service? Certain expenditure for weapon destruction is indeed included in Russian military expenditure. For other countries, such expenditure may or may not be included in their reported military expenditure.

VI. Conclusions

Four questions were formulated in section I. Is quantitative information available? What are its qualitative features? Has there been any notable change in transparency over the years? To what extent can such changes be attributed to policy or demands from the public? The answer is that data are available but they rarely meet all the quality tests of availability, reliability, comprehensiveness, comparability and disaggregation for each of the phases.[106] There are no general grounds for confidence in the quality and validity of government information, and it can only be evaluated once the definitions, sources and methods used for compilation and calculations are known. As noted above, there are variations between countries in the definitions that determine what they include and exclude in their reported data. The problem of definition is increasing, while the activities of arms producers remain partly beyond the control of the citizens of countries where they operate. The multivalent nature of many current innovations in science and technology is making it both more important, and harder, to pin down and compare amounts devoted to specifically military R&D.

The lack of internationally agreed definitions, or adherence to existing definitions, poses obvious problems for international comparisons. The effort devoted by SIPRI over the years to making data on military expenditure, arms production and arms transfers reliable and internationally comparable illus-

---

[104] The OSCE in 2000 adopted a far-reaching document on the control of SALW. A special report in 2004 pointed to many remaining difficulties; 'Disposal of surplus small arms: a survey of policies and practices in OSCE countries', Bonn International Center for Conversion (BICC), British American Security Information Council (BASIC), Saferworld and Small Arms Survey, Jan. 2004, URL <http://www.basicint.org/pubs/Joint/2004OSCE.htm>. The national cases were Belarus, Bulgaria, Germany, Norway, Poland, Romania, Russia, Switzerland, the UK and the USA. See also Bailes, A. J. K., Melnyk, O. and Anthony, I., *Relics of Cold War: Europe's Challenge, Ukraine's Experience*, SIPRI Policy Paper no. 6 (SIPRI: Stockholm, Nov. 2003), URL <http://www.sipri.org/>.

[105] Lachowski, Z. and Dunay, P., 'Conventional arms control and military confidence building', *SIPRI Yearbook 2005* (note 12), p. 661.

[106] A further issue is timeliness: since quantitative information is typically available only in retrospect (except for military expenditure forecasts, which turn out to be inaccurate for many reasons), it does not in itself guarantee any real-time public consultation and control.

trates the amount of time and resources needed for such work. Despite those efforts and despite the rise in the number of military and defence journals, especially between 1950 and 1980 (as well as many other relevant publications),[107] there is still no systematic, reliable, valid and global—or in most cases, even regional—set of quantitative data on the topics discussed in this chapter. Persistent government preferences for secrecy are part of the explanation, as illustrated by the limited transparency in national arms inventories in general and nuclear and biological weapons in particular. Although some progress has been made since the late 1960s towards greater transparency in nuclear arsenals, there remain large uncertainties about global inventories of nuclear weapons and weapon-usable fissile materials. For biological weapons, as suggested above, transparency could even be decreasing.

More positive trends have been noted regarding data on chemical weapons, military expenditure and arms transfers. Chemical weapons destroyed as well as remaining stockpiles are reported in detail by the OPCW. Increasing transparency on arms transfers is partly the result of public demand, as seen in the publication of the Annual Report on the EU Code of Conduct on Arms Exports. This increase is also a result of governments' willingness to release more and better data. Data on military expenditure—an important share of public finance in many countries—have become, among other things, part of the policy debate about development assistance, and the changing character of threats and armed conflicts has also increased the demand for data on internal security expenditure and on the balance between expenditure for internal and external security. Such demands come not only from governments and their development assistance agencies, but also from foreign investors and NGOs. The Small Arms Survey illustrates the increasing political relevance of all aspects of small arms and light weapons. In addition, public transparency can be a by-product of the growing multilateralization of peace operations and of institutional and regional programmes for capability enhancement. However, the existence of national forces and stocks of weapons abroad, as well as access to foreign bases, makes it hard to keep track of the exact size and deployment of national inventories at a given time, let alone to assess operational military capability in a particular regional setting.

The sustained and systematic work needed to increase, or simply maintain, the public transparency of the arms life cycle makes for a daunting task. Making the whole life cycle more transparent will call for major additional resources. Meeting that demand is a challenge to all governments and other organizations that count public transparency among their highest aims.

---

[107] Thanks are due to Nenne Bodell, SIPRI Head Librarian, for an overview of existing and former major military/defence journals from the earliest US and Indian journals in the late 19th century until 2005.

7. Military expenditure data: a 40-year overview

WUYI OMITOOGUN and ELISABETH SKÖNS

1. Introduction

Systematic gathering of data on the resources committed to military activities by a large number of countries did not start until the late 1960s. SIPRI was one of the pioneers of this important endeavour. The aim of the SIPRI Yearbook, as stated in the first edition, was to bring together in one place 'an account of recent trends in world military expenditure, the state of the technological arms race, and the success or failure of recent attempts at arms limitation or disarmament'.[1] The rationale for establishing SIPRI and, by implication, its Military Expenditure Project was to produce a 'factual and balanced account of a controversial subject—the arms race and attempts to stop it'.[2] Collection, standardization and analysis of impartial and accurate data were a necessity if this objective was to be achieved and they have remained at the heart of the Military Expenditure Project. Through its regular publication of military expenditure data for a large number of countries in all the geographic regions of the world, SIPRI not only helped point out the dangers inherent in accelerating military spending during the cold war years but also made possible the large-scale testing of propositions regarding the relationship between security and development in the developing world.[3] In addition, up-to-date worldwide study of military expenditure trends in different geographic regions became feasible, which facilitated discussions between states about meeting their common security needs and helped researchers of peace and defence economics to articulate their views.

Military expenditure is primarily an economic indicator since it is a measure of economic input. It is a means of measuring the economic resources devoted by states to military activities. As such, it can be used for assessing relative government priorities between military and non-military sectors, for showing the economic burden of military spending and for indicating the opportunity costs of investing in the military. The relationship between military expenditure and military output is at best indirect, owing to a number of intervening variables. There is no clear relationship between the input of economic

---

[1] Neild, R., 'Preface', *SIPRI Yearbook of World Armaments and Disarmament 1968/69* (Almqvist & Wiksell: Stockholm, 1969), p. 5.

[2] Neild (note 1).

[3] West, R. L., 'Background note on military expenditure: sources and price conversion procedures', eds G. Lamb with V. Kallab, *Military Expenditure and Economic Development: A Symposium on Research Issues*, World Bank Discussion Papers no. 185 (World Bank: Washington, DC, 1992), pp. 147–51.

resources and military strength or military activity. The link between military expenditure and security is naturally even weaker since security depends on the broader security environment, not just on military expenditure, military strength or even military security.[4]

One of the main challenges that data-gathering organizations face in gathering, analysing and reporting military expenditure statistics is how to standardize the data produced by different countries with different definitions and different bureaucratic traditions. A number of organizations have developed standardized definitions of military expenditure, the most common being those of the North Atlantic Treaty Organization (NATO),[5] the International Monetary Fund[6] and the United Nations (UN) Department for Disarmament Affairs.[7] These definitions are in many ways similar to each other, the major difference being the inclusion or exclusion of military aid, paramilitary forces and military pensions.[8] While large international organizations like these have the authority to request standardized data from their member countries, research institutes such as SIPRI, the International Institute for Strategic Studies (IISS)[9] and World Priorities,[10] which do not have that authority, depend largely on information in open sources, including budgets and other official statistics from national governments and the international organizations.[11] It is difficult, and in most cases impossible, for these research institutes to apply a common definition of military expenditure to all countries because of weaknesses inherent in the data. Furthermore, it is unclear whether, when reporting to international organizations, countries are able to apply the appropriate definitions in detail. Military expenditure data are therefore not suitable for close comparison between individual countries and are more appropriately used for

---

[4] On the concept of military expenditure and its relationship to military output see Brzoska, M., 'World military expenditures', eds K. Hartley and T. Sandler, *Handbook of Defense Economics*, vol. 1 (Elsevier: Amsterdam, 1995), pp. 46–67; and Sköns, E. et al., 'Military expenditure and arms production', *SIPRI Yearbook 1998: Armaments, Disarmament and International Security* (Oxford University Press: Oxford, 1998), pp. 187–88.

[5] See Brzoska (note 4); and Stålenheim, P. 'Sources and methods for military expenditure data', *SIPRI Yearbook 2005: Armaments, Disarmament and International Security* (Oxford University Press: Oxford, 2005), p. 373.

[6] International Monetary Fund (IMF), *Government Finance Statistics Manual 2001* (IMF: Washington, DC, 2001), pp. 82–83.

[7] United Nations, 'Objective information on military matters, including transparency of military expenditures', Report of the Secretary-General, UN document A/53/218, 4 Aug. 1998, URL <http://disarmament.un.org/cab/milex.html>.

[8] For a useful table of the coverage of the respective definitions see Brzoska (note 4), pp. 48–49. See also Brzoska, M., 'The reporting of military expenditures', *Journal of Peace Research*, vol. 18, no. 3 (1981), pp. 261–75.

[9] The IISS publishes *The Military Balance* annually. International Institute for Strategic Studies, *The Military Balance* (Brassey's: London, 1992–1994; Oxford University Press: Oxford, 1996–2004; Routledge: Abingdon, 2005–).

[10] World Priorities published 16 editions of its report on military and social expenditures. Sivard, R. L., *World Military and Social Expenditures* (World Priorities: Washington, DC, 1974–96).

[11] On the problems faced by data-gathering organizations in accessing military expenditure data from many countries and the inherent weaknesses that diminish the quality and utility of the available data see chapter 6 in this volume,

comparisons over time and as an approximate measure of the economic resources devoted to military activities.[12]

Some of the general problems of military expenditure data that have been pointed out in the literature include: (*a*) lack of uniformity in the definition of military expenditure owing to individual country preferences or budget traditions; (*b*) lack of detail in some of the data, especially those from developing countries;[13] (*c*) deliberate manipulation of data by countries (including off-budget spending); (*d*) the use of resources assigned a cost below their market value (e.g., conscripts) or at no monetary cost (e.g. direct allocation of natural resources), which is a special case of off-budget allocation; and (*e*) exchange rate conversion for comparisons in dollar terms.[14] The weaknesses are related to various aspects of the data, especially collection and standardization.

There is a broad range of users of military expenditure data, including military planners, defence analysts, academics, policy makers, peace activists and, recently, donors of economic aid. The data are used for a number of purposes and in a number of different contexts by these groups. The most common are: (*a*) for making threat assessments; (*b*) as an approach to disarmament; (*c*) in the context of international development cooperation; (*d*) for the purpose of transparency; (*e*) for academic research on their determinants and economic and political impact; and (*f*) for national defence planning. Some of these users acknowledge that military expenditure is simply an input of economic resources to finance military establishments. Other users interpret military expenditure data as indicating output in terms of military capability or military strength, even though there is no close relation between monetary allocations and military output.

This chapter examines the use of military expenditure data in different political contexts and some of the consequences of misuse and misinterpretation of the data. It focuses on use for international comparisons or by the international community and examines how data availability and quality have evolved in the past four decades. It does not cover the use of military expenditure data in the context of academic research or in defence planning and programming, except for some international purposes such as measuring burden sharing. The chapter highlights what has and has not changed, with a view to assessing the relevance of military expenditure data for the analysis of peace- and security-related issues in a changing security environment.

The analysis is divided into three periods: the cold war period (section II), the post-cold war period (section III) and the period since 11 September 2001 (section IV). Conclusions are given in section V.

---

[12] 'Sources and methods for the world military expenditure data', *World Armaments and Disarmament: SIPRI Yearbook 1979* (Taylor & Francis: London, 1979), p. 58.

[13] Brzoska (note 8); Goertz, G. and Diehl, P. F., 'Measuring military allocations: a comparison of different approaches', *Journal of Conflict Resolution*, vol. 30, no. 3 (1986), pp. 553–81; Brzoska (note 4); and Ball, N., *Security and Economy in the Third World* (Princeton University Press: Princeton, N.J., 1988).

[14] On the problems with exchange rate conversions see appendix 8E in this volume.

II. Military expenditure during the cold war

In the cold war period, 1947–89, characterized by rivalry between the Soviet Union and the United States, world military expenditure grew rapidly and reached an unprecedentedly high level.[15] More economic resources were used for military purposes after World War II than ever before; during the 1980s the level of world military spending was more than 10 times higher than in the period 1925–38.[16] This was primarily because of the trends in military expenditure by the two superpowers and, to some extent, by their respective allies. By the end of the cold war, the Soviet Union and the USA accounted for 20 and 36 per cent, respectively, of total world military spending.[17] Trends in military spending in the developing world were also affected by the cold war in that each bloc supported its partners in other regions and supplied them with weapons. Demand from the developing world for arms imports during the cold war was mostly fuelled by conflicts, but aspirations for the status of a regional power and the domestic status of the military were also important factors.[18] For all these reasons, total arms imports by developing countries increased greatly, especially during the 1970s. In particular, the Middle East became a large and expanding arms market in the 1970s and 1980s owing largely to: the rise in oil incomes after 1973–74, which generated an abundance of foreign exchange in many countries; a number of intense conflicts in the region; and strong interest and increased involvement in the region by the Soviet Union and the USA.[19] Arms imports by developing countries were to a great extent made possible through the superpowers' widespread credit financing of such imports, which subsequently aggravated the debt burden of these countries.[20] Nevertheless, while some arms imports were financed with large amounts of military aid, more were paid for from the budgets of the developing countries themselves, as reflected in their surging military expenditure.

Availability of data

During the cold war, the newly established independent data-gathering organizations suffered from a significant dearth of military expenditure data from developing countries, not because such information was not published, but because of the difficulty of accessing it. Instead, most information on these

---

[15] A 1949–85 time series of SIPRI military expenditure data is presented in Thee, M. (ed.), 'Arms and disarmament: SIPRI findings', *Bulletin of Peace Proposals* special issue, vol. 17, nos 3–4 (1986), p. 229.

[16] Sköns, E., 'Trends in military expenditure and arms transfers', eds R. Thakur, R. and E. Newman, *New Millennium, New Perspectives: The United Nations, Security and Governance* (United Nations University Press: Tokyo, 2000), p. 80.

[17] The data are for 1990. Sköns et al., 'Tables of military expenditure', *SIPRI Yearbook 1998* (note 4), pp. 214, 223, 226.

[18] Brzoska, M. and Ohlson, T., SIPRI, *Arms Transfers to the Third World, 1971–85* (Oxford University Press: Oxford, 1987), p. 36.

[19] Brzoska and Ohlson (note 18), especially chapter 2.

[20] Brzoska, M., 'The military related external debt of Third World countries', *Journal of Peace Research*, vol. 20, no. 3 (1983), pp. 271–77.

countries came from secondary sources. Data availability for developing countries increased gradually towards the end of the cold war as data-gathering organizations became more established and better equipped to gather statistics on distant countries. However, access to primary data was still limited.

Quality of data

The quality of the data was a more serious problem than the availability. Reliance on national governments for data, the countries' politicization of data on military spending and a lack of independent means of verifying data were identified in the literature as some of the main problems affecting data quality during the cold war.[21] These were problems over which the data-gathering organizations had no control.

The problems were different for different categories of country, although all tended to manipulate military expenditure data to suit their specific needs. Most attention was devoted to the quality of data on the Soviet Union, which published only a figure for its total defence budget without providing any further detail about its content or coverage. Furthermore, the size of the official Soviet defence budget was so low that it could not credibly represent total Soviet defence spending. The same was true, although to a lesser extent, for other members of the Warsaw Treaty Organization (WTO). This lack of credibility and the lack of information on the Soviet defence budget gave rise to a virtual science in methodologies for estimating Soviet military expenditure (see below).

There were also problems in the quality and comparability of data for the NATO countries. The need to meet the financial obligations demanded by membership of the alliance had consequences for military expenditure data as countries presented different data to different constituencies. For example, the Federal Republic of Germany (West Germany) published different military expenditure figures for domestic use, for NATO and for the Conference on Security and Co-operation in Europe (CSCE),[22] while the United Kingdom did not include the cost of major programmes in its defence budget.[23] Although this was a potential source of problem for data-gathering organizations, it was resolved by using the data published by NATO, which at least was based on a common definition.

While the above examples show that data manipulation was not confined to developing countries, it was certainly more widespread there than in industrialized countries.[24] It can be argued that this manipulation was largely a

---

[21] Brzoska (note 8); Goertz and Diehl (note 13); Brzoska (note 4); and Ball (note 13).

[22] Brzoska (note 8).

[23] Blackaby, F. and Ohlson, T., 'Military expenditure and the arms trade: problems of the data', ed. C. Schmidt, *Economics of Military Expenditures: Military Expenditure, Economic Growth and Fluctuations* (Macmillan: Basingstoke, 1987), pp. 3–24.

[24] Ball, N., 'Measuring Third World security expenditure: a research note', *World Development*, vol. 12, no. 2 (Feb. 1984), pp 157–64.

result of bureaucratic preference when categorizing expenditure items[25] and a lack of appreciation of the importance of proper record keeping,[26] rather than a deliberate attempt at manipulation.[27] The fact that during the cold war the two superpowers directly and indirectly encouraged their allies among the developing countries to invest in military hardware meant that the former had little motive to probe the details of military expenditure data. Moreover, the internal pressure for reduced military spending in developing countries was not strong enough during this period to warrant any manipulation of data. Whatever the motive, the lack of detail in the budgets was a major limitation in the utility of the data.

Uses of data

During the cold war, one of the most common uses of military expenditure data was as a tool to assess military potential in the arms race between the two superpowers and their respective allies. The data were also used as a basis for disarmament negotiations in the context of the UN's call for reductions of military budgets and as a tool for monitoring 'militarization' in developing countries.

Threat assessments

There was a contentious debate during the cold war about the reliability of the official military expenditure data of the Soviet Union and other WTO countries, as discussed above. In the absence of credible official data for the Soviet Union, there were efforts to estimate actual military expenditure. The main estimates were those produced by the US Central Intelligence Agency (CIA)[28] and the US Defense Intelligence Agency (DIA), which were subsequently reported to the US Congress,[29] and the US Arms Control and Disarmament Agency (ACDA).[30] These estimates were used by the USA and its allies to justify increased military spending in response to perceived increased spending by the WTO countries.

---

[25] Brzoska (note 4), pp. 49–50.

[26] Ball (note 13), p. 84.

[27] Looney, R. E., 'The political economy of Third World military expenditures: impact of regime type on the defence allocation process', *Journal of Political and Military Sociology*, vol. 16, no. 1 (spring 1988), pp. 21–39.

[28] E.g., Central Intelligence Agency (CIA), *A Dollar Cost Comparison of Soviet and US Defense Activities, 1967–77*, SR78-10002 (CIA: Washington, DC, Jan. 1978); and CIA, National Foreign Assessment Center, *Estimated Soviet Defense Spending: Trends and Prospects*, SR78-10121 (CIA: Washington, DC, June 1979).

[29] E.g., US Congress, *Allocation of Resources in the Soviet Union and China—1979*, Hearings before the Subcommittee on Priorities and Economy in Government of the Joint Economic Committee (Government Printing Office: Washington, DC, 1979).

[30] The ACDA published these in its annual report, *World Military Expenditure and Arms Transfers* (WMEAT). Since 2000 WMEAT has been published by the US Department of State's Bureau of Verification and Compliance; see URL <http://www.state.gov/t/vci/rls/rpt/wmeat/>.

The method used for estimating Soviet military expenditure was the so-called 'building-block' method.[31] This approach was not universally accepted as being methodologically sound, the critique being that it used US costs and thus also relative prices to estimate the costs in the Soviet Union, where cost conditions and relative prices were fundamentally different. It was argued that this produced an exaggeration of Soviet military spending because of the so-called 'index number' problem.[32] As SIPRI argued in those years, 'There is no doubt that the process of valuing Soviet military output at US prices is, by itself, a wholly invalid procedure for making any sensible comparison of US and Soviet military effort. Yet this invalid procedure is the basis of the statement, which is widespread among political commentators in Western countries, that it is a "known fact" that Soviet military expenditure exceeds that of the United States.'[33]

A second, more complex, issue is how the economic analysis of Soviet military expenditure figures was used to suggest a much increased threat when it actually suggested the opposite. Initially, the CIA assumed that the Soviet arms industry had a much higher level of productivity and general efficiency than the civil sector. In 1976 it changed this assumption and decided that there was, after all, no big difference in productivity. As a consequence, the CIA's estimate of the Soviet military sector's share of Soviet national output went up from 6–8 per cent to 10–15 per cent.[34] There was no change in the CIA estimate of the size of the Soviet Union's military effort nor of its military spending: the change in the estimate of productivity simply implied that the military burden on the Soviet economy was much greater than had previously been assumed. The clear conclusion is that the Soviet Union was weaker, not stronger, than previously thought. As a former SIPRI Director noted, 'The message that reached the public, and the legislators, was the exact opposite of this—that the CIA had doubled its estimate of Soviet military expenditure.'[35] With hindsight it may well be that, although the USA overestimated Soviet military strength, the economic burden of Soviet military spending was underestimated.

Those exaggerated and misinterpreted figures were then used to demand an increase in military spending in the West. They formed part of the basis for

---

[31] For a description of the building-block methodology see, e.g., US Arms Control and Disarmament Agency (ACDA), 'Soviet military expenditure', *World Military Expenditures and Arms Transfers 1968–1977* (ACDA: Washington, DC, Oct. 1979), pp. 13–15.

[32] Holzman, F. D., 'Are the Soviets really outspending the US on defense?', *International Security*, vol. 4, no. 4 (spring 1980), pp. 86–104; and Holzman, F. D., 'Soviet military spending: assessing the numbers game', *International Security*, vol. 6, no. 4 (spring 1982), pp. 78–101.

[33] 'World military expenditure', *SIPRI Yearbook 1979* (note 12), pp. 29–30.

[34] The revised estimate was produced by CIA Team B, which was appointed by the CIA Director, George H. W. Bush (with Paul Wolfowitz on its advisory panel) to revisit the CIA assessments of Soviet military strength, including its military expenditure. Hessing Cahn, A., *Killing Détente: The Right Attacks the CIA* (Pennsylvania University Press: University Park, Pa., 1998); and Hessing Cahn, A., 'Team B: the trillion-dollar experiment', *Bulletin of the Atomic Scientists*, vol. 49, no. 3 (Apr. 1993), pp. 24–27.

[35] Blackaby, F., 'How SIPRI began', *SIPRI: Continuity and Change, 1966–1996* (SIPRI: Stockholm, 1996), p. 37.

decisions by the administrations of US presidents Gerald Ford, Jimmy Carter and Ronald Reagan to massively increase US military spending from the mid-1970s to the mid-1980s.[36] They also led to NATO's decision in 1977 to call for a 3 per cent annual real increase in the defence expenditures of its members,[37] a target which NATO retained throughout the 1980s.[38]

The lesson to be learned from this episode in the use of military expenditure is that, when data on military expenditure are used as a measure of output in terms of military strength or threat, there are reasons to be sceptical, if not suspicious, of the conclusions drawn.[39]

Disarmament

Military expenditure was used in disarmament discussions throughout the cold war period, but with few practical results. Beginning in the 1950s, proposals were made in the UN General Assembly for the reduction of military budgets, based on the conviction that such measures would facilitate the disarmament process and help release resources for economic and social development. This was in line with Article 26 of the UN Charter, according to which member states committed themselves to measures 'to promote the establishment and maintenance of international peace and security with the least diversion for armaments of the world's human and economic resources'.

The first UN General Assembly resolution to use reduction of military budgets as an approach to disarmament was adopted in 1973, based on a proposal by the Soviet Union for a 10 per cent reduction in the military expenditure of the permanent members of the UN Security Council and the transfer of 10 per cent of the money saved to international development programmes.[40] The 10th Special Session of the UN General Assembly, in 1978, which was entirely devoted to disarmament, agreed a comprehensive programme of action to implement the principles and goals of disarmament that had been defined in a number of UN resolutions during the previous 30 years.[41] One of the many approaches to disarmament agreed was to consider 'Gradual reduction of military budgets on a mutually agreed basis, . . . particularly by nuclear-weapon States and other militarily significant States' in order to 'contribute to the curbing of the arms race and . . . increase the possibilities of

---

[36] 'World military expenditure and arms production', *World Armaments and Disarmament: SIPRI Yearbook 1982* (Taylor & Francis: London, 1982), pp. 103–109.

[37] 'World military expenditure, 1979', *World Armaments and Disarmament: SIPRI Yearbook 1980* (Taylor & Francis: London, 1980), p. 21.

[38] Deger, S. and Sen, S., SIPRI, *Military Expenditure: The Political Economy of International Security* (Oxford University Press: Oxford, 1990), pp. 8–9.

[39] In 1983 the CIA revised its assessment of the growth trend in Soviet military expenditure, but this had no major impact on US and NATO threat perceptions. Rather, it produced a controversy between the CIA and the DIA, which disputed the revised CIA estimates. Sköns, E. and Tullberg, R., 'World military expenditure', *World Armaments and Disarmament: SIPRI Yearbook 1984* (Taylor & Francis: London, 1984), pp. 88–94.

[40] United Nations, General Assembly Resolution 3093 (XXVIII), 7 Dec. 1973, URL <http://www.un.org/documents/ga/res/28/ares28.htm>.

[41] 'The UN Special Session on Disarmament: an analytical review', *SIPRI Yearbook 1979* (note 12), pp. 490–523, especially 'Reduction of military expenditures', pp. 507–509.

reallocation of resources now being used for military purposes to economic and social development, particularly for the benefit of the developing countries'.[42]

However, it was not until December 1980 that the UN General Assembly introduced the UN system for standardized reporting of military expenditure.[43] It was based on the recommendations of a group of experts in the field of military budgets, which had developed a detailed definition of military expenditure and designed an elaborate standardized matrix, the Instrument for Reporting Military Expenditures. Since then, the UN Secretary-General has annually requested all UN member states to report their military expenditure to the Department for Disarmament Affairs. However, reporting of military expenditure data remained relatively low during the cold war period, averaging 23 countries annually.[44]

International development cooperation

During the cold war military expenditure data were also used to estimate the extent of resources that developing countries committed to arms acquisition, which was thought to be fuelled by the arms race between the superpowers.[45] Many developing countries had begun to build their military forces to reflect their new status as independent states from the 1960s and 1970s. At the same time they faced enormous development challenges for which their limited resources were inadequate. The military expenditure of developing countries grew at a much higher rate than that of industrialized countries. Between 1960 and 1987 military expenditure in the developing countries grew at an average annual rate of 7.5 per cent, compared with 2.8 for the industrialized countries.[46] Most of the money was believed to have been spent on arms bought from the major powers.[47]

Since the structure of the international economic order was believed to be the source of the developing world's problems, there were calls by developing countries and well-meaning individuals and groups in the developed world for

[42] United Nations, 'Final document of the Tenth Special Session of the General Assembly', UN document A/RES/S-10/2, 30 June 1978, section III, 'Programme of Action', paragraph 89. Reproduced in *SIPRI Yearbook 1979* (note 12), p. 537.

[43] United Nations, General Assembly Resolution 35/142, 12 Dec. 1980, URL <http://www.un.org/documents/ga/res/35/ares35.htm>.

[44] Statistics on reporting are available on the website of the UN Department for Disarmament Affairs, URL <http://disarmament.un.org/cab/milex.html>. See also United Nations, Department for Disarmament Affairs, 'Transparency in armaments: United Nations Instrument for Reporting Military Expenditures, global and regional participation 1981–2002', New York, N.Y., 2003, URL <http://disarmament.un.org/cab/milex.html>, p. 8; and Sköns, E. and Nazet, N., 'The reporting of military expenditure data', *SIPRI Yearbook 2005* (note 5), p. 380.

[45] Luckham, R., 'Militarization in Africa', *World Armaments and Disarmament: SIPRI Yearbook 1985* (Taylor & Francis: London, 1985), pp. 295–328.

[46] United Nations Development Programme, *Human Development Report 1994: Capturing the Peace Dividend* (Oxford University Press: New York, N.Y., 1994), URL <http://hdr.undp.org/>; and West, R. L., 'Patterns and trends in the military expenditures of developing countries', eds Lamb with Kallab (note 3), pp. 19–34.

[47] Sen, S., 'Debt, financial flows and international security', *SIPRI Yearbook 1990: World Armaments and Disarmament* (Oxford University Press: Oxford, 1990), p. 210.

a reordering that paid attention to the needs of developing countries.[48] Military expenditure statistics served to point out the increasing resources that developing countries were committing to the military at a time when they were faced with great developmental challenges and were calling for an increased resource flow from the developed world. Already in 1961, the US Foreign Assistance Act was amended to make it mandatory for the US president to consider a country's level of military expenditure and amount spent on military acquisitions before granting economic assistance. Such data were produced by the US Agency for International Development (USAID) for this purpose.[49] However, military expenditure data are not the best indicator of the amount of resources committed to arms imports by developing countries, as such spending is rarely included in the military budget.[50]

At the same time, military assistance played a critical role in the relationship between the major powers (not just the superpowers) and their supporters in the developing countries during the cold war. As noted above, a large part of the increase in foreign debt in many of these countries was caused by repayable military aid.[51]

Transparency

Military expenditure data were little used in the context of transparency during the cold war, although transparency in military expenditure began to be seen as a confidence-building measure (CBM) during the period. CBMs are usually defined as tools that adversaries can use to reduce tensions and avert the possibility of military conflict. These tools include communication, constraints, transparency and verification measures.[52] In Europe, CBM negotiations initially focused on prior notification of military manoeuvres and movements and the occasional presence of military observers.

CBMs are most often used in a regional or bilateral context. During the cold war the CSCE conducted long and difficult negotiations on CBMs for Europe. The first rudimentary CBMs were contained in the 1975 Helsinki Final Act within the framework of the CSCE (in 1995 renamed the Organization for

---

[48] To address the problem of economic imbalance and poverty in the developing world, the Brandt Commission, an independent commission headed by former West German Chancellor Willy Brandt, was set up in 1977. Among other recommendations, it called for a redirection of resources from the arms race to development in the developing world. Brandt, W. (chairman), *North–South: A Programme for Survival*, Report of the Independent Commission on International Development Issues (Pan Books: London, 1980).

[49] E.g., US Agency for International Development (USAID), *Implementation of Section 620(s) of the Foreign Assistance Act of 1961, As Amended: A Report to Congress for 1984* (Department of State: Washington DC, Nov. 1985).

[50] This has been shown by a number of studies, e.g., Ball (note 13), pp. 107–108.

[51] Brzoska, M., 'Military trade, aid, and developing country debt', eds Lamb with Kallab (note 3), pp. 79–111.

[52] Meek, S., 'Confidence-building measures as tools for disarmament and development', *African Security Review*, no. 1, vol. 14 (2005), URL <http://www.iss.co.za/pubs/ASR/14No1/Cmeek.htm>.

Security and Co-operation in Europe, OSCE),[53] and the first major agreement on confidence- and security-building measures (CSBMs) was included in the 1986 Document of the Stockholm Conference on Disarmament in Europe, which focused on regulating the activities of military forces.[54] Neither of these made any reference to military expenditure.

Military expenditure as an indicator for burden sharing

Within military alliances, military expenditure data were used to show how military spending was shared among the allies. While there was no transparency in the burden-sharing system of the WTO, burden sharing was a prominent topic in NATO political debate on resource allocation. Collection of standardized military expenditure data was, and remains, an integral part of defence planning in NATO and subject to review at the annual meetings of NATO defence ministers. NATO has published these data since 1963. When new defence strategies were being adopted and allocations increased as a consequence, burden sharing was a contentious issue and data on military expenditure inevitably figured in the debate. This was the case with the adoption in 1978 of the Long-Term Defence Programme, which involved a commitment by NATO member states to increase their military expenditure at the rate of 3 per cent annually in real terms.[55]

III. Military expenditure in the post-cold war period

With the end of the cold war in 1989 there was a dramatic change in the security environment and in perceptions of security threats. Initially, there were high hopes for far-reaching disarmament after the disintegration of the Soviet Union and the dissolution of the WTO and the consequent vanishing of the Soviet military potential from Western threat perceptions. There was a change in focus towards arms reduction and the conversion of resources and facilities from military to civil use, with the expectation of a major peace dividend. There were discussions of a new world order and whether it should be characterized by uni- or multipolarity. Global systemic changes were on the agenda, in the political sphere with the spread of democratization and in the economic sphere with the spread of the market economy. Focus also gradually shifted from the North to the South. Measures to stop or prevent armed conflict in developing countries were discussed, such as peace missions and military intervention for humanitarian purposes. At the same time, some new external threats were identified. The perception of a threat from a militarily growing China remained a concern of the USA. Eventually, other threat

---

[53] Darilek, R. E., 'The future of conventional arms control in Europe, a tale of two cities: Stockholm, Vienna', *World Armaments and Disarmament: SIPRI Yearbook 1987* (Oxford University Press: Oxford, 1987), p. 340.

[54] Darilek (note 53), p. 341.

[55] Greenwood, D., 'NATO's three per cent solution', *Survival*, vol. 23, no. 6 (Nov.–Dec. 1981), pp. 254–55.

scenarios were brought onto the agenda, under the USA's rubric of 'rogue states'.

During the first 10 years after the cold war, 1989–98, world military spending fell by more than one-third in real terms.[56] It was a period of disarmament, marked by the downsizing and restructuring of the armed forces in many countries in combination with cuts in arms procurement. However, there was a wide variation between regions and countries. The deepest cuts took place in Russia and other former WTO countries. By 1998 the military expenditure of Russia and the other former Soviet republics had fallen to 6 per cent of that of the Soviet Union in 1989. Substantial reductions in military expenditure also took place in Africa (cuts of 25 per cent) and the Americas (30 per cent, primarily in the USA) during the first post-cold war decade. In Western Europe the reduction during the same period was only 14 per cent, while military spending continued to rise in Asia (by 27 per cent) and the Middle East (by 17 per cent).[57]

Gradually, new pressures emerged for increased military expenditure, motivated by the development of military technology in the context of the 'revolution in military affairs' and the transformation of military forces as they became increasingly involved in peacekeeping and peace enforcement. World military expenditure began to increase again from 1999.[58]

Availability of data

Data availability problems eased slightly after the end of the cold war as data on the former WTO countries were now available more regularly. This was due in part to the new openness in these countries but more to the aspiration of some of those countries to join Western organizations. Countries in the developing world remained more problematic since data-gathering organizations had limited access to government publications, including budget documents. The problem of access was caused by the fact that most of the countries did not give publicity to the published data through the media. Thus, the data were never reported in the West, which is where most of the data-gathering organizations at this time were located, and the researchers did not have the means to visit the countries to obtain published data. This problem was compounded by the increased use of data on military expenditure to determine eligibility for aid, as explained below. As a result, although a number of developing countries produced budget documents, these were exclusively for government use and did not represent significant progress in transparency.

---

[56] Sköns, E. et al., 'Military expenditure', *SIPRI Yearbook 1999: Armaments, Disarmament and International Security* (Oxford University Press: Oxford, 1999), p. 269.

[57] Sköns et al. (note 56), pp. 269–70.

[58] See appendix 8A in this volume.

Quality of data

The problem of data quality, which existed during the cold war in all parts of the world, became increasingly a problem of the developing countries in the post-cold war period. One reason for this was the political significance that aid donors gave to the data from developing countries when judging the recipients' degree of good governance. The impact was a further reduction in the quality, and by implication the utility, of data through deliberate manipulation, especially through resort to off-budget expenditure, by either hiding defence expenditure under other budget headings such as internal affairs or not reporting it at all.[59] Some countries presented the defence budget only as a one-line budget item when other categories of expenditure in the budget were disaggregated. In this way, while being ostensibly open, these countries provided as little information on defence as possible. In addition, during this period military expenditure data continued to suffer from a lack of proper classification. Although this was not a deliberate attempt to manipulate data, it nonetheless diminished the validity of the data as the amount of resources used by defence was not fully captured.

A more important problem for data availability and quality in the immediate post-cold war period was the increased number of states experiencing intrastate conflict. These countries' input of financial resources into war efforts could not be captured by military expenditure data. A large part of the direct and indirect costs of such conflicts are excluded from military budgets, owing in part to the nature of the means of financing, both orthodox and unorthodox, that are adopted during wars, especially in some of the more recent ones.[60] Most of these means are clearly off budget and are sometimes outside the official economy. Some attempts have been made to estimate the costs of armed conflict in a way that captures all these factors,[61] but much research remains to be done. Furthermore, the fact that intra-state conflicts involve a large number of non-state armed actors means that government data on military expenditure do not reflect the overall picture of resources consumed for armed conflict.

[59] On such practices see Hendrickson, D. and Ball, N., 'Off-budget military expenditure and revenue: issues and policy perspectives for donors', Conflict, Security and Development Group Occasional Papers no. 1, King's College, London, Jan. 2002, URL <http://www.grc-exchange.org/info_data/record.cfm?Id=295>.

[60] For some unorthodox means of financing wars see Ballentine, K. and Sherman J., The Political Economy of Armed Conflict: Beyond Greed and Grievance (Lynne Rienner: Boulder, Colo., 2003); Berdal, M. and Malone, D. M. (eds), Greed and Grievance: Economic Agendas and Civil Wars (Lynne Rienner: Boulder, Colo., 2000); and Cooper, N. et al., War Economies in a Regional Context: Challenges of Transformation (Lynne Rienner: Boulder, Colo., 2004).

[61] Brown, M. E. and Rosecrance, R. N. (eds), The Costs of Conflict: Prevention and Cure in the Global Arena (Rowman and Littlefield: Lanham, Md., 1999); Collier, P. and Hoeffler, A., 'The challenge of reducing the global incidence of civil war', Copenhagen Consensus Challenge Paper, Apr. 2004, URL <http://www.copenhagenconsensus.com/Default.asp?ID=221>; and Bohnstedt, A., 'Why civil wars are costly—and what could be done to reduce these costs', World Markets Research Centre, London, Nov. 2004. These attempts are summarized in Sköns, E., 'Financing security in a global context', SIPRI Yearbook 2005 (note 5), pp. 294–95.

In developed countries, new approaches to public procurement—for example, private financing initiatives (PFIs) as a means of public–private partnership—and changes in government budget accounting (from a cash basis to a resource basis) that began to be introduced during the 1990s may also have had an impact on the quality of military expenditure data. Under PFIs, with the aim of increasing efficiency and reducing costs, private companies pay for the production of an asset and then rent the finished product to the public sector.[62] However, while PFI deals may allow the government to procure new goods and facilities at a lower cost in the short term, they can incur a higher cost over a longer time period. As well as making government accounts less transparent and more difficult to interpret, the use of PFIs disrupts traditional accountability structures.[63] Resource-based accounting is founded on the principle of including in annual accounts the resources consumed during the year, rather than the actual cash outlays and thus does not reflect annual spending.

There was an improvement in the quality of data in one respect. As several countries in Europe replaced conscript forces with professional forces, data on military spending better reflected the true cost of military personnel.

Uses of data

With the end of the cold war, the role of military expenditure data was reduced in the context of threat assessments and disarmament, while they continued to be used as measures of transparency and confidence building. In the changed security environment, it was also gradually deemed legitimate for donor countries to raise military-related issues with developing countries in the context of development cooperation. The increased focus on armed conflict in developing countries also led to efforts to develop models of early warning of conflict, of which military expenditure data constituted one element.

Threat assessments

Since the end of the cold war the pre-eminence of the USA as the world's only superpower has not been contested. However, in spite of this acknowledgement and the great disparity in military technology and spending between the USA and its allies on the one hand and China on the other, the latter has been a major concern for the USA and other Western powers. The use of military expenditure data for threat assessment in the immediate aftermath of the cold

---

[62] An example of a military PFI project is the contract awarded in 2003 by the British Ministry of Defence to the French company Thales to provide management and support of combat aircraft training at 10 RAF sites over a 13-year period, including about 20 simulators and 64 part-task trainers. Thales, 'Focus: PFI (private finance initiative)', 2005, URL <http://www.thales-is.com/services/home_market_focus.html>.

[63] Gosling, T., 'Openness survey paper', Institute for Public Policy Research, London, Feb. 2004. URL <http://www.ippr.org.uk/uploadedFiles/projects/Openness survey final.pdf>. See also Penman, D., 'IPPR: PFI failing schools and hospitals', The Guardian, 10 Dec. 2002, URL <http://politics.guardian.co.uk/thinktanks/story/0,10538,857519,00.html>.

war has thus continued, especially in the case of China. Since official Chinese data are believed to underreport the actual military expenditure of China,[64] governments and researchers have produced estimates of Chinese military expenditure, some of which are three times higher than the official figure.[65]

It has also been suggested that, in post-conflict states, military expenditure often serves as a signal of central government's commitment to implement agreed peace settlements.[66] Where military expenditure rises, it could be seen by rebel groups as a sign of the government's intention to rearm while peace is being maintained or while rebel capabilities are weak; whereas low military expenditure would signal the government's intention to adhere to the terms of the peace settlement. This use of military expenditure to explain government intention is simplistic since post-conflict states need to re-equip the military, rebuild military infrastructure damaged during the war and demobilize some of their forces, all of which will, at least temporarily, boost military expenditure. Nonetheless, it is significant that military expenditure data are used in such cases as a measure of the extent of threat that former protagonists in a war constitute. By and large, the use of military expenditure for threat assessment declined significantly after the end of the cold war.

Disarmament

The high military spending associated with the cold war was widely expected to be reduced at the end of that period. Indeed, from its peak in 1987, military spending started to decline even before the actual end of the cold war. The peace dividend, as the expected savings were called, was expected to come mainly from the developed world, where over 85 per cent of world military spending was made, but also from developing countries, which in spite of their comparatively low share of world military spending bore a disproportionate share of the military burden owing to their relative poverty. The peace dividend was expected to be used for civil purposes, especially human development.[67] Military expenditure data have been useful in estimating the expected size of the peace dividend from both developed and developing countries.[68] One of the early efforts to capture the real value of the peace dividend was described in the United Nations Development Programme's (UNDP) *Human*

[64] Wang, S., 'Military expenditure of China, 1989–98', *SIPRI Yearbook 1999* (note 56), pp. 334–50.

[65] US Department of Defense, *The Military Power of the People's Republic of China 2005*, Report to Congress pursuant to the National Defense Authorization Act, fiscal year 2000 (Department of Defense: Washington, DC, 2005), URL <http://www.defenselink.mil/news/Jul2005/d20050719china.pdf>, especially chapter 6, 'Resources for force modernization', pp. 20–25. See also chapter 8 and, on international comparisions of military expenditure, appendix 8E in this volume.

[66] Collier, C. and Hoeffler, A., 'Military expenditure in post-conflict societies', Working Paper no. 2004-13, Centre for the Study of African Economies, Oxford University, 8 Apr. 2004, URL <http://www.csae.ox.ac.uk/workingpapers/wps-list.html>.

[67] United Nations Development Programme (note 46), especially chapter 3, 'Capturing the peace dividend', pp. 47–60.

[68] See, e.g., Barker, T., Dunne, P. and Smith, R., 'Measuring the peace dividend in the United Kingdom', *Journal of Peace Research*, vol. 28, no. 4 (1992), pp. 345–58; and Heo, U. and Eger, R. J., 'Paying for security: the security–prosperity dilemma in the United States', *Journal of Conflict Resolution*, vol. 49, no. 5 (Oct. 2005), pp. 792–817.

Development Report 1994: it estimated that the industrialized countries cumulatively saved $810 billon and developing countries $125 billion over the eight-year period 1987–94. The UNDP estimated that, based on an annual reduction of military spending by 3 per cent, there would be a peace dividend of about $460 billion in 1995–2000, which it recommended be spent on human development.[69]

The initial savings made in 1987–94 were thought to have gone into budget deficit reductions in most industrialized countries.[70] The strong focus in this debate on the financial side of the peace dividend has been criticized for being simplistic since, when considering the impact of military expenditure, the non-military budget items as well as the revenue side of the budget must also be considered.[71] Reductions in military expenditure do not necessarily translate into increases in other budget items. Many analysts argue that the peace dividend was much lower than expected and that the reason for this was a lack of policy to translate savings into productive investment or social welfare.[72] The peace dividend also had inherent costs caused, for example, by unemployment in parts of the defence sector or the need to reduce overall budget deficits that had been built up in the cold war years.[73]

With the ending of the superpower rivalry, the reduction of military spending became an issue in the developing world,[74] and military expenditure data became a tool for those advocating a reduced level of spending. In many post-conflict states, where high personnel costs made military expenditure a great burden, donors—especially multilateral donors such as the World Bank and the UNDP—organized demobilization programmes in conjunction with host countries to downsize armed forces. The financial costs of the programmes were borne by the donors.[75]

International development cooperation

Towards the end of the cold war, the burden that military expenditure constituted for the economies of most developing countries had already become obvious.[76] While the discussions of the peace dividend focused on the

[69] United Nations Development Programme (note 46), p. 59.

[70] Bonn International Center for Conversion (BICC), 'The peace dividend: lost or lasting', *Conversion Survey 1996: Global Disarmament, Demilitarization and Demobilization* (Oxford University Press: Oxford, 1996), pp. 43–73.

[71] Bonn International Center for Conversion (note 70), p. 61.

[72] Gleditsch, N. P., Cappelen, A., Bjerkholt, R., Smith, R. and Dunne, J. P. (eds), *The Peace Dividend* (Elsevier: Amsterdam, 1996).

[73] Bonn International Center for Conversion (note 70).

[74] Dunne, J. P., 'Economic effects of military expenditure in developing countries: a survey', eds Gleditsch et al. (note 72), pp. 439–64.

[75] Colletta, N. J., Kostner, M. and Wiederhofer, I., *Case Studies in War-to-Peace Transition: The Demobilization and Reintegration of Ex-Combatants in Ethiopia, Namibia and Uganda*, World Bank Discussion Paper no. 331 (World Bank: Washington, DC, 1996), URL <http://web.worldbank.org/servlets/ECR?contentMDK=20412470&sitePK=407546>.

[76] McNamara, R. S., 'The post-cold war world: implications for military expenditure in the developing countries', eds L. H. Summers and S. Shah, *Proceedings of the World Bank Annual Conference on Development Economics 1991* (World Bank: Washington, DC, 1991), pp. 95–125.

developed world and how to use the money saved from reduced military expenditure, there were also calls for reductions in military spending in developing countries.[77] The advocates of reduced military spending included major multilateral and bilateral donors who seized the opportunity of the end of the cold war to raise the issue of 'excessive' military expenditure in their dialogues with recipient countries.[78] At issue were the crowding out of other categories of expenditure, especially for the social sector, and the fungibility of economic aid within the budget (i.e., the risk that money given for development might release funds that could be diverted to the military).[79] The tying of development aid to low military expenditure was one major way to enforce a reduction in military spending in recipient countries that was advocated by multilateral and bilateral donors—especially the Organisation for Economic Co-operation and Development (OECD), the largest group of bilateral donors—and by an independent commission set up to look into the issue of resource flows to developing countries.[80]

The decision to make development aid conditional on low military expenditure gave a new significance to military expenditure data for both donors and recipients. While donors sought military spending statistics for developing countries when taking decisions on whether to offer assistance, recipients, who were the primary producers of the data, became politically alert to the importance of the data they produced. This had (and continues to have) implications for the quality of the data (see below). As a result, the data needed to support decisions on whether a state's military spending was 'excessive' and so needed to be curbed by means of aid conditionality were either not available or were not accurate enough to support such an important decision.

While the level of military assistance and the number of countries receiving such assistance have diminished significantly since the end of the cold war, it continues to be provided to countries and regions where the Western powers, especially the USA, have a major interest—such as the Middle East, Eastern Europe, Latin America, South Asia and Africa. In contrast to the cold war, when opposition and rebel groups were given military assistance, support in the post-cold war period has been mainly to governments. Consequently, the costs of this support are easily traceable to the donor government's military or foreign assistance budgets.

---

[77] For a review of some of these calls see Ball, N., 'Transforming security sectors: the IMF and World Bank approaches', *Conflict, Security and Development*, vol. 1, no. 1 (Apr. 2001), pp. 45–66. See also Omitoogun, W., 'The processes of budgeting for the military sector in Africa', *SIPRI Yearbook 2003: Armaments, Disarmament and International Security* (Oxford University Press: Oxford, 2003), pp. 261–78.

[78] Ball (note 77).

[79] Deverajan, S. and Swaroop, V., 'The implications of foreign aid fungibility for development assistance', Working Paper Series no. 2022, World Bank, Washington, DC, Oct. 1998, URL <http://www.worldbank.org/html/dec/Publications/Workpapers/instnspubsect.html>.

[80] United Nations Development Programme (note 46); and Schmidt, H. (Chairman), *Facing One World: Report by an Independent Group on Financial Flows to Developing Countries* (Hamburg, June 1989). For a review of the calls to tie aid to low military expenditure see Ball (note 77).

Transparency

During the post-cold war period, the UN Instrument for Reporting Military Expenditures has been gradually transformed into a transparency instrument. The item 'reduction of military budgets' has not been on the agenda of the UN Disarmament Commission since 1990. In 1992 the UN General Assembly endorsed a set of guidelines and recommendations for objective information on military matters. These were intended to encourage openness and transparency in military matters, to facilitate the process of arms limitations, reduction and elimination, as well as to assist verification of compliance with obligations undertaken by states in these fields.[81]

With the de-linking of the UN reporting instrument from its original purpose—reduction of military expenditure as a measure of disarmament and to release resources for development—it also lost much of its political momentum and reporting continued to be low during the first 10 years of the post-cold war period, averaging 32 countries annually in 1990–99.[82] However, since transparency also constitutes a confidence-building measure, the UN reporting instrument can also be seen as a CBM or CSBM at the global level, and this is indeed one of the factors used to justify the instrument in General Assembly resolutions. Similar initiatives to exchange information on military expenditure as a CBM have subsequently been initiated regionally, including in South America between Argentina and Chile.[83] The exchange of military budget figures between members of the OSCE has been a CSBM since 1991.[84]

Transparency in military expenditure is also used as an indicator of good governance in aid recipient countries. Donors call for military expenditure statistics to be produced as part of the routine government budget process for the use of parliament in its oversight function and for the general public.

Military expenditure as an indicator for burden sharing

NATO burden sharing once more became an issue following the adoption of a new NATO strategy and the associated Defence Capabilities Initiative (DCI) at the 1999 Washington Summit.[85] While the DCI involved commitments in terms of physical resources (equipment and personnel) rather than monetary allocations, military expenditure still remained an issue in the debate. This was the case in particular when assessing the 'transatlantic gap' in military capabil-

---

[81] United Nations, General Assembly Resolution 47/54, 9 Dec. 1992, URL <http://www.un.org/Depts/dhl/res/resa47.htm>, section B.

[82] United Nations (note 44), pp. 8–10.

[83] For a review of CBMs in Latin America see Bromley, M. and Perdomo, C., 'CBMs in Latin America and the effect of arms acquisitions by Venezuela', Working Paper 41/2005, Real Instituto Elcano, Madrid, Sep. 2005, URL <http://www.realinstitutoelcano.org/documentos/216.asp>.

[84] This was one of the provisions of the Vienna Document 1990. The requirement remains in the Vienna Document 1999. On the Vienna Document 1999 see annex A in this volume. See also Lachowski, Z., *Confidence- and Security-Building Measures in the New Europe*, SIPRI Research Report no. 18 (Oxford University Press: Oxford, 2004).

[85] North Atlantic Treaty Organization, 'Defence Capabilities Initiative', Press Release NAC-S(99)69, 25 Apr. 1999, URL <http://www.nato.int/docu/pr/1999/p99s069e.htm>.

ities, with the general perception being that there was a strong imbalance in favour of the USA.

However, there was no consensus on the best indicator to use when making comparisons of contributions to collective defence: for example, military expenditure growth trends, its share of gross domestic product (GDP) or per capita spending. Furthermore, the changing security environment made it increasingly clear that assessments of contributions to the NATO common defence could not be based exclusively on allocations to national defence—other ways of promoting security had to be included. Third, an increasingly common issue was whether national military expenditure was a relevant measure of commitment to NATO as such—the different nature of security policies also had to be taken into account, the USA's strategy being global while its allies' strategies were not.[86] This was reflected in a 2001 report by the US Congressional Budget Office, which produced a number of alternative or complementary indicators of burden sharing, including: (a) military expenditure as a share of GDP, (b) military expenditure per capita, (c) military personnel as a share of the labour force, (d) contributions to NATO's rapid reaction forces, (e) contributions to peacekeeping missions and (f) economic aid to Central and East European countries.[87] Eventually, the debate on the measure of burden sharing changed focus from military expenditure data to the transatlantic gap in military technology and in interoperability.[88]

IV. Military expenditure after September 2001

The attacks on the USA on 11 September 2001 marked a significant turning point in the international security environment. On the one hand, they shattered the sense of security felt in most of the developed world and created the urgent need for security measures to prevent a recurrence of the attacks in either the USA or other parts of the Western world. On the other hand, the new threat provided a focus for national security strategies that had been lacking in most industrialized countries since the end of the cold war.[89]

---

[86] Quantitative criteria for assessing burden sharing have been critically assessed in a number of studies including Cooper, C. and Zycher, B., *Perceptions of NATO Burden-Sharing*, RAND Report R-3750-FF/RC (RAND: Santa Monica, Calif., 1989); and Sandler, T. and Murdoch, J. C., 'On sharing NATO defence burdens in the 1990s and beyond', *Fiscal Studies*, vol. 21, no. 3 (Sep. 2000), URL <http://www.ifs.org.uk/publications.php?publication_id=2205>, pp. 297–327.

[87] US Congressional Budget Office (CBO), *NATO Burdensharing After Enlargement* (CBO: Washington, DC, Aug. 2001), URL <http://www.cbo.gov/showdoc.cfm?index=2976>, pp. 1–2. The results of the comparison according to each of these indicators are summarized in Sköns, E. et al., 'Military expenditure', *SIPRI Yearbook 2002: Armaments, Disarmament and International Security* (Oxford University Press: Oxford, 2002), pp. 255–56.

[88] The enlargement of NATO in 1999 also involved some focus on military expenditure data since NATO called for increases in military expenditure in accession countries from the mid-1990s. However, this was more as an indicator of their military commitment and modernization than in the context of burden sharing as such. Sloan, S., 'Transatlantic relations: stormy weather on the way to enlargement?', *NATO Review*, vol. 45, no. 5 (Sep./Oct. 1997), URL <http://www.nato.int/docu/review/>, pp. 12–16; and Sköns et al. (note 87), pp. 209–13.

[89] Barry, T., 'Toward a new grand strategy for US foreign policy', International Relations Center (IRC) Strategic Dialogue no. 3, IRC, Silver City, N.Mex., Dec. 2004, URL <http://www.irc-online.org/

The most immediate effect was the US-led attack on Afghanistan in October 2001. In 2002 the USA adopted a new National Security Strategy, which envisaged pre-emptive attacks on any state if it is judged to pose 'sufficient threat' to the US national security, even if 'uncertainty remains as to the time and place of the enemy's attack'.[90] The purpose would be 'to eliminate a specific threat to the United States or [its] allies and friends'.[91] The phrasing of this security strategy, which informed the attack on Iraq in March 2003, allowed for a flexible interpretation of whether and how the USA might act.

The wars in Afghanistan and Iraq have been responsible for the rapid increase in the USA's military expenditure since 2001. The USA also established the Department for Homeland Security to guard against future attacks on the country. The new focus on internal security was taken up by the European Union and other regional groups and countries, highlighting in the process that defence against terrorism is best conducted by non-military means.[92] Complex implications for the role of armed forces in security matters follow from the increasing blurring of the dividing line between internal security and external defence as a result of the overlap between the tasks performed by agencies such as the US Department of Homeland Security and those of the armed forces.[93] The new conceptualization of security to cover economic and environmental challenges further highlights the diminishing importance of the military sector in tackling new security issues.

Meanwhile, in the developing countries the events of September 2001 led to the consolidation of certain trends that had already emerged. First, the calls on industrialized countries to help alleviate poverty in the developing countries, especially in conflict and post-conflict states, and to tackle the phenomenon of weak states—which had not received adequate attention in the immediate post-cold war period—received a new impetus as poverty was identified as one of the sources of international terrorism. This helped to emphasize the reality of North–South interdependence in terms of security.[94] Second, a greater number of donors, having realized that lack of security in recipient countries undermined the effectiveness of their aid, had come to accept the link between security and development. They were consequently more willing to support countries affected by internal armed conflict in re-establishing the state's monopoly of force. The majority of donors even agreed to assist in reforming the security sector of recipient countries through the Security

content/dialogue/2004/03.php>. The consensus in this discussion is that until Sep. 2001 US foreign and military policy lacked a focus.

[90] The White House, 'The National Security Strategy of the United States of America', Washington, DC, Sep. 2002, URL <http://www.whitehouse.gov/nsc/nss.html>, p. 15.

[91] The White House (note 90), p. 16.

[92] Brozska, M., 'New security concepts required', *BICC Bulletin*, no. 24 (1 July 2002), URL <http://www.bicc.de/publications/bulletin/bulletin.php>, pp. 1–2.

[93] On the blurring of the dividing line between internal and external security see Andreas, P. and Price, R., 'From war fighting to crime fighting: transforming the American national security state', *International Studies Review*, vol. 3, no. 3 (fall 2001), pp. 31–52.

[94] Bailes, A. J. K., 'Global security governance: a world of change and challenge', *SIPRI Yearbook 2005* (note 5), pp. 1–27.

System Reform framework developed by the OECD's Development Assistance Committee.[95] Third, the broadening of the concept of security also had implications for developing countries. The new focus on human security—freedom from fear and from want, which places the needs of the individual, rather than the state, at the core of security concerns—presupposes a focus on internal rather than external security. Thus, in the aftermath of September 2001, countries in both the North and the South have addressed a broader and more internally focused security agenda with either a decreasing focus on the military or a re-categorization of the military as part of the larger security sector in need of reform.

World military spending has increased rapidly since September 2001. Between 2001 and 2005 it increased by 25 per cent in real terms. Most of the increase is accounted for by the USA—which accounted for 48 per cent of world military spending in 2005—owing largely to the rapid increase in US supplementary allocations to prosecute the 'global war on terrorism'.[96]

Uses of data

Military expenditure data in the post-September 2001 period continue to be used in contexts similar to those in the earlier post-cold war period: less for threat assessment and disarmament and, in the development cooperation context, more as a measure of good governance than as a basis for aid conditionality. Such data also continue to be used as a tool of transparency.

Threat assessments

The use of military expenditure as a tool for threat assessment has diminished considerably since the end of the cold war and particularly since September 2001. Terrorists do not use traditional military methods, so military expenditure data do not help to identify the threat that they pose (nor, indeed, a country's real capacity to respond to that threat). In addition, the unreliability of the defence budget figures of states that could serve as breeding grounds for terrorist groups means that the available data on military expenditure cannot be used as a credible indicator in threat assessment for these countries.

The one instance in which military expenditure continues to be used as a threat assessment tool is in the measurement of Chinese military expenditure. This is in spite of the equally unreliable detail in the official Chinese military expenditure figures.[97]

---

[95] Organisation for Economic Co-operation and Development (OECD), Development Assistance Committee (DAC), *Security System Reform and Governance: Policy and Good Practice*, DAC Guidelines and Reference Series (OECD: Paris, 2005), URL <http://www.oecd.org/dataoecd/8/39/31785288.pdf>.

[96] See chapter 8 and appendix 8A in this volume.

[97] US Department of Defense (note 65). See also US–China Economic and Security Review Commission (USCC), *The National Security Implications of the Economic Relationship between the United States and China*, Report to the US Congress (USCC: Washington, DC, July 2002), URL <http://www.uscc.gov/researchpapers/2000_2003/reports/anrp02.htm>. See also chapter 8 in this volume.

Disarmament

Although the size of military budgets continues to be an issue, there have been few references to reductions in military budgets as a means of disarmament in international disarmament negotiations since September 2001. However, in 2002 there was an initiative to restore the link between reductions in military expenditure and the release of resources for development: the UN General Assembly requested the Secretary-General, with the assistance of a group of governmental experts, to prepare a report reappraising the relationship between disarmament and development in the current international context. The report, submitted in 2004, 'reiterates the importance of exercising restraint in military expenditure, so that human and financial resources can be used for the ongoing effort to eradicate poverty and achieve the Millennium Development Goals'.[98] This was the first review of this issue since the adoption of the Final Document by the International Conference on the Relationship between Disarmament and Development in 1987. A December 2004 General Assembly resolution requested the Secretary-General to take action for the implementation of the action programme adopted at 1987 conference.[99]

International development cooperation

Military expenditure data continue to be used by donors of economic aid as a tool for assessing the seriousness with which governments in developing countries address critical issues of development. While donors now recognize that developing countries have genuine security needs, some still use the lowering of military expenditure as a condition for providing assistance. This is in spite of the fact that the Security System Reform framework that members of the OECD's Development Assistance Committee have adopted as the basis of their development work in crisis states clearly argues against donor pre-occupation with levels of spending in recipient countries.[100] Instead, donor countries are encouraged to emphasize good governance in the security sector, through transparency, accountability and effective oversight, using the so-called process approach.[101] At the same time, however, the pressure to support the global war on terrorism is encouraging increased spending in areas such as intelligence and internal security and the USA has provided extra military aid in cash and kind to the states it sees as bulwarks against terrorism in

[98] United Nations, 'The relationship between disarmament and development in the current international context', Report of the Group of Governmental Experts on the Relationship between Disarmament and Development, UN General Assembly document A/59/119, New York, N.Y., 23 June 2004, URL <http://www.un.org/ga/59/documentation/list1.html>, p. 4.

[99] United Nations, General Assembly Resolution 59/78, 17 Dec. 2004. See also United Nations, 'Relationship between disarmament and development', Report of the Secretary-General, UN General Assembly document A/60/94, New York, N.Y., 5 July 2005, URL <http://www.un.org/ga/60/documentation/list.html>.

[100] Organisation for Economic Co-operation and Development, Development Assistance Committee (note 95), p. 33.

[101] See, e.g., Omitoogun, W. and Hutchful, E. (eds), SIPRI, *Budgeting for the Military Sector in Africa: The Processes and Mechanisms of Control* (Oxford University Press: Oxford, 2006).

various regions.[102] These factors reintroduce the risk of truly disproportionate spending increases and make it harder for the outside world to track them because so many relatively unfamiliar kinds of data need to be compiled. If donors stick to the process approach when determining their aid policies for developing countries, then the political significance of military expenditure data might be reduced and the credibility of the data improved.

Transparency

The annual UN General Assembly resolution asking the Secretary-General to request data on military expenditure now omits the goal of reducing the spending and includes reference only to 'promoting further openness and transparency in all military matters', with the conviction that such transparency 'is an essential element for building a climate of trust and confidence between States worldwide' and 'can help to relieve international tension and is therefore an important contribution to conflict prevention'.[103] The reporting instrument is now perceived as primarily a general transparency measure which can help to build confidence and prevent conflict.

Since 2001 the UN Department for Disarmament Affairs has been engaged in efforts to encourage and facilitate reporting by member states. It has held regional and sub-regional workshops to increase familiarity with the reporting instrument and to raise awareness regarding the transparency-building process.[104] After this revival of the instrument as a transparency measure, the number of reporting countries increased to 76–82 per year in 2002–2005.[105] A simplified reporting instrument has also been introduced, but few countries have chosen to report using this version.[106]

Implications for the relevance of military expenditure data

It is difficult to identify any direct effect of the events of September 2001 on the availability of military expenditure data. In general, accessibility and availability of data have grown with the increased use of the Internet and this trend did not stop in September 2001. More of the developing countries post their budgets on the Internet, which has greatly aided access by data-reporting organizations. Even in Africa, where access to data used to be particularly difficult, there has been a marked improvement, although data for countries in

[102] E.g., US Department of State, 'Foreign operations, export financing and related programs (foreign operations)', *FY 2007 International Affairs (Function 150) Budget Request* (Department of State: Washington, DC, Feb. 2006), URL <http://www.state.gov/s/d/rm/rls/iab/2007/>, pp. 45–47.

[103] United Nations, General Assembly Resolution 60/44, 6 Jan. 2006, URL <http://www.un.org/Depts/dhl/resguide/r60.htm>.

[104] United Nations, Department for Disarmament Affairs (note 44), p. 3.

[105] United Nations, Department for Disarmament Affairs, 'Participation graph: UN instrument for reporting military expenditures 1992–2005', 1 Jan. 2006, URL <http://disarmament.un.org/cab/milex.html>.

[106] The simplified version is reproduced in Sköns and Nazet (note 44). For statistics on reporting using the simplified version see appendix 8D in this volume.

conflict continue to be lacking and, since the data are from primary documents, they can be very disaggregated. One region that continues to be particularly problematic is the Middle East, and Central Asian countries also pose significant data problems. In general, the increased level of availability still needs to be matched by improved quality, in particular accuracy.

Since the events of September 2001 most OECD member states have linked development assistance to the willingness of aid recipients to support the global war on terrorism.[107] This has implications for the quality of military expenditure data. On the one hand, it reduces the incentives for aid-dependent states to falsify their military spending data because less emphasis is placed on the level of spending. On the other hand, it encourages a change in the coverage of military expenditure to include various non-military security functions, with the added difficulties for definitions and data collection that are noted above. This further complicates disaggregation, which has always been a major problem for developing countries' military expenditure data. Without a breakdown of military expenditure data into their component parts, they remain of limited value.

Given the emerging changes in the international security environment, with the primacy of internal security and human security, the diminishing significance of military means to address these issues and the blurring of the dividing line between internal and external security, are military expenditure data still of any relevance in debates on peace and security? Clearly, the relevance of such information has been affected by the changes in the security environment in several ways. First, the blurring of the dividing line between military and internal security, in particular within the context of civil war and social unrest that threatens the state, makes it important to produce data not only on military expenditure but also on certain internal security activities in order to arrive at a comprehensive picture of total security expenditure. However, these two data series must be kept separate since the constitutional mandates of these two security sectors are different in most countries.

More importantly, data on military expenditure have lost some relevance both as an indicator of threats to security and as an indicator of the provision of security. As regards threats to security, the birth of the concept of human security and its increased use and political relevance have created the need for a data series that indicates the level of spending on human security. As a first step to develop such indicators, a stringent definition of the concept is required. So far there have been two competing concepts of human security,[108] but there are new efforts to develop a unified concept, incorporating both dimensions of the UN Millennium Declaration—freedom from fear and free-

---

[107] Organisation for Economic Co-operation and Development (OECD), Development Assistance Committee (DAC), *A Development Co-operation Lens on Terrorism Prevention: Key Entry Points for Action*, DAC Guidelines and Reference Series (OECD: Paris, 2003), URL <http://www.oecd.org/dataoecd/17/4/16085708.pdf>.

[108] Krause, K., 'Is human security "more than just a good idea"?', eds M. Brzoska and P. J. Croll, *Promoting Security: But How and for Whom?*, Bonn International Center for Conversion (BICC) Brief no. 30 (BICC: Bonn, Oct 2004). URL <http://www.bicc.de/publications/briefs/brief30/content.php>, pp. 43–46.

dom from want.[109] With the decreased relevance of the use of military force to address contemporary security problems, other indicators are needed. The development of such indicators needs to be based on a relatively broad consensus on the main components of the contemporary security environment and the proper means to address these. In this regard, reports such as that of the UN High-level Panel on Threats, Challenges and Change could provide some guidance.[110] However, it is not at all clear what consensus will develop.

Thus, in many ways data on military expenditure have lost some of their relevance to the analysis of the new security environment and need to be complemented by other data sets. However, military expenditure data are likely to remain important in this analysis. Furthermore, since the military sector represents the state's monopoly on violence, it will remain important to continue monitoring trends in military expenditure and to make such data available to a broader public.

V. Continuity and change: the use of military expenditure data over the past 40 years

Military expenditure data are used in a variety of political contexts. This chapter reviews different types of use over the past 40 years in three different international security environments and relates these uses to the availability, quality and relevance of military expenditure data. The review identifies two fundamental shifts in the use of military expenditure data. First, there has been a shift of focus from military expenditure in the countries belonging to the military blocs in the North during the cold war to that of the developing countries in the South in the post-cold war period. This shift occurred as it become legitimate for donor countries to raise the issue of military expenditure in the context of international development cooperation. The implications for the use of military expenditure data of the evolving North–South security relationship since September 2001 have not yet fully taken shape.

Second, in the United Nations there has been a shift in the aims of the use of military expenditure data from disarmament and, to a lesser extent, development to transparency. This reflects broader changes in the international peace and security community, where the idea of disarmament as a direct path to development has lost ground, while the idea of promoting security through approaches such as confidence building, conflict prevention and active regional peacekeeping has gained ground. Furthermore, increased awareness of the interdependence of security and development is resulting in new ideas on how to promote both. This will hopefully lead to increased use of non-military resources for security provision in the future. However, the picture is

---

[109] Picciotto, R., Olonisakin, F. and Clarke, M., *Global Development and Human Security: Towards a Policy Agenda*, Global Development Studies no. 3 (Swedish Ministry for Foreign Affairs, Expert Group on Development Issues: Stockholm, 2006), URL <http://www.egdi.gov.se/>.

[110] United Nations, 'A more secure world: our shared responsibility', Report of the High-level Panel on Threats, Challenges and Change, UN documents A/59/565, 4 Dec. 2004, and A/59/565/Corr. 1, 6 Dec. 2004, URL <http://www.un.org/ga/59/documentation/list5.html>.

mixed since the first half-decade of the 21st century was dominated by the opposite practice: the application of huge military resources in the name of defending and promoting democracy.

In general, it appears that data availability and accessibility have tended to improve over time, especially in terms of access to primary sources for developing countries. This is in part because of the general tendency for improved transparency, including the increasing use of the Internet by developing countries, and is possibly also promoted by the efforts of the UN, the international donor community and the data-gathering organizations. However, in spite of the improved access to data, the quality of the data remains unsatisfactory. Data on military expenditure have never been very accurate, and the quality of data has remained problematic throughout the past 40 years. In some areas there have been improvements while new problems have emerged elsewhere. Some components of military expenditure, in particular arms imports, are not always included in official data on military expenditure, especially in developing countries, including China. A main challenge is thus to encourage governments to report all military-related items in their military expenditure statistics. Tracking states' conflict-related expenditure is also a major challenge. The industrialized countries' new modes of financing procurement through private finance require further understanding in order to assess their implications for data quality.

The relevance of military expenditure data for the analysis of peace and security issues has been a perpetual issue throughout the 40-year period. The use of military expenditure data to assess military strength or other types of output, in spite of the fact that such data by their nature are an input measure, tends to lead to misconceptions, as the cold war experience demonstrates.

The relevance of military expenditure data is further challenged in the current security environment, with fundamental questions posed by the increased focus on internal security and the changing concept of security. Human security, with its focus on the individual rather than the state, and the blurring of the dividing line between internal security and external defence mean that military expenditure data are of less relevance as an indicator in this emerging security scenario. The resource consumption of non-state actors, which is financed entirely outside the government sector, leaves a big gap in what military expenditure data capture. As a result, such data have lost some relevance for the analysis of peace and security. This does not mean that data on military expenditure are of no utility, but rather that they need to be complemented by other types of data series in order to capture the dimensions of internal security and human security.

8. Military expenditure

PETTER STÅLENHEIM, DAMIEN FRUCHART,
WUYI OMITOOGUN and CATALINA PERDOMO

I. Introduction

World military expenditure in 2005 is estimated to have reached $1001 billion at constant (2003) prices and exchange rates, or $1118 billion in current dollars. This represents 2.5 per cent of world gross domestic product (GDP)[1] and $173 per capita.[2] The trend in world military expenditure, an increase in real terms of 3.4 per cent since 2004 and 34 per cent since 1996, is mainly determined by the rapidly increasing military spending of the United States, which is by far the biggest spender in the world, accounting for 48 per cent of the world total.

Together, the 15 countries with the highest military spending in 2005 account for 84 per cent of the world total. In spite of pressure on national budgets, it is likely that at least four of the five highest spenders will increase their military expenditure in the coming years. The USA, France and the United Kingdom are all involved in costly overseas military operations that demand resources in both the short and long terms. In addition, France and the UK are in the midst of military reform processes and have also sought new, private, ways of financing or deferring the cost of major procurement deals. China is engaged in a long-running modernization of the People's Liberation Army (PLA) that has caused a rapid increase in military spending since 1998 and that shows little sign of slowing down.

A striking trend during the past few years has been that of countries with rising revenues from natural resources, such as gas, oil and metals, that have formally or informally diverted these funds into military spending, in particular into arms purchases. This is probably why the Middle East, together with North America, was the region with the greatest increase in military expenditure in 2005. Eastern Europe also increased its military spending in 2005 while in Western Europe a general downward trend can be observed.

This chapter analyses military expenditure for 2005 and sets it in the context of the main developments during the past decade.[3] Section II analyses trends

---

[1] This share of GDP is based on a projected figure for world GDP in 2005 of $43 886 billion at market exchange rates. International Monetary Fund (IMF), *World Economic Outlook, September 2005: Building Institutions* (IMF: Washington, DC, 2005), URL <http://www.imf.org/external/pubs/ft/weo/2005/02/>, Statistical appendix, table 1, 'Summary of world output', p. 205.

[2] This per capita average is based on an estimated total world population of 6465 million in 2005. United Nations Population Fund (UNFPA), *State of the World Population 2005* (UNFPA: New York, N.Y., 2005), URL <http://www.unfpa.org/swp/>.

[3] Developments in the uses and availability of military expenditure data over the past 40 years are described in chapter 7 in this volume.

in military expenditure by organization and income group. In section III the spending of the 15 countries with the highest military expenditure is analysed, with a focus on the top five. Section IV looks at recent developments in the different regions of the world and sets their military expenditure in an economic and security context. Section V contains brief conclusions.

Appendix 8A presents SIPRI data on military expenditure for 166 countries for the 10-year period 1996–2005. World and regional totals in constant (2003) US dollars are provided in table 8A.1. Country data are provided in three formats: in local currency at current prices (table 8A.2); in constant (2003) US dollars (table 8A.3); and as a share of GDP (table 8A.4). Appendix 8B presents spending by members of the North Atlantic Treaty Organization (NATO) disaggregated into procurement and personnel expenditure by country for the period 2000–2005. Appendix 8C presents the sources and methods for SIPRI's military expenditure data and appendix 8D provides statistics on governments' reporting of their military expenditure to SIPRI, the United Nations (UN) and other organizations. Appendix 8E discusses problems involved in the conversion of economic data into dollars and the choice between purchasing power parity (PPP) rates and exchange rates for this conversion, a choice that can make up to a tenfold difference in a country's (apparent) spending levels.

II. Military expenditure by region, organization and income group

SIPRI military expenditure data and estimates of world and regional military expenditure as presented in appendix 8A and table 8.1 reflect information as reported by governments. The estimates of world and regional military expenditure are underestimates. There are four major reasons for this. First and perhaps most significantly, not all entities that spend money for military purposes are included in the SIPRI estimates. SIPRI military expenditure data do not include spending by non-governmental actors, and spending by some governments is also left out owing to lack of data or lack of consistent data.[4] Second, rather than not disclosing their military spending at all, some states conceal parts of it, causing underreporting.[5] Inaccuracies can also be caused by lack of capacity within the government, a weakness that is prevalent in developing countries.[6] Third, some armed forces generate their own quite substantial revenues that are not always accounted for in the budget and some-

---

[4] Some countries are excluded because of lack of data or of consistent time series data. In Africa, Angola, Benin, Equatorial Guinea and Somalia are excluded; in the Americas, Cuba, Haiti, and Trinidad and Tobago are excluded; in Asia, Myanmar and Viet Nam are excluded; and in the Middle East, Iraq and Qatar are excluded. World totals exclude all these countries.

[5] On transparency in the arms life cycle, including military expenditure, see chapter 6 in this volume.

[6] Omitoogun, W., *Military Expenditure Data in Africa: A Survey of Cameroon, Ethiopia, Ghana, Kenya, Nigeria and Uganda*, SIPRI Research Report no. 17 (Oxford University Press: Oxford, 2003); and Omitoogun, W. and Hutchful, E. (eds), SIPRI, *Budgeting for the Military Sector in Africa: The Processes and Mechanisms of Control* (Oxford University Press: Oxford, 2006).

times lie outside government and parliamentary control. This type of off-budget revenue for the armed forces is often connected to the illegal sale of natural resources, drug trade and trafficking or other types of illegal activity, but it can sometimes also reflect quite legal commercial earnings or farming. Fourth, reported figures, at least for the most recent year, only reflect budgeted expenditure. It is common for actual expenditure to be markedly higher than was originally budgeted, but the opposite occasionally occurs as well. When data on actual expenditure become available, the SIPRI data are updated; consequently, the reader is advised to always consult the latest edition of the SIPRI Yearbook.

World military spending in 2005 amounted to $1001 billion when converted to US dollars using 2003 prices and exchange rates. This represents a real-terms increase over 2004 of 3.4 per cent and of 34 per cent since 1998, when military expenditure was at its lowest level since the end of the cold war. The region where military expenditure increased most in absolute terms in 2005 was North America because of the continued rapid increases in the USA, officially owing to the 'global war on terrorism' and the conflicts in Afghanistan and Iraq.[7] The USA accounted for about 80 per cent or $26 billion of the total $33 billion increase in world military expenditure in 2005. Over the decade 1996–2005, US spending increased by $160 billion and the world total by $254 billion. The rise of 165 per cent in Chinese military expenditure over the same period only equated to a rise of $25.5 billion in constant (2003) US dollars.

The region with the highest relative spending increase in 2005 was the Middle East, mostly influenced by a massive increase in Saudi Arabia's defence budget. Total military spending in the Middle East would be substantially higher if the military expenditure of Iraq and Qatar were not excluded owing to lack of consistent data.

The only region with a decrease in military expenditure in 2005 was Europe, with a 1.7 per cent decrease. This reduction was mainly attributable to Western Europe, where spending declined by $6 billion, or 2.8 per cent. The level of Central European military expenditure did not change while in Eastern Europe it increased by 8.9 per cent; but, as West European military spending accounts for about 86 per cent of total European spending, the result is still a tangible decrease for the whole region. All five West European countries with military expenditure high enough to rank them among the 15 major spenders in 2005 (see table 8.3 below) decreased their defence budgets in 2005. The biggest decreases were in Italy and the UK. Over the 10-year period 1996–2005, however, military expenditure in Europe increased by 8.2 per cent. The only region where total military expenditure has decreased over the decade is Central America, which shows a decrease of 2.5 per cent. Since Mexico accounts for 87 per cent of Central American military spending, the country's

---

[7] Steve Kosiak claims that a large part of the increase in US spending is accounted for by procurement of military equipment that has very little to do with the war on terrorism. Kosiak, S., 'FY 2006 defense budget request: DOD budget remains on upward trajectory', Center for Strategic and Budgetary Assessment, Washington, DC, 4 Feb. 2005, URL <http://www.csbaonline.org/>.

Table 8.1. World and regional military expenditure estimates, 1996–2005

Figures are in US$ b., at constant (2003) prices and exchange rates. Figures in italics are percentages. Figures do not always add up to totals because of the conventions of rounding.

Region[a]	1996	1997	1998	1999	2000	2001	2002	2003	2004	2005	Change 96–05
Africa	**8.6**	**8.7**	**9.4**	**10.5**	**11.1**	**11.1**	**12.1**	**11.9**	**12.6**	**12.7**	*+48*
North	3.5	3.7	3.8	3.9	4.3	4.4	4.8	5.0	5.6	5.5	*+58*
Sub-Saharan	5.1	5.0	5.6	6.6	6.8	6.6	7.3	6.9	(7.0)	(7.2)	*+42*
Americas	**347**	**349**	**340**	**341**	**353**	**358**	**399**	**447**	**485**	**513**	*+48*
Caribbean	..	..	..	..	..	..	..	..	..	..	..
Central	3.3	3.4	3.3	3.5	3.6	3.7	3.5	3.4	3.2	3.2	*–2*
North	328	327	319	320	332	335	375	425	463	489	*+49*
South	15.7	18.1	17.5	17.1	17.8	19.9	20.4	18.3	18.9	20.6	*+31*
Asia, Oceania	**116**	**118**	**119**	**122**	**126**	**132**	**138**	**144**	**152**	**157**	*+36*
Central	0.5	0.5	(0.5)	0.5	..	(0.6)	(0.6)	(0.6)	(0.7)	(0.8)	*(+77)*
East	91.0	91.9	92.4	92.9	95.5	101	107	112	116	120	*+32*
Oceania	8.6	8.8	9.1	9.6	9.5	9.9	10.3	10.6	11.1	11.5	*+32*
South	15.5	16.5	17.1	19.2	19.9	20.5	20.6	21.2	23.9	25.0	*+61*
Europe	**236**	**239**	**234**	**238**	**243**	**243**	**249**	**256**	**260**	**256**	*+8*
Central	11.6	11.7	11.7	11.4	11.5	12.1	12.3	12.8	12.7	11.7	*+10*
Eastern	15.6	17.5	11.5	11.9	15.8	17.3	19.1	20.4	21.4	23.3	*+50*
Western	209	210	210	214	215	214	218	223	226	220	*+5*
Middle East	**39.0**	**43.4**	**46.5**	**45.8**	**51.5**	**55.0**	**52.6**	**55.0**	**58.9**	**(63.0)**	*(+61)*
World	**747**	**756**	**748**	**757**	**784**	**800**	**851**	**914**	**969**	**1 001**	*+34*
Change (%)		*1.3*	*–1.1*	*1.2*	*3.6*	*2.0*	*6.4*	*7.5*	*5.9*	*3.4*	

( ) = Total based on country data accounting for less than 90 per cent of the regional total; .. = Available data account for less than 60 per cent of the regional total.

[a] For the country coverage of the regions, see appendix 8A, table 8A.1. Some countries are excluded because of lack of data or of consistent time series data. Africa excludes Angola, Benin, Equatorial Guinea and Somalia; Americas excludes Cuba, Haiti and Trinidad and Tobago; Asia excludes Myanmar and Viet Nam; and the Middle East excludes Iraq and Qatar. World totals exclude all these countries.

Source: Appendix 8A, tables 8A.1 and 8A.3.

2.0 per cent decrease over the period makes a deep impression on the overall trend, but most of the other countries in the region have also reduced their spending.

It is noteworthy that the members of the Organization of the Petroleum Exporting Countries (OPEC) increased their military spending by 11.2 per cent in 2005, facilitated by extra revenues from high oil prices during the past few years. This trend of resource-facilitated increases can also be seen in Peru and Russia, where a large portion of the increasing national revenue comes from oil and gas, while increasing military expenditure in Chile was almost totally driven by increasing revenues from copper exports. Peru followed in the footsteps of Chile, with a legally mandated allocation of a certain share of revenues from gas production to military spending (see section IV below).

Table 8.2. Military expenditure estimates, 1996–2005, by organization and income group

Figures are in US $b., at constant (2003) prices and exchange rates. Figures in italics are percentages.

Organization/ income group[a]	2000	2001	2002	2003	2004	2005	Change, 1996– 2005 (%)	Military expenditure 2004	
								Per capita ($)	% GDP
Organization									
ASEAN	11.1	11.7	12.4	13.3	13.3	13.1	*+8.2*	32.2	*1.9*
CIS	16.4	17.9	19.7	21.1	22.1	24.1	*+50.4*	89.5	*3.4*
European Union	196	196	199	206	219	212	*+11.0*	478.5	*1.9*
NATO	539	541	585	642	687	706	*+34.5*	794.4	*2.9*
NATO Europe	207	207	211	217	224	217	*+10.5*	416.6	*2.0*
OECD	622	625	670	727	768	789	*+29.6*	659.9	*2.5*
OPEC	37.1	39.6	36.3	38.0	42.0	46.7	*+72.4*	81.6	*4.0*
Income group (by 2003 gross national income per capita)									
Low	24.3	24.6	25.4	25.6	28.3	29.5	*+64.2*	13.2	*2.7*
Lower middle	90.5	99.0	105	109	114	122	*+59.2*	43.4	*2.5*
Upper middle	42.2	45.2	42.5	43.9	46.7	51.0	*+47.7*	137.9	*2.3*
High	627	631	678	736	780	799	*+29.3*	810.7	*2.6*

ASEAN = Association of South East Asian Nations; CIS = Commonwealth of Independent States; GDP = Gross domestic product; NATO = North Atlantic Treaty Organization; OECD = Organisation for Economic Co-operation and Development; OPEC = Organization of the Petroleum Exporting Countries; OSCE = Organization for Security and Co-operation in Europe.

[a] For the country coverage of the organizations and income groups see appendix 8A, table 8A.1. Afghanistan, Brunei, Cuba, Haiti, Iraq, North Korea, Romania, Serbia and Montenegro, Somalia, Turkmenistan and Uzbekistan are excluded from the per capita figures because of lack of data on population.

Sources: Appendix 8A, tables 8A.1; **Population**: International Monetary Fund, *International Financial Statistics* database.

Table 8.2 shows that the middle-income countries—further divided into lower-middle and upper-middle incomes—had the highest relative increase in military expenditure in 2005, with increases of 6.7 and 9.1 per cent, respectively. At the same time low- and high-income countries increased spending by 4.1 and 2.5 per cent, respectively. Over the 10-year period 1996–2005, the low-income countries had the highest percentage increase, 64.2 per cent. Even if the 131 low- and middle-income countries are those that are increasing their military expenditure most in relative terms, their total spending accounts for only one-fifth of total world spending while the 35 high-income countries account for four-fifths. At the same time, most of the major armed conflicts are fought in developing countries.[8]

[8] See chapter 2 in this volume.

As reflected in table 8.2, high-income countries have higher military spending per capita than low-income countries. Since richer countries have more spare resources and often have smaller populations than poorer countries, their marginal cost of investing resources in the military decreases. In densely populated countries with small, developing economies, the marginal cost of increasing military expenditure can be very high while per capita spending is still very low. Such a country's economic outlay is quite small when divided by a large population figure. Hence, diverting $1 from each person to the military sector is quite expensive for the economy at large—both in aggregate and for each individual—because it takes resources that could have been spent on other social and personal priorities. In contrast, the USA has a large population, but its economic output is large enough to sustain a high level of income for the average individual while simultaneously investing large amounts per capita in the military.

III. The 15 major spenders

World military expenditure is extremely unevenly distributed between countries. Table 8.3 shows the 15 countries that spent most on their military forces in 2005, as measured in 2003 prices and converted to US dollars using 2003 market exchange rates. These 15 countries account for 84 per cent of all world spending and the remaining 151 countries for a mere 16 per cent. The USA, with its 48 per cent of total world military expenditure, stands out even among the major spenders. The next four biggest spenders, the UK, France, Japan and China, each account for 4–5 per cent of the total.

As can be seen from table 8.3, military expenditure per capita varies considerably between the major spenders. While the populous China and India spend only $31.2 and $18.5, respectively, per capita, the USA spends $1604 and Israel spends $1430. There is a remarkable difference between the pattern of world military spending and that of world population. While the five major spenders account for 65 per cent of world military spending, they account for only 29 per cent of world population.

Table 8.3 also presents an alternative ranking based on military expenditure data converted to dollars using GDP level PPP rates. This ranking is provided as an illustration of a major problem encountered in international comparison of economic data—the choice of conversion method has a major impact on the figures. The table demonstrates the large difference between economic estimates converted using the two methods. Major discrepancies can be seen in the cases of China, India and Russia, countries with large domestic economies or large shadow economies. However, even if the PPP-converted military expenditure figures better reflect the economic burden of the military on society, they do not reflect what could have been bought on the international market with the same national funds. In particular, PPP-converted figures cannot capture the technological level of the equipment that a given state can afford to buy. While military expenditure data converted using market exchange rates usually underestimate the economic burden that the armed forces constitute to society, when converted using PPP rates the data in many cases overestimate what the armed forces could buy on the world market and, to a greater extent, the level of capabilities that the cash input can produce when translated into capability. Both the theoretical underpinning and practical implications of these differences are discussed in appendix 8E.

The United States

Military expenditure by the USA increased in 2005 by $25.6 billion to $478.2 billion, at constant 2003 prices. This 5.7 per cent rise also increased the US share of world military expenditure from 47 to 48 per cent. Since 1998, when the post-cold war downward trend in US military expenditure changed to an upward one, US military spending has increased by 55 per cent or $169 billion in constant 2003 prices. The major part of this increase has occurred since 2001, largely through supplemental appropriations for the US war on terrorism and other military operations.

Public discussions of US military expenditure are impeded not so much by secrecy as by the number of different estimates that various government agencies and other organizations present to the public. As shown in table 8.4, the headline figure of $419.3 billion for the financial year (FY) 2006 defence budget is by no means the largest estimate available from official sources. The highest published figures can be almost 50 per cent higher than the lowest. There are two main reasons for this variation. The first relates to the phase of the budgeting process from which the figures originate—the president's budget request to Congress; the authorization or appropriation bills of the House of Representatives and Senate; the authorization or appropriation acts passed by Congress, where substantial changes and reallocations can be introduced; or actual outlays as presented, for instance, in the historical series of the next budget.

The second main cause of variation is the coverage of the figures, which depends in turn on the agenda of the organization that presents or uses them. The first choice is whether to cite only spending by the Department of Defense (DOD) or to include military spending by other agencies. In order to arrive at the budget item 'National Defense', expenditure such as that by the Department of Energy on the military nuclear programme and other miscellaneous spending need to be included. Winslow Wheeler of the Center for Defense Information suggests that total US spending on 'National Security' should include spending on homeland security, veterans' affairs and international security in addition to defence spending. Using this definition, the DOD accounts for only about three-quarters of the FY 2006 national security budget.[9]

---

[9] Wheeler, W., 'Defense budget tutorial #1: what is the actual size of the 2006 defense budget?', 19 Jan. 2006, Center for Defense Information, URL <http://www.cdi.org/program/document.cfm?DocumentID=3268>. Recent work has also been done by the Task Force on a Unified Security Budget for the United States to present a more comprehensive view of US security spending. Corbin, M. and

Table 8.3. The 15 countries with the highest military expenditure in 2005 in market exchange rate terms and purchasing power parity terms

Spending figures are in US$, at constant (2003) prices and exchange rates.

Military expenditure in MER dollar terms					Military expenditure in PPP dollar terms[a]		
			Spending	World share (%)			
		Spending	per capita				Spending
Rank	Country	($ b.)	($)	Spending	Popul.	Rank	Country	($ b.)
1	USA	478.2	1 604	*48*	*5*	1	USA	478.2
2	UK	48.3	809	*5*	*1*	2	China	[188.4]
3	France	46.2	763	*5*	*1*	3	India	105.8
4	Japan	42.1	329	*4*	*2*	4	Russia	[64.4]
5	China	[41.0]	[31.2]	*[4]*	*20*	5	France	45.4
Sub-total top 5		**655.7**		*65*	*29*	**Sub-total top 5**		**882.3**
6	Germany	33.2	401	*3*	*1*	6	UK	42.3
7	Italy	27.2	468	*3*	*1*	7	Saudi Arabia[b, c]	35.0
8	Saudi Arabia[b, c]	25.2	1 025	*3*	*0*	8	Japan	34.9
9	Russia	[21.0]	[147]	*[2]*	*2*	9	Germany	32.7
10	India	20.4	18.5	*2*	*17*	10	Italy	30.1
Sub-total top 10		**782.7**		*78*	*51*	**Sub-total top 10**		**1 057.2**
11	Korea, South	16.4	344	*2*	*1*	11	Brazil	24.3
12	Canada[c]	10.6	327	*1*	*0*	12	Iran[b]	23.8
13	Australia[c]	10.5	522	*1*	*0*	13	South Korea	23.4
14	Spain	9.9	230	*1*	*1*	14	Turkey	17.8
15	Israel[c]	9.6	1 430	*1*	*0*	15	Taiwan	13.4
Sub-total top 15		**839.8**		*84*	*53*	**Sub-total top 15**		**1 159.8**
World		**1 001**	**155**	*100*	*100*	**World**		**..**

MER = Market exchange rate; PPP = Purchasing power parity; [ ] = Estimated figure.

[a] The figures in PPP dollar terms are converted at PPP rates (for 2003), calculated by the World Bank, based on comparisons of gross national product.

[b] Data for Iran and Saudi Arabia include expenditure for public order and safety and might be a slight overestimate.

[c] The populations of Australia, Canada, Israel and Saudi Arabia each constitute less than 0.5% of the total world population.

Sources: **Military expenditure**: Appendix 8A; **PPP rates**: World Bank, *World Development Report 2005: A Better Investment Climate for Everyone* (World Bank: Washington, DC, 2004), URL <http://econ.worldbank.org/wdr/>, table 1, 'Key indicators of development', pp. 256–57, and table 5, 'Key indicators for other economies', p. 264; **2005 Population**: United Nations Population Fund (UNFPA), *State of the World Population 2005* (UNFPA: New York, N.Y., 2005), URL <http://unfpa.org/swp/>.

To some degree, the discussion is also obfuscated by confusion between total spending—which includes both discretionary and mandatory spending—and mandatory spending alone. As mandatory spending is regulated by law and can be changed easily only marginally, some analysts prefer to consider only discretionary spending. It is there that the administration's policies can have their main effect and that budget cuts and increases will be found. Considering also mandatory spending gives a figure that better captures the actual burden on the economy. In the FY 2006 budget, President George W. Bush asked certain congressional committees to find ways to cut mandatory spending. The result is the Spending Reconciliation Bill, which will reduce the budget deficit by $5 billion if enacted.[10]

In addition, supplemental appropriations and budget amendments can be made that increase, or reduce, the original allocations. The majority of the costs of running military operations in Afghanistan and Iraq are financed through supplemental appropriations requested by the President.[11] In FY 2006 most of the supplemental appropriations and budget amendments were for disaster relief, following hurricanes Katrina and Rita in 2005.[12] While supplementary funding is by definition not included in the original budget proposal, both the Senate and House included in their appropriation bills all supplementary funding related to Afghanistan and Iraq, some $50 billion, that had been previously suggested by the President.[13] Finally, some estimates refer to total security spending rather than to military spending and hence also include expenditure on homeland security, adding about 20 per cent.[14]

In the interest of comparability, the figures on US military expenditure reported in appendix 8A follow the NATO definition rather than any of the USA's own budgetary definitions. In the language of the US budget, the expression 'Total Outlays on National Defense' probably comes the closest to the definition used in SIPRI military expenditure data.

Pemberton, M., 'Report of the Task Force on a Unified Security Budget for the United States, 2006', Center for Defense Information and Foreign Policy in Focus, Washington, DC, May 2005, URL <http://www.cdi.org/pdfs/Unified-Security-Budget-2006.pdf>.

[10] Congressional Budget Office, *The Budget and Economic Outlook: Fiscal Years 2007 to 2016* (US Congress: Washington, DC, Jan. 2006), URL <http://www.cbo.gov/ftpdoc.cfm?index=7027>, p. 8.

[11] Sköns, E. et al., 'Military expenditure', *SIPRI Yearbook 2005: Armaments, Disarmament and International Security* (Oxford University Press: Oxford, 2005), pp. 321–24. In Feb. 2006 President Bush requested $72.4 billion in emergency supplemental appropriations for the global war on terrorism for the remaining part of FY 2006. Of this amount, $65.3 billion will be allocated to the DOD. Office of Management and Budget, 'FY 2006 emergency supplemental (various agencies): ongoing military, diplomatic, and intelligence operations in the global war on terror; stabilization and counter-insurgency activities in Iraq and Afghanistan; and other humanitarian assistance', Estimate no. 3, Washington, DC, 16 Feb. 2006, URL <http://www.whitehouse.gov/omb/budget/amendments.htm>.

[12] Congressional Budget Office (note 10), p. 12.

[13] Dagget, S., 'Defense: FY2006 authorization and appropriations', Library of Congress, Congressional Research Service, Washington, DC, 29 July 2005, URL <http://fpc.state.gov/fpc/c15293.htm>, p. 16; and Kosiak, S., 'Comparison of the FY 2006 House and SASC defense authorization bills', Center for Strategic and Budgetary Assessment, Washington, DC, 5 Oct. 2005, URL <http://www.csbaonline.org/>; and Kucera, J., 'Congress asks for more oversight of Pentagon', *Jane's Defence Weekly*, 4 Jan. 2006, p .8.

[14] Wheeler (note 9).

Table 8.4. Different presentations of US military expenditure, financial year 2006

Figures are in US$ b., at current prices.

	Discretionary spending	Total spending[a]
Original budget authority		
DOD[b]	419.3	421.1
National Defense[c]	438.8	441.8
Outlays (estimated in the mid-session review)		
DOD[b]	..	492.3
National Defense[c]	488.8	513.9
Memorandum item		
National Security[d]	..	616.4

[a] Total spending is the sum of discretionary and mandatory spending.

[b] DOD spending includes all military spending under the Department of Defense (DOD).

[c] National Defense includes, in addition to DOD expenditure, expenditure by the Department of Energy for the US military nuclear programme and other miscellaneous spending.

[d] National security includes spending on homeland security, veterans' affairs and international security.

Sources: **Original budget authority**: Office of Management and Budget, *Budget of the United States Government, Fiscal Year 2006* (The White House: Washington, DC, 7 Feb. 2005), URL <http://www.whitehouse.gov/omb/budget/fy2006/budget.html>; **Outlays**: Office of Management and Budget, 'Fiscal year 2006, Mid-session review, Budget of the U.S. Government', The White House, Washington, DC, 13 July 2005, URL <http://www.white house.gov/omb/budget/fy2006/>; and **Memorandum item**: Wheeler, W., 'Defense budget tutorial #1: what is the actual size of the 2006 defense budget?', 19 Jan. 2006, Center for Defense Information, URL <http://www.cdi.org/program/document.cfm?DocumentID= 3268>, where 'National Security' is termed 'Defense and Security spending'.

Financial year 2006 budget and appropriations

Military expenditure in the USA has increased rapidly following the September 2001 terrorist attacks on New York and Washington, and the subsequent launch of a global war on terrorism. In the budget for FY 2003 it became clear that, instead of focusing resources on the war on terrorism, the administration had decided to embark on all alternatives for future equipment programmes at the same time. In 1999 US military spending had increased slightly, by 0.3 per cent, rising to 3.9 in 2000, breaking with a decade-long near-continuous total fall of 32.1 per cent since the end of the cold war. The 2001 terrorist attacks only exacerbated this new trend, triggering a spending spree that has continued almost unquestioned for three years.

Ahead of the presidential budget request for FY 2006, leaked government documents and leading analysts suggested that the trend would at least subside somewhat and that US security spending would be redirected to address future security threats.[15] When the President eventually submitted the budget to Con-

[15] For a more detailed analysis of the FY 2006 budget see Sköns, E. et al. (note 11), pp. 320–29; and Kosiak, S. M., 'Analysis of the FY 2006 defense budget request', Center for Strategic and Budgetary Assessments, Washington, DC, May 2005, URL <http://www.csbaonline.org/>.

gress, most of the expected changes were not to be found, and he merely suggested that spending levels not be increased as much as had earlier been planned.[16]

In the Authorization Bill, Congress reduced spending on the President's initial military budget proposal by $4.4 billion, or less than 1 per cent. However, Congress also introduced some other important changes to the budget, which give it greater control over US military spending. As has been the rule since the start of the war in Afghanistan, the administration's FY 2006 budget did not include funding for ongoing military operations; as noted above, these are funded through supplemental appropriations. Two arguments have been raised in favour of this practice: first, that the estimate of how much is actually needed can be more precise if made nearer to the time of use, and second, that the funds can be released faster through an ad hoc procedure. Critics claim that the monthly costs of the operations in Afghanistan and Iraq have become so predictable that they now belong in the main defence budget. Taking account of the cap on total spending, both the Senate and the House decided to include at least the known supplemental appropriations in their bills.[17] In an attempt to gain more control over the defence budget, demands for extensive reporting back to Congress were added to the bill, including on any programme with cost overruns in excess of 50 per cent of the planned cost and a requirement that certain programmes be certified as necessary before major tranches of their funding are released.[18]

Owing to the ongoing military operations and the war on terrorism, the US military budget is likely to continue to rise in the foreseeable future. However, the growing budget deficit and ageing population will probably mean that the rate of increase will be lower than in recent years. It is also likely that the tug-of-war between the White House and Congress over control of the way the DOD spends its money will continue.

The cost of the global war on terrorism and the conflict in Iraq

The funding for the global war on terrorism constitutes a major burden on the US economy. According to a January 2006 report by the Congressional Budget Office (CBO), the US Congress and the President have made $323 billion available in appropriations for DOD activities in support of the war on terrorism, in which the CBO includes the military operations in Afghanistan and Iraq, since 11 September 2001.[19] In 2005 alone, the outlays for operations related to the war on terrorism—operations Iraqi Freedom, Enduring Freedom (in Afghanistan) and Noble Eagle (in the USA)—are estimated to amount to $90 billion. This, however, is only a portion of the full appropriations for these operations. The report explicitly states that it has excluded financial obligations for classified activities and coalition support; however, extra costs

[16] Corbin and Pemberton (note 9), p.10.
[17] Dagget (note 13), p. 22; and Kosiak (note 13).
[18] Kucera (note 13), p. 8.
[19] Congressional Budget Office (note 10).

imposed on other parts of society should also be included. An example is the budget amendment and subsequent emergency supplemental appropriation for veterans' affairs: these are intended as compensation for the greater number of veterans seeking medical assistance, largely as a result of current military operations.[20] The costs of post-conflict reconstruction have not been included in the CBO's estimates, but a report by the Center for Strategic and Budgetary Assessment states that up to January 2006 Congress had provided about $32 billion in non-DOD funding for reconstruction in Afghanistan and Iraq.[21]

The conflict in Iraq takes the greatest share of the costs of US military operations. However, how much this conflict is costing the US economy is subject to dispute. According to a March 2005 estimate by the Congressional Research Service, the total cost of the conflict in Iraq up to the end of FY 2005 (on 30 September 2005) could be $192 billion, and the combined costs for the military operations could amount to $458 billion in FYs 2005–2014.[22]

In a recent study Linda Bilmes and Joseph Stiglitz suggest that the actual cost of the conflict in Iraq will be a lot higher than earlier estimates.[23] They include not only actual running costs for the operations but also current and future costs for casualties, rehabilitation and pensions for veterans, replacement of used equipment as well as more indirect costs such as the price of recruitment and loss of economic growth. Their 'conservative' estimate of the total cost of the conflict in Iraq is at least $1 trillion and their 'moderate' estimate is up to $1.8 trillion. Direct budgetary costs are estimated at $750–1269 billion. These estimates stand in stark contrast to those of the CBO, which suggest a total cost of approximately $500 billion.[24]

France and the United Kingdom

France and the UK together account for about 37 per cent of European military expenditure and each for 5 per cent of world spending. While they both budgeted for increased military spending in 2005, SIPRI standard sources— NATO data for France and data from the Defence Analytical Service Agency (DASA) of the British Ministry of Defence for the UK—suggest that military

[20] Office of Management and Budget, 'FY 2005 supplemental: Department of Veterans Affairs (veterans health administration)', Estimate no. 7, Washington, DC, 30 June 2005, URL <http://www.white house.gov/omb/budget/05amendments.htm>.

[21] Kosiak, S., 'The cost of military operations in Iraq and Afghanistan through fiscal year 2006 and beyond', Center for Strategic and Budgetary Assessments, 4 Jan. 2006, URL <http://www.csbaonline. org/>.

[22] Belasco, A., 'The cost of operations in Iraq, Afghanistan and enhanced security', Library of Congress, Congressional Research Service, Washington, DC, 14 Mar. 2005, URL <http://fpc.state.gov/fpc/ c14409.htm>.

[23] Bilmes, L. and Stiglitz, J., 'The economic cost of the Iraq war: an appraisal three years after the beginning of the conflict', Paper presented at the Allied Social Sciences Association Annual Conference, Boston, Mass., Jan. 2006, URL <http://www2.gsb.columbia.edu/faculty/jstiglitz/Cost_of_War_in_Iraq. pdf>.

[24] Congressional Budget Office, 'An alterative budget path assuming continued spending for military operations in Iraq and Afghanistan and in support of the global war on terrorism', Washington, DC, Feb. 2005, URL <http://www.cbo.gov/showdoc.cfm?index=6067>.

expenditure in 2005 decreased by 2.2 per cent in France and 5.4 per cent in the UK. Since both countries have ongoing major equipment modernization programmes, it is likely that this decrease is temporary and may have been partly the result of a combination of budget technicalities and the non-inclusion of 'un-programmed' spending for military operations for 2005.

Trends in British military expenditure in recent years have been somewhat difficult to assess because of a conversion from cash accounting to resource-based accounting. The change has meant that comparison over time is obscured, particularly since the transition has been undertaken in two steps, introducing breaks in the series between FYs 2000/2001 and 2001/2002 and between FYs 2002/2003 and 2003/2004. An additional difficulty in making reliable estimates of British military expenditure for the latest years is that figures for spending on un-programmed operations and conflict prevention are not available at the same time as the final figures for the main budget and thus cannot be aggregated. Un-programmed spending includes provisions for activities in Afghanistan, Bosnia and Herzegovina, Iraq and Kosovo as well as conflict prevention and has varied between £500 million and £2000 million ($816–3265 million) annually in FYs 2001/2002–2003/2004.[25] When the total costs of un-programmed operations for 2005 are eventually included, the overall decrease in spending will probably be somewhat smaller than the above figure of 5.4 per cent. The conflict in Iraq alone cost £3.1 billion ($4.8 billion) in the three years up to 31 March 2005. In FY 2004/2005, £910 million ($1402 million) was spent, which is still about £400 million ($616 million) less than spending on the conflict in FY 2003/2004. In FY 2004/2005 the forces in Afghanistan cost £67 million ($103 million) and those in the Balkans £87 million ($134 million).[26] The ongoing military campaigns also account for the rise in capital spending from 20 to 22 per cent of total spending in 2005, as they have caused an increase in the rate of replacement of equipment.

An additional factor in the rising cost of capital spending by the UK is the Future Capabilities Programme, a supplement to the 2003 Defence White Paper on modernizing and equipping the armed forces for future security challenges.[27] The programme is a costly one: in order to afford its frontline high-technology equipment, staff levels have been cut and equipment retired early. Officially, the envisaged cuts and reductions only concern personnel and equipment that are no longer needed to face current and future threats. However, the project has met criticism from those who fear it might create a

---

[25] British Ministry of Defence, 'The government's expenditure plans 2005–06 to 2006–07', Command Paper 6532, London, 27 Oct. 2005, URL <http://www.mod.uk/DefenceInternet/AboutDefence/CorporatePublications/BusinessPlans/GovernmentExpenditurePlans/>, p. 27; and Defence Analytical Service Agency, *UK Defence Statistics 2005* (Ministry of Defence: London, 2005), URL <http://www.dasa.mod.uk/natstats/ukds/2005/ukds.html>, tables 1.1 and 1.4, pp. 13, 17.

[26] 'Iraq conflict, aftermath has cost Britain 3.1 billion pounds', *Defense News*, 28 Oct. 2005, URL <http://www.defensenews.com/story.php?F=1209914>.

[27] British Ministry of Defence, 'Delivering security in a changing world: Future Capabilities', Command Paper 6269, London, July 2004, URL <http://www.mod.uk/DefenceInternet/AboutDefence/CorporatePublications/PolicyStrategy/>.

capability gap in the period before the new equipment has been delivered and put into service. A March 2005 report by the House of Commons Defence Committee emphasized that such a gap would leave the British armed forces at risk.[28] John Reid, the Secretary of State for Defence, rejected these claims in evidence given to the committee.[29]

Since 2002 France has been moving from conscription towards the goal of a fully professional force by 2008 in order to face new threats and to be able to participate fully in and lead European out-of-area military operations. The Law on Military Planning 2003–2008 provides for this transformation with annual increases in military spending and a growing share of spending devoted to procurement.[30] At the same time, France is required by the European Union (EU) Stability and Growth Pact to keep its national budget deficit below 3 per cent of GDP.[31] Several approaches have been proposed to reconcile the increase in military spending with the cap on the deficit. In June 2005 the Minister of Defence, Michèle Alliot-Marie, spoke in favour of using the military economy as a driving force for economic growth, arguing that higher defence budgets in Europe would be the boost that the stagnant European economies needed.[32] President Jacques Chirac also argued that certain types of spending, among them spending on research and development and on defence, should be exempt from the Stability and Growth Pact requirements.[33]

Both France and the UK are looking for ways to bridge the gap between requirements and available resources. Both are exploring alternative methods of paying for procurement programmes traditionally covered by the state that would shift the financial burden of current military purchases into the future.[34] Such methods have had varying degrees of success. France's public–private initiative for financing 17 frigates was cancelled in January 2005 in favour of more traditional financing from the military budget. According to Alliot-Marie, the reason for this was the high cost of using private capital for the

[28] British House of Commons Defence Committee, 'Future Capabilities: fourth report', Reports HC45-I and HC45-II, London, 17 Mar. 2005, URL <http://www.publications.parliament.uk/pa/cm200405/cmselect/cmdfence/cmdfence.htm>, p. 72; and Skinner, T., 'UK armed forces at risk of future capability gaps', *Jane's Defence Weekly*, 23 Mar. 2005, p. 4.

[29] British House of Commons Defence Committee, 'Minutes of evidence: oral evidence taken before the Defence Committee on Tuesday 1 November 2005', London, 17 Jan. 2006, URL <http://www.publications.parliament.uk/pa/cm200506/cmselect/cmdfence/556/5110101.htm>.

[30] The text of Loi no. 2003-73 du 27 janvier 2003 relative à la programmation militaire pour les années 2003 à 2008 [Law no. 2003-73 of 27 January 2003 on military planning for the years 2003 to 2008] is available at URL <http://www.legifrance.gouv.fr/WAspad/UnTexteDeJorf?numjo=DEFX0200133L/>.

[31] The Stability and Growth Pact was adopted in July 1997 to ensure budgetary discipline by the EU member states participating in Economic and Monetary Union. See URL <http://europa.eu.int/comm/economy_finance/about/activities/sgp/sgp_en.htm>.

[32] 'After French and Dutch "no" to constitutional treaty, Michèle Alliot-Marie hopes to resume initiative and reinforce defence industry in France and Europe', *Atlantic News*, 10 Jun. 2005, p. 3; and Bennhold, K., 'A French call for the EU to raise military outlays', *International Herald Tribune*, 10 June 2005, URL <http://www.iht.com/articles/2005/06/09/news/defense.php>.

[33] Agence France Press, 'France's Chirac wants exceptions under Stability Pact for some expenses', 9 Feb. 2005, Translation from French, World News Connection, National Technical Information Service (NTIS), US Department of Commerce.

[34] On the private financing of arms acquisitions see also chapters 7 and 9 in this volume.

purchase.[35] However, France has not abandoned the idea of using private funds for military procurement: a 10- to 15-year deal for helicopter flight training is being investigated as a candidate for private financing. The French Government is also looking increasingly favourably at cooperation with the UK in a privately financed project for tanker aircraft.[36]

The British Government's Private Finance Initiative (PFI) for the financing of military procurement is an attempt to reduce the current cost of equipment that is going to be in service over a very long period of time. The idea is also that the involvement of private financers will improve the efficiency of the procurement process and the timely delivery of equipment, as they will want to ensure that their investment pays off. Several projects are already running on lease contracts with private owners and financiers of military equipment.[37] Even though the British PFI system is more developed than the French one, it has been heavily criticized for inefficiency and for wasting taxpayers' money. In March 2005, the Ministry of Defence established a PFI unit to oversee the initiative. This is said to have increased efficiency and transparency as well as taxpayers' return on PFI deals. However, at the same time, two major PFI deals were cancelled in 2005, to be replaced by more traditional financing schemes.[38]

China and Japan

China and Japan rank highest in East Asia for military spending, together accounting for almost 70 per cent of the region's military expenditure. Both in real terms and as a proportion of its GDP, Japan's military spending has been largely stable over the past decade, rising by only 1.9 per cent since 1996. This stability in the level of spending together with its very significant volume— 4.9 trillion yen ($42 billion) in 2005—has acted as ballast against volatile fluctuations elsewhere in East Asia. Nonetheless, the rapid increase in China's military spending is countering this effect, and Japan's share of total East Asian military expenditure has fallen from 45 per cent in 1996 to 35 per cent in 2005.

The slight real-terms decrease in Japan's military expenditure in the past two years (by 0.8 per cent in 2004 and by 0.7 per cent in 2005) is attributable to continued financial difficulties. The trend in military spending—which has consistently been approximately 6 per cent of the national budget since 1999—follows that of the rest of Japan's budget.[39] The Japan Defense Agency (JDA) had called for a 1.5 per cent annual increase in its budget, but this was

---

[35] Lewis, J. A. C., 'France abandons private funding', *Jane's Defence Weekly*, 9 Feb. 2005, p. 27.

[36] Murphy, J., 'France looks at link-up with UK on tankers', *Jane's Defence Weekly*, 6 July 2005, p. 20.

[37] Skinner (note 28).

[38] Walker, K., 'U.K. scraps Private Finance Initiative for army training', *Defense News*, 20 June 2005, p. 4; Skinner, T., 'UK forces training stays on track', *Jane's Defence Weekly*, 29 June 2005, p. 14.

[39] Matthews, R. and Zhang, N., 'Japan faces security challenges with smaller defence budget', *Asia–Pacific Defence Reporter*, Sep. 2005, p. 41; and Japan Defense Agency (JDA), [Defense of Japan 2005] (JDA: Tokyo, 2005), URL <http://jda-clearing.jda.go.jp/hakusho_data/2005/w2005_00.html>, p. 373.

Table 8.5. Annual change in Chinese military expenditure, gross domestic product and military expenditure as a share of gross domestic product, 1996–2005

Figures for change in military expenditure and GDP are percentage change over previous year; figures for change in military expenditure as a share of GDP are percentage values for the stated year.

	1996	1997	1998	1999	2000	2001	2002	2003	2004	2005
Change in military expenditure	[10.7]	[1.3]	[14.6]	[12.2]	[9.9]	[18.0]	[17.9]	[10.7]	[10.2]	[8.8]
Change in GDP	9.6	8.8	7.8	7.1	8.0	7.5	8.3	9.5	9.5	9.0
Change in military expenditure as a share of GDP	[1.8]	[1.7]	[1.9]	[2.0]	[2.0]	[2.2]	[2.3]	[2.3]	[2.4]	. .

GDP = Gross domestic product; [ ] = Estimated figure.

Source: Appendix 8.A, tables 8A.3 and 8A.4; **GDP**: International Monetary Fund, World Economic Outlook Database, Sep. 2005, URL <http://www.imf.org/external/pubs/ft/weo/2005/02/data/>.

turned down by the Ministry of Finance, with the support of the Prime Minister, Junichiro Koizumi, because of financial constraints.[40] Instead, the government intends to reduce the planned 25.01 trillion yen ($216 billion) 2005–2009 defence build-up programme by 900 billion yen ($7.8 billion). In addition, the Ministry of Finance has insisted that the mounting costs of military transformation and the ballistic missile defence programme be borne by the JDA's reduced budget through savings from reductions in the number of troops, combat vehicles, warships and aircraft.

In contrast, China has shown a rapid and sustained boost in military spending over the past decade, with real-terms growth in excess of 10 per cent in most years. This constant increase has built up a significant 165 per cent rise in military expenditure since 1996.[41] In all but two years in the period 1996–2005, China's annual increase in military spending has outpaced its already substantial GDP growth (see table 8.5). While the increase in 2005, at 8.8 per cent, was sharp, it was not on the same scale as in the previous seven years and is less than half of the increases in 2001 and 2002. The proportion of GDP spent on the military has risen from 1.8 per cent in 1996 to 2.4 per cent in 2004—a significant increase considering China's high rate of economic growth.

China's official defence budget is not comprehensively disaggregated.[42] Public data on official provisions and spending do not, for example, include

[40] Matthews and Zhang (note 39).

[41] China revalued the yuan on 21 July 2005, pegging it to a basket of currencies rather than only the US dollar. This increased the yuan's initial rate by 2.1% against the dollar with the effect that Chinese expenditure expressed in US dollars appears slightly increased when compared to the expenditure of previous years. On international comparisons of expenditure see appendix 8E.

[42] On how SIPRI arrives at its estimate of Chinese military expenditure and how off-budget items have been evaluated see Wang, S., 'The military expenditure of China, 1989–98', *SIPRI Yearbook 1999:*

defence investment, weapon and equipment production or funds for weapon purchases abroad. Nor do they reveal expenditure by sub-national governments.[43] Further opacity is added to Chinese military expenditure by activities such as military conversion, export of arms and past commercial activities, which have generated additional off-budget funding for the PLA.[44] Nonetheless, even according to China's own admissions, the rapid increase in military expenditure is unmistakable.

China justifies its rising military expenditure by reference to its 1998–2004 Defence White Papers. According to the policy outlined there, the increase in military spending has the aim of raising the salaries of military personnel in step with the country's overall rise in per capita income and developing their social insurance.[45] The 2004 White Paper includes plans to provide additional funds to support structural and organizational reform, boosting equipment acquisition and investing in gifted personnel.[46] There are reports of hundreds of newly trained soldiers with doctoral or master's degrees, some gained abroad.[47] Keen interest in the 'revolution in military affairs' in general and in information-intensive technology and warfare in particular is evidenced in public documents, where the authorities call for 'informationization' of China's military capability.[48] In order to finance improved high-tech equipment, the PLA freed funds by reducing the army to 2.3 million troops in December 2005 from 2.5 million in 2003.[49]

The political power of the military establishment has always been influential in determining its budgetary allocation. President Hu Jintao needs to retain the loyalty of senior PLA personnel by ensuring that the military also benefits from the country's prosperity.[50] Early accelerations in China's military spending over the past decade are attributable to a major structural overhaul in funding for the military, as the PLA's profitable commercial ventures were scaled back and finally discontinued in 1998. Initially intended to supplement an inadequate defence budget, these enterprises became a source of corruption

Armaments, Disarmament and International Security (Oxford University Press: Oxford, 1999), pp. 334–49.

[43] Shambaugh, D., *Modernizing China's Military: Progress, Problems, and Prospects* (University of California Press: Berkeley, Calif., 2002), pp. 215–22; and Tsao, Y. S., 'China's defence budget: arrangement and implication', *Chinese Military Update*, vol. 2, no. 8 (May 2005), p. 5.

[44] Kondapalli, S., 'Transparency with Chinese characteristics: China's 2004 White Paper on defence', *Chinese Military Update*, vol. 2, no. 9 (2005), p. 8.

[45] E.g., Central People's Government of the People's Republic of China, [Chinese national defence], Beijing, July 1998, URL <http://www.gov.cn/zwgk/2005-05/26/content_1107.htm>, especially the subheading [Defence spending] of section 3, [Establishing defence].

[46] Central People's Government of the People's Republic of China, [2004 Chinese national defence], Beijing, Dec. 2004), URL <http://www.gov.cn/zwgk/2005-05/27/content_1540.htm>, especially section 4, [Defence spending and defence assets].

[47] Tsao (note 43), p. 7.

[48] Central People's Government of the People's Republic of China (note 46), especially section 1, [Security situation]; see also section 2, [National defence policy].

[49] 'China military "lean, responsive" after cutbacks', *International Air Letter*, 10 Jan. 2006, p. 5; Bezlova, A., 'Dragon lady Rice tackles China', Asia Times Online, 24 Mar. 2005, URL <http://www.atimes.com/atimes/China/GC24Ad05.html>; and Bezlova, A., 'China's army leaner and meaner', Asia Times Online, 25 Jan. 2006, URL <http://www.atimes.com/atimes/China/HA25Ad01.html>.

[50] Hu, T., 'Country briefing: China', *Jane's Defence Weekly*, 13 Apr. 2005, p. 25.

and a hindrance to military professionalism.[51] The banning of these activities caused a significant loss of earnings for the PLA; in response, the state raised military spending above the losses in order to boost living standards for military personnel.[52]

In addition to structural remodelling, strategic considerations play a key role in the observable trends of China's military spending. Of these, none is more prominent than the status of Taiwan. Over the period covered by the two most recent five-year plans, 1996–2005, the PLA has greatly enhanced its capabilities, especially in the areas of amphibious warfare, ballistic missile forces and information-based operations relevant to contingencies involving Taiwan.[53] In addition, the PLA's practice beach assaults and amphibious landings in mock invasions of Taiwan reinforce the perception that Taiwan is the focus of the mobilization of China's military resources.[54] This trend has been all the more pronounced since President Hu assumed the chairmanship of the Central Military Commission in 2004.[55] The Anti-Secession Law adopted in March 2005 essentially gives legislative backing to China's long-standing threat of military action in the event that Taiwan declares independence but does not present any significant de facto shift in policy.[56]

IV. Regional survey

Africa

Military expenditure in Africa rose by less than 1 per cent in 2005. However, over the 10-year period 1996–2005, military spending in the region increased by 48 per cent in real terms (see table 8.1 above). This trend was mainly determined by the spending of the four countries of North Africa—Algeria, Libya, Morocco and Tunisia, which together accounted for almost half of the increase—along with a few countries in Sub-Saharan Africa. In 2005, four countries—Algeria, Morocco, Nigeria and South Africa—accounted for 62 per cent of Africa's military spending. Angola is another big spender: its expenditure has continued to rise in spite of the end of its civil war in 2002.[57] However, inconsistencies in its expenditure figures mean that Angola is not

[51] Cheung, T. M., *China's Entrepreneurial Army* (Oxford University Press: Oxford, 2001), pp. 26–58.

[52] Cheung (note 51), p. 245; and Central People's Government of the People's Republic of China, [2000 Chinese national defence], Beijing, 16 Oct. 2000, URL <http://www.gov.cn/zwgk/2005-05/26/content_1224.htm>, especially section 3, [Establishing defence].

[53] Hu (note 50), p. 23.

[54] Shambaugh (note 43), p. 4.

[55] FitzGerald, M. C., 'China plans to control space and win the coming information war', *Armed Forces Journal*, Nov. 2005, p. 41.

[56] The text of the Anti-Secession Law, adopted at the 3rd Session of the 10th National People's Congress on 13 Mar. 2005, is available at URL <http://www.gov.cn/ziliao/flfg/2005-06/21/content_8265.htm>. An English translation is available on the website of *The People's Daily*, URL <http://english.people.com.cn/200503/14/eng20050314_176746.html>. See in particular Article 8.

[57] Economist Intelligence Unit (EIU), *Country Report: Angola* (EIU: London, Dec. 2004), p. 18. See also EIU, *Country Profile 2005: Angola* (EIU: London, 2005).

included in the SIPRI world and regional totals and the rate of increase is difficult to determine.[58]

While the rest of the continent accounts for a small proportion of regional spending, military expenditure still constitutes a great burden for many other African countries (see table 8.6). Particularly affected are countries at war, such as Burundi and the Democratic Republic of the Congo (DRC),[59] or those where war has recently ended, such as Eritrea and Ethiopia.[60] Botswana also has a relatively high military burden. This is caused by its military reform and modernization programme, which appears to be coming to an end as evidenced by the decline in spending of 19 per cent in 2005.

In contrast, the region's biggest spender, South Africa, spends a relatively modest share of its GDP on the military—1.4 per cent in 2004. This can be explained by the size of its economy, which is big enough to accommodate its military spending. Algeria and Morocco have relatively high burdens, but the governments of both countries have the resources to finance their respective military budgets. Algeria has received a boost in income from high oil prices. In Nigeria, spending increased by 14 per cent in real terms in 2005 as a result of the government's purchase of 12 combat aircraft from China.[61] The increase was also a result of the additional internal role that the military is increasingly called to play, especially in the Niger Delta area, where the armed forces have the task of protecting oil workers and installations from attacks by local dissident groups.[62] In spite of the increase, Nigerian military spending did not exceed 2 per cent of GDP in 1996–2004 and was usually nearer to 1 per cent.

Military reforms continue to be a major driver of military spending in Africa. Programmes for the professionalization of the armed forces and the modernization of equipment that began a few years ago are continuing but appear to be coming to an end in a number of countries.[63] The military reforms in both Algeria and Morocco are continuing and are responsible for the ongoing rise in Algeria's military expenditure. In contrast, spending in Morocco declined by 4.5 per cent in 2005, probably signalling an end to the rising trend that started in 1999. In Angola, spending is likely to continue to

---

[58] Both the official figures from the Angolan Government in response to a SIPRI questionnaire and those in the media indicate a rising trend, but these figures are difficult to relate to other economic data on Angola and so they are not used in SIPRI calculations.

[59] The DRC has not been included in table 8.6 because relatively reliable data on the country only started to emerge from about 2004. In 2004 the country's military expenditure was 3.0% of its GDP. On the conflict in the DRC see chapter 2 in this volume; and on peace-building efforts in Burundi, the DRC and elsewhere in Africa see chapter 3 in this volume.

[60] Eritrea has the highest defence burden in the world. See table 8A.4 in appendix 8A.

[61] 'Nigeria spends $251m for Chinese F-7 fighters after oil deals', *Defense Industry Daily*, 30 Sep. 2005, URL <http://www.defenseindustrydaily.com/2005/09/nigeria-spends-251m-for-chinese-f7-fighters-after-oil-deals/>.

[62] 'Navy acquires anti-terrorism boats', *The Guardian* (Lagos), 20 June 2005. See also 'Nigerian rebels vow new oil raids', BBC News Online, 20 Jan. 2005, URL <http://news.bbc.co.uk/1/4633644.stm>.

[63] On the changes taking place in the military sector in Africa and, in particular, the ways in which African countries budget for the military see eds Omitoogun and Hutchful (note 6). See also Williams, R., 'National defence reform and the African Union', *SIPRI Yearbook 2004: Armaments, Disarmament and International Security* (Oxford University Press: Oxford, 2004), pp. 231–50.

Table 8.6. Countries with the highest defence burdens in Africa, 1996–2004

Figures are military expenditure as a percentage of gross domestic product.

Countries	1996	1997	1998	1999	2000	2001	2002	2003	2004
Algeria	3.1	3.6	4.0	3.8	3.5	3.5	3.7	3.3	3.4
Angola	[9.0]	[10.3]	[5.2]	[9.9]	[2.2]	[1.4]	[1.6]	[2.2]	[4.2]
Botswana	3.3	3.3	4.0	4.0	3.9	3.7	4.2	4.1	[3.8]
Burundi	5.8	6.4	6.6	6.3	6.0	8.0	7.6	7.3	6.3
Eritrea	22.0	12.8	35.3	37.6	36.4	24.8	24.2	19.6	..
Ethiopia	1.8	3.4	6.7	10.7	9.6	6.2	5.5	4.4	..
Lesotho	3.0	2.8	3.1	3.7	3.6	3.0	2.7	2.6	2.3
Libya	..	4.1	5.3	3.8	3.2	2.9	2.4	2.3	2.0
Morocco	4.0	3.9	3.7	4.0	4.1	4.1	4.3	4.2	4.5
Namibia	1.9	2.3	2.3	3.2	3.4	2.8	2.9	2.9	3.1
Rwanda	5.3	4.1	4.3	4.3	3.4	3.3	2.9	2.4	2.2
Uganda	2.1	1.9	2.3	2.4	2.2	2.1	2.4	2.4	2.3
Zimbabwe	3.1	3.2	2.5	4.5	4.9	2.6	2.3	2.6	..

Source: Appendix 8A, table 8A.4.

rise until all the former rebel soldiers have been either demobilized or integrated into the national army and military debts have been repaid. In South Africa, the 1999–2010 Strategic Defence Procurement programme is progressing as planned. Conflict remains another main driver of military spending in Africa, but to a lesser extent. The rising military expenditure in Burundi and the DRC are a result of the conflicts in those countries.

Latin America and the Caribbean

Military expenditure in Latin America and the Caribbean in 2005 increased by 7.2 per cent in real terms and over the 10-year period 1996–2005 by 25.6 per cent, representing an annual average increase of 2.8 per cent. Total military spending in 2005 in the region was $24 billion (in constant 2003 dollars), which represents 2.4 per cent of world military expenditure. All three of the region's major spenders—Brazil, Chile and Colombia—are in South America, where they account for three-quarters of the sub-regional total. In Central America, Mexico alone accounts for more than 85 per cent of the sub-region's military expenditure. Among Caribbean countries, the Dominican Republic is a big spender, but data are unavailable for many countries, including Cuba. Generally, military expenditure in Latin America and the Caribbean does not constitute a very large economic burden (see table 8.7). In Chile, military spending was 3.9 per cent of GDP in 2005, the highest military burden in the region. Although Brazil's military expenditure is the highest in the region—it is more than 2.7 times larger than the second biggest spender—the size of its economy means that this represents only 1.5 per cent of its GDP.

Whereas Central American military expenditure fell by 1.3 per cent in 2005, South America's rose by 8.6, an increase largely attributable to four of the biggest spenders in the sub-region: Brazil, Chile, Colombia and Venezuela.[64] Even though Chile and Venezuela do not have the highest relative increases in Latin America and the Caribbean—Uruguay, Ecuador and Peru had the largest relative increases—their increase in real terms caught the attention of many countries in the region. It is worth bearing in mind that rises in Chile and Venezuela in 2005 were lower than their 2004 increases, which were 26 and 24 per cent, respectively. During 2005, both Chile and Venezuela were engaged in significant efforts to modernize their armed forces. In both cases, concerns have been expressed that their arms acquisitions could lead to a destabilizing arms race or result in illicit flows of weapons to armed groups. However, such fears have to some degree been allayed by formal and informal military transparency measures that have been developed in the region.[65]

As 10 per cent of export revenues from Chile's state copper company goes directly to military procurement, the increase in Chile's military budget was largely funded by rises in copper prices.[66] These funds have been used to finance an ongoing military modernization programme.[67] Chile's acquisitions are, for the most part, replacements for systems that have either been or will soon be decommissioned.[68] The purchases indicate a significant qualitative leap, particularly when compared to the armed forces of other countries in the region.[69] This modernization process is occurring at such a pace that by 2010 Chile could be the first country in Latin America to possess 'NATO-standard' military forces.[70] To a greater degree than elsewhere in the region, Chile's arms procurement process is almost entirely under the armed forces' control and takes place with little or no civilian political involvement.[71] Hence, the Chilean military is able to purchase the most advanced equipment available at times of increased copper revenue.

[64] Argentina has a larger military budget than Venezuela's, but spending in Argentina decreased by 1.6% in real terms in 2005. Venezuela is the 5th-largest spender, after Argentina.

[65] On recent arms purchases by Venezuela and the development of confidence-building measures in the region see Bromley, M. and Perdomo, C., 'CBMs in Latin America and the effect of arms acquisitions by Venezuela', Working Paper no. 41/2005, Real Instituto Elcarno, 22 Sep. 2005, URL <http://www.realinstitutoelcano.org/documentos/216.asp>. See also Rosas, M., 'Latin America and the Caribbean: security and defence in the post-cold war era', *SIPRI Yearbook 2005* (note 11), pp. 251–82.

[66] According to the Ley Reservada del Cobre [Restricted law on copper], Law no. 13 196 of 29 Oct. 1958 (most recently modified in 1987), 10% of total revenue from copper exports is set aside to finance military acquisitions.

[67] 'Chile's first F-16 rolled out', *Defense News*, 25 Apr. 2005, p. 26; Hewson, R., 'Chile bolsters fighter force', *Jane's Defence Weekly*, 5 May 2004, p. 31; and Higuera, J., 'Chile's rise in copper fortunes allows arms buys', *Jane's Defence Weekly*, 18 May 2005, p. 8.

[68] E.g., Scorpene submarines will replace two Oberon Class submarines commissioned in 1976 and planned helicopter purchases will replace ageing Puma, Lama and MD-530F systems. Higuera (note 67); and Agüera, M., 'Chilean sub order sees 1st delivery', DefenseNews.com, 12 June 2005.

[69] Osacar, I., 'Los Leopard II de Chile y el equilibrio regional' [Chile's Leopard II and the regional balance], *Nueva Mayoría*, 17 Jan. 2006, URL <http://www.nuevamayoria.com/ES/INVESTI GACIONES/defensa/060117.html>.

[70] Gonzalez Cabrera, P., 'Chilean military plans to be NATO-standard force by 2010', *El Mercurio*, 18 July 2005, Translation from Spanish, Forecast International Inc., Market Alert News Center.

[71] Rojas Aravena, F., 'Chile', ed. R. P. Singh, SIPRI, *Arms Procurement Decision Making*, vol. 2, *Chile, Greece, Malaysia, Poland, South Africa and Taiwan* (Oxford University Press: Oxford, 2000), p. 17.

Table 8.7. Military expenditure in Latin America and the Caribbean, 2002–2005

Figures for military expenditure and military expenditure per capita are in US$, at constant (2003) prices and exchange rates.

	Military expenditure ($ b.)				Military expenditure as share of GDP (%)			Military expenditure per capita ($)		
	2002	2003	2004	2005	2002	2003	2004	2002	2003	2004
Caribbean*a*	..	..	..	..	..	..	..	..	..	..
Central America	3.5	3.4	3.2	3.2	*0.5*	*0.5*	*0.4*	25.1	24.1	22.4
South America	20.4	18.3	18.9	20.6	*2.1*	*1.9*	*1.8*	56.8	50.3	51.3
Total	**24.2**	**21.9**	**22.3**	**23.9**	*1.5*	*1.3*	*1.2*	**47.2**	**42.2**	**42.3**

a There are insufficient data for the Caribbean to calculate regional totals.

Sources: Appendix 8A, tables 8A.2 and 8A.4; **Population**: International Monetary Fund, *International Financial Statistics* database.

The large increases in Chilean military expenditure have caused some concern in the region, particularly from neighbouring Peru.[72] This was one of the reasons behind Peru's adoption in December 2004 of a law to create an acquisition, modernization and repair fund for the country's defence equipment.[73] This fund will be financed by 40 per cent of the revenues of the gas production company Camisea, plus any interest accrued.[74] This law is similar to Chile's Copper Law with the significant difference that a committee with representatives of different ministries, including the Ministry of Defence, and the president will administer the fund. Even though this law is less secretive than Chile's Copper Law, it drastically reduces the level of transparency in Peru's military budgetary process. The comptroller-general will supervise the correct use of the fund, while the Peruvian Parliament will have no say in the acquisitions. In addition, the exact amount of money allocated to this fund will be difficult to track, since the fund is to be kept in an account separate from that for defence.

Rising government revenues are also supporting growing military expenditure in Venezuela, in this case resulting from rises in international oil prices. In Latin America, Venezuela had the fourth highest increase in relative terms in 2005—12.4 per cent—and the third largest in constant dollar terms, after Brazil and Chile. In 2005 the Venezuelan Government announced a new strategic plan for the 'integral defence' of the country. The new defence strategy has three features: 'Strengthening the country's military apparatus', 'Strengthening the civic–military union' and 'Increasing the people's participation in

---

[72] 'Peru: government unhappy over Chilean arms purchases', *Latinnews Daily*, 18 Apr. 2005; and Osacar (note 69).

[73] The text of the Ley que crea el Fondo para las Fuerzas Armadas y la Policía [Law creating funds for the armed forces and national police], Law no. 28 455 of 16 Dec. 2004, is available at URL <http://www.minem.gob.pe/hidrocarburos/normas_inicio.asp>.

[74] However, exceptionally, in 2005 only 20% of Camisea's revenues was allocated to the fund.

the defence of the nation'.[75] 'Strengthening the civil–military union' will involve the military taking part in civil technical, academic and social projects, the expansion of the country's military reserves from 50 000 to 100 000, and the creation of 'people's defence units'. To strengthen the military apparatus, Venezuela has signed several arms acquisition deals.[76] However, concern has been raised that some of these acquisitions will have a destabilizing effect on the regional military balance.[77] In addition, fears were expressed that the purchase of AK-103/AK-194 rifles might result in surplus weapons falling into the hands of armed groups in Colombia. The Venezuelan Government maintains that the rifles would support the newly expanded military reserves.[78]

Despite Chile's and Venezuela's large procurement deals, there is little sign of the emergence of competitive arms acquisitions in the region. To a certain extent, this is attributable to the range of formal and informal confidence-building measures developed in Latin America and the Caribbean.[79]

Asia and Oceania

The military expenditure of Asia and Oceania rose by 3.5 per cent in real terms in 2005, showing a slight sign of levelling off in comparison to its increases of 5.2 per cent in 2004 and 4.1 per cent in 2003. The region's military spending has increased by 35.3 per cent in real terms over the past decade, with a noticeable slowdown during the Asian financial crisis in 1997 and 1998 when spending rose by only 1.8 and 1.2 per cent, respectively (see table 8.1 above). The trends in Asia and Oceania's military expenditure are heavily influenced by the major regional powers, China, Japan and India, as together these three countries spent 66 per cent of the region's military expenditure in 2005. Their total spending has risen by 4.5 per cent since 2004 and by over 50 per cent since 1996.[80]

While East Asia's military expenditure stagnated in the wake of the financial crisis in 1997–98, that of South Asia, buoyed by India's high spending

[75] 'Venezuela: Chávez plans for "integral defence"', *Latin American Security & Strategic Review*, Feb. 2005, URL <http://www.latinnews.com/lss/LSS5626.asp>, pp. 6–7.

[76] The acquisitions include Super Tucano light attack aircraft, Russian helicopters, transport and surveillance C-295 aircraft, patrol boats and corvettes, and a number of AK-103/AK-194 assault rifles. Forero, J., 'Arms buying by Venezuela worries U.S.', *New York Times*, 15 Feb. 2005, p. 14; ITAR-TASS, 'Russia to supply military helicopters to Venezuela', 11 June 2005, Translation from Russian, BBC Monitoring International Reports; Agüera, M., 'Spain draws fire for sale of material to Venezuela', *Defence News*, 25 Apr. 2005, p. 13; and Gentile, C., 'Venezuela formalizes Russian arms deal', ISN Security Watch, 20 May 2005, URL <http://www.isn.ethz.ch/news/sw/details.cfm?id=11325>.

[77] Webb-Vidal, A., 'Chávez goes shopping for guns and MIGs as Colombia looks on nervously', *Financial Times*, 30 Nov. 2004.

[78] McDermott, J., 'Venezuela eyes Russian arms', *Jane's Defence Weekly*, 8 Dec. 2004, p. 6; and 'Venezuela: Chávez plans for "integral defence"' (note 75). See also Bromley and Perdomo (note 65).

[79] E.g., the 1999 Inter-American Convention on Transparency in Conventional Weapons Acquisitions and the 1997 Inter-American Convention against the Illicit Manufacturing of and Trafficking in Firearms, Ammunition, Explosives, and Other Related Materials. On these conventions see annex A in this volume. On regional reporting systems see appendix 8D.

[80] Caution should be taken when considering India's military expenditure, as lack of transparency in its nuclear programme means that its defence spending figures are underreported.

figures, did not. India's spending has increased by 82.8 per cent since 1996, with a peak increase of 16.2 per cent in 2004. At a total of 1025 billion rupees ($20.4 billion) in 2005, India's military spending is 81.7 per cent of South Asia's total. The rise in India's military expenditure is, to some extent, a reflection of the country's economic prosperity.[81] It also reflects drives to strengthen the military as an element in shaping foreign policy and to establish India as a regional power by modernizing its arsenal.[82] However, the 2005 increase in the defence budget was curbed owing to pressure from India's communist parties to invest in development projects instead and, according to senior Ministry of Defence officials, in reaction to peace initiatives with both China and Pakistan.[83]

Although still very modest in comparison, neighbouring Nepal's military spending over the past decade has shown the most dramatic rise in South Asia: it has more than tripled in real terms since 1996. One reason is the expansion of the army since 2001 in response to its failure to make inroads against Maoist rebel groups.[84] The Royal Nepalese Army almost doubled in size in 2001–2005.[85] The 6.7 per cent rise in military spending in 2005 is attributable to Kathmandu's efforts to further bolster its offensive against the rebels.[86]

The largest part of Asia and Oceania's military expenditure was accounted for by the sub-region East Asia, with 69.4 per cent of the regional total. This is largely because of the spending of China and Japan (see section III above). South Korea, Asia's fourth biggest spender, increased its military expenditure by 7.2 per cent in 2005, as the country is expediting its military build-up plans in response to US force reductions on the Korean peninsula. The USA is planning to reduce its presence in South Korea from 37 500 troops in early 2004 to 25 000 by 2008.[87] In the face of this redeployment, President Roh Moo-hyun has expressed his ambition for a greater self-defence capability and has pushed for an increase in the military budget.[88]

After Taiwan's military spending peaked in 1997 at $9.0 billion, when the acquisition of major weapons platforms was completed, there was an overall

[81] 'India', *Asian Defence Yearbook 2005* (Syed Hussain Publications: Kuala Lumpur, 2005), p. 40.

[82] 'India's military spending up 7.8%', *Asian Defence Journal*, Mar. 2005, p. 66; Raghhuvanshi, V., 'Indian budget includes shipyard upgrade funds', *Defense News*, 21 Mar. 2005, p. 24; and Schaffer, T. C. and Mitra, P., 'India as a global power?', Deutsche Bank Research, Frankfurt am Main, 16 Dec. 2005, URL <http://www.dbresearch.com/servlet/reweb2.ReWEB?rwkey=u1067110>, p. 16.

[83] Bedi, R., 'Indian budget shows "modest" rise', *Jane's Defence Weekly*, 9 Mar. 2005, p. 15.

[84] Mehta, A. K. and Kanwal, G., 'Nepalese military gears up to counter escalating insurgency', *Jane's Intelligence Review*, vol. 17, no. 9 (Sep. 2005), pp. 31–33.

[85] Davis, A., 'Nepal buys ammunition from China, Pakistan', *Jane's Defence Weekly*, 5 Oct. 2005, p. 12.

[86] Sharma, S., 'Big rise in Nepal defence budget', BBC News Online, 14 Jan. 2005, URL <http://news.bbc.co.uk/2/4174269.stm>.

[87] 'Seoul to raise defence budget', *Asian Defence Journal*, June 2005, p. 60.

[88] Baker, R. W. and Morrison, C. E. (eds), 'Republic of Korea', *Asia Pacific Security Outlook 2005* (Japan Center for International Exchange: Tokyo, 2005), p. 104–11, and National Institute for Defense Studies, 'The Korean Peninsula: changing security environments', *East Asian Strategic Review 2005* (Japan Times: Tokyo, 2005), pp. 79–82.

downward trend until 2003, when spending began to rise again.[89] Military expenditure peaked again in 2004, when it was a significant 9.9 per cent above its 2002 low, but fell in 2005 by 2.3 per cent. The economic slump over the past decade has influenced Taiwan's military budget, which has had to compete with other economic and social priorities.[90] The Taiwanese Government has been pushing for the purchase of a $16 billion package of advanced weapons from the USA through a special budget (rather than through the ordinary military budget), but the Procedure Committee of the opposition-dominated Taiwanese Parliament has repeatedly turned down the proposal.[91] The arms package has been a contentious issue in both Taiwan and mainland China since US President Bush agreed to it in 2001, but it returned to prominence when China's adoption of the Anti-Secession Law in March 2005 rekindled the debate in Taiwan on the need for greater defence capabilities. However, the opposition parties, courted by the mainland, have warned against joining an arms race with China which some have characterized as being lost in advance.[92]

Both East and South Asia were severely affected by the Indian Ocean tsunami in December 2004, in which some 230 000 people died.[93] In addition to the human and material loss, the tsunami destroyed army camps in Sri Lanka and caused great damage to the Royal Thai Navy and a key Indian Air Force base in the Nicobar Islands.[94] Nonetheless, this natural catastrophe has not yet had any obvious or significant effect on military spending in Asia, whether in the reallocation of funds for relief work or in creating major defence programmes aimed at countering the consequences of such disasters.

Trends in the military spending of Oceania are determined by Australia, since it accounts for 92.0 per cent of the sub-region's military expenditure. In its 2000 Defence White Paper, the Australian Government committed itself to a 3 per cent real-terms annual increase in military spending for 10 years in order to keep up with personnel and operating costs, invest in new capabilities and increase readiness.[95] While substantial, this planned rise was overtaken by Australia's reactions to the new terrorism-centred security agenda after 2001 and the decision to support the US-led operations in Afghanistan and Iraq. Actual military spending rose by over 5 per cent in 2002 and 2004, and by nearly 4 per cent in 2001 and 2003, before settling back to a 3.1 per cent rise in 2005. Some of the funds have gone towards large increases in the intelli-

---

[89] Australian Defence Intelligence Organisation, *Defence Economic Trends in the Asia–Pacific 2000* (Defence Publishing Services: Canberra, 2000), p. 36.

[90] Chase, M. S., 'Defense reform in Taiwan: problems and prospects', *Asian Survey*, vol. 45, no. 3 (May/June 2005), p. 372.

[91] 'Taiwan and America: still waiting', *The Economist*, 6 Oct. 2005.

[92] E.g., 'Ma fears "confrontation" with China', *China Post*, 22 Mar. 2006, URL <http://www.china post.com.tw/i_latestdetail.asp?id=36632>.

[93] 'Asia's tsunami: relief but little rebuilding', *The Economist*, 20 Dec. 2005, URL <http://www.economist.com/displaystory.cfm?story_id=5327849>.

[94] Karniol, R., 'Indian Ocean militaries survey tsunami damage', *Jane's Defence Weekly*, 12 Jan. 2005, p. 4.

[95] Australian Department of Defence, *Defence 2000: Our Future Defence Force* (Commonwealth of Australia: Canberra, 2000), URL <http://www.defence.gov.au/whitepaper/>, pp. 119–21.

gence budget.[96] The Australian Defence Force's sustained deployment has depreciated its hardware and driven up replacement and maintenance costs, while the price of 'state of the art' military equipment has kept rising. Added to this, personnel and operating costs have continued to rise at rates that exceed inflation.[97]

Europe

Military expenditure in Europe decreased by 1.7 per cent in 2005, returning to 2003 levels (see table 8.1 above). This is the result of two contrasting developments: first, a steady increase in Russian military expenditure, and second, a major reduction in that of the other major European powers. With the exception of Russia, all those European states which figure among the world's 15 biggest spenders—France, Germany, Italy, Spain and the UK—reduced their spending in 2005, by a total of $7854 million. Repeating the pattern witnessed in 2004, military expenditure decreased in the sub-regions Central and Western Europe and increased in Eastern Europe. An interesting contrast can be seen between the old and new NATO members. Of the 17 pre-2004 European NATO members, seven increased their spending, nine decreased theirs and one, Iceland, has no military forces of its own. Of the seven states that joined NATO in 2004, six increased their military spending.

In several speeches and interviews in 2005, the NATO Secretary General, Jaap de Hoop Scheffer, cautioned the European allies against continuing the general downward trend in their defence budgets, encouraging them to spend more on converting old-fashioned territorial defence capabilities to more mobile and easily deployable forces. In a statement to NATO defence ministers in September 2005 he also suggested that the member states should increase the number of jointly funded operational activities in order to better share the cost burden and not dissuade any member from contributing troops on the basis of economic cost.[98]

In contrast to France (see section III above), both Germany and Italy have accepted the consequences of their large budget deficits and stagnant economies and have adhered to the rules of the EU Stability and Growth Pact. Hence, to the dismay of de Hoop Scheffer among others, they reduced their military expenditure in 2005. Italy's 10.4 per cent real-terms reduction in 2005 took its military expenditure below 2 per cent of GDP. With over 10 000 Ital-

---

[96] Thomson, M., *Pay Your Money & Take Your Pick: Defence Spending Choices for Australia* (Australian Strategic Policy Institute: Canberra, Dec. 2003), URL <http://www.aspi.org.au/22845pay money/>, p. 8; and Thomson, M., *Your Defence Dollar: The 2004–05 Defence Budget* (Australian Strategic Policy Institute: Canberra, July 2004), URL <http://www.aspi.org.au/17867defence_dollar/>, p. 7.

[97] Australian Department of Defence, *Australia's National Security: A Defence Update 2005* (Commonwealth of Australia: Canberra, 2005), URL <http://www.defence.gov.au/update2005/>, p. 25.

[98] See, e.g., 'A transforming alliance', Speech by NATO Secretary General Jaap de Hoop Scheffer at the NATO Parliamentary Assembly Spring Session Ljubljana, Slovenia, 31 May 2005, URL <http://www.nato.int/docu/speech/2005/s050531b.htm>; Baughman, A., 'Interview: Gisbert (Jaap) de Hoop Scheffer, NATO Secretary General', *Jane's Defence Weekly*, 30 Mar. 2005, p. 34; and 'Joint press point by NATO Secretary General, Jaap de Hoop Scheffer and the German Defence Minister, Peter Struck', Berlin, 13 Sep. 2005, URL <http://www.nato.int/docu/speech/2005/s050913e.htm>.

ian personnel stationed abroad, there is little room for cutting operational expenditure. Consequently, the procurement budget has suffered the greatest cuts and the focus of the procurement programme has been reoriented towards army needs, as required for the troops deployed in Afghanistan and Iraq.[99] Germany, having gone through major economic restructuring in order to tackle its huge budget deficit, has shown a trend of declining military expenditure for the past six years. In 2005 German military spending decreased by 2.3 per cent, contributing to the 10.6 per cent overall fall since 1996. At the same time, the German armed forces have been undergoing reforms as well as having been deployed to Afghanistan, their first combat mission on foreign soil since World War II.

Russia, by far the biggest spender in Eastern Europe, increased its military spending by 8.8 per cent in real terms in 2005, continuing a trend that began in 1998. At the presentation of the 2005 budget, the Minister of Defence, Sergei Ivanov, said that for the first time since 1991 the Russian budget fully reflected the needs of the military.[100] Since its post-cold war low in 1998, Russian military expenditure has more than doubled. However, this massive increase follows a decade-long decrease, and spending levels in 2005 were still much lower than at the end of the cold war.[101] The main driving force behind Russia's rapidly rising military expenditure has been the military reform programme aimed at boosting Russia's ability to combat terrorism, restore global power projection and consolidate influence in 'the near abroad' (i.e., the former Soviet states).[102] The procurement budget shows a growing focus on counterinsurgency and nuclear deterrence as well as an increased and transformed presence in Central Asia and the Caucasus.[103] Russia's rising oil and gas revenues have made this possible but these revenues must continue if future increases in military spending and continued military reform are to be realized.

The three Caucasian states, Armenia, Azerbaijan and Georgia, all increased their military expenditure massively in 2005. Georgia, with its 143 per cent increase, had the world's highest rate of increase in military expenditure in 2005. Azerbaijan and Armenia were also among the countries whose spending increased most in relative terms, at 51.1 and 22.5 per cent, respectively. Azerbaijan's military build-up is as much driven by the fact that it can afford it, owing to high oil and gas revenues, as by the search for greater leverage in

---

[99] Valpolini, P., 'Italian budget set for major cut', *Jane's Defence Weekly*, 26 Jan. 2005, p. 12; and Kington, T., 'Italy trims budget: frigate funds found; aircraft, vehicles delayed', DefenseNews.com, 17 Oct. 2005.

[100] Trifonov, D., 'Briefing: Russian defence reform', *Jane's Defence Weekly*, 8 June 2005, pp. 27–33.

[101] Cooper, J., 'Military expenditure in the 2005 and 2006 federal budgets of the Russian Federation', Research note, SIPRI, Stockholm, Jan. 2006, URL <http://www.sipri.org/contents/milap/cooper_russia_20060130>.

[102] Trifonov (note 100).

[103] Trifonov (note 100); ITAR-TASS, 'Defense ministry building infrastructure for 2 mountain', 15 July 2005, World News Connection, NTIS, US Department of Commerce; and Mukhin, V., 'Collective Security Treaty Organization arithmetic: military spending far exceeds the political dividends', *Nezavisimaya Gazeta*, 12 Apr. 2005, Translation from Russian, World News Connection, NTIS, US Department of Commerce.

negotiations with Armenia over disputed territories. Armenia's rising military expenditure can be seen as a direct reaction to the Azerbaijani increase. Georgia is building a new, smaller and more mobile force with help from Turkey and the USA at the same time as it is establishing a new reserve force. The official explanation for the huge increase in Georgian military expenditure is the country's wish to join NATO and the consequent need to bring its armed forces up to NATO standards. Others argue that the ultimate objective is to regain control over the renegade regions of Abkhazia and South Ossetia over which tension with Russia grew dramatically in late 2005.[104]

The Middle East

Military expenditure in the Middle East increased by 7 per cent in real terms in 2005. This represents a continuation of the trend of the past 10 years, during which the only decline was in 2002 (see table 8.1 above). In the 10-year period 1996–2005, military spending in the region increased by 61 per cent in real terms. For a region that is rich in oil, the increase in 2005 was modest given the unusually high and sustained oil prices throughout the year.

With relatively static—and in many cases decreasing—levels of military expenditure in almost all Middle Eastern countries, the region's increase is almost wholly attributable to Saudi Arabia, the Middle East's biggest spender—in 2005 its military expenditure increased by $4.6 billion (or 21 per cent) in constant dollar terms while the region's total spending increased by $4.1 billion. While Saudi Arabia's increase in 2005 is very high, it is below the country's record 36 per cent increase of 1997 and was restrained by the need to focus on mounting internal social problems and huge debts.[105] Unemployment has increased among Saudi Arabia's growing youth population and debts, resulting from previous budget deficits, stood at 100 per cent of GDP by 2000.[106] The windfall from oil has therefore been primarily directed at paying off debts, improving social welfare, including raising civil servants' salaries across the board for the first time in 20 years, and creating employment opportunities for the estimated 20 per cent of its population that is unemployed.[107] Nevertheless, the increased focus of the Saudi Government on internal security in the aftermath of terrorist attacks, and the plan to build an industry that would produce spare parts for the Saudi military and other security forces,[108] ensured that the defence and security sector still received a big, if not the lion's, share of the budget. Kuwait faced fewer internal problems than Saudi Arabia and, in spite of the oil windfall, its military expend-

---

[104] Fuller, L. and Giragosian, R., 'Why should Georgia need a larger army?', *RFE/RL Caucasus Report*, 24 July 2005, URL <http://www.rferl.org/reports/caucasus-report/archive2005.asp>.

[105] 'Saudi Arabia expects budget surplus to double in 2005', Gulfnews.com, 13 Dec. 2005, URL <http://archive.gulfnews.com/articles/05/12/13/10004468.html>.

[106] 'Oil producers' surpluses: recycling the petrodollars', *The Economist*, 10 Nov. 2005, URL <http://www.economist.com/displayStory.cfm?story_id=5136281>.

[107] 'Oil producers' surpluses' (note 106).

[108] Middle East Newsline, 'Saudi Arabia seeks to develop arms industry', Independent Media Review Analysis, 4 Jan. 2006, URL <http://www.imra.org.il/story.php3?id=28055>.

iture increased modestly, by only 0.5 per cent in 2005. This followed a 13 per cent rise in 2004.

Military expenditure in Iran increased by 3.9 per cent in 2005.[109] This was a modest rise in comparison to the rises of 17.3 and 14.9 per cent in 2003 and 2004, respectively. The increase in 2005 was against the background of mounting international pressure on the country over its nuclear programme.[110] While there is little information linking the rise in spending to either the tension or the nuclear programme itself, there are indications that the trend will continue following the assurance given by President Mahmoud Ahmadinejad to Iran's parliamentary Committee on Security and Defence that he would increase spending on defence.[111]

In contrast to the increased spending in the oil-producing states, the official military expenditure of Israel declined by 5 per cent in 2005, after a 3 per cent increase in 2004. However, the decline in the Israeli military expenditure figure has been queried by the State Comptroller, who criticized the government for submitting defence budgets with reduced spending to the Israeli Parliament while implementing an entirely different budget with increased expenditure.[112] In 2004, for instance, there was a divergence of 10.3 per cent between official expenditure figures and the amount actually spent.[113] The same may be the case for 2005, when expenditure was reported to exceed the approved sum because of the costs of disengagement from occupied territories and the upgrading of the barrier along the border with the Gaza Strip.[114] Indications are that these two programmes will lead to increased military expenditure in 2006. This is in contrast to the general reduction in spending which is envisaged for the rest of the budget unless the USA provides financial support for the disengagement plan which is now estimated at 8 billion shekels ($1.7 billion).[115] Israel receives military assistance from the USA amounting to about $2.2 billion annually and this constitutes part of the country's total military expenditure. Egypt receives about $1.8 billion annually in military assistance from the USA. Owing to lack of transparency in Egyptian military expenditure, the extent to which this is included in the country's officially reported military expenditure is unknown.

[109] SIPRI's military expenditure data for Iran include spending on public order and safety (internal security).

[110] Kendall, B., 'Diplomatic furore at Iran remarks', BBC News Online, 27 Oct. 2005, URL <http://news.bbc.co.uk/1/4383856.stm>. See also Kile, S. N. (ed.), *Europe and Iran: Perspectives on Non-proliferation*, SIPRI Research Report no. 21 (Oxford University Press: Oxford, 2005).

[111] 'Iran MP says 2006–7 budget does not fully meet defence sector needs', *Aftab-e Yazd*, 29 Jan. 2005, Translation from Farsi, World News Connection, NTIS, US Department of Commerce.

[112] O'Sullivan, A., 'State Comptroller reveals shadow defense funding', *Jerusalem Post*, 1 Sep. 2005, p. 1.

[113] O'Sullivan (note 112).

[114] Klein, Z., 'Defense spending rose to 25% of all gov't spending in July', *Rishon Leziyyon Globes* (online), 4 Aug. 2005.

[115] Klein, Z., 'Budget cut will total NIS 3.6', *Rishon Leziyyon Globes* (online), 2 Aug. 2005.

V. Conclusions

World military expenditure increased again in 2005, continuing an unbroken upward trend since 1999. The USA is responsible for a sizeable proportion of this increasing trend, with the result that US expenditure in 2005 accounts for almost half the world total and is 10 times higher than that of the UK, the second biggest spender. The process of concentration in military expenditure also continued in 2005, with an increasing proportion of world military spending attributable to the 15 biggest spenders. Most of these are industrialized countries, but China and India are also among the top spenders following a continued increase in expenditure in line with their growing economic power.

A salient factor that has facilitated the upward trend in military expenditure is the high and rising world market prices of minerals and fossil fuels. This is especially the case for Algeria, Azerbaijan, Russia and Saudi Arabia, where increased proceeds from oil and gas exploitation have boosted government revenues and freed up funds for military spending. The boost in the military expenditure of Peru and Chile is directly resource driven, as their military spending is linked by law to profits from the exploitation of key natural resources.

Just as world military expenditure is not evenly distributed, different countries and regions also contributed differently to the increase in world total military expenditure in 2005. In the Middle East, the increase in Saudi Arabia single-handedly raised overall spending in a region that would otherwise have shown a fall in military expenditure. Although Europe is a major spender on the world stage, rather than contributing to the global increase in military expenditure, the region actually reduced military spending in 2005. Tentative moves by France and the UK to solicit private funding for military procurement are having the effect of deferring spending.

Looking ahead, increasing trends in world military expenditure show little sign of abating in the near future. The observable increase in global spending depends to a large extent on the USA's costly military operations in Afghanistan and Iraq that are still far from conclusion. Added to that, the continued rapid economic growth of China and India that has sustained their rising military spending and their drive toward military modernization over the past decade is likely to continue unimpeded at least in the short term. For France and the UK, the dip in military spending in 2005 has been an aberration in their current trends, as they are engaged in an ongoing modernization programme based on future increases in military expenditure. In these circumstances, there is a strong likelihood that the current upward trend in world military spending will be sustained in 2006.

Appendix 8A. Tables of military expenditure

PETTER STÅLENHEIM, DAMIEN FRUCHART,
WUYI OMITOOGUN and CATALINA PERDOMO*

Table 8A.1 presents military expenditure by region, by certain international organizations and by income group for the period 1996–2005 in US dollars at constant 2003 prices and exchange rates, and also for 2005 in current US dollars. Military expenditure by individual countries is presented in table 8A.2 in local currency and at current prices for the period 1996–2005 and in table 8A.3 in US dollars at constant 2003 prices and exchange rates for the period 1996–2005 and for 2005 in current US dollars. Table 8A.4 presents military expenditure for the period 1996–2004 as a percentage of countries' gross domestic product. Sources and methods are explained in appendix 8C. Notes and explanations of the conventions used appear below table 8A.4.

Military expenditure data from different editions of the SIPRI Yearbook should not be combined because of data revision between editions. Revision can be significant; for example, when a better time series becomes available the entire SIPRI series is revised accordingly. Revisions in constant dollar series can also originate in significant revisions in the economic statistics of the International Monetary Fund that are used for these calculations. When data are presented in local currency but not in US dollars or as a share of GDP, this is owing to a lack of economic data.

* Contribution of military expenditure data, estimates and advice are gratefully acknowledged from Julian Cooper (Centre for Russian and East European Studies, University of Birmingham), David Darchiashvili (Center for Civil–Military Relations and Security Studies, Tbilisi), Dimitar Dimitrov (University of National and World Economy, Sofia), Paul Dunne (University of the West of England, Bristol), Armen Kouyoumdjian (Country Risk Strategist, Valparaiso), Pavan Kumar Nair (India Together, Pune), Elina Noor (Institute of Strategic and International Studies, Kuala Lumpur), Tamara Pataraia (Caucasus Institute for Peace, Democracy and Development, Tbilisi), Jamie Polanco (Ministry of National Defence, Bogotá), Thomas Scheetz (Lincoln University College, Buenos Aires), Ron Smith (Birkbeck College, London) and Ozren Zunec (University of Zagreb).
SIPRI Intern Anna Ritter assisted with the preparation of this appendix.

Table 8A.1. Military expenditure by region, by international organization and by income group, in constant US dollars for 1996–2005 and current US dollars for 2005

Figures are in US$ b., at constant 2003 prices and exchange rates except in the right-most column, marked *, where they are in current US$ b. Figures do not always add up to totals because of the conventions of rounding.

	1996	1997	1998	1999	2000	2001	2002	2003	2004	2005	2005*
World total	**747**	**756**	**748**	**757**	**784**	**800**	**851**	**914**	**969**	**1 001**	**1 118**
Geographical regions											
Africa	8.6	8.7	9.4	10.5	11.1	11.1	12.1	11.9	12.6	12.7	14.9
North Africa	3.5	3.7	3.8	3.9	4.3	4.4	4.8	5.0	5.6	5.5	6.1
Sub-Saharan Africa	5.1	5.0	5.6	6.6	6.8	6.6	7.3	6.9	(7.0)	(7.2)	(8.8)
Americas	347	347	340	341	353	358	399	447	485	513	551
Caribbean	:	:	:	:	:	:	:	:	:	:	:
Central America	3.3	3.4	3.3	3.5	3.6	3.7	3.5	3.4	3.2	3.2	3.5
North America	328	326	319	320	332	335	375	425	463	489	520
South America	15.7	18.1	17.5	17.1	17.8	19.9	20.4	18.3	18.9	20.6	27.4
Asia and Oceania	116	118	119	122	126	132	138	144	152	157	176
Central Asia	0.5	0.5	(0.5)	0.5	:	(0.6)	(0.6)	(0.7)	(0.7)	(0.8)	(1.0)
East Asia	91.0	91.9	92.4	92.9	95.5	101	107	112	116	120	132
Oceania	8.6	8.8	9.1	9.6	9.5	9.9	10.3	10.6	11.1	11.5	14.4
South Asia	15.5	16.5	17.1	19.2	19.9	20.5	20.6	21.2	23.9	25.0	28.8
Europe	236	239	234	238	243	243	249	256	260	256	308
Central Europe	11.6	11.7	11.7	11.4	11.5	12.1	12.3	12.8	12.7	11.7	16.2
Eastern Europe	15.6	17.5	11.5	11.9	15.8	17.3	19.1	20.4	21.4	23.3	31.8
Western Europe	209	210	210	214	215	214	218	223	226	220	260
Middle East	39.0	43.4	46.5	45.8	51.5	55.0	52.6	55.0	58.9	(63.0)	(67.3)

Organizations

ASEAN	12.1	12.0	11.0	11.0	11.1	11.7	12.4	13.3	13.3	13.1	14.0
CIS	16.1	18.1	12.0	12.4	16.4	17.9	19.7	21.1	22.1	24.1	32.8
European Union	191	191	191	195	196	196	199	206	219	212	251
NATO	525	521	515	527	539	541	585	642	687	706	779
NATO Europe	197	196	196	207	207	207	211	217	224	217	259
OECD	609	608	601	607	622	625	670	727	768	789	873
OPEC	27.1	31.9	33.7	32.4	37.1	39.6	36.3	38.0	42.0	46.7	49.6
OSCE	564	564	552	557	575	579	624	682	724	745	829

Income group (by 2003 gross national income per capita)

Low (≤$765)	18.0	19.3	20.5	23.8	24.3	24.6	25.4	25.6	28.3	29.5	34.1
Lower middle ($766–$3035)	76.4	80.8	76.5	79.9	90.5	99.0	105	109	114	122	148
Upper middle ($3036–$9385)	34.5	39.8	41.6	40.2	42.2	45.2	42.5	43.9	46.7	51.0	55.6
High (≥$9386)	618	618	610	613	627	631	678	736	780	799	880

( ) = Total based on country data accounting for less than 90% of the regional total; [ ] = Total based on country data accounting for less than 60% of the regional total; . . = Available data account for less than 60% of the regional total; ASEAN = Association of Southeast Asian Nations; CIS = Commonwealth of Independent States; NATO = North Atlantic Treaty Organization; OECD = Organisation for Economic Co-operation and Development; OPEC = Organization of the Petroleum Exporting Countries; OSCE = Organization for Security and Co-operation in Europe.

The world total and the totals for regions, organizations and income groups in table 8A.1 are estimates, based on data in table 8A.3. When military expenditure data for a country are missing for a few years, estimates are made, most often on the assumption that the rate of change in that country's military expenditure is the same as that for the region to which it belongs. When no estimates can be made, countries are excluded from the totals. The countries excluded from all totals in table 8A.1 are Angola, Benin, Cuba, Equatorial Guinea, Haiti, Iraq, Myanmar, Qatar, Somalia, Trinidad and Tobago and Viet Nam.

Totals for geographical regions add up to the world total and sub-regional totals add up to regional totals. Totals for regions and income groups cover the same groups of countries for all years, while totals for organizations cover only the member countries in the year given.

The country coverage of income groups is based on figures of 2003 gross national income (GNI) per capita as calculated in World Bank, *World Development Report 2005: A Better Investment Climate for Everyone* (Oxford University Press: New York, 2004), URL <http://econ.worldbank.org/wdr/>.

Africa: Algeria, Angola, Benin, Botswana, Burkina Faso, Burundi, Cameroon, Cape Verde, Central African Republic, Chad, Congo (Republic of), Congo (Democratic Republic of, DRC), Côte d'Ivoire, Djibouti, Equatorial Guinea, Eritrea, Ethiopia, Gabon, Gambia, Ghana, Guinea, Guinea-Bissau, Kenya, Lesotho, Liberia, Libya, Madagascar, Malawi, Mali, Mauritania, Mauritius, Morocco, Mozambique, Namibia, Niger, Nigeria, Rwanda, Senegal, Seychelles, Sierra

Leone, Somalia, South Africa, Sudan, Swaziland, Tanzania, Togo, Tunisia, Uganda, Zambia, Zimbabwe. *Sub-Saharan Africa*: Angola, Benin, Botswana, Burkina Faso, Burundi, Cameroon, Cape Verde, Central African Republic, Chad, Congo (Republic of), Congo (Democratic Republic of DRC), Côte d'Ivoire, Djibouti, Equatorial Guinea, Eritrea, Ethiopia, Gabon, Gambia, Ghana, Guinea, Guinea-Bissau, Kenya, Lesotho, Liberia, Madagascar, Malawi, Mali, Mauritania, Mauritius, Mozambique, Namibia, Niger, Nigeria, Rwanda, Senegal, Seychelles, Sierra Leone, Somalia, South Africa, Sudan, Swaziland, Tanzania, Togo, Uganda, Zambia, Zimbabwe.

Americas: Argentina, Bahamas, Barbados, Belize, Bolivia, Brazil, Canada, Chile, Colombia, Costa Rica, Cuba, Dominican Republic, Ecuador, El Salvador, Guatemala, Guyana, Haiti, Honduras, Jamaica, Mexico, Nicaragua, Panama, Paraguay, Peru, Trinidad and Tobago, Uruguay, USA, Venezuela. *Caribbean*: Bahamas, Barbados, Cuba, Dominican Republic, Haiti, Jamaica and Trinidad and Tobago. *Central America*: Belize, Costa Rica, El Salvador, Guatemala, Honduras, Mexico, Nicaragua, Panama. *North America*: Canada, USA. *South America*: Argentina, Bolivia, Brazil, Chile, Colombia, Ecuador, Guyana, Paraguay, Peru, Uruguay, Venezuela.

Asia and Oceania: Afghanistan, Australia, Bangladesh, Brunei, Cambodia, China, Fiji, India, Indonesia, Japan, Kazakhstan, New Zealand, North Korea, South Korea, Kyrgyzstan, Laos, Malaysia, Mongolia, Myanmar (Burma), Nepal, Pakistan, Papua New Guinea, Philippines, Singapore, Sri Lanka, Taiwan, Tajikistan, Thailand, Turkmenistan, Uzbekistan, Viet Nam. *Central Asia (CIS Asia)*: Kazakhstan, Kyrgyzstan, Tajikistan, Turkmenistan, Uzbekistan. *East Asia*: Brunei, Cambodia, China, Indonesia, Japan, North Korea, South Korea, Laos, Malaysia, Mongolia, Myanmar (Burma), Philippines, Singapore, Taiwan, Thailand, Viet Nam. *South Asia*: Afghanistan, Bangladesh, India, Nepal, Pakistan, Sri Lanka. *Oceania*: Australia, Fiji, New Zealand, Papua New Guinea.

Europe: Albania, Armenia, Austria, Azerbaijan, Belarus, Belgium, Bosnia and Herzegovina, Bulgaria, Croatia, Cyprus, Czech Republic, Denmark, Estonia, Finland, France, Georgia, Germany, Greece, Hungary, Iceland, Ireland, Italy, Latvia, Lithuania, Luxembourg, Macedonia (Former Yugoslav Republic of, FYROM), Malta, Moldova, Netherlands, Norway, Poland, Portugal, Romania, Russia, Serbia and Montenegro, Slovakia, Slovenia, Spain, Sweden, Switzerland, Turkey, UK, Ukraine. *Central Europe*: Albania, Bosnia and Herzegovina, Bulgaria, Croatia, Czech Republic, Estonia, Hungary, Latvia, Lithuania, Macedonia (Former Yugoslav Republic of, FYROM), Poland, Romania, Serbia and Montenegro, Slovakia, Slovenia. *Eastern Europe (CIS Europe)*: Armenia, Azerbaijan, Belarus, Georgia, Moldova, Russia, Ukraine. *Western Europe*: Austria, Belgium, Cyprus, Denmark, Finland, France, Germany, Greece, Iceland, Ireland, Italy, Luxembourg, Malta, Netherlands, Norway, Portugal, Spain, Sweden, Switzerland, Turkey, UK.

Middle East: Bahrain, Egypt, Iran, Iraq, Israel, Jordan, Kuwait, Lebanon, Oman, Saudi Arabia, Syria, United Arab Emirates, Yemen.

ASEAN: Brunei, Cambodia (1999–), Indonesia, Laos (1997–), Malaysia, Myanmar (Burma) (1997–), Philippines, Singapore, Thailand, Viet Nam.

CIS: Armenia, Azerbaijan, Belarus, Georgia, Kazakhstan, Kyrgyzstan, Moldova, Russia, Tajikistan, Turkmenistan, Ukraine, Uzbekistan.

European Union: Austria, Belgium, Cyprus (2004–), Czech Republic (2004–), Denmark, Estonia (2004–), Finland, France, Germany, Greece, Hungary (2004–), Ireland, Italy, Latvia (2004–), Lithuania (2004–), Luxembourg, Malta (2004–), Netherlands, Poland (2004–), Portugal, Slovakia (2004–), Slovenia (2004–), Spain, Sweden, UK.

NATO: Belgium, Bulgaria (2004–), Canada, Czech Republic (1999–), Denmark, Estonia (2004–), France, Germany, Greece, Hungary (1999–), Iceland, Italy, Latvia (2004–), Lithuania (2004–), Luxembourg, Netherlands, Norway, Poland (1999–), Portugal, Romania (2004–), Slovakia (2004–), Slovenia (2004–), Spain, Turkey, UK, USA. *NATO Europe*: Belgium, Bulgaria (2004–), Czech Republic (1999–), Denmark, Estonia (2004–), France, Germany,

Greece, Hungary (1999–), Iceland, Italy, Latvia (2004–), Lithuania (2004–), Luxembourg, Netherlands, Norway, Poland (1999–), Portugal, Romania (2004–), Slovakia (2004–), Slovenia (2004–), Spain, Turkey, UK.

OECD: Australia, Austria, Belgium, Canada, Czech Republic, Denmark, Finland, France, Germany, Greece, Hungary, Iceland, Ireland, Italy, Japan, South Korea, Luxembourg, Mexico, Netherlands, New Zealand, Norway, Poland, Portugal, Slovakia (2000–), Spain, Sweden, Switzerland, Turkey, UK, USA.

OPEC: Algeria, Gabon, Indonesia, Iran, Iraq, Kuwait, Libya, Nigeria, Qatar, Saudi Arabia, United Arab Emirates, Venezuela.

OSCE: Albania, Armenia, Austria, Azerbaijan, Belarus, Belgium, Bosnia and Herzegovina, Bulgaria, Canada, Croatia, Cyprus, Czech Republic, Denmark, Estonia, Finland, France, Georgia, Germany, Greece, Hungary, Iceland, Ireland, Italy, Kazakhstan, Kyrgyzstan, Latvia, Lithuania, Luxembourg, Macedonia (Former Yugoslav Republic of, FYROM), Malta, Moldova, Netherlands, Norway, Poland, Portugal, Romania, Russia, Serbia and Montenegro (2000–), Slovakia, Slovenia, Spain, Sweden, Switzerland, Tajikistan, Turkey, Turkmenistan, UK, Ukraine, USA, Uzbekistan.

Low-income countries (GNI/capita ≤$765 in 2003): Afghanistan, Angola, Bangladesh, Benin, Burkina Faso, Burundi, Cambodia, Cameroon, Central African Republic, Chad, Congo (Republic of), Congo (Democratic Republic of, DRC), Côte d'Ivoire, Equatorial Guinea, Eritrea, Ethiopia, Gambia, Ghana, Guinea, Guinea-Bissau, Haiti, India, Kenya, North Korea, Kyrgyzstan, Laos, Lesotho, Liberia, Madagascar, Malawi, Mali, Mauritania, Moldova, Mongolia, Mozambique, Myanmar (Burma), Nepal, Nicaragua, Niger, Nigeria, Pakistan, Papua New Guinea, Rwanda, Senegal, Sierra Leone, Somalia, Sudan, Tajikistan, Tanzania, Togo, Uganda, Uzbekistan, Viet Nam, Yemen, Zambia, Zimbabwe.

Lower-middle income countries (GNI/capita: $766–$3035 in 2003): Albania, Algeria, Armenia, Azerbaijan, Belarus, Bolivia, Bosnia and Herzegovina, Brazil, Bulgaria, Cape Verde, China, Colombia, Cuba, Djibouti, Dominican Republic, Ecuador, Egypt, El Salvador, Fiji, Georgia, Guatemala, Guyana, Honduras, Indonesia, Iran, Iraq, Jamaica, Jordan, Kazakhstan, Macedonia (Former Yugoslav Republic of, FYROM), Morocco, Namibia, Paraguay, Peru, Philippines, Romania, Russia, Serbia and Montenegro, South Africa, Sri Lanka, Swaziland, Syria, Thailand, Turkey, Turkmenistan, Tunisia, Ukraine.

Upper-middle income countries (GNI/capita: $3036–$9385 in 2003): Argentina, Barbados, Belize, Botswana, Chile, Costa Rica, Croatia, Czech Republic, Estonia, Gabon, Hungary, Latvia, Lithuania, Lebanon, Libya, Malaysia, Mauritius, Mexico, Oman, Panama, Poland, Saudi Arabia, Seychelles, Slovakia, Trinidad and Tobago, Uruguay, Venezuela.

High-income countries (GNI/capita: ≥$9386 in 2003): Australia, Austria, Bahamas, Bahrain, Belgium, Brunei, Canada, Cyprus, Denmark, Finland, France, Germany, Greece, Iceland, Ireland, Israel, Italy, Japan, South Korea, Kuwait, Luxembourg, Malta, Netherlands, New Zealand, Norway, Portugal, Singapore, Slovenia, Spain, Sweden, Switzerland, Taiwan, United Arab Emirates, UK, USA.

Table 8A.2. Military expenditure by country, in local currency, 1996–2005

Figures are in local currency at current prices and are for calendar years, unless stated otherwise.

Country	Currency	1996	1997	1998	1999	2000	2001	2002	2003	2004	2005
Africa											
North Africa											
Algeria‡	m. dinars	79 519	101 126	112 248	121 597	141 576	149 468	167 000	170 764	201 929	210 000
Libya	m. dinars	. .	577	675	535	556	496	575	700	740	. .
Morocco[1]	m. dirhams	12 890	12 476	12 666	13 921	14 639	15 643	16 994	17 722	20 134	19 606
Tunisia	m. dinars	387	396	417	424	456	483	491	525	540	555
Sub-Saharan Africa											
Angola[2]	b. kwanzas	[0.1]	[0.2]	[0.1]	[1.7]	[2.0]	[2.8]	[7.5]	[22.2]	[66.4]	[144]
Benin	m. CFA francs	. .	. .	. .	. .	. .	. .	. .	. .	. .	. .
Botswana	m. pula	467	586	808	855	974	1 055	1 325	1 482	[1 504]	[1 310]
Burkina Faso	m. CFA francs	19 000	22 500	23 300	25 700	26 100	27 000	33 400	31 960	34 700	40 173
Burundi§	m. francs	15 408	21 800	26 300	28 500	30 500	44 200	44 200	47 000	47 300	51.8
Cameroon§	m. CFA francs	59 819	69 288	80 969	89 095	87 598	91 118	101 500	109 556	116 808	117 670
Cape Verde	m. escudos	352	382	443	518	814	572	530	554	586	. .
Central Afr. Rep.[3]	m. CFA francs	6 239	. .	. .	. .	. .	. .	7 445	8 729	7 979	8 121
Chad	m. CFA francs	12 681	9 700	9 500	12 900	15 200	18 200	19 300	22 700	23 800	26 000
Congo, Republic of	m. CFA francs	. .	. .	. .	. .	. .	. .	. .	28 374	. .	. .
Congo, DRC[4]	m./b. francs	44.8	110	42.8	600	2 901	. .	. .	48.0	78.0	71.0
Côte d'Ivoire	b. CFA francs	52.5	54.6	. .	. .	. .	. .	. .	124	. .	. .
Djibouti	m. francs	3 712	4 019	4 042	4 053	3 979	4 045	4 500	. .	. .	. .
Equatorial Guinea	m. CFA francs	. .	. .	. .	. .	. .	. .	. .	. .	. .	. .
Eritrea[5]	m. nakfa	968	634	1 936	2 225	2 220	1 884	2 104	2 020	. .	. .
Ethiopia[6]	m. birr	803	1 512	3 263	5 589	5 075	3 154	3 000	3 000	3 000	3 000
Gabon	b. CFA francs	. .	. .	. .	. .	. .	66.0	66.0	63.0	62.0	61.0
Gambia‡	m. dalasis	38.5	42.6	43.1	40.1	42.5	44.6	44.6	45.0	45.1	45.3
Ghana§	m. cedis	72 644	93 148	132 812	158 060	277 269	231 740	297 800	439 200	636 097	726 111

Guinea	m. francs	..	48 600	55 700	76 600	80 300	171 100	185 000	..	..	..
Guinea-Bissau[7]	m. CFA francs	770	1 061	1 711	..	6 786	4 533	..	..	..	..
Kenya	m. shillings	9 756	10 327	10 381	10 684	12 614	15 349	16 844	18 676	20 158	20 632
Lesotho	m. maloti	122	132	154	208	212	201	206	221	218	217
Liberia	m. dollars	..	..	..	..	..	(1 990)	(2 590)	..	..	..
Madagascar[8]	b. ariary	40.2	53.5	54.9	56.6	63.9	85.7	..	..	..	..
Malawi	m. kwacha	309	434	450	635	698	916	1 136	1 276	..	..
Mali	b. CFA francs	27.1	31.3	32.2	36.0	41.4	43.8	44.7	47.3	49.4	52.0
Mauritania[‡]	b. ouguiyas	3.7	3.7	4.0	4.1	4.2	4.4	4.9	4.8	4.8	4.8
Mauritius	m. rupees	233	206	203	228	246	262	285	304	319	363
Mozambique[9]	b. meticais	[407]	[485]	[585]	722	843	1 048	1 267	1 422	1 780	2 073
Namibia[10]	m. dollars	286	383	435	660	786	736	880	893	1 036	1 187
Niger	b. CFA francs	8.9	10.1	13.0	14.5	14.3	18.2	14.4	14.3	17.2	..
Nigeria[11]	m. naira	15 350	17 920	25 162	45 400	37 490	63 472	108 148	82 413	85 047	111 869
Rwanda[12]	b. francs	22.6	23.3	27.2	27.0	23.9	25.2	24.3	23.0	24.0	26.0
Senegal[13]	m. CFA francs	40 809	41 324	44 300	48 200	44 400	50 500	51 829	56 293	56 819	65 469
Seychelles	m. rupees	52.4	57.3	55.5	59.3	59.0	64.8	64.1	66.1	87.6	69.0
Sierra Leone	m. leones	17 119	(9 315)	..	..	[55 000]	37 868	33 371	40 774	35 243	39 270
Somalia	shillings	..	..	..	..	..	..	..	..	..	..
South Africa	m. rand	11 143	11 131	10 716	10 678	13 128	15 516	18 138	19 579	19 516	21 697
Sudan[14]	b. dinars	13.3	15.4	52.2	109	151	100	128	104	..	..
Swaziland	m. emalangeni	[130]	137	163	180	186	184	..	..	..	..
Tanzania[15]	b. shillings	52.8	61.2	..	..	97.0	118	138	137	133	146
Togo	m. CFA francs	..	..	..	..	..	..	..	16 757	16 757	17 532
Uganda[‡]	b. shillings	135	139	181	212	203	214	255	297	324	..
Zambia[16]	b. kwacha	56.9	90.8	114	73.7	[58.0]	..	..	..	..	..
Zimbabwe[17]	m. dollars	2 742	3 441	3 710	10 068	15 361	16 208	34 403	123 100	815 000	..
Americas											
Caribbean											
Bahamas	m. dollars	21.1	27.1	27.0	43.0	31.9	29.8	30.2	32.8	37.6	39.2
Barbados	m. dollars	30.7	33.0	37.9	40.4	43.6	47.0	47.2	46.9	..	..

Country	Currency	1996	1997	1998	1999	2000	2001	2002	2003	2004	2005
Cuba	pesos	..	..	..	..	..	..	..	..	..	..
Dominican Rep.	m. pesos	1 149	1 682	1 818	2 005	2 872	3 742	4 440	3 578	4 093	[5 336]
Haiti	gourdes	..	..	..	..	..	..	..	..	..	..
Jamaica	m. dollars	1 587	1 951	1 741	1 762	1 873	2 133	2 755	3 167	[3 701]	[4 337]
Trinidad & Tobago	dollars	..	..	..	..	..	..	..	..	..	..
Central America											
Belize	th. dollars	15 932	18 790	..	..	..	..	..	..	..	..
Costa Rica[18]	m. colones	..	..	..	..	..	..	..	..	..	..
El Salvador	m. US dollar	96.4	97.5	96.3	99.8	112	109	109	106	[106]	106
Guatemala	m. quetzales	784	801	894	914	1 225	1 546	1 239	1 420	913	1 001
Honduras[†][19]	m. lempiras	..	..	..	..	516	646	898	919	928	1 004
Mexico[†§]	m. pesos	14 637	18 306	20 950	25 825	28 335	31 298	31 224	31 730	31 821	32 638
Nicaragua	m. córdobas	266	286	278	318	390	389	501	537	505	565
Panama[20]	m. balboas	101	118	104	112	..	..	..	..	..	..
North America											
Canada	m. dollars	11 748	11 001	11 495	12 199	12 326	12 972	13 332	13 952	14 749	15 379
USA[21]	m. dollars	271 417	276 324	274 278	280 969	301 697	312 743	356 720	415 223	464 675	507 089
South America											
Argentina	m. pesos	3 888	3 769	3 782	3 852	3 739	3 638	3 784	4 433	[4 803]	5 156
Bolivia	m. bolivianos	682	896	1 195	969	933	1 214	1 213	1 373	1 414	1 426
Brazil[22]	m. reais	[13 301]	[17 440]	[16 960]	[16 408]	18 617	23 062	28 620	25 590	25 620	30 450
Chile[22]	b. pesos	[965]	1 114	1 249	1 367	1 502	1 615	1 765	1 743	2 216	2 442
Colombia[23]	b. pesos	[2 786]	3 537	4 356	5 372	5 935	7 228	7 405	[8 823]	[9 790]	[10 588]
Ecuador[24]	m. US dollars	419	499	549	249	266	384	558	641	708	881
Guyana	m. dollars	780	..	..	..	..	..	..	..	..	..
Paraguay	b. guaranies	[220]	[284]	[294]	[266]	[283]	284	296	345	310	341
Peru[25]	m. nuevos soles	2 426	2 224	2 671	2 773	3 228	3 486	2 496	2 695	2 807	3 270
Uruguay	m. pesos	[3 220]	[3 812]	[4 114]	4 501	4 246	4 375	4 330	4 755	4 377	5 629
Venezuela	b. bolivares	306	753	716	927	1 030	1 524	1 388	1 706	2 571	3 351

Asia and Oceania

Central Asia

Kazakhstan[26]	b. tenge	16.3	17.9	19.0	17.2	20.4	32.5	37.7	47.5	58.0	[80.8]
Kyrgyzstan[26]	m. soms	699	955	912	1 309	1 864	1 733	2 055	2 404	2 688	..
Tajikistan[26]	th. somoni	3 977	10 713	17 562	18 723	21 496	29 577	70 700	106 500	134 000	..
Turkmenistan[27]	b. manats	158	440	436	582	..	..	..	..	..	..
Uzbekistan[26]	m. sum	(6 900)	[13 700]	..	34 860	..	41 115	..	53 018	..	..

East Asia

Brunei[28]	m. dollars	474	555	614	[520]	[485]	[548]	507	..	..	..
Cambodia[29]	b. riel	434	447	481	474	455	417	407	411	423	452
China, P. R.[30]	b. yuan	[126]	[131]	[149]	[165]	[182]	[216]	[253]	[283]	[324]	[363]
Indonesia	b. rupiah	[8 400]	8 336	10 349	10 254	13 945	16 416	19 291	21 904	[25 274]	[25 656]
Japan[†][31]	b. yen	4 815	4 922	4 942	4 934	4 935	4 950	4 956	4 954	4 916	4 868
Korea, North	b. won	..	..	(2.9)	(2.9)	(3.0)	(3.1)	(3.3)	(3.9)	(4.2)	(4.8)
Korea, South[†][33]	b. won	12 243	13 102	13 594	13 337	14 477	15 497	16 672	17 707	18 941	20 823
Laos	b. kip	49.2	53.0	66.5	224	278	325	..	..	..	..
Malaysia	m. ringgit	6 091	5 877	4 547	6 321	5 826	7 351	8 504	10 950	10 419	9 399
Mongolia	m. togrogs	11 850	14 830	16 749	18 416	26 126	25 384	28 071	27 899	33 329	..
Myanmar	b. kyats	27.7	29.8	37.3	43.7	58.8	63.9	73.1	..	..	..
Philippines	m. pesos	30 978	29 212	31 512	32 959	36 208	35 977	38 907	44 440	43 847	44 193
Singapore	m. dollars	5 782	6 618	7 475	7 616	7 466	7 721	8 108	8 230	8 526	9 100
Taiwan[†]	b. dollars	288	302	299	258	243	248	225	228	251	250
Thailand	m. baht	100 220	98 172	86 133	74 809	71 268	75 413	76 724	77 774	77 067	81 171
Viet Nam	dong	..	..	..	..	..	..	..	..	..	..

South Asia

Afghanistan	m. afghani	..	..	..	..	..	..	..	29 376	33 958	36 042
Bangladesh	m. taka	23 076	25 863	28 436	31 277	33 377	34 020	34 105	36 150	39 630	42 175
India[35]	b. rupees	351	416	492	598	642	689	717	761	918	1 025
Nepal	m. rupees	2 242	2 471	2 789	3 240	3 650	4 837	6 640	7 970	9 321	10 511
Pakistan	m. rupees	123 550	131 803	139 818	146 931	153 795	169 761	188 426	208 031	218 916	219 922
Sri Lanka[36]	b. rupees	38.1	37.1	42.5	40.1	56.9	54.2	49.2	47.0	[56.3]	62.8

Country	Currency	1996	1997	1998	1999	2000	2001	2002	2003	2004	2005
Oceania											
Australia	m. dollars	10 005	10 207	10 799	11 496	11 975	12 995	14 077	14 965	16 119	17 055
Fiji	m. dollars	51.2	47.0	48.0	49.0	73.0	86.0	71.0	[70.0]	[55.0]	. .
New Zealand	m. dollars	1 356	1 344	1 363	1 380	1 422	1 428	1 411	1 468	1 524	1 563
Papua New Guinea	m. kina	68.0	92.6	86.0	80.0	85.0	85.5	66.3	68.8	78.7	81.9
Europe											
Albania[37]	m. leks	4 777	4 442	5 067	5 891	6 519	7 638	8 220	9 279	9 643	11 827
Armenia	b. drams	21.7	31.4	33.7	36.5	36.7	36.8	36.8	44.3	49.6	61.0
Austria	m. euros	1 576	1 600	1 619	1 662	1 742	1 666	1 664	1 760	1 801	1 810
Azerbaijan	b. manat	305	353	388	436	485	532	605	679	[740]	[1 260]
Belarus[†§]	m. roubles	2 266	6 079	9 834	38 740	115 250	247 012	366 189	475 410	679 168	792 636
Belgium	m. euros	3 256	3 267	3 297	3 378	3 463	3 393	3 344	3 434	3 570	3 696
Bosnia–Herzegov.[38]	m. marka							501	351	316	274
Bulgaria[†]	m. leva	34.5	372	512	595	677	805	859	895	930	1 006
Croatia[39]	m. kunas	7 760	7 000	7 500	6 084	4 510	4 336	4 355	4 089	3 585	3 649
Cyprus	m. pounds	141	185	169	106	118	142	100	101	107	91.3
Czech Republic[40]	m. koruny	26 817	27 582	33 570	37 210	39 807	44 842	47 308	51 982	50 507	52 794
Denmark	m. kroner	17 896	18 521	19 071	19 428	19 339	21 017	21 269	21 110	21 495	21 307
Estonia[§]	m. krooni	499	736	843	1 083	1 329	1 640	2 028	2 376	2 585	2 569
Finland	m. euros	1 644	1 555	1 715	1 494	1 647	1 631	1 674	1 751	1 842	1 887
France	m. euros	36 188	36 756	36 012	36 510	36 702	37 187	38 681	40 684	42 690	42 502
Georgia[41]	m. lari	85.5	[57.1]	[57.1]	[52.4]	[37.2]	[49.4]	74.6	91.5	135	365
Germany	m. euros	29 998	29 451	29 822	30 603	30 554	30 648	31 168	31 060	30 610	30 435
Greece	m. euros	3 942	4 433	5 061	5 439	5 921	5 986	6 085	6 309	[7 031]	[8 120]
Hungary	m. forint	103 132	146 820	151 215	191 485	226 041	272 426	279 569	314 380	310 731	289 116
Iceland	krónur	0	0	0	0	0	0	0	0	0	0
Ireland	m. euros	580	623	644	677	734	835	841	874	914	923
Italy	m. euros	18 680	19 987	21 052	22 240	24 325	24 592	25 887	26 795	27 476	25 107
Latvia[42]	m. lats	21.0	22.1	24.8	33.1	42.4	54.6	91.0	108	124	153

Lithuania	m. litai	169	302	553	479	760	805	884	917	1 042	1 280
Luxembourg	m. euros	109	119	129	132	139	179	192	205	[222]	[273]
Maced. (FYROM)†	m. denar	5 223	4 163	4 302	3 769	4 602	15 397	6 841	6 292	6 683	6 265
Malta†	th. liri	12 002	12 020	11 297	11 164	11 109	12 205	12 317	12 874	13 968	14 121
Moldova† 43	m. lei	70.7	80.5	57.0	63.0	63.3	76.7	94.7	109	113	115
Netherlands	m. euros	5 989	6 056	6 154	6 595	6 482	6 929	7 149	7 404	7 782	7 957
Norway	m. kroner	22 813	23 010	25 087	25 809	25 722	26 669	32 461	31 985	32 945	31 346
Poland	m. zlotys	[8 655]	[10 489]	12 133	12 800	13 763	14 864	15 400	16 854	17 689	17 538
Portugal	m. euros	2 001	2 089	2 098	2 259	2 393	2 598	2 765	2 792	[3 057]	[3 164]
Romania44	m. new lei	[270]	[770]	[1 113]	1 465	2 031	2 864	3 491	4 151	5 010	6 070
Russia45	m. roubles	[82 485]	[105 034]	[85 574]	[164 658]	[271 024]	[365 374]	[470 055]	[568 468]	[655 629]	[808 806]
Serbia–Montenegro	m. dinars	3 950	[5 406]	6 441	8 600	21 292	33 060	43 695	42 070	48 275	47 782
Slovakia†	m. koruny	19 665	16 792	14 009	13 532	15 760	19 051	19 947	22 965	22 944	25 550
Slovenia	m. tolars	44 666	46 434	50 030	49 958	49 518	65 903	78 552	86 346	99 700	110 288
Spain46	m. euros	6 560	6 750	6 756	7 092	7 599	7 972	8 414	8 587	9 132	9 330
Sweden47	m. kronor	27 015	39 726	40 801	42 541	44 542	42 639	42 401	42 903	40 527	41 614
Switzerland†§	m. francs	4 782	4 634	4 532	4 416	4 503	4 476	4 461	4 437	4 381	4 410
Turkey48	m. new liras	612	1 183	2 289	4 168	6 248	8 844	12 108	13 553	13 386	15 716
UK49	m. pounds	22 107	21 792	22 261	22 548	23 307	24 217	25 718	29 845	32 217	31 358
Ukraine50	m. hryvnias	2 680	3 851	3 442	3 890	6 184	5 848	6 266	7 615	8 963	[10 400]
Middle East											
Bahrain	m. dinars	109	109	111	123	121	126	126	176	180	: :
Egypt51	m. pounds	7 573	7 986	8 154	8 312	9 124	9 975	10 717	11 824	13 476	[15 100]
Iran52	b. rials	6 499	8 540	10 624	17 757	31 113	38 310	35 362	48 291	63 684	75 954
Iraq	m. dinars	: :	: :	: :	: :	: :	: :	: :	: :	: :	: :
Israel53	b. new shekels	28.4	31.4	34.3	37.4	39.5	40.6	47.4	44.7	45.8	43.9
Jordan54	m. dinars	417	445	491	512	531	537	551	649	653	691
Kuwait	m. dinars	971	745	696	696	827	824	864	1 126	1 291	1 354
Lebanon	b. pounds	[1 156]	[1 044]	1 052	1 251	1 327	1 383	1 222	[1 177]	[1 232]	
Oman55	m. rials	737	760	676	687	809	933	958	1 010	1 144	1 148
Qatar	m. riyals	: :	: :	: :	: :	: :	: :	: :	: :	: :	: :

Country	Currency	1996	1997	1998	1999	2000	2001	2002	2003	2004	2005
Saudi Arabia[56]	m. riyals	50 025	67 975	78 231	68 700	74 866	78 8509	69 382	70 303	78 414	95 146
Syria	b. pounds	40.7	42.8	46.1	45.0	[49.6]	[61.4]	[62.6]	[74.4]	: :	: :
UAE[57]	m. dirhams	[8 292]	8 629	8 712	8 790	8 688	8 796	9 139	9 236	: :	[9 179]
Yemen	b. rials	39.2	51.3	52.2	61.5	76.6	[91.1]	130	148	[156]	[162]

Table 8A.3. Military expenditure by country, in constant US dollars for 1996–2005 and current US dollars for 2005

Figures are in US$ m., at constant 2003 prices and exchange rates, and are for calendar years. Figures in the right-most column, marked *, are in current US$ m.

Country	1996	1997	1998	1999	2000	2001	2002	2003	2004	2005	2005*
Africa											
North Africa											
Algeria[‡]	1 273	1 531	1 620	1 709	1 984	2 009	2 214	2 206	2 519	2 545	2 862
Libya	: :	371	419	323	346	338	435	541	585	: :	: :
Morocco[1]	1 501	1 437	1 420	1 550	1 600	1 699	1 796	1 851	2 072	1 978	2 256
Tunisia	365	361	368	364	381	396	392	408	404	409	434
Sub-Saharan Africa											
Angola[2]	[1 076]	[809]	[288]	[1 054]	[297]	[153]	[195]	[298]	[668]	[1 137]	[1 620]
Benin	: :	: :	: :	: :	: :	: :	: :	: :	: :	: :	: :
Botswana	161	186	240	236	247	251	299	292	[284]	230	[261]
Burkina Faso	37.9	43.9	43.3	48.3	49.2	48.4	58.6	55.0	59.9	64.5	78.1
Burundi	30.8	33.3	35.7	37.4	32.2	42.7	45.6	43.4	38.6	: :	: :
Cameroon[§]	120	132	150	162	163	162	176	189	200	199	229
Cape Verde	4.4	4.4	4.9	5.5	8.9	6.0	5.5	5.7	6.1	: :	: :
Central African Republic[3]	12.1	: :	: :	: :	: :	: :	13.3	15.0	14.0	13.9	15.8
Chad	29.0	21.0	18.4	26.7	30.3	32.3	32.6	39.1	43.2	45.9	50.5
Congo, Republic of	: :	: :	: :	: :	: :	: :	: :	: :	48.8	: :	: :
Congo, DRC[4]	68.7	56.6	17.0	62.0	46.1	: :	: :	118	185	136	142

Côte d'Ivoire	113	113						213			
Djibouti	23.9	25.2	24.8	24.4	23.4	23.4	25.8	..	..	..	..
Equatorial Guinea											
Eritrea[5]	171	109	328	316	263	195	186	146	321	301	345
Ethiopia[6]	117	215	453	719	648	438	411	349			
Gabon						116	116	108	106	104	119
Gambia[‡]	2.0	2.2	2.1	2.0	2.1	2.0	1.9	1.6	1.4	1.4	1.6
Ghana[8]	33.4	33.5	41.6	44.1	61.8	38.8	43.5	50.6	65.1	64.1	80.0
Guinea		35.2	38.4	50.4	49.5	100	105				
Guinea-Bissau[7]	2.3	2.1	3.2		12.0	7.8					
Kenya	210	200	188	183	197	226	244	246	238	220	271
Lesotho	27.9	27.9	30.1	37.5	36.0	32.0	29.3	29.2	27.4	26.2	34.7
Liberia						(43.8)	(50.8)				
Madagascar[8]	54.3	69.2	66.9	62.7	63.2	79.2					
Malawi	13.0	16.7	13.4	13.0	11.1	11.8	12.8	13.1			
Mali	51.7	59.9	59.3	67.0	77.6	78.1	75.9	81.4	87.7	89.0	101
Mauritania[‡]	19.4	18.5	18.5	18.4	18.3	18.3	19.6	18.2	16.5	14.3	18.1
Mauritius	12.4	10.3	9.4	9.9	10.3	10.4	10.6	10.9	10.9	11.8	12.4
Mozambique[9]	[31.2]	[34.7]	[41.2]	49.4	51.2	58.4	60.4	59.8	67.4	68.1	94.5
Namibia[10]	67.6	83.3	89.0	124	136	116	125	118	132	143	190
Niger	17.4	19.2	23.6	27.0	25.8	31.6	24.4	24.6	29.5		
Nigeria[11]	247	267	340	585	422	632	954	638	572	653	845
Rwanda[12]	57.4	52.9	58.1	59.1	50.2	51.4	48.4	42.8	39.9	38.6	46.7
Senegal[13]	77.2	77.0	81.5	88.0	80.5	88.8	89.1	96.9	97.3	112	127
Seychelles	12.4	13.5	12.7	12.8	12.0	12.4	12.3	12.2	15.6	12.3	12.1
Sierra Leone	16.0	(7.6)			[24.9]	16.8	15.3	17.4	13.1	13.3	13.5
Somalia											
South Africa	2 314	2 128	1 917	1 816	2 120	2 371	2 538	2 588	2 544	2 741	3 469
Sudan[14]	134	106	307	550	724	449	527	398	..	..	..
Swaziland	[30.2]	29.6	32.6	34.0	31.3	29.2					
Tanzania[15]	83.6	83.5			103	119	138	132	128	130	132

Country	1996	1997	1998	1999	2000	2001	2002	2003	2004	2005	2005*
Togo	..	..	..	..	..	..	..	28.8	28.7	28.1	34.1
Uganda‡	88.3	84.6	110	122	113	117	140	151	159	..	..
Zambia[16]	53.6	68.7	69.2	35.3	[22.1]	..	..	..	..	..	..
Zimbabwe[17]	300	317	259	444	435	259	229	177	260	..	..
Americas											
Caribbean											
Bahamas	23.9	30.3	29.7	46.6	34.3	31.1	31.3	32.8	37.4	38.3	39.2
Barbados	17.7	17.7	20.6	21.6	22.8	23.9	24.0	23.4	..	..	..
Cuba	..	..	..	..	..	..	..	..	..	..	..
Dominican Republic	70.9	95.8	98.8	102	136	163	184	116	87.7	[108]	[197]
Haiti	..	..	..	..	..	..	..	..	..	..	..
Jamaica	47.4	53.2	43.7	41.7	41.0	43.6	52.6	54.8	[56.4]	[58.8]	[70.0]
Trinidad and Tobago	..	..	..	..	..	..	..	..	..	..	..
Central America											
Belize	8.4	9.8	..	..	..	..	..	..	..	..	..
Costa Rica[18]	..	..	..	..	..	..	..	..	..	..	..
El Salvador	115	111	107	110	121	113	111	106	[101]	97.5	105
Guatemala	157	147	153	150	189	222	165	179	107	108	132
Honduras†[19]	..	..	..	..	37.9	43.2	55.7	53.0	49.5	49.1	53.1
Mexico†§	2 828	2 933	2 895	3 061	3 067	3 186	3 026	2 941	2 817	2 772	3 003
Nicaragua	31.7	31.2	26.8	27.6	30.3	28.2	34.9	35.6	30.8	31.6	33.8
Panama[20]	109	125	110	116	..	..	..	..	..	..	..
North America											
Canada	9 687	8 931	9 242	9 642	9 483	9 730	9 781	9 959	10 338	10 568	12 837
USA[21]	318 420	316 789	309 447	310 326	322 309	324 908	364 819	415 223	452 559	478 177	507 089
South America											
Argentina	1 881	1 813	1 803	1 858	1 821	1 791	1 480	1 528	[1 586]	1 560	1 797
Bolivia	114	143	177	140	129	165	164	179	177	169	176

Brazil	[7 116]	[8 726]	[8 223]	[7 587]	8 042	9 323	10 670	8 317	7 811	8 687	12 598
Chile[22]	[1 823]	1 984	2 115	2 240	2 371	2 461	2 625	2 521	3 172	3 401	4 399
Colombia[23]	[2 028]	2 173	2 255	2 508	2 537	2 862	2 757	[3 066]	[3 212]	[3 309]	[4 595]
Ecuador[24]	474	542	597	385	444	466	602	641	689	840	881
Guyana	5.7	. .	. .	. .	. .	. .	. .	. .	. .	. .	. .
Paraguay	[64.4]	[77.7]	[72.1]	[61.1]	[59.6]	55.8	52.6	53.7	46.3	48.4	55.1
Peru[25]	911	769	861	864	970	1 027	734	775	778	893	1 011
Uruguay	[238]	[235]	[229]	237	214	211	183	169	142	175	233
Venezuela	1 006	1 650	1 156	1 211	1 158	1 522	1 132	1 062	1 314	1 477	1 604
Asia and Oceania											
Central Asia											
Kazakhstan[26]	205	191	190	159	166	245	268	318	363	[469]	[610]
Kyrgyzstan[26]	39.8	44.1	38.1	40.2	48.3	42.0	48.7	55.1	56.7	. .	. .
Tajikistan[26]	10.7	15.4	17.6	14.7	12.7	12.6	26.9	34.8	40.9	. .	. .
Turkmenistan[27]	112	169	143	155	. .	. .	. .	. .	. .	. .	. .
Uzbekistan[26]	(98.0)	[114]	. .	172	. .	91.9	. .	71.5	. .	. .	. .
East Asia											
Brunei[28]	275	316	351	[298]	[274]	[308]	292	. .	. .	. .	. .
Cambodia[29]	139	138	130	123	119	110	104	103	103	103	111
China, P. R.[30]	[15 500]	[15 700]	[18 000]	[20 200]	[22 200]	[26 200]	[30 900]	[34 200]	[37 700]	[41 000]	[44 300]
Indonesia	[2 738]	2 558	2 005	1 649	2 162	2 282	2 397	2 554	2 774	[2 607]	[2 663]
Japan[†][31]	41 298	41 497	41 391	41 468	41 755	42 180	42 627	42 729	42 395	42 081	45 324
Korea, North[32]	. .	. .	(19.5)	(20.0)	(20.0)	(20.9)	(22.0)	(26.0)	(27.9)	. .	. .
Korea, South[†][33]	13 175	13 494	13 026	12 672	13 450	13 828	14 487	14 860	15 344	16 448	20 728
Laos	44.6	37.7	24.8	36.6	36.2	39.3	. .	. .	. .	. .	. .
Malaysia	1 886	1 772	1 302	1 762	1 600	1 991	2 263	2 882	2 703	2 363	2 487
Mongolia	20.9	19.1	19.8	20.2	25.7	23.5	25.7	24.3	26.9	. .	. .
Myanmar[34]	. .	. .	. .	. .	. .	. .	. .	. .	. .	. .	. .
Philippines	826	738	729	719	760	707	743	820	763	714	795
Singapore	3 461	3 884	4 398	4 481	4 334	4 437	4 678	4 724	4 814	5 132	5 545
Taiwan[†]	8 679	9 009	8 783	7 565	7 017	7 160	6 525	6 616	7 168	7 003	7 813

Country	1996	1997	1998	1999	2000	2001	2002	2003	2004	2005	2005*
Thailand	2 924	2 713	2 202	1 907	1 789	1 861	1 883	1 875	1 808	1 823	2 031
Viet Nam	. .	. .	. .	. .	. .	. .	. .	. .	. .	. .	. .
South Asia											
Afghanistan								9.8	11.3	. .	. .
Bangladesh	548	582	591	612	639	639	620	622	661	660	655
India[35]	11 182	12 378	12 915	15 009	15 487	16 027	15 977	16 334	18 988	20 443	23 674
Nepal	42.0	44.5	45.1	48.8	53.6	69.2	92.2	105	119	127	149
Pakistan	3 016	2 889	2 885	2 911	2 920	3 125	3 358	3 602	3 528	3 241	3 682
Sri Lanka[36]	699	621	651	586	784	655	542	487	[543]	539	625
Oceania											
Australia	7 684	7 820	8 203	8 606	8 581	8 921	9 382	9 705	10 214	10 535	13 258
Fiji	33.3	29.6	28.6	28.6	42.1	47.6	39.0	[36.9]	[28.2]	. .	. .
New Zealand	887	869	870	882	885	866	834	853	865	864	1 119
Papua New Guinea	42.0	55.0	44.9	36.4	33.4	30.8	21.3	19.3	21.6	22.0	26.4
Europe											
Albania[37]	70.6	49.3	46.6	54.0	59.7	67.9	67.8	76.1	77.4	92.6	120
Armenia	50.6	64.4	63.5	68.4	69.3	67.3	66.5	76.6	80.2	98.5	134
Austria	1 983	1 987	1 993	2 034	2 083	1 940	1 904	1 987	1 992	1 957	2 305
Azerbaijan	63.4	71.0	78.5	96.5	105	114	126	138	[141]	[213]	[265]
Belarus[†§]	97.7	160	150	150	166	220	229	232	280	292	367
Belgium	4 137	4 085	4 083	4 137	4 136	3 954	3 834	3 876	3 947	3 971	4 708
Bosnia and Herzegovina[38]	. .					. .					179
Bulgaria[†]	359	335	388	440	453	502	506	516	505	522	653
Croatia[39]	1 491	1 291	1 299	1 019	718	659	650	610	516	509	626
Cyprus	334	423	378	233	249	294	201	195	202	169	202
Czech Republic[40]	1 293	1 225	1 347	1 462	1 505	1 619	1 680	1 843	1 741	1 791	2 259
Denmark	3 192	3 232	3 268	3 248	3 142	3 337	3 297	3 204	3 225	3 140	3 641
Estonia[§]	51.4	68.5	72.6	90.2	106	124	148	171	181	173	209

Finland	2 092	1 956	2 128	1 832	1 954	1 886	1 906	1 976	2 075	2 107	2 405
France	44 981	45 145	43 936	44 308	43 796	43 667	44 564	45 917	47 177	46 150	54 143
Georgia[41]	63.4	[39.6]	[38.2]	[29.4]	[20.1]	[25.5]	36.4	42.6	59.5	146	202
Germany	37 124	35 768	35 886	36 612	36 021	35 432	35 546	35 055	33 980	33 187	35 771
Greece	5 776	6 155	6 707	7 022	7 410	7 245	7 111	7 120	[7 712]	[8 600]	[10 344]
Hungary	903	1 086	980	1 128	1 212	1 338	1 304	1 402	1 297	1 165	1 502
Iceland	0	0	0	0	0	0	0	0	0	0	0
Ireland	829	878	886	916	941	1 021	982	986	1 010	997	1 176
Italy	24 727	25 928	26 785	27 833	29 690	29 201	29 998	30 242	30 341	27 196	31 983
Latvia[42]	47.2	45.8	49.1	64.0	79.9	100	164	189	204	238	275
Lithuania	64.5	106	184	159	249	261	285	300	336	403	473
Luxembourg	140	151	162	164	168	211	221	231	[245]	[295]	[348]
Macedonia (FYROM)	112	88.3	90.7	80.5	92.2	293	127	116	123	117	130
Malta	37.2	36.2	33.2	32.1	31.2	33.3	32.9	34.1	36.0	35.4	41.7
Moldova†[43]	14.4	15.6	9.7	7.7	5.9	6.5	7.6	7.9	7.2	6.5	9.1
Netherlands	8 148	8 065	8 036	8 426	8 037	8 246	8 239	8 356	8 676	8 732	10 136
Norway	3 812	3 749	3 997	4 018	3 886	3 911	4 699	4 518	4 632	4 332	4 991
Poland	[3 660]	[3 855]	3 991	3 925	3 813	3 925	3 991	4 334	4 391	4 258	5 480
Portugal	2 784	2 845	2 782	2 927	3 015	3 135	3 223	3 151	[3 371]	[3 411]	[4 031]
Romania[44]	[1 328]	[1 489]	[1 353]	1 221	1 162	1 219	1 212	1 250	1 349	1 498	2 166
Russia[45]	[14 100]	[15 700]	[10 000]	[10 400]	[14 100]	[15 700]	[17 400]	[18 500]	[19 300]	[21 000]	[28 814]
Serbia and Montenegro	654	[756]	695	653	952	774	844	730	765	656	
Slovakia†	903	727	568	496	516	581	589	625	580	631	717
Slovenia	359	344	343	323	294	361	400	417	465	502	845
Spain[46]	8 949	9 031	8 876	9 108	9 434	9 555	9 784	9 691	10 004	9 898	586
Sweden[47]	3 627	5 295	5 456	5 660	5 875	5 490	5 343	5 306	4 993	5 105	11 885
Switzerland†§	3 737	3 603	3 523	3 405	3 419	3 365	3 333	3 294	3 226	3 212	5 761
Turkey[48]	10 008	10 427	10 926	12 064	11 675	10 703	10 108	9 030	8 212	8 907	3 627
UK[49]	42 877	40 945	40 450	40 344	40 533	41 356	43 212	48 728	51 088	48 305	11 762
Ukraine[50]	1 203	1 490	1 205	1 110	1 377	1 163	1 237	1 429	1 542	[1 567]	57 622

Country	1996	1997	1998	1999	2000	2001	2002	2003	2004	2005	2005*
Middle East											
Bahrain	298	292	299	334	332	345	340	468	456	. .	. .
Egypt[51]	1 635	1 648	1 620	1 602	1 712	1 830	1 914	2 021	2 070	[2 205]	[2 608]
Iran[52]	2 234	2 502	2 641	3 676	5 626	6 225	5 026	5 894	6 772	7 035	8 474
Iraq	. .	. .	. .	. .	. .	. .	. .	. .	. .	. .	. .
Israel[53]	8 202	8 320	8 620	8 935	9 330	9 489	10 484	9 816	10 098	9 579	9 943
Jordan[54]	667	689	739	766	789	784	790	915	891	920	975
Kuwait	3 576	2 726	2 542	2 470	2 865	2 815	2 928	3 777	4 280	4 300	4 638
Lebanon	[885]	[741]	715	848	903	945	821	[781]	[793]		
Oman[55]	1 835	1 902	1 706	1 727	2 056	2 397	2 477	2 622	2 960	2 966	2 986
Qatar	. .	. .	. .	. .	. .	. .	. .	. .	. .	. .	. .
Saudi Arabia[56]	12 951	17 588	20 314	18 083	19 930	21 227	18 635	18 772	20 824	25 206	25 393
Syria	3 710	3 829	4 150	4 209	[4 826]	[5 800]	[5 857]	[6 628]	[6 626]		
UAE[57]	[2 676]	2 705	2 678	2 646	2 580	2 543	2 566	2 517	2 327	[2 254]	[2 499]
Yemen	366	469	451	488	581	[618]	782	807	[753]	[710]	[844]

Table 8A.4. Military expenditure by country as a percentage of gross domestic product, 1996–2004

Country	1996	1997	1998	1999	2000	2001	2002	2003	2004
Africa									
North Africa									
Algeria‡	3.1	3.6	4.0	3.8	3.5	3.5	3.7	3.3	3.4
Libya	..	4.1	5.3	3.8	3.2	2.9	2.4	2.3	2.0
Morocco[1]	4.0	3.9	3.7	4.0	4.1	4.1	4.3	4.2	4.5
Tunisia	2.0	1.9	1.8	1.7	1.7	1.7	1.6	1.6	1.5
Sub-Saharan Africa									
Angola[2]	[9.0]	[10.3]	[5.2]	[9.9]	[2.2]	[1.4]	[1.6]	[2.2]	[4.2]
Benin	..	..	..	..	..	..	..	..	..
Botswana	3.3	3.3	4.0	4.0	3.9	3.7	4.2	4.1	[3.8]
Burkina Faso	1.3	1.4	1.3	1.4	1.4	1.3	1.5	1.3	1.3
Burundi	5.8	6.4	6.6	6.3	6.0	8.0	7.6	7.3	6.3
Cameroon	1.2	1.3	1.5	1.5	1.3	1.3	1.3	1.4	1.4
Cape Verde	0.8	0.8	0.9	0.8	1.3	0.8	0.7	0.7	0.7
Central African Republic[3]	1.2	..	..	..	..	..	1.0	1.3	1.2
Chad	1.5	1.1	0.9	1.4	1.5	1.5	1.4	1.5	1.0
Congo, Republic of	..	..	..	..	..	..	..	1.4	..
Congo, DRC[4]	1.5	1.4	0.4	1.2	1.0	..	..	2.1	3.0
Côte d'Ivoire	0.9	0.8	..	..	..	..	..	1.5	..
Djibouti	4.2	4.5	4.4	4.3	4.1	4.0	4.3	..	..
Equatorial Guinea	..	..	..	..	..	..	..	..	..
Eritrea[5]	22.0	12.8	35.3	37.6	36.4	24.8	24.2	19.6	..
Ethiopia[6]	1.8	3.4	6.7	10.7	9.6	6.2	5.5	4.4	..
Gabon	..	..	..	..	..	2.0	2.0	1.8	1.7
Gambia‡	1.0	1.0	1.0	0.8	0.8	0.7	0.6	0.4	0.4
Ghana	0.6	0.7	0.8	0.8	1.0	0.6	0.6	0.7	0.8
Guinea	..	1.2	1.3	1.6	1.5	2.9	2.9	..	..

Country	1996	1997	1998	1999	2000	2001	2002	2003	2004
Guinea-Bissau[7]	0.6	0.7	1.4	:	4.4	3.1	:	:	:
Kenya	1.8	1.7	1.5	1.4	1.3	1.5	1.6	1.6	1.6
Lesotho	3.0	2.8	3.1	3.7	3.6	3.0	2.7	2.6	2.3
Liberia	:	:	:	:	:	(7.7)	(7.5)	:	:
Madagascar[8]	1.2	1.5	1.3	1.2	1.2	1.4	0.8	:	:
Malawi	0.9	1.0	0.8	0.8	0.7	0.7	1.9	0.7	1.9
Mali	1.9	2.0	1.9	2.0	2.2	2.0	1.9	1.9	1.4
Mauritania[‡]	2.5	2.3	2.2	2.1	1.9	1.9	1.9	1.6	0.2
Mauritius	0.3	0.2	0.2	0.2	0.2	0.2	0.2	0.2	1.3
Mozambique[9]	[1.2]	[1.2]	[1.2]	1.4	1.4	1.4	1.3	1.2	3.1
Namibia[10]	1.9	2.3	2.3	3.2	3.4	2.8	2.9	2.9	1.1
Niger	0.9	0.9	1.1	1.2	1.2	1.4	1.0	1.0	1.0
Nigeria[11]	0.5	0.6	0.9	1.4	0.8	1.3	1.9	1.1	2.2
Rwanda[12]	5.3	4.1	4.3	4.3	3.4	3.3	2.9	2.4	1.4
Senegal[13]	1.6	1.5	1.5	1.5	1.3	1.4	1.4	1.4	2.3
Seychelles	2.1	2.0	1.7	1.8	1.7	1.8	1.7	1.7	1.2
Sierra Leone	2.0	(1.1)	:	:	[4.1]	2.4	1.7	1.8	:
Somalia	:	:	:	:	:	:	:	:	1.4
South Africa	1.8	1.6	1.4	1.3	1.4	1.5	1.6	1.6	:
Sudan[14]	1.3	1.0	2.5	4.3	5.1	3.1	3.4	2.4	1.1
Swaziland	[2.3]	2.1	2.2	2.1	1.9	1.7	:	1.3	1.6
Tanzania[15]	1.4	1.3	:	:	1.3	1.4	1.5	1.6	2.3
Togo	:	:	:	:	:	:	:	1.6	
Uganda[‡]	2.1	1.9	2.3	2.4	2.2	2.1	2.4	2.4	
Zambia[16]	1.4	1.8	1.9	1.0	[0.6]	:	:	:	
Zimbabwe[17]	3.1	3.2	2.5	4.5	4.9	2.6	2.3	2.6	:
Americas									
Caribbean									
Bahamas	0.7	0.8	0.7	1.0	0.7	0.6	0.6	0.7	0.7

Barbados	:	0.8	0.9	0.9	0.8	0.8	0.8	0.7	0.8
Cuba	:	:	:	:	:	:	:	:	0.6
Dominican Republic	0.5	0.7	1.1	1.0	0.9	0.7	0.8	0.8	0.8
Haiti	:	:	:	:	:	:	:	:	:
Jamaica	[0.7]	0.7	0.7	0.6	0.6	0.6	0.6	0.7	0.7
Trinidad and Tobago	:	:	:	:	:	:	:	:	:
Central America									
Belize	:	:	:	:	:	:	:	1.4	1.2
Costa Rica[18]	0.0	0.0	0.0	0.0	0.0	0.0	0.0	0.0	0.0
El Salvador	[0.7]	0.7	0.8	0.8	0.9	0.8	0.8	0.9	0.9
Guatemala	0.4	0.7	0.7	0.9	0.8	0.7	0.7	0.7	0.8
Honduras[†19]	0.7	0.8	0.8	0.7	0.6	:	:	:	:
Mexico[†]	0.7	0.5	0.5	0.5	0.5	0.6	0.5	0.6	0.6
Nicaragua	0.4	0.9	0.9	0.7	0.8	0.7	0.7	0.9	0.9
Panama[20]	0.7	:	:	:	:	1.0	1.0	1.2	1.1
North America									
Canada	1.1	1.1	1.2	1.2	1.1	1.2	1.3	1.2	1.4
USA[21]	4.0	3.8	3.4	3.1	3.1	3.0	3.1	3.3	3.5
South America									
Argentina	[1.1]	1.2	1.2	1.4	1.3	1.4	1.3	1.3	1.4
Bolivia	2.0	2.2	2.1	2.3	1.8	2.0	2.6	2.2	1.8
Brazil	1.5	1.6	2.1	1.9	1.7	[1.7]	[1.9]	[2.0]	[1.7]
Chile[22]	3.9	3.4	3.8	3.7	3.7	3.7	3.4	3.2	[3.1]
Colombia[23]	[3.8]	[3.8]	3.6	3.8	3.4	3.5	3.1	2.9	[2.8]
Ecuador[24]	2.4	2.4	2.3	1.8	1.7	1.5	2.4	2.1	2.0
Guyana	:	:	:	:	:	:	:	:	0.8
Paraguay	0.7	0.9	0.9	1.0	[1.1]	[1.1]	[1.3]	[1.4]	[1.1]
Peru[25]	1.2	1.3	1.3	1.9	1.7	1.6	1.6	1.4	1.8
Uruguay	1.2	1.5	1.7	1.8	1.7	1.9	[1.8]	[1.9]	[2.0]
Venezuela	1.2	1.3	1.3	1.7	1.3	1.6	1.4	1.8	1.0

Country	1996	1997	1998	1999	2000	2001	2002	2003	2004
Asia and Oceania									
Central Asia									
Kazakhstan[26]	1.2	1.1	1.1	0.8	0.8	1.0	1.0	1.1	1.0
Kyrgyzstan[26]	3.0	3.1	2.7	2.7	2.9	2.3	2.7	2.9	2.9
Tajikistan[26]	1.3	1.7	1.7	1.4	1.2	1.2	2.1	2.2	2.2
Turkmenistan[27]	2.0	4.0	3.1	2.9	. .	. .	. .	. .	. .
Uzbekistan[26]	(1.2)	[1.4]	. .	1.6	. .	0.8	. .	0.5	. .
East Asia									
Brunei[28]	6.4	7.3	9.4	[7.3]	[6.5]	[7.3]	6.6	. .	. .
Cambodia[29]	4.7	4.4	4.1	3.5	3.2	2.8	2.5	2.4	2.2
China, P. R.[30]	[1.8]	[1.7]	[1.9]	[2.0]	[2.0]	[2.2]	[2.3]	[2.3]	[2.4]
Indonesia	[1.6]	1.3	1.1	0.9	1.0	1.0	1.0	1.1	1.1
Japan† [31]	0.9	0.9	1.0	1.0	1.0	1.0	1.0	1.0	1.0
Korea, North	. .	. .	. .	. .	. .	. .	. .	. .	. .
Korea, South† [33]	2.9	2.7	2.8	2.5	2.5	2.5	2.4	2.4	2.4
Laos	2.9	2.4	1.6	2.2	2.0	2.1	. .	. .	. .
Malaysia	2.4	2.1	1.6	2.1	1.7	2.2	2.4	2.8	2.3
Mongolia	1.8	1.8	2.0	2.0	2.6	2.3	2.3	2.0	2.0
Myanmar	3.5	2.7	2.3	2.0	2.3	1.8	1.3	. .	. .
Philippines	1.4	1.2	1.2	1.1	1.1	1.0	1.0	1.1	0.9
Singapore	4.4	4.7	5.4	5.4	4.7	5.0	5.1	5.1	4.7
Taiwan†	3.8	3.6	3.4	2.8	2.5	2.6	2.3	2.3	2.5
Thailand	2.2	2.1	1.9	1.6	1.4	1.5	1.4	1.3	1.2
Viet Nam	. .	. .	. .	. .	. .	. .	. .	. .	. .
South Asia									
Afghanistan	. .	. .	. .	. .	. .	. .	. .	. .	. .
Bangladesh	1.4	1.4	1.4	1.4	1.4	1.3	1.2	1.2	1.2
India[35]	2.6	2.7	2.8	3.1	3.1	3.0	2.9	2.8	3.0
Nepal	0.8	0.8	0.8	0.9	0.9	1.1	1.5	1.6	1.7

Pakistan	5.1	4.9	4.8	3.9	3.7	3.9	3.9	3.8	3.4
Sri Lanka[36]	5.0	4.2	4.2	3.6	4.5	3.9	3.1	2.7	[2.8]
Oceania									
Australia	1.9	1.9	1.9	1.9	1.8	1.9	1.9	1.9	1.9
Fiji	1.7	1.5	1.5	1.3	2.1	2.2	1.8	[1.6]	[1.2]
New Zealand	1.4	1.3	1.3	1.3	1.2	1.2	1.1	1.1	1.0
Papua New Guinea	1.0	1.3	1.1	0.9	0.9	0.9	0.6	0.6	0.6
Europe									
Albania[37]	1.5	1.4	1.2	1.2	1.2	1.3	1.3	1.3	1.2
Armenia	3.3	3.9	3.5	3.7	3.6	3.1	2.7	2.7	2.6
Austria	0.9	0.9	0.9	0.8	0.8	0.8	0.8	0.8	0.8
Azerbaijan	2.2	2.2	2.3	2.3	2.1	2.0	2.0	1.9	[1.8]
Belarus†	1.2	1.7	1.4	1.3	1.3	1.4	1.4	1.3	1.4
Belgium	1.6	1.5	1.5	1.4	1.4	1.3	1.3	1.3	1.3
Bosnia and Herzegovina[38]	:	:	:	:	:	:	4.3	2.9	2.5
Bulgaria†	2.0	2.1	2.3	2.5	2.5	2.7	2.7	2.6	2.4
Croatia[39]	7.2	5.7	5.5	4.3	3.0	2.6	2.4	2.1	1.7
Cyprus	3.3	4.1	3.5	2.0	2.1	2.3	1.6	2.1	1.5
Czech Republic[40]	1.6	1.5	1.7	1.8	1.9	1.9	2.0	2.0	1.8
Denmark	1.7	1.7	1.7	1.6	1.5	1.6	1.6	1.5	1.5
Estonia	0.9	1.1	1.1	1.3	1.4	1.6	1.7	1.9	1.8
Finland	1.7	1.5	1.5	1.2	1.3	1.2	1.2	1.2	1.2
France	2.9	2.9	2.7	2.7	2.5	2.5	2.5	2.6	2.6
Georgia[41]	2.2	[1.2]	[1.1]	[0.9]	[0.6]	[0.7]	1.0	1.1	1.4
Germany	1.6	1.5	1.5	1.5	1.5	1.5	1.5	1.4	1.4
Greece	4.4	4.5	4.7	4.8	4.8	4.5	4.2	4.1	[4.2]
Hungary	1.5	1.7	1.5	1.7	1.7	1.8	1.7	1.7	1.5
Iceland	0.0	0.0	0.0	0.0	0.0	0.0	0.0	0.0	0.0
Ireland	1.1	1.0	0.9	0.8	0.8	0.8	0.7	0.7	0.7
Italy	1.9	1.9	2.0	2.0	2.1	2.0	2.1	2.1	2.0
Latvia[42]	0.7	0.6	0.6	0.8	0.9	1.1	1.6	1.7	1.7

Country	1996	1997	1998	1999	2000	2001	2002	2003	2004
Lithuania	0.5	0.8	1.2	1.1	1.7	1.7	1.7	1.6	1.7
Luxembourg	0.8	0.8	0.8	0.7	0.7	0.8	0.8	0.9	[0.9]
Macedonia (FYROM)	3.0	2.2	2.2	1.8	1.9	6.6	2.8	2.5	2.6
Malta	1.0	0.9	0.8	0.8	0.7	0.7	0.7	0.7	0.8
Moldova[†] [43]	0.9	0.9	0.6	0.5	0.4	0.4	0.4	0.4	0.4
Netherlands	1.9	1.8	1.7	1.8	1.6	1.6	1.6	1.6	1.7
Norway	2.2	2.1	2.2	2.1	1.8	1.7	2.1	2.0	2.0
Poland	[2.1]	[2.1]	2.1	2.0	1.9	2.0	2.0	2.1	2.0
Portugal	2.4	2.3	2.2	2.1	2.1	2.1	2.1	2.1	[2.3]
Romania[44]	[2.5]	[3.0]	[3.0]	2.7	2.5	2.5	2.3	2.2	2.1
Russia[45]	[4.1]	[4.5]	[3.3]	[3.4]	[3.7]	[4.1]	[4.3]	[4.3]	[3.9]
Serbia and Montenegro	:	[4.8]	4.4	4.5	5.6	4.3	4.4	3.5	3.4
Slovakia[†]	3.1	2.4	1.8	1.6	1.7	1.9	1.8	1.9	1.7
Slovenia	1.6	1.5	1.4	1.3	1.2	1.4	1.5	1.5	1.6
Spain[46]	1.4	1.4	1.3	1.3	1.2	1.2	1.2	1.1	1.1
Sweden[47]	1.5	2.1	2.1	2.0	2.0	1.9	1.8	1.8	1.6
Switzerland[†]	1.3	1.2	1.2	1.1	1.1	1.1	1.0	1.0	1.0
Turkey[48]	4.1	4.1	4.4	5.4	5.0	5.0	4.4	3.8	3.1
UK[49]	2.9	2.7	2.6	2.5	2.4	2.4	2.5	2.7	2.8
Ukraine[50]	3.3	4.1	3.4	3.0	3.6	2.9	2.8	2.9	2.6
Middle East									
Bahrain	4.7	4.6	4.8	4.9	4.0	4.2	4.0	4.9	4.4
Egypt[51]	3.3	3.1	2.8	2.7	2.7	2.8	2.8	2.8	[2.8]
Iran[52]	2.6	2.9	3.2	4.1	5.4	5.7	3.8	4.4	4.5
Iraq	:	:	:	:	:	:	:	:	:
Israel[53]	9.0	8.8	8.7	8.7	8.4	8.5	9.6	8.9	8.7
Jordan[54]	8.5	8.7	8.8	8.9	8.9	8.5	8.2	9.2	8.2
Kuwait	10.3	8.1	8.8	7.6	7.3	7.9	7.5	8.2	7.9
Lebanon	[5.7]	[4.3]	4.1	4.9	5.3	5.4	4.4	[3.9]	[3.8]

Oman[55]	12.5	12.5	12.5	11.4	10.6	12.2	12.3	12.1	12.0
Qatar	..	..	..	..	..	..	..	..	..
Saudi Arabia[56]	8.5	11.0	14.3	11.4	10.6	11.5	9.8	8.7	8.3
Syria	5.9	5.7	5.8	5.5	[5.5]	[6.4]	[6.3]	[7.2]	[6.6]
UAE[57]	[5.1]	4.8	5.1	4.5	3.5	3.6	3.5	3.0	2.4
Yemen	5.3	5.8	6.2	5.2	5.0	[5.6]	7.2	7.1	[6.3]

( ) = Uncertain figure; [ ] = SIPRI estimate; | = Change of multiple of currency; † = Figures for these countries do not include military pensions; ‡ = Figures for these countries are for recurrent spending only; § = Figures for these countries are for the adopted budget rather than actual expenditure.

1 Figures for Morocco for 1998–2003 are for adopted budget rather than for actual expenditure.

2 The figures for Angola should be seen in the context of highly uncertain economic statistics due to the impact of conflict on the Angolan economy. Figures are for Defence, Public Order and Security.

3 The figures for the Central African Republic are for current expenditure only. Investment expenditure for 2005 amounted to 775 000 CFA francs.

4 Until 1997 the Democratic Republic of the Congo (DRC) was known as Zaire.

5 Figures for Eritrea in 1995 include expenditure for demobilization. Eritrea changed currency during the period. All figures have been converted to the most recent currency.

6 The figure for Ethiopia in 1999 includes an allocation of 1 billion birr in addition to the original defence budget. Figures for 2002–2005 are for adopted budget.

7 An armed conflict broke out in Guinea-Bissau in 1998, which led to a substantial increase in defence expenditure, especially in 2000/2001. According to the International Monetary Fund (IMF), the increase was financed by a credit from the banking system, as well as by promissory notes. Guinea-Bissau changed currency during the period. All figures have been converted to the most recent currency.

8 Figures for Madagascar include expenditure for the gendarmerie and the National Police. Madagascar changed currency during the period. All figures have been converted to the most recent currency.

9 Figures for Mozambique include expenditure for the demobilization of government and RENAMO soldiers and the formation of a new unified army. The demobilization process ended in 1998/99. Figures are for security and public order from 1999.

10 Figures for Namibia in 1999 refer to the budget of the Ministry of Defence only. In addition to this the 1999 budget of the Ministry of Finance includes a contingency provision of N$104 million for the Namibian military presence in the DRC. The figure for 2002 includes a supplementary allocation of N$78.5 million.

11 Figures for Nigeria before 1999 are understated because of the military's use of a favourable specific dollar exchange rate.

12 The figure for Rwanda for 1998 is the official defence budget. According to the IMF there are additional sources of funding for military activities, both within budget and extra-budgetary. Alternative estimates put Rwanda's military expenditure at twice the official figure.

13 Figures for Senegal do not include expenditure for paramilitary forces, which in 1998 amounted to 21 100 million CFA francs.

14 Sudan changed currency during the period. All figures have been converted to the most recent currency.

15 Figures for Tanzania from 2003–2004 are for defence and security.

16 Figures for Zambia are uncertain, especially those for constant dollars and share of GDP, because of very high inflation and several changes in the currency.

17 The figure for Zimbabwe in 1999 includes a supplementary allocation of Zw$1800 million.

18 Costa Rica has no armed forces. Expenditure for paramilitary forces, border guard, and maritime and air surveillance is less than 0.05% of GDP.

19 Figures for Honduras do not include military pensions or arms imports.

20 The Panamanian defence forces were disbanded in 1990 and replaced by the National Guard, consisting of the national police and the air and maritime services.

21 Figures for the USA are for financial years (1 Oct.–30 Sep.) rather than calendar years.

22 Figures for Chile are for adopted budget. They include direct transfers from the state-owned copper company Corporacion Nacional del Cobre (CODELCO) for military purchases. In 2004–2005 these transfers increased owing to rising copper prices. In June 2005 copper export revenues, at $1.53 billion, were 55% higher than in June 2004.

23 Figures for Colombia in 2002–2004 includes a special allocation of 2.6 billion pesos from a war tax decree of 12 Aug. 2002.

24 Ecuador changed currency from the sucre to the US dollar on 13 Mar. 2000, at a rate of $1 to 25 000 sucres. Current price figures for 1996–2000 represent the dollar value of military expenditure at the market exchange rate for that year. Figures for 2002–2004 are for the adopted budget.

25 The figure for Peru in 2005 does not include the transfer of 20% of gas production revenues from the state-owned company CAMISEA for the armed forces and national police.

26 For the Central Asian countries purchasing power parity (PPP) rates were used for conversion to constant dollars up to and including the 2002 edition of the SIPRI Yearbook.

27 The coverage of the series for Turkmenistan varies over time due to classification changes in the Turkmenistan system of public accounts. PPP rates were used for converting local currency figures to constant dollars up to and including the 2002 edition of the SIPRI Yearbook.

28 Figures for Brunei are current expenditure on the Royal Brunei Armed Forces.

29 Figures for Cambodia are for defence and security, including the regular police force.

30 Figures for China are for estimated total military expenditure. On the estimates in local currency and share of GDP for the period 1989–98 see Wang, S., 'The military expenditure of China, 1989–98', *SIPRI Yearbook 1999: Armaments, Disarmament and International Security* (Oxford University Press: Oxford, 1999), pp. 334–49. The estimates for the years 1999–2002 are based on the percentage change in official military expenditure and on the assumption of a gradual decrease in the commercial earnings of the People's Liberation Army.

31 Figures for Japan are for adopted budget, include the Special Action Committee on Okinawa (SACO) and exclude military pensions.

32 Dollar figures for North Korea are in current dollars owing to the lack of reliable consumer price index data.

[33] The figures for South Korea do not include military pensions, arms imports or paramilitary forces.

[34] Figures for Myanmar are not presented in constant US dollar terms owing to the extreme variation in stated exchange rates between the kyat and the US dollar.

[35] Figures for India include expenditure on paramilitary forces of the Border Security Force, Central Reserve Police Force, Assam Rifles and Indo-Tibetan Border Police, but exclude spending for military nuclear activities.

[36] Figures for Sri Lanka are for current expenditure only. A special allocation in 2000 of Rs28 billion for war-related expenditure is therefore not fully reflected in the official figure.

[37] Figures for Albania for 2001–2003 are for the adopted budget. The figures for 2004 and 2005 are projections made by the Albanian authorities. Figures for Albania do not include expenditure on paramilitary forces.

[38] The figures for Bosnia and Herzegovina include expenditure on both the Army of the Federation of Bosnia and Herzegovina and the Army of the Republika Srpska. The former is divided into 2 components, Bosniac and Croat. The local currency since Jan. 1998 has been the convertible mark, set at 1 convertible mark = 1 Deutsche Mark.

[39] Figures for Croatia exclude military pensions of 448 million kunas for 2000, 428 million kunas for 2001, 433 million kunas for 2002 and 430 million kunas for 2003.

[40] Figures for the Czech Republic up to 2000 do not include military pensions.

[41] Figures for Georgia in 2002–2005 are for budgeted expenditure. During the period 1997–2001 the implementation rate for the defence budget fluctuated between 56% and 90%. The budget figure for 2003 is believed to be an underestimation of actual spending due to the political turmoil during the year.

[42] Figures for Latvia do not include: allocations for military pensions paid by Russia, which averaged 27 million lats per year over the 3 years 1996–98; or expenditure on paramilitary forces, which amounted to 98.5 million lats in 1999.

[43] Figures for Moldova exclude expenditure on military pensions and paramilitary forces. Adding all military items in the budget would give total military expenditure for 2003 of 361 million lei instead of 109 million lei and 432 million lei instead of 113 million lei in 2004.

[44] Romania changed currency during the period. All figures have been converted to the most recent currency.

[45] For sources and methods of the military expenditure figures for Russia see Cooper, J., 'The military expenditure of the USSR and the Russian Federation, 1987–97', SIPRI Yearbook 1998: Armaments, Disarmament and International Security (Oxford University Press: Oxford, 1998), pp. 243–59. Up to and including SIPRI Yearbook 2002, PPP rates were used for Russia for converting local currency figures to constant dollars.

[46] Figures for Spain do not include a major part of government military research and development expenditure, which is financed by the Ministry of Industry.

[47] Sweden changed its accounting system in 2001, giving rise to a series break between 2000 and 2001. This break means that the decrease in military expenditure between 2000 and 2001 is overestimated by 1.4 percentage points.

[48] Figures for Turkey are in new Turkish lira. The Turkish lira was redenominated in 2005 at the rate of 1 new Turkish lira = 1 million Turkish lira.

[49] The series for the UK has a break between 2000 and 2001 because in 2001 the UK changed its accounting system for defence expenditure from a 'cash basis' to a 'resource basis'. It is not clear what impact this change had on the trend in UK military expenditure.

[50] Figures for Ukraine are for the adopted budget for the Ministry of Defence, military pensions and paramilitary forces. Actual expenditure is reportedly 95–99% of budgeted figures for 1996–99.

[51] Figures for Egypt include military aid from the USA of approximately $1.3 billion annually.

[52] Figures for Iran include expenditure on public order and safety.

[53] Figures for Israel include military aid from the USA of approximately $2 billion annually.

[54] Figures for Jordan are expenditure on defence and security.

[55] Figures for Oman are for current expenditure on defence and national security.

[56] Figures for Saudi Arabia are for defence and security.

[57] Figures for the UAE exclude the local military expenditure of each of the 7 emirates that form the United Arab Emirates.

Source: SIPRI Military Expenditure Database.

Appendix 8B. Table of NATO military expenditure by category

PETTER STÅLENHEIM

Table 8B.1. NATO military expenditure on personnel and equipment, 2000–2005

Figures are in US$ m. at 2003 prices and exchange rates. Figures in italics are percentage changes from the previous year.

Country	Item	2000	2001	2002	2003	2004	2005
North America							
Canada	Personnel	4 155	4 241	4 428	4 533	4 779	4 885
	Personnel change		*2.1*	*4.4*	*2.4*	*5.4*	*2.2*
	Equipment	1 174	1 097	1 364	1 373	1 436	1 515
	Equipment change		*-6.5*	*24.4*	*0.6*	*4.6*	*5.5*
USA	Personnel	121 593	117 645	131 525	149 896	155 680	147 844
	Personnel change		*-3.3*	*11.8*	*14.0*	*3.9*	*-5.0*
	Equipment	70 636	83 408	100 067	101 730	111 330	114 446
	Equipment change		*18.1*	*20.0*	*1.7*	*9.4*	*2.8*
Europe							
Belgium	Personnel	2 722	2 718	2 741	2 822	2 944	2 982
	Personnel change		*-0.1*	*0.8*	*3.0*	*4.3*	*1.3*
	Equipment	240	282	272	205	205	254
	Equipment change		*17.9*	*-3.8*	*-24.4*	*-0.1*	*23.8*
Bulgaria	Personnel					299	291
	Personnel change						*-2.9*
	Equipment					*44.5*	71.2
	Equipment change						*60.1*

Country	Item	2000	2001	2002	2003	2004	2005
Czech Republic	Personnel	717	752	783	794	870	901
	Personnel change		4.9	4.0	1.4	9.7	3.6
	Equipment	376	333	300	372	320	210
	Equipment change		-11.6	-9.7	23.9	-14.1	-34.2
Denmark	Personnel	1 715	1 746	1 715	1 647	1 658	1 639
	Personnel change		1.8	-1.8	-3.9	0.7	-1.1
	Equipment	464	560	445	516	616	565
	Equipment change		20.6	-20.6	16.0	19.4	-8.3
Estonia	Personnel					52.8	55.7
	Personnel change						5.5
	Equipment					20.4	23.9
	Equipment change						17.4
France	Personnel	26 460	26 436	27 057	27 045	27 080	26 813
	Personnel change		-0.1	2.3	-0.0	0.1	-1.0
	Equipment	8 262	8 466	8 520	9 413	9 860	9 830
	Equipment change		2.5	0.6	10.5	4.7	-0.3
Germany	Personnel	21 853	21 371	21 124	21 068	20 150	19 680
	Personnel change		-2.2	-1.2	-0.3	-4.4	-2.3
	Equipment	4 867	4 970	4 996	4 838	5 029	5 011
	Equipment change		2.1	0.5	-3.2	4.0	-0.4
Greece	Personnel	4 686	4 690	3 827	3 585	4 034	4 429
	Personnel change		0.1	-18.4	-6.3	12.5	9.8
	Equipment	1 336	1 114	741	515	396	465
	Equipment change		-16.6	-33.5	-30.5	-23.1	17.4

Hungary						
Personnel	592	641	642	684	641	621
Personnel change		8.2	0.2	6.5	-6.3	-3.1
Equipment	150	141	145	144	154	104
Equipment change		-6.6	3.1	-0.4	6.9	-32.8
Italy						
Personnel	21 187	21 125	22 202	21 986	22 846	21 403
Personnel change		-0.3	5.1	-1.0	3.9	-6.3
Equipment	4 257	3 012	3 716	3 901	3 550	2 910
Equipment change		-29.3	23.4	5.0	-9.0	-18.0
Latvia						
Personnel					68.6	86.3
Personnel change						25.7
Equipment					11.6	13.4
Equipment change						15.9
Lithuania						
Personnel					142	154
Personnel change						8.2
Equipment					34.3	40.0
Equipment change						16.7
Luxembourg						
Personnel	128	144	149	157	162	164
Personnel change	7.8	12.9	3.6	4.9	3.6	1.3
Equipment		25.5	12.8	14.7	17.1	33.2
Equipment change		226.6	-49.9	15.1	16.4	94.1
Netherlands						
Personnel	4 086	3 960	4 221	4 395	4 321	4 331
Personnel change		-3.1	6.6	4.1	-1.7	0.2
Equipment	1 370	1 375	1 308	1 245	1 423	1 528
Equipment change		0.4	-4.9	-4.8	14.3	7.4
Norway						
Personnel	1 585	1 527	1 781	1 821	1 913	1 806
Personnel change		-3.6	16.6	2.2	5.1	-5.6
Equipment	755	828	1 114	983	1 061	975
Equipment change		9.7	34.5	-11.8	7.9	-8.1

Country	Item	2000	2001	2002	2003	2004	2005
Poland	Personnel	2 328	2 455	2 453	2 563	2 543	2 559
	Personnel change		5.5	-0.1	4.5	-0.8	0.6
	Equipment	327	337	420	492	613	687
	Equipment change		3.0	24.7	17.1	24.5	12.1
Portugal	Personnel	2 467	2 535	2 042	1 858	1 876	1 880
	Personnel change		2.7	-19.5	-9.0	1.0	0.2
	Equipment	193	167	100	175	192	292
	Equipment change		-13.8	-40.0	75.0	9.9	51.8
Romania	Personnel					680	765
	Personnel change						12.4
	Equipment					344	298
	Equipment change						-13.3
Slovakia	Personnel					296	315
	Personnel change						6.4
	Equipment					69.1	71.9
	Equipment change						4.0
Slovenia	Personnel					272	290
	Personnel change						6.6
	Equipment					81.8	85.9
	Equipment change						5.0
Spain	Personnel	6 031	6 059	6 103	6 021	6 021	6 071
	Personnel change		0.5	0.7	-1.4	0.0	0.8
	Equipment	1 221	1 209	2 590	2 400	2 547	2 315
	Equipment change		-1.0	114.3	-7.4	6.1	-9.1

Turkey						
Personnel	5 264	4 781	4 634	4 118	4 082	4 258
Personnel change		–9.2	–3.1	–11.1	–0.9	4.3
Equipment	3 303	3 527	3 185	3 459	2 702	3 287
Equipment change		6.8	–9.7	8.6	–21.9	21.6
UK						
Personnel	15 636	16 461	16 835	17 082	17 081	16 814
Personnel change		5.3	2.3	1.5	–0.0	–1.6
Equipment	10 530	10 069	10 025	9 835	9 785	10 536
Equipment change		–4.4	–0.4	–1.9	–0.5	7.7
NATO Europe						
Personnel	117 457	117 401	118 310	117 644	120 034	118 309
Personnel change		–0.0	0.8	–0.6	2.0	–1.4
Equipment	37 662	36 414	37 889	38 507	39 076	39 605
Equipment change		–3.3	4.0	1.6	1.5	1.4
NATO Europe (16 pre-2004 members)						
Personnel	117 457	117 401	118 310	117 644	118 222	116 352
Personnel change		–0.0	0.8	–0.6	0.5	–1.6
Equipment	37 662	36 414	37 889	38 507	38 470	39 001
Equipment change		–3.3	4.0	1.6	–0.1	1.4
NATO total						
Personnel	243 204	239 286	254 263	272 072	280 493	271 039
Personnel change		–1.6	6.3	7.0	3.1	–3.4
Equipment	109 471	120 919	139 320	141 610	151 841	155 566
Equipment change		10.5	15.2	1.6	7.2	2.5
NATO total (18 pre-2004 members)						
Personnel	243 204	239 286	254 263	270 072	278 681	269 082
Personnel change		–1.6	6.3	7.0	2.4	–3.4
Equipment	109 471	120 919	139 320	141 610	151 235	154 961
Equipment change		10.5	15.2	1.6	6.8	2.5

Notes: The figures in this table were calculated, based on NATO statistics on the distribution of total military expenditure by category, by applying the shares for personnel and equipment to the figures for total military expenditure and converted to constant 2003 US dollars using consumer price indices from the International Monetary Fund's publication *International Financial Statistics*. A country's data are included in the totals for NATO Europe and NATO from the year of accession: this is 2004 for Bulgaria, Estonia, Latvia, Lithuania, Slovakia and Slovenia. In order to show the trend for a consistent group of countries, additional series are provided for the totals of the states that have been members throughout the period 2000–2005 (16 in NATO Europe and 18 in NATO).

In 2004 the NATO member states agreed on a change in the definition of military expenditure. For all countries except France, Italy, Luxembourg and the Netherlands, figures from 2002 onwards are reported according to the new definition, which excludes 'Other Forces' not 'realistically deployable'. France, Italy and Luxembourg still report according to the old definition and the Netherlands has reported figures according to their approved 2004 defence budget. For Greece, Hungary, Portugal and Turkey the change in definitions has made a big difference. All data are reported according the old definition up to and including 2002 and for personnel shares up to 2003, creating two breaks in all series except for the countries that have yet not changed definitions, one between 2001 and 2002 and one between 2002 and 2003.

Source: NATO, 'NATO–Russia compendium of financial and economic data relating to defence', Press Release (2005)161, 9 Dec. 2005, URL <http://www.nato.int/docu/pr/2005/p05-161e.htm>.

Appendix 8C. Sources and methods for military expenditure data

PETTER STÅLENHEIM

I. Introduction

This appendix describes the sources and methods for the SIPRI military expenditure data provided in the tables in chapter 8 and appendices 8A and 8B, and on the SIPRI website, URL <http://www.sipri.org/contents/milap/>. For a more comprehensive overview of the conceptual problems and sources of uncertainty involved in all sets of military expenditure data, the reader is referred to other sources.[1] The data in this Yearbook should not be linked with the SIPRI military expenditure series in earlier editions because data are continuously revised and updated. This is true in particular for the most recent years as data for budget allocations are replaced by data for actual expenditure. In some cases entire series are revised as new and better data become available.[2] Consistent series dating back to 1988 are available on the SIPRI website and on request from SIPRI. These series cannot always be combined with the SIPRI series for the earlier years, 1950–87, since SIPRI conducted a major revision of the data for many countries for the period beginning in 1988. Changes in base years and method of currency conversion also hinder comparison between editions of the SIPRI Yearbook. In the current edition, the base year for the constant dollar series is 2003. Conversion to constant US dollars has been made by the use of market exchange rates (MERs) for all countries (for details, see section IV and appendix 8E).

II. Purpose of the data

The main purpose of the data on military expenditure is to provide an easily identifiable measure of the scale of resources absorbed by the military. Military expenditure is an input measure which is not directly related to the 'output' of military activities, such as military capability or military security.[3] Long-term trends in military expenditure and sudden changes in trend may be signs of a change in military output, but such interpretations should be made with caution.

Military expenditure data as measured in constant dollars (table 8A.3) are an indicator of the trend in the volume of resources used for military activities with the pur-

---

[1] Such overviews include Brzoska, M., 'World military expenditures', eds K. Hartley and T. Sandler, *Handbook of Defense Economics*, vol. 1 (Elsevier: Amsterdam, 1995); and Ball, N., 'Measuring third world security expenditure: a research note', *World Development*, vol. 12, no. 2 (1984), pp. 157–64. For African countries see Omitoogun, W., *Military Expenditure Data in Africa: A Survey of Cameroon, Ethiopia, Ghana, Kenya, Nigeria and Uganda*, SIPRI Research Report no. 17 (Oxford University Press: Oxford, 2003).

[2] One example is the military expenditure of India presented in this Yearbook. As a result of access to new information, figures have been revised to include spending on some paramilitary forces. This means that the figures for India in this edition are on average *c.* 11% higher than those in *SIPRI Yearbook 2005*.

[3] See Hagelin, B. and Sköns, E., 'The military sector in a changing context', *SIPRI Yearbook 2003: Armaments, Disarmament and International Security* (Oxford University Press: Oxford, 2003), pp. 282–300.

pose of allowing comparisons over time for individual countries and comparisons between countries. Military expenditure as a share of gross domestic product (GDP) (table 8A.4) is an indicator of the proportion of national resources used for military activities, and therefore of the economic burden imposed on the national economy.

III. Coverage of the data

The military expenditure tables in appendix 8A cover 166 countries. This edition of the Yearbook covers the 10-year period 1996–2005.

Total military expenditure figures are calculated for three country groupings—by geographical region, by membership in international organizations and by income per capita. The coverage of these groupings is provided in the notes to table 8A.1.

Definition of military expenditure

The definition of military expenditure adopted by SIPRI is used as a guideline. Where possible, SIPRI military expenditure data include all current and capital expenditure on: (a) the armed forces, including peacekeeping forces; (b) defence ministries and other government agencies engaged in defence projects; (c) paramilitary forces, when judged to be trained and equipped for military operations; and (d) military space activities. Such expenditure should include: (a) military and civil personnel, including retirement pensions of military personnel and social services for personnel; (b) operations and maintenance; (c) procurement; (d) military research and development; and (e) military aid (in the military expenditure of the donor country). Civil defence and current expenditure for past military activities, such as for veterans' benefits, demobilization, conversion and weapon destruction, are excluded.

In practice it is not possible to apply this definition for all countries, since this would require much more detailed information than is available about what is included in military budgets and about off-budget military expenditure items. In many cases SIPRI is confined to using the national data provided, regardless of definition. Priority is then given to the choice of a uniform time series for each country to achieve consistency over time, rather than to adjusting the figures for single years according to a common definition. In cases where it is impossible to use the same source and definition for all years, the percentage change between years in the deviant source is applied to the existing series in order to make the trend as correct as possible. Such figures are shown in square brackets. In the light of these difficulties, military expenditure data are not suitable for close comparison between individual countries and are more appropriately used for comparisons over time.

IV. Methods

Estimation

SIPRI data reflect the official data reported by governments. As a general rule, SIPRI assumes national data to be accurate until there is evidence to the contrary. Estimates are predominantly made either when the coverage of official data does not correspond to the SIPRI definition or when there is no consistent time series available. In the first case, estimates are made on the basis of an analysis of official government budget and expenditure accounts. The most comprehensive estimates of this type, those for China and Russia, have been presented in detail in previous Yearbooks.[4] In the second case, differing time series are linked together. In order not to introduce assumptions into the military expenditure statistics, estimates are always based on empirical evidence and never on assumptions or extrapolations. Thus, no estimates are made for countries that do not release any official data, and these countries are displayed without figures. SIPRI estimates are presented in square brackets in the tables (these are most often used when two different series are linked together). Round brackets are used when data are uncertain for other reasons, such as the reliability of the source or the economic context.

Data for the most recent years include two types of estimate, which apply to all countries. First, figures for the most recent year or years are for adopted budget, budget estimates or revised estimates, and are thus more often than not revised in subsequent years. Second, the deflator used for the last year in the series is an estimate based on part of a year or as provided by the International Monetary Fund (IMF). Unless exceptional uncertainty is involved, these estimates are not bracketed.

The totals for the world, regions, organizations and income groups in table 8A.1 are estimates because data are not available for all countries in all years. These estimates are most often made on the assumption that the rate of change in an individual country for which data are missing is the same as the average in the region to which it belongs. When no estimate can be made, countries are excluded from the totals.

Calculations

The SIPRI military expenditure figures are presented on a calendar-year basis with one exception. For the USA, SIPRI follows the reporting format of the source—a financial-year basis. To calculate calendar-year data for the USA, data for the last financial year would have to be collected from sources not comparable to the NATO statistics.[5] Calendar-year data for other countries are calculated on the assumption of an even rate of expenditure throughout the financial year. The ratio of military expenditure to GDP (table 8A.4) is calculated in domestic currency at current prices and for calendar years.

The original data are provided in local currency at current prices (table 8A.2). In order to enable comparisons between countries and over time, these are converted to US dollars at constant prices (table 8A.3). The *deflator* used for conversion from current to constant prices is the consumer price index of the country concerned. This choice of deflator is connected to the purpose of the SIPRI data—it should be an indicator of resource use on an opportunity-cost basis.[6] In order to better facilitate comparison to other current economic measures, often expressed in current dollar terms,

---

[4] Cooper, J., 'The military expenditure of the USSR and the Russian Federation, 1987–97', *SIPRI Yearbook 1998: Armaments, Disarmament and International Security* (Oxford University Press: Oxford, 1998), pp. 243–59; and Wang, S., 'The military expenditure of China, 1989–98', *SIPRI Yearbook 1999: Armaments, Disarmament and International Security* (Oxford University Press: Oxford, 1999), pp. 334–49.

[5] Up to and including *SIPRI Yearbook 2005*, figures for Canada and the United Kingdom were presented on a financial-year basis.

[6] A military-specific deflator would be a more appropriate choice if the objective were to measure purchasing power in terms of the amount of military personnel, goods and services that could be bought for the monetary allocations for military purposes.

the right-most column in tables 8A.1 and 8A.3 also provides military expenditure for 2005 in current US dollars.

Beginning in *SIPRI Yearbook 2003*, *conversion to dollars* has been done for all countries using the annual average MER. Previously, data for countries in transition and for North Korea were converted by use of the purchasing power parity (PPP) conversion rate.[7] The change to using MERs instead of PPPs resulted in a significant shift downward in the reported level of military expenditure for these countries. For example, at base year 2003, Russian military expenditure converted using PPP rates ($71.7 million in 2005) is 3.4 times higher than in MER dollars ($21.0 million in 2005). In the most extreme of cases, conversion using PPPs instead of the MER can result in a tenfold increase in the dollar value of a country's military expenditure.[8]

As argued in appendix 8E, the PPP rate is in many ways a more appropriate conversion factor than the MER for international comparison of national economic data, especially for countries in transition and developing countries. Considering opportunity cost, the ideal approach would be to use PPP rates for all countries. However, this is not possible since currently available PPP data are not sufficiently reliable for all countries in the SIPRI database. Therefore, for the sake of consistency and simplicity, MERs will be used for all countries until more reliable, regularly updated PPP data become available.[9]

The choice of base year for the constant dollar series also has a significant impact on cross-country comparisons of expenditure data because different national currencies move against the dollar in different ways. Beginning in *SIPRI Yearbook 2005*, the base year was changed to 2003, having previously been 2000. This also has an impact on the regional shares of total world military expenditure. The most extreme example is Europe because of the relative increase of the European currencies against the dollar: the shift in base year from 2000 to 2003 has resulted in an increase of approximately 4 percentage points in the region's share of world military spending.

V. Limitations of the data

A number of limitations are associated with the data on military expenditure. They are of three main types: reliability, validity and comparability.

The main problems of reliability are due to the limited and varying definitions of expenditure. The coverage of official data on military expenditure varies significantly between countries and over time for the same country. In many countries the official data cover only part of military expenditure. Important items can be hidden under non-military budget headings or can even be financed entirely outside the government budget. A multitude of such off-budget mechanisms are employed in practice.[10]

---

[7] The PPP dollar rate of a country's currency is defined as 'the number of units of a country's currency required to buy the same amount of goods and services in the domestic market as a U.S. dollar would buy in the United States'. World Bank, *World Development Indicators 2003* (World Bank: Washington, DC, 2003), p. 285. On the problems of international comparison of military expenditure and currency conversion can be found in appendix 8E. For a methodological description of the problems see 'Sources and methods for military expenditure data', *SIPRI Yearbook 1999* (note 4), pp. 327–33.

[8] Table 8.2 in chapter 8 shows the impact of using PPP rates rather than MERs on the level of military expenditure in dollar terms for the 15 countries with the highest military expenditure in 2005.

[9] A new round of benchmark surveys of price levels used for producing PPP rates was started in 2003. The ambition is that this will produce more reliable PPP rates.

[10] For an overview of such mechanisms see Hendrickson, D. and Ball, N., 'Off-budget military expenditure and revenue: issues and policy perspectives for donors', Conflict, Security and Development

Furthermore, in some countries actual expenditure may be very different from budgeted expenditure—it is most often higher, but in some cases it may be significantly lower. These factors limit the utility of military expenditure data.

A second reason for their limited utility is the very nature of expenditure data. The fact that they are merely input measures limits their utility as an indicator of military strength or capability. Just as military expenditure has an impact on military capability, so do many other factors such as the technological level of military equipment, the state of maintenance and repair, and so on. The most appropriate use of military expenditure data, even when reliably measured and reported, is therefore as an indicator of the economic resources consumed for military purposes.

For the purpose of international comparison, a third complicating factor is the method used for conversion into a common currency, usually the US dollar. As illustrated above, the choice of conversion factor makes a great difference in cross-country comparisons of military expenditure. This is a general problem in international comparisons of economic data, which is not specific to military expenditure. Nonetheless, it does represent a major limitation, and it should be borne in mind when using military expenditure data converted by different types of conversion rate.

VI. Sources

The sources for military expenditure data are, in order of priority: (*a*) primary sources, that is, official data provided by national governments, either in their official publications or in response to questionnaires; (*b*) secondary sources which quote primary data; and (*c*) other secondary sources.

The first category consists of national budget documents, defence White Papers and public finance statistics as well as responses to a SIPRI questionnaire which is sent out annually to the finance and defence ministries, central banks, and national statistical offices of the countries in the SIPRI database. It also includes government responses to questionnaires about military expenditure sent out by the United Nations and, if made available by the countries themselves, the Organization for Security and Co-operation in Europe.

The second category includes international statistics, such as those of the North Atlantic Treaty Organization (NATO) and the IMF. Data for the 16 pre-1999 NATO member states has traditionally been taken from NATO military expenditure statistics published in a number of NATO sources. The introduction of a new definition by NATO has made it necessary to rely on other sources for some NATO countries for the most recent years. Data for many developing countries are taken from the IMF's *Government Finance Statistics Yearbook*, which provides a defence heading for most of the IMF's member countries, and from Country Reports by IMF staff. This category also includes publications of other organizations that provide proper references to the primary sources used, such as the Country Reports of the Economist Intelligence Unit.

The third category of sources consists of specialist journals and newspapers.

The main sources for economic data are the publications of the IMF: *International Financial Statistics*, *World Economic Outlook* and Country Reports by IMF staff. The source for PPP rates is the World Bank's *World Development Report 2006*.

Group (CSDG) Occasional Papers no. 1, CSDG, King's College London, Jan. 2002, URL <http://www.grc-exchange.org/info_data/record.cfm?Id=295>.

Appendix 8D. The reporting of military expenditure data

CATALINA PERDOMO and ÅSA BLOMSTRÖM

I. Introduction

The United Nations (UN) in its latest General Assembly resolution on objective information on military matters asserts that 'a better flow of objective information on military matters can help to relieve international tension and is therefore an important contribution to conflict prevention' and that transparency in military issues as the essential element for building trust among countries.[1] It also encourages international and regional organizations to promote measures for transparency of military expenditure in regular and standardized way.[2]

Obtaining primary and comparable data on official military expenditure has been an important project for both SIPRI and the UN Department of Disarmament Affairs (DDA). SIPRI has collected and published official data on military expenditure since 1969 and has sent out requests to governments to report their data by filling in a standardized form since 1993.[3] Annually since 1981 the UN has requested that its member states (now 191) report their military expenditure using the UN's Standardized Instrument for Reporting Military Expenditures.[4] Both the UN and SIPRI have also engaged in facilitating the understanding of the relevance and purpose of transparency in military expenditure, particularly through regional workshops.[5] Other international bodies, such as the Organization for Security and Co-operation in Europe (OSCE), have promoted the reporting of military spending as part of confidence- and security-building measures (CSBMs). These differ from the SIPRI questionnaire and the UN Standardized Instrument, since the reports are only available to the countries participating in the CSBM, not the general public. Section II of this appendix presents the response rates by governments to the UN and SIPRI reporting systems in 2005, while section III describes some other international bodies' reporting initiatives in the framework of CSBMs.

---

[1] United Nations, General Assembly Resolution A/RES/60/44, 8 Dec. 2005, URL <http://www.un.org/Depts/dhl/resguide/r60.htm>.

[2] On transparency in the arms life cycle, including military expenditure, see chapter 6 in this volume.

[3] Data requests were initially sent only to countries for which data were most difficult to get. However, since 2002 requests have been sent to most of the governments included in the SIPRI Military Expenditure Database.

[4] For a description of the UN and SIPRI reporting systems, including reproductions of their respective standardized forms for reporting of military expenditure, see Sköns, E. and Nazet, N., 'The reporting of military expenditure data', *SIPRI Yearbook 2004: Armaments, Disarmament and International Security* (Oxford University Press: Oxford, 2004), pp. 376–77.

[5] During 2005 the UN held workshops in Fiji, Kenya and the USA. SIPRI held workshops in Ethiopia and Nigeria in the framework of its project Budgeting for the Military Sector in Africa.

II. Reporting of military expenditure data to SIPRI and the UN in 2005

In 2005 a total of 81 countries reported data on military expenditure either to the UN or to SIPRI (see table 8D.1, column 7). The same number reported data in 2004. In addition, 14 countries submitted reports to the UN with no data, 'nil reports' (see table 8D.1, column 5) giving a total of 95 countries that submitted reports in response to a request for military expenditure data. The account below focuses on the countries that actually reported data and disregards the nil reports, which, with the exceptions of Bolivia and Tonga, were submitted by countries that have no or minimal defence forces.

In 2005 the number of reports received by SIPRI increased to 65 (see table 8D.1, column 2). This was an increase from the 61 countries that reported in 2004. However, since SIPRI increased the number of country to which it sent requests from 159 in 2004 to 167 in 2005, the response rate was virtually constant—39 per cent in 2005 against 38 per cent in 2004.[6]

The number of countries reporting data to the UN decreased from 68 in 2004 to 62 in 2005 (table 8D.1, column 6). Including the nil reports, the total number of reports to the UN decreased from 79 in 2004 to 76 in 2005. The data reports in 2005 (excluding the nil reports) represent a response rate of 32 per cent of member states, a fall from 36 per cent in 2004.[7]

On a regional basis, table 8D.1 shows that seven *African* countries—Angola, Burkina Faso, Mauritius, Namibia, the Seychelles, South Africa and Zimbabwe—reported to SIPRI, whereas only one country—Zimbabwe—reported to the UN. In *North America* only the USA reported to SIPRI, while both Canada and the USA reported to the UN. Four of the eight *Central American* countries reported to SIPRI—Guatemala, Honduras, Mexico and El Salvador—while three countries—Guatemala, Honduras and Mexico—reported data to the UN. In *South America* five out of the 11 countries covered reported to SIPRI—Argentina, Bolivia, Brazil, Colombia, and Uruguay. Three South American countries—Argentina, Brazil and Ecuador—reported data to the UN.

No *Central Asian* country reported to SIPRI in 2004 or 2005. The only Central Asian country that reported to the UN in 2005 was Kazakhstan. Five out of 16 countries in *East Asia* reported to SIPRI—Cambodia, China, Japan, South Korea and Taiwan. Six East Asian countries reported data to the UN—Cambodia, Indonesia, Japan, South Korea, Malaysia and Thailand. In *South Asia* three countries—India, Pakistan and Sri Lanka—reported to SIPRI and two—Bangladesh and Nepal—to the UN. In *Oceania* Australia and New Zealand reported both to SIPRI and the UN.

In 2005 most of the European countries submitted reports to both SIPRI and the UN. In *Western Europe* 17 out of 21 countries reported to SIPRI and 20 to the UN.[8]

[6] SIPRI expanded its country coverage to 170 countries in 2005 by including the Caribbean countries in the SIPRI Military Expenditure Database; however, owing to a combination of the countries' small size and the lack of data, not all of these countries have been included in the military expenditure tables in appendix 8A. Requests for data were not sent to 3 countries: Costa Rica, because of its exceptionally small defence forces; and Rwanda and Somalia owing to a lack of contact information.

[7] For a graph of the trend in reporting military expenditure to the UN reports on during 1992–2005 see the website of the UN Department of Disarmament Affairs, URL <http://disarmament.un.org/cab/milex.html>.

[8] The total number of countries in Western Europe that responded to either SIPRI or the UN was 21 out of 21 since Iceland returned a nil report to the UN.

Table 8D.1. Reporting of military expenditure data to SIPRI and the United Nations, by region, 2005

Figures are numbers of countries.

Region/ sub-region[a]	SIPRI requests (1)	SIPRI reports (2)[b]	UN requests (3)	UN data reports (4)[c]	UN nil reports (5)[d]	Total UN reports (6)	SIPRI + UN reports (7)[e]
Africa	48	7	50	1	(0)	1	7
America, North	2	1	2	2	(0)	2	2
America, Central	7	4	8	3	(2)	5	4
America, South	11	5	11	3	(1)	4	6
Caribbean	7	1	5	1	(0)	1	2
Asia, Central	5	0	5	1	(0)	1	1
Asia, East	16	5	17	6	(0)	6	8
Asia, South	6	3	6	2	(0)	2	5
Oceania	4	2	4	2	(0)	2	2
Europe, West	21	17	21	19	(1)	20	20
Europe, Central	15	14	15	14	(0)	14	15
Europe, East	7	4	7	5	(0)	5	6
Middle East	14	2	14	2	(0)	2	2
Small states[f]	4	0	26	1	(10)	11	1
Total	**167**	**65**	**191**	**62**	**(14)**	**76**	**81**

[a] In order to make the SIPRI and UN reporting systems comparable, the countries above have been grouped according to the geographical regions in the SIPRI military expenditure database. See notes in table 8A.1, appendix 8A.

[b] The countries reporting data to SIPRI were: Angola, Argentina, Armenia, Australia, Austria, Belarus, Belgium, Bolivia, Bosnia and Herzegovina, Brazil, Bulgaria, Burkina Faso, Cambodia, China, Colombia, Croatia, Cyprus, Czech Republic, Denmark, Dominican Republic, El Salvador, Estonia, Finland, France, Georgia, Germany, Greece, Guatemala, Honduras, Hungary, India, Italy, Japan, Jordan, South Korea, Latvia, Lebanon, Lithuania, Luxembourg, Macedonia (Former Yugoslav Republic of, FYROM), Malta, Mauritius, Mexico, Moldova, Namibia, Netherlands, New Zealand, Norway, Pakistan, Poland, Romania, Serbia and Montenegro, Seychelles, Slovakia, Slovenia, South Africa, Spain, Sri Lanka, Sweden, Switzerland, Taiwan, Turkey, Uruguay, USA and Zimbabwe.

[c] The countries reporting data to the UN were: Albania, Argentina, Armenia, Australia, Austria, Bangladesh, Belarus, Belgium, Bosnia and Herzegovina, Brazil, Bulgaria, Cambodia, Canada, Croatia, Cyprus, Czech Republic, Denmark, Ecuador, Estonia, Finland, Georgia, Germany, Greece, Guatemala, Honduras, Hungary, Indonesia, Ireland, Italy, Jamaica, Japan, Jordan, Kazakhstan, South Korea, Latvia, Lebanon, Lithuania, Luxemburg, Malaysia, Malta, Mexico, Nepal, Netherlands, New Zealand, Norway, Poland, Portugal, Romania, Russia, San Marino, Serbia and Montenegro, Slovakia, Slovenia, Spain, Sweden, Switzerland, Thailand, Turkey, Ukraine, UK, USA and Zimbabwe. The following 7 reported their data using a simplified UN questionnaire: Cambodia, South Korea, Lebanon, Malaysia, Nepal, San Marino and Zimbabwe.

[d] 12 UN member states submitted nil reports: Andorra, Bolivia, Costa Rica, Iceland, Kiribati, Liechtenstein, Marshall Islands, Monaco, Panama, Samoa, Solomon Islands and Tonga. In addition, 2 non-UN members submitted nil reports: Cook Islands and Holy See.

[e] Column 7 shows the total number of countries that submitted reports with military expenditure data (excluding the nil reports). Totals may be smaller than the sums of columns 2 and 4 because the same country may appear in both columns.

f These are very small UN member states with no or only minimal defence forces.

Sources: Submitted filled-in SIPRI questionnaires; and United Nations, 'Objective information on military matters, including transparency of military expenditures', Report of the UN Secretary-General, UN document A/60/159, 25 July 2005; and United Nations, 'Objective information on military matters, including transparency on military expenditures', Report of the UN Secretary-General, UN document A/60/159/Add. 1, 20 Sep. 2005, and A/60/159/Add. 2, 27 Dec. 2005, URL <http://disarmament2.un.org/cab/milex.html>.

In *Central and Eastern Europe* all but one country covered by the SIPRI Military Expenditure Database—Albania—reported to SIPRI, while only the Former Yugoslav Republic of Macedonia did not report to the UN. Of the seven European states belonging to the *Commonwealth of Independent States* (CIS), four reported to SIPRI—Armenia, Belarus, Georgia and Moldova—and five to the UN—Armenia, Belarus, Georgia, Russia and Ukraine.

In the *Middle East* the response rate was very low, as it has been in previous years. Two countries—Jordan and Lebanon—reported to both SIPRI and the UN. However, several Middle Eastern governments have begun to provide defence budget data on their government websites, which is a sign of progress in the level of openness.

In 2005 SIPRI expanded its coverage with the inclusion of 11 Caribbean countries.[9] Of these 11 states, one reported data to SIPRI—the Dominican Republic—and one—Jamaica—reported to the UN.

III. Reporting of military expenditure data to other international bodies

As established by the UN General Assembly, sharing information on military expenditure is a way of promoting confidence and trust among countries. There are two international instruments for the reporting of military spending to international bodies under the framework of CSBMs. These two bodies are the OSCE and the UN Economic Commission for Latin America and the Caribbean (ECLAC). However, unlike the reporting to the UN and SIPRI, these two mechanisms are only available to the participating countries, and not to the public.

The OSCE members agreed to exchange information on military budgets on an annual basis in the Vienna Document 1990.[10] This initiative promoted the confidence needed to negotiate and then ratify the 1990 Treaty on Conventional Armed Forces in Europe (CFE Treaty).[11] The Vienna Document chose the UN Standardized Instrument for Reporting Military Expenditures as the reporting format. There is a substantial regional variation in the level of transparency in the military budgeting processes of OSCE member states. While European countries are relatively open about their military spending, Central Asian states are in the process of making their defence budgets more transparent.

A decade later, in 1999, the UN began the promotion, through the ECLAC, of the Common Standardized Methodology for the Measurements of Defence Spending

[9] Those 11 countries are Antigua and Barbuda, Bahamas, Barbados, Bermuda, Cuba, Dominican Republic, Grenada, Haiti, Jamaica, Suriname and Trinidad and Tobago.
[10] The requirement remains in the Vienna Document 1999, on which see annex A in this volume.
[11] Lachowski, Z., *Confidence- and Security-Building Measures in the New Europe*, SIPRI Research Report no. 18 (Oxford University Press: Oxford, 2004). On the CFE Treaty see annex A in this volume.

between Argentina and Chile.[12] This reporting system, which was extended to include Peru in 2001, has been credited as playing a role in reducing the potential tensions of arms acquisitions in the region.[13] The Andean Community of Nations has examined the possibility of adopting a similar mechanism, but no concrete advances have been made yet.[14] Similarly, a recent study by the ECLAC has suggested extending this methodology to the rest of the region.[15] Controversially, two of the three countries participating in the methodology—Chile and Peru—do not have a very transparent military financing process.

In 2005, 86 per cent of the 55 OSCE member states reported their military spending to the UN using either the standardized or the simplified instruments, whereas 67 per cent reported to SIPRI. Of the OSCE countries reporting to the UN, 72 per cent also reported to SIPRI. While all European countries reported to either SIPRI or the UN, the five Central Asian countries reported to neither SIPRI nor the UN. Of the three participants in the ECLAC initiative, only Argentina made its military expenditure public through SIPRI and as well the UN; the other two disclosed their spending to neither organization.

[12] United Nations, Economic Commission for Latin America and the Caribbean, *A Common Standardized Methodology for the Measurement of Defence Spending* (United Nations: Santiago, Nov. 2001), URL <http://www.eclac.cl/cgi-bin/getProd.asp?xml=/publicaciones/xml/1/8771/P8771.xml>. On this methodology see Sheetz, T., 'Una evaluación del documento cepalino: "Metodología estandarizada común para la medición de los gastos de defensa"' [An assessment of the CEPAL document: 'A Common Standardized Methodology for the Measurement of Defence Spending'], *Revista Fuerzas Armadas y Sociedad*, vol. 18, nos 1–2 (Jan.–June 2004), URL <http://www.fasoc.cl/php/fasoc.php?seccion=articulo&id_articulo=37>, pp. 107–21.

[13] 'Chilean foreign minister denies "arms" race with Peru, furthers stability in Ecuador', *El Comercio*, 13 Aug. 2005, Translation from Spanish, World News Connection, National Technical Information Service (NTIS), US Department of Commerce. See also chapter 8.

[14] Organization of American States, Committee on Hemispheric Security, 'Draft Declaration of Miami on Confidence and Security Building Measures', Meeting of Experts on Confidence and Security Building Measures', Document CP/CSH-528/02 rev. 3, 28 Jan. 2003, URL <http://www.oas.org/csh/english/csbmreports.asp>, p. 3.

[15] United Nations, Economic Commission for Latin America and the Caribbean, 'Methodology for the comparison of military expenditures', Santiago, July 2005, URL <http://www.eclac.cl/cgi-bin/getProd.asp?xml=/publicaciones/xml/9/22549/P22549.xml>, p. 49.

Appendix 8E. International comparisons of military expenditures: issues and challenges of using purchasing power parities

MICHAEL WARD

I. Introduction

Analysts encounter significant problems when trying to compare one country's expenditure on a group of products, expressed in its own currency, with another country's outlays on the same products valued in a different currency. In the case of military outlays, the problem of comparisons is compounded by the difficulty of identifying the total scope and coverage of official expenditure on 'defence' or 'the military' and obtaining meaningful values for the various items that this comprises.

This section continues with a discussion of why international comparisons are useful and necessary, how they have been undertaken and the specialized nature of military expenditure.[1] Section II looks at how economically relevant international comparisons can be made and compares and assesses the use of exchange rates and purchasing power parities (PPPs) against a historical and theoretical background. In section III the conceptual and empirical issues that need to be resolved to estimate meaningful PPPs are outlined. Sections IV and V look specifically at the problem of comparing military expenditures and relative military burdens in this context and considers the applicability of different comparison methods. Some of the complex practical problems of identifying national military outlays and their composition, and how their absolute size and share of gross domestic product (GDP)—and hence relative absorption of each country's resources—should be calculated, are discussed. Section VI presents the conclusions.

There are a number of reasons why governments and supranational agencies want to make international comparisons. For cross-country poverty analysis and income-related studies, where relative economic well-being, policy priorities and appropriate resource allocations are considered, the reasons are mostly self-evident. In the more political arena of national security and military spending, where economic issues have to be weighed against security concerns, the matter is less clear. The nature of the comparison depends on whether the main interest is in an individual country's capacity to produce military goods, in its total military strength or in how much its government spends on the military each year. Defence analysts want to understand whether comparative assessments of so-called military potential are aligned with a

---

[1] See also Kravis, I. B. and Lipsey, R. E., *Toward an Explanation of National Price Levels*, Princeton Studies in International Finance no. 52 (Princeton University, International Finance Section: Princeton, N.J., Nov. 1983); Kravis, I. B., Heston, A. W. and Summers, R., *International Comparisons of Real Product and Purchasing Power* (Johns Hopkins University Press: Baltimore, Md., 1978); Kravis, I. B., Heston, A. and Summers, R., *World Product and Income: International Comparisons of Real Gross Domestic Products* (Johns Hopkins University Press: Baltimore, Md., 1982); and Kravis, I. B., Kenessey, Z. and Heston, A. W., *A System of International Comparisons of Gross Product and Purchasing Power* (Johns Hopkins University Press: Baltimore, Md., 1975).

country's capacity to wage war. Others are concerned with how military spending impacts on the economy and the burden it places more broadly on living standards.

Historically, different approaches have been taken to measure comparative military strength. The most traditional has been straight number counts: the total personnel under arms, the number of tanks and guns of a certain type, the number of aircraft in the air force, and so on. Defence analysts have used these to undertake assessments of the relative merits of the armed forces and their equipment. A second approach is to take the value of military expenditure in local currencies and to convert these into US dollar terms using the published exchange rate (defined as the average principal exchange rate relating to the period in question). Exchange rates are subject, however, to the various demand and supply forces, including speculative capital flows, that affect the value of currencies. A third way is to apply purchasing power parities. These effectively transform values in local currencies onto a common price basis using a standard international unit of account. PPP conversions generally work well with most items of expenditure comprising the GDP. International comparisons of, for example, food expenditure by households (often taken as a proxy for actual consumption) can be handled in an undistorted fashion. However, the identification of relevant PPPs and their use to convert more complex categories such as military expenditure into a common international price basis pose both practical and conceptual difficulties.

The specialized nature of military expenditure

Military spending is often unidentified or deliberately obfuscated by governments.[2] Even the overall budget allocated to defence may be a closely guarded state secret. Some outlays on the armed forces may be posted 'off-budget' and some may be secreted away in spending on civil militia, part-time territorial forces, coastguard or customs services and counter-terrorism activities. Some spending in areas such as education, vocational training and medical research may also hide spending on the military. The procedures and practices to account for military expenses vary from country to country. The activities of non-government organizations that sponsor armed forces and guerrilla groups can lead to underestimation of the total extent of a country's military spending.

The focus of this appendix is on comparisons of military expenditure. It describes a more appropriate basis for analysing national expenditures across countries than that afforded by conventional exchange rate comparisons. It advocates the use of purchasing power parities to compare real outlays and argues, implicitly, for the more systematic definition and classification of military spending to ensure that the scope and methodology of comparison are consistent. The objective of the conversion into comparative dollar values is to enable comparison of money spent. Such data can be used to measure the priority that a government attaches to the military or to assess the domestic resources that are devoted to supporting the military. However, since they are input measures, these data carry little information about the output, such as military strength or the capacity to wage war, and cannot be used to assess these outputs, not least because of the wide variation between countries in the input–output relationship for military spending and the intangible nature of critical inputs such as training.

---

[2] On the transparency and availability of military expenditure data see chapters 6 and 7 in this volume.

Military expenditure is unique among the expenditures reported in GDP or gross national product (GNP) since it does not directly and immediately contribute to any equivalent increase in the economic welfare of households. The reported value of any military outlay is determined by prices that generally reflect the cost incurred directly by government or reimbursed to suppliers to provide what the country's leaders deem to be in the interests of national security and necessary to protect its citizens and their collective assets. Unlike most other items of expenditure, the prices underlying these outlays are not assessed by the market. Costs tend to be determined by recognized institutional processes (such as contract tendering and equipment procurement rules) and historical precedent (the military list). Customarily, an agreed rate of return to the supplier will be added.

II. Features of international comparisons

Two basic problems have to be overcome before reliable estimates of national military expenditures can be produced in internationally comparable terms. The first—a methodological problem that applies to all international comparisons of expenditures—concerns the criteria for choosing an appropriate statistical procedure for converting any reported values expressed in national currencies into some uniform international standard unit of account. The second problem concerns the difficulties surrounding the identification of the scope of military expenditure. This is a question not only of quantities but also of how to determine the prices embodied in officially reported military values, especially given the absence of market prices and equivalent market comparators for many specific and often unique military goods and services.

Methods of international comparison involve: (a) comparing actual expenditures and (b) comparing the respective shares of such expenditures to some national benchmark, usually GDP or GNP.[3] The former is a pure measure of equivalent money values. The latter is an apparently value-neutral indicator of the national resources that have been devoted to providing a defined outlay. While this may be interesting for internal analysis, it is invalid for international comparisons of relative resource use.

The use of exchange rates and their limitations

Historically, comparisons between countries of goods and services valued in monetary terms have been performed using quoted exchange rates. Outlays, recorded in national currencies, are converted into a commonly recognized international denominator. The US dollar has usually been used as this benchmark.

Exchange rates—specifically, a country's principal official exchange rate—have been adopted because of their convenience. Timely data are always available and the process is clear. The daily behaviour of a country's 'principal exchange rate' is on record in most countries over an extended time period. Foreign exchange data are nominally transparent, effectively independent because they are largely the outcome of financial market forces and, in a sense, neutral. For the purposes of international

---

[3] GNP—now more correctly referred to as gross national income (GNI)—differs from GDP by adding incomes earned abroad by residents and deducting incomes earned by non-residents in the domestic economy.

comparisons of real economic phenomena, however, exchange rates are not appropriate because they are volatile.

History, particularly in the second half of the 20th century, has shown that exchange rates are unreliable conversion factors for standardizing currency-based variables to a consistent numeraire. Following World War II exchange rates and absolute and relative prices were often in disarray because of resource shortages and different policy stances. New ideas about the respective roles of the public and private sectors in economic affairs had a significant impact on prices and exchange rates. Major currency devaluations (against the US dollar) and other currency depreciations took place among many of the former combatants. However, international trade surged and domestic economies boomed in the period of post-war reconstruction and renewal. Despite a worldwide 'dollar shortage', post-war optimism ran reasonably high in European countries. Most of these countries depended heavily on the machinery produced by a US economy that was relatively less disrupted by the war and each sought expansion through trade- and export-led growth. Exchange rates were not exclusively determined, at least in the short term, by economic events. They became a key policy variable in balancing desires to protect the domestic economy against the need to secure an international competitive advantage. The International Monetary Fund (IMF) tried to establish a regime of fixed exchange rates but throughout the 1950s and 1960s there were regularly devaluations of leading currencies, including the pound sterling, the Italian lira and the French franc. By the early 1970s it was clear that the system of fixed exchange rates had been seriously undermined and could not be continued. In 1974, following the first oil crisis, the IMF formally abandoned the system.

Nevertheless, some countries still pegged their currencies to the dollar, franc or sterling. Sometimes this was for reasons of historical ties and institutional relationships, particularly in the banking network. Some single-currency pegs were later abandoned as the major currencies themselves moved sharply in value, especially when the US dollar began to appreciate strongly in the early 1980s. Instead, a number of countries set the value of their currencies according to a basket of the currencies of their main trading partners weighted to reflect the respective value of their trade. This was a strategy pursued by many developing countries then facing rampant inflation. Capital flight, an outcome of political uncertainty and weaknesses in foreign exchange markets, became more common. Runs on currencies, reflecting speculative and precautionary motives, emerged as a serious problem. In the 1980s the situation gave rise to significant depreciations against the dollar of the currencies of many developing countries. Whenever this happened, dollar-denominated GNP per capita measures published by, for example, the United Nations (UN), the World Bank and the IMF created a 'new' perception about the relative level of development and ranking of countries.

The relevance of exchange rate conversions is now argued mainly on the ground that they depict long-term economic trends. However, economists have customarily attributed more importance to economic 'fundamentals' and international factors in the determination of both the level and movement of a country's exchange rate. Exchange rates do not reflect, consistently and coherently, the structural price differentials that lie at the core of every internationally based value comparison. Even for the 'baseline' country in the denominator, reported exchange rates may fluctuate, as evidenced by the significant fluctuations in the value of the US dollar against most other major currencies from the early 1980s to the present. These fluctuations represent a major drawback to the usefulness of exchange rates in converting local currencies into a uniform benchmark. The World Bank has devised, for its own operational guidelines, a variant of the standard exchange rate approach to arrive at its published GNP per capita 'Atlas' measures denominated in US dollars.[4] These numbers are widely used but take no account of national price levels, serving only to dampen down observed volatility in exchange rates over the three-year period up to the year in question.

The nature of foreign exchange regimes has changed considerably over the past three decades. In 1975, 87 per cent of all developing countries operated some type of pegged exchange rate. By 1996 this had fallen to well below 50 per cent.[5] Between 1975 and 1996, the exchange rate of various national currencies fell by at least 25 per cent within a year in 116 separate cases. Nearly half of these were countries operating flexible exchange rate regimes.[6] Several countries give only formal recognition to the official principal exchange rate. The IMF regularly notes in its monthly *International Financial Statistics* that some countries operate 'secondary' and 'tertiary' rates that are applicable to certain types of foreign transaction, such as government imports or tourism exchange. Since the behaviour of exchange rates is only loosely related to theory and internal economic conditions, there is little rationale for using them as a basis for making real economic comparisons between countries or over time. For the most part, exchange rate comparisons are appropriate only for international portfolio assessments, bilateral transfers, current financial transactions and international debt settlement. The exchange rate thus determines the real domestic opportunity costs that have to be faced by a given country when meeting any external financial obligation.

Purchasing power parities

Purchasing power parities are the 'shadow' conversion rates that indicate how much, hypothetically, it would cost in a particular country to acquire exactly the same goods and services as $1 buys in the United States (or in whichever country or group of countries is chosen as the baseline reference). Unlike exchange rates, comparisons based on purchasing power parity have the virtue of being base-country invariant. They are also transitive; that is, a country will stand in the same relationship to another country whether a comparison is drawn directly between them or indirectly via a third country. The core principle underlying PPPs is simple: national average expenditures are divided by national average prices to obtain estimates of quantities directly and the quantities in each country are then revalued at uniform average international prices. The practical application of the methodology, however, poses significant problems. An enormous volume of micro price and quantity data pertaining to all categories of private and public goods and services must be collected to perform the requisite calculations and an appropriate aggregation formula has to be chosen.[7]

---

[4] World Bank, *World Bank Atlas*, 36th edn (World Bank: Washington, DC, 2004).

[5] Caramazza, F. and Aziz, J., *Fixed or Flexible?: Getting the Exchange Rate Right in the 1990s*, Economic Issues no. 13 (International Monetary Fund: Washington, DC, Apr. 1998), URL <http://www.imf.org/external/pubs/ft/issues13/>, p. 2.

[6] Caramazza and Aziz (note 5), p. 5.

[7] Ward, M., *Purchasing Power Parities and Real Expenditures in the OECD* (Organisation for Economic Co-operation and Development: Paris, 1985).

Purchasing power parities and exchange rates

The calculation of PPPs opened up an entirely new way of looking at comparative economic size and national well-being. When introduced, it challenged long-held perceptions about country rankings in economic development—based on exchange rates converted to the US dollar. Partly for this reason, the approach of using PPPs still encounters considerable opposition, even in institutions with an international mandate.

International comparability remains a key objective of the UN statistical system. Clear concepts, conventions and standards of data compilation such as the System of National Accounts (SNA) and classification of goods and services have been laid down.[8] PPPs form part of these standards and, compared with exchange rates, they reflect how prices impact on reported values through differences in price levels within and between countries.

To understand which countries, overall, may be deemed 'cheap' and which are 'expensive', it is only necessary to divide the respective PPP for GDP by the corresponding exchange rate. For example, if the PPP between the United Kingdom and the USA is £1 = $2.15 and the corresponding official exchange rate is £1 = $1.85, then the price level (i.e., 2.15/1.85 = 1.16) indicates that, in general, prices in the UK for equivalent goods are 16 per cent higher than in the USA.

When calculated at a level below that of GDP, PPP ratios can also be considered as measures of the relative price levels of differently defined groups of commodities, such as food or military goods and services. PPPs for different groups of commodities vary and are often quite different from the overall PPP for GDP, another important distinction from the generality of the single exchange rate. The further a specific PPP ratio for a defined spending category is from 1, the more the price level will deviate from the international average for GDP or the relevant subset of GDP expenditures.

PPPs relate to differences in price levels at a particular time (a given state) while a price index measures changes in prices over time (flows).[9] PPPs only provide a measure of comparative real values applicable to a certain time period, such as a year. As such, they represent the spatial, cross-country dimension of price differences at a sector and expenditure category level. In the case of PPPs the economic 'distance' between any two observations, such as between the USA and Kenya, is not fixed, whereas in a conventional price index changes are measured sequentially with reference to fixed reporting dates and ordered chronological intervals. Because disparate and disjoint magnitudes are associated with economic size in cross-section income comparisons since different baskets of goods and services are involved, this factor can give rise to potentially greater problems of distortion in PPP price level estimates than in conventional time series price index measurements. The size of the economic gap helps explain why the GDP of low-income countries rises substantially when PPPs are used rather than exchange rates.

---

[8] United Nations, Department of Economic and Social Development, *Handbook of the International Comparison Programme* (United Nations: New York, N.Y., 1992), URL <http://siteresources.world bank.org/ICPINT/Resources/icphbeng.pdf>. The SNA is an international statistical standard for the compilation of national accounts and the measurement of the market economy. The current SNA 1993 will be replaced by the revised SNA 2006. For more information see the website of the United Nations Statistical Division, URL <http://millenniumindicators.un.org/unsd/nationalaccount/method.htm>.

[9] Ahmad, S., 'Harmonization of CPI and PPP: problems and prospects', Eurostat, *Improving the Quality of Price Indices: International Seminar, Florence, December 18–20, 1995* (Office for Official Publications of the European Communities: Luxembourg, 1996), pp. 449–54.

Purchasing power parities and national incomes

Although based on use rather than output, PPP-converted GDP estimates provide an aggregate measure of current production and of the real size of various economies. Evidence from past enquiries shows that, based on international price levels, the real GDPs of poorer countries are much higher than those officially reported in exchange rate terms. Sometimes their economies turn out to be three or four times larger.[10] Because these countries generally have very low price levels in respect of most major categories of expenditure, when an 'average' international price is applied to revalue their goods and services, GDP values are significantly uplifted. The implication is that countries like China and India, with low price levels, in reality manage much larger economies than would be apparent from a current official exchange rate comparison. It also means that important sectors and components of spending in these countries—such as government and, specifically, the military—may be considerably bigger in real PPP terms than is indicated by exchange rates. Significantly, disparities across countries in GDP and constituent spending categories also narrow with the use of international prices.

The difference consequently impacts on measures of 'real income per head'. Even allowing for size of population and differing age and sex components, the inhabitants of some countries which were previously understood to be among the very poorest (including China) are now considered on a PPP basis to be not only much better off but also significantly wealthier than other countries in real terms.[11] These findings are consistent with what is known about relative differences in growth rates over extended time periods and with what has been observed in terms of achievements in social progress independently measured by value-free social indicators.

III. The use of purchasing power parities

The calculation of purchasing power parities

Purchasing power parities are calculated from the combination of binary price ratios between countries of closely similar goods or services. Because weights do not exist for attaching importance to any item, expenditures on similar items are aggregated to form a 'basic heading'. This comprises a common group of like types of goods and services that form a well-defined basket of expenditures making up GDP. The combination of price ratios is then related to the expenditures on these basic headings. The price ratios reflect the corresponding average exchange ratios between countries for that collection of items. As a group, they can be weighted by their respective values in GDP.

Successively, calculations can be made of (*a*) initial item price ratios, (*b*) ratios for generic groups of goods and services, (*c*) ratios for basic expenditure headings and then (*d*) ratios for aggregate consumption categories—such as 'the total final consumption of households', 'the collective consumption of government' and 'gross fixed capital formation'. Progressively, according to all the separate categories of

---

[10] E.g., the World Bank measures the GNI of China to have been $1416.8 billion in 2003 in exchange rate terms (using its Atlas method) and $6410 billion in PPP terms. World Bank, *World Development Indicators 2005* (World Bank: Washington, DC, 2005), URL <http://devdata.worldbank.org/wdi2005/>, tables 1.1 and 5.7.

[11] World Bank (note 10).

GDP, a structure of cross-country price relationships representing the real rate of price exchange between all types of goods and services of a specific description can be built up. Each spending category is weighted according to its respective importance in a country's GDP, as measured by the respective expenditure outlays. Ultimately, the overall PPP for the whole economy, namely GDP, can be generated in this way. The choice of the formula depends on the primary objectives of the comparison.[12]

The above refers to comparisons in binary form while in practice the calculations are based on a 'multilateralization' of all possible direct and indirect binary ratios between all countries engaged in the comparison for every item in question.

Comparability and 'representativity'

The above methodology deviates from the original PPP notion of pricing an exactly identical basket of items in each country. The relevant 'basket' relates to each respective country's GDP and to the revealed utility preferences and unique structure of spending of final users. This is because comparing a basket containing the same items and pricing it in both Sweden and the UK poses problems. Such a basket would not be characteristic of normal expenditures, as reflected in the actual outlays of either country's GDP. Clearly, going beyond high-income Europe it would be difficult and unrepresentative to price the same bundle of consumption items in a country like China.

This is not just a question of coverage and the necessity for comprehensive pricing. At the core is the more basic issue of the economic relationship between prices and quantities. Prices and the corresponding quantities purchased are normally inversely related, whether it is a question of movements over time or differences in levels. Where a particular item is popular and people thus buy greater quantities of it, the price will tend to be relatively cheaper than other close substitutes. Comparable packets of frozen cod fingers, for example, may be found in both China and Sweden, but in China they will be relatively more expensive because they are neither popular nor bought in large quantities and they are not commonly found in many shops.

This problem also extends to the actual unit size of the quantities bought. It is clear that prices must be related to identically comparable quantities but this cannot be estimated in simple average unit value terms. The price per kilogram of the same quality of rice is quite different depending on whether it is customarily sold in 10-, 25- or 40-kg bags, as is common in Asia, or in 1- or 2-kg packets, as is generally the case in Europe and the USA. Since it is necessary when calculating PPPs to identify items

---

[12] If, as in the case of military spending, it is important to show respective shares of GDP, then the Geary–Khamis method should be applied at the aggregation level above the basic headings. If it is only necessary to compare internationally what is spent on a specific defence 'item', such as military personnel, then what is known as an EKS aggregation formula can be used. The EKS formula is a multilateral method developed by Ödön Éltető, Pál Köves and Bohdan Szulc that computes the nth root of the product of all possible Fisher price indexes between n countries. It has been used at the detailed heading level to obtain heading parities and also at the GDP level. Refinements to the EKS method, beginning with the decision to give greater weight to direct binary comparisons and to balanced comparisons of characteristic products in each pair of countries, have been progressively introduced by Eurostat and the Organisation for Economic Co-operation and Development. Éltető, Ö. and Köves, P., 'Egy nemzetközi összehasonlításoknál fellépő indexszámítási problémáról' [On an index number computation problem in international comparison], *Statisztikai Szemle*, vol. 42, no. 5 (1964), pp. 507–18; and Szulc, B. J., 'Price indices below the basic aggregation level', eds R. Turvey et al., *Consumer Price Indices: An ILO Manual* (International Labour Office: Geneva, 1989).

that are representative of people's expenditure choices, there is clearly a conflict between inter-country comparability and what is referred to as national 'characteristicity' and 'representativity' of the items that the statisticians decide to price.

It is essential that exactly the same quantities and qualities are compared when determining each country's respective prices and that derived unit values for specified quantities are not affected by bulk purchases and special packaging. It is also important that there are no obvious or intrinsic quality differences between the various items in the comparison. The ultimate objective is to define the average annual unit price (or value) underlying the different bundles of goods and services expenditures that make up GDP.

IV. International comparisons of military expenditure

This section considers how PPPs can be used for the cross-country comparison of military expenditures. It does not, and cannot, consider comparisons of total military strength or the capacity to wage war. The most that a consideration of military expenditure can do is compare the priorities that governments attach to the military or the domestic resources that are absorbed by the militaries of different countries.

Analysis of military spending

Common to all countries and corresponding to the standard distinction observed in national accounts for other official expenditures, military outlays comprise two main categories: (a) direct expenditure on the armed forces and their support personnel, plus expenditure on related consumable items including repairs and maintenance; and (b) spending on equipment and buildings. As indicated in these descriptions, each of these categories can be broken down into two component sub-categories. By convention, it is standard national accounting practice to regard all military construction and hardware spending, irrespective of its nature and durability, as current expenditure rather than 'investment' (or, more accurately, gross fixed capital formation). Outlays on buildings that can be used for civil purposes, like military hospitals and schools for the children of military personnel, may be treated differently in the national accounts, although the relevant expenditure will still appear under 'defence' in the annual budget accounts. Strictly speaking, because war is primarily concerned with conquering an opponent and destroying its capacity to wage war, all military equipment—such as guns, tanks, aircraft, ships and so on—should be considered 'expendable'. In a time of war, construction works like blockhouses, gun emplacements, military airfields and dockyards are of strategic significance and subject to destruction. Few military structures or equipment contribute economically to any direct increase in a country's productive potential. Although it could be argued that outlays on military equipment and structures help protect a country, and thus its productive potential, no obvious alternative civil use exists for these items.

Military expenditure of a current nature refers, on the one hand, to payments to armed personnel and support staff and, on the other, to the routine costs of maintaining the military. The first sub-category refers to personal emoluments such as salaries, actual and imputed pensions, benefits, and all other income in kind paid to the regular armed forces and their support staff. Conscripted manpower (usually paid much less) should also be included. Subsidized private accommodation and family housing and any other transfers of a directly personal nature made to the armed forces should also be added. The second sub-category covers the recurring expenses of housing, feeding and clothing the armed forces on the bases where they are billeted, plus military administration and communications, training and supplies. It includes all forms of regular repair and maintenance and the supply of utility services like electricity and water. Together these two types of outlay constitute the bulk of what the SNA 1993 refers to as 'current government expenditure on defence'.

The second main category of military spending covers what would be regarded elsewhere as capital outlays. In the current SNA these items are 'consumption goods', but there is strong pressure to move them into the capital formation category in the proposed SNA 2006. The category comprises: (*a*) equipment, mostly of a purely military nature, but also computers and vehicles; and (*b*) buildings such as strategic nerve centres, bases and parade grounds, silos, airfields, and storage facilities. The distinction between equipment and buildings is important for calculating relevant PPPs because the respective methodologies are different and because of the need to establish appropriate reference comparisons with other countries. When reference to the military is made under current government expenditure, the latter has to be further divided between the 'collective expenditure of government' and the 'individual household expenditure of government'. Because the role of government varies significantly between countries, particularly in the official provision of social services, consistency dictates that for international comparisons statisticians should distinguish between 'who uses' and 'who pays for' government services. Thus, all government spending on behalf of households gets added to total household consumption while government spending on the military refers only to its public collective responsibility.

In total and in terms of its component structure, military spending is affected by the respective size and strategic location of different countries as well as their allegiance to regional pacts and defence treaties. Such alliances may involve the provision or receipt of military equipment, the engagement of advisers and the use of foreign bases. Traditionally, for example, a portion of the forces of members of the North Atlantic Treaty Organization (NATO) have been stationed abroad. Peacekeeping operations pose a further complication. Inevitably, too, some (imported) equipment used by the home forces will be provided under token cost arrangements or a soft lend-lease procurement agreement that influences the cost of providing defence services.

History and how countries see their military role is also a factor. Countries such as China, which is bordered by 14 other countries, maintain large land forces because they are wary of the potential threats posed by neighbouring countries. The perspective is both domestic and regional. Others, such as the USA, see their role more globally. The USA has only two neighbours but has a long experience of overseas operations as in World War II, the cold war in Europe, and hostilities in Korea, Viet Nam and the Middle East. It has thus tended to focus on maintaining a long-range strategic capability and global mobility that depends heavily on military hardware and maintaining the capacity to strike across vast distances.

Under the present methodology of the World Bank's International Comparison Program (ICP),[13] the government sector, specifically that relating to 'collective' outlays, is taken as a whole, with the consequence that PPPs for military outlays are

---

[13] The ICP produces internationally comparable price levels, expenditure values and PPP estimates; for more information see the ICP website at URL <http://www.worldbank.org/data/icp/>.

indistinguishable from current government expenditures in general. This creates a potential for distortion, especially if the defence component is large and represents an important part of total government spending, as in the case of both China and the USA. The structure of expenditure on salaries, on the one hand, and goods and services, on the other, is potentially quite different in the case of military outlays compared with the rest of government spending, and even more so if all military spending on equipment and construction works is treated as 'current consumption'. Complications also arise if the average payments made to members of the armed forces, plus the structure of those payments across personnel and ranks, differ significantly from the salary scales of the civilian branches of government.

Quality and efficiency differences

'Quality' differences, broadly defined, are one of the biggest problems encountered when trying to compare military equipment or the skill levels of enlisted personnel in different countries. Given the desire of military leaders to keep one step ahead of potential enemies, quality improvements in military equipment and trained personnel occur continuously. These improvements will be more rapid in rich and technologically advanced countries. The relative professionalism, training and skills of the military forces, however, may be difficult to quantify. When overlaid by such real but unquantifiable factors as nationalism, patriotism and dedication, the question becomes even more problematic. Military effectiveness and readiness cannot be easily proxied by comparisons of real salaries for people of similar age, grade and 'experience', as is the procedure for other government employees. In a different but similar context, the ratio of the price or cost of the standard US rifle, the M-16, cannot be directly compared with the Chinese equivalent, the locally produced Soviet-designed AK-47. Indeed, some military experts argue that, although the AK-47 is simple, it can prove more reliable and robust than its nominally superior but more expensive US counterpart.

Which purchasing power parity rates to use?

There are basically three possible approaches to using PPPs in comparing military outlays between countries. The choice of approach will depend primarily on the availability of data but also on the purpose of the comparison: whether it be the measurement of the resources consumed by the military, opportunity cost of military expenditure or military purchasing power.

1. *Adopt the PPP at the overall GDP level.* This is the intuitive counterpart to applying the official exchange rate covering all goods and services.
2. *Apply a specific PPP for government expenditure.* This may prove more relevant on the grounds that salaries in both government spending as a whole and in the military make up the bulk of the current outlays (two-thirds or more in some cases[14]).
3. *Derive a specific PPP for military spending.* In practice, this can be done by calculating separate PPPs for all the major (and very disparate) elements of military

---

[14] See, e.g., Omitoogun, W., *Military Expenditure Data in Africa: A Survey of Cameroon, Ethiopia, Ghana, Kenya, Nigeria and Uganda*, SIPRI Research Report no. 17 (Oxford University Press: Oxford, 2003), p. 90.

expenditure, including the use of exchange rates for the purchase of imported military hardware.

The third of these methods is the best for comparing specific expenditures, especially if the expenditures can be decomposed into their major economic categories: personal emoluments, current goods and services (military supplies, transport and communications), purchases of capital-type goods (such as ships and aircraft, both domestic and imported) and defence buildings and construction. Obtaining such detail may not be possible—at least in the same statistical and analytical framework for all countries engaged in the comparison. It would still be necessary to use the GDP- and government-level PPPs to derive share estimates of the real absorption of resources for military purposes.

In the absence of a specific military PPP, the use of a government-level PPP as a proxy for real military outlays is likely to be less satisfactory because the pattern of government collective expenditures in total, except in the case of labour shares, may not match well that of the military. This will be especially the case where annual military spending falls heavily on equipment; to a large extent, this will depend on the strategic perspective of each country. This second method can be useful if the intention is to measure the opportunity cost of military expenditure. It measures what military outlays could have bought if they had been diverted to another area, such as education.

Least satisfactory would be the use of a GDP-level PPP, unless there is some underlying belief that military expenditure represents a national protection 'insurance' cost for preserving national well-being. Nevertheless, in almost all cases this method is still preferable to the use of exchange rates since the difference in real values could be as high as a factor of 4 or even 5.[15] A large difference would undoubtedly occur in a comparison between US and Chinese military spending. The use of the GDP-level PPP would indicate, in real terms, aggregate military outlays in China that are at least three times higher than when expressed in exchange rate terms. This higher figure does not mean that China's military output is that much higher; rather, it means that the real cost to China is higher. As regards the economic burden, the share of national resources devoted to military outlays might not be so different from that calculated using exchange rates.[16]

The way forward with international comparisons seems to be to use relevant PPPs for comparisons of well-defined expenditures and, in the case of military spending, to explore methods for obtaining more detailed information on military outlays in domestic prices. The problem is complicated by the increasing complexity of military procedures, the growing use of weapon systems, and the continually improving quality of military equipment and trained personnel. In some respects, however, this question may be little different from the general one posed by high-technology industry or specialized medical procedures, where similar challenges are faced in comparing their products.

[15] World Bank (note 10).

[16] Kravis, I. B., 'An approximation of the relative real per capita GDP of the Peoples' Republic of China', *Journal of Comparative Economics*, vol. 5, no. 1 (Mar. 1981), pp. 60–78.

Expenditure or output comparisons?

Purchasing power parity calculations are based on the expenditure components of the GDP aggregate. This is primarily because the concern is with the 'equivalent purchasing power' of a country's currency; that is, with how much local 'income' is used in acquiring the goods and services in question. The expenditure method is adopted because it is decomposable, practical and statistically more transparent. Clearly, knowing the share of GDP and national resources that is being allocated to the annual production of military items is also an important concern. The measurement of this phenomenon is conceptually clear in that it requires the calculation of real net output from an estimate of gross output valued in relevant international prices and the deduction of the corresponding intermediate inputs used up by each sector (transacted at a different set of international prices). However, the degree of statistical detail required to perform the calculations is monumental.[17]

The limitations of purchasing power parities for international comparisons of military expenditure

The limitations of PPPs for international comparisons are more practical than conceptual.[18] The problems of using PPPs are both general and specifically related to comparisons of military expenditure as reported in government accounts. They are general because it is not always easy to choose items to be priced for any set of outlays and, particularly for a given basic heading, to price these items at the same types of outlets. The problem is essentially to decide how best to target the process of accurately estimating the average annual unit value underlying the defined group of national expenditures. This means identifying the sources from which people buy most of their goods and services. In the case of military goods, government-owned or -controlled factories set their own prices based on costs while private firms operate within guidelines set by the government. The process of linking relevant prices to such values is far from transparent.

Countries need to resolve a number of sampling and selection issues and agree a common approach. This may be difficult to achieve in the case of the supply and delivery of military goods to foreign governments where transactions are confidential. Furthermore, within any GDP comparison in PPP terms, exchange rates are still used to convert the values of a country's imports and export of goods and services.

Specific problems of defining PPPs for the military concern the difficulty of identifying the items to be priced and then finding the appropriate price for them. There is probably less difficulty in determining the salary of an infantryman with a given number of years of service. A greater problem is identifying the salary of a conscripted soldier and who pays for his services. The real difficulty in pricing, however, relates to the costs of different types of military equipment and construction work and how to define these outlays comparably with other countries. The problem is more

---

[17] See also the work of the Growth and Development Centre of the University of Groningen under the direction of Professor Angus Maddison. E.g., Ark, B. van and Maddison, A., 'The international comparison of real product and productivity', eds A. Maddison, D. S. Prasada Rao and W. F. Shepherd, *The Asian Economies in the Twentieth Century* (Edward Elgar: Cheltenham, 2002).

[18] For a fuller review of the issues see Castles, I., 'The OECD–EUROSTAT PPP Program: review of practice and procedures', Organisation for Economic Co-operation and Development, Paris, 1997; and Ryten, J., 'Evaluation of the International Comparison Programme', United Nations, Economic and Social Council, Statistical Commission, 16 Nov. 1998, URL <http://unstats.un.org/unsd/methods/icp/>.

complicated the more sophisticated and 'customized' the equipment and facilities. In principle, it might be argued that a MiG-29 or F-16 combat aircraft used in different air forces is the same, but, like many types of modern military hardware, they form part of an overall weapon-delivery system. Even where the equipment is purchased from another country, the true acquisition cost is often concealed. Where identified, the domestic cost of imported military equipment is, by convention, determined using a country's principal exchange rates. However, this is one area where a special exchange rate may be applied to makes the goods in question cheaper for the purchasing country.

While military experts continually weigh up the relative merits of various weapons—the longbow against the crossbow, the Spitfire against the Messerschmitt 109, the MiG-15 against the Sabre F-86—they are not directly comparable Determining a PPP price ratio for any item chosen as a representative product relies on it being possible to price exactly the same item in at least one other country. This is not possible for many items of military hardware because, for strategic reasons, military forces prefer to use their own specific equipment.

There is a greater possibility, both in principle and in practice, that construction work and buildings can be compared. This is because the comparisons can be based on the cost components of common inputs and uniform 'building blocks'. Information about salaries and material costs for standard elements of work such as foundations (footings), skeleton steel frames and retaining walls then forms the basis for such comparisons. In the private sector, where there are many and varied buildings, a detailed bill of quantities can be specified for a standard prototypical building that each country can be asked to price in order to determine, hypothetically, the cost of construction in its own currency.

In current global PPP exercises, military goods and services, military equipment, and defence structures and buildings are not identified separately. In practice, the salaries of military personnel are considered along with the salaries paid to other government employees. The daily running costs of the military and its supplies are also treated like any other government current outlay and are converted as if they represent a mini cross section of all other goods and services used in the economy; that is, they are converted into international values using the PPP at the GDP or government level. The values of imported military goods are converted at the annual exchange rate and this shows up in the country's rest-of-the-world balance. The biggest outstanding problem, however, relates to comparing the costs of domestically produced structures and equipment of a capital nature, such as ships and aircraft. If these are considered in the accounts as government consumption items, then, implicitly, they will be converted into international values using the GDP-level PPP. This is not an exact conversion and it is clearly subject to significant error, although it may not be exposed to any easily discernible bias. This is an area that is currently being researched by the ICP and national accounts experts and recommendations to change existing procedures are expected in the revised SNA 2006.

V. International comparisons of military burden

The choice of currency conversion method influences cross-country comparisons of the economic burden represented by spending on the military. At the level of GDP, PPP converted values show higher levels of national expenditure for lower-income countries than would be indicated by an exchange rate conversion. These differences are proportionately larger the lower the absolute economic size and average income (GNP per capita) of a country. The same effect will be seen if PPP rates are used for lower component levels of GDP and its sub-aggregates. This means that, if an 'additive' aggregation procedure such as the Geary–Khamis formula—where PPP-adjusted components are summed consistently to give a PPP-adjusted GDP—is used to compile PPPs, the resulting pattern of real outlays in international price terms will diverge from the structure of an economy as understood in its own domestic price terms. These differences are sometimes of considerable strategic importance, as in the case of investment and public administration and, perhaps particularly, military expenditure.

When reviewing spending shares, the use of official exchange rates to similarly convert both GDP and a specific expenditure component will conceal the relative amount of domestic resources absorbed in generating that outlay. Such 'money unit' ratios may appear 'unit free' but they are not 'value free' in an international context. Even within the same country over time, such comparisons may not be relevant to any analysis of real economic change since absolute price levels and the price movements underlying the various expenditure categories may change in different ways. In some cases, price levels may differ also between final users and socio-economic classes.[19]

Comparisons of expenditure sub-components

In calculating PPPs for a country, GDP is divided into approximately 150 well-defined 'basic headings'.[20] In the richer and more complex advanced economies, even more commodity groups may be identified. Below the basic heading level, reliable information about detailed expenditure weights is generally not available. For presentational purposes and to obtain greater reliability, detailed basic heading data are usually condensed into about 50 higher-level expenditure 'groups'.[21] The consolidation of basic headings into larger categories helps to reduce the effects of volatility and errors in individual measurements.

Analysts can determine how much in real terms is allocated to each expenditure sub-component. Separate PPPs related to the underlying international price level of any identified item or group of items, such as the salaries of government personnel or the cost of private motor vehicles, can be calculated. The derivation of PPP-based component shares of GDP provides a realistic insight into the true opportunity costs of that category of spending. Thus, if the ratio of military expenditure to GDP in PPP terms is greater than the same ratio valued in national prices, then it is clear that the country is devoting more of its real resources to that activity than to other types of

[19] Biru, Y., 'The purchasing power of the poor in Zambia', Paper presented at the World Bank Seminar on Prices and Purchasing Power Parities, Washington, DC, Jan. 1999; and Decoster, R., 'Proposal for comparative poverty assessment using purchasing power parities for low income households', Paper prepared for the Development Economics and Data Group, World Bank, Jan. 1999.

[20] E.g., the ICP uses 155 headings. International Comparison Program, 'GDP and the main expenditure aggregates', ICP 2003–2006 Handbook (World Bank: Washington, DC, 2004), URL <http://www.worldbank.org/data/icp/>.

[21] E.g., the ICP has 61 groups above the level of its basic headings. International Comparison Program (note 20).

Table 8E.1. Comparison of military burden calculated using different currency conversion methods for select countries, 2000

Figures give military expenditure as a percentage of gross domestic product (GDP) in terms of market exchange rate (MER) and purchasing power parity (PPP).

Country	MER terms[a]	PPP terms[b]	Country	MER terms[a]	PPP terms[b]	Country	MER terms[a]	PPP terms[b]
Africa			China	2.04	3.76	Greece	4.87	4.22
Algeria	3.45	5.77	India	2.35	6.58	Italy	2.09	1.75
Argentina	1.32	1.67	Japan	0.96	0.94	Russia	3.74	3.56
Burundi	5.96	10.69	Mauritius	0.21	0.19	Turkey	5.02	6.12
Ethiopia	9.57	17.81	Pakistan	4.49	8.44	UK	2.48	2.40
Zimbabwe	4.68	4.22	Malaysia	1.70	4.33	*Middle East*		
Americas			Sri Lanka	4.52	13.29	Iran	5.36	6.36
Brazil	1.69	1.84	*Europe*			Israel	8.39	7.48
Canada	1.16	0.84	Armenia	3.56	7.92	Jordan	8.87	18.35
USA	3.07	2.39	Austria	0.83	0.69	Lebanon	5.37	11.38
Asia and Oceania			Bulgaria	2.53	4.51	Syria	5.53	12.84
Australia	1.85	1.64	France	2.58	2.34	Yemen	4.98	16.13

[a] These figures are calculated using the MER for both military expenditure and GDP data, i.e., as if calculated in local currency.

[b] These figures are calculated using government-level PPP rates for the conversion of military expenditure data and GDP-level PPP rates for the conversion of GDP data.

Sources: **PPP rates and exchange rates**: Heston, A., Summers, R. and Aten, B., Penn World Table, Version 6.1, Center for International Comparisons, University of Pennsylvania, Philadelphia, Penn., Oct. 2002, URL <http://pwt.econ.upenn.edu/php_site/pwt_index.php>; **GDP data**: International Monetary Fund, International Financial Statistics Database, URL <http://ifs.apdi.net/imf/>; **Military expenditure data**: Appendix 8A.

spending (see table 8E.1, which presents the military burden of select countries calculated using exchange rates and using purchasing power parities).[22]

Before PPP information became available, when researchers wanted to make international comparisons of detailed expenditure shares they used the price ratios of their own country or measures implicitly based on exchange rates. The same conversion factor used for the country as a whole was thus applied to the lower-level categories of expenditure. However, for categories below the level of GDP, expenditures and prices in each country tend to be determined by very different institutional and market conditions. The use of only one exchange rate in this context to determine the relative importance of these different types of outlays is thus inappropriate.

Government spending

The most important area where the calculation of PPPs has thrown up significant differences in comparative values is government current expenditure and the func-

---

[22] Summers, R. and Heston, A., 'The Penn World Table (Mark 5): an expanded set of international comparisons 1950–1988', *Quarterly Journal of Economics*, vol. 106, no. 2 (May 1991), pp. 327–68. The Penn World Tables are updated regularly by the Center for International Comparisons at the University of Pennsylvania; URL <http://pwt.econ.upenn.edu/>.

tional allocation of outlays to different departments. This has affected perceptions about the extent of public administration (the bureaucracy), defence (the military) and social services (society building). In these three core areas, direct comparisons using national income shares in national prices are meaningful only in an internal budgeting sense. The degree of involvement of various governments in the provision of, for example, health and education compared with the military varies significantly between countries and so government accounts need to be adjusted from a public 'spending' to a private 'use' basis to provide a more standardized coverage. This can then permit more robust measures of (a) the share of government 'proper' in GDP and (b) the share of major components of government, like military spending, in total government outlays. This is especially important when considering comparisons between China and the USA because the roles of government and their respective level of involvement in the national economy are clearly very different.

Not surprisingly, it has been found that government's share of GDP tends to be higher in poor countries when PPPs are used because of the dominant role of services and the relatively lower salaries paid in the public sector. In evaluating comparative military outlays, the level of domestic costs significantly affects estimates of the real amount of defence capacity produced each year. It is important to emphasize that PPP calculations are made only with respect to the 'running costs' of the military and not to any comparative evaluation of the total 'stock' of military goods and services; that is, the existing capacity of the military. One important element of the 'stock', however, is the current number of people in the armed forces and this component has to be paid for each year.

In general, the use of PPPs at two different benchmark periods raises other questions of interpretation because the purchasing capacity over the same unit of goods and services changes with changing relative prices during the intervening years and pure time–space consistency in price measurement is difficult to achieve. Such comparisons are also affected by changes in the number and composition of countries involved in the benchmark studies.

VI. Conclusions

This appendix outlines some of the issues involved in trying to compare, in real terms, what is spent each year by countries and, specifically, their governments, on military goods and services. It explains why it is important to use PPP conversion factors in preference to exchange rates to provide real international comparisons when assessing the resource use and the economic burden of military spending. The discussion suggests that, although PPPs can be used for most international comparisons of national expenditures, given the present limited scope and coverage of national data on military outlays and the problems of adjusting these for different quality factors, there are some serious weaknesses in existing PPPs as a basis for comparing military spending. The issue is further complicated by certain lacunae and ambiguities in the conceptual structure of the System of National Accounts relating to the definition of military expenditure. These are being looked at in the revision of the SNA due to be completed in 2006. The drawbacks to PPPs apply particularly to any comparisons involving China or, for that matter, India and any other country not directly involved in the last, 1999/2000 phase of international comparisons where data for missing countries had to be estimated econometrically. This situation is likely to improve in the foreseeable future when the results of the current round of the International Comparison Program are published in 2006. These will be based on the careful collection and selection of detailed micro data for a wide range of countries, including China and India. Since the ICP's inception in 1975, its country coverage and processes of data compilation have improved considerably.[23]

In the meantime, what should be done to compare annual military outlays? In the specific case of a China–USA comparison where China's exchange rate, although nominally free to float, remains effectively linked to the US dollar within a narrow band of fluctuation, the use of GDP- and government-level PPPs is still preferable to the application of an economically unrepresentative fixed dollar–yuan exchange rate. The fundamental difference is so large that it swamps all other considerations. Better still would be to calculate unique PPPs for each separate component of military spending and apply these to all the relevant expenditure categories. An assessment of the relative resources devoted to the military by the two countries might be better served by a direct binary comparison rather than through a full multilateral PPP exercise. In general, whichever PPP estimates are used, they will probably be less exposed to evident bias than they are subject to significant margins of error. Certainly, comparable estimates of military spending will be less reliable than other similarly deflated components of national expenditure; but this is due as much to the inherent difficulties of identifying military outlays as it is a problem of applying PPPs. Obtaining better estimates of military outlays is the clear priority.

Although PPP conversion is—at least in principle—the preferred method of conversion of military expenditure data to dollar values for purposes of comparisons of resource consumption, it is largely irrelevant for comparisons of military capacity or effectiveness. Assessments of the latter type require more qualitative and detailed analysis, where military expenditure may constitute only one of many variables.

---

[23] For research in earlier periods see Gilbert, M. and Kravis, I. B., *An International Comparison of National Products and the Purchasing Power of Currencies: A Study of the United States, the United Kingdom, France, Germany and Italy* (Organisation for European Economic Co-operation: Paris, 1954); Gilbert, M. et al., *Comparative National Products and Price Levels: A Study of Western Europe and the United States* (Organisation for European Economic Co-operation: Paris, 1958); and Kenessey, Z., 'International Comparison Program in the 1980's and 1990's', eds D. S. Prasada Rao and J. Salazar-Carrillo, *International Comparisons of Prices, Output and Productivity* (Elsevier Science Publishers: Amsterdam, 1996), pp. 3–29.

9. Arms production

J. PAUL DUNNE and EAMON SURRY*

I. Introduction

Arms sales by the 100 largest arms-producing companies (the 'SIPRI Top 100') increased again during 2004, although the increase was less dramatic than in the previous year. Sales by US companies continued to account for the bulk of this increase. While there was significant merger and acquisition activity in 2005, this was at a slower pace than in 2004. Another round of consolidation may follow which will see moves into other sectors to gain increasingly valuable skills and services and the continuing move by non-US firms into the lucrative, growing and now more accommodating US market.

While the post-cold war restructuring of the international arms industry has shown some signs of subsiding, important changes are still taking place. Consolidation among European companies continues and is likely to be reinforced by the increased political commitment in the European Union (EU) to harmonize rules for arms procurement and by the adoption of the 2005 Code of Conduct on Defence Procurement, which accepts competition in arms procurement among member states.[1] At the same time, the consequences of the 'global war on terrorism', including added emphasis on homeland security, and the experiences in Iraq are creating demands for new, private industrial services and products, and in turn are drawing new kinds of suppliers into the international arms market.

This chapter describes developments in the major arms-producing companies in 2004 and 2005. In addition, it looks at the development of the arms industry since the end of the cold war. Section II considers the data on the 100 largest arms-producing companies in the world (excluding China) in 2004.[2] In section III the long-term trends in arms production are described

---

[1] European Defence Agency, The Code of Conduct on Defence Procurement of the EU Member States Participating in the European Defence Agency, 21 Nov. 2005, URL <http://www.eda.eu.int/reference/eda/EDA - Code of Conduct - European Defence Equipment Market.htm>. Denmark does not participate in the Code of Conduct. See also 'EU agrees to open defence market', BBC News Online, 21 Nov. 2005, URL <http://news.bbc.co.uk/1/4458014.stm>; and chapter 16 in this volume.

[2] SIPRI has focused on the top 100 arms-producing companies annually in an effort to capture the trends in the overall arms industry. The choice of the top 100 companies was motivated by the fact that this is the highest number for which it was deemed realistically possible to gather data. This group of companies is fairly representative of the arms industry, accounting for roughly three-quarters of the value of global arms production in 1996. Chinese companies are excluded because of lack of data. See Sköns, E. and Weidacher, R., 'Arms production', SIPRI Yearbook 1999: Armaments, Disarmament and International Security (Oxford University Press: Oxford, 1999), pp. 389, 409; and Sköns, E. and

* The authors are grateful to Elisabeth Sköns for comments and guidance and to Jurgen Brauer, Ron Smith and Herbert Wulf for comments on earlier drafts.

Table 9.1. Regional and national shares of arms sales for the SIPRI Top 100 arms-producing companies in the world excluding China, 2004 compared to 2003

Arms sales figures are in US$ b., at current prices and exchange rates. Figures do not always add up because of the conventions of rounding.

Number of companies	Region/ country	Arms sales (US$ b.)[a]		Change in arms sales, 2003–2004 (%)		Share of total arms sales, 2004 (%)
		2003	2004	Nominal[b]	Real[c]	
41	**North America**	**147.7**	**170.3**	*15*	*12*	*63.5*
40	USA	147.3	169.8	*15*	*12*	*63.3*
1	Canada	0.5	0.5	*2*	*−7*	*0.2*
40	**Europe**	**71.0**	**82.1**	*16*	*2*	*30.6*
11	UK	26.3	32.4	*23*	*7*	*12.1*
8	France	17.6	19.8	*12*	*0*	*7.4*
1	Trans-European[d]	8.0	9.5	*18*	*6*	*3.5*
3	Italy	5.6	6.6	*19*	*6*	*2.5*
6	Germany	5.7	5.2	*−8*	*−18*	*1.9*
4	Russia[e]	3.1	3.1	*2*	*−14*	*1.2*
2	Sweden	2.3	2.3	*11*	*1*	*0.9*
2	Spain	1.7	1.7	*27*	*12*	*0.6*
1	Switzerland	0.7	0.7	*6*	*−3*	*0.2*
1	Norway	0.4	0.4	*−7*	*−12*	*0.1*
1	Finland	0.4	0.4	*64*	*49*	*0.1*
9	**Other OECD**	**8.2**	**8.2**	*11*	*3*	*3.1*
6	Japan	6.5	6.5	*12*	*5*	*2.4*
2	Korea, South[e]	1.3	1.3	*3*	*−4*	*0.5*
1	Australia	0.4	0.4	*19*	*2*	*0.2*
10	**Other non-OECD**	**7.8**	**7.8**	*6*	*1*	*2.9*
4	Israel	3.5	3.5	*0*	*−1*	*1.3*
3	India	2.3	2.7	*15*	*8*	*1.0*
1	Singapore	0.9	0.9	*−3*	*−8*	*0.3*
1	South Africa	0.5	0.5	*0*	*−16*	*0.2*
1	Brazil	0.3	0.4	*38*	*23*	*0.1*
100	**Total**	**233.4**	**268.3**	*15*	*8*	*100.0*

OECD = Organisation for Economic Co-operation and Development.

[a] Arms sales include both sales for domestic procurement and export sales.

[b] This column gives the percentage change in arms sales in 2003–2004 calculated in current dollars.

[c] This column gives the percentage change in arms sales in 2003–2004 calculated in constant dollars.

[d] The company classified as trans-European is EADS, which is based in three countries—France, Germany and Spain—and registered in the Netherlands.

[e] Data for Russian and South Korean companies are uncertain.

Source: Appendix 9A, table 9A.1.

along with the SIPRI Arms Production Project's analysis of these trends. Section IV provides some conclusions. Appendices 9A and 9B include tables of the Top 100 arms-producing companies in 2004 and acquisitions in the North American and West European arms industry in 2005. Appendix 9C provides an analysis of developments in the Russian arms industry.

II. Recent trends

The SIPRI Top 100 arms-producing companies, 2004

The value of the combined arms sales of the SIPRI Top 100 arms-producing companies in the world (excluding China) in 2004 was $268 billion (see table 9.1).[3] Companies in the United States and Western Europe accounted for most of this amount. The dominance of US companies is particularly striking. Of the total arms sales of the Top 100 companies, 63.3 per cent was accounted for by 40 US companies; and 29.4 per cent by 36 West European companies. Four Russian companies accounted for 1.2 per cent of the total value.

There was a marked expansion in total arms sales of the Top 100 in 2004 compared to 2003. However, this increase of 15 per cent (in nominal terms) was not as dramatic as in the previous year: the increase in 2003 over 2002 was 25 per cent.[4] Indeed, owing to the continued deterioration of the value of the US dollar during 2004, the increase in 2004 over 2003 was even smaller in real terms: just over 8 per cent. This is still a significant increase, especially since it followed a year of great increase, and suggests that the decline in arms sales by the largest arms-producing companies that occurred during the 1990s has ended.

The composition of firms on the Top 100 for 2004 did not change a great deal (see table 9.2), but the companies that entered and exited the list are interesting for several reasons. Four companies left the Top 100 in 2004. Two of these were Russian: Uralvagonzavod, which dropped from a ranking of 98 to 136, and MMPP Salyut, which fell less dramatically from 96 to 109. While Uralvagonzavod's arms sales decreased in 2004, its total sales increased by more than 60 per cent between 2001 and 2004 as a result of a strong increase in civil sales. Most of this increase is from building rolling stock for Russian Railways,[5] but the company also produces, for example, road-building equipment and consumer commodities that are increasingly exported.[6] The third company to exit the SIPRI Top 100 list for 2004 was the Japanese company

---

Weidacher, R., 'The economics of arms production', ed. L. Kurtz, *Encyclopedia of Violence, Peace and Conflict* (Academic Press: San Diego, Calif., 1999), p. 137.

[3] There may also be other companies that are large enough to appear in the Top 100 list but for which insufficient data are available.

[4] Sköns, E. and Surry, E., 'Arms production', *SIPRI Yearbook 2005: Armaments, Disarmament and International Security* (Oxford University Press: Oxford, 2005), pp. 383–416.

[5] Lantratov, K., 'Airplanes give way to submarines', *Kommersant*, 9 June 2005, URL <http://www.kommersant.com/doc.asp?id=584099>.

[6] 'The "steel flow" of Urals tanks', *Diplomat*, no. 5 (133), 2005, URL <http://www.diplomatrus.ru/200505/uk/02-06.php>.

Table 9.2. Companies that entered and exited the SIPRI Top 100 list of arms-producing companies in 2004

Rank 2004	Rank 2003	Company	Country	Rank 2004	Rank 2003	Company	Country
Entering companies				*Exiting companies*			
99	106	Embraer	Brazil	106	97	Komatsu	Japan
68	S	MTU Aero Engines	Germany	109	96	MMPP Salyut	Russia
100	116	Patria	Finland	136	98	Uralvagonzavod	Russia
71	142	Armor Holdings	USA	S	65	Alvis	UK

S = Subsidiary company.

Source: SIPRI Arms Industry Database.

Komatsu, which slipped marginally from rank 97 to rank 106. However, arms sales data for the Japanese companies in the Top 100 represent new military contracts rather than arms sales. Because money for these contracts may be paid out over several years, these data can provide only a rough estimate of arms sales for the year.[7] The fourth company, the British tank maker Alvis, lost its independent ranking in the list after its $651 million acquisition in 2004 by BAE Systems.

The German company MTU Aero Engines 'entered' the list as an independently ranked company, having previously been listed as a subsidiary of DaimlerChrysler. The company was sold to private equity firm Kohlberg Kravis Roberts & Co. in late 2003.[8] The rapid increase in arms sales by Armor Holdings, which climbed in ranking from 142 to 71, is indicative of the financial windfall from the conflict in Iraq for companies that supply body and vehicle armour. Armor Holdings' total sales increased from $365 million in 2003 to $980 million in 2004, with revenues from its Aerospace and Defense Division expanding by 560 per cent over the same 12 months. The company produced 3945 reinforced or 'up-armoured' high-mobility, multi-purpose wheeled vehicles (HMMWVs) in 2004, compared to 873 in 2003.[9] Patria, the Finnish producer of armoured vehicles, increased its arms sales by 64 per cent (or 49 per cent in real terms) from $220 million in 2003 to $358 million in 2004. Patria's Defence Material and Maintenance business accounted for 75 per cent of total sales in 2003 and 83 per cent in 2004. The Brazilian aircraft producer Embraer entered the list for 2004 at rank 99. This is likely to be the result of the start of deliveries in December 2003 of a light attack version

---

[7] There is a low level of transparency in Japan in data on arms production. Surry, E., *Transparency in the Arms Industry*, SIPRI Policy Paper no. 12 (SIPRI: Stockholm, Jan. 2006), URL <http://www.sipri.org/>.

[8] MTU Aero Engines, 'KKR Acquires MTU from DaimlerChrysler AG', Press release, 21 Nov. 2003, URL <http://www.mtu.de/en/press/Press_Archive/pressearchiv_2003/>.

[9] Armor Holdings, '2004 Annual Report', Jacksonville, Fla., URL <http://ccbn.mobular.net/ccbn/7/1067/1126/>, p. 6.

of the Super Tucano aircraft to the Brazilian Air Force.[10] There also appears to have been a decision by the company's management to refocus its priorities on defence. The company more than doubled its arms sales (both in value and as a percentage of total sales) in 2003 over 2002. In the mid-1990s the percentage of Embraer sales that were arms sales was as high as 30 per cent. By 2000 it had declined to just 3 per cent of total sales. In 2003 the percentage had risen again to 12 per cent, and for 2004 the share was 10 per cent.[11] However, Embraer's increase in arms sales cannot be seen as a sign of any broader resurgence in the Brazilian defence industry, which collapsed in the late 1980s and early 1990s.[12]

Mergers and acquisitions in 2005

Acquisition activity continues in the world arms industry, albeit at a less rapid pace than during the 1990s. One major difference from that period is that the largest arms-producing companies have order backlogs and are currently 'awash in cash'.[13] Companies may have been using, and will continue to use, some of this free cash flow for spending on acquisitions.[14]

Two factors continue to drive further consolidation in the arms industry. The first is the rush into those sectors of the arms industry that company managers and investors consider to be expanding. These are primarily the military services sector, which supplies services and logistical support to armed forces, and the information technology (IT) sector, which provides products and services in support of network-centric programmes. In order to succeed in these sectors, companies continue to seek to acquire smaller companies that have particular skills that they lack.[15] The second factor is the desire of non-US-

---

[10] Johan, S., 'Flying training & trainer aircraft', *Asian Defence Journal*, Jan./Feb. 2005, p. 17.

[11] In 2004 a company spokesperson indicated that Embraer wants to increase its military revenues to 20% of gross revenues. 'ACS win good new for Embraer, analysts say', *International Air Letter*, 9 Aug. 2004, p. 5.

[12] A major factor in the collapse—when 2 major Bazilian arms producers, Engesa and Avibras, filed for bankruptcy—was the end of the 1980–88 Iraq–Iran War. Perlo Freeman, S., 'Offsets and the development of the Brazilian arms industry', eds J. Brauer and J. P. Dunne, *Arms Trade and Economic Development: Theory, Policy and Cases in Arms Trade Offsets* (Routledge: London, 2004), pp. 187–204. Also see Brauer, J., 'The arms industry in developing nations: history and post-cold war assessment', eds J. Brauer and J. P. Dunne, *Arming the South: The Economics of Military Expenditures, Arms Production and Trade in Developing Countries* (Palgrave: Hampshire, 2002), pp. 101–27.

[13] Wayne, L., 'Cash puts U.S. military contractors in bind', *New York Times*, 13 May 2005, URL <http://www.iht.com/articles/2005/05/12/business/contract.php>.

[14] According to one estimate, 'free cash flow'—the amount of cash that a company has left after paying all its expenses, including investments—at the world's 8 largest defence companies grew from $8.9 billion to $17.75 billion in 2004. The analysis was conducted by J. P. Morgan and reported in Ratnam, G., 'Industry's full pockets: surplus cash, tight U.S. budgets may mean wave of acquisitions', *Defense News*, 16 May 2005, p. 16.

[15] Another incentive for acquiring a company that has employees with official security clearance is that the acquiring company avoids delays (of 2 years or more) in getting these itself. Interview with Frank Lanza, Chairman and Chief Executive of L-3, in Ratnam, G., 'DOD expected to let L-3 buy Titan', *Defense News*, 6 June 2005, p. 4.

based companies to access the lucrative US market by acquiring (either directly or through a local subsidiary) a US arms-producing company.[16]

Five very large acquisitions that were concluded in 2005, each with a deal value close to or greater than $2 billion, make it a particularly significant year for arms industry consolidation.[17] In 2004 there was only one acquisition of comparable size.[18] By far the largest and most strategically noteworthy acquisition of 2005 was that of United Defense (USA) by BAE Systems (UK) for $4192 million.[19] This was the largest ever acquisition of a US defence company by a non-US company. An extraordinary result is that a British company is now the sixth-largest contractor for the US Department of Defense (DOD).[20] The deal may also have an impact on the still-fragmented European land systems market and lead to consolidation in Europe.[21] Three of the large acquisitions in 2005 were in the IT sector. L-3 Communications (USA) acquired the Titan Corporation (USA) in a deal valued at $2650 million.[22] General Dynamics (USA) announced an agreement to acquire Anteon International (USA) for approximately $2200 million; and DRS Technologies (USA) spent $1970 million to acquire Engineered Support Systems (USA).[23] The fifth significant arms industry acquisition for 2005 was that of MTU Friedrichshafen (Germany) from DaimlerChrysler (Germany) by the private equity group EQT (Sweden). This transaction, which had been a source of considerable controversy and political debate in Germany,[24] also included the Off-Highway Division of Detroit Diesel (USA) and was valued at approximately $1900 million. With the sale of MTU Aero Engines to a US private equity firm in late 2003,[25] DaimlerChrysler has thus divested itself of all its major arms-producing activities other than its 30.9 per cent share in EADS.[26]

[16] Chuter, A. and Tran, P., 'UK firms flex muscles in US market', *Defense News*, 22 Aug. 2005, p. 16.

[17] See appendix 9B.

[18] This was the acquisition by Finmeccanica of GKN's 50 per cent share in AgustaWestland.

[19] BAE Systems, 'BAE Systems completes acquisition of United Defense Industries; creates global land systems enterprise', Press release, 24 Jun. 2005, URL <http://www.uniteddefense.com/pr/pr_2005 0624b.htm>.

[20] Rothman, A. and Lococo, E., 'BAE buys United Defense to tap U.S. military sales', Bloomberg.com, 7 Mar. 2005, URL <http://www.bloomberg.com/apps/news?pid=10000102&sid=aBEULP6o GE.Y>.

[21] Some analysts have argued that the deal will make smaller European land systems companies 'relatively weaker' in terms of their ability to compete for large contracts. This may encourage them to consolidate. Ratnam, G. and Chuter, A., 'BAE to buy United Defense, shaking land market', *Defense News*, 14 Mar. 2005, p. 1.

[22] L-3 Communications, 'L-3 Communications completes acquisition of the Titan Corporation, completes related debt offerings and tender offer', Press release, 29 July 2005, URL <http://www.titan.com/ investor/press-releases/press_releases_display_2005.html?id=33&select=5>.

[23] DRS Technologies, 'DRS Technologies to acquire Engineered Support Systems', Press release, 22 Sep. 2005, URL <http://www.drs.com/press/archivelist.cfm>.

[24] The German Government threatened to veto the sale in order to protect local defence production capabilities. Agüera, M., 'Germany tightens rules on foreign ownership', *Defense News*, 19 Sep. 2005, p. 20; and Agüera, M., 'Battle entangles MTU sale', *Defense News*, 22 Aug. 2005, p. 22.

[25] MTU Aero Engines (note 8).

[26] On a smaller scale, the company continues to produce heavy vehicles, including trucks used by militaries.

BAE Systems' acquisition of United Defense highlights an important development in the industry: BAE Systems is not alone in its strategy of gaining access to the US market by acquiring a US company. For example, another British company, QinetiQ, acquired two US aerospace and defence companies in 2004 and another two in 2005.[27] VT Group (UK) also acquired a US company, the Cube Corporation, and announced its intention to double the size of its business in the USA by 2008.[28] Other major non-US arms producers that have publicly stated their intention to increase their sales in the USA, possibly through acquisitions of US companies, include Thales[29] and Finmeccanica.[30] Efforts by non-US companies to access a greater part of the large US procurement budget in this way have been characterized as an 'uphill battle', however, because of the ongoing political debates in the USA about the procurement of foreign military equipment.[31]

III. Developments in the arms industry since the end of the cold war

The challenges at the end of the cold war

The cold war arms industry reflected what is now seen to have been a very specific set of international and domestic forces. Post-cold war developments have transformed the global military economy, not least as a result of trends in military expenditure and technology that have reinforced US dominance. Unlike that of most other countries, US military spending has been growing rapidly.[32] The fixed costs of research and development (R&D) for major systems continue to grow, both for platforms and for the infrastructure (e.g., satellites and strategic air assets) and information systems needed to support network-centric warfare. All states but the USA thus face structural disarmament, in the sense that they cannot afford to produce a comprehensive range of their own weapon systems because of the fixed costs of replacing conventional military capability with modern systems comparable to those of the USA. This is a particular problem for the other powers that aspire to a military capacity of global significance, in particular the other permanent

---

[27] QinetiQ's strategy is 'to focus on defence and security markets, especially in the US which represents [the company's] greatest opportunity for expansion'. QinetiQ, 'US expansion strategy delivers for QinetiQ', Press release, 6 July 2005, URL <http://www.qinetiq.com/home/newsroom/news_releases_homepage/2005/3rd_quarter/QinetiQ_annual_results_summary.html>

[28] Anderson, G., 'VT aims to double US growth in three years', *Jane's Defence Industry*, vol. 22, no. 7 (July 2005), p. 12.

[29] Tran, P., 'Thales plans to double U.S. sales', *Defense News*, 10 June 2005.

[30] Finmeccanica's Chief Operating Officer, Remo Pertica, has said the company is 'specifically interested in a company that would act as a bridgehead into the US Department of Defense'. Vogel, B., 'Finmeccanica aims for US market', *Jane's Defence Industry*, vol. 22, no. 7 (July 2005), p. 15.

[31] Vogel (note 30).

[32] US military expenditure increased by 50% in real terms in 1996–2005. China and Russia have also increased their military expenditure tremendously in recent years (by 165% and 49%, respectively, in 1996–2005). See appendix 8A in this volume.

members of the United Nations Security Council: China, France, Russia and the United Kingdom.

Current developments in the arms industry include the increasing internationalization of production, the increasing importance of IT companies within the defence sector and the 'privatization' of services that were once provided by the military.[33] These have led to important compositional change in the industry. The information in previous editions of the SIPRI Yearbook provides an insight into the changes that have taken place over the years. Indeed, the factors other than arms control that were specifically raised in SIPRI Yearbook 1990—the budget environment, changing technologies, West European integration, changes in military doctrine and the emergence of new producers[34]—could all be used to discuss the present situation, although the discussion would be rather different.

Work on arms production at SIPRI during the 1980s was concerned with the growth in arms production in the developing world, which was a cause for concern for some commentators.[35] The SIPRI studies concluded, however, that the attempts to establish self-sufficiency in these countries were unlikely to be successful.[36] At the end of the cold war, as domestic demand for military equipment fell, the concern was the risk of increased arms exports and its likely impact on international security. The focus of research thus shifted to the major arms-producing companies in the West.

The SIPRI Arms Production Project was set up in the environment of the ending of the cold war: there were political changes in Eastern Europe, negotiations on conventional arms control (in the Conference on Security and Co-operation in Europe and negotiations on the Treaty on Conventional Armed Forces in Europe, the 1990 CFE Treaty), changing technologies, over-capacities, expansion of the number of producers, and the cascade[37] of weapon systems within the North Atlantic Treaty Organization (NATO).[38] Although the Soviet Union still existed in 1990, the analysis in SIPRI Yearbook 1990 predicted the need for restructuring of the international arms industry and the

[33] Sköns, E., Bauer, S. and Surry, E., 'Arms production', SIPRI Yearbook 2004: Armaments, Disarmament and International Security (Oxford University Press: Oxford, 2004), p. 389.

[34] Anthony, I. et al., 'Arms production', SIPRI Yearbook 1990: World Armaments and Disarmament (Oxford University Press: Oxford, 1990), pp. 319–21.

[35] E.g., a 1981 RAND report predicted that: 'If borne out in future research, one would predict arms production in growing numbers of countries in an economically developing world.' Alexander, A. J., Butz, W. P., and Mihalka, M., 'Modeling the production and international trade of arms: an economic framework for analyzing policy alternatives', RAND Note, RAND Corporation, Santa Monica, Calif., 1981, p. 17.

[36] Brzoska, M. and Ohlson, T., SIPRI, Arms Production in the Third World (Taylor & Francis: London, 1986); Wulf, H., 'Developing countries', eds N. Ball and M. Leitenberg, The Structure of the Defense Industry: An International Survey (Croom Helm: London, 1983); and Anthony et al. (note 34).

[37] In the early 1990s NATO planned a large internal arms transfer programme to compensate for the removal of equipment under the terms of a possible CFE agreement. Second-hand equipment from the more developed member countries would be transferred to the less developed members, who would then destroy equipment which was already planned for replacement.

[38] Anthony et al. (note 34). See also Anthony, I., Allebeck, A. C. and Wulf, H., SIPRI, West European Arms Production (Oxford University Press: Oxford, 1990); Brzoska, M. and Lock, P. (eds), SIPRI, Restructuring of Arms Production in Western Europe (Oxford University Press: Oxford, 1992); and Wulf, H. (ed.), SIPRI, Arms Industry Limited (Oxford University Press: Oxford, 1993).

likely difficulties, suggesting that: 'On balance, these trends are likely to lead to a reduction in the size of the world industrial arms base. Difficulties are likely to be encountered by private companies (mainly in the United States and Western Europe) as well as by state-owned factories (mainly in the Soviet Union) that are heavily dependent on arms production.'[39]

Issues of conversion—the use of military resources for civil purposes—were a focus of attention, with considerable debates on how changes could be achieved.[40] In this context the purpose of the 1990 Yearbook chapter was: 'to describe the trends affecting the arms industrial base and to present data on the size and characteristics of the arms industry in the East and West'.[41] The authors also stated that 'Since over-capacities already exist—with additional capacities in the stage of installation in Third World countries and Japan— governments in the West should seriously plan for conversion of parts of the arms industry; otherwise corporations may truly consider themselves as "victims of peace".'[42] Such statements represent an impressive insight into the issue that would dominate the sector over the next decade, although the authors could not know the degree to which changing geopolitical, techno- logical and social drivers would restructure the industry.

There have been limitations to the coverage of the SIPRI Arms Production Project, caused by the lack of both data availability and reliability. A network of experts with local knowledge assisted the SIPRI team, but there were prob- lems with coverage of the Soviet Union and its allies because of lack of reporting by governments. While state ownership in Western countries also limited transparency, it was nevertheless easier to get information on member countries of the Organisation for Economic Co-operation and Development (OECD), and these accounted for most of the data in the tables. Consistency has increased over the years. One way of overcoming the lack of comparable information for major producers has been to include special studies by country experts, who could use a wider range of information to evaluate the changes taking place.[43]

---

[39] Anthony et al. (note 34), p. 317.

[40] E.g., Brzoska, M., 'Success and failure in defense conversion in the "long decade of dis- armament"', eds K. Hartley and T. Sandler, *Handbook of Defense Economics*, vol. 2 (Elsevier: Amster- dam, forthcoming 2007); Southwood, P. 'Disarming military industries' (Macmillan: London, 1991); Markusen, A. and Yudken J., *Dismantling the Cold War Economy* (Basic Books: New York, N.Y., 1992); Hartley, K., *Economic Aspects of Disarmament: Disarmament as an Investment Process* (UNIDIR: Geneva, 1993); Dumas, L. J. (ed.), *The Socioeconomics of Conversion from War to Peace* (ME Sharpe: New York, N.Y., 1995); Gansler, J. S. *Defence Conversion: Transforming the Arsenal of Democracy* (MIT Press: Cambridge, Mass., 1995); and Dunne, P., 'Conversion in Europe: challenges and experiences', eds B. Moller and L. Voronkov, *Defensive Doctrines and Conversion* (Dartmouth Publishing Co.: Aldershot, 1996), pp. 56–62.

[41] Anthony et al. (note 34), p. 317.

[42] Anthony et al. (note 34), p. 368.

[43] The Soviet Union and Russia have had such treatment. E.g., Cooper, J., 'Russian military expend- iture and arms production', *SIPRI Yearbook 2001: Armaments, Disarmament and International Security* (Oxford University Press: Oxford, 2001), pp. 313–22; and appendix 9C.

The cold war arms industry

The defence industry had unique characteristics during the cold war. The high level of military expenditure in the period after World War II encouraged corporate involvement in lucrative defence orders, while the high R&D expenditure influenced the structure and performance of the companies. High R&D expenditure also influenced the trend in costs, making them higher than civil costs, and the nature of production—with short production runs, technologically advanced and concerned with performance rather than cost minimization—limited the potential for economies of scale and learning.[44] While other large companies were similar in structure, the products produced by defence firms and the sub-systems they integrated had different technological forms and requirements. Thus, civil and military products and production processes differed, as did the nature of capital equipment, with labour skills and the organization of production becoming increasingly specific to the sector.

The monopsonistic[45] structure of the market and the nature of the product led to an emphasis on the performance of high-technology weaponry rather than on cost; the financial risk was borne by government, which often financed R&D and in some cases provided investment in capital and infrastructure. The characteristics of the industry also led to elaborate rules and regulations on contracts, which were seen as necessary in the absence of a competitive market and to assure public accountability.[46] In addition, military contingency planning for the worst case led to ever-increasing demand to modernize equipment, with cost only a minor concern. In such an environment, close relations developed between contractors, procurement executives and the military, leading to a 'revolving door' through which military and civil servants moved to defence contractors with which they had dealings and defence contractors moved into the bureaucracy.[47] It was not surprising that the vested interests in military production formed a powerful interest group, the 'military–industrial complex', which was capable of pushing for increases in expenditure when there was no obvious change in threats to security.[48]

---

[44] Ball, N. and Leitenberg, M., *The Structure of the Defense Industry: An International Survey* (Croom Helm: London, 1983); Melman, S., *The Permanent War Economy* (Simon and Schuster: New York, N.Y., 1985); Dunne, P., 'The political economy of military expenditure: an introduction', *Cambridge Journal of Economics*, vol. 14, no. 4 (Dec. 1990), pp. 395–404, and Lovering, J., 'Military expenditure and the restructuring of capitalism: the military industry in Britain', *Cambridge Journal of Economics*, vol. 14, no. 4 (Dec 1990), pp. 453–68.

[45] While in a monopoly situation there are many customers but only one supplier, in a monopsony there are many suppliers (in this case, national arms producers) but only one customer (the national government).

[46] Dunne, J. P., 'The defence industrial base', eds K. Hartley and T. Sandler, *Handbook of Defense Economics*, vol. 1 (Elsevier: Amsterdam, 1995), pp. 592–623.

[47] Adams, G., *The Iron Triangle: The Politics of Defense Contracting* (Council on Economic Priorities: New York, N.Y., 1981); and Higgs, R. (ed.), *Arms Politics and the Economy: Historical and Contemporary Perspectives* (Holmes and Meier: New York, N.Y., 1990).

[48] Dunne, J. P., 'The changing military industrial complex in the UK', *Defence Economics*, vol. 4, no. 2 (Mar. 1993), pp. 91–112; and Lovering, J., 'Restructuring the British defence industrial base after

These characteristics tended to favour those firms that specialized in defence work over other potential competitors. They knew their way around the red tape and had the contacts and links within the state. These firms became experts at getting money out of government, rather than being successful in commercial markets. The companies sought involvement in the development programmes for technologically advanced weapon systems as the best means of obtaining the subsequent production contracts. In some cases this led to 'buy ins', where firms understated risk or cost in order to win initial contracts and made up the losses later. In addition, some programmes saw 'gold plating', where the military continually asked for additions or technological improvements over the contract period. This allowed renegotiation of contracts or additional payments, usually to the advantage of the contractor.[49]

As a result of the structure of the market there were barriers to both entry and exit (market-related, technological and procedural). This led to the cold war defence industrial base being remarkably stable in the composition of main contractors. Moreover, unlike most other manufacturing industries, which went multinational, the arms industry remained national. Smaller countries, which could not afford the large fixed costs, imported major weapon systems.[50]

The post-cold war arms industry

Trends in world military spending can be divided into two major periods in the post-cold war period: a marked decline from the cold war peak in 1987, then a bottoming out around 1998 and an increase in 1998–2005. Indeed, world military spending in 2005 exceeded (in real terms) the peak of spending during the cold war.[51] The USA, which became the major superpower, has been the main contributor to the upward trend in world military expenditure. In 2005 the USA accounted for 48 per cent of world military expenditure, with the combined expenditure of next five largest spenders—the UK, France, Japan, China and Germany—less than half that of the USA. The 26 members of just one military alliance, NATO, account for 70 per cent of world military expenditure in 2005.[52]

With the fall in demand following the end of the cold war, the ability of even the major powers to maintain a domestic defence industrial base was

the cold war: institutional and geographical perspectives', *Defence Economics*, vol. 4, no. 2 (Mar. 1993), pp. 123–39.

[49] Dunne (note 46).

[50] Dunne (note 46); and Renner, M., *Economic Adjustment After the Cold War: Strategies for Conversion* (Dartmouth Publishing Co.: Aldershot, 1992).

[51] See chapter 8 in this volume.

[52] A further issue of increasing importance is the 'hidden' defence spending that appears in national accounts under headings other than defence. E.g., major actions are paid for from contingency funds; in the new environment of the war against terrorism, what was once defence expenditure appears elsewhere; and there is increased use of civil companies to undertake what would have been the work of the armed forces, but not necessarily recognized as defence, such as post-conflict reconstruction in Iraq. Brauer, J., 'United States military expenditure', Unpublished manuscript, College of Business, Augusta State University, Feb. 2005, URL <http://www.aug.edu/~sbajmb/paper-US_milex.pdf>.

called into question.[53] Governments had to decide whether to allow mergers and acquisitions which would reduce competition and, in particular, whether to allow mergers and acquisitions which involved foreign partners. In Europe, the UK led the way to the degree that its government definition of the national defence industrial base was concerned only with the location of production and not with the ownership of the firm.[54] Some smaller European producers, such as Belgium and Norway, followed the UK. In France and Germany the issue was much more controversial and continues to be so.[55] The change in the security environment made it harder to justify previous levels of support for the industry and so competitive procurement policies aimed at value for money were introduced in a number of countries.[56]

The end of the cold war produced not just a quantitative change in the number of weapons required, but a qualitative change in the types required.[57] During the cold war, planning was straightforward—it was fairly clear where, how and with whom war would be fought if it came. After the cold war there was much less certainty. As Western governments considered the new geo-political environment, it became apparent that the cold war weapons that made up the bulk of the NATO inventory were unlikely to be what was now required.[58] Given the long lead times and the commitments made by government bodies, research teams and companies, there are still pressures to continue to produce these weapon systems and to find roles for them. There has, however, been a clear and important qualitative change in the nature of technology as civil technology became increasingly important for weapon systems.[59] This was a marked change since, from the end of World War II to the 1980s, military technology had tended to be ahead of civil technology. By

[53] Dunne, J. P., Garcia-Alonso, M., Levine, P. and Smith, R., 'Concentration in the international arms industry', Discussion paper no. 03/01, School of Economics, University of the West of England, Bristol, Jan. 2003, URL <http://carecon.org.uk/DPs/>; Markusen, A. R. and Costigan, S. S., 'The military industrial challenge', eds A. R. Markusen and S. S. Costigan, *Arming the Future: A Defense Industry for the 21st Century* (Council on Foreign Relations Press: New York, N.Y., 1999), pp. 3–34

[54] The first clear and explicit statement of the change in British policy was made in British Ministry of Defence, 'Defence industrial policy', Ministry of Defence Policy Paper no. 5, Oct. 2002, URL <http://www.mod.uk/DefenceInternet/AboutDefence/CorporatePublications/PolicyStrategy/>, p. 9.

[55] Serfati, C. et al. (eds), *The Restructuring of the European Defence Industry: Dynamics of Change*, European Commission, Directorate General for Research, COST Action A10 (Office for Official Publications of the European Communities: Luxembourg, 2001), in particular Mampaey, L., 'Ownership and regulation of the defence industrial base: the French case', pp. 123–144; and 'Germany tightens rules on foreign ownership', *Defense News*, 19 Sep. 2005, p. 20. For a discussion of the 'strong influence of the French Government on the French defence industry' see Lundmark, M., 'To be or not to be: the integration and the non-integration of the French defence industry', Base data report FOI-R-1291-SE, Swedish Defence Research Agency (FOI), Stockholm, July 2004, URL <http://www.foi.se/FOI/templates/PublicationPage____171.aspx>, pp. 16–17; Mussington, D., *Arms Unbound: the Globalization of Defense Production* (Brassey's: Washington, DC, 1994); and Kapstein, E. B. (ed.), *Global Arms Production: Policy Dilemmas for the 1990s* (Harvard University Press: Cambridge, Mass., 1992).

[56] On the UK see Dunne, J. P. and Macdonald, G., 'Procurement in the post cold war world: a case study of the UK', eds Serfati et al. (note 55), pp. 101–22.

[57] See chapter 15 in this volume.

[58] Bailes, A. J. K., Melnyk, O. and Anthony, I., *Relics of Cold War: Europe's Challenge, Ukraine's Experience*, SIPRI Policy Paper no. 6 (SIPRI: Stockholm, Nov. 2003), URL <http://www.sipri.org/>.

[59] Branscomb, L. M. et al., *Beyond Spinoff: Military and Commercial Technologies in a Changing World* (Harvard Business School Press: Cambridge, Mass., Apr. 1992).

the 1990s in many areas, particularly electronics, military technology lagged behind civil technology, and military technology was often obsolete before it came into service. Whereas in the past the spin-off of military technology to the civil sector tended to be an important argument for the value of military production, the focus is now more on 'spinning-in' civil technology to the military. Many areas of technology that were once the preserve of the military and security services, such as cryptography, now have primarily commercial applications. In addition, the use of standard commercial components is an increasing feature of the arms industry: many components of major weapon systems are commercial off-the-shelf products, produced by manufacturers that would not consider themselves part of the arms industry. The major contractors have become increasingly systems integrators, retaining the characteristics of defence specialized firms.[60]

In the post-cold war world the arms industry's size, structure and trade are still determined by government policy, as the national government is the main customer and regulates exports. However, there have been clear changes in the structure and nature of the industry. The reduction in demand has led to a situation in which, outside the USA, many companies have become national champions, in many cases monopolies or close to it, with a consequent need for cross-border restructuring.[61]

Concentration

The most striking change in industrial policy was in the USA. During the cold war, industrial planning was undertaken through the DOD, although not explicitly. This changed in 1993: a merger wave was stimulated when the Deputy Secretary of Defense, William J. Perry, addressed a dinner attended by defence industry executives and openly encouraged consolidation—this became known as the 'last supper'.[62] The presence of financiers at this meeting illustrates the increasing role of financial capital in the arms industry.[63] To promote the consolidation, the DOD allowed companies to write off restructuring costs against military contracts, with the expectation of large costs savings which never materialized.[64] The policy ended when the DOD

---

[60] Dunne, J. P., Garcia-Alonso, M., Levine, P. and Smith, R. P., 'The evolution of the international arms industry', Unpublished manuscript, School of Economics, University of the West of England, Bristol, Aug. 2005, URL <http://carecon.org.uk/Armsproduction/Evolution2forWolfram.pdf>; and Markusen, A. R., 'The post-cold war persistence of defense specialized firms', eds G. I. Susman and S. O'Keefe, *The Defense Industry in the Post Cold War Era* (Elsevier: Oxford, 1998), pp. 121–46.

[61] The situation also meant that any introduction of competition would need to be from foreign firms. This can be implicit rather than explicit, by creating contestable markets with potential competition from abroad, although there may be problems of making incumbents believe that these external competitors would enter the market. Dunne (note 46).

[62] Perry is reported to have said that he hoped several aircraft firms, 3 of the 5 satellite firms, and 1 of the 3 missile companies would disappear through mergers. Markusen (note 60), p. 138. A description of the meeting is in Turpak, J. A., 'The distillation of the defence industry', *Airforce Magazine*, vol. 81, no. 7 (July 1998), URL <http://www.afa.org/magazine/July1998/>.

[63] Sköns and Surry (note 4), p. 387. For an analysis of the role of Wall Street in the restructuring of the US arms industry during the 1990s see Markusen (note 60).

[64] Sköns and Weidacher, 'Arms production' (note 2), p. 397.

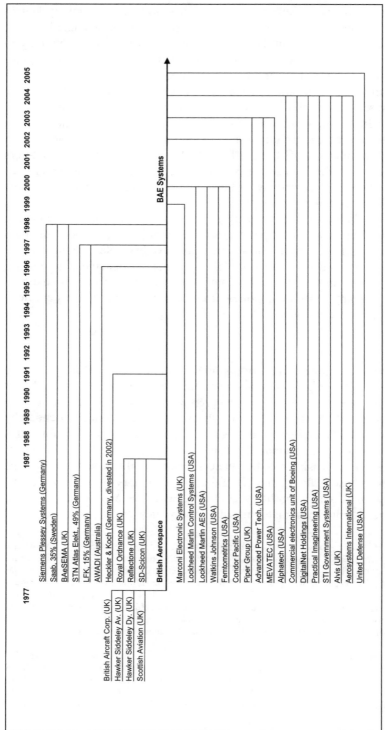

Figure 9.1. The formation and major acquisitions of BAE Systems, 1977–2005

This diagram ignores BAE System's civil acquisitions of the 1980s and focuses on it path to defence specialism. The full complexity of these mergers and acquisitions cannot be represented. For more details see the SIPRI Arms Production Project website, URL <http://www.sipri.org/contents/milap/>.

decided it had gone far enough and blocked the merger of Lockheed Martin with Northrop Grumman in early 1997.[65] This left four major US contractors in 1998: Boeing, Lockheed Martin, Northrop Grumman and Raytheon—which are now four of the top five companies in the SIPRI Top 100 for 2004.[66]

In Europe the process of post-cold war adjustment was more complicated, since restructuring necessarily involved cross-border mergers, which raised political issues.[67] The major players in Europe also had quite different owner-ship structures than those in the USA. For example, in France, Italy, Portugal and Spain there was a high degree of state ownership of companies at the end of the cold war. This made the kind of financially driven merger boom that took place in the USA more difficult in Europe. Nonetheless, the driving forces in Europe were similar and led to an increase in concentration. There have been recent moves to integrate European defence markets and further consolidate the sector.[68]

There were three waves of activity in the evolution of BAE System's defence activities (see figure 9.1). First was the consolidation in 1977–87 of the British companies that made up British Aerospace. Then came the acqui-sitions of European defence interests and of Marconi's defence business in the late 1990s. Finally, the focus moved to acquisitions of US companies. In this phase the change in name to BAE Systems reflected the company's aim of internationalization and its intention to enter the US market. The evolution of Thales reflects the different experience of the European industry, with con-tinued government ownership and, until recently, opposition to cross-European consolidation (see figure 9.2). There was a short wave of acqui-sitions in the early 1990s, then a major wave of acquisitions across the world in the late 1990s. The company's name was changed from Thomson CSF to Thales in 2000 following the acquisition of the British company Racal. With this acquisition, Thales became the second largest contractor to the British Ministry of Defence (after BAE Systems).[69] The change in European govern-ment attitudes is further reflected in the evolution of EADS (the European Aeronautics, Defence and Space Company; see figure 9.3), which was formed in 2000 from DASA (a subsidiary of Daimler) of Germany, Aérospatiale Matra of France and CASA of Spain. EADS developed its defence position through acquisitions in the early 2000s.

---

[65] Markusen and Costigan (note 53), p. 4.

[66] Sköns and Weidacher, 'Arms production' (note 2), pp. 394–98, in particular figure 10.1. The Brit-ish company BAE Systems is 4th in the Top 100. The 6th, General Dynamics, adopted the strategy of spinning off defence divisions which specialized in areas in which it was not dominant and concentrating on those where it was, becoming a smaller firm in the process. Markusen (note 60).

[67] Ripley, T., 'Western European industry ownership jigsaw', *Defence Systems Daily*, 31 May 2005, URL <http://defence-data.com/ripley/pagerip1.htm>. The current structure of the European defence industry is described as a 'spaghetti bowl' in Vlachos-Dengler, K., *Off Track?: The Future of the Euro-pean Defense Industry* (RAND: Santa Monica, Calif., 2004).

[68] Valasek, T., 'EU wants more defense competition, lower costs', ISN Security Watch, 1 Dec. 2005, <http://www.isn.ethz.ch/news/sw/details.cfm?id=13686>.

[69] Defence Manufacturers Association, 'Thales UK PLC', Member listings, URL <http://www.the-dma.org.uk/Secure/Groups/NonMemberDets.asp?ID=817>.

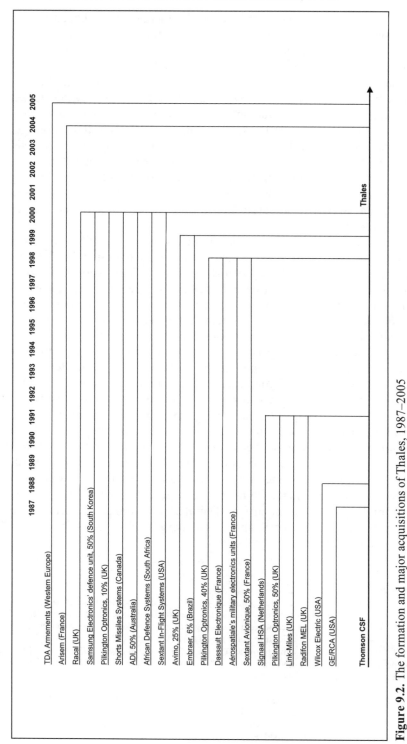

Figure 9.2. The formation and major acquisitions of Thales, 1987–2005

The full complexity of these mergers and acquisitions cannot be represented. For more details see the SIPRI Arms Production Project website, URL <http://www.sipri.org/contents/milap/>.

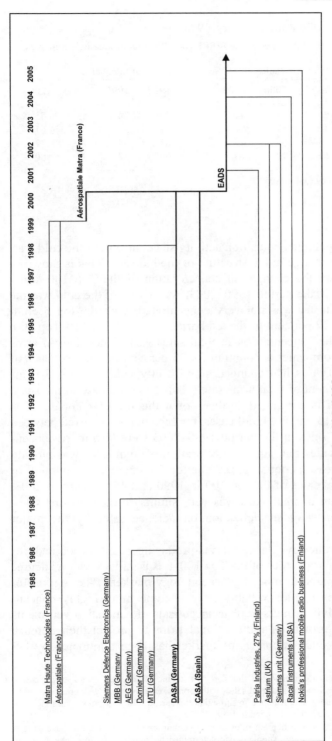

Figure 9.3. The formation and major acquisitions of EADS, 1985–2005

The full complexity of these mergers and acquisitions cannot be represented. For more details see the SIPRI Arms Production Project website, URL <http://www.sipri.org/contents/milap/>.

Table 9.3. Concentration of the arms industry, 1990–2003

Figures are percentage shares of the sales of the SIPRI Top 100 arms-producing companies.

	Share of total arms sales				Share of total sales			
	1990	1995	2000	2003	1990	1995	2000	2003
Top 5	22	28	41	44	33	34	43	45
Top 10	37	42	57	61	51	52	61	61
Top 15	48	53	65	69	61	64	71	72
Top 20	57	61	70	74	69	72	79	80

Source: SIPRI Arms Industry Database.

Structural changes

As a result of the merger and acquisition activity since the end of the cold war, there has been a clear change in the structure of the industry. This is shown in table 9.3, which shows the changes in concentration of the Top 100 arms-producing companies in the period 1990–2003. At the end of the cold war the international arms industry was not very concentrated, with the top 5 companies accounting for 22 per cent of the total arms sales of the SIPRI Top 100. It is noticeable that the concentration in total sales was higher than in arms sales, with the top 5 companies accounting for 33 per cent of the total sales of the Top 100. By 2003 this had changed significantly, with the top 5 firms accounting for 44 per cent of total arms sales. This large increase in the share of the top companies is continued further down the list of companies, as shown for the top 10, 15 and 20. In all cases, the big change occurred between 1995 and 2000. Total sales in the period 1990–2003 were also more concentrated in a few companies but, since concentration of total sales was already high in 1990, the increase is not so great. The top 5 companies accounted for 33 per cent of the total sales of the top 100 in 1990 and 45 per cent in 2003. By 2003, concentration of total sales was very similar to that of arms sales. This may reflect increasing specialization on defence sales by the major players.[70]

Although by 2003 the five largest arms-producing firms accounted for 44 per cent of the total arms sales of the Top 100, this is still a very low degree of concentration compared to other high-technology markets. The market for major weapon systems would probably have become more highly concentrated, like those for civil airliners or pharmaceuticals, if national governments had not inhibited the growth of multinational firms to protect their defence industrial base.[71] The international arms market has been dominated by US

---

[70] Computing the coefficient of variation of the Top 100 for the same years shows an increasing spread of the size distribution for arms and total sales, with arms sales having a lower spread than total sales in 1988 but increasing more. The results also show that the spread of arms shares across the companies was constant until 1998 and then declined in 1998–2003.

[71] Until the 1970s government procurement rules in many countries restricted the purchase of telecommunications equipment from foreign suppliers and determined the number of firms. The easing of

companies. BAE Systems is the only European company to have consistently been in the top 5 of the Top 100, having made a successful push for sales in the US market and gaining special status in bidding for US contracts.[72] European companies are important, however, with Thales, EADS and Finmeccanica in the top 10. Nearly all arms-producing companies have shown a rise in arms sales between 1998 and 2003 and, apart from the rise of Halliburton, the top 20 companies are relatively stable.

The process of significant concentration in the arms industry since the end of the cold war evolved in phases. The most intensive period of concentration was between 1993 and 1998. The process has continued, but slowed down, since then. This is clearly illustrated by figure 9.4, which shows the cumulative shares of the total sales of the Top 100 companies in 1988, 1993, 1998 and 2003. The curves for 1988 and 1993 almost overlap, showing almost no change in the size distribution, but there is a clear increase in concentration between 1993 and 1998, and a further, although smaller, increase between 1998 and 2003.

Company strategies

Faced with the reduction in demand for arms after the cold war, a number of strategic options were open to companies. They could convert their plants to civil production, diversify to produce additional civil products or other military products, divest from military production, cooperate with other companies or increase military specialization. They also had the option of increasing their exports, whether through new sales and marketing strategies or by finding new markets. However, their choices were constrained by government policy towards their national defence industrial base and by the nature of the financial systems within which they operated. In principle, the conversion of plants producing military products to producing civil products was an option, but there are very few examples of a successful conversion strategy in this narrow sense in this period. There were more examples of attempts to convert at company, rather than plant, level and of diversification into civil production, but these also had limited success. Some argue that this was a result of firms' internal political battles being won by the advocates of 'downsizing and focus-

---

procurement rules that followed the liberalization of the telecommunications market led to very rapid concentration in the world telecommunications industry. This is what might be expected to happen if governments ceased to interfere in the market structure of the arms industry. Sutton, J., *Technology and Market Structure* (MIT Press: Cambridge, Mass., 1998).

[72] The special status of BAE Systems Inc., as the US unit is known, dates to the later years of the administration of US President Bill Clinton, when the company became the only subsidiary of a foreign defence contractor to win a blanket 'national interest determination' from the DOD, giving it streamlined handling of approvals to work on classified contracts. The parent company does not enjoy the same level of trust. The special security status and track record of Rockville, a BAE Systems subsidiary, allows it to compete on contracts and buy companies more easily than other foreign units. 'Hands—and arms—across the sea', *Business Week*, 14 Nov. 2005, URL <http://www.businessweek.com/magazine/content/05_46/b3959161.htm>.

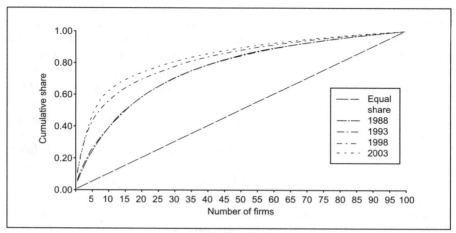

Figure 9.4. Size distribution of the SIPRI Top 100 arms-producing companies in 1988, 1993, 1998 and 2003

Each curve shows the cumulative share of the total arms sales of the Top 100: the first point on each curve is the share of the largest company; the second point is the total share of the top 2; the third point the total share of the top 3, and so on. If all companies in the Top 100 had an equal share of the total, then the line would be straight; the further the curve deviates from the straight line, the greater the concentration.

ing' or 'diversifying further into defence' over the advocates of 'convert and diversify into civil', rather than a failure of conversion per se.[73]

The experience of the companies certainly varied as they developed their policies to counter the reduction in the demand for arms.[74] Diversification involved developing new commercial activities either through the organic growth of new businesses or by acquiring existing businesses. It had more chance of success where the firm could build synergies between the military and civil parts of the business, which was more likely to be in firms with relatively low shares of arms sales. Probably the most impressive diversification was that of the British defence company Racal, which built, and then spun off, the Vodafone mobile phone business. The remaining defence components of Racal were ultimately sold to Thomson CSF of France to form the multi-national Thales. There are more examples of unsuccessful diversification. British Aerospace bought a construction company, a property company and an automobile company. There were plausible tactical justifications for each acquisition, but they did not work. British Aerospace divested each of them and became more focused as a defence company.[75] Some companies, for

[73] Markusen (note 60).

[74] Dunne et al. (note 60); Smith, R. and Smith, D., 'Corporate strategy, corporate culture and conversion; adjustment in the defence industry', *Business Strategy Review*, vol. 3, no. 2 (summer 1992), pp. 45–58. See also note 40.

[75] Some argue that British Aerospace Enterprises, the company's venture capital arm, had a potential for success that was never achieved because of the change in corporate strategy. Feldman, J., 'The rise and fall of British Aerospace Enterprises', Mimeo, National Institute for Working Life, Stockholm,

example, Daimler Benz, made acquisitions of smaller companies to develop the conglomerate into a broad-based technology company and so reduced their dependency on arms production.[76] For a time, there was also a widespread belief that synergies were possible between automobiles and aerospace, particularly defence aerospace, something on which Saab had based its advertising. The automobile companies Ford, General Motors and Daimler had all acquired defence units. Ford and General Motors subsequently sold them and Daimler spun off its defence unit, DASA, into the merger with Aérospatiale Matra and CASA to form the multinational EADS.[77]

After the consolidation that followed the 1993 'last supper', the remaining US arms producers no longer based their business plans on a broad-based and diversified product range but on specialization in defence products. This was reinforced by Wall Street transactions, which encouraged companies to concentrate on what the stock market called 'pure play' and 'core competences'.[78] Where competition regulations made it possible, selling defence divisions to competitors was an attractive proposition in a number of cases, since they were worth more to the competitor, who gained increased monopoly power. In the USA, General Dynamics was an early exponent of this strategy and shrank itself rapidly and profitably. In the UK, GEC sold its defence divisions to British Aerospace in 1999 and turned itself into a purely commercial company, renamed Marconi, which proved to be a disaster.[79]

Cooperation has always been common among aerospace and defence companies. They can use collaboration, joint ventures and strategic alliances to cut costs—by sharing high R&D and other overhead costs and pooling orders to increase production runs—without losing independence.[80] Joint ventures are partnerships or conglomerates, often formed to share risk or expertise, where two or more businesses agree to share profit, loss and control in a specific enterprise. They are seen as a good way for companies to combine without having to merge. However, joint ventures can be difficult to manage and companies generally prefer direct control, when they can get it. One of the success stories in military aerospace is the longstanding link between the partly state-owned French aero-engine company Snecma and General Electric of the

2000. That process of change is described in Evans, R. and Price, C., *Vertical Take-off* (Nicolas Brealey Publishing: London, 1999).

[76] Stephan, M., 'An evolutionary perspective on corporate diversification', Paper prepared for the Workshop on Evolutionary Economics, Buchenbach, 14–17 May 2003, URL <http://www.infokom. tu-dresden.de/papiere buchenbach 2003/CorporateDiversificationPatternsVersion2April2003.pdf>; and Renner (note 50).

[77] James, A. D., 'Comparing European responses to defense industry globalization', *Defence & Security Analysis*, vol. 18, no. 2 (June 2002), pp. 123–43. See also 'Big 3 no longer major players in U.S. defense', *Automotive News*, 31 Mar. 2003, URL <http://www.autonews.com/apps/pbcs.dll/article? AID=/20030331/FREE/303310763>.

[78] Markusen, A. (note 60); Dunne et al. (note 60); Oden, M., 'Cashing in, cashing out, and converting: restructuring of the defense industrial base in the 1990s', eds Markusen and Costigan (note 53), pp. 74–105.

[79] Marconi was hit by the end of the high-tech boom and ended up effectively bankrupt. 'Q&A: Marconi refinancing deal', BBC New Online, 29 Aug. 2002, URL <http://news.bbc.co.uk/2/2219039.stm>.

[80] Hartley, K., 'Aerospace: the political economy of an industry', ed. H. W. de Jong, *The Structure of European Industry*, 2nd edn (Kluwer: Dordrecht, 1988), pp. 329–54.

Table 9.4. Company strategies and analysis of arms-producing companies that survived in the periods 1990–2003 and 1990–98

Fate of the 1990 SIPRI Top 100 arms-producing companies			
Had exited by 2003	18		
Had merged or been acquired by 2003	25		
No data for 2003	4		
Survivors in 2003	53		

Analysis of companies in 2003[a]	Arms sales an increased or constant share of total sales	Arms sales a decreased share of total sales	Total
Winners	12	13	25
Diversifiers	2[b]	13	15
Rearmers	7	0	7
Losers	4	2	6
Total survivors	**25**	**28**	**53**

Analysis of companies in 1998[a]	Arms sales an increased or constant share of total sales	Arms sales a decreased share of total sales	Total
Winners	2	9	11
Diversifiers	0	33	33
Rearmers	6	0	6
Losers	4	3	7
Total survivors	**12**	**45**	**57**

[a] 'Winners' are companies that increased arms sales and increased civil sales; 'diversifiers' are those that decreased arms sales and increased civil sales; 'rearmers' are those that increased arms sales and decreased civil sales; and 'losers' are those that decreased arms sales and decreased civil sales.

[b] For these 2 companies, arms sales as a share of total sales remained constant.

Source: SIPRI Arms Industry Database.

USA.[81] Strategic alliances are arrangements between companies that pool, exchange or integrate selected business resources for mutual benefit, while remaining separate entities. Strategic alliances are less complicated than joint ventures. They take many forms and have become more sophisticated and flexible over the past few years. Companies may choose an alliance that involves simple market exchanges or cross-licensing agreements, or they may form a more complicated partnership that includes cooperative manufacturing arrangements or joint-equity ventures. All of these variants have been adopted by arms companies over the past two decades.[82]

The specializing companies, which acquired the defence divisions others divested and often shed civil activities, have also tended to diversify into other

[81] Wood, P. C. and Sorenson, D. S. (eds), *International Military Aerospace Collaboration* (Ashgate Publishing: Aldershot, 2000). In May 2005 Snecma merged with Sagem to form SAFRAN.

[82] Dussage, P. and Garrette, B. 'Industrial alliances in aerospace and defence: an empirical study of strategic and organizational patterns', *Defence Economics*, vol. 4, no. 1 (Jan. 1992), pp. 45–62.

weapon systems so that they can market a full product range. Such companies realized the need to internationalize and acted upon it. Even before the current wave of restructuring, companies were expanding supply chains internationally, building international joint ventures and taking strategic shares in foreign companies as an alternative to ownership. This trend has clearly accelerated with the support of governments and has led to marked changes in ownership structures. BAE Systems now sells more to the US DOD than to the British Ministry of Defence, and the French company Thales is the second largest defence contractor in the UK.[83]

Another means of replacing domestic demand was through increased exports. Governments, mindful of the need to keep costs down by maintaining or increasing the scale of production of domestic arms producers, supported and encouraged the search for orders abroad. Arms exports became heavily subsidized, both directly and indirectly, through diplomatic pressure, aid, insurance provision, assistance with offset arrangements and so on.[84] This led to increased competition among arms producers but failed to prevent the inevitable consolidation within the industry.

The different strategies adopted can be identified by considering the company data.[85] The companies can be classified as: (a) winners, with increased arms sales and increased civil sales; (b) diversifiers, with declined arms sales and increased civil sales; (c) rearmers, with increased arms sales and decreased civil sales; and (d) losers, with decreased arms sales and decreased civil sales. Diversifiers could have converted plants or diversified through organic growth, acquisitions or divestment. In table 9.4 the civil production of the sample—the Top 100 arms-producing companies for 1990—was estimated and the frequency distribution for these four categories considered both for those companies with increasing arms shares and for those with decreasing arms shares.

Of the 53 companies that still existed in 2003, the largest group is the winners, about half of whom had a decreased share of their total sales represented by arms sales, meaning that arms sales became less important to the company. While the results for the period 1990–2003 are interesting, they cover a relatively long time period. Since there could have been changes over the period in the strategies and success of companies, it is useful to consider the results over a shorter period, 1990–98. In 1998 there were a similar number of survivors, but a much smaller proportion of these had increased their arms sales (as would be expected in the short term) and there are fewer

[83] James (note 77). The USA now accounts for 40% of BAE Systems' annual sales. 'Hands—and arms—across the sea' (note 72). Thales employs 12 000 people at 70 locations in the UK. Armed Forces, 'Thales UK', Defence Suppliers Directory, 2006, URL <http://www.armedforces.co.uk/companies/raq 400d01d167144>.

[84] Cooper, N., *The Business of Death* (Taurus Academic Studies: London, 1997); Jackson, B., *Gunrunners' Gold* (World Development Movement: London, 1995); and Ingram, P. and Davis, I., *The Subsidy Trap: British Government Financial Support for Arms Exports and the Defence Industry* (Oxford Research Group: Oxford, 2001).

[85] Brzoska, M., Wilke, P. and Wulf, H., 'The changing civil military production mix in Western Europe', eds Markusen and Costigan (note 53), pp. 371–405.

Table 9.5. Regional distribution of the SIPRI Top 100 arms-producing companies, 1990 and 2003

Region/country[a]	Share of total arms sales (%)		Number of companies	
	1990	2003	1990	2003
North America	**60.8**	**63.2**	**49**	**39**
USA	*60.2*	*63.0*	47	38
Canada	*0.6*	*0.2*	2	1
Western Europe	**33.1**	**29.2**	**40**	**36**
UK	*10.4*	*11.4*	13	12
France	*12.0*	*7.5*	11	9
FRG/Germany	*5.0*	*2.2*	8	5
Italy	*3.4*	*2.7*	3	3
Switzerland	*1.1*	*0.3*	2	1
Sweden	*0.3*	*0.9*	2	2
Spain	*0.9*	*0.6*	1	2
Norway	–	*0.2*	–	1
Trans-European	–	*3.4*	–	1
Other OECD	**3.2**	**3.3**	**5**	**10**
Japan	*3.2*	*2.6*	5	7
South Korea	–	*0.5*	–	2
Australia		*0.2*	–	1
Other non-OECD	**3.0**	**4.6**	**6**	**15**
Israel	*1.2*	*1.5*	3	4
India	*1.1*	*1.0*	2	3
Singapore	–	*0.4*	–	1
South Africa	*0.7*	*0.2*	1	1
Russia	–	*1.5*	–	6

FRG = Federal Republic of Germany; OECD = Organisation for Economic Co-operation and Development.

[a] This table refers only to parent companies: the arms sales of foreign subsidiaries are included in the sales of the parent company, not in the country where the production actually takes place. The Top 100 for 1990 covered only OECD member states and developing countries (excluding *inter alia* China and Russia). By 2003, the Top 100 covered most of the world, but still excluded China.

Sources: Anthony, I., Claesson, P, Sköns, E. and Wezeman, S. T., 'Arms production and arms trade', *SIPRI Yearbook 1993: World Armaments and Disarmament* (Oxford University Press: Oxford, 1993), table 10.3, p. 428; and Sköns, E. and Surry, E., 'Arms production', *SIPRI Yearbook 2005: Armaments, Disarmament and International Security* (Oxford University Press: Oxford, 2005), table 9.1, p. 384.

winners and more diversifiers. While these figures show a high degree of diversification, they tend to understate the degree of conversion overall, as companies that successfully moved out of arms production became less visible—they leave the Top 100 and so do not count as 'survivors'—and gradual policy changes may not make headlines. In addition, according to the Bonn International Center for Conversion (BICC), it is possible that the less visible, small- and medium-sized companies have been more successful diversifiers than the large companies among the Top 100.[86]

Looking at the changes in the regional distribution of the Top 100 arms-producing companies (see table 9.5), the dominance of US-listed companies is consistent: they made up 60 per cent of arms sales in 1990 and 63 per cent in 2003. The share for European companies declined from 33 per cent to 29 per cent over the same period. Interestingly, the USA saw a decline in the number of firms in the Top 100 from 49 to 39, while for Europe the decline was only from 40 to 36, reflecting the very different nature of the industry and the restructuring experience in the USA and Europe.[87]

Increasing internationalization of the supply chains is changing the organization of production. Apart from cross-country purchases of finished goods, companies are also changing their supply chain, an example being BAE Systems' purchases in South Africa.[88] The growth of offsets deals has encouraged this development and given importing countries the opportunity to develop niche markets, by being part of the supply chain of a major international producer.[89] Arms-producing companies are determining preferred suppliers from a wider range of companies.[90] While the companies rely on domestic support through procurement and support for exports, and so are not truly 'transnational', they have internationalized. Governments are increasingly willing to recognize that the costs of high-technology defence R&D and smaller national production runs mean that economies of scale need to be met through international collaboration and industrial restructuring. This is very different from a few decades ago, when governments aimed to maintain a comprehensive national defence industrial base. Major non-US defence companies are also buying defence contractors in the USA as a means of entering the US market, as discussed in section II above.

Acquisitions activity in the arms industry in 1988–89 and in 2005 can be compared by considering the tables of acquisitions in this volume and *SIPRI Yearbook 1990*.[91] There is much less activity in the earlier period, with 18 transactions noted for 1988–89 and 54 for 2005. This may possibly be attributed to better data collection for 2005, but the change in the level of

[86] This is argued in Bonn International Center for Conversion, *Conversion Survey 1998: Global Disarmament, Defense Industry Consolidation and Conversion* (Oxford University Press: Oxford, 1998), p. 232.

[87] Note that the US-based subsidiaries of European companies have their arms sales registered in the table as those of the European parent company.

[88] Dunne, J. P. and Lamb, G., 'Defence industrial participation: the experience of South Africa', eds Brauer and Dunne, *Arms Trade and Economic Development* (note 12), pp. 284–298; and J. P. Dunne, 'The making of arms in South Africa', *Economics of Peace and Security Journal*, vol. 1, no. 1 (Jan. 2006), URL <http://www.epsjournal.org.uk/Vol1/No1/issue.php>, pp. 40–48.

[89] There is concern over the cost and sustainability of such policies. Dunne (note 88); and Brauer, J., 'Arms trade, arms industries and developing countries', eds Hartley and Sandler (note 40).

[90] Hartley, K., Dowdall, P. and Braddon, D., 'Defence industry supply chain literature and research review', Department of Trade and Industry, London, Oct. 2000; Braddon, D., 'The matrix reloaded: what future for the defence firm?' *Defence and Peace Economics*, vol. 15, no. 6 (Dec. 2004), pp. 499–507; and Dowdall, P., 'Chains networks and shifting paradigms: the UK defence industry supply system', *Defence and Peace Economics*, vol. 15, no. 6 (Dec. 2004), pp. 535–50.

[91] See table 9B.1 in appendix 9B; and Anthony et al. (note 34), table 8.7, p. 336.

activity and the range of countries involved as acquirer and acquired are striking. The attempt by European firms to move into the US market is very clear, with seven transatlantic acquisitions of US companies in 2005.[92]

The period covered by the SIPRI Arms Industry Database has been one of considerable change and restructuring in the arms industry. While the concentration of major arms producers seems to have stopped in the USA in 1997, it is still continuing at the level of the smaller companies and in the supply chain. Unlike earlier consolidation, which was driven by the need to survive in a declining market, the recent activity seems to be driven more by the need to acquire technology than by the desire for growth.[93] While there has been some activity in Europe, there is still some way to go in terms of restructuring and increasing concentration. A major driver of restructuring is the growing transatlantic nature of the industry, in terms of both the European companies' aspirations to become major players in the US market and the USA's acceptance that 'interoperability requirements, the benefits of cooperative defense programs, and an increasingly global industrial infrastructure require that the [US DOD] be prepared to accept the benefits offered by access to the most innovative, efficient, and competitive suppliers worldwide'.[94]

The changing nature of the arms industry

There have been marked changes in the structure of the international arms industry since 1990 and there are likely to be changes in the future. Future prospects for the industry are shaped by a range of factors, including the following.

1. *The changing nature of warfare.* It seems unlikely that the USA and Europe (that is, NATO) will face an enemy that can provide a symmetric response; asymmetric conflict is most likely. This can change the nature of warfare and lead to more informal, guerrilla-type conflicts with implications for the weapon systems required.[95]

2. *The rate of obsolescence of some major weapon systems, such as fighter aircraft.* Recent commentators have suggested that many fighter aircraft are coming to the end of their life and will need to be replaced.[96]

---

[92] This is also discussed in Jones, S. G., 'The rise of Europe's defense industry', US–Europe Analysis Series, Brookings Institution, Washington, DC, May 2005, URL <http://www.brookings.edu/fp/cuse/analysis/>.

[93] Sköns, Bauer and Surry (note 33). See also section II above.

[94] US Department of Defense, 'Annual arms industrial capability report to Congress', Washington, DC, Feb 2004, URL <http://www.acq.osd.mil/ip/ip_products.html>, p. ii.

[95] Dunay, P. and Lachowski, L., 'Euro-Atlantic security and institutions', *SIPRI Yearbook 2005* (note 4), p. 5

[96] According to one report, 'by 2011, the [global fighter aircraft] market will reach a new post-cold war peak, with deliveries reaching $16 billion'. Report by the Teal Group (a US consulting firm) reported in Fabey, M., 'U.S. JSF casts long shadow on fighter market', *Defense News*, 6 June 2005, p. 18. See also Frost & Sullivan, 'Future fighter aircraft requirements in emerging economies', Press release, 30 Mar. 2005, URL <http://www.prnewswire.co.uk/cgi/news/release?id=142913>. There is also an increased use of unmanned air vehicles (UAVs) and the establishment of a network-centric warfare

3. *The new security environment and its demands for new types of military missions.* There is likely to be an increasing role for NATO and EU troops in crisis management and peacekeeping roles around the world.[97] This changes both the nature and structure of the required armed forces and the type of weapon systems they need.

4. *The new technologies introduced as a result of the war on terrorism.* The 'global war on terrorism', which confronts an uncertain enemy, and US homeland security have stimulated the demand for communication and surveillance technologies. Where companies do not have these technologies, they are acquiring them.[98]

5. *The degree of outsourcing of services from the military sector (armed forces and defence ministries).* Defence ministries (particularly the US DOD) are increasingly using private companies to undertake tasks that would have been done by the military in the past.

On the other hand, long lead times and large capital investment in major weapon systems result in considerable inertia. Indeed, the military have always been relatively conservative, fighting battles with the weapons of the last war, leading to considerable inertia in procurement and planning. There are still weapon systems coming into service that were designed for the cold war, for example, the Eurofighter Typhoon.[99]

An important remaining question is how much the nature of the industry has changed. It is still greatly influenced by political pressures, both domestic and international. Governments dominate the demand for the products of the sector, and their spending and direct influence inevitably determine industrial structure: governments still decide where to buy, how to buy and what to buy, although they may now make different decisions than they would have in the past. They can still influence the size and structure of the industry, entry to and exit from the industry, efficiency and ownership, and the level of technology and exports, although they now have less control over prices and profits. In most countries the state still provides infrastructure. However, pressure groups and lobbyists are increasingly important in the governance of the industry, with Europe following in the footsteps of the USA as European state ownership and control are reduced.[100] In Europe the increased privatization of defence companies, the reduced barriers to foreign ownership and greater non-domestic procurements all continue to influence the industry.

---

environment. Jensen, D., 'Avionics outlook 2006: rising expectations', *Avionics Magazine*, Jan. 2006, URL <http://www.defensedaily.com/cgi/av/show_mag.cgi?pub=av&mon=0106>.

[97] Dunay and Lachowski (note 95), p. 6.

[98] Sköns and Surry (note 4), p. 387.

[99] The delays are outlined and the experience of other fighters discussed in Dane, B., 'Bumpy road for fighters', *Aviation Week & Space Technology*, 17 Jan. 2005, URL <http://www.aviationnow.com/media/pdf/sb05_fighters.pdf>, pp. 20–24. See also Forsberg, R. (ed.), *The Arms Production Dilemma* (MIT Press: Cambridge, Mass., 1994).

[100] See, e.g., Slijper, F., 'The emerging EU military–industrial complex: arms industry lobbying in Brussels', Transnational Institute Briefing Series no. 2005/1, Amsterdam, May 2005, URL <http://www.tni.org/pubs-docs/briefings.htm>.

The major defence contractors, or at least their defence sections, still differ from civil companies. While less risk is now borne by government and there is less emphasis on performance at the expense of cost, defence contractors still face elaborate rules and regulations in procurement and government's close links with procurers have been replaced by less formal but not necessarily less effective mechanisms (e.g., lobbying). Non-defence specialists continue to face considerable barriers to entering and exiting the market—marketing, procedural or technological. However, the technological barriers remain high only for specialists in particular areas.

While companies have been internationalized in terms of markets and their supply chains, they seem loyal to their home base. Incumbents are still favoured by the way in which contracts are set up and the major contractors remain expert at getting money out of governments. Governments have overhauled their procurement practices to try to deal with the 'gold plating' and the cost and time overruns of the cold war industry. As a consequence, they involve companies earlier in the development of equipment to meet particular security needs. The European Defence Agency (EDA) was established to help EU member states develop their defence capabilities for crisis-management operations under the European Security and Defence Policy. The EDA is intended to encourage EU governments to spend defence budgets on meeting future challenges, rather than past (cold war) threats, and to help identify common needs and promote collaboration.

As defence budgets declined, companies and governments made greater efforts to export weapons, particularly to developing countries. More recently, importing countries have used offsets to justify arms purchases, and arms-exporting countries and companies have thereby become involved in a process of questionable value that could potentially increase the number of producers and exacerbate the problems of overcapacity in certain areas.[101]

It would seem, therefore, that many of the characteristics of the old defence industrial base remain in spite of the extent of changes in the industry's structure. However, the clear internationalization of production, the changes in ownership, the 'spin-in' of civil technologies (such as IT and communications technology) and the increased number of civil companies in the supply chains all make this look like a very different industry. It is also one that is less easy to define and much more difficult to research, meaning that there is some concern as to how transparent the processes of procurement and production will be in the future.

With the growth of privatization across Europe it is likely that the financial sector will become increasingly important in the arms industry, as it has in the UK and the USA. The differences between the financial and corporate governance systems in most European countries and those in the UK and the USA have influenced the ways in which the respective industries have restructured. The 'last supper' in the USA involved financiers as well as companies, and

---

[101] eds Brauer and Dunne, *Arms Trade and Economic Development* (note 12)

Wall Street played an important role in the restructuring that followed.[102] Similarly, in the UK the financial sector and shareholders aided restructuring through their influence on company policies. In Europe the greater government ownership and the 'hands-on' involvement of institutional shareholders and bankers in company policy through their positions on boards of directors reduced the degree and speed of restructuring. The involvement of banks, investment firms and holding companies in the restructuring currently taking place in the European arms industry suggests that the process will speed up in Europe.[103] While most of the British defence industry was privatized in the past two decades, in much of the rest of Europe the state still owns a lot of the defence industrial base, although this is changing. Privatization of the major contractors is increasingly taking place in Europe and, together with the increase in foreign ownership and non-domestic procurements, is likely to have a major influence on the European industry.[104] In addition, there are previously civil companies involved in communications and IT that are feeding off demand from the 'revolution in military affairs' and the war on terrorism and expanding the international defence industrial base.

The privatization of defence services and support is a further important trend. This has been made apparent in Iraq, with companies taking on support roles that in the past the armed forces would have undertaken, even in areas of conflict. A big growth area is the provision of security—guarding people and buildings. There is a new periphery of private security companies with government contracts and 'homeland security' business and a new group of civil companies that are becoming involved in defence production.[105] The trad-

---

[102] Markusen (note 62).

[103] See section II above; and Sköns and Surry (note 4), p. 387. Financial companies involved include the Carlyle Group, TCG Financial Partners and Veritas Capital.

[104] Under the British Government's Private Finance Initiative (or Public–Private Partnerships) the public sector contracts to purchase services on a long-term basis in order to take advantage of private sector management skills, while it is private finance that is at risk. These services include concessions and franchises, where a private sector firm takes on the responsibility for providing a public service, including maintaining, enhancing or constructing the necessary infrastructure. This initiative is having an important impact on state–industry relations in the UK and is influencing government policy abroad. It could also lead to new entrants into the defence market. On the impact of private financing on military expenditure data see chapters 7 and 8 in this volume.

[105] For an analysis of the new developments see Wulf, H., *Internationalizing and Privatizing War and Peace* (Palgrave Macmillan: Basingstoke, 2005). Wulf distinguishes between private military companies—companies supplying consulting and planning, logistics and support, technical services and repairs, training, peacekeeping and humanitarian assistance—and private security companies—companies supplying property protection, crime prevention and correctional services (pp. 43–47). There are no detailed estimates of the size or value of these sectors, only rough approximations of their general magnitude. Peter Singer has estimated the annual revenues of the private military industry at c. $100 billion. Singer, P. W., *Corporate Warriors: The Rise of the Privatized Military Industry* (Cornell University Press: Ithaca, N.Y., 2003). The OECD has similarly made a rough estimate of the annual turnover of the private security sector, at $100–120 billion. Organisation for Economic Co-operation and Development (OECD), *The Security Economy* (OECD: Paris, 2004), URL <http://www.oecdbookshop.org/oecd/display.asp?SF1=DI&ST1=5LMQCR2JFHKB>, p. 8. If these estimates are accurate, then these 2 types of companies would have combined annual sales of c. $200 billion. See also Holmqvist, C., *Private Security Companies: The Case for Regulation*, SIPRI Policy Paper no. 9 (SIPRI: Stockholm, Jan. 2005), URL <http://www.sipri.org/>; and Brauer, J., 'An economic perspective on mercenaries, military companies, and the privatisation of force', *Cambridge Review of International Affairs*, vol. 13, no. 1 (Apr. 2000), pp. 130–46.

itional arms producers have discovered this new market and are buying up some of the start-up companies, the so-called private military firms.[106] The changing security environment is likely to have a further impact on this wider security industry, but there is at present little available information on the development of the relevant companies. The increasing privatization of defence and post-conflict reconstruction services could be producing a group of influential, profit-chasing companies that have a vested interest in conflict. This could lead to pressures on governments to extend conflicts or initiate new ones. In the past the arms-producing companies had a vested interest in the production of weapons and in increasing demand for them, but they did not necessarily benefit from actual conflict. As Herbert Wulf argues, there is a need for an international governance structure to deal with the erosion of the state monopoly of force.[107]

The developing world

While these changes were taking place in the developed world, adjustments were also taking place in the developing world. Research at SIPRI in the 1980s had correctly assessed that the observed fast growth in arms production capacity in developing countries would be inadequate to permit self-sufficiency or create competition for the developed world.[108] The end of the cold war and the superpower confrontation removed much of the pressure and support for the maintenance of high military burdens in the developing world. The lack of superpower involvement generally reduced tensions, military and military-related aid, and the scale of conflicts (although the number of conflicts increased).

While the large arms industries in China and India are to a great extent insulated from external competition, some other relatively more advanced arms-producing countries in the developing world have also sustained their arms production, for domestic procurement as well as for exports. During the five-year period 2000–2004, there were seven developing countries among the 30 largest exporters of major weapons: China, Israel, South Korea, Brazil, Indonesia, South Africa and North Korea.[109] India comes further down on the list in spite of its large arms industry. It has a strong import dependency and its rate of self-reliance in arms procurement is only 30 per cent.[110]

Among the remaining developing countries, by the late 1990s, 20–30 were engaged in some form of arms production and arms exports or re-exports.[111] Indigenous arms production efforts are often justified on economic grounds, providing spill-over or spin-off effects on civil industry and foreign exchange

---

[106] Wulf (note 105), p. 194.

[107] Wulf (note 105), p. 207. See also Holmqvist (note 105).

[108] Brzoska and Ohlson (note 36).

[109] Wezeman, S. T. and Bromley, M., 'The volume of transfers of major conventional weapons: by recipients and suppliers, 2000–2004', *SIPRI Yearbook 2005* (note 4), table 10A.2, pp. 453–54.

[110] Markusen, A. R., DiGiovanni, S. and Leary, M. C. (eds), *From Defense to Development: International Perspectives on Realizing the Peace Dividend* (Routledge: London, 2003), p. 191.

[111] Brauer (note 12).

earnings through exports, although there is no convincing economic argument or evidence that such economic benefits exist.[112] Offset arrangements and licensed production have often been seen as a means of promoting domestic production and improving the technological level of the systems produced, although some countries now seek the technical know-how to be an intelligent customer rather than aiming to become a producer.[113] Producing small arms and relatively unsophisticated weapon systems is an achievable goal for most developing economies with some industrial base, but developing an arms industry capable of producing large advanced weapon systems is no longer feasible.[114]

These trends were reflected in the SIPRI Top 100 arms-producing companies: although a number of companies based in developing countries have shown some potential of becoming international players, none has made it so far. Indeed, the changing nature of arms production and the restructuring of the market have reduced the opportunities for less-established companies to become more than links in the supply chains of the major international players.

IV. Conclusions

In 2004 there was yet another substantial increase in arms sales by the Top 100 arms-producing companies, although the increase was less pronounced than in 2003. The USA continues to dominate the industry and the companies in the list are little changed. There was some important merger and acquisition activity in 2005, but at a slower pace than in 2004. Further consolidation and restructuring are likely, particularly in Europe, and the industry is likely to continue to expand its supply chain, across both industries and countries. Governments will focus more on capability than on production. Non-US companies will continue to attempt to access the US market and the industry is likely to continue to internationalize.

There have been marked changes in the international arms industry since the end of the cold war and further change can be expected. The arms market continues to have a set of unique characteristics, such as the considerable barriers to entry and exit. Some companies have 'survived' from the traditional cold war arms market while others have managed to exit or enter the new market. A noteworthy trend has been the privatization of defence services and support, which has expanded the security services industry as a periphery around the core arms industry. This could have implications in terms of accountability and transparency and certainly has implications for SIPRI's Arms Production Project. While the project has been a valuable source of

---

[112] Brauer (note 12); and Brzoska and Ohlson (note 36). Brauer argues that the evidence suggests that the arms industries in developing countries depended crucially on already established civil capacities and there in no evidence that arms exports provided net foreign exchange.

[113] Brauer, J. and Dunne, J. P., 'Arms trade offsets and development', *Africanus*, vol. 35, no. 1 (2005), pp. 14–24.

[114] eds Markusen et al. (note 110).

impartial information, data and research, which has greatly improved the understanding of the post-cold war arms industry, these changes present new challenges. Meeting them will require further data collection and research activities in order to capture the changing nature, extent and visibility of the international arms and security industry.

Appendix 9A. The 100 largest arms-producing companies, 2004

EAMON SURRY and THE SIPRI ARMS INDUSTRY
NETWORK*

I. Selection criteria and sources of data

Table 9A.1 lists the world's 100 largest arms-producing companies (excluding Chinese companies), ranked by their arms sales in 2004. The table contains information on the companies' arms sales in 2003 and 2004 and their total sales, profit and employment in 2004. It includes public and private companies, but excludes manufacturing or maintenance units of the armed services. Only companies with manufacturing activities in the field of military goods and services are listed, not holding or investment companies. Chinese companies are excluded because of the lack of data. Companies from other countries might also have been included at the lower end of the list had sufficient data been available.

Publicly available information on arms sales and other financial and employment data of the arms industry worldwide are limited. The sources of data for table 9A.1 include: company annual reports and websites; a SIPRI questionnaire; and news published in the business sections of newspapers, in military journals and by Internet news services specializing in military matters. Press releases, marketing reports, government publications of prime contract awards and country surveys were also consulted. Where no data are available from these sources, estimates have been made by SIPRI. The scope of the data and the geographical coverage are largely determined by the availability of information. All data are continuously revised and updated and may change between different editions of the SIPRI Yearbook.

The source for the dollar exchange rates is the International Monetary Fund (IMF), as provided in its *International Financial Statistics*.

II. Definitions

Arms sales. Arms sales are defined by SIPRI as sales of military goods and services to military customers, including both sales for domestic procurement and sales for export. Military goods and services are those which are designed specifically for military purposes and the technologies related to such goods and services. They exclude sales of general-purpose goods (e.g., oil, electricity, office computers, cleaning services, uniforms and boots). They include all revenue related to the sale of military equipment, that is, not only for the manufacture but also for the research and development, maintenance, servicing and repair of the equipment. This definition serves as a

* Participants in the network for this yearbook were: Ken Epps (Project Ploughshares, Waterloo, Ontario), Jean-Paul Hébert (Centre Interdisciplinaire de Recherches sur la Paix et d'Études Stratégiques, Paris), Reuven Pedatzur (Tel Aviv University), Giovanni Gasparini (Istituto Affari Internazionali, Rome), Gülay Günlük-Senesen (Istanbul University) and Julian Cooper (Centre for Russian and East European Studies, University of Birmingham).

guideline; in practice it is difficult to apply. Nor is there any good alternative, since no generally agreed standard definition of 'arms sales' exists. The data on arms sales in table 9A.1 often reflect only what each company considers to be the defence share of its total sales. The comparability of company arms sales in table 9A.1 is therefore limited.

Total sales, profit and employment. Data on total sales, profit and employment are for entire companies, not for arms-producing divisions alone. All data are for consolidated sales, including those of national and foreign subsidiaries. The profit data represent profit after taxes. Employment data are year-end figures, except for those companies which publish only a yearly average. All data are presented on the financial year basis reported by the company in its annual report.

III. Calculations

Arms sales are sometimes estimated by SIPRI. In some cases SIPRI uses the figure for the total sales of a 'defence' division, although the division may also have some, unspecified, civil sales. When the company does not report a sales figure for a defence division or similar entity, estimates can sometimes be made based on data on contract awards, information on the company's current arms production programmes and figures provided by company officials in media or other reports.

The data for arms sales are used as an approximation of the annual value of arms production. For most companies this is realistic. The main exception is shipbuilding companies. For these companies there is a significant discrepancy between the value of annual production and annual sales because of the long lead (production) time of ships and the low production run (number). Some shipbuilding companies provide estimates of the value of their annual production. These data are then used by SIPRI for those companies.

All data are collected in local currency and at current prices. For conversion from local currencies to US dollars, SIPRI uses the IMF annual average of market exchange rates. The data in table 9A.1 and most of the tables in chapter 9 are provided in current dollars. Changes between years in these data are difficult to interpret because the change in dollar values is made up of several components: the change in arms sales, the rate of inflation and, for sales conducted in local currency, fluctuations in the exchange rate. Sales on the international arms market are often conducted in dollars. Fluctuations in exchange rates then do not have an impact on the dollar values but affect instead the value in local currency. If the value of the dollar declines, then the company's revenue in local currency falls and, if its production inputs are paid for in local currency—which most often is the case—this has a negative impact on the company's profit margins. Calculations in constant dollar terms are difficult to interpret for the same reasons. Without knowing the relative shares of arms sales derived from domestic procurement and from arms exports, it is impossible to interpret the exact meaning and implications of the arms sales data. These data should therefore be used with caution. This is particularly true for countries with strongly fluctuating exchange rates.[1]

---

[1] On the benefits of using purchasing power parity rates rather than market exchange rates when converting currencies in the case of military expenditure see appendix 8E in this volume.

Table 9A.1. The 100 largest arms-producing companies (excluding China), 2004

Figures in columns 6, 7, 8 and 10 are in US$ m., at current prices and exchange rates.

1	2	3	4	5	6	7	8	9	10	11
Rank[a]					Arms sales		Total sales, 2004	Column 6 as % of column 8	Profit 2004	Employment 2004
2004	2003	Company (parent company)	Country/region	Sector[b]	2004	2003				
1	2	Boeing[c]	USA	Ac El Mi Sp	27 500	24 370	52 457	52	1 872	159 000
2	1	Lockheed Martin[d]	USA	Ac El Mi Sp	26 400	24 910	35 526	74	1 266	130 000
3	3	Northrop Grumman	USA	Ac El Mi SA/A Sh Sp	25 970	22 720	29 853	87	1 084	125 400
4	4	BAE Systems[e]	UK	A Ac El Mi SA/A Sh	19 840	15 760	24 687	80	−855	90 000
5	5	Raytheon	USA	El Mi	17 150	15 450	20 245	85	417	79 400
6	6	General Dynamics	USA	A El MV Sh	15 150	13 100	19 178	79	1 227	70 200
7	8	EADS[f]	Europe	Ac El Mi Sp	9 470	8 010	39 455	24	1 280	110 660
8	7	Thales	France	El Mi SA/A	8 950	8 350	12 780	70	246	55 480
9	9	United Technologies, UTC	USA	El Eng	6 740	6 210	37 445	18	2 788	209 700
10	11	L-3 Communications	USA	El	5 970	4 480	6 897	87	382	44 200
11	10	Finmeccanica	Italy	A Ac El MV Mi SA/A	5 640	4 550	10 764	52	681	51 030
12	13	SAIC[g]	USA	Comp (Oth)	4 670	3 700	7 187	65	409	42 400
13	12	Computer Sciences Corp., CSC[h]	USA	Comp (Oth)	4 330	3 780	14 059	31	810	79 000
S	S	MBDA (BAE Systems, UK/ EADS, Europe/ Finmeccanica, Italy)	Europe	Mi	3 850	2 710	3 851	100	..	10 000
14	14	Rolls Royce[i]	UK	Eng	3 310	3 020	10 877	30	375	35 400
15	18	DCN[j]	France	Sh	3 240	2 150	3 240	100	260	12 280
16	23	Halliburton[k]	USA	Comp (Oth)	3 100	1 790	20 466	15	−979	97 000
S	S	KBR (Halliburton)	USA	Comp (Oth)	3 100	1 790	12 468	25	..	..
17	17	General Electric	USA	Eng	3 000	2 400	152 866	2	16 819	307 000
S	S	Pratt & Whitney (UTC)	USA	Eng	2 990	3 030	8 300	36	..	34 180

1	2	3	4	5	6	7	8	9	10	11
Rank[a]					Arms sales		Total sales, 2004	Column 6 as % of column 8	Profit 2004	Employment 2004
2004	2003	Company (parent company)	Country/region	Sector[b]	2004	2003				
18	15	Honeywell International	USA	El	2 810	2 560	25 601	11	1 281	109 000
19	16	Mitsubishi Heavy Industries[l]	Japan	Ac MV Mi Sh	2 500	2 430	23 945	10	37	34 310
20	24	ITT Industries	USA	El	2 410	1 790	6 764	36	432	44 000
21	20	GKN	UK	Ac	2 400	2 020	8 145	29	1 020	36 600
22	19	United Defense, UD	USA	MV	2 290	2 050	2 292	100	166	7 700
23	25	Groupe Snecma	France	Eng	1 950	1 750	8 462	23	291	39 490
24	26	Saab	Sweden	Ac El Mi	1 930	1 700	2 429	79	148	11 940
25	28	Alliant Techsystems	USA	SA/A	1 740	1 460	2 801	62	154	14 000
26	21	Rheinmetall	FRG	A El MV SA/A	1 720	1 810	4 240	41	125	18 280
27	27	CEA	France	Oth	1 720	1 540	3 878	44	333	14 940
S		Rheinmetall DeTec (Rheinmetall)	FRG	A El MV SA/A	1 720	1 810	1 719	100	..	6 799
S		Sikorsky (UTC)	USA	Ac	1 690	1 520	2 500	68	..	8 980
28	22	Groupe Dassault Aviation	France	Ac	1 670	1 810	4 297	39	383	12 040
S		Eurocopter Group (EADS)	France	Ac	1 620	1 440	3 453	47	..	..
29	36	Harris	USA	El	1 550	1 170	2 519	62	133	10 900
30	34	Rockwell Collins	USA	El	1 540	1 270	2 930	52	301	15 800
S		Dyncorp (CSC)[m]	USA	Comp (Oth)	1 430	1 660	..	..	..	..
31	32	Goodrich	USA	Comp (Ac)	1 420	1 320	4 725	30	172	21 300
32	38	QinetiQ	UK	Comp (Oth)	1 390	1 110	1 598	87	129	10 400
33	33	Israel Aircraft Industries	Israel	Ac El Mi	1 370	1 310	2 050	67	82	14 570
34	30	Kawasaki Heavy Industries[l]	Japan	Ac Eng Mi Sh	1 320	1 370	11 476	12	106	28 680
35	29	Textron	USA	Ac El Eng MV	1 300	1 400	10 242	13	365	44 000
36	40	Titan Corporation	USA	Comp (Oth)	1 290	1 010	2 047	63	–38	12 000
37	41	DRS Technologies	USA	El	1 280	940	1 309	98	61	5 660
38	39	Smiths[n]	UK	El	1 240	1 100	4 852	26	390	26 730

39	31	Sukhoi[o]	Russia	Ac	1 200	1 370	1 262	95	42	32 810
40	35	Ordnance Factories	India	A SA/A	1 150	1 190	1 357	85	..	..
41	43	Anteon	USA	Comp (Oth)	1 130	920	1 268	89	62	8 800
42	47	Groupe Sagem	France	El	1 090	830	4 435	25	166	15 370
43	48	New Izar[p]	Spain	Sh	1 090	830	1 366	80	..	5 560
44	46	VT Group	UK	Sh	1 040	840	1 362	76	49	11 000
45	37	ThyssenKrupp, TK	FRG	Sh	1 030	1 110	48 872	2	1 123	184 360
S	S	Alenia Aeronautica (Finmeccanica)	Italy	Ac	1 030	620	1 333	77	2	6 950
46	55	EDS	USA	Comp (Oth)	990	690	20 669	5	158	117 000
47	50	Mitsubishi Electric[l]	Japan	El Mi	950	820	31 524	3	658	97 660
48	44	Elbit Systems	Israel	El	940	900	940	100	53	5 500
49	52	Almaz-Antei[o]	Russia	Mi	930	750	1 327	70	55	93 000
50	56	Cobham	UK	Comp (Ac El)	900	680	1 800	50	155	9 860
51	59	Hindustan Aeronautics	India	Ac Mi	880	650	976	90	95	..
52	53	URS Corporation	USA	El	880	720	3 382	26	62	27 500
S	S	EG&G (URS Corporation)	USA	Comp (El Oth)	880	720	1 130	78	..	11 600
53	45	ST Engineering[q]	Singapore	Ac El MV SA/A Sh	860	890	1 744	49	212	11 620
54	73	NEC[l]	Japan	El	840	490	43 395	2	-227	145 810
55	69	Engineered Support Systems	USA	El	840	540	884	95	76	3 280
56	57	Samsung[r]	S. Korea	A El MV Mi Sh	800	670	121 700	1	11 800	222 000
57	75	AM General Corporation[s]	USA	MV	800	490	..	..	..	..
58	68	CACI International	USA	Comp (Oth)	770	540	1 146	67	64	9 300
59	60	ManTech International	USA	Comp (Oth)	770	640	842	92	25	5 500
60	58	Oshkosh Truck	USA	MV	770	660	2 262	34	113	7 800
61	51	Rafael	Israel	Ac Mi SA/A Oth	760	790	801	95	45	5 170
62	54	Krauss-Maffei Wegmann	FRG	MV	750	710	752	100	..	2 500
63	49	GIAT Industries	France	A MV SA/A	730	820	733	100	-100	5 000
64	66	Devonport Management[t]	UK	Sh	720	570	745	96	42	4 950
65	70	Babcock International Group	UK	Sh	700	520	1 392	50	38	9 090
66	62	RUAG	Switzerland	A Ac Eng SA/A	660	620	1 003	66	23	5 560

1	2	3	4	5	6	7	8	9	10	11
Rank[a]					Arms sales		Total sales, 2004	Column 6 as % of column 8	Profit 2004	Employment 2004
2004	2003	Company (parent company)	Country/ region	Sector[b]	2004	2003				
67	61	Diehl	FRG	Mi SA/A	650	630	1 975	33	..	10 730
68	S	MTU Aero Engines	FRG	Eng	620	500	2 383	26	16	7 680
69	77	Bharat Electronics	India	El	620	460	709	87	98	12 390
S	S	Samsung Techwin (Samsung)	S. Korea	A El Eng MV	620	520	1 729	36	23	4 140
70	71	Indra	Spain	El	610	510	1 347	45	106	6 520
71	–	Armor Holdings	USA	Comp (MV Oth)	610	90	980	62	81	4 310
72	76	Irkut[o]	Russia	Ac	570	480	622	92	68	14 020
S	65	Alvis (BAE Systems)[u]	UK	MV Oth	570	570	..	..	..	..
73	64	Fincantieri[u]	Italy	Sh	560	570	2 704	21	124	9 270
74	82	Stewart & Stevenson	USA	MV	550	450	1 157	48	5	3 000
75	93	ARINC	USA	Comp (El)	530	350	734	72	9	3 000
S	S	United States Marine Repair (UD)	USA	Comp (Sh)	530	510	573	93	..	..
76	63	Korea Aerospace Industries[w]	S. Korea	Ac	510	600	571	89	6	2 920
77	72	Aerospace Corporation[x]	USA	Comp (Oth)	510	510	..	..	..	..
78	94	Curtiss-Wright Corporation	USA	Comp (Ac)	480	350	955	50	65	5 600
79	85	EDO	USA	El	480	410	536	89	29	2 550
80	79	CAE[y]	Canada	El	460	450	758	61	..	4 800
81	99	Ishikawajima-Harima HI[l]	Japan	Eng Sh	460	310	10 066	5	20	7 390
82	84	Mitre[z]	USA	Oth	460	430	871	53	..	5 900
83	81	Denel	S. Africa	A Ac El MV Mi SA/A	450	450	586	76	–248	9 940
84	89	Ultra Electronics	UK	El	450	370	586	77	43	2 680
85	90	Cubic Corporation	USA	Comp (El Oth)	450	370	722	63	37	5 950
86	88	Tenix	Australia	El SA/A Sh	440	370	646	68	..	3 000
87	42	DaimlerChrysler, DC[aa]	FRG	Eng	440	920	176 471	..	3 063	384 720
88	80	Avio	Italy	Eng	440	450	1 516	29	–47	4 770

89	74	Aerokosmicheskoe Oborudovanie^o	Russia	El	440	490	583	76	36	42 400
S	S	ADI (Transfield Group/Thales)	Australia	El SA/A Sh	440	420	..	..	..	..
S	S	MTU Friedrichshafen (DC)	FRG	Eng	440	380	1 677	26	..	5 850
90	92	Moog	USA	Comp (El Mi)	430	360	939	46	57	5 780
91	86	Ericsson	Sweden	El	410	400	17 958	2	2 589	50 530
S	S	Ericsson Microwave (Ericsson)	Sweden	El	410	400	418	99	..	1 660
S	S	Land Systems Hägglunds (BAE Systems)^bb	Sweden	MV	410	290	410	100	..	1 030
92	91	SMA	France	Comp (Ac)	400	360	401	100	−1	3 310
93	78	Israel Military Industries	Israel	A MV SA/A	400	460	450	90	..	2 400
94	83	Kongsberg Gruppen	Norway	El Mi SA/A	400	430	955	42	5	4 020
95	–	Meggitt	UK	Oth	390	290	878	45	63	4 420
96	67	Jacobs Engineering Group^cc	USA	Comp (Oth)	390	560	4 594	9	129	24 400
97	95	Toshiba^l	Japan	El Mi	380	340	53 942	1	426	165 000
98	100	Orbital Sciences Corporation	USA	Sp	370	300	676	54	200	2 450
99	–	Embraer	Brazil	Ac	360	260	3 505	10	429	14 650
100	–	Patria Industries	Finland	Ac MV SA/A	360	220	430	83	32	1 880

^a Companies are ranked according to the value of their arms sales in 2004. Companies with the designation S in column 1 or 2 are subsidiaries. A dash (−) in column 2 indicates either that the company did not make arms sales in 2003 or that it did not rank among the 100 largest companies in 2003. Company names and structures are listed as they were on 31 Dec. 2004. Information about subsequent changes is provided in these footnotes. The 2003 ranks may differ from those published in SIPRI Yearbook 2005 owing to the continual revision of data, most often because of changes reported by the company itself and sometimes because of improved estimations. Major revisions are explained in these footnotes.

^b Key to abbreviations: A = artillery, Ac = aircraft, El = electronics, Eng = engines, Mi = missiles, MV = military vehicles, SA/A = small arms/ammunition, Sh = ships, Sp = space and Oth = other. Comp (. . .) = components, services or anything less than final systems in the sectors within the parentheses; it is used only for companies that do not produce final systems.

^c Figures for Boeing arms sales are for the Total Integrated Defense Systems unit, excluding the sales of the largely civilian Launch and Orbital Systems unit. Beginning in 2003 Boeing changed the way in which they report their market segments.

^d Figures for Lockheed Martin arms sales include management fees from the US Department of Energy for the management of nuclear weapons programmes.

e Figures for BAE Systems arms sales are for total non-commercial sales. The sales reported by the company for their 'Commercial Aerospace' business group are primarily accounted for by their 20% interest in Airbus. In addition, data for BAE Systems' arms sales include an estimate of $330 million for the arms sales of Alvis in the first 7 months of the year. Alvis was acquired by BAE Systems in Aug. 2004.

f EADS (the European Aeronautic Defence and Space Company) is 30.09% owned by DaimlerChrysler (Germany), 30.09% by Lagardère (France) together with French financial institutions and Sogepa (a French state holding company), and 5.5% by SEPI (Sociedad Estatal de Participaciones Industriales, a Spanish state holding company). EADS is registered in the Netherlands.

g The figure for SAIC total sales does not include $874 million for Telcordia, a telecommunications subsidiary sold on 15 Mar. 2005. In their annual report for financial year (FY) 2005, SAIC provides reclassified data to reflect Telcordia as a discontinued operation.

h The figure for CSC total sales does not include revenue for DynCorp International, classified by CSC in their 2005 annual report as 'discontinued operations'. DynCorp International was divested by CSC in Feb. 2005. Figures for CSC's 2004 arms sales include both its reported sales to the US Department of Defense (DOD) and the value of contracts awarded to DynCorp International by the US DOD during FY 2004.

i Figures for Rolls Royce arms sales are for their 'Defence' business division and an estimate of 45% of their 'Marine' business division.

j Figures for DCN are for sales revenue rather than value of production.

k Arms sales for Halliburton are an estimate based on one-third of their 'government and infrastructure division' sales. In the *SIPRI Yearbook 2005* Top 100 list for 2003, US DOD prime contract awards were listed as an approximation of arms sales.

l For Japanese companies figures in the arms sales column represent new military contracts rather than arms sales.

m Figures for Dyncorp represent US DOD prime contracts awarded rather than arms sales.

n Data for Smiths arms sales are for 60% of their 'Aerospace Division', in addition to an estimate of some limited defence work done within their 'Specialty Engineering' division.

o This is the third year that Russian companies have been covered by the SIPRI Top 100. There may be other companies that should be in the list, but insufficient data are available. The situation in the Russian arms industry is still very fluid, and company names are likely to change as they are restructured. Irkut and Sukhoi provide detailed information on their websites, and all data are from their own consolidated financial statements. For all other Russian companies in the list, figures for total sales and profits in 2004 are from Expert RA, the Russian rating agency, while figures for arms sales share estimates and employment are from the Centre for Analysis of Strategies and Technologies. The arms sales share estimate for Almaz-Antei is from the *Defense News* Top 100 List of Companies.

p The military shipbuilding activities of Izar were transferred to a new company, 'New Izar', on 31 Dec. 2004. The company was subsequently launched with the name Navantia on 2 Mar. 2005. The Spanish state holding company SEPI is the sole shareholder.

q ST Engineering was previously a subsidiary of Singapore Technologies Pte Ltd, which was dissolved on 31 Dec. 2004. As of 1 Jan. 2005, all companies that were under the control of Singapore Technologies Pte Ltd, including ST Engineering, came under the direct control of Temasek Holdings, an investment holding company of the Singapore Government.

r Figures for Samsung arms sales are for the estimated arms sales of Samsung Techwin and 50% of the sales of Samsung Thales.

[s] Limited financial data are publicly available for AM General. The SIPRI estimate of arms sales is based on a 3-year average of US DOD prime contract awards plus an estimate of their exports.

[t] Devonport Management Limited is owned by Halliburton KBR (51%), Balfour Beatty (24.5%) and the Weir Group (24.5%).

[u] The figure for Alvis's arms sales in 2004 is based on available data for 2003. Alvis was acquired by BAE Systems in Aug. 2004 and integrated into their Land Systems business.

[v] Fincantieri is owned by Fintecna, which was formed in Nov. 2002 from the Institute for Industrial Reconstruction, an Italian state holding company which had been in a process of liquidation since 2000.

[w] Korea Aerospace Industries was established in 1999 through the consolidation of Samsung Aerospace, Daewoo Heavy Industries and Hyundai Space and Aircraft Company.

[x] The Aerospace Corporation operates a Federally Funded Research and Development Center for the US DOD. Figures are for 2003, as the company did not produce an annual report for 2004.

[y] Data for CAE arms sales include an estimate of $101 million for their divested Marine business.

[z] Mitre operates 3 Federally Funded Research and Development Centers for the US DOD.

[aa] Figures for DaimlerChrysler arms sales are for the arms-producing activities of MTU Friedrichshafen and exclude DaimlerChrysler's 30.1% share in EADS.

[bb] Hägglunds Vehicle was a subsidiary of Alvis during the first 7 months of 2004. Alvis was acquired by BAE Systems in Aug. 2004.

[cc] Figures for Jacobs Engineering Group arms sales represent US DOD prime contracts awarded.

Appendix 9B. Table of acquisitions, 2005

EAMON SURRY

Table 9B.1 lists major acquisitions in the North American and West European arms industry that were announced or completed between 1 January and 31 December 2005. It is not an exhaustive list of all acquisition activity, but gives a general overview of strategically significant and financially noteworthy transactions.

Table 9B.1. Major acquisitions in the North American and West European arms industry, 2005

Figures are in US$ m., at current prices.

Buyer company (country/region)	Acquired company (country)	Seller company (country)[a]	Deal value ($ m.)[b]
Within North America (between USA-based companies unless indicated otherwise)			
CAE (Canada)	Terrain Experts Inc.	. .	10
CACI International Inc.	National Security Research Inc.	Employee-owned	. .
DRS Technologies	Codem Systems	. .	29
DRS Technologies	Engineered Support Systems	. .	1970
EDO Corporation	EVI Technology LLC	Privately held	. .
Engineered Support Systems	Mobilized Systems	. .	17
General Dynamics	Anteon	. .	2 200
General Dynamics	Itronix Corporation	Privately held	. .
General Dynamics	MAYA Viz	. .	. .
General Dynamics	Tadpole Computer Inc.	Privately held	. .
Goodrich Corporation	Sensors Unlimited Inc.	. .	60
L-3 Communications	BAI Aerosystems Inc.	. .	. .
L-3 Communications	EOTech Inc.	. .	49
L-3 Communications	Joseph Sheairs Associates	. .	. .
L-3 Communications	Sonoma Design Group	. .	. .
L-3 Communications	Titan Corporation	. .	2 650
Lockheed Martin	Coherent Technologies Inc.	. .	. .
Lockheed Martin	SYTEX Group	. .	440
ManTech International	Gray Hawk Systems Inc.	. .	100
Northrop Grumman	Integic Corporation		. .
SAIC	Object Sciences Corporation	. .	. .
SAIC	IMAPS	. .	. .
Teledyne Technologies	Benthos Inc.		41
Teledyne Technologies	Microwave Technical Solutions assets	Avnet Inc.	. .
Titan Corporation	Intelligence Data Systems	Employee owned	43
United Defense	Engineered Plastic Designs	. .	8
United States Marine Repair	Corrosion Engineering Services	. .	. .

Buyer company (country/region)	Acquired company (country)	Seller company (country)[a]	Deal value ($ m.)[b]
United Technologies	Rocketdyne Propulsion & Power	Boeing	..
Veritas Capital	MZM Inc.	Privately held	..
Within Western Europe			
Avio Group (Italy)	Philips Aerospace Electronics (Netherlands)	Royal Philips (Netherlands)	..
EADS (W. Europe)	Professional Mobile Radio business	Nokia (Finland)	..
EQT (Sweden)[c]	MTU Friedrichshafen (Germany) and the off-highway division of Detroit Diesel Corporation (USA)	DaimlerChrysler (Germany)	1 900
Finmeccanica (Italy)[d]	Datamat SpA (Italy)	..	171
Krauss-Maffei Wegmann (Germany)	MAN-Mobile Bridges (Germany)	MAN Technologies (Germany)	..
MBDA (W. Europe)	LFK (Germany)	EADS (W. Europe)	..
Rheinmetall (Germany)	Arges (Austria)	..	..
Smiths Group (UK)	Farran Technology (Ireland)	..	31
Snecma (France) [e]	Sagem (France)	..	..
Thales (France)[f]	TDA Armements (W. Europe)	EADS (W. Europe)	..
ThyssenKrupp Technologies (Germany) and EADS (W. Europe)[g]	Atlas Elektronik (Germany)	BAE Systems	172

Transatlantic: West European acquisitions of companies based in Canada and the USA

BAE Systems (UK)	United Defense (USA)	..	4 192
Chelton Microwave Corporation (UK)[h]	Defense & Space unit	Remec Inc.	260
EADS (W. Europe)[i]	Talon Instruments	..	..
Kongsberg (Norway)	Gallium Software (Canada)	..	26
QinetiQ (UK)	Apogen Technologies (USA)	..	288
QinetiQ (UK)[j]	Planning Systems Inc. (USA)	..	42
Ultra Electronics (UK)	Audiopack (USA)	Privately held	60
VT Group (UK)[k]	Cube Corporation (USA)	..	26

Transatlantic: US and Canadian acquisitions of West Europe-based companies

Carlyle Group (USA)	NP Aerospace (UK)	Reinhold Industries (UK)	54
Eaton Corporation (USA)	Aerospace fluid and air division	Cobham (UK)	270
L-3 Communications (USA)	SAM Electronics (Germany)	..	150
Lockheed Martin (USA)[l]	INSYS Group Limited (UK)	..	..
Rockwell Collins (USA)	Teldix (Germany)	Northrop Grumman (USA)	22
Stewart & Stevenson Services (USA)	Automotive Technik (UK)	..	47

[a] In the 'Seller company' column, '. .' indicates that the ownership of the acquired company was not specified in the company press release. The company may have been either privately held or publicly listed.

[b] In cases where the deal value was not available in US dollars, currency conversion was made using the International Monetary Fund average exchange rate for the calendar month in which the transaction was made. Companies do not always disclose the value of transactions.

[c] EQT is a private equity group.

[d] Finmeccanica agreed to acquire a controlling stake of 52.7% of Datamat, subject to approval by competition authorities.

[e] In May 2005 Sagem and Snecma merged to become SAFRAN.

[f] The 50% share in TDA Armements held by EADS was sold to Thales, making Thales the 100% shareholder in the company.

[g] ThyssenKrupp Technologies will hold 60 per cent and EADS will hold 40 per cent of Atlas Elektronik.

[h] The Chelton Microwave Corporation is a member of the Chelton Group. The Chelton Group is a part of Cobham plc, a British aerospace and defence company.

[i] EADS acquired Talon Instruments through its North American subsidiary, EADS North America.

[j] QinetiQ acquired Planning Systems Inc. through their wholly owned North American subsidiary, Foster-Miller, Inc.

[k] VT Group acquired the Cube Corporation through its US subsidiary, VT Griffin Services.

[l] Lockheed Martin U.K. Holdings Ltd., a subsidiary of the Lockheed Martin Corporation (USA), acquired INSYS Group Limited.

Source: The SIPRI Arms Industry Files on mergers and acquisitions.

Appendix 9C. Developments in the Russian arms industry

JULIAN COOPER

I. Introduction

It is now more than a decade and a half since the size of the vast arms industry of the Soviet Union began to contract, at first in terms of output and employment, and later with respect to the number of production and research facilities. Since the collapse of the Soviet Union in 1991, the administrative structures responsible for the management and oversight of the military sector in Russia have undergone frequent and at times far-reaching change. Over time, Russian military production has become increasingly dependent on export orders, with only modest domestic procurement for the needs of the Russian armed forces. Since Vladimir Putin was elected President of Russia in 2000, military output has recovered to some extent and funding for procurement and research and development (R&D) has increased at a rapid pace. However, this expansion of monetary outlays has not been matched by a corresponding increase in the number of new weapons reaching the armed forces. The principal factor accounting for these developments has been the state of the economy. Notwithstanding substantial earnings from oil and gas exports and an annual average rate of growth of gross domestic product (GDP) of some 7 per cent since Putin took office,[1] the economy remains weak and for the past decade the Russian Government has not been prepared to put economic expansion at risk by increasing the share of GDP devoted to defence. Starved of resources for almost 15 years, the Russian arms industry is now facing some extremely serious structural problems and further contraction is now almost inevitable.

Overall trends of development of the Russian arms industry between the final years of the Soviet Union and 2004 are shown in table 9C.1. It can be seen that the industry has undergone very substantial contraction and its role in the economy as a whole has diminished to a significant degree, whether measured in terms of employment or of output. The size of the industry's labour force has been in relentless decline since the late 1990s while the average age of the remaining personnel continues to rise and is now 54 years. In research institutes the average age is even higher, at 57 years, and 90 per cent of personnel are over 50.[2] A major factor in the industry's inability to recruit new workers is inadequate reward for skilled and responsible work. In Soviet times the military sector offered some of the best employment opportunities and pay; today, while wages have recovered from the very low rates characteristic of the mid-1990s, they are still far below the average for industry as a whole.

---

[1] Rosstat, 'Dinamika real'nogo ob"ema pronzvedennogo VVP' [Dynamic of real volume of produced GDP], URL <http://www.gks.ru/bgd/free/b01_19/IssWWW.exe/Stg/d000/i000040r.htm>.

[2] Solov'ev, V. and Ivanov, V., Gosprogramma vooruzhenii na 2002–2006 gody provalena [State programme of armaments for 2002–2006 has failed], *Nezavisimoe Voennoe Obozrenie*, 29 July 2005, URL <http://nvo.ng.ru/wars/2005-07-29/>. The retirement age in Russia is 60 for men and 55 for women.

Table 9C.1. The Soviet and Russian military economies, 1990–2004

	Soviet Union, 1990	Russian Federation		
		1990–92	Mid-1990s	2004
Arms industry employment:[a]	7 840 000[b]	4 889 000[b]	2 663 000[b]	1 800 000
Working in industry	6 425 000	3 990 000	2 107 000	1 340 000
Working in R&D	1 415 000	880 000	550 000	452 000
Employment in the arms industry as a share of total employment in the economy (%)	6.7	6.8	4.0	2.7
Employment in the arms industry as a share of total industrial employment (%)	17.8	18.7	12.9	9.5
Average age of arms industry employees (years)	..	39[c]	..	54
Average monthly wage in the arms industry as a share of the average industrial wage (%)	97[d]	85[e]	59[f]	78
Investment in the arms industry (as an index, 1992 = 100)	..	100[g]	7.5[g]	15.5[g]
Share of investment in the defence industry funded by the budget (%)	..	55.5	20.0	14.2
Arms industry output (as an index, 1991 = 100):	..	100[e]	20.1[h]	52.5
Military	..	100	13.9	40.5
Civilian	..	100	28.5	65.7
Arms industry output as a share of total industrial output (%)	12[i]	8.4[i]	7.7[i]	5.8[i]
Military output as a share of total industrial output (%)	6[i]	3.2[i]	2.2[i]	3.4[i]
Share of production equipment:				
Under 10 years old (%)	63	..	..	25[j]
Over 15/20 years (%)	16[k]	..	..	30[j l]
Use of production capacity (%)	..	64[m]	15.7[m]	31.2[m]
Arms exports[n] ($ m.)	16 000	4 800	3 050	5 770
as a share of total exports (%)	17.6	9.4	3.0	3.2
Share of total military production exported (%)	..	~20[o]	35–40[o]	74.6[o]
Number of *voenpredy* (military representatives)	130 000[p]	..	..	24 000

Note: This table was compiled from diverse sources and the data are often ill defined. It is presented here in order to illustrate the overall trends of development since 1990.

[a] Total employment figures for the Russian Federation refer to the arms industry excluding the nuclear industry. In some cases the total includes a few thousand 'other' employees.

[b] These figures are for 1988, 1992 and Sep. 1996, respectively.

[c] This figure is for 1990.

[d] In 1985 the share was 105%.

[e] This figure is for 1991.

[f] This figure is for June 1995, when it reached its lowest point.

[g] These figures are for 1992, 1997 and 2002, respectively.

ʰ This figure is for 1997.
ⁱ These figures are for 1990, 1991, 1993 and 2003, respectively.
ʲ This figure is for 2001.
ᵏ This figure is for equipment over 15 years old.
ˡ This figure is for equipment over 20 years old.
ᵐ These figures are for 1993, 1997 and 2003, respectively.
ⁿ These are official Soviet/Russian figures.
ᵒ These figures are for 1993–94, 1995–96 and 2003, respectively.
ᵖ No year is given for this figure; it is the maximum number reached in the Soviet period.

Sources: **Employment, 1988**: V. E. Genin (ed.), *The Anatomy of Russian Defense Conversion* (Vega Press: Walnut Creek, Calif., 2001), p. 58; International Labour Office, 'Disarmament and employment programme', Working Paper no. 16, Geneva, Mar. 1990, p. 12; industry and R&D calculated using shares of 1991 in *Moscow News*, no. 7, 1992, p. 7; **1992**: *Segodnya*, 1 Feb. 1994; **1996**: TS-VPK, Nov. 1997, URL <http://server.vpk.ru/www-vpk/reports/>; **2004**: calculated from estimated 2000 data and known decline in 2000–2004; data for 2000 calculated from TS-VPK, URL <http://ia.vpk.ru/vpkrus/kadri/>, and known employment in 2000 in aviation and shipbuilding industries, TS-VPK, URL <http://i.vpk.ru/vpkrus/otrasli>, and *Krasnaya Zvezda*, 12 Jan. 2002, URL <http://www.redstar.ru/2002/01/12_01/>; decline in 2000–2004 from *Problemy Prognozirovaniya*, no. 6, 2003, p. 72 and TsEK, *Rossiya*, no. 1, 2005, p. 63; industry and R&D, using data for 2003, TS-VPK, *VPK Rossii: strukturnye pokazateli 2003* [MIC of Russia: structural indicators 2003] (TS-VPK: Moscow, 2005), URL <http://ia.vpk.ru/local fonds/vpk_struct_demo/2003/>; **Share of total employment and total industrial employment, 1988**: Goskomstat SSSR, *Narodnoe khozyaistvo SSSR v 1990 g.* [National economy of the USSR in 1990] (Finansy i statistika: Moscow, 1991), p. 100; **1992, 2004**: Goskomstat Rossii, URL <http://www.gks.ru/bgd/regl/brus05/IswPrx.dll/Stg/06-03.htm>; **1996**: Goskomstat Rossii, *Rossiiskii statisticheskii ezhegodnik 2000* (Goskomstat Rossii: Moscow, 2001), p.112; **Average age, 1990**: TS-VPK, Kadrovyi potentsial VPK v 2000 godu [Cadre potential of the MIC in 2000], URL <http://ia.vpk.ru/sbornik_2000/kadri/kadri.htm>; **2004**: Solov'ev, B. and Ivanov, B, 'Gosprogramma vooruzhenii na 2002–2006 gody provalena' [State programme of armaments for 2002–2006 has failed], *Nezavisimoe Voennoe Obozrenie*, 29 July 2005, URL <http://nvo.ng.ru/wars/2005-07-29/>; **Average monthly wage as % average wage in industry, 1985, 1990**: *Voprosy Ekonomiki i Konversii*, no. 4, 1991, p. 95; **1991**: *Komsomolskaya Pravda*, 14 Apr. 1993; **1995**: *Krasnaya Zvezda*, 23 Sep. 1995; **2004**: TsEK, *Rossiya*, no. 1, 2005, p. 63; **Investment index**: TS-VPK, *VPK Rossii: strukturnye pokazateli 2002* (as above); **Share of budget-funded investment, 1992, 1997**: TS-VPK, 25 Jan. 2003, URL <http://i.vpk.ru/fin/>; **2002**: TS-VPK, *VPK Rossii: strukturnye pokazateli 2002* (above); **Output index, 1991, 1997**: Institute of Economics of the Transition Period, *Rossiiskaya ekonomika v 2001 godu: tendentsii i perspektivy* [Russian economy in 2001: tendencies and perspectives] (Institute of Economics of the Transition Period: Moscow, Mar. 2002), section 2.7; **2004**: TsEK, *Rossiya: ekonomicheskaya kon"yunktura* [Russia: economic conjuncture], various issues (TsEK: Moscow, 2000–2005); **Arms industry output as share of industrial output and military share, 1990**: *Nezavisimaya Gazeta*, 9 Oct. 1991, p. 4 and Goskomstat USSR, *Narodnoe khozyaistvo SSSR v 1990 g.* (above), p. 5; and *Izvestiya*, 17 Oct. 1991, p. 2; **1991**: calculated from the known 2001 share, TS-VPK, *VPK Rossii: strukturnye pokazateli 2001* (as above); **1993**: BBC, Summary of World Broadcasts, SU/2154 S1/6, 16 Nov. 1994; **2003**: TS-VPK, *VPK Rossii: strukturnye pokazateli 2003* (above); **Age of production equipment, 1990**: ed. Genin (above), p. 60; **2001**: TS-VPK, 'Proizvodstvennyi potentsial VPK Rossii v 2001 godu' [Production potential of the MIC in 2001], URL <http://ia.vpk.ru/sbornik_2001/proizvodst/page_5_3.htm>; **Use of production capacity, 1993**: TsEK, *Rossiya*, no. 1, 1998, p. 134; **1997, 2003**: TS-VPK, *VPK Rossii: strukturnye pokazateli 2002* (above) **Arms exports, 1990**: *Delovye Lyudi*, no. 3, 1999, p. 32; **1991**: TS-VPK, 6 Apr. 2004, URL <http://www.vpk-news.ru/>; **1995**: *Profil'*, no. 4, 2004, pp. 82–88 (CAST data); **2004**: ITAR-TASS news agency, 15 June 2005; **Share of total exports, 1990**: *Rossiiskii Ekonomicheskii Zhurnal*, no. 1, 1993, p. 58; **1991**: Goskomstat Rossii, *Rossiiskii statisticheskii ezhegodnik 1994* (Goskomstat Rossii: Moscow, 1995), p. 421; **1995, 2004**: Goskomstat Rossii, URL <http://www.gks.ru/bgd/regl/brus05/IswPrx.dll/Stg/25-03.htm>; **Share of total military production exported, 1993–94, 1995–96**: *Finansy*, no. 9, 1999, p. 4; **2003**: TS-VPK, URL <http://ts.vpk.ru/>, 23 Jan. 2004; **Number of military representatives, peak**: Babkin, A., 'Voennaya priemka otkryvaet tainy' [Military acceptance reveals its secrets], *Nezavisimoe Voennoe Obozrenie*, 29 July 2005, URL <http://nvo.ng.ru/armaments/2005-07-29/1_secret.html>; **2004**: Inter-regional Foundation for Information Technologies (MFIT), Obzor po materialam VPK no. 23 (4–11 June 2004), URL <http://www.mfit.ru/defensive/obzor/ob11-06-04-1.html/>.

Table 9C.2. Administrative structures of the Russian arms industry, 1991–2004

Years	Structure
1991	Nine Soviet arms industry ministries, including the Ministry of Atomic Power and Industry (nuclear weapons)
1991–92	Ministry of Industry (with defence industry departments); Minatom[a]
1992–93	Roskomoboronprom[b]; Minatom[a]
1993–96	Goskomoboronprom[c]; Minatom[a]
1996–97	Minoboronprom[d]; Minatom[a]
1997–98	Minekonomiki[e]; Minatom[a]
1999–2004	Two-tiered system: Minekonomiki[e]; later Minpromnauki[f] plus 5 agencies (Aerospace, Conventional Arms, Munitions, Shipbuilding and Control Systems); Minatom[a]
2004–	Two-tiered system: Minpromenergo[g] plus two federal agencies, Rosprom[h] and Roskosmos[i]; Rosatom[j]

[a] Minatom is the ministry of atomic energy.
[b] Roskomoboronprom is the Russian committee of the defence industry.
[c] Goskomoboronprom is the state committee of the defence industry.
[d] Minoboronprom is the ministry of defence industry.
[e] Minekonomiki is the ministry of economy.
[f] Minpromnauki is the ministry of industry and science.
[g] Minpromenergo is the ministry of industry and energy
[h] Rosprom is the federal agency for industry.
[i] Roskosmos is the federal space agency.
[j] Rosatom is the federal agency for atomic energy

Source: Burenok, V. M., Babkin, G. V. and Kosenko, A. A., 'Oboronno–promyshlennyi kompleks: sostoyanie i perspektivy razvitiya' [Defence–industrial complex: state and perspectives of development], *Voennaya Mysl'*, no. 6, 2005, p. 36.

While the rate of renewal of production equipment has shown some increase during the past five years, funded to a large extent by export earnings, there is much worn and obsolete machinery, making it difficult to meet present-day quality standards. According to a source in the Defence–Industrial Complex Department of the Russian ministry of industry and energy, Minpromenergo, 70 per cent of the basic assets of the arms industry are worn out.[3] In the past much arms industry investment was funded from the state budget, but today budgetary sources account for less than 15 per cent of all investment. There are no data on the rate of use of production capacity in Soviet times, but there is no doubt that it was substantially higher than today since the level is currently only half that of 1993. With substantial unused capacity, enterprises have high overhead costs and, with limited production runs for weapons, unit costs have risen sharply. Many enterprises of the arms industry have experienced severe financial problems. In 2003, 35 per cent of industrial enterprises and over 10 per cent of R&D organizations were loss making, while 90 enterprises were sub-

---

[3] Inter-regional Foundation for Information Technologies (MFIT), 'Voenno–promyshlennyi kompleks: sostoyanie i perspektivy' [Military–industrial complex: state and perspectives], Obzor po materialam SMI no. 32 (20–26 Aug. 2005), URL <http://www.mfit.ru/defensive/obzor/ob26-08-05-1.html#o3>.

ject to official bankruptcy procedures.[4] The output of the arms industry has been recovering since 1999 but remains far below the level of 1991, which in turn was below the peak Soviet output of 1987–88. However, exports of military goods have shown an impressive increase and have played a major role in securing the survival of facilities vital to the future of the Russian arms industry.[5]

Procurement for the domestic armed forces has contracted to a very considerable extent. One indirect indicator of this is the number of military representatives (*voen-predy*) employed at enterprises to oversee the fulfilment of contracts for the Ministry of Defence (MOD). The precise number in Russia in 1991 is not known, but it must have been at least 90 000 (i.e., 75 per cent of the Soviet Union total of 130 000). Now little more than one-quarter of this number of representatives remain.[6]

The principal factors responsible for the contraction of the Russian arms industry can be readily identified. Most significant has been the serious economic decline associated with post-communist transformation, which has given rise to severe pressure on government spending. There has also been considerable institutional flux, not least because of the process of rapid, wholesale privatization in the early 1990s. Military requirements have changed as the Russian armed forces have been reduced in scale and security priorities have been reassessed. At various times the Russian Government has attempted to implement policies designed to restructure the arms industry to meet the country's new requirements, but these initiatives have had little success. Inadequate funding has played a significant role, as has the limited administrative capability of the government—exacerbated by frequent changes in the management structures responsible for the arms industry, which have led to a progressive weakening of central control.

Since 1991 there have been frequent reforms of the government's administrative structures for managing the arms industry. The principal changes are shown in table 9C.2. Almost every restructuring has resulted in a reduction in the number of government officials involved with the military sector and the incessant reorganizations have greatly complicated the pursuit of a coherent state policy. One important government ministry has undergone relatively modest change and has probably been the single most important actor determining the fate of the Russian arms industry: the Ministry of Finance. With the backing of successive presidents and prime ministers, this ministry has for over a decade maintained very strict limits on expenditure on defence and arms procurement.

II. The Russian arms industry and its administration today

With the reorganization of the Russian Government following the appointment of Mikhail Fradkov as prime minister in March 2004, the administrative arrangements for the arms industry underwent yet another change. The five agencies that had overseen the industry since 1999 were abolished and most of the state-owned enterprises were transferred to a new federal agency for industry, Rosprom. This new agency, under the leadership of Boris Alyoshin, has responsibility for the oversight of almost

---

[4] TS-VPK, *VPK Rossii: strukturnye pokazateli 2003* [Military–industrial complex (MIC) of Russia: structural indicators 2003] (TS-VPK: Moscow, 2005), URL <http://ia.vpk.ru/localfonds/vpk_struct_demo/2003/>, section 8.1.

[5] See chapter 10 in this volume.

[6] See table 10C.1. Russia accounted for 70% of the Soviet Union's arms industry output and 90% of its military R&D. *Inzhernaya Gazeta*, no. 51 (Apr. 1992).

all Russian industry, the military sector being only a part of its very large portfolio. Within the agency, which has a staff of 495, are departments for the main branches of the arms industry, based on the five former agencies and often with some of the same personnel. Rosprom is subordinated to Minpromenergo, under Viktor Khristenko, whose Defence–Industrial Complex Department is headed by the former head of the Aerospace Agency, Yury Koptev. Minpromenergo, which has a staff of 920, is responsible for the development of policy for the arms industry; implementation is in the hands of Rosprom.[7] In addition, there is a separate federal space agency, Roskosmos, with a staff of 210. Headed by Anatoly Perminov, who has a military background, Roskosmos is responsible for enterprises and R&D organizations of the space and missile industry.[8] Minatom, the former ministry of atomic energy, has been converted into a lower-status federal agency, Rosatom, under Aleksandr Rumyantsev, with a total staff of 500. Rosatom continues to be responsible for the development and production of nuclear warheads and devices.[9] It has two directorates concerned with the nuclear weapon industry, overseen by Ivan Kamenskikh, deputy director of the agency.[10] Both Roskosmos and Rosatom answer directly to the prime minister.

These changes mean that the number of government officials with responsibility for the arms industry is now at a new low. Whereas in Soviet times the nine arms industry ministries probably employed over 10 000 personnel, today the equivalent number appears to be little more than 500. Since the adoption of these new administrative arrangements, there have been frequent complaints that the state has effectively lost control of the arms industry; it is alleged that the agencies are understaffed and that there is a lack of clarity as to the respective responsibilities of Minpromenergo and Rosprom.[11]

In addition, the ministry of economic development and trade, Minekonomrazvitiya, under German Gref, retains responsibility for a number of important military economic activities, including the system of mobilization planning in the event of war and the elaboration and implementation of the annual State Defence Order (Gosudarstvennyi Oboronnyi Zakaz, abbreviated as Gosoboronzakaz or GOZ) for arms development and procurement. Within Minekonomrazvitiya is the Department for the Economics of Programmes of Defence and Security, with a staff of up to 194 headed by a military officer, Vladimir Putilin, who answers directly to Gref.[12] Under the MOD are the Federal Agency for Military Technical Cooperation, headed by Mikhail Dimitriev; the federal service responsible for the GOZ, Rosoboronzakaz, which is

---

[7] Minpromenergo, News item, 10 Oct. 2005, URL <http://www.minprom.gov.ru/>.

[8] Roskosmos, News item, 10 Oct. 2005, URL <http://www.roscosmos.ru/>.

[9] This downgrading is deeply resented by many in the nuclear industry. Sergei Brezkun, a leading member of the Sarov Research Institute of Experimental Physics, Russia's leading nuclear weapon centre, is not alone in calling for a rapid restoration of ministerial status. He also calls for resumption of nuclear testing. Brezkun, S., 'Kraeugol'nyi kamen' nezavisimosti Rossii" [The cornerstone of Russia's independence], *VPK*, 24–30 Aug. 2005, URL <http://www.vpk-news.ru/article.asp?pr_sign=archive.2005.98.articles.weapon_02>. In Nov. 2005 Rumyantsev was replaced by Sergei Kirienko, who served as prime minister for a few months in 1998.

[10] Rosatom, News item, 10 Oct. 2005, URL <http://www.minatom.ru/>.

[11] When challenged that the 2004 administrative reform had paralysed the management of the arms industry, Boris Alyoshin denied it but did acknowledge that the reform had created problems. In his view, the difficulties arose mainly from the limited number of personnel now involved. Nikol'skii, A., 'Deistvuyushchie litsa. Interv'yu: Boris Aleshin, rukovoditel' Federal'nogo agenstva po promyshlennosto' [Dramatis personae. Interview: Boris Alyoshin, leader, Federal Agency for Industry], *Vedomosti*, 19 July 2005.

[12] Minekonomrazvitiya, News item, 10 Oct. 2005, URL <http://www.economy.gov.ru/>.

headed by Andrei Belyaninov, the former head of the arms exports company Rosvooruzhenie; and the Federal Agency for Technical and Export Controls. Rosoboronzakaz is concerned with orders for conventional arms and other military hardware, oversees competitive tenders and plays a growing role in quality management and control.

Rosprom and Roskosmos are now responsible for the oversight of all the enterprises and R&D organizations of the arms industry that was previously undertaken by five agencies; the number of facilities that the two agencies are responsible for appears to be much the same, although there is a lack of detailed data.[13] However, not all the facilities are involved in military work and over time there has been a gradual conversion to civilian production. Rosprom and Roskosmos now devote more attention to a set of enterprises and organizations that are directly involved in arms-related work. These are listed in a summary register of facilities involved directly in arms development, manufacture, testing and repair, the latest edition of which was approved in September 2004. Details are shown in table 9C.3.

In November 2005 the administrative arrangements for the arms industry underwent an unexpected change: Sergei Ivanov, while retaining his post as minister of defence, was appointed deputy prime minister with responsibility for oversight of the arms industry and its relations with the armed forces. There was speculation that Ivanov would replace Fradkov as chair of the Commission of the Government for Military–Industrial Questions, a body which meets rather infrequently to consider policy issues facing the arms industry, but this did not happen.[14] However, in March 2006 there was a significant new development: Putin approved the formation of a Military–Industrial Commission (Voenno–Promyshlennaya Komissiya, VPK) of the Russian Government. Ivanov was appointed chair, although he retains his other posts and day-to-day leadership will be exercised by the first deputy chair of the VPK, Vladislav Putilin, who until then, as noted above, had headed the military economic activities of Minekonomrazvitiya. The VPK is to be a permanent body exercising oversight of the overall development of the arms industry, the mobilization system and the production of arms for export orders.[15] At the time of writing the terms of reference and staff numbers of the VPK have yet to be agreed by the government, but it appears that it will have supra-ministerial authority similar to that exercised by its Soviet-era counterpart of the same name.

In 2001 the Russian Government adopted the Programme for the Reform and Development of the Defence–Industrial Complex in 2002–2006.[16] This sets out ambitious plans to reorganize the arms industry on the basis of so-called 'integrated structures' in the form of vertically integrated holding companies. According to the original plan, over 70 such structures were to be created, but implementation has been extremely slow. The number of structures actually created is given variously as three

[13] In 2003 there were 1487 enterprises and organizations under the 5 agencies and a further 24, considered to be part of the arms industry, under the Ministry of Industry, Science and Technology. TS-VPK (note 4), section 1.1.

[14] Petrov, N., 'VPK obrel superlobbista' [The VPK has a super-lobbyist'], Strana.ru, 16 Nov. 2005, URL <http://www.strana.ru/stories/02/11/14/3206/265199.html>.

[15] Russian Federation, Presidential Decree no. 231, 20 Mar. 2006, URL <http://document.kremlin.ru/doc.asp?ID=032784>

[16] Federal Special Purpose Programmes, 'Programma "Reformirovanie i razvitie oboronno-promyshlennogo kompleksa (2002–2006 gody)"' [Programme 'reform and development of the defence industrial complex (2002–2006)'], 2001, URL <http://www.programs-gov.ru/cgi-bin/index.cgi?prg=125>

Table 9C.3. Numbers of registered enterprises and organizations of the Russian military–industrial complex, 2005

Sector	All	Form of property		Type of activity		
		State	JSC[a]	Production	R&D	Other[b]
Defence industry[c]:	933	404	529	492	412	29
Aviation	191	38	153	104	77	10
Space and missile	97	72	25	34	58	5
Armaments	101	44	57	48	49	4
Munitions	104	83	21	63	34	7
Shipbuilding	112	49	63	72	39	1
Radio[d]	135	41	94	63	71	1
Communications	92	45	47	44	47	1
Electronics	96	27	69	62	34	0
'Special purpose'[e]	5	5	0	2	3	0
Nuclear industry[f]	63	53	10	27	27	9
Ministry of Defence[g]	190	190	0	141	30	19
Civilian industry[c h]	55	24	31	33	16	6
Total	**1 241**	**671**	**570**	**693**	**485**	**63**

JSC = Joint stock company; R&D = Research and development.

[a] Some JSCs have majority state share holdings.

[b] 'Other' activities are test facilities, training centres, information agencies and centres for design of industrial facilities.

[c] The 'defence industry' and 'civilian industry' sectors cover enterprises and organizations subordinated to or overseen by Rosprom, the federal agency for industry, and Roskosmos, the federal space agency.

[d] The 'radio' sector includes air defence and radar systems.

[e] Some cross-branch enterprises and institutes are designated as 'special purpose'.

[f] The 'nuclear industry' sector covers enterprises and organizations subordinated to or overseen by Rosatom, the federal agency for atomic energy.

[g] This sector appears to include most, if not all, of the industrial and research organizations under the Ministry of Defence, including some that are not concerned with weapons but with, e.g., cartography, food supply and construction.

[h] The 'civilian industry' sector includes mainly military vehicles, electrical equipment, instruments, chemicals and materials.

Source: TS-VPK, 'Reestr predpriyatii VPK Rossii (demo-versiya)' [Register of enterprises of the Russian MIC (demonstration version)], 29 June 2005, form 1.S, URL <http://ia.vpk.ru/localfonds/reestr_demo/enterprises/forms/form_1_s.htm>. Register as approved by Minprom-energo in Sep. 2004. As of Oct. 2005 the register included 1279 organizations.

or five.[17] The obstacles have been numerous, including clashes between privately owned and state-owned companies, disputes with regional authorities, the weakness

[17] According to Igor Garivadsky of Minpromenegro, of 75 integrated structures to be created during 2002–2004 only 3 'fully formed' structures were created. Babakin, A., 'Oboronno–promyshlennyi kompleks: krizis ili vyzdorovleniee' [Defence–industrial complex: crisis or recovery], *Nezavisimoe Voennoe Obozrenie*, 22 July 2005, URL <http://nvo.ng.ru/armament/2005-07-22/>. According to another report, of the 40 to be created in 2002–2004, only 5 existed in 2005. Samarova, E., 'Marsh-brosok: strategiya razvitiya oboronno–promyshlennogo kompleksa nuzhno bystrymi tempami' [Forced march: a strategy of

of the former agencies overseeing the arms industry and a lack of clarity on the type of structures required. Alyoshin, the head of Rosprom and a leading advocate of the creation of corporate structures, claims that when implementation of the programme started in 2002 vertically integrated structures were favoured, but even then he and others thought that horizontally integrated holding companies were preferable.[18] Now Alyoshin is the lead promoter of the most ambitious corporate structure to date, the Unified Aircraft Corporation, intended to bring together all the country's main companies for building fixed-wing aircraft, both military and civilian, together with the main design bureaux. It is envisaged that the state will initially own 75 per cent of the shares of the holding company, but this stake may later be reduced to 51 per cent.[19] This project is proving difficult to realize since it is coming up against powerful vested interests. It may also create problems for some of the privately owned companies set to be included. Not least of these is Irkut, the most successful of all Russian aircraft builders, in which the European Aeronautic Defence and Space Company (EADS) has active involvement and in late 2005 acquired a 10 per cent ownership stake.[20] A separate holding company is being created for helicopter production in a project led by Oboronprom, the joint-stock investment company of the state-owned arms export firm Rosoboroneksport. According to Sergei Chemezov, general director of Rosoboroneksport, the state export company now intends to take an ownership stake in all the newly created integrated companies of the arms industry.[21] In his view this participation is needed in order to secure the successful completion of export orders in terms of time and quality.[22]

In creating new holding companies the intention is to retain a state ownership stake of at least 51 per cent.[23] This reflects what appears to be a growing determination that the state must retain control of companies of the arms industry that are considered vital to the country's security. In 2004, of the 1462 enterprises comprising the arms industry, 594 were entirely state owned, 74 had state holdings of 50–99 per cent, 177 had state holdings of 25–49 per cent, and the remaining 617 had state holdings of less than 25 per cent.[24] According to analysis undertaken by the Centre for Analysis of Strategies and Technologies, Moscow, the 20 largest arms companies in terms of sales in 2004 had total revenues of $8529 million, of which no less than 71 per cent ($6070 million) was earned by wholly state-owned firms. In 2002 the equivalent share was 59 per cent.[25]

---

development of the defence–industrial complex needs a rapid pace], Minpromenergo, 25 Oct. 2005, URL <http://www.minprom.gov.ru/activity/defence/pub/0/>.

[18] Nikol'skii (note 11).

[19] TS-VPK, 18 Oct. 2005, URL <http://ia.vpk.ru/>.

[20] EADS paid over $65 million for the 10% stake. 'Evropeiskaya aerokosmicheskaya korporatsiya poluchila 10% Irkuta i davit Aeroflot' [European aerospace corporation has obtained 10% of Irkut and will put pressure on Aeroflot], Open Economy, 19 Dec. 2005, URL <http://www.opec.ru/news_doc.asp?d_no=59099>.

[21] TS-VPK, 19 Aug. 2005, URL <http://ia.vpk.ru/>.

[22] Gertsev, O., 'Pyatiletie "Rosoboroneksporta": dostizheniya i perspektivy' [Five years of 'Rosoboroneksport': achievements and prospects], VPK, 26 Oct.–1 Nov. 2005, URL <http://www.vpk-news.ru/article.asp?pr_sign=archive.2005.107.articles.company_01>.

[23] Reis, A., Minpromenergo deputy minister, cited by TS-VPK, 14 Nov. 2005, URL <http://ia.vpk.ru/>.

[24] These 1462 enterprises are those formerly under the 5 agencies and Minpromnauki, the ministry of industry, science and technology. Centre for Analysis of Strategies and Technologies, 'Ownership structure in Russian defense industry', Moscow Defense Brief, no. 2, 2005, URL <http://mdb.cast.ru/mdb/2-2005/facts/owner/>.

[25] Centre for Analysis of Strategies and Technologies (note 24).

Table 9C.4. Output, employment and investment in the Russian arms industry, 1991–2004

Figures are given as an index, set as 100 in 1991 for output and employment and as 100 in 1992 for investment, all at constant prices.

	1991	1992	1993	1994	1995	1996	1997	1998	1999	2000	2001	2002	2003	2004	2005
Output:	100	78.7	63.6	39.1	31.4	23.1	20.1	21.7	28.8	36.1	37.8	43.8	50.9	52.5	54.1
Military	100	62.6	49.3	30.3	25.1	18.8	13.9	16.6	22.7	29.4	29.1	35.8	42.4	40.5	43.1
Civilian	100	96.4	82.9	51.0	39.9	28.9	28.5	28.3	36.4	43.8	49.0	51.7	58.6	65.7	64.2
Employment	100	90.3	77.1	64.9	54.5	46.9	41.0	36.0	33.4	34.1	33.5	31.8	30.7	29.4	..
Investment	–	100	53.1	28.3	16.2	11.3	7.5	7.0	8.9	11.7	15.3	15.5	..	..	..

Sources: **Total, military and civilian output, 1991–2000**: TS-VPK data, as presented in Institute of Economics of the Transition Period, *Rossiiskaya ekonomika v 2001 godu: tendentsii i perspektivy* [Russian economy in 2001: tendencies and perspectives] (Institute of Economics of the Transition Period: Moscow, Mar. 2002), section 2.7; **2005**: Calculated from Minekonomrazviya data in *Ob itogakh sots'ialno-ekonomicheskogo razvitiya RF za 2005 god i zadachakh ekonomicheskoi politiki Pravitel'stvo RF na 2006 god* [On the results of socio-economic development of RF in 2005 and tasks of economic policy of the government of RF for 2006] (Minekonomrazvitiya: Moscow, 22 Feb. 2006), URL <http://www.economy.gov.ru/wps/portal/law/docmert>, p. 149; **Total and civilian output, 2001–2004**: TsEK, *Rossiya: ekonomicheskaya kon"yunktura* [Russia: economic conjuncture], various issues (TsEK: Moscow, 2000–2005); **Military output, 2001–2004**: calculated from total and civilian output data using a civilian : military ratio of 40 : 60 for each year (based on TsEK and Minekonomrazvitiya data suggesting civilian output fluctuated between 37 and 42 per cent of total output); **Employment, 1992–2002**: TS-VPK, *VPK Rossii: strukturnye pokazateli 2002* [MIC of Russia: structural indicators 2002] (TS-VPK: Moscow, 2005), URL <http://ia.vpk.ru/local fonds/vpk_struct_demo/2002/>, section 5.1; **Employment, 2002–2004**: TsEK data in *Rossiya*, no. 1, 2005, p. 63; **Investment, 1992–2002**: TS-VPK, *VPK Rossii: strukturnye pokazateli 2002* [MIC of Russia: structural indicators 2002] (TS-VPK: Moscow, 2005), URL <http://ia. vpk.ru/localfonds/vpk_struct_demo/2002/>, section 8.1.

III. The output of the arms industry

Since the early 1990s there have been two principal sources of data on the output of the Russian arms industry: the Teleinformatsionnoi Seti Voenno–Promyshlennogo Kompleksa (TS-VPK, the teleinformation network of the military–industrial complex), the industry's information agency; and the Tsentr Ekonomicheskoi Kon'yuntury Pri Pravitel'stve Rossiiskoi Federatsii (TsEK, the economic conjuncture centre of the government of the Russian Federation), the government's economic conjucture centre. The two series of data have been reasonably consistent, but neither organization has provided information on the methodologies employed for what are presented as constant price data. Nothing is known about the price deflators employed. However, given that Rosstat, the federal state statistics service, publishes data on producer prices for the individual branches of civilian industry, it is likely that similar price series are produced for each branch of the arms industry. In recent years access to the TS-VPK data has been limited; they are now available only to subscribers, a change that appears to be designed—at least in part—to restrict access by foreigners. In the case of TsEK data, since 2001 information has been provided only on total and civil production, making it necessary to estimate the trend of military output using scattered and not always consistent data on military and civil shares. What is thought to be a reasonably consistent and accurate series derived from these data is presented in table 9C.4.

Since the 1998 financial crisis in Russia the economy has recovered and from 2000 has grown at an average annual rate of approximately 7 per cent.[26] The arms industry's output has also recovered, although with considerable variation between sectors. The total output of the arms industry (both military and civilian) increased by more than 80 per cent in 1999–2004. The most rapid growth was shown by the shipbuilding industry, boosted by orders from China and India, which increased by 150 per cent, and the radio industry, which increased by 140 per cent. The least rapid growth in 1999–2004 was in the munitions industry, which grew by 20 per cent and is now in serious crisis, while the aviation industry grew by 70 per cent and the space and missile industry by 60 per cent.[27] However, as noted above, employment continues to decline, and investment—which fell to a more dramatic extent than either output or employment—had by 2002 recovered only modestly, severely limiting possibilities for the renewal of the industry's seriously degraded production base.

IV. Arms procurement in Russia

The leadership of the Russian military has become accustomed to seeing the latest products of the arms industry sold abroad in substantial quantities while few, if any, of the same weapons are delivered to the domestic forces. Instead, the Russian military has to rely on diminishing stocks of Soviet-era equipment. As noted above, funding for arms procurement has been increasing rapidly since Putin became President, but the volume of new weapons actually reaching the forces has increased only modestly. This state of affairs has become an issue of lively debate.

Domestic arms procurement, military-related R&D, and the repair and modernization of arms and other military equipment take place within the framework of the annual State Defence Order, the GOZ. This is approved by the government and president soon after the adoption of the federal budget for each year. The GOZ is drawn up on the basis of the State Programme of Armaments (Gosudarstvennyi Program Vooruzheniya, GPV), a document covering a 10-year period but drawn up in detail only for the first five years. The GPV is elaborated by the MOD, in consultation with other armed forces outside the MOD, and is based on an economic forecast supplied by Minekonomrazvitiya. The GPV sets annual targets for the scale of procurement and R&D and outlines policy and plans for armaments for each branch of the armed forces. The first such programme was adopted in the Soviet Union in 1984 and covered the period 1986–95. A successor programme for 1991–2000 was drafted but never adopted. In Russia, the first programme was for the period 1996–2005 (GPV-2005) and was approved by President Boris Yeltin in November 1996.[28] The GPV-2005 was fatally flawed from the outset: it was based on an extraordinarily overoptimistic macroeconomic forecast and provided for spending on defence of over 5 per cent of GDP. The annual GOZ diverged from the programme almost immedi-

---

[26] Rosstat (note 1).

[27] TsEK, *Rossiya: ekonomicheskaya kon"yunktura* [Russia: economic conjuncture], various issues (TsEK: Moscow, 2000–2005).

[28] Moskovskii, A., 'Uvernnost' v zavtrashnem dne' [Confidence in tomorrow], *VPK*, 10–16 Mar. 2004, URL <http://www.vpk-news.ru/article.asp?pr_sign=archive.2004.26.articles.weapon_01>.

Table 9C.5. Planned expenditure on the State Defence Order of the Russian Ministry of Defence, 1992–98 and 2003–2006[a]

Figures in roubles are given in current prices. Figures in US$ are in constant 2003 prices.

Year	Total expenditure		Procurement[b]		Research and development	
	m. roubles	US$ m.	m. roubles	share (%)	m. roubles	share (%)
1992[c]	191	1 571	115	60.2	76	39.8
1993[c]	795	1 841	570	71.7	225	28.3
1994	10 875	10 637	8 442	77.6	2 433	22.4
1995	15 211	11 250	10 275	67.5	4 936	32.5
1996	19 688	10 489	13 213	67.1	6 475	32.9
1997	35 538	7 431	20 963	59.0	11 575	41.0
1998	27 848	3 660	17 048	61.2	10 800	38.8
2003	109 817	3 578	64 331	58.6	45 486	41.4
2004	137 677	4 010	85 777	62.3	51 900	37.7
2005	187 783	5 013	127 646	66.4	63 137	33.6
2006	236 700	..	164 000	69.3	72 700	30.7

[a] Equivalent data for 1999–2002 are not available.

[b] Procurement includes repairs and modernization. In 2005 these amounted to 42 115 million roubles, 22.4% of total expenditure.

[c] There was extremely high inflation in 1992 and 1993 and the budgets were approved without account of it.

Sources: **1992–93**: *Vedomosti Syezda Narodnykh Deputatov Rossiiskoi Federatsii i Verkhovnogo Soveta Rossiiskoi Federatsii* [Proceedings of the Congress of People's Deputies and the Supreme Soviet of the Russian Federation], no. 22, 1993, article 794; and no. 34, 1992, article 197942; **1994–98, 2003**: *Sobranie zakonodatelstva Rossiiskoi Federatsii* [Collection of legislative acts of the Russian Federation], no. 52, 2002, article 5132, appendix 32; no. 13, 1998, article 1464; no. 9, 1997, article 1012; no. 1, 1996, article 21; no. 14, 1995, article 1213; and no. 10, 1994, article 1108; **2004–2005**: Russian Ministry of Finance, Federal'nyi Byudzhet [Federal budget], URL <http://www.minfin.ru/budjet/budjet.htm>; **2006**: *Izvestia*, 17 Jan. 2006, p. 5.

ately and was soon abandoned. The MOD has estimated that during 1996–2000 actual spending on procurement and R&D was just 23 per cent of that planned in the GPV-2005.[29]

The next armaments programme, GPV-2010, was approved by President Putin in January 2002 and was apparently based on much more realistic assumptions.[30] The level of funding fell far below the MOD's expectations. Given this, the GPV-2010 focused on R&D for the development of new weapons and the repair and modernization of the existing stock of arms in the expectation that the volume production and

[29] Korotchenko, I., 'Minfin gotovit sekvestr oboronnogo byudzheta' [Minfin is planning sequestration of the defence budget], *Nezavisimoe Voennoe Obozrenie*, 11 July 2003, URL <http://nvo.ng.ru/armament/2003-07-11/>; Burenok, V. M., Babkin, G. V. and Kosenko, A. A., 'Oboronno-promyshlennyi kompleks: sostoyanie i perspektivy razvitiya' [Defence industrial complex: state and prospects for development], *Voennaya Mysl'*, no. 6, 2005, pp. 37–38; and Bulavinov, I. and Safronov, I., 'Novosti: Prezident zaprogrammiroval vooruzheniya na 2.1 trln rublei' [News: President has programmed armaments to 2.1 trillion roubles], *Kommersant-Daily*, 24 Jan. 2002, p. 2.

[30] Bulavinov and Safronov (note 29).

procurement of new systems will take place after 2006.[31] At first the annual GOZ was much in line with the targets of the GPV-2010, but the MOD now claims that substantial underfunding is beginning to appear.[32] Work is under way on drafting the GPV-2015, but progress has been delayed by the lack of an agreed long-term economic forecast. The new programme is expected to be approved in the first half of 2006.[33]

While the funding of the annual GOZ may not correspond to the spending outlined in the longer-term GPV, this is not the only problem. In establishing a level of funding for procurement and R&D—and budget spending on defence as a whole—the Ministry of Finance is obliged to base its calculations on a forecast rate of inflation set by Minekonomrazvitiya. There is no specific price deflators for total spending on defence or the purchase of weapons; instead, the consumer price index is used. In reality, year after year, the rate of price increases for activities covered by the annual GOZ is far in excess of the forecast level. This has clearly been a major factor in the failure to secure anything beyond a modest increase in the number of weapons procured; but there are other factors. As Igor Garivadsky, the former deputy head of Rosprom and at the time responsible for oversight of the arms industry, has acknowledged, cost increases arise also because of 'the natural striving of enterprises to include in the price of finished goods outlays on the maintenance of non-working capacities'.[34] Almost certainly, this applies not only to the enterprises and R&D establishments of the arms industry, with their substantial underused capacity, but also to the repair works of the MOD, to which a sizeable proportion of the annual GOZ is allocated. There is also evidence that a large number of worthless research projects are funded in order to maintain the staff of R&D institutes.[35] Thus, money intended for arms procurement and R&D is being used in part to maintain facilities that are of a scale beyond the country's ability to sustain them.

In the early 1990s, as funding contracted sharply, the impact of the cuts was experienced most acutely in R&D. In line with the priorities of the GPV-2010, the share of resources devoted to R&D increased from 2001, but now, as shown in table 9C.5, the trend is once again in a direction favouring procurement, repairs and modernization.[36] This trend may threaten some of the current high-priority development programmes. There is already evidence that the fifth-generation combat aircraft project, led by the Sukhoi holding company, is being delayed by funding problems that are exacerbated

---

[31] Tul'ev, M, 'Perspektivy gosoboronzakaza' [Perspectives of the state defence order], *VPK*, 18–24 Feb. 2004, URL <http://www.vpk-news.ru/article.asp?pr_sign=archive.2004.23.articles.defence_01>.

[32] Inter-regional Foundation for Information Technologies (MFIT), 'Voenno–promyshlennyi kompleks: sostoyanie i perspektivy' [Military–industrial complex: state and perspectives], Obzor po materialam SMI no. 23 (18–24 June 2005), URL <http://www.mfit.ru/defensive/obzor/ob24-06-05-1.html#o3>. According to Aleksei Moskovsky, the MOD's head of armament, underfunding over the past 5 years amounts to 160–70 billion roubles ($5.5–5.9 billion).

[33] Inter-regional Foundation for Information Technologies (note 32); and TS-VPK, 12 Aug. 2005, URL <http://ia.vpk.ru/>.

[34] Babakin (note 17) (author's translation).

[35] Poroskop, N., 'Nikakoe real'noe voennoe stroitel'stvo v Rossiy ne vedetsysa' [No real military construction is being undertaken in Russia], *Vremya Novostei*, 9 Aug. 2005.

[36] Data on the structure of the annual GOZ for 1999–2002 are incomplete, but according to MOD sources the R&D share was just over 25% in 2000, rising to 41% in 2001. Scientific Research Institute of the Economics of Planning and Management (NIIÉPU), 28 Dec. 1999, URL <http://www.avias.com/news/>; and *Krasnaya Zvezda*, 19 Feb. 2002, URL <http://www.redstar.ru/2002/02/19_02/>, p. 1.

by the fact that few, if any, complete Sukhoi combat aircraft were exported in 2005.[37] Another priority is the new submarine-launched ballistic missile, the R-30 Bulava,[38] being developed by the Moscow Institute for Thermal Technology (MITT). The MITT is also responsible for the land-based Topol-M intercontinental ballistic missile, now entering service at a stable rate of six or seven a year and a major claimant on the procurement budget.[39] It is planned that the latter missile will be adopted for the Russian Navy by the end of 2007, but construction of the first submarines in which it is to be installed has yet to be completed.[40] Other priority development programmes include the S-400 Triumf air defence missile system developed by Almaz-Antei, to be available for procurement with its full range of missiles by 2008,[41] and the X-555 long-range non-nuclear cruise missile developed by the Takticheskoe Raketnoe Vooruzhenie (TRV, tactical missile armament) Corporation for the Tu-160 bomber aircraft and tested successfully in 2005.[42]

V. Problems of quality and foreign dependence

The MOD's Armaments Directorate and Rosoboronzakaz, the recently created federal service for the GOZ, have signalled mounting concern that the Russian arms industry is increasingly unable to supply high-quality weapons and that the new systems being developed incorporate a growing share of imported components. The quality-management systems of most enterprises are clearly inadequate: only 1 per cent of enterprises on the official register have the ISO 9001 international certificate of quality, which is increasingly essential if export orders are to be secured.[43] There may be reluctance on security grounds to undergo the independent audit required for ISO 9001 certification. Many enterprises appear to prefer quality-management certification under voluntary domestic schemes, in particular the Military Register system operated by the MOD since 2000, the Oboronsertifika system set up the former State Committee of the Defence Industry in 1994 and the Russian Register certification

---

[37] Pronina, L., 'No Sukhoi fighters to be delivered this year', *Moscow Times*, 18 Oct. 2005, URL <http://moscowtimes.ru/stories/2005/08/18/051.html>. The SIPRI Arms Transfers Project estimates that 5 Su-27 combat aircraft were delivered to Eritrea in 2005.

[38] The US designation for the R-30 is SS-N-30 or SS-NX-30, with X standing for 'experimental' since the missile is not yet in production. The Bulava is also known under the Russian industrial designation 3M14.

[39] The US designation for the Topol-M is SS-27. The R-30 is a submarine-launched version of the Topol-M. In 2006, 7 of the new mobile version of the Topol-M are to be procured. It has been reported that the cost of the Topol-M missile has increased by 250% since 2000. TS-VPK, 2 Sep. 2005, URL <http://ia.vpk.ru/cgi-bin/ia/chronicle/>. The Moscow Institute for Thermal Technology is now the sole developer of intercontinental ballistic missile in Russia; the Soviet Union had 4 such organizations.

[40] Kedrov, I., 'Pervoe popadanie "Bulavy"' [First strike of 'Bulava'], *VPK*, 5–11 Oct. 2005, URL <http://www.vpk-news.ru/article.asp?pr_sign=archive.2005.104.articles.army_01>

[41] The US designation for the S-400 Triumf is SA-21 or SA-X-21. It sometimes referred to as the SA-20 in Western sources.

[42] Inter-regional Foundation for Information Technologies (MFIT), 'Razrabotka, modernizatsiya i ispytaniya vooruzhenii i voennoi tekhniki' [Development, modernization and testing of armaments and military hardware], Obzor po materialam SMI no. 28 (23–29 July 2005), URL <http://www.mfit.ru/defensive/obzor/ob29-07-05-3.html#o4>; and *Izvestiya*, 4 Oct. 2005, p. 5.

[43] Samarova (note 17). In general, Russian firms and organizations have been relatively slow in adopting ISO 9001 certification: as of Dec. 2004 there were 3816 certifications, compared with 50 884 in the United Kingdom and 132 926 in China. International Organization for Standardization (ISO), *The ISO Survey of Certifications 2004* (ISO: Geneva, 2005), pp. 9–10; a summary is available at URL <http://www.iso.org/iso/en/commcentre/pressreleases/2005/Ref967.html>.

association.[44] As output fell in the 1990s, many enterprises appear to have run down their quality-management systems. Issues of quality were addressed at a major conference of the arms industry and the MOD at Rostov-on-Don in February 2005. According to Aleksandr Rakhmanov, deputy chief of the Russian armed forces' Armaments Directorate, 21 per cent of the output of arms industry enterprises is rejected: 9 per cent by the enterprises' own quality-control systems and a further 12 per cent by the MOD's military representatives.[45] The MOD's discontent has been voiced by Ivanov, the minister of defence. In his words, some enterprises of the arms industry boast that their products correspond to the world level, but 'not infrequently this is a myth'. He added that the MOD's relations with the military–industrial complex were 'far from peaceful'.[46] As deputy prime minister, Ivanov will now be expected to improve this relationship.

There is evidence that Russia is having to depend to an increasing extent on foreign-sourced components in the development and production of new armaments. This is strongly disapproved of by the military establishment, which has always insisted on entirely domestic supply or—since the disintegration of the Soviet Union—supply from countries considered totally dependable, in particular Belarus. In 2003 Rakhmanov noted that 22 000 different components were then being imported from other member countries of the Commonwealth of Independent States.[47] While he welcomed the positive relations, he also observed that it was necessary to secure maximum independence for the Russian arms industry in the manufacture of the basic types of armaments.[48] Growing dependence applies above all to electronic components. Recognizing this reality, the MOD has established its own centre for certifying foreign-produced components and materials for use in domestically built weapons; it is based at the MOD's 22nd Central Scientific Research and Testing Institute at Mytishchi, near Moscow.[49] The events in Ukraine in 2004–2005 appear to have prompted some reconsideration of the wisdom of depending on what is perceived to be an unreliable neighbour for the supply of key inputs. In July 2005, for example, it was decided that gas turbines for ships, previously a Ukrainian monopoly, would be built in Russia by a consortium headed by the Saturn works in Rybinsk, better known as a leading supplier of aircraft engines.[50] It is notable that, in its latest long-term forecast of the development of the Russian economy to 2020, the respected Centre for Macroeconomic Analysis and Short-term Forecasting acknowledges a serious risk that after 2010 the high-technology sector of the economy, above all the arms industry, will

[44] See the websites of the Military Register at URL <http://www.voenreg.ru/> (in Russian); Oboronsetifika at URL <http://www.center-qualitet.ru/> (in Russian); and the Russian Register at URL <http://www.rusregister.ru/eng/>.

[45] Lenta.ru, 15 Feb. 2005, URL <http://www.lenta.ru/>.

[46] Knyaz'kov, S., '"Bulava" derzhavy'' ['Bulava' of the state], Krasnaya Zvezda, 27 Aug. 2005, URL <http://www.redstar.ru/2005/08/27_08/1_03.html> (author's translation).

[47] The member states of the Commonwealth of Independent States are listed in the glossary in this volume.

[48] 'Bolee 20 tys. komplektuyushchikh dlya sozdaniya Rossiiskogo oruzhiya zavozitsya iz strany SNG—ekspert' [More than 20 thousand components for creation of Russian armaments are imported from CIS countries—an expert], Defence Express, 4 Apr. 2003, URL <http://www.defense-ua.com/rus/news/?id=5976>.

[49] Borisov, A. A., '22-mu Tsentral'nomu nauchno-issledovatel'skomu ispytatel'nomu institutu MO RF: 50 let'' [The 22nd Central Scientific Research and Testing Institute of the MOD of the Russian Federation: 50 years], Voennaya Mysl', no. 6, 2005, p. 79.

[50] '"Saturn" v nebesakh i na more' ['Saturn' in the sky and on the sea], Krasnaya Zvezda, 9 July 2005, URL <http://www.redstar.ru/2005/07/09_07/4_02.html>.

have exhausted its inherited stock of technological possibilities and Russia will find itself excluded from traditional arms markets and unable to enter new ones. It adds that 'the production of Russian armaments will become critically dependent on the import of major components'.[51]

Over the past decade the attitudes of both Russian authorities and the public towards foreign participation in the Russian arms industry appear to have hardened. In a nationwide poll undertaken in July 2005, 80 per cent expressed the view that there should be no foreign ownership stake in any company of the arms industry and only 2 per cent considered it acceptable to have no limits on ownership.[52]

In May 2005 President Putin called for new legislation on limiting access of foreign investors to strategic sectors of the economy, including the arms industry. The law was to have been elaborated by Minpromenergo before 1 November 2005, but was delayed by disagreements with Minekonomrazvitiya, which argues for a more liberal approach.[53] However, the outcome is likely to be strict limits on foreign firms' ownership of companies in the Russian arms industry.

VI. Transparency in relation to the military economy

It was only in the final years of the Soviet Union, under President Mikhail Gorbachev, that the almost impenetrable veil of secrecy over the military economy began to be cautiously lifted. Since 1991 there has been much greater transparency in relation to the arms industry, arms exports and military expenditure, but progress has been uneven, with occasional reverses. Today the situation is much improved but there are still limits and Russia still has some way to go to meet the standards of transparency typical of developed democratic countries. In particular, much military expenditure, especially that relating to procurement and R&D, is still classified and details are only available to those members of the Federal Assembly, Russia's parliament, who have security clearance. Official information on arms exports is still strictly controlled, and data on the arms industry are still relatively inaccessible to outside observers. New commercial secrecy considerations to some extent reinforce the traditional inclination to restrict the availability of information.[54] Russia continues to report annually to the United Nations on conventional arms exports and military expenditure, but with a minimum of detail in the case of arms exports and no explanation of the meaning and scope of the data provided on expenditure, which are difficult to reconcile with data published in other sources.[55]

---

[51] Belousov, A. R., *Dolgosrochnye trendy Rossiiskoi ekonomiki: stsenary ekonomicheskgo razvitaya Rossy do 2020 goda* [Long-term trends of the Russian economy: scenarios of economic development of Russia to 2020] (Centre for Macroeconomic Analysis and Short-term Forecasting: Moscow, Oct. 2005), p. 104 (author's translation).

[52] Balatskii, E., 'Svoe–chuzhoe: spravimsya sami' [Our own–foreign: let's manage it ourselves], *Vedomosti*, 29 Aug. 2005, URL <http://www.vedomosti.ru/newspaper/article.shtml?2005/08/29/96336>.

[53] Smirnov, K., 'No place for investment', *Kommersant Vlast'*, 31 Oct. 2005, URL <http://www.kommersant.com/doc.asp?idr=528&id=622328>.

[54] E.g., Irkut states in its financial report for 2002 and 2003 that its operations 'related to the construction and sale of military aircraft are subject to the Law of the Russian Federation on State Secrets signed by the President of the Russian Federation on July 21, 1993.' Irkut, 'Consolidated financial statements December 31, 2003 and 2002', 27 Aug. 2004, URL <http://www.irkut.com/en/for_investors/reports/>, p. 8.

[55] For the UN Register of Conventional Arms (UNROCA), there are missing data on Russian export deliveries, in particular to China, and few details are provided of the type of arms delivered. However, in

One significant step forward is the fact that all government agencies in Russia are now expected to provide information on their websites. The websites of Minekonomrazvitiya, Minpromenergo, Roskosmos and Rosprom provide much useful material relating to military economic issues, but other government agencies have been less forthcoming.[56] In October 2005 in a landmark legal decision a local court in St Petersburg upheld a complaint by the Institute for the Development of Freedom of Information that some federal executive bodies were in breach of a government decree of February 2003 obliging them to create official websites and provide on them information on their activities according to a specified list.[57] In the military economic field, agencies identified as having purely formal websites not meeting the terms of the decree included Rosoboronzakaz and the Federal Agency for Military Technical Cooperation.[58] The Institute for the Development of Freedom of Information has already achieved success in court in relation to other government bodies, so this latest court decision may well lead to greater transparency. Finally, one significant advance in transparency that should not be overlooked is the fact that many leading firms of the Russian arms industry now have their own informative websites: good examples include those of Almaz-Antei, Irkut, Saturn and the TVR Corporation.[59]

VII. Conclusions: further reforms?

While Russian military spending has been increasing in recent years and the output of the Russian arms industry has shown rapid growth, recovering some of the ground lost during the 1990s, there remains considerable anxiety about the state of the industry and its future prospects. The ambitious plans of 2001 for creating large corporate structures have not been realized. There is also mounting awareness that, with an ageing labour force and much obsolete equipment, it will be difficult to secure volume production of new weapons of a high technological level and quality when conditions finally permit domestic procurement on a scale adequate for a meaningful

these respects Russia is not alone and it could be argued that it is to Russia's credit that reports are still being submitted to this voluntary register when such countries as China and Iran do not. In reporting spending, it is not made explicit whether the data refer to actual or planned outlays; spending on the development and procurement of nuclear warheads and devices is omitted; and some spending, especially on R&D, is clearly neither actual nor budgeted but simply allocated between services on a percentage basis without change of the shares over a number of years. On transparency in military economic matters in present-day Russia see Cooper, J., 'Society–military relations: the economic dimension', eds S. L. Webber and J. G. Mathers, *Military and Society in Post-Soviet Russia* (Manchester University Press: Manchester, forthcoming 2006). See also chapter 7, appendix 9D and chapter 11 in this volume.

[56] See the websites of Minekonomrazvitiya, URL <http://www.economy.gov.ru/>; Minpromenergo, URL <http://www.minprom.gov.ru/>; Roskosmos, URL <http://www.roscosmos.ru/>; and Rosprom, URL <http://www.rosprom.gov.ru/>.

[57] Press service of the Russian Committee for the UNESCO Programme Information for All, 'Sud postanovil, chto organov vlasti otkryvayutsya ne "dlya galochki"' [Court has decreed that the sites of organs of power are opened not for 'ticking boxes'], 18 Oct. 2005, URL <http://www.nacbez.ru//article.php?id=1390>.

[58] At the time of writing the website of Rosoboronzakaz, URL <http://www.fsoz.gov.ru/>, is a purely 'Potemkin village' site, with virtually no content of any value. The website of the Federal Agency for Military Technical Cooperation, URL <http://www.fsvts.gov.ru/>, provides limited information but is improving.

[59] See the websites of Almaz-Antei, URL <http://www.almaz-antey.ru/> (in Russian); Irkut, URL <http://www.irkut.com/en/>; Saturn, URL <http://www.nposaturn.ru/default/>; and the TVR Corporation, URL <http://www.ktrv.ru/>.

re-equipment of the armed forces. Recognizing that the 2001 Programme for the Reform and Development of the Defence–Industrial Complex in 2002–2006 has achieved only modest results,[60] Minpromenergo is now finalizing a new federal state programme for the period to 2010, the FGP-2010, which will have a sub-programme for the nuclear industry. It is intended that the new programme will be fully compatible with the new armaments programme, the GPV-2015. The main goals of the FGP-2010 will be: (*a*) the completion of the reorganization of the core of the arms industry into 40–45 holding companies, embracing about half the enterprises and organizations in the register of the military–industrial complex; (*b*) the technical re-equipment of the industry and creation of production capacities for the manufacture of new weapons; and (*c*) the retention and development of critical technologies considered vital for the GPV-2015. It is envisaged that the implementation of the new programme will create conditions that allow the volume production of new armaments to commence in 2011. According to Koptev, head of the Defence–Industrial Complex Department of Minpromenergo, both the FGP-2010 and the GPV-2015 should be adopted by the second quarter of 2006. However, there are already concerns that inadequate funding will delay the start of the arms industry programme until 2007.[61]

It is now over 15 years since President Gorbachev started the process of halting the growth of the Soviet military economy and then, at first cautiously, began to reduce its scale. This process gathered momentum in the new conditions of post-communist Russia but an end point is still not in sight. It can now be concluded that, whereas the Soviet Union had a highly militarized economy, the same cannot be said of contemporary Russia. However, in some respects the Soviet legacy is still apparent: the Russian arms industry remains relatively isolated from the rest of the world with an evident reluctance at the official level to establish transnational partnerships for the development and production of weapons, let alone permit any sizeable foreign ownership stake in the domestic industry. While the arms industry and military economic issues in general are more open than in the past, the level of transparency still lags behind that accepted as normal in democratic countries.

---

[60] Federal Special Purpose Programmes (note 16).

[61] Mikhailov, V., 'Pyatiletka dlya "oboronki"' [A five-year plan for the defence industry], *VPK*, 24–30 Aug. 2005, URL <http://www.vpk-news.ru/article.asp?pr_sign=archive.2005.98.articles.weapon_01>; Samarova (note 17); and TS-VPK (note 33).

10. International arms transfers

BJÖRN HAGELIN, MARK BROMLEY and
SIEMON T. WEZEMAN

I. Introduction

The SIPRI Arms Transfers Project identifies trends in international transfers (i.e., deliveries) of major conventional weapons using the SIPRI trend-indicator value (TIV).[1] This makes it possible to describe changes in the international market for major weapons since 1950. According to five-year moving averages, the global downward trend was reversed in 2005 as a result of the continuous annual increase in deliveries from 2002 (figure 10.1).[2] The change in trend is also visible in the financial values of global arms exports according to national reporting (table 10.2).

One of the most marked aspects of major arms transfers over time is the stable composition of the group of major suppliers, with the Soviet Union/ Russia and the United States comprising a category of their own. The volume of arms deliveries peaked in 1982, when the Soviet Union, the USA, France, the United Kingdom and Italy accounted for about 82 per cent of the world total (see figure 10.1). In 2005 the five largest suppliers—the USA, Russia, France, Germany and the Netherlands—still accounted for about 82 per cent of total deliveries, although the total global volume was only 51 per cent of that of 1982, reflecting the post-cold war decline in transfers of major weapons. The major suppliers and recipients are discussed in section II.

In contrast, the group of major recipients has varied more over the years. Relative to the major suppliers, the major recipients account for a small share of the total market owing to the large number of minor recipients. In 1982 the five largest recipients—Iraq, Libya, Egypt, Saudi Arabia and India—accounted for 30 per cent of total imports, while in 2005 China, the United Arab Emirates (UAE), India, Israel and Greece accounted for 41 per cent of all imports. This can be partially explained by a shift in major import markets from the Middle East to Asia.

---

[1] SIPRI data on arms transfers refer to actual deliveries of major conventional weapons. To permit comparison between the data on deliveries of different weapons and to identify general trends, SIPRI uses a *trend-indicator value*. This value is only an indicator of the volume of international arms transfers and not of the financial values of such transfers. The method for calculating the TIV is described in appendix 10C and on the project website, URL <http://www.sipri.org/contents/armstrad/atmethods.html>. The figures in this chapter may differ from those given in previous editions of the SIPRI Yearbook as the arms transfers database is constantly updated.

[2] As the types and volumes of equipment delivered as well as delivery schedules vary over time, a single year is too short a period for reliable conclusions or comparisons. To reduce short-term fluctuations, SIPRI calculates a global 5-year average TIV.

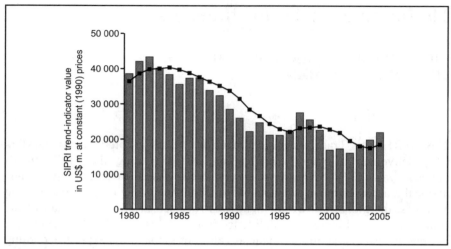

Figure 10.1. The trend in international transfers of major conventional weapons, 1980–2005

Note: The bar graph shows annual totals and the line graph denotes the five-year moving average. Five-year averages are plotted at the last year of each five-year period.

Some suppliers have a low TIV because they export goods that are not covered by the SIPRI database, such as most types of component. However, their arms exports may be financially significant, especially vis-à-vis certain recipients. Section II also discusses some smaller suppliers and includes a case study of Iraq as recipient. Section III surveys international arms embargoes in force during 2005, and section IV reports on developments in national and international arms transfer transparency.[3] Section V is a summary of the conclusions.

It should be noted that the SIPRI Arms Transfers Project has modified its methodology. First, the calculation of the TIV for military equipment manufactured under a foreign licence has been revised, generally resulting in an increased TIV. Second, to capture one aspect of multinational cooperation in arms production—that many weapons include major components that are imported by the producing or recipient country—transfers of certain engines have been added to the database. The methodology and the changes to it are explained in more detail in appendix 10C. Appendix 10A contains tables showing the volume of transfers of major conventional weapons, by recipients and suppliers, for 2001–2005. Appendix 10B lists details of the equipment that was delivered and received.

II. International arms transfers

Major suppliers and recipients

The rank order of the five largest suppliers in the period 2001–2005 was Russia, the USA, France, Germany and the UK. *Russia* accounted for 31 per

---

[3] See also chapter 6 in this volume.

cent of global transfers. Its position is partly the result of how the TIV is calculated, as Russia sells many weapons more cheaply than other major suppliers. Despite growing military expenditure in Russia, its arms industry remains dependent on exports.[4] In the period 2001–2005 exports to China and India accounted for 43 and 25 per cent respectively of Russian deliveries (see table 10.1). These two countries are expected to remain Russia's major arms markets, not least owing to licensed manufacture,[5] although deliveries are likely to reflect the general shift in Russian arms transfers towards naval equipment.[6]

The joint Russian military manoeuvres in 2005 with China and with India may be seen as 'operational marketing' of Russian weapons.[7] However, during the past few years India has increasingly turned to Western suppliers.[8] The new Indian Government, led by the Congress Party, cancelled several previous contracts with various countries in favour of international competition and announced a new acquisition policy from July 2005 that placed added emphasis on attaining military offsets.[9] Continued Russian defence cooperation with India hinged on India signing a formal intellectual property rights agreement,[10] which was finalized in December 2005.[11] This reflects another trend in Russian arms transfers—an increasing insistence on controlling technology transfers and being involved in after-sales support. The latter is the purpose of Rosoboronservice India Ltd, established in 2005 as a subsidiary of the main Russian arms export agency, Rosoboronexport.[12] Despite adminis-

---

[4] Butowski, P., 'Drop in Russian aircraft sales to hit industry hard', *Jane's Defence Weekly*, 13 July 2005, p. 21. See also appendix 9C in this volume.

[5] S. Chemezov, Director-General of Rosoboronexport, quoted in 'Russian official says India, China to remain top buyers', *Agentstvo Voyennykh Novostey*, 9 Feb. 2005, Translation from Russian, World News Connection, National Technical Information Services (NTIS), US Department of Commerce.

[6] 'Rosoboronexport: volume of Russian arms exports to stay at 2004 level in 2005', *Agentstvo Voyennykh Novostey*, 18 Aug. 2005, Translation from Russian, World News Connection, NTIS, US Department of Commerce; Novichkov, N., 'Chinese fighters to get Russian engines', *Jane's Defence Weekly*, 18 May 2005, p. 6; and Hewson, R., 'China boosts its air assets with Ilyushin aircraft', *Jane's Defence Weekly*, 21 Sep. 2005, p. 16.

[7] 'Russia/China: Russia seeks to step up military cooperation with China', *Atlantic News*, 8 Sep. 2005, p. 2; 'Russia demonstrates arms of paratroopers at point exercise with India', ITAR-TASS, 11 Oct. 2005, Translation from Russian, World News Connection, NTIS, US Department of Commerce.

[8] Raghuvanshi, V., 'India OKs Russian royalty demands', *Defense News*, 9 May 2005, p. 22.

[9] Raghuvanshi, V., 'New policy aims to boost India's exports', *Defense News*, 20 June 2005, p. 19; and Makienko, K., 'Financial results of Russian arms trade with foreign states in 2004', *Moscow Defense Brief*, no. 1, 2005, p. 11.

[10] Sahay T. S., 'Russia trips over Indian defense ties', *Asia Times* (Internet edn), 26 Oct. 2005, URL <http://www.atimes.com/atimes/South_Asia/GJ26Df02.html>.

[11] Murphy, J., 'Russia, India sign accord on intellectual property', *Jane's Defence Industry*, vol. 23, no. 1 (Jan. 2006), p. 1; and 'IPR pact signed, India to push Russia on technology transfer', *Indian Express Online*, 22 Dec. 2005.

[12] Mathews, N., 'Wheels and deals', *Aviation Week & Space Technology*, 19 Sep. 2005, p. 45; and Raghuvanshi, V., 'Russian firm to focus on Indian needs', *Defense News*, 26 Sep. 2005, p. 14. The creation of an aircraft service centre in Malaysia reflects the same tendency. 'Ambassador says Russia–Malaysia warplane contract making good progress', ITAR-TASS, 28 Nov. 2005, Translation from Russian, World News Connection, NTIS, US Department of Commerce.

Table 10.1. Transfers of major conventional weapons from the 10 largest suppliers to the 38 largest recipients, 2001–2005

Figures are trend-indicator values expressed in US$ m. at constant (1990) prices. Figures may not add up to totals because of the conventions of rounding.

Recipient	Supplier											
	Russia	USA	France	Germany	UK	Ukraine	Canada	Netherlands	Italy	Sweden	Other	Total
Africa	**2 551**	**209**	**244**	**569**	**152**	**524**	**4**	**15**	**62**	**–**	**948**	**5 278**
Algeria	941	119	16	–	–	88	4	3	–	–	213	1 381
South Africa	–	7	50	407	143	–	–	–	26	–	–	636
Sudan	549	–	–	–	–	–	–	–	–	–	26	575
Other	1 061	83	178	162	9	436	–	12	36	–	709	2 686
Americas	**215**	**1 512**	**716**	**197**	**1 363**	**50**	**1 464**	**227**	**613**	**127**	**1 145**	**7 629**
Brazil	–	307	409	–	4	–	46	–	111	80	67	1 024
Canada	–	277	1	31	960	–	:	–	98	–	12	1 379
Chile	–	25	255	1	196	–	–	204	26	–	85	792
Colombia	41	454	–	–	–	–	–	–	11	–	46	552
Peru	157	100	–	–	–	–	–	–	343	–	3	603
USA	:	–	–	–	181	50	1 409	–	18	12	533	2 213
Other	17	349	51	165	12	–	9	23	6	35	399	1 066
Asia	**22 333**	**6 933**	**1 355**	**833**	**505**	**912**	**60**	**190**	**395**	**139**	**3 164**	**36 819**
China	12 535	–	62	79	82	489	–	–	3	–	93	13 343
India	7 339	56	289	48	94	299	–	75	36	–	1 119	9 355
Indonesia	272	24	109	72	–	–	4	14	–	–	115	610
Japan	–	1 432	11	–	70	–	5	–	16	10	–	1 539
Malaysia	67	45	18	312	147	–	–	–	62	–	172	828
Pakistan	180	189	459	–	–	14	–	–	254	19	950	2 065
Singapore	9	1 165	–	–	–	–	–	–	–	102	106	1 382
South Korea	164	1 639	340	195	43	–	51	66	–	–	63	2 561
Taiwan	–	1 927	55	–	–	–	–	–	–	–	–	1 982
Thailand	–	335	–	103	23	–	–	16	10	8	109	604
Viet Nam	724	–	–	16	–	–	–	–	–	–	36	776
Other	1 043	121	12	8	46	110	–	19	14	–	401	1 774

											Total
Europe	932	11 283	1 808	3 188	879	247	112	1 239	664	1 318	1 848	23 590
Czech Republic	251	134	–	..	7	–	36	–	105	387	–	883
Germany	–	392	–	276	38	–	40	197	–	16	38	681
Greece	455	2 857	1 146	125	45	60	–	609	239	184	169	6 105
Italy	–	1 369	30	201	75	–	–	–	..	7	1	1 606
Netherlands	–	635	–	505	40	–	–	..	12	–	–	890
Poland	2	220	–	125	–	–	21	5	6	99	218	1 121
Romania	–	67	12	213	415	–	18	227	–	–	61	907
Spain	–	576	93	573	–	–	–	–	–	4	37	1 032
Turkey	–	1 318	347	425	33	–	–	39	91	–	427	2 800
UK	–	2 374	–	–	–	–	–	30	63	73	25	2 927
Other	224	1 341	180	745	226	187	85	132	148	548	622	4 638
Middle East	2 956	7 233	4 279	524	546	496	105	157	77	–	1 247	17 620
Egypt	–	2 274	–	151	–	45	–	155	–	–	276	2 901
Iran	1 707	–	–	5	–	162	–	–	–	–	269	2 143
Israel	–	2 565	–	309	–	–	–	–	–	..	–	2 873
Jordan	–	227	–	12	415	–	4	–	–	–	106	764
Saudi Arabia	–	369	1 185	5	–	–	98	–	68	–	3	1 728
United Arab Emirates	–	1 516	3 034	38	4	226	–	2	–	–	47	4 867
Yemen	1 117	–	–	–	–	63	–	–	–	–	196	1 376
Other	132	282	60	4	127	–	3	–	9	–	351	968
Oceania	1 070	–	176	295	493	–	155	44	49	160	114	2 556
Australia	991	–	176	295	485	–	75	–	49	160	112	2 343
Other	79	–	–	–	8	–	80	44	–	–	2	213
Other[a]	–	–	–	2	–	–	–	–	–	18	4	24
Total	28 982	28 236	8 573	5 603	3 933	2 226	1 971	1 868	1 858	1 760	8 506	93 516

Note: The SIPRI data on arms transfers refer to actual deliveries of major conventional weapons. To permit comparison between the data on such deliveries and identification of general trends, SIPRI uses a *trend-indicator value*, which is an indicator of the volume of international arms transfers and not of the actual financial values of such transfers. Trend-indicator values are not comparable to economic statistics such as gross domestic product or export figures.

[a] Other recipients include the UN and NATO (as organizations, not as combinations of all member states) and unknown recipients.

Source: SIPRI Arms Transfers Database.

trative and other problems,[13] sales of spare parts for Russian equipment are reported to have increased substantially in the past few years.[14]

China's interest in buying Russian weapons remains strong. It has ordered 38 Il-76 long-range transport and Il-78 tanker/transport aircraft via Russia (the aircraft are produced in Uzbekistan and fitted with Russian engines), and China and Russia are reported to be negotiating a renewal of Chinese licensed production of Sukhoi combat aircraft.[15] Russia has offered Sukhoi Su-33 and Su-35 combat aircraft to China for use on aircraft carriers.[16] The offer is significant because the aircraft are still in development, which suggests that Russia is willing to share its latest technology with China.

Both China and India have become all the more important to arms exporters as both countries are in a position to become economic powers and leaders in technology applications. Saturation of Russia's Chinese and Indian military markets may be expected in the long term,[17] and Russia's other markets, such as Iran, Viet Nam and Yemen, are relatively small. In March 2006 it was reported that Russia had signed a series of contracts with Algeria with a potential value of $7.5 billion; the deals are reputed to include combat aircraft, tanks and surface-to-air missiles (SAMs). Depending on how the deal evolves, it could have a major impact on the value of Russia's arms exports.[18]

Rosoboronexport has opened a new office in Brussels in an attempt to improve its sales in European markets.[19] Russia is also making greater efforts to market its arms in South America,[20] as well as to other members of the Collective Security Treaty Organization and the Shanghai Cooperation Organization.[21] Russia also has an ambition to become a main supplier to Iraq (see also section III below).[22]

---

[13] 'Russia should have one arms trader', Interfax, 24 Oct. 2005, Translation from Russian, World News Connection, NTIS, US Department of Commerce.

[14] 'Naval products now account for over half Russian arms exports', RIA Novosti, 4 Nov. 2005, Translation from Russian, World News Connection, NTIS, US Department of Commerce; and 'Combat materiel, arms spare parts export increase five-fold in 3 years', Interfax-AVN, 11 Nov. 2005, Translation from Russian, World News Connection, NTIS, US Department of Commerce.

[15] 'Il-76/78 pour la Chine' [Il-76/78 for China], Air & Cosmos, 16 Sep. 1005, p. 18.

[16] Butowski, P., 'La Chine s'intéresse au Su-33 embarqué' [China interested in ship-borne Su-33], Air & Cosmos, 16 Sep. 2005, p. 19.

[17] Interview with A. Brindikov, Rosoboronexport representative, 'Russian arms exports are changing direction', Izvestiya, 19 June 2005, Translation from Russian, World News Connection, NTIS, US Department of Commerce.

[18] 'Algerian arms deal brings Russia $7.5 billion, gas market leverage', Defense Industry Daily, 3 Mar. 2006, URL <http://www.defenseindustrydaily.com/2006/03/algerian-arms-deal-brings-russia-75-billion-gas-market-leverage/index.php>.

[19] Chemezov, S. V., General Director of Rosoboronexport, 'This is Rosoboronexport', NATO's Nations and Partners for Peace, vol. 50, no.2 (2005), p. 73.

[20] According to Rosoboronexport, sales of defence equipment to Latin America have been worth $30–40 million a year. The firm hopes to raise this to $100 million over the coming few years. See 'Venezuela and Peru shop for arms in Russia', Latin American Security & Strategic Review, Dec. 2004, p. 11.

[21] Trefinov, D., 'Reversing decline', Jane's Defence Weekly, 8 June 2005, p. 27; 'Sergei Ivanov to discuss military contacts with Kyrgyzstan', ITAR-TASS, 19 Sep. 2005, Translation from Russian, World News Connection, NTIS, US Department of Commerce; and 'Russia's Putin wants emphasis on arms trade with CIS countries', Interfax, 17 Oct. 2005, Translation from Russian, World News Con-

Many Russian industrialists are open about the problems facing Russia's arms industry. The risk of losing its position to Western competitors unless the quality improves, for instance through international cooperation, has been noted.[23] In 2005 an arms trade decree was issued aimed at introducing flexibility and liberalization for companies involved in what Russia defines as 'military–technical cooperation' (MTC).[24] However, attempts to restrict foreign investment in industries of strategic importance may prove counterproductive to such an ambition.[25]

Alexander Denisov, first Deputy Director of the Federal Service for MTC, has described Russia's arms export policy in a way that can be understood as 'commercial pragmatism': as long as a country is not under a United Nations (UN) embargo, Russia will in the national interest permit arms exports.[26] His statement was made in view of the decision in January 2005 to forgive a large part of Syria's debt as a prelude to future arms deals.[27] President Vladimir Putin himself defended Syrian orders for vehicle-mounted SAMs during his visit to Israel in April 2005,[28] and it seems, although there were conflicting reports, that the deal went through.[29] If it was cancelled this could be an indication that Russia's policy is influenced by more than just international arms embargoes. However, in late 2005 Russia is reputed to have signed a $1 bil-

nection, NTIS, US Department of Commerce. Members of the Collective Security Treaty Organization and the Shanghai Cooperation Organization are listed in the glossary in this volume.

[22] 'Putin to allow Russian firms to sell weapons to Iraq', *Defense Aerospace*, Voice of America, issued 30 Aug. 2004, URL <http://www.newdefenceagenda.org/news_detail.asp?ID=238>; and 'The expert 400: the defense industry', *Gateway to Russia*, 17 Nov. 2004, URL <http://www.gateway2russia.com/st/art_257174.php>.

[23] Rapoport, B., Director-General of Alfa-Integrator in 'Company chief says Russian arms exporters face loss of world market share', *Agentstvo Voyennykh Novostey*, 16 Mar. 2005, Translation from Russian, World News Connection, NTIS, US Department of Commerce.

[24] The decree is an updated version of a Dec. 2000 law. See 'Russian arms trade decree to be ready soon', Interfax, 7 Sep. 2005, Translation from Russian, World News Connection, NTIS, US Department of Commerce. Rosoboronexport is likely to remain the main arms exporter, as other companies are mainly suppliers of parts and sub-systems. Ivanov, V., 'Arms can be sold, but only in parts', *Nezavisimaya Gazeta*, 9 Sep. 2005, Translation from Russian, World News Connection, NTIS, US Department of Commerce; and interview with S. Chemezov, Director-General of Rosoboronexport, 'Arms trade is no business for dilettantes', *Military Technology*, no. 4, 2005, pp. 46–48.

[25] Vogel, B., 'Russia drafts laws limiting foreign investment in defence industry', *Defence Industry*, Nov. 2005, p. 5. See also chapter 9 in this volume.

[26] 'Russia not to cut arms sales to Syria, Iran', Interfax, 30 Nov. 2005, Translation from Russian, World News Connection, NTIS, US Department of Commerce.

[27] Kahwaji, R., 'Russia, Syria revive ties with dept reduction', *Defense News*, 31 Jan. 2005, p. 10. Negotiations for SAM systems, anti-tank weapons and surface-to-surface missiles (SSMs) to Syria were reportedly ongoing with competition from China, Belarus, Iran, North Korea and the Czech Republic; and Hughes, R., 'Syria's dilemma', *Jane's Defence Weekly*, 7 Sep. 2005, pp. 34–36.

[28] In April 2005 Russia and Singapore discussed future arms sales. 'Russia: Singapore ambassador to discuss military–technical cooperation', *Interfax*, 5 April 2005, Translation from Russian, World News Connection, NTIS, US Department of Commerce.

[29] According to the head of Rosboronexport, the deal was cancelled because it conflicted with a US–Russian agreement signed in Feb. 2005 on sharing information on and controlling man-portable air defence systems (MANPADs) sales. See 'Russian head of arms exports denies sale of Igla defence systems to Syria', Text of report by Russia TV, translated from Russian by BBC Monitoring International Reports, 2 Nov. 2005; 'Russia, US sign deal on shoulder-fired missiles', *Air Letter*, 26 Feb. 2005, p. 5. However, other sources state that the missiles were delivered. See Myasnikov, V., 'Rosoboronexport is doubling sales', Agency WPS (Internet edn), 10 Feb. 2006.

lion deal with Iran for SAMs despite criticism from the USA and the European Union (EU).[30]

In the period 2001–2005 *the USA* accounted for 30 per cent of global deliveries of arms. With more relatively large foreign markets than Russia, the four largest recipients—Greece, Israel, the UK and Egypt—accounted for 36 per cent of US deliveries in 2001–2005.[31] The year 2005 was important for US bilateral arms relations with three countries in particular—India, Israel and Japan.

US relations with India are today labelled 'strategic'. The USA's policy towards India is designed to keep India and Japan strong in order to offset China's rising regional influence.[32] While the present volume of US transfers of major weapons to India is low, the USA is prepared to offer advanced weaponry, such as the F/A-18E and an advanced version of the F-16 to meet the Indian requirement for 126 combat aircraft, and the Patriot SAM in its PAC-3 version.[33] US arms policy towards India may also embrace technology transfers, including the possible co-development of weapons ordered by India.[34] US helicopter producer Bell has offered technology transfers if it wins the competition for an order for 197 light helicopters. Should either the F-16 or the F/A-18E be selected, the USA seems willing to accept cooperation,[35] and India has expressed an interest in the new P-8A anti-submarine warfare/ maritime patrol (ASW/MP) aircraft for which the USA would like to find partners for joint development.[36]

However, India has been exposed to US arms embargoes that stopped the delivery of US weapons and US spare parts for non-US weapons, most recently in 1998. India reacted to this by demanding that its other suppliers do not use US parts. The USA will have to convince India that the risk of a future embargo is low or non-existent.[37] In addition, the USA's willingness to supply

---

[30] Jahn, G., 'EU decries Russia–Iran missile deal', *Philadelphia Inquirer*, 16 Dec. 2005.

[31] A 2005 report was very critical of US arms deliveries post 2001. See Berrigan, F., Hartung, W. D., and Heffel, L., *US Weapons at War 2005: Promoting Freedom or Fuelling Conflict?* (World Policy Institute: New York, June 2005), URL <http://www.worldpolicy.org/projects/arms/reports/wawjune 2005.html>.

[32] Ratnam, G., 'US vows to make India "world power"', *Defense News*, 4 Apr. 2005, p. 1; and Sirak, M., 'US signs defence pact with India', *Jane's Defence Weekly*, 13 July 2005, p. 15. On US–Indian civil nuclear cooperation see appendix 13B in this volume.

[33] 'Patriot pour l'Inde' [Patriot for India], *Air & Cosmos*, 16 Sep. 2005, p. 18; *Air & Cosmos*, 25 Nov. 2005, p. 9; and Murphy, J., 'India, Russia move to resolve IPR dispute', *Jane's Defence Weekly*, 26 Oct. 2005, p. 21.

[34] Competitors have offered technology transfers, licensed production and even marketing rights; e.g., France offers technology transfers and is willing to negotiate marketing rights as part of its offer of the Mirage 2000-5 to India for its planned acquisition of 126 combat aircraft. See Kaura, G. S., 'France ready to give Mirage "marketing rights" to India', *The Tribune*, 5 May 2005, URL <http://www.tribune india.com/2005/20050505/main8.htm>.

[35] Johnson, J., 'Indians greet US declaration of strategic relationship with cynicism', *Financial Times* (USA edition 2), 5 Apr. 2005, p. 2.

[36] Bedi, R., 'New Delhi in talks to acquire USN maritime patrol craft', *Jane's Defence Weekly*, 17 Aug. 2005, p. 17.

[37] Mathews, N., 'Edging closer', *Aviation Week & Space Technology*, 8 Aug. 2005, p. 37; and Nayan, R., 'Emerging frontiers of US dual-use export control laws', *Strategic Analysis*, vol. 29, no. 1, (2005), pp. 143–45.

Pakistan with advanced weaponry may further undermine the USA's chances of securing large orders from India.[38]

A long-running dispute between the USA and Israel over Israeli transfers to China reached a head in 2005 after Israel's sale of Harpy unmanned air vehicles (UAVs) to China in 2000 and follow-on sales of spare parts in 2002. The US Government claimed that it was not informed of the follow-on sales and feared that Israel might have modernized the UAVs instead of merely overhauling them.[39] This, in turn, would have given China military capabilities that could have posed 'a credible threat to other modern militaries operating in the region'.[40] In early 2005 the USA imposed sanctions on Israel's arms industry and withheld technical assistance and information sharing in relation to a number of projects, including the Joint Strike Fighter (JSF) combat aircraft.

Cooperation was partly restored following an August 2005 agreement under which Israel agreed to inform the USA of all its future arms export plans and to take the US position into account when formulating these plans.[41] Specifically, Israel agreed to observe the 1996 Wassenaar Arrangement control list and to engage in 'a process for consultation' with the US Government on arms sales.[42] The obligations on Israel to take account of US policy considerations are not limited to deliveries to China.[43] In October 2005, following US pressure, Israel froze a $100 million contract with Venezuela to modernize its US-delivered F-16 combat aircraft.[44] (On Israeli arms transfers see also below.)

[38] Pakistan was granted the status of 'major non-NATO ally' in Mar. 2005. See Ratnam, G. and Raghuvanshi, V., 'Subcontinental tightrope', *Defense News*, 29 Mar. 2005, p. 1.

[39] Ben-David, A., 'US pressure threatens Israel–China trade', *Jane's Defence Weekly*, 12 Jan. 2005, p. 22.

[40] US Department of Defense, 'Annual report on the military power of the People's Republic of China 2005: FY04 report to Congress on PRC military power', Washington, DC, 2005, URL <http://www.defenselink.mil/pubs/d20040528PRC.pdf>.

[41] Opall-Rome, B., 'Israel accelerates its export control drive', *Defense News*, 12 Sep. 2005, p. 6. See also Pomper, M. A., 'US, Israel reach China arms deal', *Arms Control Today*, Sep. 2005, p. 34.

[42] US Department of Defense, Office of the Assistant Secretary of Defense (Public Affairs), 'US Department of Defense—Israeli Ministry of Defense joint press statement', Defenselink, Press release, no. 846-05, 16 Aug. 2005, URL <http://www.defenselink.mil/releases/2005/nr20050816-4442.html>; Gertz, B., 'US to restart arms technology transfers to Israel', *Washington Times* (Internet edn), 17 Aug. 2005, URL <http://www.washingtontimes.com/national/20050817-121710-1862r.htm>; and Anthony, I. and Bauer, S., 'Transfer controls', *SIPRI Yearbook 2005: Armaments, Disarmament and International Security* (Oxford University Press: Oxford, 2005), esp. pp. 705–707. On the Wassenaar Arrangement see chapter 16 in this volume.

[43] 'US–Israeli pact may hurt Turkish defense procurement', *Turkish Daily News* (Internet edn), 23 Aug. 2005, URL <http://www.turkishdailynews.com.tr/article.php?enewsid=21450>. Reflecting the strong US political attitude against helping Chinese armament, the US House of Representatives International Relations Committee passed the 2005 East Asia Security Act including sanctions against any country or firm that sell arms to China. See Snyder, C., 'US House acts on China arms sales', *Taipei Times* (Internet edn), 2 July 2005, URL <http://www.taipeitimes.com/News/front/archives/2005/07/02/2003261859>.

[44] 'US roadblocks re: the Venezuela–Israel F-16 upgrade: politics or protectionism?', *Defense Industry Daily*, 26 Oct. 2005, URL <http://www.defenseindustrydaily.com/2005/10/us-roadblocks-re-the-venezuelaisrael-f16-upgrade-politics-or-protectionism/index.php>. Israeli defence officials have claimed that US attempts to control Israel's arms exports are at least partly motivated by a desire to protect US markets. See 'Israeli officials accuse US of trying to "reserve" arms market', *Voice of Israel*, 21 Oct. 2005, Translation from Hebrew by BBC Monitoring Middle East.

US military relations with Japan are in a process of change, not only with regard to the presence of US forces and arms pre-positioning, but also as a result of changes in Japan's policy.[45] In December 2004 Japan decided to allow exports of military components to the USA in support of the development of US missile defence systems. This was the result of a revision of Japan's established defence policy since World War II that emphasized pacifism and effectively banned all arms exports. The review began during the 1990s as a result of Japan's increasing international engagement and insecurities created by the policies and conduct of China and North Korea.[46]

Consequently changes could be seen in Japan's military policy on arms imports and exports. Japan will continue to have a unique relationship with the USA, but Japan is also likely to engage in military cooperation with India, given that limited Japanese deliveries of military equipment to countries other than the USA are permitted.[47] Imports of major combat equipment to Japan from non-US suppliers may increase because Japan cancelled plans for additional indigenous F-2 combat aircraft, meaning that it might purchase replacement aircraft from Europe.[48]

The recent enlargement of the *European Union* has increased its importance as an arms exporter. The combined exports from EU countries accounted for 27 per cent of total global exports in the period 2001–2005 making it the third largest exporter of major conventional weapons.[49] In the same period, *France*, *Germany*, *the UK* and *the Netherlands* were the largest European exporters of major conventional weapons—accounting for 9, 6, 4 and 2 per cent of the global market, respectively—followed by Italy and Sweden.

Winning orders in today's competitive major arms market is not only a matter of financing but is increasingly linked to an ability to offer a package of platform, armaments and technology. France's offer to combine its Exocet anti-ship missiles with its Scorpene submarines was one of several factors in India's decision to order six submarines in 2005. The German competitor

---

[45] 'The sun also rises', *Armed Forces Journal*, Dec. 2005, pp. 14–23. See also chapter 6 in this volume; and Lachowski, Z., *Foreign Military Bases in the Euro-Asian Region*, SIPRI Policy Paper (SIPRI: Stockholm, forthcoming 2006).

[46] See, e.g., Deming, R., 'Japan's constitution and defense policy: entering a new era?', *Strategic Forum*, no. 213 (Nov. 2004); Karniol, R., 'Shifting gear', *Jane's Defence Weekly*, 23 Mar. 2005, pp. 27–29; and Cooney, K., 'Alternative visions of Japanese security', *Asian Perspective*, vol. 29, no. 3 (2005), pp. 127–54.

[47] 'Japanese general in India', *Defense News*, 19 Sep. 2005, p. 3; and Gregory, J., 'Japan looks at exporting missiles', *Financial Times* (Internet edn), 16 July 2005. For a critical review of Japan's 'no arms' export policy, see Ballantyne, R., 'Japan's hidden arms trade', *Japan Focus*, 'URL <http://www.japanfocus.org/article.asp?id=459>.

[48] 'JASDF F-4EJ replacement', *Air Forces Monthly*, Oct. 2005, p. 22.

[49] This figure includes the combined deliveries of all 25 EU member states for the period 1 Jan. 2001–31 Dec. 2005. The inter-EU market may change as EU members, through the European Defence Agency (EDA), have agreed on a voluntary code of conduct on defence procurement to reduce the impact of Article 296 of the Treaty on European Union, which allows states to buy military equipment without following the rules of an open EU market. See European Defence Agency, The Code of Conduct on Defence Procurement of the EU Member States Participating in the European Defence Agency, 21 Nov. 2005, URL <http://www.eda.eu.int/reference/eda/EDA - Code of Conduct - European Defence Equipment Market.htm>.

could not present such a ship–missile package since the appropriate missiles are not produced in Germany.[50]

The year 2006 could be decisive for Europe's combat aircraft manufacturers. In 2005 France and the UK competed over a prospective deal to export almost 100 combat aircraft to Saudi Arabia—the UK offering the Eurofighter Typhoon and France the Dassault Rafale.[51] France's recent loss of contracts for combat aircraft in South Korea, Singapore and Indonesia raised demands for a more concerted approach to supporting arms transfers.[52] However, by the end of 2005 Saudi Arabia had selected the Typhoon, while France seemed to have received an agreement 'in principle' with Saudi Arabia on a border surveillance programme (Project Miksa) worth up to €7 billion.[53] Another major competition involving France, Sweden, Russia and the USA is the potential Indian order for 126 combat aircraft, mentioned above. Market analysts seem to regard European combat aircraft programmes as having a competitive edge because they are not exposed to the same uncertainties as the major US programmes.[54]

Technology transfer controversies also inflamed transatlantic relations in 2005 as the US Congress continued to block the implementation of the US Government's International Traffic in Arms Regulations (ITAR) waiver policy, designed to speed up and simplify foreign purchases of unclassified US military equipment.[55] There were also indications that there would be complications in the technology transfers for the JSF project if the EU lifted its arms embargo on China, drawing concern from political and industrial interests, not least in the UK.[56] In 2005 the USA stated that it intended to prohibit the re-transfer of US technology used in C-295 transport aircraft that Spain was to sell to Venezuela.[57] Such decisions and threats strengthen European arguments for harmonization and cooperation in regional weapons-acquisition policies, including shared military research and development (R&D) in the

---

[50] Bombeau, B., 'SM-39 Exocet pour l'Inde' [SM-39 Exocet for India], *Air & Cosmos*, 14 Oct. 2005, p. 45; and Lewis, J. A. C., 'India to confirm Scorpene deal', *Jane's Defence Weekly*, 14 Sep. 2005, p. 32. An offer by the German producer to integrate Russian missiles was rejected by India.

[51] 'Arabie Saoudite' [Saudi Arabia], *Air & Cosmos*, 14 Oct. 2005, p. 6.

[52] 'More export support?', *Aviation Week & Space Technology*, 17 Oct. 2005, p. 13; Mathews, N., 'India market', *Aviation Week & Space Technology*, 17 Oct. 2005, p. 62; and Raghuvanshi, V., 'French, Indian leaders to discuss cooperation', *Defense News*, 12 Sep. 2005, p. 72.

[53] 'Saudi Arabia: Al Yamamah III', *Defence News Analysis*, 2 Jan. 2006, p. 1; 'Saudi Arabia commits to Eurofighter Typhoon', *Air Letter*, 23 Dec. 2005, p. 4.

[54] Dupont, J., 'Dans les serres de l'aigle Américain' [In the claws of the American eagle], *Air & Cosmos*, 28 Oct. 2005, pp. 18–31.

[55] Spiegel, P., 'UK denied waiver on US arms technology', *Financial Times* (Internet edn), 22 Nov. 2005; Interview with Lincoln Bloomfield, former US Assistant Secretary of State for Political–Military Affairs, *Defense News*, 31 Jan. 2005, p. 22.

[56] Mulholland, D., 'Dropping EU embargo may jeopardize JSF', *Jane's Defence Weekly*, 2 Mar. 2005, p. 20; Barrie, D., 'Goodbye, waiver', *Aviation Week & Space Technology*, 20 June 2005, p. 42; Anderson, G., 'UK's restricted access to JSF technology is a "very serious issue"', *Jane's Defence Industry*, Aug. 2005, p. 10; Sharman, A., Interview with Director General, UK Defence Manufacturers Association, *Jane's Defence Weekly*, 28 Sep. 2005, p. 29.

[57] 'US blocks Israeli arms sale to Venezuela—report', Reuters, 20 Oct. 2005, URL <http://www.alertnet.org/thenews/newsdesk/L20659759.htm>; and Matthews, W., 'US holds up sale of C-295s to Venezuela', *Defense News* (Internet edn), 24 Oct. 2005.

European Defence Agency (EDA). Some European acquisition decisions could, in response, go against US equipment, partly in order to avoid US export control considerations.

Minor suppliers

China has been notable for its exports of major weapons to countries that are considered by European countries and the USA to be controversial recipients. Israel's position as an arms exporter is due not so much to its transfers of major weapons as to its exports of components and modernization of foreign weapons. India, Brazil and South Africa hold long-standing ambitions to increase their arms export capacity. In recent years they have moved towards cooperation to regain or improve their respective shares of the international arms market.

China

In 1987 China was the third-largest exporter of major conventional weapons, accounting for 9 per cent of global deliveries. Its increase in arms transfers during the late 1980s was based largely on sales to both sides in the 1980–88 Iraq–Iran War. In common with other suppliers in the developing world that benefited from sales during this war, such as Brazil, China struggled to maintain its market share after the conflict ended. The demand for Chinese weapons also suffered when the 1991 Gulf War demonstrated the superiority of Western weaponry and because of the growing availability of cheaper, more advanced Russian weapons during the 1990s.[58] In the period 2001–2005 China accounted for less than 2 per cent of global major arms transfers.

However, reinforced by cooperation with Russia, various European countries and Israel (and extensive reverse engineering), China's military technical competence has advanced.[59] In April 2005 Pakistan signed a contract for four frigates estimated to be worth $600–750 million,[60] and in September 2005 Nigeria bought 15 F-7 combat aircraft for $251 million.[61] Russia, however, has made it clear that it will not allow China to export certain combat aircraft with Russian engines, leaving the planned export of some 150 JF-17/FC-1 combat

---

[58] Byman, D. and Cliff R., *China's Arms Sales: Motivations and Implications* (RAND Corporation: Santa Monica, 1999), URL <http://rand.org/publications/MR/MR1119>, p. vii.

[59] Kogan, E., 'Russia–China aerospace cooperation', International Relations and Security Network: Security Watch, Center for Security Studies, Zurich, 6 Oct. 2004, URL <http://www.isn.ethz.ch/news/sw/details.cfm?ID=9869>. For more on China's recent development of military systems see Wezeman, S. and Bromley, M., 'International arms transfers', *SIPRI Yearbook 2005* (note 42), pp. 422–25.

[60] 'Pak-China deal on frigates after finalising loan modalities: CNS', *The News* (Karachi), 16 Sep. 2004, URL <http://jang.com.pk/thenews/sep2004-daily/16-09-2004/main/main12.htm>; 'Shaikh, S., 'Pakistan to buy four Chinese warships', *The News* (Karachi), 5 April 2005, URL <http://www.jang.com.pk/thenews/apr2005-daily/05-04-2005/main/main4.htm>; and 'Pak to get Chinese frigates by 2013', *The Nation* (Lahore), 8 July 2005, URL <http://nation.com.pk/daily/july-2005/8/index9.php>.

[61] 'Nigeria spends $251m for Chinese F-7 fighters after oil deals', *Defense Industry Daily*, 30 Sep. 2005, URL <http://www.defenseindustrydaily.com/2005/09/nigeria-spends-251m-for-chinese-f7-fighters-after-oil-deals>.

aircraft to Pakistan indefinitely deferred. Indeed, many advanced Chinese weapons include Russian major components, notably engines and electronics. A test of China's progress in developing and marketing advanced indigenous weapon systems will be the deployment of the J-10 combat aircraft. If and when the system is ready for export, China will be in direct competition with Russia for sales of advanced combat aircraft to middle-income countries.[62]

China's arms sales policy, which in the cold war period was at least partly geared towards supporting revolutionary movements, is today a means of strengthening strategic relations with, for example, Pakistan, Iran and Egypt, the three largest recipients of exports from China in 2001–2005. China's economic growth has also led to an increasing dependency on imported raw materials, especially oil and gas, and recent Chinese arms sales to Cambodia, Nigeria and Sudan are seen as part of a policy to secure access to needed resources.[63]

China's future role as an arms supplier is, as for many other suppliers including Russia,[64] based on a paradox. China's best chance of increasing its arms exports lies in exporting to countries that have been shunned by Western suppliers. At the same time, in order to develop weapon systems that can compare with Russian and Western equipment it is dependent on access to foreign technologies. This access may be refused if China exports to destinations that are under international embargoes or restricted by national export policies of Western suppliers.[65]

Zimbabwe, which has been under EU and US arms embargoes since 2000, has been unable to secure spare parts for the five Hawk trainer/light combat aircraft that it bought from the UK in the early 1990s.[66] In April 2005 Zimbabwe announced that it was buying six K-8 aircraft, a Chinese aircraft similar to the Hawk aircraft.[67] In December 2005 the USA imposed sanctions on nine foreign companies, six of them Chinese companies that allegedly supplied military equipment or technology to Iran.[68]

---

[62] Donnan, S. and Dickie, M., 'Jakarta in missile deal with Beijing', *Financial Times* (Internet edn), 31 July 2005. Middle-income countries are listed in appendix 8A in this volume.

[63] Byman and Cliff (note 58), pp. 2–6.

[64] The use of foreign components in Russian armaments is increasing. See appendix 9C in this volume.

[65] Jones, S., 'China reforms its strategic exports control regime', *Jane's Intelligence Review*, Apr. 2005, pp. 30–34. See also Grimmett, R. F., Library of Congress, Congressional Research Service (CRS), *Conventional Arms Transfers to Developing Nations 1997–2004*, CRS Report for Congress RL33051 (US Government Printing Office: Washington, DC, 29 Aug. 2005), p. 9.

[66] 'Purchase of jets from China wise', *Africa News*, 1 July 2005.

[67] Hartnack, M., 'Mugabe buys fighter jets', *Mail and Guardian* (Internet edn), 13 April 2005, URL <http://www.mg.co.za/articledirect.aspx?articleid=215053>.

[68] Murphy, J., 'US imposes sanctions on companies alleged to have sold equipment to Iran', *Jane's Defence Industry*, Feb. 2006, p. 7. An unnamed Iranian diplomat is quoted as saying that Iran intends to meet its military aviation requirements from China and other friendly countries. See Vogel, B., 'Iran/China discuss aircraft purchase', *Jane's Defence Industry*, Feb. 2006, p. 7.

Israel

Although Israel has gained an international reputation in the field of military exports, the level of its performance is difficult to establish. In the period 2001–2005 Israel was a smaller supplier of major weapons than China. Most Israeli exports consist of small arms, ammunition, electronics and modernized weapons, for which there are no reliable data.[69] Exports are also difficult to identify because non-Israeli companies market Israeli-made goods or produce them under licence. Israeli companies establish partnerships with European companies, partly to penetrate protected markets, but also because buying weapons from Israel may be politically controversial. According to Rafael, the producer of the Spike anti-tank missile, it is 'more comfortable for European customers to buy from Eurospike than from Israeli Rafael'. Finland, the Netherlands, Poland and Romania ordered Spike missiles from Eurospike, established in 1997 by Rafael and German Diehl and Rheinmetall.[70] Rafael also sells its Litening targeting system via Zeiss, a German company.[71]

As Israel has long experience of security threats similar to those faced by the coalition forces in Iraq, the ongoing conflict there has provided a number of export opportunities for Israel. Equipment such as armour and other protection for vehicles has proved lucrative: in 2004–2005, orders worth $84 million were placed by the USA to protect infantry fighting vehicles (IFVs).[72] Israel and Turkey also established close military cooperation during the 1990s, partly because Turkey felt exposed to insurgency threats. In 2005 Turkey placed several orders for Israeli equipment, including a $183 million order for UAVs.[73]

India is one of Israel's main markets, especially since sales to China were blocked (see above).[74] According to the Indian Minister of Defence, Pranab Mukherjee, India and Israel have signed contracts worth $2.76 billion over the past three years.[75] Sources claim that sales of missiles and modernization packages alone have been worth about $900 million a year.[76] Included in bilateral discussions have been the Israeli Arrow anti-ballistic missile, Heron

---

[69] E.g., AMI has signed a $300 million ammunition order with the USA. Ben-David, A., 'Israeli government decides fate of IMI', *Jane's Defence Weekly*, 7 Sep. 2005, p. 22.

[70] Ben-David, A., 'Partner power', *Jane's Defence Weekly*, 23 Nov. 2005, pp. 22–23.

[71] Sariibrahimoglu, L., 'Turkey to buy Litening III targeting pods', *Jane's Defence Weekly*, 13 July 2005, p. 13.

[72] Ben-David, A., 'Israel to supply extra ERA kits', *Jane's Defence Weekly*, 3 Aug. 2005, p. 20.

[73] Turkey has shown a renewed interest in several other large orders such as the modernization of Turkish combat aircraft and tanks, air-to-ground missiles and the Arrow-2 ABM system. See Ben-David, A., 'Israeli industry is "back to business" with Turkey', *Jane's Defence Weekly*, 18 May 2005, p. 15.

[74] Pomper, M. A., 'US, Israel seek to cut deal on China arms sales', *Arms Control Today*, July–Aug. 2005, pp. 31–32; There are also a number of smaller Israeli markets. Viet Nam in autumn 2005 signed a deal for electronic warfare equipment while negotiations were ongoing for the sale of production technology for artillery shells with cluster sub-munitions. See Karniol, R., 'Israel bolsters EW business in Vietnam', *Jane's Defence Weekly*, 5 Oct. 2005, p. 7. Unmanned surface vehicles (USV) are among Israel's most exported products, and in 2004 Israel sold several Protector USVs to Singapore. See Scott, R., 'Singapore reveals Protector USV buy', *Jane's Defence Weekly*, 25 May 2005, p. 5.

[75] This would make Israel the second-largest supplier to India after Russia. Bedi, R., 'Indian conventional defence purchases soar', *Jane's Defence Weekly*, 14 Sep. 2005, p. 42.

[76] Russian sales to India are estimated at some $1.5 billion per year. Bedi (note 75).

UAVs, laser target designators, anti-tank missiles and a joint development of an extended-range Barak SAM for India and Indian-made Dhruv helicopters.[77] The Dhruv is being jointly marketed by India and Israel.[78] Israel also cooperates with foreign—especially Russian and Ukrainian—companies that sell to or modernize weapons in India.[79]

Indian arms acquisition policy is torn between pursuing domestic military production or increasing imports of arms. Many domestic projects have faced technical difficulties and been delayed. The Indian Government has stated that it might increase direct imports to quicken military deployment even though such a course runs contrary to its preference for a policy of self-reliance.[80] Should Israel become an increasingly important arms supplier and military–industrial partner to India—which is especially likely if it is acting in tandem with the USA—it is possible that Russia's trade with one of its major arms markets will be drastically reduced.[81]

Brazil, South Africa and India—competition or cooperation?

Brazil was in the 1980s an important exporter, with reported exports per year of $1.5 billion.[82] Today this has shrunk to some $400 million. In 2005 the Brazilian Government announced that it was a priority to increase the value of its arms exports, both for financial reasons and to support its aspirations to play a larger role in the world. The armed forces and private industries have drawn up a national defence industry programme designed to boost industrial capacity and increase exports with tax incentives, credits and joint research projects with universities and the private sector.[83]

South Africa's indigenous arms industry developed during the international embargo against the apartheid policy.[84] The country achieved moderate levels

---

[77] Ben-David, A. and Bedi, A., 'Equipment deals strengthen Israel–India ties', *Jane's Defence Weekly*, 19 Jan. 2005, p. 7.

[78] Ben-David, A. 'IAI and HAL pitch for US helicopter contract', *Jane's Defence Weekly*, 1 June 2005, p. 19.

[79] E.g., Israeli company Elbit joined Aviant of the Ukraine to modernize a large number of Indian An-32 transport aircraft for around $70 million. Novichkov, N., 'Aviant in line to upgrade Indian An-32s', *Jane's Defence Weekly*, 4 May 2005, p. 15.

[80] That statement was countered by a call from the Federation of Indian Chambers of Commerce and Industry to create more jobs by reducing imports. Anderson, G., 'India may purchase globally in order to "counter security threats"', *Jane's Defence Industry*, July 2005, p. 5; and Anderson, G., 'India faces calls to reduce military imports', *Jane's Defence Industry*, Aug. 2005, p. 11.

[81] Blank, S., 'Arms sales and technology transfer in Indo-Israeli relations', *Journal of East Asian Affairs*, vol. 19, no. 1 (2005), pp. 200–41; and Menon, R. and Pandey, S., 'An axis of democracy?', *The National Interest*, no. 80 (2005), pp. 29–36.

[82] Lehman, S., 'Brazil plans comeback of its once-lucrative defense industry', Associated Press, 7 Mar. 2005. However, according to SIPRI data, Brazil's deliveries never exceeded $250 million annually in the 1980s and were mostly based on sales to both sides in the Iraq–Iran War.

[83] 'Brazil looks for weapons export gains', *Jane's Defence Weekly*, 4 May 2005, p. 10. In Mar. 2005 Air Force General Antonio Hugo Pereira Chaves, Director of the Brazil MOD Logistics Department, said that 'a country without a strong defense industry is a country without a voice'. Lehman (note 82).

[84] Batchelor, P. and Willett, S., SIPRI, *Disarmament and Defence–Industrial Adjustment in South Africa* (Oxford: Oxford University Press, 1998).

of military deliveries in the 1980s and early 1990s. From the mid-1990s the main South African export products have been light and medium-weight armoured vehicles as well as new or modernized surplus equipment delivered to countries and organizations involved in peacekeeping operations.

In contrast to South Africa, *India* has not been successful in marketing its arms internationally. It has a large arms industry but imports over 70 per cent of its military equipment. A 2005 report by an independent committee set up in May 2004 by the new government made suggestions for improving Indian industrial performance, including a national offset policy, more private industries and increasing arms exports.[85]

As part of a wider policy of cooperation, Brazil, India and Israel have sought to coordinate or even pool their arms industrial resources to increase their respective capacities and arms exports. The India–Brazil–South Africa Dialogue Forum (IBSA) was inaugurated with the Declaration of Brasília, signed in June 2003 by the countries' three foreign ministers. The initiative is designed to allow for an exchange of views on regional and international issues and promote cooperation.[86] The countries have declared their commitment to 'cooperation in defence production, co-development, trade and joint marketing', and 'to explore coordination among the defence research institutions in the three countries and of their respective defence industries to provide inputs for the identification of concrete cooperation projects.'[87] One example is Brazil's industrial involvement in South Africa's development of the A-Darter air-to-air missile, which was selected by the Brazilian Air Force in early 2006.[88]

The prospects for the cooperation initiative were dealt a significant blow in October 2005 when India cancelled all contracts with South Africa's Denel company after a five-month investigation into allegations that the company had paid bribes to win Indian contracts.[89] Meanwhile, in all three countries domestic support for the principle of trilateralism seems limited. On the political left, the project's natural constituency, attitudes are divided between support, based on Southern solidarity, and strong resistance because of the project's advocacy of economic liberalization. In Brazil, right-wing parties, liberal camps within the Ministry of Foreign Affairs, and academics and representatives of business and agricultural sectors argue that the countries' inter-

[85] Bedi, 'Report urges kick-start to Indian defence sector', *Jane's Defence Weekly*, 20 Apr. 2005, p. 21.

[86] Alden, C., and Antonio Vieira, M., 'The new diplomacy of the South: South Africa, Brazil, India and trilateralism', *Third World Quarterly*, vol. 26, no. 7 (2005), pp. 1077–95.

[87] India–Brazil–South Africa (IBSA) Dialogue Forum Trilateral Commission Meeting, 'New Delhi agenda for cooperation and plan of action', URL <http://www.southcentre.org/info/southbulletin/bulletin75/bulletin75-05.htm>.

[88] 'Brazil picks A-Darter', *Flight International* (Internet edn), 14 Feb. 2006.

[89] Phasiwe, K., 'Denel bribe row deals blow to SA arms trade', *Business Day* (Internet edn), 4 Oct. 2005, URL <http://www.businessday.co.za/PrintFriendly.aspx?ID=BD4A98377>. The decision annulled a 3-year-old order for 400 anti-materiel rifles and a deal for the Bhim, a 155-mm tracked self-propelled gun, produced in India with Denel's support. The decision also affects Denel's involvement in the competition for 180 towed guns. See Helmoed-Römer, H., 'India backs off from Denel contracts', *Jane's Defence Weekly*, 12 Oct. 2005, p. 20.

ests would be better served by focusing on relations with the developed world.[90] In fact, the prospects for deeper cooperation are hampered by the fact that the defence industries of all three countries, particularly South Africa, cooperate with and sell military equipment to major arms-producing countries. For instance, in 2005 South African light armoured vehicles were sold in large numbers to Sweden, Italy and the USA. Some of these sales are the result of offset agreements tied to large South African arms imports. Others are a consequence of joint bidding on foreign contracts and transnational mergers and acquisitions involving South African and, not least, European companies.[91]

Iraq as recipient

Prior to the August 1990 Iraqi invasion of Kuwait, Iraq was among the most significant importers of major arms. Its five largest suppliers in the period 1970–90 were the Soviet Union, France, China, Czechoslovakia and Poland. After the invasion the UN Security Council (UNSC) put strict sanctions in place, banning countries from supplying Iraq with military equipment. With the revision of the arms embargo in June 2004, Iraq's government again became a legitimate customer. According to SIPRI data, Iraq was the 23rd largest recipient of major weapons in 2005, accounting for 1 per cent of the global volume. Despite this low figure, this brief survey of major orders and deliveries is warranted for two reasons. First, there is a good possibility that Iraq may regain its position as one of the region's largest importers of military equipment. Iraqi military forces are today almost exclusively reliant on arms imports, so a brief look at which companies and countries have been exporting weapons to Iraq since 2004 may give an indication of who might be the major suppliers in the future. Second, the USA's ability to fulfil its stated aim of withdrawing its forces from frontline combat and transferring security duties to Iraqi forces depends upon the development of adequately trained and equipped Iraqi forces.[92]

Recent procurement

Aside from salvaging equipment from the large pre-2003 Iraqi inventories, Iraq has since June 2004 obtained military equipment in three main ways: through purchases made by the Multinational Force command; from donations made by other countries; and via contracts issued by the Iraqi Government.[93] Prior to the transfer of sovereignty on 28 June 2004 the Coalition Provisional Authority administered contracts for the purchase of military equipment for Iraqi forces. Following the transfer of sovereignty, the Project and Contracting Organization (PCO) within the US embassy has managed the $18 billion in

[90] Alden and Antonio Vieira (note 86), p. 1091.

[91] Heitman, H-R., 'Opportunity knocks', *Jane's Defence Weekly*, 3 Aug. 2005, pp. 24–29.

[92] On the conflict in Iraq and the training of the Iraqi Security Forces see chapter 2 in this volume.

[93] Mroue, B., 'Iraqi military investigating bad purchases: officials open corruption probe', *Washington Times*, 10 Aug. 2005, p. 12.

assistance on behalf of Iraqi government agencies.[94] The Multinational Security Transition Command–Iraq (MNSTC–I) handles the task of training and equipping the Iraqi Security Forces.[95]

Among the largest contracts issued by the USA was a $259 million award in May 2004 to a Virginia-based company, Anham Joint Ventures, to equip and train the new Iraqi Army. The contract covered the delivery of various ground vehicles, handguns, and heavy and light machine guns.[96] In April 2005 it emerged that a consortium that had been awarded a $174.4 million contract by the US Army to supply weapons and communications equipment to the Iraqi Army had, with US approval, awarded a $29 million sub-contract to a Chinese state-owned company. In 1996 the same company was indicted in California in connection with the smuggling of 2000 AK-47 rifles into the USA.[97]

In addition, the Iraqi Government has received military aid from many countries. The UAE has donated 44 M-3 APCs to the Iraqi Army and Jordan has given 16 UH-1H helicopters.[98] The Coalition Military Assistance Training Team (CMATT) agreed to pay for the aircraft to be refurbished. Announced in February 2005, among the largest donations from Europe has been a gift of 77 second-hand T-72 tanks from Hungary under the auspices of the NATO Training Mission–Iraq (NTM-I). The US company Defense Solutions subsequently agreed a $3.4 million contract with the Iraqi Government to overhaul the tanks. The cost is likely to be covered by US military aid.[99]

Following the transfer of sovereignty in June 2004 the Iraqi Government began issuing its own contracts for military equipment. Poland again seems to be one of the largest suppliers. As of July 2005 the Iraqi Ministry of Defence (MOD) had reportedly awarded the Polish company Bumar 35 contracts worth $400 million.[100] These contracts included a $120–132 million agreement for 20 W-3 helicopters and another for $105 million covering the delivery of 24 second-hand Mi-8MTV helicopters.[101] However, when it became clear that the delivery of the W-3 would take several years, the order was reduced to two

[94] Pappalardo, J., 'US moves to rearm Iraq', *National Defense*, Oct. 2004, URL <http://www.nationaldefensemagazine.org/issues/2004/oct/US_Moves.htm>, p. 14.

[95] MNSTC–I, URL <http://www.mnstci.iraq.centcom.mil/mission.htm>.

[96] Scully, M., 'US company wins $259m deal to equip Iraqi army', *Defense News*, 31 May 2004, p. 22. According to press reports 'Ukrainian companies will supply 65 per cent of the contracted equipment, including some 1,500 16-soldier troop carriers and 2,000 six-soldier wagons'. See Warner, T., 'Ukraine will be main equipment supplier to army', *Financial Times*, 18 June 2004, p. 8; and 'Ukraine to supply 2,000 trucks to Iraq', Kiev Interfax-Ukraine, 14 July 2004, Foreign Broadcast Information Service (FBIS), FBIS-SOV-2004-0714, 14 June 2004.

[97] Landay, J. S., 'Chinese firm picked by US to arm Iraq tied to smuggling', *Pittsburgh Post-Gazette*, 28 Apr. 2005, p. A4.

[98] Baranauskas, T., 'Germany and the UAE helping equip new Iraqi military', *Forecast International Government & Industry Group*, 20 Dec. 2004, URL <http://www.forecast1.com>; and 'Air corps evolves from Jordan to back army in Iraq', *Jane's Defence Weekly*, 24 Mar. 2004, p. 14.

[99] Lockwood, D., 'Defense Solutions LLC to rebuild surplus Hungarian T-72 tanks for Iraq', *Forecast International Military Vehicles Forecast*, 10 May 2005; and 'UK supplies more equipment to Iraq', *Jane's Defence Weekly*, 8 June 2005, p. 18.

[100] Lockwood, D., 'Iraq orders armored vehicles from Poland', *Forecast International Military Vehicles Forecast*, 25 July 2005.

[101] 'Iraq's shopping spree in Poland', *Jane's Defence Weekly*, 22 Dec. 2004, p. 7.

helicopters and a new order for 10 Mi-17 helicopters from Russia was placed via Bumar.[102] During 2005 Poland also granted export licences for the sale of armoured personnel carriers (APCs) to Iraqi forces.

Poland's contracts with the Iraqi Government appear to be attributable in part to Poland's contribution of troops to the coalition forces stationed in Iraq.[103] Poland was largely unsuccessful in its attempts to win US-funded contracts for military equipment, which were mainly awarded to US-based companies. However, having a presence in the country and an experience of submitting bids gave Poland an advantage compared with its experience in 2004. Poland also reportedly benefited from the fact that the minister in charge of armaments in Iraq after the transfer of sovereignty, Ziad Cattan, had studied in Poland.[104]

Main issues

The USA has played an instrumental role in dictating the size and make-up of the future Iraqi security forces via its close involvement in all three methods of procurement.[105] This control is particularly apparent in the issuing of contracts for military equipment and the modernization and shipping of weapons donated by other states. US influence is also evident in the contracts issued by the Iraqi Government, since many of these were signed by the interim administration, a body whose members were largely chosen by the USA.[106]

Since the fall of Saddam Hussein's government the slow pace of the rearmament of Iraqi forces has been a consistent target of criticism.[107] According to Professor Andrew Terrill of the Strategic Studies Institute at the US Army War College, the USA was initially unwilling to transfer heavy equipment to Iraqi forces. The US plan was for an 'extremely weak Iraqi military' unable to threaten neighbours or to launch a coup against a US-backed Iraqi government.[108] However, many domestic issues influenced the creation of the Iraqi force, and by 2005 the initial fears had been overridden by an acknowledgement of the need to create an Iraqi force that was strong enough to survive a US withdrawal. Evidence of this was provided by the US-funded creation of an Iraqi heavy division, including two battalions of T-72 tanks, two of T-55

---

[102] Nikolsky, A., 'Russia will make some money from the war in Iraq', *Vedomosti* (Internet edn), 2 Aug. 2005.

[103] 'Iraq contract ban angers US allies', *International Herald Tribune*, 11 Dec. 2003, p. 1.

[104] Baczynski, N. R., Bumar CEO, 'Polish businesses afraid of doing business in Iraq, one arms sector exception', *Polityka* (Warsaw), 13 Nov 2004, translated from Polish by BBC Monitoring.

[105] Pappalardo, J., 'US moves to rearm Iraq', *National Defense*, Oct. 2004, URL <http://www.nationaldefensemagazine.org/issues/2004/oct/US_Moves.htm>, p. 14.

[106] Cockburn, P., 'What has happened to Iraq's missing $1bn?', *The Independent* (Internet edn), 19 Sep. 2005, URL <http://news.independent.co.uk/world/middle_east/article313538.ece>.

[107] Cordesman, A. H., *The Critical Role of Iraqi Military, Security, and Police Forces: Necessity, Problems, and Progress*, (Center for Strategic and International Studies: Washington, D.C., Oct. 2004), URL <http://www.csis.org/component/option,com_csis_pubs/task,view/id,1241>, p. 13.

[108] Grant, G., 'T-72s to bolster Iraqi military,' *Defense News* (Internet edn), 24 Oct. 2005.

tanks and five of BMP-1 IFVs. The bulk of this equipment was taken from Iraqi stocks.[109]

Even now there is a dearth of equipment, particularly of armoured vehicles, but the reasons for this are not clear. It might be a consequence of continued US resistance to supplying certain types of equipment,[110] or it may stem from troubles at the Iraqi MOD. In mid-2005 it emerged that the Iraqi procurement process may have been beset by corruption resulting in the theft of funds and the acquisition of outdated, inappropriate or non-functioning equipment.[111] Most of the alleged corruption relates to money allocated to purchase arms from Pakistan and Poland.[112]

In August 2005 the Swiss Government froze a sale to the UAE of 180 second-hand M-113 IFVs that were to be donated to Iraq. The Swiss authorities stated that the deal could not proceed until Iraq guaranteed that the vehicles would not be used in combat operations.[113] In October 2005 the UAE cancelled the deal, arguing that they could wait no longer for the delivery of the vehicles.[114] There are signs of similar qualms in other West European governments over the export of weapons to Iraq, a country in a state of conflict whose government has been frequently accused of human rights abuses. As long as individual European countries are in control of their arms export policies, the largest military suppliers to Iraq might include Central and East European countries such as Poland.

III. International arms embargoes

There were 21 international arms embargoes in force in 2005,[115] of which nine were mandatory UN embargoes and 12 were embargoes by smaller groups of states. Of these latter 12, nine were imposed by the EU, one by the Organization for Security and Cooperation in Europe (OSCE), one by the African Union (AU) and one by the Economic Community of West African States

---

[109] Grant (note 108).

[110] In Aug. 2005 the commander of the Iraqi ground forces, General Abdul Qader Mohammed Jassim, was reported as stating that his troops needed helicopters and artillery, weapons that US authorities claimed they did not require. See Smith, C. S., 'US wary of supplying heavy weapons to Iraq', New York Times, 29 Aug. 2005, p. 5.

[111] Cockburn (note 106); 'Iraqi arms buying rife with corruption', Knight Ridder, 15 July 2005; Allam, H., 'Audit of Iraqi arms deals finds widespread fraud', Philadelphia Inquirer, 14 Aug. 2005.

[112] In Oct. 2005 the Iraqi Government issued arrest warrants for a former defence minister and 22 other current and former officials, accusing them of involvement in the misappropriation of funds. There was more confusion when one of the accused claimed that only 4 or 5 officials deserved to be indicted. According to the director of human resources at the MOD, Mumtaz al-Obeidi, the remaining warrants were part of a bid by the 2 main Shiite parties to seize key MOD positions from independents and Sunnis. See Martin, P., 'Iraq accuses 23, cites graft in defense deals', Washington Times, 12 Oct. 2005, p. 1.

[113] 'Switzerland freezes armored vehicle deal with Iraq', Defense News (Internet edn), 15 Aug. 2005, URL <http://www.defensenews.com>.

[114] 'Tanks-for-Iraq deal cancelled', Swiss Information Service, 6 Oct. 2005, URL <http://www.defense-aerospace.com>.

[115] An international arms embargo is defined here as an embargo established by an international organization or a group of states. Embargoes imposed by single states are not discussed in this chapter.

(ECOWAS). The non-mandatory UN embargo on Afghanistan, established in 1996, has not been lifted, but it has not been observed since 2001.[116]

In 2005 ECOWAS and the AU for the first time established arms embargoes. On 19 February ECOWAS put in place a 'complete arms embargo' against *Togo* after Faure Gnassingbé, with the help of the armed forces, illegally became Togo's president following the death of his father.[117] The Commission of the AU first asked members on 20 February 2005 to support the ECOWAS sanctions; the AU then adopted the embargo itself on 25 February 2005.[118] The ECOWAS sanctions were lifted on 26 February, after Gnassingbé stepped down.[119] However, the AU sanctions remained in force until 28 May after Gnassingbé won the presidential elections.[120] Since these embargoes lasted for only a short period, it is not possible to assess whether non-ECOWAS and non-AU members would have abided by them.

UN embargoes

In 2005 no new UN embargoes were imposed and none was lifted. In July the UN Security Council rejected calls by the AU and the Intergovernmental Authority on Development (IGAD) to lift the arms embargo against *Somalia*. The AU and IGAD wanted the embargo to be lifted to enable them to deploy an armed peacekeeping force. However, the Security Council wanted Somalia's Transitional Federal Government, established as part of the 2004 peace agreement, to present a detailed plan on the country's security before it would consider lifting the embargo.[121] In the meantime, weapons were smuggled into Somalia. The president and head of the Transitional Federal Government boasted that he was procuring weapons for his forces, and the UN identified groups on the opposition side that were acquiring weapons, including larger systems such as anti-aircraft guns.[122]

---

[116] A full list of international arms embargoes is available at the SIPRI Arms Transfers Project web page, URL <http://www.sipri.org/contents/armstrad/embargoes.html>.

[117] 'ECOWAS imposes sanctions on Togo', *Xinhuanet*, 19 Feb. 2005, URL <http://news.xinhuanet.com/english/2005-02/20/content_2595727.htm>.

[118] 'Togo prepares elections, Gnassingbé stays in power', *Afrol News*, 21 Feb. 2005, URL <http://www.afrol.com/articles/15678>; 'AU calls for wider Togo sanctions', BBC News Online, 25 Feb. 2005, URL <http://news.bbc.co.uk/2/4297183.stm>; 'AU slaps Togo with sanctions', *IOL* (Internet), 25 Feb. 2005, URL <http://www.iol.co.za>; and 'African Union demands Togo guarantee fair elections after president resigns', Associated Press, 26 Feb. 2005, URL <http://www.signonsandiego.com/news/world/20050226-1030-togo.html>. The AU, however, does not have any formal announcement on the imposition of an arms embargo on its website.

[119] 'Ecowas lifts Togo sanctions', *News24.com*, 26 Feb. 2005, URL <http://www.news24.com/News24/0,,2-11-1447_1668384,00.html>.

[120] Blunt, E., 'African Union lifts Togo embargo', BBC News Online, 27 May 2005, URL <http://news.bbc.co.uk/2/4588281.stm>. However, the 27 May communiqué from the AU does not explicitly mention lifting the AU sanctions. African Union, Communiqué of the 30th meeting of the Peace and Security Council, Addis Ababa, 27 May 2005, URL <http://www.africa-union.org/psc/30th/30th Communiqué _Eng.pdf>.

[121] Blanch, E., 'Renewed civil war feared in Somalia', *Jane's Intelligence Review*, vol. 17, no. 8 (Aug. 2005), p. 4; and Kucera, J., 'Somalia likely to get fewer peacekeepers', *Jane's Defence Weekly*, 5 Oct. 2005, p. 6.

[122] Blanch (note 121).

The UN embargo on the *Democratic Republic of the Congo* (DRC) was, according to a Security Council expert group, repeatedly broken. The group's January 2005 report accused Uganda of having sold weapons in 2004 in exchange for minerals. Uganda denied supplying weapons to anyone in the DRC.[123] Evidence was also found of breaches of the embargo on *Côte d'Ivoire*, with a Danish-registered ship delivering 22 'military vehicles' for Ivorian forces. The UN forces confiscated the vehicles, but their origin was unclear.[124]

EU embargoes

Nine EU embargoes were in effect in 2005.[125] On 14 November *Uzbekistan* became the target of an EU embargo after its government refused to allow an independent international investigation of the violent suppression of peaceful anti-government demonstrations in May 2005.[126]

The heated inter-EU and Euro-Atlantic discussions about a possible lifting of the EU embargo against *China* cooled in 2005. There remained much debate in the first half of the year, with the USA arguing to keep the embargo and threatening to restrict exports of arms and other sensitive technologies to any country exporting arms to China, and to prohibit US Government agencies from doing business with any company that sells arms to China for five years.[127] However, by mid-2005 developments in UK and German domestic politics had more or less edged the issue from the EU agenda.

IV. Reporting and transparency in arms transfers

The financial value of the international arms trade

The SIPRI trend-indicator value was not developed to assess the economic magnitude of national arms markets or of the global market.[128] However, by adding financial data released by supplier governments it is possible to arrive at a rough estimate of the financial value of the global arms trade. That value for 2004, the most recent year for which data are available, is estimated at $44–53 billion. This accounts for 0.5–0.6 per cent of total world trade.[129] The

---

[123] 'Operation Kisanja', *Africa Confidential*, 4 Feb. 2005, p. 5.

[124] 'Arms embargo breach threatens Ivory Coast truce', *Sunday Telegraph*, 17 July 2005, p. 27.

[125] The EU embargo against Bosnia and Herzegovina was lifted in Jan. 2006.

[126] Council of the European Union, 'Council Common Position 2005/792/CFSP of 14 November 2005 concerning restrictive measures against Uzbekistan', *Official Journal of the European Union*, L299 (16 Nov. 2005), URL <http://europa.eu.int/eur-lex/lex/JOIndex.do>.

[127] E.g., the US Department of Defense report on China's military power gave several arguments to keep the embargo, all related to military power, not to human rights. US Department of Defense (note 42); and Murphy, J., 'US warns EU over risks of lifting arms on China', *Jane's Defence Weekly*, 27 July 2005, p. 19.

[128] See note 1.

[129] Total world exports in 2004 amounted to $9045 billion. International Monetary Fund, International financial statistics online, URL <http://ifs.apdi.net/imf>.

comparability of these national data is limited because of differences in data collection methodologies and conflicting definitions of 'arms' and 'military equipment'.

For the first time in several years this chapter includes a table of government and industry data on the financial value of countries' arms exports (table 10.2).

International transparency

The two main international mechanisms for public transparency in arms transfers are the UN Register of Conventional Arms (UNROCA), introduced in 1992, and the Annual Report according to Operative Provision 8 of the 1998 EU Code of Conduct on Arms Exports, produced since 1999.

The UN Register of Conventional Arms

The total number of UNROCA responses in 2005 was approximately 120, a similar figure to previous years.[130] The regions from which there was the lowest response were the same as in recent years: the Middle East (where almost no country reported), Africa, and North-East Asia, where China has not reported since 1998. North Korea has never reported, and the UN does not ask Taiwan to report.

The UNROCA showed large discrepancies in reported data between exports and imports. Furthermore, the criteria that different countries used to decide which weapons to report and how a 'transfer' is defined remain at variance. Some states, for example Australia and Sweden, continue to refuse to report the number of imported and/or exported Category VII items—that is, missiles and missile launchers, which since 2003 include man-portable defence systems (MANPADS)—or those in the national inventory. Others, such as the UK, reported numbers of at least some UNROCA-defined missiles and launchers, albeit not all and not always clearly specifying whether numbers of missiles or numbers of launchers were being reported.[131]

There are signs of political fatigue with regard to UNROCA reporting, visible even among some strong supporters of the principle of transparency in arms transfers. For instance, the British report was in several respects a return to less transparency.[132] Private discussions between the authors and officials in several European countries revealed that many see limited value in transparency mechanisms like the UNROCA.

---

[130] Data reported to the UNROCA since 1992 are available at URL <http://disarmament.un.org/cab/register.html>.

[131] The UK reported numbers of several types of missiles. The air-launched missiles it reported are known from other sources as those in use with the British Royal Air Force. Numbers of SAMs reported were for launchers only, not for missiles. The UK did not report ship-launched missiles in service (e.g., the Harpoon anti-ship missile or the BGM-109 land-attack missile).

[132] No data were provided on imports, the export data were partly wrong (the delivery of 24 Hawk Mk-132 aircraft to India was noted, even though these aircraft had not been produced as of the end of 2005), and data on procurement from national production was noted as included but is actually missing.

Table 10.2. The financial value of arms exports according to national government and industry sources, 1998–2004

Figures are in US$ m., at constant (2003) prices.

Country[a]	1998	1999	2000	2001	2002	2003	2004	Stated data coverage
Australia	10	368	23	53	..	..	..	Shipments of military goods (covers 1 July to 30 June)
Austria	262	465	554	359	226	278	19	Licences for arms exports
Belgium	815	732	767	789	1 106	752	658	Licences for arms exports
Brazil	79	441	191	301	171	49	278	Defence exports
Canada	320	323	344	397	442	..	..	Shipments of military goods (excluding exports to the USA)
Czech Republic	115	106	86	56	74	94	109	Arms exports
Denmark	..	..	..	71	109	90	123	Licenses issued for weapons exports
Finland	39	47	23	37	52	55	51	Arms exports
France	7 422	4 457	2 671	2 947	4 265	4 854	8 667	Deliveries of arms and associated services
Germany	858	1 711	670	341	307	1 505	1 366	Exports of 'weapons of war'
Greece	..	51	21	47	50	126	18	Licences for arms exports
India	38	19	..	..	48	94	66	Military export earnings (covers 1 Apr. to 31 Mar.)
Ireland	25	71	31	50	35	40	33	Licences for arms exports
Israel	2 120	1 774	1 885	2 078	2 045	2 350	2 532	Defence export deliveries
Italy	131	1 043	595	515	470	711	581	Deliveries of military equipment
Korea, South	166	218	59	208	..	240	409	Arms exports
Lithuania	0	0	0	0	13	..	4	Licences for arms exports
Netherlands	542	431	411	605	434	1 299	755	Export licences for military goods
Norway	155	174	129	185	294	427	291	Actual deliveries of defence materiel
Pakistan	..	33	43	83	102	100	97	Arms exports
Portugal	19	13	13	10	6	28	18	Arms exports
Romania	63	74	41	26	45	70	41	Arms exports
Russia	2 933	3 744	3 931	3 849	4 929	5 400	5 629	Exports of military equipment
Slovakia	41	61	47	97	32	42	75	Licences granted for the export of military material
Slovenia	7	1	3	4	2	2	1	Arms export licences
South Africa	132	198	213	210	249	410	..	Export permits issued

Spain	206	166	136	215	265	432	491	Exports of defence materiel
Sweden	499	488	510	308	361	801	966	Actual deliveries of military equipment
	629	521	666	503	690	1 182	1 371	Exports of military and other goods, services and software to military users
Switzerland	166	171	135	159	182	281	315	Exports of war materiel
Taiwan	0	0	<1	<1	2	<1	<1	Weapons exports
Turkey	90	93	131	139	254	331	191	Arms exports
UK	3 676	1 753	2 781	2 292	1 444	1 621	2 481	Exports of military equipment
	11 264	7 515	7 121	6 302	6 317	7 427	9 208	Deliveries of defence materiel and other aerospace equipment and services
Ukraine	338	..	534	519	511	500	..	Arms exports
USA	19 428	19 947	13 855	10 049	10 528	13 327	18 071	Arms deliveries
	14 869	19 375	11 657	13 321	10 821	12 043	17 822	Foreign military sales deliveries added to licensed commercial exports (covers 1 Oct. to 30 Sep.)
World total[b]	37 720–48 789	37 025–45 202	32 785–35 589	27 001–33 897	29 290–38 407	37 207–43 041	44 219–53 271	

.. = No data available.

Note: Conversion to constant (2003) US$ is made using the market exchange rates of the reporting year and the US consumer price index (CPI). National arms export data are not entirely reliable or comparable. Data are collected using different criteria: in certain cases, data are based on information supplied by industry on the value of their arms exports. In other cases they are based on the value of goods identified as military equipment that pass through customs in a given year. Secondly, the list of goods covered by the data collection mechanism can differ drastically. For instance, the German figure on the value of 'weapons of war' covers only a subset of licensed exports of military equipment from Germany.

[a] Countries have only been included in the table if official data are available for at least 4 of the 7 years covered.

[b] According to the SIPRI Arms Transfers Database, the countries covered in this table account for over 90% of the total volume of deliveries of major conventional weapons. By adding together the financial value of their arms exports it is possible to estimate the financial value of the global arms trade. Because certain countries release more than one figure on the value of their arms exports, this estimate can only be a range, including the aggregates of the lowest and the highest reported values. For certain countries and certain years official data are unavailable and estimates have been made on the assumption that the rate of change in a country for which data are missing is the same as the average in the sample as a whole. Before calculating the world total, all national figures have been converted to calendar years, assuming equal distribution during relevant years.

Source: Data are based on reports by, direct quotes from, or direct communication with, governments or official industry bodies. For certain countries data on the value of arms export licences have been used because these are the only figures available. For the list of sources used, and all available financial data on arms exports, see URL <http://www.sipri.org/contents/armstrad/at_gov_ind_data.html>.

The EU Code of Conduct on Arms Exports

In December 2005 the EU published its Seventh Annual Report on the implementation of the EU Code of Conduct on Arms Exports.[133] In 2004 member states agreed that 'breakdowns of licences and actual exports by [EU] Military List category (if available) should also be included in the report'.[134] The number of states submitting data on the financial value of either licences granted or actual exports per destination, disaggregated by the 22 categories of the EU Common Military List, rose from 11 in the Sixth Annual Report to 20 in the Seventh Annual Report. Of those 20 countries, 13 submitted disaggregated data on both licences granted and actual exports while the rest submitted data on only one of the two categories.

The 10 states that joined the EU in May 2004 all submitted financial data on either the value of licences granted or the value of national exports, disaggregated by EU Military List categories and by country of destination. This is a notable achievement, given that this is only the second year that these states have been asked to submit data to the EU Annual Report and only the first year that they have been obliged to do so.[135] It is also a significant improvement in both the comprehensiveness and the comparability of national data in the EU Annual Report. Even so, the question remains regarding the usefulness of financial data, as opposed to descriptions of the goods involved, for assessing how states are interpreting and applying the criteria of the Code.[136]

National transparency

In February 2005 *Estonia* published its first annual report on arms exports, detailing activities in 2004. The report, published in Estonian and English, provides information on licences granted for the import, export and transit of military equipment and dual-use goods. It details the category of the goods, their value and their destination.[137] In February 2005 *Bosnia and Herzegovina* published its first report on arms exports. Available in Bosnian with an English summary, the report provides information on licences granted for the import, export and transit of military equipment. The report gives the category

[133] Council of the European Union, 'Seventh Annual Report according to Operative Provision 8 of the European Union Code of Conduct on Arms Exports', *Official Journal of the European Union*, C328 (23 Dec. 2005), URL <http://europa.eu.int/eur-lex/lex/JOIndex.do>.

[134] Working Party on Conventional Arms Exports (COARM), Operational conclusions of the meeting of 22 June 2004.

[135] The Sixth Annual Report, released in 2004, covered export licences issued and actual exports in 2003. Cyprus, the Czech Republic, Estonia, Hungary, Latvia, Lithuania, Malta, Poland, Slovakia and Slovenia, who joined the EU on 1 May 2004, were therefore not obliged to submit data. Rather, they were invited to submit figures for 2003 if they were available, which 8 of them did.

[136] See Bauer, S. and Bromley, M., *The European Code of Conduct on Arms Exports: Improving the Annual Report*, SIPRI Policy Paper no. 8 (SIPRI: Stockholm, Nov. 2004), URL <http://www.sipri.org>.

[137] Estonia Ministry of Foreign Affairs, 'Strategic Goods Commission activity report year 2004', 10 Feb. 2005, URL <http://www.vm.ee/eng/kat_153>. For this report and other national data on arms transfers see the SIPRI website, URL <http://www.sipri.org/contents/armstrad/atlinks_gov.html>.

of the goods, a brief description and their destination.[138] In June 2005 *Slovakia* passed a new arms export control law. The law gave the Ministry of Economy a mandate to produce an annual report on arms exports. The first report, covering activities during 2004, was released to the public in January 2006.[139]

Ukraine also published its first report on arms exports in January 2006. The report, covering activities during 2004, is available only in Ukrainian. It reproduces Ukraine's submission to the UNROCA; provides details on the number of small arms and light weapons (SALW) exported worldwide, broken down by category and destination; and gives the total number of import, export and transit licences granted for military and dual-use goods.

As illustrated by the UK's case above, 2005 also provided evidence that advances made in national transparency in one year may be reversed and that maintaining existing levels of openness requires an ongoing commitment by governments.[140] In September 2003 the Government of *Belgium* transferred powers over granting export licences for military equipment from the federal level to the three regional governments (Wallonia, Flanders and Brussels).[141] It also transferred responsibility for reporting on arms exports to these bodies, so there are now three separate reports on arms exports. In certain areas the change led to an increase in the level of transparency. For example, the Flanders report on arms exports is published more often than the Belgian national report was and includes more detail. However, the three reports do not cover the same time periods and use different methods of reporting. In addition, the Wallonian and Brussels reports are not as complete and informative as some Belgian national reports have been and are harder to access since they are not published on the Internet. It may therefore be concluded that there has been a decrease in the overall transparency of Belgian arms exports.

To increase comparability with the rest of Europe, the annual report of *Sweden* began classifying Swedish arms export data according to the EU Common Military List.[142] However, the 22 categories of the EU List are far broader than the 36 categories of Sweden's Military Equipment Classification List, which the report previously employed. It has therefore become harder to identify which weapons are being licensed for export and are exported.

Canada has not published an annual report since that of December 2003, which detailed exports in 2002.[143] Similarly, *Australia* has not published an

---

[138] Bosnia and Herzegovina Ministry of Foreign Trade and Economic Relations. *Informacija o ozdatim dozvolama za izvoz/uvoz naoružanja i vojne opreme u 2004. godini* [Report on arms export control 2004]. This report, as well as all other national, regional and international reporting mechanisms, are available at URL <http://www.sipri.org/contents/armstrad/atlinks_gov.html>.

[139] Dlhopolcekova, J., Slovak Ministry of Economy, Communication with the authors, 26 Jan. 2006. Available at URL <http://www.sipri.org/contents/armstrad/atlinks_gov.html>.

[140] See chapter 6 in this volume.

[141] Anthony, I. and Bauer, S., 'Transfer controls and destruction programmes', *SIPRI Yearbook 2004: Armaments, Disarmament and International Security* (Oxford University Press: Oxford, 2004), p. 750.

[142] Swedish Ministry of Foreign Affairs, 'Sweden's export control policy in 2004', Government communication 2004/05:114, 17 March 2005, URL <http://www.isp.se/sa/node. asp?node=528>, p. 42,

[143] Canadian Export Controls Division, Export and Import Controls Bureau, Department of Foreign Affairs and International Trade, 'Export of military goods from Canada: annual report 2002', Dec. 2003, URL <http://www.dfait-maeci.gc.ca/trade/eicb/military/milit_tech-en.asp>.

annual report since February 2003.[144] In both cases, delays are a result of logistical rather than policy constraints and new reports are expected in 2006. However, in August 2005 it was revealed that the *South African* report on arms exports in 2003 and 2004 had been classified and released only to members of the South African Parliament's Portfolio Committee on Defence, 'because some contracting countries do not want their purchases publicised'.[145]

V. Conclusions

For the past three years there has been an increase in the volume of major arms transfers as reflected in the SIPRI trend-indicator value and in arms exports according to aggregated national statistics. Russia and the USA in the period 2001–2005 each accounted for roughly 30 per cent of global deliveries of major weapons.

The experiences of Brazil, India and South Africa suggest that cooperation among minor suppliers to strengthen their international market positions is easier said than done. Deliveries of major weapons to Iraq further suggest that smaller suppliers outside Europe and North America have been unsuccessful in that market and may continue to be so. Poland, however, may remain an important European supplier to Iraq.

The search for new markets and the drive to maintain existing markets sharpen international competition. In some cases this supports 'commercial pragmatism' in national implementations of export policy, that is, markets that are not under international embargoes are open markets. Pragmatic attitudes may also be hardened by US attempts to make other arms suppliers accept its basic export control policy. Suppliers in Europe, Israel and China were in 2005 exposed to US re-export controls or sanctions.

There is evidence of political fatigue in some governments with regard to their commitment to transparency and the UNROCA mechanism. Moreover, the use of the categories of the Military List in national reporting by EU member states means that difficulties will remain in assessing how states interpret and apply the criteria of the Code of Conduct. It would be detrimental to developments in transparency if a tendency towards commercial pragmatism in national arms export policy should spread and reduce political willingness to report on national arms exports. There is also a danger that the ambition to achieve greater multinational harmonization in the format of reporting could inadvertently cloud understanding of the data reported.

---

[144] Australian Department of Defence, Defence Trade Control and Compliance Division, *Annual Report: Exports of Defence and Strategic Goods from Australia 2001/2002*, Feb. 2003, URL <http://www.defence.gov.au/strategy/dtcc/reports.htm>.

[145] According to Dumisani Dladla, acting director of the Conventional Arms Control Directorate, quoted in Honey, P., 'Arms sales kept "secret"', *Sunday Times* (Johannesburg, Online edn), 11 Aug. 2005, URL <http://www.suntimes.co.za/zones/sundaytimesNEW/business/business1123753234.aspx>.

Appendix 10A. The volume of transfers of major conventional weapons: by recipients and suppliers, 2001–2005

BJÖRN HAGELIN, MARK BROMLEY
and SIEMON T. WEZEMAN

Table 10A.1 The recipients of major conventional weapons, 2001–2005

The table includes all countries and non-state actors with imports of major conventional weapons in the five-year period 2001–2005. Ranking is according to the 2001–2005 aggregate imports. Figures are SIPRI trend-indicator values expressed in US$ m. at constant (1990) prices. Figures may not add up because of the conventions of rounding.

Rank order								
2001–2005	2000–2004[a]	Recipient	2001	2002	2003	2004	2005	2001–2005
1	1	China	3 142	2 647	2 096	2 761	2 697	13 343
2	2	India	875	1 655	2 883	2 471	1 471	9 355
3	3	Greece	709	495	2 131	1 656	1 114	6 105
4	8	UAE	178	194	791	1 323	2 381	4 867
5	4	UK	1 263	675	698	197	94	2 927
6	5	Egypt	819	598	520	368	596	2 901
7	13	Israel	147	239	333	732	1 422	2 873
8	6	Turkey	389	871	570	224	746	2 800
9	7	South Korea	508	336	401	772	544	2 561
10	9	Australia	657	459	471	360	396	2 343
11	12	USA	232	432	654	508	387	2 213
12	10	Iran	491	455	473	321	403	2 143
13	11	Pakistan	364	574	615	351	161	2 065
14	14	Taiwan	434	314	116	341	777	1 982
15	20	Saudi Arabia	56	538	120	544	470	1 728
16	17	Italy	262	165	516	439	224	1 606
17	18	Japan	333	307	351	298	250	1 539
18	19	Singapore	184	227	61	487	423	1 382
19	16	Algeria	531	221	188	292	149	1 381
20	15	Canada	455	369	129	314	112	1 379
21	21	Yemen	92	603	40	352	289	1 376
22	22	Poland	71	276	427	251	96	1 121
23	23	Spain	183	249	113	206	281	1 032
24	24	Brazil	522	165	74	121	142	1 024
25	52	Romania	19	16	18	275	579	907
26	25	Netherlands	159	279	172	151	129	890
27	54	Czech Republic	71	58	115	9	630	883
28	46	Malaysia	23	135	122	81	467	828
29	37	Chile	44	73	176	43	456	792
30	40	Viet Nam	71	123	32	259	291	776
31	26	Jordan	155	122	290	174	23	764

Rank order

2001–2005	2000–2004[a]	Recipient	2001	2002	2003	2004	2005	2001–2005
32	30	Germany	146	68	44	207	216	681
33	89	South Africa	22	4	2	2	606	636
34	28	Indonesia	24	61	356	150	19	610
35	32	Thailand	121	149	133	103	98	604
36	56	Peru	161	5	22	47	368	603
37	33	Sudan	146	57	102	270	–	575
38	31	Colombia	254	161	115	11	11	552
39	55	Eritrea	60	2	–	202	276	540
40	35	Denmark	125	57	71	206	78	537
41	68	Portugal	15	–	60	44	406	525
42	48	Switzerland	53	53	98	172	144	520
43	42	Myanmar (Burma)	170	238	62	–	20	490
44	29	Mexico	144	42	30	224	35	475
45	34	Sweden	163	74	63	48	104	452
46	27	Finland	10	16	222	78	77	403
47	41	Angola	322	29	2	8	22	383
48	39	Ethiopia	–	20	193	162	–	375
49	50	Libya	145	–	145	74	–	364
50	83	Iraq	–	–	–	53	290	343
51	49	Kazakhstan	31	83	62	46	68	290
52	43	Bangladesh	164	39	9	26	27	265
53	36	Norway	148	90	4	6	9	257
54	45	Argentina	2	16	12	160	67	257
55	59	Oman	16	62	21	41	98	238
56	79	Tunisia	11	49	–	–	156	216
57	61	New Zealand	45	17	100	42	8	212
58	53	Morocco	5	168	–	–	32	205
59	60	Afghanistan/NA[b]	203	–	–	–	–	203
60	57	France	16	38	53	89	3	199
61	62	Austria	15	66	42	55	21	199
62	111	Bulgaria	–	–	2	12	158	172
63	58	Venezuela	86	50	13	14	7	170
64	51	Kuwait	48	18	49	–	55	170
65	47	Sri Lanka	117	11	12	16	8	164
66	63	Armenia	–	–	–	151	–	151
67	67	Cyprus	121	11	8	–	–	140
68	66	Azerbaijan	–	140	–	–	–	140
69	65	Macedonia	133	–	–	–	–	133
70	64	Belgium	33	35	27	17	–	112
71	70	Côte d'Ivoire	–	29	66	14	–	109
72	44	Bahrain	31	58	6	10	–	105
73	72	Croatia	70	2	24	8	–	104
74	74	Ireland	42	23	–	28	4	97
75	81	Philippines	7	5	8	37	38	95
76	73	Georgia	80	–	2	12	–	94
77	75	Slovenia	56	2	15	15	2	90
78	71	Congo, DRC	39	14	15	–	14	82
79	76	Lithuania	15	7	1	48	9	80

Rank order

2001– 2005	2000– 2004[a]	Recipient	2001	2002	2003	2004	2005	2001–2005
80	38	Syria	13	13	40	13	–	79
81	69	Nigeria	7	6	52	10	–	75
82	78	Latvia	13	8	28	15	7	71
83	87	Afghanistan	–	31	17	–	22	70
84	77	Uganda	–	22	19	26	–	67
85	80	Nepal	11	8	9	32	–	60
86	103	Ecuador	–	1	–	19	33	53
87	92	Namibia	18	11	–	13	–	42
88	94	Ghana	8	1	4	27	–	40
89	86	Qatar	12	12	10	–	–	34
90	93	Laos	34	–	–	–	–	34
91	90	North Korea	23	3	3	3	2	34
92	130	Albania	–	–	2	–	31	33
93	95	Zimbabwe	8	–	23	–	–	31
94	88	Estonia	–	1	15	5	10	31
95	91	Dominican Republic	1	–	3	27	–	31
96	97	Turkmenistan	–	–	20	10	–	30
97	107	Uruguay	–	11	–	–	18	29
98	96	Hungary	14	–	–	3	12	29
99	84	Botswana	12	1	7	9	–	29
100	100	Serbia and Montenegro	27	–	–	–	–	27
101	98	Slovakia	–	27	–	–	–	27
102	101	El Salvador	–	16	9	–	–	25
103	141	Kenya	–	–	–	–	25	25
104	104	Unknown country[c]	20	–	–	3	–	23
105	144	Burkina Faso	–	–	–	–	19	19
106	140	Malta	–	–	–	–	18	18
107	110	Kyrgyzstan	–	–	9	5	3	17
108	105	Equatorial Guinea	8	–	–	8	–	16
109	108	Chad	15	–	–	–	–	15
110	114	Paraguay	6	–	–	4	1	11
111	113	Uzbekistan	5	5	–	–	–	10
112	106	Bolivia	–	–	–	1	9	10
113	118	Lesotho	6	–	–	1	–	7
114	119	Gambia	–	–	–	7	–	7
115	120	Cameroon	1	6	–	–	–	7
116	121	Guyana	6	–	–	–	–	6
117	102	Guinea	5	–	1	–	–	6
118	122	Benin	–	6	–	–	–	6
119	123	Tanzania	–	–	5	–	–	5
120	124	Gabon	–	–	–	5	–	5
121	125	Burundi	1	4	–	–	–	5
122	127	Brunei	4	–	–	–	–	4
123	128	Djibouti	–	2	–	–	–	2
124	131	Lebanon/Hizbollah[b]	–	–	–	1	–	1
125	99	Zambia	–	1	–	–	–	1
126	112	Trinidad and Tobago	1	–	–	–	–	1
127	129	Swaziland	1	–	–	–	–	1

Rank order								
2001– 2005	2000– 2004[a]	Recipient	2001	2002	2003	2004	2005	2001–2005
128	132	Mozambique	–	–	1	–	–	1
129	116	Mali	–	1	–	–	–	1
130	133	Luxembourg	–	–	1	–	–	1
131	126	Lebanon	–	–	–	–	1	1
132	136	Unknown rebel group[c]	–	–	–	–	–	–
133	137	Uganda/LRA[b]	–	–	–	–	–	–
134	138	Macedonia/NLA[b]	–	–	–	–	–	–
135	85	United Nations[d]	–	–	–	–	–	–
136	109	Rwanda	–	–	–	–	–	–
137	139	Panama	–	–	–	–	–	–
138	115	Mauritania	–	–	–	–	–	–
139	117	Liberia	–	–	–	–	–	–
140	142	Congo	–	–	–	–	–	–
141	134	Cape Verde	–	–	–	–	–	–
142	135	Belize	–	–	–	–	–	–
143	143	Bhutan	–	–	–	–	–	–
144	82	Bahamas	–	–	–	–	–	–
		Total	**17 334**	**16 136**	**18 245**	**19 836**	**21 965**	**93 516**

– = between 0 and 0.5.

[a] The rank order for recipients in 2000–2004 differs from that published in *SIPRI Yearbook 2005* (pp. 449–52) because of subsequent revision of figures for these years.

[b] Non-state actor/rebel group: NA = Northern Alliance (UFSA, United Islamic Front for the Salvation of Afghanistan); LTTE = Liberation Tigers of Tamil Eelam; NLA = National Liberation Army.

[c] One or more unknown recipient(s).

[d] Non-state actor/international organization.

Note: The SIPRI data on arms transfers relate to actual deliveries of major conventional weapons. To permit comparison between the data on such deliveries of different weapons and to identify general trends, SIPRI uses a *trend-indicator value*. This value is only an indicator of the volume of international arms transfers and not of the financial values of such transfers. Thus, it is not comparable to economic statistics such as gross domestic product or export/ import figures. The method for calculating the trend-indicator value is described in appendix 10C and on the SIPRI Arms Transfers Project website, URL <http://www.sipri.org/ contents/armstrad/atmethods.html>.

Source: SIPRI Arms Transfers Database.

Table 10A.2. The suppliers of major conventional weapons, 2001–2005

The list includes all countries and non-state actors with exports of major conventional weapons in the period 2001–2005. Ranking is according to the 2001–2005 aggregate exports. Figures are SIPRI trend-indicator values expressed in US$ m. at constant (1990) prices. Figures may not add up because of the conventions of rounding.

Rank order								
2001–2005	2000–2004[a]	Supplier	2001	2002	2003	2004	2005	2001–2005
1	2	Russia	5 548	5 656	5 567	6 440	5 771	28 982
2	1	USA	5 516	4 662	5 139	5 818	7 101	28 236
3	3	France	1 133	1 259	1 268	2 514	2 399	8 573
4	4	Germany	640	632	1 639	837	1 855	5 603
5	5	UK	1 070	708	567	797	791	3 933
6	6	Ukraine	702	281	536	519	188	2 226
7	7	Canada	110	351	568	577	365	1 971
8	11	Netherlands	190	249	339	250	840	1 868
9	12	Italy	185	332	310	204	827	1 858
10	10	Sweden	459	114	271	324	592	1 760
11	8	China	408	472	428	146	129	1 583
12	9	Israel	264	354	292	401	160	1 471
13	14	Uzbekistan	–	73	340	170	–	583
14	13	Belarus	299	53	80	50	–	482
15	15	Spain	7	120	158	73	113	471
16	20	Poland	70	36	70	55	124	355
17	16	South Korea	165	–	114	20	38	337
18	19	Norway	45	91	83	64	13	296
19	21	Switzerland	29	15	39	119	74	276
20	17	Czech Republic	89	58	65	–	10	222
21	35	Belgium	21	20	–	–	173	214
22	18	Slovakia	73	44	–	79	–	196
23	26	Australia	43	30	40	2	50	165
24	22	Georgia	22	120	–	7	–	149
25	31	Brazil	–	31	–	56	62	149
26	23	North Korea	77	45	13	13	–	148
27	25	South Africa	25	13	30	37	39	144
28	27	Turkey	2	23	38	28	28	119
29	24	Austria	23	81	3	3	3	113
30	30	Indonesia	16	49	–	25	8	98
31	33	Finland	12	18	23	23	22	98
32	29	Kyrgyzstan	–	–	92	–	–	92
33	32	Bulgaria	4	32	48	–	–	84
34	28	Unknown country[b]	19	28	–	4	20	71
35	34	Singapore	–	2	–	66	3	71
36	66	Hungary	–	–	–	–	70	70
37	37	Jordan	–	–	–	47	15	62
38	36	Libya	–	11	38	–	–	49
39	38	Lebanon	–	45	–	–	–	45
40	43	Romania	–	–	22	–	17	39
41	65	Saudi Arabia	–	–	–	–	36	36
42	42	Pakistan	–	9	9	8	9	35
43	39	India	2	–	4	22	–	28

Rank order

2001–2005	2000–2004[a]	Supplier	2001	2002	2003	2004	2005	2001–2005
44	44	Egypt	25	–	–	–	–	25
45	40	Denmark	–	6	2	6	2	16
46	45	Peru	4	5	–	5	–	14
47	41	Kazakhstan	9	–	–	5	–	14
48	57	UAE	–	–	–	2	10	12
49	46	Thailand	–	–	5	5	–	10
50	47	Malta	–	–	–	10	–	10
51	48	Greece	2	–	8	–	–	10
52	49	Moldova	5	–	–	–	4	9
53	50	Serbia and Montenegro	7	–	–	–	–	7
54	51	Taiwan	6	–	–	–	–	6
55	53	Bosnia and Herzegovina	–	4	–	–	–	4
56	52	Argentina	4	–	–	–	–	4
57	55	Lithuania	–	3	–	–	–	3
58	54	New Zealand	–	1	–	1	–	2
59	56	Chile	–	2	–	–	–	2
60	59	Bahrain	2	–	–	–	–	2
61	60	Venezuela	–	–	–	1	–	1
62	63	Iran	–	–	–	1	–	1
63	64	Angola	–	1	–	–	–	1
64	61	Uruguay	–	–	–	–	–	–
65	62	Malawi	–	–	–	–	–	–
66	58	Croatia	–	–	–	–	–	–
		Total	**17 332**	**16 139**	**18 248**	**19 834**	**21 961**	**93 514**

– = between 0 and 0.5.

[a] The rank order for suppliers in 2000–2004 differs from that published in *SIPRI Yearbook 2005* (pp. 453–54) because of subsequent revision of figures for these years.

[b] One or more unknown supplier(s).

Note: The SIPRI data on arms transfers relate to actual deliveries of major conventional weapons. To permit comparison between the data on such deliveries of different weapons and to identify general trends, SIPRI uses a *trend-indicator value*. This value is only an indicator of the volume of international arms transfers and not of the financial values of such transfers. Thus, it is not comparable to economic statistics such as gross domestic product or export/ import figures. The method for calculating the trend-indicator value is described in appendix 10C and on the SIPRI Arms Transfers Project website, URL <http://www.sipri.org/ contents/armstrad/atmethods.html>.

Source: SIPRI Arms Transfers Database.

Appendix 10B. Register of transfers of major conventional weapons, 2005

BJÖRN HAGELIN, MARK BROMLEY and SIEMON T. WEZEMAN

Table 10B.1 lists major weapons delivered or on order during 2005, including licensed production. In cases where the recipient is directly involved in the production of weapons received or ordered (through the production of components or through local assembly or licensed production), the supplier is listed as 'licenser' in a separate section of the recipient's record. Sources and methods for the data collection, and the conventions, abbreviations and acronyms used, are explained below the table and in appendix 10C. Entries in the table are arranged alphabetically, by recipient, supplier and licenser. 'Year(s) of deliveries' includes aggregates of all deliveries and licensed production since the beginning of the contract. 'Deal worth' values in the Comments column refer to real monetary values as reported in sources, not to SIPRI trend-indicator values. The data presented are as of February 2006. For current or previous years' data and for registers of suppliers, consult the SIPRI Arms Transfers Project website, URL <http://www.sipri.org/contents/armstrad/at_data.html>.

Table 10B.1. Register of transfers of major conventional weapons, 2005, by recipients

Recipient/ supplier (S) or licenser (L)	No. ordered	Weapon designation	Weapon description	Year of order/ licence	Year(s) of deliveries	No. delivered/ produced	Comments
Afghanistan							
S: Russia	(4)	Mi-8/Mi-17/Hip-H	Helicopter	(2005)	2005	(4)	Probably ex-Russian; part of $30 m aid; designation uncertain
USA	6	TV-3	Turboshaft	2004	2005	6	Spares for Mi-24 combat helicopters
	(79)	M-113	APC	(2004)	2005	(79)	Ex-US; aid; M-113A2 version; incl M-577A2 CP version
Albania							
S: Germany	12	Bo-105C	Light helicopter	2005	2005	(12)	Ex-German; aid
Italy	7	Bell-205/UH-1H	Helicopter	2003	2005	(7)	Ex-Italian; AB-205A1 version; aid
Turkey	2	MRTP-33	Patrol craft	2004	2005	(2)	

Recipient/ supplier (S) or licenser (L)	No. ordered	Weapon designation	Weapon description	Year of order/ licence	Year(s) of deliveries	No. delivered/ produced	Comments
Algeria							
S: Canada	12	PW-100	Turboprop	2004	2005	(4)	For 6 C-295 transport aircraft from Spain; PW-127 version
France	(12)	AS-355/555	Light helicopter	(2003)	2005	(12)	AS-355N version; possibly incl 4 for police
Russia	(36)	MiG-29SMT/Fulcrum	FGA ac	(2005)	. .	. .	Part of $4 b deal; probably incl MiG-29UBT; contract probably not yet signed
	22	Su-24MK/Fencer-D	Bomber ac	2000	2001–2005	(22)	Ex-Russian; $120 m deal; probably modernized before delivery
	(28)	Su-30MK/Flanker	FGA ac	(2005)	. .	. .	Part of $4 b deal; contract probably not yet signed
	3	Drum Tilt	Fire control radar	(1997)	2000	1	For modernization of 3 Koni (Mourad Rais) frigates
	3	Garpun/Plank Shave	Air surv radar	(1997)	2000	1	For modernization of 3 Nanuchka (Hamidou) corvettes
	6	Pozitiv-ME1.2	Air/sea surv radar	(1997)	2000	2	For modernization of 3 Koni (Mourad Rais) frigates and 3 Nanuchka (Hamidou) corvettes
	(96)	Kh-35 Uran/SS-N-25	Anti-ship missile	1998	2000–2005	(36)	For modernized Nanuchka (Hamidou) corvettes
	. .	R-77/AA-12 Adder	BVRAAM	(2005)	. .	. .	For MiG-29SMT and Su-30MK combat aircraft; status uncertain
	(24)	TEST-71	AS/ASW torpedo	(1997)	2000	(8)	For modernized Koni (Mourad Rais) frigates; desig uncertain
Spain	6	C-295	Transport ac	2004	2005	(2)	€130 m ($170 m) deal
Angola							
S: Israel	(6)	Bell-212/UH-1N	Helicopter	(2004)	2004–2005	(6)	Ex-Israeli
Moldova	1	An-32/Cline	Transport ac	(2004)	2005	1	Second-hand
Netherlands	1	C-130H-30 Hercules	Transport ac	2005	2005	1	Second-hand (from Dutch Antilles); L-100-30 version; bought by air force after many years (at least since 1993) lease by Angolan airlines

Argentina

S:							
France	1	Ouragan	AALS	2004	2005	1	Ex-French
	1	Ouragan	AALS	2005	2005	1	Ex-French; delivery 2007
USA	12	TFE-731	Turbofan	(2001)		..	For 12 AT-63 trainer aircraft produced in Argentina; TFE-731-2C-2N version
L:	20	Bell-205/UH-1 Huey-2	Helicopter	2004	2005	(10)	Argentinian UH-1H rebuilt to Huey-2; 19 assembled from kits in Argentina

Australia

S:							
France	12	TSM-2633 Spherion-B	ASW VDS sonar	1989	1996–2005	8	For modernization of 4 Perry (Adelaide) and for 8 MEKO-200 (Anzac) frigates from Germany; Spherion-B Mod-5 version
Israel	17	Vampyr	Air surv system	2005	2005	..	For modernization of 8 MEKO-200 (Anzac) frigates
	18	EL/M-2022	MP ac radar	1995	2002–2005	(18)	Part of $372–495 m 'Project Air-5276' for modernization of 18 P-3C ASW/MP aircraft to AP-3C Sea Sentinel by US company
	37	Litening	Ac El/Op system	2005	2005	..	Litening-AT version; for F/A-18 combat aircraft; ordered via USA; from US production line; delivery 2006–2007
Sweden	8	9LV	Fire control radar	(1991)	1996–2005	7	For 8 MEKO-200 (Anzac) frigates from Germany; 9LV453 version; incl for use with Sea Sparrow SAM
	8	Sea Giraffe-150	Air/sea surv radar	1991	1996–2005	7	For 8 MEKO-200 (Anzac) frigates from Germany SEK150 m ($18 m) deal (part of SEK600 m 'Project Land-19 Phase-6'); Bolide version; delivery 2003–2006
	(170)	RBS-70 Mk-2	Portable SAM	2003	2003–2005	(130)	
USA	3	King Air-350/C-12S	Light transport ac	2005	2005	(1)	10-year lease (bought and owned by Australian company); incl for surveillance
	11	SH-2G Super Seasprite	ASW helicopter	1997	2001–2003	(10)	Ex-US SH-2F rebuilt to SH-2G(A); $421–769 m 'Project Sea-1411' (incl $67 m for 10-year support); mission systems fitted several years after delivery
	8	Mk-45 127mm	Naval gun	(1989)	1996–2005	7	For 8 MEKO-200 (Anzac) frigates from Germany; Mk-45 Mod-2 version

Recipient/ supplier (S) or licenser (L)	No. ordered	Weapon designation	Weapon description	Year of order/ licence	Year(s) of deliveries	No. delivered/ produced	Comments
	59	M-1A1 Abrams	Tank	2004	..	..	Part of $420–475 m 'Project Land-907'; ex-US M-1A1 rebuilt to M-1A1AIM(D) version; delivery 2006
	7	M-88A2 HERCULES	ARV	2004	..	..	Ex-US; part of $420–475 m 'Project Land-907'; delivery from 2007
	150	6V-53	Diesel engine (AV)	1998	2002–2005	(150)	For 150 Piranha/LAV-25 (ASLAV) APC and IFV from Canada; 6V-53T version
	299	CAT-3126	Diesel engine (AV)	(1999)	2004–2005	(210)	For 299 Bushmaster APC produced in Australia
	8	LM-2500	Gas turbine (SH)	(1989)	1996–2005	7	For 8 MEKO-200 (Anzac) frigates from Germany
	8	AN/SPS-49	Air surv radar	1993	1996–2005	7	AN/SPS-49V(8) version; for 8 MEKO-200 (Anzac) frigates from Germany
	5	PSTAR-ER	Air surv radar	2003	2004–2005	(4)	Part of AUD110 m ($73 m) 'Project Land-19 Phase-6'; for use with RBS-70 SAM
	..	AGM-114K HELLFIRE	Anti-tank missile	(2004)	2005	(10)	AGM-114K and AG-114M versions; for AS-665 Tiger helicopters
	(260)	AGM-158 JASSM	ASM	(2005)	..	..	AUD350–450 m ($270–350 m) 'Project Air-5418'; for F/A-18 combat aircraft; delivery by 2009
	(400)	AIM-120B AMRAAM	BVRAAM	(2000)	2001–2005	(375)	'Project Air-5400'; for F/A-18A combat aircraft
	(676)	Javelin	Anti-tank missile	2003	2005	(200)	$60–110 m 'Project Land-40-1'; delivery 2005–2007
	..	Mk-48 Mod-5 ADCAP	AS/ASW torpedo	(2003)	..	..	AUD465 m ($280 m) 'Project Sea-1429'; for Collins submarines; delivery from 2006
	64	RGM-84L Harpoon	Anti-ship missile	2002	2004–2005	(20)	AUD170 m ($96 m) 'Project Sea-1348'; RGM-84L Harpoon Block-2 version; for MEKO-200 (Anzac) frigates
	(576)	RIM-162 ESSM	SAM	2002	2003–2005	(300)	For MEKO-200 (Anzac) and modernized Perry (Adelaide) frigates
	(175)	RIM-66M Standard-2	SAM	(2005)	..	..	'Project Sea 1390-4b'; for modernized Perry (Adelaide) frigates; contract possibly not yet signed

Supplier	No.	Weapon designation	Weapon description	Year of order	Year(s) of delivery	No. delivered	Comments
L: Canada	(69)	Piranha	APC	1998	2002–2005	(69)	Part of $180–210 m 'Project Land-112 Phase-3' or 'ASLAV programme Phase-3'; incl 7 ambulance, 11 ARV, 14 CP, 15 radar reconnaissance and 11 repair version; Australian desig ASLAV
	(81)	Piranha/LAV-25	IFV	1998	2003–2005	(81)	Part of $180–210 m 'Project Land-112 Phase-3' or 'ASLAV programme Phase-3'; Australian desig ASLAV-25
France	22	AS-665 Tiger	Combat helicopter	2001	2004–2005	(7)	AUD1.3 b ($670–981 m) 'Project Air-87' (offsets incl production of components and assembly of 18 in Australia and production of EC-120 helicopter for Asian market); Aussie Tiger version; delivery 2004–2008
	..	MU-90 Impact	ASW torpedo	2003	2005	(10)	€150 m 'Joint Project-2070 Djimindi Phase-3' (incl up to 35% of components produced in Australia)
Germany	259	Waran	APC	2002		..	Part of AUD500 m ($280 m) 'Project Land-106 Phase-2'; Australian M-113A1 APCs rebuilt to Waran; assembled from kits in Australia; Australian desig M-113AS4; delivery delayed from 2004–2009 to 2006–2011
	8	MEKO-200ANZ	Frigate	1989	1996–2005	7	$2.7 b deal; Australian desig Anzac; delivery 1996–2006
South Korea	1	Delos	Tanker	2004		..	AUD50 m ($35 m) deal; delivery 2006 after AUD60 m modification in Australia to oiler/support ship; Australian desig Sirius
Multiple sellers	5	A-330 MRTT	Tanker/transport ac	2004		..	AUD1.4 b ($1.1 b) 'Project Air-5402'; 4 assembled in Australia; delivery from 2008/2009
	12	NH-90 TTH	Helicopter	2005		..	AUD1 b ($760 m) 'Project Air-9000/Phase-2' (offsets at least $233 m incl assembly of 8 in Australia); MRH-90 version; delivery 2007–2009
UK	61	MSTAR	Ground surv radar	1999	2002–2005	(61)	$32 m 'Project NINOX'; 55 assembled in Australia; Australian desig AMSTAR
USA	4	Boeing-737-7ES	AEW&C ac	2000		..	$1.6–1.8 b 'Wedgetail' programme; Australian desig A-30; 2 assembled in Australia; delivery 2006–2007

Recipient/ supplier (S) or licenser (L)	No. ordered	Weapon designation	Weapon description	Year of order/ licence	Year(s) of deliveries	No. delivered/ produced	Comments
	2	Boeing-737-7ES	AEW&C ac	2004		..	AUD326 m ($224 m) 'Wedgetail' programme; Australian desig A-30; assembled in Australia; delivery 2008
	4	AN/TPS-77	Air surv radar	1998	2004–2005	(4)	AUD125–150 m ($68–90 m) 'Project Air-5375'
	3	Burke	Destroyer	(2005)		..	AUD6 b ($4.56 b) 'Project Sea-4000' for 'Air Warfare Destroyer' (incl AUD455 m for design and construction of shipyard); modified version; for delivery 2013–2015; contract not yet signed
Austria							
S: Germany	18	Eurofighter/Typhoon	FGA ac	2003		..	€1.95 b (c. $2.4 b) deal (offsets $4.7 b incl UK order for Austrian trucks); delivery 2007–2009
	20	Dingo-2	APC/ISV	2004	2004–2005	(20)	Mainly for use in peacekeeping operations
	(112)	MTU-199	Diesel engine (AV)	1999	2001–2005	(112)	For 112 Ulan (ASCOD) IFV produced in Spain
Italy	2	RAT-31S/L	Air surv radar	(2005)		..	€50 m ($60 m) deal; RAT-31DL version
Switzerland	12	F-5E Tiger-2	FGA ac	2004	2004–2005	(12)	Ex-Swiss; €52 m 4-year lease; interim until new Eurofighter delivered
Bahrain							
S: Oman	6	Nimer-1	APC/ISV	2005		..	Recipient uncertain
UK	6	Hawk-100	Trainer/combat ac	2003		..	Hawk-129 version; possibly option on 6 more; delivery 2006
USA	1	AN/TPS-59	Air surv radar	2004		..	$44 m deal; AN/TPS-59(V)3 version; delivery 2008
Bangladesh							
S: Pakistan	19	T-37B	Trainer ac	2003	2004–2005	(19)	Ex-Pakistani; T-37C version
Russia	3	Mi-8/Mi-17/Hip-H	Helicopter	2004	2005	(3)	Mi-171 armed version

	No. ordered	Weapon designation	Weapon description	Year of order	Year(s) of deliveries	No. delivered	Comments
Belarus							
S: Russia	(2)	S-300PM/SA-10B	SAM system	2005		..	Ex-Russian; partly financed by Russia; delivery by 2006
Belgium							
S: Multiple sellers	10	NH-90 TTH	Helicopter	(2005)		..	€300 m deal; incl for SAR; contract not yet signed
Netherlands	2	Doorman/M	Frigate	2005		..	Ex-Dutch; €200 m 'MPEV' programme; delivery 2007–2008
Switzerland	170	Piranha-3	APC	(2005)		..	Part of €800 m deal; incl 24 CP, 12 ambulance, 17 ARV and 18 AEV version; delivery 2007–2015; contract not yet signed
	72	Piranha-3	IFV	(2005)		..	Part of €800 m deal; incl 32 IFV (30mm) and 40 FSV (90mm) version; delivery 2007–2015; contract not yet signed
USA	242	C-9	Diesel engine (AV)	(2005)		..	For 242 Piranha APC/IFV from Switzerland
L: Germany	220	Dingo-2	APC/ISV	2005	2005	1	€170 m ($222 m) 'MPPV' programme (offsets incl production of components in Belgium); option on 132 more; delivery 2005–2011
Bolivia							
S: Brazil	8	MB-326GB	Trainer/combat ac	2004	2005	(8)	Ex-Brazilian; EMB-326 Xavante version; aid
	6	Universal-1	Trainer ac	2005	2005	(6)	Ex-Brazilian; gift
Brazil							
S: Canada	76	PT-6	Turboprop	(2001)	2003–2005	(52)	For 76 EMB-314 (ALX or A-29/AT-29) trainer/combat aircraft produced in Brazil; PT-6A-68B version
	24	PW-100	Turboprop	2005		..	For 12 C-295 transport aircraft from Spain; PW-127 version

Recipient/ supplier (S) or licenser (L)	No. ordered	Weapon designation	Weapon description	Year of order/ licence	Year(s) of deliveries	No. delivered/ produced	Comments
France	12	Mirage-2000	FGA ac	2005		..	Ex-French, €80 m ($96 m) deal (incl €60 m for aircraft and €20 m for spares); modernized before delivery; interim solution after 'F-X' programme for new combat aircraft delayed; Mirage-2000C version; incl some Mirage-2000B; delivery 2006–2008
	8	Ocean Master	MP ac radar	(2005)		..	Part of €320 m ($415 m) 'P-X' programme for modernization of 8 P-3A ASW/MP aircraft to P-3AM (P-3BR); desig uncertain; delivery 2008–2010
Germany	(8)	MM-40 Exocet	Anti-ship missile	(1995)	2002	(1)	For Barroso frigate
	2	MTU-1163	Diesel engine (SH)	1994		..	For 1 Barroso frigate produced in Brazil
Italy	46	Grifo	Ac radar	2000	2005	(12)	For $285 m 'F-5BR' modernization programme of F-5E combat aircraft to F-5EM/FM; Grifo-F version
	7	RAN-20S	Air/sea surv radar	1995	2001–2005	(6)	Part of $112 m deal; for 1 Barroso frigate produced in Brazil and modernization of 6 Niteroi frigates
	13	RTN-30X	Fire control radar	1995	2001–2005	(12)	Part of $112 m deal; for 1 Barroso frigate produced in Brazil and modernization of 6 Niteroi frigates
	(53)	SCP-01 Scipio	Ac radar	2004		..	Part of $400 m modernization of 53 AMX combat aircraft
Saudi Arabia	9	F-5E Tiger-2	FGA ac	2005	2005	(9)	Ex-Saudi Arabian; bought via US company; interim solution after modernization of Brazilian F-5E delayed; incl 4 F-5F
Spain	12	C-295	Transport ac	2005		..	€238 m (c. $303 m) 'CL-X' programme (part of 'Phoenix' programme; offsets 10% or 100%); delivery 2006–2009
USA	24	Bell-205/UH-1 Huey-2	Helicopter	2003	2004–2005	(24)	Brazilian UH-1H rebuilt to Huey-2
	..	Cessna-208 Caravan	Light transport ac	(2005)		..	

No.	Weapon designation	Weapon description	Year of order	Year(s) of deliveries	No. delivered	Comments
8	P-3A Orion	ASW/MP ac	2002	..		Ex-US; $10 m deal (incl 4 more for spares; part of $425 m 'P-X' programme incl modernization in Spain to P-3AM); delivery from 2008–2010
10	S-70A/UH-60L	Helicopter	(2005)	..		$250 m deal; contract possibly not yet signed
1	LM-2500	Gas turbine (SH)	(1994)	..		For 1 Barroso frigate produced in Brazil
7	EDO-997	Sonar	(1995)	2001–2005	(6)	For 1 Barroso frigate produced in Brazil and for modernization of 6 Niteroi frigates; EDO-997F version
L: Germany						
1	Type-209/1400	Submarine	1995	..		Brazilian desig Tikuna; 1 more planned but cancelled; delivery probably 2006
Brunei						
S: France						
(36)	MM-40 Exocet	Anti-ship missile	2000	..		For Brunei frigates; MM-40 Block-2 version
Indonesia						
3	CN-235MP	ASW/MP ac	(1995)	..		CN-235MPA version; status uncertain
UK						
(96)	Sea Wolf	SAM	(2001)	..		For Brunei frigates
3	Brunei	Frigate	1998	..		Delivery delayed due to disgreement over contract
USA						
8	CT-7	Turboprop	(1995)	1997	2	For 1 CN-235 transport and 3 CN-235MPA MP aircraft from Indonesia; CT-7-9C3 version
Bulgaria						
S: Belgium						
1	Wielingen	Frigate	2004	2005	1	Ex-Belgian; €23 m ($28 m) deal; transferred to Bulgaria direct after modernization for Belgium finished
France						
6	AS-365/AS-565 Panther	Helicopter	2004	..		Part of €358 m deal (offsets €354 incl €105 m indirect); AS-565MB Panther version; delivery from 2007
(12)	AS-532 Cougar/AS-332	Helicopter	2004	..		Part of €358 m deal (offsets €354 incl €105 m indirect); AS-532AL version; incl some for CSAR; option on 7 more; delivery 2006–2007
Italy						
5	C-27J Spartan	Transport ac	(2005)	..		€91 m ($109 m) deal; option on 3 more; delivery 2007–2011
USA						
10	AE-2100	Turboprop	(2005)	..		For 5 C-27J transport aircraft from Italy

Recipient/ supplier (S) or licenser (L)	No. ordered	Weapon designation	Weapon description	Year of order/ licence	Year(s) of deliveries	No. delivered/ produced	Comments
Burkina Faso							
S: Russia	2	Mi-24P/Mi-35P/Hind-F	Combat helicopter	2005	2005	2	Mi-35 version
Canada							
S: South Africa	50	RG-31 Nyala	APC/ISV	(2005)		..	Ordered via USA; from US production line; M-777 version
UK	6	UFH/M-777 155mm	Towed gun	2005	2005	6	
USA	66	LPT 105mm	AV turret	(2005)		..	Part of CAD600–700 m deal; for 66 Piranha-3 LPTAG from Switzerland
	66	CAT-3126	Diesel engine (AV)	(2005)		..	For 66 Piranha-3 LPTAG from Switzerland; desig uncertain
	80	AN/APG-73	Ac radar	2001	2003–2005	(58)	For modernization of 80 CF-18 (F/A-18) combat aircraft to CF-18IMP; delivery 2003–2006
	16	AN/APS-143(V)	MP ac radar	(2003)		..	For 'AIMP' modernization programme of 16 P-3 (CP-140A) ASW/MP aircraft to CP-140M version; delivery from 2008
	(97)	AIM-120C AMRAAM	BVRAAM	2004	2005	(10)	CAD146 m deal; AIM-120C5 version
	(3 000)	BGM-71F TOW-2B	Anti-tank missile	2004		..	$136 m deal; 2000 TOW-2A, 600 TOW-2B and 400 anti-bunker version; status uncertain
	(288)	RIM-162 ESSM	SAM	2001	2004–2005	(75)	For modernized Halifax frigates; delivery 2004–2010
	12	RIM-66M Standard-2	SAM	2002		..	$19 m deal
L: France	5	Sperwer	UAV	(2005)		..	CAD15 m deal; assembled from kits in Canada; delivery 2006
Switzerland	66	Piranha-3 LPTAG	FSV	(2005)		..	Part of CAD600–700 m deal; delivery from 2008; contract not yet signed
USA	28	H-92 Superhawk	ASW helicopter	2004		..	CAD4.2 b ($3 b) 'MHP' programme (incl CAD2.7 b for 20 year support and training; offsets incl production of components and assembly in Canada; Canadian desig Cyclone; delivery from 2008

152	M-113A3	APC	2000	2002–2005	(92)	Part of CAD215 m 'Life Extended M-113A3/MTVL' programme; Canadian M-113 APC rebuilt to M-113A3; delivery 2002–2007
147	MTVL	APC	2000	2003–2005	(87)	Part of CAD215 m 'Life Extended M-113A3/MTVL' programme; Canadian M-113 APC rebuilt to MTVL; delivery 2003–2007

Chile

S: France

(8)	AS-355/555	Light helicopter	(2004)		..	Second-hand; modernized before delivery
1	Scorpene	Submarine	1997	2005	1	Part of $400–460 m 'Neptune' programme (incl 1 from Spain); Chilean desig O'Higgins
Germany						
8	MTU-396	Diesel engine (AV)	1997	2005	4	For 2 Scorpene submarines from France and Spain
Israel						
..	Derby	BVRAAM	2003	2005	..	For F-16C combat aircraft
..	Python-4	BVRAAM	2003	2005	..	For F-16C combat aircraft
Italy						
..	Black Shark	AS torpedo	(2003)	2005	(10)	For Scorpene (Hyatt) and modernized Type-209 (Thomson) submarines
Netherlands						
18	F-16C	FGA ac	2005	2005	..	Ex-Dutch; $100 m deal; F-16AM version; incl 7 F-16BM (F-16D); delivery 2006–2007
(72)	AIM-7M Sparrow	BVRAAM	(2004)	2005	(36)	For Heemskerck frigates; RIM-7M Sea Sparrow (SAM) version; status uncertain
200	RIM-66B Standard-1MR	SAM	2004	2005	(100)	Ex-Dutch; for Heemskerck frigates
2	Doorman/M	Frigate	2004	2005	..	Ex-Dutch; part of $350–380 m deal; delivery 2006–2007
2	Van Heemskerck/L	Frigate	2004	2005	1	Ex-Dutch; part of $350–380 m deal; delivery 2005–2006
Spain						
1	Scorpene	Submarine	1997		..	Part of $400–460 m 'Neptune' programme (incl 1 from France); Chilean desig O'Higgins
Switzerland						
24	M-109A1 155mm	Self-propelled gun	2004	2005	(24)	Ex-Swiss; M-109A1 version; modernized before delivery
UK						
1	Mk-8 114mm	Naval gun	2005		..	For modernization of Boxer (Almirante Williams) frigate
3	Duke/Type-23	Frigate	2005		..	Ex-UK; deal worth $350 m (incl $225 m for ships and $125 m for logistics); delivery 2006–2008

Recipient/ supplier (S) or licenser (L)	No. ordered	Weapon designation	Weapon description	Year of order/ licence	Year(s) of deliveries	No. delivered/ produced	Comments
USA	10	F-16C	FGA ac	2003		..	$660 m 'Peace Puma', 'Caza-2000' or 'F-2000' progamme (not including engines; offsets 100%); F-16C Block-50/52 version; incl 4 F-16D; delivery 2006
	(20)	RGM-84L Harpoon	Anti-ship missile	(2005)		..	$50 m deal; contract not yet signed
L: Germany	2	Fassmer OPV	OPV	2005		..	$50 m 'Proyecto Danubio-4'
Multiple sellers	(3)	A-400M	Transport ac	(2005)		..	$250 m deal (offsets incl production of components for all A-400M in Chile; delivery 2018–2022; contract not yet signed
China							
S: Germany	14	MTU-1163	Diesel engine (SH)	(1987)	1994–2005	14	For 4 Luyang, 1 Luhai and 2 Luhu destroyers produced in China
	(44)	MTU-396	Diesel engine (AV)	(2000)	2001–2005	(40)	For 11 Type-039G (Song) submarines produced in China; possibly produced in China
	..	MTU-883	Diesel engine (AV)	(1989)	1998–2005	(160)	For Type-98 (ZTZ-98) and Type-99 (ZTZ-99) tanks produced in China; Incl 150HB883 version
Russia	(3)	A-50U/Mainstay	AEW&C ac	(2003)		..	No. could be up to 6 (possibly incl lease of 2); ordered after Israel (under US pressure) refused delivery of ordered AEW&C aircraft; delivery possibly from 2006
	24	Mi-8/Mi-17/Hip-H	Helicopter	2005		..	$200 m deal; Mi-17 version; delivery 2006
	54	AL-31FN	Turbofan	2000	2001–2005	(54)	For J-10 combat aircraft (including for prototypes)
	100	AL-31FN	Turbofan	2005	2005	(20)	$300 m deal; for J-10 combat aircraft; delivery 2005–2006
	200	D-30	Turboprop	2005		..	$300 m deal; for 30 Il-76 transport and 8 Il-78 tanker/transport aircraft from Uzbekistan; D-30KP version

No.	Designation	Description	Year of order	Year(s) of deliveries	No. delivered	Comments
100	RD-33/RD-93	Turbofan	2005	2005	..	$267 m deal; RD-93 version; for FC-1/JF-17 combat aircraft produced in China; sold under condition not to re-export by China
1	64N6/Tombstone	Air surv radar	2004	2004	..	Part of $980 m deal; 64N6E2 version; for use with S-300PMU2 (SA-10) SAM systems; delivery 2006
(4)	Fregat/Top Plate	Air surv radar	(2001)	2004	2	For 2 Type-051C and 2 Type-052B (Luyang-1) destroyers produced in China
..	MR-90/Front Dome	Fire control radar	(2001)	2004	8	For use with SA-N-12 SAM on 2 Type-052B (Luyang-1) and with SA-N-6 SAM on 2 Type-051C destroyers produced in China
8	S-300PMU-2/SA-10E	SAM system	2004	2004	..	Part of $980 m deal; delivery 2006
..	Zhuk	Ac radar	(2005)	2005	..	For FC-1/JF-17 combat aircraft produced in China
..	3M-54E1 Klub/SS-N-27	Anti-ship missile	2002	2002	..	For modernized and new Kilo submarines; probably incl 3M14E land-attack version
(144)	48N6/SA-10 Grumble	SAM	(2002)	2002	..	For 2 Type-051C destroyers produced in China
(297)	48N6E2/SA-10	SAM	2004	2004	..	Part of $980 m deal; for S-300PMU2 (SA-10) SAM systems; delivery 2006
(212)	9M311/SA-19 Grison	SAM	(2002)	2005	(106)	For Kashtan AD system on Sovremenny destroyers
(264)	9M317/SA-17 Grizzly	SAM	(2001)	2005	(66)	SA-N-12/9M317 version for Type-052B and Sovremenny destroyers; desig uncertain
..	Kh-31A1/AS-17	Anti-ship missile	(1997)	2003–2005	(125)	For Su-30MKK, J-8MIIM and/or JH-7 combat aircraft; possibly assembled/produced in China
..	Kh-31P1/AS-17	Anti-radar missile	(1998)	2001–2005	(189)	Incl for Su-30MKK and JH-7A combat aircraft; possibly produced in China as KR-1 or YJ-91
..	Kh-59M/AS-18 Kazoo	ASM	(1999)	2004–2005	(100)	Incl for Su-30MKK combat aircraft
..	Kh-59M2/AS-18	Anti-ship missile	(2005)	2005	..	For Su-30MK2 combat aircraft; developed for China
(32)	Moskit/SS-N-22	Anti-ship missile	(2001)	2005	(16)	P-270 Moskit (3M80MBE) version; for Sovremenny destroyers
..	R-73/AA-11 Archer	SRAAM	(1995)	1996–2004	(1 800)	For Su-27SK and Su-30MKK combat aircraft
..	R-77/AA-12 Adder	BVRAAM	(2000)	2002–2004	(300)	For Su-27SK and Su-30MKK combat aircraft
8	Kilo/Type-636E	Submarine	2002	2005	(2)	$1.5–1.6 b deal; delivery 2005–2007
2	Sovremenny	Destroyer	2002	2005	1	$1–1.4 b deal; Type-956EM version; option on 2 more; delivery 2005–2006

Recipient/ supplier (S) or licenser (L)	No. ordered	Weapon designation	Weapon description	Year of order/ licence	Year(s) of deliveries	No. delivered/ produced	Comments
UK	140	Spey	Turbofan	(1988)	1997–2005	(66)	For JH-7 combat aircraft produced in China; incl some 80 ex-UK; probably more to be produced in China as WS-9
	(6)	Searchwater	AEW ac radar	1996	1999–2001	(2)	$62–66 m deal; for Y-8 AEW and MP aircraft; no. may be up to 8; uncertain if all delivered or used in operational AEW aircraft
Ukraine	(8)	DT-59	Gas turbine (SH)	(2001)	2004–2005	8	For 4 Luyang (Type-052B/C) destroyers produced in China; DA-80 version
	(1 260)	R-27/AA-10 Alamo	BVRAAM	(1995)	1996–2005	(1 000)	For Su-27SK and Su-30MKK combat aircraft; some could be from Russia
	(1 260)	R-27E/AA-10 Alamo	BVRAAM	(1995)	1996–2005	(1 000)	For Su-27SK and Su-30MKK combat aircraft; some could be from Russia
Uzbekistan	30	Il-76M/Candid-B	Transport ac	2005		..	$0.85–1.5 b deal; ordered via Russia; Il-76TD version; delivery 2006–2010
	8	Il-78M/Midas	Tanker ac	2005		..	$0.85–1.5 b deal; ordered via Russia; delivery 2006–2010
L: France	..	AS-350/550 Fennec	Light helicopter	(1992)	1995–2005	(22)	Chinese desig Z-11; incl Z-11W armed version
	..	AS-365/AS-565	Helicopter	1988	1992–2005	(14)	Chinese desig Z-9A or Z-9A-100 Haitun and Z-9B/G; incl WZ-9 anti-tank version
	..	AS-365F/565SA Panther	ASW helicopter	(1980)	1989–2005	(25)	Chinese desig Z-9C Haitun
	12	PA-6	Diesel engine (SH)	(2001)	2004–2005	8	For 3 Jiangkai frigates produced in China; desig uncertain
Germany	(4 000)	BF-8L	Diesel engine (AV)	(1981)	1982–2005	(3 900)	For YW-531/Type-63, YW-531H/Type-85, YW-534/Type-89, YW-535/Type-90, WZ-551 and WMZ-551 APC (incl IFV and other versions) and Type-85 self-propelled gun produced in China; BF8L413 and BF8L513 versions
Russia	(95)	Su-27SK/Flanker-B	FGA ac	1996	1998–2005	(95)	Part of $1.5–2.5 b deal for 200 but rest cancelled; assembled from kits in China as J-11

	No. ordered	Weapon designation	Weapon description	Year of order	Year of delivery	No. delivered	Comments
Colombia							
S: Brazil	25	EMB-314 Super Tucano	Trainer ac	2005		..	$235 m deal (loan from Brazilian banks); mainly for combat role (against FARC and ELN rebels); delivery 2006–2008
Canada	22	PT-6	Turboprop	2005		..	For 22 EMB-314 (ALX) trainer/combat aircraft from Brazil; PT-6A-68A version
Spain	(2)	C-212 Aviocar	Transport ac	2004	2005	2	Ex-Spanish; aid (symbolic €200 paid); C-212-100 medical evacuation version
	1	C-212 Aviocar	Transport ac	2005	2005	1	Ex-Spanish; aid (symbolic €100 paid); medical evacuation version
USA	3	BT-67	Transport ac	2004	2005	(2)	Aid; for police anti-narcotics operations; possibly Colombian C-47 transport aircraft rebuilt to BT-67 in USA
	8	S-70A/UH-60L	Helicopter	(2005)		..	$100 m deal; incl for use against 'narco-terrorists'
Congo, Democratic Republic of the							
S: Belgium	1	Mi-26/Halo	Helicopter	2003	2005	1	Second-hand
Czech Republic							
S: Austria	199	Pandur-2	IFV	(2005)		..	€828 m deal; option on 35 more; delivery 2007–2012; contract not yet signed
Italy	2	RAT-31S/L	Air surv radar	2002	2005	(1)	Part 'NATO ACCS' programme; for 'NADGE' air-surveillance network; RAT-31DL version
Russia	10	Mi-24V/Mi-35/Hind-E	Combat helicopter	2004	2005	(8)	$184–250 m deal (payment for debt); delivery 2005–2006
	16	Mi-8/Mi-17/Hip-H	Helicopter	2004	2005	(16)	Part of $184–250 m deal (payment for debt); Mi-171S/Mi-171Sh version
Sweden	14	JAS-39 Gripen	FGA ac	2004	2005	14	Originally produced for Sweden but declared surplus; CZK19.7 b (c. $775 m) 10-year lease (option to buy after lease; offsets 130%); JAS-39C version; incl 2 JAS-39D
	3	ARTHUR	Arty locating radar	2004		..	CZK1.8 b ($78 m) deal; ARTHUR Mod-B version; delivery 2006–2007

Recipient/ supplier (S) or licenser (L)	No. ordered	Weapon designation	Weapon description	Year of order/ licence	Year(s) of deliveries	No. delivered/ produced	Comments
	(200)	RBS-70	Portable SAM	2004	2005	(15)	SEK204 m ($29 m) deal (incl 15–16 launchers; offsets 100%); delivery 2005–2007
UK	36	Condor CV-12	Diesel engine (AV)	2002	2003–2005	(35)	For modernization of 30 T-72M1 to T-72CZ-M4
USA	14	F-404	Turbofan	2004	2005	14	For 14 JAS-39C combat aircraft from Sweden; RM-12 version (from Swedish production line)
	199	ISC-350	Diesel engine (AV)	(2005)		..	For 199 Pandur-2 APC/IFV from Austria
	(24)	AIM-120C AMRAAM	BVRAAM	2005		..	CZK700 m deal; AIM-120C-5 version; for JAS-39 combat aircraft; delivery 2006
	100	AIM-9M Sidewinder	SRAAM	2002	2002–2005	100	$15–20 m deal (incl $2 m 'FMF' aid for first 20); for L-159 trainer/combat and JAS-39 combat aircraft
Denmark							
S: Germany	4	MTU-8000	Diesel engine (SH)	(2001)	2004–2005	4	For 2 Absalon (FSS) frigates/support ships produced in Denmark
Netherlands	5	SMART	Air surv radar	2004	2004–2005	2	For 3 PS frigates and 2 Absalon (FSS) frigates/support ships produced in Denmark; SMART-S Mk-2 version
Sweden	36	Archer 155mm	Self-propelled gun	2005		..	Delivery from 2008
	(2)	CEROS-200	Fire control radar	(2004)	2004–2005	(2)	For 2 Absalon (FSS) frigates/support ships; incl for use with RIM-162 ESSM SAM and Millennium CIWS
Switzerland	85	Eagle	Reconnaissance veh	2005		..	Eagle-4 version
USA	1	C-130J-30 Hercules	Transport ac	2004		..	DKR525 m ($88 m) deal; delivery 2007
	2	Mk-45 127mm	Naval gun	2002	2004–2005	2	Ex-US; $30 m deal; modernized to Mk-45 Mod-4 before delivery; for 2 Absalon (FSS) frigates/support ships produced in Denmark
	2	AN/TPS-77	Air surv radar	2005		..	$40 m deal
	(60)	AIM-9X Sidewinder	SRAAM	2004		..	
	40	AIM-9X Sidewinder	SRAAM	2005		..	$7 m deal

No.	Designation	Description	Year of order	Year of delivery	No. delivered	Comments
(442)	RIM-162 ESSM	SAM	2002	2004–2005	(72)	For 2 Absalon (FSS) frigates/support ships, 3 PS frigates and 2 OPV
(72)	RIM-66M Standard-2	SAM	(2005)		..	SM-2 Block-3A version; for 3 PS frigates; contract not yet signed
L: Sweden						
45	CV-9035	IFV	2005		..	SEK1.7 b deal (incl production of turret and assembly in Denmark); CV-9035DK (CV-9035 Mk-3) version; delivery 2007–2009
6	SF-Mk-2	Patrol craft	(2005)		..	Ordered via Danish company and fitted out in Denmark; delivery 2006–2007
Switzerland						
22	Piranha-3	APC	2003	2005	(22)	$30 m deal; Piranha-3C version; incl 11 ambulance version; assembled from kits in Denmark
69	Piranha-3	APC	2004	2005	(10)	Part of DKR650 m ($108 m) deal (incl 22 ordered in 2003; incl DKR150 m components produced in Denmark); Piranha-3C version, incl CP, ambulance and reconnaissance versions; delivery 2005–2007
UK						
14	EH-101-400	Helicopter	2001	2005	(3)	$329 m deal (offsets incl production of components in Denmark for Danish and other EH-101); incl for SAR; delivery 2005–2006
Dominican Republic						
S: Brazil						
10	EMB-314 Super Tucano	Trainer ac	(2005)		..	Incl for combat role (anti-narcotics operations); status uncertain
Canada						
10	PT-6	Turboprop	(2005)		..	For 10 EMB-314 (ALX) trainer/combat aircraft from Brazil; PT-6A-68A version
Ecuador						
S: Brazil						
5	HS-748	Transport ac	2004	2005	(5)	Ex-Brazilian; possibly gift
Spain						
2	C-212 Aviocar	Transport ac	2004	2005	2	Part of $30 m deal; C-212-400 version
1	CN-235	Transport ac	2004	2005	1	Part of $30 m deal; CN-235-300M version
3	Vigilante	Patrol craft	2004		..	$32 m deal (partly financed by Spain); designed in UK; for coast guard
USA						
4	CT-7	Turboprop	2003	2004–2005	4	For 1 CN-235MP and 1 CN-235 transport aircraft from Spain; CT-7-9C3 version

Recipient/ supplier (S) or licenser (L)	No. ordered	Weapon designation	Weapon description	Year of order/ licence	Year(s) of deliveries	No. delivered/ produced	Comments
Egypt							
S: Netherlands	431	AIFV	IFV	2004	2005	(431)	Ex-Dutch; incl APC and other versions
Ukraine	3	An-74/Coaler-B	Transport ac	2004	2005	(3)	$34 m deal; An-74TK-200A version; incl for VIP transport; option on 6 more
USA	201	M-109A1 155mm	Self-propelled gun	(2003)	2004–2005	(201)	Ex-US; $44 m deal; M-109A2 and M-109A3 versions
	200	M-109A1 155mm	Self-propelled gun	(2005)	..	..	Ex-US; $181 m deal; M-109A5 version; contract possibly not yet signed
	(80)	TFE-731	Turbofan	1999	2001–2005	(80)	For 80 K-8E trainer aircraft from China
	5	AN/APS-145	AEW ac radar	1999	2005	(2)	Part of $138 m deal (not incl $36 m for installation); for modernization of 5 E-2C AEW&C aircraft to Hawkeye-2000; delivery 2005–2007
	6	AN/SPS-48	Air surv radar	2001	2005	(3)	$143 m deal; AN/SPS-48E version; delivery by 2006
	4	Mk-15 Phalanx	CIWS	2001	2004–2005	(3)	Ex-US; $32 m deal; modernized to Phalanx Block-1B before delivery; delivery 2004–2006
	414	AIM-9M Sidewinder	SRAAM	2003	2005	(207)	$38 m or $50 m deal; AIM-9M-2 version; delivery by 2006
	25	RGM-84L Harpoon	Anti-ship missile	2003		..	RGM-84L-4 version; land-attack capability removed before delivery after Israeli pressure
	..	RIM-116A RAM	SAM	2005		..	Part of $565 m deal; for 3 Ambassador FAC
	(3)	Ambassador	FAC(M)	(2005)		..	$450–565 m deal; Ambassador Mk-3 or King Cobra version; contract not yet signed
L: China	80	K-8 Karakorum-8	Trainer/combat ac	1999	2001–2005	(80)	$345 m deal; K-8E version; 70 assembled from kits in Egypt
USA	100	M-1A1 Abrams	Tank	2001	2004–2005	(100)	$590 m deal; assembled from kits in Egypt
	125	M-1A1 Abrams	Tank	2003	2005	(5)	$267–920 m deal; assembled from kits in Egypt; delivery 2005–2008
	21	M-88A2 HERCULES	ARV	2004		..	Assembled from kits in Egypt

INTERNATIONAL ARMS TRANSFERS 501

	No.	Weapon designation	Weapon description	Year of order	Year(s) of deliveries	No. delivered	Comments
El Salvador							
S: USA	..	Bell-205/UH-1 Huey-2	Helicopter	(2004)		..	Salvadoran UH-1H rebuilt to Huey-2
Eritrea							
S: Russia	(6)	MiG-29SMT/Fulcrum	FGA ac	2002	2005	2	Incl Su-27UB
	(10)	Su-27SK/Flanker-B	FGA ac	2003	2004–2005	(10)	
	80	9M133 Kornet/AT-14	Anti-tank missile	2005	2005	(80)	$0.17 m deal; Kornet-E version
Estonia							
S: Czech Republic	1	VERA-E	Air surv system	2005	2005	1	CZK100 m ($4 m) deal
Finland	60	XA-180	APC	2004		..	Ex-Finnish; EEK173 m ($14 m) deal (not incl EEK62 m for overhaul and EEK25 m for armament); delivery 2006
Finland							
S: Germany	4	TRS-3D	Air/sea surv radar	(2004)		..	For 4 Hamina FAC produced in Finland
Israel	6	Ranger	UAV	2003	2005	(6)	$20 m deal; ordered via Swiss company; Ranger-2 version
	..	Spike-ER	Anti-tank missile	2002		..	$22 m deal; for coastal defence; from German EuroSpike production line
	..	Spike-MR/LR	Anti-tank missile	2000	2005	(50)	$30 m deal; from German EuroSpike production line; Spike-2.5 or Spike-MR version
Netherlands	4	Scout	Sea surv radar	1998	1998–2003	2	For 4 Hamina FAC produced in Finland
South Africa	..	Umkhonto-1R	SAM	2002	2004–2005	(15)	$17 m deal; for Hamina FAC
Sweden	4	CEROS-200	Fire control radar	2003	2004–2005	(2)	SEK85 m ($10 m) deal; for 4 Hamina FAC produced in Finland
	(16)	HARD	Air surv radar	2002		..	Part of $120 m deal; for ASRAD-R SAM systems from Germany
	..	RBS-15 Mk-3	Anti-ship missile	2001	2003–2005	(15)	$50 m deal (incl modernization of Finnish RBS-15 missiles to RBS-15 Mk-3); Finnish desig RBS-15SF-3
	(128)	RBS-70 Mk-2	Portable SAM	2002	2005	(42)	$30 m deal (part of $120 m deal for ASRAD-R SAM systems)

Recipient/ supplier (S) or licenser (L)	No. ordered	Weapon designation	Weapon description	Year of order/ licence	Year(s) of deliveries	No. delivered/ produced	Comments
L: France	(10)	NH-90 TTH	Helicopter	2001	2004–2005	(2)	Part of $350 m deal (for 20 NH-90 from France and Italy; $520 m incl support; offsets incl assembly of 18 for Finland and some 28 for Norway and Sweden in Finland); delivery 2004–2008
Germany	2	TRML-CS	Air/sea surv radar	2002	2004–2005	(2)	For 2 Hamina FAC produced in Finland
Italy	(10)	NH-90 TTH	Helicopter	2001	2005	(2)	Part of $350 m deal (for 20 NH-90 from France and Italy; $520 m incl support; offsets incl assembly of 18 for Finland and some 28 for Norway and Sweden in Finland); delivery 2005–2008
Sweden	57	CV-9030	IFV	2000	2003–2005	(57)	$176 m 'TA-2000' project (offsets incl production of components in Finland); CV-9030FIN version
	45	CV-9030	IFV	2004		..	€120 m ($145 m) deal (offsets 50% incl production of components in Finland); CV-9030FIN version; delivery 2006–2007
France							
S: Austria	2	A-340	Transport ac	2005		..	Second-hand; 'TLRA' programme; 5–9-year lease (with option to buy) via French and Portugese company; A-340-211 version; delivery 2006–2007
Israel	3	Eagle	UAV	2001	2005		'SIDM' programme, delivery by 2006
Italy	2	NA-25XM	Fire control radar	(2000)		(2)	For 2 Forbin (Horizon) destroyers produced in France; for use with 76mm guns
Netherlands	2	SMART-L	Air/sea surv radar	(2001)		..	S-1850M version; for 2 Forbin (Horizon) destroyers produced in France; French desig DRBV-27 Astral
USA	(4)	LM-2500	Gas turbine (SH)	(2000)		..	For 2 Horizon (Forbin) destroyers produced in France; from Italian production line
Germany							
S: Austria	112	M-16	Diesel engine (AV)	2002	2003–2004	31	For 112 Bv-206S APC from Sweden

Supplier	No.	Designation	Description	Year of order	Year(s) of deliveries	No. delivered	Comments
France	(30)	Ocean Master	MP ac radar	2000		..	For 30 NH-90 NFH ASW helicopters produced in Germany
Italy	2	RAT-31S/L	Air surv radar	2005		..	RAT-31DL/M version; delivery 2007
Netherlands	8	P-3CUP Orion	ASW/MP ac	2004	2005	(1)	Ex-Dutch; €324 m ($250 m) 'MPA-2000' or 'MPA-R' programme (incl €24 m ($18 m) for training and €29 m ($22 m) for spare parts); transfered to Germany direct after modernization in USA for Netherlands finished; delivery 2005–2006
	3	APAR	Multi-function radar	(1997)	2004–2005	3	For 3 Sachsen (F-124/Type-124) frigates produced in Germany
	3	SMART-L	Air/sea surv radar	(1997)	2004–2005	3	For 3 Sachsen (F-124/Type-124) frigates produced in Germany
	3	Sirius	Ship El/Op system	(1999)	2004–2005	3	For 3 Sachsen (F-124/type-124) frigates produced in Germany
Sweden	81	Bv-206S	APC	2005		..	€67 m ($45 m) deal; incl CP version; delivery 2006–2009
	5	Ericsson SAR	Satellite radar	(2000)			For SAR-Lupe reconnaissance satellite produced in Germany
USA	4	LM-2500	Gas turbine (SH)	(1999)	2002–2005	3	For 4 Sachsen (F-124/Type-124) frigates produced in Germany
	(200)	MIM-104 PAC-3	SAM	(2005)		..	Contract probably not yet signed (offsets 100%)
	(144)	RIM-162 ESSM	SAM	(2002)	2004–2005	(144)	For Sachsen (F-124/Type-124) frigates
	108	RIM-66M Standard-2	SAM	2001	2003–2005	(108)	For Sachsen (F-124/Type-124) frigates; SM-2 Block-3A version
L: Israel	..	Litening	Ac El/Op system	(2000)	2003–2005	(15)	For Tornado combat aircraft
Sweden	30	RBS-15 Mk-3	Anti-ship missile	2005		..	€68 m deal (€37 m offsets incl production of components and/or assembly in Germany); for K-130 corvettes; delivery 2007–2009
USA	(4)	RQ-4A Global Hawk	UAV	(2005)		..	Possibly €600 m deal (incl sensors from Germany and other European companies); for ELINT; Euro Hawk version; delivery 2007; contract not yet signed
	(30)	HELRAS	Dipping sonar	2000		..	For 30 NH-90 NFH ASW helicopters produced in Germany

Recipient/ supplier (S) or licenser (L)	No. ordered	Weapon designation	Weapon description	Year of order/ licence	Year(s) of deliveries	No. delivered/ produced	Comments
Greece							
S: Brazil	4	EMB-145AEW&C	AEW&C ac	1999	2004–2005	(4)	Part of $476–676 m deal (incl PS-890 Erieye radar fitted in Sweden); EMB-145H version; option on 2 more
Canada	2	CL-415MP	MP ac	1999	2004–2005	2	Part of $380 m deal; CL-415GR CSAR version; 8 more CL-415GR version delivered for fire-fighting
France	2	AS-532 Cougar/AS-332	Helicopter	2003		..	AS-532A2 CSAR version
	25	Mirage-2000-5	FGA ac	2000	2004–2005	(25)	Part of €1.6 b deal; Mirage-2000-5 Mk-2 version; incl 10 Greek Mirage-2000EG rebuilt to Mirage-2000-5 Mk-2; option on 8 more
	20	NH-90 TTH	Helicopter	2003	2005	(1)	€657 m ($716–755 m) deal (offsets 120%); possibly incl some delivered from Germany and/or Italy; option on 14 more; delivery 2005–2009
	(70)	VBL	Reconnaissance veh	(2002)	2004–2005	(70)	
	(100)	MICA	BVRAAM	2004			Possibly MICA-IR version
	27	MM-40 Exocet	Anti-ship missile	2000	2004–2005	(27)	$55 m deal (offsets 160%); for Super Vita (Rousen) FAC; MM-40 Block-2 version
	..	MM-40 Exocet	Anti-ship missile	(2003)		..	For Super Vita (Rousen) FAC; MM-40 Block-2 version
Germany	(34)	Storm Shadow/SCALP	ASM	2004		..	
	(4)	Bergepanzer-1	ARV	2005		..	Ex-German; part of €270 m ($333 m) deal
	10	BrPz-1 Biber	ABL	2005		..	Ex-German; part of €270 m ($333 m) deal
	150	Leopard-1A5	Tank	2005		..	Ex-German; gift as part of order for new and ex-German Leopard-2 tanks
	183	Leopard-2A4	Tank	2005		..	Ex-German; part of €420 m deal (Incl €150 m for modernization of 130 in Germany and 53 in Greece)
	415	Marder	IFV	(2005)		..	Ex-German; €247 deal (incl 30 more for spares) Marder-1A3 version

No.	Designation	Description	Year of order	Year(s) of deliveries	No. delivered	Comments
35	AN/APG-65	Ac radar	1997	2003–2005	(35)	Part of $315–336 m 'Peace Icarus-2000' modernization programme of 35 F-4E combat aircraft
Italy						
(95)	RIM-116A RAM	SAM	(2003)	2004–2005	(95)	Part of $25 m deal; for Super Vita (Rousen) FAC
(63)	RIM-116A RAM	SAM	(2003)			For Super Vita (Rousen) FAC
1	RAT-31S/L	Air surv radar	(2002)	2005	1	Part 'NATO ACCS' programme; for 'NADGE' air-surveillance network; RAT-31DL version
Netherlands						
(6)	X-TAR	Surveillance radar	(2003)		..	For use with Skyguard (Velos) SAM system
(7)	LIROD	Fire control radar	2000	2003–2005	(7)	For 3 Super Vita (Rousen) from UK and 4 Osprey-55 (Pyrpolitis) FAC from Denmark
11	MIRADOR	Air surv system	2000	2004–2005	3	For 5 Super Vita (Rousen) FAC from UK and for modernization of 6 Kortenaer (Elli) frigates
3	MW-08	Air surv radar	2000	2004–2005	3	For 3 Super Vita (Rousen) FAC from UK
2	MW-08	Air surv radar	2003		..	For 2 Super Vita (Rousen) FAC from UK
3	STING	Fire control radar	2000	2004–2005	3	For 3 Super Vita (Rousen) FAC from UK
6	STING	Fire control radar	2003		..	For 2 Super Vita (Rousen) FAC from UK and modernization of 4 Combattante-3 (Laskos)) FAC
3	Scout	Sea surv radar	2000	2004–2005	3	For 3 Super Vita (Rousen) FAC from UK; Scout Mk-2 version
6	Scout	Sea surv radar	2003		..	Scout Mk-2 version; part of $353 m deal for modernization of 6 Kortenaer (Elli) frigates
6	Scout	Sea surv radar	2003		..	For 2 Super Vita (Rousen) FAC from UK and modernization of 4 Combattante-3 (Laskos) FAC; Scout Mk-2 version
(10)	Variant	Air/sea surv radar	2000	2003–2005	(10)	For 3 Super Vita (Rousen) FAC from UK, 4 Osprey-55 (Pyrpolitis) FAC from Denmark and 3 Saar-4 patrol craft from Israel
Russia						
19	Tor-M1/SA-15	Mobile SAM system	(2002)	2005	(10)	$400 m or $700 m deal (offsets $1.3 b)
(323)	9M338/SA-15 Gauntlet	SAM	(2002)	2005	(323)	For Tor-M1 SAM systems
Sweden						
1	Pomornik/Type-1232.2	ACV/landing craft	2002	2005	1	$64 m deal; Greek desig Kefallinia
2	Ericsson SLAR	AGS radar	(1998)	2004–2005	2	For 2 CL-415GR (CL-415CSAR) MP aircraft from Canada

Recipient/ supplier (S) or licenser (L)	No. ordered	Weapon designation	Weapon description	Year of order/ licence	Year(s) of deliveries	No. delivered/ produced	Comments
	4	PS-890 Erieye	AEW ac radar	1999	2004–2005	(4)	Part of $476–676 m deal (incl 4 EMB-145H AEW aircraft from Brazil; radars fitted in Sweden); option on 2 more
USA	4	AH-64D Apache	Combat helicopter	2003		..	Part of $675–703 m deal (offsets $845 m); option on 4 more; delivery 2007
	8	AH-64D Apache	Combat helicopter	2003		..	Part of $675–703 m deal (offsets $845 m); option on 4 more; delivery 2007
	30	F-16C	FGA ac	2005		..	$2 b 'Peace Xenia-4' deal (offsets 132%); F-16 Block-52+ version; option on 10 more; delivery by 2009–2010
	2	S-70B/SH-60F Seahawk	ASW helicopter	(2003)		..	$107 m deal; S-70B-6 Aegean Hawk version
	24	AE-2100	Turboprop	2003	2005	(16)	For 12 C-27J transport aircraft from Italy; AE-2100D-3 version
	8	AE-3007	Turbofan	1999	2004–2005	(8)	For 4 EMB-145 AEW aircraft from Brazil
	(53)	AIM-120C AMRAAM	BVRAAM	2004	2005	(53)	Part of $53 m deal; AIM-120C-5 version
	432	FIM-92C Stinger	Portable SAM	2000	2005	(216)	$48 m deal; for ASRAD SAM systems from Germany
	..	MIM-104 PAC-3	SAM	(1999)		..	For Patriot SAM systems
	..	RIM-162 ESSM	SAM	(2003)		..	For modernized Kortenaer (Elli)
L: Germany	12	Buffel	ARV	2003		..	Part of €1.7 b ($1.9 b) deal (offsets incl 40% in production of components in Greece); Buffel-2 version; delivery 2005/2006–2009
	170	Leopard-2A5	Tank	2003		..	Part of €1.7 b ($1.9 b) deal (offsets incl 40% in production of components and assembly of 140 in Greece); Leopard-2HEL (Leopard-2A6EX) version; delivery 2006–2009
	(350)	IRIS-T	SRAAM	(2004)		..	Greece funds 8% of IRIS-T programme incl production of components in Greece; option on 100 more; delivery from 2006

No.	Weapon designation	Weapon description	Year of order	Year(s) of delivery	No.	Comments
3	Type-214	Submarine	2000		..	$0.9–1.3 b deal (offsets 115% incl setting up of submarine production in Greece and $224 m in assembly of 2 from kits in Greece); Greek desig Katsonis; delivery 2005–2009
Italy 1	Type-214	Submarine	2002		..	Part of €700 m ($700 m) deal (incl modernization of 3 Type-209 submarines); assembled from kit in Greece; delivery 2009/2010
12	C-27J Spartan	Transport ac	2003	2005	(8)	€297 m (c. $350 m) deal (offsets 360% incl production of components in Greece); delivery 2005–2006
UK 2	Super Vita	FAC(M)	2003		..	€200–270 m ($227–325 m) deal; Greek desig Rousen; delivery 2006–2007
3	Super Vita	FAC(M)	2000	2004–2005	3	€440–580 m ($497–580 m) deal; Greek desig Rousen
Hungary						
S: Italy 3	RAT-31S/L	Air surv radar	2002	2005	(1)	Part 'NATO ACCS' programme; for 'NADGE' air-surveillance network; RAT-31DL version
Sweden 14	JAS-39 Gripen	FGA ac	2001		..	$924 m 10-year lease (to be bought after lease; offsets 110%); ex-Swedish aircraft rebuilt to JAS-39EBS HU; incl 2 JAS-39D; delivery 2006–2007
USA 40	AIM-120C AMRAAM	BVRAAM	(2004)		..	$25–38 m deal; AIM-120C-5 version; for JAS-39 combat aircraft; delivery 2006–2007
India						
S: France 6	PA-6	Diesel engine (SH)	(1999)	2005	(2)	For 3 Shivalik (Projekt-17) frigates produced in India; PA-6-STC version
4	ATAS	Sonar	(1992)	2000–2005	4	For 1 Delhi (Project-15) destroyer and 3 Brahmaputra (Project-16A) frigates produced in India
(36)	SM-39 Exocet	Anti-ship missile	2005		..	Possibly $150 m deal; SM-39 Block-2 version; for Scorpene submarines
Germany (24)	MTU-396	Diesel engine (AV)	2005		..	For 6 Scorpene submarines from France
155	MTU-838	Diesel engine (AV)	(1990)	2004–2005	(40)	For 124 Arjun tanks produced in India
Israel (30)	Heron-2	UAV	(2005)		..	$200–266 m deal; Eagle version; no. may be up to 50; contract possibly not yet signed

Recipient/ supplier (S) or licenser (L)	No. ordered	Weapon designation	Weapon description	Year of order/ licence	Year(s) of deliveries	No. delivered/ produced	Comments
	(4)	Heron-2	MP UAV	(2003)	2005	(4)	
	28	EL/M-2022	MP ac radar	(2000)	2001–2005	(17)	For 28 Do-228MP MP aircraft from Germany; fitted up to 4 years after aircraft delivered
	(2)	EL/M-2032	Ac radar	(1999)	2004–2005	(2)	For 2 Jaguar-IM (Maritime Jaguar) combat aircraft from UK
	10	EL/M-2032	Ac radar	1999	1999–2005	(10)	$16 m deal; for modernization of 10 Jaguar-M combat aircraft
	(14)	EL/M-2032	Ac radar	2005		..	Part INR4.76 b deal; for modernization of 14 Sea Harrier combat aircraft
	3	EL/M-2075 Phalcon	AEW ac radar	2004		..	Part worth $1.1 b deal (incl $350 m advance payment); for 3 A-50EhI AEW&C aircraft from Uzbekistan (ordered via Russia and fitted with radar in Israel); delivery 2007–2009
	6	EL/M-2221	Fire control radar	(2002)	2003–2005	(4)	For 3 Delhi and 3 Bangalore destroyers produced in India; for use with Barak SAM
	5	EL/M-2221	Fire control radar	(2003)	2004–2005	(4)	For 3 Brahmaputra frigates produced in India and modernization of 2 Godavari frigates; for use with Barak SAM
	2	Green Pine	Air surv radar	2002		..	Status uncertain
	(144)	Barak	SAM	(2002)	2003–2005	(72)	For Delhi and Bangalore destroyers
	(60)	Barak	SAM	(2003)	2004–2005	(60)	For Brahmaputra and modernized Godavari frigates
	20	Derby	BVRAAM	2005		..	$25 m deal; for modernized Sea Harrier combat aircraft
	30	Popeye-1	ASM	2001	2004–2005	(4)	INR2.7 b ($63 m) deal; for Mirage-2000 combat aircraft; Indian desig Crystal Maze
Italy	3	RAN-30X	Air surv radar	(1993)	2000–2005	3	For 3 Brahmaputra (Project-16A) frigates produced in India
	6	Seaguard TMX	Fire control radar	1993	2000–2005	6	For 3 Brahmaputra (Project-16A) frigates produced in India; assembled/produced in India as Shikari

No.	Designation	Description	Year of order	Year of delivery	No. delivered	Comments
6	Seaguard TMX	Fire control radar	(2001)	2005	(2)	For 3 Shivalik (Project-17) frigates produced in India; assembled/produced in India as Shikari
(72)	A-244/S	ASW torpedo	(1993)	2000–2005	(48)	For Brahmaputra (Project-16A) and Shivalik (Project-17) frigates; possibly produced in India as NST-58
2	Il-38/May	ASW/MP ac	2005	..	..	Ex-Russian; modernized to Il-38SD version before delivery; delivery 2006–2007
(3)	Ka-27PL/Helix-A	ASW helicopter	2004	..	..	Ka-28 version
(5)	Ka-31/Helix	AEW helicopter	2004	..	..	$700–740 m deal; for use on Gorshkov aircraft-carrier; incl 4 MiG-29KUB; option on 30 more; delivery 2007–2009
16	MiG-29K/Fulcrum-D	FGA ac	2005	..	..	
(4)	140mm RL	Naval MRL	(1992)	1997	(2)	For 2 Magar landing ships produced in India; desig uncertain
3	AK-100 100mm	Naval gun	(2003)	..	..	For 3 Bangalore (Project-15A) destroyers produced in India
(28)	BM-9A52 Smerch	MRL	2005	..	..	$450–500 m deal; originally more planned but reduced after Russia refused technology transfers; delivery from 2006–2007/2008
12	PS-90A	Turbofan	2004	..	..	For 3 A-50EhI AEW&C aircraft from Uzbekistan
250	V-46	Diesel engine (AV)	(2002)	2004–2005	(100)	For modernization of 250 T-72M1 tanks
308	V-46	Diesel engine (AV)	2002	2002–2005	(160)	For 308 WZT-3 ARV from Poland; possibly from Polish production line
6	Fregat/Top Plate	Air surv radar	(1999)	2005	(1)	For 3 Bangalore (Project-15A) destroyers and 3 Shivalik (Project-17) frigates produced in India
6	Kashtan/CADS-N-1	CIWS/SAM system	(1999)	2005	(2)	For 3 Shivalik (Project-17) frigates produced in India
3	Kite Screech	Fire control radar	(2003)	..	..	For 3 Bangalore (Project-15A) Class destroyers produced in India
(125)	Kopyo	Ac radar	1996	2001–2005	(125)	Part of $428–630 m deal for modernization of 125 MiG-21bis combat aircraft to MiG-21UPG Bison (MiG-21I or MiG-21-93); option on 50 more not used
6	MR-123/Bass Tilt	Fire control radar	(2003)	..	..	For 3 Bangalore (Project-15A) destroyers produced in India

Russia

Recipient/ supplier (S) or licenser (L)	No. ordered	Weapon designation	Weapon description	Year of order/ licence	Year(s) of deliveries	No. delivered/ produced	Comments
	30	MR-90/Front Dome	Fire control radar	(1999)	2005	(4)	For 3 Bangalore (Project-15A) destroyers and 3 Shivalik (Project-17) frigates produced in India
	(19)	Zmei/Sea Dragon	MP ac radar	2000	2005	1	Part of $205 m deal; for modernization of 5 Il-38 ASW/MP aircraft to Il-38SD and some 14 Ka-28 ASW helicopters
	(168)	3M-54E1 Klub/SS-N-27	Anti-ship missile	(1998)	2001–2005	(108)	For Talwar and Shivalik (Project-17) frigates, Bangalore (Project-15A) destroyers and Kilo submarines; possibly incl 3M14 land-attack version
	(288)	9M311/SA-19 Grison	SAM	(2005)		..	9M311 (SA-N-11) version; for Kashtan CIWS on 1 Gorshkov aircraft-carrier
	(288)	9M311/SA-19 Grison	SAM	(1999)	2005	(96)	9M311 (SA-N-11) version for Kashtan CIWS systems on 3 Shivalik (Project-17) frigates
	(3 000)	9M133 Kornet/AT-14	Anti-tank missile	(2003)		..	INR1.5 b deal (incl over 250 launchers); Kornet-E version; status uncertain
	(216)	9M317/SA-17 Grizzly	SAM	(2002)		..	9M317ME (SA-N-12) version; for Bangalore (Project-15A) destroyers
	(108)	9M38/SA-11 Gadfly	SAM	(2000)	2005	(36)	9M38M1 (SA-N-7) version; for Shivalik (Project-17) frigates
	(1 140)	R-27E/AA-10 Alamo	BVRAAM	1996	1997–2005	(450)	For Su-30MKI combat aircraft
	(3 900)	R-73/AA-11 Archer	SRAAM	(1996)	1997–2005	(1 400)	For Su-30MKI, MiG-21UPG (modernized MiG-21bis) and probably for MiG-29 and modernized MiG-27ML combat aircraft
	(750)	R-77/AA-12 Adder	BVRAAM	(2000)	2002–2005	(425)	For Su-30MKI, MiG-21UPG (modernized MiG-21bis) and possibly for MiG-29 and modernized MiG-27ML combat aircraft
	2	Akula-2	Nuclear submarine	(2005)		..	$700 m or $1.4 b deal (possibly lease); option on 1 more; possibly to be armed with Indian nuclear weapons; delivery possibly 2006/2007–2008/2009; contract possibly not yet signed

No. ordered	Weapon designation	Weapon description	Year of order	Years of deliveries	No. delivered	Comments
Ukraine						
1	Gorshkov	Ac-carrier	2004	..	..	Ex-Russian; $625–675 m deal (incl modernization and modification to conventional take off/landing (CTOL) carrier); Indian desig Vikramaditya; delivery 2008
12	DT-59	Gas turbine (SH)	(2003)	..	..	For 3 Bangalore (Project-15A) destroyers produced in India
USA						
(1 140)	R-27/AA-10 Alamo	BVRAAM	(1996)	1997–2005	(686)	For Su-30MKI combat aircraft; desig uncertain
17	F-404	Turbofan	2004			$105 m deal; for Tejas (LCA) combat aircraft produced in India; F404-GE-IN20 version; ordered after Indian Kaveri engine delayed
40	F-404	Turbofan	2001	..	..	For Tejas (LCA) combat aircraft produced in India, F-404-GE-F2J3 version
(6)	LM-2500	Gas turbine (SH)	(1999)	2005	(2)	For 3 Shivalik (Project-17) frigates produced in India; possibly from Italian production line
4	LM-2500	Gas turbine (SH)	(2004)	..	..	For 1 ADS aircraft-carrier produced in India; possibly from Italian production line
122	TPE-331	Turboprop	1983	1986–2005	(98)	For 61 Do-228 MP aircraft from Germany
8	AN/TPQ-37 Firefinder	Arty locating radar	2002	2005	(6)	Part of $142–190 m deal; orginally planned for 1998 but embargoed by USA after Indian nuclear tests in 1998; AN/TPQ-37(V)3 version
4	AN/TPQ-37 Firefinder	Arty locating radar	2003	..	..	Part of $142–190 m deal; AN/TPQ-37(V)3 version; delivery probably 2006
1	Austin	AALS	(2005)	..	..	Ex-US; status uncertain
3	A-50EhI	AEW&C ac	2004	..	..	Part of $1.1 b deal (incl $350 m advance payment); with Phalcon AEW system from Israel; ordered via Israel and Russia; delivery via Israel 2006–2009
L: France						
(230)	SA-315B Lama	Light helicopter	1971	1977–2005	(230)	Produced in India as Cheetah
..	TM-333 Ardiden	Turboshaft	(2001)	..	..	TM-333-2C2 Ardiden-1H version; for Dhruv LCH combat helicopter produced in India; assembled in India as Shakti
..	MILAN	Anti-tank missile	(1981)	1984–2005	(54 000)	MILAN-2 version; incl for BMP-2 IFV
6	Scorpene	Submarine	2005	..	..	€2.4 b 'Project-75' (incl €900 m for French designing company); delivery 2012–2017

Recipient/ supplier (S) or licenser (L)	No. ordered	Weapon designation	Weapon description	Year of order/ licence	Year(s) of deliveries	No. delivered/ produced	Comments
Germany	61	Do-228MP	MP ac	1983	1986–2005	(49)	Incl 7 ordered 2000 for $72 m and 11 ordered 2005 for INR7.62 b; 57 produced in India; incl 36 for Coast Guard;
Netherlands	4	DA-05	Air surv radar	(1989)	1995–2005	(4)	For modernization of 1 Viraat aircraft-carrier and for 3 Brahmaputra (Project-16A) frigates produced in India; Indian desig RAWS, RAWS-03 or PFN-513
	3	DA-08	Air surv radar	1999	2000–2005	3	For 3 Brahmaputra (Project-16A) frigates produced in India; Indian desig RAWS-03
	7	LW-08	Air surv radar	(1989)	1997–2005	(7)	For modernization of 1 Viraat aircraft-carrier and for 3 Delhi (Project-15) destroyers and 3 Brahmaputra (Project-16A) frigates; Indian desig RALW, RAWL-2 or PLN-517
	6	LW-08	Air surv radar	(2003)	2005	(1)	For 3 Bangalore (Project-15A) destroyers and 3 Shivalik (Project-17) frigates produced in India; Indian desig RAWL or RAWL-02
	(12)	ZW-06	Sea surv radar	(1989)	1997–2005	(11)	For modernization of 1 Viraat aircraft-carrier and for 3 Delhi (Project-15) destroyers and 3 Brahmaputra (Project-16A) and 3 Shivalik (Project-17) frigates produced in India; Indian desig Rashmi
Poland	228	WZT-3	ARV	2004	2004–2005	(80)	$202 m deal (18–40% of components produced in India); delivery 2004–2007
Russia	140	Su-30MK/Flanker	FGA ac	2000	2004–2005	(9)	$3–5 b deal; Su-30MKI version; delivery 2004–2017/2018
	310	T-90S	Tank	2001	2001–2005	(310)	$600–700 m deal (incl 55% advance payment); reaction on Pakistani acquisition of 320 T-80UB tanks; 124 assembled from kits in India
	(300)	T-90S	Tank	(2005)		..	Delivery possibly from 2007/2008; contract not yet signed

No.	Weapon designation	Weapon description	Year of order	Year(s) of deliveries	No. delivered	Comments
250	AL-55	Turbofan	2005		..	$350 m deal; most assembled/produced in India; option on 1000 more; for HJT-36 trainer and HJT-39 trainer/combat aircraft produced in India
9	Garpun/Plank Shave	Air surv radar	(1998)	2000–2005	(4)	For 3 Bangalore (Project-15A) destroyers and 3 Brahmaputra (Project-16A) and 3 Shivalik (Project-17) frigates produced in India; for use with SS-N-25 missiles; assembled in India as Aparna
..	9M113/AT-5 Spandrel	Anti-tank missile	(1988)	1992–2005	(6 300)	For BMP-2 IFV; ordered from Soviet Union and produced under Russian licence after break-up of Soviet Union; incl 9M113M version from 2003
UK 66	Hawk-100	Trainer/combat ac	2004		..	£1.1 b ($1.7 b) 'Advanced Jet Trainer' (AJT) programme (incl £800m for aircraft); 50 assembled/produced in India; Hawk-132 version; delivery from 2007
17	Jaguar International	FGA ac	1999	2003–2005	(17)	Jaguar-B version; for night-attack role; possibly incl 2 Jaguar-IM (Maritime Jaguar); Indian desig Shamsher
20	Jaguar International	FGA ac	(2000)	2005	(1)	Jaguar International-IS version; Indian desig Shamsher; delivery 2005–2007
Indonesia						
S: Canada						
5	PT-6	Turboprop	2005		..	For 5 KT-1B trainer aircraft from South Korea; PT-6A-62A version
France						
5	TB-9 Tampico	Light ac	2004	2004–2005	5	$2.5 m deal; TB-10 Tobago-GT version; for training
(6)	Makila	Turboshaft	(2000)	2004–2005	(6)	For modernization of 3 Indonesian SA-330L (NSA-330L) helicopters to NSA-330SM; Makila-1A1 version
1	Master-T	Air surv radar	2004		..	
(2)	Master-T	Air surv radar	2005		..	
(9)	Ocean Master	MP ac radar	1996	2000–2005	(6)	For 6 C-212MP (NC-212MP) MP aircraft from Spain and 3 Bo-105 (NBo-105) helicopters from Germany
Germany						
12	MTU-4000	Diesel engine (SH)	(2000)	2000–2005	(12)	For modernization of 6 Parchim (Patimura) corvettes
12	TBD-620	Diesel engine (SH)	(1999)	2000–2005	(12)	For modernization of 6 Parchim (Patimura) corvettes
South Korea						
5	KT-1 Woong-Bee	Trainer ac	2005		..	Delivery from 2007; option on 8 more

Recipient/ supplier (S) or licenser (L)	No. ordered	Weapon designation	Weapon description	Year of order/ licence	Year(s) of deliveries	No. delivered/ produced	Comments
Netherlands	2	SIGMA-90	Frigate	2004		..	$340 m deal (payment spread over 3 years); delivery 2007
Poland	2	SIGMA-90	Frigate	2005		..	Delivery 2008
	3	M-28 Skytruck	Light transport ac	2005		..	Part of $75 m deal (financed with Polish loan); delivery 2006
	7	M-28B Bryza-1R	MP ac	2005		..	Part of $75 m deal (financed with Polish loan); delivery 2006
	1	Kobra	SAM system	2005		..	Part of $35 m deal (incl 15% paid direct + $30 m with Polish loan); delivery by 2007
	..	GROM-2	Portable SAM	2005		..	Part of $35 m deal (incl 15% paid direct + $30 m with Polish loan); for Kobra SAM system; delivery by 2007
USA	5	NS-935	Patrol craft	2005		..	Part of $145 m deal; for police
	8	CAT-3516	Diesel engine (SH)	(2000)	2002–2005	(8)	For modernization of 4 Parchim (Patimura) corvettes
	16	AN/APG-66	Ac radar	1996	1999	10	For 16 Hawk-200 combat aircraft from UK; status of last 6 uncertain after US arms embargo against Indonesia
L: South Korea	4	LPD-122m	AALS	2004		..	$150 m deal; incl 2 assembled/produced in Indonesia; incl 1 for use as command ship; delivery from 2007
Spain	(6)	C-212MP Aviocar	MP ac	1996	2005	(3)	Part of $50 m 'On Top-2' programme; NC-212-200MP version; assembled from kits in Indonesia
Iran							
S: Germany	..	BF-8L	Diesel engine (AV)	(1996)	1997–2005	(150)	For Boraq APC produced in Iran; probably from Chinese production line
Russia	(29)	Tor-M1/SA-15	Mobile SAM system	2005	2005	(4)	$700m deal (part of $1 b deal) ; incl for protection of Iranian nuclear plant; delivery 2005–2007/2008
	35	Zhuk	Ac radar	2005	2005	(12)	For modernization of 35 MiG-29 combat aircraft to MiG-29SMT

No. ordered	Weapon designation	Weapon description	Year of order	Year(s) of deliveries	No. delivered	Comments
(493)	9M338/SA-15 Gauntlet	SAM	2005	2005	(75)	For Tor-M1 (SA-15) SAM systems
L: China						
..	C-802/CSS-N-8 Saccade	Anti-ship missile	2005	1994–2005	(240)	Incl for Hudong (Thondor) and modernized Combattante-2 (Kaman) FAC and possibly incl air-launched version; Iranian desig Tondar or Noor
..	FL-6	Anti-ship missile	(2000)	2002–2005	(85)	Developed or copied by China from Italian Sea Killer anti-ship missile supplied by Iran to China; Iranian desig Fajr-e Darya; incl for SH-3D helicopters
Russia						
..	TL-10/FL-8	Anti-ship missile	(2002)	2004–2005	(20)	TL-10A and possibly TL-10B version
..	TL-6/FL-9	Anti-ship missile	(2003)	2005	(10)	Iranian desig probably Nasr
1 500	BMP-2	IFV	(1991)	1993–2005	(725)	Part of $2.2 b deal; Iranian desig possibly BMT-2
(1 000)	T-72M1	Tank	(1991)	1993–2005	(756)	Part of $2.2 b deal; T-72S1 version
(15 000)	9M111/AT-4 Spigot	Anti-tank missile	(1991)	1993–2005	(9 000)	For BMP-2 and Boraq IFV
..	9M113/AT-5 Spandrel	Anti-tank missile	(1998)	1999–2005	(1 200)	Iranian desig probably Towsan-1
..	9M14M/AT-3 Sagger	Anti-tank missile	(1995)	1996–2005	(2 500)	Iranian desig RAAD; incl 1-RAAD version
Iraq						
S: Canada						
8	CH-2000	Light ac	2004	2004–2005	(8)	$5.8 m deal; SAMA CH-2000 version; ordered via USA; assembled in Jordan; for surveillance
8	CH-2000	Light ac	(2005)	2005	(8)	$6.2 m deal; SAMA CH-2000 version; ordered via USA; assembled in Jordan; for surveillance; status uncertain
Germany						
8	MTU-956	Diesel engine (SH)	1981		..	For 2 Assad corvettes from Italy
Hungary						
66	BTR-80	APC	2005	2005	(33)	Ex-Hungarian; part of $30 m deal; ordered via Polish company; modernized (probably in Ukraine) before delivery; delivery 2005–2006
77	T-72	Tank	(2005)	2005	77	Ex-Hungarian; aid ($3.4 m overhaul financed by USA)
Italy						
(4)	VT-55	ARV	(2005)	2005	(4)	Second-hand; supplier uncertain; aid
2	Assad	Corvette	1981		..	Handed over unfinished to Iraq 1986 but delivery embargoed 1990 after Iraqi invasion of Kuwait until 2004; 4 more ordered but confiscated by Italy after 1990 and sold to Malaysia; delivery 2006

Recipient/ supplier (S) or licenser (L)	No. ordered	Weapon designation	Weapon description	Year of order/ licence	Year(s) of deliveries	No. delivered/ produced	Comments
Jordan	16	Bell-205/UH-1H	Helicopter	2004	2005	(4)	Ex-Jordanian; aid
	2	C-130B Hercules	Transport ac	2004		..	Ex-Jordanian; aid
	100	M-113	APC	2004	2005	(100)	Ex-Jordanian; M-113A1 version; aid
	100	Spartan	APC	2004	2004–2005	(100)	Ex-Jordanian; aid
Poland	2	W-3 Sokol	Helicopter	2004		..	Originally 20 ordered but changed to 2
	600	Dzik	APC/ISV	2005	2005	(22)	$80 m deal; Dzik-3 version; delivery 2005–2008
Russia	24	Mi-8/Mi-17/Hip-H	Helicopter	2004	2005	24	Ex-Russian; $50–105 m deal; ordered via Polish company; Mi-17V-1 version
	10	Mi-8/Mi-17/Hip-H	Helicopter	2005	2005	10	Ordered via Polish company; Mi-17V-5 version; incl 1 for VIP transport
Turkey	(573)	Akrep/Scorpion	Reconnaissance veh	(2005)	2005	(100)	Part of $88 m deal; desig uncertain; delivery 2005–2006
UAE	4	Bell-206/OH-58	Light helicopter	2004	2005	(4)	Ex-UAE; aid; Bell-206B version
UK	72	Shorland	APC/ISV	2004	2005	72	Ex-UK; modernized before delivery; aid
Unknown country	100	BMP-1	IFV	2005	2005	(50)	Second-hand; aid; originally 500 offered as aid but only 100 accepted
	(49)	BTR-80	APC	2005	2005	(25)	Second-hand; part of $30 m deal; ordered via Polish company from a former Soviet republic; probably modernized (probably in Ukraine) before delivery; delivery 2005–2006
USA	16	Bell-205/UH-1 Huey-2	Helicopter	2005		..	Iraqi UH-1H rebuilt to Huey-2
	3	C-130E Hercules	Transport ac	(2004)	2005	3	Ex-US; aid
	43	ASV-150/M-1117	APC	2004	2004–2005	(43)	$50 m deal; incl 2 CP version
Ireland							
S: Germany	2	EC-135/EC-635	Helicopter	2005	2005	2	Incl for training; EC-135P-2 version
Italy	4	AB-139	Helicopter	2004		..	€49 m ($64 m) deal; option on 2 more; delivery 2006–2007
USA	36	Javelin	Anti-tank missile	2003		..	$12.5 m deal

Israel

	No.	Designation	Description	Year of order	Years of delivery	No. delivered	Comments
S: Germany	..	MTU-883	Diesel engine (AV)	(2000)	2002–2005	(115)	For Merkava-4 tanks produced in Israel; possibly from US production line
	2	Dolphin/Type-800	Submarine	(2005)		..	$0.7–1.2 b deal (33% financed by Germany); contract not yet signed
USA	12	AH-64D Apache	Combat helicopter	2001	2005	(11)	$509 m deal (financed by US 'FMF' aid); incl 3 Israeli AH-64A rebuilt to AH-64D; Israeli desig Sharaf
	6	AH-64D Apache	Combat helicopter	2004		..	Deal worth $200 m; Israeli desig Saraf
	18	Bonanza	Light ac	2004	2004–2005	(18)	$11 m deal; option on 6 more
	50	F-16I	FGA ac	1999	2004–2005	(50)	$2.5 b 'Peace Marble-5 Phase-1' deal (financed by US 'FMF' aid; offsets 25%); Israeli desig Suefa
	52	F-16I	FGA ac	2001		..	$2 b 'Peace Marble-5 Phase-2' deal (incl $1.3 b for aircraft and $300 m for engines; offsets $800 m); Israeli desig Suefa; delivery 2006–2008
	(200)	AGM-114K HELLFIRE	Anti-tank missile	(2004)		..	Part of $50 m deal; AGM-114K and AGM-114M versions
	(480)	AGM-114L HELLFIRE	Anti-tank missile	(2000)	2005	(240)	AGM-114L3 version; for AH-64D helicopters
L:	(4)	Gulfstream-5	Transport ac	2003		..	Part of $473 m deal (partly financed by US 'FMF' aid); G-550 version; modified in Israel to Nahshon/Etam AEW aircraft; option on 2 more; delivery from 2007
	3	Gulfstream-5	Transport ac	2001	2005	1	$174–206 m deal (partly financed by US 'FMF' aid); G-550 version; modified in Israel to G-550 SEMA Nahshon/Shavit ELINT aircraft, delivery from 2005

Italy

	No.	Designation	Description	Year of order	Years of delivery	No. delivered	Comments
S: Austria	148	M-16	Diesel engine (AV)	2000	2001–2005	(42)	For 148 Bv-206S APC from Sweden
France	4	PA-6	Diesel engine (SH)	(2000)		..	For 2 Doria (Horizon) destroyers produced in Italy
	..	Ocean Master	MP ac radar	2000		..	For 46 NH-90 NFH ASW helicopters produced in Italy
	..	Vampyr	Air surv system	(2000)		..	For 2 Doria (Horizon) destroyers produced in Italy

Recipient/ supplier (S) or licenser (L)	No. ordered	Weapon designation	Weapon description	Year of order/ licence	Year(s) of deliveries	No. delivered/ produced	Comments
Netherlands	2	SMART-L	Air/sea surv radar	(2001)		..	S-1850M version; for 2 Doria (Horizon) destroyers produced in Italy
Sweden	112	Bv-206S	APC	2003	2004–2005	(40)	€57 m ($68 m) deal (offsets for Swedish NH-90 helicopter order); delivery 2004–2007
	34	Bv-206S	APC	2003		..	Part of €24 m ($29 m) deal (offsets for Swedish NH-90 helicopter order); delivery from 2007
UK	120	Gem	Turboshaft	(1979)	1990–2005	(120)	For 60 A-129 combat helicopters produced in Italy; Gem Mk-1004 version
USA	200	Storm Shadow/SCALP	ASM	1999	2004–2005	(25)	$275 m deal
	4	C-130J-30 Hercules	Transport ac	2000	2004–2005	(4)	For 12 C-27J transport aircraft produced in Italy
	24	AE-2100	Turboprop	2002	2004–2005	(8)	For modernization of A-129 combat helicopters
	..	T-800	Turboshaft	(2005)		..	
	2	AN/TPS-77	Air surv radar	2002		..	AN/TPS-117 version
	46	HELRAS	Dipping sonar	(2000)		..	For 46 NH-90 NFH ASW helicopters produced in Italy; probably from German production line
L: Germany	70	PzH-2000 155mm	Self-propelled gun	2002	2003–2005	(19)	$455–510 m deal; 68 assembled in Italy; delivery 2003–2008
	(444)	IRIS-T	SRAAM	(2003)		..	Italy funds 19% of IRIS-T programme incl production of components in Italy; delivery probably from 2006
	2	Type-212	Submarine	1997	2005	1	Italian desig Todaro; option on 2 more; delivery 2005–2006
USA	4	KC-767	Tanker/transport ac	2002		..	$619 m deal (offsets up to $1.1 b incl assembly of 3 in Italy); option on 2 more; delivery 2006–2008
	(8)	LM-2500	Gas turbine (SH)	(2000)		..	For 1 Cavour aircraft-carrier and 2 Doria (Horizon) destroyers produced in Italy
	232	T-700	Turboshaft	(2003)		..	For 70 NH-90 TTH transport and 46 NH-90 NFH ASW helicopters produced in Italy; T-700-T-6E1 version

No.	Designation	Description	1997	2001–2005	No. del.	Comments
Japan						
S: France						
60	T-700	Turboshaft			(60)	For 20 EH-101 helicopters produced in Italy; T-700-T-6A/3 version
2	EC-225/EC-725	Helicopter	2005		..	For coast guard SAR
(14)	Ocean Master	MP ac radar	1996	2004	(2)	For 14 US-2 (US-1AKai) MP aircraft produced in Japan
Italy						
5	Compact 127mm	Naval gun	(1999)	2003–2004	3	For 5 Takanami frigates produced in Japan
Netherlands						
(2)	LIROD	Fire control radar	(2004)		..	For 2 FD aircraft-carriers produced in Japan
Sweden						
2	Saab 340B SAR-200	MP ac	2005		..	Second-hand Saab-340B rebuilt to SAR-200 version; for coast guard SAR; delivery 2006
USA						
(8)	Stirling AIP	AIP engine	2005		..	For 2 Improved Oyashio submarine produced in Japan
4	KC-767	Tanker/transport ac	2003		..	'KC-X' programme; delivery 2006–2010
(20)	King Air-350/C-12S	Light transport ac	1997	1999–2005	(9)	Incl for reconnaissance; Japanese desig LR-2
(56)	AE-2100	Turboprop	(1996)	2004	(8)	For 14 US-2 (US-1AKai) MP aircraft produced in Japan; AE-2100J version
..	F-110	Turbofan	(1987)	2000–2005	(68)	For F-2 combat aircraft produced in Japan; F-110-GE-129 version
(13)	AN/APS-145	AEW ac radar	2000	2004–2005	(5)	For modernization of 13 E-2C AEW&C aircraft to Hawkeye-2000
6	AN/SPG-62	Fire control radar	(2002)		..	For 2 Improved Kongou destroyers produced in Japan; for use with Standard SAM
2	AN/SPY-1D	Air surv radar	2002		..	For 2 Improved Kongou destroyers produced in Japan
(38)	Mk-15 Phalanx	CIWS	(1993)	1996–2005	32	For 2 Improved Kongou destroyers, 9 Murasame and 5 Takanami frigates and 3 Oosumi AALS produced in Japan; incl some Block-1B version
16	MIM-104 PAC-3	SAM	2005		..	Part of $6.5–9.3 b anti-ballistic missile defence system; delivery by 2006 or 2010
..	RIM-162 ESSM	SAM	2004		..	For Takanami and Murasame frigates
40	RIM-66M Standard-2	SAM	(2005)		..	Part of $104 m deal; SM-2 Block-3B version; contract possibly not yet signed
18	RIM-66M Standard-2	SAM	(2003)		..	Part of $482 m deal; SM-2 Block-3B version

Recipient/ supplier (S) or licenser (L)	No. ordered	Weapon designation	Weapon description	Year of order/ licence	Year(s) of deliveries	No. delivered/ produced	Comments
L: France	..	MO-120-RT-61 120mm	Mortar	1992	1993–2005	(354)	Incl for Type-96 mortar carrier produced in Japan
UK	14	EH-101-400	Helicopter	2003	..	..	$518 m 'MCH-X' programme; 13 assembled from kits in Japan; incl for mine-sweeping; delivery from 2006
	(30)	Spey	Gas turbine (SH)	(1991)	1995–2005	28	For 5 Takanami and 9 Murasame frigates and 1 Kashima training ship produced in Japan
USA	(60)	AH-64D Apache	Combat helicopter	2001	..	..	'AH-X' programme; AH-64DJP version; delivery from 2006
	(21)	BAe-125-800	Light transport ac	1995	1998–2005	(17)	'H-X' programme; RH-800 or Hawker-800 version; modified in Japan for SAR; Japanese desig U-125A
	86	CH-47D Chinook	Helicopter	1984	1986–2005	(76)	CH-47J and CH-47JA version; 84 assembled/produced in Japan
	(67)	S-70A/UH-60L	Helicopter	1988	1990–2005	(52)	S-70A-12/UH-60J version
	(80)	S-70A/UH-60L	Helicopter	1995	1998–2005	(30)	$2.7 b deal; UH-60JA version
	(126)	S-70B/SH-60J Seahawk	ASW helicopter	1988	1991–2005	(113)	Incl SH-60K version
	(90)	M-270 MLRS	MRL	1993	1995–2005	(87)	
	2	Mk-45-4 127mm	Naval gun	2003	..	..	For 2 Improved Kongou destroyers produced in Japan
	(62)	LM-2500	Gas turbine (SH)	(1988)	1993–2005	44	For 2 FD aircraft-carriers, 4 Kongou and 2 Improved Kongou destroyers, 5 Takanami and 9 Murasame frigates and 1 Asuka research ship produced in Japan
	(80)	T-64	Turboprop	(1970)	1975–2005	(80)	For 20 US-1A MP aircraft produced in Japan, T-64-IHI-10J version
	(27)	Sea Vue	MP ac radar	1992	1995–2005	(23)	For 27 BAe-125-800/RH-800 (U-125A) SAR aircraft from UK and USA
	(336)	AIM-7M Sparrow	BVRAAM	1993	1996–2005	(303)	For Murasame and Takanami frigates; RIM-7M Sea Sparrow (SAM) version; incl production of components and assembly in Japan
	(9)	RIM-66/SM-3	SAM	(2005)	..	..	Part of $6.5–9.3 b anti-ballistic missile defence system; SM-3 Block-1 version; for Kongou

destroyers; incl production of components in Japan; contract probably not yet signed

Jordan

S:	No.	Designation	Description	Year order	Year delivery	Delivered	Comments
Germany	4	EC-135/EC-635	Helicopter	(2005)		(..)	EC-635T-1 version; for border patrol and VIP transport; delivery 2006–2007
Netherlands	3	F-16C	FGA ac	(2005)		(..)	Ex-Dutch; delivery 2006; contract probably not yet signed
Russia	8	PS-90A	Turbofan	2005		(..)	For 2 Il-76MF transport aircraft from Uzbekistan; PS-90A-76 version
South Africa	(200)	Ratel-20	IFV	2004	2004–2005	(150)	Ex-South African; delivery 2004–2006
UAE	(10)	AS-350/550 Fennec	Light helicopter	2005	2005	(10)	Ex-UAE (but only few years old); AS-350B-3 version; for training
USA	8	S-70A/UH-60L	Helicopter	2004			$220 m deal; UH-60L version; delivery 2006
	232	6V-53	Diesel engine (AV)	(2000)	2004–2005	(132)	For 100 AIFV (ACV-300) APC from Turkey and modernization of 132 M-113A1APC to M-113A2 Mk-1J
	17	AN/APG-66	Ac radar	2004			Part of $87 m deal; for modernization of 17 Jordanian F-16ADF combat aircraft to F-16AM in Turkey; delivery 2006–2009
	50	AIM-120C AMRAAM	BVRAAM	(2004)		(..)	$39 m deal; contract not yet signed
	2	Il-76MF/Candid	Transport ac	2005		(..)	Ordered via Russia; option on 2 more; delivery 2006
L: Turkey	100	AIFV-APC	APC	(2004)		(..)	$42 m deal; assembled from kits in Jordan; contract probably not yet signed

Kazakhstan

S:	No.	Designation	Description	Year order	Year delivery	Delivered	Comments
South Korea	3	Sea Dolphin	Patrol craft	2005		(..)	Ex-South Korean; aid; delivery 2006
Russia	20	Mi-8/Mi-17/Hip-H	Helicopter	2004	2004–2005	(14)	$100 m deal; Mi-17 version; for anti-terrorist and anti-narcotics operations; delivery 2004–2006
	(38)	Su-27S/Flanker-B	Fighter ac	(1995)	1996–2003	(26)	Ex-Russian; payment for debt; status uncertain

Recipient/ supplier (S) or licenser (L)	No. ordered	Weapon designation	Weapon description	Year of order/ licence	Year(s) of deliveries	No. delivered/ produced	Comments
Kenya							
S: Spain	1	Gondan OPV	OPV	2003	2005	1	KES4.1 b ($54 m) deal (not incl KES2 b for armament); ordered and delivered as civilian ship but armed in Kenya; delivery delayed due to corruption investigation
North Korea							
L: Russia	..	9M111/AT-4 Spigot	Anti-tank missile	(1987)	1992–2005	(3 350)	Ordered from Soviet Union and produced under Russian licence after break-up of Soviet Union
	..	Igla-1/SA-16 Gimlet	Portable SAM	(1989)	1992–2005	(1 300)	Probably ordered from Soviet Union and produced under Russian licence after break-up of Soviet Union
South Korea							
S: Canada	(105)	PT-6	Turboprop	(1995)	2000–2005	(90)	For 85 KT-1 trainer and 20-40 KO-1 combat/reconnaissance aircraft produced in South Korea; PT-6A-62A version
France	4	PC-2.5	Diesel engine (SH)	(2002)		..	For 1 Dodko (LPX) AALS produced in South Korea; possibly produced in South Korea
Germany	(750)	MTU-881	Diesel engine (AV)	(1998)	1999–2005	(220)	For K-9 self-propelled guns produced in South Korea
	6	MTU-956	Diesel engine (SH)	(1999)	2003–2005	6	For 3 KDX-2 frigates produced in South Korea
	3	DSQS-23	Sonar	(1999)	2003–2005	3	For 3 KDX-2 frigates produced in South Korea
Netherlands	3	Goalkeeper	CIWS	1999	2003–2005	3	For 3 KDX-2 frigates produced in South Korea
	5	Goalkeeper	CIWS	2003		..	$54 m deal; for 1 LPX AALS and 3 KDX-3 destroyers produced in South Korea
Russia	(23)	Il-103	Light ac	2002	2005	(3)	$9 m deal (incl $4.5 m debt payment); part of $534 m 'Bul-Gom' or 'Red Bear-2' deal (incl $267 m debt payment); for training; delivery 2005–2006
	(37)	BMP-3	IFV	2002	2005	(37)	Part of $534 m 'Bul-Gom' or 'Red Bear-2' deal (incl $267 m debt payment)

Supplier	No. ordered	Weapon designation	Weapon description	Year of order	Year(s) of deliveries	No. delivered/produced	Comments
	(10)	T-80U	Tank	2002	2005	(2)	Part of $534 m 'Bul-Gom' or 'Red Bear-2' deal (incl $267 m debt payment); delivery by 2006
	(2 000)	9M131/AT-13 Saxhorn	Anti-tank missile	2002	2003–2005	(1 500)	Part of $534 m 'Bul-Gom' or 'Red Bear-2' deal (incl $267 m debt payment); delivery 2003–2006
	3	Murena/Type-1206	Landing craft	2002	2005	(1)	Part of $534 m 'Bul-Gom' or 'Red Bear-2' deal (incl $267 m debt payment); delivery 2005–2007
USA	8	P-3B Orion	ASW/MP ac	2005		..	Ex-US; $493 m deal (incl $66 m for aircraft and $427 m for modernization after delivery); 1 more for spares only; delivery 2007–2009
	27	F-404	Turbofan	(2003)		..	$80 m deal; for 25 T-50 trainer aircraft produced in South Korea; F-404-GE-102 version
	6	LM-2500	Gas turbine (SH)	(1999)	2003–2005	6	For 3 KDX-2 frigates produced in South Korea
	(44)	AN/APG-67	Ac radar	(2003)		..	AN/APG-67(V)4 version; for 44 T-50 LIFT/A-50 trainer/combat aircraft produced in South Korea; contract possibly not yet signed
	3	AN/SPS-49	Air surv radar	(1999)	2003–2005	3	For 3 KDX-2 frigates produced in South Korea; AN/SPS-49(V)5 version
	3	AN/SPY-1D	Air surv radar	(2002)		..	For 3 KDX-3 destroyers produced in South Korea
	(40)	Tiger Eyes	Ac radar	2002	2005	(4)	$164 m deal; for F-15K combat aircraft
	(45)	AGM-84H SLAM-ER	ASM	(2003)	2005	(5)	$70 m deal; for F-15K combat aircraft
	..	AIM-9X Sidewinder	SRAAM	2002		..	Part of $110 m deal; for F-15K combat aircraft
	(150)	Mk-46 Mod-5 NEARTIP	ASW torpedo	(1995)	1998–2005	(150)	For KDX-1 (Kwanggaeto the Great) frigates and for ASROC ASW missiles on KDX-2 frigates
	64	RIM-116A RAM	SAM	2001	2003–2005	(64)	For KDX-2 frigates
	(125)	RIM-116A RAM	SAM	(2004)		..	For KDX-3 destroyers and LPX AALS
	..	RIM-66/SM-3	SAM	(2004)		..	For KDX-3 Class destroyers; contract not yet signed
	110	RIM-66M Standard-2	SAM	2000	2003–2005	(110)	$159 m deal; for KDX-2 frigates; SM-2MR Block-3A version
L: France	(48)	Crotale-NG	SAM system	(1997)	1999–2005	(48)	Part of Chun Ma (Pegasus) SAM system produced in South Korea (with South Korean missiles); assembled in South Korea

Recipient/ supplier (S) or licenser (L)	No. ordered	Weapon designation	Weapon description	Year of order/ licence	Year(s) of deliveries	No. delivered/ produced	Comments
Germany	3	Type-214	Submarine	2000		..	$1.1 b 'KSS-2' programme (incl $711 m import from Germany); assembled from kits in South Korea; delivery 2007–2009
Netherlands	3	MW-08	Air surv radar	1999	2003–2005	3	For 3 KDX-2 frigates produced in South Korea
	(41)	MW-08	Air surv radar	(2003)		..	For 40 PKM-X FAC and 1 LPX AALS produced in South Korea
	6	STIR	Fire control radar	1999	2003–2005	6	For 3 KDX-2 frigates produced in South Korea; STIR-240 version
Sweden	(9)	CEROS-200	Fire control radar	2003		..	SEK114 m ($14 m) deal; for 9 PKX FAC produced in South Korea; delivery from 2006/2007
USA	40	F-15E Strike Eagle	Fighter/bomber ac	2002	2005	4	$4.2 b 'F-X' programme (offsets 65–83% incl production of components for 32 F-15K and all production of AH-64 combat helicopter fuselages in South Korea); F-15K Slam Eagle version; option on 40 more; delivery 2005–2008
	3	Mk-45 127mm	Naval gun	1999	2003–2005	3	$22 m deal; for 3 KDX-2 frigates produced in South Korea; Mk-45 Mod-4 version
	67	LVTP-7A1/AAV-7A1	APC	2000	2001–2005	(58)	$99–120 m deal; assembled from kits in South Korea as KAAV (Korean Armoured Amphibious Vehicle); delivery 2001–2006
Kuwait							
S: France	2	AS-365/AS-565 Panther	Helicopter	(2002)	2005	2	For police
Germany	8	Condor	APC	(2003)	2005	(8)	For National Guard; Condor-2 version
USA	8	AH-64D Apache	Combat helicopter	2002	2005	(1)	Part of $868 m deal (incl $213 m for airframes and $46 m for Longbow radars; part of $2.1 b deal); sold on condition to be used for defensive operations only; delivery 2005–2008
	8	AH-64D Apache	Combat helicopter	2002	2005	(1)	Part of $868 m deal (incl $213 m for airframes and $46 m for Longbow radars; part of $2.1 b deal); sold

Recipient/supplier (S)	No. ordered	Weapon designation	Weapon description	Year of order	Year(s) of deliveries	No. delivered	Comments
							on condition to be used for defensive operations only; delivery 2005–2008
	1	L-88 LASS	Air surv radar	2003	2005	1	$85 m deal
	(188)	AGM-114K HELLFIRE	Anti-tank missile	2002	2005	(10)	Part of $868 m deal (part of larger $2.1 b deal); AGM-114K3 version; for AH-64D helicopters; delivery 2005–2008
	(96)	AGM-114L HELLFIRE	Anti-tank missile	2002	2005	(10)	Part of $868 m deal (part of larger $2.1 b deal); AGM-114L3 version; for AH-64D helicopters; delivery 2005–2008
Kyrgyzstan							
S: Russia	1	Mi-8/Mi-17/Hip-H	Helicopter	(2005)	2005	1	Probably ex-Russian; part of $3 m aid (in return for Russian access to Kyrgyz air base)
Latvia							
S: Netherlands	5	Tripartite	MCM ship	2005		..	Ex-Dutch; €57 m ($71 m) deal; delivery 2006–2008
Russia	2	Mi-8/Mi-17/Hip-H	Helicopter	(2003)	2004–2005	2	Mi-8MTV-1 version; incl for SAR
Sweden	(2)	Giraffe-40	Air surv radar	2004		..	Ex-Swedish; for use with RBS-70 SAM systems; delivery 2006–2007
	..	RBS-70	Portable SAM	2004		..	EK185 m ($28 m) deal (incl ex-Swedish launchers as aid); delivery 2006–2007
Lebanon							
S: USA	(2)	R44	Helicopter	(2003)	2005	(2)	R44 Raven-2 version; for training
Libya							
S: Italy	10	A-109K	Light helicopter	(2005)		..	€80 m ($97 m) deal; for border patrol; delivery from 2006
USA	8	C-130H Hercules	Transport ac	1973		..	$70 m deal; ordered 1973 but embargoed 1974–2005 (paid for and owned by Libya but stored in USA)

Recipient/ supplier (S) or licenser (L)	No. ordered	Weapon designation	Weapon description	Year of order/ licence	Year(s) of deliveries	No. delivered/ produced	Comments
Lithuania							
S: Norway	(5)	Giraffe-40	Air surv radar	2004	2004–2005	(5)	Ex-Norwegian; part of LTL135 m (c. $50 m) aid
	(260)	RBS-70	Portable SAM	2004	2004–2005	(260)	Ex-Norwegian; part of LTL135 m (c. $50 m) aid; deal incl also 21 launchers
USA	2	AN/MPQ-64	Air surv radar	2002		..	Part of $31 m deal; for use with FIM-92 SAMs; delivery 2006
	54	FIM-92A Stinger	Portable SAM	2002		..	Part of $31 m deal; deal incl also incl 8 launchers; delivery 2006
Malaysia							
S: Canada	10	PT-6	Turboprop	(2005)		..	For 10 PC-7 Mk-2 trainer aircraft from Switzerland; PT-6A-25C version
France	40	SM-39 Exocet	Anti-ship missile	2002		..	For Scorpene submarines; delivery 2007–2008
	1	Agosta	Submarine	2002		..	Ex-French; incl for 4-year training of Malaysians in France; status uncertain
	1	Scorpene	Submarine	2002		..	Part of €1.2 b (c. $1.05 b) deal (incl 1 more from Spain; incl over 50% barter); delivery 2009
Germany	32	D-2848	Diesel engine (AV)	2004	2004–2005	(32)	Part of $10 m deal for modernization of 32 K-200 KIFV APC to K-200A1; from South Korea production line
	2	TRML-CS	Air/sea surv radar	2005		..	€20 m deal; option on 1 more; TRML-3D version; delivery 2008
Indonesia	2	CN-235	Transport ac	2002	2005	(1)	$34 m deal; possibly ex-Indonesian; incl for VIP transport
Italy	6	Seaguard TMX	Fire control radar	(2000)	2005	(2)	For 6 MEKO-A100 (Kedah) frigates from Germany; desig uncertain
Multiple sellers	(30)	Black Shark	AS torpedo	2002		..	For Scorpene submarines
	4	A-400M	Transport ac	2005		..	MYR2.8 b (c. €600 m/$630 m) deal (offsets at least MYR1 b); delivery 2013–2014

	No.	Designation	Category	Order	Delivery	(No.)	Comments
Poland	3	MID-M	AEV	2003	2005	(1)	Part of $368–400 m deal (offsets $111 m); delivery 2005–2006
	5	PMC-90	ABL	2003	2005	(1)	Part of $368–400 m deal (offsets $111 m); PMC Leguan version; delivery 2005–2006
	48	PT-91	Tank	2003	2005	(5)	Part of $368–400 m deal (offsets $111 m); PT-91M version; delivery 2005–2006/2007
	6	WZT-4	ARV	2003	2005	(1)	Part of $368–400 m deal (offsets $111 m); PT-91M version; delivery 2005–2006
Russia	10	Mi-8/Mi-17/Hip-H	Helicopter	2003		..	$70–120 m deal; Mi-171Sh armed version; for CSAR; delivery from 2006
	18	Su-30MK/Flanker	FGA ac	2003		..	$900 m deal (offsets over 33% incl $270 m as barter and incl space technology transfer and training of Malaysian astronaut); Su-30MKM version; delivery 2006/2007–2008
	..	R-77/AA-12 Adder	BVRAAM	(1997)		..	For MiG-29N and Su-30MKM combat aircraft; status uncertain
Spain	1	Scorpene	Submarine	2002		..	Part of €1.2 b (c. $1.05 b) deal (incl 1 more from France; incl over 50% barter); delivery 2009
Switzerland	10	PC-7 Turbo Trainer	Trainer ac	(2005)	2005	..	CHF70 m deal; PC-7 Mk-2 version; delivery 2007
UK	(15)	Jernas	SAM system	2002	2005	(5)	Part of £220 m ($400 m) deal (offsets incl production of components in Malaysia); delivery from 2005
	..	Rapier Mk-2	SAM	2002	2005	(50)	Part of £220 m ($400 m) deal (offsets incl production of components in Malaysia); for Jernas SAM systems
USA	..	CT-7	Turboprop	2002	2005	(2)	For 2 CN-235 transport aircraft from Indonesia; CT-7-9C3 version
	12	Caterpillar-3616	Diesel engine (SH)	2000	2005	(4)	For 6 MEKO-A100 (Kedah) frigates from Germany
L: Germany	6	MEKO-A100	Frigate	1999	2005	(2)	$1.4 b 'New Generation Patrol Vessel' (NGPV) programme (offsets incl production of at least 30% of components and assembly of 4 in Malaysia); MEKO-100RMN version; Malaysian designaton Kedah; delivery 2005–2008/2009

Recipient/ supplier (S) or licenser (L)	No. ordered	Weapon designation	Weapon description	Year of order/ licence	Year(s) of deliveries	No. delivered/ produced	Comments
Italy	11	A-109K	Light helicopter	2003	2005	(2)	$70–75 m deal (offsets incl assembly of some in Malaysia and technology transfer); A-109LOH armed version
Malta S: Italy	1	Diciotti	Patrol craft	2004	2005	1	€17 m ($20 m) deal (mainly financed by Italy)
Mauritius S: India	1	Druhv/ALH	Helicopter	2005	..	..	Desig uncertain; possibly ex-Indian
	1	SDB Mk-2	Patrol craft	2005	..	..	
Mexico S: Denmark	4	SCANTER-2001	Sea surv radar	(2003)	2004–2005	(4)	For 4 Oaxaca OPV produced in Mexico
France	2	AS-365/AS-565 Panther	Helicopter	2003	2005	2	AS-565SB version; option on 8 more
Israel	(2)	S-65/Yasur-2000	Helicopter	(2005)	2005	2	Ex-Israeli
USA	24	Caterpillar-3616	Diesel engine (SH)	(1997)	1998–2005	24	For 4 Sierra, 4 Durango and 4 Oaxaca OPV produced in Mexico
	8	Sea Vue	MP ac radar	2002	2003–2005	(6)	For modernization of 8 C-212 MP aircraft
Morocco S: France	(27)	RDY	Ac radar	2005		..	Part of €350 m ($420 m) deal for modernization of 27 Moroccan Mirage F-1 combat aircraft; RC-400 version
	..	MICA	BVRAAM	2005		..	Part of €350 m ($420 m) deal; for modernized Mirage F-1 combat aircraft
Russia	(6)	2S6M Tunguska	AAV(G/M)	2005	2005	(2)	No. could be 12
	(96)	9M311/SA-19 Grison	SAM	2005	2005	(32)	For 2S6 AAV(G/M)
Spain	..	M-60A3 Patton-2	Tank	2005		..	Ex-Spanish; aid

Myanmar (Burma)

S:	No. ordered	Weapon designation	Weapon description	Year of order	Year of deliveries	No. delivered	Comments
India	1	BN-2 Islander	Light transport ac	2005		..	Second-hand; gift; status uncertain after UK warns India delivery may affect Uk arms sales to India
Ukraine	..	BTR-3U Guardian	IFV	(2003)	2003	10	No. ordered may be up to 1000; possibly assembled from kits in Myanmar; status uncertain
	(60)	R-27E/AA-10 Alamo	BVRAAM	(2002)	2003–2005	(60)	For MiG-29 combat aircraft

Namibia

S:							
Brazil	1	Grajau	Patrol craft	2004			Part of $35 m deal

NATO

S:							
Multiple sellers	(5)	A-321	Transport aircraft	(2005)			Part of $3.15–4.8 b 'NATO AGS' programme; for modification to AGS aircraft; contract not yet signed; delivery possibly from 2010
USA	(7)	RQ-4A Global Hawk	UAV	(2005)			Part of $3.15–4.8 b 'NATO AGS' programme; contract not yet signed; delivery possibly from 2010

Nepal

S:							
India	1	Druhv/ALH	Helicopter	2004			Aid; probably armed version

Netherlands

S:							
France	12	Ocean Master	MP ac radar	2000		..	For 12 NH-90 NFH ASW helicopters
Germany	57	PzH-2000 155mm	Self-propelled gun	2002	2004–2005	(10)	$420 m deal (offsets 100%); 18 to be sold immediately after delivery to Netherlands; delivery 2004–2009
	4	DSQS-24	Sonar	(1993)	2002–2005	4	For 4 De Zeven Provincien frigates produced in Netherlands; DSQS-24C version
	3	TRS-3D	Air/sea surv radar	2004		..	'FGBADS Phase-1' programme worth €35 m ($44 m); TRS-3D/32 version; delivery 2007
Italy	4	Compact 127mm	Naval gun	1996	2002–2005	4	Ex-Canadian guns sold back to producer and modernized before delivery; for 4 De Zeven Provincien frigates produced in Netherlands
Sweden	74	BvS-10	APC	2005		..	SEK570 m ($77 m) deal; incl CP, ARV and ambulance versions; delivery 2006–2007

Recipient/supplier (S) or licenser (L)	No. ordered	Weapon designation	Weapon description	Year of order/ licence	Year(s) of deliveries	No. delivered/ produced	Comments
UK	8	Spey	Gas turbine (SH)	(1993)	2002–2005	8	For 4 De Zeven Provincien frigates produced in Netherlands; Spey SM-1C version
USA	2	C-130H Hercules	Transport ac	2005		..	Ex-US; €54 m deal; EC-130Q version modernized before delivery; delivery 2007
	5	CH-47D Chinook	Helicopter	(2005)		..	Part of €250–290 m ($300–340 m) deal; CH-47F version; contract not yet signed; delivery 2007–2011
	74	BTA-5.9	Diesel engine (AV)	2005		..	For 74 BvS-10 APC from Sweden
	24	AN/APG-78 Longbow	Ac radar	(2004)		..	For modernization of 24 AH-64D helicopters; contract not yet signed
	12	HELRAS	Dipping sonar	2000		..	For 12 NH-90 NFH ASW helicopters; probably from German production line
	32	MIM-104 PAC-3	SAM	2005		..	Delivery by 2006
	(240)	RIM-162 ESSM	SAM	2002	2003–2005	(150)	For De Zeven Provincien frigates
	(164)	RIM-66M Standard-2	SAM	(2002)	2003–2005	(164)	For De Zeven Provincien frigates
L: Israel	2 400	Spike-MR/LR	Anti-tank missile	2001	2005	(10)	$150–225 m deal (offsets incl production of components in Netherlands); from German Eurospike production line; Spike-MR version
Multiple sellers	12	NH-90 NFH	ASW helicopter	2000		..	Originally 20 NFH version ordered but changed to 12 NFH and 8 TTH version; 5% of components produced in Netherlands
Sweden	8	NH-90 TTH	Helicopter	(2004)		..	5% of components produced in Netherlands
	184	CV-9035	IFV	2004		..	€749–891 m ($939–992 m) deal (offsets 100% incl production of components and assembly in Netherlands); CV-9035NL (CV-9035 Mk-3) version; incl 34 CP version; delivery 2007–2010

Supplier (S) / Licenser (L)	No.	Weapon designation	Weapon description	Year of order	Year(s) of deliveries	No. delivered	Comments
New Zealand							
S: Israel	6	EL/M-2022	MP ac radar	2005		...	Part of NZD352 m modernization of 6 P-3K ASW/MP aircraft; EL/M-2022(V)3 version; delivery 2008–2010
Multiple sellers	(8)	NH-90 TTH	Helicopter	(2005)		...	'Project Warrior'; contract not yet signed; delivery from 2009
Netherlands	2	PAGE	Air surv radar	2004		...	Part of NZD10–15 m deal; for use with Mistral SAM; delivery 2006
	1	MRV	AALS	2004		...	Part of NZD500 m ($317 m) 'Project Protector'; ordered via Australian company; delivery 2006
UK	60	Pinzgauer 6x6	APC/ISV	2004	2005		Part of NZD93 m 'LOV' programme (incl 261 unarmoured version); incl CP version
USA	(164)	Javelin	Anti-tank missile	2003		60	Part of NZD27 m ($18 m) 'Project Crossbow' (incl 24 launchers); delivery 2006
L: Australia	2	Tenix-1600	OPV	2004		...	Part of NZD500 m ($317 m) 'Project Protector'; designed in UK; partly produced in New Zealand and assembled in Australia; delivery 2007
	4	Tenix-340	Patrol craft	2004		...	Part of NZD500 m ($317 m) 'Project Protector'; delivery 2007–2008
Nigeria							
S: China	12	F-7M Airguard	Fighter ac	2005		...	$220 m deal; F-7NI version; incl 3 FT-7NI; delivery from 2006
	20	PL-9	SRAAM	2005		...	Part of $32 m deal; PL-9C version; for F-7NI combat aircraft; delivery from 2006
Italy	1	G-222	Transport ac	2005		...	Ex-Italian; part of €60 m (75 m) deal; modernized before delivery; delivery 2006–2008
Norway							
S: France	6	FLASH	Dipping sonar	(2001)		...	For 6 NH-90NFH ASW helicopters
	6	MRR-3D	Air surv radar	2003		...	MRR-3D(NG) version; for 6 Skjold FAC produced in Norway; delivery 2006–2009
	6	Ocean Master	MP ac radar	2001		...	For 6 NH-90 NFH ASW helicopters

Recipient/ supplier (S) or licenser (L)	No. ordered	Weapon designation	Weapon description	Year of order/ licence	Year(s) of deliveries	No. delivered/ produced	Comments
	5	TSM-2633 Spherion	ASW sonar	(2000)		..	For 5 Nansen frigates from Spain; TSM-4131S (MRS-2000) version
Germany	10	MTU-183	Diesel engine (AV)	2003		..	For 5 Skjold FAC produced in Norway
	4	TRS-3D	Air/sea surv radar	2005		..	$12.2 or $25 m deal; for modernization of 4 Coast Guard Svalbard OPV
Sweden	6	CEROS-200	Fire control radar	2004		..	SEK155 m ($16 m) deal; for 6 Skjold FAC produced in Norway; delivery 2006–2009
USA	5	LM-2500	Gas turbine (SH)	(2000)		..	For 5 Nansen frigates from Spain
	10	ST-18	Gas turbine (SH)	2003		..	For 5 Skjold FAC produced in Norway
	10	ST-40	Gas turbine (SH)	2003		..	For 5 Skjold FAC produced in Norway
	5	AN/SPY-1F	Air surv radar	2000		..	Part of $500 m deal; part of AEGIS combat system for 5 Nansen frigates from Spain
	6	PANTERA	Ac El/Op system	2004		..	For F-16 combat aircraft
	(240)	RIM-162 ESSM	SAM	(2000)		..	For Nansen frigates
L: Germany	150	IRIS-T	SRAAM	(2003)	2005	(50)	Norway funds 4% of IRIS-T programme incl production of components in Norway; delivery 2005–2007
Multiple sellers	6	NH-90 NFH	ASW helicopter	2001		..	Part of $425 m deal (assembled in Finland; offsets incl production of components in Norway); ordered from France, Germany and Italy; delivery 2005–2008
	8	NH-90 TTH	Helicopter	2001		..	Part of $425 m deal (assembled in Finland; offsets incl production of components in Norway); for coast guard; for SAR; ordered from France, Germany and Italy; option on 10 more; delivery 2005–2008/2009
Spain	5	Nansen/F-100	Frigate	2000		..	Part of $1.5 b deal (offsets 100% in 10 years incl production of components and production of 2 in Norway and Spanish order of NASAMS SAM systems and Penguin missiles); delivery 2006–2009

Supplier/Recipient	No.	Weapon designation	Weapon description	Year of order	Year of delivery	No. delivered	Comments
USA	526	Javelin	Anti-tank missile	2004		..	$86 m deal (incl 90 launchers; offsets incl production of components in Norway); delivery 2006–2007
Oman							
S: Multiple sellers	20	NH-90 TTH	Helicopter	2004		..	€600–800 m ($720–960 m) deal; incl for SAR; delivery from 2008
UAE	1	Mahmal	Landing craft	2005		..	'Project Mahmal'
UK	16	Super Lynx-300	Helicopter	2002	2004–2005	(16)	Super Lynx-300/Lynx Mk-120 version
USA	12	F-16C	FGA ac	2002	2005	2	$224 m deal (part of $1.1 b deal); F-16C Block-50 version; delivery 2005–2006
	32	T-800	Turboshaft	2000	2004–2005	(32)	For 16 Super Lynx-300 helicopters from UK
	7	PANTERA	Ac El/Op system	2003		..	For F-16 combat aircraft
	80	AGM-65D Maverick	ASM	(2002)		..	Part of $1.1 b deal; AGM-65D/E version; for F-16C combat aircraft
	50	AIM-120C AMRAAM	BVRAAM	2002		..	Part of $1.1 b deal; for F-16C combat aircraft
	(100)	AIM-9M Sidewinder	SRAAM	2002		..	Part of $1.1 b deal; AIM-9M-8/9 version; for F-16C combat aircraft
	(100)	Javelin	Anti-tank missile	2005		..	$15–20 m deal
	20	RGM-84 Harpoon	Anti-ship missile	2003		..	$22 m deal (part of deal worth $1.1 b); AGM-84D version; for F-16C combat aircraft
Pakistan							
S: China	(4)	Z-9C/AS-565	ASW helicopter	(2005)		..	Contract probably not yet signed
	2	Type-347G	Fire control radar	(2003)	2004	1	For 2 Jalalat FAC produced in Pakistan
	(16)	C-802/CSS-N-8 Saccade	Anti-ship missile	(2003)	2004	(8)	For Jalalat FAC
	(32)	C-803	Anti-ship missile	(2005)		..	For Jiangwei (F-22P) frigates
	(64)	FM-80/HQ-7	SAM	(2005)		..	For Jiangwei (F-22P) frigates
	..	PL-12/SD-10	BVRAAM	(2004)		..	For JF-17 and possibly modernized Mirage-3/5 combat aircraft; contract not yet signed
France	8	SA-316B Alouette-3	Light helicopter	2005		..	Ex-French; SA-319B version
	(96)	F-17P	AS torpedo	(1996)	1999–2005	(84)	F-17P Mod-2 version; for Agosta-90B (Khalid) submarines
Germany	(24)	SM-39 Exocet	Anti-ship missile	1994	1999–2005	(23)	$100 m deal; for Agosta-90B (Khalid) submarines
	59	DM-2A4 533mm	AS torpedo	2005		..	$59 m deal; for Agosta-90B (Khalid) submarines

Recipient/ supplier (S) or licenser (L)	No. ordered	Weapon designation	Weapon description	Year of order/ licence	Year(s) of deliveries	No. delivered/ produced	Comments
Indonesia							
Sweden	4	CN-235	Transport ac	2005	..	..	SEK8.3 b ($1.1 b) deal; contract not yet signed; delivery possibly from 2009
	(7)	Saab-2000 AEW	AEW&C ac	(2005)		..	
Ukraine	(80)	5TDF	Diesel engine (AV)	(2000)	2004–2005	(80)	For modernization of Type-59 tanks to Al Zarrar
	315	6TD	Diesel engine (AV)	2002		..	$150 m deal; for MBT-2000 Al Khalid tanks produced in Pakistan
USA	40	Bell-205/UH-1H	Helicopter	(2004)		..	Ex-US; status uncertain
	(40)	Bell-209/AH-1F	Combat helicopter	(2004)		..	Ex-US; possibly all or some for spares only; status uncertain
	26	Bell-412	Helicopter	2004	2004–2005	(26)	$230 m deal (probably 'FMF' aid); from Canadian production line; for use in 'war on terrorism'; incl some for police; Bell-412EP version
	6	C-130E Hercules	Transport ac	2004	2005	1	Ex-Australian aircraft sold back to US producer and sold to Pakistan; $64 m deal; modernized before delivery; 1 more delivered for spares only
	2	F-16A	FGA ac	2005	2005	(2)	Ex-US (but only used 2 years); originally produced for Pakistan but delivery embargoed and delivered to USA; aid
	8	P-3C Orion	ASW/MP ac	2005		..	Ex-US; gift; modernized before and after delivery (paid with US aid worth up to $970 m); delivery from 2006
	2	SA-316B Alouette-3	Light helicopter	2005		..	Second-hand; SA-319B version
	115	M-109A5 155mm	Self-propelled gun	(2005)		..	Ex-US; $56 m deal; contract not yet signed
	..	CT-7	Turboprop	2005		..	For 4 CN-235 transport aircraft from Indonesia; CT-7-9C3 version
	6	AN/TPS-77	Air surv radar	(2005)		..	$89 m deal
	(6)	L-88 LASS	Air surv radar	(2003)		..	$155 m deal; for surveillance of border area with Afghanistan; status uncertain
	6	Mk-15 Phalanx	CIWS	(2004)		..	Part of $155 m deal (incl modernization of 6 Pakistani Phalanx); status uncertain

No. ordered	Weapon designation	Weapon description	Year of order	Year(s) of deliveries	No. delivered/produced	Comments
(300)	AIM-9M Sidewinder	SRAAM	(2005)	..		$29 m or $46 m deal; AIM-9M1 and AIM-9M2 version
2 014	BGM-71 TOW	Anti-tank missile	(2004)	..		$82 m deal; TOW-2A version; for AH-1 helicopters; contract possibly not yet signed
50	RGM-84L Harpoon	Anti-ship missile	2005	..		$61 m deal; incl 40 AGM-84 version; contract possibly not yet signed
L: China						
(150)	JF-17	FGA ac	1999	..		Developed for Pakistan; incl production of components and assembly in Pakistan; delivery possibly from 2006/2007
(22)	K-8 Karakorum-8	Trainer/combat ac	2005	..		Incl production of components and assembly in Pakistan
..	QW-1 Vanguard	Portable SAM	(1993)	1994–2005	(950)	Pakistani desig Anza-2
..	Red Arrow-8	Anti-tank missile	1989	1990–2005	(13 600)	Pakistani desig Baktar Shikan
4	Jiangwei	Frigate	2005	..		$500–750 m deal; F-22P version; incl assembly/production in Pakistan; delivery 2008–2013
France						
3	Agosta-90B	Submarine	1994	1999–2003	2	$750 m deal (+ $200 m for modernization of Pakistan Naval Dockyard to build submarines); 2 assembled from kits in Pakistan; incl 1 with air-independent propulsion system; Pakistani desig Khalid; delivery 1999–2006
Italy						
(57)	Grifo	Ac radar	(2002)	2004–2005	(35)	Grifo-7PG version; for 57 F-7MG (F-7PG) combat aircraft from China
Sweden						
(150)	MFI-17 Supporter	Trainer ac	(2001)	2001–2005	(56)	Super Mushshak version
..	RBS-70	Portable SAM	(1985)	1988–2005	(450)	Assembled from kits in Pakistan
Palestinian Authority						
S: Russia						
2	Mi-8/Mi-17/Hip-H	Helicopter	2005	..		Mi-17 version; possibly ex-Russian; aid; status uncertain
50	BTR-70	APC	2005	..		Probably ex-Russian; aid; desig uncertain; status uncertain

Recipient/ supplier (S) or licenser (L)	No. ordered	Weapon designation	Weapon description	Year of order/ licence	Year(s) of deliveries	No. delivered/ produced	Comments
Paraguay							
S: Brazil	6	Universal-1	Trainer ac	2005	2005	(6)	Ex-Brazilian; gift
Peru							
S: Germany	24	MTU-595	Diesel engine (SH)	(1999)	2000	12	For modernization of 6 PR-72P (Velarde) FAC
Italy	2	Lupo	Frigate	(2004)	2005	2	Ex-Italian; $30 m deal; modernized before delivery
	2	Lupo	Frigate	2005		:	Ex-Italian; modernized before delivery; delivery 2006
Russia	5	An-32/Cline	Transport ac	(2005)		:	Part of $140 m deal
	5	Mi-24V/Mi-35/Hind-E	Combat helicopter	(2005)		:	Part of $140 m deal
USA	16	Bell-205/UH-1 Huey-2	Helicopter	(2003)	2004-2005	(16)	Ex-US UH-1H rebuilt to Huey-2 before delivery; aid for police anti-narcotics operations
Philippines							
S: South Korea	2	Sea Dolphin	Patrol craft	(2002)		:	Desig uncertain; probably ex-South Korean; delivery 2006
Singapore	(7)	Bell-205/UH-1H	Helicopter	2003	2004-2005	(7)	Ex-Singaporean; part of $12 m deal; modernized before delivery
Unknown country	(6)	Bell-205/UH-1H	Helicopter	2003	2004-2005	(6)	Second-hand; part of $12 m deal; ordered and delivered via Singapore; modernized in Singapore before delivery
USA	20	Bell-205/UH-1H	Helicopter	2003	2005	(20)	Ex-US; part of $30 m aid (incl 10 more delivered for spares)
	(7)	Bell-205/UH-1H	Helicopter	2003	2004-2005	(7)	Second-hand; part of $12 m deal; ordered and delivered via Singapore; modernized in Singapore before delivery
	6	Bell-205/UH-1H	Helicopter	2003	2005	(3)	$8.2 m deal; delivery 2005/2006
	4	C-130H Hercules	Transport ac	(2002)		:	Ex-UK C-130K version sold back to US producer; $41 m deal; modernized before delivery; incl for MP
	48	M-113	APC	(2003)		:	Ex-US; aid

No.	Weapon designation	Weapon description	Year of order	Year(s) of deliveries	No. delivered	Comments
L: USA	2	Bell-205/UH-1 Huey-2	Helicopter		2005	(2)	Philippine UH-1H rebuilt to Huey-2; assembled from kits in Philippines
Poland						
S: Canada	16	PW-100	Turboprop	2001	2003–2005	16	For 8 C-295 transport aircraft from Spain; PW-127 version
Italy	3	RAT-31S/L	Air surv radar	(2002)		..	$38 or $90 m deal; part of 'NATO ACCS' programme; for 'NADGE' air-surveillance network; RAT-31DL version; delivery 2006–2007
Multiple sellers	..	MU-90 Impact	ASW torpedo	(2002)		..	€30 m deal; incl for Mi-14PL and SH-2G helicopters and MEKO-A100 and Perry (Pulaski) frigates; ordered from Germany, Italy or France
Netherlands	3	STING	Fire control radar	2001	2003	1	For modernization of 3 Orkan corvettes; delivery 2003–2006
Russia	(200)	9M120 Vikhr/AT-9	Anti-tank missile	(2004)		..	For modernized Mi-24PL helicopters
Spain	8	C-295	Transport ac	2001	2003–2005	8	$212 m deal (offsets 100%); option on 4 more
Sweden	(128)	Eagle-1	Fire control radar	(2001)	2004	(1)	For Loara AAV(G) produced in Poland; status uncertain
	3	Giraffe AMB-3D	Air surv radar	2001	2003	1	Sea Giraffe AMB version; for modernization of 3 Orkan corvettes; delivery 2003–2006
	(60)	RBS-15 Mk-3	Anti-ship missile	(2001)	2003–2005	(24)	For 3 Orkan corvettes and probably for 2 MEKO-A100 frigates
USA	5	C-130H Hercules	Transport ac	(2004)		..	Ex-UK aircraft returned to US producer and tranferred to Poland; 'FMF' aid worth orginally $72 m but increased to $120 m (incl modernization before delivery); C-130K version; incl 1 C-130K Hercules C-3 version; delivery delayed from 2006–2007 to 2011–2012 due to extensive modernization
	48	F-16C	FGA ac	2003		..	$3.5 b 'Peace Sky-1' deal ($4.7 b incl interest; offsets $6 b or $12.5 b); delivery 2007–2008
	11	MSTAR	Ground surv radar	2004	2005	11	$2.7 m deal
	22	PANTERA	Ac El/Op system	2003		..	For F-16 combat aircraft
	360	AGM-65G Maverick	ASM	2004		..	$78 m deal; AGM-64G2 version; delivery by 2007
	(126)	AIM-120C AMRAAM	BVRAAM	2004		..	AIM-120C-5 version

Recipient/ supplier (S) or licenser (L)	No. ordered	Weapon designation	Weapon description	Year of order/ licence	Year(s) of deliveries	No. delivered/ produced	Comments
	178	AIM-9X Sidewinder	SRAAM	2004	2004–2005	..	For F-16C combat aircraft
	..	RIM-162 ESSM	SAM	(2003)		..	For MEKO-A100 frigates; contract not yet signed
L: Finland	313	XC-360 AMV	IFV	2003	2004–2005	(13)	Part of PLN4.9 b (c. $1.45 b) 'Suhak' programme (incl $308 m for turrets from Italy; offsets 133%); XC-360P version; Polish desig Rosomak; delivery 2004–2013
	377	XC-360 AMV	APC	2003	2004–2005	(46)	Part of PLN4.9 b (c. $1.45 b) 'Suhak' programme (offsets 133%); XC-360P version; incl 32 reconnaissance version; Polish desig Rosomak; delivery 2004–2013
Germany	2	MEKO-A100	Frigate	2001		..	Polish desig Project-621 Gawron-2; option on 2–5 more; delivery from 2006
Israel	(2 675)	Spike-MR/LR	Anti-tank missile	2003	2004–2005	(270)	PLN1.49b (c. $425 m) deal (incl $250–260 m for Israeli producer; offsets $826 m incl production of components and assembly in Poland; incl 264 launchers); Spike-LR version; delivery 2004–2013
UK	(78)	AS-90 turret	Turret	(2004)		..	For use on Polish chassis as Chrobry or Krab self-propelled gun; incl assembly/production in Poland; contract not yet signed
Portugal							
S: Canada	24	PW-100	Turboprop	2005		..	For 12 C-295 transport aircraft from Spain; PW-127 version
France	12	EC-120B Colibri	Light helicopter	2003	2004–2005	(12)	
Germany	2	Type-214	Submarine	2004		..	€846 m ($970 m) deal (offsets 100%); Type-209PN version; option on 1 more; delivery 2009–2010

Recipient/Supplier	No.	Weapon designation	Weapon description	Year of order	Year of deliveries	No. delivered	Comments
Italy	12	EH-101-400	Helicopter	2002	2004–2005	(11)	$287–315 m deal (incl 2 financed by EU for fishery protection); incl for SAR and CSAR; delivery 2004–2006
	. .	Black Shark	AS torpedo	2005		. .	€47 m ($62 m) deal; for Type-214 (Type-209PN) submarines
Netherlands	3	P-3C Orion Update-2.5	ASW/MP ac	2004		. .	Ex-Dutch; part of €70 m or €223 m ($85 m or $265 m) deal
	2	P-3CUP Orion	ASW/MP ac	2004		. .	Ex-Dutch P-3C sold to Portugal while being modernized to P-3CUP in USA for Netherlands; part of €70 m or €223 m ($85 m or $265 m) deal
Spain	12	C-295	Transport ac	2005		. .	€278 m deal
	1	S763-LANZA	Air surv radar	2004		. .	€18 m ($22 m) deal; option on 3 more
UK	260	ISC-350	Diesel engine (AV)	2005		. .	For 260 Pandur-2 APC/IFV from Austria
USA	36	RTM-322	Turboshaft	2002	2004–2005	(33)	For 12 EH-101 helicopters from Italy
	12	AIM-120C AMRAAM	BVRAAM	(2002)	2005	(6)	
	(96)	MIM-72F Chaparral	SAM	(2004)		. .	Ex-US; aid; MIM-72G version; status uncertain
L: Austria	30	Pandur-2	IFV	2005		. .	Part of €365 m (c. $480 m) deal (incl €21 m for spare parts; offsets 150% in 9 years incl assembly of most in Portugal); delivery 2006–2009
	230	Pandur-2	APC	2005		. .	Part of €365 m (c. $480 m) deal (incl €21 m for spare parts; offsets 150% in 9 years incl assembly of most in Portugal); incl ambulance, ARV, CP and anti-tank version; delivery 2006–2009
USA	20	F-16C	FGA ac	1998	2003–2005	(13)	$268 m 'Peace Atlantis-2' deal (incl aircraft as aid; 5 more for spares); ex-US F-16OCU version modernized to F-16AM (F-16C) in Portugal with US kits; incl 4 F-16B; delivery 2003–2006
Romania							
S: Germany	36	Gepard	AAV(G)	1998	2004–2005	(21)	Ex-German; aid (worth $37 m); modernized before delivery (7 more delivered for spares only)
Israel	(1 000)	Spike-ER	Anti-tank missile	(1998)	1999–2005	(1 000)	For SA-330 (IAR-330) helicopters modernized to IAR-330 SOCAT

Recipient/ supplier (S) or licenser (L)	No. ordered	Weapon designation	Weapon description	Year of order/ licence	Year(s) of deliveries	No. delivered/ produced	Comments
	..	Spike-MR/LR	Anti-tank missile	(2005)	2005	(50)	For modernized MLI-84 IFV; from German EuroSpike production line
Netherlands	8	I-HAWK	SAM system	2004	2005	8	Ex-Dutch; €24 m ($32 m) deal; possibly HAWK PIP-3 version or modernized to PIP-3 version after delivery
UK	(288)	MIM-23B HAWK	SAM	2004	2005	(288)	Ex-Dutch
	2	Boxer/Type-22	Frigate	2003	2004–2005	2	Ex-UK; £116 m ($187 m) deal (offsets 80–90%); modernized before delivery; Romanian desig Regele Ferdinand
USA	1	C-130H Hercules	Transport ac	2004	2005	1	Ex-Italian aircraft sold back to US producer; $7.8 m deal (part of $55 m deal incl modernization of 4 Romanian C-130B and $16 m 'FMF' aid); modernized before delivery
	21	AN/TPS-73 MMSR	Air surv radar	2003	2004–2005	(8)	Delivery 2004–2008
L: UK	9	Viper	Turbojet	2000	2002–2005	(9)	For 9 IAR-99C trainer aircraft produced in Romania; Viper-632-41M version
Saudi Arabia							
S: France	3	La Fayette/F-3000S	Frigate	1994	2002–2005	3	Part of $3.4 b 'Sawari-2' deal (offsets 35%); also designated Modified La Fayette; Saudi desig Al Riyadh
Germany	100	Deutz V-10	Diesel engine (AV)	(1995)	1998–2005	(100)	For 100 AF-40-8-1 APC produced in Saudi Arabia
Pakistan	20	MFI-17 Supporter	Trainer ac	(2003)	2005	(20)	$34 m deal; Super Mushshak version
UK	(72)	Eurofighter/Typhoon	FGA ac	(2005)		..	Part of up to $16 b 'Al Yamamah-3' deal; contract not yet signed
USA	4	Cessna-550 Citation-2	Light transport ac	(2005)	2005	2	Delivery 2005–2006
	523	6V-53	Diesel engine (AV)	1997	2003–2005	(300)	Part of $413 m modernization of 523 M-113 APC to M-113A3; 6V-53T version

No. ordered	Weapon designation	Weapon description	Year of order	Year(s) of deliveries	No. delivered	Comments
..	AN/AAQ-13 LANTIRN	Ac El/Op system	(2005)		(..)	For Tornado combat aircraft; contract probably not yet signed
..	AN/AAQ-14 LANTIRN	Ac radar	(2005)		(..)	For Tornado combat aircraft; contract probably not yet signed
500	AIM-120C AMRAAM	BVRAAM	2000	2003–2005	(331)	$475 m deal; for F-15 combat aircraft
150	AIM-9M Sidewinder	SRAAM	2005		(..)	$17 m deal; delivery 2006/2007
Singapore						
S: Denmark						
12	SCANTER-2001	Sea surv radar	(2002)		(..)	For 6 La Fayette (Formidable) frigates from France
France						
5	EC-120B Colibri	Light helicopter	2005		(..)	Part of SGD120 m (€60 m) deal (owned by and leased for 20 years from Singaporean company); for training
(288)	ASTER-15 SAAM	SAM	(2001)			Part of $1.6 b 'Project Delta'; for La Fayette (Formidable) frigates
Germany						
24	MTU-8000	Diesel engine (SH)	(2000)		(..)	For 6 La Fayette (Formidable) frigates from France; MTU-8000-M90 version
Russia						
..	Igla/SA-18 Grouse	Portable SAM	(2001)	2005	(100)	Possibly incl assembly/production in Singapore; incl for use on Igla M-113 SAM system produced in Singapore
Sweden						
2	Västergötland/A-17	Submarine	2005		(..)	Ex-Swedish; SEK1 b ($128 m) deal; modernized (incl with AIP engines) before delivery; delivery 2010
USA						
12	AH-64D Apache	Combat helicopter	2001	2005	(12)	$617 m 'Peace Vanguard' deal; stationed in USA until 2006
12	F-15E Strike Eagle	Fighter/bomber ac	2005		(..)	$1 b 'NFRP' programme; F-15SG version; option on 8 more; delivery 2008–2009
20	F-16C	FGA ac	(2000)	2004–2005	(20)	'Peace Carvin-4' deal; F-16D Block-52 version
6	S-70B/SH-60B Seahawk	ASW helicopter	2005		(..)	SH-70(N) version; delivery 2008–2010
54	M-109 chassis	Gun chassis	(2001)	2001–2005	(54)	For use as chassis of Primus self-propelled gun produced in Singapore (with Singaporean 155mm gun turret)
18	AN/AAQ-14 LANTIRN	Ac radar	2001	2004–2005	(18)	For F-16 combat aircraft
(192)	AGM-114K HELLFIRE	Anti-tank missile	(2001)	2005	(192)	For AH-64D helicopters
(60)	AGM-154 JSOW	ASM	(2005)		(..)	For F-15SG combat aircraft; contract not yet signed
50	AIM-120C AMRAAM	BVRAAM	2004		(..)	$25 m deal; AIM-120C5 version

Recipient/ supplier (S) or licenser (L)	No. ordered	Weapon designation	Weapon description	Year of order/ licence	Year(s) of deliveries	No. delivered/ produced	Comments
L: France	(200)	AIM-120C AMRAAM	BVRAAM	(2005)	2005	..	For F-15SG combat aircraft; contract not yet signed
	(200)	AIM-9X Sidewinder	SRAAM	(2005)	2005	..	For F-15SG combat aircraft; contract not yet signed
L: France	6	La Fayette/F-3000	Frigate	2000		..	$750 m deal (part of $1.6 b 'Project Delta'); 5 assembled/produced in Singapore; Singaporean desig Formidable; delivery 2007–2009
Israel	..	Spike-MR/LR	Anti-tank missile	1999	2001–2005	(900)	Probably Spike-LR version
Slovenia							
L: Austria	36	Pandur	APC	2003	2004–2005	(18)	Slovenian desig Valuk
South Africa							
S: France	4	MRR-3D	Air surv radar	(2000)	2005	(1)	For 4 MEKO-A200 (Valour) frigates from Germany
	4	TSM-2633 Spherion-B	ASW VDS sonar	(1999)	2005	(1)	For 4 MEKO-A200 (Valour) frigates from Germany; TSM-4132 Kingklip version
	17	MM-40 Exocet	Anti-ship missile	2000	2005	17	For MEKO-A200 (Valour) frigates; originally 32 planned but reduced to 17 after budget cut
Germany	3	Type-209/1400	Submarine	2000	2005	1	€748 m (c. $875 m) deal (offsets 375–430%); Type-209/1400MOD version; delivery 2005–2007
Netherlands	2	PAGE	Air surv radar	2003	2005	(1)	Part of $117 m 'Ground Based Air Defence System (GBADS) Phase-1' programme
Sweden	19	JAS-39 Gripen	FGA ac	(2000)		..	Part of $1.2 b deal (offsets $8.7 b incl $1.5 b for arms industry); JAS-39C version; for delivery 2009–2011/2012
	9	JAS-39 Gripen	FGA ac	1999		..	Part of $1.2 b deal (offsets $8.7 b incl $1.5 b for arms industry); JAS-39D version; for delivery 2008–2009
UK	4	Super Lynx-300	Helicopter	2003		..	$107 m deal (offsets $173 m incl $88 m for arms industry); option on 2 more; delivery 2007
	(72)	Starstreak	Portable SAM	2003	2005	(36)	$13 m deal (part of $117 m 'Ground Based Air Defence System (GBADS) Phase-1' programme)

Supplier	No.	Weapon designation	Weapon description	Year of order	Year of delivery	No. delivered	Comments
USA	9	F-404	Turbofan	1999		..	For 9 JAS-39D combat aircraft from Sweden; RM-12 version from Swedish production line
	19	F-404	Turbofan	(2000)		..	For 19 JAS-39C combat aircraft from Sweden; RM-12 version from Swedish production line
	4	LM-2500	Gas turbine (SH)	(1999)	2005	(1)	For 4 MEKO-A200 (Valour) frigates from Germany
	8	T-800	Turboshaft	2003		..	For 4 Super Lynx-300 helicopters from UK
	4	AN/APS-143(V)	MP ac radar	2003		..	For 4 Super Lynx-300 helicopters from UK
L: Germany	4	MEKO-A200	Frigate	(2000)	2005	(1)	$0.8–1.12 b deal (offsets $3.2 b incl $403 m for arms industry incl South African weapons and equipment fitted in South Africa); South African desig Amatola; delivery 2005–2006
Italy	30	A-109K	Light helicopter	1999	2005	(10)	$240–254 m deal (offsets $977 m incl $191 m for arms industry; incl assembly of 25 in South Africa and production of A-109 and A-119 in South Africa for export); A-109LUH version; option on 10 more; delivery 2005–2006
Multiple sellers	8	A-400M	Transport ac	2005		..	€830 m deal (offsets €400–430 m incl production of components in South Africa for south African and other A-400); delivery 2010–2014
UK	12	Hawk-100	Trainer/combat ac	2002		..	Part of $620 m deal (offsets inc assembly in South Africa; Hawk-100LIFT/Hawk-120 version; delivery 2006
	12	Hawk-100	Trainer/combat ac	1999	2005	(12)	Part of $1.2 b deal (offsets $8.7 b incl $1.5 b for arms industry incl assembly of 11 in South Africa); Hawk-100LIFT/Hawk-120 version
Spain							
S: Canada	18	PW-100	Turboprop	1999	2001–2005	(18)	For 9 C-295 transport aircraft produced in Spain; PW-127 version
France	..	Mistral	Portable SAM	(2003)		..	For AS-665 Tiger helicopters
Germany	(212)	MTU-183	Diesel engine (AV)	2003	2005	(35)	For 212 Pizarro (ASCOD) IFV produced in Spain
	1	Patriot	SAM system	2004	2005	1	Ex-German; €40–50 m deal

Recipient/ supplier (S) or licenser (L)	No. ordered	Weapon designation	Weapon description	Year of order/ licence	Year(s) of deliveries	No. delivered/ produced	Comments
	40	DM-2A4 533mm	AS torpedo	2005		..	€76 m deal; for Scorpene (S-80) submarines
	43	Taurus KEPD-350	ASM	2005		..	€57 m deal
Israel	2 600	Spike-MR/LR	Anti-tank missile	(2005)		..	€250 m deal (incl 260 launchers); contract not yet signed
Italy	5	RAN-12L/X	Air/sea surv radar	(1996)	2002–2005	4	For 5 De Bazán (F-100) frigates produced in Spain
Norway	(20)	Penguin-2	Anti-ship missile	(2000)	2005	(5)	$26 m deal (offsets for Norwegian order for 5 frigates); Penguin-2 Mod-7 version; for S-70/SH-60B helicopters; option on more
USA	5	Mk-45 127mm	Naval gun	1999	2002–2005	4	Ex-US; modernized before delivery; for 5 De Bazán (F-100) destroyers produced in Spain; Mk-45 Mod-2 version
	8	CT-7	Turboprop	(2005)		..	For 4 CN-235MP MP aircraft produced in Spain; CT-7-9C3 version
	10	LM-2500	Gas turbine (SH)	1996	2002–2005	8	For 5 De Bazán (F-100) destroyers produced in Spain
	4	AN/MPQ-64	Air surv radar	(2000)	2004	(1)	Ordered via Norway as part of 4 NASAMS SAM systems
	10	AN/SPG-62	Fire control radar	(1996)	2002–2005	8	AN/SPG-62 Mk-99 version; for use with Standard and ESSM SAMs on 5 De Bazán (F-100) destroyers produced in Spain
	4	AN/SPY-1F	Air surv radar	1996	2002–2005	4	Part of $750 m deal; for 4 De Bazán (F-100) frigates produced in Spain
	1	AN/SPY-1F	Air surv radar	2005	2002–2005	..	Part of $550 m deal; for 1 De Bazán (F-100) frigate produced in Spain
	5	DE-1160	ASW sonar	1996	2002–2005	4	For 5 De Bazán (F-100) frigates produced in Spain; DE-1160LF version (possibly older Spanish DE-1160B modernized to DE-1160F)
	..	AGM-114K HELLFIRE	Anti-tank missile	(2003)		..	For SH-60B helicopters; for anti-ship role; contract not yet signed
	..	AIM-120A AMRAAM	BVRAAM	(2000)	2004–2005	(50)	For NASAMS SAM systems from Norway
	226	Javelin	Anti-tank missile	(2001)		..	$25 m deal (incl 12 launchers); status uncertain

	No. ordered	Weapon designation	Weapon description	Year of order	Year of deliveries	No. delivered	Comments
	(384)	RIM-162 ESSM	SAM	(2003)		..	For De Bazán (F-100) frigates; contract possibly not yet signed
	(94)	RIM-66B Standard-1MR	SAM	(2005)		..	$41 m deal; for Perry (Santa Maria) frigates; status uncertain
L: France	24	AS-665 Tiger	Combat helicopter	2003		..	€1.4 b deal; incl 6 HAP (later modernized to HAD) and 18 HAD version; incl assembly/production of 18 HAD version in Spain; delivery 2006/2007–2011
Germany	16	Buffel	ARV	1998	2003–2005	(7)	Part of €1.9 b ($2.2 b) deal (offsets 80% incl production of 12 in Spain)
	219	Leopard-2A5+	Tank	1998	2003–2005	(40)	Part of €1.9 b ($2.2 b) deal (offsets 80% incl production of 189 in Spain); Leopard-2A5E version; delivery 2005–2008
	(700)	IRIS-T	SRAAM	(2004)		..	Spain funds 5% of IRIS-T programme incl production of components in Spain; delivery possibly from 2006
Italy	62	B-1 Centauro	Armoured car	2002	2004–2005	(38)	€219 m ($185 m) deal (offsets incl production of components in Spain); Spanish desig VRC-105; delivery 2004–2006
Multiple sellers	45	NH-90 TTH	Helicopter	2005		..	€1.3 b deal; contract not yet signed; delivery from 2010
USA	10	Caterpillar-3616	Diesel engine (SH)	(1996)	2002–2005	8	For 5 De Bazán (F-100) frigates produced in Spain; probably assembled in Spain
Sri Lanka							
S: China	(3)	CEIEC-408C	Air surv radar	2004		..	Desig uncertain
Israel	1	Kfir C-7	FGA ac	(2004)	2005	1	Ex-Israeli; part of $25 m deal; probably modernized before delivery
Sweden							
S: Canada	(11)	Hydra	Sonar	(1995)	2004–2005	(3)	For 5 Visby corvettes produced in Sweden and for modernization of 4 Göteborg and 2 Stockholm FAC
France	5	FLASH	Dipping sonar	(2001)		..	For 5 NH-90NFH ASW helicopters
Germany	10	MTU-N-90	Diesel engine (SH)	(1995)	2005	(4)	For 5 Visby corvettes produced in Sweden

Recipient/ supplier (S) or licenser (L)	No. ordered	Weapon designation	Weapon description	Year of order/ licence	Year(s) of deliveries	No. delivered/ produced	Comments
Italy	20	A-109K	Light helicopter	2001	2005	(2)	€130 m ($113 m) deal (incl components made in South Africa as offsets for South African order for JAS-39 combat aircraft); A-109LUH (A-109M) version; Swedish desig Hkp-15; 2 more on loan from 2002 for training; delivery 2005–2007
South Africa	200	RG-32 Scout	APC/ISV	2005	2005	(10)	Part of offsets for South African order for JAS-39 combat aircraft
USA	20	TF-50	Gas turbine (SH)	(1995)	2005	(8)	For 5 Visby corvettes produced in Sweden; TF-50A version
	5	AN/APS-143(V)	MP ac radar	2002		..	$7.6 m deal; for 5 NH-90 NFH ASW helicopters
	(53)	AIM-120C AMRAAM	BVRAAM	2004	2005	(53)	Part of $53 m deal; AIM-120C-5 version
L: Germany	(250)	IRIS-T	SRAAM	(2004)		..	Sweden funds 18% of IRIS-T programme incl production of components in Sweden; delivery from 2009
Multiple sellers	5	NH-90 NFH	ASW helicopter	2001		..	Part of $660 b deal (most assembled in Finland; offsets 100% incl $220 m production of parts for 200 NH-90 in Sweden); Swedish desig Hkp-14; delivery 2007–2009
	13	NH-90 TTH	Helicopter	2001		..	Part of $660 b deal (most assembled in Finland; offsets 100% incl $220 m production of parts for 200 NH-90 in Sweden); NH-90TTT version; incl 3 for SAR; Swedish desig Hkp-14; option on 7 more; delivery 2007–2009
USA	(190)	F-404	Turbofan	(1982)	1993–2005	(168)	For JAS-39 Gripen combat aircraft produced in Sweden; F-404-GE-400/RM-12 version

	No. ordered	Weapon designation	Weapon description	Year of order	Year(s) of deliveries	No. delivered/ produced	Comments
Switzerland							
S: Germany	(18)	EC-135/EC-635	Helicopter	(2005)		..	Part of SFR310 m 'HTLF' programme; EC-635 version (2 more EC-135 ordered for VIP transport; incl for training; contract probably not yet signed
USA	(15)	PiPz-3 Kodiak	AEV	(2002)	(2002)	..	Delivery from 2007; status uncertain
	(222)	AIM-9X Sidewinder	SRAAM	2002	2002	..	SFR104 m ($80 m) deal (offsets 100%); for F/A-18C combat aircraft; delivery probably from 2006/2007
L: Germany	25	Buffel	ARV	2001	2004–2005	(25)	$63–70 m deal (10.5% of components produced in Switzerland)
Sweden	186	CV-9030	IFV	2000	2001–2005	(186)	SEK4 b ($424 m) 'Schutzenpanzer-2000' programme (offsets 100% incl 40% in production of components and assembly in Switzerland); CH-9030CH (CH-9030 Mk-2) version; incl 32 CP version; option on 124 more
UK	(2 000)	Rapier Mk-2	SAM	(2002)	2004–2005	(750)	Delivery 2004–2007
Syria							
S: Russia	(14)	Su-27SK/Flanker-B	FGA ac	(1999)		..	Status uncertain
	..	Igla/SA-18 Grouse	Portable SAM	2005		..	For use on vehicles/helicopters/ships (not with portable launchers after Israeli and US pressure); status uncertain
Taiwan							
S: France	1	ROCSAT-2	Optical surv satellite	1999	2005	1	$70 m deal; after Chinese pressure fitted with limitations to surveillance of Chinese territory
USA	2	E-2C Hawkeye-2000	AEW&C ac	1999	2005	2	$400 m deal; E-2T/Hawkeye-2000 version
	3	S-92/H-92 Superhawk	Helicopter	(2005)		..	For SAR; contract not yet signed
	54	LVTP-7A1/AAV-7A1	APC	2003	2005	(15)	$64–156 m deal; ex-US AAV-7A1 rebuilt to AAV-7A1RAM/RS; incl 4 CP and 2 ARV version; delivery from 2005
	(1 400)	C-9	Diesel engine (AV)	(2005)	2004–2005	..	For 1400 CM-32 APC/IFV produced in Taiwan
	1	AN/BOND	Air surv radar	2005		..	Part of $752 m deal; delivery by 2009
	11	AN/TPS-77	Air surv radar	2002	2004–2005	(6)	Incl 4 AN/TPS-117

Recipient/ supplier (S) or licenser (L)	No. ordered	Weapon designation	Weapon description	Year of order/ licence	Year(s) of deliveries	No. delivered/ produced	Comments
	(449)	AGM-114K HELLFIRE	Anti-tank missile	(2004)		..	Part of $50 m deal; AGM-114M3 version
	5	AIM-7M Sparrow	BVRAAM	2005		..	Part of $280 m deal; for training in USA
	182	AIM-9M Sidewinder	SRAAM	2003		..	$17 m deal; AIM-9M-2 version; delivery by 2006
	10	AIM-9M Sidewinder	SRAAM	2005		..	Part of $280 m deal; for training in USA
	360	Javelin	Anti-tank missile	(2002)	2005	(360)	$51 m deal (incl 40 launchers)
	(22)	RGM-84L Harpoon	Anti-ship missile	(2003)	2005	(8)	RGM-84L Block-2 version; for Kidd (Keelung) destroyers
	(148)	RIM-66M Standard-2	SAM	(2003)	2005	(74)	SM-2 Block-3A version; for Kidd (Keelung) destroyers
	4	Kidd	Destroyer	(2003)	2005	2	Ex-US; $740 m deal; Taiwanese desig Keelung; delivery 2005–2007
Thailand							
S: China	(97)	WZ-551	APC	2005		..	THB1.9–2 b deal (barter with Thai fruit); no. may be up to 133; incl for police; WZ-551B version
Germany	2	OPV-95	Frigate	2002	2005	1	€75–80 m ($66–95 m) deal
	(97)	BF-8L	Diesel engine (AV)	2005		..	For some 97 WZ-551B APC from China; probably from Chinese production line
Italy	2	RAN-30X	Air surv radar	(2002)	2005	1	For 2 OPV-95 frigates from China
	2	Seaguard TMX	Fire control radar	(2002)	2005	1	For 2 OPV-95 frigates from China
Netherlands	8	Flycatcher	Fire control radar	2004	2005	(8)	Ex-Dutch; for use with 40mm AA guns
UK	22	L-118 105mm	Towed gun	2004	2005	(11)	L-119 version
	4	20RK-270	Diesel engine (SH)	(2002)	2005	2	For 2 OPV-95 frigates from China
Unknown country	..	Bell-212/UH-1N	Helicopter	(2005)		..	Second-hand; contract probably not yet signed
USA	7	Bell-209/AH-1F	Combat helicopter	2005		..	Ex-US; aid (Thailand to pay THB300 m ($7.1 m) for overhaul and transport)
	(4)	S-70A/UH-60L	Helicopter	2003	2004–2005	(4)	THB3 b deal
	2	S-70A/UH-60L	Helicopter	(2005)		..	$46 m deal; bought after 2004 natural disaster as reaction to lack of helicopters for SAR; contract possibly not yet signed

Supplier	No. ordered	Weapon designation	Weapon description	Year of order	Year(s) of deliveries	No. delivered/ produced	Comments
	3	Sea Vue	MP ac radar	(2005)	2005	(1)	For modernization of 3 P-3T ASW/MP aircraft

Tunisia

Supplier	No. ordered	Weapon designation	Weapon description	Year of order	Year(s) of deliveries	No. delivered/ produced	Comments
S: Germany	6	Albatros/Type-143	FAC(M)	2004	2005	6	Ex-German; €34 m (c. $43 m) deal; Type-143B version
USA	(15)	Bell-205/UH-1H	Helicopter	(2004)		..	Ex-US; aid; status uncertain
	(30)	M-106 107mm	APC/mortar carrier	(2003)		..	Ex-US; aid; M-106A2 version; status uncertain
	(92)	M-113	APC	(2003)		..	Ex-US; aid; M-113A2 version; M-577A2 CP version; status uncertain

Turkey

Supplier	No. ordered	Weapon designation	Weapon description	Year of order	Year(s) of deliveries	No. delivered/ produced	Comments
S: Canada	20	PW-100	Turboprop	2005		..	For 10 ATR-72MP ASW/MP aircraft from Italy; PW-127 version
France	19	Ocean Master	MP ac radar	2002		..	Part of $400 m deal; part of 'Meltem' programme; for 9 CN-235MPA and 10 ATR-70 MP aircraft from Spain and Italy
Germany	298	Leopard-2A4	Tank	2005		..	Ex-German; €365 m ($430 m) deal (incl €70 m for Germany and €295 m for German industry for technology transfers); delivery 2006–2007
	470	MTU-881	Diesel engine (AV)	(2001)	2003–2005	(55)	For 170 Sabra-3 (modernized M-60) tanks from Israel and 300 K-9 self-propelled guns from South Korea
	40	DM-2A4 533mm	AS torpedo	(1999)	2004–2005	(40)	$40 m deal; for Type-209/1400 (Preveze) submarines
Israel	10	Heron-2	UAV	2005		..	$183 m deal (offsets 30%); delivery 2007
	170	Sabra-3	Tank	(2002)	2005	1	$688 m deal; Turkish M-60A3 tanks rebuilt to Sabra-3
Italy	10	ATR-72MP	ASW/MP ac	2005		..	'Meltem' or 'Uzun Ufuk' programme worth €180 m (c. $220 m; offsets $752–775 m incl producton of components in and assembly in Turkey); ATR-70 or ATR-72ASW version; delivery 2009/2010–2012
	5	Bell-412	Helicopter	2005		..	AB-412EP version; for Coast Guard; delivery 2006 or 2007–2008
	4	RAT-31S/L	Air surv radar	2002		(2)	Part 'NATO ACCS' programme; for 'NADGE' air-surveillance network; RAT-31DL version
Netherlands	6	LIROD	Fire control radar	2001	2004–2005	(3)	For 6 Kilic FAC from Germany
	6	MW-08	Air surv radar	2001	2004–2005	(3)	For 6 Kilic FAC from Germany

Recipient/ supplier (S) or licenser (L)	No. ordered	Weapon designation	Weapon description	Year of order/ licence	Year(s) of deliveries	No. delivered/ produced	Comments
USA	6	STING	Fire control radar	2001	2004–2005	(3)	For 6 Kilic FAC from Germany
	4	Boeing-737-7ES	AEW&C ac	2003		..	$1.5 b 'Peace Eagle' programme (offsets $500 m); option on 2 more; delivery 2007–2008
	12	S-70B/SH-60B Seahawk	ASW helicopter	2005		..	Part of $340–389 m deal (mainly financed with US loan); option on 5 more; delivery from 2008
	(117)	AN/APG-68	Ac radar	(2005)		..	Part of $1.1 b 'Peace Onyx-3' modernization of 117 Turkish F-16C combat aircraft; AN/APG-68(V)9 version; delivery by 2012
	8	AN/MPQ-64	Air surv radar	2002	2005	(8)	For use with 8 modernized I-HAWK SAM systems
	8	I-HAWK	SAM system	2002	2005	(8)	Ex-US; $100 m deal; modernized (partly in Norway) to I-HAWK PIP-3 before delivery
	127	AIM-9X Sidewinder	SRAAM	(2005)		..	$36 m deal; delivery by 2008
	(175)	MIM-23B HAWK	SAM	(2002)	2005	(175)	Ex-US; aid
L: Germany	6	Frankenthal/Type-332	MCM ship	1999	2005	1	$625 m deal; 5 produced in Turkey; Turkish desig Alanya; delivery 2005–2008
	6	Kiliç	FAC(M)	2000	2004–2005	(3)	5 produced in Turkey; delivery 2004–2007
	4	Type-209/1400	Submarine	1998	2003–2005	2	$556 m deal; assembled from kits in Turkey; Turkish desig Gur; delivery 2003–2007
South Korea	(300)	K-9 Thunder 155mm	Self-propelled gun	2001	2003–2005	(54)	$1–1.2 b deal (incl $60–70 m for first 8–20); Turkish desig Firtina/TUSpH Storm; delivery 2003–2013
UK	840	Rapier Mk-2	SAM	1999	2002–2005	(325)	$130–150 m deal; for use with Rapier SAM systems modernized to Rapier B1X; delivery 2002–2010
Turkmenistan S: Georgia	..	Su-25T/Frogfoot	Ground attack ac	(2003)		..	Payment for debt; Su-25KM version; status uncertain (possibly modernization of Turkmeni aircraft in Georgia)

United Arab Emirates

S:	No.	Designation	Description	Year of order	Year of delivery	No. delivered	Comments
Canada	8	PW-100	Turboprop	(2001)	..	..	For 4 C-295MPA ASW/MP aircraft from Spain; PW-127 version
Denmark	6	SCANTER-2001	Sea surv radar	2004	..	..	For 4 Baynunah corvettes from France
France	(62)	Mirage-2000-5 Mk-2	FGA ac	1998	2003–2005	(44)	$3.4 b deal; ordered after USA refused sale of F-16 combat aircraft with long-range ASM capability; Mirage-2000-9 version; incl 30 UAE Mirage-2000 rebuilt to Mirage-2000-9; delivery 2003–2007
	46	Leclerc DNG	ARV	1993	1997–2004	(28)	Part of $3.4 b deal (offsets 60%); last 18 possibly to be converted to AEV before delivery
	4	Ocean Master	MP ac radar	(2001)	..	..	For 4 CN-295MPA MP aircraft from Spain
	(1 134)	MICA	BVRAAM	1998	2003–2005	(700)	For Mirage-2000-9 combat aircraft
	(96)	MM-40-3 Exocet	Anti-ship missile	(2004)	..	..	For Baynunah corvettes
	500	R-550 Magic-2	SRAAM	(1998)	2003–2005	(300)	For Mirage 2000-9 combat aircraft
	(600)	Storm Shadow/SCALP	ASM	1998	2003–2005	(260)	Black Shaheen version (with reduced range to fall below 300km MTCR limits); for Mirage-2000-9 combat aircraft
Germany	32	Tpz-1 Fuchs	APC	2005	..	..	€160 m ($205 m) deal; Fuchs-2 version; incl 16 NBC and 8 biological warfare reconnaissance, and 8 CP version; delivery 2007–2010
	85	BF-6M	Diesel engine (AV)	2003	2004–2005	(85)	For modernization of 85 M-109L-47 self-propelled guns; BF-6M-1015CP version
	(24)	MTU-595	Diesel engine (SH)	(2003)	..	..	For 6 Baynunah corvettes from France
	436	MTU-883	Diesel engine (AV)	1993	1994–2004	(418)	For 390 Leclerc tanks and 46 Leclerc ARV from France
Italy	8	AB-139	Helicopter	2005	..	..	$83–84 m deal; incl 6 for SAR and 2 for VIP transport
	12	NA-25XM	Fire control radar	2004	..	..	For 6 Baynunah corvettes from France
Libya	(12)	CH-47C Chinook	Helicopter	2003	..	..	Ex-Libyan; modernized in Italy before delivery 2006
Romania	10	SA-330 Puma	Helicopter	2001	2005	(3)	Part of $125 m deal (incl modernization of 15 UAE SA-330); IAR-330SM version; for Abu Dhabi; delivery 2005–2007

Recipient/ supplier (S) or licenser (L)	No. ordered	Weapon designation	Weapon description	Year of order/ licence	Year(s) of deliveries	No. delivered/ produced	Comments
Russia	50	96K9 Pantzyr-S1	Mobile SAM system	2000		..	$800 m deal (incl development partly funded by UAE); incl 26 wheeled and 24 tracked version; delivery delayed from 2003–2005 to 2006–2008
	(1 008)	9M311/SA-19 Grison	SAM	2000		..	For 96K9 Pantzyr-S1 SAM systems
South Africa	28	RG-31 Nyala	APC/ISV	2005		..	$11 m deal; RG-31 Mk-3A version; delivery 2006
Spain	4	C-295MPA	ASW/MP ac	(2001)		..	$114–140 m 'Shaheen-1' programme; for Abu Dhabi
Sweden	6	Giraffe AMB-3D	Air surv radar	2004		..	For 6 Baynunah corvettes from France
USA	80	F-16E	FGA ac	2000	2004–2005	(39)	$5 b deal (incl $400 m for engines; incl $3 b advance payments incl for development of avionics and radar; part of $6.8 b deal); incl 25 F-16F; delivery 2004–2007
	49	AGM-114K HELLFIRE	Anti-tank missile	(2002)	2005	(49)	AGM-114M3 version; for AH-64D helicopters
	240	AGM-114L HELLFIRE	Anti-tank missile	(2002)	2005	(240)	AGM-114L3 version; for AH-64D helicopters
	(1 163)	AGM-65D Maverick	ASM	(2003)		..	For F-16E combat aircraft; incl AGM-65G version; contract not yet signed
	159	AGM-88 HARM	Anti-radar missile	2001	2004–2005	(60)	For F-16E combat aircraft; AGM-88C version
	..	AIM-120B AMRAAM	BVRAAM	(2003)		..	For F-16E combat aircraft; contract possibly not yet signed
	(267)	AIM-9M Sidewinder	SRAAM	2002	2004–2005	(125)	For F-16E combat aircraft
	1 000	Javelin	Anti-tank missile	(2005)		..	$135 m deal (incl 100 launchers); contract not yet signed
	52	RGM-84 Harpoon	Anti-ship missile	(2003)		..	$40 m deal; AGM-84 version for F-16E combat aircraft; contract probably not yet signed
	(237)	RIM-162 ESSM	SAM	(2004)		..	$245 m deal; for Baynunah corvettes and probably for modernized Kortenear frigates
L: France	4	Baynunah	Corvette	2003		..	$500–545 m 'Project Baynunah' (incl $205 m for French ship producer); 3 assembled in UAE; for Abu Dhabi; delivery from 2008

No.	Designation	Description	Year of order	Year of deliveries	No. delivered	Comments
2	Baynunah	Corvette	2005	1999	..	Part of 'Project Baynunah'; assembled in UAE
United Kingdom						
S: Canada						
5	BD-700 Global Express	Transport ac	1999		..	Part of $1.3 b deal (offsets 100%); for modification to Sentinel R-1 AGS aircraft in USA and UK with ASTOR radars from USA; delivery from 2006
Denmark						
1	SCANTER-2001	Sea surv radar	(2005)		..	Scanter-4001 version; for 1 River OPV produced in UK; delivery 2007
Germany						
10	BR-710	Turbofan	1999		..	For 5 BD-700/Sentinel AGS aircraft from Canada and USA
Israel						
20	Litening	Ac El/Op system	2005		..	£15 m deal; Litening-3 version; bought via UK company; for Eurofighter combat aircraft
Netherlands						
6	SMART-L	Air/sea surv radar	(2002)		..	S1850M version; for 6 D (Type-45) destroyers produced in UK
USA						
1	C-17A Globemaster-3	Transport ac	(2004)		..	Contract not yet signed
(1 717)	BTA-5.9	Diesel engine (AV)	1997	1999–2005	(1 217)	For 110 BvS-10 APC from Sweden and modernization of some 1607 Scimitar and Sabre reconnaissance vehicles and Spartan and FV-432 APC
(150)	AIM-120B AMRAAM	BVRAAM	2004	2004	..	$144 m deal
64	BGM-109 Tomahawk	SLCM	2004	2005	(32)	£70 m ($126–129 m) deal; BGM-109 Tomahawk Block-IV (Tactical Tomahawk) version; for Swiftsure and Trafalgar submarines;
L: Israel						
..	Hermes-450	UAV	2005		..	Part of £700 m ($1.2 b) 'Watchkeeper' programme (incl £300m for producer of Hermes-450); most produced in UK; UK desig WK-450; delivery from 2010
Italy						
401	MLV	APC/ISV	2003	2004–2005	(7)	£166 m ($282 m) 'Future Command and Liason Vehicle' (FCLV) programme; armour and other components produced in UK; UK desig Panther; option on 400 more; delivery 2004–2009

Recipient/ supplier (S) or licenser (L)	No. ordered	Weapon designation	Weapon description	Year of order/ licence	Year(s) of deliveries	No. delivered/ produced	Comments
Netherlands	2	Enforcer	AALS	2000	2005	(1)	£224 m 'LSD(A)' programme (original £140 m increased 2005 with £84 m to compensate UK producer for additional costs due to delay); UK desig Bay; delivery 2005–2006
	2	Enforcer	AALS	2001	2005	(1)	£140 m 'LSD(A)' programme (original £120 m increased 2005 by £20 m to compensate UK producer for additional costs due to delay); UK desig Bay; delivery 2005–2006
Sweden	110	BvS-10	APC	2000	2001–2005	(110)	SEK700 m (c. $95 m) deal; armour produced in UK; incl 31 CP and 6 ARV version; UK desig Viking
USA	5	ASTOR	AGS radar	1999		..	Part of $1.3 b deal (offsets 100%); for modification of 5 BD-700 transport aircraft from Canada to AGS aircraft; 4 produced in UK; delivery from 2006
	..	GMLRS	SSM	2005		..	£31 m deal ($55 m); 12.5% of developement financed by UK; warhead and other components produced in UK; for use with MLRS and LIMAWS(R) MRLs; delivery by 2007
	3 871	Javelin	Anti-tank missile	2003	2005	(500)	£300 m ($459–490 m) 'LFATGWS' programme (offsets 100% incl production of components in UK)
	..	Javelin	Anti-tank missile	2004		..	£100 m ($179 m) deal (offsets 100% incl production of components in UK); delivery from 2007
United States							
S: Canada	(782)	PT-6	Turboprop	1996	1999–2005	(269)	For 782 PC-9 (T-6A) trainer aircraft ('JPATS' programme) from Switzerland; PT-6A-62 version
France	(69)	MO-120-RT-61 120mm	Mortar	2004		..	'EFSS' programme
Germany	(1 013)	MTU-883	Diesel engine (AV)	(2003)	2005	(1)	For 1013 EFV IFV produced in USA; MTU-883Ka-523 version; possibly produced in USA

Recipient/Supplier	No. ordered	Weapon designation	Weapon description	Year of order	Year(s) of deliveries	No. delivered/produced	Comments
	5	TRS-3D	Air/sea surv radar	2004		..	For 2 LCS Flight-0 frigates, 1 WMSL (MSCL or NSC) OPV and 1 land-based site; TRS-3D/16 version; option on 3 more
Israel	..	CARDOM 120mm	Mortar	(2003)	2004–2005	(75)	For Piranha-3 (Stryker) mortar carrier
New Zealand	17	A-4K Skyhawk-2	FGA ac	2005		..	Ex-New Zealand; part of NZD155 m ($110 m) deal; for US company for training of US armed forces
	17	MB-339C	Trainer/combat ac	2005		..	Ex-New Zealand; part of NZD155 m ($110 m) deal; for US company for training of US armed forces
South Africa	148	RG-31 Nyala	APC/ISV	2005	2005	(148)	$78 m deal; mainly for use in Iraq
Spain	2	CN-235MP	ASW/MP ac	2004		..	$87 m deal; part of Coast Guard 'Deepwater-2000' programme; CN-235M-300M/C-235ER version; option on 6 more; assembled/produced in USA; delivery 2006
Switzerland	32	F-5E Tiger-2	FGA ac	2003	2003–2005	(19)	Ex-Swiss; $19 m deal; for use as 'enemy' in training; US desig F-5N; delivery 2003–2007
UK	27	Seaspray	MP ac radar	2005		..	Seaspray-7500E version; for modernization of 27 Coast Guard HC-130H MP aircraft; delivery by 2012
L: Australia	1	LCS	Frigate	2005		..	$100–135 m deal; part of 'LCS' programme; LCS Flight-0 (prototype) version
Canada	(204)	Piranha-3 LPTAG	FSV	2000	2002–2005	(33)	Part of $4 b 'IAV' programme; Stryker MGS version
	(1 837)	Piranha/LAV-25	IFV	2000	2002–2005	(1 406)	Part of $4 b 'IAV' programme; LAV-3 (LAV-25/Stryker) version; incl APC and mortar carier version; delivery 2002–2008
France	(200)	FLASH	Dipping sonar	(2005)		..	For 200 SH-60R ASW helicopters produced in USA
Israel	..	Litening	Ac El/Op system	(2001)	2002–2005	(40)	Litening-2 and Litening-ER versions; for F-16 and AV-8B combat aircraft; US desig AN/AAQ-28
	(24)	Litening	Ac El/Op system	2005		..	Litening-AT version; for F/A-18 combat aircraft; US desig AN/AAQ-28
	(250)	Popeye-1/AGM-142	ASM	1998	2000–2005	(250)	US desig AGM-142 Raptor or Have Nap
Switzerland	(782)	PC-9/T-6A Texan-2	Trainer ac	1996	1999–2005	(269)	$7 b 'JPATS' programme (incl $4.7 b for aircraft only); delivery 1999–2017

Recipient/ supplier (S) or licenser (L)	No. ordered	Weapon designation	Weapon description	Year of order/ licence	Year(s) of deliveries	No. delivered/ produced	Comments
UK	187	Hawk/T-45A Goshawk	Trainer ac	1981	1990–2005	(181)	'VTXTS' or 'T-45TS' programme; T-45A and T-45C Goshawk version; delivery 1990–2006
	(591)	UFH/M-777 155mm	Towed gun	(2000)	2002–2005	(62)	$970 m deal (incl $135 m for first 94 and $834 m for remaining 495); US desig M-777; delivery 2002–2009
Unknown country							
S: Israel	3	SPYDER	Mobile SAM system	(2005)	..	..	Recipient is an Asian country (possibly Singapore)
Uruguay							
S: Brazil	1	AS-355/555	Light helicopter	2005	2005	1	Ex-Brazilian; AS-355F2 version
Germany	1	Lüneburg/Type-701	Support ship	2005	2005	1	Ex-German; $1 m deal; Uruguayan desig General Artigas
Spain	2	Descubierta/F-30	Frigate	(2005)	..	..	Ex-Spanish; $20 m deal; contract not yet signed
Venezuela							
S: Brazil	12	AMX	FGA ac	(2002)	..	..	AMX-ATA version; incl 4 AMX-E EW version; status uncertain
China	3	JYL-1	Air-surv radar	2005	..	..	Part of $150 m programme for military-civilian air-surveillance system
France	8	AS-350/550 Fennec	Light helicopter	2003	2004–2005	(8)	$50 m deal; AS-550C2 Fennec version
Israel	12	EL/M-2032	Ac radar	(2002)	..	..	For 12 AMX-ATA trainer/combat aircraft from Brazil
	5	Mi-24P/Mi-35P/Hind-F	Combat helicopter	2005	..	..	$81 m deal; Mi-35M version; delivery 2006
Russia	1	Mi-26/Halo	Helicopter	2005	..	..	Part of $120 m deal; possibly (also) for civilian use; delivery 2006
	(9)	Mi-8/Mi-17/Hip-H	Helicopter	2005	..	..	Part of $120 m deal; Mi-17-1V armed version; delivery 2006
Spain	10	C-295	Transport ac	2005	..	..	Part of €1.3–1.6 b deal; delivery from 2006
	2	CN-235MP	ASW/MP ac	2005	..	..	Part of €1.3–1.6 b deal; delivery by 2010

	No. ordered	Weapon designation	Weapon description	Year of order	Year(s) of deliveries	No. delivered	Comments
	20	PW-100	Turboprop	2005		..	For 10 C-295 transport aircraft from Spain; PW-127 version
	4	Navantia-1700t	OPV	2005		..	Part of €1.3–1.6 b deal; delivery by 2010
	4	Serviola	OPV	2005		..	Part of €1.3–1.6 b deal; delivery by 2010
UK	2	Shorts-360	Transport ac	(2005)	2005	2	Second-hand
	..	Spey	Turbofan	2000			For AMX combat aircraft from Brazil; Spey-807 version; probably from Italian production line
USA	4	CT-7	Turboprop	(2005)		..	For 2 CN-235 MP aircraft from Spain; CT-7-9C3 version
Viet Nam							
S: Czech Republic	10	Su-22/Fitter-H/J/K	FGA ac	(2004)		..	Ex-Czech; modernized in Ukraine (for anti-ship operations) before delivery
Germany	4	MTU-8000	Diesel engine (SH)	(1996)	2001–2005	4	For 2 BPS-500 FAC from Russia; desig uncertain
Poland	2	M-28B Bryza-1R	MP ac	2003	2005	2	For coast guard; delivered without MP system (still to be ordered); option on 8 more
Russia	4	W-3 Sokol	Helicopter	2005		..	W-3RM Anakonda SAR version; delivery by 2007
	2	S-300PMU-1/SA-10D	SAM system	2003	2005	(2)	Part of $200–380 m deal
	(72)	48N6/SA-10 Grumble	SAM	2003	2005	(72)	Part of $200–380 m deal; for S-300PMU-1 (SA-10) SAM systems
	..	Igla-1/SA-16 Gimlet	Portable SAM	(1996)	2001–2005	(50)	SA-N-10 version for BPS-500 (Ho-A) and Svetlyak FAC
Ukraine	(32)	Kh-35 Uran/SS-N-25	Anti-ship missile	(1996)	2001–2005	(32)	For BPS-500 (Ho-A) FAC
	(2)	Svetlyak/Type-1041Z	Patrol craft	(2003)		..	
	24	DR-76	Gas turbine (SH)	(2003)		..	For 12 Tarantul FAC from Russia
	24	DR-77	Gas turbine (SH)	(2003)		..	For 12 Tarantul FAC from Russia
L: Russia	(2)	BPS-500/Type-1241A	FAC(M)	1996	2001–2005	(2)	Assembled from kits in Viet Nam; Vietnamese desig Ho-A
	(12)	Tarantul-1/Type-1241	FAC(M)	(2003)		..	Probably Tarantul-4 version; 10 assembled from kits in Viet Nam; status uncertain

Recipient/ supplier (S) or licenser (L)	No. ordered	Weapon designation	Weapon description	Year of order/ licence	Year(s) of deliveries	No. delivered/ produced	Comments
Yemen							
S: Australia	10	Bay	Patrol craft	2003	2005	10	AUD90 m ($55–70 m) deal
Russia	12	Ka-52/Hokum-B	Combat helicopter	2005		..	Deal worth $150 m; status uncertain
	8	MiG-29SMT/Fulcrum	FGA ac	2003	2004–2005	(8)	Incl 2 MiG-29UBT version
	180	BMP-2	IFV	2004	2004–2005	(180)	BMP-2D version
	(50)	Kh-29/AS-14 Kedge	ASM	(2003)	2004–2005	(50)	For MiG-29SMT combat aircraft
	(176)	R-73/AA-11 Archer	SRAAM	(2001)	2002–2005	(176)	For MiG-29SMT combat aircraft
	(88)	R-77/AA-12 Adder	BVRAAM	(2003)	2004–2005	(88)	For MiG-29SMT combat aircraft
Zimbabwe							
S: China	6	K-8 Karakorum-8	Trainer/combat ac	2005		..	$120 m deal; bought after UK refused to sell spare parts for Hawk trainer/combat aircraft in service in Zimbabwe
Ukraine	(6)	AI-25/DV-2	Turbofan	2005		..	For 6 K-8 trainer aircraft from China

Conventions

. .	Data not available or not applicable
( )	Uncertain data or SIPRI estimate
m	million (10^6)
b	billion (10^9)

Three-letter currency abbreviations (other than for the US dollar, $, the euro, €, and the pound sterling, £) follow international conventions.

'Contract not yet signed' is used in the Comments field when sources indicate that preliminary agreements have been signed, but the final contract has not yet been signed.

'Status uncertain' is used in the Comments field when sources are contradictory about the (continued) existence of the reported deal.

'Unknown country' is used in cases where it has not been possible to identify a supplier or recipient with an acceptable degree of certainty.

'Multiple sellers' is used in cases where the weapon is a co-production of two or more countries and where it has not been possible to identify the final supplier; the co-producing countries are mentioned in the comments field and the final supplier will be known when actual deliveries will take place.

Acronyms and abbreviations

AALS	Amphibious assault landing ship		EU	European Union
AAV	Anti-aircraft vehicle		FAC	Fast attack craft
ABL	Armoured bridge-layer		FGA	Fighter/ground attack
ac	Aircraft		FMF	Foreign Military Funding (US)
ACV	Air-cushion vessel (hovercraft)		(G)	Gun-armed
AEV	Armoured engineer vehicle		IFV	Infantry fighting vehicle
AEW	Airborne early-warning		incl	Including/include(s)
AEW&C	Airborne early-warning and control		(M)	Missile-armed
AGS	Airborne ground-surveillance		MCM	Mine countermeasures
ALV	Armoured logistic vehicle		MP	Maritime patrol
AMV	Anti-mine vehicle		MRL	Multiple rocket launcher
APC	Armoured personnel carrier		NBC	Nuclear, biological and chemical
arty	Artillery		no.	Number
ARV	Armoured recovery vehicle		OPV	Offshore patrol vessel
AS	Anti-ship		SAM	Surface-to-air missile
ASM	Air-to-surface missile		SAR	Search and rescue
ASW	Anti-submarine warfare		SLCM	Submarine-launched cruise missile
BVRAAM	Beyond visual range air-to-air missile		SRAAM	Short-range air-to-air missile
CIWS	Close-in weapon system		SSM	Surface-to-surface missile
CP	Command post		surv	Surveillance
CSAR	Combat SAR		UAE	United Arab Emirates
desig	Designation		UAV	Unmanned air vehicle (drone)
ELINT	Electronic intelligence		VIP	Very important person

Appendix 10C. Sources and methods for arms transfers data

BJÖRN HAGELIN, MARK BROMLEY and
SIEMON T. WEZEMAN

The SIPRI Arms Transfers Project reports on international flows of conventional weapons. Since publicly available information is inadequate for the tracking of all weapons and other military equipment, SIPRI covers only what it terms *major conventional weapons*. Data are collected from open sources in the SIPRI arms transfers database and presented in a register that identifies the suppliers, recipients and weapons delivered, and in tables that provide a measure of the trends in the total flow of major weapons and its geographical pattern. SIPRI has developed a unique trend-indicator value (TIV) system. This value is not comparable to financial data such as gross domestic product, public expenditure and export/import figures.

The database covers the period from 1950. Data collection and analysis are continuous processes. As new data become available the database is updated for all years included in the database.[1]

I. Revisions to sources and methods in 2005

New published information on arms transfers often includes new delivery data. This is also true for data on individual systems, which may necessitate a new calculation of their TIV. From time to time, however, more significant and generic modifications are introduced to reflect the changing reality of arms transfers or to make use of new sources of information. For example, in the 1980s radar systems were added to the database. In 2005 several generic changes were introduced into the coverage of the database while the calculation of the SIPRI TIV for production under licence was reviewed and modified. These changes have been made retroactively for the entire database in order to preserve a meaningful time series from 1950.

Revisions to the range of coverage

In 2005 the coverage of the database was expanded to include: (*a*) engines for military aircraft, for example, combat-capable aircraft, larger military transport and support aircraft, including helicopters; (*b*) engines for combat ships, such as fast attack craft, corvettes, frigates, destroyers, cruisers, aircraft carriers and submarines; (*c*) engines for most armoured vehicles—generally engines of more than 200 horsepower (hp) output; and (*d*) anti-submarine warfare (ASW) sonar systems for ships. None of these systems are standalone, but rather components belonging to platforms

---

[1] Thus, data from several editions of the SIPRI Yearbook or other SIPRI publications cannot be combined or compared. Readers who require time-series TIV data for periods before the years covered in this volume or who require updated registers should contact SIPRI, preferably via the website at URL <http://www.sipri.org/contents/armstrad/>.

classified by SIPRI as 'major weapons'. As such they are similar to many of the radar systems added to the SIPRI coverage in the 1980s.

These sub-systems are only included when they are supplied from a country other than the supplier of the platform on which the systems are mounted; for example, a K-8 trainer aircraft transferred from China to Egypt would also lead to an entry for the transfer of a TPE-731 engine from the United States. However, the transfer of an F-16 combat aircraft from the USA to Oman would not lead to an entry for an engine, since that is also supplied from the USA. The above systems are also included when used for modernization of existing platforms. Generally, the number of items is derived from the number of platforms, but where available, exact numbers of ordered and delivered items are used. These sub-systems are included because they provide a more complete picture of arms transfer relations between suppliers and recipients, and because they are for the most part technically advanced systems and as such important (and often export controlled), and because major platforms are becoming more and more dependent on such components supplied from other countries. It also makes it possible to capture at least part of the trend for 'cooperative' weapons. They can be included because they are discrete items that can be identified from open sources as a specific 'measurable' component.

With regard to the register, this means that additional information is available on some of the major components of conventional weapons. For the TIV tables the value of the platform would be reduced by the value of the components, and the TIV of the components would show up as coming from a supplier different to the supplier of the platform. Alternatively, in cases of components supplied for indigenous platforms, the TIV of the component would be listed where previously nothing would have been listed.

Revisions to the SIPRI trend-indicator value

The SIPRI TIV for weapons produced under licence was reviewed in 2005 and many systems previously listed as 'produced under licence' had their status changed to 'direct delivery'. Only weapons with a low input from the licenser (below 50 per cent) are now regarded as licensed production and calculated as such. The systems with a higher input from the licenser are considered as being 'assembled' and are given the full TIV. This change was introduced because the previous calculation of the percentage of input from the licenser was always problematic and margins of error large, especially in cases with a high input from the licenser.

II. Selection criteria and coverage

Selection criteria

SIPRI uses the term 'arms transfer' rather than 'arms trade' since the latter is usually associated with 'sale'. SIPRI covers not only sales of weapons, including manufacturing licences, but also other forms of weapon supply, including aid and gifts.

The weapons transferred must be destined for the armed forces, paramilitary forces or intelligence agencies of another country. Weapons supplied to or from rebel forces in an armed conflict are included as deliveries to or from the individual rebel forces, identified under separate 'recipient' or 'supplier' headings. Supplies to or from international organizations are also included and categorized in the same fashion. In cases where deliveries are identified but it is not possible to identify either the supplier or the recipient with an acceptable degree of certainty, transfers are registered as coming from 'unknown' suppliers or going to 'unknown' recipients. Suppliers are termed 'multiple' only if there is a transfer agreement for weapons that are produced by two or more cooperating countries and if it is not clear which country will make the delivery.

Weapons must be transferred voluntarily by the supplier. This includes weapons delivered illegally—without proper authorization by the government of the supplier or the recipient country—but excludes captured weapons and weapons obtained from defectors. Finally, the weapons must have a military purpose. Systems such as aircraft used mainly for other branches of government but registered with and operated by the armed forces are excluded. Weapons supplied for technical or arms procurement evaluation purposes only are not included.

Major conventional weapons: the coverage

SIPRI covers only what it terms *major conventional weapons*, defined as:

1. *Aircraft*: all fixed-wing aircraft and helicopters, including unmanned reconnaissance/surveillance aircraft, with the exception of microlight aircraft, powered and unpowered gliders and target drones.

2. *Armoured vehicles*: all vehicles with integral armour protection, including all types of tank, tank destroyer, armoured car, armoured personnel carrier, armoured support vehicle and infantry fighting vehicle.

3. *Artillery*: naval, fixed, self-propelled and towed guns, howitzers, multiple rocket launchers and mortars, with a calibre equal to or above 100 millimetres (mm).

4. *Radar systems*: all land-, aircraft- and ship-based active (radar) and passive (e.g., electro-optical) surveillance systems with a range of at least 25 kilometres (km), with the exception of navigation and weather radars, and all fire-control radars, with the exception of range-only radars. In cases where the system is fitted on a platform (vehicle, aircraft or ship), the register only notes those systems that come from a different supplier from the supplier of the platform.

5. *Missiles*: all powered, guided missiles and torpedoes with conventional warheads. Unguided rockets, guided but unpowered shells and bombs, free-fall aerial munitions, anti-submarine rockets and target drones are excluded.

6. *Ships*: all ships with a standard tonnage of 100 tonnes or more, and all ships armed with artillery of 100-mm calibre or more, torpedoes or guided missiles, with the exception of most survey ships, tugs and some transport ships.

7. *Engines*: (*a*) engines for military aircraft, for example, combat-capable aircraft, larger military transport and support aircraft, including helicopters; (*b*) engines for combat ships, such as fast attack craft, corvettes, frigates, destroyers, cruisers, aircraft carriers and submarines; (*c*) engines for most armoured vehicles—generally engines of more than 200 hp output; and (*d*) ASW and anti-ship sonar systems for ships.

The statistics presented refer to transfers of weapons in these six categories only. Transfers of other military equipment—such as small arms and light weapons, trucks, artillery under 100-mm calibre, ammunition, support equipment and components, as well as services or technology transfers—are not included.

III. The SIPRI trend indicator

The SIPRI system for the valuation of arms transfers is designed as a *trend-measuring device*. It permits the measurement of changes in the total flow of major weapons and its geographical pattern. The trends presented in the tables of SIPRI trend-indicator values are based only on *actual deliveries* during the year or years covered in the relevant tables and figures, not on orders signed in a year.

The trend-indicator value system, in which similar weapons have similar values, reflects both the quantity and the quality of the weapons transferred. The value reflects the transfer of *military resources*. The SIPRI TIV does not reflect the financial value of (or payments for) weapons transferred. This is impossible for three reasons. First, in many cases no reliable data on the value of a transfer are available. Second, even if the value of a transfer is known, it is in almost every case the total value of a deal, which may include not only the weapons entered in the SIPRI database but also other items related to these weapons (e.g., spare parts, armament or ammunition) as well as support systems (e.g., specialized vehicles) and items related to the integration of the weapon in the armed forces (e.g., software changes to existing systems or training). Third, even if the value of a transfer is known, there remains the problem that important details about the financial arrangements of the transfer (e.g., credit or loan conditions and discounts) are usually not known.[2]

Measuring the military implications of transfers would require a concentration on the value of the weapons as a military resource. Again, this could be done from the actual money values of the weapons transferred, assuming that these values generally reflect the military capability of the weapon. However, the problems enumerated above would still apply (e.g., a very expensive weapon may be transferred as aid at a 'zero' price, and therefore not show up in financial statistics, but still be a significant transfer of military resources). The SIPRI solution is a system in which military resources are measured by including an evaluation of the technical parameters of the weapons. The tasks and performance of the weapons are evaluated and the weapons are assigned a value in an index. These values reflect the military resource value of the weapon in relation to other weapons. This can be done under the condition that a number of benchmarks or reference points are established by assigning some weapons a fixed place in the index. These are the core of the index, and all other weapons are compared to these *core weapons*.

In short, the process of calculating the SIPRI trend-indicator value for individual weapons is as follows. For a number of weapon types (noted in the register as the 'weapon designation') it is possible to find the actual average unit acquisition price in open sources. It is assumed that such real prices roughly reflect the military resource value of a system. For example, a combat aircraft bought for $10 million may be assumed to be a resource twice as great as one bought for $5 million, and a submarine bought for $100 million may be assumed to be 10 times the resource a $10 million combat aircraft would represent. Those weapons with a real price are used as the core weapons of the valuation.

Weapons for which a price is not known are compared with core weapons. This comparison is made in the following steps.

---

[2] It is possible to present a very rough idea of the economic factors from the financial statistics now available from most arms-exporting countries. However, most of these statistics lack sufficient detail.

1. The description of a weapon is compared with the description of the core weapon. In cases where no core weapon exactly matches the description of the weapon for which a price is to be found, the closest match is sought.

2. Standard characteristics of size and performance (weight, speed, range and payload) are compared with those of a core weapon of a similar description. For example, a 15 000-kg combat aircraft would be compared with a combat aircraft of similar size.

3. Other characteristics, such as the type of electronics, loading or unloading arrangements, engine, tracks or wheels, armament and materials, are compared.

4. Weapons are compared with a core weapon from the same period.

Weapons delivered in second-hand condition are given a standard value of 40 per cent of the value assigned to the new weapon; second-hand weapons that have been significantly refurbished or modified by the supplier before delivery (and have thereby become a greater military resource) are given a value of 66 per cent of the new value. In reality there may be huge differences in the military resource value of a second-hand weapon depending on its condition after use and the modifications during the years of use.

The SIPRI trend indicator does not measure military value or effectiveness. It does not take into account the conditions under which a weapon is operated (e.g., an F-16 combat aircraft operated by well-balanced, well-trained and well-integrated armed forces has a much greater military value than the same aircraft operated by a developing country; the resource is the same but the effect is very different). The trend indicator also accepts the prices of the core weapons as genuine rather than reflecting costs that, even if officially part of the programme, are not exclusively related to the weapon itself. For example, funds that appear to be allocated to a particular programme could be related to optional add-ons and armament or to the development of basic technology that will be included (free of cost) in other programmes. Such funds could also act, in effect, as government subsidies to keep industry in business by paying more than the weapon is worth.

IV. Sources

A variety of sources are used for the data presented in the arms transfer register—newspapers; periodicals and journals; books, monographs and annual reference works; and official national and international documents. The common criterion for all these sources is that they are open; that is, published and available to the public.

Such open information cannot, however, provide a comprehensive picture of world arms transfers. Published reports often provide only partial information, and substantial disagreement between them is common. Order and delivery dates and exact numbers, or even types, of weapons ordered and delivered, or the identity of suppliers or recipients, may not always be clear from the sources. The exercise of judgement and the making of estimates are therefore important elements in compiling the SIPRI arms transfers database. Estimates are kept at conservatively low levels (and may very well be underestimates).

All sources of data as well as calculations of estimates, while not published by SIPRI, are documented in the SIPRI database.

11. The security dimension of European collective efforts in space

THERESA HITCHENS and TOMAS VALASEK

I. Introduction

Europe, both collectively and nationally, has long been a major power in outer space, with countries maintaining an array of facilities for satellite launches, satellite production and research. Like many other elements of European power, however, space capability is not a fully unified project, but rather arises through the accumulation of a confused mixture of national and multinational entities and efforts. As might be expected, the major national players in space are the four European states with the largest economies: France, Germany, Italy and the United Kingdom. At the collective level, there are two premier organizations: the 25-state European Union (EU) and the 17-state European Space Agency (ESA). In addition, other joint European projects involve sets and subsets of national governments and multinational organizations.

While European space activities have focused on civil and commercial applications, over the past several years European countries and Europe collectively have recognized the need to add a security dimension to their space programmes. This has been a slow and halting process. Even today, European states jealously guard their military space capabilities; they are often wary of inter-European cooperation and more so of collective endeavours. That mindset is beginning to change, spurred in large part by the revolution in military space power in the United States, where the increased exploitation of space assets for both tactical and strategic purposes has provided the country with an undisputed edge on the battlefield.

The pressures for more cooperation in military space activities also stem from the general evolution of European military thinking: primarily, the trend towards collectivism in foreign affairs and defence policy that began with the articulation of the EU Common Foreign and Security Policy (CFSP), established in 1992 and expanded in 1997, and its subordinate European Security and Defence Policy (ESDP), established in 1999. European militaries cooperate ever more closely on the ground, on the seas and in the air. The creation of joint units such as EU battle groups,[1] in turn, drives member states to integrate their space policies and assets, without which much of modern warfare would be impossible.

[1] See chapter 1 in this volume.

Another, but no less important, driver has been Europe's desire to build capabilities that are independent of the USA—a trend that has its roots in the end of the cold war but which has hastened in recent years as European views about US unilateralism have hardened and US restrictions on space technology transfer have tightened. A March 2005 report to the European Commission by a panel of space experts concluded that 'Europe can no longer assume a fortuitous coincidence of interest with the USA'.[2] While European states have a growing desire for information about a wide range of issues from sources other than the USA, no European country could itself hope to finance a space programme that could deliver such information. The EU is therefore increasingly becoming a locus for new space efforts.

All this said, some important factors limit Europe's current collective ambitions in space. First, European countries have different types of cooperation arrangements with the USA as regards space in general and its security dimension in particular. Second, EU policy makers have never contemplated a collective missile defence project of the sort that has driven a number of developments of systems based in and using space in the US military technology programme—although the subject of a theatre missile shield for Europe remains under discussion in the North Atlantic Treaty Organization (NATO).[3] On a related point, the policies of EU members on the use of space generally oppose such aspects of the 'militarization' of space as the development of anti-satellite (ASAT) systems and technologies. Last, and more broadly, EU policy on the development of space assets for the Union's own collective military purposes is constrained by the important formal limits that exist on those purposes: operations under the ESDP are still limited to various tasks of crisis management (and various kinds of military support for civilian needs, e.g., in emergency response), rather than being fully engaged with the defence of Europe's own territory and the high-intensity operations that would involve.

Section II of this chapter examines the emerging EU space policy from the perspective of its potential security implications. Section III surveys the main collective organizations engaged in space policy, and section IV gives an overview of national space programmes that have a security dimension.[4] Section V presents the conclusions.

II. The emerging security dimension in EU space policy

While the collective engagement of European countries in space programmes pre-dates the creation of the European Union, the EU is now increasingly the

---

[2] European Commission, 'Report of the Panel of Experts on Space and Security', Brussels, Mar. 2005, URL <http://europa.eu.int/comm/space/news/article_2262.pdf>, p. 38.

[3] The limited evidence of purely national programmes in Europe for missile defence that involve space assets, and British, Norwegian and Danish (Greenland) involvement in the USA's own ballistic missile defence programme, are referred to below in section IV.

[4] For comprehensive, up-to-date information on developments in space programmes in Europe and worldwide see GlobalSecurity.org's 'World Space Guide' at URL <http://www.globalsecurity.org/space/world>.

focal point for a rapidly developing security policy in which space-based and associated terrestrial infrastructure already play a substantial role.[5]

Given Europe's multi-dimensional approach to security, differentiation between a purely military space infrastructure for traditional military purposes and a wider space infrastructure and systems relevant to security is becoming more and more difficult. As noted by the European Commission, 'The Council of the EU has recognized that space assets could contribute both to making the EU more capable in the field of crisis management and to fighting other security threats. It has therefore approved the idea that identified and agreed upon ESDP requirements should be reflected in the global EU space policy and European space programme.'[6]

The 'militarization' of European space programmes has come slowly, but over the past several years the EU has quietly breached a number of taboos by fully embracing the use of space for security purposes. The change has been more psychological than substantive: extant space assets, which often take decades to move from drawing boards to orbits, have naturally changed very little. However, the new course of discussions in Europe points to potentially significant changes in the future. EU member states are now openly talking about using common civilian assets for military purposes, and about managing the next generation of military space assets at a European, rather than national, level. A November 2004 EU Council document on European Space Policy discusses the possibility in the long term of launching military space programmes 'supported or possibly managed by the [European Defence Agency (EDA)] on behalf of member states'.[7] Already, the new emphasis on exploring the use of EU space assets for security has translated into the establishment of a Space Assets Group within the European Capabilities Action Plan (ECAP) process,[8] aimed at identifying and filling gaps in military software and hardware programmes.

The driving forces behind the growing EU role in space are both military and political. As for the first category, space itself is becoming indispensable for modern security and military operations. European member states have been pooling their military assets on a number of levels, and a move towards cooperation in space grew out of these efforts. In one example, space will play a role in sourcing and relaying data in real time at virtually every step of the deployment of the EU's new battle groups: from identification of a threat (surveillance/early warning) to operational planning (observation/surveillance) to deployment (communication/satellite navigation) to operation (satellite navi-

---

[5] For a broad introduction to satellite terminology, technology and applications see the chapter 'Military satellites', *SIPRI Yearbook 1977* (Almqvist &Wessell: Stockholm, 1977); and Jasani, B. (ed.), *Outer Space: A New Dimension of the Arms Race* (Taylor & Francis: London, 1982). For a comprehensive history of the development of military space technology see the relevant chapters in the *SIPRI Yearbooks 1973–92*.

[6] European Commission, 'European space policy', Brussels, 2005, URL <http://europa.eu.int/comm/space/themes/intro_space_en.html>.

[7] Council of the European Union, 'European space policy: ESDP and space', document 11616/3/04 REV3, Brussels, 16 Nov. 2004.

[8] European Commission (note 2).

gation/communication/observation). The associated work overseen by the EU Military Committee and the EDA to identify military needs and coordinate the development of capabilities has naturally included a closer look at how existing and future space assets can help support EU military efforts.[9]

The use of satellite technology for civilian purposes, such as earth imaging, meteorology and communications, also feeds into military operations. These and other applications of space-based data are also relevant for the EU's development of non-military policies, for example, civil emergency response, border management, and safety of transport and communications. At the same time, moves towards developing EU space assets for military purposes must not be viewed in a purely technical light. Space, while important for modern warfare, is not at the top of the list of EU capability priorities, which is dominated by more immediate needs such as airlift, sealift and transport helicopters. Of the 64 categories listed in the Council's May 2005 Capability Improvement Chart,[10] only five directly involve space; and even in those categories (such as imagery and early warning), non-space alternatives exist.

Interest in the EU's use of space for military purposes is driven in equal measure by political imperatives set by member states. Common technological projects, of which space is just one example, have become a symbol of collective European achievement and, as such, a driver for further policy development. Projects like Galileo and Global Monitoring for Environment and Security (GMES) continue the tradition of European technology projects such as the CERN particle accelerator:[11] they help generate support for further and deeper cooperation among member states. When space and security are used as symbols of integration, commonality of approach is just as important as the substance of the project itself. At the same time, the growing military need for space helps build the case for stronger EU involvement. Thus, the political and military imperatives are inseparable.

Last but not least, use of space by the EU for security is heavily influenced by the desire in Europe for strategic autonomy. The EU today has become both more active in foreign and security policy and more likely to act independently of the USA. The EU's civilian and military planning activities as well as its growing range of operations require extensive use of information gleaned from space. However, a declining proportion of EU missions abroad now involve day-to-day cooperation with NATO and the USA, which have provided the lion's share of intelligence and other space support needed in the past. Current EU needs are met by national European and non-European assets, but the limitations of these are increasingly at odds with the Union's

---

[9] European Commission (note 2).

[10] The Capability Improvement Chart is a twice-yearly report prepared by the Council of the European Union in order to monitor member states' progress in fulfilling EU military readiness goals. Council of the European Union, 'European Security and Defence Policy—Capability Improvement Chart I/2005', 23 May 2005, URL <http://www.eu2005.lu/en/actualites/documents_travail/2005/05/23pesd>.

[11] Pasco, X., 'Space for security: a European perspective', Paper presented at the conference Space: Key to Europe's Security and Defence Capabilities?, Wilton Park, 7 Sep. 2005.

foreign policy ambitions. This realization, too, is fuelling the drive to shift more responsibility for the use of space for security purposes to the EU.

Transatlantic relations

The evolution of EU plans for space brings both benefits and difficulties to the relationship with the USA. For example, since capabilities such as imagery are in high demand, more European assets generate more options to which the USA—either directly or through NATO—has a measure of access. However, Europe's ability to independently verify US satellite intelligence potentially reduces US influence over European foreign policy choices. Given the fallout from the faulty intelligence on Iraqi weapons of mass destruction, this is not a secondary consideration for either Europe or the USA.

More immediately, the plans for the European Galileo satellite navigation system (discussed below) have already proved contentious. The USA raised two issues in particular. First, the original frequency planned for Galileo's highest-quality signal, the Public Regulated Service (PRS), overlapped with the new M-signal of the US military's Global Positioning System (GPS). This posed a difficulty for the US Department of Defense (DOD): if Galileo were used against the USA in a future conflict, the overlap would impede its ability to jam all signals except its own encrypted GPS code.[12] After years of sometimes tense negotiations, in June 2004 the EU agreed to move the encrypted PRS signal from the original frequency band.

The second US concern focused on preventing Galileo technology from falling into the wrong hands. The participation of China, the largest non-European country involved in the Galileo project, raised particular concerns in the USA. The EU vowed to scrutinize the security implications of Galileo contracts with the greatest care. It is now proceeding on two levels: limiting non-EU member states' access to Galileo's most sensitive signals, and creating mechanisms for interrupting those signals if they are used against EU interests. A July 2004 regulation by the Council of the European Union created a supervisory authority including a special Safety and Security Committee with a mandate 'to ensure the safety and reliability of the system against attacks (malicious or otherwise) and to prevent its use for purposes that run counter to the interests of the EU and its member states'.[13] The supervisory authority scrutinizes each of Galileo's features (such as its range of signals) and communicates with outside countries regarding the security implications. EU officials have repeatedly said that China will not gain access to PRS technology.

A separate Joint Action of the European Council also gave the Secretary-General of the Council, Javier Solana, the right to disable Galileo 'in exceptional cases, where the urgency of the situation is such that it requires immedi-

---

[12] Biever, C., 'US and Europe to combine satellite navigation', *New Scientist*, 24 June 2004, URL <http://www.newscientist.com/article.ns?id=dn6068>.

[13] Council Regulation (EC) no. 1321/2004, *Official Journal of the European Union*, L246 (12 July 2004), URL <http://europa.eu.int/eur-lex/en/archive>.

ate action'.[14] While the regulation refers specifically to threats against EU member states rather than allies, the legislation does in theory create a tool for blocking unauthorized use of Galileo against US interests.

III. European organizations

The European Space Agency

The 17-member ESA, an intergovernmental agency established in 1975, is responsible for coordinating the official European space programme.[15] ESA is independent from the EU, although the two organizations have signed a framework agreement for cooperation (see below). The Agency's work includes research into the earth sciences, the near-space environment, the solar system and deep space; developing satellite-based technologies and services; and promoting Europe's space industry. ESA is also the leading European space launch service group: it builds the Ariane rocket series used for commercial and civil payloads and is a partner with European firm EADS and the Russian Space Agency on the (Russian-built, but jointly owned) Soyuz rockets. ESA further manages Europe's primary launch facility, the Guiana Space Centre at Kourou, French Guiana.

ESA's budget, funded by its member states, was set at €2.9 billion for 2006, and its staff numbers at about 1900.[16] ESA has four associated centres, each of which has different responsibilities: (a) the European Space Research and Technology Centre (ESTEC), which is the design hub for most ESA spacecraft and technology development, based in Noordwijk, the Netherlands; (b) the European Space Operations Centre (ESOC), responsible for controlling ESA satellites in orbit, based in Darmstadt, Germany; (c) the European Astronaut Centre (EAC), which trains astronauts for future missions, based in Cologne, Germany; and (d) ESA's European Space Research Institute (ESRIN), based in Frascati, Italy. ESRIN's responsibilities include collecting, storing and distributing earth-observation satellite data to ESA's partners, and acting as the Agency's information technology centre.[17]

ESA's activities run the gamut from launch technology research to participation in the International Space Station (ISS) and planetary exploration. ESA's current launch fleet consists of three primary rockets: (a) the heavy-lift

---

[14] Council Joint Action 2004/552/CFSP, *Official Journal of the European Union*, L246 (20 July 2004), URL <http://europa.eu.int/eur-lex/en/archive>.

[15] ESA member states are: Austria, Belgium, Denmark, Finland, France, Germany, Greece, Ireland, Italy, Luxembourg, the Netherlands, Norway, Portugal, Spain, Sweden, Switzerland and the UK. Canada, the Czech Republic and Hungary also participate in some projects under cooperation agreements, with the latter 2 countries preparing for full membership. ESA further has a framework cooperative agreement with the Russian Space Agency and is increasingly involved in cooperative projects with the Chinese Space Agency. ESA was set up in 1975 as a successor to the European Space Research Organisation (ESRO) and the European Launcher Development Organisation (ELDO), both established in 1964.

[16] European Space Agency, 'ESA facts and figures', URL <http://www.esa.int/esaCP/GGG4SXG3 AEC_index_0.html>.

[17] European Space Agency (note 16).

Ariane 5 ECA, successfully launched by Arianespace (ESA's contractor for space launches) for the first time in February 2005, and capable of lifting 6–10 tonnes to geosynchronous orbit (GEO) and 21 tonnes to low earth orbit (LEO);[18] (b) the jointly owned Soyuz medium launch vehicle, capable of lifting 3 tonnes to GEO and which is due to enter into ESA service in 2007; and (c) the small launch vehicle Vega, capable of lifting 1.5 tonnes to LEO and currently planned for first launch in 2007.[19]

In December 2005 the ESA ruling council approved a budget of €8.26 billion—nearly the entire €8.8 billion proposed by ESA—to fund the planned ESA programme in 2006–2010.[20] The ministers on the council also approved a resolution to give preference to European-built launchers for ESA space launches, although they did not rule out non-European options.[21]

The European Union

ESA cannot be the vehicle for developing EU space policy as such, given the different memberships. Two ESA members—Norway and Switzerland—are not members of the EU, while none of the 10 countries that recently joined the Union is in ESA (although the Czech Republic and Hungary cooperate in certain ESA projects and will eventually become members). In November 2004 all 27 EU and ESA countries met at the first European Space Council, in Brussels. At that meeting, the exploitation of space was identified as a shared competence of the EU. A formal European Space Policy has, however, yet to be established, although it was debated in 2005 on the basis of a discussion paper prepared by the British EU Presidency.[22]

In November 2003 the European Commission presented a first White Paper on European Space Policy with the intention of providing a point of reference for the development of EU space policy. It included an action plan containing a list of recommended actions. The White Paper represented the first clear articulation of the relationship of space to Europe's common security and defence policy, as well as outlining the key space-related requirements necessary for European security. It stated:

Space technology, infrastructure and services are an essential support to one of the most rapidly evolving EU policies—the Common Foreign and Security Policy including European Security and Defence Policy. Most space systems are inherently cap-

[18] GEO is about 36 000 km in altitude, where most communications satellites orbit. LEO is generally defined as orbits up to 1000 km in altitude, where many earth-observation satellites orbit.

[19] European Space Agency, 'The first stone for Vega at Europe's Spaceport', 4 Nov. 2005, URL <http://www.esa.int/SPECIALS/Launchers_Home/SEM4AU0A90E_0.html>; 'ESA proceeds with Vega launch vehicle', SPACEandTECH, 8 Jan. 2001, URL <http://www.spaceandtech.com/digest/sd2001-01/sd2001-01-005.shtml>.

[20] De Selding, P. B., 'Ministers approve 8.26 billion euro package for ESA', Space News, 12 Dec. 2005, p. 6.

[21] Strohecker, K., 'Europe increases funds for space research', MSNBC, URL <http://www.msnbc.msn.com/id/10352128/from/RL.2>; and De Selding (note 20).

[22] European Commission, 'Third Space Council focuses on GMES', Press release, 28 Nov. 2005, URL <http://europa.eu.int/comm/space/news/article_2291_en.html>.

able of multiple use and the credibility of the above polices will be significantly strengthened by taking better advantage of space applications. EDSP needs access to suitable space-based systems and services, both because of their strategic capabilities and because they confer a capacity for autonomous decision-making.[23]

Following publication of the White Paper on 11 November 2003, the Commission and ESA agreed on respective EU and ESA roles and the planned cooperation between them. The division of labour places the EU as the political driver for setting Europe-wide priorities, promoting and enabling cooperation, providing research funding and ensuring a favourable EU-wide regulatory regime governing space activities. ESA, by contrast, is to develop space technology to meet EU-wide requirements, spearhead innovative research and advise the EU on requirements to ensure access to space services.

The White Paper further recommended the establishment of a Panel of Experts on Space, Security and Defence to examine European capabilities. The panel was launched in June 2004 and its final report was published in March 2005. The report made it clear that Europe still has a long way to go in developing a common approach to space for security and military purposes. It identified three primary gaps in capability: (a) lack of a common agreed architecture and interface standards for the user ground segment of earth-observation systems;[24] (b) lack of European space surveillance capabilities; and (c) lack of very high or high data rate mobile telecommunications.[25]

The panel highlighted a number of improvements in space capabilities that are required by the EU, including: improved performance and interoperability of earth-observation systems; improved collection of critical data from earth-observation systems, communications satellites, signals intelligence satellites, space-based early-warning satellites, and positioning and navigation systems; improved access to, and dissemination of, data from space surveillance systems; and harmonization of operational standards for all satellite systems.[26] The panel recommended that a new forum be established to tackle these issues. Its main tasks would be: (a) establishing a network between the users;[27] (b) determining how existing capabilities could be considered in multiple-use systems to fulfil these needs; (c) refining capability gaps; (d) translating user needs into requirements; and (e) assessing how space capabilities can match the requirements.[28]

[23] 'White Paper, Space: a new European frontier for an expanding the Union; an action plan for implementing the European space policy', European Commission document COM(2003)673, Brussels, 11 Nov. 2003, URL <http://europa.eu.int/comm/space/whitepaper/pdf/whitepaper_en.pdf>.

[24] The user ground segment is the land-based technical facilities that provide information to the users of the satellite system.

[25] European Commission (note 2), pp. 35, 38–39.

[26] European Commission (note 2), pp. 38–39.

[27] Users of satellite systems for security purposes include critical infrastructure services such as transportation authorities, authorities responsible for civil protection and search and rescue, police and intelligence services, border surveillance authorities, crisis management teams, and humanitarian aid organizations and governmental authorities. See European Commission (note 2), pp. 18–19.

[28] European Commission (note 2), pp. 41–42.

Europe's collective space ambitions, both civil and military, continue to be plagued by budgetary troubles as EU member states dispute priorities for collective research in the medium-term planning period 2007–2013.[29] In the spring of 2005 the European Commission released the seventh framework programme, which outlined proposed EU research efforts and a funding package for that period. In that proposal, the Commission called for €3.96 billion to be spent on security and space, which was the first occasion that Commission security and space funding had been lumped into a single category. However, officials have said that the funding will again be split into roughly equal parts. The proposal would represent an increase of the Commission's space budget from 2006, which was set at €235 million.[30] As of November 2005, however, no final decision had been made on the allocations under the seventh framework programme because of a major disagreement among EU member states about the Commission's priorities.[31] Consequently, the Commission has been unable to fulfil its promises of funding for collective programmes.

The Commission has, however, funded at least one new programme under its Preparatory Action in the field of Security Research (PASR) effort for 2004–2006. The Advanced Space Technologies to Support Security Operations (ASTRO+) programme, funded largely by the EU budget but with input from a number of industry partners, is studying how earth-observation, reconnaissance, navigation and telecommunications satellites can improve European military operations, particularly operations abroad. In part, the aim of the project is to convince EU security officials of the positive role that space capabilities can play in military operations.[32] The ASTRO+ effort is also aimed at developing a research and technology innovation roadmap for security-related space capabilities. The project is estimated to cost €2.9 million.[33] The initial plenary session of ASTRO+ took place on 31 August 2005 in Paris.[34]

European institutions, programmes and projects

While there is currently no single body that gives direction to space policy at the European level, there are a number of collective institutions, programmes and projects in which most or all EU member states participate.

[29] European Commission, 'Proposal for a decision of the European Parliament and of the Council concerning the seventh framework programme of the European Community for research, technological development and demonstration activities (2007 to 2013)', COM (2005) 119 final, 6 Apr. 2005, URL <http://europa.eu.int/comm/research/future/basic_research/brp_era_en.htm>.

[30] De Selding, P. B., 'European Commission unveils space spending plan', *C⁴ISR*, 25 Apr. 2005, URL <http://isr.dnmediagroup.com/story.php?F=807586>.

[31] De Selding, P. B., 'ESA seeks major earth-observation funding', *Space News*, 17 Oct. 2005, p.12.

[32] Institute of International Affairs, 'Advanced space technologies to support security operations: ASTRO+', Rome, 3 Feb. 2005, URL <http://www.iai.it/sections_en/ricerca/difesa_sicurezza/ASTRO/ASTRO+.asp>.

[33] 'Advanced space technologies to support security operations', Grant Agreement no. SEC4-PR-00960, URL <http://europa.eu.int/comm/enterprise/security/doc/astro_en.pdf>.

[34] European Commission, 'Space and European security', Brussels, 2005, URL <http://europa.eu.int/comm/space/themes/security_en.html>.

The European Organization for the Exploitation of Meteorological Satellites

The 18-state European Organization for the Exploitation of Meteorological Satellites (EUMETSAT) is an intergovernmental organization that serves as Europe's meteorological satellite agency.[35] It was founded in 1986. Weather forecasting data and images from the EUMETSAT fleet of Meteosat satellites are provided to the national meteorological services of member and partner countries, which in turn provide funding. EUMETSAT works with ESA, and the two agencies often jointly fund projects. EUMETSAT is also a key player in the ESA–European Commission GMES programme.

The European Union Satellite Centre

The European Union Satellite Centre (EUSC) became operational in January 2002 as an agency of the Council of the European Union under a July 2001 Council joint action.[36] Located in Torrejón de Ardoz, Spain, the centre was established as the Western European Union (WEU) Satellite Centre, but was adapted to its new status and transferred to the EU in 2001 as part of the launch arrangements for the ESDP. The EUSC's primary mission is to provide the EU with imagery analysis and data from European earth-observation satellites to support the CFSP and the ESDP. Data provided by the centre can be used by the various EU bodies, EU member countries, third-party countries and international organizations to support: (*a*) general security surveillance; (*b*) humanitarian and rescue, peacekeeping, crisis management and peacemaking (the so-called Petersberg Tasks);[37] (*c*) treaty verification; (*d*) arms and proliferation control efforts; (*e*) maritime surveillance; and (*f*) environmental monitoring.[38]

In practice, the work of the centre is supervised by the EU High Representative for the Common Foreign and Security Policy, Javier Solana. Among the EU users of EUSC imagery are the Commission's Directorate-General for External Relations as well as the EU Military Staff and Situation Centre within the Council apparatus. Despite its clear mandate vis-à-vis Europe's collective security, the EUSC's role in GMES and in coordinating imagery from national military assets remains somewhat hazy. The centre's budget is only some €10 million a year and its staff is just 20 strong, at a time when demand for imagery analysis is growing.[39] The EUSC is largely forced to pay

[35] EUMETSAT members are: Austria, Belgium, Denmark, Finland, France, Germany, Greece, Ireland, Italy, Luxembourg, the Netherlands, Norway, Portugal, Spain, Sweden, Switzerland, Turkey and the UK. Another 11 countries have signed cooperation agreements with the agency: Bulgaria, Croatia, the Czech Republic, Hungary, Latvia, Lithuania, Poland, Romania, Serbia and Montenegro, Slovakia and Slovenia.

[36] European Union Satellite Centre, 'The Centre', URL <http://www.eusc.org/centre.html>.

[37] The Petersberg Tasks are the range of crisis management missions first agreed by the WEU in 1992 at the Hotel Petersberg near Bonn, Germany, and later incorporated into the EU Treaty and ESDP funding documents.

[38] European Union Satellite Centre, 'Mission', URL <http://www.eusc.org/html/centre_mission.html>.

[39] Tigner, B., 'EU tries to assess compatibility problems: fixing a disconnect', *Defense News*, 31 Oct. 2005, URL <http://www.defensenews.com>.

for available imagery from civil and commercial systems.[40] The EUSC's agreement with France in 2003 on sharing data from the French military imagery satellite, Helios I, has yet to be put into force. Meanwhile, a French-led coalition that is funding the follow-on Helios II system has reached an internal agreement to share a limited amount of that system's data with the EUSC, but a final accord may prove difficult.[41] The EUSC is also exploring how it might provide analysis to the EU Military Committee.[42]

Galileo

Galileo is arguably the most ambitious of the European security-related collective space programmes. This effort to develop an alternative to the US GPS and the Russian GLONASS satellite navigation and positioning systems was officially launched on 26 May 2003, by the EU and ESA, although studies of such a network began as early as 1998. Galileo is designed primarily for civilian use and will be civilian controlled, in contrast to GPS, which—even though its civilian usage has exploded over the past decade—is owned and operated by the US military. However, Galileo's signals do offer a wide range of security applications, and at least some governments have invariably regarded it as a military tool. In fact, US and British concerns that Galileo represented a misallocation of European military resources held up the project for several years. Galileo, in effect, became part of a wider transatlantic debate on the need for Europe to improve its military capabilities.

Galileo is intended to provide users with: greater precision than is currently available from GPS or GLONASS; improved coverage of satellite signals at northern latitudes; and guaranteed availability and reliability for customers even in times of war.[43] In addition, Galileo's signals will be compatible with both GLONASS and GPS to provide enhanced services for specific applications.

Galileo is described by EU and ESA officials as a wholly civilian system, but as noted above it will have military applications (although European militaries have been loath to specify them) as well as applications for homeland security and public security, such as firefighting. GPS, for example, is currently widely used by European and US militaries to steer precision-guided munitions to their targets and for navigation purposes.

Development of the network of 30 satellites (27 active and three spares), with an estimated cost of €1.1 billion, is being financed jointly by ESA and the European Commission. Private industry is pledged to provide two-thirds of the approximately €2.5 billion required to deploy the network, recouping this

---

[40] Fiorenza, N., 'French, German sats to widen intelligence capabilities', *C⁴ISR*, 6 Dec. 2005, URL <http://isr.dnmediagroup.com/story.php?F=328012>.

[41] De Selding, P. B., 'Red tape hinders EU military space cooperation', *C⁴ISR*, 12 May 2005, URL <http://isr.dnmediagroup.com/story.php?F=844999>.

[42] Tigner, B., 'EU tries to assess compatibility problems: fixing a disconnect,' *Defense News*, 31 Oct. 2005.

[43] European Space Agency, 'What is Galileo?', 17 Mar. 2005, URL <http://www.esa.int/esaNA/GGGMX650NDC_index_0.html>.

investment by charging for services outside the free core service (designed for general public applications such as navigation systems in vehicles); the remainder will be provided by ESA and the EU. The development programme is managed by the Galileo Joint Undertaking, which includes representatives of the European Commission and ESA, but ultimately may include private companies and the European Investment Bank.[44] In addition, a number of international partners—China, India, Israel, Morocco, Saudi Arabia and Ukraine—are contributing funds in exchange for data. Talks are also ongoing with Argentina, Australia, Brazil, Canada, Chile, Souh Korea, Malaysia, Mexico, Norway and South Korea.[45]

The network is expected to provide an array of services with different levels of accuracy.[46] Aside from an open service and commercial pay-for-use service, the functions most relevant for security will be: an encrypted PRS reserved for EU governments and public security authorities, such as police forces, intelligence services and militaries; a safety-of-life service aimed at public safety applications such as air traffic control and shipping; and a search and rescue service able to detect and broadcast signals globally from the international search and rescue satellite-aided tracking system, COSPAS-SARSAT,[47] and thus to serve as part of the Global Maritime Distress Safety System (GMDSS).

It was originally planned that Galileo would be fully deployed and operational by 2008. However, the schedule has slipped considerably owing to disputes among the European partners over funding, work shares and the location of the network's ground facilities. The first Galileo test satellite, called GIOVE-A (Galileo In-Orbit Validation Element), was launched on 28 December 2005; the second, GIOVE-B, is scheduled to be launched in the spring of 2006. Both are designed to demonstrate basic technologies, including atomic clocks and the simultaneous use of two signal transmission channels.[48] Four more satellites are scheduled to be launched in 2008 to complete the testing phase, which was originally to have been completed by 2006.[49] It is still unclear when the full network of satellites will be deployed and operational.

---

[44] European Union Directorate-General for Energy and Transport, 'Galileo European satellite navigation system', URL <http://europa.eu.int/comm/dgs/energy_transport/galileo/programme/index_en.htm>.

[45] Spongenberg, H., 'EU unveils first Galileo satellite', Associated Press, 9 Nov. 2005, URL <http://abcnews.go.com/Technology/wireStory?id=1296543>.

[46] European Space Agency, 'Galileo services, Galileo specifications', URL <http://www.esa.int/esaNA/SEMTHVXEM4E_galileo_0.html>.

[47] COSPAS-SARSAT was founded in 1988 by Canada, France, the Soviet Union and the USA. See URL <http://www.cospas-sarsat.org/MainPages/indexEnglish.htm>.

[48] De Selding, P. B., 'ESA's Galileo system faces key milestones over next 12 months', *Space News*, 28 Nov. 2005, p.10; and European Space Agency, 'First Galileo signals transmitted by GIOVE-A', Press release, 12 Jan. 2006, URL <http://www.esa.int/SPECIALS/Galileo_Launch/SEMQ36MZCIE_0.html>.

[49] European Space Agency, 'Europe's first Galileo satellite named "Giove"', Press release, 11 Nov. 2005, URL <http://www.spaceflightnow.com/news/n0511/11giove>; and European Space Agency (note 46).

Global Monitoring for Environment and Security

The massive and highly complex GMES earth-observation programme grew out of a 1998 plan devised by ESA and the EU to improve Europe's capabilities in environmental monitoring.[50] It also has direct security and military applications, specifically tasked to support the CFSP and the ESDP. GMES could markedly improve the capacity of European militaries to independently generate mapping, weather prediction and targeting data. According to a February 2004 EU–ESA report, GMES will be used 'in support of conflict prevention and crisis management: monitoring of international treaty [treaties] for preventing the proliferation of nuclear, chemical and biological weapons; monitoring population; assessment of sensitive areas for early warning; [and] rapid mapping during crisis management'.[51]

While there has been an EU decision to support GMES and an implementation plan drawn up, many uncertainties dog the programme. A key question is what role national satellites, such as the French SPOT, will play; even stickier is the question of what data from military satellites, such as France's Helios or Germany's SAR-Lupe, will be shared and how. Funding is also uncertain, with no Commission budget established as of the end of 2005. However, ESA found strong support during its December ministerial meeting: ESA had proposed spending €200 million on the programme over the period 2006–2010, but ministers pledged a total of €235 million.[52]

The current GMES action plan was approved in November 2001.[53] It consists of two phases: an 'Initial Period', 2001–2003, and an 'Implementation Period', 2004–2008. In parallel, the ESA–EU high-level framework agreement that entered into force on 28 May 2004 identifies GMES as one of its key priorities for short-term action.[54] The first goal of the GMES implementation phase—reiterated by a ministerial-level meeting of the Space Council on 28 November 2005[55]—is to launch three so-called fast-track services by 2008.

---

[50] A call for a collective European earth-observation network first came from a high-level ESA meeting at Baveno, Italy, in May 1998: 'Global monitoring for environmental security: a manifesto for a new European initiative', also known as the Baveno Manifesto. See *GMES Forum*, URL <http://www.gmesforum.com/workingfor.htm>. GMES is intended to be a European contribution to the Global Earth Observation System of Systems, launched by the USA in 2003 at the Earth Observation Summit to improve sharing of imaging and data for climate research and to monitor and respond to natural disasters.

[51] European Union and European Space Agency, 'Global Monitoring for Environment and Security: final report for the GMES initial period (2001–2003)', Brussels, 10 Feb. 2004, URL <http://www.gmes.info/115.0.html>, p. 18.

[52] De Selding (note 20), p. 6.

[53] Management of GMES is provided by 2 separate bodies: the GMES Advisory Council and the GMES Programme Office. The Advisory Council serves as a coordinating body with national governments and the various user communities. The Programme Office consists of national experts and officials of involved international organizations, including the European Commission and ESA. See URL <http://www.gmes.info>.

[54] 'Earth and space—Europe sets its sights on GMES', *RTDinfo*, no. 44 (Feb. 2005), URL <http://europa.eu.int/comm/research/rtdinfo/44/01/print_article_2027_en.html>.

[55] The Space Council is a joint and concomitant meeting of the ESA Council and the EU Competitiveness Council at the level of ministers. The 28 Nov. 2005 meeting was the third such annual meeting and focused on GMES issues. For a report of the meeting see European Commission (note 22).

These are the Emergency Management Service, aimed at reinforcing Europe's capacity to predict and respond to disasters; the Land Monitoring Service, providing information on land use and land cover; and the Marine Service, providing information on the marine environment.[56]

Additional services are to be added between 2009 and 2013. According to ESA sources, the GMES implementation budget was set at €2.7 billion for the space component and its associated ground infrastructure, with another €150 million per year estimated for the services segment.[57] The total cost over a 10-year timeframe is estimated at €5 billion.[58] Currently, it is agreed that ESA will fund the first segment of the programme, running from 2006 to 2012, 'with the possibility of incorporating [a European Commission] contribution as it becomes available'; the second segment, 2008–2013, is expected to be co-funded.[59]

Besoins Opérationnels Communs

In 2002 Belgium, France, Germany, Italy and Spain sought to develop Common Operational Requirements for a European Global System of Observation by Satellite—usually known as Besoins Opérationnels Communs (BOCs). Greece joined the effort in 2003. The process is intended to define the elements of a dedicated, independent European military earth-observation system to support future peacekeeping missions and joint operations. The sponsoring states have said that the EU will be granted access to the network.[60] A key obstacle for BOCs, however, has been developing ground systems that allow participating governments to link into each other's satellite networks, and protocols for what data would be exchanged.[61] Reflecting the sensitivity of this last point, a French military expert has noted that 'the EU will not own the system, because strategic intelligence is not shared, it is exchanged'.[62]

The proposed European space surveillance system

While several European countries operate radar and optical telescopes to locate and track objects orbiting in space, Europe is fundamentally dependent on the USA for the data necessary for detection and routine tracking. The US Air Force's Space Surveillance Network is the only global system capable of providing more or less comprehensive tracking data on satellites and space debris,

---

[56] 'Global monitoring for environment and security: first concrete steps', *SpaceRef*, 16 Nov. 2005, URL <http://www.spaceref.com/news/viewsr.html?pid=18704>.

[57] European Commission, 'Volker Liebeg, ESA's earth-observation head, speaks about GMES', European Space Policy, 3 Feb. 2005, URL <http://europa.eu.int/comm/space/news/article_2048_en.html>.

[58] 'Earth and Space—Europe sets its sights on GMES', *RTDinfo*, no. 44 (Feb. 2005), URL <http://europa.eu.int/comm/research/rtdinfo/44/01/print_article_2027_en.html>.

[59] European Space Agency, 'Discovery and competitiveness: the keywords in Europe's policies and programmes for space', 28 Nov. 2005, URL <http://www.esa.int/esaCP/Pr_2_2005_i_EN.html>.

[60] De Selding, P. B., 'Europe pools space spy efforts', *Defense News*, 1–7 July 2002, p. 18.

[61] European Commission (note 2), p. 33.

[62] Quoted in De Selding, P. B., 'One European space system unlikely for foreseeable future', *Space News*, 11 Oct. 2004, <http://www.space.com/spacenews/archive04/futurearch_101804.html>.

and such data are used to 'prime' current European surveillance assets. There is growing European interest in an independent space surveillance capability both for security and military purposes and to better predict, and avoid, collisions with dangerous space debris. Most recently, the Panel of Experts on Space and Security asserted in its March 2005 final report: 'The lack of a European Space Surveillance Capability is identified as a serious capability gap that must be one of the priority [priorities] of the future European Space Programme. Beyond the security of the European space assets, this system must contribute to the control of the application of International Space Treaties and to the evaluation of the activities of the space-faring nations or organizations.'[63]

The European Space Operations Centre laid out a design study for a future independent European Space Surveillance System in 2002 and subsequently awarded a contract to a team led by France's Office National d'Études et de Recherches Aérospatiales (ONERA, National Aerospace Research Centre), to provide options for achieving such a system.[64] The study, presented in 2004, found that a network able to provide detection and tracking capabilities roughly equivalent to the USA's would cost around €330 million to develop by 2015.[65] Such a network, although requiring several new sensors, would primarily be based on linking current European assets. Despite support from ESA, the European Commission and France, no specific development plan has yet been put forward, and the issue is highly sensitive politically.

IV. Major national programmes

France, Germany, Italy and the UK are the dominant European national players in space, but France is the undisputed leader. France's Centre National d'Études Spatiales (CNES, National Centre for Space Study) is a civilian agency that also handles military space programmes via cooperation with the Ministry of Defence (MOD). France's space budget was about €1.7 billion in 2005—including its contribution to ESA—the largest of any European state.[66] Of all the European countries only France has a dedicated military space budget.

While joint (bilateral or multilateral) projects are becoming more common, mainly because of the need for cost sharing, there is no mechanism to develop common military space requirements and no Europe-wide apparatus for sharing current military capabilities. Instead, there exists a patchwork of collective European, national, bi-national and multinational projects that often fail to work together effectively, leaving major gaps in European military space capabilities.

[63] European Commission (note 2), p. 36.

[64] Donath, T. et al., 'European space surveillance system study—final report', Document no. DPRS/N/158/04/CC, ESOC, 12 Oct. 2004, p. 6.

[65] Donath et al. (note 64), pp. 2, 18, 23.

[66] Center for Non-Proliferation Studies, 'Current and future space security: France', Monterey, Calif., 2006, URL <http://cns.miis.edu/research/space/france>.

Total European spending on military space is estimated at about €1 billion per year, versus about €5.5 billion spent annually on civil space projects.[67] The USA spends six times more than Europe on space and 30 times more on military space.[68]

European national space projects related to security and defence include earth-observation systems, satellite communications networks and very limited space surveillance assets. Of the other primary assets required for a robust military space capability—signals intelligence and missile early warning—the only ongoing efforts are planned French experiments.

Earth-observation assets

While France currently operates the only dedicated military earth-observation satellites, the Helios series (the current generation, Helios II, is designed to provide a day-and-night capability, with an estimated best resolution of 0.5 metres),[69] that is set to change over the next five years. The British MOD has orbited a low-cost, experimental microsatellite, TopSat, and is considering a follow-on programme. In 2006 Germany will launch SAR-Lupe, a synthetic-aperture radar (SAR) constellation of five satellites for military reconnaissance, expected to provide a best resolution of 0.5 m.[70] In addition, Italy is planning a dual-use cooperative venture with France to replace the venerable SPOT civilian system, under a programme called ORFEO (Optical and Radar Federated Earth Observation). France will provide Pleiades, a two-satellite optical military reconnaissance system;[71] and Italy will provide the dual-use Constellation of Small Satellites for Mediterranean Basin Observation (COSMO-SkyMed), comprising four high-resolution-radar satellites.[72]

The trend in Europe towards embracing earth-observation satellites for military applications is accompanied by improvements in the capabilities of such systems to allow for their use as tactical battlefield assets. Earth-observation satellite systems are used by militaries to make detailed maps, monitor troops in the field (both friendly and enemy), look for suspicious activities (such as the construction of nuclear facilities), and provide geo-

---

[67] New Defence Agenda, 'Tracking European space policies—have we got the civil/military balance right?', <http://www.forum-europe.com/publication/NDA_SOD_18Oct2005.pdf>.

[68] New Defence Agenda (note 67), p. 7.

[69] De Selding, P. B., 'France debuts Helios IIA recon satellite images', C^4ISR, 29 Mar. 2005, URL <http://isr.dnmediagroup.com/story.php?F=750641>.

[70] Sell, D., OHB-System AG, Communication with the authors, 28 Nov. 2005; Embassy of France in the USA, 'Fifth Franco-German Council of Ministers, Statement by the Franco-German Defence and Security Council', 26 Apr. 2005, URL <http://www.ambafrance-us.org/news/statmnts/2005/franco_germany_defense042605.asp>; De Selding, P. B., 'German military prepares for 2005 SAR-Lupe deployment', C^4ISR, URL <http://isr.dnmediagroup.com/story. php?F=327973>; and OHB-System AG, 'SAR-Lupe', URL<http://www. ohb-system.de/Security/sarlupe.html>.

[71] France and Italy signed a memorandum of understanding in Jan. 2001, under which each country would pay for its own space system but the costs of ground systems to use the satellites would be shared. See 'Pleiades (high resolution optical imaging constellation of CNES)', *eoPortal*, URL <http://directory. eoportal.org/pres_PleiadesHRHighResolutionOpticalImagingConstellationofCNES.html>.

[72] Alenia Spazio, 'Cosmo-Skymed', URL <http://www.alespazio.it/earth_observation_page.aspx?Id Prog=23>.

graphic data to missiles and other weapon systems for use in targeting and so on. To be useful in a conflict or crisis, high-resolution images must be taken repeatedly at the shortest time intervals possible, and data relayed and analysed as quickly as possible. All these capabilities are being sought under planned European programmes.

As noted above, the key political question that remains unresolved is whether and how these assets, including GMES, will be integrated into collective European operations. There continues to be strong antipathy among European military leaders towards sharing imagery and analysis.

Satellite communications

Communications satellites are of increasing importance to militaries around the world for global communication and data transfer, allowing an unprecedented degree of networking of forces and commanders. In the short term, European governments and institutions, including NATO, will have access to at least 20 different commercial, military and dual-use communications satellite systems.[73]

Most of the world's militaries rely on commercial satellite networks for the bulk of their communications needs. However, commercial satellites do not provide the same level of security (via encrypted signals, component hardening, anti-jam techniques, etc.), as those built to military specifications; thus several European countries have chosen to pursue dedicated military satellites. The UK currently operates five Skynet IV satellites, and two Skynet V satellites will be launched in 2006/2007.[74] Italy has one SICRAL satellite with an upgraded version, SICRAL 1B, to be launched in early 2007 and the more capable SICRAL 2 by 2009.[75] France's Syracuse IIIA was launched in October 2005 and Syracuse IIIB will be in orbit in 2006.[76] Spain's planned SPAINSAT is also due for launch in 2006, and XTAR-EUR, a US–Spanish satellite, was launched in February 2005.[77] Germany plans to have two SATCOMBw Stufe 2 satellites in orbit by 2008.[78] NATO's two operational NATO IV satellites are being replaced by NATO SATCOM Post 2000, which comprises services from three SKYNETS, one Syracuse and one SICRAL under agreements with France, Italy and the UK.[79]

[73] Donath et al. (note 64), p. 30.

[74] Donath et al. (note 64), p. 30.

[75] Donath et al. (note 64), p. 30; Dutch Space, 'Sicral', URL <http://www.dutchspace.nl/pages/business/content.asp?id=200&LangType=1033>, p. 31; and European Commission (note 2).

[76] Donath et al. (note 64), p. 30; and 'Syracuse III', Alcatel Space, May 2003. URL <http://www.alcatel.com/space/pdf/telecom/syracusegb.pdf>. In addition, the older Syracuse II remains operational.

[77] Donath et al. (note 64), p. 30; and Loral Space and Communications, 'XTAR-EUR enters full commercial service, beginning a new era of military satellite communications', Press release, 4 Apr. 2005, URL <http://www. loral.com/inthenews/050404.html>.

[78] De Selding, P. B., 'Two firms win tentative German milcom sat contracts', *C⁴ISR*, 11 May 2005, URL <http://isr.dnmediagroup.com/story.php?F=842556>.

[79] Howell, R. R. N., 'International leaders call for strategies and changes that support a stronger NATO', *Signal*, URL <http://www.afcea.org/signal/articles/anmviewer.asp?a=1010&z=8>.

Electronic intelligence

Electronic intelligence (ELINT) satellites are designed to intercept electromagnetic signals such as radio communications. France is the only European
country known to be currently operating a standalone ELINT system, Essaim
(meaning swarm), which itself is only a demonstration programme. The
French Government hopes that this demonstration will convince other European governments of the value of an independent European ELINT system.[80]
Essaim is a network of four satellites, launched in December 2004 and operational since May 2005.[81] It 'analyze[s] the electromagnetic environment on
the ground in a number of frequency bands that are used exclusively for military communications'.[82] A follow-on, tentatively named Elint, is being
planned for launch in 2008 or 2009. It would comprise an LEO constellation
of three small satellites to monitor radar signals and radio communications,.

Missile warning

The French MOD is financing Spirale, a system designed to demonstrate an
initial capability to detect missiles during their boost phase.[83] The experiment
involves two micro-satellites carrying advanced, high-resolution infrared
payloads.[84] Two satellites are to be launched in 2008.

Space surveillance

There are about a dozen European radar facilities with potential applicability
to space surveillance and a handful of optical telescopes.

The European Incoherent Scatter Scientific Association's incoherent scatter
radar network should be noted here, even though it is a multinational programme. At its main facility in Tromsø, Norway, a project is under way to try
to routinely piggyback surveillance of objects in LEO with the network's primary job of atmospheric and ionospheric research.

The French MOD's GRAVES, a radar 'fence' that detects objects passing
through its beam, is the only European system that can independently detect
and track space objects down to a size of about 1 m in diameter at altitudes of
up to 1000 km.[85]

---

[80] De Selding, P. B., 'CNES, DGA to fund demonstration satellite', C^4ISR, URL <http://isr.dnmedia group.com/story.php?F=842558>.

[81] Malik, T., 'Ariane 5 successfully orbits France's Helios 2A satellite', *Space*, 18 Dec. 2004, URL <http://space.com/missionlaunches/ariane5_helios_launch_041218.html>.

[82] EADS, 'ESSAIM, micro-satellites in formation', 6 June 2005, URL <http://eads.net>.

[83] EADS, 'Astrium selects Arianespace to launch Spirale', Press release, 17 Oct. 2005, URL <http:// www.space.eads.net/press-center/press-releases/eads-astrium-selects-arianespace-to-launch-spirale>.

[84] 'French Spirale to launch aboard Ariane 5', *Space News*, 24 Oct. 2005, p. 8.

[85] 'Imminent delivery of French space surveillance system' *France ST*, no. 75 (24 Aug. 2005), URL <http://www.fitscience.org/media/upload/FranceST_075.pdf>.

The UK maintains the most powerful space surveillance radar in Europe, located at Fylingdales Air Base and operated by the British MOD under agreement with the US DOD and US Air Force. Fylingdales has traditionally been used for early warning of ballistic missile launches, but it also has a secondary role as a so-called collateral sensor as part of the US space surveillance network (SSN).[86] While Fylingdales is being upgraded to perform ballistic missile tracking as well as detection under a February 2003 agreement with the USA,[87] the UK has shown no interest in incorporating it into, or providing data for, any future European network. The nature of Fylingdales's relationship with the US DOD would make doing so extremely complicated if not impossible. No data are currently made available to other European space agencies.[88]

Another facility that is part of the SSN is the Globus II radar at Vardø, Norway, operated by the Norwegian Intelligence Service under a 1997 agreement with the USA. It has operated since 2002 with sub-metre resolutions.[89] In addition, the Danish Government controls a similar radar at Thule Airbase in Greenland that is part of the SSN, and like Globus, it will be upgraded to play a role in the planned US missile defense launch-warning network.[90] The German Research Establishment for Applied Science operates the tracking and image radar (TIRA) system at Wachtberg, Germany, which has been used to provide data on potential collision hazards to ESA satellites.[91]

Optical systems for GEO tracking include ESA's Space Debris Telescope at the Teide Observatory in the Canary Islands, the British MOD's three PIMS telescopes, and the French ROSACE and TAROT telescopes.

V. Conclusions

For Europe, the move to entrust the EU with using space for military purposes carries much significance, at least in terms of future aspirations. With the exceptions of Galileo, GMES and the EU Satellite Centre the control of the vast majority of assets with clear military and security applications remains in the hands of individual European countries and the USA; however, there are undeniable signs of convergence under the EU umbrella. The integration of European military assets, in its early stages but evident in projects such as the EU battle groups, points in this direction, as does the desire of many member states to endow the EU with true foreign and security policy tools, independ-

[86] 'Fylingdales: radar on the moors', BBC News Online, 14 Dec. 2002, URL <http://news.bbc.co.uk/2/2575759.stm>.

[87] Spring, B., 'Congress should commend Britain on missile defense upgrade', Heritage Foundation, Executive Memorandum #861, 21 Feb. 2003, URL <http://www.heritage.org/Research/NationalSecurity/em861.cfm>.

[88] Klinkrad, H., 'Monitoring space—efforts made by European countries', Paper presented at the International Colloquium on Europe and Space Debris, Académie Nationale de l'Air et de l'Espace, Toulouse, 27–28 Nov. 2002, URL <http://www.fas. org/spp/military/program/track/klinkrad.pdf>.

[89] Klinkrad (note 88).

[90] Boese, W., 'Greenland Radar Cleared for US Missile Defense', *Arms Control Today*, July/August 2004, URL <http://www.armscontrol.org/act/2004_07-08/GreenlandRadar.asp>.

[91] Klinkrad (note 88).

ent of the USA. Many EU member states clearly share a sense that their foreign policy influence, when acting alone, is inherently limited, and that the future requires greater pooling of all foreign policy and security tools. The strong US influence over national space surveillance networks in Europe is also a driver for greater EU common action in this area.

With the lead-in time to the launch of new space assets measured in decades rather than years, decisions made today are not likely to translate into common projects in the near future. However, the practical expressions of this trend are already visible. The framework agreement between ESA and the EU brings the technological dimension of European space projects closer to the EU's political heart. The military organs and staffs of the EU are brainstorming for ways in which space can add to the effectiveness of future collective military action. Debate within EU institutions has moved on from downplaying the security implications of projects formerly billed as purely civilian, such as Galileo, to discussing the possibility of the EU's actually managing the next generation of military satellites.

It would be wrong to claim that this trend is inevitable. Space is the ultimate high ground, the enabler of most security and military operations taking place on earth. It is the key to building the political case for use of force as well as to the planning and implementation of any modern military operation. As such, the military use of space is probably more akin to nuclear weapons than conventional arms in terms of its international significance. The EU's member states will probably continue to guard their ability to make independent judgements based on national assets and selective partnerships. However, the more the EU becomes the tool of choice for the security and military operations of its member states, and the more it seeks to profile itself as a global actor, the further it will be driven towards the use of space for security and military purposes. If the trend continues, the Union will most probably progress from operating dual-use assets and distributing data from national networks to deploying collectively owned technology for the exploitation of space for security purposes.

Part III. Non-proliferation, arms control and disarmament, 2005

12. Reflections on continuity and change in arms control

IAN ANTHONY

I. Introduction

In asserting that law and diplomacy could have a role in building security, the pioneers of modern arms control in the 1950s were making a conscious effort to overcome the bitter (and at the time very recent) experience that security depended, above all, on military capability based in large part on superior technology.

During the cold war, arms control was necessary given the risk (albeit remote) that bipolar political confrontation would spill over into a war that would, because of the presence of nuclear weapons, be even more catastrophic than those of the past. Whether arms control can play a useful role in managing security problems is again a topical question today. The United States has become so powerful relative to its peers that it is tempted to seek national security by framing international political dialogue in ways that suit US national interests (as determined unilaterally), underpinned by a predominant military power based on an overwhelming superiority in military technology. Whereas war avoidance was the main US priority during the cold war, after its end the use of force has not by any means been excluded as a tool to shape international politics.

This chapter argues that the objectives of arms control, which were set by major power interests during the cold war, have changed significantly and that these changes by and large reflect the trends in thinking about international security in the USA. An example of this tendency is the relatively much greater emphasis placed on strengthening controls to prevent the emergence of new nuclear weapon capabilities without a parallel obligation for properly verified and irreversible nuclear arms reductions. However, there are also some cases where arms control initiatives that are not under the leadership of the United States have been developed, notably in regard to certain types of anti-personnel landmines.

During the cold war, bilateral Soviet–US arms control helped manage the relationship that was the most important single element of the global security environment. After the end of the cold war the strategic objectives that were previously dominant in arms control have been supplemented by a focus on achieving humanitarian goals and attempts to develop instruments that can address the increased concern about threats from non-state actors. Some changes in thinking about what arms control is for are examined in section II of this chapter.

Multilateral arms control efforts led to a number of treaties, including the 1968 Treaty on the Non-proliferation of Nuclear Weapons (Non-Proliferation Treaty, NPT)[1] and the 1972 Biological and Toxin Weapons Convention (BTWC).[2] However, approaches to cooperation, reciprocity and inclusivity in arms control agreements have changed recently. Section III discusses the way in which thinking about the appropriate legal form for arms control has altered. In its cold war variant, arms control was seen as a binding contract between parties. This approach was not only intended to underline that parties should do what they promised, which is true for agreements of any kind, but to indicate that sanctions (albeit of an unspecified kind) could flow from a proven failure to live up to obligations.

Closely connected to the discussion of legal form has been the relative emphasis placed on verifying whether or not the parties to an agreement actually live up to their obligations. Verification provisions have sometimes, but by no means always, been a feature of arms control treaties. Strong verification provisions have tended to be a key element in those treaties that major powers perceive as touching on the most critical security issues. The issues of verification and compliance are also taken up in section III.

One key aspect of arms control is determining the scope of what is to be controlled by any agreement. This judgement has always been made in the context of the objectives of the agreement, which has been based on either a strategic assessment or humanitarian grounds. Recently, states have examined how arms control might contribute to counter-terrorism, and in particular the effort to reduce the risk of mass impact terrorism. Section IV discusses the impact of this change on thinking about the technologies that should be subject to control. Section V draws conclusions from the preceding sections.

II. The objectives of arms control

Modern arms control was initiated in the mid-1950s at a time of great tension between two ideologically opposed blocs which were just embarking on what became a long period of competitive armament. Whereas a number of discussions about general and complete disarmament had taken place previously, arms control was conceived in the USA as a mechanism that could provide some predictability and (hopefully) moderate and make more stable a strategic competition that threatened to take on new and more dangerous proportions after the Soviet Union tested its first nuclear weapon in 1949.

Thomas C. Schelling and Morton H. Halperin identified the specific objectives of arms control as being to help prevent war, to make war less destructive

---

[1] For a description of the main provisions of the NPT and a list of the parties see annex A in this volume. The full text of the NPT is available at URL <http://disarmament.un.org/wmd/npt/npttext.html>. See also chapter 13 in this volume.

[2] The Convention on the Prohibition of the Development, Production and Stockpiling of Bacteriological (Biological) and Toxin Weapons and on Their Destruction is reproduced on the SIPRI Chemical and Biological Warfare (CBW) Project website, URL <http://www.sipri.org/contents/cbwarfare/>. The site includes complete lists of parties, signatories and non-signatories to this convention. See also annex A in this volume. On the BTWC see chapter 14 in this volume.

should prevention fail and to reduce the financial costs of effective deterrence.[3] However, it has been argued persuasively that the main benefit of Soviet–US arms control was not primarily to curb armaments but to provide a channel of communication and a 'safety valve' between two adversaries which otherwise had few non-confrontational contacts with one another.[4] Arms control was a mechanism at a general level for reducing the risk that war could start either by accident or as a result of misperception or misunderstanding. At a more directly operational level, the establishment in 1963 of a 'hotline' system for emergency communication between the leaders of the two cold war blocs in a crisis had the same purpose.

At the regional level in Europe strategic objectives were predominant in arms control negotiation after 1973, when talks aimed at achieving force reductions in conventional forces were initiated. These discussions and negotiations were between the two armed blocs, the North Atlantic Treaty Organization (NATO) and the Warsaw Treaty Organization (WTO, or Warsaw Pact). Here, too, the opportunity to communicate was at least as important as the effort to create balanced sets of forces—an objective that was recognized to be unachievable at an early stage given the asymmetries in geography, technology and doctrine of the two blocs and the inherent difficulties of measuring capability.[5]

Initially, it appeared as if the new objective of multilateral arms control after the end of the cold war would be to alleviate serious humanitarian concerns over the indiscriminate effect of weapons, rather than being related to the strategic balance in any particular location or among any particular group of states.

This approach probably influenced the decision to ban chemical weapons. While a ban on chemical weapons had been discussed since the 1960s, international agreement on the text of the 1993 Chemical Weapons Convention (CWC)[6] could not be reached until 1992—when these weapons were no longer earmarked by the major powers for battlefield use in Europe. The humanitarian impulse was triggered in the early 1990s by events in Iraq. While Iraq had used chemical weapons on the battlefield as early as 1984, in the context of the 1980–88 Iraq–Iran War, the international reaction to this use was limited. International reaction was much stronger after 1988, when Saddam Hussein ordered the use of chemical weapons to attack Halabja, a town of about 80 000 predominantly Kurdish inhabitants. The assault on Halabja included a series of attacks mounted over many hours and involved

[3] Schelling, T. C. and Halperin, M. H., *Strategy and Arms Control* (Twentieth Century Fund: New York, N.Y., 1961), p. 2.

[4] This point is made in Carter, A., SIPRI, *Success and Failure in Arms Control Negotiations* (Oxford University Press: Oxford, 1989), pp. 6–7.

[5] Epstein, J. M., *Measuring Military Power: The Soviet Air Threat to Europe* (Princeton University Press: Princeton, N.J., 1984).

[6] The Convention on the Prohibition of the Development, Production, Stockpiling and Use of Chemical Weapons and on their Destruction (corrected version), 8 Aug. 1994, is available on the SIPRI CBW Project website (note 2). The site includes complete lists of parties, signatories and non-signatories to this convention. See also annex A in this volume. On the CWC see chapter 14 in this volume.

the use of a number of different chemical agents. The same or greater destructive effect could have been achieved using conventional weapons, given that the population of the town was defenceless and captive. It was arguably the abhorrent nature of the attack—in effect using the civil population for large-scale weapon testing—rather than its destructiveness that provided a political impulse leading to the successful conclusion of the CWC in conditions where the great powers no longer had any strategic imperative to retain chemical weapons.

Another category of weapon that was examined with a view to reaching a global arms control instrument and where the humanitarian impulse was combined with a declining military utility was that of anti-personnel landmines.[7] A provision of international humanitarian law that had been agreed in 1981, the Convention on Prohibitions or Restrictions on the Use of Certain Conventional Weapons which may be Deemed to be Excessively Injurious or to have Indiscriminate Effects (CCW Convention, or 'Inhumane Weapons' Convention),[8] was examined in the mid-1990s with a view to strengthening it. However, in 1996 the parties to those negotiations agreed to limited amendments to the part of the convention dealing with landmines (Protocol II). Subsequently, a group of states that wished to go further negotiated a complete ban on certain types of landmines, which resulted in the 1997 Convention on the Prohibition of the Use, Stockpiling, Production and Transfer of Anti-Personnel Mines and on their Destruction (APM Convention).[9] This complete ban underlined that for the countries concerned the negative humanitarian impact of using these kinds of landmines outweighed any potential military utility.

A number of arms control processes have been re-examined to see whether and how they might contribute to denying capabilities to non-state groups that may be planning acts of mass impact terrorism. It has not proved possible to adapt the BTWC, the CWC or the NPT. However, states that participate in export control regimes have discussed how to adapt controls to take the risk of mass impact terrorism into account.[10] The need to prevent acts of mass impact terrorism has also led to new approaches to arms control within the United Nations (UN). Several UN Security Council resolutions have created obligations on states to put in place national laws and procedures to implement them in an effort to address terrorist threats.[11]

---

[7] On arms control efforts related to anti-personnel landmines see also chapter 15 in this volume.

[8] For the parties to and basic information on the CCW Convention and Protocols see annex A in this volume.

[9] For the parties to and basic information on the APM Convention see annex A in this volume.

[10] On export control regimes see chapter 16 in this volume.

[11] UN Security Council Resolution 1333, 19 Dec. 2000, established an arms embargo on Usama bin Laden and his associates. UN Security Council Resolution 1373, 28 Sep. 2001, required states to refrain from providing any form of support, active or passive, to entities or persons involved in terrorist acts, including by eliminating the supply of weapons to terrorists. The provisions of UN Security Council Resolution 1540, 28 Apr. 2004, are discussed further below. UN resolutions are available at URL <http://www.un.org/Docs/sc/index.html>. On Resolution 1540 see also Anthony, I., 'Arms control and non-proliferation; the role of international organizations', *SIPRI Yearbook 2005: Armaments, Disarmament and International Security* (Oxford University Press: Oxford, 2005), pp. 542–47.

Cooperation, symmetry and reciprocity in arms control

During the cold war, arms control efforts at the global, regional and bilateral levels had certain common characteristics that contrast somewhat with contemporary approaches. Notably, arms control was conceived during the cold war as something that states would do in cooperation, even in conditions where they were heavily armed adversaries in what was sometimes a bitter ideological struggle.

The US analyst Robert Jervis perhaps best captured this notion with the expression 'cooperation under the security dilemma'.[12] Jervis meant that if a unilateral policy intended to increase the security of one state is perceived by other states to diminish their security, then they will work to defeat it. This made it a common interest of states to make other states understand the non-threatening and defensive intent behind their national programmes even if those programmes, on the face of it, appeared offensive.

Bilateral arms control was nevertheless viewed as part of, and not isolated from, the cold war conflict, and the approach was not based on an imperative to compromise. However, cooperation was never taken to imply that reaching agreement was of paramount importance. The underlying thinking was summarized from a US perspective by Secretary of State James A. Baker in December 1989, when he noted that 'our mission must be to press the search for mutual advantage. Where we find Soviet agreement, we'll both be better off. Where we meet Soviet resistance, we'll know that we have to redouble our efforts so that Moscow practices, not just preaches, the new thinking'.[13]

Multilateral arms control also took place during the cold war but, whereas bilateral Soviet–US arms control talks and the conventional arms talks between the two military blocs that faced one another in Europe dealt with limited sub-sets of the total inventories of arms held by the negotiating parties, multilateral arms control dealt with all of the weapons in a particular class that could be isolated and defined according to technical parameters.

The obligations established in the NPT apply to nuclear weapons or nuclear explosive devices. Similarly, the BTWC applies to 'microbial or other biological agents, or toxins whatever their origin or method of production, of types and in quantities that have no justification for prophylactic, protective or other peaceful purposes'.[14] The obligations established in the BTWC also apply to any weapons, equipment or means of delivery that are designed to use such agents or toxins for hostile purposes or in armed conflict. In contrast, the Soviet–US bilateral arms control treaties applied to some, but by no means all, nuclear weapon delivery systems. The obligations in the 1990 Treaty on Con-

---

[12] Jervis, R., 'Cooperation under the security dilemma', *World Politics*, vol. 30, no. 2 (1978), pp. 167–214

[13] Baker, J. A., 'U.S.–Soviet relations: a discussion of perestroika and economic reform', *US Department of State Bulletin*, vol. 89 (Dec. 1989), URL <http://www.findarticles.com/p/articles/mi_m1079/is_n2153_v89/ai_8528187>.

[14] BTWC (note 2), Article I.

ventional Armed Forces in Europe (CFE Treaty)[15] applied to a limited number of categories of conventional weapon, and not all of the delivery systems in those categories held in the inventories of the signatories were treaty-limited items.

One feature of the approach to arms control in the past was an assumption that the outcome of negotiations among parties will be to create reciprocal obligations that will be applied in a symmetrical manner to the military capacities of those states that are parties to arms control agreements.[16] Furthermore, universal adherence to multilateral treaties was put forward as an arms control objective. After the end of the cold war these assumptions were challenged and there is growing evidence that neither symmetry nor reciprocity are universally regarded as prerequisites for arms control.

This tendency away from symmetry has been expressed by US President George W. Bush in regard to Russian–US arms control. President Bush observed in 2001:

I think it's interesting to note that a new relationship based upon trust and cooperation is one that doesn't need endless hours of arms control discussions . . . I've announced a level that we're going to—that we'll stick by. To me, that's how you approach a relationship that is changed, and different . . . I looked the man in the eye and shook his hand, and if we need to write it down on a piece of paper, I'll be glad to do that. But that's what our government is going to do over the next 10 years. And we don't need an arms control agreement . . . to reduce our weaponry in a significant way.[17]

In the event, Russian President Vladimir Putin expressed a preference for codifying an agreement, and the Treaty on Strategic Offensive Reductions (SORT) was signed on 24 May 2002.[18] Although it is a treaty, SORT has been characterized by analysts as 'a codification of unilateral statements made by the presidents'.[19] Unlike past strategic arms control agreements, the manner of reducing arsenals in an irreversible, verified manner is not laid down in the treaty. Each side can decide how to carry out the reductions and, without violating the terms of the treaty, delivery systems and the materials that are the essential elements of warheads may be held in storage. Thus, parts of the 'reduced' arsenal could be reconstituted rather quickly.

---

[15] For the text of the CFE Treaty and Protocols see Koulik, S. and Kokoski, R., SIPRI, *Conventional Arms Control: Perspectives on Verification* (Oxford University Press: Oxford, 1994), pp. 211–76; and the OSCE website at URL <http://www.osce.org/docs/english/1990-1999/cfe/cfetreate.htm>. The parties to the CFE Treaty are listed in annex A in this volume. See also chapter 15 in this volume.

[16] One exception to this was the acceptance in the NPT of 5 so-called 'recognized' nuclear weapon states. The NPT did not confer permanent nuclear weapon state status on the 5 countries, but a pragmatic acknowledgement was made that a period of time would be needed during which the 5 states could negotiate the conditions under which they could reduce and then eliminate their nuclear forces.

[17] The White House, 'President announces reduction in nuclear arsenal', Press Conference by President Bush and Russian President Vladimir Putin, News release, Washington, DC, 13 Nov. 2001, URL <http://www.whitehouse.gov/news/releases/2001/11/20011113-3.html>.

[18] SORT was signed by Russia and the USA; it entered into force on 1 June 2003 and is available at URL <http://www.state.gov/t/ac/trt/18016.htm>. See also annex A in this volume.

[19] Miasnikov, E., 'Status of U.S.–Russian negotiations on strategic arms reduction', 9 Aug. 2002, URL <http://www.armscontrol.ru/start/nuc-cuts.htm>.

Therefore, SORT maintains the legal form of a treaty but abandons the notion of symmetry. It does, however, retain the idea of reciprocity, at least in broad form, in that the treaty obliges each party to reduce the numbers of its strategic nuclear warheads to 1700–2200. In a number of other recent initiatives that must be considered as part of modern arms control the idea of reciprocity is absent.

The reciprocal model could be contrasted with some current thinking about arms control, which emphasizes how states can control the military capabilities of third parties. Moreover, a number of political initiatives have been launched by groups of states to explore how they can work together to make the instruments used to restrict the capabilities of others more effective— although each restrictive measure is still applied unilaterally. One example of this tendency has been the transformation and revitalization after 1990 of multilateral cooperation to apply general rules and guidelines effectively through national controls that criminalize the export of specified items without prior authorization. Governments have increasingly come to see export controls as a valuable part of the overall effort to combat proliferation partly because of their preventive aspect. Authorities assess the risk that a specified item will be used in a nuclear, biological or chemical (NBC) weapon programme of concern or in a missile that would be used to deliver such weapons before granting or refusing permission for that item to be exported. Moreover, export controls provide one of the few linkages between the business and scientific community and arms control. Efficient export control authorities have usually developed methods for conducting a systematic dialogue with industry which involves a reciprocal exchange of information that is valuable in combating proliferation. Another recent example where the principle of reciprocity is absent is the 2003 Proliferation Security Initiative (PSI), which is intended to facilitate cooperation among states to prevent specific shipments of certain weapons, their delivery systems or related materials from taking place.[20]

A change in the approach to symmetry and reciprocity can also be seen in the conditions under which a comprehensive nuclear test ban will enter into force, which require participation by the most relevant parties. A 'standstill agreement' on nuclear testing was proposed by Indian Prime Minister Jawaharlal Nehru in 1954, but was not endorsed by the Soviet Union, the United Kingdom and the USA until 1958. After a permanent arms control negotiating forum was established in Geneva in 1959, one of its first agenda items was to negotiate a comprehensive ban on testing of nuclear weapons. The negotiations on a global test ban reflected the interest of nuclear powers that had completed their own testing to limit the possibility that an unspecified number of new nuclear weapon states would emerge. However, the Compre-

---

[20] US Department of State, Bureau of Nonproliferation, 'Proliferation Security Initiative: frequently asked questions', Fact sheet, 26 May 2005, URL <http://www.state.gov/t/isn/rls/fs/32725.htm>. On PSI see also Ahlström, C., 'The Proliferation Security Initiative: international law aspects of the Statement of Interdiction Principles', *SIPRI Yearbook 2005* (note 11), pp. 743–48.

hensive Nuclear-Test-Ban Treaty (CTBT)[21] could not be agreed until 1996—the point at which China and France completed the programme of nuclear testing that they considered necessary. The arrangements for entry into force of the CTBT specify that, while the treaty is open to any state, it cannot enter into force until it has been ratified by 44 specified countries that have nuclear research or nuclear power reactors on their territory. Three of these 44 states—India, North Korea and Pakistan—have not signed the treaty and 8, including China, Egypt, Iran, Israel, Russia and the USA, have signed but not ratified it.

Non-state actor participation in arms control

Arms control has traditionally been carried out exclusively by states. However, participation in arms control is beginning to extend beyond states to include a variety of non-state actors.

The APM Convention was achieved in part through the effective political actions of non-governmental organizations (NGOs), which coordinated their activities in an international network that could both spread information and apply political pressure to governments. This coalition made extremely skilful use of modern media and campaigning techniques adapted from the private sector (mainly from the world of advertising). While this innovation, facilitated by the development of wide-area computer networks and in particular by the growth of the Internet, proved extremely effective in shaping opinions in open and democratic societies, its effectiveness in closed and authoritarian societies is more difficult to evaluate.

A similar international NGO network has tried to build momentum behind another campaign to develop a global legal instrument to control small arms and light weapons (SALW). In 2001 the UN adopted the Programme of Action to Prevent, Combat and Eradicate the Illicit Trade in Small Arms and Light Weapons in All Its Aspects. The programme is not a legal instrument and it addresses only illicit trade, rather than other aspects of the production, acquisition and use of SALW. However, it can be asserted with confidence that NGOs played a part in the development and adoption of the programme.

Arms control was traditionally an activity confined to the weapons held in the armed forces of states and for use in international conflicts. After the end of the cold war thought was given to whether arms control might also be applied to shape the capabilities of state armed forces when used in internal conflicts. This discussion was most active in Europe, where a Code of Conduct on Politico-Military Aspects of Security was adopted by the Conference on Security and Co-operation in Europe (CSCE)—the forerunner of the Organization for Security and Co-operation in Europe (OSCE)—in December 1994.[22] The code is a politically binding measure (although it does refer to

---

[21] The CTBT was opened for signature in 1996 and had been ratified by 132 states by 1 Mar. 2006. For a description of the treaty and a list of the states parties see annex A in this volume.

[22] Organization for Security and Co-operation in Europe, OSCE Code of Conduct on Politico-Military Aspects of Security (COC), OSCE document DOC.FSC/1/95, 3 Dec. 1994, URL <http://www.osce.org/item/883.html>. This document was adopted at the 91st Plenary Meeting of the Special Committee of the CSCE Forum for Security Co-operation in Budapest on 3 Dec. 1994.

international legal agreements related to politico-military affairs) that incorporates existing norms on the democratic control and use of armed forces. The code also lays down guidelines for the personal responsibility and accountability of individual members of the armed forces.

The OSCE code does not apply to the non-state actors that would be engaged in internal conflicts and this remains to a large extent an arms control lacuna, with the exception of the voluntary measures that some non-state armed groups have accepted under agreements reached through non-governmental processes.[23] In a more positive context, a different set of non-state actors—the private sector—is becoming engaged in shaping and implementing export controls. More widely there is evidence of a private sector awareness of the need to be active partners in security building.[24]

Regional, sub-regional and country-specific arms control

Recent history suggests that at present states have great difficulty in agreeing on the objectives of multilateral arms control in so far as it applies to the armed forces and the military capabilities of states. The fact that the Conference on Disarmament (CD) has now failed to agree on a programme of work for nine consecutive years can also be taken as an illustration of this point. In the absence of political convergence around either strategic or humanitarian objectives, further multilateral arms control initiatives should not be expected.

The same difficulty has constrained further progress in arms control at the regional level. In Europe the Agreement on Adaptation was negotiated to adapt the CFE Treaty to conditions where there were no longer two military blocs in Europe.[25] However, the adapted treaty regime has not entered into force. Outside Europe there have been a number of arms control proposals and, in the Middle East in particular, some discussions have occurred among governments about the need for regional arms limitation agreements. There are five treaties that establish nuclear weapon-free zones (NWFZs) in Africa, Antarctica, Latin America, South-East Asia and the South Pacific.[26] Three of these zones have been agreed since the end of the cold war. In addition, Mongolia has declared its territory to be an NWFZ and has, in addition to enacting national legislation to that effect, worked to achieve international

---

[23] Under a process facilitated by Geneva Call, a Swiss NGO, a number of armed non-state groups have agreed to abide by the provisions of the APM Convention. See the Geneva Call website at URL <http://www.genevacall.org>.

[24] Bailes, A. J. K. and Frommelt, I. (eds), *Business and Security: Public–Private Sector Relationships in a New Security Environment* (Oxford University Press: Oxford, 2004).

[25] For the text of the Agreement on Adaptation see *SIPRI Yearbook 2000: Armaments, Disarmament and International Security* (Oxford University Press: Oxford, 2000), pp. 627–42; and the OSCE website at URL <http://www.osce.org>. See also chapter 15 in this volume.

[26] On the 1959 Antarctic Treaty; the 1967 Treaty for the Prohibition of Nuclear Weapons in Latin America and the Caribbean (Treaty of Tlatelolco); the 1985 South Pacific Nuclear Free Zone Treaty (Treaty of Rarotonga); the 1995 Treaty on the Southeast Asia Nuclear Weapon-Free Zone (Treaty of Bangkok); and the 1996 African Nuclear-Weapon-Free Zone Treaty (Treaty of Pelindaba) see annex A in this volume. The Treaty of Pelindaba has not entered into force.

recognition of that status. The text for a treaty establishing an NWFZ in Central Asia was drafted in 2002.

Another tendency has been to supplement global approaches to controlling arms with instruments tailored to particular sub-regions or to define country-specific measures. For example, issues raised by North Korea's violation of its safeguards agreement with the International Atomic Energy Agency (IAEA)—directly linked to the NPT under Article III.1 of the treaty—have not been addressed by the UN Security Council, although this is envisaged in Article XII of the IAEA Statute.[27] Instead, North Korea's nuclear weapon programme has been addressed through a series of initiatives tailored to the specific conditions of the Korean peninsula. While the most recent of these, the Six-Party Talks, involves China, Japan, North Korea, South Korea, Russia and the USA as participants, only the programmes of North Korea are the subject of discussion. The objective of the talks is to bring North Korea, which is the only country to have withdrawn from the NPT, back into the treaty as a non-nuclear weapon state and to ensure that this decision is irreversible.

The IAEA has been seeking to provide assurances about the peaceful nature of Iran's nuclear programme, about which uncertainties remain with regard to its scope and nature. In parallel with intensive scrutiny of Iran's nuclear programme by the IAEA, after October 2003 three European Union (EU) member states (France, Germany and the UK) negotiated with Iran in an attempt to persuade Iran to modify its nuclear programme.[28] The objective of the 'E3' was to persuade Iran to permanently suspend uranium enrichment and to cancel plans to build a heavy water reactor.[29] The E3–Iran negotiations took place in circumstances where Iran (which still has not been found to be in non-compliance with the NPT) had not been found to be in non-compliance with its safeguards agreement—something that only occurred in September 2005.

In each of these cases the objective of the targeted initiative is being sought through the application of a package of measures tailored to the specific conditions in Iran and North Korea, respectively.

III. Arms control form and process: beyond legal instruments

The relationship between international law and arms control has been redefined as the objectives of arms control have changed. In particular, the tendency to make restricting the capabilities of third parties the purpose for cooperation has altered thinking about the appropriate legal form for arms control. In the past arms control would have been seen as an aspect of international law, but in a modern understanding legal instruments are viewed as one among several elements that, taken collectively, constitute arms control.

---

[27] The IAEA Statute is available at URL <http://www.iaea.org/About/statute_text.html>.

[28] Kile, S. N. (ed.), *Europe and Iran: Perspectives on Non-proliferation*, SIPRI Research Report no. 21 (Oxford University Press: Oxford, 2005). See also chapter 13 in this volume.

[29] See the discussion in chapter 13.

The characteristics normally associated with law-making were important when agreements were negotiated by adversaries or when there was a low level of trust that other parties would make good faith efforts to comply with any obligations established in an agreement. Legal agreements create rights and obligations between parties to them, either specified in the agreement itself or established by recognized and accepted international legal practice and principles. One important characteristic of legal agreements is that the parties understand that violating them could lead to remedies that are either laid down in the agreement or that are recognized under general treaty law. The possibility of remedies being taken leads states to insist on a text that minimizes the risk of being found to be non-compliant—by seeking precise language to establish a common understanding of obligations contained in the agreement, for example.

In cases where groups of states have a long history of cooperation, are broadly like-minded and perhaps are partners in politico-military alliances, an approach based on an assumed risk of cheating and the possibility that non-compliance could trigger sanctions might not be thought appropriate. Precise language about what an agreement calls for would still be valuable, but in order to avoid misunderstanding rather than in order to avoid sanctions.

The cooperation between groups of states to make their national export controls more effective that is noted above has taken the form of ad hoc political arrangements, rather than being codified in legal agreements establishing obligations for the participating states. This was the case during the cold war, when the USA and its allies used the Coordinating Committee for Multilateral Export Controls (COCOM) to manage an embargo on the transfer of many nuclear items, munitions and industrial goods with potential military applications to the Soviet Union and its allies. When the decision to abolish COCOM was taken in 1993, multilateral export control cooperation was transformed into an effort to agree rules that all participating states would apply to all destinations through their national laws.

During the 1990s this system of international cooperation to develop high and uniform export control standards to be applied nationally was revitalized and extended. More states now participate in the activities of the main cooperation arrangements—the Australia Group (AG), the Missile Technology Control Regime (MTCR), the Nuclear Suppliers Group (NSG) and the Wassenaar Arrangement on Export Controls for Conventional Arms and Dual-Use Goods and Technologies (WA)—and participation continues to grow. The AG has 40 participants (39 states and the European Commission); 45 states participate in the NSG; the MTCR has 34 participants; and 40 states participate in the WA.[30]

In spite of these developments, the issue of which states are needed for the cooperation arrangements to function effectively has been discussed extensively. As the groups have expanded, and in the absence of a very specific objective, there is a feeling that the sense of 'like-mindedness' that character-ized COCOM has been lost. At the same time, there are a growing number of sources of supply for proliferation-sensitive materials, technologies, equip-ment and knowledge. The increasing number of sources of supply is under-mining the effectiveness of approaches carried out by groups with limited par-ticipation. In these circumstances, a number of influential actors have pointed to the possible need to apply legal agreements in the area of export control and to move away from a more ad hoc approach based on understandings reached between officials and experts at the working level.

The Director General of the IAEA, Mohammed ElBaradei, has drawn atten-tion to the fact that export controls would be more effective if they were based on a legal agreement by all parties under which observance of the established rules would guarantee countries access even to proliferation-sensitive mater-ials and equipment. If countries conclude that they will be denied specific items regardless of their status under legal agreements, this will undermine their commitment to compliance. ElBaradei has argued that:

the nuclear export control system should be binding rather than voluntary, and should be made more widely applicable, to include all countries with the capability of manu-facturing sensitive nuclear related items. It should strike a balance between ensuring effective control and preserving the rights of states to peaceful nuclear technology. The aim should be easier access to non-sensitive technology and stronger control over the most sensitive parts.[31]

In September 2004 Jack Straw gave public support to the idea of an arms trade treaty. While Straw is the British Foreign Secretary, his support was given at a political rally of the Labour Party, rather than on a government plat-form. However, in September 2005 Straw included on the agenda of an EU foreign ministers' meeting a proposal from the UK and Finland for an inter-national arms trade treaty to cover the traffic in SALW. The foreign ministers discussed reaching a common position inside the EU that could serve as the basis for a proposal to be taken forward in the United Nations in 2006.[32]

While these proposals might lead to a new discussion of the appropriate legal form for export controls, other initiatives have underlined that ad hoc and political approaches can be extremely effective under certain conditions. In 1998 the EU made a political declaration on the Code of Conduct on Arms Exports.[33] The Code has two main elements. The first is a normative compon-ent consisting of guidelines that were based on eight criteria for arms exports

---

[31] ElBaradei, M., 'Nuclear non-proliferation: global security in a rapidly changing world', Speech to the Carnegie International Non-proliferation Conference, Washington, DC, 21–22 June 2004, URL <http://www.ceip.org/files/projects/npp/resources/2004conference/home.htm>.

[32] The proposal was not accompanied by any details of the scope or objectives of such a treaty. However, non-governmental groups have been advocating such a treaty since at least 1993, when a coa-lition of academics and lawyers put forward a Draft Convention on the Monitoring and Reduction of Arms Production, Stockpiling and Transfers. The essence of the 1993 proposal was mandatory registra-tion and reporting of arms production, stockpiling and transfers accompanied by criminalization of trans-fers of non-registered items.

[33] Council of the European Union, European Union Code of Conduct on Arms Exports, Brussels, 5 June 1998, URL <http://ue.eu.int/uedocs/cmsUpload/08675r2en8.pdf>.

agreed in 1991 in meetings of the five permanent members of the UN Security Council. The second element comprises operative provisions including: an exchange of information about export licence applications that have been denied for reasons related to the Code, consultations on potential 'undercuts' that could occur if an EU member state exports an essentially identical item to an end-user that has been denied a licence by another member state, and a mechanism for reporting on EU Code implementation.

Although it is based on a political declaration, the Code of Conduct has become the cornerstone of EU export control cooperation on conventional arms. Officials from EU member states have elaborated a User's Guide which has become a handbook that is used on a daily basis by licensing officers in carrying out their work.[34] The reporting mechanism has been developed to the point where it now provides unprecedented transparency in EU arms exports.[35]

Since the end of the cold war many programmes have developed to provide financial, economic and technical assistance to states (in the first instance the Russian Federation) which lack the means to implement shared disarmament, non-proliferation and counter-terrorism objectives. The USA's Cooperative Threat Reduction (CTR) programme is probably the best known programme of this kind. Managed by the Department of Defense, CTR was initially an emergency programme responding to the rapid collapse of the Soviet Union. Subsequent CTR projects have helped implement commitments contained in arms control agreements—the first bilateral 1991 Treaty on the Reduction and Limitation of Offensive Arms (START I)[36] and the CWC. Moreover, the 1991 legislation that established the CTR Programme (usually known as the Nunn–Lugar Act) was revised in 1997 and 2003 to allow funds to be spent on a broader range of activities. Further revisions were made in 2005 to widen the scope of the activities captured by CTR even further, so that virtually all geographical and functional restrictions on the use of funds will be lifted.

International non-proliferation and disarmament assistance (INDA) differs from the traditional approach to arms control. As noted above, the traditional approach depends on each state party to a treaty or an agreement implementing its obligations in good faith and at its own initiative and expense. INDA consists of practical assistance measures that are jointly implemented on the territory of one state by a coalition of parties that may include states, international organizations, local and regional government, NGOs and the private sector. Through initiatives like the Global Partnership Against Weapons and Materials of Mass Destruction, agreed in 2002 by the Group of Eight (G8) leading industrial nations, more countries are becoming engaged as either

---

[34] Council of the European Union, User's Guide to the European Union Code of Conduct on Arms Exports, Document 5179/05, Brussels, 11 Jan. 2006, URL <http://ue.eu.int/cms3_fo/showPage.asp?id=408&lang=en&mode=g>.

[35] 'Seventh Annual report according to operative provision 8 of the European Union Code of Conduct on Arms Exports', 14 Nov. 2005, Official Journal of the European Union, C328 (23 Dec. 2005), p. 1.

[36] The START I Treaty was signed by the USA and the Soviet Union; it entered into force on 5 Dec. 1994 for Russia and the USA (under the 1992 Lisbon Protocol, which entered into force on 5 Dec. 1994, Belarus, Kazakhstan and Ukraine also assumed the obligations of the former Soviet Union under the treaty). For the treaty see URL <http://www.state.gov/www/global/arms/starthtm/start/toc.html>.

donors or recipients of assistance.[37] As the geographical and functional scope of INDA has expanded, this is becoming an important part of the modern understanding of arms control.

In a recent innovation, the UN Security Council passed Resolution 1540 in April 2004.[38] This resolution introduced a requirement for states to introduce a number of national measures intended to reduce the risk that groups planning mass impact terrorism could gain access to NBC weapons or missile delivery systems for them. The resolution was not adopted in response to a particular event but was viewed as a preventive measure. The resolution, which was discussed briefly and by a limited number of states prior to its adoption, creates binding obligations on all UN member states to amend their national laws and regulations or create new ones. It therefore represents an innovative legal approach to arms control from a number of angles.

Verification, safeguards and transparency

In conditions where parties to arms control agreements have little reason to trust one another, few such agreements can be considered 'self-executing' in the sense that all parties have such an evident self-interest in compliance as more or less to exclude cheating. Therefore, the question of how to verify that parties to an agreement respect their obligations has been an important feature of arms control.

Allan S. Krass has defined verification as 'the process of determining the compliance of treaty partners based on the results of monitoring and on judgements of their significance in the existing military and political context'.[39] Paula de Sutter has noted that 'verification, compliance assessment and compliance enforcement are the three components of a policy process wherein information about a state's actions is weighed against its obligations and commitments, and if it is determined that the state is not fulfilling its obligations and commitments, steps are identified and taken to induce or enforce compliance'.[40] The determination must usually be made by each of the parties to an agreement individually because there is usually no mechanism for collective judgement about compliance with most arms control treaties.

---

[37] See also Anthony, I., 'Arms control in the new security environment', *SIPRI Yearbook 2003: Armaments, Disarmament and International Security* (Oxford University Press: Oxford, 2003), pp. 567–70; and Anthony, I. and Bauer, S., 'Transfer controls and destruction programmes', *SIPRI Yearbook 2004: Armaments, Disarmament and International Security* (Oxford University Press: Oxford, 2004), pp. 758–61. On the Global Partnership see Anthony and Bauer (note 30), pp. 699–719. See also Anthony, I. and Fedchenko, V., 'International non-proliferation and disarmament assistance', *SIPRI Yearbook 2005* (note 11), pp. 675–98.

[38] UN Security Council Resolution 1540 (note 11).

[39] Krass, A. S., *The United States and Arms Control: The Challenge of Leadership* (Praeger: Westport, Conn., 1997), p. 68. See also Krass, A. S., SIPRI, *Verification: How Much is Enough?* (Taylor & Francis: London, 1985).

[40] de Sutter, P., US Department of State, Assistant Secretary for Verification and Compliance, 'Verification, compliance and compliance enforcement', Remarks to the UN General Assembly, New York, 22 Oct. 2004.

For most of the cold war the opportunities to carry out verification were restricted by the fact that the adversaries were not in a position to enforce compliance. The negotiation of verification provisions proved a stumbling block to both bilateral and multilateral arms control.

The development of IAEA safeguards illustrates that, even when verification measures were developed for cold war arms control, they could only be limited in their scope. Although safeguards are sometimes referred to as the verification mechanism of the NPT, this is not an accurate characterization. The concept of safeguards pre-dates the NPT and was first applied in Europe in the framework of the 1957 Treaty Establishing the European Atomic Energy Community (Euratom Treaty). Article III of the NPT contains the requirement that:

each non-nuclear-weapon State Party to the Treaty undertakes to accept safeguards, as set forth in an agreement to be negotiated and concluded with the International Atomic Energy Agency in accordance with the Statute of the International Atomic Energy Agency and the Agency's safeguards system, for the exclusive purpose of verification of the fulfilment of its obligations assumed under this Treaty with a view to preventing diversion of nuclear energy from peaceful uses to nuclear weapons or other nuclear explosive devices.[41]

Three observations follow from this. First, comprehensive safeguards are the means by which the IAEA independently verifies the declarations made by states about their nuclear material and activities. Therefore they are limited in the information that they can provide in that they apply only to materials declared by the state subject to the safeguards. Safeguards cannot provide information about undeclared materials. Second, there is no obligation under the NPT for nuclear weapon states to apply safeguards at all, including to their civil nuclear activities. Third, the NPT is usually said to rest on three 'pillars' and no verification standard has been established for two of those pillars—the right in Article IV of peaceful use of nuclear technology, and the commitment of nuclear weapon states in Article VI to pursue disarmament in good faith.

When the cold war ended, it appeared as if this situation in regard to verification could change. A number of treaties negotiated at that time—the 1987 Treaty on the Elimination of Intermediate-Range and Shorter-Range Missiles (INF Treaty),[42] START I, the CFE Treaty and the CWC—had an elaborate verification apparatus and a mechanism for judging compliance and discussing issues of non-compliance. In each of these cases the verification regimes were based in part on extremely intrusive inspection regimes.

A new safeguards regime was also negotiated after 1993, embodied in a model Additional Protocol to bilateral safeguards agreements. Darryl Kimball and Paul Kerr have described the essence of the Additional Protocol as reshaping the safeguards regime:

---

[41] NPT (note 1).
[42] For basic information on the INF Treaty see annex A in this volume.

from a quantitative system focused on accounting for known quantities of materials and monitoring declared activities to a qualitative system aimed at gathering a comprehensive picture of a state's nuclear and nuclear-related activities, including all nuclear-related imports and exports. The Additional Protocol also substantially expands the IAEA's ability to check for clandestine nuclear facilities by providing the agency with authority to visit any facility (declared or not) to investigate questions about or inconsistencies in a state's nuclear declarations.[43]

Three nuclear weapon states (France, the UK and the USA) have signed and ratified an Additional Protocol with the IAEA.

During the cold war, states went to great lengths to find out as much as they could about the military capacities of actual and potential adversaries, using all available means of collecting information. A parallel effort was undertaken by states to prevent information about their own military capabilities from leaking. This meant that secrecy was a strong characteristic of state attitudes towards security matters for most of the period during which arms control was being developed.

What seemed to be a new approach to verification was triggered by a change in the Soviet Union, where President Mikhail Gorbachev altered the secrecy paradigm. One of the most important aspects of the new approach was its emphasis on transparency as a unilateral, voluntary act by the government of a state that had previously made secrecy one of its main priorities. This 'official openness' was the opposite of official secrecy and had a powerful effect on international perceptions of the Soviet Union.[44]

The new approach to openness proved to be short lived. In implementing the verification provisions of the CWC inspectors have not been able to use the most up-to-date equipment available. In nuclear arms control, modern methodologies and equipment for non-intrusive monitoring of nuclear materials have not been applied in verification. The collapse of the effort to provide a verification system for the BTWC and the uncertainty about the need for a verification provision in a treaty to ban the production of fissile material for military purposes are also signs that there are still strict limits to the willingness of states to open themselves to inspection.

Dealing with non-compliance

There will inevitably be a spillover from changing approaches to verification into issues of arms control compliance assessment and enforcement. In the absence of a verification standard, collective judgements about treaty non-compliance depend on the quality of information available through national

[43] Kimball, D. and Kerr, P., Arms Control Association, 'The 1997 IAEA Additional Protocol at a glance', Fact sheet, Jan. 2005, URL <http://www.armscontrol.org/factsheets/IAEAProtocol.asp>.

[44] Ann Florini has noted that while 'Secrecy means deliberately hiding your actions; transparency means deliberately revealing them. This element of volition makes the growing acceptance of transparency much more than a resigned surrender to the technologically facilitated intrusiveness of the Information Age. Transparency is a choice, encouraged by changing attitudes about what constitutes appropriate behavior'. Florini, A., 'The end of secrecy', *Foreign Policy*, 22 June 1998. See also chapter 6 in this volume.

means and the degree to which states share assessments of that information. This places a premium on the 'like-mindedness' among states vis-à-vis the state that is the object of verification and in essence makes verification a reflection of political relationships.

The recent case of Iraq has underlined the difficulty of managing a rule-based international response in conditions where a state is suspected to be developing NBC weapons. In the nuclear weapon-related realm Pierre Goldschmidt, former Deputy Director General of the IAEA, has described the difficulty of dispelling suspicions, even taking into account the great progress that has been made in developing more effective safeguards.[45] Where a state has been found to be in non-compliance with safeguards agreements, these suspicions will be heightened, and any lack of clarity about future nuclear ambitions carries a risk that concerned states will seek to resolve this problem outside a rule-based international framework. To reduce the risk of this occurring, Goldschmidt has urged the UN Security Council to adopt a generic binding resolution that would establish peaceful measures for containing crises when the IAEA finds a state to be in non-compliance with its safeguards obligations.[46]

IV. The impact of technology

Arms control is an effort to reduce the risk of clashes between organized armed forces under the control of states and armed with weapons that were designed and developed for battlefield use. Within this frame of reference it is not enough for a particular item to be lethal or destructive in order to be considered a weapon. In order to be attractive to a military user a material needs to be stable enough to resist a reduction of its effect during handling and storage, as it is unlikely to be used immediately after production. The results of using the weapon should be predictable under different climatic and geographical conditions and against different kinds of targets. Once the material to be used in the weapon has been identified, it must be possible to produce, process and shape it into forms that can be filled into munitions or other delivery systems, or into forms that can be held ready for such filling. It must be possible to carry out this process of filling and storing weapons and then transporting them and using them without too great a risk to the possessor.

These factors have also shaped the decisions about the items that should be subject to arms control measures. For example, in the case of radiological dispersal devices (RDDs or 'dirty bombs') it was decided in the 1970s that because there was no battlefield use for such devices in cold war military plan-

---

[45] International Atomic Energy Agency (IAEA), Pierre Goldschmidt, IAEA Deputy Director General, Head of the Department of Safeguards, 'Present status and future of international safeguards', International Forum for Peaceful Utilization of Nuclear Energy, Tokyo, 12 Feb. 2003, URL <http://www.iaea.org/NewsCenter/Statements/DDGs/2003/goldschmidt12022003.html>.

[46] Goldschmidt, P., 'The urgent need to strengthen the nuclear non-proliferation regime', Carnegie Endowment for International Peace, *Policy Outlook*, Jan. 2006, URL <http://www.carnegieendowment.org/files/PO25.Goldschmidt.FINAL2.pdf>.

ning, agreements related to them were superfluous. Recently, however, the need for and the feasibility of controlling high-activity radioactive sources that could be used to make dirty bombs has attracted much greater attention in the light of the efforts to adapt arms control to different kinds of threats, including mass impact terrorism. Radiological terrorism requires little technical knowledge and could involve a much wider range of relatively easily accessible materials.[47] Nuclear terrorism—obtaining or constructing a device that produces a nuclear explosion—requires great technical expertise and access to specific types of material (highly enriched uranium or certain types of plutonium) that are not easy to obtain. These factors are to a degree shaping the choice about which materials to make the focus of control.

When defining the scope of measures aimed to combat terrorism, none of the above factors might apply when thinking about which materials should be subject to control. In thinking about a mass impact terrorist attack, the choice of item to be used as a 'weapon' may be only loosely connected to the technical characteristics noted above and becomes heavily dependent on the intentions of the actor that acquires it (whose identity could be unknown in advance of an attack).

Roger Roffey has observed that because of their properties, threats from biological agents should be seen as risks to be managed rather than problems to be solved.[48] Roffey has also pointed out that since micro-organisms are self-replicating, maintaining and updating a catalogue of agents would be a formidable challenge because extremely small quantities are required to permit mass production given the right growth conditions. Furthermore, the approaches for handling biological material are frequently somewhat different for human, animal and plant pathogens and for toxins. Therefore, if the threat of malicious use is extended beyond attacks against people to include attacks against plants and animals, the magnitude of the task becomes even greater.

The nature of biological agents and their use means that there is no comprehensive inventory of locations where biological agents are being isolated, produced, held and used. Roffey has noted that dangerous pathogens are distributed globally and that they are held in thousands of laboratories, clinical facilities or commercial companies. The biological agents and toxins can be present in a number of places in a facility if they are used or being studied, in addition to the places where pure cultures are stored in freezers and the like.

---

[47] Maurizio Martellini and Kathryn McLaughlin of the Landau Network-Centro Volta have explained that 'there are hundreds of thousands of radiological sources currently in use in scientific and commercial activities worldwide, ranging from nuclear medicine and pharmaceuticals to geological activities. These sources pose varying degrees of proliferation risk according to their level of radioactivity and their relative sizes'. In some cases redundant radioactive sources are simply abandoned without further control and these could be recovered by groups with malicious intent. Martellini, M. and McLaughlin, K., Landau Network-Centro Volta, 'The security of high-activity radioactive sources', Background paper 3 presented at the Conference on Strengthening European Action on WMD Non-proliferation and Disarmament: How Can Community Instruments Contribute?, Brussels, 7–8 Dec. 2005, URL <http://www.sipri.org/contents/expcon/euppconfmaterials.html>.

[48] Roffey, R., 'From bio threat reduction to cooperation in biological proliferation prevention', Background paper 4 presented at the Conference on Strengthening European Action on WMD Non-proliferation and Disarmament: How Can Community Instruments Contribute? (note 47). On the need for a global approach to bio-security see appendix 14A in this volume.

Apart from these stocks—which in theory could be catalogued, although this would be a large task—biological agents can, in many cases, be isolated from nature.

Many common industrial chemicals that are in widespread use around the world have been identified with a risk of terrorist use, including ammonia, chlorine, oxides of nitrogen and sulphur dioxide. Heavy restriction of the use of these chemicals, which are produced in many places and in large quantities, would be a serious impediment to the civil chemical industry and could add significantly to the cost of many common products.

Recently, a number of initiatives have been undertaken that are intended to impact on the capabilities that a non-state actor might find attractive when planning to commit acts of mass impact terrorism. In March 2002 the IAEA approved a Plan of Activities to Protect Against Nuclear Terrorism. Since then the IAEA has carried out a review of its nuclear security plan. At the General Conference in September 2005 the IAEA Governing Board approved a new Nuclear Security Plan to cover the period 2006–2009.[49] The new plan envisages activities in three areas: needs assessment, analysis and evaluation; prevention; and detection and response. The instruments available under the plan are the provision of nuclear security guidance, assistance with the application of that guidance, evaluation services, human resource development, and research and development on enhanced security technology. However, the IAEA Director General has stressed that the new plan will give greater emphasis to the implementation of new and existing instruments—such as the revised 1980 Convention on the Physical Protection of Nuclear Materials and the 2001 Code of Conduct on the Safety and Security of Radioactive Sources. Moreover, analyses by the IAEA have underlined that there are still significant gaps in the application of existing nuclear security measures. Another area of emphasis for the new nuclear security plan will be to give greater prominence to 'coordinated efforts to work towards universal application of harmonized standards based on international instruments'.[50]

Elements of UN Security Council Resolution 1540 are also devoted to the need to control proliferation-sensitive items. Resolution 1540 requires states to establish domestic controls to prevent the proliferation of NBC weapons and their means of delivery, including by establishing 'appropriate effective measures to account for and secure such items in production, use, storage or transport' and 'appropriate effective physical protection measures'.[51]

[49] International Atomic Energy Agency (IAEA), 'Nuclear security: measures to protect against nuclear terrorism, progress report and nuclear security plan for 2006–2009', Report by the Director General IAEA document GC(49)/1, 23 Sep. 2005, URL <http://www.iaea.org/About/Policy/GC/GC49/Documents/gc49-17.pdf>.

[50] ElBaradei, M., 'Nuclear terrorism: identifying and combating the risks', Statement to the International Conference on Nuclear Security: Global Directions for the Future, London, 16 Mar. 2005, URL <http://www.iaea.org/NewsCenter/Statements/2005/ebsp2005n003.html>.

[51] UN Security Council Resolution 1540 (note 11).

V. Conclusions

This chapter underlines that, although there have been some significant changes in thinking about arms control and although the evolution of arms control continues, legal and diplomatic means are still considered to be essential elements in security building. One main objective of arms control—to facilitate a dialogue on international politico-military aspects of security—remains valid and necessary. Other characteristics of arms control in the cold war no longer seem to have the same importance to states at present. Three aspects of cold war arms control—symmetry, reciprocity and universal participation—are absent from a number of recent processes. However, UN Security Council Resolution 1540 does have these features.

Nevertheless, several new processes are having an important effect on the policies and practices of states and may, working in conjunction with one another, represent a new international arms control regime. The multilateral arms control treaties form one part of this emerging regime, but the treaties are increasingly being supplemented and supported by a number of other measures.

Gains in verification and a tendency towards greater transparency facilitated arms control agreements during a short period after the end of the cold war. These gains have now been lost. The changing view on the desirability and feasibility of verification has complicated arms control compliance assessment and enforcement and will continue to do so in future.

Arms control was traditionally focused on items specially designed and developed for military use. Some recent initiatives have focused on items that can have civil as well as military uses. However, a strategy based on the elimination or complete denial of access to dual-use items is neither feasible nor desirable. Dual-use technology is not a threat in and of itself, and denial of access to dual-use technology is only sought when the technology concerned is going to be misapplied or when the risk that it will be misapplied is unacceptably high.

Arms control was traditionally an activity confined to states. However, recent thinking has focused on how the capabilities available to non-state groups that may be planning acts of mass impact terrorism can be controlled and access to them denied on a selective basis. In a more positive context, non-state actors, including the private sector, are becoming engaged in security building.

13. Nuclear arms control and non-proliferation

SHANNON N. KILE

I. Introduction

In 2005 the global nuclear non-proliferation regime continued to face a number of serious challenges from both inside and outside the regime. The effectiveness and viability of its principal legal and normative foundation, the 1968 Treaty on the Non-Proliferation of Nuclear Weapons (Non-Proliferation Treaty, NPT), were called into question by the deadlock among the states parties that arose at the seventh five-yearly NPT Review Conference.[1] The conference failed to produce a final report containing any substantive decisions on treaty implementation issues. During 2005 there continued to be international concern about the scope and nature of Iran's nuclear fuel cycle programme. The International Atomic Energy Agency (IAEA) provided further detail about Iran's failures to declare important nuclear activities, in contravention of its NPT-mandated nuclear safeguards agreement with the Agency. In East Asia, little progress was made in the multilateral negotiations on the fate of the nuclear programme of the Democratic People's Republic of Korea (DPRK, or North Korea), which in February 2005 declared for the first time that it possessed nuclear weapons. In addition to these controversies, further details emerged about the activities of the clandestine network of scientists and private companies centred around Pakistani scientist Abdul Qadeer Khan and involving the illicit transfer of nuclear weapon-related materials and equipment. This led to growing international support for voluntary and ad hoc measures, outside the framework of the NPT regime, aimed at addressing proliferation risks and challenges posed by non-state actors.

This chapter reviews the main developments in nuclear arms control and non-proliferation in 2005. Section II outlines some of the reasons for the meagre results of the 2005 NPT Review Conference. Section III describes developments related to Iran's nuclear programme and summarizes the IAEA's findings about the country's past and current nuclear activities. Section IV summarizes developments in the Six-Party Talks and the diplomatic impasse over North Korea's nuclear programme. Section V describes international initiatives aimed at enhancing the safety and custodial security of nuclear materials and facilities and preventing nuclear terrorism. Section VI presents the conclusions.

---

[1] For a description of the main provisions of the NPT and a list of the parties see annex A in this volume. The full text of the NPT is available at URL <http://disarmament.un.org/wmd/npt/npttext.html>. On the Review Conference see section II of this chapter.

Appendix 13A provides tables of data on world nuclear forces and on the nuclear forces of the United States, Russia, the United Kingdom, France, China, India, Pakistan and Israel. Appendix 13B describes an initiative that was announced in 2005 for civil nuclear cooperation initiative between the USA and India; the appendix evaluates its compatibility with US obligations under the NPT and the Nuclear Suppliers Group Guidelines. Appendix 13C examines the renewed interest in proposals for establishing multilateral arrangements for control of the nuclear fuel cycle and describes the main approaches that are under consideration.

II. The 2005 Non-Proliferation Treaty Review Conference

The 2005 NPT Review Conference (RevCon) was held at UN Headquarters in New York on 2–27 May 2005. Delegations from 153 of the 188 states parties to the NPT participated. Ambassador Sérgio de Queiroz Duarte, of Brazil, served as the conference president.[2]

The RevCon opened against a background of deep differences between the parties, primarily between the five treaty-defined nuclear weapon states (NWS) parties on the one hand, and the majority of the 183 non-nuclear weapon states (NNWS) parties on the other.[3] These divisions had been starkly highlighted during the 2004 Preparatory Committee (PrepCom) meeting of the states parties, which was the third and final session scheduled to be held before the 2005 RevCon.[4] Under the 'enhanced' strengthened review process adopted at the 2000 RevCon, the main purpose of the third PrepCom session was to produce recommendations for the next review conference on a range of treaty-related issues, taking into account the deliberations and results of the two previous sessions.[5] However, the 2004 PrepCom meeting failed to produce a report with any substantive recommendations,[6] nor did it adopt an agenda for the 2005 conference. This outcome disappointed proponents of the 'enhanced', more effective, strengthened review process, who had hoped that it would promote greater accountability among the states parties in implement-

---

[2] United Nations, 'Nuclear Non-proliferation Treaty Review Conference opens at headquarters; Secretary-General says regime has worked, but is now under "great stress"', Press release DC/2955, 2 May 2005, URL <http://www.un.org/News/Press/docs/2005/dc2955.doc.htm>.

[3] As defined in Article IX of the NPT, only states that manufactured and exploded a nuclear device before 1 Jan. 1967 are recognized as nuclear weapon states. By this definition, China, France, Russia, the UK and the USA are the nuclear weapon states parties to the treaty.

[4] The 1995 NPT Review and Extension Conference had sought to strengthen the review process by requiring that PrepCom meetings be held in each of the 3 years leading up to the 5-yearly Review Conferences. The purpose of the meetings is to 'consider principles, objectives and ways in order to promote the full implementation of the Treaty, as well as its universality, and to make recommendations thereon to the Review Conference'. 'Strengthening the review process for the Treaty', NPT/CONF.1995/32 (Part I), New York, 11 May 1995, URL <http://disarmament2.un.org/wmd/npt/1995dec1.htm>.

[5] 'Improving the effectiveness of the strengthened review process for the treaty', NPT/CONF.200/28 (Part I), New York, 19 May 2000, URL <http://disarmament2.un.org/wmd/npt/finaldoc.html>.

[6] Johnson, R., 'Report on the 2004 NPT PrepCom', *Disarmament Diplomacy*, no. 77 (May/June 2004), URL <http://www.acronym.org.uk/dd/dd77/77npt.htm>; and Boese, W., 'NPT meeting marked by discord', *Arms Control Today*, vol. 34, no. 5 (June 2004), pp. 28–29.

ing the treaty. It also led to numerous warnings that the integrity of the treaty regime was being undermined by the parties' selective approach to fulfilling their obligations.[7]

Issues and concerns

The 2005 Review Conference was opened by UN Secretary-General Kofi Annan on 2 May. The first seven days of the conference were devoted to a general debate on the implementation of the NPT and the promotion of its principles and objectives. More than 90 states parties delivered prepared statements, either on a national basis or as part of groups of states, that raised a number of perennial issues. These included ways of helping to bring the 1996 Comprehensive Nuclear Test-Ban Treaty (CTBT) into force;[8] opening negotiations on a global treaty banning the production of fissile material for military purposes; enhancing transparency in nuclear weapon inventories and production complexes; establishing a nuclear weapon-free zone in the Middle East; and concluding a global treaty on negative security assurances—that is, on a legally binding commitment by the NWS not to use, or threaten to use, nuclear weapons against NNWS parties to the NPT.[9]

The general debate revealed a clear division in the parties' views about the nature of the main implementation and compliance challenges facing the treaty regime. Many of the NNWS emphasized the need for greater 'balance' in implementing the treaty's disarmament and non-proliferation obligations, which they argued were interdependent and mutually reinforcing pillars of the NPT.[10] This was a leitmotif running through many of the presentations made by NNWS during the general debate. The parties that are members of the Non-Aligned Movement (NAM)[11] were particularly critical of what they saw as the failure of the NWS to make sufficient progress towards fulfilling their commitment to work towards nuclear disarmament, codified in Article VI of the treaty.[12] They argued that this posed at least as serious a threat to the viability of the NPT regime as so-called horizontal proliferation by NNWS.[13]

---

[7] Timerbaev, R., 'What's next for the NPT?', *IAEA Bulletin*, vol. 46, no. 2 (Mar. 2005), pp. 4–7; and Middle Powers Initiative, *Atlanta Consultation II: The Future of the NPT* (Global Security Institute: San Francisco, Calif., Feb. 2005), pp. 3–8.

[8] The CTBT was opened for signature in 1996 and had been ratified by 127 states by 1 Jan. 2006. For a brief description of the treaty and a list of the states that have ratified it see annex A in this volume.

[9] For further detail about the debate over negative security assurances see du Preez, J., 'Security assurances against the use or threat of use of nuclear weapons: is progress possible at the NPT Prepcom?', Monterey Institute of International Studies, Centre for Nonproliferation Studies (CNS), 28 Apr. 2003, URL <http://cns.miis.edu/research/npt/nptsec.htm>.

[10] See, e.g., 'Statement by H. E. Ms. Laila Freivalds, Minister for Foreign Affairs of Sweden, to the 2005 Review Conference of the parties to the Treaty on the Non-proliferation of Nuclear Weapons', 3 May 2005, URL <http://www.un.org/events/npt2005/statements/npt03sweden.pdf>.

[11] For a list of the members of NAM see the glossary in this volume.

[12] Article VI commits the parties to 'pursue negotiations in good faith on effective measures relating to cessation of the nuclear arms race at an early date and to nuclear disarmament'.

[13] 'Statement by the Hon. Syed Hamid Albar, Minister of Foreign Affairs of Malaysia, on behalf of the non-aligned states parties to the Treaty on the Non-proliferation of Nuclear Weapons, at the general

Among the nuclear weapon states, the USA took the lead in attempting to play down Article VI compliance questions, claiming that it had made significant reductions in its deployed nuclear forces as well as in its stocks of weapon-usable fissile material.[14] US officials sought to focus instead on NNWS parties known or believed to be developing nuclear weapons, in contravention of articles I and II of the NPT.[15] They identified four serious cases of non-compliance by NNWS over the past decade: Iraq, Libya, Iran and North Korea. While the first two cases had been resolved,[16] they claimed that Iran and North Korea were both pursuing long-running nuclear weapon programmes that posed direct challenges to the treaty regime. Furthermore, US officials warned that there were growing proliferation risks from non-state actors, including transnational terrorist groups, which required innovative responses going beyond the NPT framework, such as the Proliferation Security Initiative (PSI) and UN Security Council Resolution 1540.[17] They noted that the discovery of the global black market network in nuclear technology, equipment and expertise centred around the Pakistani nuclear engineer A. Q. Khan was particularly worrying, since the network's activities circumvented many of the existing legal, regulatory and technical measures intended to curb the proliferation of weapons of mass destruction (WMD).[18]

Many other parties also expressed concern about the emergence of new challenges, from both inside and outside the treaty regime, since the last review conference. North Korea's withdrawal from the NPT in 2003 was the motivation for a number of proposals for reconsidering a party's rights and obligations in withdrawing from the NPT.[19] Among these were a European Union (EU) proposal to prohibit a state party withdrawing from the treaty from using 'nuclear materials, facilities, equipment and technologies acquired from a third country prior to withdrawal'; these would have to be 'frozen, with

debate of the 2005 Review Conference of the parties to the Treaty on the Non-proliferation of Nuclear Weapons', 2 May 2005, URL <http://www.un.org/events/npt2005/statements/npt02malaysia.pdf>.

[14] 'US implementation of Article VI and the future of nuclear disarmament', Statement by Ambassador Jackie W. Sanders, Special Representative of the President for the Nonproliferation of Nuclear Weapons, to the 2005 Review Conference of the Treaty on the Nonproliferation of Nuclear Weapons, 20 May 2005, URL <http://www.state.gov/t/np/rls/rm/46603.htm>.

[15] 'Statement by Stephen G. Rademaker, United States Assistant Secretary of State for Arms Control, to the 2005 Review Conference of the Treaty on the Non-proliferation of Nuclear Weapons', 2 May 2005, URL <http://www.un.org/events/npt2005/statements/npt02usa.pdf>.

[16] On the Libyan case see Hart, J. and Kile, S. N., 'Libya's renunciation of nuclear, biological and chemical weapons and ballistic missiles', *SIPRI Yearbook 2005: Armaments, Disarmament and International Security* (Oxford University Press: Oxford, 2005), pp. 629–48. On the Iraq case see chapter 14 in this volume.

[17] Rademaker (note 15). On the PSI see Ahlström. C., 'The Proliferation Security Initiative: international law aspects of the Statement of Interdiction Principles', *SIPRI Yearbook 2005* (note 16), pp. 741–65, and for the list of states participants see the glossary in this volume. For UN Security Council 1540, 28 Apr. 2004, see URL <http://www.un.org/Docs/sc/unsc_resolutions04.html>, and on the resolution see also chapter 12 in this volume.

[18] On the activities of the Khan network see Kile, S. N., 'Nuclear arms control and non-proliferation', *SIPRI Yearbook 2005* (note 16), pp. 552–55.

[19] Under NPT Article X, a state party has 'the right to withdraw from the Treaty if it decides that extraordinary events, related to the subject matter of this Treaty, have jeopardized the supreme interests of its country'. A party must give 3 months' advance notice of its withdrawal to all other parties and to the UN Security Council.

a view to having them dismantled and/or returned to the supplier State, under IAEA control'.[20] There was also interest in strengthening export controls on nuclear material and sensitive equipment and technologies. Several states proposed making the acceptance of the NPT Additional Safeguards Protocol a condition for any new supply contract with a NNWS recipient.[21] In addition, revelations about the activities of the Khan network led to calls for the parties to tighten their controls on nuclear material and sensitive technologies.

The controversies over the nuclear programmes of Iran and North Korea were largely responsible for one 'old' idea that gained renewed currency at the 2005 Review Conference: proposals for establishing multilateral arrangements for control of the nuclear fuel cycle activities of greatest proliferation concern—uranium enrichment and plutonium reprocessing, as well as spent fuel management and waste disposal.[22] The main objective of such measures would be to limit these activities to a small number of fully transparent facilities, operating under international or multilateral control. The interest in this idea reflected the concern of some states parties about a perceived structural weakness in the NPT—that Article IV, which gives NNWS parties an 'inalienable right' to import and develop materials and technologies for use in nuclear energy programmes, potentially allows those states to put in place the sensitive fuel cycle facilities for producing nuclear weapons under the cover of civil nuclear programmes.[23]

However, some NNWS strongly opposed any proposal seen as infringing upon either the letter or the spirit of Article IV. Iran emphasized its right and intention to 'pursue all legal areas of nuclear technology, including [uranium] enrichment, exclusively for peaceful purposes'.[24] It also denounced what it called the discriminatory double standard of some states aimed at restricting the transfer of nuclear technology to developing countries—a complaint that found considerable support among other NAM countries. South Africa put for-

[20] 'Withdrawal from the Treaty on the Non-Proliferation of Nuclear Weapons: Working Paper submitted by Luxembourg on behalf of the European Union', NPT/CONF.2005/WP.32, 10 May 2005, URL <http://www.un.org/events/npt2005/working%20papers.html>, pp. 2–3.

[21] 'Article III and preambular paragraphs 4 and 5, especially in their relationship to Article IV and preambular paragraphs 6 and 7 [Export Controls]: Working Paper for submission to Main Committee II by Australia, Austria, Canada, Denmark, Hungary, Ireland, the Netherlands, New Zealand, Norway, and Sweden', NPT/CONF.2005/WP.14, 26 Apr. 2005, URL <http://www.un.org/events/npt2005/working %20papers.html>. For a list of the states with NPT safeguards agreements and Additional Safeguards Protocols in force with the IAEA see annex A in this volume.

[22] The IAEA presented an expert group's report assessing options for multilateral arrangements to control the nuclear fuel cycle. 'Report of The Expert Group on Multilateral Approaches to the Nuclear Fuel Cycle submitted to the Director General of the International Atomic Energy Agency: submitted by the International Atomic Energy Agency', NPT/CONF.2005/18, 9 May 2005, URL <http://www.un.org/events/npt2005/reports.html>. On the report and approaches under consideration see appendix 13C.

[23] 'Articles III (3) and (IV), preambular paragraphs 6 and 7, especially in their relationship to Article III (1), (2) and (4) and preambular paragraphs 4 and 5 [Approaches to the nuclear fuel cycle]: Working paper for submission to Main Committee III by Australia, Austria, Canada, Denmark, Hungary, Ireland, the Netherlands, New Zealand, Norway and Sweden', 26 Apr. 2005, NPT/CONF.2005/WP.12, URL <http://www.un.org/events/npt2005/working%20papers.html>.

[24] 'Statement by H. E. Dr Kamal Kharrazi, Minister for Foreign Affairs of the Islamic Republic of Iran, to the Seventh NPT Review Conference', 3 May 2005, URL <http://www.un.org/events/npt 2005/statements/npt03iran.pdf>, p. 4.

ward a similar objection. It said that it could not support 'unwarranted restrictions on the NPT's guaranteed access to . . . nuclear capabilities for peaceful purposes' because the imposition of 'additional restrictive measures on some NPT states parties while allowing others to have access to such capabilities' exacerbated the 'inequalities' inherent in the NPT.[25]

Procedural disputes

Adoption of an agenda

The substantive work of the conference was stalled from the outset by the inability of the states parties to agree an agenda. The main dispute was over whether to frame the treaty review explicitly in terms of agreements adopted by consensus at previous review conferences, including the 1995 Principles and Objectives for Nuclear Non-proliferation and Disarmament and the 13-step Programme of Action on Nuclear Disarmament, adopted in 2000. Many of the NNWS attached particular importance to reaffirming the Programme of Action. This included commitments by the states parties to work for the treaty's universality (i.e., the accession to the NPT by all UN-recognized states); to ratify and bring into force at an early date the CTBT; observe a moratorium on all nuclear explosions; to conclude within five years a treaty banning the production of fissile material for military purposes; to establish a subsidiary body in the Conference on Disarmament (CD) to deal with nuclear disarmament; and to negotiate deeper reductions in existing nuclear arsenals.[26] As one of the 13 steps, the NWS had reaffirmed their commitment to work towards nuclear disarmament by undertaking specific measures to reduce the role of, and eventually eliminate, their nuclear arsenals.[27]

The dispute over the agenda was primarily between the NWS, led by the USA, and the NAM countries, with Egypt, Indonesia and Malaysia in the forefront. The latter insisted that the agenda refer to specific agreements adopted at previous review conferences.[28] These included the 1995 Resolution on the Middle East, which had called for the establishment of a nuclear

---

[25] 'Statement by the Republic of South Africa during the general debate of the 2005 Review Conference of the states parties to the Treaty on the Nonproliferation of Nuclear Weapons', 3 May 2005, URL <http://www.un.org/events/npt2005/statements03may.html>, p. 4.

[26] 2000 Review Conference of the Parties to the Treaty on Non-proliferation of Nuclear Weapons, 'Final Document: review of the operation of the treaty, taking into account the decisions and the resolution adopted by the 1995 Review and Extension Conference', 19 May 2000, NPT/CONF2000.28, URL <http://disarmament2.un.org/wmd/npt/finaldoc.html>, vol. I, part I, pp. 13–15. For the Principles and Objections and other documents of the 1995 Review and Extension Conference see *SIPRI Yearbook 1996: Armaments, Disarmament and International Security* (Oxford University Press: Oxford, 1996), pp. 590–93.

[27] The NWS undertook to: increase transparency in their nuclear arsenals; further reduce their inventories and deployments of non-strategic nuclear weapons; lower the operational status of the nuclear forces; diminish the role of nuclear weapons in their security policies; and work towards the complete elimination of their nuclear weapons. NPT/CONF2000.28, vol. I, part I (note 26) p. 15.

[28] 'Working paper presented by the members of the Group of Non-Aligned Movement states parties to the Treaty on the Non-Proliferation of Nuclear Weapons', NPT/CONF.2005/WP.8, 26 Apr. 2005, URL <http://www.un.org/events/npt2005/working%20papers.html>, p. 1.

weapon-free zone in the region,[29] and the 13-step Programme of Action on Nuclear Disarmament. This was strongly supported by the seven members of the New Agenda Coalition (NAC), which had played a crucial role at the 2000 RevCon in formulating and securing the adoption of the Programme of Action.[30] In contrast, the USA resisted efforts to frame the 2005 treaty review in terms of the progress made towards implementing the 13 steps. The dispute was complicated by US efforts to link any reference to past agreements to explicit text on developments after the 2000 RevCon. This in turn raised objections from Iran, which believed that the USA was attempting to use the ongoing controversy over Iran's compliance with its NPT-mandated safeguards agreement to unfairly cast it in a negative light.[31]

At the end of the first week of the conference, a compromise statement put forward by the conference president appeared to have resolved the agenda dispute. Duarte's statement was associated with agenda item 16, 'Review of the operation of the Treaty'. It stated that the 2005 review 'would be conducted in light of the decisions and the resolutions of previous Conferences, and allow for discussion of any issue raised by States Parties'.[32] The USA indicated that this wording was acceptable, since it did not mention previous review conferences by date. On 6 May, however, Egypt rejected Duarte's statement and insisted that it be amended to state that the review would 'take into account' the specific 'outcomes' as well as the decisions and resolutions of previous conferences.[33] This led to a renewed diplomatic stalemate and raised concern that Duarte might be forced to suspend the conference.

Following intensive negotiations, on 11 May the states parties finally adopted an agenda for the conference. Duarte's statement, which was not amended, was linked to item 16 by an asterisk.[34] Egypt and the other NAM states parties declared that the asterisk also linked the agenda item to a statement made by Malaysia on behalf of the group. This statement reaffirmed the commitment of the NAM states to implementing the obligations and resolutions adopted at the 1995 and 2000 review conferences and urged all states parties to do the same.[35] The linkage of the two statements made it possible for

[29] 'Resolution on the Middle East', NPT/CONF.1995/32 (Part I), Annex, 11 May 1995, URL <http://disarmament.un.org/wmd/npt/1995RESME.htm>.

[30] 'Working paper on nuclear disarmament for Main Committee I: recommendations submitted by New Zealand on behalf of Brazil, Egypt, Ireland, Mexico, South Africa and Sweden as members of the New Agenda Coalition', NPT/CONF.2005/WP.27, 4 May 2005, URL <http://www.un.org/events/npt2005/working%20papers.html>, pp. 1–2.

[31] Johnson, R., 'Decisions, resolution and outcomes: frustration as agenda is thwarted', *Acronym Report* (Acronym Institute), 7 May 2005, URL <http://www.acronym.org.uk/npt/05rep03.htm>.

[32] Applegarth, C., 'Divisions foil NPT Review Conference', *Arms Control Today*, vol. 35, no. 5 (June 2005), p. 39.

[33] Johnson (note 31). Egypt's insistence on this language was motivated in part by its desire to recall the 1995 resolution supporting the establishment of a nuclear weapon-free zone in the Middle East (see note 29).

[34] 'Agenda', NPT/CONF.2005/30, 11 May 2005; and 'Statement by the President in connection with the adoption of the agenda (item 16)', NPT/CONF.2005/31*, 11 May 2005, URL <http://www.un.org/events/npt2005/reports. html>.

[35] 'Statement by the delegation of Malaysia, on behalf of the Group of Non-Aligned States Parties to the Treaty on the Non-Proliferation of Nuclear Weapons, at the plenary of the 2005 Review Conference

the conference to adopt the agenda, but in the closing days it was challenged by the British delegation. The secretariat eventually removed the NAM statement from the technical report of the conference, while keeping the president's statement.[36]

Adoption of a work programme

The attention of the delegations then turned to another contentious procedural issue—adoption of a work programme for the Review Conference. Following the practice of previous review conferences, the secretariat had established three Main Committees (MCs) that were responsible for conducting the conference's substantive work: MC I, on nuclear disarmament; MC II, on safeguards and regional issues; and MC III, on nuclear safety and the peaceful uses of nuclear energy.[37] The principal point of contention was over how to divide these committees into subsidiary bodies that would then consider specific issues in greater detail.

The main obstacle to adopting a work programme was a disagreement over the issue of negative security assurances. The dispute was between the USA and several other Western states, on the one hand, and the NAM countries, on the other. The latter group strongly supported calls for concluding a global treaty on negative security assurances that would make legally binding the unilateral declarations made by the NWS in 1995.[38] The NAM countries proposed the establishment of a subsidiary body (SB) on security assurances as well as a separate body on practical disarmament measures. This proposal appeared to be acceptable to most delegations but was rejected by the USA, which strongly opposed the establishment of a separate subsidiary body on security assurances.[39]

The impasse was broken on 18 May, when the NAM countries reluctantly withdrew their proposal. This paved the way for consensus agreement on a work programme that established a single subsidiary body under each of the Main Committees and allocated the issues to be discussed.[40] The subsidiary body under MC I covered practical disarmament steps, including security assurances. The subsidiary body under MC II covered regional issues, includ-

---

of the Parties to the Treaty on the Non-Proliferation of Nuclear Weapons, concerning the adoption of the agenda', New York, 12 May 2005, NPT/CONF.2005/32, URL <http://www.un.org/events/npt2005/reports.html>.

[36] Johnson, R., 'Day 25, or "my objection is bigger than your objection"', *Acronym Report*, 26 May 2005, URL <http://www.acronym.org.uk/npt/05rep11.htm>.

[37] The chairpersons of the Main Committees were: MC I, Sudjadnan Parnohadinigrat (Indonesia); MC II, Laszló Mólnár (Hungary); and MC III, Elisabet Borsiin-Bonnier (Sweden).

[38] In 1995, the UN Security Council recognized the unilateral political declarations, made by each of the 5 NWS parties to the NPT, providing negative assurances to the NNWS parties. 'Security assurances', UN Doc S/RES/984 (1995), URL <http://www1.umn.edu/humanrts/resolutions/SC95/984SC95.html>.

[39] Successive US administrations have maintained a policy of 'strategic ambiguity' by refusing to rule out the use of nuclear weapons in response to attacks from NNWS involving biological or chemical weapons. See du Preez (note 9).

[40] 'Allocation of items to the Main Committees of the Conference', NPT/CONF.2005/DEC.1, 18 May 2005, URL <http://www.un.org/events/npt2005/decisions.html>.

ing implementation of the 1995 Resolution on the Middle East, while the subsidiary body under MC III considered 'other provisions of the treaty', including withdrawal from the NPT.[41]

Work of the Main Committees and subsidiary bodies

The adoption of the work programme 17 days into the conference left the Main Committees with less than six days in which to discuss the working papers submitted by the delegations on a wide range of substantive issues. Main Committee I, on nuclear disarmament, and its subsidiary body on practical disarmament steps, completed the only report to be transmitted to the conference presidency.[42] The report included an annex containing a working paper from the chairman of MC I, reviewing the implementation of articles I and II of the NPT,[43] and one from the chairman of SB I, focusing on Article VI and practical steps towards nuclear disarmament. However, the report noted that the committee had not been able to reach a consensus on the text of the working papers, since the proposals contained in them did not 'reflect fully the views of all States parties'.[44] As a result, the conference president decided not to forward the text of the report to the Drafting Committee.

The other two Main Committees failed to send reports to the presidency. The report from MC II, on nuclear safeguards, was blocked by a disagreement in the subsidiary body that dealt with regional issues (SB II), including the Middle East. Iran objected to a paragraph calling for it to respect the resolutions adopted by the IAEA Board of Governors and to continue to observe its self-imposed moratorium on uranium conversion and enrichment activities, arguing that this amounted to unwarranted criticism of its peaceful nuclear activities.[45] The USA opposed a paragraph calling for the NPT states parties to take additional measures to induce Israel to accede to the treaty as a non-nuclear weapon state.[46] The report from MC III, on nuclear energy and institutional issues, was blocked by the USA after Egypt refused to accept

[41] 'Decision on subsidiary bodies', NPT/CONF.2005/DEC.2, 18 May 2005, URL <http://www.un.org/events/npt2005/decisions. html>.

[42] 'Report of Main Committee I', NPT/CONF.2005/MC.I/1, 25 May 2005, URL <http://www.un.org/events/npt2005/main%20committee%20documents.html>.

[43] Article I requires the NWS not to transfer possession or control of nuclear weapons or other nuclear explosive devices to any recipient and not to assist, encourage, or induce any non-nuclear weapon state to acquire nuclear weapons. Under Article II, NNWS parties undertake not to 'manufacture or otherwise acquire' nuclear weapons or 'seek or receive any assistance in the manufacture' of nuclear weapons.

[44] Among other disagreements, the USA objected to most of the section on negative security assurances contained in the chairman's working paper from the subsidiary body, in particular its call for 'the conclusion of multilaterally negotiated legally binding security assurances for all non-nuclear weapon States Parties'. NPT/CONF.2005/MC.I/1 (note 42), p. 13.

[45] Johnson, R., 'Day 23: closed meetings and bracketed texts', *Acronym Report*, 24 May 2005, URL <http://www.acronym.org.uk/npt/05rep09.htm>.

[46] Johnson (note 45), The proposed measures included a commitment 'not to transfer nuclear-related material, technology and information to Israel, notwithstanding prior engagements'. The draft text of the subsidiary body report is available at URL <http://www.acronym.org.uk/npt/MCII_SB_may24.pdf>.

annexation of the text of SB III: this text sought to clarify the states parties' rights and obligations under NPT Article X.[47]

In addition to the deadlocks in MCs II and III and their respective subsidiary bodies, there were disagreements between the members of key informal and formal groupings of states parties. The five permanent members of the UN Security Council, which are also the five legally defined nuclear weapon states, were unable to agree on a joint statement. This was due primarily to the United States' opposition to Russia's insistence that the statement should support calls for early entry into force of the CTBT.[48] The NAC states also failed to agree on a final statement. In contrast to 2000, the NAC made little substantive contribution to the 2005 Review Conference, amid signs of serious strains between Egypt and several other NAC members.[49] The European Union (EU) was also hampered by internal divisions, despite having adopted a Common Position on the NPT prior to the conference.[50] The EU produced several working papers for the Main Committees and helped to forge the procedural compromises on the agenda and work programme. However, its effectiveness was limited by the long-standing tensions between the interests of the EU nuclear and non-nuclear weapon state members. Some observers criticized the UK for allegedly using its position as the coordinator of the Western Group to support the obstructionist positions of the USA.[51]

The results and an assessment

The 2005 Review Conference closed on 27 May with the perfunctory adoption by consensus of a Final Document. It was devoted exclusively to procedural matters and did not contain any substantive decisions building on the consensus agreements reached at previous conferences, including recommendations for promoting the implementation of the treaty and improving its operation.[52]

While such a meagre outcome had been widely expected, the reasons for it were the subject of debate. Some participants placed part of the blame on dysfunctional rules of procedure that allowed the intransigence of a few states

[47] Johnson (note 45). Egypt refused to allow the SB III text to be annexed to the report following the committee's rejection of informal paper on universality that it had put forward.

[48] Article XIV of the CTBT requires ratification of the treaty by 44 named states for it to enter into force. US President Bill Clinton signed the CTBT in 1996 but the US Senate voted to reject US ratification in 1999. Although the Bush Administration is continuing with the US nuclear test moratorium that was adopted in 1992, it has made clear its opposition to the CTBT. For the current status of the treaty and the list of 44 states see annex A in this volume.

[49] Müller, H., 'The 2005 NPT Review Conference: reasons and consequences of failure and options for repair', Working Paper No. 31, Weapons of Mass Destruction Commission, Stockholm, URL <http://www.wmdcommission.org/files/no31.pdf>, p. 12.

[50] Council Common Position relating to the 2005 Review Conference of the Parties to the Treaty on the Non-Proliferation of Nuclear Weapons, 2005/329/PESC, Brussels, 25 Apr. 2005, URL <http://europa.eu.int/eur-lex/lex/LexUriServ/site/en/oj/2005/l_106/l_10620050427en00320035.pdf>.

[51] Müller (note 49), p. 4.

[52] 'Final Document: 2005 Review Conference of the Parties to the Treaty on the Non-Proliferation of Nuclear Weapons (Organization and work of the Conference)', NPT/CONF.2005/57 (Part I), 27 May 2005, URL <http://www.un.org/events/npt2005/reports.html>.

on particular issues to override the preferences of the majority. These included long-standing practices, such as requiring all decisions to be taken by consensus and dividing the conference into caucus groups.[53] According to Canadian Ambassador Paul Meyer, at the 2005 conference a 'handful of states' were able to take advantage of 'consensus rules to prevent, not just the result of a negotiation from being adopted, but the mere initiation of discussion of issues dear to the policy aims of the vast majority of states'.[54] In this regard, Egypt came under widespread criticism for allegedly impeding the work of the Main Committees and their subsidiary bodies.

Many of the NAM countries assigned the primary blame for the conference's unsatisfactory outcome to the USA. They complained that US-led procedural manoeuvres, which in some instances were supported by other NWS, had prevented the consideration of a number of important disarmament measures and allowed the NWS to avoid scrutiny of their compliance with their treaty commitments. They also complained that the US Administration had undermined the review process by explicitly repudiating some of the 13 steps towards nuclear disarmament that were agreed in 2000. In their view, the US action called into question the status of consensus agreements reached at previous conferences.

The closing session of the conference was accompanied by numerous expressions of regret that the states parties had 'lost the opportunity to make realistic progress' towards addressing the pressing challenges facing the NPT.[55] However, some observers speculated that, in the light of the deep divisions at the conference, a number of delegations may have welcomed the adoption of a Final Document confined to procedural matters. The NWS avoided undertaking any new disarmament obligations, while the NAM and other NNWS parties prevented the package of agreements reached at the 1995 and 2000 review conferences from being replaced by a new set of weaker, lowest-common-denominator commitments.[56]

At the same time, the outcome clearly frustrated many of the states parties, especially the NNWS, which were already disenchanted by the lack of progress towards nuclear disarmament. They made it clear that, as long as the USA and the other nuclear weapon states were not working in a serious way towards fulfilling their legally binding disarmament commitment, they were not prepared to agree to proposals—such as reinterpreting Article IV—aimed at strengthening the non-proliferation side of the so-called NPT bargain. One noteworthy development at the conference was the public scepticism towards

[53] For an assessment of procedural weaknesses in the NPT review conferences and possible remedies see Müller (note 49), pp. 3–4.

[54] Quoted in Middle Powers Initiative, '28 states participate in inaugural "Article VI forum"', Middle Powers Initiative Report and Brief, Nov. 2005, URL <http://www.middlepowers.org/mpi/pubs/ArticleVI _Report.pdf>.

[55] 'Closing statement by South Africa at the 2005 NPT Review Conference: delivered by Mr Abdul Samad Minty', 27 May 2005, URL <http://www.reachingcriticalwill.org/legal/npt/RevCon05/GD statements/SAfrica27.pdf>.

[56] Boese, W., 'Nuclear nonproliferation treaty meeting sputters', Arms Control Today, vol. 35, no. 6 (July/Aug. 2005), p. 23.

the NPT expressed by some of the regime's erstwhile strongest supporters, such as Egypt and South Africa. This suggested that the NPT is not only facing a 'crisis of compliance', as described by US officials, but a broader crisis of legitimacy. This in turn calls into question the effectiveness and viability of a treaty regime that relies heavily on the parties' voluntary compliance with its underlying norms.

III. Iran and nuclear proliferation concerns

In 2005 the international controversy over the scope and nature of Iran's nuclear programme intensified.[57] The controversy has centred on revelations by the IAEA that Iran had failed over an extended period of time to declare important nuclear activities, in contravention of its NPT-mandated full-scope safeguards agreement with the Agency.[58] Iran insists that its nuclear programme is intended solely for peaceful purposes and that any safeguards violations were inadvertent. However, in Europe, the USA and elsewhere, there is concern that Iran is attempting to put into place, under the cover of a nuclear energy programme, the fuel-cycle facilities needed to produce fissile material—plutonium and highly enriched uranium (HEU)—for a secret nuclear weapon programme.[59] Since the end of 2003, three EU member states—France, Germany and the United Kingdom, the 'E3'—have taken the lead in attempting to resolve the controversy through negotiations with Iran. These negotiations have also involved the participation of the High Representative for the EU's Common Foreign and Security Policy, Javier Solana.[60]

In 2005 Iran reaffirmed its plans to develop a complete nuclear fuel cycle, including an indigenous uranium enrichment capability, as part of a long-term energy policy to make up for the expected depletion of its fossil fuel reserves. In May, the Majlis (parliament) approved a new programme to construct, over the next 20 years, nuclear power plants with a total capacity of 20 000 megawatts-electric (MW(e)).[61] Outside experts argued that Iran's plans

[57] For a description of the origins of the nuclear controversy see Kile, S. N., 'Nuclear arms control and non-proliferation', *SIPRI Yearbook 2004: Armaments, Disarmament and International Security* (Oxford University Press: Oxford, 2004), pp. 604–07. See also Kile, S. N. (ed.), *Europe and Iran: Perspectives on Non-Proliferation*, SIPRI Research Report No. 21 (Oxford University Press: Oxford, 2005).

[58] Iran acceded to the NPT on 2 Feb. 1970. Its full-scope safeguards agreement with the IAEA (INFCIRC/214) entered into force on 15 May 1974. The text of the agreement is available at URL <http://www.iaea.org/Publications/Documents/Infcircs/Others/infcirc214.pdf>.

[59] The nuclear fuel cycle consists of front-end steps (milling and mining of uranium ore, uranium conversion and enrichment, fuel fabrication) that lead to the preparation of uranium for use as fuel for reactor operation and back-end steps that are necessary to safely manage, prepare and dispose of the highly radioactive spent nuclear fuel. See also appendix 13C.

[60] European and Iranian views on the nuclear controversy and related issues are presented in ed. Kile, (note 57).

[61] Islamic Republic News Agency (IRNA), 'Iran's parliament approves bill on access to peaceful N-technology', 15 May 2005, URL <http://www.irna.ir/en/news/view/line22/0505150260114226.htm>. In 2002 Iran had announced plans to construct nuclear power plants with a total capacity of 6000 MW(e), in addition to the 1000-MW(e) plant under construction at Bushehr.

for its nuclear fuel cycle made little economic sense in the light of the current global surplus of enriched uranium.[62] Iran emphasized that its long-term goal was to achieve self-sufficiency in fuel manufacture, pointing out that the USA had sought to disrupt every major deal with foreign suppliers in the past—in violation of Iran's legal rights under Article IV of the NPT. The desire to achieve independence from outside assistance has been a recurring theme in Iran's justifications for pursuing sensitive fuel-cycle technologies.[63]

The Iran–E3 negotiations

In 2005 the negotiations between Iran and the E3 on Iran's sensitive nuclear fuel cycle activities broke down after having made little progress. The negotiations had been established by the Paris Agreement of November 2004.[64] They were aimed at finding a 'mutually acceptable agreement on long-term arrangements' that would provide 'objective guarantees' that Iran's nuclear programme was exclusively for peaceful purposes as well as 'firm guarantees' on nuclear, technological and economic cooperation between Europe and Iran as well as on security issues'.[65] Under the agreement, Iran had pledged, as a voluntary confidence-building measure, to suspend all enrichment-related and reprocessing activities while talks were under way.[66]

During the spring of 2005, the main point of contention in the negotiations continued to be the future of Iran's enrichment programme. The E3 insisted that Iran accept a complete and permanent cessation of the programme. They argued that this was the only meaningful 'objective guarantee' that Iran's nuclear activities were exclusively for peaceful purposes.[67] At the same time, they recognized Iran's right to develop nuclear energy and pledged to facilitate Iran's access to nuclear technology and fuel. This included a promise to

---

[62] Moreover, according to a US State Department briefing, Iran's known uranium reserves could only provide enough fuel to operate a single 1000-MW(e) power reactor for 6–7 years. US Department of State, 'Questioning Iran's pursuit of the nuclear fuel cycle—Iran's nuclear fuel cycle facilities: a pattern of peaceful intent?', Briefing slides presented to US and foreign diplomats in Vienna, Sep. 2005, URL <http://www.globalsecurity.org/wmd/library/report/2005/iran-fuel-cycle-brief_dos_2005.pdf>.

[63] 'Communication dated 1 August 2005 received from the Permanent Mission of the Islamic Republic of Iran to the Agency', reproduced in IAEA, INFCIRC7648, 1 Aug. 2005, URL <http://www.iaea.org/publications/documents/infcircs/2005/infcirc648.pdf>.

[64] The agreement between Iran and France, Germany and the UK was signed in Paris on 15 Nov. 2004; it appears in IAEA, INFCIRC/637, 26 Nov. 2004, URL <http://www.iaea.org/Publications/Documents/Infcircs/2004/infcirc637.pdf>. The Paris Agreement specified that the negotiations were to be held under the auspices of a senior-level Steering Committee, which was also given responsibility for coordinating working groups on political and security issues, technology and economic cooperation and nuclear issues.

[65] INFCIRC/637 (note 64).

[66] These activities were specified in the agreement as: the manufacture and import of gas centrifuges and their components; the assembly, installation testing or operation of gas centrifuges; work to undertake any plutonium separation, or to construct or operate any plutonium separation installation; and all tests or production at any uranium conversion installation. INFCIRC/637 (note 64).

[67] Council of the European Union, 'Text of letter to the president of the Council from Messrs Barnier, Fisher, Straw and Solana on Iran', 7222/05, 11 Mar. 2005, URL <http://register.consilium.eu.int/pdf/en/05/st07/st07222.en05.pdf>, p. 4.

support Iran's acquisition of a light-water research reactor to replace the heavy-water reactor under construction at Arak.[68]

Iranian officials categorically rejected the European demand for a permanent cessation of Iran's uranium enrichment programme. They said that the E3 had accepted in the Paris Agreement that suspension of Iran's enrichment activities was a temporary measure.[69] They also emphasized that, as a non-nuclear weapon state party to the NPT, Iran was legally entitled to develop sensitive nuclear fuel-cycle facilities, including uranium enrichment, as part of its civil nuclear programme. Iranian officials stated repeatedly that the country would restart enrichment activities, with appropriate assurances about their peaceful purpose, once the remaining safeguards issues had been resolved.[70]

With the negotiations facing serious difficulties, the E3 and the USA moved to align their policies in order to give Iran additional incentives to abandon its enrichment programme. On 11 March 2005 US Secretary of State Condoleezza Rice stated that, if Iran agreed to renounce the programme permanently, the USA would drop its objections to Iran applying to join the World Trade Organization (WTO); it would also consider, 'on a case by case basis', licensing the sale of spare parts for Iranian civilian aircraft.[71] In return for this change in US policy, the E3 agreed to actively support US efforts to refer Iran to the Security Council if it resumed uranium enrichment.[72] European officials had previously opposed the US calls for a prompt referral, arguing that this move would be premature and possibly counterproductive since it could spur Iran to disengage altogether from its cooperation with the IAEA.

The convergence of the US and European approaches had little effect on Tehran. Iranian officials rejected the US offer as insufficient and emphasized that the USA did not have a role to play in Iran's talks with the E3.[73] They indicated that Iran would restart operations at its uranium conversion plant and eventually move ahead with its uranium enrichment programme, although they added that Iran would not resume enrichment as long as a meaningful dialogue was under way.[74]

---

[68] Council of the European Union (note 67), p. 3. Heavy-water reactors are suitable for producing weapon-grade plutonium.

[69] Mehr News Agency, 'Iran will not be bound to commitments if EU officially demands halt to enrichment: Govt', *Tehran Times*, 5 Mar. 2005, pp. 1, 15.

[70] Reuters, 'Iran says determined to resume uranium enrichment', 24 Apr. 2005, URL <http://www.iranvajahan.net/cgi-bin/news.pl?l=en&y=2005&m=04&d=24&a=1>.

[71] US Department of State, Bureau of Public Affairs, 'US support for the EU-3', Statement of Secretary of State Condoleeza Rice, Washington, DC, 11 Mar. 2005, URL <http://www.state.gov/secretary/rm/2005/43276.htm>.

[72] Sanger, D. and Weisman, S., 'US and European allies agree on steps in Iran dispute', *New York Times* (Internet edn), 11 Mar. 2005, URL <http://www.nytimes.com/2005/03/11/ politics/11iran.html>.

[73] Islamic Republic News Agency (IRNA), 'Asefi says incentives will not persuade Iran to forsake rights', 12 Mar. 2005, URL <http://www.irna.ir/en/news/view/line-22/0503120791143125.htm>.

[74] IRNA, 'Iran to quit talks if Europe turns out to be dishonest: Rowhani', 20 Apr. 2005, URL <http://www.irna.ir/en/news/view/line-22/0504200895153401.htm>.

Iran's proposal for a general framework agreement

On 3 May 2005 Iran proposed a four-phase 'general framework' for resolving the nuclear controversy.[75] Under the proposal Iran would be allowed to resume operations at the uranium conversion facility (UCF) at Esfahan and to begin assembly, installation and testing of 3 000 gas centrifuges at the pilot-scale enrichment plant at Natanz.[76] At the same time, Iran would implement additional transparency and confidence-building measures, beyond those mandated by its Additional Safeguards Protocol, in order to provide 'objective guarantees' about the peaceful nature of its enrichment activities. Iran pledged to immediately convert all enriched uranium to fuel rods to preclude the technical possibility of further enrichment; ratify the Additional Protocol while continuing to abide by the Protocol's provisions prior to its entry into force; allow continuous on-site presence of IAEA inspectors at the Esfahan and Natanz facilities; and commit itself to having an open nuclear fuel cycle (i.e., one that does not involve plutonium reprocessing).

In return, the E3 would agree to sell light-water nuclear power reactors (which are more proliferation-resistant) to Iran; provide 'firm guarantees' on the supply of nuclear reactor fuel to supplement Iranian domestic production; loosen export control regulations on the sale of advanced technology to Iran; and give greater access to the EU market for Iranian goods. In addition, the Iranian proposal called for the establishment of joint task forces on strategic cooperation and defence requirements as well as for a 'joint commitment to principles' governing Iran–EU relations.

European negotiators promptly rejected the proposed framework's central bargain: namely, that Iran be allowed to maintain a limited uranium enrichment capability in exchange for new, intrusive transparency measures.[77] They refused to deviate from their position that Iran must permanently suspend all enrichment-related activities, including uranium conversion. However, the E3 reportedly struggled to put together a package of inducements essentially aimed at buying out Iran's fuel cycle programme without compromising on this position.[78] Their dilatory response to the Iranian proposal led to complaints from Tehran that the E3 states were protracting the negotiations in

---

[75] 'General framework for objective guarantees, firm guarantees and firm commitments', 3 May 2005, URL <http://abcnews.go.com/images/international/iran_eu_objectives.pdf>.

[76] For a description of Iran's nuclear fuel cycle infrastructure see International Institute for Strategic Studies (IISS), *Iran's Strategic Weapons Programme: A Net Assessment* (Routledge: Abingdon, 2005), pp. 33–51.

[77] Sciolino, E., 'Europe gets Iran to extend freeze in nuclear work', *New York Times* (Internet edn), 26 May 2005, URL <http://www.nytimes.com/2005/05/26/international/europe/26iran.html>; and Traynor, I., 'EU warns Iran: no talks if freeze ends', *The Guardian* (Internet edn), 3 Aug. 2005, URL <http:// www.guardian.co.uk/iran/story/0,12858,1541351,00.html>.

[78] Dombey, D., Smyth, G. and Fidler, S., 'US fires warning shot over Iran nuclear talks', *Financial Times*, 25 May 2005, p. 9; and Nuclear Threat Initiative, 'Chirac urges softening of EU stance on Iran', Global Security Newswire, 14 Apr. 2005, URL <http://www.nti.org/d_newswire/issues/2005/4/14/ 3af87c7e-dee5-46be-98ca-e768ff55dac5.html>.

order to keep Iran's enrichment suspension in place long enough to make its permanent cessation a *fait accompli*.[79]

The E3 proposal for a long-term framework agreement

On 5 August 2005 the E3 proposed a framework for a long-term agreement consisting of linked packages of incentives on nuclear energy, technology cooperation, and political and security issues.[80] The central pillar of the framework involved providing assurances to Iran that it would have access to international nuclear fuel services at market prices. These assurances would consist of the following elements: an Iran–E3 'ad hoc mechanism', to be used in the event that a contracted supplier was not able to provide nuclear fuel to Iran for non-commercial reasons; a buffer store of fuel, sufficient to maintain supplies at the contracted rate for five years, to be located in a mutually acceptable third country; and cooperation with the IAEA to develop new multilateral approaches to the nuclear fuel cycle. In addition, the E3 pledged to support Iran's acquisition of a research reactor and to cooperate with Iran in the fields of nuclear safety and security.[81]

In return, the E3 proposal called for Iran to take a series of steps. These included making a 'binding commitment not to pursue fuel cycle activities other than the construction and operation of light water power and research reactors'; committing itself to full cooperation and transparency with the IAEA to resolve all remaining safeguards issues and ratify the Additional Protocol by the end of 2005; making a legally binding commitment not to withdraw from the NPT and to keep all nuclear facilities under IAEA safeguards; promising to return all spent fuel to the original supplier after the minimum necessary cooling down period for safe transport; and halting construction of the planned heavy-water reactor at Arak.[82]

With regard to political and security issues, the E3 proposal called for enhanced cooperation in countering terrorism; joint programmes to combat illicit drug production and trafficking; and establishment of an EU–Iran regional security dialogue. In the area of technology and economic cooperation, the proposal confirmed European support for Iran's accession to the WTO and called for cooperation in a variety of areas, including scientific research, civil aviation, railway and shipping transport, petrochemicals and communications.[83]

---

[79] IAEA, 'Communication dated 1 August 2005 received from the Permanent Mission of the Islamic Republic of Iran', INFCIRC/648, Vienna, 1 Aug. 2005, p. 5, URL <http://www.iaea.org/Publications/Documents/Infcircs/2005/infcirc648.pdf>.

[80] IAEA, 'Communication dated 8 August 2005 received from the Resident Representatives of France, Germany and the United Kingdom to the Agency', INFCIRC/651, Vienna, 8 Aug. 2005, URL <http://www.iaea.org/Publications/Documents/Infcircs/2005/infcirc651.pdf>.

[81] INFCIRC/651 (note 80).

[82] INFCIRC/651 (note 80).

[83] INFCIRC/651 (note 80). The proposal also called for cooperation in a variety of areas, including scientific research, civil aviation, railway and shipping transport, petrochemicals and communications.

Iran's newly inaugurated president, Mahmoud Ahmadinejad, immediately rejected the E3 proposal as 'an insult to the nation'.[84] Iranian negotiators complained that the proposal sought to 'establish a subjective, discriminatory and baseless set of criteria' that would lead to the dismantlement of most of Iran's nuclear infrastructure.[85] Moreover, it did not include any 'firm commitments' on economic and technology cooperation with Iran, other than to repeat 'vague, conditional and partial restatements' of previous offers. Iran's harsh language in rejecting the proposal suggested that the new nuclear negotiating team put in place by Ahmadinejad intended to take a tougher approach to the nuclear talks with the E3 than its predecessor. Both Ahmadinejad and the new secretary of the Supreme National Security Council, Ali Larijani, had denounced the negotiations during their campaigns leading up to the June 2005 presidential election. More generally, some analysts have argued that there is a growing belief within the Iranian leadership that they are negotiating from a position of strength vis-à-vis the USA and its allies, making it possible for them to be more forthright in pursuing their goals.[86]

Iran's resumption of uranium conversion operations

On 8 August 2005 Iran announced that it had begun preparations to resume uranium conversion activities at the Esfahan facility, under IAEA monitoring.[87] While emphasizing that the decision was non-negotiable, Iran stated that it would continue to observe its moratorium on uranium enrichment after restarting operations at Esfahan, as specified in phase one of its May 2005 framework proposal.

Iran's resumption of uranium conversion prompted the E3 to cancel the next round of talks, scheduled for the end of August.[88] It also elicited sharp warnings from the three capitals that they were prepared to support US calls for Iran to be referred to the Security Council if Tehran did not immediately reinstate a freeze on all enrichment-related activities. At an emergency meeting of the IAEA Board of Governors on 9 August 2005, the European Union denounced the move as a 'flagrant disregard for the Board's repeated calls on Iran to suspend all enrichment related and reprocessing activities as a

---

[84] Mehr News Agency, 'EU proposal an insult to Iranian nation, Ahmadinejad tells Annan', 9 Aug. 2005, URL <http://www.mehrnews.com/en/NewsDetail.aspx?newsid=216526>.

[85] 'Response of the Islamic Republic of Iran to the framework agreement proposed by the EU3/EU' (undated), available at URL <http://www.basicint.org/countries/iran/Iranresponse.pdf>.

[86] Giacomo, C., 'US policy on Iran called ineffective', Reuters, 4 Dec. 2005, URL <http://www.iiss.org/news-more.php?itemID=1834>.

[87] Mehr News Agency, 'Operations at Isfahan UCF restarted', 8 Aug. 2005, URL <http://www.mehrnews.com/en/newsdetail.aspx?NewsID=216032>; and IAEA, 'Iran starts feeding uranium ore concentrate at uranium conversion facility', Press release, PR 2005/09, Vienna, 8 Aug. 2005, URL <http://www.iaea.org/NewsCenter/PressReleases/2005/prn200509.html>.

[88] Bennhold, K., 'Europeans call off next round of nuclear talks with Tehran', *International Herald Tribune*, 24 Aug. 2005, p. 3.

confidence building measure'.[89] At the end of the meeting, the IAEA Board of Governors adopted a unanimous resolution urging Iran to 're-establish full suspension of all enrichment-related activities'.[90]

Iran's decision to resume uranium conversion activities, despite the diplomatic costs involved, may have been motivated in part by the desire of the Atomic Energy Organization of Iran (AEOI) to address serious technical problems that reportedly had emerged at the UCF. According to accounts in nuclear industry trade journals, the uranium hexafluoride produced at Esfahan was contaminated with metal particles that rendered it unsuitable for use as gas centrifuge feedstock.[91] To the extent that this problem posed a long-term technical challenge, it represented a major obstacle to Iran's development of an indigenous uranium enrichment capability.

The IAEA Director General's assessment of Iran's nuclear programme

On 2 September 2005 the IAEA Director General, Mohamad ElBaradei, sent to the Agency Board of Governors the seventh in a series of written reports on progress in verifying Iran's implementation of its safeguards agreement.[92] This was the Director General's first report to the Board since in November 2004, when he issued a comprehensive assessment that included detailed summaries of the IAEA findings that Iran had failed to report or declare a wide range of nuclear activities, including uranium conversion and enrichment experiments, as required under its safeguards agreement.[93]

ElBaradei's new report identified two main safeguards compliance questions that the IAEA was working with Iran to resolve.[94] The first had to do with the origins of low-enriched uranium (LEU) and HEU particles discovered in environmental samples taken by inspectors at various sites in Iran.[95] There has been speculation that the LEU particles were produced in undeclared enrichment experiments inside Iran.[96] According to ElBaradei's report, the

---

[89] 'Statement by the United Kingdom on behalf of the European Union at the IAEA Board of Governors, 9 August 2005', Vienna, 9 Aug. 2005, URL <http://www.iaea.org/NewsCenter/Focus/IaeaIran/bog092005_statement-eu.pdf>.

[90] IAEA, 'Implementation of the NPT Safeguards Agreement in the Islamic Republic of Iran and related Board resolutions: Resolution adopted on 11 August 2005', Vienna, 11 Aug. 2005, URL <http://www.iaea.org/Publications/Documents/Board/2005/gov2005-64.pdf>, p. 2.

[91] Hibbs, M., 'Intelligence estimates vary widely on Iran's timeline to purify UF6', *Nuclear Fuels*, vol. 30, no. 18 (29 Aug. 2005), p. 1; and Hibbs, M., 'Iran can be producing impure UF6, trying to solve upstream process issues', *Nuclear Fuels*, vol. 30, no. 17 (15 Aug. 2005), p. 1.

[92] IAEA, 'Implementation of the NPT safeguards agreement in the Islamic Republic of Iran', Report by the Director General to the IAEA Board of Governors, GOV/2005/67, Vienna, 2 Sep. 2005, URL <http://www.iaea.org/Publications/Documents/Board/2005/gov2005-67.pdf>.

[93] IAEA, 'Implementation of the NPT safeguards agreement in the Islamic Republic of Iran', Report by the Director General to the IAEA Board of Governors, GOV/2004/83, Vienna, 15 Nov. 2004, URL <http://www.iaea.org/Publications/Documents/Board/2004/gov2004-83.pdf>.

[94] For further detail see Kile and Hart (note 16), pp. 558–60.

[95] HEU is uranium enriched to 20% or above in the isotope uranium-235 (U-235); LEU is uranium enriched to 0.72–20% U-235. Weapons-grade uranium is uranium enriched to more than 90% U-235.

[96] Albright, D. and Hinderstein, C., 'The centrifuge connection', *Bulletin of the Atomic Scientists*, vol. 60, no. 2 (Mar./Apr. 2004), pp. 62–63.

results of the environmental samples taken in Pakistan in the summer of 2005 'tended, on balance, to support Iran's statement' attributing the presence of the enriched uranium particles to contamination from centrifuge components imported through 'foreign intermediaries' (i.e., the A. Q. Khan nuclear smuggling network).[97] However, the IAEA had yet to establish a definitive conclusion with respect to all of the contamination, particularly the LEU contamination.[98]

The second main issue had to do with the chronology of Iran's work on advanced centrifuge designs. The IAEA was continuing to investigate Iran's claims about its research and development (R&D) work on an advanced centrifuge design, known as the P-2 centrifuge. Iran has admitted to the IAEA that it received Pakistani design plans for the P-2 centrifuges through foreign intermediaries in 1995; however, because of a 'shortage of professional resources', it did not begin manufacturing work and mechanical testing of the centrifuge's composite rotors until 2002. IAEA investigators questioned this account, citing the investment made by Iran in obtaining the design drawings and the country's technical capabilities. They also expressed doubt about the feasibility of carrying out centrifuge tests based on the P-2 design—which required the procurement of magnets, bearings and other parts from abroad as well as the manufacture of casings and centrifuge components—within the stated period of less than a year. They have sought additional documentation in order to verify Iran's claim that it did not work on the P-2 centrifuge design in 1995–2002.[99]

ElBaradei's report gave further detail about other transactions between Iran and the Khan network. Papers made available to IAEA inspectors by Iran in January 2005 included a copy of a handwritten, one-page document reflecting an offer allegedly made by a foreign intermediary in 1987 to sell centrifuge components and equipment to Iran.[100] Iran stated that only components from one or two disassembled centrifuges, and supporting drawings and specifications, had been delivered by the intermediary. The inspectors repeatedly asked to have access to original documentation related to the 1987 offer, but Iran maintained that the only existing paper reflecting the offer was the one-page document.[101]

In addition to these issues, ElBaradei reported that the IAEA was still assessing other aspects of Iran's nuclear programme, including the dates of plutonium separation experiments; the purpose of experiments involving the

[97] GOV/2005/67 (note 92), p. 11.

[98] The environmental samples revealed that domestically manufactured components were contaminated mainly with LEU, while imported components showed both LEU and HEU contamination; some of the imported components, along with associated assembly equipment and work areas, were contaminated with particles of c. 36% U-235 and others with c. 54% U-235. GOV/2004/83 (note 94), p. 9.

[99] GOV/2005/67 (note 92), p. 11.

[100] GOV/2005/67 (note 92), p. 5. The document contained drawings and specifications for the production of centrifuges; drawings, specifications and calculations for a 'complete' centrifuge plant; and lists of materials for manufacturing 2 000 centrifuges. The document also referred to uranium reconversion and casting capabilities, which Iran said it had not requested from the foreign intermediaries.

[101] GOV/2005/67 (note 92), p. 11.

isotope polonium-210; and certain activities at the Gchine uranium mine. The IAEA also continued to press for expanded access to two sites outside Tehran where undeclared nuclear weapon-related activities may have taken place. The first was the Parchin military complex, which is dedicated to the development and production of ammunition and high explosives.[102] Traditionally, military sites are considered off limits to IAEA inspectors, whose mandate is to monitor civilian nuclear facilities. In November 2005, after lengthy discussions, Iran granted IAEA inspectors access to buildings in an area of the complex chosen by the inspectors and allowed them to take environmental samples there. With regard to the second site, at Lavisan-Shian, ElBaradei reported that the IAEA was still awaiting permission to undertake additional inspections of relevant military-owned workshops and dual-use equipment associated with the Physics Research Centre previously located there.[103]

Iran as a special verification case

ElBaradei's report to the Board of Governors painted a mixed picture of the results achieved by the IAEA's special safeguards inspections. It stated that inspectors were able to verify that none of the declared nuclear material inside Iran had been diverted to prohibited activities. However, the IAEA was still not in a position to conclude that there were no undeclared nuclear materials or activities in Iran. ElBaradei told the Board that, in the light of Iran's 'past concealment efforts over many years', its full transparency was 'indispensable and overdue'.[104] He urged Iran to adopt additional transparency measures extending beyond the formal requirements of its comprehensive safeguards agreement and Additional Protocol. These would include granting IAEA inspectors unhindered access to key personnel, workshops and R&D sites as well as making available all original documentation related to the procurement of dual-use equipment and sensitive technologies. Other experts, including Pierre Goldschmidt, who was the IAEA's Deputy Director for Safeguards until July 2005, have argued that the Agency cannot fully reconstruct the history and assess the current capabilities of Iran's nuclear programme without expanded investigative powers authorized by the Security Council.[105]

The IAEA Board of Governors resolution

On 24 September 2005 the IAEA Board of Governors passed a resolution stating that 'Iran's many failures and breaches of its obligations to comply'

---

[102] Some reports have suggested that a separately secured site for the testing of high explosives within the complex could be part of a programme to develop conventional explosives for a nuclear warhead. See Albright, D. and Hinderstein, C., 'Parchin: possible nuclear weapons-related site in Iran', Institute for Science and International Security (ISIS), *ISIS Issue Brief*, 17 June 2004, URL <http://www.isis-online.org/publications/iran/parchin.html>.

[103] GOV/2005/67 (note 92), p. 10.

[104] GOV/2005/67 (note 92), p. 11.

[105] Goldschmidt, P., 'Decision time on Iran', *New York Times*, 14 Sep. 2005, URL <http://www.iranfocus.com/modules/news/article.php?storyid=3708>.

with its safeguards agreement, as described in previous reports by Director General ElBaradei, 'constitute non-compliance in the context of Article XII.C of the Agency's Statute'.[106] The resolution was drafted by the E3, in consultation with the USA. However, under pressure from China and Russia, the E3 dropped a demand contained in an earlier draft that would have forced the Board to immediately report Iran to the Security Council.[107] Instead, the version approved by the Board stated that Iran's concealment for 18 years had resulted in the 'absence of confidence' that its nuclear programme was exclusively for peaceful purposes and had 'given rise to questions that are within the competence of the Security Council'.[108] The resolution obligated the Board to report Iran to the Council but left open when this would happen.

Iran reacted angrily to the resolution, with the foreign minister denouncing it as 'illegal and illogical'.[109] Officials in Tehran argued that, since Iran had accepted inspections of unprecedented intrusiveness and cooperated fully with the IAEA to remedy past safeguards breaches, it was now in compliance with its obligations under the NPT. They also argued that the divided vote on the Board of Governors—22 member states in favour, with 12 abstentions (including Russia and China) and one rejection (by Venezuela), rather than the customary consensus—demonstrated that the resolution had the backing only of Western countries and was politically motivated.[110] They warned that Iran might respond to the Board's resolution by restarting uranium enrichment and suspending its adherence to the unratified Additional Protocol. The Majlis subsequently passed legislation requiring the government to block international inspections of the country's nuclear facilities if the IAEA Board reported Iran to the Security Council.[111]

Postponement of the referral decision by the IAEA Board of Governors

The Board's adoption of the resolution stating that Iran was in non-compliance with its safeguards agreement gave rise to expectations that the USA and the E3 would push at the next meeting of the Board, in November 2005, for Iran to be referred to the UN Security Council. However, prior to the meeting, US and European officials indicated that they would postpone calling for a referral

[106] IAEA, 'Implementation of the NPT safeguards agreement in the Islamic Republic of Iran', Resolution adopted by the IAEA Board of Governors, GOV/2005/77, Vienna, 24 Sep. 2005, URL <http://www.iaea.org/Publications/Documents/Board/2005/gov2005-77.pdf>, p. 1. According to Article XII of the IAEA Statute, the 'Board shall call upon the recipient State or States to remedy forthwith any [safeguards] non-compliance which it finds to have occurred. The Board shall report the non-compliance to all members and to the Security Council and General Assembly of the United Nations'.

[107] Landler, M., 'Nuclear agency expected to back weaker rebuke to Iran', New York Times (Internet edn), 24 Sep. 2005, URL <http://www.nytimes.com/2005/09/24/international/middleeast/24iran.html>.

[108] GOV/2005/77 (note 106), p. 2.

[109] Associated Press, 'Iran rejects UN resolution', 25 Sep. 2005, URL <http://www.cbsnews.com/stories/2005/09/25/world/main882946.shtml>.

[110] Mehr News Agency, 'International consensus against Iran fails', MehrNews.com, 24 Sep. 2005, URL <http://www.mehrnews.com/en/NewsDetail.aspx?newsid=233325>.

[111] Dareini, A., 'Iran votes to block nuclear inspections', Associated Press, 20 Nov. 2005, URL <http://www.breitbart.com/news/2005/11/20/D8E0B9IO0.html>.

in order to give Iran more time to consider a compromise proposal for ending the diplomatic impasse that had been put forward by Russia.[112] Their decision reportedly reflected an acknowledgement that such a call lacked broad support from the Board, including key member states such as China and Russia.[113]

The Board's deliberations were complicated by a new report from Director General ElBaradei, issued on 18 November 2005, on safeguards implementation in Iran. Among other findings, the report noted that IAEA inspectors had discovered a document, dating from 1987, on 'the casting and machining of enriched, natural and depleted uranium metal into hemispherical forms'.[114] This discovery attracted considerable media attention, since uranium metal hemispheres can be used in making the core of an implosion-type nuclear weapon.[115] According to ElBaradei's report, Iran stated that it had never requested this information and had been given it by a foreign intermediary. Officials in Tehran also asserted that the fact that they turned over the document demonstrated their commitment to full transparency.

Although the document did not contain detailed design or engineering information, its discovery heightened international concern about Iran's nuclear activities. Speaking on behalf of the EU, the ambassador of the UK to the IAEA warned that the document was an 'indication of weaponisation', since it showed that Iran was interested in acquiring, starting at least 18 years before, the technologies and expertise relevant to building a nuclear weapon.[116] This warning came in the wake of a US claim, made public earlier in 2005, that Iran had a secret programme to develop a compact re-entry vehicle for its Shahab intermediate-range ballistic missile that could carry a nuclear warhead.[117] The discovery of the document also raised questions about whether there were other documents in Iran's possession which were relevant to IAEA investigations and which Iran had neglected to turn over.[118]

---

[112] 'More time for Iran in nuclear row', BBC News Online, 21 Nov. 2005, URL <http://news.bbc.co.uk/1/4457772.stm>; and Jahn, G., 'US, Europe won't push for move on Iran', Associated Press, 21 Nov. 2005, URL <http://www.apnews.myway.com/article/20051121/D8E13P400.html>.

[113] Dinmore, G. and Bozorgmehr, N., 'Rice fails to win support for Iran referral to Security Council', *Financial Times*, 17 Oct. 2005, p. 4.

[114] IAEA, 'Implementation of the NPT safeguards agreement in the Islamic Republic of Iran', Report by the Director General to the IAEA Board of Governors, GOV/2005/87, Vienna, 18 Nov. 2005, URL <http://www.iaea.org/Publications/Documents/Board/2005/gov2005-87.pdf>, p. 3.

[115] Heinrich, M. and Murphy, F., 'Iran gives UN bomb part instruction', Reuters, 18 Nov. 2005, URL <http://www.iranfocus.com/modules/news/article.php?storyid=4475>.

[116] 'Statement by UK Ambassador Peter Jenkins to the IAEA Board of Governors', 24 Nov. 2005, URL <http://www.iranwatch.org/IAEAgovdocs/uk-fco-statement-iaea-board-112405.htm>.

[117] In 2004, the USA allegedly obtained 1000 pages of Persian-language documents—including computer simulations and accounts of experiments—related to a missile warhead that US officials maintained was designed to carry a nuclear weapon. Broad, W. and Sanger, D., 'Relying on computer, US seeks to prove Iran's nuclear aims, *New York Times*, 13 Nov. 2005, URL <http://www.mezomorf.com/technology/news-11854.html>.

[118] 'Statement by UK Ambassador Peter Jenkins to the IAEA Board of Governors' (note 116).

Resumption of the Iran–E3 talks

Shortly after the conclusion of the Board meeting, European Union foreign ministers agreed to an Iranian request to resume talks on the country's nuclear programme.[119] The subsequent 'talks about holding talks' were held in Vienna on 21 December 2005 and ended with the parties agreeing to meet again in January 2006. The negotiators reportedly deferred any substantive discussion of Iran's enrichment programme until the next meeting, amid signs that the two sides remained far apart on the issue.[120] The political climate for the resumed talks had deteriorated following a series of vitriolic anti-Israel remarks made by President Ahmadinejad. His comments elicited sharp rebukes from many governments and were formally condemned at a European Council meeting in Brussels on 15 December 2005.[121]

One of the main subjects to be taken up by Iranian and European negotiators was Russia's informal proposal for it to establish a joint venture with Iran to produce nuclear fuel.[122] In general terms, the proposal called for Iran to outsource to Russia the most sensitive part of its enrichment programme. Iran would be permitted to continue converting uranium ore into uranium tetrafluoride (an intermediate step in the production of uranium hexafluoride) at the Esfahan facility, under IAEA safeguards and with appropriate transparency measures. The uranium tetrafluoride would then be shipped to a facility in Russia for conversion into uranium hexafluoride and subsequent enrichment into LEU fuel for nuclear power plant; this facility could operate under joint Iranian–Russian ownership. Iran would return the spent reactor fuel to Russia for long-term storage and disposition, as it had already agreed to do with the Russian-supplied fuel for the Bushehr plant.

The initial reaction of Iranian officials to the Russian proposal was negative. A spokesman of the Iranian Foreign Ministry insisted that any fuel supply deal would have to guarantee that the nuclear fuel cycle remained inside Iran.[123] Larijani told a news conference in early December 2005 that he saw 'no need' for the proposed fuel services deal with Russia and reaffirmed that Iran intended to produce nuclear fuel domestically.[124] He did not specify when this might occur, but he emphasized that Iran preferred to do it as a result of negotiations, which might take several months. Senior Iranian officials subse-

---

[119] Associated Press and Agence France-Presse, 'EU offers to resume nuclear negotiations with Iran', *International Herald Tribune* (Internet edn), 28 Nov. 2005, URL <http://www.iht.com/articles/2005/11/28/news/iran.php>.

[120] Nuclear Threat Initiative, 'No progress made on Iran's nuclear program', Global Security Newswire, 22 Dec. 2005, URL <http://www.nti.org/d_newswire/issues/2005_12_22.html#8C17BDDF>.

[121] Nuclear Threat Initiative, 'EU condemns Iranian President's anti-Israel comments, warns Tehran on nuclear program', Global Security Newswire, 16 Dec. 2005, URL <http://www.nti.org/d_newswire/issues/2005_12_16. html#54C8DF8A>.

[122] Nuclear Threat Initiative, 'Russia wants nuclear fuel deal with Iran', Global Security Newswire, 3 Nov. 2005, URL http://www.nti.org/d%5Fnewswire/issues/2005/11/3/683cea4e%2Dfcea%2D4882 %2D902e%2D40ad8cb344f7.html >.

[123] 'EU offers to resume nuclear negotiations with Iran' (note 119).

[124] Agence France-Presse, 'Iran will NPT give up uranium enrichment programme says Larijani', SpaceWar, 5 Dec. 2005, URL <http://www.spacewar.com/news/iran-05zzzzzzzf.html>.

quently offered a more positive public assessment of the Russian proposal, but they insisted that Iran's policy to have a domestic uranium enrichment capability had not changed.[125]

On 3 January 2006, Iran informed the IAEA that it 'has decided to resume from 9 January 2006 those R&D [activities] on the peaceful nuclear energy programme which has been suspended as part of its expanded voluntary and non-legally binding suspension'.[126] Iran did not immediately specify which enrichment R&D activities it planned to resume. The announcement, which was criticized by ElBaradei, appeared to set the stage for an imminent collision between Iran and the E3 and the USA.[127] The EU had previously said that any decision by Iran to resume work on its uranium enrichment programme would be a 'red line' that would end their attempts to negotiate differences with Iran.[128] As 2006 began, however, it was unclear whether a tougher approach to addressing concerns about Iran's nuclear fuel cycle activities, including a referral of the issue to the Security Council for possible sanctions, would be acceptable to Russia, China and other states.[129]

IV. North Korea's nuclear programme and the Six-Party Talks

During 2005 the protracted confrontation over North Korea's nuclear programme showed no sign of abating. It had entered into a new, more perilous phase in 2002, when a series of tit-for-tat moves by Pyongyang and Washington resulted in the collapse of the 1994 Agreed Framework.[130] In April 2003 North Korea further raised the stakes in the crisis by formally withdrawing from the NPT.[131] North Korea is widely believed to have produced

---

[125] Nuclear Threat Initiative, 'Iran pledges to study compromise nuclear proposal, Global Security Newswire, 3 Jan. 2006, <http://www.nti.org/d_newswire/issues/2006_1_3.html#1E575FA9>; and IRNA, 'Asefi says nuclear talks with Russia positive', 8 Jan. 2006, URL <http://www.irna.ir/en/news/view/line-22/0601081605 141451.htm>.

[126] IAEA, 'Iran to resume suspended nuclear research and development', Press release 2006/01, Vienna, 3 Jan. 2006, URL <http://www.iaea.org/NewsCenter/PressReleases/2006/prn200601.html>.

[127] Jahn, G., 'Iran rebuffs IAEA chief', Associated Press, 5 Jan. 2006, URL <http://www.washingtonpost.com/wp-dyn/content/article/2006/01/05/AR2006010500877.html>.

[128] Dareini, A., 'Iran plans to resume nuclear research', Associated Press, 3 Jan. 2005, URL <http://www.washingtonpost.com/wp-dyn/content/article/2006/01/03/AR2006010300303.html>.

[129] Russia's announcement in early Dec. 20005 that it would sell new air defence missiles to Iran elicited sharp criticism from both Europe and the United States. Jahn, G., 'EU protests Russian–Iran missile deal', Associated Press, 15 Dec. 2005, URL <http://www.forbes.com/business/services/feeds/ap/2005/12/15/ap2395314.html>.

[130] On the 1994 Agreed Framework between North Korea and the USA, and the events leading up to its breakdown, see Kile, S. N., 'Nuclear arms control, non-proliferation and ballistic missile defence', *SIPRI Yearbook 2003: Armaments, Disarmament and International Security* (Oxford University Press: Oxford, 2003), pp. 578–92. For the text of the Agreed Framework see URL <http://www.kedo.org/pdfs/AgreedFramework.pdf>.

[131] North Korea's withdrawal from the treaty, which it announced on 10 Jan. 2003 for reasons of 'supreme national interest', took effect on 10 Apr. 2003. North Korea's safeguards agreement (INFCIRC/403) was considered to have lapsed on that date as well.

and separated enough plutonium from the spent fuel of its 5-MW(e) research reactor at Yongbyon to build a small number of nuclear warheads.[132]

In 2005 there were two new rounds of the Six-Party Talks between China, Japan, North Korea, South Korea, Russia and the USA aimed at resolving the diplomatic impasse over North Korea's nuclear programme. The talks, organized by China, had been suspended for more than a year after the third round ended in June 2004 with North Korea rejecting a US proposal for a nuclear deal and announcing that it would not participate in further rounds.[133] The prospects for resuming the talks were complicated when, on 10 February 2005, North Korea announced for the first time that it had developed operational nuclear weapons.[134] In addition, in April 2005 there was speculation within the US intelligence community that North Korea was preparing to carry out a nuclear explosive test near Kilju, on the country's north-east coast.[135]

At the same time, in the spring of 2005 North Korea indicated that it was prepared to return to the talks if the USA agreed to end its 'hostile policy' and treat it with appropriate respect.[136] For its part, the US Administration showed greater diplomatic flexibility in responding to overtures from Pyongyang, including by holding informal discussions with North Korean officials at the United Nations.[137] The shift in US policy was motivated in part by a desire to allay the concerns of some regional allies that the administration was not interested, for ideological reasons, in holding serious negotiations with North Korea.[138]

On 10 July 2005 North Korea announced that it would return to the Six-Party Talks. According to a foreign ministry spokesman, the decision had been taken after the USA gave assurances that it recognized the North as a sovereign state, had no intention of invading it and would hold bilateral talks within the framework of the multilateral negotiations.[139] In addition, China and South Korea reportedly had strongly encouraged North Korea to end its boycott of the talks. Following the announcement, South Korea said that it had

[132] According to one non-governmental assessment, in mid-2005 North Korea possessed 15–38 kg of separated plutonium, which would be enough to build 3–9 nuclear weapons. Institute for Science and International Security (ISIS), 'The North Korean plutonium stock, mid–2005', *ISIS Issue Brief*, 7 Sep. 2005, URL <http://www.isis-online.org/publications/dprk/dprkplutoniumstockmid05.pdf>.

[133] The first round of the Six-Party Talks had been held on 27–29 Aug. 2003, the second on 25–28 Feb. 2004 and the third round on 23–26 June 2004.

[134] Korea Central News Agency (KCNA), 'DPRK FM on its stand to suspend its participation in Six-Party Talks for indefinite period', 10 Feb. 2005, URL <http://www.kcna.co.jp/item/2005/200502/news02/11.htm#1>

[135] Sanger, D., 'What are Koreans up to? US agencies can't agree', *New York Times* (Internet edn), 12 May 2005, URL <http://www.nytimes.com/2005/12/politics/12intel.html>.

[136] KCNA, 'DPRK Foreign Ministry spokesman on denuclearization of Korea', 31 Mar. 2005, URL <http://www.kcna.co.jp/item/2005/200504/news04/01.htm#17>.

[137] Sanger, D. and Shanker, T., 'North Korea is reported to hint at nuclear talks', *New York Times* (Internet edn), 6 June 2005, URL <http://www.nytimes.com/2005/06/06/international/asia/06korea.html>.

[138] Eckert, P., 'US should renew focus on N. Korea talks—analysts', Reuters, 25 Jan. 2005, URL <http://www.reuters.ch/newsArticle.jhtml?type=reutersEdge&storyID=7429557>.

[139] KCNA, 'Spokesman for DPRK FM on contact between heads of DPRK and US dels', 10 July 2005, URL <http://www.kcna.co.jp/item/2005/200507/news07/11.htm#1>.

offered to supply the 2000 MW of electric power to North Korea if it returned to the talks and pledged to eliminate its nuclear weapon programme.[140]

The North Korean–US Joint Statement

The fourth round of the Six-Party Talks was held in Beijing, China, on 26 July–7 August 2005 and, following a recess, on 13–19 September 2005. It ended with the parties issuing a Joint Statement on principles guiding future talks aimed at the 'verifiable denuclearization of the Korean Peninsula in a peaceful manner'.[141] In the Joint Statement, North Korea and the USA undertook a number of specific commitments. North Korea pledged to 'abandon all nuclear weapons and existing nuclear programs' and to return, at an early date, to the NPT and to IAEA safeguards. The USA affirmed that it had no nuclear weapons on the Korean Peninsula and had 'no intention to attack or invade' North Korea with nuclear or conventional weapons. The two countries also undertook to 'respect each other's sovereignty' and to 'take steps to normalize their relations subject to their respective bilateral policies'. In addition to these commitments, China, Japan, South Korea, Russia and the USA declared their willingness to provide energy assistance to North Korea.[142] They also 'expressed their respect' for North Korea's statement that it had the right to peaceful uses of nuclear energy and 'agreed to discuss, at an appropriate time, the subject of the provision of a light water reactor' to the North.[143]

Although the signing of the Joint Statement was hailed by some diplomatic observers as a breakthrough, it left unsettled a number of key questions and points of contention that had emerged in the Six-Party Talks. North Korea's commitment to 'abandon' its nuclear weapons and existing nuclear programmes in exchange for aid and security guarantees appeared to fall short of the USA's insistence in the talks that Pyongyang agree to verifiably dismantle all of its nuclear facilities. North Korea was also unwilling to admit that it had a secret uranium enrichment programme—something which the US intelligence community suspects that it is developing, in addition to the declared plutonium reprocessing facility. At the same time, the Joint Statement did not include a long-standing North Korean demand: that the USA provide North Korea with formal security guarantees, including a non-aggression treaty.

Immediately after the statement was issued, the two main antagonists presented conflicting views about what had actually been agreed. The fundamental difference between North Korea and the USA continued to be over the timing, or sequencing, of a possible deal. US negotiators emphasized

---

[140] Brinkley, J., 'South Korea offers power if North Korea quits arms program', *New York Times* (Internet edn), 13 July 2005, URL <http://www.nytimes.com/2005/07/13/international/asia/13diplo.html>. The energy offered was equal to the combined capacity of the 2 light-water nuclear power reactors that were promised to North Korea under the 1994 Agreed Framework.

[141] US Department of State, Office of the Spokesman, 'Joint Statement of the Fourth Round of the Six-Party Talks', 19 Sep. 2005, URL <http://www.state.gov/r/pa/prs/ps/2005/53490.htm>.

[142] South Korea reaffirmed its July 2005 offer to provide the North with 2 million MW of electric power.

[143] US Department of State (note 141).

that they had not moved away from insisting on a 'complete, verifiable and irreversible' end to all of North Korea's nuclear activities. In their view, the 'appropriate time' to discuss providing a nuclear power reactor to North Korea would come only after it had met two conditions: the prompt elimination of all nuclear weapons and nuclear programmes, to be verified by international inspections; and full compliance with the obligations of a non-nuclear weapon state party to the NPT, including its safeguards agreement with the IAEA.[144] For its part, North Korea warned that the USA 'should not even dream of the issue of the DPRK's dismantlement of its nuclear deterrent' before providing it with a light-water reactor as a 'physical guarantee for confidence-building'.[145] North Korean officials subsequently clarified that the delivery of the reactor was a precondition for North Korea to rejoin the NPT as a non-nuclear weapon state and readmit IAEA inspectors.[146]

Little progress was subsequently made towards resolving the diplomatic impasse, against the background of a hardening of the positions of both Pyongyang and Washington.[147] The fifth round of the Six-Party Talks, which were held in Beijing on 9–11 November 2005, ended inconclusively. On 11 December North Korea announced that it had suspended 'for an indefinite period' its participation in the talks.[148] It declared it that would not return until Washington first lifted financial sanctions imposed against the North over its suspected involvement in a number of illegal activities, including money laundering, counterfeiting and weapon smuggling. In addition, Pyongyang continued to insist that it should receive political and economic compensation for the cancellation of the two light-water power reactors to be built in North Korea as part of the Agreed Framework.[149] On 23 November 2005 the USA and its partners in the Korean Peninsula Energy Development Organization decided to terminate the project, which had been suspended since 2002.[150]

---

[144] Statement by Assistant Secretary of State Christopher R. Hill to the Closing Plenary of the Fourth Round of the Six-Party Talks, US Department of State, Office of the Spokesman, 19 Sep. 2005, URL <http://www.state.gov/r/pa/prs/ps/2005/53499.htm>.

[145] KCNA, 'Spokesman for DPRK Foreign Ministry on Six-Party Talks', URL <http://www.kcna.co.jp/item/2005/200509/news09/21.htm#1>.

[146] Nuclear Threat Initiative, 'North Korea demands energy reactor as precondition to resuming international inspections', Global Security Newswire, 7 Oct. 2005, URL <http://www.nti.org/d_newswire/issues/2005_10_7.html# BEDD96F5>.

[147] Sanger, D., 'US widens campaign on North Korea', New York Times (Internet edn), 24 Oct. 2005, URL <http://www.nytimes.com/2005/10/24/international/asia/24korea.html>.

[148] Agence France-Presse, 'Nuclear talks suspended indefinitely: N. Korea', SpaceWar, 11 Dec. 2005, URL <http:// www.spacewar.com/news/korea-05zzzzzze.html>.

[149] KCNA, 'DPRK FM spokesman demands US compensate for political and economic losses', 28 Nov. 2005, URL <http://www.kcna.co.jp/item/2005/200511/news11/29.htm>.

[150] Nuclear Threat Initiative, 'North Korea reactor project terminated', Global Security Newswire, 23 Nov. 2005, URL <http://www.nti.org/d_newswire/issues/2005_11_23.html>; and Kim, K-T., 'North Korea demands that US lifts sanctions', The Guardian (Internet edn), 6 Dec. 2005, URL <http://www.guardian.co.uk/worldlatest/story/0,1280,-5460734,00.html>.

V. International cooperation to secure nuclear materials and facilities

International concern about the dangers of nuclear material falling into the hands of non-state actors that could use them in act of terrorism has been accompanied by a growing awareness that national measures for protecting nuclear material and facilities are uneven in their substance and application. As a result, a number of international non-proliferation and disarmament assistance (INDA) programmes have been launched in recent years aimed at securing and accounting for fissile and other hazardous radiological materials and reducing the potential for their theft.[151] During 2005 the European Union discussed how Community instruments could contribute to securing global stocks of nuclear material stocks as part of the EU's Strategy to Prevent the Proliferation of Weapons of Mass Destruction.[152] In the USA, the Bush Administration requested a significant increase in funding in financial year (FY) 2006 for the Department of Energy's material protection control and accounting programmes, designed to enhance the security of nuclear materials in the former Soviet Union and elsewhere in the world.[153] The request for increased funding reflected growing concern in Congress about nuclear security in Russia and the risks of terrorist acquisition of nuclear or radiological weapons.[154]

US–Russian cooperation on nuclear security

On 24 February 2005, at a summit meeting in Bratislava, Slovakia, US President Bush and Russian President Vladimir Putin agreed to expand and deepen bilateral cooperation aimed at combating nuclear terrorism.[155] The two presidents pledged to accelerate projects to upgrade the security of Russian nuclear facilities and develop a plan of work through and beyond 2008. To facilitate this work, they established the US–Russian Senior Interagency Group for cooperation on nuclear security, including the disposal of fissile

---

[151] For a summary of current INDA activities see Fedchenko, V., Maerli, M. and Anthony, I., 'Nuclear security: reinforcing EU co-operative threat reduction programmes, Background Paper 2 to the Interim Report, *Strengthening European Action on WMD Non-proliferation and Disarmament: How Can Community Instruments Contribute?* (Stockholm: SIPRI, Dec. 2005), URL <http://www.sipri.org/contents/expcon/BP2.pdf>, pp. 22–39.

[152] In 2005 a pilot project was initiated to provide independent recommendations for the use of Community resources within the framework of the EU's WMD Strategy during the budget period 2007–13. See SIPRI, 'EU Pilot Project conference materials', URL <http://www.sipri.org/contents/expcon/euppconfmaterials.html>.

[153] Ruppe, D., 'White House threat reduction budget stresses Energy Department activities', Global Security Newswire, 8 Feb. 2005, URL <http://www.nti.org/d_newswire/issues/2005_2_8.html#1 FA28A1A>. The administration's FY 2006 budget request proposed an increase for the Department of Energy's overall threat reduction activities from $439 million to $526 million.

[154] Pincus, W. and Baker, P., 'US–Russia pact aimed at nuclear terrorism', *Washington Post* (Internet edn), 24 Feb. 2005, URL <http://www.washingtonpost.com/wp-dyn/articles/A48465-2005Feb23.html>.

[155] The White House, 'US–Russia Joint Fact Sheet: Bratislava Initiatives', News release, 24 Feb. 2005, URL <http://www.whitehouse.gov/news/releases/2005/02/20050224-7.html>.

material no longer needed for defence purposes. In addition, the presidents undertook to work jointly to develop LEU fuel for use in any US- and Russian-designed research reactors in third countries currently using HEU fuel and to repatriate fresh and spent HEU from these reactors.[156] The closer bilateral cooperation envisioned by the Bratislava initiative came at a time when the US and Russian security establishments were clashing over sensitive INDA activities. Some observers pointed out that it failed to address several important outstanding issues, such as the controversy over allowing US access to Russian nuclear material nuclear warhead storage sites, and did not provide for sustaining nuclear security improvements with Russian resources after international assistance is phased out.[157]

In July 2005 the US and Russian governments reached an agreement in principle on the resolution of a lengthy legal dispute over liability issues that had blocked implementation of the 2000 US–Russian Plutonium Management and Disposition Agreement.[158] The dispute centred on the level of protection that US officials and contractors should receive from lawsuits arising from their work to implement assistance projects in Russia, in particular in the area of plutonium disposition.[159] Resolution of the dispute was also expected to facilitate the extension of the 1992 Cooperative Threat Reduction programme's 'umbrella agreement', which serves as the basis for most US-funded nuclear projects in Russia and is scheduled to expire in June 2006.[160] At the same time, however, no final agreement had been reached on funding the project to build a Russian mixed-oxide (MOX) fuel plant to convert excess plutonium from weapons into civil nuclear reactor fuel.[161]

In 2005 progress was made in implementing the US-funded Global Threat Reduction Initiative (GTRI) programme. The purpose of this programme, which was launched under the auspices of the US Department of Energy's National Nuclear Security Administration (NNSA) in May 2004, is to 'consolidate, accelerate, and expand existing efforts to remove potential nuclear weapon-usable material from vulnerable sites' and to 'identify and prioritize nuclear materials and equipment of proliferation concern not being addressed

[156] The White House (note 155).

[157] See Bunn, M. and Weir, A., *Securing the Bomb 2005: The New Global Imperatives*, Project on Managing the Atom, Belfer Center for Science and International Affairs, Kennedy School of Government, Harvard University, May 2005, URL <http://www.nti.org/e_research/report_cnwm update2005.pdf>, p. 22.

[158] Under the terms of the agreement, each party must dispose of at least 34 tonnes of weapon-grade plutonium declared to be in excess of defence needs by irradiating it as fuel in reactors or by immobilizing it with high-level radioactive waste and thereby rendering it suitable for geological disposal. The text of the agreement is available at URL <http://www.nnsa.doe.gov/na-20/docs/ 2000_Agreement.pdf>.

[159] Saradzhyan, S., 'Key nuclear dispute is resolved', *Moscow Times*, 20 July 2005, p. 2, URL <http://themoscowtimes.com/stories/2005/07/20/010.html>.

[160] Pincus and Baker (note 154); and Antonov, A., Address to the Centre for Policy Studies in Russia (PIR Centre) Advisory Board [in Russian], 13 July 2005, URL <http://www.pircenter.org/cgi-bin/pirnews/getinfo.cgi?ID=1954>.

[161] Francis, D., 'Washington, Moscow come to liability agreement for US-backed nuclear projects in Russia', Global Security Newswire, 9 Nov. 2005, URL <http://www.nti.org/d_newswire/issues/2005_ 11_9.html>.

by existing threat reduction efforts'. The creation of the programme reflected growing concerns in the USA and elsewhere about the proliferation risks posed by the existence of large number of unsecured sites with civilian nuclear materials.[162] As part of a global 'nuclear clean-out', the USA is working with Russia, the IAEA and other partners to convert the cores of civilian research reactors that use HEU fuel to LEU fuel and to repatriate from locations around the world all fresh and spent HEU fuel of Russian or US origin.[163] On 27 September 2005 the NNSA announced that 14 kg of HEU had been removed from the Czech Technical University's VR-1 Sparrow research reactor, in Prague, and returned to a secure facility in Dimitrovgrad, Russia, where the material will be down-blended to LEU. This marked the eighth shipment of Russian-origin HEU reactor fuel back to Russia under the GTRI programme.[164] In November 2005 the NNSA announced that the Czech research reactor was the first Russian-supplied reactor to successfully convert HEU to LEU fuel.[165]

IAEA initiatives

In 2005, concern about the dangers of nuclear material falling into the hands of terrorists led to the adoption of an amendment strengthening the 1980 Convention on the Physical Protection of Nuclear Material.[166] The convention, which is the only multilateral treaty in force that deals with physical protection issues, obligates the parties to make specific arrangements and meet defined standards for the protection of nuclear material in international transport or storage incidental to such transport. On 8 July 2005 delegations from 89 states parties voted in favour of amending the convention to make it legally binding for the parties to protect nuclear facilities and material in domestic use, transport and storage.[167] The amendment requires parties to establish and maintain a legislative and regulatory framework to govern physical protection according to a set of fundamental principles. In addition, it provides for

---

[162] For an overview of these concerns, see Bleek, P., *Global Cleanout: an Emerging Approach to the Civil Nuclear Material Threat*, Project on Managing the Atom, Belfer Center for Science and International Affairs, Kennedy School of Government, Harvard University, Sep. 2004, URL <http://www.bcsia.ksg.harvard.edu/publication.cfm?program=STPP&ctype=paper&item_id=464>.

[163] IAEA, 'IAEA welcomes US new Global Threat Reduction Initiative' 27 May 2004, URL <http://www.iaea.org/NewsCenter/News/2004/GTRI_Initiative.html>.

[164] US Department of Energy, National Nuclear Security Administration, 'Highly enriched uranium recovered from Czech Technical University', Press release no. NA-05-22, 27 Sep. 2005, URL <http://www.nnsa.doe.gov/docs/newsreleases/2005/PR_2005-09-27_NA-05-22.htm>. As of Sep. 2005, fresh Russian-origin HEU fuel had also been repatriated to Russia from Bulgaria, the Czech Republic, Latvia, Libya, Romania, Serbia and Montenegro, and Uzbekistan.

[165] US Department of Energy, National Nuclear Security Administration, 'NNSA completes Czech research reactor conversion', Press Release No. NA-05-28, 4 Nov. 2005, URL <http://www.nnsa.doe.gov/docs/newsreleases/2005/PR_2005-11-04_NA-05-28.htm>.

[166] The text of the convention is available at URL <http://www.iaea.org/Publications/Documents/Infcircs/Others/inf274r1.shtml>.

[167] IAEA, 'States agree on stronger physical protection regime', Press Release 2005/03, 8 July 2005, URL <http://www.iaea.org/NewsCenter/PressReleases/2005/prn200503.html>. The amendments will take effect once they have been ratified by two-thirds of the currently 112 parties to the convention.

expanded cooperation between states in rapidly locating and recovering stolen or smuggled nuclear material.[168]

In September 2005 the IAEA Board of Governors adopted a Nuclear Security Plan covering the period 2005–2009.[169] The new plan builds on the Plan of Activities to Protect against Nuclear Terrorism adopted by the Board in March 2002.[170] It is intended to increase worldwide protection against acts of terrorism involving fissile and other radioactive nuclear materials by assisting countries working at the national level to upgrade physical protection of their nuclear material and nuclear facilities, detect illicit nuclear trafficking across borders and improve control of radioactive sources.

Global measures

On 13 April 2005 the UN General Assembly adopted, by consensus, the International Convention for the Suppression of Acts of Nuclear Terrorism, addressing the unlawful possession or use of nuclear devices or materials by non-state actors.[171] The purpose of the convention is to complement existing UN instruments against other manifestations of terrorism by providing a legal basis for international cooperation in the investigation, prosecution, and extradition of those who commit terrorist acts involving radioactive material or a nuclear device. The Nuclear Terrorism Convention calls for states to develop appropriate legal frameworks criminalizing nuclear terrorism-related offences. With its focus on the investigation and prosecution of individuals, the convention also addresses to a limited extent the treatment of detainees and extradition policies. The treaty was opened for signature on 14 September 2005 and will enter into force 30 days after it has been ratified by 22 states.

VI. Conclusions

The year 2005 was marked by a number of failures, or missed opportunities, to solve some of the pressing challenges coming from within and outside the nuclear non-proliferation regime. Most notably, the 2005 NPT Review Conference concluded without producing a final report containing any substantive decisions on issues of treaty implementation. The deadlock at the conference

---

[168] For the text of the amendment see 'Nuclear security measures to protect against nuclear terrorism: amendment to the Convention on the Physical Protection of Nuclear Material', Report by the Director General to the Board of Governors General Conference, GOV/INF/2005/10-GC(49)/INF/6, Vienna, 6 Sep. 2005, URL <http://www.iaea.org/About/Policy/GC/GC49/Documents/gc49inf-6.pdf>.

[169] IAEA, 'Nuclear security: measures to protect against nuclear terrorism', Resolution adopted by the 49th IAEA General Conference, GC(49)/res/10, 30 Sep. 2005, URL <http://www.iaea.org/About/Policy/GC/GC49/documents/gc49res10.pdf>.

[170] IAEA, 'IAEA Board of Governors approves IAEA Action Plan to combat nuclear terrorism', Press Release PR2002/04, 19 Mar. 2002, URL <http://www.iaea.org/NewsCenter/PressReleases/2002/prn0204.shtml>.

[171] International Convention for the Suppression of Acts of Nuclear Terrorism, UN General Assembly A/59/766, 13 Apr. 2005, URL <http://www.un.int/usa/a-59-766.pdf>. As of 31 Dec. 2005, the convention had been signed by 99 states but none had ratified it.

highlighted the long-standing—and deepening—division between the nuclear 'have' and 'have not' states over the nature and purpose of the NPT, and it raised doubts about the future viability of the treaty regime. While there was general consensus among the states parties at the conference that the regime was becoming dangerously debilitated, they did not agree on the causes or on solutions. As one participant lamented, the conference's lack of results reflected 'the broader malaise and paralysis that abounds in multilateral disarmament diplomacy under its various current configurations'.[172]

Developments in 2005 suggested that recent innovations in multilateral approaches to preventing the spread of nuclear weapon-usable materials and technologies are likely to be controversial for some time to come. Many states acted during the year to implement the legal and regulatory measures mandated by UN Security Council Resolution 1540, and more states cooperated within the US-organized Proliferation Security Initiative. There was also growing interest in the idea of repairing alleged shortcomings or loopholes in the NPT by limiting civil uranium enrichment and plutonium reprocessing programmes to a handful of fully transparent nuclear fuel cycle facilities, operating under multinational or international control.

At the same time, however, considerable concern was expressed by some states about the consequences of a paradigmatic shift, led by the USA, from treaty-based disarmament to ad hoc counter-proliferation approaches involving self-selecting coalitions of the willing. This shift was criticized as intruding on the sovereign rights of individual states as well as undermining the existing legal and normative foundations of international efforts for combating the spread of WMD. While acknowledging that there was an urgent need for the international community to work to revitalize and strengthen the non-proliferation regime, the NAM states and many other non-nuclear weapon states argued that achieving this goal required, above all, a renewed commitment by all states to fully implement their arms control and disarmament commitments within the existing multilateral treaty framework.

[172] Closing statement made by Tim Caughley, Ambassador for Disarmament of New Zealand, at the 2005 Review Conference on the Treaty on the Non-proliferation of Nuclear Weapons, 27 May 2005, URL <http://www.reachingcriticalwill.org/legal/npt/RevCon05/GDstatements/index.html>.

Appendix 13A. World nuclear forces, 2006

SHANNON N. KILE, VITALY FEDCHENKO and
HANS M. KRISTENSEN

I. Introduction

While world attention is focused on the nuclear programmes of Iran and North Korea, eight states possess about 12 100 operational nuclear weapons (see table 13A.1).[1] Several thousand nuclear weapons are kept on high alert, ready to be launched within minutes. If all nuclear warheads are counted—operational warheads, spares, and those in both active and inactive storage—the United States, Russia, the United Kingdom, France, China, India, Pakistan and Israel together possess a total of more than 27 000 warheads.

None of the five legally recognized nuclear weapon states, as defined by the 1968 Non-Proliferation Treaty (NPT), appears to be planning to disarm its nuclear arsenal in the foreseeable future.[2] Russia and the USA are in the process of reducing their operational nuclear forces as a result of two bilateral treaties—the 1991 Strategic Arms Reduction Treaty (START I Treaty) and the 2002 Strategic Offensive Reductions Treaty (SORT).[3] In the USA, implementation of the 2001 Nuclear Posture Review (NPR)[4] has begun on all aspects of the nuclear postures. This includes a reduction by 'almost half' of the total stockpile by 2012 and the development of new ballistic missiles, strategic submarines, long-range bombers, new or modified nuclear weapons, nuclear weapon production facilities, nuclear command and control systems, and modified nuclear war plans. Similarly, Russia has announced its plan to reduce mainly land-based strategic missiles but also to retain for another decade, rather than dismantling, intercontinental ballistic missiles (ICBMs) equipped with multiple, independently targetable re-entry vehicles (MIRVs). A new ICBM, a new class of strategic submarines and a new cruise missile are being introduced. Tables 13A.2 and 13A.3 show the composition of the deployed nuclear forces of the USA and Russia, respectively.

---

[1] On developments in world nuclear forces see Kile, S. N. and Kristensen, H. M., 'World nuclear forces, 2005', *SIPRI Yearbook 2005: Armaments, Disarmament and International Security* (Oxford University Press: Oxford, 2005), pp. 578–602, and previous editions of the SIPRI Yearbook. For a discussion of the national governance of nuclear weapons in these 8 states see chapter 5 in this volume.

[2] According to the NPT, only states that manufactured and exploded a nuclear device prior to 1 Jan. 1967 are recognized as nuclear weapon states. By this definition, China, France, Russia, the UK and the USA are the nuclear weapon states parties to the NPT.

[3] The Treaty on the Reduction and Limitation of Strategic Offensive Arms (START I Treaty) was signed in 1991 by the USA and the USSR; it entered into force on 5 Dec. 1994 for Russia and the USA (under the 1992 Lisbon Protocol, which entered into force on 5 Dec. 1994, Belarus, Kazakhstan and Ukraine also assumed the obligations of the former USSR under the treaty). For the treaty see URL <http://www.state.gov/www/global/arms/starthtm/start/toc.html>. SORT was signed by Russia and the USA in 2002; it entered into force on 1 June 2003 and is available at URL <http://www.state.gov/t/ac/trt/18016.htm>. On the implications of SORT see 'Special Section', *Arms Control Today*, vol. 32, no. 5 (June 2002), pp. 3–23.

[4] See 'Nuclear Posture Review [excerpts], submitted to Congress on 31 December 2001', 8 Jan. 2002, URL <http://www.globalsecurity.org/wmd/library/policy/dod/npr.htm>.

Table 13A.1. World nuclear forces, by number of deployed warheads, January 2006

Country[a]	Strategic warheads	Non-strategic warheads	Total number of warheads
USA	5 021	500	**5 521**[b]
Russia	3 352	2 330	**5 682**[c]
UK	185[d]	–	**185**
France	348	–	**348**
China	~130	?[e]	**~130**
India	–	–	**~50**[f]
Pakistan	–	–	**~60**[f]
Israel	–	–	**100–200**[f]
Total			**~12 100**

 [a] North Korea claimed in 2005 that it had developed nuclear weapons, although there is no public information to verify this claim.

 [b] The total US stockpile, including reserves, contains c. 10 000 warheads. In addition, 5000 plutonium cores (pits) are in storage as a strategic reserve, while another 7000 pits make up most of 34 tons of weapon-grade plutonium declared in excess of military needs.

 [c] The total Russian stockpile contains roughly 16 000 warheads, of which c. 10 100 are in storage and/or awaiting dismantlement.

 [d] Some warheads on British strategic submarines have sub-strategic missions.

 [e] The existence of operational Chinese non-strategic warheads is uncertain.

 [f] The stockpiles of India, Pakistan and Israel are thought to be only partly deployed.

The nuclear arsenals of China, the UK and France are considerably smaller than those of the USA and Russia. Data on their delivery vehicles and nuclear warhead stockpiles are presented in tables 13A.4–13A.6. China is about to deploy a new generation of strategic missiles, but it remains unclear whether it intends to deploy a significantly larger strategic nuclear force or a more modern force of relatively the same size. France is currently engaged in developing and deploying a new generation of nuclear-powered ballistic-missile submarines (SSBNs), submarine-launched ballistic missiles (SLBMs) and air-launched nuclear weapons, although the number of operational warheads may decrease somewhat with the introduction of the new SLBM around 2010. Unlike any of the other nuclear weapon states, France continues to deploy nuclear weapons on its surface fleet in peacetime. The British nuclear weapon stockpile has levelled out at about 200 warheads: the UK is the only one of the five nuclear weapon states that is not known to have new nuclear weapon systems under development. Yet, the UK appears to have begun a multi-year programme to extend the service life of the warhead on the Trident II (D-5) SLBM, and it will soon face a decision about the future of its nuclear deterrent after the Trident system reaches the end of its scheduled service life.

It is particularly difficult to obtain public information about the nuclear arsenals of the three states that are not parties to the NPT—India, Pakistan and Israel. The information that is available is limited and often contradictory. India and Pakistan are both expanding their operational nuclear strike capabilities, while Israel appears to be waiting to see how the situation in Iran develops. Tables 13A.7–13A.9 provide information about the status of the Indian, Pakistani and Israeli nuclear arsenals.

The figures in the tables are estimates based on public information and contain some uncertainties, as reflected in the notes.

II. US nuclear forces

As of January 2006, the USA maintained an estimated stockpile of approximately 5500 active or operational nuclear warheads,[5] consisting of more than 5000 strategic and 500 non-strategic warheads. Another 215 warheads are spares. More than 4200 inactive warheads are in reserve, for a total stockpile of about 10 000 warheads.

Of the current US stockpile, more than 4000 warheads are expected to be retired for dismantlement by 2012 as a result of the 2004 Nuclear Weapons Stockpile Plan. Most of these warheads will come from the large reserve of inactive warheads, while a smaller number will come from warheads removed from operational status as a result of SORT implementation. This will leave a stockpile of nearly 6000 warheads.

Because SORT does not include verification measures, and because the START I Treaty expires in 2009, monitoring the development of Russian and US strategic nuclear forces will be increasingly difficult. Much like during the cold war, satellite surveillance and human intelligence will once again be the primary means with which the world's two largest nuclear weapon powers monitor—and potentially misunderstand—each other's nuclear force developments.

In parallel with adjusting the nuclear forces, the US Department of Defense (DOD) has upgraded its nuclear strike plans to reflect new presidential guidance and a transition in war planning from the Single Integrated Operational Plan (SIOP) of the cold war to a set of smaller and more flexible strike plans designed to defeat today's adversaries. The new central strategic war plan is known as OPLAN (Operations Plan) 8044. Former chairman of the Joint Chiefs of Staff General Richard B. Meyers described some of the planning changes in congressional testimony in February 2005: '[US Strategic Command] has revised our strategic deterrence and response plan that became effective in the fall of 2004. This revised, detailed plan provides more flexible options to assure allies, and dissuade, deter, and if necessary, defeat adversaries in a wider range of contingencies'.[6]

One example of this adjustment is CONPLAN (Concept Plan) 8022, a plan for the quick use of nuclear, conventional, or information warfare capabilities to destroy—pre-emptively, if necessary—'time-urgent targets' anywhere in the world. Defense Secretary Donald Rumsfeld issued an Alert Order in early 2004 that directed the military to put CONPLAN 8022 into effect. As a result, the pre-emption policy of the administration of President George W. Bush is now operational for long-range bombers, strategic submarines and presumably ICBMs.

Land-based ballistic missiles

On the basis of the estimate for January 2006, the US ICBM force was reduced in 2005 by 10 missiles with the retirement of the Peacekeeper (MX) ICBM. The 500 W87 warheads from the 50 retired Peacekeeper missiles will be modified to replace W62 warheads on Minuteman ICBMs beginning in financial year (FY) 2006. With a yield of 310 kt, the W87 is nearly twice as powerful as the W62, which will

---

[5] This estimate for operational warheads is 600 warheads above the estimate for 2005 owing to new information about the composition of the active and inactive stockpiles. See Kile and Kristensen (note 1), p. 580.

[6] Myers, R. B., General, US Air Force, Chairman of the Joint Chiefs of Staff, Posture Statement before the Senate Armed Services Committee, 17 Feb. 2005, URL <http://www.senate.gov/~armed_services/statemnt/2005/February/Myers%2002-17-05.pdf>, p. 32.

broaden the range of hardened targets that can be held at risk with the Minuteman force. The W62 will be retired by 2009. During 2005 work continued on modernizing the guidance and propulsion systems of the Minuteman ICBM force.

The USA abandoned the START II Treaty in 2002 and now plans to retain a multiple warhead capability for its ICBM force. The number of warheads deployed on ICBMs will be reduced to 500 to comply with the SORT ceiling of no more than 2200 operationally deployed strategic warheads by 2012. However, hundreds of additional ICBM warheads will be retained in the 'responsive force' reserve for potential uploading onto Minuteman missiles.

Four Minuteman IIIs were test-launched in 2005 from Vandenberg Air Force Base (AFB) in California; three with a single re-entry vehicle and one with three re-entry vehicles. One of the missiles with a single re-entry vehicle (from Malmstrom AFB) was a demonstration test for adapting the W87 warhead from the retired MX/Peacekeeper for deployment on the Minuteman III.[7]

Work is continuing on designing a new ICBM to begin replacing Minuteman III missiles from 2018. The Mission Need Statement (MNS) for the new ICBM states that nuclear weapons will 'continue to play a unique and indispensable role in US security policy' and that a credible and effective land-based nuclear deterrent force 'beyond 2020' will 'prepare the US for an uncertain future by maintaining US qualitative superiority in nuclear war-fighting capabilities in the 2020–2040 time frame'.[8]

Ballistic missile submarines

The Trident I (C-4) SLBM was retired in October 2005 after 26 years of service when the USS *Alabama* offloaded the last 24 operational C-4 missiles. The *Alabama*, along with three other former C-4-equipped SSBNs, will be converted to carry the longer-range and more accurate D-5 SLBM. The USS *Alaska* and USS *Nevada* have already been converted, while USS *Henry M. Jackson* and USS *Alabama* will be converted in 2006 and 2007, respectively.

The build-up of the SSBN force in the Pacific continued in 2005 with the transfer of two more boats from Kings Bay in Georgia to Bangor in Washington. The USS *Louisiana* arrived in its new homeport at Bangor in October, followed by the USS *Maine* in November. The transfers boost the Pacific SSBN fleet to nine boats, leaving only five SSBNs in the Atlantic, the lowest number there since ballistic missile-equipped submarines were first deployed to sea, in 1961. The SSBNs are being transferred to increase targeting of China, although SSBNs in the Pacific also target Russia and North Korea.

The US Navy purchased five more D-5 SLBMs in the FY 2006 budget, and production of the missile has been extended through 2013 for a total of 561 missiles. The development of a Life Extension (LE) programme for 108 older D-5s will allow them to match the service life of the Trident SSBN force, which has been extended through 2042.

---

[7] The 2006 Quadrennial Defense Review decided to reduce the ICBM force by 50 missiles, to 450 missiles, beginning in FY 2007. US Department of Defense, Office of the Secretary of Defense, *Quadrennial Defense Review*, 6 Feb. 2006, URL <http://www.defenselink.mil/qdr/report/Report2006 0203.pdf>.

[8] US Department of the Air Force, HQ, Air Force Space Command/Data Records Management, 'Final Mission Need Statement (MNS), AFSPC 001-00: Land-Based Strategic Nuclear Deterrent', Acquisition Category One (ACAT I), 18 Jan. 2002, p. 2.

Five D-5 missiles were flight-tested in 2005, four from two US SSBNs and one from a British SSBN. The first test, carried out from the USS *Tennessee* (SSBN-734) off Florida in March, involved the launch of a missile in the shortest trajectory ever flown by a US SLBM: 1200 nautical miles (2222 km). The re-entry vehicle was equipped with an 'accuracy adjunct', using a three-axis flap system developed by Lockheed Martin, which enabled manoeuvring of the re-entry vehicle to 'GPS-like accuracy' (within 10 metres). Both nuclear and conventional warhead strikes were simulated.

The modernization of the W76 warhead continues with three specific efforts under way. One involves an LE programme that *inter alia* replaces the arming, firing and fuzing (AF&F) system on the W76/Mk4 re-entry vehicle to add a ground-burst capability that will significantly enhance the lethality of the weapon against harder targets. The modified warhead, which will be called the W76-1, may permit a reduction of the explosive yield. A second effort involves adding the 'accuracy adjunct' to the Mk4 re-entry vehicle to enhance the effectiveness of the W76-1/Mk4 and to enable deployment of conventional warheads on the Trident II (D-5) SLBM. The third effort involves a design incorporating the W76-1 on the larger Mk5 re-entry vehicle normally used for the W88 warhead in order to relax the design constraints required when using the smaller Mk4 re-entry vehicle.[9]

Long-range bombers

The size of the US bomber force remained unchanged in 2005, but the aircraft and their nuclear weapons continued to be upgraded.

The US Air Force is replacing its bombers' ultra-high frequency (UHF) and very-high frequency (VHF) radios and satellite communications (SATCOM) with a new communications system to receive beyond-line-of-sight (BLOS) voice and data. This will allow crews to review full mission plans en route to their targets. An Extremely High Frequency (EHF) satellite communication will also be added to ensure that the bombers have secure BLOS communications in its nuclear mission.

The installation of the Avionics Midlife Improvement (AMI) on the B-52H, which is the only carrier of the air-launched cruise missile (ALCM) and the advanced cruise missile (ACM), began in 2005 to improve the aircraft's navigation and nuclear weapon delivery capabilities. The installation work is expected to be completed in September 2008. The existing Air Force satellite communications (AFSATCOM) radio will also be replaced by EHF radio to improve communications in nuclear strike scenarios.

The US Air Force is studying options for a new long-range strike aircraft to eventually replace the current bomber force. It is also studying options for a next-generation nuclear cruise missile. One possibility is a multi-service enhanced cruise missile (ECM) with a nuclear payload and longer range to support global strike missions against 'targets deep within future high threat anti-access environments', according to Air Force documents. Delivery is envisioned from bombers or from various ground- or sea-based platforms.

---

[9] The 2006 Quadrennial Defense Review decided to replace nuclear warheads on 24 Trident II (D-5) missiles with conventional warheads for deployment in 2008. The intention is to mix conventional and nuclear missiles throughout the SSBN fleet—a plan which, if approved by Congress, could have a significant impact on crisis stability if the launch of a conventionally armed D-5 SLBM were misinterpreted by a nuclear adversary as a pre-emptive nuclear strike. US Department of Defense (note 7).

Table 13A.2. US nuclear forces, January 2006

Type	Designation	No. deployed	Year first deployed	Range (km)[a]	Warheads x yield	Warheads
Strategic forces						
Bombers[b]						
B-52H	Stratofortress	85/56	1961	16 000	ALCM 5–150 kt	1 000[c]
					ACM 5–150 kt	400
B-2	Spirit	21/16	1994	11 000	Bombs	555[d]
Subtotal		*106/72*				*1 955*
ICBMs[e]						
LGM-30G	Minuteman III					
	Mk-12	50	1970	13 000	3 x 170 kt	150
		150			1 x 170 kt[f]	150
	Mk-12A	300	1979	13 000	2–3 x 335 kt	750
Subtotal		*500*				*1 050*
SSBNs/SLBMs[g]						
UGM-133A	Trident II (D-5)					
	Mk-4	n.a.	1992	>7 400	6 x 100 kt	1 632
	Mk-5	n.a.	1990	>7 400	6 x 475 kt	384
Subtotal		*336*				*2 016*
Strategic subtotal						*5 021*
Non-strategic forces						
B61-3, -4, -10 bombs		n.a.	1979	n.a.	0.3–170 kt	400[h]
Tomahawk SLCM		320	1984	2 500	1 x 5–150 kt	100[i]
Non-strategic subtotal						*500*
Total						**5 521**[j]

[a] Aircraft range is for illustrative purposes only; actual mission range will vary according to flight profile and weapon loading.

[b] The first figure in the *No. deployed* column is the total number of B-52Hs in the inventory, including those for training, test and reserve. The second figure is for PMI (primary mission inventory) aircraft, i.e., the number of operational aircraft assigned for nuclear and conventional wartime missions.

[c] Another 360 ALCM warheads are in reserve.

[d] Available for both the B-52H and the B-2A.

[e] The Peacekeeper ICBM was retired in Sep. 2005. The planned downloading of all Minuteman ICBMs to a single warhead to meet the SORT-mandated force ceiling may already have taken place. The W62 (Mk-12) will be retired by 2009.

[f] Each of the 150 Minuteman III missiles of the 90th Space Wing at F.E. Warren AFB was downloaded from 3 to 1 W62 warhead in 2001.

[g] Two of 14 SSBNs are undergoing conversion from the C-4 missile, which was retired in Oct. 2005, to the D-5. Although D-5 missiles are counted under START I as carrying 8 warheads each, the US Navy completed a preliminary download in 2005 (to an average of 6 warheads per missile) and will conduct an additional download later to meet the SORT-mandated force ceiling in 2012.

[h] Approximately 440 bombs (including inactive weapons) are deployed in Europe.

[i] Another 200 W80-0s are in inactive storage. The TLAM/N is no longer deployed at sea but is stored on land.

[j] Another 215 warheads are spares and more than 4220 warheads are kept in the inactive stockpile for a total stockpile of approximately 10 000 warheads. In addition, more than 12 000 plutonium pits are stored at the Pantex Plant in Texas.

Sources: US Department of Defense, various budget reports and press releases; US Department of Energy, various budget reports; US Department of State, START I Treaty MOUs, 1990 through July 2005; US Department of Defense, various documents obtained under the Freedom of Information Act; US Navy, personal communication; 'NRDC Nuclear Notebook', *Bulletin of the Atomic Scientists*, various issues; US Naval Institute, *Proceedings*, various issues; and Authors' estimates.

Non-strategic nuclear weapons

As of January 2006, the USA retained approximately 500 active non-strategic nuclear warheads. These consisted of 400 B61 gravity bombs and 100 W80-0 warheads for Tomahawk Land-Attack Cruise Missiles (TLAM/Ns). Another 790 non-strategic warheads are in inactive storage. Despite the significant number of warheads, neither the 2001 NPR nor SORT addresses non-strategic nuclear weapons.

The most significant change in 2005 was that all of the B61-10 bombs are now considered part of the inactive stockpile. Some of these weapons are still deployed in Europe together with B61-3/4 bombs. A total of 440 B61 non-strategic nuclear bombs are forward-deployed at eight airbases in six European NATO member states (Belgium, Germany, Italy, the Netherlands, Turkey and the UK). The aircraft of non-nuclear weapon NATO countries that are assigned nuclear strike missions with US nuclear weapons include Belgian and Dutch F-16 and German and Italian Tornado combat aircraft.[10]

Only 100 W80-0 warheads for the TLAM/N are active; another 200 are in inactive storage. TLAM/Ns are earmarked for deployment on selected Los Angeles, Improved Los Angeles and Virginia Class nuclear-powered attack submarines (SSNs). The weapon is not deployed at sea under normal circumstances, but it can be redeployed within 30 days of a decision to do so.

Nuclear warhead stockpile management and modernization

The total US stockpile of roughly 10 000 warheads is organized in two categories: active and inactive warheads. The active category includes intact warheads with all components that are either deployed on operational delivery systems or are part of the 'responsive force' of reserve warheads that can be deployed on operational delivery systems in a relatively short time. The inactive category includes warheads that are held in long-term storage as a reserve with their limited life components (tritium) removed. As SORT and the 2004 Nuclear Weapons Stockpile Plan are implemented over the next six years, the 'responsive force' will contain roughly three times as many warheads as there are operationally deployed warheads. In addition to the 10 000 active and inactive warheads, the USA keeps about 5000 plutonium cores (pits) in storage at the Pantex Plant in Texas as a strategic reserve. Approximately the same number of canned assemblies (thermonuclear secondaries) are kept at the Oak Ridge Y-12 Plant in Tennessee. Another 7000 pits held at Pantex make up most of

---

[10] On the history and status of US nuclear weapons in Europe see Kristensen, H. M., 'US nuclear weapons in Europe,' Natural Resources Defense Council, Washington, DC, 2005, URL <http://www.nrdc.org/nuclear/euro.contents.asp>.

the 34 tonnes of weapon-grade plutonium previously declared in excess of military needs by the administration of President Bill Clinton. All of these 12 000 pits come from retired warheads.

III. Russian nuclear forces

Land-based ballistic missiles

The ICBMs assigned to the Strategic Rocket Forces (SRF) have traditionally made up the largest element of the Soviet/Russian strategic nuclear forces. As of January 2006, the SRF consisted of three missile armies, with a total 13 missile divisions: the 27th Guards Missile Army (headquarters in Vladimir, five divisions), the 31st Missile Army (Orenburg, three divisions) and the 33rd Guards Missile Army (Omsk, five divisions).[11] In 2005, the SRF eliminated two missile divisions and decommissioned 36 SS-18s, 14 SS-19s, 36 SS-25s and all 15 remaining SS-24 missiles.[12] According to the long-term plan for Russia's strategic forces, made public at the end of 2004, the SRF will eventually deploy only the SS-27 Topol-M missile, while all other ICBMs will be gradually decommissioned.[13]

The SS-27 Topol-M missile is a solid-propellant three-stage ICBM and has been developed in both road-mobile (RS-12M1) and silo-based (RS-12M2) versions. The latter began to be deployed in 1997 with the 60th Missile Division in Tatischevo, Saratov oblast, as a replacement for the SS-19 missiles based there. As of early 2005, this division had four regiments armed with 10 RS-12M2 missiles each. Two more Topol-Ms were added in December 2005.[14] Russia will have to deploy on average four or five missiles per year to fulfil its plan to have 64 RS-12M2 missiles on duty by 2010.[15]

According to the 2006 State Defence Order, Russia will procure six Topol-M missiles in 2006, compared with four in 2005.[16] Three of these will be road-mobile RS-12M1 missiles scheduled for deployment with the 54th Missile Division in Teikovo, Ivanovo region, by December 2006.[17] Russia plans to have 15 such missiles by 2010.[18]

On 1 November 2005 the SRF successfully launched an RS-12M1 Topol-M missile from the Kapustin Yar test range in Astrakhan' region to the Balkhash test range in Kazakhstan. The launch reportedly tested a new hypersonic re-entry vehicle (RV) that

---

[11] 'Strategic Rocket Forces', Russian Nuclear Forces Project, 17 Dec. 2005, URL <http://www.russianforces.org/eng/missiles/>.

[12] Kile and Kristensen (note 1), pp. 586–87.

[13] Poroskov, N., '"V god budem sokrachshyat' po odnoy-dve raketnye divizii"' ['We will be decommissioning one or two missile divisions a year'], *Vremya Novostey*, 6 May 2005, URL <http://www.vremya.ru/2005/78/4/124290.html>.

[14] Dolinin, A., 'Khraniteli derzhavy' [The guardians of the state], *Krasnaya Zvezda*, 31 Jan. 2006, URL <http://www.redstar.ru/2006/01/31_01/1_01.html>.

[15] Safronov, I., 'Russian missiles will die of old age', *Kommersant*, 1 Apr. 2005, URL <http://www.kommersant.com/page.asp?id=559554>.

[16] 'Fradkov distributes defense order', *Kommersant*, 1 Dec. 2005, URL <http://www.kommersant.com/doc.asp?idr=527&id=631438>; and Kile and Kristensen (note 1), p. 587.

[17] Safronov, I., 'Moskva ispytala assimetrichnyi otvet' [Moscow has tested an asymmetrical response], *Kommersant*, 2 Nov. 2005.

[18] Safronov (note 15).

is capable of manoeuvring in flight in order to penetrate missile defence systems.[19] President Vladimir Putin has stated on several occasions that Russia was developing a new nuclear missile system 'which had no counterpart elsewhere in the world' and would be able to defeat any strategic missile defence system. Many observers believe that Putin was referring to the manoeuvrable RV for the Topol-M. The commander of the SRF, Colonel-General Nikolai Solovtsov, has stated that the new RV will be deployed on Topol-M missiles beginning in 2006 and later on a new SLBM, the SS-NX-30 'Bulava' (R-30).[20] He also indicated that the Topol-M could be equipped with multiple warheads, if a decision to do so were to be made by the political leadership.[21]

The SRF plans to continue to deploy the SS-18 'Satan' (R-36M) heavy ICBM for another 10–15 years, and possibly longer. Under the terms of the abandoned START II Treaty, Russia was committed to scrapping all of its SS-18s, which can carry up to 10 warheads each. As of January 2006, Russia had on combat duty 74 SS-18s, in two versions: the R-36MUTTKh and the R-36M2 Voevoda.[22] The former was first deployed in 1979–83 and the latter in 1988–92. They are silo-based, two-stage liquid-propellant ICBMs produced by the Yuzhnoe Machine-Building Plant in Dnepropetrovsk, Ukraine.[23]

In December 2004 Russia successfully test-launched an R-36M2 missile, which had been on combat alert for 16 years, as part of a programme to extend the service life of the R-36M2. In the summer of 2005 the SRF performed additional maintenance operations, which extended the service lives of its approximately 40 R-36M2 missiles until at least 2016.[24] On 26 December 2005 Solovtsov announced that Russia and Ukraine would sign an agreement on joint work to refurbish a number of R-36M2 missiles.[25]

In the summer of 2005 the service life of the R-36MUTTKh was extended until 2007–2009, after which time the remaining missiles will be decommissioned. The decomissioning process is under way. In early 2005 the warheads were removed from the missiles of the 59th Missile Division in Kartaly, Chelyabinsk region, and moved to the storage facilities of the 12th Main Directorate of the Ministry of Defence (MOD). The missiles were sent to Surovatikha, Nizhnii Novgorod region, for dismantlement.[26] In October 2005 the disbandment of the division at Kartaly was reported to have been completed.[27]

At the beginning of 2006 the SRF had 126 SS-19 Stiletto (UR-100NUTTH) missiles deployed at Kozelsk and Tatishchevo. The SS-19 is a silo-based, two-stage, liquid-propellant ICBM, capable of carrying up to six warheads. The currently deployed version of the missile entered service in 1980. On 20 October 2005 the SRF

[19] Richardson, D., 'Russia conducts further flight test of maneuvering warhead', *Jane's Missiles & Rockets*, vol. 10, no. 1 (Jan. 2006), p. 11.

[20] Safronov (note 15). On the Bulava SLBM see also the sub-section 'Ballistic missile submarines' below.

[21] Dolinin, A., 'Strazh bezopasnosti derzhavy' [The state security guard], *Krasnaya Zvezda*, 16 Dec. 2005, URL <http://www.redstar.ru/2005/12/16_12/1_01.html>.

[22] Dolinin (note 14).

[23] Lennox, D. (ed.), *Jane's Strategic Weapon Systems* (Jane's Information Group Limited: Coulsdon, 2005), pp. 127–28.

[24] Poroskov (note 13).

[25] 'Russian commander pins hopes on missile cooperation with Ukraine', Interfax, 26 Dec. 2005.

[26] Safronov (note 15).

[27] ITAR-TASS, 'Russia disbands strategic missile division, redeploys troops', 19 Oct. 2005.

test-launched an SS-19 as part of a programme to extend the missile's service life by an additional 20 years. The dummy warhead successfully hit the target at the Kura test range at Kamchatka peninsula.[28] Of the 150 test-launches of the SS-19 carried out to date, only three are reported to have failed.[29] The Rokot satellite launch vehicle, a derivative of the SS-19, has been launched seven times since 2000, of which six launches were successful.[30] A launch failure occurred on 8 October 2005, when Rokot failed to put a European satellite, Cryosat, into orbit.[31]

The SRF deployed 270 SS-25 'Sickle' ICBMs as of January 2006. The SS-25 is a road-mobile, three-stage solid-propellant ICBM that carries a single warhead. The missile was first deployed in 1985 and production ceased in 1994.[32] According to Russian sources, 144 SS-25s are expected to be in service in 2010.[33] The missile's original 10-year service life has reportedly been extended to 19 years.[34] On 29 November the SRF successfully test-launched an SS-25 that had entered service in 1985. On the basis of the results of the test, the SRF stated that the service lives of such missiles could be extended up to 23 years, in which case they may remain operational until 2016–18.[35]

Ballistic missile submarines

In 2005 the Russian Navy deployed 13 SSBNs with the Northern and Pacific fleets. Of these, six were Delta III (Project 667BDR Kalmar) submarines.[36] Some experts suggest that the submarines of this class, which first entered service in 1982, may be retired during the next few years.[37] The Navy continues to operate seven Delta IV Class (Project 667BDRM Delfin) submarines. One SSBN has been paid off and is currently being refitted as a special-purpose submarine. The six remaining SSBNs— *Verkhotur'e*, *Yekaterinburg*, *Novomoskovsk*, *Tula*, *Bryansk* and *Kareliya*—are based in the Northern Fleet. As of January 2006, *Bryansk* and *Kareliya* were undergoing service life-extension overhauls and refitting with newly produced SS-N-23 Skiff

---

[28] 'Zapusk "Stileta" vnov' podtverdil nadezhnost' odnoy iz samykh sovershennykh MBR Rossii' [The launch of 'Stiletto' has once again confirmed the reliability of the one of Russia's most refined ICBMs'], *Izvestia*, 20 Oct. 2005, URL <http://news.izvestia.ru/community/news99862>.

[29] 'Russia to test launch ICBM on 20 Oct', ITAR-TASS, 17 Oct. 2005.

[30] 'Zapusk "Stileta"...' (note 28).

[31] 'Russia apologizes to ESA over the loss of Cryosat space probe', *Pravda*, 10 Oct. 2005, URL <http://english.pravda.ru/main/18/88/354/16280_Cryosat.html >.

[32] Lennox (note 23), p. 138.

[33] Safronov (note 15).

[34] 'S kosmodroma Plesetsk zapustili 20-letnyuyu raketu' [20-year-old missile was launched from Plesetsk cosmodrome], Strana.ru, 29 Nov. 2005, URL <http://www.strana.ru/news/266308.html>.

[35] 'Topol missile life could be extended', RIA Novosti, 29 Nov. 2005, URL <http://en.rian.ru/russia/20051129/42252655.html >.

[36] The *Petropavlovsk-Kamchatskii*, *Svyatoi Georgii Pobedonosets*, *Zelenograd* and *Podol'sk* are deployed with the Pacific Fleet, and the *Ryazan'* and *Borisoglebsk* are with the Northern Fleet. The Navy uses a seventh non-operational Delta III as a test platform.

[37] Norris, R. and Kristensen, H., 'Russian nuclear forces, 2005', *Bulletin of the Atomic Scientists*, vol. 61, no. 2 (Mar./Apr. 2005), pp. 70–72, URL <http://www.thebulletin.org/article_nn.php?art_ofn=ma05norris>; and Barabanov, M., 'Perspektivy atomnogo podvodnogo sudostroeniya v XXI veke' [Perspectives of nuclear submarines shipbuilding in XXI century], *Yadernyi Kontrol'*, vol. 10, no. 2 (summer 2004), pp. 133–54, URL <http://www.pircenter.org/data/publications/yk2-2004.pdf>.

missiles, which the others had recently completed.[38] The six Delta IVs may remain in service until 2015–20.

In addition to these submarines, the Russian Navy operates one Typhoon Class submarine, renamed the *Dmitrii Donskoi* following its overhaul and relaunching in June 2002, as a test platform for new SS-NX-30 Bulava missile.[39] The sea trials of *Dmitrii Donskoi* were successfully completed on 6 December 2004.[40] Russian military officials indicated in 2005 that *Dmitrii Donskoi* and the two remaining Typhoon Class submarines—*Arkhangel'sk* and *Severstal'*, which were laid up in 2004 for financial reasons—are to be upgraded by replacing their obsolete SS-N-20 Sturgeon SLBMs with the new SS-NX-30 Bulava.[41]

Russia is building a new class of SSBN, the Project 955 Borei, which so far does not have a NATO designation. Three submarines of this class are scheduled to be commissioned by 2010, with three more to follow. The first ship in the class, *Yurii Dolgorukii*, was laid down in November 1996 at the Severnoye Mashinostroitel'noye Predpriyatiye (Sevmash) shipyard in Severodvinsk in northern Russia.[42] The commissioning of this submarine was postponed several times because of financial problems and the decision to arm it with the SS-NX-30 Bulava SLBM instead of the previously planned SS-NX-28 Bark.[43] In November 2005, the Commander-in-Chief of the Russian Navy, Admiral Vladimir Masorin, stated that *Yurii Dolgorukii* will be commissioned in 2007.[44] The second ship in the class, *Aleksandr Nevskii*, was laid down at Sevmash on 19 March 2004. The construction of the third ship, tentatively named *Vladimir Monomakh*, is scheduled to begin in March 2006.[45] Each of these submarines will be armed with 12 SS-NX-30 Bulava missiles.[46]

Russia's SLBM force consists of two types of missile. The SS-N-18 Stingray missile (RSM-50), which first entered service in 1977, is deployed on Delta III Class submarines. The SS-N-18 M1 has two liquid-fuelled stages and carries three war-

[38] Norris and Kristensen (note 37); and Saunders, S. (ed.), *Jane's Fighting Ships 2005-2006* (Jane's Information Group Limited: Coulsdon, UK, 2005), p. 602); and Bondarenko, A., and Emel'yanenkov, A., 'Prishla "Tula" s novym "samovarom"' ['Tula' came with the new 'samovar'], *Rossiiskaya Gazeta*, 12 Jan. 2006.

[39] The Soviet Union built a total of six Typhoon Class (Project 941 Akula) SSBNs in 1976–89. Russia decommissioned three of the Typhoons in 1996.

[40] 'APL "Dmitrii Donskoi" zavershila hodovye ispytaniya' [SSBN 'Dmitry Donskoy' has finished sea trials], ITAR-TASS, 6 Dec. 2004, URL <http://www.a-submarine.ru/news/main/viewPrintVersion?id=10113&idChannel=418>.

[41] Tul'ev, M., 'V interesah triady' [In the interest of the triad], *Voenno-Promyshlennyi Kur'ier*, 11 May 2005; 'Russian defense minister on plans to equip new submarines with Bulava missiles', Agentstvo Voennykh Novostei, 28 Sep. 2005.

[42] Plugatarev, I., '"Topol-M" vytesnyaet "Molodtsa" i "Voevodu"'["Topol-M" replaces "Molodets" and "Voevoda"], *Nezavisimoe Voennoe Obozrenie*, 28 Jan. 2005, URL <http://nvo.ng.ru/printed/forces/2005-01-28/1_topol.html>.

[43] Kile and Kristensen (note 1), pp. 587–88; and Litovkin, V., '"Bulava" idet maketom' [The model of 'Bulava'], *Moskovskie Novosti*, 15 Oct. 2004, URL <http://www.mn.ru/issue.php?2004-39-16>.

[44] Ustinov, E. and Fomishenko, R., 'Novye kalibry "Astrakhani"' [New calibers of "Astrakhan"'], *Krasnaya Zvezda*, 17 Nov. 2005, URL <http://www.redstar.ru/2005/11/17_11/1_02.html>.

[45] 'V Rossii postroyat novuyu submarinu' [New submarine will be built in Russia], *Kommersant*, 25 Jan. 2006, URL <http://www.kommersant.ru/index-news-y.html?id=93941>.

[46] Safronov, I., '"Alexandr Nevskii" strategicheskogo naznacheniya' ['Alexander Nevsky' of strategic purpose], *Kommersant*, 19 Mar. 2004.

Table 13A.3. Russian nuclear forces, January 2006

Type	NATO designation	No. deployed	Year first deployed	Range (km)[a]	Warheads x yield	Warheads
Strategic offensive forces						
Bombers						
Tu-95MS6	Bear-H6	32	1981	6 500–10 500	6 x AS-15A ALCMs, bombs	192
Tu-95MS16	Bear-H16	32	1981	6 500–10 500	16 x AS-15A ALCMs, bombs	512
Tu-160	Blackjack	14	1987	10 500–13 200	12 x AS-15B ALCMs or AS-16 SRAMs, bombs	168
Subtotal		*78*				*872*
ICBMs[b]						
SS-18	Satan	74	1979	11 000–15 000	10 x 500–750 kt	740
SS-19	Stiletto	126	1980	10 000	6 x 500–750 kt	756
SS-25	Sickle	270	1985	10 500	1 x 550 kt	270
SS-27	(Topol-M)	42	1997	10 500	1 x 550 kt	42
Subtotal		*512*				*1 808*
SLBMs[b]						
SS-N-18 M1	Stingray	96	1978	6 500	3 x 200 kt (MIRV)	288
SS-N-23	Skiff	96	1986	9 000	4 x 100 kt (MIRV)	384
Subtotal		*192*				*672*
Total strategic offensive forces		**782**				**3 352**
Strategic defensive forces						
ABMs						
SH-11/ SH-08	Gorgon/ Gazelle	100	1989/1986		1 x 1000/10 kt	100
SA-10	Grumble[c]	1900	1980		1 x low kt	600[c]
Non-strategic forces						
Land-based non-strategic						
Bombers						
Tu-22M Backfire		116	1974		2 x AS-4 ASM, bombs	
Su-24 Fencer		371	1974		2 x bombs	
Subtotal		*487*				*974[d]*
Naval non-strategic						
Attack aircraft						
Tu-22M Backfire		58	1974		2 x AS-4 ASM, bombs	
Su-24 Fencer		58	1974		2 x bombs	
Subtotal		*116*				*232[d]*
SLCMs						
SS-N-12, SS-N-19, SS-N-21, SS-N-22						266
ASW and SAM weapons						
SS-N-15/16, torpedoes, SA-N-3/6						158
Total defensive and non-strategic						**2 330**
Total						**5 682**

a Aircraft range is for illustrative purposes only; actual mission range will vary according to flight profile and weapon loading.

b US designations are used in this column for Russian ICBMs and SLBMs.

c The SA-10 Grumble may have some capability against some ballistic missiles. Only a third of 1900 deployed SA-10s are counted as nuclear.

d Figure includes warheads for all the land-based and naval aircraft, respectively.

Sources: US Department of State, START I Treaty Memoranda of Understanding (MOU), 1990 through January 2006; US Air Force, National Air and Space Intelligence Center (NASIC), *Ballistic and Cruise Missile Threat* (NAIC: Wright-Patterson Air Force Base, Ohio, August 2003), URL <http://www.nukestrat.com/us/afn/NAIC2003rev.pdf>); US Central Intelligence Agency, National Intelligence Council, 'Foreign missile developments and the ballistic missile threat through 2015' (unclassified summary), Dec. 2001, URL <http://www.cia.gov/nic/pubs/other_products/Unclassifiedballisticmissilefinal.pdf>; US Department of Defense, *Proliferation: Threat and Response,* Jan. 2001; US Foreign Broadcast Information Service (FBIS), various issues; 'Russia: General Nuclear Weapons Developments', Nuclear Threat Initiative/Monterey Institute's Center for Nonproliferation Studies, URL <http://www.nti.org/db/nisprofs/russia/weapons/gendevs.htm>; Russianforces.org; International Institute for Strategic Studies, *The Military Balance 2004–2005* (Routledge: London, 2004); Cochran, T. B. et al., *Nuclear Weapons Databook Volume IV: Soviet Nuclear* Weapons (Harper & Row: New York, N.Y., 1989); *Proceedings*, US Naval Institute, various issues; 'NRDC Nuclear Notebook', *Bulletin of the Atomic Scientists*, various issues; and Authors' estimates.

heads.[47] Apart from commercial launches, in 2005 the Russian Navy conducted two launches of this missile. On 30 September the *Svyatoi Georgii Pobedonosets* launched an SS-N-18 from a submerged position in the Okhotsk Sea. All three dummy warheads successfully hit the target at the Chizha test range in north-western Russia. On 8 October an SS-N-18 was successfully launched in the Barents Sea from the *Borisoglebsk* Delta III submarine.[48] This submarine had experienced a widely reported launch failure during a strategic forces exercise in 2004 observed by President Putin.

The three-stage SS-N-23 Skiff (RSM-54) missile is a successor to the SS-N-18 and was first test-launched in 1983. The current version of the missile, which carries four warheads, is deployed on Delta IV SSBNs.[49] As reported in September 2005, the missile underwent a modernization programme in 1996–2002, which included the development of an improved warhead.[50] There were three successful test-launches of modernized SS-N-23s from a Delta IV submarine, *Yekaterinburg,* in the Barents Sea on 29 June 2004, 8 September 2004 and 17 August 2005. In all of the tests the warheads reportedly hit their targets at the Kura test range on the Kamchatka peninsula.[51]

[47] Lennox (note 23), p. 147.

[48] Safronov, I., '"Svyatoi Georgii Pobedonosets" reabilitiroval "Volnu"' ['Svyatoi Georgii Pobedonosets' rehabilitated 'Volna'], *Kommersant*, 1 Oct. 2005; and 'Volna SLBM hits target in Kamchatka', RIA Novosti, 8 Oct. 2005.

[49] Lennox (note 23), p. 153; and US Department of State, START I Treaty Memorandum of Understanding (MOU), July 2005.

[50] Kontareva, E., 'Ofitsial'no. Gosudarstvo vysoko otsenilo vklad yuzhnoural'tsev v modernizatsiyu odnogo iz luchshikh strategicheskikh kompleksov Voenno-Morskogo Flota Rossii' [Officially. The state highly appreciated the contribution of the people of South Urals to modernization of the one of the best strategic missile complexes of the Russian Navy], Ural-Press-Inform News Agency, 23 Sep. 2005, URL <http://uralpress.ru/show_article_print.php?id=82055>.

[51] 'Ballistic missile successfully fired from a nuclear-powered submarine of the Russian Northern Fleet', ITAR-TASS, 29 June 2004; 'Russian submarines launch ballistic missiles', RIA Novosti, 8 Sep.

As noted above, Russia is developing a new three-stage, solid-propellant SLBM, the SS-NX-30 Bulava (R-30). The missile reportedly will have a maximum range of 8300 km. Russia has declared that the Baluva will be counted under START I rules as carrying six warheads.[52] The first tests of the Bulava—unpowered 'pop-up' launches—were conducted from the *Dmitrii Donskoi* Typhoon Class submarine in December 2003 and September 2004.[53] In 2005 the Russian Navy conducted two flight-tests of the Bulava. On 27 September the *Dmitrii Donskoi* launched a Bulava from a submerged position in the White Sea.[54] The missile carried a single warhead that hit a designated target at the Kura range in Kamchatka.[55] On 21 December the *Dmitrii Donskoi* successfully launched another Bulava while the submarine was moving under water. Following this, Defence Minister Sergey Ivanov stated that Bulava tests would continue in 2006 and the missile would be deployed by 2008.[56]

Strategic aviation

Russian strategic aviation units form the 37th Air Army of the Supreme High Command (Strategic) of the Russian Air Force, which includes two heavy bomber divisions of Tu-160 and Tu-95MS aircraft. The 22nd Guards Heavy Bomber Division is based in Engels, Saratov oblast, and the 326th Heavy Bomber Division is based in Ukrainka, Khabarovsk kray. The 37th Air Army also includes four divisions of Tu-22M3 Backfire C bombers.[57] The Russian Ministry of Defence announced in November 2004 that it planned to have a total of 75 Tu-160 Blackjack and Tu-95MS Bear bombers in service by 2010.[58]

The composition of the Russian strategic bomber fleet did not change in 2005, despite declared plans to deliver two Tu-160 Blackjack long-range bombers during the year.[59] On 30 December 2005 the Air Force accepted delivery of the 15th Tu-160 bomber, which was returning to active service after modernization.[60] The aircraft will be deployed by March 2006.[61] The other 14 deployed Tu-160 bombers will undergo

---

2004; and Gordeeva, E., 'Dostizheniye tselei' [Achievement of goals], *Vremya Novostey*, 18 Aug. 2005, URL <http://www.vremya.ru/2005/150/4/132369.html>.

[52] US Department of State, START I Treaty Memorandum of Understanding (MOU), Jan. 2006.

[53] 'First test launch of Bulava missile to be held late this year', ITAR-TASS, 28 Mar. 2005.

[54] 'Defense minister praises Bulava missile system tests', RIA Novosti, 28 Sep. 2005, URL <http://en.rian.ru/russia/20050928/41538033.html>.

[55] 'Update: Strategic ballistic missile launched in White Sea—defense ministry', RIA Novosti, 27 Sep. 2005, URL <http://en.rian.ru/russia/20050927/41525719.html>.

[56] 'Bulava missile launch successful—defense minister', RIA Novosti, 21 Dec. 2005, URL <http://en.rian.ru/russia/20051221/42609288.html>.

[57] 'Strategic Aviation', Russian Nuclear Forces Project, 2 Nov. 2005, URL <http://www.russianforces.org/eng/aviation/>; and Khudoleev, V., '37-ya derzhit kurs' [37th Army is following the course], *Krasnaya Zvezda*, 23 Dec. 2005, URL <http://www.redstar.ru/2005/12/23_12/1_02.html>.

[58] 'Mnogoletnie plany Minoborony' [Long-term plans of the defence ministry], *Kommersant*, 18 Nov. 2004, p. 3.

[59] Kristensen and Kile (note 1), pp. 586, 588.

[60] Khudoleev (note 57).

[61] 'Modernizirovannyi strategicheskii bombardirovshchik Tu-160 v kontse dekabrya byl prinyat na vooruzheniye VVS RF' [Modernized strategic bomber Tu-160 was added to the arsenal of the Russian Air Force in the end of December], ARMS-TASS, 17 Jan. 2006, URL <http://armstass.su/?page=article&aid=22369&cid=25>; and 'Dva samoleta v tri goda' [Two airplanes in three years], *Izvestia*, 17 Jan. 2006, URL <http://izvestia.ru/armia2/article3054737>.

similar modernization in the future.[62] The 2006 State Defence Order allocates funds to pay for one new Tu-160.[63] According to the Commander of the 37th Air Army, Major General Igor Khvorov, this will be a modernized bomber with new weapon systems and 'radio-electronic equipment'. It is scheduled to enter active service by the end of 2006.

In 2005 Russian strategic aviation units participated in a number of military exercises. These included manoeuvres with eight countries of the Commonwealth of Independent States in April, manoeuvres with China ('Peace Mission 2005') in August and a live-fire exercise of Tu-160 Blackjack bombers, also in August.[64] In the last exercise, four ALCMs were test-fired in the presence of President Putin and hit their targets at the Pemboy firing range near Vorkuta, in northern Russia. The type of the missiles that were fired was not disclosed, but they are believed to have been the nuclear-capable AS-15B Kent-B and the Raduga Kh-555 long-range conventional cruise missile.[65] Russia is planning to test-fire at least 10 ALCMs in 2006.[66]

IV. British nuclear forces

The UK possesses an arsenal of about 185 warheads for use by a fleet of four Vanguard Class Trident SSBNs. It leases a total of 58 Trident II (D-5) SLBMs, including spares, from the US Navy. Under normal circumstances one British SSBN will be on patrol, carrying up to 48 warheads on 16 D-5 missiles. The second and third SSBNs can be put to sea fairly rapidly, with similar loadings, while the fourth would take longer because of its cycle of extensive overhaul and maintenance. With the end of the cold war, the SSBN on patrol is maintained at a level of reduced readiness with a 'notice to fire' measured in days, and its missiles are de-targeted. There are reports that some patrol coordination takes place between the UK and France.

The first British Trident submarine, HMS *Vanguard*, entered service in 1994. In December 2004 it emerged from the Devonport Naval Base after undergoing a three-year Long Overhaul Period (Refuel). On 10 October 2005 *Vanguard* successfully launched a D-5 SLBM in the final phase of its Demonstration and Shakedown Operations (DSAO).[67] The Ministry of Defence did not specify when the vessel would resume operational patrols. In January 2005, HMS *Victorious* arrived at the Devonport Naval Base for a major refit, including a refuelling of its nuclear reactor. This meant that for most of 2005 only two SSBNs in the fleet—*Vigilant* and *Vengeance*—were available for operational deployment.

---

[62] Pulin, G., 'Nam otvoditsya osnovnaya rol' v politike uprezhdeniya' [We are assigned to play a major role in the policy of pre-emption], *Voenno-Promyshlennyi Kur'ier*, 15 Feb. 2006, URL <http://www.vpk-news.ru/article.asp?pr_sign=archive.2006.122.articles.names_01>.

[63] 'Fradkov distributes defense order', *Kommersant*, 1 Dec. 2005, URL <http://www.kommersant.com/doc.asp?idr=527&id=631438>.

[64] 'CIS air defense practiced on Russia's missile carriers', *Kommersant*, 6 Apr. 2005, URL <http://www.kommersant.com/doc.asp?id=560866>; 'First China–Russia war games begin', *The Guardian*, 18 Aug. 2005, URL <http://www.guardian.co.uk/russia/article/0,,1551833,00.html>; and 'Putin takes to the skies "like in a dream"', RIA Novosti, 17 Aug. 2005, URL <http://en.rian.ru/russia/20050817/41169637.html>.

[65] 'President Putin flies a cruise-missile sortie', *Jane's Missiles & Rockets*, vol. 9, no. 10 (Oct. 2005), p. 11.

[66] Khudoleev (note 57).

[67] 'Vanguard prepares to rejoin UK Royal Navy Trident fleet', *Jane's Missiles & Rockets*, vol. 9, no. 12 (Dec. 2005), pp. 1–2.

Table 13A.4. British nuclear forces, January 2006

Type	Designation	No. deployed	Year first deployed	Range (km)[a]	Warheads x yield	Warheads in stockpile
SLBMs						
D-5	Trident II	48	1994	>7 400	1–3 x 100 kt	185[b]

[a] Aircraft range is for illustrative purposes only; actual mission range will vary according to flight profile and weapon loading.

[b] Fewer than 200 warheads are operationally available, *c.* 144 to arm 48 missiles on 3 of 4 SSBNs. The operational stockpile may consist of 185 warheads. Only 1 boat is on patrol at any time, with no more than 48 warheads.

Sources: British Ministry of Defence (MOD), Press releases and the MOD website, URL <http://www.mod.uk/issues/sdr/index.htm>; British MOD, *Strategic Defence Review* (MOD: London, July 1998); British House of Commons, *Parliamentary Debates (Hansard)*; Ormond, D., 'Nuclear deterrence in a changing world: the view from a UK perspective', *RUSI Journal*, June 1996, pp. 15–22; Norris, R. S. et al., *Nuclear Weapons Databook, vol. 5: British, French, and Chinese Nuclear Weapons* (Westview: Boulder, Colo., 1994), p. 9; 'NRDC Nuclear Notebook', *Bulletin of the Atomic Scientists*, various issues; and Authors' estimate.

The four Vanguard Class SSBNs will operate for almost two decades before their nominal retirement date. However, owing to the lengthy procurement process required for complex weapon systems (15 years in the case of the Trident system), Secretary of State for Defence John Reid told the House of Commons in July 2005 that 'decisions on any replacement of the United Kingdom's are likely to be necessary in the lifetime of the current Parliament, which will of course last some years'.[68] Reid later told the Commons Defence Committee that the government intended to retain 'Britain's minimum nuclear deterrent' for an unspecified period, pointing out that the UK 'has always maintained that as long as some other nuclear state which is a potential threat has nuclear weapons we will retain ours'.[69] Critics of the government, including some Labour Party parliamentarians, alleged that the decision had already been made to replace the Trident with a new generation of nuclear weapons— at an estimated cost of up to £20 billion ($35 billion)—without a public debate on whether the UK still needed a nuclear deterrent.[70]

The Ministry of Defence has confirmed that it is considering a range of options for replacing the Trident. These include options involving land- and air-based delivery systems as well as submarines.[71] In July 2005 the MOD announced a new, three-year,

---

[68] Reid, J., Secretary of State for Defence, Oral answers, 4 July 2005, House of Commons, *Hansard* C5, URL <http://www.publications.parliament.uk/pa/cm200506/cmhansrd/cm050704/debtext/50704-02.htm#50704-02_sbhd0>.

[69] Reid, J., Secretary of State for Defence, Oral evidence before the Select Committee on Defence, 1 Nov. 2005; as reproduced in House of Commons Paper 556-i (Session 2005-06), 17 Jan. 2006, URL <http://www.publications.parliament.uk/pa/cm200506/cmselect/cmdfence/556/5110101.htm>.

[70] McSmith, A., 'Revealed: Blair's nuclear bombshell', *The Independent* (Internet edn), 18 Oct. 2005, URL <http://news.independent.co.uk/uk/politics/article320124.ece>; and 'Labour MPs debate Trident scheme', BBC News Online, 31 Oct. 2005, URL <http://news.bbc.co.uk/1/4392050.stm>.

[71] Kirkup, J., 'UK nuclear defence up in the air', *The Scotsman* (Internet edn), 29 Oct. 2005, URL <http://news.scotsman.com/uk.cfm?id=2164822005>. For an overview of the options for a future nuclear deterrent see Willet, L., 'Questions for the debate on the future of the UK strategic deterrent', *RUSI Journal*, vol. 150, no. 6 (Dec. 2005), pp. 50–57.

£1.05 billion (€1.5 billion) investment to upgrade the Trident missile warhead facilities at the Atomic Weapons Establishment (AWE) at Aldermaston and Burghfield. The purpose of the investment is to ensure that the 'existing Trident warhead stockpile is reliable and safe' and can be 'maintained throughout its intended in-service life'.[72] MOD officials have denied reports that the facilities might be used to develop new nuclear weapons.

V. French nuclear forces

France continues to modernize and upgrade its nuclear forces. It maintains an operational arsenal of an estimated 348 nuclear warheads for delivery by SLBMs, carrier-based strike aircraft and land-based aircraft. In 2005 France allocated approximately €3 billion, or 7 per cent of its overall defence budget, to the nuclear forces.

The backbone of France's nuclear deterrent is the Force Océanique Stratégique, which consists of a fleet of four operational SSBNs of two classes: three of the new Triomphant Class SSBNs; and one L'Inflexible Class (formerly Redoubtable Class) SSBN. The remaining L'Inflexible Class SSBN will be retired when the fourth and final vessel of the Triomphant Class, Le Terrible, enters service in 2010. The French Navy's four operational SSBNs are each armed with 16 Aérospatiale M45 missiles carrying up to 6 TN-75 warheads. In 2010–15, beginning with the Le Terrible, three Triomphant Class SSBNs will be retrofitted with the M51.1 SLBM. The new missile will have a payload of six warheads and a maximum range of 8000 km.[73] Its increased range compared to the M45 will permit French SSBNs to significantly expand their patrol zones. The French Navy plans to take delivery of the improved M51.2 missile, armed with the new Tête Nucléaire Océanique (TNO) warhead, from 2015.

The air component of the French nuclear force consist of two types of aircraft: approximately 60 Mirage 2000Ns, which equip the three Air Force squadrons currently with nuclear strike roles; and about 24 Super Étendard aircraft deployed on the aircraft carrier Charles de Gaulle. Both types of aircraft carry the Air-Sol Moyenne Portée (ASMP) cruise missile. It is estimated that France has about 60 operational ASMPs, but additional missiles may be in inactive storage. A new follow-on cruise missile, designated the ASMP-A, is under development and will replace the ASMP on Mirage 2000N aircraft in 2007. Beginning in 2008, the missile will also be integrated with an unspecified number of Rafale aircraft in the Air Force and the Navy.

There has been a gradual evolution in France's nuclear doctrine since the end of the cold war. Although French officials continue to reject a no-first-use posture, they have emphasized the need for greater flexibility in meeting a widening range of plausible deterrence scenarios. Several reports in 2003 suggested that President Jacques Chirac had approved changes in the country's nuclear doctrine, similar to those in the USA, to permit the targeting of 'rogue states' armed with nuclear, biolog-

---

[72] Reid, J., Secretary of State for Defence, Oral answers, 19 July 2005, House of Commons, Hansard C60WS, URL <http://www.publications.parliament.uk/pa/cm200506/cmhansrd/cm050719/wmstext/507 19m03.htm>.

[73] 'France's nuclear-powered Le Vigilant prepares for patrol', Jane's Missiles & Rockets, vol. 9, no. 2 (Feb. 2005), p. 5.

Table 13A.5. French nuclear forces, January 2006

Type	No. deployed	Year first deployed	Range (km)[a]	Warheads x yield	Warheads in stockpile
Land-based aircraft					
Mirage 2000N	60	1988	2 750	1 x 300 kt ASMP	50
Carrier-based aircraft					
Super Étendard	24	1978	650	1 x 300 kt ASMP	10
SLBMs[b]					
M45	48	1996	6 000[c]	6 x 100 kt	288
Total					**348**

[a] Aircraft range is for illustrative purposes only; actual mission range will vary according to flight profile and weapon loading.

[b] The fourth and final Triomphant Class SSBN, *Le Terrible*, will replace *L'Inflexible*, in 2010 with the M51 SLBM.

[c] The range of M45 is listed as only 4000 km in a 2001 report from the National Defence Commission of the National Assembly.

Sources: French National Assembly, 'Bill of Law for the 2003–2008 Military Programme', 2002; French Ministry of Defence, 'Nuclear disarmament and non-proliferation', *Arms Control, Disarmament and Non-Proliferation: French Policy* (La Documentation française: Paris, 2000), chapter 3, pp. 36–56; Norris, R. S. et al., *Nuclear Weapons Databook, Vol. 5: British, French, and Chinese Nuclear Weapons* (Westview: Boulder, Colo., 1994), p. 10; *Air Actualités*, various issues; *Aviation Week & Space Technology*, various issues; 'NRDC Nuclear Notebook', *Bulletin of the Atomic Scientists*, various issues; and Authors' estimates.

ical or chemical weapons and which threatened France's vital interests.[74] However, Chirac denied at the time that that there had been any changes in nuclear doctrine.

On 19 January 2006 Chirac delivered a speech at L'Ile-Longue nuclear submarine base setting out a new rationale for France's *force de frappe* (nuclear deterrent force).[75] In the speech Chirac cited the dangers of regional instability, growing extremism and the proliferation of weapons of mass destruction and said that the country's nuclear deterrent remained the fundamental guarantor of its security. He threatened to retaliate with nuclear weapons against any state found to be supporting terrorism against France or considering the use of weapons of mass destruction. Chirac revealed that French nuclear forces had already been reconfigured to enable them to destroy the 'power centres' of any state which sponsored a terrorist attack against France.[76] This involved *inter alia* reducing the number of nuclear warheads of SLBMs to allow more precisely targeted strikes. He did not say whether France was prepared to resort to pre-emptive nuclear strikes against a country it saw as a threat.

The doctrinal change announced by Chirac was similar to one already undertaken by the UK. In 2002, an addendum to the UK's 1998 Strategic Defence Review (SDR)

---

[74] Tertrais, B., 'Nuclear policy: France stands alone', *Bulletin of the Atomic Scientists*, vol. 60, no. 4 (July/Aug. 2004), pp. 48–55.

[75] 'Speech by Jacques Chirac, President of the French Republic, during his visit to the Strategic Air and Maritime Forces at Landivisiau/L'Ile Longue', 19 Jan. 2006, URL <http://www.elysee.fr/elysee/elysee.fr/anglais/speeches_and_documents/2006/speech_by_jacques_chirac_president_of_the_french_re public_during_his_visit_to_the_stategic_forces.38447.html>.

[76] 'Speech by Jacques Chirac' (note 75).

extended the role of nuclear weapons to include deterring 'leaders of states of concern and terrorist organizations'.[77]

VI. Chinese nuclear forces

In July 2005, the annual report of the US Department of Defense on Chinese military power included an overview of the composition of China's ballistic missile force.[78] This overview and other recent information—most significantly a declaration by the Chinese Foreign Ministry in 2004 that 'China . . . possesses the smallest nuclear arsenal of all the nuclear weapon states[79]—necessitates a reduction in the estimate of the size of China's nuclear forces. It is estimated here that China deploys approximately 130 nuclear warheads for delivery by land-based missiles, sea-based missiles and bombers.[80] Additional warheads are thought to be in storage.

Notwithstanding the change in the estimate for China's nuclear forces, the size of the Chinese warhead stockpile is thought not to have changed significantly for many years. However, the delivery systems for those warheads have changed, with the gradual withdrawal of the old DF-3A (CSS-2) and conversion of some of the newer DF-21s to conventional missions. Moreover, according to US Government assessments, China will soon begin replacing its small force of medium- and intermediate-range ballistic missiles with newer, more survivable, long-range missiles.[81] This includes the DF-31 (Dong Feng, or East Wind), a new solid-propellant, road-mobile ICBM that the US DOD for a number of years has predicted was about to enter service but which the 2005 report stated is still in development. Two modifications of the DF-31, the longer-range DF-31A and the submarine-based Julang-2, are also under development. The deployment of these longer-range, mobile systems is expected to enhance the survivability of the Chinese missile force by enabling the weapons to operate over a larger area. While the DOD is concerned that the new missiles will increase the number of warheads that can reach the USA, the Chinese Government insists that the development is consistent with China's long-standing commitment to a policy of no-first use of nuclear weapons.[82]

The July 2005 DOD report predicted that the future Chinese land-based missile force will eventually consist of modernized, silo-based DF-5A (CSS-4 Mod 2) and road-moble DF-31 and DF-31A ICBMs. In addition, China will maintain a number of nuclear-armed DF-21A MRBMs 'for regional contingencies'.[83] The US intelligence

[77] British Ministry of Defence, *The Strategic Defence Review: A New Chapter*, CM 5566, vol. 1, July 2002, p. 12, URL <http://www.mod.uk/linked_files/SDR_New_Chapter.pdf>.

[78] US Department of Defense, *Annual Report to Congress: The Military Power of the People's Republic of China 2005*, 19 July 2005, URL <http://www.defenselink.mil/news/Jul2005/d20050719 china.pdf>, p. 45.

[79] Ministry of Foreign Affairs of the People's Republic of China, 'Fact Sheet: China: nuclear disarmament and reduction of [sic]', Beijing, 27 Apr. 2004, p. 1, URL <http://www.fmprc.gov.cn/eng/wjb/zzjg/jks/cjjk/2622/t93539.htm>.

[80] Some analysts have argued that only the land-based missile force is operationally deployed, in which case China's operational nuclear arsenal would be as low as *c.* 80 warheads. Lewis, J., 'The ambiguous arsenal', *Bulletin of the Atomic Scientists*, vol. 61, no. 3 (May/June 2005), pp. 52–59.

[81] US Department of Defense (note 78).

[82] Information Office of the State Council of the People's Republic of China, 'China's endeavors for arms control, disarmament and non-proliferation', Beijing, Sep. 2005, URL <http://www.china.com.cn/english/features/book/140320.htm>.

[83] US Department of Defense (note 78), p. 28.

Table 13A.6. Chinese nuclear forces, January 2006

Type	US or NATO designation	No. deployed	Year first deployed	Range (km)^a	Warheads x yield	Warheads in stockpile
Land-based missiles^b						
DF-3A	CSS-2	16	1971	3 100^c	1 x 3.3 Mt	16
DF-4	CSS-3	22	1980	>5 500	1 x 3.3 Mt	22
DF-5A	CSS-4	20	1981	13 000	1 x 4–5 Mt	20
DF-21A	CSS-5	21	1991	2 100^c	1 x 200–300 kt	21
DF-31	CSS-X-10	0	(2006)	~8 000	1 x ?	0
DF-31A	?	0	(2007–09)	~12 000	1 x ?	0
SLBM s						
Julang 1^c	CSS-NX-3	12	1986	>1 000	1 x 200–300 kt	12
Julang 2	?	0	(2008–10)	~8 000	1 x ?	0
Aircraft^d						
Hong-6	B-6	20	1965	3 100	1 x bomb	~20
Attack	(Qian-5, Others?)	?	1972–?	?	1 x bomb	~20
Strategic weapons						*~130*
Non-strategic weapons^e						
Short-range ballistic missiles (DF-15 and DF-11)						?
Total						**~130**^{f}

^{a} Aircraft range is for illustrative purposes only; actual mission range will vary according to flight profile and weapon loading.

^{b} China defines missile ranges as: short-range, <1000 km; medium-range, 1000–3000 km; long-range, 3000–8000 km; and intercontinental range, >8000 km. The range of the DF-3A and the DF-21A may be longer than is normally reported.

^{c} The JL-1 has never been fully operational and the single Xia Class SSBN has never conducted a deterrent patrol.

^{d} A small stockpile of bombs with yields between 10 kt and 3 Mt is thought to exist for delivery by aircraft. Chinese aircraft are not believed to have nuclear weapons delivery as a primary role but as a contingency mission. Figures for aircraft are for nuclear-configured versions only. The table assumes no more than 40 bombs for aircraft.

^{e} The existence of tactical warheads is highly uncertain, but several low-yield nuclear tests in 1970s and US Government statements in the 1980s and 1990s suggest that some tactical warheads may have been developed.

^{f} Additional warheads may be in storage.

Sources: US Department of Defense (DOD), Office of the Secretary of Defense, 'The Military Power of the People's Republic of China,' July 2005; US Air Force, National Air and Space Intelligence Center (NASIC), various documents; US Central Intelligence Agency, 'Foreign Missile Developments and the Ballistic Missile Threat Through 2015' (unclassified summary), Dec. 2001, URL <http://www.cia.gov/nic/pubs/other_products/Unclassifiedballistic missilefinal.pdf>; US DOD, Office of the Secretary of Defense, 'Proliferation: threat and response', Washington, DC, Jan. 2001, URL <http://www.defenselink.mil/pubs/ptr20010110. pdf>; Norris, R. S. et al., *Nuclear Weapons Databook, Vol. 5: British, French, and Chinese Nuclear Weapons* (Westview: Boulder, Colo., 1994); 'NRDC Nuclear Notebook', *Bulletin of the Atomic Scientists*, various issues; and Authors' estimates.

community has stated that China might deploy multiple warheads on its DF-5A (CSS-4) missiles to ensure the effectiveness of its deterrent against missile defence systems, but neither the DF-31 nor its two modifications are thought to be designed to carry multiple warheads.[84]

China has had great difficulty in developing a sea-based nuclear deterrent. The single Type 092 (Xia Class) SSBN, armed with the JL-1 SLBM, is not believed to have achieved full operational capability and, according to US Naval Intelligence, has never conducted a deterrent patrol. A new SSBN, the Type 094, is under construction. Press reports that the submarine had been launched in July 2004 appear to have been premature;[85] the submarine was probably the first unit of the Type 093, a replacement for the Han Class nuclear-powered attack submarine. The Type 094 is not expected to enter into service before the end of this decade at the earliest.

The missile intended for the Type 094 Class SSBN, a modified DF-31 known as the Julang-2 (JL-2), was successfully test-launched on 16 June 2005 from a submerged submarine in the Pacific Ocean near the Shandong Peninsula.[86] The submarine is believed to have been a modified Golf Class submarine. A previous test in mid-2004 failed. The DOD estimates that JL-2 will have an intercontinental range of about 7500–8000 km and that it will carry a single warhead.[87]

It is thought that China has a small stockpile of nuclear bombs for delivery by aircraft. Between 1965 and 1976, Chinese Hong-5, Hong-6 and Qian-5 aircraft dropped a total of 11 nuclear bombs in nuclear tests at the Lop Nur Test Site. The bombs detonated with yields of 8–4000 kt in four distinct ranges. The US Defense Intelligence Agency estimated in 1984 that 'a small number of the nuclear-capable aircraft probably have nuclear bombs, even though we are unable to identify airfield storage sites',[88] and in 1993 the National Security Council told Congress that China has a 'small stockpile of nuclear bombs'. Although the Chinese Air Force was not believed to have units whose primary purpose was to deliver the bombs, the NSC estimated that 'some units may be tasked for nuclear delivery as a contingency mission'.[89] The candidates for nuclear contingency missions today include the H-6 bomber, and perhaps also a fighter-bomber. China is also developing land-attack cruise missiles that may be for delivery by the H-6. The 2005 DOD report states that, once developed, there 'are no technological bars to placing on these systems a nuclear payload'.[90]

[84] A multiple re-entry vehicle system releases 2 or more RVs along the missile's linear flight path to a single target, which land in a relatively confined area at about the same time. The more sophisticated and flexible MIRV system can manoeuvre multiple RVs to several different release points to provide targeting flexibility against several independent targets over a much wider area and longer period of time.

[85] See, e.g., Gertz, B., 'China tests ballistic missile submarine', *Washington Times* (Internet edn), 3 Dec. 2004, URL <http://www.washingtontimes.com/functions/print.php?StoryID=20041202-115302-2338r>.

[86] 'China test-fires new submarine-launched missile', *Daily Yomiuri* (Internet edn), 18 June 2005, URL <http://www.yomiuri.co.jp/newse/20050618wo42.htm>; and 'China test fires long-range missile from submarine', *Jane's Missiles and Rockets*, vol. 9, no. 8 (Aug. 2005), p. 4.

[87] Norris, R. and Kristensen, H., 'Chinese nuclear forces 2003', *Bulletin of the Atomic Scientists*, vol. 59, no. 6 (Nov./Dec. 2003), URL <http://www.thebulletin.org/print.php?art_ofn=nd03norris>, pp. 77–80,

[88] US Defense Intelligence Agency, 'Nuclear weapons systems in China', DEB-49-84, 24 Apr. 1984, pp. 3–4, partially declassified and released under the US Freedom of Information Act.

[89] US National Security Council, 'Report to Congress on status of China, India and Pakistan nuclear and ballistic missile programs', n.d. [28 July 1993], p. 2, obtained under the US Freedom of Information Act by the Federation of American Scientists.

[90] US Department of Defense (note 78), p. 29.

VI. Indian nuclear forces

India is widely believed to be expanding the size of its nuclear arsenal, although little public information is available about the pace and scale of such an expansion. The conservative estimate presented here is that India possesses about 50 nuclear weapons. The figure is based on India's estimated inventory of 360–530 kg of military plutonium[91] and assessments made by the US intelligence community. The US Defense Intelligence Agency estimated in July 1999 that India possessed 10–15 nuclear weapons.[92]

There is considerable uncertainty in published estimates of the total amount of weapon-grade plutonium that India has produced and, hence, in estimates of the number of nuclear weapons that it could have built. A number of factors contribute to this. First, there are different assessments of the lifetime operating capacity (i.e., of the reliability and efficiency) of the 100-megawatt-thermal (MW(t)) Dhruva reactor and the ageing 40-MW(t) CIRUS reactor, which are dedicated to producing plutonium for military use.[93] Second, it is unclear whether India has used all of its available weapon-grade plutonium to build nuclear weapons, as some analysts have assumed. Finally, there are different views on how to take into account the losses and draw-downs of nuclear material that occur during production, processing and testing.

In addition to these factors, there continues to be a debate about whether non-weapon-grade plutonium (either in the form of reactor-grade plutonium or a mix of isotopes closer to weapon-grade plutonium) was used in one of the nuclear explosive tests carried out by India in May 1998.[94] If the test gave confidence that this material could be used for weapons, India may see the large quantity of plutonium contained in the spent fuel of its unsafeguarded power reactors as being a potential part of its military nuclear programme.

India may be working to increase its capability for producing weapon-grade plutonium.[95] Some critics of the July 2005 Civil Nuclear Cooperation Initiative (CNCI) between India and the United States have argued that, by allowing the sale of nuclear fuel for use in designated Indian civilian installations, the deal would free up India's limited domestic uranium supplies for military purposes.[96] Critics of the deal have also expressed concern about the unwillingness of India's Department of Atomic Energy to place its fast breeder reactor (FBR) programme under International Atomic

---

[91] Albright, D., 'India's military plutonium inventory, end of 2004', 7 May 2005, Institute for Science and International Security (ISIS), *Global Stocks of Nuclear Explosive Materials*, URL <http://www.isis-online.org/global_stocks/end2003/India:_military_plutonium.pdf>. The estimate of 50 warheads assumes that each warhead would require 5 kg of plutonium and that only 250 kg of the military plutonium produced by India has so far been used in assembled nuclear warheads.

[92] US Defense Intelligence Agency, 'A Primer on the Future Threat: The Decades Ahead: 1999–2020', July 1999, p. 38, reproduced in Scarborough, R., *Rumsfeld's War* (Regnery: Washington, DC, 2004), pp. 194–223.

[93] According to the World Nuclear Association, in the 1990s India's nuclear power reactors had some of the world's lowest operating capacity factors. World Nuclear Association, 'India and Pakistan', Information and Issues Brief, Nov. 2002, URL <http://www.world-nuclear.org/info/inf53.htm>.

[94] Perkovich, G., *India's Nuclear Bomb: the Impact on Global Proliferation* (University of California Press: Berkeley, Calif., 1999), pp. 428–31.

[95] Albright (note 91).

[96] Mian, Z. and Ramana, M., 'Feeding the nuclear fire', *Economic and Political Weekly* (Mumbai), 27 Aug. 2005, URL <http://www.geocities.com/m_v_ramana/nucleararticles/indo-us-deal.html>. For further detail on the Indo-US CNCI see appendix 13B in this volume.

Energy Agency safeguards, thereby raising doubt that the programme is for exclusively peaceful purposes.[97]

It is not publicly known whether India has produced highly enriched uranium (HEU) for weapon purposes. India operates two gas centrifuge facilities: a pilot scale plant at the Bhabha Atomic Research Centre (BARC) complex and a larger plant that has been reportedly operating since 1990 at Rattehalli, Karnataka. The primary purpose of the latter facility appears to be to produce HEU for an indigenous nuclear-powered submarine under development.

India's nuclear doctrine, which was published as a draft document in 1999, is 'based on the principle of a minimum credible deterrent and no-first-use'.[98] Additional guidelines, published in January 2003, state that India would use nuclear weapons to deter or retaliate against the use of chemical or biological weapons.[99] There have been no official statements specifying the size of the nuclear stockpile required for 'credible minimum deterrence'. However, according to the Indian MOD it involves 'a mix of land-based, maritime and air capabilities'.[100] Most observers believe that India maintains a recessed nuclear posture, in accordance with its no-first-use policy: that is, nuclear warheads are not mated to their delivery vehicles, and some nuclear warheads may be stored in unassembled form, with the plutonium core kept separately from the non-nuclear ignition components.

Strike aircraft

Aircraft currently constitute the core of India's nuclear strike capabilities. The Indian Air Force (IAF) has reportedly certified the Mirage 2000H Vajra ('Divine Thunder') combat aircraft for delivery of nuclear gravity bombs. The IAF deploys two squadrons of Mirage 2000H aircraft at the Gwalior Air Force Station in north-central India. In August 2005 India and Qatar suspended negotiations over India's purchase of 12 ex-Qatari Mirage 2000-5 aircraft, which could have augmented the IAF's nuclear strike capability. Some of the IAF's four squadrons of Jaguar IS Shamsher ('Sword') combat aircraft may have a nuclear delivery role.[101] Other aircraft that are potentially suitable for a nuclear role are the MiG-27 and the Su-30MKI.

Land-based ballistic missiles

The Prithvi ('Earth') was India's sole operational ballistic missile for many years and the first believed to have a nuclear capability. The Prithvi I (SS-150) is a single-stage, road-mobile ballistic missile capable of delivering a 1000-kg warhead to a maximum

[97] Albright, D. and Basu, S., 'Separating India's military and civilian nuclear facilities', Institute for Science and International Security (ISIS), *ISIS Report*, 16 Dec. 2005, URL <http://www.isis-online.org/publications/southasia/indiannuclearfacilities.pdf>; and 'Atomic Lethargy', *Indian Express* (Internet edn), 23 Jan. 2006, URL <http://www.indianexpress.com/full_story.php? content_id=86424>.

[98] Indian Ministry of External Affairs, *Draft Report of National Security Advisory Board on Indian Nuclear Doctrine*, 17 Aug. 1999, URL <http://meaindia.nic.in//disarmament/dm17Aug99.htm>.

[99] Indian Ministry of External Affairs, 'Cabinet Committee on Security reviews operationalization of India's nuclear doctrine', Press release, 4 Jan. 2003, URL <http://meaindia.nic.in/pressrelease/2003/01/04pr01.htm>.

[100] Indian Ministry of Defence, *Annual Report 2004–05*, URL <http://mod.nic.in/reports/report 05.htm>, p. 14.

[101] Norris, R. and Kristensen, H., 'India's nuclear forces', *Bulletin of the Atomic Scientists*, vol. 61, no. 5 (Sep./ Oct. 2005), pp. 73–75.

Table 13A.7. Indian nuclear forces, January 2006

Type	Range (km)[a]	Payload (kg)	Status
Ballistic missiles			
Prithvi I (P-I)	150	800	Entered service in 1994, widely believed to have a nuclear delivery role. Most recent flight-tests on 19 Mar. and 12 Dec. 2005
Agni I[b]	800	1 000	Inducted into Indian Army service in 2004
Agni II	2 000–2 500[c]	1 000	Inducted into Indian Army service in 2004
Aircraft[d]			
Mirage 2000H Vajra	1 850	6 300	Aircraft has reportedly been certified for delivery of nuclear gravity bomb
Jaguar IS Shamsher	1 400	4 760	Some of 4 squadrons may have nuclear delivery role

[a] Missile payloads may have to be reduced in order to achieve maximum range. Aircraft range is for illustrative purposes only; actual mission range will vary according to flight profile and weapon loading.

[b] The original Agni I, now known as the Agni, was a technology demonstrator programme that ended in 1996.

[c] An upgraded version (Agni III) currently under development may have a range of 3500 km, possibly with a reduced payload.

[d] Other aircraft in the Indian Air Force's inventory which are potentially suitable for a nuclear role are the MiG-27 (Bahadur) and the Su-30MKI. The Su-30MKI has an in-flight refuelling capability with the IL-78 aerial tanker.

Sources: Indian Ministry of Defence, annual reports and press releases; International Institute for Strategic Studies (IISS), *The Military Balance 2004–2005* (IISS: London, 2004); US Air Force, National Air and Space Intelligence Center (NASIC), *Ballistic and Cruise Missile Threat* (NAIC: Wright-Patterson Air Force Base, Ohio, Aug. 2003), URL <http://www.nukestrat.com/us/afn/NAIC2003rev.pdf>; US Central Intelligence Agency, 'Unclassified report to Congress on the acquisition of technology relating to weapons of mass destruction and advanced conventional munitions, 1 January through 30 June 2002', Apr. 2003, URL <http://www.cia.gov/cia/publications/bian/bian_apr_2003.htm>; US National Intelligence Council, 'Foreign missile developments and the ballistic missile threat through 2015' (unclassified summary), Dec. 2001, URL <http://www.cia.gov/nic/pubs/other_ products/Unclassifiedballisticmissilefinal.pdf>; Lennox, D. (ed.), *Jane's Strategic Weapon Systems* (Jane's Information Group, Ltd: Coulsdon, 2004); Bharat Rakshak, Consortium of Indian military websites URL <http://www.bharat-rakshak.com>; Vivek Raghuvanshi, *Defense News*, various articles; and Authors' estimates.

range of 150 km. The missile was first test flown in 1988 and entered into service with the Indian Army in 1994. It is currently deployed with the Army's 333, 444 and 555 Missile Groups. On 19 March and 12 May 2005, India conducted test-launches of Prithvi I missiles at its Integrated Test Range at Chandipur-on-Sea, in the Bay of Bengal, off the coast of the eastern state of Orissa. A number of Prithvi I missiles are widely believed to have been modified to deliver nuclear warheads, although this has never been officially confirmed.

There are two newer versions of the Prithvi missile featuring improved range, accuracy and handling characteristics. The Prithvi II (SS-250), which has entered into service with the Indian Air Force, can carry a 500- to 700-kg warhead to a maximum range of 250 km. It is not believed to have a nuclear role. The Prithvi III (SS-350), which is in development, is a two-stage, solid-fuel missile designed to deliver a 1000-kg warhead to a range of up to 350 km. Its most recent flight-tests took place in January and October 2004.

Indian defence sources indicate that the family of longer-range Agni ('Fire') ballistic missiles, which are designed to provide a short-reaction-time nuclear capability, has largely taken over the Prithvi's nuclear delivery role.[102] The original Agni missile was a technology demonstrator that was test flown several times between 1989 and 1994, up to a range of 1500 km, but never operationally deployed. The short-range Agni I is a single-stage, solid-fuel missile that can deliver a 1000-kg warhead to a maximum range of 700–800 km. The two-stage Agni II can deliver a similar payload to a range of up to 2500 km. The missiles are road and rail mobile, and both can carry nuclear as well as conventional warheads. Following several successful flight-tests in 2004, the Agni I and Agni II were inducted into service with the Indian Army's 334 and 335 Missile Groups, respectively. In May 2005, the missiles were incorporated into India's tri-service Strategic Forces Command. The Defence Research & Development Organization (DRDO) is reportedly planning to upgrade the Agni II's engines and to install decoys along with the warhead to counter defensive systems.[103]

The DRDO is developing a longer-range Agni III intermediate-range ballistic missile with a maximum range of 3500 km. The Agni III continues to experience engineering and systems integration problems, and its maiden flight-test scheduled for 2003 was again postponed in 2005.[104] Indian media reports indicate that because of the ongoing technical problems, the DRDO has decided to increase the range of the Agni II missile, initially by 300 km, as an interim measure.[105]

In 2005 the Indian press reported that the MOD wanted to move beyond the Agni III and proceed with development of an ICBM. The proposed missile reportedly will be a three-stage design, with the first two stages using solid propellant and the third stage using liquid propellant, and will have a range of 9000–12 000 km. It may carry two or three nuclear warheads with yields of 15–20 kt.[106] It is not expected to enter service until after 2015. Western analysts have speculated for some time that India was developing an ICBM, known as the Surya, based on an indigenous space-launch vehicle.[107]

India continues to develop the naval leg of its planned 'triad' of nuclear forces. The Indian Navy is acquiring a rudimentary nuclear capability with the Dhanush ('Bow') ship-based launcher system. The system uses a modified version of the Prithvi II

[102] 'Prithvi SRBM', Bharat Rakshak: consortium of Indian military websites, updated 15 Apr. 2005, URL <http://www.bharat-rakshak.com/MISSILES/Prithvi.html>.

[103] 'DRDO plans to add decoys to Agni IRBM', *Jane's Missiles & Rockets*, vol. 9, no. 12 (Dec. 2005), p. 4.

[104] Pandit, R., 'Glitches delaying Agni III test', *Times of India* (Internet edn), 3 Mar. 2005, URL <http://timesofindia.indiatimes.com/articleshow/1038860.cms>; and 'Agni III to be test fired by end of year', *Hindu* (Internet edn), 30 Mar. 2005, URL <http://www.thehindu.com/2005/03/30/stories/2005 033011851200.htm>.

[105] Dikshit, S., 'Step-up of Agni-II range planned', *The Hindu* (Internet edn), 13 Feb. 2005, URL <http://www.hindu.com/2005/02/13/stories/2005021303540900.htm>.

[106] Madhuprasad, 'India to "soon" develop intercontinental ballistic missile', *Deccan Herald* (Internet edn), 25 Aug. 2005, URL <http://www.deccanherald.com/deccanherald/aug252005/index2032552005 824.asp>.

[107] 'Indian press reports potential for ICBM development', *Jane's Missiles & Rockets*, vol. 9, no. 10 (Oct. 2005), pp. 10–11.

missile, which the MOD has stated will be capable carrying both conventional and nuclear warheads.[108] The DRDO successfully test-fired two missiles using the Dhanush launcher system mounted on a surface ship, INS *Rajput*, off the coast of Orissa on 16 April and 28 December 2005.

India appears to be developing a more advanced sea-based nuclear strike capability in the form of the Sagarika ('Oceanic') SLBM, which has sometimes been reported as being an sea-launched cruise missile (SLCM).[109] According to the US Defense Intelligence Agency, India flight-tested an SLBM for the first time in the spring of 2005.[110] Some press reports suggest that India may intend to deploy nuclear-armed missiles on the Advanced Technology Vessel, a much-delayed nuclear-powered submarine project that began in 1983.[111]

VII. Pakistani nuclear forces

The estimate presented here—that Pakistan possesses approximately 60 nuclear weapons—is a conservative one, based on the size of Pakistan's estimated military inventory of fissile material[112] and on assessments made by the US intelligence community. The US Defense Intelligence Agency estimated in July 1999 that Pakistan had up to 25 nuclear weapons.[113]

Pakistan is believed to be working to increase and diversify its nuclear forces, which are under the control of a National Command Authority that was established by the military government in 2000. In March 2005 President Pervez Musharraf pledged to upgrade the country's nuclear capability, which he said 'was here to stay' and would 'continue to receive the highest national priority'.[114] Pakistani officials have stated that the country 'subscribes to the principle of minimum credible deterrence and opposes nuclear proliferation and an arms race in the region'.[115] However, because of Pakistan's fears of being overrun by India's larger conventional forces in a military conflict, Pakistan has consistently rejected a no-first-use nuclear policy.

[108] Indian Ministry of Defence, 'Dhanush successfully test fired', Press release, New Delhi, 8 Nov. 2004, URL <http://mod.nic.in/pressreleases/content.asp?id=853>.

[109] Norris and Kristensen (note 101).

[110] Maples, M. D., Lieutenant General, US Army, Director, Defense Intelligence Agency, 'Current and projected national security threats to the United States', Statement for the Record to the Senate Armed Services Committee, 28 Feb. 2006, URL <http://www.senate.gov/~armed_services/statemnt/2006/February/Maples%2002-28-06.pdf>, p. 11.

[111] Pandit, R., 'Nuclear sub project gathers steam', *Times of India* (Internet edn), 20 July 2005, URL <http://timesofindia.indiatimes.com/articleshow/msid-1178241,prtpage-1.cms>.

[112] It is assumed that Pakistan's nuclear weapons are of solid core, implosion-type designs requiring 15–20 kg of HEU each, but it is likely that Pakistan has used only part of its inventory of military fissile material in assembled warheads. At the end of 2003 Pakistan's inventory of HEU for military programmes was estimated to be *c.* 1000–1250 kg. Albright, D., 'ISIS estimates of unirradiated fissile material produced in de facto nuclear weapon states, produced in nuclear weapon programs', revised 30 June 2005, Institute for Science and International Security (ISIS), *Global Stocks of Nuclear Explosive Material*, URL <http://www.isis-online.org/global_stocks/end2003/de_facto_nws.pdf>.

[113] US Defense Intelligence Agency (note 92).

[114] Gilani, M., 'Pakistan vows to strengthen nuclear program', Agence France-Presse, 21 Mar. 2005, URL <http://www.defensenews.com/story.php?F=735622&C=asiapac&P=true>.

[115] Shaukat Aziz, Prime Minister of Pakistan, quoted in 'PM warns of arms race in South Asia', *Dawn* (Internet edn), 25 Jan. 2006, URL <http://www.dawn.com/2006/01/25/top3.htm>.

Ballistic missiles

Pakistan will most likely remain dependent on external suppliers for its medium-range ballistic missile programmes in the short and medium terms.[116] The National Defence Complex (NDC), a subsidiary body of the National Engineering and Scientific Commission, and the Kahuta Research Laboratories have vigourous research and development and procurement programmes under way for MRBMs, based on imported missiles and production technology. Pakistan has received considerable technical assistance from China and North Korea in the past. Former Prime Minister Benazir Bhutto acknowledged in July 2004 that Pakistan had purchased missile technology from North Korea but denied that it aided the latter with nuclear technology.[117]

Pakistan has deployed three families of ballistic missiles that may have a nuclear delivery role, and it continues to develop more advanced versions. The Ghaznavi (Hatf-3) ballistic missile was formally inducted into service with the Pakistani Army in 2004. It can deliver a 500-kg payload to a maximum range of 290 km. Its single-stage, solid-propellant design, which can be transported by road on a modified Scud-B wheeled transporter–erector–launcher (TEL), is believed to be a domestically produced copy of the Chinese M-11 missile.

The Shaheen I (Hatf-4), which has been declared to be nuclear-capable, entered into service with the Pakistani Army in 2003. Analysts remain divided over whether the single-stage, solid-fuel Shaheen I is a version of the Chinese M-9 missile or an improved Chinese M-11 missile. It uses the same wheeled TEL as the Ghaznavi and has a range of 600–800 km, depending on the payload. The two-stage Shaheen II (Hatf-6) is believed to use the Shaheen I missile as its second stage and may be able to carry multiple warheads. Its reported range of 2000–3000 km means that it can reach targets across India. On 19 March 2005 Pakistan announced that it had successfully test-fired a Shaheen II ballistic missile. Pakistan said that it had given India prior notice of the test, in accordance with the informal practice that they agreed in 1999. Development flight-tests are expected to continue in 2006.

Pakistani defence officials have stated that the medium-range Ghauri missiles have a nuclear delivery role. The 1500 km-range Ghauri I (Hatf-5) missile and a longer-range variant, the Ghauri II, are based on North Korea's No-dong 1/2 missile technology and reportedly have been developed with extensive design and engineering assistance from North Korea. The Ghauri I was first successfully test-launched in April 1998. Pakistani defence sources indicate that limited production of the Ghauri began in late 2002 and that it entered into service in January 2003, although developmental work was still continuing. A Ghauri II (or Hatf-5A) missile is under development by the NDC and the KRL and will feature improved propellants and a new motor assembly. The status of the programme is unclear. Pakistan is also reportedly developing a Ghauri III missile with a design range of 3500 km, which would make it the longest-range ballistic missile in the country's inventory. In May 2004 Pakistani officials indicated that the first test-launch of the Ghauri III would be conducted in the near future; however, the test had not taken place by the end of 2005. Some ana-

---

[116] For a description of Pakistan's missile design and production capabilities see Kampani, G., 'Pakistan profile: missile overview', Nuclear Threat Initiative, Country Profiles, updated Feb. 2005, URL <http://www.nti.org/e_research/profiles/Pakistan/Missile/index_3066.html>.

[117] Takeishi, E., 'Bhutto: we bought missile technology', *Asahi Shimbun* (Internet edn), 19 July 2004, URL <http://www.asahi.com/english/world/TKY200407190155.html>.

Table 13A.8. Pakistani nuclear forces, January 2006

Type	Range (km)[a]	Payload (kg)	Status
Aircraft			
F-16A/B	1 600	4 500	32 aircraft, deployed in 3 squadrons; most likely aircraft to have a nuclear delivery role
Ballistic missiles			
Ghaznavi (Hatf-3)	290	500	Entered service with Pakistani Army in 2004. Believed to be a copy of M-11 missile acquired from China in 1990s
Shaheen I (Hatf-4)	600–800	750–1 000	Entered service with Pakistani Army in 2003
Ghauri I (Hatf-5)	1 200	700–1 000	Entered service with Pakistani Army in 2003

[a] Missile payloads may have to be reduced in order to achieve maximum range. Aircraft range is for illustrative purposes only; actual mission range will vary according to flight profile and weapon loading.

Sources: International Institute for Strategic Studies, *The Military Balance 2004–2005* (Routledge: London, 2004); US Air Force, National Air and Space Intelligence Center (NASIC), *Ballistic and Cruise Missile Threat* (NAIC: Wright-Patterson Air Force Base, Ohio, Aug. 2003), URL <http://www.nukestrat.com/us/afn/NAIC2003rev.pdf>; US Central Intelligence Agency, *Unclassified Report to Congress on the Acquisition of Technology Relating to Weapons of Mass Destruction and Advanced Conventional Munitions*, 1 January through 30 June 2002', Apr. 2003, URL <http://www.cia.gov/cia/publications/bian/bian_apr_2003.htm>; US Central Intelligence Agency, National Intelligence Council, 'Foreign missile developments and the ballistic missile threat through 2015' (unclassified summary), Dec. 2001, URL <http://www.cia.gov/nic/pubs/other_products/Unclassified ballisticmissilefinal.pdf; 'NRDC Nuclear Notebook', *Bulletin of the Atomic Scientists*, various issues; and Authors' estimates.

lysts have speculated that the Ghauri III may either be a North Korean Taepodong missile or draw extensively on components and technologies from the latter programme.[118]

On 11 August 2005 Pakistan carried out the first test-flight of a ground-launched cruise missile, designated the Babur (Hatf-7), at a new test range in Baluchistan.[119] Pakistani officials indicated that the 500-km range cruise missile was capable of carrying a nuclear warhead, although it has not been confirmed that the Babur will have a nuclear role.

---

[118] Kampani (note 116).

[119] Sharif, A., 'Pakistan test-fires its first cruise missile', *Dawn* (Internet edn), 12 Aug. 2005, URL <http://www.dawn.com/2005/08/12/top2.htm>.

Strike aircraft

The aircraft of the Pakistani Air Force that is most likely to be used in the nuclear weapon delivery role is the F-16. Other aircraft, such as the Mirage V or the Chinese-produced A-5, could also be used.

Pakistan currently maintains 32 F-16s in service, deployed in 3 squadrons. In 1988–89 Pakistan had contracted with the USA to buy 71 F-16s to augment its existing inventory of 40 F-16A/B aircraft. However, in October 1990 the US Government announced that it had embargoed any further deliveries in accordance with the Pressler Amendment.[120] As a result, only 28 of the 71 aircraft were ever built and none was delivered.

On 26 March 2005, the Bush Administration announced that it was notifying Congress of plans to sell 75 F-16s to Pakistan.[121] US officials said that the deal, which was intended to reward Pakistan for its cooperation in the war on terrorism, would not affect the military balance in the region—in part because India would probably proceed with its own purchase of advanced aircraft, either from the USA or from another supplier.[122] In August 2005 the Pakistani Air Force's Deputy Chief of Air Staff (Operations), Air Vice Marshal Shehzad Aslam Chaudary, said that the USA had offered to give Pakistan two F-16 aircraft as a goodwill gesture; they arrived in Pakistan before the end of the year. He added that the aircraft were not part of the deal to purchase 75 F-16s from the USA.[123] In November 2005 Pakistan announced that it would postpone the purchase in order to make available more financial resources to provide relief to victims of the previous month's devastating earthquake.[124]

VIII. Israeli nuclear forces

The size of the Israeli nuclear weapon stockpile is unknown but is widely suggested to contain 100–200 warheads. The Institute for Science and International Security estimated in 2004 that Israel possessed some 0.56 tonnes of military plutonium,[125] or the equivalent of about 110 warheads, each containing 5 kg of plutonium. Only part of the plutonium may have been used, however, and the US Defense Intelligence Agency estimated in 1999 that Israel had assembled 60–80 nuclear warheads.[126] Many analysts believe that Israel has a recessed nuclear arsenal (i.e., one that is stored

---

[120] Approved by the US Congress in 1984, the Pressler Amendment barred military sales to foreign countries unless the president could certify that the country was not pursuing the acquisition of nuclear weapons.

[121] Baker, P., 'Bush: US to sell F-16s to Pakistan', *Washington Post* (Internet edn), 25 Mar. 2005, URL <http://www.washingtonpost.com/wp-dyn/articles/A800-2005Mar25.html>.

[122] On international arms transfers see chapter 10 in this volume.

[123] 'F-16 deal update', PakistaniDefence.com, Aug. 2005, URL <http://www.pakistanidefence.com/news/MonthlyNewsArchive/2005/August2005.htm>.

[124] 'Musharraf postpones F-16 purchase to provide more quake relief', Voice of America (VOA) News (Internet edn), 4 Nov. 2005, URL <http://www.voanews.com/english/archive/2005-11/2005-11-04-voa10.cfm?CFID=27784474&CFTOKEN=85289695>.

[125] Albright, D. and Kramer, K., 'Plutonium Watch: tracking plutonium inventories', Institute for Science and International Security, June 2004, URL <http://www.isis-online.org/global_stocks/plutonium_watch2004.html >, p. 5.

[126] US Defense Intelligence Agency (note 92). The DOD predicted that the Israeli stockpile in 2020 would consist of 65–85 weapons, suggesting that the stockpile is not increasing in size.

Table 13A.9. Israeli nuclear forces, January 2006

Type	Range (km)^a	Payload (kg)	Status
Aircraft^b			
F-16A/B/C/D/I Falcon	1 600	5 400	205 aircraft in the inventory; some are believed to be certified for nuclear weapon delivery
Ballistic missiles^c			
Jericho II	1 500–1 800	750–1 000	c. 50 missiles; first deployed in 1990; test-launched 27 June 2001
Submarines			
Dolphin			Rumoured to be equipped with nuclear-capable cruise missiles; denied by Israeli officials

^{a} Missile payloads may have to be reduced in order to achieve maximum range. Aircraft range is for illustrative purposes only; actual mission range will vary according to flight profile and weapon loading.

^{b} Some of Israel's 25 F-15I aircraft may also have a long-range nuclear delivery role.

^{c} The Shavit space launch vehicle, if converted to ballistic missile, could deliver a 775-kg payload a distance of 4000 km. The Jericho I, first deployed in 1973, is no longer thought to be operational.

Sources: Cohen, A., *Israel and the Bomb* (Columbia University Press: New York, N.Y., 1998); Albright, D., Berkhout, F. and Walker, W., SIPRI, *Plutonium and Highly Enriched Uranium 1996: World Inventories, Capabilities and Policies* (Oxford University Press: Oxford, 1997); Lennox, D. (ed.), *Jane's Strategic Weapon Systems* (Jane's Information Group, Ltd: Coulsdon, 2003); Fetter, S., 'Israeli ballistic missile capabilities,' *Physics and Society*, vol. 19, no. 3 (July 1990), pp. 3–4 (see 'Ballistic missile primer' (unpublished) for an updated analysis, URL <http://www.puaf.umd.edu/Fetter/1990-MissilePrimer.pdf>); 'NRDC Nuclear Notebook'. *Bulletin of the Atomic Scientists*. various issues: and Authors' estimates.

but not armed, requiring some preparation before use); if true, the warheads for Israel's purported nuclear weapon delivery systems may not actually be deployed. These delivery systems are believed to be strike aircraft, land-based ballistic missiles and possibly SLCMs. There are also rumours that Isreal may have developed nuclear-capable SLCMs for its Dolphin Class submarines and non-strategic nuclear weapons such as nuclear artillery shells and atomic demolition munitions or landmines.

Appendix 13B. Legal aspects of the Indian–US Civil Nuclear Cooperation Initiative

CHRISTER AHLSTRÖM

I. Introduction

On 18 July 2005 US President George W. Bush and Indian Prime Minister Manmohan Singh launched the Civil Nuclear Cooperation Initiative (CNCI).[1] For the United States, the CNCI was designed to allow US exports of civilian nuclear technology to India, while India, in essence, pledged to prevent the proliferation of nuclear weapons to non-nuclear weapon states. The CNCI was preceded by an agreement on 28 June 2005 between the two countries' defence ministers, which stipulated *inter alia* that India and the USA would 'expand [their] collaboration relating to missile defense'.[2] The two agreements are steps in the development of a strategic partnership between India and the USA that was formally initiated in 2004 in a process called the Next Steps in Strategic Partnership (NSSP).[3] The NSSP is founded on a growing realization in the USA of the geopolitical advantages that would follow from closer ties with India. For India, the main advantage—apart from recognition of what it sees as its status as a 'responsible nuclear weapon power'—is the prospect of technical assistance for its endeavour to increase its production of nuclear energy for the rapidly growing Indian economy.[4]

The declared willingness of the USA to engage with India in the field of civil nuclear technology and missile defence has raised concerns about the impact of this move on the integrity of the nuclear non-proliferation regime. Commentators have also expressed concerns, describing the CNCI as a non-proliferation 'reality check' or a 'sea change' of policy.[5] If India and the USA carry out their declared policy, and if

---

[1] The White House, 'Joint statement between President George W. Bush and Prime Minister Manmohan Singh', News release, Washington, DC, 18 July 2005, URL <http://www.whitehouse.gov/news/releases/2005/07/20050718-6.html>.

[2] Embassy of India, 'New framework for the US–India defense relationship', Press release, Washington, DC, 28 June 2005, para. 4H, URL <http://www.indianembassy.org/press_release/2005/June/31.htm>. On transfers of ballistic missile technologies and the commitments made under the Missile Technology Control Regime see Ahlström, C., 'Arrows for India?—technology transfers for ballistic missile defence and the Missile Technology Control Regime', *Journal of Conflict and Security Law*, vol. 9, no. 1 (spring 2004), pp. 103–25.

[3] See generally Kronstadt, K. A., *US–India Bilateral Agreements in 2005* (US Library of Congress, Congressional Research Service: Washington, DC, 8 Sep. 2005), URL <http://fpc.state.gov/documents/organization/53616.pdf>.

[4] On the recent development of the bilateral relationship see Tellis, A. J., *India as a New Global Power: An Action Agenda for the United States* (Carnegie Endowment for International Peace: Washington, DC, 2005), URL <http://www.carnegieendowment.org/publications/index.cfm?fa=view&id=17079&prog=zgp&proj=zsa>.

[5] See, e.g., Kimball, D. G., 'US–India nuclear cooperation: a reality check', *Arms Control Today*, vol. 35, no. 7 (Sep. 2005), p. 3; and Gormley, D. M. and Scheinman, L., 'Implications of proposed

this prompts other states to enter into such deals, this would signify a major change in the way in which members of the non-proliferation regime engage with non-members. International non-proliferation policy has thus far been directed at denying or restricting transfers of nuclear goods and technologies to those few states that remain outside the nuclear non-proliferation agreements, primarily the 1968 Treaty on the Non-Proliferation of Nuclear Weapons (Non-Proliferation Treaty, NPT).[6] Furthermore, it has been a salient feature of policy on India to avoid taking any measure that could be interpreted as acknowledging that India has de jure status as a nuclear weapon state.

This appendix analyses some of the legal aspects of implementation of the CNCI, if it is approved by the US Congress and in India. Section II describes the main elements of the 18 July Indian–US joint statement as it pertains to cooperation in the nuclear field, followed by a discussion in section III of the implications of their proposed cooperation regarding the obligations assumed by the USA under the NPT. Most commentators have analysed the CNCI from the perspective of policy according to the Guidelines for Nuclear Transfers of the Nuclear Suppliers Group (NSG) rather than the NPT. Section IV discusses how the CNCI would affect the USA's commitments as a participant in the NSG. Implementation of the CNCI would, however, have an impact not only on international obligations and commitments but also on national legislation and policies. Section V discusses the CNCI in the light of Indian and US national legislation on exports of nuclear technology, and section VI presents the conclusions.

II. The 2005 Civil Nuclear Cooperation Initiative

In the 1950s the USA cooperated actively with India in the field of nuclear technology under the Atoms for Peace programme. The USA exported heavy water for the Canadian-supplied Canadian–Indian–US (CIRUS) research reactor and assisted in the construction of the Indian Tarapur Atomic Power Station (TAPS).[7] The detonation by India of a 'peaceful nuclear explosive device' in 1974 resulted in a shift in US policy towards discouraging other states from engaging with India in the nuclear field. In 1998, when India—and Pakistan—conducted a number of nuclear tests, the USA implemented sanctions against India. In 1998 the UN Security Council adopted Resolution 1172, stipulating *inter alia* that all UN member states should be encouraged to 'prevent the export of equipment, materials or technology that could in any way assist programmes in India or Pakistan for nuclear weapons or for ballistic missiles capable of delivering such weapons'.[8]

India–US civil nuclear cooperation', Nuclear Threat Initiative (NTI) Issue Brief, July 2005, URL <http://www.nti.org/e_research/e3_67b.html>. See also Potter, W. C., 'India and the new look of US nonproliferation policy', CNS Research Story, Monterey Institute of International Studies, Center for Nonproliferation Studies (CNS), 25 Aug. 2005, URL <http://cns.miis.edu/pubs/week/050825.htm>.

[6] The Treaty on the Non-Proliferation of Nuclear Weapons was opened for signature on 1 July 1968 and entered into force on 5 Mar. 1970; the text is available in *United Nations Treaty Series*, vol. 729 (1970), p. 161 and at URL <http://www.un.org/Depts/dda/WMD/treaty/>.

[7] For a detailed treatment of US assistance for the development of the Indian nuclear infrastructure see Perkovich, G., *India's Nuclear Bomb: The Impact on Global Proliferation* (University of California Press: Berkley, Calif., 1999); and Abraham, I., *The Making of the Indian Atomic Bomb: Science, Secrecy and the Postcolonial State* (Zed Books Ltd: London, 1998).

[8] UN Security Council Resolution 1172, 6 June 1998, URL <http://www.un.org/documents/scres.htm>, para. 8.

There has recently been a rapprochement between India and the USA. Even before the September 2001 attacks on the United States, there was a new shift in US policy as the USA began to view India as an important ally in South Asia. In 2001 the USA lifted the sanctions it had imposed on India after the 1998 nuclear tests as a consequence of India's support in the fight against terrorism. A more important reason for the current rapprochement may be the growing realization in the USA that India is 'a rising global power' that could act as a counterbalance to an increasingly powerful China.[9] It would seem as if India's significance as a de facto nuclear weapon state is secondary to this strategic consideration.

In 2001 India and the USA also stepped up their bilateral negotiations in several policy areas. This culminated in the announcement in January 2004 of the NSSP initiative,[10] under which the two countries committed themselves to closer cooperation in four areas: civilian nuclear energy, civilian space programmes, high-technology trade and missile defence. The Next Steps in Strategic Partnership programme was 'completed' in July 2005, when President Bush and Prime Minister Singh issued a joint statement that the NSSP had provided the basis for expanding their bilateral activities and commerce in space, civil nuclear energy and dual-use technology.[11] Their cooperation on civil nuclear energy is now to be developed in line with their commitments in the CNCI.

The CNCI joint statement lists the commitments made by both sides. In the document President Bush declared his view that 'as a responsible state with advanced nuclear technology, India should acquire the same benefits and advantages as other such states'. He committed the US Administration to 'work to achieve full civil nuclear energy cooperation with India': it will accordingly 'seek agreement from Congress to adjust US laws and policies, and the United States will work with friends and allies to adjust international regimes to enable full civil nuclear energy cooperation and trade with India, including but not limited to expeditious consideration of fuel supplies for safeguarded nuclear reactors at Tarapur'. The Bush Administration also promised to consult with US partners on India's participation in the International Thermonuclear Experimental Reactor (ITER) consortium and support India's part in the work to develop advanced nuclear reactors.[12]

India, for its part, pledged to 'reciprocally' agree to assume the same 'responsibilities and practices', and thereby acquire the same 'benefits and advantages', as other countries with advanced nuclear technology. These 'responsibilities and practices' are defined in the joint statement as:

identifying and separating civilian and military nuclear facilities and programs in a phased manner and filing a declaration regarding its civilian nuclear facilities with the International Atomic Energy Agency (IAEA); taking a decision to place voluntarily its civilian nuclear facilities under IAEA safeguards; signing and adhering to an Additional Protocol with respect

[9] Burns, R. N. (US Under Secretary for Political Affairs) and Joseph, R. G. (US Under Secretary for Arms Control and International Security), 'The US and India: an emerging entente?', Remarks as prepared for the House International Relations Committee, Washington, DC, 8 Sep. 2005, URL <http://www.state.gov/p/us/rm/2005/52753.htm>.

[10] US Department of State, 'Next Steps in Strategic Partnership with India', Statement by the President, Washington, DC, 12 Jan. 2004, URL <http://www.state.gov/p/sa/rls//pr/28109.htm>.

[11] US Department of State, 'United States and India successfully complete Next Steps in Strategic Partnership', Washington, DC, 18 July 2005, URL <http://www.state.gov/p/sa/rls/fs/2005/49721.htm>.

[12] US Department of State, 'US–India civilian nuclear cooperation', Fact sheet, Office of the Spokesman, Washington, DC, 22 July 2005, URL <http://www.state.gov/r/pa/prs/ps/2005/49969.htm>. On the ITER see URL <http://www.iter.org> and appendix 13C.

to civilian nuclear facilities; continuing India's unilateral moratorium on nuclear testing; working with the United States for the conclusion of a multilateral Fissile Material Cut Off Treaty; refraining from transfer of enrichment and reprocessing technologies to states that do not have them and supporting international efforts to limit their spread; and ensuring that the necessary steps have been taken to secure nuclear materials and technology through comprehensive export control legislation and through harmonization and adherence to Missile Technology Control Regime (MTCR) and Nuclear Suppliers Group (NSG) guidelines.[13]

In the joint statement President Bush 'welcomed' Prime Minister Singh's 'assurance'. They decided to establish a working group 'to undertake on a phased basis in the months ahead the necessary actions mentioned above to fulfill these commitments', and they agreed to review progress towards fulfilment of their commitments during the US President's visit to India in early 2006.

The CNCI thus provides for 'full civil nuclear energy cooperation' between India and the USA in return for a number of commitments related to certain aspects of the nuclear non-proliferation regime. The main thrust of the commitments made by India relates to the identification and separation of civilian and military nuclear facilities and programmes—which would seem to be a sine qua non for civilian nuclear energy cooperation in the first place. India maintains a significant nuclear infrastructure that comprises 15 operating nuclear power reactors, with an additional 8 reactors under construction and another 24 proposed.[14] Furthermore, the country has a large number of facilities that operate on the front-end as well as the back-end of the nuclear fuel cycle.[15] India's nuclear infrastructure has not been developed with a clear separation between military and civilian programmes. Commentators have noted the problems involved in separating the two.

[A]ttempts to separate military and civil nuclear programs in the five internationally acknowledged nuclear weapon states, as defined by the NPT, have been fraught with difficulty. In practice, the effective separation of military and civil nuclear programs has required additional steps that are largely absent from the US/India agreement. . . . India's extensive military and civil nuclear programs are often connected, sharing personnel and infrastructure. In addition, some facilities currently have both a military and civilian purpose.[16]

Concerns have been expressed that the Indian authorities may try to limit the number of facilities and programmes that they will declare as civilian because India's military nuclear programme would rely at least partly on the former for fissile material: 'The prospect that the nuclear bureaucracy in India will seek to minimize the undertakings with respect to international safeguards, and to avoid having to fully separate civil and military activities (*inter alia* for cost considerations of having to build dedicated facilities for the latter alone) suggests that reaching closure on a mutually acceptable arrangement will not be easy'.[17] India's plan to separate civilian and military nuclear facilities has been the subject of bilateral discussions with the

[13] The White House (note 1), p. 2.

[14] See appendix 13C, table 13C.1.

[15] See, e.g., Cirincione, J. with Wolfsthal, J. B. and Rajkumar, M., *Deadly Arsenals: Tracking Weapons of Mass Destruction* (Carnegie Endowment for International Peace: Washington, DC, 2002), pp. 191–205. On the nuclear fuel cycle see appendix 13C.

[16] Albright, D., 'Testimony before the House Committee on International Relations Hearing on the US–India "Global Partnership" and its impact on non-proliferation', Institute for Science and International Security, Washington, DC, 26 Oct. 2005, URL <http://www.isis-online.org/publications/south asia/abrighttestimonyoctober262005usindiadeal.pdf>.

[17] Gormley and Scheinman (note 5).

USA: the intention was to finalize the plan before President Bush's March 2006 visit to India. These discussions have been carried out with the understanding that a credible separation between civilian and military nuclear installations will play a vital role in helping to secure the endorsement of both the participants in the NSG and members of the US Congress of this shift in US policy. Information revealed in early 2006 indicated that there are differences between the USA and India as to the scope of the separation—regarding the number of reactors placed under safeguards and the duration of the safeguards.[18]

After identifying its civilian nuclear facilities India should take a decision to voluntarily place these facilities under IAEA safeguards. India has already concluded five safeguards agreements of the INFCIRC/66 type—safeguards that are item-specific rather than comprehensive.[19] These safeguards agreements typically specify the material, facilities and equipment to be safeguarded, and under them the IAEA is required to ensure that the specified items are not used in a way that would further any military purpose. Under the CNCI India has committed itself to 'sign and adhere to' an Additional Safeguards Protocol with respect to its civilian facilities.[20] Briefly, the safeguards system under the 1997 Additional Protocol includes measures to strengthen the IAEA's access to information, *inter alia* by extending the access of IAEA inspectors under the safeguards mandate to include the detection of clandestine sites. The Protocol is additional to the NPT-type comprehensive ('full-scope') safeguards laid down in INFCIRC/153[21] (see section III below), and for many of its provisions it is presupposed that there is also such a safeguards agreement in place. As a non-party to the NPT, India does not have any safeguards agreements that meet that standard. Furthermore, the safeguards laid down in INFCIRC/153 and INFCIRC/540 could not serve their intended purpose—that is, to verify that a party to the NPT is not acting in contravention of its obligation under the treaty not to develop or acquire nuclear weapons—in this case since India would be permitted under the CNCI to retain a nuclear weapon programme. The task would rather be to retain the rationale of INFCIRC/66-type safeguards—to ensure that certain specified nuclear components and technologies are not used for military purposes.

It should be noted in this context that the IAEA Board of Governors has asked the Director General to negotiate Additional Protocols with those non-parties to the NPT that are prepared to accept measures stipulated in the Model Additional Protocol in

---

[18] 'U.S. says obstacles remain to U.S.–Indian agreement', Nuclear Threat Initiative, Global Security Newswire, 23 Jan. 2006, URL <http://www.nti.org/d_newswire/issues/2006_1_23.html>.

[19] IAEA, The Agency's Safeguards System (1965, as Provisionally Extended in 1966 and 1968), INFCIRC/66/Rev.2, 16 Sep. 1968; this and other IAEA Information Circulars discussed in this appendix are available at URL <http://www.iaea.org/Publications/Documents/Infcircs/index.html>.

[20] In 1997 the IAEA put forward a Model Additional Protocol, in INFCIRC/540, intended to strengthen existing NPT safeguards agreements. IAEA, Model Protocol Additional to the Agreement(s) Between State(s) and the International Atomic Energy Agency for the Application of Safeguards, INFCIRC/540 (Corrected), Sep. 1997.

[21] IAEA, The Structure and Content of Agreements Between the Agency and States Required in Connection with the Treaty on the Non-Proliferation of Nuclear Weapons, INFCIRC/153 (Corrected), June 1972. The term full-scope safeguards refers to safeguards that cover 'all source or special fissionable material in all peaceful nuclear activities within the territory of such State, under its jurisdiction, or carried out under its control anywhere'. The objective of such safeguards is the timely detection of the diversion of significant quantities of nuclear material from peaceful nuclear activities to the manufacture of nuclear weapons or of other nuclear explosive devices or for purposes unknown, and the deterrence of such diversion by the risk of early detection.

pursuance of safeguards effectiveness and efficiency objectives.[22] However, in conformity with the IAEA Statute, each individual Additional Protocol or other legally binding agreement requires the approval of the Board. Bearing in mind India's interest in acquiring the same benefits and advantages as the USA and other countries with advanced nuclear technology, India would probably not be prepared to accept full-scope safeguards of the type applicable to non-nuclear weapon states under the NPT. Rather, India may aim for the 'voluntary-offer' type of safeguards arrangement, similar to those in place for the states recognized as nuclear weapon states under the NPT. In voluntary-offer safeguards, the nuclear weapon state voluntarily offers to submit some or all of its civilian nuclear material and facilities to those safeguards measures that it has identified. These voluntary-offer safeguards agreements generally follow the INFCIRC/153 type of agreement, but they vary in scope. The negotiation of an Additional Protocol between the IAEA and India could become a problem for India since it is difficult to see how the Agency could negotiate such an agreement without considering India's status as a non-nuclear weapon state under the NPT (see section III below). Furthermore, since the conclusion of a voluntary-offer type of agreement with India could be viewed as de jure recognition of its current status as a de facto nuclear weapon state, it cannot be taken for granted that such an agreement would obtain the necessary support in the IAEA Board of Governors. Furthermore, the USA has declared that a voluntary-offer safeguards arrangement would not be acceptable under the terms of the CNCI.[23] Finding a generally acceptable safeguards arrangement with India will be a key issue for the realization of the CNCI but, given the diversity of interests of the actors involved, it is difficult to see how an acceptable arrangement can be devised.

Under the CNCI India pledges to continue its unilateral moratorium on nuclear testing. However, in the light of the Bush Administration's strong reluctance to ratify the 1996 Comprehensive Nuclear Test-Ban Treaty (CTBT), it is no surprise that the CNCI does not commit India to ratify the CTBT.[24] This would seem to mean that India could in the future revoke its unilateral test moratorium. In addition, under the CNCI India is committed to merely work with the USA to conclude a multilateral fissile material cut-off treaty—not to stop its production of fissile material for military purposes. Some observers have noted that the CNCI would not require India to unilaterally respect a moratorium on the production of fissile material in a manner similar to that of the five NPT-defined nuclear weapon states, none of which is believed currently to be involved in the production of fissile material for military purposes.[25] Hence, under the CNCI India is in a position to increase its stocks of fissile material and, consequently, to enlarge its arsenal of nuclear weapons, which some experts believe it is aiming to do.[26]

[22] See the foreword to INFCIRC/540 (Corrected) (note 20).

[23] Prepared remarks by Robert G. Joseph (US Under Secretary of State for Arms Control and International Security), Senate Foreign Relations Committee, Hearing on US–India Civil Nuclear Cooperation Initiative, 2 Nov. 2005, URL <http://www.state.gov/t/us/rm/55968.htm>, p. 9.

[24] Under Article XIV of the CTBT, the treaty will enter into force 180 days after the date of the deposit of the instruments of ratification by all the 44 states listed in its annex 2. India is among those 44 states, and its ratification is consequently necessary for the treaty to enter into force. The 44 states are also listed in annex A in this volume.

[25] Fiorill, J., 'Experts call for conditions on US–India agreement', Global Security Newswire, Nuclear Threat Initiative, 13 Oct. 2005, URL <http://www.nti.org/d_newswire/issues/2005_10_13.html>.

[26] See, e.g., Kile, S. N. and Kristensen, H. M., 'World nuclear forces, 2005', *SIPRI Yearbook 2005: Armaments, Disarmament and International Security* (Oxford University Press: Oxford, 2005), p. 594.

India has also committed itself to support a proposal made by the USA in February 2004 to the NSG—an export control regime in which India is not a participant. This proposal called on the NSG states to limit the transfer of enrichment and reprocessing technology, but it has faced problems in obtaining the necessary support there.[27] In any case, India's record on the non-proliferation of goods and technologies that may be used for the production of nuclear weapons is considered by many to be good, even though two Indian scientists have faced sanctions (they are barred from visiting the USA or dealing with US companies) as a result of US allegations that they provided nuclear information to Iran.[28]

Finally, it is interesting to note that under the CNCI India is not committed to subscribe to the 2002 Hague Code of Conduct against Ballistic Missile Proliferation (HCOC), the only multilateral instrument to ensure responsible policies in the field of ballistic missile non-proliferation.[29] Furthermore, the CNCI is silent on India's position vis-à-vis the most recent US initiative on non-proliferation of weapons of mass destruction, the 2003 Proliferation Security Initiative (PSI).[30]

III. The Non-Proliferation Treaty

The NPT entered into force on 5 March 1970. As of 1 March 2006 there were 189 parties—making it almost universal.[31] The USA was a driving force behind the negotiation of the NPT, and the US Government is one of its three depositaries. While the USA joined the treaty at an early stage, India remains a non-party. Hence, none of the rights or obligations of the NPT apply to India, but some of the USA's obligations under the treaty are relevant to the CNCI.

India's main argument for not joining the NPT is that it is 'discriminatory' because it distinguishes between two types of party: 'nuclear-weapon states' (NWS) and 'non-nuclear-weapon states' (NNWS). The original 'grand bargain' of the treaty can be summarized as follows: the NNWS relinquished their option to develop nuclear weapons in return for the promise of access to civilian nuclear technology as well as a general obligation on the part of the NWS to halt the cold war nuclear arms race and a more general pledge to work for disarmament. According to NPT Article IX, paragraph 3, 'a nuclear-weapon State is one which has manufactured and exploded a nuclear weapon or other nuclear explosive device prior to January 1, 1967'. This temporal delimitation signifies that only five states may have formal NWS status

---

[27] Boese, W., 'No consensus on nuclear supply rules', *Arms Control Today*, vol. 35, no. 7 (Sep. 2005), p. 41, URL <http://www.armscontrol.org/act/2005_09/NoConsensusNukeSupply.asp>.

[28] Lugar, R. G. (Senator), 'Opening statement for hearing on the India nuclear agreement', US Senate Foreign Relations Committee, 2 Nov. 2005, URL <http://lugar.senate.gov/pressapp/record.cfm?id=248133>. See also 'Delhi issues plea on US sanctions', BBC News Online, 1 Oct. 2004, URL <http://news.bbc.co.uk/2/3708250.stm>.

[29] On India's position during the negotiation of the HCOC see, e.g., Ahlström, C., 'Non-proliferation of ballistic missiles: the 2002 Code of Conduct', *SIPRI Yearbook 2003: Armaments, Disarmament and International Security* (Oxford University Press: Oxford, 2003), p. 749. For the list of participants of the HCOC see the glossary in this volume. See also Mallik, A., *Technology and Security in the 21st Century: A Demand-side Perspective* SIPRI Research Report no. 20 (Oxford University Press: Oxford, 2004).

[30] See, e.g., Ahlström, C., 'The Proliferation Security Initiative: international law aspects of the Statement of Interdiction Principles', *SIPRI Yearbook 2005* (note 26), p. 741. For the list of states participating in the PSI see the glossary in this volume.

[31] For lists of the parties to the NPT and the states with safeguards agreements and Additional Safeguards Protocols see annex A in this volume.

under the NPT—China, France, Russia (as main successor to the USSR), the United Kingdom and the United States. Because India did not detonate a nuclear explosive device before 1 January 1967 it would automatically be considered a NNWS upon joining the NPT unless this paragraph of Article IX is amended.

Under Article I of the NPT a NWS assumes a specific obligation not to assist, encourage or induce 'any non-nuclear weapon State' to manufacture or otherwise acquire nuclear weapons or other nuclear explosive devices. The key question here is the meaning of the words 'assist' and 'any'—would 'any' encompass only NNWS *parties* to the NPT, or would it have a broader material field of application so as to encompass *any* NNWS (i.e., any state not meeting the requirements of Article IX, irrespective of that country's participation in the NPT)? If so, could the CNCI be seen as allowing 'assistance' to a NNWS within the context of Article I?

The negotiation history of the NPT demonstrates that the scope of the term 'any NNWS' was not intended to apply *inter partes* only, but also to cover non-parties to the treaty. One of the major preoccupations of the drafters of the NPT was to establish a legal regime that did not contain any loopholes in its main provisions.[32] Earlier drafts of the treaty not only defined what was to be seen as a 'nuclear-weapon state', but also provided a definition of 'non-nuclear-weapon state'. In the US proposal of 21 March 1966, a NNWS was defined as 'any State which is not a "nuclear-weapon State"'.[33] The definition did not include any requirement of participation in the treaty itself. Furthermore, this interpretation is also consistent with the way in which the terms are used in Article III (see below). It should also be noted that legal doctrine is uniform in holding that the term does not only cover parties to the treaty: 'The obligation of nuclear-weapon States not to assist non-nuclear-weapon States applies to all the latter states whether they are Parties to the NPT, or not. ... [A]ny other result would constitute an inducement to non-nuclear-weapon States not to become parties'.[34] Hence there is a legal argument to be made in support of a wide material field of application of Article I and that the provision is not limited *inter partes*.

The next question is whether the nuclear cooperation promised under the CNCI could be seen as having the effect 'in any way to assist' a NNWS and would hence fall under the prohibition in NPT Article I. The drafting record of the NPT indicates that this provision was intended to have a wide scope.[35] Mason Willrich notes that 'any nuclear assistance received by a non-nuclear-weapon state could be subjectively

---

[32] Shaker, M. I., *The Nuclear Non-Proliferation Treaty: Origin and Implementation 1959–1979*, vol. 1 (Oceana Publications, Inc.: New York, N.Y., 1980), pp. 191 ff. Furthermore, it should be noted that UN General Assembly Resolution 2028 (XX), 19 Nov. 1965—laying down the main elements of a draft NPT—established that 'the treaty should be void of any loop-holes which might permit nuclear or non-nuclear Powers to proliferate, directly or indirectly, nuclear weapons in any form'.

[33] American Amendments to the Draft Treaty of 17 August 1965 submitted on 21 March 1966, Article IV, para. b, reprinted in United States Arms Control and Disarmament Agency, *International Negotiations on the Treaty on the Nonproliferation of Nuclear Weapons* (US Government Printing Office: Washington, DC, 1969), p. 140.

[34] Shaker (note 32), p. 257. Mason Willrich, a counsel of the US Arms Control and Disarmament Agency who was involved in the negotiation of the NPT, notes that '[t]he undertaking by nuclear-weapon states not to assist non-nuclear-weapon states under Article I is universal and applies with equal force to all such states, whether or not they are parties to the Treaty. Indeed, any other result would constitute an inducement to non-nuclear-weapon states not to become parties'. Willrich, M., *Non-Proliferation Treaty: Framework for Nuclear Arms Control* (Michie Co.: Charlottesville, Va., 1969), p. 95.

[35] Shaker (note 32), p. 259.

appraised as falling within the range of prohibited activity'.[36] The feature intended to allow such appraisal under the NPT was the application of safeguards under Article III, which would provide a means to 'establish and clarify the peaceful purpose of most international assistance'.[37] Little detailed information is available on the type of cooperation with India envisaged by the USA under the CNCI, other than the 'expeditious consideration of fuel supplies for safeguarded nuclear reactors at Tarapur'.[38] Could this be seen as the provision of assistance under NPT Article I? Some commentators argue that this is the case since the export of nuclear fuel for the Tarapur Atomic Power Station could free up domestic enrichment capacity in India that could be used for the production of fissile material for military purposes.[39] This would be an argument that is familiar to the USA, as it was made a few years ago against the Russian attempts to provide the same power plant with nuclear fuel. It may therefore be concluded that implementation of the CNCI—depending on the nature of the cooperation—may come into conflict with US obligations under NPT Article I. It would also involve Article III: paragraph 2 stipulates that 'Each State Party to the Treaty undertakes not to provide: (a) source or special fissionable material, or (b) equipment or material especially designed or prepared for the processing, use or production of special fissionable material, to any non-nuclear-weapon State for peaceful purposes, unless the source or special fissionable material shall be subject to the safeguards required by this article'. This provision is not particularly specific—what is meant by the terms 'source or special fissionable material' and 'equipment or material especially designed or prepared for the processing, use or production of special fissionable material'? Furthermore, the phrase 'safeguards required by this article' could be read as demanding the type of safeguards that Article III deals with—safeguards to be applied in NNWS under the NPT. The Zangger Committee—another export control regime, formed in 1971—has taken on the task of interpreting the requirements of Article III in relation to exports to non-parties of the NPT. According to the Zangger Committee Guidelines, the exporting state should require that safeguards should be applied 'to the source or special fissionable material in question'.[40] In other words, the safeguards required under this provision have been interpreted to mean safeguards of the INFCIRC/66 type—safeguards covering the *specific* source or special fissionable material exported.

There has, however, been a significant development in this interpretation over the years. During the 1970s and the 1980s it was common for nuclear supplier states party to the NPT, in their domestic legislation on nuclear exports, to demand that the recipient country should have a full-scope safeguards agreement in place as a condition for supply. Such safeguards conform with the safeguards requirements incumbent on NNWS parties to the NPT (cf. Article III, paragraph 1, and INFCIRC/153).[41] The objective of these safeguards is the timely detection of the diversion of signifi-

[36] Willrich (note 34), p. 94.

[37] Willrich (note 34), p. 94.

[38] The White House (note 1), p. 2.

[39] Ruppe, D., 'US deal would aid Indian nuclear weapons, expert says', Global Security Newswire, Nuclear Threat Initiative, 13 Oct. 2005, URL <http://www.nti.org/d_newswire/issues/2005/10/13/5b4a 539b-1a2a-44f4-b53e-a193fde69f6f.html>.

[40] IAEA, Communications of 15 November 1999 received from member States regarding the export of nuclear material and of certain equipment and other material, INFCIRC/209/Rev.2, 9 Mar. 2000.

[41] For a legal analysis of the system of safeguards agreements under the NPT see, e.g., Edwards, D. M., 'International legal aspects of safeguards and the non-proliferation of nuclear weapons', *International and Comparative Law Quarterly*, vol. 33 (1984), pp. 1–21.

cant quantities of nuclear material from peaceful nuclear activities to the manufacture of nuclear weapons or of other nuclear explosive devices or for purposes unknown, and deterrence of such diversion by the risk of early detection.

In 1992 the NSG states adopted a requirement for full-scope safeguards as a condition for supply (see below). More importantly, at the 1995 NPT Review and Extension Conference the parties to the NPT adopted a consensus document on the Principles and Objectives for Nuclear Non-Proliferation and Disarmament. Paragraph 12, under the heading 'Safeguards', states: 'New supply arrangements for the transfer of source and or special fissionable material or equipment or material especially designed or prepared for the processing, use or production of special fissionable material to non-nuclear-weapon States should require, as a necessary precondition, acceptance of IAEA full-scope safeguards and internationally legally binding commitments not to acquire nuclear weapons or other nuclear explosive devices'.[42] The formulation is clear in that, for new supply arrangements, it demands the acceptance of full-scope safeguards as well as internationally legally binding commitments not to acquire nuclear weapons. The 1995 Principles and Objectives document was 'recalled and reaffirmed' by the parties at the 2000 NPT Review Conference.[43]

Since the previous supply arrangements between India and the USA have lapsed, the CNCI should formally be viewed as a new supply arrangement.[44] However, India has not, and will not under the CNCI, accept full-scope safeguards or a legally binding obligation not to acquire nuclear weapons. Does this mean that the USA would be acting against its obligations under the NPT if it were to decide to provide nuclear materials without the required conditions? The answer to this question boils down to the legal nature of the 1995 Principles and Objectives document. Should this be viewed as a political declaration, devoid of normative impact, or as a document expressing an authoritative interpretation of the requirements of NPT Article III, paragraph 2 by the parties to the treaty? In contrast with the guidelines of the Zangger Committee and the NSG—which have been accepted by only some of the states parties to the NPT—the 1995 Principles and Objectives document as well as the Final Declaration of 2000 have been accepted by all parties to the NPT.

It is a recognized principle of international law that a treaty provision may be modified by subsequent agreement or practice, not necessarily by means of a formal amendment.[45] Anthony Aust notes that parties to a treaty may 'subsequently agree on an authoritative interpretation of its terms, and this can amount, in effect, to an amendment'.[46] Article 31, paragraph 3, of the 1969 Vienna Convention on the Law of Treaties states—on the interpretation of treaties—that the following factors shall be taken into account: '(a) any subsequent agreement between the parties regarding the

---

[42] For the Principles and Objectives document, adopted on 11 May 1995, see 'Documents on nuclear arms control and non-proliferation', *SIPRI Yearbook 1996: Armaments, Disarmament and International Security* (Oxford University Press: Oxford, 1996), pp. 591–93.

[43] Final Document, 2000 Review Conference of the Parties to the Treaty on the Non-Proliferation of Nuclear Weapons, vol. I, NPT/CONF.2000/28 (Parts I and II), p. 3.

[44] See McGoldrick, F., Bengelsdorf, H. and Scheinman, L., 'The US–India nuclear deal: taking stock', *Arms Control Today*, vol. 35, no. 8 (Oct. 2005), pp. 6–12.

[45] Sinclair, I. M., *The Vienna Convention on the Law of Treaties*, 2nd edn (Manchester University Press: Manchester, 1984), pp. 106 ff.

[46] Aust, A., *Modern Treaty Law and Practice* (Cambridge University Press: Cambridge, 2000), p. 191. See also Jennings, R. and Watts, A. (eds), *Oppenheim's International Law*, vol. 1, *Peace*, 9th edn (Longman: London, 1996), p. 1254, note 5; and Brownlie, I., *Principles of Public International Law*, 4th edn (Clarendon Press: Oxford, 1990), p. 625.

interpretation of the treaty or the application of its provisions; (*b*) any subsequent practice in the application of the treaty which establishes the agreement of the parties regarding its interpretation; (*c*) any relevant rules of international law applicable in the relations between the parties'.[47] The 1995 Principles and Objectives document could certainly qualify as a 'subsequent agreement'. It is also evident that this document has affected the practice of the parties: states have for the past 10 years shown a consistent pattern of support for the requirement of full-scope safeguards as a condition for supply.[48] Hence, an argument may be made that the provision in NPT Article III should today be interpreted to require full-scope, rather than item-specific, safeguards. This would also imply that implementation of the CNCI would conflict with US obligations under that article.

IV. The Nuclear Suppliers Group and full-scope safeguards as a condition for supply

The Nuclear Suppliers Group was formed in 1974 with the purpose of strengthening the nuclear non-proliferation regime with broader—as regards both substance and participation—multilateral export controls.[49] It is pertinent to note that the event that triggered the formation of the NSG was India's 1974 nuclear test explosion, which demonstrated the risks that could follow from purportedly 'peaceful' uses of nuclear technology. As of 1 January 2006, 45 states (and the European Commission as a permanent observer) participate in the NSG, which operates on the basis of consensus. It is important to note that cooperation in the NSG is not based on a legally binding international agreement:[50] rather, it is through the incorporation of NSG policy recommendations in national legislation that its provisions gain normative force.

In 1978 the NSG Guidelines for Nuclear Transfers were communicated to the IAEA, which subsequently published them in INFCIRC/254.[51] The guidelines state

[47] The Vienna Convention on the Law of Treaties (VCLT) was opened for signature on 23 May 1969 and entered into force on 27 Jan. 1980; it is available in *United Nations Treaty Series*, vol. 1155 (1980), p. 331 and at URL <http://www.un.org/law/ilc/texts/treaties.htm>. The VCLT has no retroactive effect and does not apply to treaties concluded prior to its entry into force (cf. Article 4). However, the International Court of Justice (ICJ) has generally viewed the VCLT as an authoritative point of departure for the assessment of customary international law on the interpretation of treaties. See, e.g., *Territorial Dispute* (Libyan Arab Jamahiriya/Chad), Judgment, *ICJ Reports 1994*, pp. 21–22, §41; *Maritime Delimitation and Territorial Questions between Qatar and Bahrain* (Qatar v Bahrain), Jurisdiction and Admissibility, Judgment, *ICJ Reports 1995*, p. 18, §33; *Oil Platforms* (Islamic Republic of Iran v United States of America), Preliminary Objection, Judgment, *ICJ Reports 1996* (II), p. 812, §23.

[48] Another example is the repeated reference to the document in the NSG itself to the effect that its outreach activities are taking place 'in accordance' with the 1995 document. On Russia's supply of fuel to India in 2001 see section IV below.

[49] On the history of the NSG see IAEA, Communication of 10 May 2005 received from the Government of Sweden on behalf of the participating governments of the Nuclear Suppliers Group, INFCIRC/539/Rev.3, 30 May 2005. For the participants of the NSG and the other export control regimes discussed in this appendix see the glossary and chapter 16 in this volume.

[50] See further Ahlström, C., *The Status of Multilateral Export Control Regimes: An Examination of Legal and Non-legal Agreements in International Cooperation* (Iustus Förlag: Uppsala, 1999); and Gualtieri, D. S., 'The system of non-proliferation export controls', ed. D. Shelton, *Commitment and Compliance: The Role of Non-binding Norms in the International Legal System* (Oxford University Press: Oxford, 2003), p. 467.

[51] IAEA, Communications Received from Certain Member States Regarding Guidelines for the Export of Nuclear Material, Equipment and Technology, INFCIRC/254, Feb. 1978, reprinted in

that suppliers 'should transfer trigger list items only when covered by IAEA safeguards'. There is no requirement for full-scope safeguards—only for safeguards on the items transferred. The revelation of a clandestine nuclear weapon programme in Iraq in 1991 served as a wake-up call for the nuclear non-proliferation regime. It led to a renaissance for the NSG, and at the 1992 plenary meeting the participants decided to implement a policy by which full-scope safeguards would be a condition for supply.[52] The requirement for full-scope safeguards is outlined in Paragraph 4(a) of the guidelines: 'Suppliers should transfer trigger list items or related technology to a non-nuclear-weapon State only when the receiving State has brought into force an agreement with the IAEA requiring the application of safeguards on all source and special fissionable material in its current and future peaceful activities'. In the absence of full-scope safeguards in the recipient state, transfers of controlled items may take place in only two situations: (a) as an exceptional case when the trigger list item is deemed essential for the safe operation of a safeguarded facility, and (b) if the transfer takes place in accordance with agreements and contracts drawn up on or prior to 3 April 1992 (the 'grandfathering clause').

The conclusion of the Model Additional Protocol in 1997 has generated proposals to expand the requirement for full-scope safeguards so as to also require the application of that instrument. As noted above, in February 2004 President Bush made a proposal according to which only states that have signed an Additional Protocol should be allowed to import nuclear equipment. This proposal has been under consideration within the NSG but has not yet been agreed by all members.[53]

It is clear that the civil nuclear cooperation between India and the USA proposed under the CNCI would not be possible to reconcile with the commitment of the USA, as an NSG participant, to insist on full-scope safeguards as a condition for supply. It should also be noted that the exemptions so far recognized would not be applicable to the present situation: there are no bilateral agreements in place between India and the USA that would 'grandfather' the requirement for full-scope safeguards. Invoking the safety exemption clause would also pose serious difficulties, given the reactions of NSG participants (including in particular the USA itself) to the recent experience of Russian transfers to India. In the autumn of 2000 Russia declared its intention to supply nuclear fuel to the TAPS. It is important to note that Russia did not challenge the validity of full-scope safeguards as a condition for supply, but rather argued that the transfer should fall under the safety exemption clause because the delivery of fuel was necessary for the safe operation of the plant. However, the other NSG participants were unconvinced by Russia's position and maintained that the proposed transfer would not be in conformity with Russia's commitments as an NSG participant. In February 2001 Russia nevertheless exported 50 tonnes of low-enriched uranium to India and was heavily criticized by other NSG participants.[54] Because of this criticism, Russia later abstained from further exports of nuclear fuel and power plants to India; instead, it initiated a discussion in the NSG on the possibility of making an

---

International Legal Materials, vol. 17 (1978), p. 220. The most recent version of the NSG Guidelines is reproduced in INFCIRC/254/Rev.7/Part 1, 23 Feb. 2005.

[52] IAEA, Statement on full-scope safeguards, INFCIRC/405, May 1992, reprinted in International Legal Materials, vol. 31 (1992), p. 1253.

[53] Boese (note 27).

[54] E.g., the USA declared that it 'deeply regrets that the Russian Federation has shipped nuclear fuel to the Tarapur power reactors in India in violation of Russia's nonproliferation commitments'. 'US deeply regrets Russian shipment of uranium fuel to India', 16 Feb. 2001, URL <http://www.us embassy.it/file2001_02/alia/a1021910.htm>.

exemption for India from the requirement of full-scope safeguards as a condition for supply.

Paragraph 10 of the NSG Guidelines for Nuclear Transfers contains a 'non-proliferation principle' which states that, 'notwithstanding other provisions of these Guidelines, suppliers should authorize transfer of items or related technology identified in the trigger list only when they are satisfied that the transfers would not contribute to the proliferation of nuclear weapons or other nuclear explosive devices or be diverted to acts of nuclear terrorism'. Given the criticism that the US nuclear cooperation with India—even with a separation between military and civilian facilities—could be seen as providing assistance to the Indian nuclear weapon programme, it is difficult to see how the USA could act in accordance with this commitment under the terms of the CNCI.

Hence, implementation of the CNCI would conflict with the USA's commitments under paragraph 4 of the NSG Guidelines and possibly also with the 'non-proliferation' principle in paragraph 10. In the 2005 Indian–US joint statement, the USA states that it will work to 'adjust international regimes' in order to allow for full civil nuclear cooperation with India. This would seem to indicate that the USA will work to amend provisions of the NSG Guidelines, but it is by no means certain that it would receive consensus support. However, recent information suggests that the USA is not seeking to bring about amendments: in November 2005, in a statement before the Senate Foreign Relations Committee, Robert G. Joseph, Under Secretary of State for Arms Control and International Security, clarified how the USA proposes to accommodate the CNCI with US commitments under the NSG.

We [have] stressed our desire that the NSG maintain its effectiveness, and emphasized that we do not intend to undercut this important nonproliferation policy tool. For this reason, *the U.S. proposal neither seeks to alter the decisionmaking procedures of the NSG nor amend the current full-scope safeguards requirement in the NSG Guidelines*. Rather, the United States proposes that *the NSG take a policy decision to treat India as an exceptional case*, given its energy needs, its nuclear nonproliferation record, and the nonproliferation commitments it has now undertaken. *We do not advocate similar treatment for others outside the NPT regime.*[55]

The USA aims to have a consensus decision in the NSG to this effect by the 2006 Plenary Meeting.

The US proposal was discussed at the October 2005 NSG Consultative Group meeting, and apparently acquired some support from France, the UK and Russia. Other participating governments, notably Austria, Sweden and Switzerland, expressed strong reservations.[56] Many other participants adopted a wait-and-see approach.[57]

The approach not to amend the NSG Guidelines and to take a policy decision to treat India as a special case has the advantage of being a quick solution. It would still, however, require consensus among the NSG states and, as noted above, at least a few participants remain unconvinced by the US proposal.[58] Moreover, the proposal

---

[55] Prepared remarks by Robert G. Joseph (note 23), p. 9 (emphasis added).

[56] Boese, W., 'Suppliers weigh Indian nuclear cooperation', *Arms Control Today*, vol. 35, no. 9 (Nov. 2005).

[57] Prepared remarks by Robert G. Joseph (note 23), p. 6.

[58] E.g., in the late autumn of 2005 critical reports in the official Chinese media claimed that the CNCI would have a 'negative impact' on the global nuclear order and non-proliferation efforts. See Mohan, C. R., 'Delhi's comrades slam India, Beijing's slam US for n-deal', *Indian Express*, 4 Nov. 2005, URL <http://www.indianexpress.com/print.php?content_id=81265>.

arguably does not take sufficient account of the nature of the NSG regime: while the NSG Guidelines are not binding under international law, they have been incorporated into national legislation by the participants and have therefore acquired a formal legal force at the national level. This implies that national licensing authorities (in the USA or elsewhere) would still have to consider the guidelines when deciding upon a proposed transfer of nuclear technology to India. As the requirement for full-scope safeguards would remain, it is difficult to see how participants could agree to a transfer without having amended the guidelines.

The NSG participants have declared that they view their cooperation as consistent with, and complementary to, the NPT. A delicate situation would arise if the members of the NPT regime were to make an exception for full-scope safeguards as a condition for supply to India, while the treaty regime at the same time has moved to elevate this principle as part of the requirements of NPT Article III. Here it should be noted that all the states participating in the NSG are also parties to the NPT and can obviously not act contrary to their international obligations under the treaty. If they nevertheless were to do so, this would most likely be viewed as undermining the integrity of the treaty—and at a time when the NPT is regarded as under severe stress.[59]

V. National legislation on nuclear exports

In the July 2005 Joint Statement, the US President declared his intention that the United States would 'seek agreement from Congress to adjust U.S. laws and policies' and India's Prime Minister committed India to implement comprehensive domestic export control legislation.[60]

US legislation

The 1954 Atomic Energy Act (AEA), as amended, is the principal US legislation governing US nuclear cooperation and exports.[61] The AEA was amended in 1978 with the adoption of the Nuclear Non-Proliferation Act (NNPA), which added nonproliferation to the criteria for US exports of nuclear equipment.[62]

Section 123(a)(2) of the AEA establishes that an 'agreement for cooperation' meeting certain criteria must be in place before the commencement of international cooperation. In the case of non-nuclear-weapon states there is a requirement 'as a condition of continued United States nuclear supply under the agreement for cooperation, that IAEA safeguards be maintained with respect to all nuclear materials in all peaceful nuclear activities within the territory of such state, under its jurisdiction, or carried out under its control anywhere'. Hence, under US domestic law there is also a requirement for full-scope safeguards as a condition for cooperation. However, the US president may exempt a proposed agreement for cooperation from any of the

[59] On the outcome of the 2005 NPT Review Conference see chapter 13, section II.

[60] The White House (note 1), p. 2.

[61] The Atomic Energy Act of 1954, 30 Aug. 1954, Public Law 83-703 (68 Stat. 919), reprinted in *Nuclear Regulatory Legislation*, NUREG-0980, vol. 1, no. 6 (US Nuclear Regulatory Commission, Office of the General Counsel: Washington, DC, June 2002), pp. 1–9.

[62] Nuclear Non-Proliferation Act of 1978, 10 Mar. 1978, Public Law 95-242 (92 Stat. 120), reprinted in *Nuclear Regulatory Legislation*, NUREG-0980 (note 61), pp. 15.1–3.

requirements of section 123 if it is determined that the inclusion of any such requirement would be 'seriously prejudicial to the achievement of United States non-proliferation objectives or otherwise jeopardize the common defense and security'. According to the 1985 Export Administration Amendment Act, an exempted agreement would not become effective unless both houses of Congress approve it.[63]

Section 128 of the AEA outlines the criteria governing US exports for peaceful nuclear uses of source material, special nuclear material, production facilities and any sensitive nuclear technology to a non-nuclear weapon state. Subparagraph (a)(1) lays down the condition that IAEA safeguards should be maintained with respect to 'all peaceful nuclear activities in, under the jurisdiction of, or carried out under the control of such state at the time of the export'. This provision also allows the US president to waive the requirement for full-scope safeguards as a condition of supply if he determines that a failure to approve an export would be seriously prejudicial to the achievement of US non-proliferation objectives or otherwise jeopardize the common defence or security. Finally, section 129 of the AEA also has a bearing on the CNCI. Under this provision no nuclear materials and equipment or sensitive nuclear technology may be exported to 'any non-nuclear-weapon state that is found by the president to have, at any time after the effective date of this section [to have] detonated a nuclear explosive device'. Also under this provision the president may waive the cessation of exports if he determines 'that cessation of such exports would be seriously prejudicial to the achievement of United States non-proliferation objectives or otherwise jeopardize the common defense and security'.

The Bush Administration has already introduced several amendments as a result of the CNCI. Amendments to the Export Administration Regulations (EAR) became effective on 30 August 2005: they removed some licence requirements for exports and re-exports to India of items controlled unilaterally for nuclear non-proliferation reasons. Furthermore, six Indian entities were removed from the Entity List of the EAR.[64] Yet, as shown above, full implementation of the CNCI would require the involvement and consent of Congress.

The initial reaction of the US Congress to the CNCI was not enthusiastic. Members of Congress have complained that they were not consulted before this major policy shift was announced.[65] A hearing of the House of Representatives International Relations Committee on 8 September 2005 revealed that many congressmen were concerned about the possible negative impact of the CNCI on the nuclear non-proliferation regime.[66] As of the late autumn of 2005 the administration had not begun formal consultations with Congress. The administration aims to forward a proposal for amendments to domestic legislation in early 2006 so as to enable civil nuclear cooperation with India. While no detailed information is available, it has been

[63] See Squassoni, S., *US Nuclear Cooperation With India: Issues for Congress* (US Library of Congress, Congressonal Research Service: Washington, DC, 29 July 2005), p. 5.

[64] *Federal Register*, vol. 70, no. 167 (30 Aug. 2005), p. 51251.

[65] Robinson, D., 'US: India nuclear accord will not harm non-proliferation effort', Voice of America, 8 Sep. 2005, URL <http://www.globalsecurity.org/wmd/library/news/india/2005/india-050908-voa01.htm>.

[66] Ruppe, D., 'Obstacles surface to proposed US–Indian nuclear deal', Global Security Newswire, Nuclear Threat Initiative, 9 Sep. 2005, URL <http://www.nti.org/d_newswire/issues/2005_9_9.html>.

suggested that amendments will be proposed to Section 129 of the AEA and to the NNPA.[67]

It remains to be seen whether the US Administration will succeed in conveying the notion to Congress that the CNCI involves a net gain for the non-proliferation of nuclear weapons and whether congressmen will accept the CNCI as it is currently formulated. It cannot be excluded that Congress may decide to add further conditions for its approval, such as Indian participation in a fissile material cut-off. Both Indian and US representatives have made it clear that any such additional conditions are likely to be seen as 'deal-breakers'.[68]

Indian legislation

India is committed under the CNCI to ensure that the necessary steps have been taken to secure its nuclear materials and technology through comprehensive domestic export control legislation and through harmonization and adherence to the guidelines of both the Missile Technology Control Regime and the NSG. India previously implemented national export controls on dual-use items, but the legislation has been described as 'a complicated patchwork'.[69] In May 2005 the Indian Government enacted the Weapons of Mass Destruction and their Delivery Systems (Prohibition of Unlawful Activities) Act, which *inter alia* criminalizes the possession and transfer of weapons of mass destruction (WMD) by unauthorized individuals and entities. The enactment of this law was motivated primarily by the obligations on all states under UN Security Council Resolution 1540,[70] which requires penal legislation as well as 'effective measures to establish domestic controls' to prevent WMD proliferation.[71] The Indian export control system still involves seven different primary laws, but it appears to be fairly comprehensive. Some commentators have argued that India needs to adopt unified, comprehensive export control legislation,[72] but that would seem to go beyond the commitments made within the context of the CNCI. For India's part, it includes among its responsibilities under the CNCI 'adherence' to the guidelines of both the NSG and the MTCR.[73] India has previously been an ardent opponent of the multilateral export control regimes but seems recently to have changed its attitude.

It should be noted that the CNCI is not uncontroversial in India. Some commentators have criticized it as a deal by which India would give up its independent policies in the nuclear field. The CNCI has also been seen as an important explanation for why India voted in favour of finding Iran in non-compliance with its safeguards obligations at the September 2005 IAEA Board of Governors meeting—a decision that

---

[67] 'Work begins on legislative changes needed to implement US–India nuclear agreement', Global Security Newswire, Nuclear Threat Initiative, 17 Aug. 2005, URL <http://www.nti.org/d_newswire/issues/2005_8_17.html>.

[68] See, e.g., 'India envoy warns on changes to US nuclear deal', *New York Times*, 22 Nov. 2005.

[69] Anthony, I. and Bauer, S., 'Transfer controls', *SIPRI Yearbook 2005* (note 26), p. 708.

[70] United Nations, Letter dated 8 August 2005 from the Permanent Representative of India to the United Nations addressed to the President of the Security Council, UN document S/2005/521, 11 Aug. 2005 (the 2005 Act is reproduced in the annex to this letter).

[71] UN Security Council Resolution 1540, 28 Apr. 2004.

[72] Gahlaut, S. and Srivastava, A., *Nonproliferation Export Controls in India—Update 2005* (Center for International Trade and Security: Athens, Ga., 2005), p. 11.

[73] The term 'adherence' in this context is typically used to describe the behaviour of a state that is not a formal participant in the export control regimes but whose export control practices conform to the guidelines of the regimes.

has generated a certain measure of domestic criticism.[74] In January 2006 US representatives hinted at a link between the successful realization of the CNCI and the position of India on the referral of Iran to the UN Security Council, although India denied that there was such a link and maintained that they were two separate issues.[75]

VI. Conclusions

The announcement of the Civil Nuclear Cooperation Initiative by India and the United States in the summer of 2005 has raised considerable interest—as well as anxiety—among states and in academic circles. It represents a paradigmatic departure from what has been seen as the conventional wisdom in the field of the non-proliferation of nuclear weapons—not to engage with an NPT 'hold-out' state. US policy on nuclear non-proliferation has so far been dominated by a desire to hinder other states from acquiring a nuclear weapon capability. The policy of technology denial and cold-shouldering has been in operation ever since India acquired its nuclear capability. However, the current US Administration seems no longer to be interested in sacrificing what it sees as its wider geopolitical, or economic, interests for the sake of consistency in its non-proliferation policies.

The present situation throws into relief a dichotomy between two perspectives on nuclear non-proliferation—a 'pragmatic' one and a 'normative' one. The former would focus on the fact that India has already managed to defeat the purpose of the multilateral nuclear non-proliferation regime: it has acquired the position of a 'technology holder' and should be treated as such. The main interest today would then be not to punish India, but to limit the potential negative effects by ensuring that India does not proliferate its nuclear technologies. To continue to insist that India should accede to the NPT as a non-nuclear weapon state would serve no useful purpose since India has repeatedly stated that it will not do so. The second perspective would remain faithful to the formal nuclear non-proliferation regime and regard India as a 'hold-out' that has managed to acquire a nuclear weapon capability and should therefore pay a political, and an economic, price. The principal objective should be to maintain the integrity of the nuclear non-proliferation regime. To engage with India in the nuclear field would only demonstrate to potential proliferators that it is possible to defeat the purpose of the Non-Proliferation Treaty, running the risk of stimulating other states to acquire a nuclear capability.

In the final analysis it may be concluded that the CNCI would be a very good bargain for India. India could reap the benefits of full civil nuclear cooperation in return for rather modest pledges that would not affect its ability to retain and expand its nuclear weapon arsenal. As this appendix shows, the CNCI raises a number of international and domestic legal issues. Accommodation of the CNCI is a question not only for the participants in the NSG and members of the US Congress, but possibly also for the parties to the NPT.

[74] 'India's foreign policy compromised: experts', *The Hindu*, 29 Oct. 2005, URL <http://www.hinduonnet.com/thehindu/thscrip/print.pl?file=2005102918391200.htm>.

[75] 'Nuclear deal could die if India fails to back U.S. position on Iran, ambassador says', Global Security Newswire, Nuclear Threat Initiative, 26 Jan. 2006, URL <http://www.nti.org/d_newswire/issues/2006_1_26.html>.

Appendix 13C. Multilateral control of the nuclear fuel cycle

VITALY FEDCHENKO*

I. Introduction

The international community recognized at an early stage that nuclear technology was inherently 'dual-use'; that is, it could be used for both civil and military applications. In 2005 the issue of how to reconcile the development of nuclear energy with the goal of nuclear weapon non-proliferation featured prominently on the international agenda. This was highlighted in October, when it was announced that the Nobel Peace Prize for 2005 would be awarded jointly to the International Atomic Energy Agency (IAEA) and its Director General, Mohammed ElBaradei, 'for their efforts to prevent nuclear energy from being used for military purposes and to ensure that nuclear energy for peaceful purposes is used in the safest possible way'.[1]

Since the early 1940s, three types of proposal have been put forward for ways to control the spread of sensitive nuclear technology and materials.[2] One type is multilateral arrangements for the joint use, development or ownership of sensitive nuclear fuel cycle facilities.[3] Under such arrangements no individual participant would have sole control over any nuclear facilities and thus could not covertly divert them to military purposes. This type of multinational arrangement may prove to be both politically and commercially viable.

The second type of proposal has involved legal and regulatory barriers to the transfer of sensitive technologies and materials. This approach shaped the non-proliferation regime that is in place today: although nuclear facilities are owned and operated nationally, most of them are subject to certain restrictions, regulations and safeguards imposed by international treaties and agreements. The legal and political foundation of this regime was laid in the 1968 Treaty on the Non-Proliferation of Nuclear Weapons (Non-Proliferation Treaty, NPT).[4] The NPT relies on the Inter-

---

[1] Norwegian Nobel Committee, 'The Nobel Peace Prize for 2005', Press release, Oslo, 7 Oct. 2005, URL <http://nobelprize.org/peace/laureates/2005/press.html>.

[2] Scheinman, L., 'Control of proliferation and the challenge of sensitive nuclear technology', *Journal of Nuclear Materials Management*, vol. 33, no. 4 (summer 2005), pp. 34–35; and Rauf, T., 'Background & report of the Expert Group on Multilateral Approaches to the Nuclear Fuel Cycle', Address to the International Conference on Multilateral, Technical and Organizational Approaches for the Nuclear Fuel Cycle Aimed at Strengthening the Non-Proliferation Regime, Moscow, 13–15 July 2005, URL <http://www.iaea.org/NewsCenter/News/PDF/rauf_report220605.pdf>.

[3] 'Nuclear fuel cycle' is defined by the IAEA as 'a system of nuclear installations and activities interconnected by streams of nuclear material'. It represents the totality of all nuclear installations and activities involved in the production of nuclear power or nuclear materials. International Atomic Energy Agency (IAEA), *IAEA Safeguards Glossary: 2001 Edition*, International Nuclear Verification Series no. 3 (2001), URL <http://www-pub.iaea.org/MTCD/publications/PDF/nvs-3-cd/PDF/NVS3_prn.pdf>, p. 37. See also section V of this appendix.

[4] On the NPT see chapter 13 and annex A in this volume. For the text of the treaty see URL <http://www.un.org/Depts/dda/WMD/treaty/>.

---

* The author would like to thank Frank von Hippel, Andrey Frolov, Shannon N. Kile, Marvin Miller and Lothar H. Wedekind for their useful comments on an early draft of this appendix.

national Atomic Energy Agency (IAEA) and its safeguards system for verification of the parties' fulfilment of their treaty obligations. The IAEA has improved its verification mechanisms over the years.[5] In addition, controls on the transfer of sensitive materials and technologies between states have been agreed by various export control regimes, including the Nuclear Suppliers Group (NSG).[6] The 2003 Proliferation Security Initiative (PSI) was launched by the United States and a group of other states to intercept illicit transfers of weapons of mass destruction (WMD), missiles and their components, including nuclear weapons and materials.[7] UN Security Council Resolution 1540 linked the nuclear non-proliferation regime and international criminal law in order to curb the access of non-state actors to sensitive materials and technologies.[8] In June 2004 the Group of Eight (G8) leading industrialized nations adopted the Action Plan on Nonproliferation, which, in particular, endorsed the work of the NSG, called for universal adherence to IAEA safeguards and reiterated the G8's commitment to the PSI.[9]

The third approach is a technical one. The known types of nuclear fuel cycle entail certain proliferation risks because they all involve the use of nuclear explosive isotopes: uranium-235, plutonium-239 or uranium-233. Many experts claim that new technologies can reduce those risks. Innovative processes are being developed that are claimed to be inherently proliferation-resistant, economically attractive and environmentally safe.

Section II examines the NPT regime and new developments in nuclear power. Section III describes the history of studies and negotiations on multilateral cooperative arrangements for the use of sensitive nuclear fuel cycle facilities. This approach was developed considerably in 2005, as described in section IV. Section V reviews proposals for the development of proliferation-resistant technologies, and section VI offers the conclusions.

II. The NPT and nuclear energy

A number of developments since 2003 have given rise to concerns about perceived weaknesses in the NPT regime. First, in early 2003 IAEA inspectors discovered that Iran had for many years failed to declare important nuclear activities, in contravention of its NPT-mandated safeguards agreement with the Agency. This led some outside observers to conclude that Iran was seeking to put into place, under the cover of a civilian nuclear power programme, the infrastructure needed to produce

---

[5] For a discussion of the development of IAEA safeguards see Zarimpas, N., 'Nuclear verification: the IAEA strengthened safeguards system', *SIPRI Yearbook 2000: Armaments, Disarmament and International Security* (Oxford University Press: Oxford, 2000), pp. 496–508. For the list of states with IAEA safeguards agreements in force see annex A in this volume.

[6] On the export control regimes and their participating states see the glossary and chapter 16 in this volume. On the NSG see also appendix 13B.

[7] On the PSI see Ahlström, C., 'The Proliferation Security Initiative: international law aspects of the Statement of Interdiction Principles', *SIPRI Yearbook 2005: Armaments, Disarmament and International Security* (Oxford University Press: Oxford, 2005), pp. 741–65; and the glossary in this volume.

[8] United Nations Security Council Resolution 1540, 28 Apr. 2005, available at URL <http://www.un.org/documents/scres.htm>; and Anthony, I., 'Arms control and non-proliferation: the role of international organizations', *SIPRI Yearbook 2005* (note 7), pp. 542–47.

[9] Group of Eight (G8), G8 Action Plan on Nonproliferation, Sea Island, Georgia, 9 June 2004, URL <http://www.g8.utoronto.ca/summit/2004seaisland/nonproliferation.html>.

nuclear weapons.[10] Second, also in 2003, North Korea became the first state party to withdraw from the NPT. It subsequently announced that it had built nuclear weapons using the infrastructure it had acquired, in compliance with the treaty, for peaceful purposes.[11] Evidence of the existence of an illicit international nuclear technology transfer network began to emerge publicly in October of that year, when Iran admitted to the IAEA that it had covertly imported sensitive components from Pakistan. Libya's decision in December to abandon its WMD capabilities and most of its advanced missile programmes resulted in the official disclosure of this network, led by Pakistan's most prominent nuclear scientist, Abdul Qadeer Khan.[12]

In October 2003 IAEA Director General ElBaradei noted that the performance of the NPT was 'less than optimal' and pointed out that controlling access to sensitive technologies has become increasingly difficult because technical barriers to proliferation have gradually eroded, because much of the hardware on the market is of a dual-use nature, and because the diversity of the technology makes it difficult to control procurement and sales.[13] In addition, some observers conclude that there is an inherent structural weakness in the NPT, because, in accordance with Article IV, a state has the right to develop sensitive nuclear fuel cycle capacities 'to develop research, production and use of nuclear energy for peaceful purposes', but it can then withdraw from the treaty without legal consequences, for example, in order to pursue a nuclear weapons option.[14] At the June 2004 meeting of the IAEA Board of Governors, ElBaradei announced that he had appointed an international Expert Group to explore innovative multilateral approaches to the secure development of nuclear energy.[15] The group published its recommendations in February 2005, and in May its findings and proposals were presented at the NPT Review Conference.[16] Implementation of some of the recommendations began in September 2005 (see section IV below).

Against the background of a 'battered' nuclear non-proliferation regime, in 2005 signals of a renewed interest in nuclear power on the part of various states became especially visible. Three factors were cited as influencing states' interest. First, soaring fossil fuel prices in 2005 prompted energy consumers to investigate alternative options for the production of electricity. Second, many states paid increased attention to the 1997 Kyoto Protocol and emissions of greenhouse gases. Fossil fuels are believed to be contributing to global warming by producing greenhouse gases, while emissions from nuclear energy are lower by two orders of magni-

[10] Kile, S. N., 'Nuclear arms control and non-proliferation', *SIPRI Yearbook 2004: Armaments, Disarmament and International Security* (Oxford University Press: Oxford, 2004), pp. 604–11.

[11] Kile, S. N., 'Nuclear arms control, non-proliferation and ballistic missile defence', *SIPRI Yearbook 2003: Armaments, Disarmament and International Security* (Oxford University Press: Oxford, 2003), pp. 578–91.

[12] Kile, S. N., 'Nuclear arms control and non-proliferation', and Hart, J. and Kile, S. N., 'Libya's renunciation of nuclear, biological and chemical weapons and ballistic missiles', *SIPRI Yearbook 2005* (note 7), pp. 551–55 and 629–48, respectively. On developments in 2005 see chapter 13.

[13] ElBaradei, M., 'Towards a safer world', *The Economist*, 18 Oct. 2003, p. 43.

[14] Kile (note 12), p. 573.

[15] IAEA, Introductory statement to the Board of Governors by IAEA Director General Dr Mohamed ElBaradei, DG/14062004, Vienna, 14 June 2004, URL <http://www.iaea.org/NewsCenter/Statements/2004/ebsp2004n003.html>.

[16] IAEA, *Multilateral Approaches to the Nuclear Fuel Cycle: Expert Group Report to the Director General of the International Atomic Energy Agency* (IAEA: Vienna, 2005), URL <http://www-pub.iaea.org/MTCD/publications/PDF/mna-2005_web.pdf>. On the 2005 NPT Review Conference see chapter 13 in this volume.

tude.[17] Finally, some governments regarded nuclear power as a way to enhance their energy independence and security of supply. As stated by ElBaradei, owing to the 'diverse global roster of stable uranium producers and the small storage space required for a long term nuclear fuel supply', nuclear power is considered to be the source of electricity that is relatively independent of the international political situation.[18] The importance of this consideration was emphasized by the dispute between Russia and Ukraine over gas prices, which resulted in the temporary curtailing of supplies of Russian natural gas to Europe in January 2006.[19] In the same month there were reports of temporary cuts in the supply to Europe of Russian gas piped via Ukraine caused by extremely cold weather conditions, and there were explosions on pipelines delivering natural gas to Georgia.[20] These incidents reinforced the arguments of advocates of nuclear power that this is the most dependable source of energy.

Analysis of data on the numbers and output of future nuclear power reactors around the world shows that Asia is, and is likely to remain, the main growth area for the nuclear industry, with China, India, Japan and South Korea leading in the number of planned and proposed reactor projects (see table 13C.1). The second largest projected area of growth is Europe, where Russia has the most ambitious construction plans. In January 2006 the head of the Russian Federal Atomic Energy Agency (Rosatom), Sergey Kirienko, put forward a plan to build 40 new nuclear power reactors within the next 25 years.[21] The USA may become the third largest area of growth in the future: the 2005 Energy Policy Act includes a considerable package of incentives to encourage the construction of new nuclear power plants in the USA.[22] President George W. Bush vowed to 'start building nuclear plants again by the end of this decade'.[23] There were also signs in 2005 of a possible change of policy in favour of nuclear power in Western Europe.[24]

As shown in table 13C.1, the combined electricity generation capacity of the 168 reactors that are now under construction or planned to be built is about

[17] Organisation for Economic Co-operation and Development (OECD), 'Nuclear energy today', OECD Policy Brief, Feb. 2005, URL <http://www.oecd.org/dataoecd/32/62/34537360.pdf>, pp. 1–3. The Kyoto Protocol to the 1992 United Nations Framework Convention on Climate Change is available at URL <http://unfccc.int/resource/docs/convkp/kpeng.html>.

[18] ElBaradei, M., 'Nuclear power: a look at the future', International Conference on Fifty Years of Nuclear Power: The Next Fifty Years, 27 June 2004, URL <http://www.iaea.org/NewsCenter/Statements/2004/ebsp2004n005.html>.

[19] White, A., 'Europe seeks home-grown power solutions', Business Week Online, 5 Jan. 2006, URL <http://www.businessweek.com/ap/financialnews/D8EUKIRG4.htm>.

[20] Warner, T., 'Gazprom accuses Ukraine of restricting supplies', Financial Times, 23 Jan. 2006, URL <http://news.ft.com/cms/s/d5800b62-8b52-11da-91a1-0000779e2340.html>; and Chivers, C. J., 'Explosions in southern Russia sever gas lines to Georgia', New York Times, 23 Jan. 2006, URL <http://www.nytimes.com/2006/01/23/international/Europe/23georgia.html>.

[21] Nikol'skii, A., '$60 mlrd na AES' [$60 billion for nuclear power plants], Vedomosti, 23 Jan. 2006.

[22] 'US energy bill favours new build reactors, new technology', Nuclear Engineering International, 12 Aug. 2005, URL <http://www.neimagazine.com/storyprint.asp?sc=2030325>.

[23] The White House, Office of the Press Secretary, 'President signs Energy Policy Act', 8 Aug. 2005, URL <http://www.whitehouse.gov/news/releases/2005/08/20050808-6.html>.

[24] MacLachlan, A., 'France's common EU energy policy would include nuclear power', Nucleonics Week, 26 Jan. 2006; Shaikh, T., 'Blair to give his blessing to nuclear reactors as only way to cut emissions', The Independent, 22 Nov. 2005, URL <http://news.independent.co.uk/uk/politics/article328586.ece>; and Krägenow, T., 'Union und SPD wollen Atomausstieg verschleppen' [Union and SPD want to delay the halt to nuclear power], Financial Times Deutschland, 20 Oct. 2005, URL <http://www.ftd.de/pw/de/26975.html>.

Table 13C.1. Number and capacity of nuclear power reactors in the world, as of January 2006[a]

Region/state	Operating No.	Operating MW(e)	Under construction No.	Under construction MW(e)	Planned No.	Planned MW(e)	Proposed No.	Proposed MW(e)
Asia	*108*	*79 590*	*16*	*11 318*	*28*	*31 932*	*47*	*32 160*
China	9	6 572	3	3 000	7	7 000	19	15 000
Taiwan	6	4 904	2	2 600	–	–	–	–
India	15	3 040	8	3 602	–	–	24	13 160
Indonesia	0	–	–	–	–	–	2	2 000
Japan	56	47 839	1	866	12	14 782	–	–
Korea, North	–	–	1	950	1	950	–	–
Korea, South	20	16 810	–	–	8	9 200	–	–
Pakistan	2	425	1	300	–	–	–	–
Viet Nam	–	–	–	–	–	–	2	2 000
Europe	*205*	*172 215*	*8*	*7 930*	*1*	*925*	*20*	*21 210*
Armenia	1	376	–	–	–	–	–	–
Belgium	7	5 801	–	–	–	–	–	–
Bulgaria	4	2 722	–	–	–	–	1	1 000
Czech Republic	6	3 368	–	–	–	–	2	1 900
Finland	4	2 676	1	1 600	–	–	–	–
France	59	63 363	–	–	–	–	1	1 600
Germany	17	20 339	–	–	–	–	–	–
Hungary	4	1 755	–	–	–	–	–	–
Lithuania	1	1 185	–	–	–	–	–	–
Netherlands	1	449	–	–	–	–	–	–
Romania	1	655	1	655	–	–	3	1 995
Russia	31	2 1743	4	3 775	1	925	8	9 375
Slovakia	6	2 442	–	–	–	–	2	840
Slovenia	1	656	–	–	–	–	–	–
Spain	9	7 588	–	–	–	–	–	–
Sweden	10	8 918	–	–	–	–	–	–
Switzerland	5	3 220	–	–	–	–	–	–
Turkey	–	–	–	–	–	–	3	4 500
UK	23	11 852	–	–	–	–	–	–
Ukraine	15	13 107	2	1 900	–	–	–	–
Middle East	*–*	*–*	*1*	*915*	*2*	*1 900*	*5*	*4 650*
Egypt	–	–	–	–	–	–	1	600
Iran	–	–	1	915	2	1 900	3	2 850
Israel	–	–	–	–	–	–	1	1 200
North America	*124*	*113 119*	*–*	*–*	*2*	*1 540*	*11*	*14 000*
Canada	18	12 599	–	–	2	1 540	–	–
Mexico	2	1 310	–	–	–	–	–	–
USA	104	99 210	–	–	–	–	11	14 000
South America	*4*	*2 836*	*1*	*692*	*1*	*1 245*	*–*	*–*
Argentina	2	935	1	692	–	–	–	–
Brazil	2	1 901	–	–	1	1 245	–	–
Africa: S. Africa	*2*	*1 800*	*–*	*–*	*1*	*165*	*24*	*4 000*
World total	**443**	**369 560**	**26**	**20 855**	**35**	**37 625**	**107**	**76 020**

[a] 'Operating' indicates that the reactor is connected to the grid; 'Under construction' means 'first concrete for reactor poured, or major refurbishment under way'; 'Planned' means 'approvals and funding in place, or construction well advanced but suspended indefinitely'; and 'Proposed' means that there is a 'clear intention but still without funding and/or approvals'.

Sources: World Nuclear Association, 'World nuclear power reactors 2004–06 and uranium requirements', 4 Jan. 2006, URL <http://www.world-nuclear.org/info/reactors.htm>; IAEA Power Reactor Information System (PRIS), 2 Mar. 2006, URL <http://www.iaea.org/programmes/a2/index.html>; and World Nuclear Association, 'Nuclear power in China', Information and Issue Brief, Dec. 2005, URL <http://www.world-nuclear.org/info/inf63.htm>.

135 gigawatts-electric (GW(e)). The construction of additional reactors will probably be announced in the near future. The total electricity generation capacity of the 443 currently operated reactors is about 370 GW(e). The fleet of operating reactors is ageing, and older reactors are being decommissioned. It remains an open question whether the future pace of construction of new reactors would be sufficient to keep up with the retirement of older plants.

III. Multilateral cooperative strategies

The idea of international control of nuclear power was first put forward in 1946, in a formal US proposal known as the Baruch Plan. The plan envisaged 'the creation of an International Atomic Development Authority, to which should be entrusted all phases of the development and use of atomic energy', including ownership or managerial control over nuclear fuel cycle activities judged to be potentially dangerous for world security, and the right to control, inspect and license all other nuclear activities.[25] This plan was dismissed, primarily by the Soviet Union, as being too far-reaching and intrusive.

The centrepiece of the Atoms for Peace plan, presented by US President Dwight D. Eisenhower at the UN General Assembly in 1953, was the creation of an international atomic energy agency 'to which the governments principally involved would make joint contributions' from their stockpiles of fissile material and natural uranium.[26] The 1956 IAEA Statute provides for the creation of an international nuclear fuel bank that could guarantee the supply of fuel to those states that need it, thus relieving them of the need to have their own facilities.[27] Article XII.A.5 of the IAEA Statute gives the Agency the right to require temporary 'deposit with the Agency of any excess of any special fissionable materials' produced for peaceful uses 'in order to prevent stockpiling of these materials'. This clause provides for the creation of an IAEA bank of plutonium or spent fuel where it could be placed under international inspection and control until it was required for use in civil nuclear power applications. Variations of these two ideas have been discussed since then.

Simultaneously with the establishment of the IAEA in 1956, the Council of Ministers of the Organisation for European Economic Co-operation approved the creation of a European reprocessing plant—Eurochemic—as a joint undertaking.[28] In the late 1950s, during the initial stages of the development of nuclear energy in European countries, international cooperation seemed to be the least risky way for the NNWS

[25] 'The Baruch Plan, Presented to the United Nations Atomic Energy Commission, June 14, 1946', NuclearFiles.org, URL <http://www.nuclearfiles.org/menu/key-issues/nuclear-weapons/issues/arms-control-disarmament/baruch-plan_1946-06-14.htm>.

[26] Fischer, D., 'History of the International Atomic Energy Agency: the first forty years', IAEA, Vienna, 1997, URL <http://www-pub.iaea.org/MTCD/publications/PDF/Pub1032_web.pdf>, p. 9.

[27] IAEA, Statute of the IAEA, URL <http://www.iaea.org/About/statute_text.html>, Articles III.A.2 and B.3, IX, XI, XII, XIII, XIV.B.2 and E–G.

[28] Fischer (note 26), pp. 61–62.

to obtain cutting-edge reactor technology. The USA was also likely to support such solutions pending the establishment of the nuclear non-proliferation regime.[29] Eurochemic was set up by 13 member states of the European Nuclear Energy Agency (which became the Nuclear Energy Agency of the Organisation for Economic Co-operation and Development in 1972) as an international shareholding company open for business participation with an objective to serve as the nucleus of a European reprocessing industry. It carried out an innovative research programme, trained a large number of specialists and operated an industrial pilot reprocessing plant in Mol, Belgium, commissioned in 1966.[30] Because of its small size and its situation in a competitive market, the plant was closed down in 1975. The Eurochemic company operated until 1990, with the Belgian Government progressively taking over its installations.

The Treaty establishing the European Atomic Energy Community (Euratom Treaty) was signed in 1957. A fundamental objective of Euratom is to encourage progress in the field of nuclear energy in the EU: the Euratom Supply Agency (ESA), established in the Euratom Treaty and operative since 1960, is to ensure the supply of ores, source materials and special fissile materials by means of a common supply policy based on the principle of equal access to sources of supply. No contract in the EU on nuclear supply, including purchases, sales, exchanges and enrichment, can be concluded without the consent of the ESA. It also has 'a right of option' on those materials produced in the territories of EU member states. Another fundamental objective of Euratom is to prevent the diversion of nuclear materials from peaceful to military use on EU territory by applying the system of Euratom safeguards.[31]

In 1970 the Treaty of Almelo was signed by the Federal Republic of Germany, the Netherlands and the United Kingdom, creating the Uranium Enrichment Company (Urenco).[32] The treaty formed the basis for cooperation between these three countries for the development and industrial exploitation of centrifuge uranium enrichment technology. Until September 1993 each party had a national company operating its own enrichment plant, which were all then brought together into a centrally managed international group of companies. In 2004 Urenco covered 19 per cent of world enrichment needs and had a turnover of €707 million.[33] However, multilateral arrangements of this kind can be misused: for example, A. Q. Khan diverted Urenco centrifuge technology to the Pakistani nuclear weapon programme.[34]

In 1973 France, Belgium, Spain and Sweden formed the joint stock company EURODIF. In 1974 EURODIF decided to build a large gaseous diffusion enrichment plant on the Tricastin nuclear site at Pierrelatte in France's Rhône valley. Sweden withdrew from the project in 1974. In 1975 Sweden's 10 per cent share in EURODIF

---

[29] Berkhout, F., *Radioactive Waste: Politics and Technology* (Routledge: London, 1991), p. 55.

[30] Organisation for Economic Co-operation and Development (OECD), Nuclear Energy Agency, *History of the EUROCHEMIC Company 1956–1990* (OECD: Paris, 1996), reviewed in OECD, Nuclear Energy Agency, Press communiqué, Paris, 26 Nov. 1996, URL <http://www.nea.fr/html/general/press/1996/1996-17.html>.

[31] The Treaty establishing the European Atomic Energy Community (Euratom Treaty) entered into force on 25 Mar. 1957; see URL <http://europa.eu.int/scadplus/treaties/euratom_en.htm>, Articles 1, 2, 52–76, 80, 86–91, 171, 195 and 197.

[32] Krass, A. S. et al., SIPRI, *Uranium Enrichment and Nuclear Weapon Proliferation* (Taylor & Francis: London, 1983), p. 31, available in full text on SIPRI's website at URL <http://www.sipri.org>.

[33] Urenco, *Urenco Annual Report and Accounts, 2004*, URL <http://www.urenco.com/im/uploaded/1125054354.pdf>.

[34] Smith, C. and Bhatia, S., 'How Dr. Khan stole the bomb for Islam', *The Observer*, 9 Dec. 1979.

went to Iran as a result of an arrangement between France and Iran. The French government subsidiary company Cogema and the Iranian Government established the Sofidif (Société franco–iranienne pour l'enrichissement de l'uranium par diffusion gazeuse) enterprise with 60 per cent and 40 per cent shares, respectively. In turn, Sofidif acquired a 25 per cent share in EURODIF, which gave Iran its 10 per cent share of EURODIF.[35] Iran's agreement with EURODIF was cancelled after the 1979 Islamic Revolution. Currently, EURODIF Production is a subsidiary of the Areva Group. In 2004 the uranium enrichment market share of EURODIF was about 25 per cent.[36]

The 1974 IAEA General Conference, prompted by India's test of a nuclear explosive device in May of that year, discussed the possibility of establishing international facilities to handle spent nuclear fuel from nuclear power plants as an alternative to the development of plutonium reprocessing technologies in individual states.[37] In the same year the IAEA started the Regional Nuclear Fuel Cycle Center (RNFC) study project to assess the feasibility and advantages of such facilities.[38] It led to the discussion of RNFCs at the 1975 NPT Review Conference, which encouraged the IAEA to continue the study and secured support for it from individual states.[39] The RNFC study, completed in 1977, provided a review of the regional cooperative projects covering the entire back-end of the fuel cycle. The study was based on the assumption that world nuclear power would soon be based largely on fast reactors, but this did not happen.[40] Partially for this reason, and because of a general lack of political will, no follow-up action was taken.

On 7 April 1977 the USA proposed an International Nuclear Fuel Cycle Evaluation (INFCE) to investigate ways of strengthening the technological base of the nuclear non-proliferation regime. The INFCE Conference opened on 19 October, with the participation of 40 state representatives. INFCE touched upon all three approaches to the problem of the dual-use nature of nuclear energy (see section I).[41] It was agreed that multinationalization has the potential to limit the number of sensitive facilities, which should have a positive impact on both non-proliferation and the economical operation of the plants. However, considerable drawbacks such as the risk of leak of sensitive know-how were highlighted. By the time of its conclusion in 1980, INFCE had failed to reach consensus on important questions, including the distribution of responsibilities between the host country and foreign shareholders and assurance of supply for foreign investors. No concrete steps stemmed from this comprehensive study, but its findings have considerably influenced the debate.

---

[35] Krass et al. (note 32), pp. 200, 215.

[36] Areva Group, *Annual Report 2004* (Areva: Paris, Apr. 2005), p. 44.

[37] Scheinman (note 2), p. 34.

[38] Lee, B. W., 'Viable scheme for regional fuel cycle center: issues and strategies', Nuclear Cooperation Meeting on Spent Fuel and High Level Waste Storage and Disposal, Las Vegas, Nev., 7–9 Mar. 2000, URL <http://eed.llnl.gov/ncm/session4/Lee_Byong_Whi.pdf>.

[39] 'Final Declaration of NPT Review Conference', *SIPRI Yearbook 1976: World Armaments and Disarmament* (Taylor & Francis: London, 1976), p. 408.

[40] A fast reactor is one that operates mainly with neutrons in the energy range above 0.1 MeV (fast neutrons) and does not need a moderator. Fast reactors are generally designed to use plutonium fuel and can produce, through the transmutation of uranium-238, more plutonium than they consume. IAEA (note 3). On the back- and front-end of the nuclear fuel cycle, see section V of this appendix.

[41] 'Nuclear fuel cycle and nuclear proliferation', *SIPRI Yearbook 1978: World Armaments and Disarmament* (Taylor & Francis: London, 1978), p. 26; and Stein, M. et al., 'Multi- or internationalization of the nuclear fuel cycle: revisiting the issue', *Journal of Nuclear Materials Management*, vol. 32, no. 4 (summer 2004), p. 54.

Among many other concepts discussed in the INFCE framework was one that envisaged an international plutonium storage facility. To continue the examination of the issue, in 1978 the IAEA established the Committee on International Plutonium Storage (IPS) to explore possibilities for implementing the INFCE concept under Article XII.A.5 of the IAEA Statute. This is different from the RNFC approach, in which control of materials and technologies was to remain with a group of states, not the IAEA. The Committee looked into the issue until 1982, when it outlined the basis for an IPS scheme in its Final Report, but disagreements over the definition of 'excess plutonium', the nature and location of storage facility, and the mechanisms determining the release of plutonium by the IAEA led to no outcome.[42] An Expert Group on Spent Fuel Storage was convened in parallel, also with no results.

The 1978 US Nuclear Non-Proliferation Act (NNPA) provided for negotiations on the establishment of an International Nuclear Fuel Authority (INFA) with responsibility for ensuring fuel supply on reasonable terms, which could have led to the creation of the backup fuel bank. However, this initiative was not pursued.[43]

In June 1980 the IAEA established the Committee on Assurances of Supply (CAS) to explore measures to ensure a guaranteed supply of nuclear material, equipment and technology to states committed to non-proliferation and to determine the IAEA's role in this context.[44] CAS discussed various emergency and backup supply mechanisms, including the idea of multinational fuel cycle centres, but was unable to reach consensus before it was disbanded in 1987.

On 5 December 1980 the UN General Assembly established the United Nations Conference for the Promotion of International Cooperation in the Peaceful Use of Nuclear Energy (UNCPICPUNE).[45] It discussed, in particular, the concerns of developing states related to nuclear safety issues, security measures to prevent diversion, and the link between non-proliferation and assurances of supply. UNPICPUNE reaffirmed the need for international cooperation on the peaceful uses of nuclear energy but failed to result in any substantive product.

The IAEA held the International Symposium on Nuclear Fuel Cycle and Reactor Strategies on 3–6 June 1997 as another follow-up to the 1980 INFCE study. IAEA Director General Hans Blix stated there that installed nuclear capacity in 2000 had turned out to be much lower than was predicted in 1980, that fast breeder technology was not commercialized and that the closed nuclear fuel cycle had not taken hold.[46] Nonetheless, the symposium concluded that the creation of a global nuclear system in which sensitive fuel cycle activities are centralized in a few locations is still feasible; that such multilateral centres can provide both economic and non-proliferation benefits; and that international cooperation in the back-end of the nuclear fuel cycle,

[42] Rauf, T., 'Perspectives on multilateral approaches to the nuclear fuel cycle', Address to the 2004 Carnegie Nonproliferation Conference, Washington, DC, 2004, URL <http://www.ceip.org/files/projects/npp/resources/2004conference/speeches/rauf.ppt>.

[43] The NNPA also sought to limit the transfer of reprocessing technology and to curb the reprocessing of US-origin fuel abroad. Nuclear Non-Proliferation Act of 1978, URL <http://www.nti.org/db/china/engdocs/nnpa1978.htm>.

[44] Bailey, E. et al., *PPNN Briefing Book*, vol. 1, 'The peaceful uses of nuclear energy', *The Evolution of the Nuclear Non-Proliferation Regime*, 6th edn (Mountbatten Centre for International Studies, Program for Promoting Nuclear Non-Proliferation (PPNN): Southampton, 2000), URL <http://www.mcis.soton.ac.uk/Bb1Chap8.pdf>, p. 48.

[45] Bailey et al. (note 44), p. 48.

[46] IAEA, 'Nuclear fuel cycle and reactor strategies: adjusting to new realities, Contributed papers, IAEA International Symposium, Vienna, 3–6 June 1997', IAEA-TECDOC-990, 18 Dec. 1997, URL <http://www-pub.iaea.org/MTCD/publications/PDF/te_990_prn.pdf>.

including centralized disposal of the spent nuclear fuel, should be encouraged. In 2003 and 2005 the IAEA again confirmed that regional spent-fuel storage facilities are technically feasible, potentially viable economically, and advantageous in terms of non-proliferation and nuclear security, and that the real challenges to their development lay in the areas of political, social and public acceptance.[47] In 2001 and 2002 the IAEA broadened its focus on multilateralization of the fuel cycle beyond reprocessing and enrichment to include repositories for spent fuel and nuclear waste. In 2004 the Agency published its conclusions on developing multinational radioactive waste repositories.[48]

IV. Multilateral approaches to the nuclear fuel cycle

In 2003 and 2004 IAEA Director General ElBaradei gave a new impetus to studies on security in the development of nuclear energy. This was first done in his statement to the IAEA General Conference in September 2003 and developed further in October 2003, when he proposed a new approach to the problem, consisting of three parts: (*a*) the restriction of operations with highly enriched uranium (HEU) and plutonium exclusively to facilities under multinational control; (*b*) a transition to new nuclear-energy systems that by design avoid the use of materials directly usable for weapons; and (*c*) the introduction of multinational approaches to the management and disposal of spent fuel and radioactive waste.[49]

The Expert Group that was established by ElBaradei in June 2004 had a threefold mandate: (*a*) to analyse issues and options relevant for multilateral nuclear approaches (MNAs) to the nuclear fuel cycle; (*b*) to provide an overview of the incentives and disincentives for cooperation in multilateral arrangements; and (*c*) to provide a brief review of the historical and current experiences and analyses relevant to the study. The group was to set out options for a solution, but not to choose or indicate any preference for one option. Any solution that was proposed was to be concrete, inclusive and without reference to the status of specific states under the NPT.

The Expert Group concluded that past initiatives for multilateral nuclear cooperation had not produced any tangible results, for several reasons. First, proliferation concerns were not strong enough in the past. Second, most of the past initiatives lacked sufficient economic incentives. Third, concerns about assurances of supply were paramount. Finally, factors such as national pride and expectations of technological and economic spin-offs played a role in negotiations on MNAs. The Expert Group agreed that 'the case to be made in favour of MNAs is not entirely straightforward', but it tried to contribute to the development of MNAs by identifying five specific options that would be possible to introduce gradually and noted a number of pros and cons for each. All these options aim at a simultaneous increase in non-proliferation assurances and assurances of supply and services relevant to the nuclear fuel cycle.[50]

---

[47] Rauf (note 42); and IAEA, 'Technical, economic and institutional aspects of regional spent fuel storage facilities', IAEA-TECDOC-1482, Nov. 2005, URL <http://www-pub.iaea.org/MTCD/publications/PDF/te_1482_web.pdf>.

[48] IAEA, 'Developing multinational radioactive waste repositories: infrastructural framework and scenarios of cooperation', IAEA-TECDOC-1413, 15 Oct. 2004, URL <http://www-pub.iaea.org/MTCD/publications/PDF/te_1413_web.pdf>.

[49] ElBaradei (note 13), pp. 43–44.

[50] IAEA (note 16).

1. The first option is to reinforce existing commercial market mechanisms using assurances provided by suppliers through long-term contracts and transparent arrangements, possibly with government backing. For the front-end of the fuel cycle this could mean, for example, that a state which decided not to pursue nuclear fuel production would be offered an arrangement whereby it could lease nuclear fuel and then give it back or one in which it would be guaranteed the provision of enrichment capacities. Commercial or intergovernmental 'fuel banks' could be envisaged. At the back-end of the fuel cycle, commercial offers to store and dispose of spent fuel are possible. The major advantages of this arrangement are that it is easy to implement, does not require new facilities or further dissemination of know-how and does not imply an extra financial burden on the IAEA. The disadvantages of this approach may come from its market nature, because the costs of required idle reserve capacities may be high. In addition, the credibility of assurances provided by private firms or even by consortia of states may not seem sufficient for some.

2. The second option is to introduce international supply guarantees with IAEA participation. This is a variation of the previous option, with the IAEA acting as a guarantor of the supply. For the front-end of the fuel cycle, for example, the IAEA either could hold title to the stock of nuclear material or may have in place the mechanism to ensure that one supplier would replace another should the first fail to perform. For the back-end of the fuel cycle this could mean essentially the revival of the old idea of International Plutonium Storage (IPS), exploiting the provisions of Article XII.A.5 of the IAEA Statute. The Expert Group noted that the failure of previous ideas of this kind was due to the reluctance of states to renounce national sovereignty over separated plutonium. The international storage of spent fuel, however, could generate more interest because it is less immediately valuable, more difficult to store and less sensitive than separated plutonium. International storage of mixed oxide (MOX) fuel is also conceivable in this framework. The advantages and disadvantages of this option are similar to those of the previous option; in addition, the participation of the IAEA gives more credibility and flexibility to the whole exercise. In the case of IPS, other difficulties apply, related to the complex setup and demanding management requirements, with attending financial implications.

3. In this option, national facilities would be put under multinational control, with the participation of all states, regardless of their relationship to the NPT. This would mean the creation of new players on the market. For the front-end of the fuel cycle, EURODIF would be the most likely model for such conversion. For the back-end there are the existing examples of Eurochemic and the reprocessing of Japanese nuclear fuel in the UK. The advantages of such an arrangement include the fact that no new construction of facilities or dissemination of know-how are required, additional safeguards may be introduced where they do not exist, and the expertise of various states may be pooled. The disadvantages, especially regarding the back-end of the fuel cycle, include the difficulties of international management, low political and public acceptance, increased transportation requirements and the fact that several multinational facilities would have to be built, in more than one country, in order to provide credible assurance of supply. However, arguments for internationalization of the efforts of the nuclear industry are visible in the adjacent area of nuclear science, with its trend to consolidate future research in a few 'centres of excellence'.[51]

---

[51] IAEA, 'New life for research reactors? Bright future but far fewer projected', IAEA Staff Report, 8 Mar. 2004, URL <http://www.iaea.org/NewsCenter/Features/ResearchReactors/reactors20040308.html>.

4. A fourth option is to create, through voluntary agreements and contracts, multinational or regional MNAs for new facilities based on joint ownership, drawing rights or co-management. Different models have been used to operate a multinational enrichment facility at the front-end of the nuclear fuel cycle. The original arrangement of Urenco entailed the sharing of technology between the partners involved. Later, Urenco evolved into the complex 'black-box' model, in which design and assembly of centrifuges are done in the Netherlands and completed centrifuges are exported to enrichment plants in partner states. Another model is used by EURODIF: the level of investment of each partner corresponds to its percentage share of the product, but the enrichment facility is operated by only one partner— France. Joint construction of a new facility for the back-end of the fuel cycle was investigated in the IAEA's RNFC study. The example of a multinational reprocessing facility is Eurochemic. There is also the conceivable option of 'fuel cycle centres', combining in one location several segments of the fuel cycle. It is believed that regional fuel cycle centres offer most of the benefits of other MNAs, in particular with regard to material security and transport. The existence of precedents and the results of studies suggest that this fourth option is feasible, although the creation of a new facility from scratch would require large human and financial resources, and additional non-proliferation and commercial issues would have to be addressed. Issues of political and public acceptance would also arise under this approach.

5. The fifth option is more remote. In the case of a further expansion of nuclear energy around the world, there may be scope for the development of a nuclear fuel cycle with stronger multilateral arrangements and broader cooperation, involving the IAEA and the international community. For example, a worldwide network of regional fuel cycle centres would minimize transport and give customers a degree of flexibility.

The Expert Group's report prompted both debate and official action. At the September 2005 IAEA General Conference, the USA officially declared that the US Department of Energy (DOE) would reserve up to 17 tonnes of HEU from materials previously declared excess to US national security needs for 'an IAEA verifiable assured supply arrangement' for states renouncing enrichment,[52] and Russia has made a similar proposal.[53] In October 2005 the Nuclear Threat Initiative (NTI) endorsed the idea of a uranium stockpile being used as 'a backstop guarantee of nuclear fuel supply' under IAEA control and assessed that the optimum size of a fully developed stockpile should be 10 per cent of annual civilian demand. The NTI announced its intention to contribute to such a stockpile low-enriched uranium (LEU) of sufficient volume to yield fuel for one standard 1000-megawatts-electric (MW(e) power reactor for three years. The NTI offered to give a $50 million grant to the IAEA to cover the cost of buying the HEU declared excessive for military purposes, its downblending to LEU, transport and storage.[54] In November 2005 Russia tried to resolve the international controversy over the scope and nature of Iran's nuclear programme by offering to establish a joint venture to produce nuclear fuel on Russian territory,

[52] IAEA, 'Communication dated 28 September 2005 from the Permanent Mission of the United States of America to the Agency', IAEA Information Circular INFCIRC/659, 29 Sep. 2005, URL <http://www.iaea.org/Publications/Documents/Infcircs/2005/infcirc659.pdf>.

[53] 'Russia proposes creating reserve stock of nuclear fuel under IAEA control', RIA Novosti, 13 July 2005.

[54] 'Catalyzing an IAEA nuclear material stockpile', Material from the NTI Governing Board Meeting, Moscow, Oct. 2005, provided by Rolf Ekéus.

effectively outsourcing the Iranian enrichment programme to Russia.[55] In January 2006 Russian President Vladimir Putin generalized this proposal and essentially endorsed the findings of the IAEA Expert Group by calling for the 'creation of a system of international centres providing nuclear fuel cycle services, including enrichment, on a non-discriminatory basis and under the control of the IAEA'.[56] In February 2006 the US DOE announced its Global Nuclear Energy Partnership (GNEP) programme, part of which is a proposal to establish 'a fuel services program that would allow developing nations to acquire and use nuclear energy economically while minimizing the risk of nuclear proliferation'.[57]

The idea of multilateral supply guarantees is thus beginning to materialize under the umbrella of the IAEA, although many practical arrangements remain to be settled. Some states are less than enthusiastic, however, because in their view such guarantees can be successful only if all parties are confident in the availability of fuel and services, regardless of political developments. An IAEA fuel bank is not acceptable to some to a large extent because they do not see sufficiently credible assurances that the IAEA would not stop supplies for reasons other than those related to the compliance of individual states with the NPT: for example, for fear that the necessary export licences would not be granted for political reasons. Various models for providing such assurances were put forward in 2005.[58]

V. Proliferation-resistant nuclear fuel cycle technologies

The nuclear fuel cycle consists of two distinctive parts. The first part, or 'front-end', is a set of stages that lead to the preparation of fuel for reactor operation. Although enrichment is not needed for some reactors and it is conceivable to use thorium instead of uranium, in most cases the front-end consists of uranium ore exploration, mining, milling, uranium conversion, enrichment and fuel fabrication.[59] After fuel has been irradiated and unloaded from the reactor, the second part of the nuclear fuel cycle, the 'back-end', begins. It may consist of three stages: intermediate fuel storage; fuel reprocessing in order to separate useful isotopes such as plutonium-239 and uranium-235 from waste; and nuclear waste disposal.[60] Fuel reprocessing may be omitted, in which case all the spent fuel is ultimately disposed as waste. It is widely recognized that two steps of the nuclear fuel cycle—enrichment and reprocessing—are especially proliferation-prone. It is relatively easy to build a crude nuclear

---

[55] See chapter 13.

[56] Official Web Portal of the President of Russia, 'Statement on the Peaceful Use of Nuclear Energy', 25 Jan. 2006, URL <http://president.kremlin.ru/eng/text/speeches/2006/01/25/1741_type82912type 82914_100665.shtml>.

[57] US Department of Energy, Office of Public Affairs, 'Department of Energy announces new nuclear initiative', Press release, Washington, DC, 6 Feb. 2006, URL <http://www.gnep.energy.gov/pdfs/gnep PressRelease020606.pdf>.

[58] Goldschmidt, P., 'Mechanisms to increase nuclear fuel supply guarantees', Carnegie International Non-Proliferation Conference, Washington, DC, 7–8 Nov. 2005, URL <http://www.carnegieendowment. org/static/npp/2005conference/presentations/Goldschmidt_fuel_supply.pdf>; Gottemoeller, R., 'One model for a fuel supply agreement', Presentation at the Workshop on International Fuel Services, Nuclear Power and Nonproliferation, Stockholm, 12 Dec. 2005; and chapter 13 in this volume.

[59] 'Enrichment' is 'an isotope separation process by which the abundance of a specified isotope in an element is increased', e.g., production of HEU or heavy water. IAEA (note 3), pp. 33, 41.

[60] Nuclear fuel 'reprocessing' is 'a chemical separation of nuclear material from fission products'. IAEA (note 3), pp. 33, 41.

explosive device once a sufficient amount of direct-use material is obtained. Enrichment and reprocessing can lead to the production of such material in the eminently suitable form of HEU or plutonium.

Uranium enrichment facilities under IAEA safeguards currently exist in Argentina, Brazil, China, Germany, Iran, Japan, the Netherlands and the UK. Furthermore, enrichment facilities that are not under safeguards exist in France, India, Pakistan, Russia and the USA. Australia, Israel and South Africa have developed technologies and processes to the point where they can be said to have a working understanding of uranium enrichment.[61] Industrial-scale uranium enrichment facilities are listed in table 13C.2.

None of the nuclear weapon states is believed to be currently reprocessing spent nuclear fuel for military purposes, although this may be under way in India, Israel, North Korea and Pakistan. Large commercial plutonium separation plants are operated in France, Russia and the UK. India operates three smaller plutonium separation facilities and one for thorium separation. Japan operates one such facility and is planning to begin commercial operation of another in the near future.[62] Details on world civilian reprocessing plants are given in table 13C.3. A significant number of other countries that pursued but subsequently abandoned military nuclear programmes have also conducted research on or developed reprocessing technologies and processes.

Many of the technologies employed in the contemporary nuclear fuel cycle were originally developed for use in military applications. For instance, gaseous diffusion technology for uranium enrichment 'was developed in an atmosphere of intense urgency and with virtually none of the normal constraints on costs, efficiency and profitability', let alone environmental, non-proliferation or sustainability considerations.[63] This has resulted in a highly distorted subsequent development of the enrichment industry and nuclear fuel cycle technologies in general. With the huge investments already made in military applications, governments around the world have been more inclined to adapt developed technologies and processes than to search for new ones that could be more suitable for the safe development of civil nuclear power. A different approach to dealing with the dual nature of nuclear energy is based on the idea of introducing new, proliferation-resistant technologies. Although they cannot make nuclear facilities absolutely proliferation-proof, new technologies could make illicit use very difficult.[64] This approach may be applied on two levels.

At one level, proposals have been made to replace individual sensitive technologies with proliferation-resistant technologies. The most successful proposal today is to replace the HEU fuel of research and isotope-producing reactors with high-density LEU fuel. The Reduced Enrichment for Research and Test Reactors (RERTR) Program was initiated by the US DOE in 1978 and is still operating successfully, with

---

[61] IAEA (note 16), pp. 133–36; and Makhijani, A., Chalmers, L. and Smith, B., 'Uranium enrichment', Institute for Energy and Environmental Research, Takoma Park, Md., 15 Oct. 2004, URL <http://www.ieer.org/reports/uranium/enrichment.pdf>.

[62] 'Summary table: production and status of military stocks of fissile material, end of 2003', URL <http://www.isis-online.org/mapproject/supplements.html>; World Nuclear Association, 'Processing of used nuclear fuel' Information and Issue Brief, London, Mar. 2005, URL <http://www.world-nuclear.org/info/inf69.htm>; and IAEA (note 16), pp. 79–81.

[63] Krass et al. (note 32), pp. 14–16.

[64] A good review of the notion of 'proliferation resistance' is given in Feiveson, H. A., 'Proliferation resistant nuclear fuel cycles', *Annual Review of Energy*, vol. 3 (Nov. 1978), pp. 357–94.

Table 13C.2. Estimated world industrial-scale uranium enrichment capacity, as of April 2005

Operator	Technology	Nominal capacity (million kgSWU per year)[a]
China		
Heping Uranium Enrichment Plant	Gaseous diffusion	0.2–0.3[b]
Lanzhou Nuclear Fuel Complex	Centrifuge	0.5
Shaanxi Uranium Enrichment Plant[c]	Centrifuge	0.5
France		
EURODIF Production	Gaseous diffusion	10.8
Germany		
Urenco Deutschland GmbH	Centrifuge	1.8
Japan		
Japan Nuclear Fuel Limited	Centrifuge	1.05
Netherlands		
Urenco Nederland BV	Centrifuge	2.6
Russia		
Angarsk Electrolysis Chemical Complex	Centrifuge	1.6
Urals Electrochemical Integrated Plant	Centrifuge	9.8
Zelenogorsk Electrochemical Plant	Centrifuge	5.8
Siberian Chemical Combine	Centrifuge	2.8
United Kingdom		
Urenco (Capenhurst) Ltd	Centrifuge	3.0
United States		
United States Enrichment Corporation	Gaseous diffusion	11.3

[a] Separative work unit (SWU) is a measure of the effort required in an enrichment facility to separate uranium of a given content of uranium-235 into 2 components, 1 with a higher and 1 with a lower percentage of uranium-235. The unit of separative work is the kilogram separative work unit (kgSWU, or SWU).

[b] Unofficial estimates. Cirincione, J., Wolfsthal, J. B. and Rajkumar M., 'China', *Deadly Arsenals: Nuclear, Biological, and Chemical Threats* (Carnegie Endowment for International Peace: Washington, DC, 2005), p. 162. Some experts believe that this facility was shut down.

[c] There are 2 facilities at this plant.

Sources: IAEA, *Multilateral Approaches to the Nuclear Fuel Cycle: Expert Group Report to the Director General of the International Atomic Energy Agency* (IAEA: Vienna, 2005), pp. 62–66; Bukharin, O., 'Understanding Russia's uranium enrichment complex', *Science and Global Security*, no. 12 (2004), p. 195; *Urenco Annual Report and Accounts, 2004*, URL <http://www.urenco.com/im/uploaded/1125054354>, p. 8; Harding, P. J. C., Urenco, 'The role of UK business in providing security of energy supply from nuclear power: BEA Workshop, London, 14 April 2005', URL <http://www.worldenergy.org/wec-geis/global/down loads/bea/BEA_WS_0405Harding.pdf>, p. 9; Nuclear Engineering International, *World Nuclear Industry Handbook 2005* (Wilmington Publishing: Sidcup, 2005), p. 216; and World Nuclear Association, 'Nuclear power in China', Information and Issue Brief, Dec. 2005, URL <http://www.world-nuclear.org/info/inf63.htm>.

a parallel programme in Russia. Proposals along these lines exist for other types of reactor using HEU, in particular for naval propulsion.[65]

Another suggestion has been to introduce the proliferation-resistant technology of chemical enrichment of uranium, which would be economically competitive with other processes while producing LEU, but would make it technically infeasible to reach a level of enrichment that is suitable for a nuclear explosive device. Variations of such technologies have been developed independently by France and Japan. On the one hand, slow kinetics and criticality limitations, the two main intrinsic features of both processes, do not allow the attainment of high uranium-235 assays and thus make them proliferation-resistant.[66] On the other hand, French chemical enrichment technology was pursued in the Iraqi clandestine nuclear programme and might have produced LEU for further enrichment in another process if more effort had been put into it.[67] The chemical enrichment process is reportedly economically competitive, relatively simple and fairly similar to processes in the petrochemistry industry, and adaptable to small- or medium-scale applications. It also involves a low level of energy consumption.[68] The technology for gaseous diffusion enrichment can also be proliferation-resistant if the plant using this technology is designed specifically to produce LEU.[69]

Proposals have also been put forward to introduce proliferation-resistant technologies to the back-end of the fuel cycle. The idea here is to develop processes for spent fuel reprocessing that would operate with mixtures of plutonium and other selected elements for preparing proliferation-resistant fuel. For example, in November 2005 the US Secretary of Energy, Samuel W. Bodman, set the goal to develop 'recycling technologies that do not produce separated plutonium'.[70] This idea was incorporated in the US DOE's Global Nuclear Energy Partnership (GNEP) programme.[71] Some experts question the value of such recycling technologies in terms of their proliferation resistance.[72]

At the second level, several more ambitious proposals have been put forward for the development of new, innovative nuclear energy systems that would be safe, sustainable, economically attractive and proliferation-resistant.

---

[65] von Hippel, F., 'A comprehensive approach to elimination of highly-enriched-uranium from all nuclear-reactor fuel cycles', *Science and Global Security*, no. 12 (2004), p. 147. Russia also proposed building floating nuclear power plants that would use an LEU-based fuel and would be available for leasing. Samoilov, O. B., 'Russian reactor development: ploughing the waves', *Nuclear Engineering International*, Jan. 2006.

[66] Krass et al. (note 32), pp. 17–21. 'Assay' refers to the level of enrichment; see, e.g., IAEA, 'Management of high enriched uranium for peaceful purposes: status and trends', IAEA-TECDOC-1452, June 2005, p. 1.

[67] Cordesman, A. H., *Iraq and the War of Sanctions: Conventional Threats and Weapons of Mass Destruction* (Praeger: Westport, Conn., 1999), p. 614.

[68] Coates, J. H. and Barré, B., 'Practical suggestions for the improvement of proliferation resistance within the enriched uranium fuel cycle', eds F. Barnaby et al., SIPRI, *Nuclear Energy and Nuclear Weapon Proliferation* (Taylor & Francis: London, 1979), pp. 49–53; and Kokoski, R., SIPRI, *Technology and the Proliferation of Nuclear Weapons* (Oxford University Press: Oxford, 1995), p. 64.

[69] Kokoski (note 68), pp. 65–66.

[70] '2005 Carnegie Non-proliferation Conference: Remarks prepared for Energy Secretary Sam Bodman', Washington, DC, 7 Nov. 2005, URL <http://www.doe.gov/engine/content.do?PUBLIC_ID=19141&TT_CODE=PRESSSPEECH>.

[71] US Department of Energy (note 57).

[72] Kang, J. and von Hippel, F., 'Limited proliferation-resistance benefits from recycling unseparated transuranics and lanthanides from light-water reactor spent fuel', *Science and Global Security*, no. 13 (2005), pp. 169–81.

Table 13C.3. World civilian spent fuel reprocessing capacity, as of April 2005

Operator (Plant)	Nominal capacity (MTHM/yr)	Reprocessing fuel type
France		
COGEMA (La Hague UP2 800)	1 000[a]	Light-water reactors
COGEMA (La Hague UP3)	1 000[a]	Light-water reactors
India		
Indira Gandhi Centre for Atomic Research (Kalpakkam Atomic Reprocessing Plant)	125	Pressurized heavy-water reactors
Nuclear Power Corporation of India, Ltd (Tarapur Power Reactor Fuel Reprocessing Plant)	100	Pressurized heavy-water reactors
Bhabha Atomic Research Centre (Trombay Plutonium Reprocessing Plant)	50	Pressurized heavy-water reactors
Japan		
Japan Nuclear Fuel Cycle Development Institute (Tokaimura Reprocessing Plant)	200	Light-water reactors
Russia		
Mayak Production Association (RT-1 Reprocessing Plant)	400	VVER-440 and RBMK power reactors; research, naval, fast, isotope-producing reactors
United Kingdom		
British Nuclear Group (Sellafield Mixed Oxide Plant)	1 500	Magnox reactors
British Nuclear Group (Thermal Oxide Reprocessing Plant)	900	Advanced gas-cooled and light-water reactors

MTHM = Metric tonnes of heavy metal.

[a] The actual maximum combined production level of all the La Hague plants does not exceed 1700 MTHM/year. Extra capacity is kept in order to maintain 'industrial flexibility to spread the workload more evenly between the 2 units, and not to increase total production'. COGEMA, 'Press release: Review of the public inquiry concerning the La Hague plant', 7 June 2000, URL <http://www.cogemalahague.fr/servlet/ContentServer?pagename=cogema_en/communique/communiqué_full_template&c=communique&cid=1039473237061&p=1039 482707003>.

Sources: IAEA, *Multilateral Approaches to the Nuclear Fuel Cycle: Expert Group Report to the Director General of the International Atomic Energy Agency* (IAEA: Vienna, 2005), pp. 79–81; Korotkevich, V. and Kudryavtsev, E., 'Spent nuclear fuel management in the Russian Federation: technology and safety', *Bulletin on Atomic Energy* (Moscow), no. 12 (Dec. 2002), p. 26, URL <http://www.minatom.ru/filereader?id=18150>; 'Processing of used nuclear fuel for recycle', World Nuclear Association Issue Brief, Dec. 2005, URL <http://www.world-nuclear.org/info/inf69.htm>; Nuclear Engineering International, *World Nuclear Industry Handbook 2005* (Wilmington Publishing: Sidcup, 2005), p. 218; and IAEA Nuclear Fuel Cycle Information System (NFCIS), URL <http://www-nfcis.iaea.org/NFCIS/NFCIS Main.asp>.

Some studies claim that it may be conceivable to develop a sustainable and proliferation-resistant (because of the specific qualities of the isotopes involved) thorium fuel cycle, although significant technical problems need to be resolved.[73] The thorium fuel cycle concept is not expected to be completely proliferation-proof, but its realization would employ technologies that would make the diversion of fissile material extremely difficult.[74] Development of the thorium nuclear fuel cycle is led by India, and studies are being carried out in Canada, Germany, Russia, the USA and other states. Indian uranium reserves are modest but India's thorium reserves are the world's second largest.[75] In 1958 the Indian Government formally adopted a long-term plan for a future closed thorium fuel cycle and for providing India with an unlimited supply of thorium–uranium-233 fuel.[76] It stipulated that India would build three distinct types of nuclear reactor in consecutive stages. Currently, India is entering the second stage of that plan and is continuing to implement it, but it is still uncertain how proliferation-resistant India's thorium fuel cycle will be.

In January 2000 the US DOE began discussions with other states on international cooperative development of so-called 'Generation IV' nuclear energy systems that comprise the entire nuclear power plant as well as facilities for the entire fuel cycle. This group, representing states with significant nuclear expertise, was formally chartered into the Generation IV International Forum (GIF) in 2001. The goal of the GIF is the research and development of innovative reactor and fuel cycle technologies that represent advances in sustainability, economics, safety, reliability and proliferation-resistance; and they should become commercially viable before 2030. To this end, GIF members selected the six most promising reactor technologies.[77] In February 2005 the USA, Canada, France, Japan and the UK signed an agreement on the joint development of such technologies,[78] with Switzerland and South Korea joining later in the year. The DOE also runs the Advanced Fuel Cycle Initiative, in

[73] Thorium is assessed to be about 3 times more abundant than uranium and about as common as lead. The only natural isotope of thorium, thorium-232, is fertile (it can be converted into a special fissionable material) like uranium-238 and can absorb slow neutrons in the reactor to produce uranium-233, which is fissile (capable of undergoing fission by neutrons of all energies) like uranium-235. Uranium-233 can be separated from the spent fuel and fed back into the reactor as part of a closed fuel cycle. Los Alamos National Laboratory, Chemical Division, 'Thorium', 15 Dec. 2003, URL <http://periodic.lanl.gov/elements/90.html>.

[74] Galperin, A., Reichert, P. and Radkowsky, A., 'Thorium fuel for light water reactors: reducing proliferation potential of nuclear power fuel cycle', *Science and Global Security*, vol. 6 (1997), pp. 265–90.

[75] World Nuclear Association, 'Thorium', Information and Issue Brief, Nov. 2004, URL <http://www.world-nuclear.org/info/inf62.htm>; and 'Thorium: statistics and information', US Department of the Interior, US Geological Survey, Minerals Information, June 2005, URL <http://minerals.usgs.gov/minerals/pubs/commodity/thorium/index.html>.

[76] Perkovich, G., *India's Nuclear Bomb: The Impact on Global Proliferation* (University of California Press: Berkeley, Calif., 1999), pp. 26–27.

[77] The members of the GIF are Argentina, Brazil, Canada, France, Japan, South Korea, South Africa, Switzerland, the UK, the USA and the EU. US DOE Nuclear Energy Research Advisory Committee and the Generation IV International Forum, 'A technology roadmap for Generation IV nuclear energy systems', Dec. 2002, URL <http://gif.inel.gov/roadmap/pdfs/gen_iv_roadmap.pdf>; and World Nuclear Association, 'Generation IV nuclear reactors', Information and Issue Brief, Apr. 2005, URL <http://www.world-nuclear.org/info/inf77.htm>.

[78] The Framework Agreement for International Collaboration on Research and Development of Generation IV Nuclear Energy Systems is available on the Generation IV International Forum website at URL <http://www.gen-4.org/PDFs/Framework-agreement.pdf>.

particular 'to develop reactor fuel and fuel cycle technologies to support Generation IV nuclear energy systems'.[79]

In 2001 the IAEA launched the International Project on Innovative Nuclear Reactors and Fuel Cycles (INPRO). The aim of the project is for IAEA member states to jointly develop innovative nuclear reactor and fuel cycle technology with certain basic features, including effectively unlimited fuel resources, nuclear and environmental safety, proliferation resistance and economic competitiveness.[80] As of the end of 2005 INPRO had developed and validated the methodology for the assessment of innovative nuclear energy systems and is conducting assessments of individual systems under development in IAEA member states in order to pursue their construction in the future. INPRO assessments include a review of the options for multilateral nuclear fuel cycles.[81] In particular, Russia's proposal for a closed nuclear fuel cycle with fast reactors is being evaluated.[82] In September 2005, at the IAEA General Conference, the USA announced that it will join INPRO.[83] This step improved cooperation between INPRO and GIF, which do very similar work.

VI. Conclusions

The only certain way to diminish the risk of the diversion of civil nuclear materials to military programmes would be to cease the use of nuclear power. Nuclear technologies for energy generation are predominantly used for the production of electricity. The sources currently discussed as possible substitutes for nuclear fission in electricity production are fossil fuels, renewable sources and nuclear fusion.[84] If restrictions on the emission of greenhouse gases or price considerations come to impose limitations on the development of fossil fuel power plants, then renewable sources would step in. The prospects for such sources to become reliable replacements for nuclear power within the next few decades are questionable, however. The

---

[79] US Department of Energy, Office of Nuclear Energy, Science and Technology, 'Advanced Fuel Cycle Initiative', Washington, DC, Nov. 2005, URL <http://www.ne.doe.gov/infosheets/afci.pdf>; and 'Advanced fuel cycle program: addressing national priorities and needs', Advanced Fuel Cycle Initiative website, URL <http://afci.lanl.gov/aboutaaa.html>.

[80] International Project on Innovative Nuclear Reactors and Fuel Cycles (INPRO), INPRO Brochure, Sep. 2004, IAEA website, URL <http://www.iaea.org/img/assets/3836/inpro_2004.pdf>, pp. 1–2.

[81] IAEA, 'Draft terms of reference for Phase-1B (second part) and Phase II International Project on Innovative Nuclear Reactors and Fuel Cycles (INPRO)', URL <http://www.iaea.org/OurWork/ST/NE/NENP/NPTDS/Downloads/INPRO/tor_phase_1b_2_rev_ys_final.pdf>.

[82] Perrera, J., 'Innovation for tomorrow', *Nuclear Engineering International*, 29 Sep. 2005, URL <http://www.neimagazine.com/story.asp?sectioncode=76&storyCode=2031487>.

[83] IAEA Information Circular INFCIRC/659 (note 52).

[84] Fusion power is useful energy generated in nuclear fusion reactions where 2 light atomic nuclei fuse together to form a heavier nucleus and release energy. The most feasible reaction is between 2 isotopes of hydrogen—deuterium and tritium. Deuterium occurs naturally in sea water (30 grams per cubic metre), which means that fusion energy, if and when it is developed, would provide a practically unlimited energy resource. Contemporary fusion research is led by the EU, Japan, Russia and the USA, with substantial programmes also under way in Brazil, Canada, China, India and South Korea. There are a number of ongoing experimental attempts to build fusion power generators, but none of them continuously generates more energy than it uses. As announced in June 2005, the first experimental reactor intended to achieve this goal, ITER, will be built at Cadarache, France, at a cost of €10 billion. Current plans for the development of fusion power show that this technology is not planned to be ready for commercial production of electricity until 2050 or even later. 'France gets nuclear fusion plant', BBC News, 28 June 2005, URL <http://news.bbc.co.uk/1/4629239.stm>; and ITER, 'Fast track to fusion', 21 Oct. 2004, URL <http://www.iter.org/fast_track.htm>.

future share of nuclear power in electricity production may vary, but it is likely that in the foreseeable future all three sources will be used, at least until (or unless) there is a breakthrough in nuclear fusion technology. This means that the goal of ensuring the security and development of nuclear power will remain important for years to come. Even though all three approaches discussed in this appendix may serve this goal well, none of them is sufficient alone. Multilateral arrangements may be misused, as can proliferation-resistant technologies. In addition, international control may be rejected because the NPT does not provide for any consequences for non-nuclear weapon states parties that withdraw from it after having acquired nuclear material and fuel cycle technologies for peaceful purposes.

It is the combination of the three approaches that seems most promising: carried out together, they may reinforce the strengths and cancel the flaws of each other. The IAEA is already combining all three approaches in its work, simultaneously conducting studies on internationalization of the nuclear fuel cycle, developing INPRO and strengthening the safeguards regime. In 2005 Russia and the USA showed that they are also pursuing all three routes simultaneously. However, the exact, optimal combination of measures in the three approaches was not defined in 2005.

14. Chemical and biological warfare developments and arms control

RICHARD GUTHRIE, JOHN HART and FRIDA KUHLAU

I. Introduction

In 2005 the states parties to the 1972 Biological and Toxin Weapons Convention (BTWC)[1] held their third annual expert and political meetings, which considered 'the content, promulgation, and adoption of codes of conduct for scientists' and started preparations for the Sixth Review Conference, to be held in 2006. The states parties to the 1993 Chemical Weapons Convention (CWC)[2] decided to extend the action plans on national implementation and universality. The US-led Iraq Survey Group (ISG) published its conclusions on past Iraqi weapon programmes at the end of its investigations in Iraq, and further information was made public about the sources that had been used for pre-war intelligence and the methodologies for handling such information. More information relating to allegations of terrorist acquisition of chemical and biological materials for hostile purposes was revealed as a consequence of the acquittals of a number of individuals accused of such activities.

Issues relating to the control of biological weapons are discussed in section II of this chapter. Developments in chemical weapons and disarmament are described in section III. Section IV discusses developments in relation to Iraq and the connected intelligence issues. Section V covers other allegations, activities and prosecutions. Section VI presents the conclusions. Appendix 14A considers means of enhancing bio-security and the need for a global strategy.

II. Biological issues

In 2005 Moldova acceded to the BTWC, meaning that, as of 31 December 2005, 155 states were parties to it. An additional 16 states have signed but not

---

[1] The Convention on the Prohibition of the Development, Production and Stockpiling of Bacteriological (Biological) and Toxin Weapons and on Their Destruction was signed on 10 Apr. 1972 and enterd into force on 26 Mar. 1975. It is reproduced on the SIPRI Chemical and Biological Warfare Project website, URL <http://www.sipri.org/contents/cbwarfare/>. The site includes complete lists of parties, signatories and non-signatories to this convention. See also annex A in this volume.

[2] The Convention on the Prohibition of the Development, Production, Stockpiling and Use of Chemical Weapons and on their Destruction (corrected version), 8 Aug. 1994 was signed on 13 Jan. 1993 and enterd into force on 29 Apr. 1997. It is available on the SIPRI Chemical and Biological Warfare Project website (note 1). The site includes complete lists of parties, signatories and non-signatories to this convention. See also annex A in this volume.

ratified the BTWC.[3] During 2005, separate from the formal meetings of the BTWC parties, a number of external activities took place such as a regional meeting of BTWC parties co-hosted by Australia and Indonesia in February.[4]

The BTWC is the only global convention prohibiting possession of a class of weapons of mass destruction (WMD) that has no formal verification and compliance mechanisms. Negotiations on a protocol that had been intended to provide such a mechanism came to an abrupt halt in 2001.[5]

The 2005 BTWC meetings: codes of conduct

In 2005 the parties to the BTWC held a Meeting of Experts and a Meeting of States Parties, following on from similar meetings held in 2003[6] and 2004.[7] The mandate for the 2005 meetings was to consider 'the content, promulgation, and adoption of codes of conduct for scientists'.[8] The meetings are the result of a decision taken by the reconvened Fifth Review Conference of the States Parties to the BTWC in 2002.[9]

The BTWC *Meeting of Experts* was held in Geneva on 13–24 June 2005.[10] In addition to the usual presentations by states parties, a novel feature was that

[3] 'List of states parties', BTWC Meeting of the States Parties document BWC/MSP/2005/MX/INF.5, 21 June 2005. Although no states are reported to have acceded later in the year, Kazakhstan indicated in 2005 that 'the appropriate internal procedures are currently taking place' to accede to the BTWC in a statement to the Conference on Disarmament (CD) in Mar., as reproduced in CD/PV.980, 17 Mar. 2005. Unless otherwise noted, all United Nations (UN), CD and BTWC meetings documents cited in this chapter are available via the UN documents website URL <http://documents.un.org>.

[4] Mathews, R. J. (ed.), *Proceedings of the Biological Weapons Convention Regional Workshop: Co-hosted by the Governments of Australia and Indonesia: 21–25 February 2005* (University of Melbourne: Melbourne, 2005).

[5] Zanders, J. P., Hart, J. and Kuhlau, F., 'Chemical and biological weapon developments and arms control', *SIPRI Yearbook 2002: Armaments, Disarmament and International Security* (Oxford University Press: Oxford, 2002), pp. 665–708.

[6] Guthrie, R. et al., 'Chemical and biological warfare developments and arms control', *SIPRI Yearbook 2004: Armaments, Disarmament and International Security* (Oxford University Press: Oxford, 2004), pp. 661–67. The 2003 meeting topics were 'the adoption of necessary national measures to implement the prohibitions set forth in the Convention, including the enactment of penal legislation' and 'national mechanisms to establish and maintain the security and oversight of pathogenic microorganisms and toxins'.

[7] Guthrie, R., Hart, J. and Kuhlau, F., 'Chemical and biological warfare developments and arms control', *SIPRI Yearbook 2005: Armaments, Disarmament and International Security* (Oxford University Press: Oxford, 2005), pp. 604–607. The 2004 meeting topics were 'enhancing international capabilities for responding to, investigating and mitigating the effects of cases of alleged use of biological or toxin weapons or suspicious outbreaks of disease' and 'strengthening and broadening national and international institutional efforts and existing mechanisms for the surveillance, detection, diagnosis and combating of infectious diseases affecting humans, animals, and plants'.

[8] Final Document of the Fifth Review Conference of the States Parties to the Convention on the Prohibition of the Development, Production and Stockpiling of Bacteriological (Biological) Weapons and on Their Destruction, BTWC Review Conference document BWC/CONF.V/17, para. 18 (a), URL <http://www.opbw.org>, p. 3.

[9] Hart, J., Kuhlau, F. and Simon, J., 'Chemical and biological weapon developments and arms control', *SIPRI Yearbook 2003: Armaments, Disarmament and International Security* (Oxford University Press: Oxford, 2003), pp. 646–50.

[10] Pearson, G. S., 'Report from Geneva: the Biological Weapons Convention new process', *CBW Conventions Bulletin*, no. 68 (June 2005), URL <http://www.sussex.ac.uk/spru/hsp/cbwcb68.pdf>, pp. 12–19. Participants from 82 states parties, 3 signatory states, 1 observer state, 8 specialized agencies and intergovernmental organizations, and 16 non-governmental organizations attended. 'List of participants', BTWC Meeting of the States Parties document BWC/MSP/2005/MX/INF.6, 24 June 2005.

formal presentations were made by a number of outside organizations, such as professional associations, invited as 'guests of the Chair'. As in 2004, an informal list of issues raised at the meeting was prepared by the chairman and appended to the report of the meeting.[11] This list of issues was distilled into a synthesis paper by the chairman before the *Meeting of States Parties*,[12] which was held in Geneva on 5–9 December.[13] The meeting recognized that, while the primary responsibility for implementing the convention rests with the states parties, codes of conduct, voluntarily adopted, can make a significant and effective contribution to combating the present and future threats posed by biological and toxin weapons and that a range of different approaches exists to develop such codes. The meeting also recognized that all those with a responsibility for, or legitimate interest in, codes of conduct should be involved in their development, promulgation and adoption.[14]

The issues addressed by these two inter-governmental meetings are challenging and require the attention not only of governments but also of the scientific community.[15] As the process of scientific study involves communication between scientists and relies on the free exchange of information between individuals and between institutions, a framework that includes codes of conduct relating to any activities that could potentially promote the hostile use of biological sciences should enhance the overall regime. While the guidance in codes might not inhibit an individual with the intent to cause harm, it would strengthen the norm and make it easier for scientists to alert others if someone were undertaking questionable activities.

Concerns have been expressed that codes of conduct are difficult to formulate precisely. However, by their nature, codes deal primarily with subject matter that cannot be clearly defined. Where there are clear dividing lines between acceptable and unacceptable practices, traditional forms of law and regulation can operate effectively, but many life science subjects deal with dual-use materials and technologies and have no such clear dividing lines. The context and circumstances of each research activity in these cases must be carefully assessed and reviewed, and this is where codes of conduct have their greatest added value.

---

[11] 'Report of the Meeting of Experts', BTWC Meeting of the States Parties document BWC/MSP/2005/MX/3, 5 Aug. 2005. The report includes a complete list of working papers and other documents from the meeting.

[12] 'Considerations, lessons, perspectives, recommendations, conclusions and proposals drawn from the presentations, statements, working papers and interventions on the topic under discussion at the Meeting of Experts', BTWC Meeting of the States Parties document BWC/MSP/2005/L.1, 16 Nov. 2005.

[13] Pearson, G. S., 'Report from Geneva: the Biological Weapons Convention Meeting of States Parties, 2005', *CBW Conventions Bulletin*, no. 69/70 (Sep.–Dec. 2005), pp. 15–27, URL <http://www.sussex.ac.uk/Units/spru/hsp/CBWCB%2069-70.pdf>. Participants from 87 states parties, 7 signatory states, 2 observer states, 6 specialized agencies and intergovernmental organizations, and 18 non-governmental organizations attended. 'List of participants', BTWC Meeting of the States Parties document BWC/MSP/2005/INF.2, 9 Dec. 2005.

[14] 'Report of the Meeting of States Parties', BTWC Meeting of the States Parties document BWC/MSP/2005/3, 14 Dec. 2005.

[15] See also appendix 14A.

Codes of conduct create a set of benchmarks by which activities can be assessed. In the context of the BTWC, the most significant benchmark that could be adopted in codes is the general purpose criterion embodied in the convention. This criterion prohibits all activities within the remit of the convention unless there is legitimate justification for an activity, including the scale of that activity. Some comparisons have been made with the Hippocratic oath traditionally taken by doctors when qualifying. However, few medical schools use the original oath; there have been a number of modern variations, and some attempts have been made to unify these newer versions.[16] Only a small proportion of professional scientific associations have a code of conduct for their members.

Other subjects of debate have included: (a) whether ethical standards should be established on a national basis, with the hope that eventually international standards will develop, or whether an international set of codes should be agreed upon which can then be adopted on a national basis; and (b) whether codes should be promulgated by governments, by professional scientific associations or by both.

Codes cannot exist in isolation but must form part of a broader package of educational measures. There is a broad consensus that scientists should receive more training to help them examine the wider consequences of their research and how it might be misused by others. Codes formulated with the cooperation of scientists would be better than codes imposed by governments which may be overly restrictive and have the effect of both hampering legitimate research and discouraging scientists from pursuing certain legitimate research areas.

The 2006 BTWC Review Conference and the inter-sessional process

The sixth five-yearly BTWC review conference is to be held within the period 20 November–8 December 2006.[17] The Preparatory Committee (PrepCom) meeting for the review conference is to be held on 26–28 April 2006 and will take the formal decision on the dates. Ambassador Masood Khan of Pakistan will chair both the PrepCom and the review conference. There is still no clear common understanding on how the outcomes of the series of annual meetings that formed the inter-sessional process will be handled during the 2006 review conference.

The inter-sessional process since 2003 has made a number of achievements. It enabled a focus on particular practical subjects; it encouraged states parties to implement the convention more effectively through a range of national measures, based on shared experience and lessons learned by other states parties; through the intergovernmental process it ensured that states maintained a political focus on biological issues and continued to employ officials special-

---

[16] E.g., a proposed 'Revised Hippocratic oath' was presented to the World Medical Association by the British Medical Association in 1997.

[17] At the time of this decision at the Meeting of States Parties there was no consensus over whether the review conference should be of 2 or 3 weeks' duration. See 'Report of the Meeting of States Parties' (note 14).

izing in the subject; and, to some extent, it mitigated the negative atmosphere existing at the time the protocol negotiations came to a halt.[18]

A number of lessons were learned from the inter-sessional process. The scale of effort that would be needed to bring all states parties up to a basic level of national implementation of BTWC obligations became apparent during the meetings. Many states had believed that national implementation would simply involve adopting laws and regulations but came away from the meetings with a better appreciation of the challenges associated with national legislation, pathogen security and disease surveillance.

Procedural questions

The same decision that established the inter-sessional process also decided that 'The Sixth Review Conference will consider the work of these meetings and decide on any further action'.[19] A measure of the value of the inter-sessional process will be how it is reflected in the proceedings of the review conference. When the inter-sessional process was established, it was assumed that there were various ways in which this might be done.

1. Ideas from the inter-sessional process could be raised during the standard article-by-article review of the convention as carried out at previous review conferences.

2. Presentations could be made to a special portion of the review conference, perhaps as one part of an approach to review by themes.

3. Some form of reporting back to the review conference could be made during the PrepCom.

The alternative to these three options would be not to have any form of input from the inter-sessional process.[20]

Lessons learned

As preparations are made for the review conference, there is an appreciation by many states of the vacuum that would have existed without the inter-sessional process between 2002 and 2006. A number of states, including the members of the European Union (EU), have made explicit calls for a comparable work programme to follow from the 2006 meeting.[21]

Further lessons may be learned from the experiences of other arms control regimes, such as the Action Plans on national implementation and universality

---

[18] See Zanders, Hart and Kuhlau (note 5), pp. 669–73.

[19] BWC/CONF.V/17, para. 18(e) (note 8).

[20] It is possible that none of the Chairs of the meetings of the inter-sessional process will be attending the review conference as all 3 individuals have moved to other posts unconnected with the convention. One early proposal had been for the Chairs of each of the inter-sessional meetings to introduce the relevant subjects being discussed.

[21] The statement by the United Kingdom on behalf of the EU and the national statement by Germany at the Meeting of the States Parties explicitly called for a follow-on work programme.

carried out under the framework of the CWC.[22] However, direct parallels cannot be drawn as there is no central institution for the BTWC equivalent to the CWC's Organisation for the Prohibition of Chemical Weapons (OPCW). As there is firm opposition to the establishment of any form of BTWC institution or secretariat, most notably from the USA, novel thinking may be required: it may be possible to create an 'action plan liaison office' in a form that would not be seen as a prototype for such an institution but could still be a useful focal point for assistance.

Preparedness and response issues

The economic and national security implications of diseases received unprecedented attention during 2005. The reasons for this included: continuing fears that terrorists might deliberately spread disease; the spread outwards from Asia of the H5N1 strain of avian influenza combined with fears that this strain may develop into another that could cause a human epidemic; and the lessons from the impact of Hurricane Katrina on New Orleans and the surrounding area, which made clear that preparations in the USA to protect civilian populations had been inadequate. A number of countries updated or introduced plans for responding to pandemic influenza,[23] and cooperative response measures were discussed in various international forums.[24]

The World Health Assembly adopted new International Health Regulations in May comprising legally binding provisions for member states of the World Health Organization (WHO) on sharing epidemiological information about the transboundary spread of infectious diseases in order to manage public health emergencies of international concern. The new rules will 'prevent, protect against, control and provide a public health response to the international spread of disease'. The original regulations, agreed in 1969, were designed to help monitor and control six serious infectious diseases—cholera, plague, relapsing fever, smallpox, typhus and yellow fever. The new rules will govern a broader range of public health emergencies of international concern, including emerging diseases, and are scheduled to take effect in 2007.[25] The new regulations allow for the WHO Director-General to form a 'determination of a public health emergency of international concern', even if the government of the territory is in disagreement with this conclusion. They also allow for greater flexibility in responding to outbreaks as the WHO may also consult unofficial reports and ask for cooperation from the relevant state in verifying

---

[22] The Action Plans are discussed in section III below.

[23] E.g., US President George W. Bush announced a national strategy in Nov. 2005. The White House, 'National strategy for pandemic influenza', News release, Washington, DC, 1 Nov, 2005, URL <http://www.whitehouse.gov/homeland/pandemic-influenza.html>.

[24] E.g., the Association of South East Asian Nations Summit in Kuala Lumpur on 14 Dec. 2005 adopted the 'East Asia Summit declaration on avian influenza prevention, control and response', URL <http://www.aseansec.org/18101.htm>.

[25] World Health Organization (WHO), 'World Health Assembly adopts new international health regulations', Press release, 23 May 2005, URL <http://www.who.int/mediacentre/news/releases/2005/pr_wha03/en/>. The regulations are contained in WHO document A58/55, 23 May 2005. On emerging diseases see appendix 14A.

them. If a state does not provide a timely response to a request from the WHO for disease outbreak verification, the WHO would be authorized to make such information public.

The European Centre for Disease Prevention and Control (ECDC) began operations in Stockholm, becoming an independent legal entity on 1 July 2005.[26] The role of the centre is to 'to identify, assess and communicate current and emerging threats to human health from communicable diseases'.[27] The ECDC was established in response to an assessment that existing arrangements were 'simply not efficient enough to protect the EU's citizens sufficiently against threats to their health posed by communicable diseases, including the possibility of the deliberate release of infectious agents ("bioterrorism")'.[28]

III. Chemical weapons and disarmament

As of December 2005, 175 states had ratified or acceded to the CWC and a further 11 states had signed but not ratified it,[29] while 8 states had neither signed nor ratified the convention.[30]

The Conference of the States Parties to the CWC

The 10th Session of the Conference of the States Parties (CSP) to the CWC met on 7–11 November 2005. It approved the OPCW 2006 budget of €75.6 million (*c.* $88.6 million), a decrease of around 0.1 per cent from the 2005 budget.[31] The CSP focused on agreeing follow-up measures to the OPCW Action Plans on national implementation measures (Article VII of the CWC) and universality (i.e., achieving universal membership to the convention). The CSP also considered the implementation of CWC provisions

[26] ECDC website, URL <http://www.ecdc.eu.int>.

[27] 'Regulation (EC) No. 851/2004 of the European Parliament and of the Council of 21 April 2004 establishing a European Centre for disease prevention and control', *Official Journal of the European Union*, L142 (30 Apr. 2004), pp. 1–11.

[28] European Commission, Health & Consumer Protection Directorate-General, 'Preparatory actions for setting up the ECDC: handover file', Brussels, 15 July 2005, URL <http://www.eu.int/comm/health/ph_overview/strategy/ecdc/ecdc_handover1_en.pdf>.

[29] Antigua and Barbuda, Bhutan, Cambodia, the Democratic Republic of the Congo, Grenada, Honduras, Niue and Vanuatu became parties to the CWC in 2005. The states that have signed, but not ratified the CWC are Bahamas, Central African Republic, Comoros, Congo, Djibouti, Dominican Republic, Guinea-Bissau, Haiti, Israel, Liberia and Myanmar.

[30] The states that had not signed or acceded to the CWC as of Dec. 2005 were Angola, Barbados, Egypt, Iraq, North Korea, Lebanon, Somalia and Syria.

[31] One area in which cost savings have been realized is with the implementation, on a trial basis, of an on-call inspector scheme in 2004–2005 whereby inspectors are based in their home countries, rather than at the OPCW headquarters in The Hague. See 'Note by the Technical Secretariat: the trial phase of the on-call-inspector scheme', OPCW document S/523/2005, 29 Sep. 2005. OPCW costs will tend to rise as the number of operational chemical weapon destruction facilities (CWDFs) increases. Starting in 2004 additional costs were incurred as a consequence of the implementation of the OPCW's 7-year tenure policy that affects most OPCW Secretariat staff. Additional training and recruitment costs have resulted. Annual contributions by states parties are expected to decrease by almost 1.3% because of improved recovery of Article IV and Article V inspection costs.

pertaining to the declaration and inspection of chemical industry facilities and the implementation of the CWC's provisions on economic and technological development (Article XI).[32]

In its official statement, the Africa Group of states parties to the CWC urged the OPCW to open a regional office in Africa.[33] Supporters of the proposal noted that not all of the African parties to the CWC have permanent diplomatic representation in The Hague and argued that the establishment of a regional office would promote universality of adherence to and effective implementation of the CWC by states in the region.[34] The proposal, which has been considered at least informally for a number of years, was resisted by some states partly because of uncertain cost implications and the possibility that other geographical regions of the CWC regime might also push for the establishment of their own regional offices. The CSP recommended to the Executive Council that an ad hoc, open-ended working group be established to examine the proposal.[35]

The CSP also authorized the Executive Council to establish a working group to prepare for the Second Special Session of the Conference of the States Parties to Review the Operation of the Chemical Weapons Convention (Second Review Conference), which will be held no later than 2008.[36] In addition, the CSP re-elected by acclamation OPCW Director-General Ambassador Rogelio Pfirter of Argentina to a second, and final, term that will start on 25 July 2006 and end on 24 July 2010.[37] The CSP adopted a decision on implementing a common understanding of 'captive use', a chemical industry implementation matter relating to whether and how chemicals that appear in the CWC's Annex on Chemicals should be declared.[38] Finally, the CSP endorsed a proposal to establish 29 April, the day the CWC entered into force, as a day of remembrance for victims of chemical warfare and that a memorial to its victims be established in The Hague.[39]

---

[32] See Hart, J., Verification Research, Training and Information Centre (VERTIC), *Chemical Industry Inspections under the Chemical Weapons Convention*, Verification Matters Research Report no. 1 (VERTIC: London, 2001).

[33] 'Statement by the African Group of States Parties to the CWC at the 10th Session of the Conference of States Parties, 7–11 November 2005', 10th Conference of the States Parties to the CWC, The Hague, 7–11 Nov. 2005.

[34] In most cases, the nearest permanent diplomatic representation is located in Brussels.

[35] Organisation for the Prohibition of Chemical Weapons (OPCW), 'Decision, establishment of an OPCW office in Africa', OPCW document C-10/DEC.13, 10 Nov. 2005.

[36] Organisation for the Prohibition of Chemical Weapons, 'Report of the tenth session of the Conference of the States Parties, 7–11 November 2005', OPCW document C-10/5, 11 Nov. 2005, para. 23.1.

[37] Organisation for the Prohibition of Chemical Weapons, 'Decision, renewal of the appointment of the Director-General', OPCW document C-10/DEC.7, 10 Nov. 2005.

[38] Organisation for the Prohibition of Chemical Weapons, 'Decision, understanding relating to the concept of "captive use" in connection with declarations of production and consumption under Part VI of the Verification Annex to the convention', OPCW document C-10/DEC.12, 10 Nov. 2005. For background on captive use and the OPCW's 2004 decision on the issue, see Guthrie, Hart and Kuhlau (note 7), pp. 610–11.

[39] Organisation for the Prohibition of Chemical Weapons (note 36), para. 23.3.

Action Plans

In 2003 the OPCW began to carry out a two-year 'plan of action' to ensure that the parties to the CWC have effectively enacted their obligations in the area of national implementation measures. This included the adoption of penal legislation that prohibits individuals and groups under a party's jurisdiction or control from carrying out activities banned by the CWC.[40] In the same year the OPCW also began to implement a plan of action to promote universality of the CWC. Both plans expired when the 10th Conference of the States Parties to the CWC met.

With respect to the *Action Plan on national implementation measures*, as of 17 October 2005, 147 of the parties (84 per cent) had established or designated a National Authority; 105 parties (60 per cent) had reported the adoption of general domestic legislative or administrative measures to the OPCW Secretariat; and 59 parties (34 per cent) had adopted and reported national legislation covering all key areas required by the CWC.[41]

The main concern behind the discussions on the Article VII Action Plan on national implementation measures was the extent to which follow-on measures should be of a cooperative, as opposed to a more coercive, nature. These discussions focused on three areas: (*a*) agreeing a suitable time frame for achieving specific objectives; (*b*) the extent to which any follow-up measures should be taken up under Article XII (Measures to redress a situation and to ensure compliance, including sanctions); and (*c*) the extent to which any follow-up measures should be handled by the United Nations (UN). There was a strong reluctance by some parties to include references to Article XII and the UN.[42] These discussions also highlighted differences in understanding among the parties of when a violation of a technical or administrative nature should be considered a fundamental violation. The discussion on possible referral of non-compliance with the Action Plan to the UN focused on whether non-implementation of Article VII obligations should fall under UN Security Council Resolution 1540 or under the 2000 OPCW–UN relationship agreement.[43]

[40] Organisation for the Prohibition of Chemical Weapons, 'Decision, plan of action regarding the implementation of Article VII obligations', OPCW document C-8/DEC.16, 24 Oct. 2003.

[41] Organisation for the Prohibition of Chemical Weapons, 'Note by the Director General, report on the plan of action regarding the implementation of Article VII obligations', OPCW document C-10/DG.4/rev.1, 2 Nov. 2005, pp. 5, 11. At the time these figures were compiled, there were 174 parties to the CWC.

[42] E.g., the African Group stated: 'The African Group acknowledges the delay by some of its members to notify the Organization of their National Authorities at the time the Convention entered into force for them. We are, however, of the view that this issue is not one of those prohibited by the Convention. This issue is therefore, in our view, neither of serious gravity nor does it call for invoking the provisions of Article XII of the Convention'. 'Statement by the African Group of States Parties to the CWC at the 10th Session of the Conference of States Parties, 7–11 November 2005' (note 33).

[43] Agreement Concerning the Relationship between the United Nations and the Organisation for the Prohibition of Chemical Weapons, New York, 17 Oct. 2000, URL <http://www.opcw.org/html/db/legal/rel_agree.html>. The relationship agreement was delayed for several years to a large extent over the question of whether and how information can be transferred to the UN without violating the OPCW confidentiality policy. In principle, there is a significant degree of flexibility in the interpretation of the relationship agreement to allow for essentially open-ended consultations. On the implementation of

The CSP agreed language that strongly urged a process of focused engagement among the parties and the Technical Secretariat to identify and resolve specific difficulties, partly through the further exchange of information and the continued involvement of the Executive Council. The CSP decided to review the implementation of the Article VII Action Plan during the 11th CSP, in 2006, 'to consider and decide on any appropriate measures to be taken, if necessary, in order to ensure fulfillment' by the parties of their Article VII obligations.[44]

With respect to the *Action Plan on universality*, the CSP called on all states not party to the CWC to join the convention 'without delay', particularly in cases where states' 'non-adherence' to the CWC is a 'cause for concern'. The CSP urged the parties and the OPCW Secretariat to intensify their efforts to achieve universality of membership to the CWC by attempting to ensure that the membership to the convention is at least 180 by the end of 2006 and that the CWC achieve universal membership by the time the 12th CSP convenes in 2007, 10 years after the entry into force of the convention.[45]

Assisting Iraq to become a party to the CWC

On 6–9 July 2005 the OPCW convened a CWC implementation training workshop in The Hague for nine representatives of the Government of Iraq. While there was no official indication of when Iraq would accede to the CWC, the Iraqi delegation affirmed its country's intention to accede to the CWC and an observer from Iraq attended the 10th CSP.[46] The workshop, which was funded by a voluntary contribution by Japan, was designed to ensure that the convention is effectively applied upon Iraq's accession to the CWC and was attended by representatives of interested member states, including Japan, the Netherlands, the United Kingdom and the USA. The topics considered included the preparation of declarations, the establishment and efficient operation of a National Authority, and the enactment of national implementing legislation.[47]

The factors related to Iraq's accession to the CWC include the fact that the current and future governments of Iraq will not have complete access to pertinent information and records about past programmes and activities.[48] The

Resolution 1540, see chapter 12 in this volume. UN Security Council Resolution 1540, 28 Apr. 2004, URL <http://www.un.org/Docs/sc/unsc_resolutions04.html>.

[44] Organisation for the Prohibition of Chemical Weapons, 'Decision, follow-up to the plan of action regarding the implementation of Article VII obligations', OPCW document C-10/DEC.16, para. 14.

[45] Organisation for the Prohibition of Chemical Weapons, 'Decision, universality of the Chemical Weapons Convention and the implementation of the universality Action Plan', OPCW document C-10/DEC.11, 10 Nov. 2005, paras 1, 4.

[46] For background, see Zanders, J. P. et al., *The Relevance of the Chemical Weapons Convention for Cases of Non-compliance: Lessons from and for Iraq?*, SIPRI Policy Paper no. 5 (SIPRI: Stockholm, Oct. 2003), URL <http://www.sipri.org/>.

[47] Organisation for the Prohibition of Chemical Weapons, 'OPCW trains Iraqi officials in CWC implementation', OPCW Press release no. 32, 11 July 2005, URL <http://www.opcw.org>.

[48] The CWC requires that facilities that produced chemical weapons at any time since 1 Jan. 1946 be declared and verifiably destroyed or converted for peaceful purposes. It is not clear how comprehensive any past records may be because many developments seem to have been unrecorded and many records were deliberately destroyed by past governments or were destroyed as a consequence of military action.

Iraqi Government also has limited or no access to or control over the scientists and technicians who were involved with the former programmes for weapons that were prohibited by the UN.[49] During the period when Iraq was under UN sanctions, the UN Special Commission on Iraq (UNSCOM) and the International Atomic Energy Agency (IAEA) had provided Iraq with model legislation to assist with the implementation of relevant UN Security Council resolutions, including through the adoption and implementation of laws prohibiting any legal person or entity under Iraq's jurisdiction or control from developing, producing or storing UN-prohibited weapons.[50] Iraq's new constitution makes specific reference to similar prohibitions on these types of weapons.[51]

The 'assistex' exercise

An important aspect of CWC implementation relates to OPCW assistance and protection under Article X for those attacked with or threatened by chemical weapons. On 9–13 October 2005 the OPCW conducted its second 'assistex' field exercise (Joint Assistance 2005) in Ukraine to help develop and maintain the organization's readiness to fulfil the provisions of this article. (The first exercise was held in Croatia in 2002.) The 2005 exercise, which was conducted jointly with the Government of Ukraine and the North Atlantic Treaty Organization (NATO) Euro-Atlantic Disaster Response Coordination Centre, consisted of a simulated chemical attack by terrorists.[52] The participants assessed the nature and type of contamination that might result and implemented procedures for decontaminating affected areas and individuals, disseminating information to the public and evacuating local inhabitants.[53] The OPCW also rehearsed procedures for investigating alleged use of chemical weapons.[54] Confidence in the CWC regime could be significantly undermined if the OPCW were not able to give a credible response in this area.

---

[49] Four Corners Australian Broadcasting Corporation, 'Secrets and lies', Transcript, 15 Feb. 2005, URL <http://www.abc.net.au/4corners/content/2005/s1302767.htm>; and Global Security Newswire, 'Former inspectors want release of Iraqi scientists', 18 July 2005, URL <http://www.nti.org/d_newswire/issues/2005_7_18.html#DB36F26F>. The number of scientists and technical experts from the former Iraqi chemical and biological weapon programmes remaining in the custody of coalition forces is unknown.

[50] Blix, H., 'Briefing the Security Council, 19 December 2002: inspections in Iraq and a preliminary assessment of Iraq's weapons declaration', Presentation by UNMOVIC Executive Chairman to the UN Security Council, 19 Dec. 2002, URL <http://www.unmovic.org>.

[51] The relevant section of the draft reads: 'The Iraqi Government shall respect and implement Iraq's international commitments regarding the non-proliferation, non-development, non-production and non-use of nuclear, chemical, and biological weapons. Associated equipment, material, technologies and communications systems for use in the development, manufacture, production and use of such weapons shall be banned.' As included in a speech by Ambassador Majid H. Al-Anbaki of Iraq to the UN General Assembly First Committee, 17 Oct. 2005, reproduced in UN document A/C.1/60/PV.13, 17 Oct. 2005.

[52] Organisation for the Prohibition of Chemical Weapons, 'Note by the Technical Secretariat, final exercise instructions "Joint Assistance 2005"', OPCW document S/511/2005/Rev. 1, 6 Oct. 2005.

[53] North Atlantic Treaty Organizaion, Euro-Atlantic Disaster Response Coordination Centre, 'Joint Assistance exercise 2005', 17 Oct. 2005, URL <http://www.nato.int/eadrcc/2005/ukraine/index.html>.

[54] Organisation for the Prohibition of Chemical Weapons, 'Chemical terrorism protection and assistance exercise "Joint Assistance 2005" concludes in Ukraine', Press release no. 60, 13 Oct. 2005, URL <http://www.opcw.org/html/global/press_releases/2005/PR60_2005.html>.

Consultations, cooperation and fact finding

One of the least understood but, nevertheless, most important aspects of the implementation of the CWC has been the implementation of the provisions of Article IX on consultations, cooperation and fact finding regarding concerns about non-compliance. Although no challenge inspection has been requested,[55] the other provisions of the article have been regularly implemented since the CWC's entry into force in 1997. In 2005 a US Department of State report noted that the USA has used the bilateral consultation provisions of this article to 'resolve numerous compliance concerns' and that recent US bilateral discussions with other parties to the CWC under the article had been 'well received' and were 'useful in laying the groundwork for judging compliance'.[56]

Destruction of chemical weapons

The states that declared the possession of chemical weapons at the time the CWC entered into force for them are Albania, India, Libya, Russia, the USA and 'another state party', not identified at its request but widely understood to be South Korea. As of 31 December 2005, of approximately 71 373 agent tonnes of declared chemical weapons, about 12 434 agent tonnes had been verifiably destroyed; of approximately 8.68 million declared items, about 2.4 million munitions and containers had been destroyed.[57] As of the same date, 12 states[58] had declared 64 chemical weapon production facilities,[59] of which 37 had been certified by the OPCW as being destroyed and 14 as being converted for purposes not prohibited under the CWC. While information on the stockpiles of India and the unnamed state party is limited, both states are said to be on schedule to meet their final CWC destruction deadlines.

Albania's chemical weapon stockpile consists of approximately 16 tonnes of agent—mainly sulphur mustard but also reportedly adamsite, lewisite and sulphur mustard–lewisite mixtures—stored in bulk at a single location near Tirana.[60] Destruction of the stockpile is set to begin in 2006 using a portable incinerator provided by the US Cooperative Threat Reduction programme.[61]

---

[55] See Hart, J., 'Political and technical aspects of challenge inspections under the Chemical Weapons Convention', Paper presented at the EU seminar on 'challenge inspections' in the framework of the CWC, Vienna, 24–25 June 2004, URL <http://www.sipri.org/contents/cbwarfare/Publications/Publications/cbw-papersfactsheets.html>.

[56] US Department of State, 'Adherence to and compliance with arms control, nonproliferation and disarmament agreements and commitments', Washington, DC, Aug. 2005, URL <http://www.state.gov/t/vci/rls/rpt/51977.htm>, p. 5.

[57] Organisation for the Prohibition of Chemical Weapons, 'Inspection activity', URL <http://www.opcw.org>.

[58] The 12 states were Bosnia and Herzegovina, China, France, India, Iran, Japan, South Korea, Libya, Russia, Serbia and Montenegro, the UK and the USA.

[59] Article II, para. 8, of the CWC defines a chemical weapon production facility as any facility that was designed, constructed or used to produce chemical weapons at any time since 1 Jan. 1946.

[60] Guthrie, Hart and Kuhlau (note 7), pp. 611–12.

[61] On the Cooperative Threat Reduction programme see chapter 12 in this volume.

Albania has reportedly not uncovered any paperwork about or found eyewitnesses willing to discuss the origin of the stockpile that was discovered in an unused military bunker in 2003.[62] There were further reports stating that many of the estimated 600 containers have Chinese-language labels that describe the contents.[63]

The CSP granted *Libya*, in principle, a further extension of its intermediate deadlines for destroying its Category 1 chemical weapon stockpiles.[64] The specific dates will be determined by the Executive Council, which will then submit a report on the matter to the 11th CSP in 2006.[65]

The *Russian* chemical weapon stockpile consists of about 40 000 agent tonnes and is stored at seven locations.[66] As of December 2005, Russia had destroyed approximately 4 per cent of this stockpile. In 2005 destruction operations were carried out at Gorny; these operations were scheduled to be completed by the end of 2005, while the destruction facility at Kambarka was expected to become operational by the end of the year (see table 14.1).[67]

In October 2005 Russia issued a revised chemical weapon destruction plan which places the total cost of the destruction programme at 160.4 billion roubles (*c.* $5.6 billion) and states that the total amount of international financial and technical assistance required will be 34.2 billion roubles (*c.* $1.2 billion).[68] The plan also estimates that up to 0.6 billion roubles (*c.* $21 million)

---

[62] Albania's post-World War II Communist regime constructed numerous and now mostly unused bunkers throughout the country.

[63] Warrick, J., 'Albania's chemical cache raises fears about others', *Washington Post*, 10 Jan. 2005, URL <http://www.washingtonpost.com/wp-dyn/articles/A61698-2005Jan9.html>, p. A01.

[64] The CWC's Annex on Chemicals consists of 3 'schedules'. Schedule 1 chemicals consist of chemicals and their precursors judged to have few, if any, peaceful applications. Chemicals listed in schedules 2 and 3 have wider peaceful, including commercial, applications. The definition of chemical weapon categories, which is partly based on what schedule a chemical may be listed under, is given in CWC, Part IV(A) of the Verification Annex, para. 16.

[65] Organisation for the Prohibition of Chemical Weapons, 'Decision, request by the Libyan Arab Jamahiriya for extensions of the intermediate deadlines for the destruction of its Category 1 chemical weapons stockpiles', OPCW document C-10/DEC.10, 10 Nov. 2005. For background see Hart, J. and Kile, S., 'Libya's renunciation of nuclear, biological and chemical weapons and ballistic missiles', *SIPRI Yearbook 2005* (note 7), pp. 643–45; and 'Khimicheskaya bomba obezvrezhena: voennyie khimiki unichtozhili pervuyu tonn boevikh otravlyayushchikh veshchstv' [The chemical bomb rendered harmless: military chemists have destroyed the first 1000 tonnes of military poisonous substances], Interview with Valery Petrovich Kapashin, head of the Federal Directorate on Safety, Storage and Destruction of Chemical Weapons, *Rossiiskaya Gazeta*, 26 Sep. 2005, URL <http://www.rg.ru/2005/09/26/kapashin.html>.

[66] The 7 locations are Kambarka, Udmurtia Republic (planned destruction capacity 2500 tonnes/year); Gorny, Saratov oblast (390 tonnes/year); Kizner, Udmurtia Republic (1900 tonnes/year); Maradikovsky, Kirov oblast (1200 tonnes/year); Pochep, Bryansk oblast (2000 tonnes/year); Leonidovka, Penza oblast (2000 tonnes/year); and Shchuchye, Kurgan oblast (1900 tonnes/year). For background on Russian chemical weapon destruction see Hart, J. and Miller, C. D. (eds), *Chemical Weapon Destruction in Russia: Political, Legal and Technical Aspects*, SIPRI Chemical & Biological Warfare Studies, no. 17 (Oxford University Press: Oxford, 1998); and *Khimicheskoe Razoruzhenie* [Chemical disarmament], URL <http://www.chemicaldisarmament.ru/>.

[67] For background see Hart, J., 'Assistance for the destruction of chemical weapons in the Russian Federation: political and technical aspects', Paper presented at the Conference on Strengthening European Action on WMD Non-proliferation and Disarmament: How Can Community Instruments Contribute?, Brussels, 7–8 Dec. 2005.

[68] On assistance see Hart (note 67); Global Green USA, Green Cross Switzerland and Institute for Urban Economics, 'Deadly weapons and dire needs: exploring the intersection of social infrastructure

Table 14.1. Schedule of chemical weapon agent destruction in Russia, 2004–12

Year	Quantity
2004	692
2005	304
2006	5 202
2007	3 000
2008	5 970
2009	7 787
2010	7 720
2011	6 047
2012	3 244

Source: 'Changes to be included in the Special Federal Programme Destruction of Chemical Weapons in the Russian Federation, approved by Resolution no. 305, dated 21 March 1996, for the Russian Federation', Resolution of the Government of the Russian Federation no. 639, 24 Oct. 2005 (in Russian).

can be recovered by reusing destruction by-products such as purified arsenic and decontaminated scrap metal.[69] Contracts with donors totalling approximately 10.5 billion roubles (*c.* $364 million) had been signed by mid-2005.[70]

The stockpile of chemical weapons in *the United States* is stored at eight locations.[71] As of December 2005, approximately 36 per cent of the USA's 31 280-tonne chemical weapon stockpile had been destroyed.[72] In 2005 destruction operations were carried out at the Aberdeen, Anniston, Edgewood, Pine Bluff, Tooele and Umatilla facilities. In February 2005 the last of the sulphur mustard agent stored at Aberdeen Proving Ground was destroyed and the destruction facility will be shut down once the decontamination of the bulk containers and the destruction of any residual gelled sulphur-containing sludge ('heels') remaining within the storage containers are completed.[73] In 2005 destruction operations were temporarily suspended at three facilities owing to

and weapons demilitarization in Shchuch'ye, a struggling chemical weapons community', Zurich, Sep. 2005, URL <http://www.globalgreen.org/>; and Ember, L. R., 'The Shchuch'ye dilemma: civil unrest could undermine construction of a Russian chemical arms disposal facility', *Chemical & Engineering News*, vol. 83, no. 45 (7 Nov. 2005), pp. 19–24. See also Anthony, I. and Fedchenko, V., 'International non-proliferation and disarmament assistance', *SIPRI Yearbook 2005* (note 7), pp. 675–98.

[69] 'Changes to be included in the Special Federal Programme Destruction of Chemical Weapons in the Russian Federation, approved by Resolution no. 305, dated 21 March 1996, for the Russian Federation', Resolution of the Government of the Russian Federation no. 639, 24 Oct. 2005 (in Russian).

[70] 'Failure to comply with chemical weapons liquidation program will cost Russia dearly', *RIA Novosti*, 21 July 2005, URL <http://en.ria.ru/russian/20050721/40945404.html>.

[71] The US chemical weapon stockpiles are located at Aberdeen Proving Ground, Md.; Anniston Army Depot, Ala.; Lexington-Blue Grass Army Depot, Ky.; Newport Chemical Depot, Ind.; Pine Bluff Arsenal, Ark.; Pueblo Chemical Depot, Colo.; Deseret Chemical Depot, Utah; and Umatilla Chemical Depot, Oreg.

[72] Types and quantities of the US chemical weapon stockpile are given in Zanders, J. P., Eckstein, S. and Hart, J., 'Chemical and biological weapon developments', *SIPRI Yearbook 1997: Armaments, Disarmament and International Security* (Oxford University Press: Oxford, 1997), pp. 449–51.

[73] US Army Chemical Materials Agency, 'Last mustard agent container is removed from the APG chemical agent storage yard for destruction', Press release no. 05–02, 4 Feb. 2005.

operational problems: Newport, Umatilla and Pine Bluff.[74] As of December 2005 it was not clear when destruction operations at the Blue Grass and Pueblo sites might start.[75] The delay is partly the result of political and technical difficulties surrounding long-standing opposition, including by the areas' congressional representatives, to incineration at these sites. Concern was also expressed over a study funded by the US Army to consider the feasibility of transporting the chemical weapons stockpiled at the Blue Grass and Pueblo sites to the Tooele destruction facility for disposal.[76] Under current US law, chemical weapon stockpiles must be destroyed on site. There was also concern that funding thought to be earmarked for these two sites was being improperly transferred to the other sites to support the destruction operations at these sites.

Meeting the final CWC destruction deadline

The continuing difficulties with chemical weapon destruction mean that it is becoming increasingly unlikely that all states will meet the destruction deadline (29 April 2012) mandated under the CWC. If one or more states need extra time to complete their destruction, having shown good faith in their destruction efforts, this may seem of little consequence. However, the precedent could be set that weapon destruction deadlines under international treaties are flexible.[77]

Some of these issues were highlighted in a senior official's testimony to the US Senate on the implications of a chemical weapon possessor not meeting the final CWC stockpile destruction deadline.[78] The official stated: 'if current

[74] Neutralization of VX at the Newport facility was stopped in June when tests showed the hydrolysate to be flammable due to the presence of diisopropylamine (DIPA). The neutralization process was modified to reduce the level of DIPA to an acceptable level and destruction operations were resumed. There was also opposition in the US Congress and elsewhere to the shipping of VX hydrolysates off-site. The Centers for Disease Control and Prevention (CDC) and the Department of Health and Human Services (DHHS) were asked to study the matter. Operations were also suspended at Newport after approximately 114 litres accumulated in a containment area due to a faulty valve. Destruction operations at the Umatilla and Pine Bluff facilities were temporarily suspended following the outbreak of fires in an explosive containment chamber where sarin-filled M-55 rockets are cut into pieces ('guillotined'). Fires have occasionally occurred during destruction operations since 1990. However, operations were suspended to investigate further methods to minimize their occurrence. 'Army studying chemical arms fires', *Chemical & Engineering News*, vol. 83, no. 24 (13 June 2005), p. 22; 'VX spill at disposal facility', *Chemical & Engineering News*, vol. 83, no. 25 (20 June 2005), p. 22; Ember, L., 'Army halts VX destruction', *Chemical & Engineering News*, vol. 83, no. 28 (11 July 2005), p. 13; and Ember, L., 'Army resumes disposal of VX nerve gas', *Chemical & Engineering News*, vol. 83, no. 39 (26 Sep. 2005), p. 13. See also DHHS and CDC, 'Review of the U.S. Army proposal for off-site treatment and disposal of caustic VX hydrolysate from the Newport Chemical Agent Disposal Facility', Apr. 2005, URL <http://www.cdc.gov/nceh/demil/reports/VX/vxreporttoc.htm>.

[75] See the US Army Chemical Materials Agency website, URL <http://www.cma.army.mil/>; and the Program Manager, Assembled chemical weapons alternatives website, URL <http://www.pmacwa.army.mil/>.

[76] 'Army considers shipping chemical arms to Utah for disposal', *Chemical & Engineering News*, vol. 83, no. 4 (24 Jan. 2005), p. 24.

[77] Flexibility of deadlines reduces pressure to ensure that they are achieved. As well as reducing pressure to keep to the chemical weapon destruction timetable, this might make future negotiations on agreements to destroy other classes of weapon more difficult.

[78] Mahley, D. A., Deputy Assistant Secretary for Arms Control Implementation, US Department of State, 'Chemical weapons demilitarization', Statement before the Subcommittee on Emerging Threats

assumptions hold' and the USA becomes non-compliant for not having completed destruction of its chemical weapon stockpile by the final deadline, some countries will argue that the USA has 'lost the right to offer opinions' on the chemical weapon-related activities of other countries. In addition, Russia could seize any US destruction delays past the 2012 deadline 'as an excuse to further submerge its own destruction program in competing budget priorities, and to justify its own failure to meet the treaty deadline'.

The official strongly recommended against any attempt by the USA to modify the CWC provisions to allow for a further extension because: (a) doing so would result in the chemical weapon destruction obligation becoming 'essentially open-ended' and the political priority given to chemical weapon destruction within states that possess chemical weapons would therefore be reduced; (b) other parties to the CWC could propose amendments of their own with uncertain consequences; and (c) any amendments not of an 'administrative or technical nature' can be vetoed by a single vote.[79] Such a case of US non-compliance, he said, should not be viewed as an attempt by the USA to evade its legal obligations to destroy its stockpile or of its commitment to the rule of law and should not automatically result in a loss of voting rights or of a seat on the Executive Council. However, he stated that the possibility for those with 'a particular political agenda' to 'seek to exploit the situation'—either at the OPCW or elsewhere—could not be ruled out. [80]

It is important that the parties with chemical weapon stockpiles remain actively engaged in order to ensure that political and technical difficulties associated with their destruction programmes are resolved. Where appropriate, the possibilities for taking advantage of international expertise and assistance should also be actively considered.

Old and abandoned chemical weapons

As of December 2005 three countries had declared that abandoned chemical weapons (ACWs) were present on their territories, and 11 countries had declared that they possessed old chemical weapons (OCWs).[81]

---

and Capabilities, Senate Armed Services Committee, 11 Apr. 2005, URL <http://www.state.gov/t/ac/rls/rm/44633.htm>. The CWC requires that all stockpiles be destroyed no later than 10 years after the convention enters into force, a deadline that can be extended by agreement of the states parties to 15 years. For provisions regarding 'order of destruction' and intermediate and final deadlines for the destruction of chemical weapons see CWC, Verification Annex, Part IV(A), paras 15–28.

[79] Two types of amendment are possible. Those of an administrative or technical nature can be taken by a majority vote of parties attending a Conference of the States Parties. Amendments not of an administrative or technical nature can be voted down by a single party to the CWC. The question of whether a proposed amendment is of an administrative or technical nature can also be determined by a majority vote. See CWC, Article XV.

[80] Mahley (note 78).

[81] The countries that have declared ACWs to the OPCW are China, Italy and Panama. The countries that have declared OCWs to the OPCW are Australia, Belgium, Canada, France, Germany, Italy, Japan, Russia, Slovenia, the UK and the USA. ACWs are defined as chemical weapons that were abandoned by a state after 1 Jan. 1925 on the territory of another state without the permission of the latter. CWC, Article II, para. 6. OCWs are defined as chemical weapons that were produced before 1925 or chemical weapons produced between 1925 and 1946 that have deteriorated to such an extent that they are no

In 2005 *China* and *Japan* reportedly agreed to start construction in China of a chemical weapon destruction facility, which will cost an estimated 97.3 billion yen (*c*. $815 million), to eliminate chemical weapons abandoned in China by Japan in the 1930s and 1940s.[82]

In *Russia* it was reported that seven chemical rounds dating from World War II were found near the town of Balakovo (Saratov oblast) inside a concrete and iron container, and a number of identical rounds were discovered near the village of Ivanovka (Balakov region). Russian officials declined to confirm the type of chemical weapon agent contained in the munitions, but the report indicated that they contained sulphur mustard, phosgene or an organophosphorus nerve agent. It was suggested that the weapons may have been located at a secret munitions storage facility in the region since military combat apparently did not occur in the region during the war.[83]

In *the USA*, the Department of Health and Human Services issued a further report on possible adverse effects of World War I-era chemical munitions located in Spring Valley, in the District of Columbia.[84] The report concluded that the state of health of the local population does not detectably differ from that of the people who live in the surrounding regions and that demonstrating any possible adverse health effects caused by the chemical weapon-related materials is problematic. In 2005 remediation work focused on an area where at least 15 sealed glass bottles were recovered which were found to contain suspected degradation products of sulphur mustard.[85] Clean-up operations were expected to cost approximately $165 million and continue until 2010.[86]

Codes of conduct

In 2005 a joint OPCW–International Union of Pure and Applied Chemistry (IUPAC) Project on Education and Outreach Regarding Chemical Weapons met twice. The meetings complemented and paralleled the consideration in

longer usable in the manner in which they were designed. CWC, Article II, para. 5. For information on countries not discussed in this chapter see CBW chapters in previous editions of the SIPRI Yearbook.

[82] 'Estimates cost of chemical weapons disposal facility at almost $1 billion', *Sankei Shimbun*, 17 Oct. 2005, Translation from Japanese, World News Connection, National Technical Information Service (NTIS), US Department of Commerce; and 'Japan, China agree on chemical arms disposal facility', *Japan Today*, 29 Apr. 2005.

[83] Bocharova, S., 'Khimicheskie bomby plokho okhranyali' [Chemical bombs were poorly protected], *Nezavisimaya Gazeta*, 4 Oct. 2005, p. 9.

[84] Federal Facilities Assessment Branch, Division of Health Assessment and Consultation and Agency for Toxic Substances and Disease Registry, *Health Consultation: Spring Valley Chemical Munitions, Washington, District of Columbia, Public Health Evaluation for the Spring Valley Community* (US Department of Health and Human Services: Washington, DC, 7 Sep. 2005), URL <http://www.atsdr. cdc.gov/>. The 268-hectare area in north-west Washington, DC, was used for field testing of weaponry during and shortly after World War I (the area was then called the American University Experiment Station), and clean-up operations and sampling and analysis operations have been under way there since 1993 when chemical weapons were first uncovered. See Hart, Kuhlau and Simon (note 9), pp. 658–59.

[85] US Army Corps of Engineers, 'Spring Valley, Washington, DC, project overview', URL <http:// www.nab.usace.army.mil/projects/WashingtonDC/springvalley/overview.htm>.

[86] Levine, S., 'Spring Valley toxins report sounds an almost all-clear', *Washington Post*, 20 Mar. 2005, p. C03.

2005 of codes of conduct by the parties to the BTWC.[87] The participants agreed that there is a need for chemists to develop their own codes of conduct and recommended that educational material be developed that describes the CWC and its obligations. The project, which was scheduled to issue a final report in 2006, considered it important to place the CWC in the context of the beneficial uses and misuses of chemicals and to raise awareness of multiple uses of the same substances as otherwise the perceived relevance of the CWC to chemists and chemistry students would be lessened.[88]

IV. Investigations and intelligence relating to Iraq

In 2005 the US-led Iraq Survey Group closed its investigation into the past chemical and biological weapon programmes in Iraq. The United Nations Monitoring, Verification and Inspection Commission (UNMOVIC) remained excluded from Iraq but continued to monitor and analyse past and current issues according to its mandate in UN Security Council resolutions.[89] The outcome of the investigation concerning the mismanagement of the Oil-for-Food Programme (OFFP) impacts on the continued work of UNMOVIC, which has hitherto been funded from that source, as well as on the entire UN structure.[90]

The last of the major official inquiries into the issues of pre-war intelligence relating to Iraq was published in 2005.[91] The Commission on the Intelligence Capabilities of the United States Regarding Weapons of Mass Destruction was established in February 2004 and submitted its final report to the US Government on 31 March 2005.[92] The report concluded that the 'Intelligence Community's Iraq assessments were . . . riddled with errors'.[93]

---

[87] See section II above.

[88] International Union of Pure and Applied Chemistry, 'A joint OPCW–IUPAC project on education and outreach regarding chemical weapons', Project no. 2004-048-1-020, URL <http://www.iupac.org/projects/2004/2004-048-1-020.html>.

[89] See, in particular, UN Security Council Resolution 1284, 17 Dec. 1999, which established UNMOVIC, but also previous resolutions describing the tasks of inspection that remain in place.

[90] The OFFP was established by UN Security Council Resolution 986, 14 Apr. 1995, in order for Iraq to sell oil in exchange for purchasing humanitarian goods and other UN-approved materials. It was intended to enable the meeting of humanitarian needs in Iraq while the country remained under international sanctions for failing to comply fully with UN Security Council Resolution 687, 3 Apr. 1991, which, specified the terms for the cessation of hostilities between Iraq and the UN coalition forces that began as a result of Iraq's 1990 invasion of Kuwait. The programme was discontinued on 31 May 2004. In Oct. 2005 the UN Security Council independent enquiry, chaired by Paul A. Volcker, issued the final report on its investigation into the administration and management of the OFFP, including allegations of corruption and fraud within the UN. The report concluded that Iraq derived $228.8 million of illicit income through its manipulation of the OFFP, while a total of $1.8 billion was misspent. See reports Independent Inquiry Committee, 'The management of the United Nations Oil-for-Food programme', vol. I, p. 60, 7 Sep. 2005, URL <http://www.iic-offp.org/Mgmt_Report.htm>; and Independent Inquiry Committee, 'Report on programme manipulation: summary of report on programme manipulation', 27 Oct. 2005, URL <http://www.iic-offp.org/story27oct05.htm>.

[91] For background on the intelligence reports during 2004 see Guthrie, Hart and Kuhlau (note 7), pp. 622–26. See also chapter 1 in this volume.

[92] United States, 'Final report of the Commission on the Intelligence Capabilities of the United States Regarding Weapons of Mass Destruction', 31 Mar. 2005, URL <http://www.wmd.gov/report/>.

[93] United States (note 92), p. 9.

The final Iraq Survey Group report and unresolved concerns

In March 2005 the ISG released a series of addenda to its 2004 report on the search for Iraqi chemical and biological weapons.[94] These addenda officially closed the ISG investigation and concluded that the investigation had 'gone as far as feasible'.[95] In 2005 a small group of inspectors continued to operate in Iraq, although after more than 18 months of ISG inspections no evidence of active chemical or biological warfare programmes had been found, indicating that such programmes no longer existed at the time of the military action in 2003. The report concluded that, while Iraq's chemical and biological physical infrastructure did not pose a proliferation concern, some missing dual-use equipment could contribute to chemical and biological weapon production by insurgents or terrorists.[96] The addenda also warned of the risk of the proliferation of weapon expertise to countries of concern, to terrorists and to insurgent groups and of the possibility that small numbers of degraded chemical weapons remain in Iraq.[97] The ISG considered it 'unlikely that an official transfer of WMD material from Iraq to Syria took place'.[98]

UNMOVIC: present and future activities

Although its inspectors have not been involved in searching for weapons and programmes on the ground, UNMOVIC continues to collect information on Iraq using satellite imagery. According to UNMOVIC, imagery has been examined for 378 of the 411 sites inspected from November 2002 to March 2003, including those considered to be most important. On this basis, analysts have concluded that 120 sites have been 'cleaned' (i.e., equipment or materials removed, to varying degrees).[99] UNMOVIC has also made progress on the compendium[100] of Iraq's proscribed weapons and programmes, the first draft of which was compiled in March 2005. The draft contains lessons learned from the experience gained in the verification process by UN inspectors. Issues include VX nerve agent, missile monitoring and determining the final status of biological warfare agent production facilities.[101] Since the main compendium contains sensitive information on technological details of research

---

[94] Iraq Survey Group (ISG), 'Addenda to the comprehensive report of the special advisor to the DCI on Iraq's WMD', Mar. 2005, URL <http://www.cia.gov/cia/reports/iraq_wmd_2004/addenda.pdf>. For background on the Oct. 2004 ISG final report findings see Guthrie, Hart and Kuhlau (note 7), p. 617.

[95] Iraq Survey Group (note 94), 'Iraqi detainees: value to investigation of Iraq WMD and current status', p. 3.

[96] Iraq Survey Group (note 94), 'Residual proliferation risk: equipment and material', p. 1.

[97] Iraq Survey Group (note 94), 'Residual pre-1991 CBW stocks in Iraq', p. 1.

[98] Iraq Survey Group (note 94), 'Pre-war movement', p. 1.

[99] UN Security Council, 'UNMOVIC's 22nd quarterly report', S/2005/545, 30 Aug. 2005, p. 2; and UN Security Council, 'UNMOVIC's 23rd quarterly report', S/2005/742, 29 Nov. 2005, URL <http://www.unmovic.org>, p. 3.

[100] For background see Guthrie, Hart and Kuhlau (note 7), pp. 619–20.

[101] UN Security Council, 'UNMOVIC's 21st quarterly report', S/2005/351, 27 May 2005, URL <http://www.unmovic.org>, pp. 13–18.

and production, a summary providing a general description of proscribed programmes and lessons learned is being produced and will be made public.[102]

The debate about the future of UNMOVIC continued in 2005.[103] Iraq has called for UNMOVIC to be terminated and support for this position has been growing in the UN Security Council.[104] One outstanding issue is to make the final judgement on whether Iraq has met its disarmament obligations under remaining relevant UN Security Council resolutions. This decision will require a new Security Council resolution.[105] Criteria need to be established in order to finalize the work and to lift the standing resolutions.[106] There are also indications that Iraq will not in future accept the special constraints or continued intrusive monitoring that UNMOVIC is mandated for.[107] One suggestion is that UNMOVIC, together with the IAEA, should evaluate the technical information and methodologies that have been developed for future reference and, after this is done, UNMOVIC should be disbanded.[108]

Several states have proposed that UNMOVIC's capacities and expertise be used to permanently enhance the UN's verification capability, and some states consider it an opportunity to obtain such a capacity with respect to biological weapons and missiles, where international verification is lacking. Some analysts have gone further, suggesting that all UNMOVIC's capabilities be absorbed into the international system.[109] The question of whether and how UNMOVIC's institutional expertise could be used to strengthen the UN Secretary-General's mechanisms to investigate alleged breaches of the 1925 Geneva Protocol[110] also continued to be considered in 2005. By the end of 2005, no formal decision on UNMOVIC's future had been taken.

---

[102] Extracts of summaries and lessons learned are provided in UNMOVIC's quarterly reports 21 (note 101), 22 and 23 (note 99), URL <http://www.unmovic.org>. The finalized summary of the compendium will be published on the UNMOVIC website.

[103] Guthrie et al. (note 6), pp. 689–91; and Guthrie, Hart and Kuhlau (note 7), pp. 620–21.

[104] Reuters, 'UN eyes shutting down Iraq arms inspection agency', 8 June 2005, URL <http://www.nti.org/e_research/profiles/Iraq/Nuclear/2121_4595.html>.

[105] Iraq has a continued obligation to submit reports and notifications under various Security Council resolutions. The Iraq counterpart to UNMOVIC, the Iraqi National Monitoring Directorate, was asked in Sep. 2005 to clarify its functions and competences and its relevant point of contact. The readiness of UNMOVIC to assist Iraq in fulfilling its obligations and in particular in developing an appropriate national monitoring system was repeated. A response has not yet been received. See UN Security Council, 'UNMOVIC's 23rd quarterly report' (note 99).

[106] Kerr, P., 'New reports cite looting at Iraqi sites; UNMOVIC future discussed', Arms Control Today, vol. 35, no. 3 (Apr. 2005), pp. 36–37.

[107] Barry, J., 'Iraq: stepped-up scrutiny', Newsweek, 22 Aug. 2005, URL <http://msnbc.msn.com/id/8940843/site/newsweek/>.

[108] United States Institute for Peace (USIP), 'Deterring death and destruction: catastrophic terrorism and the proliferation of nuclear, chemical, and biological weapons', American Interests and UN Reform: Report of the Task Force on the United Nations (USIP: Washington, DC, 2005), URL <http://www.usip.org/un/report/>, p. 79.

[109] Findlay, T., 'Looking back: the UN Monitoring, Verification and Inspection Commission', Arms Control Today, vol. 35, no. 7 (Sep. 2005), URL <http://www.armscontrol.org/act/2005_09/Looking Back-UNMOVIC.asp>, pp. 45–48.

[110] On the Geneva Protocol see annex A in this volume.

The funding of UNMOVIC

UNMOVIC currently has an annual budget of about $12 million.[111] Although the OFFP was terminated in 2003,[112] UNMOVIC continues to receive funding from Iraqi oil revenues. It holds an 'escrow account', created under UN Security Council Resolution 1284, which held $345.9 million on 31 December 2004, and the UN Secretary-General wrote to the President of the Security Council requesting the release of $220 million from this account.[113] The Security Council agreed to this request, allowing $200 million to be transferred to the Iraqi-administered Development Fund for Iraq and the remainder of the request 'to be credited against assessments issued in respect of the obligations of the Government of Iraq for regular budget, peacekeeping and tribunal activities and the capital master plan of the [UN]'.[114]

V. Other allegations of chemical and biological warfare activities and related prosecutions

Significant information relating to alleged and confirmed past and present activities in the chemical and biological warfare field became public in 2005.

The US Department of State published its assessment of 'Adherence to and compliance with arms control, nonproliferation and disarmament agreements and commitments' covering the years 2002 and 2003.[115] The report is highly nuanced and reveals disagreements between analysts. For example, in relation to *Cuba*, the report states that 'the Intelligence Community unanimously held that it was unclear whether Cuba has an active offensive biological warfare effort now, or even had one in the past'. Yet, 'On the basis of the same reporting, the policy community believes that the compliance judgment of the [previous report] that Cuba has "at least a limited, developmental offensive [biological warfare] research and development effort" remains correct'.

According to the report, *China* maintains 'some elements' of an offensive biological warfare capability 'in violation of its BWC obligations', 'has not acknowledged past transfers of chemical weapons' and may not have declared all relevant chemical facilities. *Iran* is reported to have 'an offensive biological weapons program in violation of the BWC' and 'is acting to retain and modernize' key infrastructure elements to include an offensive chemical warfare research and development capability. *North Korea* is alleged to have 'a dedicated, national-level effort to develop a [biological warfare] capability and

---

[111] Ridolfo, K., Radio Free Europe/Radio Liberty, 'Iraq: UN chief seeks mission extension, amid corruption allegations against former Oil-for-Food head', 8 Aug. 2005, URL <http://www.rferl.org/features article/2005/08/77a012bb-6da8-4597-9e73-2dc3b3cc0b30.html>.

[112] UN Security Council Resolution 1483, 22 May 2003, URL <http://www.un.org/Docs/sc/ unsc_resolutions03.html>, para. 16.

[113] The letter, dated 20 June 2005, is reproduced in UN document S/2005/406, 24 June 2005.

[114] UN Security Council, Provisional verbatim records of the 5214th meeting, 24 June 2005, UN document S/PV.5214. This decision was communicated to the Secretary-General via a letter reproduced in UN document S/2005/407, 24 June 2005.

[115] US Department of State (note 56). The previous report in the series was published in June 2003.

has developed, produced, and may have weaponized for use, [biological warfare] agents in violation of the BWC'. The report claims that *Russia* 'continues to maintain an offensive [biological warfare] program in violation of the Convention' and 'is in violation of its CWC obligations because its CWC declaration was incomplete with respect to declaration of production and development facilities, and declaration of chemical agent and weapons stockpiles'; and *Syria* is 'developing an offensive biological warfare capability that would constitute a violation of the BWC if Syria were a State Party'. In a change from earlier policy, the report states that the 'United States lacks sufficient evidence to determine whether *Sudan* is in violation of its CWC obligations'.

A survey of proliferation threats and responses which summarized returns from 85 international security experts was published by Richard Lugar, Chairman of the Senate Foreign Relations Committee.[116] Asked to give an assessment of the probability of a biological terrorist attack inflicting numerous casualties in the next five years, the average response was 19.7 per cent with the median response being 10 per cent. When the period was extended to 10 years the average response was 32.6 per cent with the median response being 20 per cent. The equivalent response figures for similar questions on the probability of a major chemical weapon terrorist attack were on average 20.1 per cent (median 15 per cent) over 5 years and on average 30.5 per cent (median 15 per cent) over 10 years.

Allegations and prosecutions relating to state activities

In *the Netherlands*, Frans van Anraat was convicted of supplying chemicals for *Iraq*'s chemical warfare programme in the 1980s. It had been alleged that, between 25 October 1984 and 12 January 1989, the defendant had arranged 36 shipments of materials to Iraq totalling 2360 tonnes of chemicals.[117] Van Anraat, a Dutch national, was given a 15-year jail sentence for complicity in war crimes (the maximum sentence for the charge) but was acquitted on genocide charges relating to attacks on Kurdish villages in the late 1980s. The Dutch court stated that it considered the Kurdish population an ethnic group under the 1948 Genocide Convention[118] and that 'The court has no other conclusion than that these attacks were committed with the intent to destroy the Kurdish population of Iraq'. The judges ruled that van Anraat was not aware of the 'genocidal intentions' of the Iraqi regime when he sold the chemicals.[119]

---

[116] Lugar, R., 'The Lugar survey on proliferation threats and responses', 22 June 2005, URL <http://www.lugar.senate.gov/reports/NPSurvey.pdf>.

[117] Karskens, A., 'De Ondergang van Nederlands Grootste Oorlogsmisdadiger' [The demise of the greatest Dutch war criminal], *Nieuwe Revu*, no. 51 (Dec. 2004), pp. 20–24. Van Anraat was initially arrested in 1989 in Italy. Jumping bail, he escaped to Iraq where he lived until 2003. He was arrested in Dec. 2004 in the Netherlands.

[118] Convention on the Prevention and Punishment of the Crime of Genocide, available at URL <http://www.icrc.org/>.

[119] 'Killing of Iraq Kurds "genocide"', BBC News Online, 23 Dec. 2005, URL <http://news.bbc.co.uk/2/hi/europe/4555000.stm>.

The Constitutional Court of *South Africa* delivered its verdict on an appeal relating to the earlier prosecution of Wouter Basson, who was involved in that country's past chemical warfare programme.[120] During the earlier case, certain allegations had been considered by the trial judge as outside the jurisdiction of the court because they concerned activities outside South Africa: namely, conspiracy to murder using toxic substances. The Constitutional Court found that such charges were within the jurisdiction of the lower court and so should be reinstated, but left open whether this would amount to 'double jeopardy', the issue of which 'will have to be considered by a trial court'. The prosecuting authorities subsequently decided not to pursue the reinstated charges on the grounds of 'double jeopardy' so the issue will not be decided by a court.[121]

In *the United Kingdom* more information was revealed about LSD tests on humans in the 1950s suggesting that the intelligence services as well as the military had been behind testing policy.[122] Separately, the Ministry of Defence won a High Court appeal on 19 April enabling it to challenge an inquest's verdict of 'unlawful killing'[123] in the case of Ronald Maddison, a Royal Air Force serviceman who died during nerve agent exposure tests in 1953.[124]

Allegations that *the United States* had used toxic materials in its military action in Fallujah, Iraq, in November 2004 were repeated during 2005 and focused on suggestions that, in particular, white phosphorus devices were employed against civilian targets.[125] The main allegations related to the suggestion that the white phosphorus munitions were being used to cause burns on human flesh rather than as a screening smoke. While the burns might be caused by a chemical reaction, this manner of operation would fall outside the definition of a chemical weapon. Some later allegations suggested that the white phosphorus was actually being used to exploit the effects of the smoke produced, which has an irritant effect on those who inhale it. If white phosphorus is being used in lieu of riot control agents and employed as a method of warfare, this activity would be contrary to the terms of the CWC.[126]

---

[120] South Africa, Constitutional Court, Case CCT 30/03, The State versus Basson, 9 Sep. 2005, URL <http://www.constitutionalcourt.org.za/site/basson.htm>. Details of the original trial can be found in Zanders, J. P. et al., 'Chemical and biological weapon developments and arms control', *SIPRI Yearbook 2000: Armaments, Disarmament and International Security* (Oxford University Press: Oxford, 2000), pp. 536–37.

[121] Menges, W., '"Dr Death" is off the hook in South Africa', *The Namibian*, 24 Oct. 2005

[122] Evans, R., 'MI6 ordered LSD tests on servicemen', *The Guardian*, 22 Jan. 2005, URL <http://www.guardian.co.uk/print/0,3858,5109714-111400,00.html>

[123] Guthrie, Hart and Kuhlau (note 7), p. 627.

[124] Press Association, as reproduced in 'MoD to challenge Porton Down verdict', *The Guardian*, 19 Apr. 2005, URL <http://politics.guardian.co.uk/print/0,3858,5174609-110247,00.html>

[125] Guthrie, Hart and Kuhlau (note 7), p. 627.

[126] The definition of 'chemical weapons' in the CWC is deliberately broad. Aside from issues of legitimate industrial uses, items and materials that might fall within the definition of chemical weapons under the convention might be considered to lie within 4 groupings relating to human exposure: (*a*) items or materials that have no purpose other than as chemical weapons and so the possession of them is clearly prohibited except for some clearly defined activities such as defensive research (e.g., specialized delivery systems and chemicals such as VX or sarin); (*b*) materials that can be used as chemical weapons but have other uses that would be rarely confused with use as a chemical weapon (e.g., nitrogen mustard which is used as an anti-cancer drug under the names mustine and chlormethine); (*c*) chemicals that operate through a deliberate toxic effect but which have specific uses not prohibited by the CWC, such as domestic law enforcement (e.g., tear gases); and (*d*) materials that do not rely on their toxic

Allegations and prosecutions relating to non-state activities

Allegations of possible terrorist acquisition of biological weapons were repeated in 2005. At a conference on bio-terrorism convened by Interpol in March, French Interior Minister Dominique de Villepin stated that, after the fall of the Taliban in Afghanistan, al-Qaeda cells relocated to the Pankisi Gorge region of *Georgia* to produce biological agents.[127] No supporting evidence was supplied for this assertion. The Russian authorities stated that they took these allegations very seriously.[128] The Georgian authorities countered by asserting that the problem in Pankisi had been resolved and no threat of terrorism currently existed in that region.[129] In an effort to reduce the controversy, the French ambassador to Georgia suggested that de Villepin's statement 'concerned the situation in the gorge which existed several years ago'.[130]

In *the United Kingdom* a court case claiming a terrorist conspiracy for the production of ricin concluded with one defendant, Kamel Bourgass, found guilty and eight co-defendants found not guilty on 8 April, leading to the abandoning of a second conspiracy trial.[131] Although the arrests leading to the case in January 2003, at a flat in London, had been cited many times as evidence that terrorists were actually acquiring biological materials for hostile uses, the prosecution evidence to the court showed that no evidence of ricin production had been found. The court heard that, although an early test had indicated the possible presence of ricin when investigators entered the flat, subsequent detailed chemical analysis had shown that there was no ricin

properties for their primary purpose (such as a screening smoke) during which use they would not cause 'chemical casualties', but which, if deliberately targeted against humans, would cause injury through their toxic properties and hence, if used in this way, would come under the CWC definition of 'chemical weapon'.

[127] Gecker, J., Associated Press, as reproduced in 'Official: U.S. prepared to fight anthrax', *The Guardian*, 1 Mar. 2005. The allegations were essentially those in the presentation by US Secretary of State Colin Powell to the UN Security Council on 5 Feb.2003. Powell stated: 'We also know that Zarqawi's colleagues have been active in the Pankisi Gorge, Georgia, and in Chechnya, Russia. The plotting to which they are linked is not mere chatter: members of Zarqawi's network say their goal was to kill Russians with toxins.' Presentation as reproduced in UN document S/PV.4701, 5 Feb. 2003.

[128] Russian Ministry of Foreign Affairs, 'Alexander Yakovenko, the spokesman of Russia's Ministry of Foreign Affairs, answers a media question regarding French Interior Minister Dominique de Villepin['s] statement concerning chemical and bacteriological weapons being made by terrorists in Pankisi Gorge, Georgia', 1 Mar. 2005 <http://www.ln.mid.ru/brp_4.nsf/sps/DAAB52A44925D929C3256FB8003C8160>.

[129] Georgian authorities carried out extensive actions to clear terrorist groups from the Pankisi Gorge with assistance from other states during 2002 and 2003. In 2003 Georgia declared the gorge clear of terror groups. If biological or chemical activities had been discovered, it is implausible that such a discovery would not have been publicized.

[130] 'Georgia's authorities doubt possibility of biological weapons development in [P]ankisi', *RIA Novosti*, 1 Mar. 2005, URL <http://en.rian.ru/onlinenews/20050301/39698523.html>.

[131] Campbell, D., 'The ricin ring that never was', *The Guardian*, 14 Apr. 2005, URL <http://politics.guardian.co.uk/print/0,3858,5170380-108933,00.html>. This story was removed from *The Guardian* website and later reinstated with certain details removed relating to government scientists who carried out the ricin analysis. See also Mayes, I., 'Open door: The readers' editor on . . . the welcome restoration of a report to the website', *The Guardian*, 24 Oct. 2005, URL <http://www.guardian.co.uk/Columnists/Column/0,5673,1599273,0.html>. See also Summers, C., 'Questions over ricin conspiracy', BBC News Online, 13 Apr. 2005, URL <http://news.bbc.co.uk/2/4433499.stm>.

present at the location.[132] In the words of one analysis, 'There was no UK poison cell linked to al Qaida or [Abu Musab] al Zarqawi. There was no ricin with which to poison London, only notes and 22 castor seeds. There was no one who even knew how to purify ricin'.[133] Bourgass was found guilty of 'conspiring to commit a public nuisance by the use of poisons and/or explosives to cause disruption, fear or injury'[134] but was not found guilty of conspiracy to commit murder by the same methods.

VI. Conclusions

Although there had been many initial doubts about the usefulness of the BTWC inter-sessional process, there is now a broad consensus that the series of meetings have been productive. It will be important for the 2006 Review Conference of the convention to build on this, and the most obvious way to do so would be through the adoption of a further programme of work up to the time of the following review conference in 2011. Many lessons may be drawn from the successes of the Action Plans carried out under the CWC and from the work under UN Security Council Resolution 1540. The lack of an institution or mechanism for the BTWC limits the ability of the states parties to carry out similar activities and presents a continuing challenge.

The magnitude of terrorist threat in the chemical and biological field remains unclear. Two of the most often cited cases relating to terrorist acquisition of chemical and biological materials for hostile purposes are the London 'ricin conspiracy' and the Pankisi Gorge allegations. In both cases, the initial claims and the final results were very different. The other high-profile 'bioterrorism' case was the anthrax letters in the USA in late 2001, since which time there has been no repetition, only hoaxes. The longer the time before this happens, the more uncertain it becomes that there is a large number of people with the capability or the intent to carry out similar actions.

However, this should not lead to complacency. There is still a need to prevent the inappropriate use of biological and chemical materials. While such inappropriate use might be either through deliberate or accidental actions, many of the mechanisms for prevention or response are similar in either case.[135] While the magnitude of biological and chemical dangers may be hard to quantify, the scale will inevitably change over time, sometimes for the better, sometimes for the worse. It would be prudent to ensure that effective bio-safety and bio-security measures are adopted as soon as is practicable.

---

[132] 'Ricin results not told to police', BBC News Online, 15 Sep. 2005, URL <http://news.bbc.co.uk/2/4249516.stm>.

[133] Smith, G., 'UK terror trial finds no terror: not guilty of conspiracy to poison London with ricin', *National Security Notes*, 11 Apr. 2005, URL <http://www.globalsecurity.org/org/nsn/nsn-050411.htm>

[134] British Crown Prosecution Service, 'Crown Prosecution statement on convictions of Kamel Bourgass', 13 Apr. 2005, URL <http://www.cps.gov.uk/news/pressreleases/121_05.html>. Bourgass had been convicted at an earlier trial of the murder of a police officer with a knife at the time of his arrest.

[135] See appendix 14A.

Appendix 14A. Enhancing bio-security: the need for a global strategy

ROGER ROFFEY and FRIDA KUHLAU

I. Introduction

In order to prevent the spread of biological weapon programmes from countries where they previously existed and to prevent terrorists from acquiring biological agents, materials and know-how, so-called threat reduction activities have been undertaken that include eliminating biological weapon-relevant equipment and infrastructure and redirecting the efforts of former weapon scientists to peaceful activities.[1] One important aim of these activities has been to enhance safety when working with pathogens (bio-safety); another is to improve security at facilities where such work is carried out in order to preclude unauthorized access to agents, materials and knowledge (bio-security). Emerging and re-emerging diseases pose a threat to humankind,[2] and global bio-security measures are an essential element of the efforts to decrease the risk of the use of biological agents for bio-terrorism.

Section II of this appendix discusses the increased perceived threat of bio-terrorism, which has led to enhanced international awareness of the need to improve bio-security worldwide at facilities that deal with dangerous pathogens. Proposals to develop international standards or guidelines for bio-security are also addressed. Section III presents the concept of bio-security and the measures required to achieve adequate laboratory bio-security. Section IV describes the global risks of natural or deliberately induced outbreaks of infectious diseases and the need for a global, coordinated strategy of preventive measures, such as enhancing bio-safety and bio-security. Section V outlines the challenges presented by the proliferation of biological weapons, related materials and know-how and notes the current shift in threat reduc-

---

[1] For approximately 10 years the United States has provided the main funding for threat reduction programmes which have covered the biological area and which have focused on Russia and the other former Soviet states. Recently, other Western countries have initiated projects in this area. Such support has, however, focused on biological research and redirecting the efforts of former weapon scientists to peaceful activities through assistance channelled via the international science and technology centres in Moscow and Kyiv. See International Science and Technology Center, Moscow, URL <http://www.istc.ru/>; and Science and Technology Center, Kyiv, URL <http://www.stcu.int/>. On threat reduction activities see Roffey, R., 'From bio threat reduction to cooperation in biological proliferation prevention', and Kuhlau, F., 'From bio threat reduction to cooperation in biological proliferation prevention: overview of ongoing international activities aimed towards preventing proliferation of biological technology, material and expertise that may be used for hostile purposes', Papers presented at the Conference on Strengthening European Action on WMD Non-proliferation and Disarmament: How Can Community Instruments Contribute?, Brussels, 7–8 Dec. 2005, URL <http://www.sipri.org/contents/expcon/euppconfmaterials.html>.

[2] 'An emerging infectious disease is either a newly recognised, clinically distinct infectious disease, or a known disease whose reported incidence within the past two decades is increasing in a given place or among a specific population.' British Health Protection Agency, *CDR Weekly: The Communicable Disease Report Weekly*, vol. 15, no. 6 (10 Feb. 2005), URL <http://www.hpa.org.uk/cdr/archives/2005/cdr0605.pdf>. Re-emerging diseases are those infections that have reappeared after a significant decrease in incidence.

tion activities towards taking a wider geographical approach and towards measures that address the prevention of bio-terrorism. The public health and environmental aspects of bio-security are also discussed. The conclusions are presented in section VI.

II. The increased perceived risk of bio-terrorism and enhanced international bio-security awareness

In the 1990s the issues of the proliferation of biological weapons and the threat of bio-terrorism became the focus of international attention for a number of reasons, including the discovery of Iraq's biological weapon programme,[3] revelations about the massive offensive biological weapon programme of the Soviet Union[4] and the perceived increased threat of bio-terrorism. Recent incidents have illustrated the threat that terrorism poses to international peace and security.[5] Another important factor in this context has been the rapid progress in biotechnology. If misused to develop more efficient biological weapons, biotechnology could become a driving force in promoting biological weapon programmes by creating new possibilities for future, potential military applications.[6] An analysis of potential threats from the present to 2020 indicates that most terrorists will continue to use primarily conventional methods, but there is concern that smaller, well-informed terrorist groups might use biological agents to cause mass casualties.[7] The risk of bio-terrorism cannot be disregarded, although it is difficult to identify which groups could and would use bio-terrorism and what would be the most likely targets.[8]

The World Health Organization (WHO) has expressed serious concern about the threat to civilian populations presented by the deliberate use of biological, chemical or radiological agents, including via the contamination of food. The WHO has requested that its director-general provide tools and support to the WHO member states, in particular developing countries, in order to strengthen their national response systems.[9]

---

[3] Pearson, G. S., *The Search for Iraq's Weapons of Mass Destruction: Inspection, Verification and Non-Proliferation* (Palgrave MacMillan: Basingstoke, 2005).

[4] Alibek, K., *Biohazard: The Chilling True Story of the Largest Covert Biological Weapons Program in the World, Told From Inside by the Man Who Ran It* (Random House: New York, N.Y., 1999); and Domaradskij, I. V. and Orent, W., *Biowarrior: Inside the Soviet/Russian Biological War Machine* (Prometheus Books: New York, N.Y., 2003).

[5] These incidents include the 11 Sep. 2001 terrorist attacks on the USA and other terrorist incidents causing mass casualties (e.g., in Bali, in Oct. 2002; in Madrid, in Mar. 2004; in Beslan, Russia, in Sep. 2004; and in London, in July 2005).

[6] Roffey, R., 'Biological weapons and potential indicators of offensive biological weapon activities', *SIPRI Yearbook 2004: Armaments, Disarmament and International Security* (Oxford University Press: Oxford, 2004), pp. 557–71. See also US National Research Council, Committee on Advances in Technology and the Prevention of their Application to Next Generation Biowarfare Threats, *Globalization, Biosecurity, and the Future of the Life Sciences* (National Academies Press: Washington, DC, 2006).

[7] National Intelligence Council, 'Mapping the global future', Report of the National Intelligence Council's 2020 Project, Dec. 2004, URL <http://www.cia.gov/nic/NIC_2020_project.html>.

[8] Interpol, 'Bio-terrorism conference opens with warning of major threat: Interpol member countries seek co-ordinated global response', Media release, 1 Mar. 2005, URL <http://www.interpol.int/Public/ICPO/PressReleases/PR2005/PR200510.asp>.

[9] World Health Organization (WHO), 'Global public health response to natural occurrence, accidental release or deliberate use of biological and chemical agents or radionuclear material that affect health', Fifty-fifth World Health Assembly, Resolution WHA 55.16, 18 May 2002, URL <http://www.who.int/gb/ebwha/pdf_files/WHA55/ewha5516.pdf>; and WHO, Food Safety Department, 'Terrorist threats to

The 2004 Report of the United Nations (UN) High-level Panel on Threats, Challenges and Change stressed that future biological threats and bio-security are key security concerns.[10] Improving global disease-monitoring capabilities may be a means to counter new, emerging infectious diseases; defend against the threat of biological terrorism; and build effective and responsible states. The report calls on the states parties to the 1972 Biological and Toxin Weapons Convention (BTWC) to resume the negotiation of a credible verification protocol and to initiate negotiations on a new bio-security protocol.[11] The report also draws attention to the overall deterioration of the global health system, and it highlights both the promise and the peril of the advances in biotechnology.[12]

The 2003 BTWC Meeting of Experts discussed bio-safety and bio-security issues, and the parties acknowledged the need for risk assessment as a tool for designing appropriate and balanced legislation.[13] They also noted that self-regulation of bio-security by facilities, including those for research or production, was unlikely to be adequate and that formal, governmental oversight arrangements, including legislation, would probably be necessary. The key elements of national bio-security programmes emerged from the discussions, and it was recognized that some states are more vulnerable to unauthorized access to facilities that possess dangerous pathogens owing to the lack of appropriate legislation and security.[14] The meeting noted that only a small number of countries have enacted legislation that specifically addresses bio-security. There was, however, no common understanding or recommendation on how to proceed on this issue because of the current lack of political agreement about specific efforts to strengthen the BTWC.

Developing bio-security standards

Proposals have also been made to develop international bio-security standards or agree a legal protocol in order to prevent proliferators and terrorists from acquiring biological warfare agents and know-how and in order to simplify the tracing of agents used in bio-terrorism attacks. Such an approach could include legal commitments by states, a set of universal standards and an oversight mechanism. It could also comprise emergency response plans in the event of bio-security breaches; a mechanism for accounting and controlling pathogens and toxins when storing, using or transfer-

---

food guidance for establishing and strengthening prevention and response systems', 2002, URL <http://www.who.int/foodsafety/publications/general/en/terrorist.pdf>.

[10] United Nations, 'A more secure world: our shared responsibility', Report of the High-level Panel on Threats, Challenges and Change, UN documents A/59/565, 4 Dec. 2004, and A/59/565/Corr.1, 6 Dec. 2004, URL <http://www.un.org/ga/59/documentation/list5.html>.

[11] United Nations (note 10), para. 27, p. 102, and para. 137, pp. 45–46. On the BTWC see chapter 14 and annex A in this volume.

[12] United Nations (note 10), p. viii.

[13] In the final document of the 2002 Fifth Review Conference of the BTWC the states parties agreed to hold 3 annual meetings before the Sixth Review Conference in 2006 in order to discuss and promote common and effective action on a variety of subjects. Each meeting of the states parties was to be preceded by a 2-week preparatory Meeting of Experts, which would prepare factual reports describing their work. BTWC website, URL <http://www.opbw.org/new_process/new.htm>. See also chapter 14.

[14] Hersh, M., 'A view to the BWC 2006 Review Conference: a focus on risk', Draft paper presented at the Conference on Meeting the Challenges of Bioterrorism: Assessing the Threat and Designing Biodefence Strategies, Füringen, Switzerland, 22–23 Apr. 2005; and Pearson, G., 'Maximizing the security and improving oversight of pathogenic microorganisms and toxins', *Strengthening the Biological Weapons Convention*, Briefing Paper no. 5 (2nd series), University of Bradford, Department of Peace Studies, July 2003, URL <http://www.brad.ac.uk/acad/sbtwc/briefing/BP_5_2ndseries.pdf>.

ring them; registration and licensing of facilities and personnel working with dangerous pathogens; and physical security measures. Negotiated global bio-security standards would reduce threats while reinforcing the legal prohibitions of the BTWC. It has been suggested that such a regime should include transparency measures for national bio-defence programmes and for the transfer of technology to developing countries in order to enhance their levels of bio-safety and bio-security.[15] This regime should be incorporated into the framework of the BTWC and include the active participation of the scientific and public health organizations, such as the WHO, the UN Food and Agriculture Organization (FAO) and the World Organization for Animal Health (Office International des Epizooties, OIE).

III. The concept of bio-security

An effective strategy for biological security will differ significantly from corresponding strategies to curtail the spread of chemical or nuclear weapons. Bio-security not only is a matter of physical security, but also includes all the measures necessary to raise awareness of the risks involved and the measures to keep know-how, technology and dangerous pathogens or toxins from falling into the hands of those who would use them for criminal acts such as bio-terrorism or biological warfare. The concept of bio-security is relatively new, however, which explains why there is still no generally accepted definition.[16]

A bio-security system should include elements of preparedness and response in the event of bio-safety or bio-security breaches. An essential part of a bio-security system is a programme of epidemiological surveillance that is effective, responds rapidly and is carried out at the local, regional and national levels of a state. This is crucial in order to enable early detection of possible releases of biological agents. Directly connected to this requirement is the ability to quickly identify potential disease-causing pathogens using rapid, reliable, standardized and internationally accepted diagnostic methods that enable confirmation of suspected cases of infectious disease outbreaks, identification of breaches of bio-safety or bio-security and characterization of the agent involved. Enforceable national legislation and regulations that cover the relevant areas are also essential. 'Bio-security' is sometimes inappropriately used to refer to a broader range of measures to prevent and respond to possible biological attacks (e.g., bio-defence, public health and law enforcement). Some bio-security measures overlap with policies on bio-safety, food safety, agricultural security, biodiversity and counter-terrorism measures. In the United States, for example, the term bio-security is used to motivate increased funding for bio-defence research, thereby draining resources from public health research. Such a broad definition of bio-security is inappropriate and should be avoided.

---

[15] Atlas, R. and Reppy, J., 'Globalizing biosecurity', *Biosecurity and Bioterrorism: Biodefense Strategy, Practice, and Science*, vol. 3, no. 3 (Mar. 2005), pp. 51–60; Tucker, J. B., 'Preventing terrorist access to dangerous pathogens: the need for international biosecurity standards', *Disarmament Diplomacy*, no. 66 (Sep. 2002), URL <http://www.acronym.org.uk/dd/dd66/66op2.htm>; and Tucker, J., 'A strategy for international harmonization of biosecurity standards under SCR 1540', Workshop on UN Security Council Resolution 1540 as it Pertains to Biological Weapons, Geneva, 3 Dec, 2004.

[16] States interpret the term 'bio-security' in different ways, which complicates attempts to agree on terminology. E.g., in Australia and New Zealand bio-security refers to measures to protect agriculture from the risks posed by imported pests. In Russian there is no word for bio-security; only the term bio-safety is used, with its meaning dependent on the context.

Bio-security affects the international community, governments, industries and laboratories as well as individuals, and guidelines are badly needed. The WHO and other relevant international organizations have begun to define the concept of bio-security and to develop standards and guidelines for laboratories and production facilities. According to the draft WHO definition, laboratory bio-security refers to institutional and personal security measures adopted in laboratories that are designed to prevent unauthorized access to and the loss, theft, misuse, diversion or intentional release of valuable biological materials, thereby increasing their protection and accountability.[17]

Laboratory bio-security is primarily achieved through 'administrative and procedural requirements that clearly identify the threats to be addressed, the materials to be protected, the responsibilities of workers and the measures that restrict access to these materials by unauthorized individuals'.[18] Bio-security practices should be a logical extension of good laboratory bio-safety procedures and good management practices. Laboratory bio-security and bio-safety are both essential to good laboratory practice. The WHO defines laboratory bio-safety as the containment principles, technologies and practices that are implemented to prevent unintentional exposure to pathogens or their accidental release as well as the containment of pathogens in a limited space or area. High levels of laboratory bio-safety can be achieved through the implementation of various laboratory measures that increase containment, thereby safeguarding workers, biological material and the environment.[19] The WHO has urged its member states to promote improved bio-safety at laboratories.[20]

Bio-safety measures should be integrated with bio-security as a component of the overall improvement of proliferation prevention measures. Thousands of production facilities and laboratories around the world carry out work involving dangerous pathogens or toxins. It is not known how many or which of these pathogens or toxins could be of potential interest to states or non-state actors (i.e., terrorists) who wish to acquire a biological weapon capability. In many cases, these facilities and research centres are aware of the need for bio-safety measures to protect their personnel and to prevent accidental releases. However, they are usually unaccustomed to considering the need for enhanced security measures on site. Often such measures are perceived by scientists as ineffective, intrusive, too costly or as an obstruction to free research, which has created scepticism about their value.

The need for laboratory and facility bio-security

Essential to the concept of bio-security is a system of laboratory bio-security that includes components such as risk assessment, physical security, personnel manage-

---

[17] According to their owners, users or those who retain them, valuable biological materials are biological materials that require administrative oversight and specific protective, monitoring and tracking measures. Valuable biological materials can include pathogens and toxins as well as culture collections, vaccine strains, food and genetically modified organisms, cell components, genetic elements, etc. World Health Organization (WHO), Department of Communicable Disease Surveillance and Response, 'Laboratory biosecurity: WHO guidance', WHO document WHO/CDS/CRS/LYO, Draft 9, 2005; and WHO official, Communication with Roffey, 15 Dec. 2005.

[18] Chyba, C. F., 'Towards biological security', *Foreign Affairs*, vol. 81, no. 3 (May/June 2002), p. 122.

[19] World Health Organization (WHO), *Laboratory Biosafety Manual*, 3rd edn (WHO: Geneva, 2004), URL <http://www.who.int/csr/resources/publications/biosafety/WHO_CDS_CSR_LYO_2004_11/en/>.

[20] World Health Organization, 'Enhancement of laboratory biosafety', Fifty-eighth World Health Assembly, 25 May 2005, URL <http://www.who.int/csr/labepidemiology/WHA58_29-en.pdf>.

ment, control and handling of dangerous pathogens and toxins, the secure transfer of infectious materials between facilities, internal and cross-border accountability, information security, licensing and accreditation, programme management, scientific oversight, and well-developed standards and codes of practice.[21] Bio-security is also promoted by instituting a culture of responsibility and accountability among those handling, using, transporting and overseeing work with dangerous pathogens and other valuable biological materials.

Assessing the risk

The approaches to handling biological material differ for human, animal and plant pathogens and for toxins. Standards and procedures for the safe and secure storage, transfer, handling and disposal of dangerous pathogens should be developed by each facility. Identifying risks and listing the assets which the security system should protect based on plausible threat scenarios would facilitate this process.[22] The classification of risk should be based on the type of asset in need of protection. The highest classification level should be assigned to material whose misuse would have national or international security consequences. When making such a classification, risk factors such as the probability of terrorist use should be considered together with the possible consequences of such use.[23] The category of risk that an agent represents will not necessarily correspond to its bio-safety risk level. Most microbiological agents would be evaluated as posing minimal security risk.

Management and control

The obvious approaches to physical security would be to install video cameras for monitoring purposes and to erect a physical barrier around a facility in order to limit access to all or part of it to authorized personnel only, to detect unauthorized access and to respond to security breaches. It is important that the facility's management carefully selects personnel and promotes a security culture that is based on shared perceptions about security and the conviction that the security measures taken or proposed are important.[24] Security is vital as regards the access to and the handling of dangerous pathogens or toxins; and serious consideration should be given to the control, registration and licensing of facilities and of individuals working with or handling them.[25]

---

[21] Sandia National Laboratories, 'Laboratory biosecurity implementation guidelines', Sandia Report SAND2005-2348P, Apr. 2005, URL <http://www.biosecurity.sandia.gov/documents/LBIG.pdf>; and Chyba (note 18), p. 122.

[22] Salerno, R. M. and Estes, D. P., 'Biosecurity: protecting high consequence pathogens and toxins against theft and diversion', Sandia Report 2003-4274P, Oct. 2003, URL <http://www.biosecurity.sandia.gov/documents/sand2003-4274p.pdf>, p. 8.

[23] Kwik, G. et al., 'Biosecurity: responsible stewardship of bioscience in an age of catastrophic terrorism', *Biosecurity and Bioterrorism: Biodefence Strategy, Practice, and Science*, vol. 1, no. 1 (2003), URL <http://www.liebertonline.com/doi/pdfplus/10.1089/15387130360514805>, pp. 27–36; and Steinbruner, J. et al., 'Controlling dangerous pathogens: a prototype protective oversight system', *CISSM Working Paper*, 1 Sep. 2005, URL <http://www.cissm.umd.edu/documents/pathogensmonograph.pdf>.

[24] Khripunov, I. and Holmes, J. (eds), *Nuclear Security Culture: The Case of Russia* (Center for International Trade and Security, University of Georgia: Atlanta, Ga., Dec. 2004), URL <http://www.uga.edu/cits/home/index.htm>.

[25] Tucker, J., 'Preventing the misuse of pathogens: the need for global biosecurity standards', *Arms Control Today*, June 2003, URL <http://www.armscontrol.org/act/2003_06/tucker_june03.asp>.

Many states control the import and export as well as transfer within the country of dangerous human, animal or plant pathogens. In some cases, in order to further reduce risks, dangerous pathogens or toxins can only be transferred between approved or licensed facilities. Several internationally agreed standards regulate the transport of dangerous pathogens and toxins and include requirements for the containers and packaging used for such transport. The UN Model Regulations define suitable packaging that affords a level of safety appropriate to the degree of risk.[26]

Codes of conduct and practice

In conjunction with other bio-security measures, codes of conduct and practice for scientists and technicians can affect how current and future threats from the use of biological materials are handled. The advances and benefits of the rapid developments in biotechnology, including genetic engineering, are immense, but they can also pose risks when mistakes or misuse occur.[27] Individual responsibility, an increased awareness of how research could be misused and a culture of integrity and responsibility—including through scientific oversight, peer review, pre-publication review and whistle-blowing mechanisms—could be important in this context.[28] The Interacademy Panel on International Issues in 2005 issued a statement on bio-security that addresses five fundamental issues that should be taken into account when formulating codes of conduct for scientists: awareness, safety and security, education and information, accountability and oversight.[29] 'Codes of practice' refers to practical guidance and advice on how to achieve a certain standard. Such codes are considered enforceable, in contrast to 'codes of conduct'—which are often interpreted to be advisory and to apply to individuals only.[30] A code of good manufacturing practice is, for example, already used in the pharmaceutical industry.[31]

[26] World Health Organization (WHO), 'Transport of infectious substances: background to the amendments adopted in the 13th revision of the United Nations Model Regulations guiding the transport of infectious substances', WHO document WHO/CDS/CSR/LYO/2004.9, 2004, URL <http://www.who.int/csr/resources/publications/WHO_CDS_CSR_LYO_2004_9/en/>; and United Nations, 'UN recommendations on the transport of dangerous goods: model regulations', 13th revised edn, 2003, URL <http://www.unece.org/trans/danger/publi/unrec/rev13/13files_e.html>.

[27] Examples include the reconstruction of Spanish influenza virus, the synthesis of poliovirus and the inadvertent creation of a lethal mouse pox virus. Hart, J. and Kuhlau, F., 'Codes of conduct for scientists in the biological field', Paper presented at the Conference on Meeting the Challenges of Bioterrorism: Assessing the Threat and Designing Biodefence Strategies (note 14); and Chyba, F. and Greninger, A. L., 'Biotechnology and bioterrorism: an unprecedented world', *Survival*, vol. 46, no. 2 (2004), pp. 143–44.

[28] Meeting of the States Parties to the BTWC, 'Synthesis of considerations, lessons, perspectives, recommendations, conclusions and proposals drawn from the presentations, statements, working papers and interventions on the topic under discussion at the Meeting of Experts', BWC/MSP/2005/L.1, Geneva, 16 Nov. 2005.

[29] Hart and Kuhlau (note 27); Somerville, M. A. and Atlas, R., 'Ethics: a weapon to counter bioterrorism', *Science*, 25 Mar. 2005, pp. 1881–82; and Interacademy Panel on International Issues, A Global Network of Science Academies, 'Statement on biosecurity', 30 June 2005, URL <www.knaw.nl/nieuws/pers_pdf/IAP_Biosecurity_statement.pdf>. A version endorsed by 68 national academies of science from all regions of the world was presented in Geneva on 7 Dec. 2005 at the Meeting of the States Parties to the BTWC. See Interacademy Panel on International Issues, 'IAP Statement on Biosecurity', 7 Nov. 2005, URL <http://www4.nationalacademies.org/iap/iaphome.nsf>.

[30] University of Exeter and University of Bradford, 'Biological weapons and codes of conduct', URL <http://www.ex.ac.uk/codesofconduct/Examples/>; and Hart and Kuhlau (note 27), p. 8.

[31] World Health Organization (WHO), 'Good manufacturing practices and inspections', *Quality Assurance of Pharmaceuticals: A Compendium of Guidelines and Related Materials*, vol. 2, updated edn (WHO: Geneva, 2004), URL <http://www.who.int/medicines/areas/quality_safety/quality_assurance/inspections/en/>.

IV. Infectious diseases: a threat to health and security

Despite medical advances, communicable diseases are still major threats to human health in both the technologically advanced and in the developing regions of the world. Outbreaks of infectious diseases continue to have significant consequences for public health, agriculture and the global economy.[32] Measures to reduce the global risks caused by accidental and deliberately induced outbreaks of infectious disease require a coordinated global strategy, and it is well known that it is extremely difficult initially to distinguish one kind of outbreak from the other.[33] Many disease-control strategies focus on the response to an outbreak, but bio-safety and bio-security are preventive measures that counter risks before they lead to outbreaks of disease. Emerging and re-emerging infectious diseases are global problems and should be addressed by a global strategy. Of immediate concern are the infectious disease situation, the deficiencies of the epidemiological disease surveillance system and weaknesses in diagnostic abilities, preparedness and response capacities. Improving preparedness and enhancing global public health efforts on a broad scale are essential. A disease outbreak in one country can spread internationally in a matter of hours or days. Many experts believe that there is a risk of a new influenza pandemic that could kill millions of people.[34] The consequences of an outbreak of infectious disease resulting from the deliberate use of a pathogenic micro-organism could be at least as damaging as naturally occurring infections, and possibly more so. The 2001 attacks in the USA using letters that were filled with dried anthrax spores had a relatively modest health impact, with 5 deaths among the 22 people exposed to the letters, but the attacks caused enormous social disruption and economic damage.[35]

Disease caused by leaks and accidents: a lack of oversight

In recent years it has been increasingly recognized that bioscience facilities are potential sources from which terrorists could obtain pathogens and toxins or knowledge that could be misused to create weapons. Bio-security in the sense of preventing theft is therefore a relatively new issue that only some Western countries, including only a few European Union (EU) members, have begun to consider seriously. In December 2005 the EU listed as a priority the promotion through funding of the physical secur-

---

[32] The outbreak of foot-and-mouth disease in the United Kingdom in 2001 caused economic losses of about €11 billion. The outbreak of severe acute respiratory syndrome in 2003 infected over 8000 people, killed almost 800 and had considerable impact on economies in the Pacific Rim and Canada. Outbreaks of avian influenza in 2004 inflicted losses in Asia estimated at €400 million. World Health Organization (note 17); and Njuguna, J. T., 'The SARS epidemic: the control of infectious diseases and biological weapon threats', *SIPRI Yearbook 2004* (note 6), pp. 697–712.

[33] Dando, M., Kriz, B. and Pearson, G., University of Bradford, *Scientific and Technical Means of Distinguishing Between Natural and Other Outbreaks of Disease: Proceedings of the NATO Advanced Research Workshop, Prague, Czech Republic, 18–20 October 1998* (Kluwer: Dordrecht, 2001).

[34] Enserink, M., 'Looking the pandemic in the eye', *Science*, vol. 306, issue 5695 (15 Oct. 2004), pp. 392–94; and 'WHO warns of bird flu pandemic', BBC News Online, 23 Feb. 2005, URL <http://news.bbc.co.uk/2/4289637.stm>.

[35] Zanders, J. P., Hart, J. and Kuhlau, F., 'Chemical and biological warfare developments and arms control', *SIPRI Yearbook 2002: Armaments, Disarmament and International Security* (Oxford University Press: Oxford, 2002), p. 699; Zanders, J. P., 'Weapons of mass disruption', *SIPRI Yearbook 2003: Armaments, Disarmament and International Security* (Oxford University Press: Oxford, 2003), pp. 683–90; and Greene. C. M. et al., 'Epidemiologic investigations of bioterrorism-related anthrax, New Jersey, 2001', *Emerging Infectious Diseases*, vol. 8, no. 10 (Oct. 2002).

ity of laboratories in Ukraine and other countries.[36] There are large numbers of laboratories in the world that possess dangerous pathogens or toxins or conduct work on them, but there are no data on exactly how many such laboratories exist because an international inventory has not been conducted. Few countries even have a national inventory. It is known, however, that about 1500 state-owned and commercial culture collections exist worldwide—in addition to culture collections of various types at universities, hospitals, laboratories or commercial companies which do not trade in agents.[37] For instance, an inventory of laboratories disclosed that 160 000 laboratories in 152 countries possess poliovirus.[38]

Leaks from laboratories and accidents involving the release of pathogens have already occurred. In 2004, in Boston, Massachusetts, scientists mistakenly worked with live tularaemia strains when they thought they were working on a harmless vaccine strain. The mistake was first detected when the scientists displayed influenza-like symptoms.[39] It is also known that in Beijing, Singapore and Taipei the severe acute respiratory syndrome (SARS) virus leaked in four cases from laboratories,[40] and a case of Ebola haemorrhagic fever infection occurred because of an accident at the State Research Centre of Virology and Biotechnology (Vector) in Koltsovo, Russia.[41] In 2004 a laboratory in the USA accidentally sent out proficiency tests that included pandemic influenza virus to 3750 laboratories around the world and then urgently had to ask the laboratories to destroy the samples. It proved difficult to track down all the samples and some seemed to have gone missing. The mistake was not discovered until one month after the samples had been distributed, when a patient was mistakenly diagnosed as having influenza because of the contamination from the proficiency test kit sample.[42]

There is no information on the scale of global transfers of dangerous pathogens or on the quantity of such pathogens that are transferred and not covered by current regulations. As far as can be determined from publicly available information, there are also few cases of theft or illicit transfer of dangerous pathogens. The means to detect illicit transfers across borders are few and the task is difficult since the small quantities that would be required in order to have an effect can be easily concealed.

---

[36] Council of the European Union, 'Implementation of the EU Strategy against proliferation of WMD: six-monthly progress report on the implementation of Chapter III of the EU Strategy against the Proliferation of Weapons of Mass Destruction, and updated list of priorities for a coherent implementation of the EU WMD Strategy', document 14520/05, Brussels, 5 Dec. 2005, URL <http://tradeinfo.cec.eu.int/doclib/docs/2005/december/tradoc_126701.en05.pdf>.

[37] Tucker (note 25).

[38] Walgate, R., 'SARS labs unsafe, says WHO: scientific advisors call for international regime to regulate pathogen biocontainment', The Scientist, 3 June 2004, URL <http://www.the-scientist.com/news/20040603/03>.

[39] Shane, S., 'Exposure at germ lab reignites a public health debate', New York Times, 24 Jan. 2005.

[40] Walgate, R., 'SARS escaped Beijing lab twice: laboratory safety at the Chinese Institute of Virology under close scrutiny', The Scientist, 26 Apr. 2004, URL <http://www.the-scientist.com/article/display/22139/>.

[41] Walgate (note 40).

[42] World Health Organization, 'International response to the distribution of a H2N2 influenza virus for laboratory testing: risk considered low for laboratory workers and the public', 12 Apr. 2005, URL <http://www.who.int/csr/disease/influenza/h2n2_2005_04_12/en/index.html>; 'Labs race to destroy flu virus after test kit mistake', Financial Times, 14 Apr. 2005; and 'Virus scare shows need for better disease-control methods', Vancouver Sun, 15 Apr. 2005.

Naturally emerging infectious diseases: avian influenza

After the SARS epidemic in 2003,[43] attention focused on avian influenza and the risk of pandemic influenza. The WHO has repeatedly warned of the rapid spread of avian influenza virus (H5N1).[44] The EU has agreed new guidelines for surveillance and has called for intensified bio-security and other disease prevention and control measures.[45] The first recorded case of avian influenza occurred in 1997 in Hong Kong.[46] According to the WHO, the avian influenza virus moved from domestic poultry to ducks and then to migrating birds in China.[47] Since 2003 the virus has spread westward, reaching Turkey;[48] of the 184 reported human cases, 103 had died from the virus as of 23 March 2006. The virus has also led to the death of around 140 million birds.[49] Confirmed reported human cases of infection have been detected in eight countries: Azerbaijan, Cambodia, China, Indonesia, Iraq, Thailand, Turkey and Viet Nam.[50] The EU has banned the import of chickens, other poultry and birds from 14 countries,[51] and it has urged increased surveillance by member states.[52] Experts agree that even a complete global ban on the import and export of poultry will only slow the spread of the virus, not stop it.[53]

---

[43] See Njuguna (note 32).

[44] Avian influenza, commonly known as 'bird flu', is an infectious disease of birds caused by type A strains of the influenza virus. The disease occurs worldwide and all birds are thought to be more or less susceptible to infection. There are a number of avian strains of the virus and, apart from H5N1 (the most severe strain), the H9N2 and H7N7 strains have also caused cases of mild illness in humans. See World Health Organization, 'Avian influenza', Fact sheet, URL <http://www.who.int/mediacentre/factsheets/avian_influenza/en/>.

[45] European Union, 'Conclusions of the Standing Committee on the Food Chain and Animal Health working group meeting on avian influenza', Press release, Brussels, 25 Aug. 2005, URL <http://www.europa.eu.int/rapid/pressReleasesAction.do?reference=MEMO/05/285&format=HTML&aged=0&language=EN&guiLanguage=en>.

[46] Liu, J. et al., 'Highly pathogenic H5N1 influenza virus infection in migratory birds', *Science*, vol. 309, issue 5738 (19 Aug. 2005), p. 1206, URL <http://www.sciencemag.org/cgi/content/abstract/1115273>.

[47] South East Asian Nations Infectious Diseases Outbreak Surveillance Network, 'WHO repeats warning of rapid bird flu spread', 7 Sep. 2005, URL <http://www.asean-disease-surveillance.net/ASN News_Detail.asp?ID=3340>.

[48] European Commission, 'Avian influenza in Turkey: EU takes further import measures and joint expert team starts work on the ground', Press release, 9 Jan. 2006, URL <http://www.europa.eu.int/comm/dgs/health_consumer/dyna/influenza/index.cfm>.

[49] US Department of Health and Human Services, 'Statement by Mike Leavitt, Secretary of Health and Human Services, International Partnership on Avian and Pandemic Influenza, United Nations General Assembly', Press release, Washington, DC, 15 Sep. 2005, URL <http://www.hhs.gov/news/press/2005pres/20050915a.html>.

[50] World Health Organization, 'Confirmed human cases of avian influenza A(H5N1)', URL <http://www.who.int/csr/disease/avian_influenza/country/en/index.html>.

[51] The countries affected by the ban are Cambodia, China, Croatia, Indonesia, Kazakhstan, North Korea, Laos, Malaysia, Pakistan, Romania, Russia, Thailand, Turkey and Viet Nam.

[52] European Commission, 'Avian influenza: adjustments to import bans and to biosecurity requirements agreed', Press release, Brussels, 23 Nov. 2005, URL <http://www.europa.eu.int/rapid/press ReleasesAction.do?reference=IP/05/1460&format=HTML&aged=0&language=EN>; European Commission, 'Avian influenza in Romania and Turkey: Commission takes further action', Press release, Brussels, 13 Oct. 2005; European Union, 'EU Business: EU calls for ban on bird imports from Russia, Kazakhstan', 8 Aug. 2005, URL <http://www.eubusiness.com/Health/050808102229.zi87uoei>; and European Commission, 'Avian influenza: Commission asks member states to step up surveillance', Press release, Brussels, 25 Aug. 2005, URL <http://www.europa.eu.int/rapid/pressReleasesAction.do?reference=IP/05/1068&format=HTML&aged=0&language=EN&guiLanguage=en>.

[53] Doyle, S., 'No stopping a flu pandemic, officials say: even a "global shutdown" would only buy time', *National Post*, 24 Aug. 2005.

There are indications that the avian influenza virus currently is not easily transmitted from birds to humans. So far there is no evidence of human-to-human transmission of the virus.[54] The fear among health officials is, however, that if the virus combines with the human influenza virus it may be highly infectious and lead to a global influenza pandemic.[55] Recent publication of the complete sequence of the 1918 Spanish influenza virus has shown that it was an avian influenza virus strain that adapted to humans.[56] The potential risks of publishing complete sequences of dangerous pathogens should not be ignored. By using this sequence, scientists have recreated the virus and studied its effects in mice. It has been demonstrated that only 10 amino acid changes in the polymerase proteins consistently differentiate the 1918 and subsequent human influenza virus sequences from avian influenza virus sequences. Notably, a number of the same changes have been found in the H5N1 virus.[57]

In the EU it is estimated that 2–3 million deaths could occur in the event of a pandemic influenza epidemic. More than 40 million people died in the last three global pandemics, in 1918, 1957 and 1968. As of November 2005, approximately 120 (62 per cent) of the 194 WHO member states had preparedness plans for a pandemic or were drawing up such plans; this is an increase of more than 70 countries since May 2005.[58] Preparedness for and the response to pandemic influenza were important issues for the Sixth Ministerial Meeting of the Global Health Security Initiative, held in November 2005.[59] The EU has updated and revised its preparedness plans,[60] and the WHO has presented its strategic approach.[61] The European Commission and China hosted an international pledging conference on avian and human influenza in Beijing in 2006.[62] The international community has pledged $1.9 billion,

[54] World Health Organization, 'Avian influenza: frequently asked questions', URL <http://www.who.int/csr/disease/avian_influenza/avian_faqs/en/index.html>.

[55] Osterholm, M. T., 'Preparing for the next pandemic', *Foreign Affairs*, vol. 84, no. 4 (July/Aug. 2005), URL <http://www.foreignaffairs.org/20050701faessay84402-p0/michael-t-osterholm/preparing-for-the-nextpandemic.html>; and 'Indonesia bird flu toll increases', BBC News Online, 26 Sep. 2005, URL <http://news.bbc.co.uk/2/4281794.stm>.

[56] The 1918–19 'Spanish flu' pandemic killed an estimated 20–50 million people worldwide. Tumpey, T. M. et al., 'Characterization of the reconstructed 1918 Spanish influenza pandemic virus', *Science*, vol. 310 (7 Oct. 2005), pp. 77.

[57] Tumpey et al. (note 56), pp. 77–80; and Taubenberger, J. K. et al., 'Characterization of the 1918 influenza virus polymerase genes', *Nature*, vol. 437 (6 Oct. 2005), URL <http://www.nature.com/nature/journal/v437/n7060/full/nature04230.html>, pp. 889–93.

[58] World Health Organization (WHO), 'Perspectives from WHO: status of human health preparedness & response', Presentation by Dr Mike Ryan, Director, Epidemic and Pandemic Alert and Response (CDS/EPR), Meeting on Avian Influenza and Human Pandemic Influenza, Geneva, 7–9 Nov. 2005, URL <http://www.who.int/mediacentre/events/2005/avian_influenza_meeting_presentations/en/index.html>.

[59] US Department of State, 'Sixth Ministerial Meeting on the Global Health Security Initiative', Rome, 18 Nov. 2005, URL <http://www.state.gov/g/oes/rls/or/57804.htm>.

[60] European Commission, 'Communication from the Commission to the Council, the European Parliament, the European Economic and Social Committee and the Committee of the Regions on pandemic influenza preparedness and response planning in the European Community', Brussels, COM(2005) 607 final, 28 Nov. 2005, URL <http://www.europa.eu.int/comm/health/ph_threats/com/Influenza/keydo_influenza_en.htm>.

[61] UN Development Group, 'Avian and human pandemic influenza: UN system contributions and requirements, a strategic approach', 13 Jan. 2006, URL <http://siteresources.worldbank.org/PROJECTS/Resources/40940-1136754783560/UNSIC-Strategy.pdf>.

[62] European Commission, 'European Commission to co-host International Pledging Conference on Avian and Human Influenza in Beijing', Press release, Brussels, 22 Dec. 2005, URL <http://www.europa.eu.int/rapid/pressReleasesAction.do?reference=IP/05/1686>; and World Bank, 'Program framework document for proposed loans/credits/grants in the amounts of US $500 million equivalent for a

of which $260 million was pledged by the EU.[63] A global influenza pandemic could result in severe economic losses, estimated at $550 billion for high-income countries alone.[64] Concern about an influenza pandemic has led to international initiatives such as the proposal to initiate a global influenza vaccine programme by the Group of Eight (G8) industrialized nations and the establishment of a new International Partnership on Avian and Pandemic Influenza announced by US President George W. Bush.[65] Twenty-seven countries possess stockpiles of anti-virus drugs in amounts sufficient to cover 2 per cent of the world's population.[66] Nine states produce most of the world's vaccine.[67] Europe's production amounts to 70 per cent of the global total. There is great concern that, in an emergency, the states with vaccine production facilities will limit or ban exports to other states.[68]

Other major infectious diseases: requests for international cooperation

Another major global threat from infectious disease is the spread of HIV/AIDS, which has killed more than 25 million people since 1981.[69] Sub-Saharan Africa has been more severely affected by AIDS than any other part of the world. The UN has reported that 25.8 million adults and children are infected with HIV in the region, where about 10 per cent of the world's population lives and where two-thirds of the total of HIV-infected people also live.[70] AIDS has surpassed malaria as the leading cause of death in Africa, and it kills more Africans than conflict.[71] In addition, and because of the HIV/AIDS epidemic, there are around 8.5 million diagnosed cases of tuberculosis, and 2 million people die of the disease every year. The HIV/AIDS epidemic is also growing in other regions in the world, particularly in Eastern Europe and Central Asia where the HIV-infected population has increased by one-quarter, to 1.6 million, since 2003 and the number of deaths almost doubled to 62 000. Another affected region is East Asia, where the number of infected people increased by

global program for avian influenza control and human pandemic preparedness and response', Report no. 34386, 5 Dec. 2005, URL <http://siteresources.worldbank.org/PROJECTS/Resources/40940-113675 4783560/Avian-Flu-PAD.pdf>.

[63] European Commission, Markus Kyprianou European Commissioner for Health and Consumer Safety, 'Remarks at the concluding press conference, International Pledging Conference on Avian and Human Pandemic Influenza', Press release, Beijing, 18 Jan, 2006, URL <http://europa.eu.int/rapid/press ReleasesAction.do?reference=SPEECH/06/14>.

[64] Brahmbhalt, M., 'Avian influenza: economic and social impacts', World Bank, 23 Sep. 2005, URL <http://web.worldbank.org/WBSITE/EXTERNAL/NEWS/0,,contentMDK:20663668~pagePK:34370~pi PK:42770~theSitePK:4607,00.html>.

[65] 'Pandemic project needed, expert says: flu pandemic would drain the world's economy and trigger universal panic, author warns', *Vancouver Sun*, 5 May 2005. The G8 programme is discussed below. See also The White House, 'President addresses United Nations high-level plenary meeting', UN Headquarters, Press release, New York, 14 Sep. 2005, URL <http://www.whitehouse.gov/news/releases/ 2005/09/20050914.html>.

[66] Kvankom, A. and Tangwisutijit, N., 'Not enough drugs to fight a new pandemic', *The Nation*, 23 Aug. 2005.

[67] The states are Australia, Canada, France, Germany, Italy, Japan, the Netherlands, the UK and the USA.

[68] Osterholm (note 55); and 'Preparing for a pandemic: more vaccine is needed to prepare the world for an influenza pandemic', *The Economist*, 22 Sep. 2005, p. 95.

[69] Joint UN Programme on HIV/AIDS and the World Health Organization, 'AIDS epidemic update', Dec. 2005, URL <http://www.unaids.org>, pp. 1–3. See also the Introduction in this volume.

[70] Joint UN Programme on HIV/AIDS and the WHO (note 69), pp. 1–3.

[71] Copson, R. W., 'AIDS in Africa', *CRS Issue Brief for Congress*, 3 Oct. 2003, URL <http://www. law.umaryland.edu/marshall/crsreports/crsdocuments/IB10050a.pdf>.

one-fifth, to 870 000, between 2003 and 2005. The total number of HIV-infected people reached 40.3 million in 2005.[72]

Owing to lack of funding and resources, new strains of tuberculosis have developed that are more difficult to treat. The recent SARS outbreak illustrated how the spread of disease can be limited when states cooperate closely and with international institutions.[73] UN agencies estimate that about $35 billion is needed to fight preventable diseases such as AIDS, malaria and tuberculosis, which together kill 2–3 million children every year.[74] In addition, livestock agriculture is the most important industry in sub-Saharan Africa, and diseases are its biggest constraint. Crop diseases and pests pose major threats to Africa's food security.[75]

V. International efforts to prevent biological weapon proliferation

Parallel to naturally occurring diseases and their sudden outbreaks, other major challenges and threats have emerged, such as the risk of the proliferation of biological weapons or the intentional use of disease by terrorists. The security measures required to address these threats should take into account the dual-use nature of biological materials and equipment, the small amounts of agent initially needed to cause an outbreak of disease, the relative ease with which such agents can be produced, their availability as the result of natural outbreaks and the dynamic nature of biotechnology.

The international community has attempted to prevent the proliferation of biological weapons, related materials and know-how but with limited success. Arms control and disarmament actions in the biological area have proved more difficult than for other weapon of mass destruction categories not only for political reasons, but also owing to practical factors such as the relative ease of acquiring dual-use materials and technologies. The obstacles to progress include the extreme secrecy surrounding work in biological weapon-related areas; the difficulty of identifying prohibited activities, especially by non-state actors; and the technical and political challenges of verifying that materials or activities are not being used for hostile purposes.[76] Threat assessments and intelligence are crucial in order to monitor biological weapon capabilities, and the inherent limitation of intelligence information in this area was recently demonstrated again by the intelligence failure in Iraq.[77]

State contributions to enhance bio-security

Thus far most international bio-security-related activities have been carried out under the US threat reduction programmes in Russia and the other former Soviet states. The

[72] Joint UN Programme on HIV/AIDS and the World Health Organization (note 69).

[73] United Nations (note 10), p. viii.

[74] Agence France-Presse, 'Experts urge G8 to help wipe out preventable diseases', 9 June 2005.

[75] British Department of Trade and Industry, 'Infectious diseases in Africa using science to fight the evolving threat', *Foresight Report*, Office of Science and Technology, Feb. 2005, URL <http://www.foresight.gov.uk>.

[76] Roffey (note 6).

[77] Guthrie, R., Hart, J. and Kuhlau, F., 'Chemical and biological warfare developments and arms control', *SIPRI Yearbook 2005: Armaments, Disarmament and International Security* (Oxford University Press: Oxford, 2005), pp. 622–26.

changed international security environment has resulted in the need for broader non-proliferation and disarmament activities that are intended to deal with global problems such as the risks posed by bio-terrorism and outbreaks of infectious diseases. The focus of activities has moved from threat reduction to terrorism prevention, public health-related issues and environmental protection.[78] These changes raise the question of whether there is a need to further modify current threat reduction approaches. Support should be refocused from the nuclear to the biological area and expanded beyond the former Soviet Union.

Compared to the budgets for assistance in, for example, the nuclear field, the contribution to improving bio-security is minimal.[79] The USA is by far the largest contributor in the biological area: its annual funding is estimated to be approximately $90–100 million, although most of the funding is not allocated to bio-security.[80] Other states contribute mainly through the G8 Global Partnership against the Spread of Weapons of Mass Destruction or, in the case of the EU member states, through the Technical Assistance to the Commonwealth of Independent States (TACIS) programme.[81] These contributions primarily fund the science centres in Russia and Ukraine that were established to engage former Soviet weapon scientists in peaceful research.[82] The funding for bio-security enhancement is limited in the former Soviet states. However, states such as Canada, France and the United Kingdom are becoming increasingly involved in bio-security-related activities there.

New international approaches to prevent biological proliferation

The BTWC is the natural framework in which bio-security issues could be developed and agreed upon in a multilateral setting, but since the negotiations on a verification protocol for the treaty stalled in 2001 little has been achieved.[83] The lack of a concrete outcome from the discussions in the BTWC framework has spurred a range of activities designed to promote bio-security in organizations such as the Organisation for Economic Co-operation and Development (OECD) and the WHO and among non-governmental organizations. These organizations play important roles in developing the concept of bio-security, in raising global awareness of the issues involved and in highlighting the need to engage various actors to prevent proliferation. Lack of coordination of these initiatives, however, has made it difficult to harmonize bio-security measures, and their impact has been limited so far.

The International Science and Technology Center (ISTC) in Moscow and the Science and Technology Center (STCU) in Kyiv play central roles in promoting non-proliferation in the former Soviet Union by facilitating cooperation between scientists

---

[78] US National Research Council, *Biological Science and Biotechnology in Russia: Controlling Diseases and Enhancing Security* (National Academies Press: Washington, DC, 2005).

[79] Anthony, I., *Reducing Threats at the Source: A European Perspective on Cooperative Threat Reduction*, SIPRI Research Report no. 19 (Oxford University Press: Oxford, 2004).

[80] Roffey (note 1); and Kuhlau (note 1).

[81] The states that are involved in significant bio-security support activities are Canada, Finland, France, Sweden, the UK and the USA.

[82] International Science and Technology Center (note 1); and Science and Technology Center (note 1).

[83] Zanders, Hart and Kuhlau (note 35), pp. 666–77; and Hart, J., Kuhlau, F. and Simon, J., 'Chemical and biological warfare developments and arms control', *SIPRI Yearbook 2003* (note 35), pp. 646–650.

and Western states.[84] Other international organizations such as the FAO, the OECD, the OIE and the WHO act from their different perspectives to enhance bio-security through the development of guidelines, standards and principles.[85] The WHO has also taken action to help its member states improve their preparedness against bio-terrorism.[86] The World Bank continues to support the improvement of epidemio-logical surveillance systems and the development of medical countermeasures and ways to handle disease outbreaks.[87] The OECD is also actively pursuing the establish-ment of a global network of biological resource centres (BRCs), which will operate as focal points and serve as repositories to permit the safe and secure exchange of microbial cultures among its members.[88] The national centres will have the key func-tion of safeguarding valuable culture collections for the life sciences and the biotech-nology industry and will provide global coordination in the form of a BRC network to increase efficiency and transparency and to facilitate the international exchange of these cultures in a safe and secure manner.[89]

As noted, the G8 Global Partnership has played an important role in addressing non-proliferation, disarmament and counter-terrorism issues with a focus on the former Soviet Union.[90] However, the funding committed and allocated for the bio-logical area is minimal and the contributions pledged by some states in the G8 frame-work have not yet been honoured.[91] Another partnership, the Global Health Security Initiative, includes the G7 states plus the European Commission and Mexico.[92] It aims to improve global health security and meet the threats of chemical, biological, radiological and nuclear terrorism as well as pandemic influenza.[93] In the biological field, its goals are to build joint surveillance networks, to develop approaches for enhancing national and international preparedness, to prepare the response to out-breaks of disease and to strengthen public health emergency response and detection.[94] It also aims to achieve common standards and promote cooperation among labora-

---

[84] International Science and Technology Center (note 1); and Science and Technology Center (note 1).

[85] Roffey (note 1); and Kuhlau (note 1).

[86] World Health Organization (WHO), *Public Health Response to Biological and Chemical Weapons: WHO Guidance* (WHO: Geneva, 2004).

[87] On these projects see the World Bank database 'Projects and operations', URL <http://www.worldbank.org/>.

[88] Organisation for Economic Co-operation and Development, 'Biological resource centres: underpin-ning the future of life sciences and biotechnology', Mar. 2001, pp. 41–47. See also Tucker (note 25).

[89] Organisation for Economic Co-operation and Development (note 88); and Tucker (note 25).

[90] Reports from G8 summit meetings are available at URL <http://www.g8.gov.uk/>. The members of the G8 are listed in the glossary in this volume.

[91] In addition to the G8, 13 states—Australia, Belgium, the Czech Republic, Denmark, Finland, Ireland, South Korea, the Netherlands, New Zealand, Norway, Poland, Sweden and Switzerland—joined the Global Partnership in 2003–2004. The EU is also a member.

[92] The G7 states are Canada, France, Germany, Italy, Japan, the UK and the USA. The European Commission and Mexico participate in the Global Health Security Initiative.

[93] Foreign Affairs Canada and the International Trade Canada, 'Canada and the US: a global security partnership', Keynote speech by the Deputy Minister of Foreign Affairs Peter Harder, CIIA annual meeting, Halifax, 11 Mar. 2005, URL <http://www.fac-aec.gc.ca/department/deputy-minister-speeches-2005-03-11-en.asp>.

[94] Global Health Security Initiative (G7 and Mexican ministers of health), 'Sixth ministerial meeting on health security and bioterrorism', Rome, 18 Nov. 2005, URL <http://www.g8.utoronto.ca/health/rome2005.html>.

tories,[95] and the Global Health Security Action Group has been created to improve linkages between laboratories.[96]

Challenges to current non-proliferation approaches

The non-proliferation approach has so far focused on threat reduction activities, but such activities have had a limited focus on biological issues in general and bio-security in particular. After a decade of assistance in Russia and the other former Soviet states, new geographical regions, such as Africa and parts of Asia, should also be prioritized. Proliferation risks are high in these regions and concern exists with regard to their potential as favourable environments for terrorists seeking to acquire biological agents and develop biological weapon capabilities. In order to prevent proliferation and enhance bio-security in these regions, it is necessary to rethink non-proliferation approaches. In most African states, bio-security, or even bio-safety, would be considered a luxury and is given lower priority than basic needs such as secure access to food and water and combating infectious diseases. A new approach is needed in order to prevent proliferation and improve the level of bio-security. The urgent need to strengthen the public health infrastructure can be used to make the case for also increasing bio-safety and bio-security in order to combat disease. A well-coordinated and well-developed international strategy is needed to assist primarily Africa, but also parts of Asia, to cope with threats to health and security by putting in place efficient epidemiological surveillance systems, diagnostic capabilities and crucial bio-security components for laboratories and facilities that deal with dangerous pathogens and toxins. Such a strategy would also increase the control of pathogens and the awareness of which pathogens exist and would enhance preparedness and the response to naturally occurring diseases as well as those deliberately induced. The public health approach would be useful as a point of entry in other regions of the world as well.

The first meeting to deal with bio-terrorism and bio-security issues in sub-Saharan Africa was held in Kampala, Uganda, in September 2005. Ideas for an African initiative for a Global Bargain on Bio-security and Bioscience were developed that will be presented to the African Union (AU) if there is adequate support. In order to promote human security and protect against misuse of the biological sciences, the African states would make certain commitments—including in the area of enhancing bio-security—in exchange for assistance in a number of areas such as public health infrastructure and capacities; development programmes for vaccines and other capabilities to protect against diseases like AIDS, malaria and tuberculosis; disease monitoring; notification and surveillance systems; and strengthening African universities. The AU has also identified terrorism as a priority and has established the Centre for the Study of and Research on Terrorism, in Algiers.[97] The potential use of biological agents might have more serious consequences in Africa than in other parts of the world because large parts of the population have a decreased immune defence

---

[95] G7 health ministers, 'Statement of G7 health ministers' meeting', London, 14 Mar. 2002, URL <http://www.g8.utoronto.ca/health/london2002.html>.

[96] G7 health ministers, 'Statement of G7 health ministers' meeting', Ottawa, 7 Nov. 2001, URL <http://www.g8.utoronto.ca/health/ottawa2001.html>.

[97] 'AU anti-terrorism center inaugurated', *African Terrorism Bulletin*, issue 1 (Dec. 2004), URL <http://www.iss.org.za/pubs/Newsletters/Terrorism/0104.htm>.

owing to HIV infection. In addition, the public health infrastructure is weak, and there is a lack of medicines and other essential items.

VI. Conclusions: general bio-security trends

In the past decade the world has confronted new biological challenges because of a combination of emerging and re-emerging infectious diseases, rapid advances in bio-technology and a perceived increased bio-terrorism threat. It is now also generally accepted that security measures to prevent proliferation and bio-terrorism are needed in the biological field. The current limited international approach of enhancing bio-safety and bio-security through measures developed under the threat reduction umbrella has prevailed for a decade in assistance programmes in the former Soviet Union. Bio-security has to be seriously considered when developing a broader approach to the new global threats. Current methods, approaches and ways of carry-ing out support programmes demand modification to address the changing global security environment and the increased awareness of other geographical regions of concern.

Recent outbreaks of infectious disease have highlighted the global challenge they present. Emerging and re-emerging infectious diseases have developed from being merely public health and foreign aid issues to a prioritized issue on the global security agenda. The security implications of disease have become the focus of attention because diseases such as AIDS, malaria and tuberculosis have had devastating social, economic, health and security effects in many parts of the world, not least Africa, for a considerable period of time.

A well-coordinated international strategy for coping with the threats posed by dis-ease outbreaks, whether naturally occurring or deliberately induced, should be devel-oped, taking into account the need to prevent unauthorized access to dangerous pathogens and toxins. Global discussion of these issues is needed in order to achieve a well-balanced and realistic approach to them. Such an approach should be developed in a multilateral framework such as the BTWC in close cooperation with international organizations such as the FAO, the OECD, the OIE and the WHO. Pre-vention efforts will have limited practical effect unless there is a common inter-national understanding of the problem and its global scale and of what assistance is required and where. Immediate steps could be taken to strengthen the public health infrastructure through well-focused aid programmes in regions like Africa where the immense scale of the need in this area is clear. The next step would be to enhance preparedness, oversight and the general level of biological security at facilities that deal with dangerous pathogens or toxins. Such work should also be concentrated at fewer facilities worldwide. By enhancing preparedness, control and transparency, particularly in regions of concern, the global ability to prevent proliferation in the biological area would increase and the ability to prevent and limit the spread of future infectious diseases would be enhanced.

15. Conventional arms control

ZDZISLAW LACHOWSKI

I. Introduction

The year 2005 marked the 15th anniversary of the signing of the 1990 Treaty on Conventional Armed Forces in Europe (CFE Treaty). Any inclination to celebrate the event was dampened by the fact that the updating of Europe's 'hard' conventional arms control regime is still stalled by disagreements between Russia and the West over texts adopted at the 1999 Istanbul Summit of the Organization for Security and Co-operation in Europe (OSCE).[1] As a result, entry into force of the 1999 Agreement on Adaptation of the CFE Treaty remained hostage to Russia's completion of its promised military pull-outs from Georgia and Moldova. In Georgia the May 2005 agreement on the closing of Russian military bases and other facilities in the country was welcomed as a promising 'step forward',[2] but in Moldova deadlock persists over the presence of Russian personnel and equipment.

In 2005 the OSCE participating states continued to evaluate, adjust and develop certain arms control-related endeavours, including confidence- and security-building measures (CSBMs) and other arrangements, in order to better meet the common and regional risks and challenges facing Europe. Globally, the problem of 'inhumane weapons' continued to engage the international community.

This chapter analyses the major issues and developments relating to conventional arms control. Section II reviews the challenges that this process has encountered in Europe and elsewhere since the end of the cold war. Section III deals with critical elements of the implementation of the CFE Treaty in 2005. Section IV discusses arms control-related efforts to promote confidence, render assistance and foster stability in the OSCE area. The Open Skies Treaty regime is dealt with in section V.[3] The issue of mines and unexploded ord-

---

[1] On conventional arms control in Europe before 1999 see the relevant chapters in previous editions of the SIPRI Yearbook. For the text of the CFE Treaty and Protocols see Koulik, S. and Kokoski, R., SIPRI, *Conventional Arms Control: Perspectives on Verification* (Oxford University Press: Oxford, 1994), pp. 211–76; and the OSCE website at URL <http://www.osce.org/documents/chronological.php>. For the text of the Agreement on Adaptation see *SIPRI Yearbook 2000: Armaments, Disarmament and International Security* (Oxford University Press: Oxford, 2000), pp. 627–42; and the OSCE website. The parties to the CFE Treaty and the signatories of the Agreement on Adaptation are listed in annex A in this volume. On the CFE limits and holdings of the individual states parties see the Facts on International Relations and Security Trends (FIRST) database at URL <http://first.sipri.org/>.

[2] Russian Ministry of Foreign Affairs, 'Joint Statement by the Ministers of Foreign Affairs of the Russian Federation and Georgia', 30 May 2005, URL <http://www.ln.mid.ru/brp_4.nsf/sps/BF502C 80081D8AC5C32570120056B2D2>. See also the discussion in section III below.

[3] The parties and signatories of the 1992 Treaty on Open Skies are listed in annex A in this volume. On the 2005 status of the treaty see Lachowski, Z. and Dunay, P., 'Conventional arms control', *SIPRI*

nance is addressed in section VI. Section VII presents recommendations for the advancement of conventional arms control.

II. Conventional arms control: a balance sheet, 1990–2005

Much effort has been devoted to arms control in the field of conventional weapons both globally and regionally, but arms control has failed to take firm root outside Europe. Even though Europe remains a role model in this context, because of critical security changes since 1989 it also faces serious challenges.

Conventional arms control has all but vanished from Europe's mainstream security policy agenda, falling victim in part to its own success and in part to the general demise or transmutation of the underlying assumptions of the post-cold war arms control regime.[4] Once at the centre of military cold war politics, arms control lost its prominence as a powerful security tool after the end of the bloc confrontation when the risk of a sudden, mass-scale armed attack dramatically diminished. Immediately after the cold war, however, there was still interest in containing military confrontation and distrust, creating both the opportunity and need for formal provisions on arms reductions and building confidence. In 1992–95 the CFE states parties scrapped or converted to non-military use some 50 000 items of treaty-limited equipment (TLE). In the following years they carried out further cutbacks, which officially resulted in a total decrease of more than 63 500 heavy weapons.[5] In fact, the cuts were much deeper as many states reduced their conventional armaments well below their treaty limits (see table 15.1). In parallel, a total of 6–7.6 million military personnel on both sides in 1989 had fallen to about 3 million by 2005. Equally important, albeit less spectacular and quantifiable, was the arms control-related process of military confidence building in the entire OSCE area with the series of the Vienna Document on CSBMs.[6] In the latter part of the 1990s there was a separate, internationally monitored arms control regime in the former Yugoslavia, which brought about an additional reduction of some 6600 items of heavy weapons and a substantial limitation of military manpower there.[7] In addition, endeavours were made to adapt the existing CFE

Yearbook 2005: Armaments, Disarmament and International Security (Oxford University Press: Oxford, 2005), pp. 665–68; and section V of this chapter.

[4] This does not prevent European actors from asserting that arms control and CSBMs remain an important instrument for strengthening European security. See, e.g., Organization for Security and Co-operation in Europe Permanent Council, 2005 Annual Security Review Conference, Chair's report, Working session 2: comprehensive security, OSCE document PC.DEL/814/05, 1 Aug. 2005, p. 22.

[5] Permanent Mission of the Slovak Republic to the OSCE, 'Selected data on the implementation of CFE Treaty obligations', Vienna, 19 Dec. 1995. In 1989–90 the Soviet Union had relocated tens of thousands of TLE beyond the Urals; in a political statement in 1991 it undertook to destroy or convert to civil uses an additional 14 500 items of heavy weapons.

[6] The Vienna Documents 1990, 1992, 1994 and 1999 were based on the achievements of the former era and each built on the preceding documents. They are available at URL <http://www.osce.org/documents/chronological.php>. The Vienna Documents are summarized in annex A in this volume.

[7] The 1996 Agreement on Sub-Regional Arms Control (Florence Agreement, also known as the Article IV Agreement) was signed by Bosnia and Herzegovina and its 2 entities, and by Croatia and the Federal Republic of Yugoslavia (FRY, now Serbia and Montenegro). For the text of the Florence Agreement see URL <http://www.sipri.org/contents/worldsec/eurosec.html>.

Treaty regime to the new security realities, which aimed at moving from the cold war concept of an equilibrium of forces to a balance of security interests.

In 1999 the last peak in arms control activity in Europe occurred when two major agreements were signed: the legally binding Agreement on Adaptation and the politically binding Vienna Document 1999 on CSBMs. In January 2002 the long-awaited entry into force of the 1992 Treaty on Open Skies took place.

The relevance of European arms control

In the first years of the 21st century there have been dramatic changes in the European and global security landscape—the challenges of high-impact terrorism, the proliferation of weapons of mass destruction (WMD), the increase in the number of weak and failed states, the enlargements of the European Union (EU) and the North Atlantic Treaty Organization (NATO), the intra-West divides over numerous critical security issues (including the shift of the United States from a pillar of the European status quo towards a more unilateralist and interventionist posture outside Europe), and so on. These inevitably had an impact on the role of arms control in general and conventional arms control in Europe in particular.[8] As mentioned above, the changes after the end of the cold war almost eliminated the pressure to use arms control as a way to contain the risks of generalized conflict and surprise attack. The common aim of combating terrorism ensured that relations between NATO and the USA, on the one hand, and Russia, on the other, remained essentially calm and pragmatic. However, for various reasons this state of affairs did not translate into progress on cooperative 'hard' (structural) arms control. Currently, the adapted CFE Treaty regime (i.e., the CFE Treaty and the Agreement on Adaptation) remains in limbo.

Nonetheless, specific threats and challenges in Europe, such as regional and sub-regional security crises, conflicts (including 'frozen' conflicts) and local civil wars, have reinforced in a more differentiated way the *raison d'être* of arms control. This has been illustrated by the regional arms control agreements in the Balkans resulting from the 1995 General Framework Agreement for Peace in Bosnia and Herzegovina (Dayton Agreement).[9] The general evolution of political relations in Europe towards 'common and cooperative inclusive security', and the extension of that process to Central Asia, has led to the development of new approaches and solutions that make use of the 'softer' (operational) variants of arms control and that extend such techniques to cover new aspects of security and stability.

---

[8] This section summarizes the findings of a SIPRI study. See Lachowski, Z., Dunay, P. and der Haan, J., 'The relevance of conventional arms control in Europe', 2005, URL <http://www.sipri.org/contents/worldsec/Relevance.of.armscontrol.pdf>.

[9] General Framework Agreement for Peace in Bosnia and Herzegovina (Dayton Agreement), Dayton, Ohio, 14 Dec. 1995, URL <http://www.oscebih.org/overview/gfap/eng/ >.

Table 15.1. Treaty on Conventional Armed Forces in Europe limits and holdings, 1990–2005

Holdings, Nov. 1990	Limits: CFE, Nov. 1990 and CFE-1A, July 1992	Holdings, Nov. 1995	Adapted CFE, limit, 1999	Holdings, Jan. 2005
Treaty-limited equipment				
201 005	154 712	130 813	145 653	108 516
Manpower				
6–7.6 million	5 789 181	5 470 695	–	2 993 652

CFE = Treaty on Conventional Armed Forces in Europe; CFE-1A = Concluding Act of the Negotiation on Personnel Strength of Conventional Armed Forces in Europe

Sources: Manpower data were compiled from 'On the correlation of Warsaw Treaty and North Atlantic Alliance force strengths and armaments in Europe and adjoining waters', *Pravda*, 30 Jan. 1989, p. 5; and International Institute for Strategic Studies (IISS), *The Military Balance 1989/90* (IISS: London, 1989). Harahan, J. P. and Kuhn, J. C., *On-Site Inspections Under the CFE Treaty* (US Department of Defense, On-Site Inspection Agency: Washington, DC, 1996); *Arms Control Today*, Mar. 1993, p. 28; and Treaty on Conventional Armed Forces in Europe (CFE Treaty) Joint Consultative Group, Group on Treaty Operation and Implementation, Joint Consultative Group document JCG.TOI/56/05, 29 Nov. 2005.

All this and the impressive accomplishments of arms control in Europe notwithstanding, important questions remain about the relevance of further efforts in this field. The ambitious attempts made in the first half of the 1990s to harmonize, or even merge, the individual arms control regimes in Europe came to nothing and are not likely to be revived soon. The adapted CFE Treaty is held up by extraneous, although politically valid, obstacles (regarding Russia's behaviour towards its former Soviet neighbours and the wider strategic competition in the CFE's southern flank areas). Attempts made since 1999 to move forward with further adaptation ('modernization') of the Vienna CSBM Document to the new circumstances have thus far foundered. The Treaty on Open Skies failed to make headway at its first review conference in early 2005. In sum, the main arms control agreements today are facing erosion through neglect, or at best are muddling along, rather than setting the course for new goals comparable with those of the previous decade. The OSCE, which provided the framework for past achievements, is now confronted with a broader crisis of consensus and credibility that is hampering both the application of sufficient political energy to overcome old blockages and the opening up of new paths.

However, conventional arms control does not seem to be facing an early demise. Some of its traditional cold war functions, such as the emphasis on relations between enemies, decreasing the likelihood of war or limiting damage when a strategic conflict breaks out, are objectively less urgent today, at least in Europe. However, the overall framework of arms control and confidence building in Europe retains some unique major advantages. First, it is by far the most advanced workable system of its kind in the world, rightly envied—and sometimes at least partially emulated—by states trying to build security elsewhere. Second, it continues to have a substantial stabilizing, security-building role in intra-European relations based on openness, transparency and mutual reassurance. Third, it should remain a kind of insurance policy for a worst-case scenario, in the event that the trend of history is reversed in future.

The main methods for strengthening security in Europe are unique— multilateral cooperation, persuasion, reassurance and confidence among likeminded states—as against the unilateral action, pre-emption and coercion (including the use of military force) that are prevalent elsewhere. Arms control is still part of this European agenda in an age when military capabilities and doctrines are constantly being updated for generally more active applications (e.g., for peace operations or expeditionary missions). It will remain pertinent as long as military force plays a major role in international and domestic policies and as long as traditional and new threats alike call for constraints on access to and the use of weapons and military methods generally. Even with the spread of democracy in the OSCE area and the acknowledged lesser propensity of democracies to wage wars, the tools of politico-military transparency, restraint, communication and predictability can keep their value as long as they are well-defined, effective and timely. The work of conventional arms control in Europe is not done as long as, on the one hand, Europeans believe that security should be indivisible and norms equally applied and, on the other, many places within the OSCE area manifestly do not enjoy stable and equitable security conditions.

Arms control can and should be pursued further in terms of both geographical extent and substance. As habits of active, common and cooperative security become prevalent, the focus of arms control is naturally tilting towards its 'soft' dimension, whose logic relies less on a cold war-style confrontation. The extent of this switch has, however, been exaggerated by the failure to accommodate the structural arms control regime of the treaty to the new realities, as should have been done.

New challenges and risks place strain on the status quo. Europe's security is being put to the test by regional and local crises and conflicts, mostly on its peripheries. Both operational and structural arms control approaches could have an obvious application here if properly tailored to the new forms of intrastate and global challenges (including terrorism). European states could best show their solidarity (and common sense) as a security community by finding ways to extract new value from the arms control *acquis* they have so laboriously built up in the past.

Conventional arms control is also moving and must move further out of the role of an autonomous, predominantly military instrument. Increasingly, various CSBMs are being integrated in cooperative packages or are taking on a multidimensional character themselves, the better to fulfil new tasks and missions. Most menaces to Europe's security emerge on its perimeter, and Europe increasingly needs to share, among other things, its rich experience with its non-OSCE neighbouring states as one way to create a 'ring of friends'.

Perhaps less visible, but still real, is the challenge posed for arms control by new developments in the armed forces and their modes of operation. The new missions of military (and other) personnel and the new generations of weapons and technologies used by them will sooner or later have to be addressed and checked against the existing military doctrines if the inclusive, transparent and cooperative pattern of security relations is to be preserved.

The new OSCE states have limited experience of the complex arms control and CSBM *acquis* and procedures as well as scant resources to meet all the requirements of compliance. Along with pressure and encouragement to conform, they need continued special assistance from other, more experienced and better-off participants in the regimes.

The situation in Europe after the end of the cold war has gradually brought the commitments made and the obligations assumed by various sets of participants under the adapted CFE Treaty, the 1992 Concluding Act of the Negotiation on Personnel Strength of Conventional Armed Forces in Europe (CFE-1A Agreement)[10] regime and the Vienna Document closer to each other. The Treaty on Open Skies is also in the process of adapting to new tasks and requirements. This evolution holds out hope of extending the coverage of overall arms control to the entire OSCE area. Ideally, a single comprehensive regime would offer the virtues of clarity, more streamlining in operation and the guaranteed equality of all participants. Owing to its history, diversity and actual divisions, 'OSCE Europe' is still far from that regime. The overarching choice to be made is whether to continue the practice of small steps or to revitalize the idea of 'harmonization' by applying the existing commitments more widely or—even more boldly—designing an entirely new system. In the meantime, the relevance and utility of arms control as a flexible and versatile tool in the dynamically changing environment must be maintained.[11]

The experience of other regions[12]

Outside Europe conventional arms control awaits its breakthrough. Various attempts to apply European models in other politico-military contexts have so far yielded mixed results. For the most part they do not go beyond basic confidence-building steps of a voluntary character, comparable with the first-generation measures tested in Europe in the 1970s and 1980s. The rule of a lowest common denominator has been the dominant mode. Successful experiments have been made only in regions that enjoy a relatively high degree of security dialogue, share a common purpose (e.g., military disengagement) or lack strong incentives to engage in an arms race. In regions divided by inter-

---

[10] For a brief summary of the CFE-1A Agreement see annex A in this volume.

[11] The OSCE's 2005 Annual Security Review Conference once again appeared unable to formulate a European arms control strategy, although hope was expressed that the recent reforms of security policies and doctrinal changes would allow the adaptation of the relevant instruments. Organization for Security and Co-operation in Europe Permanent Council (note 4), p. 22.

[12] On regional security cooperation see chapter 4 in this volume.

state conflicts and tensions and without the political will to overcome them, such tools either prove short-lived or cannot be applied at all.

In the Association of South East Asian Nations (ASEAN) Regional Forum framework and in Latin America, military confidence-building measures (CBMs) have been agreed within looser, broad packages that combine military and non-military steps, and the political and military authorities have incrementally endeavoured to test them. In Central Asia CSBM and arms control agreements were reached in 1996–97 by the Shanghai Five.[13] These were inspired by the CFE Treaty and the 1994 Vienna Document, but they also introduced some indigenous elements.[14] In other conflict-afflicted parts of the world, such as North-East Asia, South Asia and the Middle East, arms control ambitions have hardly gone beyond discussion and proposals by theoreticians and analysts, politically frail arrangements and abortive initiatives launched by governments.[15]

Arms control is not a phenomenon limited to democratic states, although democracy generally facilitates its operation and development.[16] Communist bloc leaders often suspected that subversive intentions lay behind European arms control efforts. The lesson of the collapse of those regimes may, rightly or wrongly, adversely affect the attitudes of authoritarian or dictatorial governments elsewhere. Outside Europe armed forces are generally perceived to be the foremost tool for enhancing state security, and competition and rivalry, let alone animosity, between local actors may make them see positive value in shaking their neighbours' confidence. Such political principles as renunciation of violence, non-violation of borders and non-intervention are not addressed in earnest in many non-European regions and are viewed more as constraining than reassuring factors in strategic calculations. Another major obstacle in pursuing arms control is the poor accountability and the associated volatility of the domestic and external policies of numerous non-European actors, which feed mutual misunderstanding and misconceptions. Last but not least, although not a critical impediment, the lack of transparency (and provision for democratic debate) over the existing arms control agreements can seriously detract from the value of this tool.[17]

---

[13] The members of the Shanghai Five were China, Russia, Kazakhstan, Kyrgyzstan and Tajikistan. The Shanghai Cooperation Organization (SCO) was founded on 15 June 2001 by the members of the Shanghai Five and Uzbekistan. On the SCO see the glossary in this volume.

[14] On Central Asian arms control and CSBM application see Trofimov, D., 'Arms control in Central Asia', A. J. K. Bailes et al., *Armament and Disarmament in the Caucasus and Central Asia*, SIPRI Policy Paper no. 3 (SIPRI: Stockholm, July 2003), URL <http://www.sipri.org/>, pp. 46–56.

[15] The most recent confidence-building agreement, which was reached by the military delegations of North and South Korea on 4 June 2004, provides for measures concerning the prevention of accidents in the Yellow Sea (West Sea) and the suspension of propaganda activities along the military demarcation line. See 'Second North–South general-level military talks held', Korean Central News Agency of DPRK, URL <http://www.kcna.co.jp/item/2004/200406/news06/05.htm#9>. The agreement has reportedly been partially implemented.

[16] See also chapter 5 in this volume.

[17] The Agreement on Mutual Reduction of Armed Forces in Border Areas, signed by China, on the one hand, and Russia, Kazakhstan, Kyrgyzstan and Tajikistan, on the other, fails to meet the European criteria of openness and transparency and is kept secret from countries that are not parties to it and other international monitoring bodies. For more on transparency issues see chapter 6 in this volume.

As 'human security' gains in importance more interest and development have been noted in the humanitarian aspects of arms control. The limitation, removal, elimination and prohibition of inhumane weapons enjoy widening support worldwide and will continue to demand the serious attention of governments of all kinds. Such weapons are addressed by the 1981 Convention on Prohibitions or Restrictions on the Use of Certain Conventional Weapons which may be deemed to be Excessively Injurious or to have Indiscriminate Effects (CCW Convention or 'Inhumane Weapons' Convention) and the 1997 Convention on the Prohibition of the Use, Stockpiling, Production and Transfer of Anti-Personnel Mines and on their Destruction (APM Convention),[18] other regional, bi- and unilateral arrangements and even relevant pledges by non-state actors.

III. The Treaty on Conventional Armed Forces in Europe

The 1990 CFE Treaty regime remains by far the most elaborate conventional arms control regime worldwide. Acclaimed as the 'cornerstone of European security', it has contributed significantly to removing the threat of large-scale military attack and has enhanced confidence, openness and mutual reassurance in Europe. The CFE Treaty process has also inspired regional arms control solutions in the Balkans and Central Asia.

The current status

The CFE Treaty set equal ceilings on the major categories of heavy conventional armaments and equipment for the two groups of states parties in the Atlantic-to-the-Urals (ATTU) zone of application.[19] The 1999 Agreement on Adaptation discarded the original, bipolar concept of an equilibrium of forces between NATO and the then defunct Warsaw Treaty Organization (WTO); introduced a new regime of arms control based on national and territorial ceilings, codified in the agreement's protocols as binding limits; increased the verifiability of its provisions; and opened the adapted treaty regime to European states that were not yet parties to the CFE Treaty in 1999. As noted, however, the agreement has not entered into force because of the refusal of the NATO members and other states to ratify it in the face of Russia's non-compliance with the commitments it made at the 1999 OSCE Istanbul Summit.[20] Of the 30 signatories of the CFE Treaty, only Belarus, Kazakhstan and Russia have ratified the Agreement on Adaptation and deposited their instruments of ratification with the depositary. Ukraine has ratified the agreement but has not deposited its ratification document. The CFE Treaty and the

---

[18] For the signatories and parties to these conventions see annex A in this volume.

[19] CFE Treaty (note 1).

[20] Organization for Security and Co-operation in Europe (OSCE), Istanbul Summit Declaration, Istanbul, 17 Nov. 1999, para. 19; OSCE, Final Act of the Conference of the States Parties to the Treaty on Conventional Armed Forces in Europe, Istanbul, 17 Nov. 1999. These texts are reproduced as appendix 10B in *SIPRI Yearbook 2000* (note 1), pp. 642–43, 645–46.

associated agreed documents and decisions therefore continue to be binding on all parties.

Treaty adaptation, operation and compliance issues

In 2005 Russia and NATO continued to cling to their positions regarding ratification of the Agreement on Adaptation of the CFE Treaty. Russia reached an agreement with Georgia during the year, but failed to remove the other stumbling block by pulling out its troops and ammunition from the breakaway Trans-Dniester region of Moldova (see below). Germany and several other NATO members made attempts to facilitate diplomatic progress on the issue, but at the end of 2005 the NATO states maintained their position.[21] In 2005 Russia continued to reject this 'artificial linkage' arguing that it had fulfilled its CFE Treaty obligations[22] and that the political commitments it made in Istanbul had been delayed by the complex situation in the two former Soviet republics. Russia further persuaded its allies in the Collective Security Treaty Organization (CSTO) to join it in exhorting the West to do 'everything possible for early implementation of the political commitment undertaken in Istanbul in 1999' (i.e., to expedite the ratification of the agreement).[23]

In August, the US Department of State's Bureau of Verification and Compliance published its report on compliance with arms control agreements and commitments in 2002–2003 (plus some updates), which also reviewed the implementation of the CFE Treaty.[24] While acknowledging that most of the provisions of the treaty had been successfully implemented, it detailed a catalogue of compliance failings by Armenia, Azerbaijan, Belarus, Russia and Ukraine. The list included unreported TLE, suspension of CFE provisions, stationed foreign forces, improper designation and exemptions of equipment, denials of access to sites, failure to meet collective obligations (in the wake of the break-up of the Soviet Union), and other issues. Russia, whose non-compliance record was the longest in the document, rejected this criticism with the backhanded argument that the CFE Treaty had lost its viability and

---

[21] North Atlantic Treaty Organization, 'Ministerial Meeting of the North Atlantic Council, Final communiqué', Press release (2005)158, Brussels, 8 Dec. 2005, URL <http://www.nato.int/docu/pr/2005/p05-158e.htm>.

[22] Russia's official view was essentially reiterated in a newspaper article by the Russian Foreign Ministry spokesman in the spring of 2005. Yakovenko, A., 'Myths and reality of the Istanbul accords', *Rossiyskaya Gazeta*, 6 Apr. 2005. Unofficial translation reproduced at Russian Ministry of Foreign Affairs, Information and Press Department, 7 Apr. 2005, URL <http://www.ln.mid.ru/brp_4.nsf/english?OpenView&Start=1.1131>. Russia's interpretation is slanted: e.g., in the flank area the Russian holdings remain below the sub-ceilings under the adapted CFE Treaty but exceed the current CFE Treaty limits.

[23] Statement by the Member States of the Collective Security Treaty Organization on the Ratification of the Agreement on Adaptation of the Treaty on Conventional Armed Forces in Europe, Moscow, 22 June 2005, URL <http://www.mid.ru/ns-rsng.nsf/3a813e35eb116963432569ee0048fdbe/432569d800221466c3257028005bbe34?OpenDocument>. The members of the CSTO are Armenia, Belarus, Kazakhstan, Kyrgyzstan, Russia and Tajikistan. On the CSTO see the glossary in this volume.

[24] US Department of State, Bureau of Verification and Compliance, 'Adherence to and compliance with arms control, non-proliferation and disarmament agreements and commitments', Washington, DC, 30 Aug. 2005, available on the GlobalSecurity.org website at URL <http://www.globalsecurity.org/wmd/library/report/2005/ac-acnpdac-report_bvc-dos_050830.htm>.

needed urgent adaptation; it threatened 'tough talk' at the 2006 CFE Third Review Conference.[25]

Several issues are pending in the run-up to the review conference. The updating of the 1990 CFE Protocol on Existing Types of Conventional Armaments and Equipment (POET) continued to be constrained by the issue of armoured combat vehicles.[26] The USA has decided to build military bases in the Eastern Balkans (the flank area),[27] and possible deployments of TLE will apparently have to be dealt with. The problem of unaccounted-for and uncontrolled treaty-limited equipment (UTLE) was not addressed in 2005. Although not adversely affecting overall European security—being more symptom than cause of the intractable conflicts in the post-Soviet space—the problem remains a significant factor in the sub-regional context. In violation of the CFE Treaty, residual amounts of Soviet/Russian TLE, which should have been destroyed or returned to Russia long ago, are still at the disposal of the self-proclaimed authorities of Trans-Dniester (Moldova), Abkhazia and South Ossetia (Georgia). The issue of UTLE in Nagorno-Karabakh (under dispute between Armenia and Azerbaijan) also continues to adversely affect the operation of the CFE Treaty. In March the presidents of Georgia and Moldova drew attention to the danger of the resulting 'black holes' in Europe, demanding among other things the speedy removal of foreign forces from the territory of both countries.[28]

The Georgian–Russian agreement on base withdrawal

After the impasse of 2001–2004 the issue of the withdrawal of Russian forces from Georgia reached a critical point in 2005. Russia had already reduced the number of its heavy ground weapons deployed on Georgian territory to the levels agreed at the Istanbul Summit, but the process of troop withdrawal progressed unevenly.[29] Since 2003 Russia has under various pretexts suspended or stalled talks on pull-out. At the Maastricht and Sofia OSCE Ministerial Council Meetings in 2003 and 2004 Russia refused to consent to political declarations and 'regional' statements (including one on Georgia) that would *inter alia* have stressed its failure to implement the Istanbul commitments.

---

[25] Russian Ministry of Foreign Affairs, Information and Press Department, 'Concerning US State Department report', Press release, Unofficial translation, Moscow, 31 Aug. 2005, URL <http://www.ln.mid.ru/brp_4.nsf/english?OpenView&Start=1.522>.

[26] The CFE Treaty specifies that POET should be updated periodically. Although this was discussed at the 1996 and 2001 review conferences, the task has not been completed.

[27] US Department of State, 'Southeast Europe ministers approve troop brigade for Afghanistan. Rumsfeld welcomes Romania basing deal; talks under way with Bulgaria', 7 Dec. 2005, URL <http://usinfo.state.gov/eur/Archive/2005/Dec/07-334213.html>.

[28] United Nations, Letter dated 4 March from the Permanent Representatives of Georgia and the Republic of Moldova to the United Nations addressed to the Secretary-General, General Assembly, 59th session, agenda items 56(n) and 105, UN document A/59/725, 7 Mar. 2005.

[29] See Lachowski, Z., 'Conventional arms control', *SIPRI Yearbook 2002: Armaments, Disarmament and International Security* (Oxford University Press: Oxford, 2002), pp. 709–35; and Lachowski, Z., 'Conventional arms control in Europe', *SIPRI Yearbook 2003: Armaments, Disarmament and International Security* (Oxford University Press: Oxford, 2003), pp. 691–711.

Various political and other factors, including the completion of the US three-year 'train-and-equip' programme in Georgia in 2004, apparently accommodated Russia's concerns and contributed to a settlement in 2005. In the early months of the year Russia reiterated its demands for financial compensation[30] and proposed eventual co-locating of the existing bases with 'anti-terrorist centres'. During the visit by the Russian Foreign Minister, Sergei Lavrov, to Tbilisi in February, Georgia expressed cautious interest in a joint Georgian–Russian anti-terrorist centre and a working group began to discuss the proposal.[31] On 10 March 2005 the Georgian Parliament passed a non-binding resolution demanding that Russia agree a timetable for closing its bases and withdraw its troops by 15 May or Russia's military presence would be declared to be illegal from 1 January 2006.[32] A meeting of the Georgian and Russian foreign ministers on 25 April 2005 brought their positions closer. Despite tension in the run-up to an agreement (e.g., Russian preconditions regarding the withdrawal deadlines, the threat of restrictions on the Russian military after 15 May, reciprocal financial demands and Georgia's subsequent boycott of Russia's celebration of the end of World War II in Europe), the diplomats continued their work. In order to facilitate the negotiations Georgia's President, Mikheil Saakashvili, declared on 26 May that, after the closure of the Russian bases, no foreign bases would be permitted on Georgian territory, which temporarily satisfied Russia.

On 30 May the ministers of foreign affairs of Georgia and Russia issued a joint statement on the closing of the Russian military bases and other military facilities and the withdrawal of Russian forces from Georgia.[33] The agreement is not legally binding. The withdrawal is to take place in stages from June 2005 until an unspecified date 'in the course of' 2008. The final stage will be the closing of the Batumi base and the Tbilisi headquarters of the Group of Russian Forces in the Transcaucasus. With regard to CFE-limited equipment, TLE from the Akhalkalaki base will be removed by the end of 2006 and the rest of the heavy military equipment stationed on Georgian territory will be withdrawn by 1 October 2007 (or if weather conditions are adverse, by the end of 2007).

It was agreed that both sides will 'cooperate in a bid' to obtain additional financing for transport costs linked to withdrawal.[34] Georgia will assist in various ways in the organization of the pull-out. Russia undertakes not to replace or replenish the weapons and military equipment withdrawn. Three supplementary agreements will 'soon' be agreed on: (a) the functioning and closure

---

[30] Russia apparently assumed that the West would pay the cost of pull-out to and redeployment in Russia. In Apr. 2005 Russian Defence Minister Sergei Ivanov estimated that the cost would be $250–300 million, but he admitted that Russia would be able to carry such a financial burden.

[31] Russia insisted, unsuccessfully, that the centre should start its work before a pull-out agreement had been reached.

[32] Mite, V. 'Georgia: Russia calls parliamentary resolution on bases "counterproductive"', Radio Free Europe/Radio Liberty, 11 Mar. 2005, URL <http://www.rferl.org/featuresarticle/2005/03/6b905aa5-e339-446a-86b1-99326b1c8ca6.html>.

[33] Russian Ministry of Foreign Affairs (note 2).

[34] This means that seeking external financing will concern only the withdrawal from Georgia but not the redeployment of forces in Russia.

of the bases in Batumi and Akhalkalaki; (*b*) the establishment and functioning of the anti-terrorist centre; and (*c*) transit through Georgian territory.[35] The agreement on the continued Russian military presence will be in line with the 1999 Istanbul Georgian–Russian joint statement, which provides for 'temporary deployment' by Russia of CFE treaty-limited equipment.[36] 'Necessary measures' are also to be taken to help determine whether Russia has completed its pull-out from the Gudauta base.[37]

The NATO states welcomed the joint statement as an 'encouraging step' towards both the fulfilment of the Istanbul commitments and the resolution of the requirement of Article IV(5) of the CFE Treaty.[38] They also called on Russia to sign the relevant agreements and resolve the outstanding issues (including the military presence in Moldova) as soon as possible. On 15 August Russia completed the first round of withdrawal of 40 units of heavy armaments, including 20 CFE-limited T-72 battle tanks. The OSCE Ljubljana Ministerial Council's statement on Georgia welcomed the joint statement, the negotiations on the agreement on the Batumi and Akhalkalaki bases, and the partial withdrawal of the Russian heavy equipment and encouraged further progress on the Gudauta base.[39]

The Georgian–Russian agreement apparently did not address the problem of UTLE in the separatist regions of Georgia. In September the Georgian Government denounced the military parade in Tskhinvali (South Ossetia) in which CFE-limited tanks, armoured combat vehicles and artillery took part.

Russian troops and ammunition in Moldova

Unlike Georgia, Moldova made no progress in its military relations with Russia in 2005. Under its 1994 constitution, Moldova is permanently neutral and refuses to host foreign forces on its territory. Withdrawal of Russian TLE was completed in 2003, but the lack of a political settlement over the separatist Trans-Dniester region caused Russia to delay the withdrawal of its 700 troops and the disposal of its roughly 20 000 tonnes of stockpiled ammunition and non-CFE-limited equipment. Disappointed by Russia's strategy to keep it divided and weak, Moldova has since 2004 sought stronger international support in its settlement talks with Russia.[40] It has also suggested that enterprises are manufacturing unreported CFE-limited equipment in the Trans-Dniester region. In September 2005, during the celebrations to commemorate

---

[35] In this context, Azerbaijan expressed concern about the transfer to Armenia of some TLE from the Russian bases in Georgia. Russia assured Azerbaijan that the equipment transferred to Armenia will not exceed the adapted CFE treaty ceilings and will remain under Russia's control.

[36] I.e., not more than 153 tanks, 241 armoured combat vehicles and 140 artillery pieces.

[37] The relevant, vaguely worded provision relates to a multinational mission to be sent to the Gudauta base to ascertain that Russia has fulfilled its withdrawal obligations. Germany is the lead state in this regard.

[38] The provision stipulates that countries belonging to the same group of states parties may locate their ground equipment within the CFE area of application 'provided that no State Party stations conventional armed forces on the territory of another State Party without the agreement of that State Party'.

[39] OSCE Ministerial Council, Statement on Georgia, OSCE document MC.DOC/4/05, 6 Dec. 2005.

[40] Lachowski and Dunay (note 3), pp. 656–58.

the proclamation of the 'Dniester Moldovan Republic' (Trans-Dniester) a military parade was held that included 6 tanks, several armoured personnel carriers, 20 missile launchers, 50 artillery guns and howitzers, and 5 helicopters (some of them apparently subject to CFE limitations).

In 2005 several initiatives attempted to advance the bogged-down negotiations with Russia. In addition to the 'five-sided' talks—involving Moldova, the OSCE, Russia, the Trans-Dniester entity and Ukraine—separate efforts were made by the OSCE and Ukraine. On 10 June, following a similar move by the Georgian Parliament, the Moldovan Parliament issued an appeal for demilitarization, calling on the international community to encourage the withdrawal of Russian troops and ammunition by the end of 2005, the reduction of the Russian 'peacekeeping' force in 2006, the dismantling of the Trans-Dniester military units, and so on.[41] However, subsequent events have made it clear that the 'Georgia scenario' is not applicable in Moldova. Discussions at the OSCE only produced proposals for a regional arrangement with arms control and confidence-building provisions (see below).

In October 2005 an enlarged '5+2' format (with the EU and the USA as observers) was agreed in another attempt to overcome the 15-month deadlock. However, the following months showed that Russia was not ready to meet its Istanbul commitments without a political settlement of the conflict, and the Russian 'peacekeeping' force will remain in the Trans-Dniester region for the indefinite future.[42] In addition, no progress was made on ammunition removal activities in 2005.

Russia's Istanbul commitments, including those related to Moldova, became the main point of disagreement on which the efforts of the Ljubljana OSCE Ministerial Meeting to agree on a political declaration foundered.[43]

IV. Building confidence and stability in Europe

The CSBM process in Europe has amassed a huge body of cooperative measures, norms and mechanisms. CSBMs were designed to help prevent preparation for an unexpected, mass-scale attack by one state or military bloc against another. However, such situations no longer exist in Europe. Little progress has been made in rethinking confidence- and stability-building approaches to

[41] OSCE Mission to Moldova, Activity report: June 2005, OSCE document SEC.FR/301/05, 13 July 2005. On peacekeeping missions see appendix 3A in this volume.

[42] Russia claims that it cannot override the objections of the Trans-Dniester authorities to the removal of the ammunition and that its troops must stay to protect the arsenals. Russia also claims that the Russian–Commonwealth of Independent States 'peacekeeping' force must remain pending a political solution. Clearly, the Russian military presence is intended to prop up the regime in Trans-Dniester.

[43] Diplomats in Ljubljana reportedly claimed that Russia's veto was sparked by the following text: 'We also note the lack of movement in 2005 on withdrawal of Russian forces from Moldova. We reaffirm our shared determination to promote the fulfilment of that commitment as soon as possible, and the entry into force of the adapted CFE Treaty'. OSCE Ministerial Council, Draft Ljubljana Ministerial Declaration, Ljubljana 2005, OSCE document MC.DD/14/05/Rev.7, 6 Dec. 2005. See also Eggleston, R., 'OSCE: final text nixed after dispute on Russian troops in Moldova', Radio Free Europe/Radio Liberty, 6 Dec. 2005, URL <http://www.rferl.org/featuresarticle/2005/12/0aace2d9-9ffd-4384-bb4a-54788321404b.html>. For analysis of the Ljubljana Meeting see Socor, V., 'OSCE year-end conference fails to adopt key documents on security', *Eurasian Daily Monitor*, vol. 2, no. 227 (7 Dec. 2005).

the kinds of menace that the international community actually faces today: combinations of intra-state violence and trans-state or global threats.

While the distinct Vienna Document framework for CSBMs has been maintained, the OSCE community is attempting to address more urgent issues through flexible voluntary approaches including measures that address only part of the OSCE area or extend beyond its limits. CSBMs are no longer perceived as a subordinate phase preceding and leading to 'real' disarmament. The latter can no longer be seen as a simple good. Fifteen post-cold war years of preoccupation with conflict management have done more to encourage 'states of good will' to rebuild than to restrain their own defence capabilities. The military legacy of the cold war also had to be re-evaluated in the wake of the profound changes on the territory of the former Soviet Union and the other WTO states. The result is that the setting for confidence- and stability-building work in Europe is now shaped by the following general tendencies: (a) the shift towards 'soft' rather than quantitative restraints; (b) the expansion of the range of actions covered by norms and standards; (c) regional 'subsidiarity'; (d) the possible 'all-weather' applications of CSBMs (i.e., including conflict prevention and post-conflict reconstruction);[44] (e) the integration of CSBMs into cooperative packages; (f) the cross-dimensionality of new measures; (g) the response to new threats, changes and developments; and (h) the sharing of arms control experience outside 'OSCE Europe'.[45] The OSCE Forum for Security Co-operation (FSC) provides the institutional framework for the implementation and coordination of all OSCE agreements on conventional arms control, ensures their continuity and works out new priorities for future arms control negotiations.

The political conditions for extending confidence-building endeavours were not favourable in 2005. Ambassador Julie Finley, the chief US delegate to the OSCE, stated that: 'A key element of this dimension should be implementation of commitments. . . . We are against negotiating new traditional style arms control/CSBMs, although we *may* be willing to consider specific proposals if there is a clear security need to be addressed'.[46] Even so, two new steps of potential significance were taken in 2005. After two years of extensive negotiations, on Turkey's initiative a statement was agreed by the FSC on prior notification of major military activities below the notification thresholds of the Vienna Document 1999.[47] The length of time devoted to the elaboration of this measure stood in stark contrast to its outcome—a non-binding, voluntary CSBM—evidencing the plight of all-European arms control. How-

---

[44] Lachowski, Z., 'Confidence- and security-building measures in Europe', *SIPRI Yearbook 2000* (note 1), pp. 615–16.

[45] On the new trends in CSBMs see Lachowski, Dunay and der Haan (note 8).

[46] Ambassador Finley also stated that: 'We would like to see better use made of the pol[itico]-mil[itary] dimension to support field missions, resolve frozen conflicts, address sub-regional tensions, and support OSCE work in other dimensions'. Statement by US Permanent Representative Ambassador Julie Finley, Morning session of the High Level Consultations, Vienna, 13 Sep. 2005, URL <http://osce.usmission.gov/archive/2005/09/septindex.html>, emphasis in the original.

[47] Organization for Security and Co-operation in Europe, Statement by the Chairperson of the Forum for Security Cooperation on prior notification of major military activities, OSCE document FSC.JOUR/467, 5 Oct. 2005. Belarus and Russia readily supported the measure.

ever, some participants hoped that its eventual success might help to overcome the wider stalemate. In their annual calendar notifications Belarus, the Czech Republic, Finland, Hungary, Latvia, Lithuania, Russia, Serbia and Montenegro, Sweden, Switzerland and Turkey provided information on their below-the-threshold major military activities to be carried out in 2006. The other significant decision was to agree to hold a high-level OSCE seminar on military doctrine in February 2006, the first such meeting since the fourth seminar, in 2001, and also the first since the 11 September 2001 terrorist attacks in the USA.[48] The meeting assessed and discussed both doctrinal and technological changes and their impact on defence structures and forces in the diametrically altered security situation.

Other notable items on the FSC agenda in 2005 were the non-proliferation of WMD and a workshop to evaluate the operation of the 1994 Code of Conduct on Politico-Military Aspects of Security.[49] However, more energy was devoted to the topics of small arms, excess ammunition and the disposal of dangerous fuel (see below).

Regional confidence building

There are more than 20 military confidence-building arrangements in Europe,[50] aiming to address specific security concerns and defuse tensions in domestic, bilateral or regional contexts. The successive waves of NATO enlargement have resulted in more such arrangements; conversely, some of the existing CSBM agreements between states which are now members of NATO may be phased out in coming years. On 19 January 2005 one such arrangement, the 1998 Hungarian–Slovakian CSBM agreement, was terminated because both countries had become members of NATO.[51] In March 2005 Hungary and Serbia and Montenegro signed a CSBM agreement regarding expansion of the scope of information exchange through notification and invitation of observers to certain military activities of land forces, military cooperation and contacts, and increased quotas of evaluation visits and inspections.

---

[48] Organization for Security and Co-operation in Europe, OSCE Decision no. 3/95, 29 June 2005.

[49] Organization for Security and Co-operation in Europe, Code of Conduct on Politico-Military Aspects of Security (COC), OSCE document DOC.FSC/1/95, 3 Dec. 1994, URL <http://www.osce.org/item/883.html>. The FSC held a special meeting on 15 June on the non-proliferation of WMD. It also encouraged dialogue on support of the implementation of UN Security Council Resolution 1540, which requires states to adopt legal measures to reduce the risk that WMD could be acquired by terrorists. UN Security Council Resolution 1540, 28 Apr. 2004. See also chapter 12 in this volume. The FSC adopted a decision supporting the effective implementation of Resolution 1540. OSCE, Decision no. 7/05, OSCE document FSC.DEC/7/05, 30 Nov. 2005. On 10th anniversary of the Code of Conduct, in Jan. 2005, a workshop was held to review the substance and implementation of the Code.

[50] For a list and summaries of regional CSBM agreements reached in 1991–2004 see Lachowski, Z., *Confidence- and Security-Building Measures in the New Europe*, SIPRI Research Report no. 18 (Oxford University Press: Oxford, 2004), pp. 138–46.

[51] On the other hand, the 1991 Hungarian–Romanian open skies agreement will continue its operation for training and trial purposes.

The agreement basically follows similar provisions contained in other bilateral agreements of this type.[52]

One of the vital tests for CSBMs is whether they are applicable in intra-state 'foul-weather' conditions (i.e., during times of crisis, conflict, war, etc.), such as the frozen conflict in Moldova. On 12 July 2005 the three mediators in the Trans-Dniester settlement process—the OSCE and the future 'guarantor states', Russia and Ukraine—presented a package of force reduction and CSBMs to the Government of Moldova and the authorities of the separatist Trans-Dniester entity.[53] The content of the plan derives from the European arms control and CSBM experience: the CFE Treaty, the Dayton arms control agreements of 1996 and the Vienna Document 1999.

The 'demilitarization' and confidence-building schemes were controversial on political and military grounds. Trans-Dniester did not participate in meetings of a working group of military experts to consider and comment on the proposed measures. Instead, the OSCE Mission to Moldova presented the CSBM package to journalists in November and to OSCE diplomats and experts in December. Both schemes were alleged to adversely affect the political settlement in Moldova by separating it from the military plan; by sanctioning the indefinite Russian military presence in Moldova in contravention of the spirit of the OSCE Istanbul commitments and Moldova's neutrality status; by bestowing on Russia a privileged status vis-à-vis the other actors and discriminating against the Government of Moldova; by legitimizing the Trans-Dniester separatist entity and its forces; by exempting the Russian 'peacekeeping' force and 'internal security forces' from reductions and inspections; by barely dealing with the problem of small arms which wreak havoc in the region, and so on.[54]

On 1 December 2005, Moldova submitted information about its military units and equipment, as required under the Protocol on exchange of information (A-1) of the arms control–CSBM package. The Trans-Dniester authorities submitted a letter that provided brief information on the number of their troops and military equipment. In effect, Russia was requested to assist Trans-Dniester in drawing up information regarding its forces and armaments in conformity with Protocol A-1 of the package.

---

[52] Organization for Security and Co-operation in Europe, Agreement on confidence- and security-building measures complementing the Vienna Document 1999 and on the development of military relations between the Government of the Republic of Hungary and the Council of Ministers of Serbia and Montenegro, 24 Mar. 2005, OSCE document FSC.DEL/133/05, 20 Apr. 2005.

[53] Organization for Security and Co-operation in Europe, Arms control–confidence and security building measures in Moldova, OSCE document SEC.GAL/178/05, 28 July 2005. The proposals were initiated by the US-led OSCE Mission to Moldova and jointly developed with Russian and Ukrainian military experts.

[54] For analysis of deficiencies of the plans see Socor, V., 'Russia–OSCE military plan for Moldova: back to a "post-Soviet security space"', and 'OSCE verification procedures provide ample opportunities to cheat', *Eurasian Daily Monitor*, vol. 2, no. 171 (15 Sep. 2005); Socor, V., 'Moldovan experts blast Russia–OSCE military plan', *Eurasian Daily Monitor*, vol. 2, no. 226 (6 Dec. 2005); and Socor, V., 'OSCE–Russia military plan for Moldova criticized in Vienna', *Eurasian Daily Monitor*, vol. 2, no. 232 (14 Dec. 2005).

Small arms and light weapons

The 2000 OSCE Document on Small Arms and Light Weapons (SALW) and other relevant documents[55] remain effective instruments for addressing SALW problems, fostering transparency and confidence among the participating states, and helping to combat terrorism and organized crime. In 2001–2004 the OSCE participating states destroyed more than 4.3 million items of small arms that were deemed surplus or that were seized from illegal possession and trafficking. In terms of the number of information exchanges, implementation has been improving in recent years, although the qualitative impact is unclear. Assistance for small arms measures is being provided to the countries of the Caucasus, Central Asia and South-Eastern Europe. Present efforts focus *inter alia* on the need for full implementation of export controls, especially on man-portable air defence systems (MANPADS), which pose a threat especially to civil aviation. Open questions involve the direction the SALW process should take in future; what implementation issues should be addressed; and how the OSCE could contribute regionally to the 2006 First Review Conference of the United Nations (UN) Programme of Action on illicit trade in SALW.[56]

Three requests have been submitted to the FSC to address problems related to SALW. The 2003 request by Belarus for assistance to destroy its surplus SALW and improve stockpile management and security was unexpectedly withdrawn in November 2005.[57] The SALW and conventional ammunition project in Tajikistan was agreed with the signature of a Memorandum of Understanding on 1 June 2005, and contributions were made or pledged by the OSCE and individual participating states. In response to Kazakhstan's December 2004 request for assistance, a workshop on SALW and conventional ammunition destruction techniques and stockpile security and management was held in June 2005 and initial assessment visits were paid to two stockpiles. Owing to the security situation in South Ossetia, the SALW project in Georgia remains suspended.

Since 1999 the EU has tackled the SALW threat with specific disarmament actions in various parts of the world.[58] Its Joint Actions, mostly of a reactive

[55] These OSCE documents include the Handbook on Best Practice Guides on SALW, Principles for export controls of man-portable air defence systems (MANPADS), Standard elements on end-user certificates and verification procedures for SALW exports, and Principles on the control of brokering in SALW. See Lachowski, Z. and Sjögren, M., 'Conventional arms control', *SIPRI Yearbook 2004: Armaments, Disarmament and International Security* (Oxford University Press: Oxford, 2004), pp. 726–30; Anthony, I. and Bauer, S., 'Transfer controls and destruction programmes', *SIPRI Yearbook 2004* (note 55), pp. 751–56; and Lachowski and Dunay (note 3). See also chapter 10 in this volume.

[56] See Organization for Security and Co-operation in Europe, FSC Chairperson's progress report to the Ministerial Council on implementation of the OSCE Document on Small Arms and Light Weapons, OSCE document MC.GAL/5/05, 30 Nov. 2005.

[57] In May 2005, in response to the request by Belarus, 14 MANPADS were destroyed. A project plan was presented in the FSC on 5 Oct. 2005. Belarus has stated that it can manage the destruction itself.

[58] 'Joint Action of 17 December 1998 adopted by the Council on the basis of Article J.3 of the Treaty on European Union on the European Union's contribution to combating the destabilising accumulation and spread of small arms and light weapons', document 1999/34/CFSP, 17 Dec. 1998, *Official Journal of the European Communities*, L9, 15 Jan. 1999, pp. 1–5; and 'Council Joint Action of 12 July 2002 on the European Union's contribution to combating the destabilising accumulation and spread of small arms

character, established principles for the resolution of armed conflicts. In 2005, in an effort to develop a comprehensive and coherent approach, the EU expanded these efforts with the additional aim of launching preventive actions to stave off the further destabilizing accumulation of SALW and reducing existing accumulations of SALW and their ammunition. The December 2005 EU Strategy to Combat Illicit Accumulation and Trafficking of SALW and their Ammunition envisaged an Action Plan to provide for universal, regional (especially in sub-Saharan Africa) and national mechanisms to counter the supply and spread of SALW and their ammunition; responses to the accumulation and the problems posed by the availability of existing stocks; measures to deal with the causes and consequences on human development of the illicit spread of SALW; and the necessary structures within the EU.[59]

The destruction of stockpiles of ammunition and toxic fuel

Unsecured or uncontrolled stockpiles of conventional ammunition and liquid rocket fuel component ('melange') pose multiple risks in the security, humanitarian, economic and environmental dimensions. Under the 2003 OSCE Document on Stockpiles of Conventional Ammunition (SCA Document),[60] any OSCE state that has identified a security risk to its surplus stockpiles and needs assistance to address such a risk may request such assistance from the international community through the OSCE.

Belarus, Kazakhstan, Russia, Tajikistan and Ukraine have submitted such requests. A further five requests for assistance to eliminate melange (altogether more than 3500 tonnes) were made by Afghanistan, Armenia, Kazakhstan, Ukraine and Uzbekistan. In response, 10 participating countries had donated or pledged funds by the end of 2005.[61] Outside the scope of the SCA Document, projects are being carried out to remove or dispose of some 21 000 tonnes of ammunition, to destroy other outdated and surplus ammunition and to upgrade ammunition storage facilities in Trans-Dniester. Georgia has requested assistance for the neutralization and conversion of some 10 tonnes of napalm.

Several countries initiated the development of best practice guides. An FSC editorial review board has reviewed both national and international experiences in the fields of stockpile management, transport, project management, and marking, registration and record-keeping. It plans to discuss other areas for additional guides. In addition to wide-ranging OSCE activities, cooper-

and light weapons and repealing Joint Action 1999/34/CFSP', document 2002/589/CFSP, 12 July 2002, *Official Journal of the European Communities*, L191, 19 July 2002, pp. 1–4.

[59] Council of the European Union, EU Strategy to Combat Illicit Accumulation and Trafficking of SALW and their Ammunition, adopted by the European Council, Document 5319/06, Brussels, 13 Jan. 2006, URL <http://register.consilium.eu.int/pdf/en/06/st05/st05319.en06.pdf>.

[60] Organization for Security and Co-operation in Europe, Document on Stockpiles of Conventional Ammunition, Forum for Security Co-operation document FSC.DOC/1/03, 19 Nov. 2003, URL <http://www.osce.org/documents/fsc/2003/11/1379_en.pdf>.

[61] Organization for Security and Co-operation in Europe, FSC Chairperson's progress report to the Ministerial Council on further implementation of the OSCE Document on Stockpiles of Conventional Ammunition, OSCE document MC.GAL/4/05, 30 Nov. 2005.

ation with other international organizations, such as NATO and the UN, and public awareness campaigns are being developed. In July 2005 a first joint NATO–OSCE technical workshop on melange was organized in Kyiv, Ukraine, and at a special FSC meeting in September the NATO representative proposed cooperation between the FSC and NATO.

Defence conversion in South-Eastern Europe

A key challenge facing South-Eastern Europe is the restructuring and downsizing of military forces in response to the new security and economic realities of the region, including the ambition of some countries to join the EU and NATO. Efforts are thus shifting from traditional arms control towards defence conversion as an integral part of security sector reform.[62] Defence conversion represents one crucial dimension of a much wider transformation process, which calls for consideration of the overall socio-economic situation, including reconstruction and social development policies. In general, the main components of defence conversion are: (a) retraining of redundant military personnel; (b) conversion of military bases and facilities; (c) addressing redundant military stockpiles, including the sale or destruction of surplus military equipment and weapons; and (d) restructuring or downsizing of military industries and the redirection of military research and development.

As the task force leader of the Stability Pact Initiative on Defence Conversion, NATO monitors programmes for the retraining of redundant military personnel and the conversion of military sites in South-Eastern Europe. Several NATO members have initiated bilateral programmes in the region to help meet these challenges, including retraining of defence sector personnel and destruction of ammunition and SALW. Numerous other international actors (e.g., the OSCE, the UN Development Programme, and some international and local non-governmental organizations, NGOs) are active particularly in the field of demobilization and retraining of redundant military personnel. In this context, the role of the Zagreb-based Regional Arms Control Verification and Implementation Assistance Centre (RACVIAC) as a regional centre for defence conversion is being strengthened.[63]

V. The Treaty on Open Skies

The first Review Conference on the Implementation of the Treaty on Open Skies, held in Vienna on 14–16 February 2005, made a positive assessment of the operation of the treaty since its entry into force in 2002 and supported the view that the treaty could still contribute to European security despite changed

---

[62] On security sector reform in the context of EU and NATO enlargement and in the Western Balkans see Caparini, M., 'Security sector reform and NATO and EU enlargement', *SIPRI Yearbook 2003* (note 29), pp. 237–60; and Caparini, M., 'Security sector reform in the Western Balkans', *SIPRI Yearbook 2004* (note 55), pp. 251–82.

[63] See Stability Pact for South Eastern Europe, 'Working table III: security issues', URL <http://www.stabilitypact.org/wt3/default.asp>. The participants are listed in the glossary in this volume.

political and other circumstances.[64] The accession to the treaty of Lithuania and Estonia in May 2005 raised the number of states parties to 34.[65]

The review conference did not address one of the most sensitive matters: the modernization of the agreed list of sensors. Owing to its technical nature, the Open Skies Consultative Commission (OSCC) agreed that the matter would be addressed at sessions of the Informal Working Group on Sensors (IWGS) in December 2005. The IWGS adopted decisions on the recording format and the exchange of data recorded on media other than photographic film, and on the logical format for the exchange of digital data among parties.[66]

During 2005 states conducted about 100 observation flights in the course of which the parties also shared single overflights. Moreover, the states continued to conduct training observation flights on a bilateral basis.[67] In 2005 the Informal Working Group on Rules and Procedures took an important decision on transit flights and flights to the point of entry and from the point of exit.[68] In preparation for the second phase of the implementation of the treaty, starting in 2006,[69] the OSCC successfully carried out the task of full distribution of the parties' active quotas for 2006.

VI. Mines and unexploded ordnance

Banning 'inhumane weapons' has long been an international, public and governmental concern. The 1981 CCW Convention has the form of an 'umbrella treaty' to which specific agreements can be added as protocols. The convention prohibits or restricts some categories of inhumane weapons, including mines, booby-traps and other devices (Protocol II).[70] Since the early 1990s the efforts of NGOs and concerned governments have mustered international public opinion against anti-personnel mines (APMs). This resulted in a significant shift in attitudes in the mid-1990s towards a total ban on such weapons. In 1996 the Amended Protocol II, which reinforces the constraints regarding landmines, was agreed. In 1997 the so-called Ottawa process led to the APM

---

[64] For discussion of the first Review Conference see Lachowski and Dunay (note 3), pp. 665–68.

[65] The long-standing application of the Republic of Cyprus remained blocked in 2005.

[66] Open Skies Consultative Commission (OSCC), Decision no. 13/05 on revision one of Decision number seventeen to the Treaty on Open Skies: the format in which data is to be recorded and exchanged on recording media other than photographic film, OSCC document OSCC.DEC/0013/05, Vienna, 12 Dec. 2005; and OSCC, Decision no. 12/05: Standardization on logical formats for the exchange of digital data among states parties, OSCC document OSCC.DEC/12/05, Vienna, 12 Dec. 2005. The discussion of the other 2 expiring decisions (nos 14 and 15) was not concluded. See Lachowski and Dunay (note 3), p. 666, fn 77.

[67] Organization for Security and Co-operation in Europe, Letter from the Chairperson of the Open Skies Consultative Commission to the Minister for Foreign Affairs of Slovenia, Chairperson of the Thirteenth Ministerial Meeting of the OSCE Ministerial Council, OSCE document MC.GAL/2/05, Vienna, 21 Nov. 2005.

[68] Open Skies Consultative Commission, Decision no. 2/05 on the conduct of transit flights and flights to the point of entry and from the point of exit, OSCC document OSCC.DEC/2/05, Vienna, 31 Jan. 2005.

[69] Treaty on Open Skies (note 3), Article XVIII, Section II, para. 6.

[70] For the parties and basic information on the CCW Convention and Protocols see annex A in this volume.

Convention, which is aimed at the elimination of all anti-personnel mines.[71] The CCW Convention Review Conference in 2001 extended the application of all its four protocols to domestic armed conflicts, and in 2003 Protocol V on explosive remnants of war (ERW) was signed.[72]

Anti-personnel mines

The APM Convention remains the most successful enterprise in worldwide conventional arms control. Widely supported by states and promoted by grassroots movements, the convention is viewed as a valuable contribution to 'human security' as well as traditional 'hard' security.

Soon after it was opened for signature in December 1997, there were 121 signatory states and 3 parties to the convention. When it entered into force, on 1 March 1999, 133 states had signed and 65 states had ratified it. By the end of 2005 the number of parties to the convention had increased to 147, and an additional 7 countries had signed but not ratified it.[73] The rate of new accessions has slowed in recent years, leaving 40 states outside the convention. The non-parties are concentrated mostly in conflict-prone or -ridden areas, such as Asia, the Middle East and the post-Soviet space.

While pointing to the growing international ostracism of landmines, the balance sheet issued by the non-governmental *Landmine Monitor Report 2005*[74] summed up the achievements of the abolition movement as: (*a*) no use of landmines by parties and signatories to the convention;[75] (*b*) decreased production of landmines; (*c*) a de facto global ban on trade in APMs; (*d*) continuous destruction of millions of stockpiled landmines; (*e*) increased transparency reporting; (*f*) expanding mine action programmes; (*g*) increasing international mine action funding;[76] and (*h*) more national funding by 'mine-affected' countries.

Today only 13 countries are identified as producing or retaining the right to produce APMs. More importantly, the global trade in landmines has virtually ceased since 2003 and, because the use of landmines has declined, so have mine casualties. Currently, 15 000–20 000 people fall victim to landmines annually compared with the number 26 000 commonly quoted at the time of

---

[71] For the parties and basic information on the APM Convention see annex A in this volume.

[72] On 28 Nov. 2003 the parties adopted Protocol V on ERW to the CCW Convention. See Lachowski and Sjögren (note 55), pp. 734–35.

[73] Bhutan, Latvia and Vanuatu joined the APM Convention in 2005; 3 states joined in 2004. In 2003, 11 states joined; 8 states joined in 2002, and 13 states joined in 2001. Reportedly, several more governments are poised to ratify or accede to the APM Convention, including Indonesia, Poland and Ukraine. See also annex A in this volume.

[74] Mines Action Canada, 'Main findings', *Landmine Monitor Report 2005: Toward a Mine-Free World*, Oct. 2005, URL <http://www.icbl.org/lm/2005/>.

[75] Almost 250 000 mines have been retained by almost half the states parties to the APM Convention for training and development; 5 states parties account for nearly one-third of these retained mines: Brazil, Algeria, Bangladesh, Sweden and Turkey. *Landmine Monitor Report 2005* (note 74).

[76] The USA, which is not party to the APM Convention, is the top donor. It has provided *c*. $1 billion to nearly 50 countries for humanitarian mine removal since 1993. The other main donors include the EU, Japan and Norway.

the Ottawa process. More than 38.3 million stockpiled landmines have been destroyed since the entry into force of the APM Convention.

On the other hand, too many (40) countries still remain outside the APM Convention, including China (possessing 110 million landmines), Russia (26.5 million)[77] and the USA (10.4 million landmines). Altogether an estimated 160 million APMs are held in stockpiles by states that have not signed the convention. Some 7 million APMs are stockpiled by signatories to the APM Convention, with Ukraine retaining 6 million and Poland 1 million APMs.[78] Disturbingly, a few states have laid new mines in areas previously free from them,[79] and a further negative trend in recent years has been the use of landmines by non-state armed groups. However, an increased number of such groups are also embracing the ban on landmines.[80]

More than 80 countries and 8 areas not internationally recognized as independent states are mine-affected. In this light, the goal of a 'mine-free world' 10 years after the entry into force of the convention (by 2009–10) appears unattainable.

Unexploded ordnance and anti-vehicle mines

Although the number of civilian casualties associated with mines other than anti-personnel mines (MOTAPMs), or anti-vehicle mines, is fewer than those resulting from the use of APMs, the presence of such devices has major humanitarian implications because it obstructs post-conflict reconstruction. Work on MOTAPMs continued in 2005 in accordance with mandates agreed in November 2004 for the Group of Governmental Experts of the States Parties to the CCW Convention. It was directed to continue addressing the issues of ERWs and MOTAPMs, to explore options to promote compliance with the convention and its protocols, and to prepare for the Third Review Conference of the States Parties, to be held in 2006.

Three sessions were held during 2005 in the ERW and MOTAPM working groups. The ERW working group studied possible preventive measures to improve the design of certain types of munitions, including sub-munitions (e.g., cluster munitions), with a view to minimizing the humanitarian risk from unexploded items of this kind.[81] In March a questionnaire on ERW and international humanitarian law was sent to the parties, with the aim of developing principles that can be applied to the use of munitions and sub-munitions that

---

[77] In 2005 for the first time Russia disclosed the number of mines in its stockpile; 23.5 million of its 26.5 million mines are scheduled to be destroyed by 2015.

[78] Ukraine's Parliament ratified the APM Convention in May 2005, but Ukraine has not deposited its ratification instrument with the UN. Poland has begun the national process of ratifying the convention.

[79] In 2005 this occurred in Myanmar, Nepal and Russia. See *Landmine Monitor Report 2005* (note 74).

[80] An NGO, Geneva Call, has taken steps since 2001 to encourage 'armed non-state actors' to commit themselves not to use landmines; 28 armed groups in Burma, Burundi, India, Iraq, the Philippines, Somalia, Sudan and Western Sahara have agreed to ban APMs using this mechanism. See Geneva Call, URL <http://www.genevacall.org/home.htm>.

[81] Information on ERWs and MOTAPMs is available at the UN Office at Geneva, News and media website, URL <http://www.unog.ch/>.

may become ERW and the ways in which states may implement these principles.[82] At the end of the year it was reported that the three main actors—China, Russia and the USA—were moving more actively towards ratifying Protocol V on ERW.[83]

With regard to MOTAPMs, the effort initiated by Denmark and the USA in 2001[84] made limited progress in 2005. The MOTAPM working group considered the matters of detectability; restrictions on the use on anti-vehicle mines; fuse design and sensors for MOTAPMs; protection of civilians, including a system of warning and mine-risk education; transfers; transparency and other confidence-building measures; issues relating to the irresponsible use of MOTAPMs; possibilities for international cooperation and assistance; and other possible recommendations (e.g., restrictions on the transfers of MOTAPMs, best practice on export control, a trust fund for humanitarian assistance, etc.).[85] A consensus has reportedly emerged with regard to three principles: (a) that all MOTAPMs should be detectable for the purposes of humanitarian de-mining; (b) that some types of anti-vehicle mines should have a limited active life; and (c) that transfers of MOTAPMs should be restricted.[86]

In order to overcome the concerns of some countries, a US-led group of states sponsored the '30-nation proposal', which proposed several compromises, including permitting the use of non-detectable anti-vehicle mines if they are used within clearly marked perimeter areas. However, the main opponents to restrictions on the use of MOTAPMs continued to block progress on various grounds such as doubts about the risks to civilians posed by MOTAPMs (Russia) and the alleged technological and financial challenges (China).[87] The USA encouraged the parties to the amended Protocol II and the CCW Convention to: (a) ban the use of all non-detectable landmines; (b) revise their policies on the continued use of persistent anti-vehicle mines; (c) negotiate a ban on the sale or export of all persistent mines (including MOTAPMs); and (d) increase their funding for mine action. The challenge remains to find the political will to turn these and other issues into treaty text.[88]

---

[82] For analysis of responses to the questionnaire see 'Explosive remnants of war: states parties' responses to "international humanitarian law and ERW" questionnaire', Nov. 2005, URL <http://www.hrw.org/doc/?t=arm>.

[83] Boese, W., 'Anti-vehicle mines proposal falters', *Arms Control Today*, Jan./Feb. 2006.

[84] For text of the proposal see URL <http://www.ccwtreaty.com/usdanishproposal.html>; see also Lachowski, *SIPRI Yearbook 2002* (note 29), p. 733.

[85] 'Proposals and ideas on MOTAPM in the Group of Governmental Experts (GGE) with the purpose to provide a basis for further work' by the Coordinator, document CCW/GGE/X/WG.2/1 of the Tenth Session of the CCW Group of Governmental Experts, Geneva, 7–11 Mar. 2005.

[86] U.S. Statement at the Opening Session by Edward Cummings, Head of the United States Delegation, Eleventh Session of the CCW Group of Governmental Experts, 2 Aug. 2005, URL <http://www.ccwtreaty.com/Aug05Cummings.htm>.

[87] Boese (note 83).

[88] US Department of State, International Information Programs, International Security, Arms Control, 'U.S. shares international aim of protecting civilians from mines', *Washington File*, 28 Nov. 2005, URL <http://usinfo.state.gov/is/Archive/2005/Nov/28-711927.html>.

VII. Looking ahead: some recommendations

In late 2005 and early 2006 the future viability of the CFE Treaty regime appeared uncertain, with Russia positioning itself for a showdown at the 2006 CFE Third Review Conference. If the discussions at the OSCE's military doctrine seminar in February 2006 are successfully followed up and the final impediments to entry into force of the adapted CFE Treaty regime can be overcome, this should give a new, admittedly limited, impetus to further steps in conventional arms control in Europe and elsewhere. Any resulting measures must, however, be well thought through, adequate and timely, and properly followed up. A serious discussion is needed on the concept of arms control and CSBMs and their place in security building, and some classical criteria of arms control will have to be reassessed in the process.

The main but not the sole forum for European arms control efforts remains the OSCE. Prospects of progress would be much enhanced if the EU engaged itself more deeply in the issue. The EU has not elaborated a conventional arms control strategy in spite of its forays into some areas (SALW, export controls and the international arms trade). However, the new mention of possible 'disarmament' and security sector reform tasks in the context of the European Security and Defence Policy, the 2003 European Security Strategy envisaging *inter alia* the building of a 'ring of friends', and the European Neighbourhood Policy all may result in a new dynamic in this field as well. Russia's legitimate concerns and perceived insecurity—its tactical manoeuvrings notwithstanding—provide a cause and opportunity for further pursuance of arms control in Europe, on the one hand, and for broader efforts to allay the anxieties both of Russia and of its smaller neighbours, on the other.

Improved synergy of multilateral and inter-institutional efforts in developing the existing and future arms control measures should be pursued. NATO and the OSCE could cooperate further in the destruction of surplus munitions; the OSCE and the EU should cooperate rather than compete in areas connected with border control; and both the EU and NATO should reflect on using the leverage they have over further accession candidates to promote local and general arms control objectives.

Currently there is resistance to the idea of a new Vienna Document or further pan-European changes. The use of 'softer', voluntary CBM arrangements (perhaps starting at the sub-regional level) or the introduction of CSBM-like measures as part of a specific functional strategy may offer an easier approach and pave the way for more advanced endeavours.

A realistic assessment of the role that the OSCE might play in resolving frozen conflicts, and in peace-building afterwards, should put special (although not exclusive) emphasis on arms control and confidence building. The political obstacles to resolving these conflicts—and that in Chechnya—now appear insurmountable, but leaving them to themselves spells an even graver danger in the changing environment. The experience of existing regional CSBMs (e.g., under the Dayton Agreement), which focus on border security management and military activities in the vicinity of the borders, should be further developed. Other non-military measures could be applied to deadlocked conflicts, either in combination or independently from CSBMs.

Risk-reduction and stabilizing measures are worth considering more intensively in the context of preventive diplomacy and early-warning mechanisms for foul-weather situations, especially those arising in local contexts. Recent and ongoing unrest in Central Asia could be considered as offering a possible 'laboratory' for such an undertaking.

The conflict prevention and crisis management functions of the Treaty on Open Skies need further elaboration and application, particularly in regional and possible non-military dimensions. An increase in the number of parties and extension of the Open Skies regime to countries in potential conflict zones in the Balkans and the eastern part of the OSCE area would help promote that goal.

It is worth considering how the experience acquired in peace-supporting activities elsewhere in the world—including lessons learned in the application of demobilization, disarmament and reintegration, and security sector reform approaches—could contribute to enhancing the possible synergy between arms control, defence conversion, CSBMs and crisis management in Europe. Another approach is to foster the cross-dimensionality of CSBMs in order to better meet the multifaceted character of current security challenges on both pan-European and regional levels.

The current circumstances on Europe's perimeter are evidence that the OSCE community cannot defer the issue interminably. Europe's arms control *acquis* could be more aggressively promoted outside the OSCE area, both in adjacent areas and on a global scale (comprehensive regimes and mutual assistance programmes for SALW, MANPADS, etc.). The question of CSBM implementation in the contiguous areas of the states which share frontiers with non-European, non-OSCE states remains outstanding. As Europe faces transnational threats, the issue of eventual extension of the CSBM provisions to areas beyond the zone of application becomes a matter not just of helping others but of deepening the protection of Europe's own security. The OSCE Partners for Co-operation[89] need to be further encouraged to follow and get involved in the CSBM and arms control processes. OSCE-inspired regional CSBM arrangements between OSCE states and their non-OSCE neighbours could be a starting point, including perhaps especially new debates on the relevance of conventional arms control—and the OSCE politico-military *acquis* in general—with partners in the Far East, the Mediterranean and the greater Middle East.

---

[89] On the Asian and Mediterranean Partners for Co-operation see URL <http://www.osce.org/ec/>.

16. Transfer controls

IAN ANTHONY and SIBYLLE BAUER

I. Introduction

This chapter surveys the main efforts to strengthen multilateral export control cooperation in 2005, both in informal arrangements and in the formal arrangements of the European Union (EU). The countries that participate in multilateral export control cooperation have placed a growing emphasis on the need for strong and effective export controls to be adopted and enforced by the largest possible number of states in order to reinforce the international non-proliferation effort. The adoption in April 2004 by the United Nations (UN) Security Council of Resolution 1540,[1] which is discussed below, was one indicator of the high priority attached to the adoption of modern and effective export controls.

In 2005 the tendency for more states to take part in multilateral efforts to strengthen national export controls continued with new states participating in the Australia Group (AG), the Nuclear Suppliers Group (NSG) and the Wassenaar Arrangement on Export Controls for Conventional Arms and Dual-Use Goods and Technologies (WA). While 11 countries attended the first meeting of the Proliferation Security Initiative (PSI), in 2003, over 100 states participated in the second anniversary meeting, in 2005—a remarkable expansion in what was regarded at first as a controversial undertaking.

Section II of this chapter focuses on transfer control cooperation through the AG, the Missile Technology Control Regime (MTCR), the NSG and the WA. The participating states in these arrangements as well as the Zangger Committee are identified in table 16.1.[2] Section III examines supply-side measures in the EU, including dual-use and defence items. It also examines a new regulation concerning trade in certain equipment and products which could be used for capital punishment, torture or other cruel, inhuman or degrading treatment or punishment that was adopted in June 2005. International efforts to strengthen controls on high-activity radioactive sources are discussed in section IV. The conclusions are presented in section V.

---

[1] UN Security Council Resolution 1540, 28 Apr. 2004, URL <http://www.un.org/Docs/sc/unsc_resolutions04.html>

[2] The Zangger Committee is not formally a part of the 1968 Treaty on the Non-proliferation of Nuclear Weapons (Non-Proliferation Treaty, NPT) regime, but its participants seek to take account of the effect of changing security aspects on the NPT and to adapt export control conditions and criteria in that light.

Table 16.1. Membership of multilateral weapon and technology transfer control regimes, as of 1 January 2006

State	Zangger Committee[a] 1974	NSG[b] 1978	Australia Group[a] 1985	MTCR 1987	Wassenaar Arrangement 1996
Argentina	x	x	x	x	x
Australia	x	x	x	x	x
Austria	x	x	x	x	x
Belarus		x			
Belgium	x	x	x	x	x
Brazil		x		x	
Bulgaria	x	x	x	x	x
Canada	x	x	x	x	x
China	x	x			
Croatia		x[c]			x[c]
Cyprus		x	x		
Czech Republic	x	x	x	x	x
Denmark	x	x	x	x	x
Estonia		x	x		x[c]
Finland	x	x	x	x	x
France	x	x	x	x	x
Germany	x	x	x	x	x
Greece	x	x	x	x	x
Hungary	x	x	x	x	x
Iceland			x	x	
Ireland	x	x	x	x	x
Italy	x	x	x	x	x
Japan	x	x	x	x	x
Kazakhstan		x			
Korea, South	x	x	x	x	x
Latvia		x	x		x[c]
Lithuania		x	x		x[c]
Luxembourg	x	x	x	x	x
Malta		x	x		x[c]
Netherlands	x	x	x	x	x
New Zealand		x	x	x	x
Norway	x	x	x	x	x
Poland	x	x	x	x	x
Portugal	x	x	x	x	x
Romania	x	x	x		x
Russia	x	x		x	x
Slovakia	x	x	x		x
Slovenia	x	x	x		x
South Africa	x	x		x	x[c]
Spain	x	x	x	x	x
Sweden	x	x	x	x	x
Switzerland	x	x	x	x	x
Turkey	x	x	x	x	x
UK	x	x	x	x	x
Ukraine	x	x	x[c]	x	x
USA	x	x	x	x	x
Total	**35**	**45**	**39**	**34**	**40**

NSG = Nuclear Suppliers Group; MTCR = Missile Technology Control Regime

Note: The years in the column headings indicate when the export control regime was formally established, although the groups may have met on an informal basis before then.

ᵃ The European Commission participates in this regime.

ᵇ The European Commission is an observer in this regime.

ᶜ These countries joined in 2005.

II. International transfer control cooperation in 2005

Prior to 1990 international cooperation in export control was defined by the cold war. The Coordinating Committee for Multilateral Export Control (COCOM) was an embargo through which the United States and its allies sought to deny the Soviet Union, its allies and like-minded countries access to items that could be of strategic relevance. The Soviet Union operated a system of planning through which it could direct the industrial capacities for the development, production and transfer of strategic products in other Warsaw Treaty Organization (WTO) participating states. The Soviet planning system (of which the Council for Mutual Economic Assistance, COMECON, was an important part) was dissolved in 1991 and the decision to end COCOM was made in March 1994.

In the first half of the 1990s, after the end of the cold war, there was extensive discussion of how to modify export controls among the group of roughly 30–35 countries (a number of which were former targets for the COCOM embargo) that wanted to cooperate in this area. In the changed circumstances of the time there was no simple approach comparable to the denial of technology to an enemy around which all countries could coalesce.

The idea of keeping the COCOM instrument but aiming it at a different target was first addressed at a time when the need to respond to Iraq's August 1990 invasion of Kuwait was fresh in every mind. Iraq had built the world's fourth-largest army with foreign arms acquisitions. Moreover, the discovery by post-war inspection teams that Iraq had easily obtained a broad range of Western industrial equipment for use in illegal weapon programmes was disquieting. The administration of US President George H. W. Bush launched two initiatives to remedy these problems. The first sought agreement from the five permanent members of the UN Security Council (the P5) to restrain arms transfers to the Middle East. The second sought agreement from the Group of Seven (G7)[3] industrialized states on limiting exports of sensitive industrial and civil goods to Iran, Iraq, Libya and North Korea. Preliminary discussions suggested that agreeing on the target countries to be denied technology would have been impossible in the absence of decisions taken in the UN framework. It quickly emerged that each supplier state had its own lists of countries that should be targeted by, and countries that should be exempt from, a strategy of denial, and that these lists were not harmonized.[4] Moreover, the extensive

---

[3] The G7 states are Canada, France, Germany, Italy, Japan, the UK and the USA.

[4] The P5 (China, France, Russia, the United Kingdom and the USA) began consultations on the implications of arms proliferation for international security with special attention to conditions in the Middle East in 1991. Principles and guidelines to be applied to conventional arms transfers were elaborated.

sanctions regime imposed on Iraq under the auspices of the UN suggested that a global framework could be a more effective setting in which to discuss this issue than a self-selecting group of states.

The small plot of common ground identified at that time was first, that export controls should aim to stop proliferation of nuclear, biological and chemical (NBC) weapons and of missile delivery systems for them; and second, that a system based on technology denial should be replaced by the evaluation of potential exports against agreed criteria, with the possibility to approve or deny exports depending on the outcome of the assessment. The multilateral export control regimes have found it difficult to progress beyond this agreement in the 1990s, and it has been left to other types of cooperation arrangement (notably the EU) to develop more ambitious common efforts—such as using a single law to control dual-use exports from 25 states, and a common approach to arms export policy contained in a code of conduct.

It is recognized that the proliferation of NBC weapons and missiles that could be used to deliver them is only taking place in a few locations, rather than being a general phenomenon. A return to the COCOM approach of denying technology to these few locations while permitting transfers to other countries is unlikely for political reasons, even though it would bring a clarity that would aid implementation and enforcement. In practice, too, since standards for export control implementation and enforcement are not uniformly high within the international community, the risk of unauthorized re-export or diversion to the country subject to denial from an intermediate party is too great. However, in what might be a sign of a change in thinking, the NSG—while underlining that its guidelines are to be applied to all exports of controlled items—has begun to name two countries (Iran and North Korea) whose nuclear programmes it regards as 'proliferation challenges'.

In chapter 12 of this volume, the case is made that the group of states participating in discussions of export control needs to be extended because of the growing number of sources of supply for proliferation-sensitive materials, technologies, equipment and knowledge. In recent years, outreach efforts towards non-members have become more prominent on the agenda of the international export control regimes. However, given the pace at which the number of sources of supply has increased, the process of expanding regime participation may be too slow to assure the effectiveness of approaches carried out by groups with limited participation.

In these circumstances, a number of influential actors have pointed to the possible need to apply legal agreements in the area of export control, and to move away from the current more ad hoc approach based on understandings reached between officials and experts at the working level. Creating a global system of export control that conforms to the highest standards has become

Originally conceived as an open-ended series of consultations, these P5 talks were suspended in 1992 after a disagreement between China and the USA over how the agreed guidelines should be applied to Taiwan. The documents produced by the P5 are available at URL <http://www.sipri.org/contents/expcon/un_d1.html>.

recognized as a major priority.[5] Efforts in this direction, such as UN Security Council Resolution 1540 and the evolution of the Proliferation Security Initiative, have made this an area of innovation within arms control as well as an arena for potential future cooperation.[6]

Resolution 1540 and the PSI were both first suggested by the United States as part of a wider set of measures intended to slow the spread of nuclear weapons in the wake of the public disclosure of the illicit nuclear trafficking network led by Pakistani nuclear scientist Abdul Qadeer Khan.[7] In the past, the USA has been recognized to have a critical role in maintaining cohesion in international export control cooperation. While the USA has placed a high value on strengthening such cooperation, it has also found it difficult at times to harmonize this with wider national foreign and security policy interests. The USA currently faces this dilemma in regard to India, where the development of civil nuclear cooperation is inconsistent with US commitments under the NSG but is being promoted as part of a wider effort to improve bilateral cooperation and partnership, including on strategic issues.[8] This has led to a discussion of the reverse side of the differentiated treatment of destinations under export control cooperation regimes: namely, preferential treatment for certain countries.

Forty years ago this discussion was focused on China, when the US foreign and security policy interest to improve relations with China clashed with the commitment to deny technology under COCOM. The USA argued that China should be treated as an exception from the general embargo applied by the committee. This exceptional status was agreed within COCOM in 1972. The technology that could be supplied to China was reviewed regularly and the licensing status of China was adjusted on a number of occasions to give further preferential treatment in comparison with other communist countries.

The USA has raised the possibility that India might also be seen as an exception to the general application of NSG Guidelines. In this regard the Chinese experience is perhaps of interest in that it contributed to a reduction in the coherence of COCOM. The granting of an exception to China made it more difficult for the USA to argue against the requests of other countries with a special interest in trading with communist countries—notably, requests from

---

[5] University of Georgia, Center for International Trade and Security, 'Strengthening multilateral export controls: a nonproliferation priority', Athens, Ga., Sep. 2002, URL <http://www.uga.edu/cits/>.

[6] Through their Chairs, export control regimes expressed their readiness to respond to calls for assistance in a 2004 letter to the Security Council's 1540 Committee. On PSI see Ahlström. C., 'The Proliferation Security Initiative: international law aspects of the Statement of Interdiction Principles', *SIPRI Yearbook 2005: Armaments, Disarmament and International Security* (Oxford University Press: Oxford, 2005), pp. 741–65. The PSI Statement of Interdiction Principles is reproduced in *SIPRI Yearbook 2005*, pp. 766–67. The members of the PSI are listed in the glossary in this volume.

[7] Progress on this set of measures proposed by President George W. Bush has been mixed. One proposal led to the adoption of UN Security Council Resolution 1540 in Apr. 2004. Another proposal, to create a special committee at the International Atomic Energy Agency (IAEA) to discuss safeguards verification and made up of governments in good standing with the IAEA, was acted on in June 2005. The White House, 'Statement on progress in achieving the President's nonproliferation proposals', News release, Washington, DC, 17 June 2005, URL <http://www.whitehouse.gov/news/releases/2005/06/20050617-6.html>.

[8] This issue is discussed further below and in detail in appendix 13B in this volume.

the Federal Republic of Germany to treat trade with the German Democratic Republic as an exception to the COCOM embargo.

The Australia Group

The Australia Group was established in 1985 following international concern about the use of chemical weapons (CWs) in the 1980–88 Iraq–Iran War. The participating states in this informal group initially cooperated to maintain and develop their national export controls to prevent the further spread of chemical exports that might be used for, or diverted to, CW programmes. The participating states seek to prevent the intentional or inadvertent supply by their nationals of materials or equipment to CW or biological weapon (BW) programmes. The AG is currently also developing measures that seek to prevent the acquisition of BW or CW by non-state actors, with a particular focus on measures aimed at individuals or groups planning to carry out terrorist attacks. When the AG first convened in Brussels in 1985, it had 15 participating states. In 2005 membership rose to 39 states (as well as the European Commission) when Ukraine participated in the group for the first time.

In April 2005 the AG marked 20 years of its activities at the plenary meeting held in Sydney. At that meeting Australian Foreign Minister Alexander Downer outlined the main challenges that participating states face in sustaining the effectiveness of export controls. Downer drew attention to the greater sophistication of efforts by proliferators to evade export controls through strategies such as the trans-shipment and re-export of items as well as the use of front companies and intermediaries to mask the true end-use of dual-use exports. He also noted that 'the rapid pace of technological change, including the spectacular growth of the biotechnology sector, makes the task of keeping lists of controlled items up to date increasingly challenging'. Finally, he pointed out that traditional approaches to export control have been challenged by the growing tendency to transfer technical data and know-how through intangible means to centres of production located close to markets, rather than to transfer materials and finished products across international borders. As Downer pointed out, 'such transactions cannot be monitored by traditional means'.[9]

The AG has agreed a series of lists that define dual-use precursor chemicals, biological agents, chemical and biological equipment, and related technology. The participating states are informally committed to ensure that these items are subject to national export controls, and they have agreed a set of guidelines to consider when assessing export licence applications. In 2005 the AG made changes to the Control List of Dual-Use Chemical Manufacturing Facilities and Equipment and Related Technology by revising the entry that controls certain pumps that can be used to make chemical weapons or AG-controlled

---

[9] Speech of the Hon. Alexander Downer, Minster for Foreign Affairs, 'Twentieth anniversary plenary of the Australia Group', 18 Apr. 2005, URL <http://www.foreignminister.gov.au/speeches/2005/050418_ag.html>. See also the AG website at URL <http://www.australiagroup.net>.

precursor chemicals. The AG also amended the Control List of Dual-Use Biological Equipment by adding certain spraying or fogging systems, spray booms or arrays of aerosol-generating units. The understanding of the technical note related to the AG Control List of Biological Agents, the AG Control List of Animal Pathogens and the AG Control List of Plant Pathogens was clarified.[10]

The AG has undertaken a wide range of outreach and assistance efforts. The AG Chair briefs a number of non-participating states with non-confidential information after plenary meetings every year. In addition, regional seminars on export licensing practices have been held dealing with issues such as intangible technology transfers, end-user verification and industry outreach. In 2005 outreach visits by the AG Chair included China, Singapore and Taiwan.

The Missile Technology Control Regime

The Missile Technology Control Regime is an informal arrangement in which countries that share the goal of preventing proliferation of unmanned delivery systems for NBC weapons cooperate to exchange information and coordinate their national export licensing processes.[11] The MTCR was formed in 1987, at which time the primary focus of its activities was on ballistic missiles able to deliver a payload weighing 500 kilograms to a range of 300 kilometres. These technical parameters were considered to be consistent with missiles likely to be used to deliver first-generation nuclear weapons. The MTCR participating states have subsequently expanded the scope of their activities to include any unmanned air vehicles (UAVs) capable of delivering NBC weapons. At present 34 states are MTCR participants.

At their annual plenary meetings the MTCR participating states make a general assessment of proliferation risks, including a discussion of missile programmes of concern to the regime. However, the participating states have stressed that the MTCR Guidelines are for general application and do not 'target' particular states. The role of export control in combating terrorism continues to be discussed in the MTCR as in other export control cooperation arrangements. The question of how to share information and intelligence—an activity that normally takes place on a bilateral basis—more effectively in order to provide the most critical information to the people that need it in real time is one important issue in this context.

A number of missile producing countries are outside the regime. A country can choose to adhere to the MTCR Guidelines without participating in the regime. A number of countries, such as China and Israel, have done so, and the MTCR participating states have encouraged all non-participating countries to take this approach. In order to further this objective, the MTCR participating states have carried out a broad dialogue on missile proliferation issues with a range of countries. The Chair has the main responsibility for outreach.

---

[10] The AG control lists are available on the AG website (note 9).
[11] See the MTCR website at URL <http://www.mtcr.info/english/>.

In 2005 the MTCR Chair visited India, Israel, Pakistan and the United Arab Emirates.

Allegations of non-compliance

In August 2005 the United States issued a report on compliance with arms control, non-proliferation and disarmament agreements that included a separate section on compliance with missile-related undertakings.[12] Although this report, known as the Non-compliance Report, is required annually under the US Arms Control and Disarmament Act, the 2005 report was the first to be submitted since 2003. It included two specific findings related to non-compliance with missile proliferation commitments by states.

While China does not participate in the MTCR—its application to join having been blocked by the USA—in November 2000 the Chinese Government gave the USA a specific undertaking on missile proliferation which included a commitment not to assist 'in any way, any country in the development of ballistic missiles that can be used to deliver nuclear weapons'.[13] The Non-compliance Report found that 'items transferred by Chinese entities contributed to Category I missile programs contrary to the Chinese Government's November 2000 missile nonproliferation commitments'.[14] The report drew attention to transfers by China of controlled materials and technology to Iran, North Korea and Pakistan.

Russia has been a participant in the MTCR since 1995. The Non-compliance Report found that 'Russian entities have engaged in transfers that, although not directly precluded by Russia's commitments under the MTCR Guidelines, raise serious missile proliferation concerns and call into question Russia's ability to implement controls on missile-related technologies. To date, Russia's efforts to prevent further transfers have been inadequate'.[15] The report drew particular attention to the supply of missile-applicable technologies to China, India and Iran by Russian entities.

The Nuclear Suppliers Group

The aim of the NSG is to prevent the proliferation of nuclear weapons through export controls of nuclear and nuclear-related material, equipment, software and technology. The export controls, which are implemented by the participating states through national legislation and procedures, are not intended to prevent or hinder international cooperation on peaceful uses of nuclear energy. At the 2005 plenary meeting of the NSG the participating states, which operate by consensus, agreed that Croatia would participate in the activities of the

---

[12] US Department of State, Bureau of Verification and Compliance, 'Adherence to and compliance with arms control, nonproliferation, and disarmament agreements and commitments', Washington, DC, 30 Aug. 2005, URL <http://www.state.gov/t/vci/rls/rpt/51977.htm>.

[13] US Department of State (note 12), p. 104.

[14] US Department of State (note 12), p. 106.

[15] US Department of State (note 12), p. 108.

group. The NSG now includes 45 countries with the European Commission as an observer.[16]

The NSG participating states have agreed two sets of guidelines that they apply when assessing applications to export controlled items. One set of guidelines is applied to items that were specially designed or developed for nuclear use, while the other set of guidelines is applied to exports of nuclear dual-use items. The NSG participating states include states in which the main exporters of nuclear technology are located, and the group recognizes that peaceful nuclear cooperation is both legitimate and necessary. The participating states share the view that its guidelines 'facilitate the development of trade in this area' by 'providing the means whereby obligations to facilitate peaceful nuclear cooperation can be implemented in a manner consistent with international nuclear non-proliferation norms'.[17]

In 2005 the NSG participating states agreed on three new elements that should be incorporated in national export control decision making. First, the NSG agreed to establish a procedure to suspend nuclear transfers to countries that are non-compliant with their bilateral safeguards agreements with the International Atomic Energy Agency (IAEA). Second, the NSG agreed that it would be desirable for the supplier and the recipient states to elaborate 'fall-back safeguards' that would be invoked if the IAEA could no longer carry out safeguards in a recipient state. Third, the NSG agreed an important change to its guidelines: namely, that the existence of effective export controls in the recipient state should be introduced as a criterion of supply for nuclear material, equipment and technology and as a factor for consideration for dual-use items and technologies. In addition, the participating states agreed to continue discussing two other proposals: the existence of an Additional Protocol[18] as a condition of nuclear supply, and the further strengthening of the NSG Guidelines with respect to enrichment and reprocessing technologies.

The proposals to strengthen guidelines for enrichment and reprocessing technologies that have been discussed would require nuclear suppliers to deny transfers of these items to an end-user that was the object of an active denial by more than one NSG party, and to make a determination that the country of final destination had a credible nuclear energy requirement and no alternative solution to fuel supply/waste management available. The failure to agree on these changes reflected reservations about prohibiting the further spread of sensitive technologies (in particular uranium enrichment) in the light of the potential demand for such technologies in the future from the civil nuclear power sector. At least some NSG participating states prefer to examine effect-

---

[16] Nuclear Suppliers Group (NSG), 'NSG Plenary Meeting, Oslo Norway, 23–24 June 2005', Press Statement, URL <http://www.nuclearsuppliersgroup.org/public.htm>.

[17] The latest versions of the NSG Guidelines as well as a statement on how they are to be applied are available at URL <http://www.nuclearsuppliersgroup.org/guide.htm>.

[18] Article 2.a.ix of the model Additional Protocol contains an export control component. A supplier state that concludes a bilateral agreement with the IAEA commits itself to report exports of trigger list items to the IAEA, and recipient states that conclude such an agreement must confirm the receipt of trigger list items to the IAEA on request.

ive controls over the end-use of nuclear items rather than adopting a prohibition on transfer.

Nuclear cooperation with and nuclear supplies to India have been discussed extensively in the NSG in the past, and the group has taken the view that such cooperation is inconsistent with elements of the NSG Guidelines. Cooperation on civil nuclear matters was one element in the Next Steps in the Strategic Partnership Initiative agreed during the Indian–US Summit in Washington, DC, on 18 July 2005.[19] In exchange for a number of measures to be undertaken by India, the USA promised, among other things, to work 'to adjust international regimes to enable full civil nuclear energy cooperation and trade with India'.[20]

The impact of the Indian–US cooperation on the application of the NSG Guidelines was discussed on 16–17 October 2005, although no specific proposal was under discussion. It was later reported that France, Russia and the United Kingdom offered conditional support to developing civil nuclear cooperation with India, provided India first took the steps outlined in its bilateral agreement with the USA. Canada is reported to have asked for an exploration of additional steps which India should be asked to take prior to any change in current NSG policy and practice, including a declaration by India that no further fissile material is being produced for nuclear weapons. Other states—Austria, Sweden and Switzerland among them—reportedly registered strong reservations to modification of the NSG Guidelines. [21]

The Wassenaar Arrangement

The decision to establish the WA was taken by 33 states in December 1995 at a meeting in Wassenaar, the Netherlands. The objective of the WA is to promote transparency, exchange of information and exchange of views on transfers of an agreed range of items with a view to promoting responsibility in transfers of conventional arms and dual-use goods and technologies and to preventing 'destabilizing accumulations' of such items.

In 2004 the WA was enlarged for the first time since its establishment with the admission of Slovenia; and five more countries (Croatia, Estonia, Latvia, Lithuania and Malta) were admitted to the WA in the spring of 2005 following inter-sessional consultations. This leaves Cyprus as the only EU member state outside the WA. During the 2005 WA plenary session, held in December, South Africa was admitted as a member, expanding membership to Africa for the first time.[22] At present 40 states participate in the WA.

[19] The White House, 'Joint statement between President George W. Bush and Prime Minister Manmohan Singh', News release, Washington, DC, 18 July 2005, URL <http://www.whitehouse.gov/news/releases/2005/07/20050718-6.html>.

[20] The wider implications of the Indian–US agreement for nuclear arms control and export control are examined in appendix 13B and the international fusion energy consortium is examined in appendix 13C.

[21] Boese, W., 'Suppliers weigh Indian nuclear cooperation', *Arms Control Today*, Nov. 2005.

[22] Wassenaar Arrangement, 'Public Statement, 2005 Plenary Meeting of the Wassenaar Arrangement on Export Controls for Conventional Arms and Dual-use Goods and Technologies', Vienna, 14 Dec. 2005, URL <http://www.wassenaar.org/publicdocuments/public131205.html>.

Any decision to expand WA participation is taken by consensus among existing participants and is based on an assessment of various criteria: whether the applicant state 'is a producer/exporter of arms or industrial equipment respectively'; whether the country adheres to 'fully effective export controls'; whether the country has 'non-proliferation policies and appropriate national policies'; and whether a country has adopted the WA control lists as a reference in its national export controls.[23]

At the 2005 plenary session, the participating states agreed an 'indicative list' of 'end-use assurances commonly used', which was based on a survey. The document lists essential and optional elements referring to: (*a*) 'parties involved in the transaction', (*b*) 'goods', (*c*) 'end-use', (*d*) 'location', (*e*) 're-export/diversion', (*f*) 'delivery verification', and (*g*) 'documentation'.[24] The WA control lists were amended to take into account technical and security developments. A number of amendments related to items of potential interest to terrorists, such as jamming equipment and certain UAVs. Changes to the WA control lists are prepared at technical meetings during the year and formally approved at the December plenary session.

In October 2005 the WA held its second outreach seminar, this time addressed to industry, in which representatives from over 50 companies participated. Speakers included government officials, academics and industry representatives.[25]

During two rounds of talks in Vienna, in April 2004 and May 2005, the WA and China exchanged views on the principles of export control of conventional weapons and related dual-use items and technologies, control lists and best practice. The two sides agreed to have a regular dialogue in the future.[26]

The possible role of the PSI in enforcing export controls

The USA has proposed extending the scope of the Proliferation Security Initiative, an initiative launched in 2003 to track and interdict proliferation-sensitive cargoes during international transport. President George W. Bush proposed expanding the PSI to include more participating states and also to expand its functional scope to address more than shipments and transfers. Bush suggested that, building on the means developed to fight terrorists, states could take direct action against proliferation networks through cooperation in law enforcement. He suggested that 'PSI participants and other willing nations should use the Interpol and all other means to bring to justice those who traffic

[23] Wassenaar Arrangement, 'Purposes, Guidelines & Procedures, including the Initial Elements, as adopted and amended by the Plenary of December 2003', URL <http://www.wassenaar.org/2003 Plenary/2003PlenaryDocs.htm>.

[24] Wassenaar Arrangement, 'End-use assurances commonly used, consolidated indicative list', updated at the 2005 WA plenary session, URL <http://www.wassenaar.org/publicdocuments/>.

[25] Wassenaar Arrangement, 'Wassenaar Arrangement outreach seminar', Press statement, Vienna, Oct. 2005, URL <http://www.wassenaar.org/publicdocuments/press031005.html>.

[26] Chinese Information Office of the State Council, 'China's endeavors for arms control, disarmament and non-proliferation', Sep. 2005, URL <http://www.china.org.cn/english/features/book/140320.htm>.

in deadly weapons, to shut down their labs, to seize their materials, to freeze their assets.'[27]

The initial meeting of the PSI in May 2003 was attended by 11 countries (Australia, France, Germany, Italy, Japan, the Netherlands, Poland, Portugal, Spain, the UK and the USA). More than 60 states, as well as representatives from the EU and NATO, participated in the first anniversary meeting of the PSI. More than 100 states were represented at the second anniversary meeting, a rapid expansion. Moreover, the functional scope of the PSI is changing. The participating states have agreed to identify law enforcement authorities and other tools or assets that could be used in support of efforts to stop proliferation facilitators and to share that information. In addition, at the meeting of Operational Experts in Omaha, Nebraska, the participants agreed on the need 'to ensure greater involvement of law enforcement agencies from all partner states' in the PSI.[28] In this regard the PSI could evolve into a practical mechanism with which to implement the commitments contained in UN Security Council Resolution 1540 requiring all states to criminalize proliferation by non-state actors and to enact effective export controls.

III. Supply-side measures in the European Union

In 2005 the EU focused on efforts to complete the revision of its 1998 Code of Conduct on Arms Exports[29] and to make the implementation of dual-use export controls more effective. Working groups under the Council of the European Union also continued to discuss a number of issues that are relevant in both the dual-use and the conventional export control context. These include controls of intangible technology transfers, a common approach to criminal sanctions for illegal export, brokering and smuggling as well as more coordinated and comprehensive export control outreach and capacity building.

Dual-use export control

The December 2003 EU Strategy against Proliferation of Weapons of Mass Destruction (WMD) identified export controls as part of the first line of defence against proliferation and committed the EU to strengthen export control policies and practices 'within its borders and beyond'.[30] The imple-

---

[27] The White House, 'President announces new measures to counter the threat of WMD', Remarks by the President on weapons of mass destruction proliferation, Fort Lesley J. McNair, National Defense University, News release, Washington, DC, 11 Feb. 2004 URL <http://www.whitehouse.gov/news/releases/2004/02/20040211-4.html>.

[28] Stephen G. Rademaker, 'The Proliferation Security Initiative (PSI): a record of success', Assistant Secretary of State for Arms Control, Testimony before the House International Relations Committee, Subcommittee on International Terrorism and Nonproliferation, Washington, DC, 9 June 2005 URL <http://www.state.gov/t/ac/rls/rm/47715.htm>.

[29] Council of the European Union, European Union Code of Conduct on Arms Exports, Brussels, 5 June 1998, URL <http://ue.eu.int/uedocs/cmsUpload/08675r2en8.pdf>.

[30] Council of the European Union, EU Strategy against Proliferation of Weapons of Mass Destruction, Brussels, 12 Dec. 2003, URL <http://ue.eu.int/cms3_applications/Applications/newsRoom/LoadDocument.asp?directory=en/misc/&filename=78340.pdf>.

mentation of EU Council Regulation 1334/2000 (the common and uniform legislative basis for dual-use export control in all member states) in an enlarged EU was reviewed in 2004.[31] The review revealed discrepancies regarding implementing legislation, industrial awareness programmes, the technical capacities available to national authorities to evaluate licence applications and classify items, and as regards the intelligence infrastructure. The review also found that the application of the dual-use regulation differed with regard to *inter alia* the use of the catch-all clause, the implementation of denial exchanges, intangible technology transfer controls, and transit and trans-shipment controls.

The General Affairs Council meeting of 13–14 December 2004 decided that recommendations put forward to address these discrepancies should be 'acted upon without delay', making strengthening export controls a key priority for 2005.[32] The recommendations, grouped in nine broad areas, were to: (*a*) 'ensure transparency and awareness of legislation implementing the EU system'; (*b*) 'minimise any significant divergence in practices amongst Member States'; (*c*) 'investigate the possibilities for adding controls on transit and transhipment'; (*d*) 'provide assistance in recognition of dual-use items subject to control'; (*e*) 'improve exchanges of information on denials, and consider the creation of a data base to exchange sensitive information'; (*f*) 'agree best practices for the enforcement of controls'; (*g*) 'improve transparency to facilitate harmonisation of implementation of controls on nonlisted items (catch-all)'; (*h*) 'enhance interaction with exporters'; and (*i*) 'agree best practices for controlling intangible transfers of technology'.

The Council Working Party on Dual-Use Goods was charged with taking forward the follow-up to the review,[33] but implementation falls to the responsible authorities of the EU member states. To minimize divergences in national licensing practices, the member states have discussed the conditions that each of them attaches to various kinds of export authorizations.

UN Security Council Resolution 1540, which the EU has strongly endorsed, requires states to establish effective transit and trans-shipment controls. However, these are not currently contained in Regulation 1334/2000. In 2005 the Commission began to gather the information needed to assess the impact of modifying Regulation 1334/2000 to include controls on dual-use goods in transit or trans-shipment.

Exporters often request advice from licensing authorities about whether or not their products require authorization prior to export. If an export has taken place that is suspected to violate export control laws and regulations, subse-

---

[31] The first stage of the peer review was described in Anthony, I. and Bauer, S., 'Transfer controls', *SIPRI Yearbook 2005* (note 6), pp. 699–719.

[32] Council of the European Union, 2630th Council Meeting General Affairs and External Relations, Brussels, 13 Dec. 2004, General Affairs, Press release no. 15460/04 (Presse 343), URL <http://www.consilium.eu.int>.

[33] On progress made in 2005 see Council of the European Union, 'Implementation of the recommendations of the peer review of member states' export control systems for dual use goods', Document 15826/05, Brussels, 15 Dec. 2005, URL <http://register.consilium.eu.int/pdf/en/05/st15/st15826.en05.pdf>.

quent legal proceedings require an authoritative statement of whether or not the item that was exported (or to be exported) was licensable. For these reasons it is necessary for governments to have a source of technical advice available to them on an 'as needs' basis. For larger countries that export many dual-use items this almost certainly requires maintaining a dedicated cadre of technical experts within the export control establishment. For smaller countries, which may need to call on such advice infrequently and at irregular times, the cost of maintaining a permanent technical resource nationally may not be justifiable. The Council Working Party on Dual-Use Goods has established a pool of technical experts who are available to assist colleagues in other countries with recognition of dual-use items subject to control. This demonstrates trust among the member states in that such a pool inevitably involves sharing information, some of which could be commercially sensitive.

Before any EU member state authorizes an export that has been denied by another member state or states for an essentially identical transaction within the previous three years, it must first consult each of the member states that issued a denial. Member states have been responsible for collecting and storing information on licence denials. The EU is establishing an electronic database to collect and record denial notices made by member states under Regulation 1334/2000 and in the international export control regimes. The design of the database has been agreed, and its construction is scheduled to be completed by mid-2006. Once it is functioning, the database is expected to enhance the capability of the member states to access and exchange information quickly.

In recent years the discussion of strengthening dual-use export control has increasingly focused on the need for effective enforcement. As one part of the response to the peer review the EU member states initiated a comprehensive review of licensing and customs practices regarding enforcement. Under Regulation 1334/2000 exporters are obliged to apply for authorization for exports that do not appear on lists of controlled items:

if the exporter has been informed by the competent authorities of the Member State in which he is established that the items in question are or may be intended, in their entirety or in part, for use in connection with the development, production, handling, operation, maintenance, storage, detection, identification or dissemination of chemical, biological or nuclear weapons or other nuclear explosive devices or the development, production, maintenance or storage of missiles capable of delivering such weapons.

Industry has drawn attention to differing interpretations of this 'catch-all' control between member states and, in response, the administration of the catch-all control was examined during the peer review and as part of its follow-up.

More broadly, it is increasingly recognized that close engagement with industry must become a more central feature of modern export controls since exporters have adopted new working practices based on greater international cooperation. The EU member states have developed a checklist that they can use to benchmark their existing practices on interaction with industry in order to achieve a higher level of awareness by the private sector and to ensure its full support and active cooperation in the fight against the proliferation of WMD.[34]

Customs security initiatives of the EU

Since 2003 the European Commission has brought together the elements of a new security-management model for the external borders of the enlarged EU based on two pillars: a set of common control standards to be used as the basis for customs procedures throughout the EU and a set of trade facilitation measures that will be available to exporters that can demonstrate a responsible approach to exporting. The elements of the model were the basis for security amendments to the Community Customs Code contained in EC Regulation 648/2005 of 13 April 2005.[35]

With these amendments the European Union introduced three important changes to the Customs Code. First, the new regulation requires traders to provide customs authorities with pre-arrival and pre-departure declarations containing information on goods prior to import to or export from the EU. Second, the new regulation introduces the status of authorized economic operator that will, once conferred, provide reliable traders with the right to receive certain trade facilitation measures. Third, the new regulation introduces a mechanism for setting uniform Community risk-selection criteria for controls, supported by computerized systems.

Subsequently, the Commission has drafted implementing provisions (published in July 2005) and managed an open consultation in order to prepare a final draft provision for discussion by EU member states in the EU Customs Code Committee.[36] It is hoped that revised implementing regulations for the Community Customs Code could enter into force in 2006. The new system is intended to help protect the internal market of the EU as well as help to secure international supply chains.[37] However, the new mechanisms being developed as part of this process can also strengthen the implementation of dual-use export controls by helping customs authorities to recognize sensitive shipments, stop them at the border and inspect them more closely. The pre-arrival and pre-departure declarations required under the new system could

---

[34] Council of the European Union, 'Outreach to industry checklist', Council document 15291/05, 5 Dec. 2005, available at URL <http://register.consilium.eu.int/>.

[35] 'Regulation (EC) No. 648/2005 of the European Parliament and of the Council of 13 April 2005 amending Council Regulation (EEC) No 2913/92 establishing the Community Customs Code', *Official Journal of the European Union*, L113 (4 May 2005), pp. 13–19.

[36] 'Preliminary Draft Commission Regulation laying down provisions for the implementation of Council Regulation (EEC) No 2913/92 establishing the Community Customs Code', Working document TAXUD/1250/2005. REV.3, Brussels, 2006.

[37] The approach being adopted by the EU is compatible with the Framework of Standards to Secure and Facilitate Global Trade being developed within the World Customs Organization (WCO). A High Level Strategic Group within the WCO has been developing global security and facilitation measures concerning the international trade supply chain since June 2004.

also provide the information needed to control the transit and trans-shipment of dual-use goods across the EU.

EU controls over trade in goods that could be used for capital punishment, torture or other cruel, inhuman or degrading treatment

The EU internal market presents a legal and practical challenge to maintaining and implementing national export controls, and there are occasions when the EU will want to place collective restrictions on exports to further its strategic and political objectives. In one example of this approach, work is ongoing to introduce EU-wide controls on the export of paramilitary equipment. In another example, in June 2005 the EU adopted Council Regulation 1236/2005, to enter into force on 30 July 2006, concerning trade in certain goods which could be used for capital punishment, torture or other cruel, inhuman or degrading treatment or punishment.[38] Whereas several EU member states already had national bans or controls on exports of equipment used in torture, the aim of the regulation, a law that directly applies in all member states, is to ensure a harmonized, agreed approach to exports of such items.

The regulation bans the export of goods that have no practical use other than for the purposes of capital punishment, torture and other cruel, inhuman or degrading treatment or punishment in certain types of trade. The regulation also introduces a requirement to control exports of certain identified items that could be used for such purposes. Its annexes include a list of goods and the supply of technical assistance related to those goods that will be banned for both import into and export from the EU; and a list of goods that may not be exported without authorization by the responsible national authorities of the member states. Each application to export is to be evaluated on a case-by-case basis, and general or global licences may not be used to authorize exports. A separate annex contains a model licence document, but the regulation also envisages that authorization may be issued by electronic means according to specific procedures established on a national basis.

Regulation 1236/2005 requires the member states to inform each other and the Commission within 30 days of licence applications that are denied. The regulation contains a 'no undercut' procedure by which a competent authority must consult a counterpart that has denied authorization for an essentially identical transaction within the previous three years. An authority may subsequently authorize the transaction, but it must then inform the EU partners of the reasons why the authorization was granted.

The regulation includes criteria for assessing applications to export goods listed in annex III. Authorization may not be granted for an export when there are reasonable grounds to believe that listed goods 'might be used for torture or other cruel, inhuman or degrading treatment or punishment, including

---

[38] 'Council Regulation (EC) no. 1236/2005 of 27 June 2005 concerning trade in certain goods which could be used for capital punishment, torture or other cruel, inhuman or degrading treatment or punishment', *Official Journal of the European Union*, L200 (30 July 2005), pp. 1–19.

judicial corporal punishment, by a law enforcement authority or any natural or legal person in a third country'. In addition, the competent authority must take two other factors into account: (a) any relevant available international court judgements; and (b) the findings of the competent bodies of the UN, the Council of Europe and the EU, including reports of the Council of Europe's European Committee for the Prevention of Torture and Inhuman or Degrading Treatment and Punishment and of the UN Special Rapporteur on Torture and Other Cruel, Inhuman or Degrading Treatment or Punishment. The regulation draws attention to other relevant information (e.g., available national court judgements, reports or other information prepared by civil society organizations and information on restrictions on exports of listed goods applied by the country of destination) that may be taken into account when considering an export application.

The 2005 regulation was based on a proposal made by the Commission in December 2002 but not all parts of the proposal were retained.[39] For example, the original Commission proposal included several chemicals on the list of goods that may not be exported without authorization that are also controlled for export by EU member states as part of their system for controlling exports of military items. The chemicals in question are contained in the Wassenaar Arrangement Military List, and Cyprus is still outside the Wassenaar Arrangement. However, the WA Military List is reproduced as the EU Common Military List, which is used by all member states as a reference list to ensure common application of the EU Code of Conduct on Arms Exports. The Code of Conduct also includes a relevant general criterion requiring export decisions to take account of the degree of respect for human rights in the country of final destination. During the discussion of the draft regulation in the EU member states the utility of a list-based approach to control was questioned given that many everyday items could in theory be misused, but practical difficulties of implementation effectively rule out compiling a very extensive control list.[40]

The Commissioner for External Relations and European Neighbourhood Policy, Benita Ferrero-Waldner, has stressed that the regulation should not be seen in isolation but judged as one of many steps that the EU is taking 'to encourage all countries that have not yet done so to abolish the death penalty, outlaw torture and follow the EU's lead in controlling trade in goods used for these purposes'.[41]

[39] 'Proposal for a Council Regulation concerning trade in certain equipment and products which could be used for capital punishment, torture or other cruel, inhuman or degrading treatment or punishment', COM(2002) 770 final, 30 Dec. 2002.

[40] British House of Lords, European Union Committee, 'Proposal to ban trade in products used for capital punishment or torture: report with evidence', HL paper 75, London, 22 Mar. 2005. URL <http://www.publications.parliament.uk/pa/ld200405/ldselect/ldeucom/ldeucom.htm>.

[41] European Commission, 'EU curbs trade of torture equipment', Press release IP/05/819, Brussels, 30 June 2005. E.g., where considered necessary, actions against torture and ill-treatment are to be reflected in relations with third countries as an element in the political dialogue with the country concerned, through démarches and public statements and as a component of bilateral and multilateral cooperation for the promotion of human rights. EU Heads of Mission in countries around the world are asked to analyse the occurrence of torture and ill-treatment and the measures taken to combat it in the country where they are located and report their findings. The Council Working Group on Human Rights (COHOM) is to combine these reports with other relevant information in order to identify situations

The European Union Code of Conduct on Arms Exports

The EU Code of Conduct on Arms Exports was adopted in June 1998.[42] Beyond its application to the 25 members of the EU, Bosnia and Herzegovina (BiH), Bulgaria, Canada, Croatia, the Former Yugoslav Republic of Macedonia (FYROM), Iceland, Norway and Romania have aligned themselves with its criteria and principles.[43] Of these states, Norway has been granted official adherent status, which *inter alia* involves some access to information about denials of export licences. In addition, a number of countries in South-Eastern Europe (BiH, Serbia and Montenegro and FYROM) have included an obligation to apply the EU Code criteria when assessing licence applications in their new export control laws adopted in 2004 and 2005. Acceding countries Bulgaria and Romania have participated in the meetings of the Council Working Party on Conventional Arms (COARM) since May 2005.

The EU Code of Conduct contains eight criteria for export licensing and operative provisions, which outline reporting procedures and mechanisms for intergovernmental denial notification and consultation. In 2000 the EU member states agreed a list of military equipment to which the Code is applied. That list has been revised several times. The 2006 version takes into account the changes to the WA Munitions List agreed in December 2005.[44]

In 2004 the EU member states initiated a review of the 1998 Code of Conduct. COARM prepared a revised Code, which includes changes to its operative provisions, eight criteria and legal status.[45] A draft 'Council Common Position defining common rules governing the control of exports of military technology and equipment' was agreed at technical level in the spring of 2005, but was still awaiting ministerial approval at the beginning of 2006.[46] This was not because of substantive objections to the revised Code but owing to a political link to the controversial arms embargo against China and the proposal for a 'toolbox'—complementing the EU Code—to enhance the transparency of transfers to countries on which arms embargoes have been lifted.[47] On 30 June

where EU actions are called for and then either to agree on further steps or to make recommendations to EU ministers. 'Guidelines to EU policy towards third countries on torture and other cruel, inhuman or degrading treatment or punishment', Adopted by the General Affairs Council, Luxembourg, 1 Sep. 2004, URL <http://ue.eu.int/uedocs/cmsUpload/TortureGuidelines.pdf>.

[42] Bauer, S. and Bromley, M., *The European Union Code of Conduct on Arms Exports: Improving the Annual Report*, SIPRI Policy Paper no. 8 (SIPRI: Stockholm, Nov. 2004), URL <http://www.sipri.org/>.

[43] 'Seventh annual report according to operative provision 8 of the European Union Code of Conduct on arms exports', *Official Journal of the European Communities*, C 328 (23 Dec. 2005), pp. 1–288.

[44] 'Common Military List of the European Union (equipment covered by the European Union Code of Conduct on Arms Exports) adopted by the Council on 27 February 2006', *Official Journal of the European Union*, C66 (17 Mar. 2006), pp. 1–28.

[45] For a summary of changes see Anthony and Bauer (note 31), pp. 715–18.

[46] Unlike a Council Declaration, a Common Position is an instrument of the Common Foreign and Security Policy, which politically obliges member states to bring their legislation and policies in line with the agreed Common Position. While a Common Position would not transform the Code of Conduct into European law or make it subject to the jurisdiction of the European Court of Justice, a Common Position has national legal implications for some member states.

[47] See Anthony and Bauer (note 31); and Anthony, I., 'Militarily relevant EU–China trade and technology transfers: issues and problems', Paper presented at the Conference on Chinese Military

2005, the EU Committee of Permanent Representatives (Coreper) endorsed the agreement reached at technical level on a draft revised Code,[48] but it failed to agree 'additional transparency and mutual control measures to be applied upon the lifting of an arms embargo, for inclusion in the User's Guide to the Council Common Position defining common rules governing the control of exports of military technology and equipment'.[49]

The User's Guide to the EU Code, first published in November 2003, has been updated at least once per year. It further defines and interprets the terms and procedures outlined in the 1998 Code of Conduct. The October 2005 version outlines best practice for the application of criterion 8, which obliges the member states in the licensing process to consider the compatibility of arms exports with the technical and economic capacity of the recipient country. Work on best practice guides for criterion 2 (human rights) and criterion 7 (end-use controls) is ongoing.[50] The latest edition, published in January 2006, introduces a common template for information to be included in national reports, and updates the list of websites for national reports on arms exports.[51]

The development of the EU Code's implementation during 2005 is documented in the seventh annual report.[52] While much of COARM's work focused on the review process, other areas of work included implementation of the 2003 Common Position on Brokering. According to the seventh annual report, legislation in 19 of the 27 member states and acceding countries was in full compliance with the Common Position.

Among COARM's stated priorities for the near future are both outreach to promote the Code's principles and criteria, and the provision of practical and technical assistance for this purpose. The EU member states are also seeking to enhance the coordination of national outreach and assistance efforts.

IV. Exports of radiological materials

Radioactive sources are in widespread use throughout the world in medicine, agriculture, research and industry. While the great majority of sources are relatively harmless—since the activity levels and the potential radiological dose hazards are relatively small—poorly protected sources that have a high level of radioactivity and a physical form that facilitates dispersion could be

---

Modernization: East Asian Political, Economic, and Defense Industrial Responses, Maui, Hawaii, 19–20 May 2005, URL <http://www.sipri.org/contents/expcon/euchinapaper>.

[48] 'EU/armaments: towards new common rules for arms export control', *Atlantic News*, no. 3693 (5 July 2005), p. 4.

[49] Dombey, D., 'EU considers binding rules on arms sales', *Financial Times*, 18 Apr. 2005, p. 2.

[50] Council of the European Union, 'User's Guide to the European Union Code of Conduct on Arms Exports', Document 5179/05, Brussels, 11 Jan. 2006, URL <http://ue.eu.int/cms3_fo/showPage.asp?id=408&lang=en&mode=g>.

[51] Council of the European Union (note 50).

[52] 'Seventh annual report according to operative provision 8 of the European Union Code of Conduct on arms exports' (note 43).

acquired by terrorists and used to construct a a 'dirty bomb'.[53] Furthermore, radioactive sources account for a far larger number of detected cases of illicit nuclear trafficking than nuclear materials that could be used to make a nuclear explosive device. Against this background, there have been a number of international efforts to counter radiological terrorism, including the development of high standards that reduce the vulnerability of radioactive sources to acquisition by terrorists.

Brian Dodd has pointed out that the number of international bodies, groups, agencies and organizations that contribute to the goals of preventing the acquisition of radioactive materials by terrorists, detecting and responding to any attempts to acquire relevant materials or responding to their actual acquisition or use is very large.[54] One initiative was the process of revising and updating the 2001 IAEA Code of Conduct on the Safety and Security of Radioactive Sources. This non-binding Code of Conduct was approved by the IAEA Board of Governors on 8 September 2003.[55]

The Code seeks to create a 'cradle-to-grave' system of regulation and safe custody for radiological sources that pose 'a significant risk to individuals, society and the environment' and to do this 'through the development, harmonization and implementation of national policies, laws and regulations, and through fostering the international co-operation'.

As part of this system for control the Code establishes specific requirements for controlling the export and import of high-risk radioactive sources in the form of a set of guidelines. These guidelines are contained in the Guidance on the Import and Export of Radioactive Sources in accordance with the IAEA Code of Conduct on the Safety and the Security of Radioactive Sources, which was approved in September 2004.

The IAEA Guidance on the Import and Export of Radioactive Sources

The IAEA Guidance on the Import and Export of Radioactive Sources was developed to supplement the import and export provisions contained in the IAEA's Code of Conduct.[56] It represents the first global framework for the control of radioactive source exports. On 24 September 2004, the IAEA General Conference endorsed the Guidance and noted that more than 30 countries had stated their intention to work towards effective import and export controls

---

[53] There have been instances of the use of radiological weapons by sub-state groups. For a discussion see Zarimpas, N., 'The illicit traffic in nuclear and radioactive materials', *SIPRI Yearbook 2001: Armaments, Disarmament and International Security* (Oxford University Press: Oxford, 2001), pp. 503–11,

[54] Dodd, B., 'International efforts in countering radiological terrorism', *Health Physics*, vol. 89 (2005), pp. 556–65.

[55] IAEA, Code of Conduct on the Safety and Security of Radioactive Sources, GOV/2000/34-GC (44)/7, 8 Sep. 2003. This code replaced the version published by the IAEA in Mar. 2001.

[56] Sowder, A. G., 'The IAEA Code of Conduct and Import/Export Control Guidance: strengthening global safety and security of radioactive sources through international coordination and assistance', 37th National Conference on Radiation Control, Conference of Radiation Control Program Directors, Kansas City, Mo., 25–28 Apr. 2005, URL <http://www.crcpd.org/AnnualMeeting-05/Abstracts/Sowder.htm>.

by 31 December 2005. The conference encouraged all states to act in accordance with the Guidance on a harmonized basis.[57]

The IAEA Guidance states that high-activity radioactive sources should only be exported to states that have an effective system for regulating their possession and use and only after the responsible authorities in the recipient country have given their assent to the transaction. A system of notification is proposed to ensure that the responsible authorities know when and where sources are entering the country and to verify receipt by the end-user. Limited exceptional circumstances are suggested under which sources can be provided to countries that do not meet the authorization criteria.[58]

In June 2005 the EU and the USA restated their objective of having effective controls applied by the end of 2005 in accordance with the IAEA Guidance.[59] However, in spite of this political commitment to a self-imposed deadline this objective was widely considered to be unrealistic in the absence of a common approach within the EU for the implementation by member states of the IAEA Guidance.[60] At an international conference held in Bordeaux, France, in mid-2005 it was noted that, although more than 30 countries had made clear their intention to work towards effective import and export controls by 31 December 2005, only three IAEA member states had subsequently notified the IAEA Director General about national measures.[61]

The EU member states have been working to implement a 2003 Council Directive on the control of high-activity sealed radioactive sources and orphan sources.[62] However, this directive establishes modern and effective controls for radioactive sources within the EU and not for exports or transfers to other parties. According to the 'progress report' on the implementation of the December 2003 EU Strategy against Proliferation of Weapons of Mass Destruction, supplementary Community legislation concerning the import and

---

[57] IAEA General Conference, Resolution GC(48)/RES/10.D, 24 Sep. 2004.

[58] The guidance is consistent with the Statement on Securing Radioactive Sources agreed by the Group of Eight (G8) industrialized states at their summit meeting in Evian, France in 2003. G8 Summit, 'Non proliferation of weapons of mass destruction: securing radioactive sources, a G8 statement', Evian, 2003, URL, <http://www.g8.fr/evian/english/>.

[59] The White House, 'Joint Statement by the European Union and United States on the Joint Programme of Work on the Nonproliferation of Weapons of Mass Destruction', News release, Washington, DC, 20 June 2005, URL <http:// www.whitehouse.gov/news/releases/2005/06/20050620. html>.

[60] It can be noted that the US Nuclear Regulatory Commission amended Title 10, part 110 of the Code of Federal Regulations (Export and Import of Nuclear Equipment and Material) on 1 July 2005 to give expression to this commitment.

[61] International Atomic Energy Agency, 'Findings of the President of the Conference', International Conference on the Safety and Security of Radioactive Sources: Towards a Global System for the Continuous Control of Sources Throughout their Life Cycle, 27 June–1 July 2005, Bordeaux, available at URL <http://www-pub.iaea.org/MTCD/Meetings/Announcements.asp?ConfID=134>.

[62] 'Council Directive 2003/122/EURATOM of 22 December 2003 on the control of high-activity sealed radioactive sources and orphan sources', *Official Journal of the European Union*, L346 (31 Dec. 2003), p. 57. At the end of 2005 the EU member states were still working to introduce the elements of this regulation into their national legislation. Council of the European Union, 'Six-monthly report on the implementation of Chapter III of the EU Strategy against the Proliferation of Weapons of Mass Destruction', Council document no. 14520/05, Brussels, 5 Dec. 2005, p. 12.

export of radioactive sources was being prepared.[63] While the requirements of the IAEA Guidance are partly met in EU law,[64] aspects related to practical implementation (including who would authorize exports and who would seek the consent of the countries of destination prior to shipment) would have to be decided nationally.

The EU and the USA have offered support to 'efforts to assist countries that need such assistance to establish effective and sustainable controls'.[65] International assistance efforts have largely been organized under the umbrella of the IAEA and financed using external contributions made into the IAEA Nuclear Security Fund.[66]

V. Conclusions

The states that participate in informal multilateral groups to enhance the effectiveness of their national export controls acknowledge that more effort is still needed to combat and, if possible, reverse the proliferation of weapons of mass destruction and their delivery systems. There is growing sensitivity to the need to include the widest possible participation in these efforts to strengthen export control, and to base future efforts on cooperation to implement agreed international standards. There is increasing recognition that the work accomplished in the past in the self-selecting export control arrangements has established a solid platform on which an international set of standards can be built.

There are indications that export controls are likely to be applied in new functional areas as part of the wider effort to adapt arms control to a changing security environment. Two efforts are reported in this chapter. The new EU regulation on trade in goods that could be used for capital punishment, torture or other cruel, inhuman or degrading treatment extends export controls beyond the realm of military or strategic products in pursuit of human rights objectives. Many of the member states of the IAEA are examining how export controls might help reduce the risk of acquisition and use of radiological weapons by non-state actors.

The need to accelerate the adoption of the highest international standards through national laws and regulations continues to stimulate demand for export control outreach and assistance. The export control regimes have all

[63] In contrast, by early 2006 the USA is only at the initial stage of discussing strengthened regulations to control high-activity radioactive sources as an aspect of homeland security.

[64] Hallemans, J.-M. and Tricas Aizpún, A., 'The European legislation on transport of radioactive materials', *International Journal of Radioactive Materials Transport*, vol. 12, no. 4 (2001), pp. 193–96.

[65] The White House (note 59).

[66] E.g., financial support from the EU has helped the IAEA carry out projects to strengthen the security of radioactive materials in non-nuclear applications, and the capabilities of states for detection and response to illicit trafficking. These projects are primarily focused on countries in South-Eastern Europe and in the Central Asia region (Kazakhstan, Kyrgyzstan, Uzbekistan, Tajikistan and Turkmenistan). 'Council Joint Action 2004/495/CFSP of 17 May 2004 on support for IAEA activities under its Nuclear Security Programme and in the framework of the implementation of the EU Strategy against Proliferation of Weapons of Mass Destruction', *Official Journal of the European Union*, L182 (19 May 2004), pp. 46–50.

continued their active outreach efforts, and both the European Union and Japan have been considering how best to help the USA finance and deliver assistance in the quantities needed and to the locations where there is demand.

The need for a broader participation in the development and implementation of international standards has been accompanied by a growing discussion of the need for discrimination, both negative and positive, between recipient countries. The long-standing support for closer scrutiny of exports to countries widely recognized to represent proliferation challenges may, at some point, tip into support for technology denial. At the same time, calls for greater efficiency in implementing export controls and for closer cooperation with industry may generate support for simplified procedures in cases of trade with countries acknowledged to have a high level of commitment to non-proliferation and control.

The high level of support in 2005 for two recent initiatives—UN Security Council Resolution 1540 and the PSI—suggests a growing awareness of the need to pay the same attention to enforcement of controls that has been paid to the development of modern and comprehensive legislation. In this regard a number of serious challenges are on the horizon for those charged with the development, management and implementation of export control. Two such issues for the immediate future appear to be how to control intangible technology transfer, and how to link export control enforcement with other parts of the effort to combat organized cross-border crime.

Annexes

Annex A. Arms control and disarmament agreements

Annex B. Chronology 2005

Annex A. Arms control and disarmament agreements

NENNE BODELL

Notes

1. The agreements are listed in the order of the date on which they were adopted, signed or opened for signature (multilateral agreements) or signed (bilateral agreements); the date on which they entered into force and the depositary for multilateral treaties are also given. Information is as of 1 March 2006 unless otherwise indicated.

2. The main source of information is the lists of signatories and parties provided by the depositaries of the treaties.

3. For a few major treaties, the substantive parts of the most important reservations, declarations and/or interpretive statements made in connection with a state's signature, ratification, accession or succession are given in footnotes below the lists. For the 1925 Geneva Protocol, only 'explicit reservations' are listed here. For 'implicit reservations' and an explanation of the categories see URL <http://www.sipri.org/contents/cbwarfare/cbw_research_doc/cbw_historical/cbw-hist-geneva-parties.html>.

4. States listed as parties have ratified, acceded or succeeded to the agreements. Former non-self-governing territories, upon attaining independence, sometimes make general statements of continuity to all agreements concluded by the former colonial power. This annex lists as parties only those new states that have made an uncontested declaration on continuity or have notified the depositary about their succession.

5. Taiwan, while not recognized as a sovereign state by some nations, is listed as a party to those agreements which it has ratified.

6. The Russian Federation confirmed the continuity of international obligations assumed by the USSR.

7. Unless stated otherwise, the multilateral agreements listed in this annex are open to all states for signature, ratification, accession or succession.

8. A complete list of UN member states, with the year in which they became members, appears in the glossary at the front of this volume. Not all the signatories and parties listed in this annex are UN members.

Protocol for the Prohibition of the Use in War of Asphyxiating, Poisonous or Other Gases, and of Bacteriological Methods of Warfare (1925 Geneva Protocol)

Signed at Geneva on 17 June 1925; entered into force on 8 February 1928; depositary French Government

The protocol declares that the parties agree to be bound by the prohibition on the use of these weapons in war.

Parties (134): Afghanistan, Albania, Algeria[1], Angola[1], Antigua and Barbuda, Argentina, Australia, Austria, Bahrain[1], Bangladesh[1], Barbados, Belgium, Benin, Bhutan, Bolivia, Brazil, Bulgaria, Burkina Faso, Cambodia[1], Cameroon, Canada, Cape Verde, Central African Republic, Chile, China[1], Côte d'Ivoire, Cuba, Cyprus, Czech Republic, Denmark, Dominican Republic, Ecuador, Egypt, Equatorial Guinea, Estonia, Ethiopia, Fiji[1], Finland, France, Gambia, Germany, Ghana, Greece, Grenada, Guatemala, Guinea-Bissau, Holy See, Hungary, Iceland, India[1], Indonesia, Iran, Iraq[1], Ireland, Israel[2], Italy, Jamaica, Japan, Jordan[3], Kenya, Korea (North)[1], Korea (South)[5], Kuwait[1], Laos, Latvia, Lebanon, Lesotho, Liberia, Libya[1], Liechtenstein, Lithuania, Luxembourg, Madagascar, Malawi, Malaysia, Maldives, Malta, Mauritius, Mexico, Monaco, Mongolia, Morocco, Nepal, Netherlands, New Zealand, Nicaragua, Niger, Nigeria[1], Norway, Pakistan, Panama, Papua New Guinea[1], Paraguay, Peru, Philippines, Poland, Portugal, Qatar, Romania, Russia, Rwanda, Saint Kitts and Nevis, Saint Lucia, Saint Vincent and the Grenadines, Saudi Arabia, Senegal, Serbia and Montenegro[1], Sierra Leone, Slovakia, Solomon Islands[1], South Africa, Spain, Sri Lanka, Sudan, Swaziland, Sweden, Switzerland, Syria, Taiwan, Tanzania, Thailand[4], Togo, Tonga, Trinidad and Tobago, Tunisia, Turkey, Uganda, UK, Ukraine, Uruguay, USA[4], Venezuela, Viet Nam[1], Yemen

[1] The protocol is binding on this state only as regards states which have signed and ratified or acceded to it. The protocol will cease to be binding on this state in regard to any enemy state whose armed forces or whose allies fail to respect the prohibitions laid down in it.

[2] The protocol is binding on Israel only as regards states which have signed and ratified or acceded to it. The protocol shall cease to be binding on Israel in regard to any enemy state whose armed forces, or the armed forces of whose allies, or the regular or irregular forces, or groups or individuals operating from its territory, fail to respect the prohibitions which are the object of the protocol.

[3] Jordan undertakes to respect the obligations contained in the protocol with regard to states which have undertaken similar commitments. It is not bound by the protocol as regards states whose armed forces, regular or irregular, do not respect the provisions of the protocol.

[4] The protocol shall cease to be binding on this state with respect to use in war of asphyxiating, poisonous or other gases, and of all analogous liquids, materials or devices, in regard to any enemy state if such state or any of its allies fails to respect the prohibitions laid down in the protocol.

[5] South Korea withdrew its reservation concerning bacteriological and toxin weapons in 2002.

Signed but not ratified: El Salvador

Treaty for Collaboration in Economic, Social and Cultural Matters and for Collective Self-defence among Western European states (Brussels Treaty)

Signed at Brussels on 17 March 1948; entered into force on 25 August 1948; depositary Belgian Government

The treaty provides for close cooperation of the parties in the military, economic and political fields.

Parties (7): *Original parties:* Belgium, France, Luxembourg, Netherlands, UK

Germany and Italy acceded through the Protocols of 1954.

See also Modified Brussels Treaty and Protocols of 1954.

Convention on the Prevention and Punishment of the Crime of Genocide (Genocide Convention)

Adopted at Paris by the UN General Assembly on 9 December 1948; entered into force on 12 January 1951; depositary UN Secretary-General

Under the convention any commission of acts intended to destroy, in whole or in part, a national, ethnic, racial or religious group as such is declared to be a crime punishable under international law.

Parties (138): Afghanistan, Albania*, Algeria*, Antigua and Barbuda, Argentina*, Armenia, Australia, Austria, Azerbaijan, Bahamas, Bahrain*, Bangladesh*, Barbados, Belarus*, Belgium, Belize, Bolivia, Bosnia and Herzegovina, Brazil, Bulgaria*, Burkina Faso, Burundi, Cambodia, Canada, Chile, China*, Colombia, Comoros, Congo (Democratic Republic of the), Costa Rica, Côte d'Ivoire, Croatia, Cuba, Cyprus, Czech Republic, Denmark, Ecuador, Egypt, El Salvador, Estonia, Ethiopia, Fiji, Finland, France, Gabon, Gambia, Georgia, Germany, Ghana, Greece, Guatemala, Guinea, Haiti, Honduras, Hungary*, Iceland, India*, Iran, Iraq, Ireland, Israel, Italy, Jamaica, Jordan, Kazakhstan, Korea (North), Korea (South), Kuwait, Kyrgyzstan, Laos, Latvia, Lebanon, Lesotho, Liberia, Libya, Liechtenstein, Lithuania, Luxembourg, Macedonia (Former Yugoslav Republic of), Malaysia*, Maldives, Mali, Mexico, Moldova, Monaco, Mongolia*, Morocco*, Mozambique, Myanmar (Burma)*, Namibia, Nepal, Netherlands, New Zealand, Nicaragua, Norway, Pakistan, Panama, Papua New Guinea, Paraguay, Peru, Philippines*, Poland*, Portugal*, Romania*, Russia*, Rwanda*, Saint Vincent and the Grenadines, Saudi Arabia, Senegal, Serbia and Montenegro*, Seychelles, Singapore*, Slovakia, Slovenia, South Africa, Spain*, Sri Lanka, Sudan, Sweden, Switzerland, Syria, Tanzania, Togo, Tonga, Trinidad and Tobago, Tunisia, Turkey, Uganda, UK, Ukraine*, United Arab Emirates, Uruguay, USA*, Uzbekistan, Venezuela*, Viet Nam*, Yemen*, Zimbabwe

* With reservation and/or declaration.

Signed but not ratified: Dominican Republic

Geneva Convention (IV) Relative to the Protection of Civilian Persons in Time of War

Signed at Geneva on 12 August 1949; entered into force on 21 October 1950; depositary Swiss Federal Council

Geneva Convention (IV) establishes rules for the protection of civilians in areas covered by war and on occupied territories. This convention was worked out at the Diplomatic Conference held from 21 April to 12 August 1949. (Other conventions adopted at the same time: Convention (I) for the Amelioration of the Condition of the Wounded and Sick in Armed Forces in the Field; Convention (II) for the Amelioration of the Condition of the Wounded, Sick and Shipwrecked Members of Armed Forces at Sea; and Convention (III) Relative to the Treatment of Prisoners of War.)

Parties (192): Afghanistan, Albania*, Algeria, Andorra, Angola*, Antigua and Barbuda, Argentina, Armenia, Australia*, Austria, Azerbaijan, Bahamas, Bahrain, Bangladesh*, Barbados*, Belarus, Belgium, Belize, Benin, Bhutan, Bolivia, Bosnia and Herzegovina, Botswana, Brazil, Brunei Darussalam, Bulgaria, Burkina Faso, Burundi, Cambodia, Cameroon, Canada, Cape Verde, Central African Republic, Chad, Chile, China*, Colombia, Comoros, Congo (Democratic Republic of the), Congo (Republic of), Cook Islands, Costa Rica, Côte d'Ivoire, Croatia, Cuba, Cyprus, Czech Republic*, Denmark, Djibouti, Dominica, Dominican Republic, Ecuador, Egypt, El Salvador, Equatorial Guinea, Estonia, Eritrea,

Ethiopia, Fiji, Finland, France, Gabon, Gambia, Georgia, Germany*, Ghana, Greece, Grenada, Guatemala, Guinea, Guinea-Bissau*, Guyana, Haiti, Holy See, Honduras, Hungary, Iceland, India, Indonesia, Iran*, Iraq, Ireland, Israel*, Italy, Jamaica, Japan, Jordan, Kazakhstan, Kenya, Kiribati, Korea (North)*, Korea (South)*, Kuwait*, Kyrgyzstan, Laos, Latvia, Lebanon, Lesotho, Liberia, Libya, Liechtenstein, Lithuania, Luxembourg, Macedonia (Former Yugoslav Republic of)*, Madagascar, Malawi, Malaysia, Maldives, Mali, Malta, Marshall Islands, Mauritania, Mauritius, Mexico, Micronesia, Moldova, Monaco, Mongolia, Morocco, Mozambique, Myanmar (Burma), Namibia, Nepal, Netherlands, New Zealand*, Nicaragua, Niger, Nigeria, Norway, Oman, Pakistan*, Palau, Panama, Papua New Guinea, Paraguay, Peru, Philippines, Poland, Portugal*, Qatar, Romania, Russia*, Rwanda, Saint Kitts and Nevis, Saint Lucia, Saint Vincent and the Grenadines, Samoa, San Marino, Sao Tome and Principe, Saudi Arabia, Senegal, Serbia and Montenegro, Seychelles, Sierra Leone, Singapore, Slovakia, Slovenia, Solomon Islands, Somalia, South Africa, Spain, Sri Lanka, Sudan, Suriname*, Swaziland, Sweden, Switzerland, Syria, Tajikistan, Tanzania, Thailand, Timor-Leste, Togo, Tonga, Trinidad and Tobago, Tunisia, Turkey, Turkmenistan, Tuvalu, Uganda, UK*, Ukraine*, United Arab Emirates, Uruguay*, USA*, Uzbekistan, Vanuatu, Venezuela, Viet Nam*, Yemen*, Zambia, Zimbabwe

* With reservation and/or declaration.

In 1989 the Palestine Liberation Organization (PLO) informed the depositary that it had decided to adhere to the four Geneva Conventions and the two Protocols of 1977.

See also Protocols I and II of 1977.

Treaty of Economic, Social and Cultural Collaboration and Collective Self-defence among Western European States (Modified Brussels Treaty); Protocols to the 1948 Brussels Treaty (Paris Agreements)

Signed at Paris on 23 October 1954; entered into force on 6 May 1955; depositary Belgian Government

The 1948 Brussels Treaty was modified by four protocols which amended the original text to take account of political and military developments in Europe, allowing the Federal Republic of Germany (West Germany) and Italy to become parties in return for controls over German armaments and force levels (annulled, except for weapons of mass destruction, in 1984). The Western European Union (WEU) was created through the Modified Brussels Treaty. The treaty contains an obligation for collective defence of its members.

Members of the WEU: Belgium, France, Germany, Greece, Italy, Luxembourg, Netherlands, Portugal, Spain, UK

Antarctic Treaty

Signed at Washington, DC, on 1 December 1959; entered into force on 23 June 1961; depositary US Government

Declares the Antarctic an area to be used exclusively for peaceful purposes. Prohibits any measure of a military nature in the Antarctic, such as the establishment of military bases and fortifications, and the carrying out of military manoeuvres or the testing of any type of weapon. The treaty bans any nuclear explosion as well as the disposal of radioactive waste material in Antarctica.

In accordance with Article IX, consultative meetings are convened at regular intervals to exchange information and hold consultations on matters pertaining to Antarctica, as well as to recommend to the governments measures in furtherance of the principles and objectives of the treaty.

The treaty is subject to ratification by the signatories and is open for accession by UN members or by other states invited to accede with the consent of all the parties entitled to participate in the consultative meetings provided for in Article IX.

Parties (45): Argentina[†], Australia[†], Austria, Belgium[†], Brazil[†], Bulgaria[†], Canada, Chile[†], China[†], Colombia, Cuba, Czech Republic, Denmark, Ecuador[†], Estonia, Finland[†], France[†], Germany[†], Greece, Guatemala, Hungary, India[†], Italy[†], Japan[†], Korea (North), Korea (South)[†], Netherlands[†], New Zealand[†], Norway[†], Papua New Guinea, Peru[†], Poland[†], Romania, Russia[†], Slovakia, South Africa[†], Spain[†], Sweden[†], Switzerland, Turkey, UK[†], Ukraine[†], Uruguay[†], USA[†], Venezuela

[†] Consultative members under Article IX of the treaty.

The Protocol on Environmental Protection to the Antarctic Treaty (**1991 Madrid Protocol**) entered into force on 14 January 1998.

Treaty Banning Nuclear Weapon Tests in the Atmosphere, in Outer Space and Under Water (Partial Test-Ban Treaty, PTBT)

Signed at Moscow by three original parties on 5 August 1963 and opened for signature by other states at London, Moscow and Washington, DC, on 8 August 1963; entered into force on 10 October 1963; depositaries British, US and Russian governments

The treaty prohibits the carrying out of any nuclear weapon test explosion or any other nuclear explosion: (*a*) in the atmosphere, beyond its limits, including outer space, or under water, including territorial waters or high seas; and (*b*) in any other environment if such explosion causes radioactive debris to be present outside the territorial limits of the state under whose jurisdiction or control the explosion is conducted.

Parties (125): Afghanistan, Antigua and Barbuda, Argentina, Armenia, Australia, Austria, Bahamas, Bangladesh, Belarus, Belgium, Benin, Bhutan, Bolivia, Bosnia and Herzegovina, Botswana, Brazil, Bulgaria, Canada, Cape Verde, Central African Republic, Chad, Chile, Colombia, Congo (Democratic Republic of the), Costa Rica, Côte d'Ivoire, Croatia, Cyprus, Czech Republic, Denmark, Dominican Republic, Ecuador, Egypt, El Salvador, Equatorial Guinea, Fiji, Finland, Gabon, Gambia, Germany, Ghana, Greece, Guatemala, Guinea-Bissau, Honduras, Hungary, Iceland, India, Indonesia, Iran, Iraq, Ireland, Israel, Italy, Jamaica, Japan, Jordan, Kenya, Korea (South), Kuwait, Laos, Lebanon, Liberia, Libya, Luxembourg, Madagascar, Malawi, Malaysia, Malta, Mauritania, Mauritius, Mexico, Mongolia, Morocco, Myanmar (Burma), Nepal, Netherlands, New Zealand, Nicaragua, Niger, Nigeria, Norway, Pakistan, Panama, Papua New Guinea, Peru, Philippines, Poland, Romania, Russia, Rwanda, Samoa (Western), San Marino, Senegal, Serbia and Montenegro, Seychelles, Sierra Leone, Singapore, Slovakia, Slovenia, South Africa, Spain, Sri Lanka, Sudan, Suriname, Swaziland, Sweden, Switzerland, Syria, Taiwan, Tanzania, Thailand, Togo, Tonga, Trinidad and Tobago, Tunisia, Turkey, Uganda, UK, Ukraine, Uruguay, USA, Venezuela, Yemen, Zambia

Signed but not ratified: Algeria, Burkina Faso, Burundi, Cameroon, Ethiopia, Haiti, Mali, Paraguay, Portugal, Somalia, Viet Nam

Treaty on Principles Governing the Activities of States in the Exploration and Use of Outer Space, Including the Moon and Other Celestial Bodies (Outer Space Treaty)

Opened for signature at London, Moscow and Washington, DC, on 27 January 1967; entered into force on 10 October 1967; depositaries British, Russian and US governments

The treaty prohibits the placing into orbit around the earth of any objects carrying nuclear weapons or any other kinds of weapons of mass destruction, the installation of such weapons on celestial bodies, or the stationing of them in outer space in any other manner. The establishment of military bases, installations and fortifications, the testing of any type of weapons and the conduct of military manoeuvres on celestial bodies are also forbidden.

Parties (106): Afghanistan, Algeria, Antigua and Barbuda, Argentina, Australia, Austria, Bahamas, Bangladesh, Barbados, Belarus, Belgium, Benin, Brazil, Brunei Darussalam, Bulgaria, Burkina Faso, Canada, Chile, China, Cuba, Cyprus, Czech Republic, Denmark, Dominica, Dominican Republic, Ecuador, Egypt, El Salvador, Equatorial Guinea, Fiji, Finland, France, Germany, Greece, Grenada, Guinea-Bissau, Hungary, Iceland, India, Indonesia, Iraq, Ireland, Israel, Italy, Jamaica, Japan, Kazakhstan, Kenya, Korea (South), Kuwait, Laos, Lebanon, Libya, Madagascar, Mali, Mauritius, Mexico, Mongolia, Morocco, Myanmar (Burma), Nepal, Netherlands, New Zealand, Niger, Nigeria, Norway, Pakistan, Papua New Guinea, Peru, Poland, Portugal, Romania, Russia, Saint Kitts and Nevis, Saint Lucia, Saint Vincent and the Grenadines, San Marino, Saudi Arabia, Seychelles, Sierra Leone, Singapore, Slovakia, Solomon Islands, South Africa, Spain, Sri Lanka, Swaziland, Sweden, Switzerland, Syria, Taiwan, Thailand, Togo, Tonga, Tunisia, Turkey, Uganda, UK, Ukraine, United Arab Emirates, Uruguay, USA, Venezuela, Viet Nam, Yemen, Zambia

Signed but not ratified: Bolivia, Botswana, Burundi, Cameroon, Central African Republic, Colombia, Congo (Democratic Republic of the), Congo (Republic of), Ethiopia, Gambia, Ghana, Guyana, Haiti, Holy See, Honduras, Iran, Jordan, Lesotho, Luxembourg, Macedonia (Former Yugoslav Republic of), Malaysia, Nicaragua, Panama, Philippines, Rwanda, Serbia and Montenegro, Somalia, Trinidad and Tobago

Treaty for the Prohibition of Nuclear Weapons in Latin America and the Caribbean (Treaty of Tlatelolco)

Original treaty opened for signature at Mexico, Distrito Federal, on 14 February 1967; entered into force on 22 April 1968. The treaty was amended in 1990, 1991 and 1992; depositary Mexican Government

The treaty prohibits the testing, use, manufacture, production or acquisition by any means, as well as the receipt, storage, installation, deployment and any form of possession of any nuclear weapons by Latin American and Caribbean countries.

The parties should conclude agreements with the IAEA for the application of safeguards to their nuclear activities. The IAEA has the exclusive power to carry out special inspections.

The treaty is open for signature by all the independent states of the region.

Under *Additional Protocol I* states with territories within the zone (France, the Netherlands, the UK and the USA) undertake to apply the statute of military denuclearization to these territories.

Under *Additional Protocol II* the recognized nuclear weapon states—China, France, Russia (at the time of signing, the USSR), the UK and the USA—undertake to respect the statute of military denuclearization of Latin America and not to contribute to acts involving a violation of the treaty, nor to use or threaten to use nuclear weapons against the parties to the treaty.

Parties to the original treaty (33): Antigua and Barbuda, Argentina, Bahamas, Barbados, Belize, Bolivia, Brazil, Chile, Colombia, Costa Rica, Cuba, Dominica, Dominican Republic, Ecuador, El Salvador, Grenada, Guatemala, Guyana, Haiti, Honduras, Jamaica, Mexico, Nicaragua, Panama, Paraguay, Peru, Saint Kitts and Nevis, Saint Lucia, Saint Vincent and the Grenadines, Suriname, Trinidad and Tobago, Uruguay, Venezuela

Amendments ratified by: Argentina, Barbados, Belize, Brazil, Chile, Colombia, Costa Rica, Cuba, Dominican Republic, Ecuador, El Salvador, Grenada, Guatemala, Guyana, Jamaica, Mexico, Panama, Paraguay, Peru, Suriname, Uruguay, Venezuela

Note: Not all the countries listed had ratified all three amendments by 1 Mar. 2006.

Parties to Additional Protocol I: France[1], Netherlands, UK[2], USA[3]

Parties to Additional Protocol II: China[4], France[5], Russia[6], UK[2], USA[7]

[1] France declared that Protocol I shall not apply to transit across French territories situated within the zone of the treaty, and destined for other French territories. The protocol shall not limit the participation of the populations of the French territories in the activities mentioned in Article 1 of the treaty, and in efforts connected with the national defence of France. France does not consider the zone described in the treaty as established in accordance with international law; it cannot, therefore, agree that the treaty should apply to that zone.

[2] When signing and ratifying Protocols I and II, the UK made the following declarations of understanding: The signing and ratification by the UK could not be regarded as affecting in any way the legal status of any territory for the international relations of which the UK is responsible, lying within the limits of the geographical zone established by the treaty. Should any party to the treaty carry out any act of aggression with the support of a nuclear weapon state, the UK would be free to reconsider the extent to which it could be regarded as bound by the provisions of Protocol II.

[3] The USA ratified Protocol I with the following understandings: The provisions of the treaty do not affect the exclusive power and legal competence under international law of a state adhering to this Protocol to grant or deny transit and transport privileges to its own or any other vessels or aircraft irrespective of cargo or armaments; the provisions do not affect rights under international law of a state adhering to this protocol regarding the exercise of the freedom of the seas, or regarding passage through or over waters subject to the sovereignty of a state. The declarations attached by the USA to its ratification of Protocol II apply also to Protocol I.

[4] China declared that it will never send its means of transportation and delivery carrying nuclear weapons to cross the territory, territorial sea or airspace of Latin American countries.

[5] France stated that it interprets the undertaking contained in Article 3 of Protocol II to mean that it presents no obstacle to the full exercise of the right of self-defence enshrined in Article 51 of the UN Charter; it takes note of the interpretation by the Preparatory Commission for the Denuclearization of Latin America according to which the treaty does not apply to transit, the granting or denying of which lies within the exclusive competence of each state party in accordance with international law. In 1974, France made a supplementary statement to the effect that it was prepared to consider its obligations under Protocol II as applying not only to the signatories of the treaty, but also to the territories for which the statute of denuclearization was in force in conformity with Protocol I.

[6] On signing and ratifying Protocol II, the USSR stated that it assumed that the effect of Article 1 of the treaty extends to any nuclear explosive device and that, accordingly, the carrying out by any party of nuclear explosions for peaceful purposes would be a violation of its obligations under Article 1 and would be incompatible with its non-nuclear weapon status. For states parties to the treaty, a solution to the problem of peaceful nuclear explosions can be found in accordance with the provisions of Article V of the NPT and within the framework of the international procedures of the IAEA. It declared that authorizing the transit of nuclear weapons in any form would be contrary to the objectives of the treaty.

Any actions undertaken by a state or states parties to the treaty which are not compatible with their non-nuclear weapon status, and also the commission by one or more states parties to the treaty of an act of aggression with the support of a state which is in possession of nuclear weapons or together with such a state, will be regarded by the USSR as incompatible with the obligations of those countries under the treaty. In such cases it would reserve the right to reconsider its obligations under Protocol II. It further reserves the right to reconsider its attitude to this protocol in the event of any actions on the part of other states possessing nuclear weapons which are incompatible with their obligations under the said protocol.

[7] The USA signed and ratified Protocol II with the following declarations and understandings: Each of the parties retains exclusive power and legal competence, to grant or deny non-parties transit and transport privileges. As regards the undertaking not to use or threaten to use nuclear weapons against the parties, the USA would consider that an armed attack by a party, in which it was assisted by a nuclear weapon state, would be incompatible with the treaty.

Treaty on the Non-proliferation of Nuclear Weapons (Non-Proliferation Treaty, NPT)

Opened for signature at London, Moscow and Washington, DC, on 1 July 1968; entered into force on 5 March 1970; depositaries British, Russian and US governments

The treaty prohibits the transfer by nuclear weapon states (defined in the treaty as those which have manufactured and exploded a nuclear weapon or other nuclear explosive device prior to 1 January 1967) to any recipient whatsoever, of nuclear weapons or other nuclear explosive devices or of control over them, as well as the assistance, encouragement or inducement of any non-nuclear weapon state to manufacture or otherwise acquire such weapons or devices. It also prohibits the receipt by non-nuclear weapon states from any transferor whatsoever, as well as the manufacture or other acquisition by those states, of nuclear weapons or other nuclear explosive devices.

The parties undertake to facilitate the exchange of equipment, materials and scientific and technological information for the peaceful uses of nuclear energy and to ensure that potential benefits from peaceful applications of nuclear explosions will be made available to non-nuclear weapon parties to the treaty. They also undertake to pursue negotiations in good faith on effective measures relating to cessation of the nuclear arms race at an early date and to nuclear disarmament, and on a treaty on general and complete disarmament.

Non-nuclear weapon states undertake to conclude safeguard agreements with the International Atomic Energy Agency (IAEA) with a view to preventing diversion of nuclear energy from peaceful uses to nuclear weapons or other nuclear explosive devices. A Model Protocol Additional to the Safeguards Agreements, strengthening the measures, was approved in 1997; such Additional Safeguards Protocols are signed by states individually with the IAEA.

A Review and Extension Conference, convened in 1995 in accordance with the treaty, decided that the treaty should remain in force indefinitely.

Parties (189): Afghanistan[†], Albania[†], Algeria[†], Andorra, Angola, Antigua and Barbuda[†], Argentina[†], Armenia[†], Australia[†], Austria[†], Azerbaijan[†], Bahamas[†], Bahrain, Bangladesh[†], Barbados[†], Belarus[†], Belgium[†], Belize[†], Benin, Bhutan[†], Bolivia[†], Bosnia and Herzegovina[†], Botswana, Brazil[†], Brunei Darussalam[†], Bulgaria[†], Burkina Faso[†], Burundi, Cambodia[†], Cameroon[†], Canada[†], Cape Verde, Central African Republic, Chad, Chile[†], China[†], Colombia, Comoros, Congo (Democratic Republic of the)[†], Congo (Republic of), Costa Rica[†], Côte d'Ivoire[†], Croatia[†], Cuba[†], Cyprus[†], Czech Republic[†], Denmark[†], Djibouti, Dominica[†], Dominican Republic[†], Ecuador[†], Egypt[†], El Salvador[†], Equatorial Guinea, Eritrea, Estonia[†], Ethiopia[†], Fiji[†], Finland[†], France[†], Gabon, Gambia[†], Georgia, Germany[†], Ghana[†], Greece[†], Grenada[†], Guatemala[†], Guinea, Guinea-Bissau, Guyana[†], Haiti, Holy See[†], Honduras[†], Hungary[†], Iceland[†], Indonesia[†], Iran[†], Iraq[†], Ireland[†], Italy[†], Jamaica[†], Japan[†],

Jordan[†], Kazakhstan[†], Kenya, Kiribati[†], Korea (South)[†], Kuwait[†], Kyrgyzstan[†], Laos[†], Latvia[†], Lebanon[†], Lesotho[†], Liberia, Libya[†], Liechtenstein[†], Lithuania[†], Luxembourg[†], Macedonia[†] (Former Yugoslav Republic of), Madagascar[†], Malawi[†], Malaysia[†], Maldives[†], Mali[†], Malta[†], Marshall Islands, Mauritania, Mauritius[†], Mexico[†], Micronesia, Moldova, Monaco[†], Mongolia[†], Morocco[†], Mozambique, Myanmar (Burma)[†], Namibia[†], Nauru[†], Nepal[†], Netherlands[†], New Zealand[†], Nicaragua[†], Niger, Nigeria[†], Norway[†], Oman, Palau, Panama, Papua New Guinea[†], Paraguay[†], Peru[†], Philippines[†], Poland[†], Portugal[†], Qatar, Romania[†], Russia[†], Rwanda, Saint Kitts and Nevis[†], Saint Lucia[†], Saint Vincent and the Grenadines[†], Samoa[†], San Marino[†], Sao Tome and Principe, Saudi Arabia, Senegal[†], Serbia and Montenegro[†], Seychelles[†], Sierra Leone, Singapore[†], Slovakia[†], Slovenia[†], Solomon Islands[†], Somalia, South Africa[†], Spain[†], Sri Lanka[†], Sudan[†], Suriname[†], Swaziland[†], Sweden[†], Switzerland[†], Syria[†], Taiwan, Tajikistan[†], Tanzania[†], Thailand[†], Togo, Timor-Leste, Tonga[†], Trinidad and Tobago[†], Tunisia[†], Turkey[†], Turkmenistan, Tuvalu[†], Uganda, UK[†], Ukraine[†], United Arab Emirates[†], Uruguay[†], USA[†], Uzbekistan[†], Vanuatu, Venezuela[†], Viet Nam[†], Yemen[†], Zambia[†], Zimbabwe[†]

[†] Party with safeguards agreements in force with the International Atomic Energy Agency (IAEA), as required by the treaty, or concluded by a nuclear weapon state on a voluntary basis.

75 Additional Safeguards Protocols in force: Afghanistan, Armenia, Australia, Austria, Azerbaijan, Bangladesh, Belgium, Bulgaria, Burkina Faso, Canada, Chile, China, Congo (Democratic Republic of the), Croatia, Cuba, Cyprus, Czech Republic, Denmark, Ecuador, El Salvador, Estonia, Finland, France, Georgia, Germany, Ghana, Greece, Haiti, Holy See, Hungary, Iceland, Indonesia, Ireland, Italy, Jamaica, Japan, Jordan, Korea (South), Kuwait, Latvia, Lithuania, Luxembourg, Madagascar, Mali, Malta, Marshall Islands, Monaco, Mongolia, Netherlands, New Zealand, Nicaragua, Norway, Palau, Panama, Paraguay, Peru, Poland, Portugal, Romania, Seychelles, Slovakia, Slovenia, South Africa, Spain, Sweden, Switzerland, Tajikistan, Tanzania, Turkey, Turkmenistan, Uganda, UK, Ukraine, Uruguay, Uzbekistan

Note: Iran and Libya have pledged to apply their Additional Safeguards Protocols pending their entry into force. Taiwan, although it has not concluded a safeguards agreement, has agreed to apply the measures contained in the 1997 Model Additional Safeguards Protocol.

Treaty on the Prohibition of the Emplacement of Nuclear Weapons and other Weapons of Mass Destruction on the Seabed and the Ocean Floor and in the Subsoil thereof (Seabed Treaty)

Opened for signature at London, Moscow and Washington, DC, on 11 February 1971; entered into force on 18 May 1972; depositaries British, Russian and US governments

The treaty prohibits implanting or emplacing on the seabed and the ocean floor and in the subsoil thereof beyond the outer limit of a 12-mile seabed zone any nuclear weapons or any other types of weapons of mass destruction as well as structures, launching installations or any other facilities specifically designed for storing, testing or using such weapons.

Parties (94): Afghanistan, Algeria, Antigua and Barbuda, Argentina[1], Australia, Austria, Bahamas, Belarus, Belgium, Benin, Bosnia and Herzegovina, Botswana, Brazil[2], Bulgaria, Canada[3], Cape Verde, Central African Republic, China, Congo (Republic of), Côte d'Ivoire, Croatia, Cuba, Cyprus, Czech Republic, Denmark, Dominican Republic, Ethiopia, Finland, Germany, Ghana, Greece, Guatemala, Guinea-Bissau, Hungary, Iceland, India[4], Iran, Iraq, Ireland, Italy[5], Jamaica, Japan, Jordan, Korea (South), Laos, Latvia, Lesotho, Libya, Liechtenstein, Luxembourg, Malaysia, Malta, Mauritius, Mexico[6], Mongolia, Morocco, Nepal,

Netherlands, New Zealand, Nicaragua, Niger, Norway, Panama, Philippines, Poland, Portugal, Qatar, Romania, Russia, Rwanda, Saint Vincent and the Grenadines, Sao Tome and Principe, Saudi Arabia, Serbia and Montenegro[7], Seychelles, Singapore, Slovakia, Slovenia, Solomon Islands, South Africa, Spain, Swaziland, Sweden, Switzerland, Taiwan, Togo, Tunisia, Turkey[8], UK, Ukraine, USA, Viet Nam[9], Yemen, Zambia

[1] Argentina precludes any possibility of strengthening, through this treaty, certain positions concerning continental shelves to the detriment of others based on different criteria.

[2] Brazil stated that nothing in the treaty shall be interpreted as prejudicing in any way the sovereign rights of Brazil in the area of the sea, the seabed and the subsoil thereof adjacent to its coasts. It is the understanding of Brazil that the word 'observation', as it appears in para. 1 of Article III of the treaty, refers only to observation that is incidental to the normal course of navigation in accordance with international law.

[3] Canada declared that Article I, para. 1, cannot be interpreted as indicating that any state has a right to implant or emplace any weapons not prohibited under Article I, para. 1, on the seabed and ocean floor, and in the subsoil thereof, beyond the limits of national jurisdiction, or as constituting any limitation on the principle that this area of the seabed and ocean floor and the subsoil thereof shall be reserved for exclusively peaceful purposes. Articles I, II and III cannot be interpreted as indicating that any state but the coastal state has any right to implant or emplace any weapon not prohibited under Article I, para. 1 on the continental shelf, or the subsoil thereof, appertaining to that coastal state, beyond the outer limit of the seabed zone referred to in Article I and defined in Article II. Article III cannot be interpreted as indicating any restrictions or limitation upon the rights of the coastal state, consistent with its exclusive sovereign rights with respect to the continental shelf, to verify, inspect or effect the removal of any weapon, structure, installation, facility or device implanted or emplaced on the continental shelf, or the subsoil thereof, appertaining to that coastal state, beyond the outer limit of the seabed zone referred to in Article I and defined in Article II.

[4] The accession by India is based on its position that it has full and exclusive rights over the continental shelf adjoining its territory and beyond its territorial waters and the subsoil thereof. There cannot, therefore, be any restriction on, or limitation of, the sovereign right of India as a coastal state to verify, inspect, remove or destroy any weapon, device, structure, installation or facility, which might be implanted or emplaced on or beneath its continental shelf by any other country, or to take such other steps as may be considered necessary to safeguard its security.

[5] Italy stated, *inter alia*, that in the case of agreements on further measures in the field of disarmament to prevent an arms race on the seabed and ocean floor and in their subsoil, the question of the delimitation of the area within which these measures would find application shall have to be examined and solved in each instance in accordance with the nature of the measures to be adopted.

[6] Mexico declared that the treaty cannot be interpreted to mean that a state has the right to emplace weapons of mass destruction, or arms or military equipment of any type, on the continental shelf of Mexico. It reserves the right to verify, inspect, remove or destroy any weapon, structure, installation, device or equipment placed on its continental shelf, including nuclear weapons or other weapons of mass destruction.

[7] In 1974, the Ambassador of Yugoslavia transmitted to the US Secretary of State a note stating that in the view of the Yugoslav Government, Article III, para. 1, of the treaty should be interpreted in such a way that a state exercising its right under this article shall be obliged to notify in advance the coastal state, in so far as its observations are to be carried out 'within the stretch of the sea extending above the continental shelf of the said state'. The USA objected to the Yugoslav reservation, which it considered incompatible with the object and purpose of the treaty.

[8] Turkey declared that the provisions of Article II cannot be used by a state party in support of claims other than those related to disarmament. Hence, Article II cannot be interpreted as establishing a link with the UN Convention on the Law of the Sea. Furthermore, no provision of the Seabed Treaty confers on parties the right to militarize zones which have been demilitarized by other international instruments. Nor can it be interpreted as conferring on either the coastal states or other states the right to emplace nuclear weapons or other weapons of mass destruction on the continental shelf of a demilitarized territory.

[9] Viet Nam stated that no provision of the treaty should be interpreted in a way that would contradict the rights of the coastal states with regard to their continental shelf, including the right to take measures to ensure their security.

Signed but not ratified: Bolivia, Burundi, Cambodia, Cameroon, Colombia, Costa Rica, Equatorial Guinea, Gambia, Guinea, Honduras, Lebanon, Liberia, Madagascar, Mali, Myanmar (Burma), Paraguay, Senegal, Sierra Leone, Sudan, Tanzania, Uruguay

Convention on the Prohibition of the Development, Production and Stockpiling of Bacteriological (Biological) and Toxin Weapons and on their Destruction (Biological and Toxin Weapons Convention, BTWC)

Opened for signature at London, Moscow and Washington, DC, on 10 April 1972; entered into force on 26 March 1975; depositaries British, Russian and US governments

The convention prohibits the development, production, stockpiling or acquisition by other means or retention of microbial or other biological agents, or toxins whatever their origin or method of production, of types and in quantities that have no justification of prophylactic, protective or other peaceful purposes, as well as weapons, equipment or means of delivery designed to use such agents or toxins for hostile purposes or in armed conflict. The destruction of the agents, toxins, weapons, equipment and means of delivery in the possession of the parties, or their diversion to peaceful purposes, should be effected not later than nine months after the entry into force of the convention for each country. According to a mandate from the 1996 BTWC Review Conference, verification and other measures to strengthen the convention are being discussed and considered in an Ad Hoc Group.

Parties (155): Afghanistan, Albania, Algeria, Antigua and Barbuda, Argentina, Armenia, Australia, Austria, Azerbaijan, Bahamas, Bahrain, Bangladesh, Barbados, Belarus, Belgium, Belize, Benin, Bhutan, Bolivia, Bosnia and Herzegovina, Botswana, Brazil, Brunei Darussalam, Bulgaria, Burkina Faso, Cambodia, Canada, Cape Verde, Chile, China, Colombia, Congo (Democratic Republic of the), Congo (Republic of), Costa Rica, Croatia, Cuba, Cyprus, Czech Republic, Denmark, Dominica, Dominican Republic, Ecuador, El Salvador, Equatorial Guinea, Estonia, Ethiopia, Fiji, Finland, France, Gambia, Georgia, Germany, Ghana, Greece, Grenada, Guatemala, Guinea-Bissau, Holy See, Honduras, Hungary, Iceland, India, Indonesia, Iran, Iraq, Ireland, Italy, Jamaica, Japan, Jordan, Kenya, Korea (North), Korea (South), Kuwait, Kyrgyzstan, Laos, Latvia, Lebanon, Lesotho, Libya, Liechtenstein, Lithuania, Luxembourg, Macedonia (Former Yugoslav Republic of), Malaysia, Maldives, Mali, Malta, Mauritius, Mexico, Moldova, Monaco, Mongolia, Morocco, Netherlands, New Zealand, Nicaragua, Niger, Nigeria, Norway, Oman, Pakistan, Palau, Panama, Papua New Guinea, Paraguay, Peru, Philippines, Poland, Portugal, Qatar, Romania, Russia, Rwanda, Saint Kitts and Nevis, Saint Lucia, Saint Vincent and the Grenadines, San Marino, Sao Tome and Principe, Saudi Arabia, Senegal, Serbia and Montenegro, Seychelles, Sierra Leone, Singapore, Slovakia, Slovenia, Solomon Islands, South Africa, Spain, Sri Lanka, Sudan, Suriname, Swaziland, Sweden, Switzerland*, Taiwan, Thailand, Timor-Leste, Togo, Tonga, Tunisia, Turkey, Turkmenistan, Uganda, UK, Ukraine, Uruguay, USA, Uzbekistan, Vanuatu, Venezuela, Viet Nam, Yemen, Zimbabwe

* With reservation.

Signed but not ratified: Burundi, Central African Republic, Côte d'Ivoire, Egypt, Gabon, Guyana, Haiti, Liberia, Madagascar, Malawi, Myanmar (Burma), Nepal, Somalia, Syria, Tanzania, United Arab Emirates

Treaty on the Limitation of Anti-Ballistic Missile Systems (ABM Treaty)

Signed by the USA and the USSR at Moscow on 26 May 1972; entered into force on 3 October 1972; no longer in force as of 13 June 2002

The parties undertook not to build nationwide defences against ballistic missile attack and limited the development and deployment of permitted strategic missile defences. The treaty prohibited the parties from giving air defence missiles, radars or launchers the technical ability to counter strategic ballistic missiles and from testing them in a strategic ABM mode.

The **1974 Protocol** to the ABM Treaty introduced further numerical restrictions on permitted ballistic missile defences.

In 1997 Russia and the USA signed a set of Agreed Statements, specifying the demarcation line between strategic missile defences, which are not permitted under the treaty, and non-strategic or theatre missile defences (TMD), which are permitted under the treaty. The set of 1997 agreements on anti-missile defence were ratified by Russia in April 2000, but because the USA did not ratify them they did not enter into force. On 13 December 2001 the USA announced its withdrawal from the ABM Treaty, which entered into effect on 13 June 2002.

Treaty on the Limitation of Underground Nuclear Weapon Tests (Threshold Test Ban Treaty, TTBT)

Signed by the USA and the USSR at Moscow on 3 July 1974; entered into force on 11 December 1990

The parties undertake not to carry out any underground nuclear weapon test having a yield exceeding 150 kilotons.

Treaty on Underground Nuclear Explosions for Peaceful Purposes (Peaceful Nuclear Explosions Treaty, PNET)

Signed by the USA and the USSR at Moscow and Washington, DC, on 28 May 1976; entered into force on 11 December 1990

The parties undertake not to carry out any underground nuclear explosion for peaceful purposes having a yield exceeding 150 kilotons or any group explosion having an aggregate yield exceeding 150 kilotons.

Convention on the Prohibition of Military or Any Other Hostile Use of Environmental Modification Techniques (Enmod Convention)

Opened for signature at Geneva on 18 May 1977; entered into force on 5 October 1978; depositary UN Secretary-General

The convention prohibits military or any other hostile use of environmental modification techniques having widespread, long-lasting or severe effects as the means of destruction, damage or injury to states party to the convention. The term 'environmental modification techniques' refers to any technique for changing—through the deliberate manipulation of natural processes—the dynamics, composition or structure of the earth, including its biota, lithosphere, hydrosphere and atmosphere, or of outer space. The understandings reached during the negotiations, but not written into the convention, define the terms 'widespread', 'long-lasting' and 'severe'.

Parties (72): Afghanistan, Algeria, Antigua and Barbuda, Argentina, Armenia, Australia, Austria, Bangladesh, Belarus, Belgium, Benin, Brazil, Bulgaria, Canada, Cape Verde, Chile, China*, Costa Rica, Cuba, Cyprus, Czech Republic, Denmark, Dominica, Egypt, Finland, Germany, Ghana, Greece, Guatemala, Hungary, India, Ireland, Italy, Japan, Kazakhstan, Korea (North), Korea (South)*, Kuwait, Lithuania, Laos, Malawi, Mauritius, Mongolia, Netherlands*, New Zealand, Niger, Norway, Pakistan, Panama, Papua New Guinea, Poland,

Romania, Russia, Saint Lucia, Saint Vincent and the Grenadines, Sao Tome and Principe, Slovakia, Slovenia, Solomon Islands, Spain, Sri Lanka, Sweden, Switzerland, Tajikistan, Tunisia, UK, Ukraine, Uruguay, USA, Uzbekistan, Viet Nam, Yemen

* With declaration.

Signed but not ratified: Bolivia, Congo (Democratic Republic of the), Ethiopia, Holy See, Iceland, Iran, Iraq, Lebanon, Liberia, Luxembourg, Morocco, Nicaragua, Portugal, Sierra Leone, Syria, Turkey, Uganda

Protocol I Additional to the 1949 Geneva Conventions, and Relating to the Protection of Victims of International Armed Conflicts
Protocol II Additional to the 1949 Geneva Conventions, and Relating to the Protection of Victims of Non-International Armed Conflicts

Opened for signature at Bern on 12 December 1977; entered into force on 7 December 1978; depositary Swiss Federal Council

The protocols confirm that the right of the parties to international or non-international armed conflicts to choose methods or means of warfare is not unlimited and that it is prohibited to use weapons or means of warfare which cause superfluous injury or unnecessary suffering.

Parties to Protocol I (163) and Protocol II (159): Albania, Algeria*, Angola[1]*, Antigua and Barbuda, Argentina*, Armenia, Australia*, Austria*, Bahamas, Bahrain, Bangladesh, Barbados, Belarus, Belgium*, Belize, Benin, Bolivia, Bosnia and Herzegovina, Botswana, Brazil, Brunei Darussalam, Bulgaria, Burkina Faso, Burundi, Cambodia, Cameroon, Canada*, Cape Verde, Central African Republic, Chad, Chile, China*, Colombia, Comoros, Congo (Democratic Republic of the), Congo (Republic of), Cook Islands, Costa Rica, Côte d'Ivoire, Croatia, Cuba, Cyprus, Czech Republic, Denmark*, Djibouti, Dominica, Dominican Republic, Ecuador, Egypt*, El Salvador, Equatorial Guinea, Estonia, Ethiopia, Finland*, France*, Gabon, Gambia, Georgia, Germany*, Ghana, Greece, Grenada, Guatemala, Guinea, Guinea-Bissau, Guyana, Holy See, Honduras, Hungary, Iceland*, Ireland, Italy*, Jamaica, Japan*, Jordan, Kazakhstan, Kenya, Korea (North)[1], Korea (South)*, Kuwait, Kyrgyzstan, Laos, Latvia, Lebanon, Lesotho, Liberia, Libya, Liechtenstein*, Lithuania, Luxembourg, Macedonia (Former Yugoslav Republic of), Madagascar, Malawi, Maldives, Mali, Malta*, Mauritania, Mauritius, Mexico[1], Micronesia, Moldova, Monaco, Mongolia, Mozambique, Namibia, Netherlands*, New Zealand*, Nicaragua, Niger, Nigeria, Norway, Oman, Palau, Panama, Paraguay, Peru, Philippines[2], Poland, Portugal, Qatar*, Romania, Russia*, Rwanda, Saint Kitts and Nevis, Saint Lucia, Saint Vincent and the Grenadines, Samoa (Western), San Marino, Sao Tome and Principe, Saudi Arabia*, Senegal, Serbia and Montenegro*, Seychelles, Sierra Leone, Slovakia, Slovenia, Solomon Islands, South Africa, Spain*, Suriname, Swaziland, Sweden*, Switzerland*, Syria*[1], Tajikistan, Tanzania, Timor-Leste, Togo, Tonga, Trinidad and Tobago*, Tunisia, Turkmenistan, Uganda, UK, Ukraine, United Arab Emirates*, Uruguay, Uzbekistan, Vanuatu, Venezuela, Viet Nam[1], Yemen, Zambia, Zimbabwe

* With reservation and/or declaration.

[1] Party only to Protocol I.
[2] Party only to Protocol II.

In 1989 the Palestine Liberation Organization (PLO) informed the depositary that it had decided to adhere to the four Geneva Conventions and the two Protocols.

Convention on the Physical Protection of Nuclear Material

Opened for signature at Vienna and New York on 3 March 1980; entered into force on 8 February 1987; depositary IAEA Director General

The convention obligates the parties to protect nuclear material for peaceful purposes while in international transport.

Parties (116): Afghanistan, Albania, Algeria*, Antigua and Barbuda, Argentina*, Armenia, Australia, Austria*, Azerbaijan*, Bangladesh, Belarus, Belgium*, Bolivia, Bosnia and Herzegovina, Botswana, Brazil, Bulgaria, Burkina Faso, Cameroon, Canada, Chile, China*, Colombia, Congo (Democratic Republic of the), Costa Rica, Croatia, Cuba*, Cyprus*, Czech Republic, Denmark, Djibouti, Dominica, Ecuador, Equatorial Guinea, Estonia, Euratom*, Finland*, France*, Germany, Ghana, Greece*, Grenada, Guatemala*, Guinea, Honduras, Hungary, Iceland, India*, Indonesia*, Ireland*, Israel*, Italy*, Jamaica, Japan, Kazakhstan, Kenya, Korea (South)*, Kuwait*, Latvia, Lebanon, Liechtenstein, Libya, Lithuania, Luxembourg*, Macedonia (Former Yugoslav Republic of), Madagascar, Mali, Malta, Marshall Islands, Mexico, Moldova, Monaco, Mongolia, Morocco, Mozambique*, Namibia, Nauru, Netherlands*, New Zealand, Nicaragua, Niger, Norway*, Oman*, Panama, Pakistan*, Paraguay, Peru*, Philippines, Poland, Portugal*, Qatar*, Romania*, Russia*, Senegal, Serbia and Montenegro, Seychelles, Slovakia, Slovenia, Spain*, Sudan, Swaziland, Sweden*, Switzerland*, Tajikistan, Tonga, Trinidad and Tobago, Tunisia, Turkey*, Turkmenistan, Uganda, UK*, Ukraine, United Arab Emirates, Uruguay, USA, Uzbekistan

* With reservation and/or declaration.

Signed but not ratified: Dominican Republic, Haiti, South Africa*

Convention on Prohibitions or Restrictions on the Use of Certain Conventional Weapons which may be Deemed to be Excessively Injurious or to have Indiscriminate Effects (CCW Convention, or 'Inhumane Weapons' Convention)

The convention, with protocols I, II and III, was opened for signature at New York on 10 April 1981; entered into force on 2 December 1983; depositary UN Secretary-General

The convention is an 'umbrella treaty', under which specific agreements can be concluded in the form of protocols. To become a party to the convention a state must ratify a minimum of two of the protocols.

The amendment to Article I of the original, 1981 convention was opened for signature at Geneva on 21 November 2001. It expands the scope of application to non-international armed conflicts. The Amended Convention entered into force on 18 May 2004.

Protocol I prohibits the use of weapons intended to injure by fragments which are not detectable in the human body by X-rays.

Protocol II prohibits or restricts the use of mines, booby-traps and other devices.

Amended Protocol II, which entered into force on 3 December 1998, reinforces the constraints regarding landmines.

Protocol III restricts the use of incendiary weapons.

Protocol IV, which entered into force on 30 July 1998, prohibits the employment of laser weapons specifically designed to cause permanent blindness to unenhanced vision.

Protocol V on Explosive Remnants of War, adopted in Geneva on 28 November 2003, recognizes the need for measures of a generic nature to minimize the risks and effects of explosive remnants of war. It will enter into force after the 20th deposit of the instruments of ratification.

Parties to the 1981 convention and original protocols (100): Albania, Argentina*, Australia, Austria, Bangladesh, Belarus, Belgium, Benin[1], Bolivia, Bosnia and Herzegovina, Brazil, Bulgaria, Burkina Faso, Cambodia, Canada, Cape Verde, Chile[1], China, Colombia, Costa Rica, Croatia, Cuba, Cyprus*, Czech Republic, Denmark, Djibouti, Ecuador, El Salvador, Estonia[1], Finland, France*, Georgia, Germany, Greece, Guatemala, Holy See, Honduras, Hungary, India, Ireland, Israel[2], Italy, Japan, Jordan[1], Korea (South)[3], Laos, Latvia, Lesotho, Liberia, Liechtenstein, Lithuania[1], Luxembourg, Macedonia (Former Yugoslav Republic of), Maldives[1], Mali, Malta, Mauritius, Mexico, Moldova, Monaco[3], Mongolia, Morocco[4], Nauru, Netherlands*, New Zealand, Nicaragua[1], Niger, Norway, Pakistan, Panama, Paraguay, Peru[1], Philippines, Poland, Portugal, Romania, Russia, Senegal[5], Serbia and Montenegro, Seychelles, Sierra Leone, Slovakia, Slovenia, South Africa, Spain, Sri Lanka, Sweden, Switzerland, Tajikistan, Togo, Tunisia, Turkey[3], Turkmenistan[2], Uganda, UK, Ukraine, Uruguay, USA[2], Uzbekistan, Venezuela

* With reservation and/or declaration.

[1] Party only to 1981 Protocols I and III.
[2] Party only to 1981 Protocols I and II.
[3] Party only to 1981 Protocol I.
[4] Party only to 1981 Protocol II.
[5] Party only to 1981 Protocol III.

Signed but not ratified the 1981 convention and original protocols: Afghanistan, Egypt, Iceland, Nigeria, Sudan, Viet Nam

Parties to the Amended Convention and original protocols (44): Argentina, Australia, Austria, Belgium, Bulgaria, Burkina Faso, Canada, China*, Croatia, Denmark, Estonia, Finland, France, Germany, Greece, Holy See*, Hungary, India, Italy, Japan, Korea (South), Latvia, Liberia, Liechtenstein, Lithuania, Luxembourg, Malta, Mexico*, Moldova, Netherlands, Norway, Panama, Peru, Romania, Serbia and Montenegro, Sierra Leone, Slovakia, Spain, Sri Lanka, Sweden, Switzerland, Turkey, UK, Ukraine

* With reservation and/or declaration.

Parties to Amended Protocol II (85): Albania, Argentina, Australia, Austria, Bangladesh, Belarus, Belgium, Bolivia, Bosnia and Herzegovina, Brazil, Bulgaria, Burkina Faso, Cambodia, Canada, Cape Verde, Chile, China, Colombia, Costa Rica, Croatia, Cyprus, Czech Republic, Denmark, Ecuador, El Salvador, Estonia, Finland, France, Germany, Greece, Guatemala, Holy See, Honduras, Hungary, India, Ireland, Israel, Italy, Japan, Jordan, Korea (South), Latvia, Liberia, Liechtenstein, Lithuania, Luxembourg, Macedonia (Former Yugoslav Republic of), Maldives, Mali, Malta, Moldova, Monaco, Morocco, Nauru, Netherlands, New Zealand, Nicaragua, Norway, Pakistan, Panama, Paraguay, Peru, Philippines, Poland, Portugal, Romania, Russia, Senegal, Seychelles, Sierra Leone, Slovakia, Slovenia, South Africa, Spain, Sri Lanka, Sweden, Switzerland, Tajikistan, Turkey, Turkmenistan, UK, Ukraine, Uruguay, USA, Venezuela

Parties to Protocol IV (81): Albania, Argentina, Australia, Austria, Bangladesh, Belarus, Belgium, Bolivia, Bosnia and Herzegovina, Brazil, Bulgaria, Burkina Faso, Cambodia, Canada, Cape Verde, Chile, China, Colombia, Costa Rica, Croatia, Cyprus, Czech Republic, Denmark, Ecuador, El Salvador, Estonia, Finland, France, Germany, Greece, Guatemala, Holy See, Honduras, Hungary, India, Ireland, Israel, Italy, Japan, Latvia, Liberia, Liechtenstein, Lithuania, Luxembourg, Maldives, Mali, Malta, Mauritius, Mexico, Moldova, Mongolia, Morocco, Nauru, Netherlands, New Zealand, Nicaragua, Norway, Pakistan,

Panama, Peru, Philippines, Poland, Portugal, Romania, Russia, Serbia and Montenegro, Seychelles, Sierra Leone, Slovakia, Slovenia, South Africa, Spain, Sri Lanka, Sweden, Switzerland, Tajikistan, Turkey, UK, Ukraine, Uruguay, Uzbekistan

Protocol V, 16 ratifications deposited: Bulgaria, Croatia, Denmark, Finland, Germany, Holy See*, India, Liberia, Lithuania, Luxembourg, Netherlands, Nicaragua, Norway, Sierra Leone, Sweden, Ukraine

* With reservation and/or declaration.

South Pacific Nuclear Free Zone Treaty (Treaty of Rarotonga)

Opened for signature at Rarotonga, Cook Islands, on 6 August 1985; entered into force on 11 December 1986; depositary Director of the Pacific Islands Forum Secretariat

The treaty prohibits the manufacture or acquisition by other means of any nuclear explosive device, as well as possession or control over such device by the parties anywhere inside or outside the zone area described in an annex. The parties also undertake not to supply nuclear material or equipment, unless subject to IAEA safeguards, and to prevent in their territories the stationing as well as the testing of any nuclear explosive device and undertake not to dump, and to prevent the dumping of, radioactive wastes and other radioactive matter at sea anywhere within the zone. Each party remains free to allow visits, as well as transit, by foreign ships and aircraft.

The treaty is open for signature by the members of the Pacific Islands Forum.

Under *Protocol 1* France, the UK and the USA undertake to apply the treaty prohibitions relating to the manufacture, stationing and testing of nuclear explosive devices in the territories situated within the zone, for which they are internationally responsible.

Under *Protocol 2* China, France, Russia, the UK and the USA undertake not to use or threaten to use a nuclear explosive device against the parties to the treaty or against any territory within the zone for which a party to Protocol 1 is internationally responsible.

Under *Protocol 3* China, France, the UK, the USA and Russia undertake not to test any nuclear explosive device anywhere within the zone.

Parties (13): Australia, Cook Islands, Fiji, Kiribati, Nauru, New Zealand, Niue, Papua New Guinea, Samoa (Western), Solomon Islands, Tonga, Tuvalu, Vanuatu

Parties to Protocol 1: France, UK; **signed but not ratified:** USA

Parties to Protocol 2: China, France[1], Russia, UK[2]; **signed but not ratified:** USA

Parties to Protocol 3: China, France, Russia, UK; **signed but not ratified:** USA

[1] France declared that the negative security guarantees set out in Protocol 2 are the same as the CD declaration of 6 Apr. 1995 referred to in UN Security Council Resolution 984 of 11 Apr. 1995.

[2] On ratifying Protocol 2 in 1997, the UK declared that nothing in the treaty affects the rights under international law with regard to transit of the zone or visits to ports and airfields within the zone by ships and aircraft. The UK will not be bound by the undertakings in Protocol 2 in case of an invasion or any other attack on the UK, its territories, its armed forces or its allies, carried out or sustained by a party to the treaty in association or alliance with a nuclear weapon state or if a party violates its non-proliferation obligations under the treaty.

Treaty on the Elimination of Intermediate-Range and Shorter-Range Missiles (INF Treaty)

Signed by the USA and the USSR at Washington, DC, on 8 December 1987; entered into force on 1 June 1988

The treaty obligates the parties to destroy all land-based missiles with a range of 500–5500 km (intermediate-range, 1000–5500 km; and shorter-range, 500–1000 km) and their launchers by 1 June 1991. A total of 2692 missiles were eliminated by May 1991. For 10 years after this date, on-site inspections were conducted to verify compliance; the inspections were ended on 31 May 2001.

Treaty on Conventional Armed Forces in Europe (CFE Treaty)

Original treaty signed at Paris on 19 November 1990; entered into force on 9 November 1992; depositary Netherlands Government

The treaty sets ceilings on five categories of treaty-limited equipment (TLE)—battle tanks, armoured combat vehicles, artillery of at least 100-mm calibre, combat aircraft and attack helicopters—in an area stretching from the Atlantic Ocean to the Ural Mountains (the Atlantic-to-the-Urals, ATTU, zone).

The treaty was negotiated and signed by the member states of the Warsaw Treaty Organization and NATO within the framework of the Conference on Security and Co-operation in Europe (from 1995 the Organization for Security and Co-operation in Europe, OSCE).

The **1992 Tashkent Agreement**, adopted by the former Soviet republics (with the exception of the three Baltic states) with territories within the ATTU zone, and the **1992 Oslo Document** (Final Document of the Extraordinary Conference of the States Parties to the CFE Treaty) introduced modifications to the treaty required because of the emergence of new states after the break-up of the USSR.

Parties (30): Armenia, Azerbaijan, Belarus, Belgium, Bulgaria, Canada, Czech Republic, Denmark, France, Georgia, Germany, Greece, Hungary, Iceland, Italy, Kazakhstan, Luxembourg, Moldova, Netherlands, Norway, Poland, Portugal, Romania, Russia, Slovakia, Spain, Turkey, UK, Ukraine, USA

The first Review Conference of the CFE Treaty adopted the **1996 Flank Document**, which reorganized the flank areas geographically and numerically, allowing Russia and Ukraine to deploy more TLE.

The **1999 Agreement on Adaptation of the CFE Treaty** replaces the CFE Treaty bloc-to-bloc military balance with individual state limits on TLE holdings and provides for a new structure of limitations and new military flexibility mechanisms, flank sub-limits and enhanced transparency; it opens the CFE regime to all the other European states. It will enter into force when it has been ratified by all the signatories. The **1999 Final Act**, with annexes, contains politically binding arrangements with regard to the North Caucasus and Central and Eastern Europe, and withdrawals of armed forces from foreign territories.

3 ratifications of the Agreement on Adaptation deposited: Belarus, Kazakhstan, Russia*

* With reservation and/or declaration.

Concluding Act of the Negotiation on Personnel Strength of Conventional Armed Forces in Europe (CFE-1A Agreement)

Signed by the parties to the CFE Treaty at Helsinki on 10 July 1992; entered into force simultaneously with the CFE Treaty; depositary Netherlands Government

The agreement limits the personnel of the conventional land-based armed forces of the parties within the ATTU zone.

Treaty on the Reduction and Limitation of Strategic Offensive Arms (START I Treaty)

Signed by the USA and the USSR at Moscow on 31 July 1991; entered into force on 5 December 1994

The treaty obligates the parties to make phased reductions in their offensive strategic nuclear forces over a seven-year period. It sets numerical limits on deployed strategic nuclear delivery vehicles (SNDVs)—ICBMs, SLBMs and heavy bombers—and the nuclear warheads they carry. In the Protocol to Facilitate the Implementation of the START Treaty (**1992 Lisbon Protocol**), which entered into force on 5 December 1994, Belarus, Kazakhstan and Ukraine also assumed the obligations of the former USSR under the treaty.

Treaty on Open Skies

Opened for signature at Helsinki on 24 March 1992; entered into force on 1 January 2002; depositaries Canadian and Hungarian governments

The treaty obligates the parties to submit their territories to short-notice unarmed surveillance flights. The area of application stretches from Vancouver, Canada, eastward to Vladivostok, Russia.

The treaty was negotiated between the member states of the Warsaw Treaty Organization and NATO. It was opened for signature by the NATO states, the states of the former Warsaw Treaty Organization and the states of the former Soviet Union (except the three Baltic states). For six months after entry into force of the treaty, any other participating state of the Organization for Security and Co-operation in Europe could apply for accession to the treaty, and from 1 July 2002 any state can apply to accede to the treaty.

Parties (34): Belarus, Belgium, Bosnia and Herzegovina, Bulgaria, Canada, Croatia, Czech Republic, Denmark, Estonia, Finland, France, Georgia, Germany, Greece, Hungary, Iceland, Italy, Latvia, Lithuania, Luxembourg, Netherlands, Norway, Poland, Portugal, Romania, Russia, Slovakia, Slovenia, Spain, Sweden, Turkey, UK, Ukraine, USA

Signed but not ratified: Kyrgyzstan

Treaty on Further Reduction and Limitation of Strategic Offensive Arms (START II Treaty)

Signed by the USA and Russia at Moscow on 3 January 1993; not in force

The treaty obligated the parties to eliminate their MIRVed ICBMs and reduce the number of their deployed strategic nuclear warheads to no more than 3000–3500 each (of which no more than 1750 may be deployed on SLBMs) by 1 January 2003. On 26 September 1997 the two parties signed a *Protocol* to the treaty providing for the extension until the end of 2007 of the period of implementation of the treaty.

Note: The START II Treaty was ratified by the US Senate and the Russian Duma and Federation Council, but the two parties never exchanged the instruments of ratification. Hence the treaty never entered into force. On 14 June 2002, as a response to the taking effect on 13 June of the USA's withdrawal from the ABM Treaty, Russia declared that it will no longer be bound by the START II Treaty.

Convention on the Prohibition of the Development, Production, Stockpiling and Use of Chemical Weapons and on their Destruction (Chemical Weapons Convention, CWC)

Opened for signature at Paris on 13 January 1993; entered into force on 29 April 1997; depositary UN Secretary-General

The convention prohibits the use, development, production, acquisition, transfer and stockpiling of chemical weapons. Each party undertakes to destroy its chemical weapons and production facilities within 10 years of the entry into force of the treaty.

Parties (178): Afghanistan, Albania, Algeria, Andorra, Antigua and Barbuda, Argentina, Armenia, Australia, Austria, Azerbaijan, Bahrain, Bangladesh, Belarus, Belgium, Belize, Benin, Bhutan, Bolivia, Bosnia and Herzegovina, Botswana, Brazil, Brunei Darussalam, Bulgaria, Burkina Faso, Burundi, Cambodia, Cameroon, Canada, Cape Verde, Chad, Chile, China, Colombia, Congo (Democratic Republic of the), Cook Islands, Costa Rica, Côte d'Ivoire, Croatia, Cuba, Cyprus, Czech Republic, Denmark, Djibouti, Dominica, Ecuador, El Salvador, Equatorial Guinea, Eritrea, Estonia, Ethiopia, Fiji, Finland, France, Gabon, Gambia, Georgia, Germany, Ghana, Greece, Grenada, Guatemala, Guinea, Guyana, Haiti, Holy See, Honduras, Hungary, Iceland, India, Indonesia, Iran, Ireland, Italy, Jamaica, Japan, Jordan, Kazakhstan, Kenya, Kiribati, Korea (South), Kuwait, Kyrgyzstan, Laos, Latvia, Lesotho, Liberia, Libya, Liechtenstein, Lithuania, Luxembourg, Macedonia (Former Yugoslav Republic of), Madagascar, Malawi, Malaysia, Maldives, Mali, Malta, Marshall Islands, Mauritania, Mauritius, Mexico, Micronesia, Moldova, Monaco, Mongolia, Morocco, Mozambique, Namibia, Nauru, Nepal, Netherlands, New Zealand, Nicaragua, Niger, Nigeria, Niue, Norway, Oman, Pakistan, Palau, Panama, Papua New Guinea, Paraguay, Peru, Philippines, Poland, Portugal, Qatar, Romania, Russia, Rwanda, Saint Kitts and Nevis, Saint Lucia, Saint Vincent and the Grenadines, Samoa, San Marino, Sao Tome and Principe, Saudi Arabia, Senegal, Serbia and Montenegro, Seychelles, Sierra Leone, Singapore, Slovakia, Slovenia, Solomon Islands, South Africa, Spain, Sri Lanka, Sudan, Suriname, Swaziland, Sweden, Switzerland, Tajikistan, Tanzania, Thailand, Timor-Leste, Togo, Tonga, Trinidad and Tobago, Tunisia, Turkey, Turkmenistan, Tuvalu, Uganda, UK, Ukraine, United Arab Emirates, Uruguay, USA, Uzbekistan, Vanuatu, Venezuela, Viet Nam, Yemen, Zambia, Zimbabwe

Signed but not ratified: Bahamas, Central African Republic, Comoros, Congo (Republic of), Dominican Republic, Grenada, Guinea-Bissau, Israel, Myanmar (Burma)

Treaty on the Southeast Asia Nuclear Weapon-Free Zone (Treaty of Bangkok)

Signed at Bangkok on 15 December 1995; entered into force on 27 March 1997; depositary Government of Thailand

The treaty prohibits the development, manufacture, acquisition or testing of nuclear weapons inside or outside the zone area as well as the stationing and transport of nuclear weapons in or through the zone. Each state party may decide for itself whether to allow visits and transit by foreign ships and aircraft. The parties undertake not to dump at sea or discharge into the atmosphere anywhere within the zone any radioactive material or wastes or dispose of radioactive material on land. The parties should conclude an agreement with the IAEA for the application of full-scope safeguards to their peaceful nuclear activities.

The zone includes not only the territories but also the continental shelves and exclusive economic zones of the states parties.

The treaty is open for all 10 states of South-East Asia.

Under a *Protocol* to the treaty China, France, Russia, the UK and the USA are to undertake not to use or threaten to use nuclear weapons against any state party to the treaty. They should further undertake not to use nuclear weapons within the Southeast Asia nuclear weapon-free zone. The protocol will enter into force for each state party on the date of its deposit of the instrument of ratification.

Parties (10): Brunei Darussalam, Cambodia, Indonesia, Laos, Malaysia, Myanmar (Burma), Philippines, Singapore, Thailand, Viet Nam

Protocol: no signatures, no parties

Agreement on Confidence- and Security-Building Measures in Bosnia and Herzegovina between Bosnia and Herzegovina, the Federation of Bosnia and Herzegovina and the Republika Srpska

Signed at Vienna on 26 January 1996; entered into force on 26 January 1996; suspended on 24 September 2004

The agreement is based largely on the 1994 Vienna Document on Confidence- and Security-Building Measures but includes additional restrictions and restraints on military movements, deployments and exercises and provides for exchange of information and data relating to major weapon systems.

African Nuclear-Weapon-Free Zone Treaty (Treaty of Pelindaba)

Signed at Cairo on 11 April 1996; not in force as of 1 January 2006; depositary Secretary-General of the African Union

The treaty prohibits the research, development, manufacture and acquisition of nuclear explosive devices and the testing or stationing of any nuclear explosive device. Each party remains free to allow visits, as well as transit by foreign ships and aircraft. The treaty also prohibits any attack against nuclear installations. The parties undertake not to dump or permit the dumping of radioactive wastes and other radioactive matter anywhere within the zone. The parties should conclude an agreement with the IAEA for the application of comprehensive safeguards to their peaceful nuclear activities.

The zone includes the territory of the continent of Africa, island states members of the African Union (AU) and all islands considered by the AU to be part of Africa.

The treaty is open for signature by all the states of Africa. It will enter into force upon the 28th ratification.

Under *Protocol I* China, France, Russia, the UK and the USA are to undertake not to use or threaten to use a nuclear explosive device against the parties to the treaty.

Under *Protocol II* China, France, Russia, the UK and the USA are to undertake not to test nuclear explosive devices anywhere within the zone.

Under *Protocol III* states with territories within the zone for which they are internationally responsible are to undertake to observe certain provisions of the treaty with respect to these territories. This protocol is open for signature by France and Spain.

The protocols will enter into force simultaneously with the treaty for those protocol signatories that have deposited their instruments of ratification.

20 ratifications deposited: Algeria, Botswana, Burkina Faso, Côte d'Ivoire, Equatorial Guinea, Gambia, Guinea, Kenya, Lesotho, Libya, Madagascar, Mali, Mauritania, Mauritius, Nigeria, South Africa, Swaziland, Tanzania, Togo, Zimbabwe

Signed but not ratified: Angola, Benin, Burundi, Cameroon, Cape Verde, Central African Republic, Chad, Comoros, Congo (Democratic Republic of the), Congo (Republic of), Djibouti, Egypt, Eritrea, Ethiopia, Gabon, Ghana, Guinea-Bissau, Liberia, Malawi, Morocco, Mozambique, Namibia, Niger, Rwanda, Sao Tome and Principe, Senegal, Seychelles, Sierra Leone, Sudan, Tunisia, Uganda, Zambia

Protocol I: ratifications deposited: China, France[1], UK[3]; **signed but not ratified:** Russia[2], USA[4]

Protocol II: ratifications deposited: China, France, UK[3]; **signed but not ratified:** Russia[2], USA[4]

Protocol III: ratifications deposited: France

[1] France stated that the Protocols did not affect its right to self-defence, as stipulated in Article 51 of the UN Charter. It clarified that its commitment under Article 1 of Protocol I was equivalent to the negative security assurances given by France to non-nuclear weapon states parties to the NPT, as confirmed in its declaration made on 6 Apr. 1995 at the Conference on Disarmament, and as referred to in UN Security Council Resolution 984.

[2] Russia stated that as long as a military base of a nuclear state was located on the islands of the Chagos archipelago these islands could not be regarded as fulfilling the requirements put forward by the Treaty for nuclear-weapon-free territories. Moreover, since certain states declared that they would consider themselves free from the obligations under the Protocols with regard to the mentioned territories, Russia could not consider itself to be bound by the obligations under Protocol I in respect to the same territories. Russia interpreted its obligations under Article 1 of Protocol I as follows: It would not use nuclear weapons against a state party to the Treaty, except in the case of invasion or any other armed attack on Russia, its territory, its armed forces or other troops, its allies or a state towards which it had a security commitment, carried out or sustained by a non-nuclear-weapon state party to the treaty, in association or alliance with a nuclear-weapon state.

[3] The UK stated that it did not accept the inclusion of the British Indian Ocean Territory within the African nuclear weapon-free zone without its consent, and did not accept, by its adherence to Protocols I and II, any legal obligations in respect of that territory. Moreover, it would not be bound by its undertaking under Article 1 of Protocol I in case of an invasion or any other attack on the United Kingdom, its dependent territories, its armed forces or other troops, its allies or a state towards which it had security commitment, carried out or sustained by a party to the treaty in association or alliance with a nuclear-

weapon state, or if any party to the treaty was in material breach of its own non-proliferation obligations under the treaty.

[4] The USA stated, with respect to Protocol I, that it would consider an invasion or any other attack on the USA, its territories, its armed forces or other troops, its allies or on a state toward which it had a security commitment, carried out or sustained by a party to the treaty in association or alliance with a nuclear-weapon state, to be incompatible with the treaty party's corresponding obligations. The USA also stated that neither the treaty nor Protocol II would apply to the activities of the UK, the USA or any other state not party to the treaty on the island of Diego Garcia or elsewhere in the British Indian Ocean Territories. No change was, therefore, required in US armed forces operations in Diego Garcia and elsewhere in these territories.

Agreement on Sub-Regional Arms Control concerning Yugoslavia (Serbia and Montenegro), Bosnia and Herzegovina, and Croatia (Florence Agreement)

Adopted at Florence and entered into force on 14 June 1996

The agreement was negotiated under the auspices of the OSCE in accordance with the mandate in the 1995 General Framework Agreement for Peace in Bosnia and Herzegovina (Dayton Agreement). It sets numerical ceilings on armaments of the former warring parties: Bosnia and Herzegovina and its two entities, Croatia and the Federal Republic of Yugoslavia. Five categories of heavy conventional weapons are included: battle tanks, armoured combat vehicles, heavy artillery (75 mm and above), combat aircraft and attack helicopters. The reductions were completed by 31 October 1997. It is confirmed that 6580 weapon items were destroyed by that date.

Comprehensive Nuclear-Test-Ban Treaty (CTBT)

Opened for signature at New York on 24 September 1996; not in force as of 1 March 2006; depositary UN Secretary-General

The treaty prohibits the carrying out of any nuclear weapon test explosion or any other nuclear explosion, and urges each party to prevent any such nuclear explosion at any place under its jurisdiction or control and refrain from causing, encouraging, or in any way participating in the carrying out of any nuclear weapon test explosion or any other nuclear explosion.

The treaty will enter into force 180 days after the date of the deposit of the instruments of ratification of the 44 states listed in an annex to the treaty. All the 44 states possess nuclear power reactors and/or nuclear research reactors.

The 44 states whose ratification is required for entry into force are: Algeria, Argentina, Australia, Austria, Bangladesh, Belgium, Brazil, Bulgaria, Canada, Chile, China*, Colombia*, Congo (Democratic Republic of the), Egypt*, Finland, France, Germany, Hungary, India*, Indonesia*, Iran*, Israel*, Italy, Japan, Korea (North)*, Korea (South), Mexico, Netherlands, Norway, Pakistan*, Peru, Poland, Romania, Russia, Slovakia, South Africa, Spain, Sweden, Switzerland, Turkey, UK, Ukraine, USA* and Viet Nam.

* States which as of 10 Mar. 2006 had not ratified the treaty.

132 ratifications deposited: Afghanistan, Albania, Algeria, Antigua and Barbuda, Argentina, Australia, Austria, Azerbaijan, Bahrain, Bangladesh, Belarus, Belgium, Belize, Benin, Bolivia, Botswana, Brazil, Bulgaria, Burkina Faso, Cambodia, Cameroon, Canada, Cape Verde, Chile, Congo (Democratic Republic of the), Cook Islands, Costa Rica, Côte d'Ivoire,

Croatia, Cyprus, Czech Republic, Denmark, Djibouti, Ecuador, El Salvador, Eritrea, Estonia, Fiji, Finland, France, Gabon, Georgia, Germany, Greece, Grenada, Guyana, Haiti, Holy See, Honduras, Hungary, Iceland, Ireland, Italy, Jamaica, Japan, Jordan, Kazakhstan, Kenya, Kiribati, Korea (South), Kuwait, Kyrgyzstan, Laos, Latvia, Lesotho, Libya, Liechtenstein, Lithuania, Luxembourg, Macedonia (Former Yugoslav Republic of), Madagascar, Maldives, Mali, Malta, Mauritania, Mexico, Micronesia, Monaco, Mongolia, Morocco, Namibia, Nauru, Netherlands, New Zealand, Nicaragua, Niger, Nigeria, Norway, Oman, Panama, Paraguay, Peru, Philippines, Poland, Portugal, Qatar, Romania, Russia, Rwanda, Saint Kitts and Nevis, Saint Lucia, Samoa, San Marino, Senegal, Serbia and Montenegro, Seychelles, Sierra Leone, Singapore, Slovakia, Slovenia, South Africa, Spain, Sudan, Suriname, Sweden, Switzerland, Tajikistan, Tanzania, Togo, Tunisia, Turkey, Turkmenistan, Uganda, UK, Ukraine, United Arab Emirates, Uruguay, Uzbekistan, Vanuatu, Venezuela, Viet Nam, Zambia

Signed but not ratified: Andorra, Angola, Armenia, Bahamas, Bosnia and Herzegovina, Brunei Darussalam, Burundi, Central African Republic, Chad, China, Colombia, Comoros, Congo (Republic of), Dominican Republic, Egypt, Equatorial Guinea, Ethiopia, Gambia, Ghana, Guatemala, Guinea, Guinea-Bissau, Indonesia, Iran, Israel, Lebanon, Liberia, Malawi, Malaysia, Marshall Islands, Moldova, Mozambique, Myanmar (Burma), Nepal, Palau, Papua New Guinea, Sao Tome and Principe, Solomon Islands, Sri Lanka, Swaziland, Thailand, USA, Yemen, Zimbabwe

Inter-American Convention Against the Illicit Manufacturing of and Trafficking in Firearms, Ammunition, Explosives, and Other Related Materials

Adopted at Washington, DC, on 13 November 1997; opened for signature at Washington, DC, on 14 November 1997; entered into force on 1 July 1998; depositary General Secretariat of the Organization of American States

The purpose of the convention is to prevent, combat and eradicate the illicit manufacturing of and trafficking in firearms, ammunition, explosives and other related materials; and to promote and facilitate cooperation and the exchange of information and experience among the parties.

Parties (26): Antigua and Barbuda, Argentina*, Bahamas, Barbados, Belize, Bolivia, Brazil, Chile, Colombia, Costa Rica, Dominica, Ecuador, El Salvador, Grenada, Guatemala, Honduras, Mexico, Nicaragua, Panama, Paraguay, Peru, Saint Kitts and Nevis, Saint Lucia, Trinidad and Tobago, Uruguay, Venezuela

* With reservation.

Signed but not ratified: Canada, Dominican Republic, Guyana, Haiti, Jamaica, Saint Vincent and the Grenadines, Suriname, USA

Convention on the Prohibition of the Use, Stockpiling, Production and Transfer of Anti-Personnel Mines and on their Destruction (APM Convention)

Opened for signature at Ottawa on 3–4 December 1997 and at New York on 5 December 1997; entered into force on 1 March 1999; depositary UN Secretary-General

The convention prohibits anti-personnel mines, which are defined as mines designed to be exploded by the presence, proximity or contact of a person and which will incapacitate, injure or kill one or more persons.

Each party undertakes to destroy all its stockpiled anti-personnel mines as soon as possible but not later that four years after the entry into force of the convention for that state party. Each party also undertakes to destroy all anti-personnel mines in mined areas under its jurisdiction or control not later than 10 years after the entry into force of the convention for that state party.

Parties (149): Afghanistan, Albania, Algeria, Andorra, Angola, Antigua and Barbuda, Argentina, Australia, Austria, Bahamas, Bangladesh, Barbados, Belarus, Belgium, Belize, Benin, Bhutan, Bolivia, Bosnia and Herzegovina, Botswana, Brazil, Bulgaria, Burkina Faso, Burundi, Cambodia, Cameroon, Canada, Cape Verde, Central African Republic, Chad, Chile, Colombia, Comoros, Congo (Democratic Republic of the), Congo (Republic of), Costa Rica, Côte d'Ivoire, Croatia, Cyprus, Czech Republic, Denmark, Djibouti, Dominica, Dominican Republic, Ecuador, El Salvador, Equatorial Guinea, Eritrea, Estonia, Ethiopia, Fiji, France, Gabon, Gambia, Germany, Ghana, Greece, Grenada, Guatemala, Guinea, Guinea-Bissau, Guyana, Haiti, Holy See, Honduras, Hungary, Iceland, Ireland, Italy, Jamaica, Japan, Jordan, Kenya, Kiribati, Latvia, Lesotho, Liberia, Liechtenstein, Lithuania, Luxembourg, Macedonia (Former Yugoslav Republic of), Madagascar, Malawi, Malaysia, Maldives, Mali, Malta, Mauritania, Mauritius, Mexico, Moldova, Monaco, Mozambique, Namibia, Nauru, Netherlands, New Zealand, Nicaragua, Niger, Nigeria, Niue, Norway, Panama, Papua New Guinea, Paraguay, Peru, Philippines, Portugal, Qatar, Romania, Rwanda, Saint Kitts and Nevis, Saint Lucia, Saint Vincent and the Grenadines, Samoa, San Marino, Sao Tome and Principe, Senegal, Serbia and Montenegro, Seychelles, Sierra Leone, Slovakia, Slovenia, Solomon Islands, South Africa, Spain, Sudan, Suriname, Swaziland, Sweden, Switzerland, Tajikistan, Tanzania, Thailand, Timor-Leste, Togo, Trinidad and Tobago, Tunisia, Turkey, Turkmenistan, Uganda, UK, Ukraine, Uruguay, Vanuatu, Venezuela, Yemen, Zambia, Zimbabwe

Signed but not ratified: Brunei Darussalam, Cook Islands, Indonesia, Marshall Islands, Poland

Inter-American Convention on Transparency in Conventional Weapons Acquisitions

Adopted at Guatemala City on 7 June 1999; entered into force on 21 November 2002; depositary General Secretariat of the Organization of American States

The objective of the convention is to contribute more fully to regional openness and transparency in the acquisition of conventional weapons by exchanging information regarding such acquisitions, for the purpose of promoting confidence among states in the Americas.

Parties (11): Argentina, Canada, Chile, Ecuador, El Salvador, Guatemala, Nicaragua, Paraguay, Peru, Uruguay, Venezuela

Signed but not ratified: Bolivia, Brazil, Colombia, Costa Rica, Dominica, Haiti, Honduras, Mexico, USA

Vienna Document 1999 on Confidence- and Security-Building Measures

Adopted by the participating states of the Organization for Security and Co-operation in Europe at Istanbul on 16 November 1999; entered into force on 1 January 2000

The Vienna Document 1999 builds on the 1986 Stockholm Document on Confidence- and Security-Building Measures (CSBMs) and Disarmament in Europe and previous Vienna Documents (1990, 1992 and 1994). The Vienna Document 1990 provided for military budget exchange, risk reduction procedures, a communication network and an annual CSBM implementation assessment. The Vienna Documents 1992 and 1994 introduced new mechanisms and parameters for military activities, defence planning and military contacts.

The Vienna Document 1999 introduces regional measures aimed at increasing transparency and confidence in a bilateral, multilateral and regional context and some improvements, in particular regarding the constraining measures.

Treaty on Strategic Offensive Reductions (SORT)

Signed by the USA and Russia at Moscow on 24 May 2002; entered into force on 1 June 2003

The treaty obligates the parties to reduce the number of their operationally deployed strategic nuclear warheads so that the aggregate numbers do not exceed 1700–2200 for each party by 31 December 2012.

Annex B. Chronology 2005

NENNE BODELL

For the convenience of the reader, key words are indicated in the right-hand column, opposite each entry. Definitions of the abbreviations can be found on page xviii. The dates are according to local time.

3 Jan.	The US Special Representative of the President and Secretary of State for Mine Action, Lincoln P. Bloomfield, Jr, announces that the USA will terminate its use of any landmines that cannot be located with standard metal detectors, following the US landmine policy announced in Feb. 2004.	USA; Mines
4 Jan.	The Governor of Baghdad, Ali al-Haidri, is killed in a roadside ambush. The violence in Iraq escalates before the parliamentary elections to be held on 30 Jan.	Iraq
9 Jan.	Meeting in Nairobi, Kenya, representatives of the Sudanese Government and the Sudan People's Liberation Movement/ Army (SPLM/A) sign the Comprehensive Peace Agreement, providing for a sharing of revenues from natural resources and for partial autonomy for the south of Sudan.	Sudan
9 Jan.	Mahmoud Abbas (also known as Abu Mazen) wins the Palestinian presidential elections, and on 15 Jan. he is inaugurated as the new Palestinian President in Ramallah, the West Bank.	Palestinian Authority
26 Jan.	Israeli officials state that Israel has stopped targeted killings of Palestinian militants, following the announcement made on 25 Jan. by two Palestinian militant groups, the Harakat al-Muqawama al-Islamiyya (Hamas) and the Islamic Jihad, that they will suspend their attacks on Israel. Israeli Prime Minister Ariel Sharon decides to lift a ban on diplomatic contacts with the new Palestinian President.	Israel/ Palestinians
30 Jan.	The first multi-party parliamentary elections in Iraq for more than 50 years are held.	Iraq
31 Jan.	Meeting in Abuja, Nigeria, the Assembly of the African Union (AU) adopts the African Union Non-aggression and Common Defence Pact, to reinforce cooperation among the AU member states in the areas of defence and security and to strengthen the Mechanism for Conflict Prevention, Management and Resolution.	AU
1 Feb.	The UN Security Council unanimously adopts Resolution 1584, strengthening the arms embargo imposed on Côte d'Ivoire in Nov. 2004; calling on the warring parties to establish comprehensive lists of the armaments they possess and their locations; and authorizing the UN Operation in Côte d'Ivoire (UNOCI), and the French forces supporting it, to monitor the implementation of the embargo.	Côte d'Ivoire; UN; Arms embargo

8 Feb.	Meeting in Sharm el-Sheikh, Egypt, Palestinian President Mahmoud Abbas and Israeli Prime Minister Ariel Sharon announce a mutual ceasefire and a pledge to break the four-year cycle of bloodshed and to restart the peace talks.	Israel/ Palestinians
9 Feb.	The second round of Asian Senior-level Talks on Non-Proliferation (ASTOP) is held in Tokyo, Japan, to discuss strengthened non-proliferation measures.	Asia; Non-proliferation
10 Feb.	The North Korean Ministry of Foreign Affairs issues a statement for the first time officially admitting that North Korea has manufactured nuclear weapons 'for self-defence' and stating its refusal to participate, for an indefinite period, in the continuation of the Six-Party Talks (between China, Japan, North Korea, South Korea, Russia and the USA) on its nuclear programme.	North Korea; Nuclear weapons
10 Feb.	The NATO defence ministers decide at an informal meeting in Nice, France, to extend the International Security Assistance Force (ISAF) into the western regions of Afghanistan.	Afghanistan; NATO
14 Feb.	Former Lebanese Prime Minister Rafik Hariri is killed together with some 15 people, and about 120 more are injured, in a car bomb attack in Beirut, Lebanon. The Lebanese Army is put on high alert after the attack. Syria is blamed for the assassination of Hariri. His death causes massive demonstrations in the streets of Beirut.	Lebanon; Syria
21–23 Feb.	Under the auspices of the Crisis Management Initiative (CMI), led by former Finnish President Martti Ahtisaari, representatives of the Government of Indonesia and the Gerakan Aceh Merdeka (GAM, Free Aceh Movement) meet in Helsinki, Finland. Discussions are held on a peaceful comprehensive settlement of the conflict in the Aceh province, including self-government for Aceh.	Indonesia/Aceh
24 Feb.	The Government of Syria announces its decision to redeploy its troops stationed in Lebanon to the eastern Bekaa Valley, closer to the Syrian border. The redeployment will be carried out in line with UN Security Council Resolution 1559 of 2 Sep. 2004.	Syria; Lebanon; UN
24 Feb.	Meeting in Bratislava, Slovakia, US President George W. Bush and Russian President Vladimir Putin issue a Joint Statement on Nuclear Security Cooperation, on the enhancement of their bilateral cooperation aimed at combating nuclear terrorism.	USA; Russia; Terrorism
27 Feb.	Israeli Prime Minister Ariel Sharon threatens to freeze peace efforts with the Palestinians following a suicide bomb attack in Tel Aviv on 25 Feb. The Israeli Cabinet decides to suspend the plan to hand over control of five West Bank towns to the Palestinian Authority and to free 400 more prisoners.	Israel/ Palestinians
28 Feb.	Over 125 people are killed and more than 140 are wounded in a massive car bomb attack in Hillah, south of Baghdad. This is the worst single attack in Iraq since the invasion of Mar. 2003.	Iraq; Terrorism

7 Mar.	Meeting in Damascus, Syria, the Lebanese and Syrian presidents, Emile Lahoud and Bashar al-Assad, respectively, sign an agreement formally approving the two-phase redeployment to the Bekaa Valley of Syrian troops stationed on Lebanese territory that was announced by Syria on 24 Feb.	Lebanon; Syria
8 Mar.	The Prime Minister of Kosovo and former commander of the Kosovo Liberation Army (KLA), Ramush Haradinaj, resigns after being charged with war crimes in the 1998–99 Kosovo conflict by the International Criminal Tribunal for the former Yugoslavia (ICTY) in The Hague, the Netherlands. Haradinaj states that he will cooperate fully with the ICTY.	Kosovo; ICTY
8 Mar.	Chechen rebel leader Aslan Maskhadov is killed in a raid by Russian Army Special Forces in Tolstoy-Yurt, Chechnya.	Russia/ Chechnya
15 Mar.	The UN Security Council unanimously adopts Resolution 1587, requesting Secretary-General Kofi Annan to re-establish the Monitoring Group to investigate the violations of the 1992 arms embargo in Somalia, including 'transfers of ammunition, single-use weapons and small arms'. On 11 Apr. the Secretary-General appoints four experts to the group.	Somalia; UN; Arms embargo
16 Mar.	Israel begins to withdraw its troops from Jericho, the West Bank, following the plan presented in Feb. 2004 by Israeli Prime Minister Ariel Sharon.	Israel/ Palestinians
20–24 Mar.	Following the disputed parliamentary elections in Feb. and in Mar., opposition demonstrators take to the streets in Jalal-Abad and in several other cities in the southern part of Kyrgyzstan. On 24 Mar. pro-government forces clash with several thousand opposition protesters in Bishkek.	Kyrgyzstan
21 Mar.	UN Secretary-General Kofi Annan presents the report on UN reforms *In Larger Freedom: Towards Development, Security and Human Rights for All* to the General Assembly (see *14–16 Sep.* and *20 Dec.*).	UN
24 Mar.	The UN Security Council unanimously adopts Resolution 1590, establishing the UN Mission in Sudan (UNMIS) for an initial period of six months. The mandate of UNMIS is to liaise and coordinate with the African Union Mission in Sudan (AMIS); to monitor and verify the ceasefire agreement; to set up a programme for disarmament, demobilization and reintegration of ex-combatants; and to promote national reconciliation and human rights.	Sudan; UN; AU
29 Mar.	The UN Security Council adopts, by a vote of 12–0, with 3 abstentions (Algeria, China and Russia), Resolution 1591, imposing sanctions on individuals committing atrocities in Darfur and strengthening the arms embargo on Sudan.	Sudan; UN; Sanctions
31 Mar.	The Commission on the Intelligence Capabilities of the United States Regarding Weapons of Mass Destruction presents its report, offering 74 recommendations for improving the US intelligence community after the failure regarding the judgements about Iraq's possession of weapons of mass destruction.	USA; WMD

31 Mar. The UN Security Council adopts, by a vote of 11–0, with 4 abstentions (Algeria, Brazil, China and the USA), Resolution 1593, deciding to refer any war crimes suspects from the Darfur region of Sudan to the International Criminal Court (ICC). The withdrawal of the US opposition to sending cases to the ICC represents a significant diplomatic change in the US policy. On 6 Apr. UN Secretary-General Kofi Annan hands to the ICC a list of 51 people who are allegedly involved in war crimes in Darfur.

Sudan; UN; ICC; USA

6 Apr. Meeting in Pretoria, South Africa, under the auspices of the African Union (AU), representatives of the government and the rebel groups of Côte d'Ivoire sign a ceasefire agreement (the Pretoria Accord), agreeing to end hostilities, to start immediate disarmament and to hold elections during 2005.

Côte d'Ivoire; AU

13 Apr. The UN General Assembly unanimously adopts the International Convention for the Suppression of Acts of Nuclear Terrorism, criminalizing the possession by non-state actors of nuclear weapons and the threat of use by non-state actors of such weapons; and strengthening the international legal framework against terrorism. The convention will be open for signature at the UN from 14 Sep. 2005 until 31 Dec. 2006 and will enter into force 30 days after the deposit of the 22nd ratification.

UN; Terrorism

16 Apr. Meeting in Bouake, army chief Philippe Mangou and the chief of staff of the New Forces rebel group, Soumaila Bakayoko, agree on a provisional timetable for disarmament, to take place between 14 May and 31 July (see also *14 May*). On 15 Apr. two ministers from the rebel groups return to the power-sharing government after a five-month absence.

Côte d'Ivoire

18 Apr. The UN Security Council unanimously adopts Resolution 1596, condemning the continued illicit flow of weapons into the Democratic Republic of the Congo (DRC) and widening the existing arms embargo to include, for violators of the embargo, a travel ban and a freeze of assets.

DRC; UN; Arms embargo

20 Apr. The Israeli Army begins moving equipment and infrastructure from its bases in the Gaza Strip in preparation for the troop withdrawal from the Palestinian territory (see *13–20 July*).

Israel/ Palestinians

21 Apr. At the NATO–Russia Council Meeting in Vilnius, Lithuania, Russian Foreign Minister Sergey Lavrov signs the Partnership for Peace Status of Forces Agreement (SOFA), providing a legal framework for movements of military personnel and support staff to and from allied countries, partner countries and Russia. The agreement is based on the 1951 NATO Status of Forces Agreement.

Russia; NATO

22 Apr.	Meeting in Chisinau, Moldova, the leaders of the GUAM states—Georgia, Ukraine, Azerbaijan and Moldova—decide to revitalize the group (established in 1997) and use it as a vehicle for integration with the Euro-Atlantic organizations outside the frameworks of the Commonwealth of Independent States (CIS) and Russia. Uzbekistan does not participate in the meeting and on 5 May announces its withdrawal from the 'GUUAM' group, from which it had suspended its participation since 2002.	GUAM; CIS; Russia; Uzbekistan
26 Apr.	The last of the Syrian troops deployed in Lebanon since the civil war of 1976 are withdrawn. A formal ceremony marking the completion of the Syrian withdrawal is held at the Rayaq Air Base in the eastern Bekaa Valley. A UN mission is sent to Lebanon to verify the withdrawal of troops, military assets and intelligence. On 23 May the UN Secretary-General, Kofi Annan, confirms that the withdrawal is completed.	Lebanon; Syria; UN
26 Apr.	The US Iraq Survey Group (ISG) is officially closed down after publishing an addendum to the Final Report on Iraq's weapons of mass destruction (WMD), issued in Oct. 2004. The Head of the ISG, Charles Duelfer, states that inquiries into WMD in Iraq have 'gone as far as feasible'.	Iraq; USA; WMD
30 Apr.	The EU Police Mission in Kinshasa in the Democratic Republic of the Congo (EUPOL Kinshasa) is launched. It is the first EU civil crisis management mission in Africa and comes under the European Security and Defence Policy (ESDP).	DRC; EU; ESDP
2–27 May	The seventh Review Conference of the Treaty on the Non-Proliferation of Nuclear Weapons (NPT) is held in New York. The conference ends without having adopted any decision or recommendation for future nuclear non-proliferation and disarmament.	NPT; Nuclear weapons
14 May	Meeting in Yamoussoukro, representatives from the Côte d'Ivoire national armed forces and the New Forces rebel group sign an agreement on the process of disarmament and demobilization of the belligerents. On 13 June the political leaders of the opposition forces issue a statement that, owing to the lack of political and technical conditions for implementation of the agreement, the disarmament plan cannot proceed as planned.	Côte d'Ivoire
26 May	Taking part in the pledging conference on financial and logistical support for the AU Mission in Sudan (AMIS), held in Addis Ababa, Ethiopia, the EU and NATO both pledge to support the mission with logistics and training. The conference raises pledges of $291 million.	Sudan; AU; EU; NATO
30 May	Meeting in Moscow, the foreign ministers of Georgia and Russia, Salome Zurabishvili and Sergei Lavrov, respectively, issue a joint statement on the closure of Russia's military bases in Akhalkalaki and Batumi, Georgia. The withdrawal of the Russian forces will be completed in 2008.	Georgia; Russia; Military bases
8 June	The EU Advisory and Assistance Mission for DRC Security Sector Reform (EUSEC DR Congo) is launched.	DRC; EU

18 June   Representatives of the Government of Sudan and the   Sudan
             opposition group National Democratic Alliance (NDA) sign, in
             Cairo, Egypt, a national reconciliation agreement under which
             the NDA is granted a place in the power-sharing administration
             set up in the Comprehensive Peace Agreement signed by the
             Sudan People's Liberation Movement/Army (SPLM/A) on 9
             Jan. The Cairo Agreement does not include the conflict in the
             Darfur region (see *5 July*).

18 June   Following the referendums in France and in the Netherlands,   France;
             which resulted in no-votes to the Treaty Establishing a Consti-   Netherlands;
             tution for Europe, the Brussels European Council adopts the   EU
             Declaration by the Heads of State or Government of the
             Member States of the European Union on the Ratification of
             the Treaty Establishing a Constitution for Europe, agreeing on
             a period of reflection on the new situation. The ratification pro-
             cess is stalled and will be discussed again in 2006.

5 July   Meeting in Abuja, Nigeria, under the auspices of the African   Sudan; AU
             Union (AU), the Sudanese Government, the Sudan People's
             Liberation Movement/Army (SPLM/A), and the Justice and
             Equality Movement (JEM) sign the Declaration of Principles
             for the Resolution of the Sudanese Conflict in Darfur, includ-
             ing democracy and regional devolution. Further negotiations
             are held, but no decisive agreements are reached.

6–8 July   The leaders of the Group of Eight (G8) leading industrialized   G8; Non-
             nations, meeting in Gleneagles, UK, issue a statement on non-   proliferation;
             proliferation, reaffirming that the proliferation of weapons of   WMD;
             mass destruction and international terrorism remain the pre-   Peacekeeping
             eminent threats to international peace and security; and agree to
             provide extra resources for Africa's peacekeeping forces, and
             that all debts owed by eligible heavily indebted countries
             should be cancelled.

7 July   In a series of coordinated attacks four bombs explode in the   UK; Terrorism;
             underground network and on a bus in London, killing at least   al-Qaeda
             38 people and wounding 700. On 14 July four suicide bombers
             are named after the finding in Leeds of explosives similar to
             those used in other attacks.

9 July   In accordance with the Comprehensive Peace Agreement   Sudan
             signed on 9 Jan., the Government of National Unity is inaug-
             urated, with former rebel leader of the Sudan People's Lib-
             eration Movement (SPLM), John Garang, as vice-president,
             and the new Sudanese constitution comes into force.

9 July   Meeting in Yamoussoukro, Côte d'Ivoire, representatives of   Côte d'Ivoire
             the Côte d'Ivoire national armed forces and the New Forces
             rebel group sign an agreement on a new timetable for disarma-
             ment, under which 40 500 rebels and 15 000 government
             troops are due to disarm before the presidential elections
             scheduled for 30 Oct. (The elections are later postponed by the
             UN Security Council owing to lack of cooperation from the
             New Forces and opposition parties, and President Gbagbo
             remains in office).

11–15 July   The UN Second Biennal Meeting of States to Consider the   UN; SALW
Implementation of the Programme of Action to Prevent, Com-
bat and Eradicate the Illicit Trade in Small Arms and Light
Weapons in All Its Aspects is held in New York.

13–20 July   Ahead of the Israeli withdrawal from Palestinian territory,   Israel/
Israeli Prime Minister Ariel Sharon orders the Gaza Strip   Palestinians
closed and forbids entry to non-residents. This also applies to
the four West Bank settlements from which Israel is due to
withdraw in mid-Aug. Anti-withdrawal activists clash with the
police and soldiers at a crossing point for Gaza settlers on the
Israeli border.

18 July   Meeting in Washington, DC, US President George W. Bush   USA; India;
and Indian Prime Minister Manmohan Singh announce the US–   Nuclear energy
India Civil Nuclear Cooperation Initiative. Under the
agreement India will receive access to US civil nuclear
technology; it will place its nuclear facilities under IAEA
safeguards; and it will adhere to the guidelines of the Nuclear
Suppliers Group and the Missile Technology Control Regime.

23 July   Three bombs explode in the tourist resort Sharm al-Sheikh,   Egypt;
killing at least 80 people and injuring some 200. Several   Terrorism
Islamist groups claim responsibility for the bombings.

26 July–   The Six-Party Talks (between China, Japan, North Korea,   North Korea;
7 Aug.   South Korea, Russia and the USA) on the North Korean   Nuclear
nuclear programme is reopened in Beijing for the fourth round.   weapons
On 7 Aug., after 13 days of deadlocked negotiations, the talks
go into recess until 13 Sep.

28 July   The Irish Republican Army (IRA) issues a statement in which   Northern
it formally orders an end to its armed campaign and declares   Ireland; IRA
that it will pursue its goals exclusively through political means.

1 Aug.   The Government of Sudan announces the death of Vice-   Sudan
President John Garang. On 30 July the helicopter he was travel-
ling in when returning to Sudan after attending meetings in
Rwakitura, Uganda, had crashed. Riots after the announcement
are reported from Khartoum and from southern Sudan.

1 Aug.   The Government of Iran states in a letter to the International   Iran; IAEA;
Atomic Energy Agency (IAEA) that it will break the seals on   Uranium
the Esfahan nuclear plant placed there by the IAEA in Nov.
2004 and resume its uranium conversion. On 10 Aug. all seals
are removed under the supervision of the IAEA, which also
installs equipment to monitor the activities.

11 Aug.   At an emergency meeting, the International Atomic Energy   Iran; IAEA;
Agency (IAEA) adopts Resolution GOV/2005/64, calling on   Uranium
Iran to halt its nuclear fuel development. Iran resumed its uran-
ium conversion at Esfahan on 10 Aug. (see *16 Nov.*).

12 Aug. The Foreign Minister of Sri Lanka, Lakshman Kadirgamar, is Sri Lanka
assassinated in a gun attack in Colombo. The government
blames the separatist group the Liberation Tigers of the Tamil
Eelam (LTTE) for the killing. The LTTE denies involvement.
On 17 Aug. the government calls for a review of the 2002
ceasefire agreement.

15 Aug. Meeting in Helsinki, Finland, representatives of the Govern- Indonesia/
ment of Indonesia and the Gerakan Aceh Merdeka (GAM, Free Aceh; ASEAN;
Aceh Movement) sign a Memorandum of Understanding, con- EU
firming the peace agreement agreed on 17 July. Under the
agreement the Aceh province is to be governed by a new law;
all non-local military and police forces are to be withdrawn; all
hostilities are to cease and the GAM is to disarm; amnesty is to
be granted to GAM members; a truth and reconciliation commission is to be established; and the Aceh Monitoring Mission
(AMM) is to be set up by ASEAN and the EU. Withdrawal of
the government troops begins on 22 Aug. (see *29 Dec.*).

15–23 Aug. The deadline for the withdrawal from the Israeli settlements in Israel/
the Gaza Strip issued by the Israeli Army on 9 Aug. expires. Palestinians
On 17 Aug. Israeli forces begin an operation to evict settlers
resisting the orders. On 23 Aug. the evacuation of settlers from
the Gaza Strip and the West Bank, in line with Prime Minister
Ariel Sharon's withdrawal plan, is completed.

28 Aug. The draft constitution of Iraq is approved by the Iraqi interim Iraq
parliament. On 15 Oct. a referendum approves the constitution
and on 15 Dec. parliamentary elections are held (see *15 Dec.*).

31 Aug. More than 600 people are killed in a stampede of Shia pilgrims Iraq; Terrorism
in Baghdad after motar rounds are fired into the crowd and
rumours spread that suicide bombers are in the crowd. No
group claims responsibility for the attack, allegedly intended to
foment sectarian tensions.

11 Sep. Israel declares a formal end to military rule in the Gaza Strip Israel/
and withdraws the remaining Israeli troops. Palestinians

14 Sep. The UN Security Council, meeting at the level of Head of State UN; Terrorism;
and Government, unanimously adopts Resolutions 1624 and Conflict
1625, calling for strengthened steps against terrorism and for a prevention
stronger role for the UN in preventing conflict, particularly in
Africa.

14 Sep. Over 150 people are killed and hundreds are injured in a series Iraq; Terrorism
of bomb attacks and shootings across Iraq in one of the most
severe outbreaks of violence since the invasion of Mar. 2003.

14–16 Sep. The 2005 World Summit, the High-level Plenary Meeting of UN
the 60th UN General Assembly, is held in New York. The
meeting is presented with the reform package drawn up by
Secretary-General Kofi Annan in his report of 21 Mar. The
Summit decides to establish a UN Peacebuilding Commission
and a Human Rights Council (see *20 Dec.*). On the questions of
non-proliferation and disarmament no decisions are taken.

18 Sep.	The first parliamentary and local elections in more than 30 years are held in Afghanistan. The final results are accepted and published on 15 Nov.	Afghanistan
19 Sep.	Meeting in Beijing on 13–19 Sep., for the reopened fourth round of the Six-Party Talks (between China, Japan, North Korea, South Korea, Russia and the USA), North Korea agrees to abandon all its nuclear weapons and existing nuclear programmes and return to the Treaty on the Non-Proliferation of Nuclear Weapons (NPT) at an early date; the USA affirms that it has no intention to attack or invade North Korea. The parties agree to hold the fifth round of the talks in early Nov. (see *9–11 Nov.*)	North Korea; Nuclear weapons; NPT
20 Sep.	North Korea states that it will not abandon its nuclear programme or return to the Treaty on the Non-Proliferation of Nuclear Weapons (NPT) unless it is given a light-water nuclear reactor, thereby undermining the agreement of 19 Sep.	North Korea; Nuclear weapons; NPT
21–23 Sep.	The fourth Conference on Facilitating the Entry into Force of the Comprehensive Nuclear-Test-Ban Treaty (CTBT) is held at the UN Headquarters, New York. A final declaration is adopted, reaffirming the international community's determination to continue to work towards early entry into force of the treaty.	CTBT
24 Sep.	Meeting in Vienna, Austria, the International Atomic Energy Agency (IAEA) Board of Governors adopts, by a vote of 22 in favour, 1 against and 12 abstentions, Resolution GOV/2005/77 on the implementation of safeguards in Iran, stating that Iran's failures and breaches constitute non-compliance and calling on Iran to return to the negotiation process.	Iran; IAEA; Safeguards
26 Sep.	The Independent International Commission on Decommissioning (IICD) announces that the Irish Republican Army (IRA) has completed the arms decommissioning initiated in May 2000.	Northern Ireland; IRA
2 Oct.	Three bomb attacks in the two tourist areas, Kuta and Jimbaran, in Bali, kill at least 26 people and injure over 50. No group claims responsibility for the bombings. The attacks come almost exactly three years after the terrorist bombings of Oct. 2002.	Indonesia; Terrorism
3 Oct.	Meeting in Islamabad, Pakistan, the Indian and Pakistani foreign ministers sign the Agreement on Pre-notification of Flight Testing of Ballistic Missiles, aiming to reduce tension between the two countries.	India/Pakistan; Missiles
4 Oct.	The Eritrean Government imposes a ban on all helicopter flights by the UN Mission in Ethiopia and Eritrea (UNMEE). On 14 Oct. further restrictions are imposed on the activities of UNMEE through limitations on night patrols.	Eritrea/ Ethiopia; UN

8 Oct.	The peace process between India and Pakistan is accelerated by the devastating earthquake that strikes the Kashmir region in Pakistan and results in a humanitarian catastrophe, killing over 55 000 people and making 3 million people homeless. After a formal request from the Government of Pakistan, on 11 Oct. NATO launches its second disaster relief operation.	Pakistan/India; NATO
13 Oct.	At least 86 people are killed in a rebel attack targeting police stations and military installations in the city of Nalchik, Kabardino-Balkaria. On 17 Oct. Chechen warlord Shamil Basayev claims responsibility for the attack.	Russia/ Chechnya; Terrorism
19 Oct.	The trial against former Iraqi President Saddam Hussein and seven other defendants opens at the Iraqi Special Tribunal (IST) in Baghdad. Hussein and his co-defendants plead not guilty to the charges of ordering the killing of 148 Shia men in Dujail in 1982.	Iraq; IST
26 Oct.	The US Director of National Intelligence releases the National Intelligence Strategy of the United States of America, establishing the strategic objectives for the US intelligence community.	USA
27 Oct.	The UN Independent Inquiry Committee (IIC), chaired by Paul A. Volcker, releases its final Report on the Manipulation of the Oil-for-Food Programme (the Volcker Report), finding instances of 'illicit, unethical and corrupt' behaviour and blaming UN Secretary-General Kofi Annan for mismanagement.	UN; Iraq
29 Oct.	Three explosions occurring in near succession in New Delhi kill over 60 people. The previously little-known group Inqilabi claims that it carried out the attacks.	India; Terrorism
9 Nov.	Three near-simultaneous suicide bomb attacks on foreign-owned hotels in Amman kill at least 56 people and injure about 100. Abu Musab al-Zarqawi, the leader of the al-Qaeda Organization in Mesopotamia, claims responsibility for the attacks.	Jordan; Terrorism; al-Qaeda
9–11 Nov.	The fifth round of the Six-Party Talks (between China, Japan, North Korea, South Korea, Russia and the USA) is held in Beijing. The meeting ends with no other progress than the reaffirmation of the parties' commitment to implement the agreement reached on 19 Sep.	North Korea; Nuclear weapons
10 Nov.	UN Secretary-General Kofi Annan appoints former Finnish President Martti Ahtisaari as the Special Envoy for the Future Status Process for Kosovo, to lead the political process to determine the future status of Kosovo in the context of Security Council Resolution 1244 (1999). Ahtisaari visits the region on 21–27 Nov.	UN; Kosovo
14 Nov.	Meeting in Brussels, the Council of the EU adopts Common Position 2005/792/CFSP concerning restrictive measures against Uzbekistan, including an arms embargo.	Uzbekistan; EU; Arms embargo
16 Nov.	Iran starts a second round of uranium conversion at the Esfahan plant despite heavy pressure from the USA and the E3 (France, Germany and the UK) to cease all its nuclear activity.	Iran; Uranium; USA; E3

23 Nov. — The UN Security Council unanimously adopts Resolution 1640, demanding that both Ethiopia and Eritrea return to the 16 Dec. 2004 level of troop deployment; demanding that Ethiopia accept fully and without further delay the final and binding decision of the Eritrea–Ethiopia Boundary Commission; and demanding that Eritrea reverse its decisions from Oct. on the restrictions imposed on the UN Mission in Ethiopia and Eritrea (UNMEE).   Eritrea/Ethiopia; UN

25 Nov. — The Rafah crossing on the Gaza Strip border with Egypt is reopened under Palestinian control and under the supervision of the EU Border Assistance Mission for the Rafah Crossing (EU BAM Rafah). The border station was closed by Israel on 7 Sep., shortly after withdrawing from the Gaza Strip, after holding it for almost 40 years.   Israel/Palestinians; EU

6 Dec. — The Government of Eritrea requests members of the UN Mission in Ethiopia and Eritrea (UNMEE) who are nationals of the USA, Canada and Europe, including Russia, to leave the country within 10 days, without giving any reason. The UN Security Council and the UN Secretary-General, Kofi Annan, condemn the decision.   Eritrea/Ethiopia; UN

7 Dec. — Former Croatian General Ante Gotovina is arrested on Tenerife, Canary Islands, Spain. He is brought to the International Criminal Tribunal for the former Yugoslavia (ICTY), The Hague, the Netherlands, on 10 Dec., indicted for the death of about 150 Serb civilians during a Croatian offensive in the Krajina region in 1995.   Croatia; ICTY

11 Dec. — North Korea announces that the Six-Party Talks (between China, Japan, North Korea, South Korea, Russia and the USA) on its nuclear programme are suspended 'for an indefinite period' unless the USA lifts the financial sanctions it has imposed on North Korea.   North Korea; Nuclear weapons; Sanctions

15 Dec. — The EU Police Advisory Team in the Former Yugoslav Republic of Macedonia (EUPAT) replaces the EU Police Mission in the Former Yugoslav Republic of Macedonia (EUPOL PROXIMA), launched in Dec. 2003.   EU; FYROM

15 Dec. — The first full-term parliamentary elections to the National Assembly since the invasion of Mar. 2003 are held in Iraq. Election officials report a high turnout of all the ethnic groups. The voting takes place amid a massive security operation with around 150 000 Iraqi soldiers and police, backed by US forces.   Iraq

20 Dec. — The UN Security Council and the UN General Assembly unanimously adopt Resolutions 1645 and 1646, and Resolution A/RES/60/180, establishing the Peacebuilding Commission originally proposed by UN Secretary-General Kofi Annan in his report of 21 Mar. and decided by the 14–16 Sep. World Summit. The commission is to be an inter-governmental advisory body to help stabilize and rebuild countries emerging from war and prevent them from relapsing into conflict.   UN

29 Dec.   In Lhokseumawe, Aceh, a ceremony takes place marking the   Indonesia/Aceh
final withdrawal of the Indonesian armed forces from Aceh. On
19 Dec. the Gerakan Aceh Merdeka (GAM, Free Aceh
Movement) decommissioned the last of the 840 weapons
referred to in the peace agreement reached between GAM and
the Indonesian Government on 15 Aug.

About the authors

Dr Christer Ahlström (Sweden) is Counsellor for legal affairs at the Swedish Embassy in The Hague, the Netherlands. He was Deputy Director of SIPRI from 2002 to 2005. Previously, he served as a Deputy Director in the Swedish Ministry for Foreign Affairs on issues related to disarmament and non-proliferation of weapons of mass destruction. He has contributed to the SIPRI Yearbook since 2003.

Dr Ian Anthony (United Kingdom) is SIPRI Research Coordinator and Leader of the SIPRI Non-proliferation and Export Controls Project. In 1992–98 he was Leader of the SIPRI Arms Transfers Project. His most recent publication for SIPRI is *Reducing Threats at the Source: A European Perspective on Cooperative Threat Reduction*, SIPRI Research Report no. 19 (2004). He is also editor of *Russia and the Arms Trade* (1998), *Arms Export Regulations* (1991) and *The Future of Defence Industries in Central and Eastern Europe*, SIPRI Research Report no. 7 (1994), and author of *The Naval Arms Trade* (1990) and *The Arms Trade and Medium Powers: Case Studies of India and Pakistan 1947–90* (Harvester Wheatsheaf, 1992). He has contributed to the SIPRI Yearbook since 1988.

Alyson J. K. Bailes (United Kingdom) has been Director of SIPRI since July 2002. She was a member of the British Diplomatic Service for 33 years, ending as British Ambassador to Finland in 2000–2002. Her other diplomatic postings include the British Delegation to Beijing, Bonn, Budapest, Oslo and NATO. She spent several periods on detachment outside the Service, including two academic sabbaticals, a two-year period with the British Ministry of Defence, and assignments to the European Union and the Western European Union. Her main analytical interests are politico-military affairs, European integration and Central European affairs. She has published widely in international journals on these subjects as well as on Chinese foreign policy. She is the author of *The European Security Strategy: An Evolutionary History*, SIPRI Policy Paper no. 10 (Feb. 2005) and co-editor of *The Nordic Countries and the European Security and Defence Policy* (2006). She has contributed to the SIPRI Yearbook since 2003.

Dr Sibylle Bauer (Germany) is a Researcher with the SIPRI Non-proliferation and Export Controls Project. Previously, she was a Researcher with the Institute for European Studies in Brussels. She has published widely on European export control and armaments issues, including chapters in *The Restructuring of the European Defence Industry* (Office for Official Publications of the European Communities, 2001), *Annuaire français de relations internationales* [French yearbook of international relations] (Bruylant, 2001) and *The Path to European Defence* (Maklu, 2003). She is co-author of *The European Union Code of Conduct on Arms Exports: Improving the Annual Report*, SIPRI Policy Paper no. 8 (Nov. 2004); and is the author of *European Arms Export Policies and Democratic Accountability* (forthcoming). She has contributed to the SIPRI Yearbook since 2004.

Åsa Blomström (Sweden) joined SIPRI in 2005 and is acting Project Secretary for the Military Expenditure and Arms Production Programme and the Arms Transfers Project. She is responsible for the electronic archive common to these three research areas, and maintains the SIPRI reporting system for military expenditure.

Nenne Bodell (Sweden) is Head of the SIPRI Library and Documentation Department and of the SIPRI Arms Control and Disarmament Documentary Survey Project. She has contributed to the SIPRI Yearbook since 2003.

Dr Hans Born (Netherlands) is a Senior Fellow in Democratic Governance of the Security Sector at the Geneva Centre for the Democratic Control of Armed Forces (DCAF). He leads DCAF's working groups on parliamentary accountability of the security sector and on legal aspects of security sector governance. He is a guest lecturer on civil–military relations at the Federal Institute of Technology (ETH) in Zurich and on the governing of nuclear weapons at the United Nations Disarmament Fellowship Programme. He is co-author of *Civil–Military Relations in Europe* (Routledge, 2006) and *Making Intelligence Accountable: Legal Standards and Best Practice for Oversight of Intelligence Agencies* (Norwegian Parliament, 2005) and lead author of *Parliamentary Oversight of the Security Sector: Principles, Mechanisms and Practices* (Inter-Parliamentary Union/DCAF, 2003). He contributed to the SIPRI Yearbook in 2005.

Mark Bromley (United Kingdom) is a Research Associate with the SIPRI Arms Transfers Project. Previously, he was a Policy Analyst for the British American Security Information Council (BASIC). While at BASIC he authored or co-authored a number of research reports and papers, including 'Secrecy and dependence: the UK Trident system in the 21st century' (BASIC, 2001) and 'European missile defence: new emphasis, new roles (BASIC, 2001). He is co-author of *The European Union Code of Conduct on Arms Exports: Improving the Annual Report*, SIPRI Policy Paper no. 8 (Nov. 2004) and has contributed to the SIPRI Yearbook since 2004.

Julian Cooper (United Kingdom) is Deputy Director of the Centre for Russian and East European Studies (CREES) and Professor of Russian Economic Studies, University of Birmingham. He is the author of many publications on the economics of the military in Russia and other former Soviet republics, including the chapters 'Russian military expenditure and arms production' in *SIPRI Yearbook 2001* and 'The arms industries of the Russian Federation, Ukraine and Belarus' in *SIPRI Yearbook 2004*.

Dr Andrew Cottey (United Kingdom) is Jean Monnet Chair in European Political Integration in the Department of Government, University College Cork. He previously worked in the Department of Peace Studies at the University of Bradford, the EastWest Institute (EWI), Saferworld and the British American Security Information Council (BASIC), and was a NATO Research Fellow, a Research Associate at the International Institute for Strategic Studies (IISS) and a visiting researcher at SIPRI. His publications include *New Security Challenges in Postcommunist Europe: Securing Europe's East* (Manchester University Press, 2002), *Democratic Control of the Military in Postcommunist Europe: Guarding the Guards* (Palgrave, 2002) and, as co-editor, *The Challenge of Military Reform in Postcommunist Europe: Building*

Professional Armed Forces (Palgrave, 2002). He is co-author of *Reshaping Defence Diplomacy: New Roles for Military Cooperation and Assistance*, Adelphi Paper 365 (Oxford University Press/IISS, May 2004). He contributed to the SIPRI Yearbook in 2003 and 2004.

Dr Pál Dunay (Hungary) is a Senior Researcher with the SIPRI Euro-Atlantic, Regional and Global Security Project. Before joining SIPRI he worked at the Geneva Centre for Security Policy between 1996 and 2004. He is co-author of *Ungarns aussenpolitik 1990–1997: zwischen westintegration, nachbarschafts- und minderheitenpolitik* [Hungarian foreign policy 1990–1997: at the crossroads of Western integration, neighbourhood and minority policy] (Nomos Verlag, 1998) and *Open Skies: A Cooperative Approach to Military Transparency and Confidence-Building* (United Nations Institute for Disarmament Research, 2004). He has contributed to the SIPRI Yearbook since 2004.

J. Paul Dunne (United Kingdom) is Professor of Economics at the University of the West of England, Bristol; Chair of the British affiliate of Economists for Peace and Security; and co-editor of the new *Economics of Peace and Security Journal*. He previously held posts at Birkbeck College, the University of Leeds, Middlesex University, the University of Warwick and Magdalene College, Cambridge. His main area of research is the economics of peace and security. He has published widely and is co-editor of *Arms Trade and Economic Development: Theory, Policy, and Cases in Arms Trade Offsets* (Routledge, 2004) and *Arming the South: The Economics of Military Expenditure, Arms Production and Trade in Developing Countries* (Palgrave, 2002). Details of his work are available at URL <http://www.carecon.org.uk>.

Vitaly Fedchenko (Russia) joined SIPRI in 2005 as a Researcher with the Reinforcing European Union Cooperative Threat Reduction Programmes Project, with responsibility for nuclear security issues and EU–Russian relations. Previously, he was a visiting researcher at SIPRI, a Researcher and Project Coordinator at the Center for Policy Studies in Russia and a Research Fellow at the Institute for Applied International Research in Moscow. He is the author or co-author of several publications on international non-proliferation and disarmament assistance and on Russian nuclear exports.

Damien Fruchart (United Kingdom) is a Research Assistant with the SIPRI Military Expenditure and Arms Production Programme, responsible for monitoring military expenditure in Asia and Oceania. He has a BA in Chinese and Japanese Studies from the University of Leeds and an MA from Uppsala University. Previously, he held an internship with the European Commission's delegation in Beijing, China.

Richard Guthrie (United Kingdom) is the Leader of the SIPRI Chemical and Biological Warfare Project. Previously, he was an independent consultant dealing with defence and security issues, with a specialization in the control of materials and technologies used to make nuclear, biological and chemical weapons. He has worked extensively with intergovernmental bodies, governments, non-governmental organizations and academic departments. He was involved in a long-term collaboration with the Harvard Sussex Program (1988–2003), where he was responsible for production of the *CBW Conventions Bulletin* and for managing data resources. He edited or co-edited the Verification Technology Information Centre (VERTIC) yearbook in

1992–97 and the VERTIC newsletter *Trust and Verify* in 1992–97. He was an adviser to British Members of Parliament in 1986–2003.

Dr Björn Hagelin (Sweden) is the Leader of the SIPRI Arms Transfers Project. Before joining SIPRI in 1998, he was Researcher and Associate Professor in the Department of Peace and Conflict Research, Uppsala University, and a security analyst at the Swedish National Defence Research Institute. His recent publications include 'From certainty to uncertainty: Sweden's armament policy in transition', *Defence Procurement and Industrial Policy: A Small Country Perspective* (Routledge, forthcoming 2006); 'Kritiken av säkerhetspolitiska kritiker: ett försök att skriva om Sveriges historia' [The criticism of security policy critics: an attempt to rewrite Sweden's history], *Internasjonal politikk*, vol. 12 (2005); 'Internationellt materielutvecklingssamarbete' [International equipment development cooperation], *Materiel för miljarder* [Materiel for billions] (Riksrevisionen, 2004); and 'Nordic offset policies: changes and challeges', *Arms Trade and Economic Development: Theory and Policy in Offsets* (Routledge, 2004). He has contributed to the SIPRI Yearbook since 1999.

Lotta Harbom (Sweden) is a Research Assistant with the Uppsala Conflict Data Program at the Department of Peace and Conflict Research, Uppsala University. She is currently working on both the Uppsala Conflict Data Program and a project on conflicts and conflict resolution in the context of Africa's weak states. She contributed to the SIPRI Yearbook in 2005.

John Hart (United States) is a Researcher with the SIPRI Chemical and Biological Warfare Project. He is a co-editor of *Chemical Weapon Destruction in Russia: Political, Legal and Technical Aspects*, SIPRI Chemical & Biological Warfare Studies no. 17 (1998). In 2005 he prepared a report for the European Union on assistance for the destruction of chemical weapons in Russia. He is the author of 'The ALSOS Mission, 1943–1945: a secret U.S. scientific intelligence unit', *International Journal of Intelligence and Counter Intelligence* (autumn 2005), and 'The Soviet biological weapons program', *Deadly Cultures: Biological Weapons since 1945* (Harvard University Press, 2006). He has contributed to the SIPRI Yearbook since 1997.

Theresa Hitchens (United States) is Director of the Center for Defense Information (CDI). She has had a long career in journalism with a focus on military, defence industry and NATO affairs, and was editor of *Defense News* between 1998 and 2000. In addition to her duties as CDI Director, she leads CDI's Space Security Project. She is the author of *Future Security in Space: Charting a Cooperative Course* (CTR/DEFENS, 2004) and continues to write on space and nuclear arms control issues for outside publications. She serves on the editorial board of *Bulletin of the Atomic Scientists* and is a member of Women in International Security and the International Institute for Strategic Studies.

Caroline Holmqvist (Sweden) is a Research Associate with the SIPRI Armed Conflict and Conflict Management Programme. She holds degrees in international relations and political science from the London School of Economics and previously worked at the Foreign Policy Centre, London. She is the author of several publications on armed conflicts and the role of non-state actors, including *Private Security Companies: The Case for Regulation*, SIPRI Policy Paper no. 9 (Jan. 2005) and 'Engaging armed non-state actors in post-conflict settings', *Security Governance and Post-conflict Peacebuilding* (Lit Verlag, 2005). She has contributed to the SIPRI Yearbook since 2004.

Shannon N. Kile (USA) is a Senior Researcher with the Non-proliferation and Export Controls Project at SIPRI, where he has worked since 1991. His principal areas of research are nuclear arms control and non-proliferation with a special interest in Iran and North Korea. He has contributed to numerous SIPRI publications, including chapters on nuclear arms control and nuclear forces and weapon technology for the SIPRI Yearbook since 1995. His recent publications include, as editor, *Europe and Iran: Perspectives on Non-proliferation*, SIPRI Research Report no. 21 (2005).

Hans M. Kristensen (Denmark) is the Director of the Nuclear Information Project at the Federation of American Scientists (FAS) in Washington, DC. He is co-author of the NRDC Nuclear Notebook column in *Bulletin of the Atomic Scientists*. His recent publications include *Global Strike: A Chronology of the Pentagon's New Offensive Strike Plan* (FAS, 2006), 'Chinese nuclear forces', *Imaging Notes* (winter 2006), *Preparing for the Failure of Deterrence* (Royal Canadian Military Institute, Nov./Dec. 2005) and 'New doctrine falls short of Bush pledge', *Arms Control Today*, (Sep. 2005). He has contributed to the SIPRI Yearbook since 2001.

Frida Kuhlau (Sweden) is a Research Associate with the SIPRI Chemical and Biological Warfare Project. In 2005 she prepared a report for the European Commission on the status of bio-threat reduction programmes in the former Soviet Union. She is a co-author of the SIPRI Fact Sheets 'Biotechnology and the future of the Biological and Toxin Weapons Convention' (2001) and 'Maintaining the effectiveness of the Chemical Weapons Convention' (2002) and of *Non-Compliance with the Chemical Weapons Convention: Lessons from and for Iraq*, SIPRI Policy Paper no. 5 (Oct. 2003). She has contributed to the SIPRI Yearbook since 2002.

Dr Zdzislaw Lachowski (Poland) is a Senior Researcher with the SIPRI Euro-Atlantic, Regional and Global Security Project. Previously, he worked at the Polish Institute of International Affairs in Warsaw. He has published widely on the problems of European military security and arms control as well as on European politico-military integration. He is the co-editor of *International Security in a Time of Change: Threats–Concepts–Institutions* (Nomos, 2004) and author of *Confidence-and Security-Building Measures in the New Europe*, SIPRI Research Report no. 18 (2004). He has contributed to the SIPRI Yearbook since 1992.

Dr Neil J. Melvin (United Kingdom) is the Leader of the Armed Conflict and Conflict Management Project. Prior to joining SIPRI, he served as Senior Adviser to the High Commissioner on National Minorities of the Organization for Security and Co-operation in Europe. He has also held various teaching and research positions at universities and policy institutes in the United States and Europe. He is the author of a number of books and articles on security and conflict in Eurasia, including *Countering Conflict in the North Caucasus*, SIPRI Policy Paper (forthcoming 2006), and co-author of 'Diaspora politics: ethnic linkages, foreign policy, and security in Eurasia', *International Security* (winter 1999/2000).

Wuyi Omitoogun (Nigeria) is a Researcher with the SIPRI Military Expenditure and Arms Production Programme. He is co-editor of *Budgeting for the Military Sector in Africa: The Processes and Mechanisms of Control* (2006) and the author of *Military Expenditure Data in Africa: A Survey of Cameroon, Ethiopia, Ghana, Kenya, Nigeria and Uganda*, SIPRI Research Report no. 17 (2003). He has contributed to the SIPRI Yearbook since 2000.

Catalina Perdomo (Colombia) is a Research Assistant with the SIPRI Military Expenditure and Arms Production Programme, responsible for monitoring military expenditure in Latin America. Previously, she worked for the Inter-American Development Bank (IADB) in Washington, DC, and at the Washington, DC, office of the Fundación Ideas para la Paz of Colombia. She is co-author of *Informe sobre la implementación de la estrategia de desarrollo subnacional* [Report on the implementation of subnational development strategy] (IADB, 2004). She is also the author of 'Methodology for international comparison of government priorities' (2004). She has contributed to the SIPRI Yearbook since 2004.

Roger Roffey (Sweden) is Research Director at the Swedish Defence Research Agency (FOI), Division of Nuclear, Biological and Chemical Defence. He has spent five years on secondment with the Swedish Ministry of Defence focusing on NBC defence policy questions. He was a technical expert for the Swedish Ministry for Foreign Affairs in the Biological and Toxin Weapons Convention disarmament negotiations in Geneva, and served in the Australia Group for 15 years and as a United Nations Special Commission on Iraq (UNSCOM) inspector. His main areas of research are international developments in arms control related to biological weapons and bioterrorism, and threat reduction initiatives in Russia and the former Soviet Union. He contributed to the SIPRI Yearbook in 2004.

Elisabeth Sköns (Sweden) is the Leader of the SIPRI Military Expenditure and Arms Production Programme. Her most recent publications outside SIPRI include papers on the costs of conflict and on the financing of peace missions for the International Task Force on Global Public Goods, chapters on defence offsets in *Arms Trade and Economic Development: Theory and Policy in Offsets* (Routledge, 2004), on the restructuring of the West European defence industry in *Mot et avnasjonalisert forsvar?* [Towards a denationalized defence?] (Abstrakt, 2005), and on financing of security in *The Statesman's Yearbook 2007* (Palgrave Macmillan, forthcoming 2006). She has contributed to the SIPRI Yearbook since 1983.

Petter Stålenheim (Sweden) was in 2005–2006 acting Leader of the SIPRI Military Expenditure and Arms Production Programme and Head of the Military Expenditure Data Sub-Project. He is responsible for monitoring data on military expenditure, with a special focus on Europe and Central Asia, and for the maintenance of the SIPRI Military Expenditure Database. He has worked as a consultant to the International Institute for Democracy and Electoral Assistance in Stockholm and lectured at the George C. Marshall Center in Germany. He is co-author of *Armament and Disarmament in the Caucasus and Central Asia*, SIPRI Policy Paper no. 3 (July 2003) and has contributed to the SIPRI Yearbook since 1998.

Eamon Surry (Australia) is a Research Associate with the SIPRI Military Expenditure and Arms Production Programme. He is responsible for maintaining the project's arms industry databases and Internet site. Prior to joining SIPRI, he worked as a Researcher for a broadcast media consultancy in London. He is the author of *Transparency in the Arms Industry*, SIPRI Policy Paper no. 12 (2006). He has contributed to the SIPRI Yearbook since 2004.

Tomas Valasek (Slovakia) is the Director of the Brussels office of the Center for Defense Information (CDI). He is the editor of *The Easternization of Europe's Security Policy* (IVO-CDI, 2004) and author of numerous articles in various newspapers and journals including *The Wall Street Journal, Jane's Defence Weekly* and *World Policy Journal*. He also serves as a defence and foreign policy analyst for the BBC Czech-language service. He is a member of the International Institute for Strategic Studies.

Professor Peter Wallensteen (Sweden) has held the Dag Hammarskjöld Chair in Peace and Conflict Research since 1985 and was Head of the Department of Peace and Conflict Research, Uppsala University, in 1972–99. He directs the Uppsala Conflict Data Program and the Stockholm Process on Targeted Sanctions. He is the author of *Understanding Conflict Resolution: War, Peace and the Global System* (SAGE, 2002) and *Making Targeted Sanctions Effective: Guidelines for the Implementation of UN Policy Options* (Uppsala, 2003). He is co-editor of *International Sanctions: Between Words and Wars in the Global System* (Frank Cass, 2005) and has contributed to the SIPRI Yearbook since 1988.

Michael Ward (United Kingdom) is an independent consultant on economic statistics and development issues. He has worked for the World Bank and the Organization for Economic Development in Europe, where he produced the first internationally comparable purchasing power parity (PPP) estimates of gross domestic product and national expenditures for the OECD countries and countries in Eastern and Central Europe. He has been involved from the start in the development of different methodologies underlying international comparisons and has published extensively on the analysis of PPP data. He is the author of *Quantifying the World: UN Ideas and Statistics* (United Nations Intellectual History Project, 2004), co-editor of *Identifying the Poor* (IOS Press, 1999) and the author of *The Measurement of Capital: The Methodology of Capital Stock Estimates in OECD Countries* (OECD, 1976). In 1999 he was awarded the International Statistical Institute's medal for outstanding services to international statistics.

Connie Wall (United States) is Head of the SIPRI Editorial and Publications Department. She has edited or contributed to the SIPRI Yearbook since 1970.

Siemon T. Wezeman (Netherlands) is a Researcher on the SIPRI Arms Transfers Project. Among his publications are several relating to international transparency in arms transfers. His most recent publication is *The Future of the United Nations Register of Conventional Arms*, SIPRI Policy Paper no. 4 (Aug. 2003). He has contributed to the SIPRI Yearbook since 1993.

Sharon Wiharta (Indonesia) is a Research Associate with the SIPRI Armed Conflict and Conflict Management Programme, working on peacekeeping and peace-building issues, particularly efforts to promote justice and to establish the rule of law in post-conflict situations. Recently, she co-led a study on local ownership and the rule of law during the peace-building process. Prior to joining SIPRI in 2001, she worked at the Center for International Affairs of the University of Washington, Seattle, where she conducted research on sustainable development issues. She is co-author of *The Transition to Order after Conflict* (Folke Bernadotte Academy Publications, 2006) and has contributed to the SIPRI Yearbook since 2002.

SIPRI Yearbook 2006: Armaments, Disarmament and International Security

Oxford University Press, Oxford, 2006, 888 pp.
(Stockholm International Peace Research Institute)
ISBN 0-19-929873-4 and 978-0-19-929873-0

ABSTRACTS

BAILES, A. J. K., 'Introduction. The world of security and peace research in a 40-year perspective', in *SIPRI Yearbook 2006*, pp. 1–30.

In the four decades since SIPRI's inauguration, the East–West confrontation has not been replaced by any one clear strategic paradigm. More dimensions of security are now recognized and more types of actors involved. Boundaries between military defence and active peace-building have been blurred, so that armaments are not automatically seen as a problem and traditional disarmament models are under threat. However, a wider range of institutions now attempt to limit conflict- and arms-related hazards by more varied means. A disturbing number of grave security problems are no nearer solution, and valuable initiatives no nearer realization, than they were 40 years ago.

DUNAY, P. and LACHOWSKI, Z., 'Euro-Atlantic security and institutions', in *SIPRI Yearbook 2006*, pp. 33–62.

Pragmatism dominated Euro-Atlantic relations in 2005. Beyond the basically unsolved rift over Iraq, the USA and EU/NATO-aligned Europe have expediently recognized their roles in global affairs as complementary rather than confrontational. Institutionally, the rivalry between the EU and NATO has entered a new phase as their geographical and functional agendas increasingly overlap. Both organizations have lost their enlargement momentum for years to come. In the former Soviet area a sharp divide remains between the countries that have embarked on transformation and those that have retained authoritarian rule or have returned to it. Central Asia, thus far less scarred by conflicts than the Caucasus, could become more vulnerable to instability as a result of the demand for regime change.

DUNAY, P., 'Status and statehood in the Western Balkans', in *SIPRI Yearbook 2006*, pp. 63–76.

The violence that prevailed in the Western Balkans in 1999–2001 has diminished. Kosovo's future status, the relationship between Serbia and Montenegro and the integrity of Bosnia and Herzegovina dominate the agenda. The resolution of these issues will shape the future of the region. Whether the ethnic composition of states and other entities will have a long-term effect on state borders is debatable. Achieving stability, however temporary, may help regional reconciliation. In order to avoid the emergence of weak states and non-functional entities, external actors, primarily the EU and the USA, should continue to support the region, help promote respect for human rights and closely monitor developments.

HOLMQVIST, C., 'Major armed conflicts', in *SIPRI Yearbook 2006*, pp. 77–107.

Notwithstanding the longevity of certain conflicts, e.g., Israel–Palestinians and Kashmir, there have been major changes in both the dynamics and understanding of conflict in the past four decades. In particular, the increasing prominence of non-state actors in conflict has led to new challenges for conflict responses. Developments in Darfur, Sudan, in 2005 illustrated how the mutability of non-state actors may complicate conflict resolution, while the conflict in Chechnya demonstrated the frequent intermingling of criminal and political elements in conflicts involving non-state actors. Continued unrest in the Democratic Republic of the Congo showed how non-state violence has persisted despite the existence of formal 'peace'. The insurgency in Iraq continued virtually unabated during 2005, and developments in formal political institutions could not halt the widening of sectarian divisions in the country.

HARBOM, L. and WALLENSTEEN, P., 'Patterns of major armed conflicts, 1990–2005', in *SIPRI Yearbook 2006*, pp. 108–19.

There were 17 major armed conflicts in 16 locations worldwide in 2005. The number of major armed conflicts and the number of conflict locations were slightly lower in 2005 than in 2004, when there were 19 major armed conflicts in 17 locations. No interstate conflicts were active in 2005, and Asia was the region with the highest number of conflicts. In the 16-year post-cold war period 1990–2005, there were 57 different major armed conflicts. There has been a steady decline in the number of conflicts since 1999, and the figure for 2005 is the lowest for the entire period.

MELVIN, N. J., 'Islam, conflict and terrorism', in *SIPRI Yearbook 2006*, pp. 123–38.

With the end of the cold war, religion has increasingly been viewed as a key element in many of the world's conflicts. In recent years, and particularly after the events of 11 September 2001 in the United States, radical Islam has been identified as a source of violence, including terrorism. While some observers have seen in the growth of religious extremism a 'clash of civilizations' in which Islamists are taking a leading role, recent research has shown a more complex picture of Muslim societies and their relationship to the rest of the world. From this perspective, internal transformation and conflict within the Muslim world as a result of globalization is promoting the emergence of new, dynamic and, in some circumstances, violent movements that are often opposed to traditional Islam. The diversity of contemporary Islamist movements and the variety of factors that shape the role of Islam within conflict suggest the need for more sophisticated development of security policies intended to prevent and terminate conflict involving individuals and groups linked to the Muslim world.

WIHARTA, S., 'Peace-building: the new international focus on Africa', in *SIPRI Yearbook 2006*, pp. 139–57.

The establishment in 2005 of the UN Peacebuilding Commission, which is tasked with coordinating the efforts of peacekeeping and development actors, underscored the sustained focus of the international peace and security agenda on post-conflict peacebuilding, with Africa figuring most prominently. Africa was also the site of 14 peace missions with over 65 000 personnel deployed in costly, multidimensional operations. Despite the allocation of considerable international assistance and resources, the struggle of the African Union and the United Nations missions in Sudan, among other missions, points to the continued severe difficulties of building peace in Africa.

BAILES, A. J. K. and COTTEY, A., 'Regional security cooperation in the early 21st century', in *SIPRI Yearbook 2006*, pp. 195–223.

Regional security cooperation has spread over large parts of the world since 1945 and developed new forms. It can contribute to conflict avoidance and management; constructive military cooperation; security cooperation in other dimensions, including against new threats or coordination of economic and functional efforts for security ends; and the advancement of human rights and democracy. The 'quality' of cooperation may be assessed using tests *inter alia* of freedom, a non-zero-sum approach, productiveness and cost-effectiveness. It seems harder for very large states to group successfully with their neighbours than for diverse or even underdeveloped ones. The world may be an uneasy mix of integrated and emerging regions, single powers and powder-keg areas for some time to come.

BORN, H., 'National governance of nuclear weapons: opportunities and constraints', in *SIPRI Yearbook 2006*, pp. 225–42.

While the international governance of nuclear weapons is a well-covered topic, the same cannot be said of the governance of nuclear weapons in nuclear weapon states. From a security-sector governance perspective it can be argued that the debate on the accountability of the control of nuclear weapons should be broadened beyond the traditional 'command and control' approach. Analysis and comparison of the governance of nuclear weapons in the five Non-Proliferation Treaty-defined nuclear weapon states—China, France, Russia, the United Kingdom and the United States—and three de facto nuclear weapon states—India, Israel and Pakistan—illustrate how nuclear weapon states, both democratic and non-democratic, balance the usability and security of nuclear weapons against political accountability.

HAGELIN, B., BROMLEY, M., HART, J., KILE, S. N., LACHOWSKI, Z., OMITOOGUN, W., PERDOMO, C., SURRY, E. and WEZEMAN, S. T., 'Transparency in the arms life cycle', in *SIPRI Yearbook 2006*, pp. 245–67.

No set of systematic, reliable, valid and global quantitative data exists on the arms life cycle, i.e., military expenditure, arms production, research and development (R&D), arms transfers, arms inventories and the disposal of arms. This is often also the case regionally. The lack of internationally agreed definitions, or adherence to existing ones, poses problems for international comparisons. Moreover, the activities of arms producers remain partly beyond the control of the countries where they operate. The dual-use nature of many recent innovations in science and technology makes it more important and more difficult to pin down and compare monies devoted to military R&D. Transparency in national arms inventories is limited generally, and large uncertainties remain about global inventories of nuclear weapons and weapon-usable fissile materials. For biological weapons, transparency could be said to have decreased, but there are more positive trends for data on chemical weapons, military expenditure and arms transfers.

OMITOOGUN, W. and SKÖNS, E., 'Military expenditure data: a 40-year overview', in *SIPRI Yearbook 2006*, pp. 269–94.

During the past 40 years in which SIPRI has gathered data on military expenditure on a global scale, the quality, availability and uses of the data have been influenced by changing international security contexts. Two fundamental shifts in the use of military expenditure data have occurred: first, from the cold war focus on countries in the North to a post-cold war focus on countries in the South; and second, a shift of the policy context in the UN system in which military expenditure data are used—from disarmament and development to transparency. The relevance of the data for analysis of peace and security issues has been further challenged by the greater focus on internal and human security in the current security environment. As a result, military expenditure data have lost some relevance. This does not mean that data on military expenditure are no longer useful, but rather that they need to be complemented by other types of data series.

STÅLENHEIM, P., FRUCHART, D., OMITOOGUN, W. and PERDOMO, C., 'Military expenditure', in *SIPRI Yearbook 2006*, pp. 295–324.

World military expenditure in 2005 is estimated to have been $1001 billion at constant (2003) prices, or $1118 billion in current dollars, a 34 per cent rise since the post-cold war low point in 1998. The high rate of growth is mainly attributable to the United States' costly campaigns in Afghanistan and Iraq and its 'global war on terrorism'. The USA accounted for about 80 per cent of the rise in global spending in 2005, and US military expenditure now makes up 48 per cent of the world total, distantly followed by the United Kingdom and France, which each account for 5 per cent. Together, the top 15 spenders account for 84 per cent of total world spending because a shrinking number of countries are responsible for a growing proportion of spending. In many countries, rising military expenditure has been facilitated by increasing revenues owing to high commodity prices.

WARD, M., 'International comparisons of military expenditures: issues and challenges of using purchasing power parities', in *SIPRI Yearbook 2006*, pp. 369–86.

Comparing one country's expenditure on the military (or any other sector) with that of another country expressed in a different currency poses significant problems. A traditional approach has been to convert currencies using market exchange rates. A preferable method is to use purchasing power parity (PPP) rates, which indicate how much, hypothetically, it would cost in one country to acquire the same (military) goods and services bought by another country, and thus allow more accurate international comparisons of the economic burden represented by the spending. However, there are conceptual and empirical issues in the estimation of PPPs that need to be resolved. In the case of military expenditure, these are further compounded by military secrecy, the coverage of military budgets, the nature of military prices and the uniqueness of military products.

DUNNE, J. P. and SURRY, E., 'Arms production', in *SIPRI Yearbook 2006*, pp. 387–418.

The combined arms sales of the SIPRI Top 100 arms-producing companies in the world (excluding China) in 2004 was $268 billion, 15 per cent higher than in 2003 in current dollars. Sixty-four per cent of the sales of these 100 companies are accounted for by 41 companies based in North America: 40 in the United States and one in Canada. Forty European companies (including 4 in Russia) accounted for 31 per cent of sales. Since the cold war the international arms industry has undergone considerable change. The share of arms sales of the top 5 in the Top 100 arms-producing companies rose from 22 to 44 per cent between 1990 and 2003. There has been increased internationalization of supply chains, encouraged by the growth of offset deals and growing privatization of defence services and support. Further change can be expected, although the arms market retains unique characteristics, including considerable barriers to entry and exit.

COOPER, J., 'Developments in the Russian arms industry', in *SIPRI Yearbook 2006*, pp. 431–48.

Since 1991 the huge Soviet arms industry has contracted markedly and the administrative structures for the management and oversight of the Russian military sector have undergone frequent and far-reaching change. Since President Vladimir Putin came to power, military output has recovered to some extent and spending on procurement and research and development has increased, but Russian military production remains dependent on exports. The Soviet legacy is still apparent: the industry remains relatively isolated from the rest of the world with a reluctance to establish transnational partnerships or permit foreign ownership. The level of transparency, while improving, is still short of that accepted as normal in democratic countries.

HAGELIN, B., BROMLEY, M. and WEZEMAN, S. T., 'International arms transfers', in *SIPRI Yearbook 2006*, pp. 449–476.

For the past three years there has been an increase in the volume of major arms transfers. The 5 largest suppliers of major conventional weapons in the 5-year period 2001–2005 were Russia, the United States, France, Germany and the United Kingdom. Russia and the USA each accounted for roughly 30 per cent of global deliveries of major weapons. Smaller suppliers outside Europe and North America have been unsuccessful in deliveries of major weapons to Iraq and may continue to be so. Poland, however, may remain a key European supplier to Iraq. Cooperation among minor suppliers to strengthen their international arms market positions has been problematic. The search for new markets and the drive to maintain existing markets have sharpened international competition, encouraging commercial pragmatism in national export policy. In some countries there is political fatigue regarding transparency mechanisms such as the United Nations Register on Conventional Arms and national annual reports. Transparency in arms transfers reporting may be at a crossroads if the tendency towards commercial pragmatism spreads and reduces political willingness to report on national arms exports.

HITCHENS, T. and VALASEK, T., 'The security dimension of European collective efforts in space', in *SIPRI Yearbook 2006*, pp. 565–84.

Europe, collectively and nationally, has long been a major power in outer space. However, like many other elements of European power, space capability is not provided in a unified manner. Instead it accrues through a confused mixture of national and multinational entities and efforts. European space activities, especially collective projects, have long focused on civil and commercial applications. In recent years, however, European countries have recognized the need to add a security dimension to their space programmes. This impetus stems from the trend towards collectivism in foreign policy, the US revolution in military affairs powered by space capability and Europe's increasing desire to act independently from the United States.

ANTHONY, I., 'Reflections on continuity and change in arms control', in *SIPRI Yearbook 2006*, pp. 587–606.

One key aim of arms control—facilitating dialogue on international politico-military aspects of security—remains valid and necessary, but other aspects of cold war arms control (e.g., symmetry, reciprocity and universal participation) are declining in importance and are absent from many recent processes. Nonetheless, these processes have an important effect on the policies and practices of states. Improved verification and transparency promoted arms control agreements after the cold war. These gains have now been lost. Changing views on verification complicate assessment and enforcement of arms control compliance. Arms control was traditionally state focused, but the recent focus has been on controlling capabilities available to non-state groups that may be planning terrorist acts. In a more positive context, non-state actors such as private businesses are becoming engaged in arms control activities. Recent arms control initiatives have focused on dual-use items not under exclusive state control. Elimination or full denial of access to dual-use items is neither feasible nor desirable. Denial of access to dual-use technology is only sought when the technology concerned might be misused or when the risk that it will be misused is unacceptably high.

KILE, S. N., 'Nuclear arms control and non-proliferation', in *SIPRI Yearbook 2006*, pp. 607–38.

In 2005 the nuclear non-proliferation regime continued to face serious challenges. The effectiveness and viability of the Non-Proliferation Treaty (NPT) were called into question by the deadlock that arose at the seventh five-yearly NPT Review Conference. The controversy over the nature of Iran's nuclear programme remained unresolved as the International Atomic Energy Agency (IAEA) provided further detail about Iran's failure to declare important nuclear activities as required by its safeguards agreement with the IAEA. No breakthrough was made in the international talks on the future of North Korea's nuclear programme, although North Korea declared for the first time that it possessed nuclear weapons. There was continued concern about the safety and custodial security of global stocks of nuclear materials. In the light of these challenges, there was renewed interest in multinational approaches to managing the global nuclear fuel cycle.

AHLSTRÖM, C., 'Legal aspects of the Indian–US Civil Nuclear Cooperation Initiative', in *SIPRI Yearbook 2006*, pp. 669–85.

In 2005 the United States and India launched the Civil Nuclear Cooperation Initiative (CNCI). For the USA, the CNCI was designed to allow US exports of civilian nuclear technology to India, while India, in essence, pledged to assume the responsibilities of a nuclear weapon state. The declared willingness of the USA to engage with India in the field of civil nuclear technology has raised concerns about the impact this would have on the nuclear non-proliferation regime. An analysis of legal aspects of the CNCI shows that there are a number of both international and domestic legal issues. The accommodation of the CNCI is a question not only for the participants in the Nuclear Suppliers Group and for members of the US Congress, but also for the parties to the 1968 Non-Proliferation Treaty.

FEDCHENKO, V., 'Multilateral control of the nuclear fuel cycle, in *SIPRI Yearbook 2006*, pp. 686–705.

The fact that the development of nuclear energy for peaceful purposes entails acquiring the means for production of nuclear weapons has been recognized for decades. The international community has developed three approaches to deal with this problem: the introduction of legal and regulatory barriers to the transfer of technology and sensitive types of materials; the promotion of multilateral arrangements for the joint use of, and development or ownership of, sensitive nuclear fuel cycle facilities; and the use of innovative proliferation-resistant nuclear technologies. Nuclear security and energy security developments in 2005 once again prompted discussion of the strengths and weaknesses of these approaches, and the importance of the latter two was emphasized.

GUTHRIE, R., HART, J. and KUHLAU, F., 'Chemical and biological warfare developments and arms control', in *SIPRI Yearbook 2006*, pp. 707–31.

In 2005 the states parties to the 1972 Biological and Toxin Weapons Convention held meetings to consider codes of conduct for scientists and started preparations for the Sixth Review Conference, scheduled for 2006. The states parties to the 1993 Chemical Weapons Convention decided to extend the action plans on national implementation and universality. The economic and national security implications of diseases received unprecedented attention during 2005. The US-led Iraq Survey Group published its conclusions on past Iraqi weapon programmes and further information was made public about pre-war intelligence sources and handling. Much information about alleged terrorist acquisition of chemical and biological materials for hostile purposes was revealed as a consequence of acquittals in significant court cases.

ROFFEY, R. and KUHLAU, F., 'Enhancing bio-security: the need for a global strategy', in *SIPRI Yearbook 2006*, pp. 732–48.

Recent outbreaks of diseases in combination with rapid developments in biotechnology and the perceived heightened risk of bio-terrorism have contributed to a focus on global public health and related security challenges. Historically, threat reduction activities have centred on Russia and the former Soviet republics, but a broader, more carefully considered global strategy to enhance bio-security is required. This can be achieved *inter alia* by raising awareness, enhancing international efforts in this area, improving bio-security worldwide at facilities that deal with dangerous pathogens, and developing legislation and standards to help prevent the acquisition of materials, technology and expertise by malicious actors. Effective epidemiological surveillance networks should be developed, and preparedness and response plans are needed in the event of security breaches and to protect public health from the threat of naturally occurring and accidentally released agents. Cooperation and discussion of these issues should be promoted on a global scale.

LACHOWSKI, Z., 'Conventional arms control', in *SIPRI Yearbook 2006*, pp. 749–74.

The year 2005 marked the 15th anniversary of the signing of the 1990 Treaty on Conventional Armed Forces in Europe (CFE Treaty). However, the updating of Europe's 'hard' conventional arms control regime remained stalled by disagreements over texts adopted at the 1999 Istanbul Summit of the Organization for Security and Co-operation in Europe (OSCE). The May 2005 agreement on the closure of Russian military bases in Georgia was a step forward, but deadlock persisted over the presence of Russian personnel and equipment in Moldova. The OSCE states continued to evaluate, adjust and make arms control-related efforts in order to better meet the common and regional risks and challenges facing Europe. Globally, the problem of 'inhumane weapons' continued to engage the international community.

ANTHONY, I. and BAUER, S., 'Transfer controls', in *SIPRI Yearbook 2006*, pp. 775–797.

The states involved in the improvement of export controls acknowledge that more must be done to combat the proliferation of weapons of mass destruction and their delivery systems, and they recognize the need for broader participation and greater cooperation on implementing international standards. There is broad agreement that past achievements in self-selecting export control arrangements are a solid platform for the development of international standards. Firm support for two recent initiatives—UN Security Council Resolution 1540 and the Proliferation Security Initiative—shows awareness of the need to pay the same attention to the enforcement of controls as has been paid to the development of legislation. Recent events indicate that export controls are likely to be applied in new areas as part of attempts to adapt arms control to a changing security environment. For example, a new EU regulation extends export controls beyond military or strategic products to human rights objectives. International Atomic Energy Agency member states are examining how export controls might help to reduce the risk of acquisition and use of radiological weapons by non-state actors. The need to accelerate the adoption of international standards through national laws and regulations continues to stimulate the demand for export control outreach and assistance.

Index